Sedative, Hypnotic, or Anxiolytic Intoxication
Delirium
Sedative, Hypnotic, or Anxiolytic Withdrawal
Delirium

Polysubstance-Related Disorder
Polysubstance Dependence

Schizophrenia and Other Psychotic Disorders
Schizophrenia
Paranoid Type
Disorganized Type
Catatonic Type
Undifferentiated Type
Residual Type
Schizophreniform Disorder
Schizoaffective Disorder
Brief Psychotic Disorder
Shared Psychotic Disorder
Psychotic Disorder Due to. . .
[Indicate the General Medical Condition]
Substance-Induced Psychotic Disorder
Psychotic Disorder NOS

Mood Disorders

Depressive Disorders
Major Depressive Disorder
Dysthymic Disorder
Depressive Disorder NOS

Bipolar Disorders
Bipolar I Disorder
Bipolar II Disorder
Cyclothymic Disorder
Bipolar Disorder NOS

Mood Disorder Due to. . .[Indicate the General
Medical Condition]
Substance-Induced Mood Disorder

Mood Disorder NOS

Anxiety Disorders
Panic Disorder Without Agoraphobia
Panic Disorder With Agoraphobia
Agoraphobia Without History of Panic Disorder
Specific Phobia
Specify type: Animal Type/Natural Environment
Type/ Blood-Injection-Injury Type/ Situational
Type/Other Type
Social Phobia
Obsessive-Compulsive Disorder
Posttraumatic Stress Disorder
Acute Stress Disorder
Generalized Anxiety Disorder
Anxiety Disorder Due to. . .[Indicate the General
Medical Condition]
Substance-Induced Anxiety Disorder (refer to
Substance-Related Disorders for substance
specific codes)
Anxiety Disorder NOS

Somatoform Disorders
Somatization Disorder
Undifferentiated Somatoform Disorder
Conversion Disorder
Pain Disorder
Hypochondriasis

Body Dysmorphic Disorder
Somatoform Disorder NOS

Factitious Disorders
Factitious Disorder
Factitious Disorder NOS

Dissociative Disorders
Dissociative Amnesia
Dissociative Fugue
Dissociative Identity Disorder
Depersonalization Disorder
Dissociative Disorder NOS

Sexual and Gender Identity Disorders

Sexual Desire Disorders
Hypoactive Sexual Desire Disorder
Sexual Aversion Disorder

Sexual Arousal Disorders
Female Sexual Arousal Disorder
Male Erectile Disorder

Orgasmic Disorders
Female Orgasmic Disorder
Male Orgasmic Disorder
Premature Ejaculation

Sexual Pain Disorders
Dyspareunia
Vaginismus

**Sexual Dysfunction Due to a General Medical
Condition**
Sexual Dysfunction NOS

Paraphilias
Exhibitionism
Fetishism
Frotteurism
Pedophilia
Sexual Masochism
Sexual Sadism
Transvestic Fetishism
Voyeurism
Paraphilia NOS

Gender Identity disorders
Gender Identity Disorder
Gender Identity Disorder NOS
Sexual Disorder NOS

Eating Disorders
Anorexia Nervosa
Bulimia Nervosa
Eating Disorder NOS

Sleep Disorders

Dyssomnias
Primary Insomnia
Primary Hypersomnia
Narcolepsy
Breathing-Related Sleep Disorder
Circadian Rhythm Sleep Disorder
Dyssomnia NOS

Parasomnias
Nightmare Disorder
Sleep Terror Disorder

Sleepwalking Disorder
Parasomnia NOS

Impulse-Control Disorders Not Elsewhere Classified
Intermittent Explosive Disorder
Kleptomania
Pyromania
Pathological Gambling
Trichotillomania
Impulse-Control Disorder NOS

Adjustment Disorders
Adjustment Disorder

Personality Disorders
Note: These are coded on Axis II
Paranoid Personality Disorder
Schizoid Personality Disorder
Schizotypal Personality Disorder
Antisocial Personality Disorder
Borderline Personality Disorder
Histrionic Personality Disorder
Narcissistic Personality Disorder
Avoidant Personality Disorder
Dependent Personality Disorder
Obsessive-Compulsive Personality Disorder
Personality Disorder NOS

Other Conditions That May Be a Focus of Clinical Intervention

Relational Problems
Relational Problem Related to a Mental Disorder or
General Medical Condition
Parent-Child Relational Problem
Partner Relational Problem
Sibling Relational Problem
Relational Problem NOS

Problems Related to Abuse or Neglect
Physical Abuse of Child
Sexual Abuse of Child
Neglect of Child
Physical Abuse of Adult
Sexual Abuse of Adult

**Additional Conditions That May be a Focus of
Clinical Attention**
Noncompliance With Treatment
Malingering
Adult Antisocial Behavior
Borderline Intellectual Functioning
Age-Related Cognitive Decline
Bereavement
Academic Problem
Occupational Problem
Identity Problem
Religious or Spiritual Problem
Acculturation Problem
Phase of Life Problem

Abnormal
Psychology

Thomas F. Oltmanns
University of Virginia

Robert E. Emery
University of Virginia

PRENTICE HALL
Englewood Cliffs
New Jersey 07632

Library of Congress Cataloging-in-Publication Data

Oltmanns, Thomas F.
  Abnormal Psychology / Thomas F. Oltmanns, Robert E. Emery.
    p.   cm.
  Includes bibliographical references and index.
  ISBN 0-13-007295-8
  1. Psychology, Pathological. 2. Mental illness. I. Emery,
Robert E. II. Title.
RC454.O44 1995
616.89—dc20   94-35274
                                              CIP

Executive editor: Peter Janzow
Editorial/production supervision: Patricia V. Amoroso
Development editor: Robert Weiss
Marketing manager: Lauren Ward
Editorial assistant: Marilyn Coco
Copy editor: Virginia Rubens
Design director: Paula K Martin
Designer: Carbone Smolan Associates
Cover art: Zita Asbaghi
Photo editor: Lorinda Morris-Nantz
Photo researchers: Barbara Scott and Eloise Marion
All portraits illustrated by Van Howell

To Gail, Sara, and Josh

TFO

To Kimberly, Maggie, and Jacey

REE

© 1995 by Prentice-Hall, Inc.
A Simon & Schuster Company
Englewood Cliffs, NJ 07632

Printed in the United States of America

10 9 8 7 6 5 4 3 2 1

ISBN 0-13-007295-8
      0-13-309857-5 (Professional copy)

Prentice Hall International (UK) Limited, *London*
Prentice-Hall of Australia Pty. Limited, *Sydney*
Prentice-Hall Canada Inc., *Toronto*
Prentice-Hall Hispanoamericana, S.A., *Mexico*
Prentice-Hall of India Private Limited, *New Delhi*
Prentice-Hall of Japan, Inc., *Tokyo*
Simon & Schuster Asia Pte. Ltd., *Singapore*
Editora Prentice-Hall do Brasil, Ltda., *Rio de Janeiro*

Brief Contents

Contents

Treatment of Psychological Disorders 70

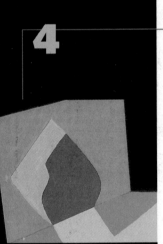

Classification and Assessment 108

Mood Disorders 150

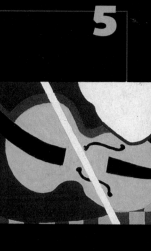

Anxiety Disorders 192

5

6

Maladaptive Responses to Stress 234

Dissociative and Somatoform Disorders 272

Personality Disorders 300

9

Alcoholism and Substance Use Disorders 336

10

11

Sexual and Gender Identity Disorders 372

12

Schizophrenic Disorders 404

Dementia, Delirium, and Amnestic Disorders   446

14 Mental Retardation and Pervasive Developmental Disorders 476

15 Psychological Problems of Childhood and Eating Disorders 512

Preface

Writing a new textbook on abnormal psychology is an intimidating task. Our endeavor has been all the more daunting, because we had two very ambitious goals for our book. First, we wanted to create a text that would not only educate but also would captivate students with both the substance and the science of abnormal psychology. Second, we wanted to anticipate the future of psychopathology, not just report on the past, and write a text that would help shape the discipline itself. We have worked toward these ends for more than 5 years, and we offer a textbook that takes a fresh, new approach to abnormal psychology both in content and in style.

INTEGRATIVE SYSTEMS APPROACH

Throughout the book, we follow an integrative systems approach, in which we combine evidence on biological, psychological, and social factors in discussing the etiology of different disorders. This biopsychosocial approach recognizes that many factors combine to cause abnormal behavior. Moreover, our systems approach highlights the reality that biological, psychological, and social theories are not necessarily incompatible. We did not want to present these or other perspectives as alternative paradigms, sweeping explanations that purport to identify the causes of all mental disorders. Rather, we wanted to convey three key points about biopsychosocial influences on abnormal behavior:

- First, biological, psychological, and social systems often combine to produce an emotional disorder, as when a difficult environmental event (a stressor) causes a genetic predisposition (a diathesis) to be expressed.

- Second, biological, psychological, and social explanations of abnormal behavior sometimes are compatible viewpoints that differ only in their level of analysis. For example, we raise the problem of reductionism in science and note that neurochemical explanations of depression are not necessarily incompatible with explanations that focus on helplessness, gender roles, and other psychosocial factors.

- Third, different psychological disorders have different causes; no single paradigm can accurately explain all psychological disturbances. We note that the most productive scientific research focuses on the specific etiology of a single disorder or a subtype of that disorder.

In addition to etiology, we extend the systems approach to cover treatment in an integrated fashion. We introduce biological, psychological, and social (and community) treatments for psychological disorders early in the text (Chapter 3).

In this discussion, we emphasize research on psychotherapy outcome and psychotherapy process. Our early introduction to treatment and our empirical focus on psychotherapy allow us in later chapters to highlight only the most promising, empirically based approaches to psychotherapy, medication, and community-based prevention.

Our dedication to the scientist-practitioner model of clinical psychology is likewise reflected in two major stylistic and pedagogical innovations in our textbook.

CASE STUDIES

The first innovation was to include detailed case studies throughout the book. In our own classes we have noted that students pay special attention to case studies during our lectures, and in evaluations at the end of the semester they plead for more cases. Our goals in presenting case studies in the text are the same as our goals in using cases in lecture: (1) to illustrate the symptoms and phenomenology of different psychological problems; (2) to demonstrate novel approaches and to raise questions about etiology and treatment; and (3) to "hook" students - to motivate them to master the scientific material that forms the core of abnormal psychology. To achieve these goals, throughout the book we systematically discuss memorable cases from our own clinical experience, together with cases from the literature.

As touched on above, for many students, case studies are among the most interesting, memorable, and motivating elements of their abnormal psychology course. Despite this, textbooks in psychopathology have traditionally introduced students to the subject by trekking through a series of historical vignettes about demons and witches, and waiting until later chapters to introduce case studies. Our Chapter 1 instead presents the central concepts of abnormal psychology in a novel and compelling manner: by highlighting four detailed case histories that illustrate the range of abnormal behaviors and raise basic questions about conceptualizing psychopathology.

We open every subsequent chapter with a thorough case study that both illustrates and raises questions about a major disorder discussed in that chapter. We often refer back to the case throughout the chapter as a means of making our scientific points more concrete – and of making it clear that science is indeed relevant to practice. Finally, in most chapters we include two or three additional brief cases to make key points or to describe the different forms of a broader category of a disorder; for example, mania as a subtype of mood disorder.

RESEARCH

Our second stylistic innovation focuses on the scientific side of the scientist-practitioner model. We have developed a unique approach to covering research methods in this textbook. Rather than relegating research methods to a single chapter or an appendix, we integrate methodology with the substance of abnormal psychology throughout the text. In every chapter, we include featured discussions titled "Research Methods" in which we introduce a new topic in scientific methodology. In Chapter 1, for example, Research Methods highlights the value – and the limitations – of the case study method. Research Methods in Chapter 2 covers the correlational study, and in Chapter 3, the discussion focuses on the experimental method. In subsequent chapters, Research Methods discussions cover more specialized topics; for example, longitudinal designs, alternative comparison groups, the heritability ratio, and base rates.

We also include another featured discussion in every chapter called "Research Close-up," a detailed presentation of a single study. We often coordinate the Research Close-up and Research Methods discussions to enhance their value to students. In Research Methods in Chapter 14, for example, we discuss the null hypothesis and the burden of proof. We draw an analogy to legal proceedings and emphasize that the burden of proof in science rests upon the scientist who offers an hypothesis. The Research Close-up, in turn, presents a study of "facilitated communication," a technique that purportedly allows children with autistic disorder to communicate in surprisingly sophisticated ways. We review a study that finds no evidence to support facilitated communication, and in this substantive context, we again note the rationale behind the null hypothesis. The burden of proof must rest with the proponent of an hypothesis; scientists assume that facilitated communication is not effective until research proves that their assumptions are wrong.

ADDITIONAL FEATURES

In addition to these special approaches to the substance of abnormal psychology and style of presentation, we have incorporated a number of additional distinguishing features in this textbook:

- Detailed coverage of developmental issues that reflect theoretical innovations from developmental psychology, the emergence of the developmental psychopathology perspective, a lifespan orientation, attachment theory, the course of abnormal behavior, detailed coverage of childhood disorders (2 chapters), aging, dementia, and family issues (including coverage of family law).

- Acknowledging the many social and demographic changes taking place in the United States and throughout North America, we systematically address ethnicity and gender issues in sections on epidemiology found in every chapter, in other parts of the text, and in several featured discussions titled "Further Thoughts."

- We emphasize research throughout the text, but we include selective coverage of specific research studies. We have not written an encyclopedia; rather we focus on ideas. This book is an investigation of the key contents, concepts, methods, questions, and controversies in abnormal psychology.

- A brief historical perspective in every chapter reviews past developments in classification, introduces key contemporary concepts and controversies, and suggests directions for future change.

- We follow consistent chapter outlines in every chapter that focuses on a psychological disorder. These outlines include major sections on typical symptoms and associated features, classification, epidemiology, etiology, and treatment. The approach provides systematic coverage of some important topics like epidemiology. The consistent outlines also help the student follow and review the substantive material.

- Our summaries of DSM-IV terminology and diagnostic criteria are based on the official, published version of the manual, which was released in the spring of 1994.

- A unique, separate chapter (16) examines normal but difficult transitions during the course of adult development that are often the focus of psychological research and treatment.

SUPPLEMENTS PACKAGE

An extensive and useful array of instructor and student supplements are available with this book:

The Instructor's Manual, written by Gordon Atlas of Alfred University, contains detailed lecture outlines and teaching suggestions for each chapter, as well as a compendium of handouts and transparency masters and a coordinated listing of video segments by chapter.

The Test Item File contains over 2000 test items written by the authors, with the assistance of Katherine Kitzmann of the University of Virginia.

Prentice Hall Test Manager 2.0 testing software for PC's and Macintoshes allows users to select or edit existing test items, insert additional questions, and provides a wide range of printing and scrambling options.

INSTRUCTIONAL VIDEOS

Two distinct types of video, providing more than 400 minutes of video material, accompany our text:

ABC News/Prentice Hall Video Libraries I and II provide more than 30 relevant segments from award-winning ABC News programs, including Nightline, 20/20, PrimeTime Live, and American Agenda. A summary of each segment and suggestions on how to incorporate the video into your classroom are included in the Instructor's Manual.

Video Cases in Abnormal Psychology: The Patients as Educators, James H. Scully, Jr., M.D., and Alan M. Dahms, Ph.D., Colorado State University. This exclusive video contains a series of 10 patient interviews illustrating a range of

disorders. Each interview is preceded by a brief history of the patient and a synopsis of some major symptoms of the disorder, and ends with a summary and a brief analysis.

Prentice Hall Color Transparencies for Abnormal Psychology.

The New York Times Abnormal Psychology Supplement. *The New York Times* and Prentice Hall are sponsoring Themes of The Times, a program designed to enhance access to current information of relevance in the classroom.

Through this program, the core subject matter provided in the text is supplemented by a collection of time-sensitive articles from one of the world's most distinguished newspapers, *The New York Times.* These articles demonstrate the vital, ongoing connection between what is learned in the classroom and what is happening in the world around us.

To enjoy the wealth of information of *The New York Times* daily, a reduced subscription rate is available. For information, call toll-free: 1-800-631-1222.

Prentice Hall and *The New York Times* are proud to co-sponsor Themes of The Times. We hope it will make the reading of both textbooks and newspapers a more dynamic, involving process.

The Study Guide, written by Patricia H. Rosenberger of Colorado State University, provides a chapter review, learning objectives, key concepts and terms (with definitions), self-tests, and activities for each chapter of the text.

Asking the Right Questions About Abnormal Psychology, Stuart M. Keeley, Bowling Green State University. Keeley presents a basic critical thinking methodology, then asks students to apply this method to a variety of classic research studies in psychopathology.

ACKNOWLEDGMENTS

Years of effort have gone into writing this book, and we are grateful to a number of people who assisted us in this arduous but fruitful task. We would like to start by expressing our appreciation to the following colleagues who wrote detailed reviews of various portions of the manuscript:

Gordon Atlas,
Alfred University

Deanna Barch,
University of Pittsburgh

Caryn L. Carlson,
University of Texas at Austin

William Edmonston, Jr.,
Colgate University

Ronald Evans,
Washburn University

John Foust,
Parkland College

Alan Glaros,
University of Missouri, Kansas City

Ian H. Gotlib,
Northwestern University

Irving Gottesman,
University of Virginia

Mort Harmatz,
University of Massachusetts

Jennifer Jenkins,
University of Toronto

Stuart Keeley,
Bowling Green State University

Carolin Keutzer,
University of Oregon

Roger Loeb,
University of Michigan, Dearborn

Carol Manning,
University of Virginia School of Medicine

Richard McFall,
Indiana University

John Monahan,
University of Virginia School of Law

Demetrios Papageorgis,
University of British Columbia

Patricia H. Rosenberger,
Colorado State University

Forrest Scogin,
University of Alabama

Janet Simons,
Central Iowa Psychological Services

Cheryl Spinweber,
University of California, San Diego

Bonnie Spring,
The Chicago Medical School

Milton E. Strauss,
Case Western Reserve University

J. Kevin Thompson,
University of South Florida

Robert H. Tipton,
Virginia Commonwealth University

Douglas Whitman,
Wayne State University

Michael Wierzbicki,
Marquette University

Robert D. Zettle,
Wichita State University

We have been fortunate to work in a stimulating academic environment that has fostered our interests in studying psychopathology and in teaching undergraduate students. We are particularly grateful to our current colleagues Irving Gottesman, Eric Turkheimer, Mavis Hetherington, John Monahan, Dan Wegner, and Mary Ainsworth for extended (and on-going) discussions of the issues that are considered in this book. Close friends and colleagues at Indiana University have also served in this role, especially Richard McFall and Alexander Buchwald. Many undergraduate and graduate students who have taken our courses at UVa and IU have helped to shape the viewpoints that are expressed in this book. They are too numerous to identify individually, but we are grateful for the intellectual challenges and excitement that they have provided over the past several years.

Many other people have contributed to the book in various important ways. Students who helped contribute to the text include Shari Miller Johnson, Robin Dolch, Katherine Kitzmann, Cynthia Moore, Peter Dillon, Jeffery Aaron, and Sarah Liebman. Kimberly Carpenter Emery did extensive legal research and helped organize Chapter 17. Carol Manning and Charles Vandenberg provided consultation on case study materials for Chapters 13 and 1. Linda Christian and Debbie Snow were diligent in helping with typing and word processing.

We would also like to express our gratitude to several people at Prentice Hall who made major contributions to this effort. We thank Susan Finnemore-Brennan and Leslie Carr for getting us started. We especially thank Pete Janzow for his tremendous effort in getting us finished and in making a commitment to produce a book with an exciting and innovative design. We thank Robert Weiss for his detailed and extremely helpful developmental editing of the manuscript. We are also grateful to Pattie Amoroso for her skillful handling of the production of our text. The visual appeal of the text reflects the efforts of Paula Martin, who contributed to the attractive design, and Barbara Scott, Eloise Marion, and Lori Morris-Nantz, who were responsible for photo research. We are also grateful to Lauren Ward for directing the marketing efforts for the book.

Finally, we give our loving thanks to our families: Gail, Sara, and Josh Oltmanns and Kimberly, Maggie, and Jacey Emery. You are the loving sources of our inspiration and our motivation.

TOM OLTMANNS

BOB EMERY

About the Authors

Thomas F. Oltmanns (right) is Professor of Psychology and Psychiatric Medicine at the University of Virginia, where he was also Director of Clinical Training from 1987 to 1993. He received his B.A. from the University of Wisconsin and his Ph.D. from the State University of New York at Stony Brook. He was on the faculty in the Department of Psychology at Indiana University from 1976 to 1986 before moving to Virginia. He was a member of the Psychopathology and Clinical Biology Research Review Committee at NIMH from 1985 to 1989 and served as Associate Editor of the *Journal of Abnormal Psychology* from 1989 to 1993. In 1993 he was elected president of the Society for a Science of Clinical Psychology. His research has been concerned primarily with the role of cognitive and emotional factors in psychopathology, especially schizophrenia. His previous books include *Schizophrenia* (1980), written with John Neale, *Case studies in abnormal psychology* (3rd ed., 1991), written with John Neale and Gerald Davison, and *Delusional beliefs* (1988), edited with Brendan Maher.

Robert E. Emery (left) is Professor of Psychology and Director of Clinical Training at the University of Virginia. He also is an associate faculty member of the Institute of Law, Psychiatry, and Public Policy at the university. He received a B.A. from Brown University in 1974 and a Ph.D. from SUNY at Stony Brook in 1982. He is on the editorial boards of seven journals and is a member of the Population and Social Sciences study section of NIMH. His research focuses on family conflict, children's mental health, and associated legal issues. His 1982 *Psychological Bulletin* paper was designated a "Citation Classic" by the Institute for Scientific Information, and a later *Child Development* paper received the Outstanding Research Publication Award from the American Association for Marriage and Family Therapy in 1989. He is the author of over 60 scientific articles and book chapters and two monographs: *Marriage, Divorce, and Children's Adjustment* (1988, Sage Publications) and *Renegotiating Family Relationships: Divorce, Child Custody, and Mediation* (1994, Guilford Press).

Abnormal Psychology

1

Examples and Definitions of Abnormal Behavior

Mental disorders touch every realm of human experience. They can disrupt the way people think, the way they feel, and the way they behave. Ultimately, they affect relationships with other people. It would be surprising if you hadn't already heard about most of the problems that will be addressed in this book, such as depression, alcoholism, and schizophrenia. In fact, you are likely to know someone—a friend or family member—who has struggled with one of these disorders. One national study begun by the President's Commission on Mental Health found that, during a specific 12-month period, one out of every five Americans exhibited active symptoms of at least one mental disorder. Almost one in three of the 20,000 men and women who were interviewed had experienced at least one kind of mental disorder at some point during their lives (Robins, Locke, & Regier, 1991). The purpose of this book is to help you become familiar with the nature of these disorders and the various ways in which psychologists are advancing knowledge of their causes and treatment.

Abnormal Psychology: An Overview

Psychology is the scientific study of behavior, cognition, and emotion. Since the late nineteenth century, psychologists have generated an extensive body of knowledge that is concerned with perception, motivation, learning, memory, problem solving, attitudes, emotions, and language, to name only a few of the most general issues that have been studied. Psychologists have also conducted research on brain mechanisms and the physiological underpinnings of these phenomena, as well as on the societal and environmental factors that influence each realm of behavior. Developmental psychologists have traced the growth of factors such as cognitive abilities, emotional responses, and personality traits from infancy to old age. Comparative psychologists have examined the same, or analogous, phenomena in other species, placing human behavior in evolutionary perspective. Taken collectively, this body of knowledge—including the research tools by which knowledge has been generated and the concepts

that have guided the search—is referred to as *psychological science*. That base of knowledge sheds crucial light on the problems that are included under the general heading of mental disorders. **Abnormal psychology** is the application of psychological science to the study of mental disorders.

Psychologists who treat people with mental disorders are often trained according to the **scientist-practitioner model,** which emphasizes the integration of science and practice (Shakow, 1960; Barlow, Hayes, & Nelson, 1984; Belar & Perry, 1992). Scientist-practitioners operate simultaneously as behavioral scientists and practicing clinicians. These are two aspects of the same professional role, regardless of whether the person happens to be doing applied clinical work—assessment and therapy with a client— or research on abnormal behavior (McFall, 1991). The way in which psychologists collect information about a clinical problem is guided by scientific principles. Hypotheses about the causes of the problem, even at the level of the individual client, are based on psychological science, and they are formulated in a testable fashion. In fact, the treatment process parallels the scientific process. Assessment leads to the formulation of a hypothesis, interventions are implemented based on that hypothesis, and the validity of the hypothesis is tested by the success or failure of the treatment. Moreover, most of the important scientific advances in abnormal psychology have been made by researchers who are working directly with clinical problems—people who are intimately familiar with the signs and symptoms of psychopathology and who simultaneously bring to bear the attitudes and methods of scientific inquiry.

We believe that the scientist-practitioner model of training should be applied to the study of abnormal psychology. Descriptions of real clinical problems must be integrated with discussions of more abstract issues. Students should be introduced to the study of abnormal psychology by learning about specific cases—people whose efforts to grapple with various behavioral, emotional, and mental difficulties bring the issues of the field to life. In this way, we hope to convey to our readers our own enthusiasm for this fascinating field.

Case studies are a useful way to raise issues and generate hypotheses, but they are only a beginning. Careful observations of the person's behaviors and the social context in which they appear *must* be followed by the formulation of testable hypotheses that can be evaluated using scientific methods. We discuss the process of scientific research throughout this book. Each chapter contains a featured discussion that will examine a special methodological issue with which people who specialize in the study of abnormal psychology must be concerned. Taken as a whole, this collection of methodological notes will help you appreciate the challenges faced by investigators who set out to test hypotheses

regarding various types of abnormal behavior.

Before we begin our first case study, we need to define a few terms. Many forms of training prepare people to provide professional assistance to those who suffer from mental disorders. The two professional groups that are mentioned in the cases in this chapter are clinical psychologists and psychiatrists. **Clinical psychology** is a field that is concerned with the application of psychological science to the assessment and treatment of mental disorders (APA, 1991). A clinical psychologist typically completes 5 years of graduate study in a department of psychology, as well as a one-year internship, before receiving a doctoral degree.[†] **Psychiatry** is the branch of medicine that is concerned with the study and treatment of mental disorders. Psychiatrists complete the normal sequence of course work and internship training in a medical school (usually 4 years) before going on to receive specialized residency training (another 4 years) that is focused on abnormal behavior. By virtue of their medical training, psychiatrists are licensed to practice medicine and are therefore able to prescribe medication. Most psychiatrists are also trained in the use of psychosocial intervention methods. The distinctions between clinical psychology and psychiatry have evolved gradually over the past 100 years, and it is likely that they will continue to evolve in the future (see Further Thoughts)[††].

Psychosis is a general term that refers to several types of severe mental disorder in which the person is considered to be out of contact

▲ **Many Americans, both past and present, have experienced some type of mental disorder. For example, Abraham Lincoln suffered episodes of severe depression. Awareness of the prevalence of emotional problems can help reduce the stigma associated with mental illness.**

[†] Within clinical psychology, there are two primary types of clinical training programs. One course of study, which leads to the Ph.D. degree (doctor of philosophy), involves a traditional sequence of graduate training lasting 4 or 5 years with a serious emphasis on research methods. The other approach to training, which culminates in a Psy.D. degree (doctor of psychology), also requires 4 or 5 years of graduate study, but it places greater emphasis on practical skills of assessment and treatment and does not require that the student conduct an independent research project for the dissertation.

[††] *Social work* is a third major profession that is concerned with helping people achieve an effective level of psychosocial functioning (Hopps & Pinderhughes, 1987). Most practicing social workers have a Master's degree in social work. In contrast to psychology and psychiatry, social work is based less on a body of scientific knowledge than on a commitment to action. The practice of social work encompasses a wide range of settings, from courts and prisons to schools, hospitals, and many other social service agencies. The emphasis in this profession tends to be on social and cultural factors, such as the effects of poverty on availability of educational and health services, rather than individual differences in personality or psychopathology. Psychiatric social workers receive training that is specialized in the treatment of mental health problems.

Legal Decisions and the Mental Health Professions

A profession is largely defined in terms of what its members do. In that sense, the mental health professions are quite similar to one another, and it is not surprising that they are often confused by the public. Clinical psychologists, psychiatrists, and social workers can all be trained to conduct psychotherapy. Some members of all three professions are actively involved in research; others become administrators in hospitals and clinics. All are licensed in their own specialties by state boards of examiners. Professions evolve, and the boundaries among them change as a function of technological advancement (such as the discovery of antipsychotic drugs), economic pressures (such as decisions by insurance companies regarding which procedures and professions will be reimbursed), legislative action, and courtroom decisions.

This has been particularly true in the field of mental health, where enormous changes have taken place over the past few decades (Reisman, 1991). Two landmark court decisions in the early 1970s, *Blue Shield of Virginia v. McCready* and *Wyatt v.*

Stickney, held that licensed clinical psychologists and social workers should be able to treat patients without the supervision of a psychiatrist. Perhaps most importantly, they ruled that these professionals were entitled to receive payments for their services from insurance companies. This ruling essentially established the legal right of patients to freedom of choice in selecting their own practitioners. In 1979, California passed a law authorizing clinical psychologists to admit patients to hospitals. Those professional privileges have subsequently been upheld by additional court rulings. At the present, some clinical psychologists are pursuing the right to prescribe medication (DeLeon, Fox, & Graham, 1991). Decisions regarding these issues all have a dramatic impact on the boundaries that separate the mental health professions. The ongoing conflict over the containment of health care costs suggests that debates over the rights and privileges of patients and their therapists will intensify in the coming years. It is therefore difficult to say with any certainty that the professions can be easily distinguished on the basis of what they do. ■

with reality.[†] There are three main types of *psychotic symptoms:* delusions, hallucinations, and disorganized speech. An idiosyncratic belief—one not shared by other members of the society—that is rigidly held in spite of its preposterous nature is known as a *delusion*. A perceptual experience in the absence of external stimulation—such as hearing voices that are not really there—is called a *hallucination*. Severe disruptions of verbal communication are called *disorganized speech*, or *formal thought disorder*. This symptom involves the form of the person's speech—the way in which a thought is expressed—rather than the content of the speech. Judgments regarding the presence of disorganized speech depend on the

listener's sense that a person's speech is exceedingly vague or difficult to understand.

In the following pages, we will describe four individuals whose behavior would be considered abnormal by mental health professionals. The problems experienced by these people are all examples of **psychopathology,** which, literally translated, means "pathology of the mind," and is generally used as a term to describe abnormal behavior. A *psychopathologist* is a person who studies psychopathology. This term can apply to people with various types of professional training, including psychologists, psychiatrists, and social workers.

[†] Another term that is often used to describe abnormal behavior is *insanity*, which does not refer to any specific type of psychopathology. This is actually a legal term that refers to judgments about whether or not a person should be held responsible for criminal behavior if he or she is also mentally disturbed (see Chapter 17).

Conceptualizing Psychopathology

The cases in this chapter illustrate several of the most important forms of abnormal behavior: schizophrenia, eating disorders, alcoholism, and depression. We use these cases to introduce several fundamental concepts and controversies that are addressed later in this book. The cases allow us to consider definitions of abnormal behavior, processes by which abnormal behaviors are classified, and ways in which psy-chopathologists think about factors that cause these disorders.

Our first case raises fundamental questions about the definition of abnormal behavior. What is the basis for the distinction between normal and abnormal behavior? What kinds of problems are associated with abnormal behavior, and in what ways do they affect a person's life?

CASE STUDY

Schizophrenia

Kevin and Joyce Warner (not their real names) had been married for 8 years when they sought help from a psychologist for their marital problems.[†] Joyce was 34 years old, worked full time as a pediatric nurse, and was 6 months pregnant with her first child. Kevin, who was 35 years old, was finishing his third year working as a librarian at a local university. Kevin's job was the most pressing of several issues that were causing problems for the couple. His 4-year contract was about to expire, and it was unlikely that it would be renewed. When he had taken the job, the library had expected that Kevin would soon complete the last hurdle for his Ph.D. in history—his dissertation. Unfortunately, Kevin had made no further progress with his writing. Joyce was extremely worried about what would happen if Kevin lost his job, especially in light of the baby's imminent arrival. The anxiety and frustration had driven Joyce almost over the edge, and she openly wondered if getting pregnant had been a mistake.

Although the Warners had come for couples therapy, the psychologist soon became concerned about certain eccentric aspects of Kevin's behavior. In the first session, Joyce described one recent event that had precipitated a major argument. One day, after eating lunch at work, Kevin had experienced sharp pains in his chest and difficulty breathing. Fearful, he rushed to the emergency room at the hospital where Joyce worked. The physician who

saw Kevin found nothing wrong with him, even after extensive testing. She gave Kevin a few tranquilizers and sent him home to rest. When Joyce arrived home that evening, Kevin told her that he suspected that he had been poisoned at work by his supervisor. He still held this belief.

Kevin's belief about the alleged poisoning raised serious concern in the psychologist's mind about Kevin's mental health. He decided to interview Joyce alone so that he could ask more extensive questions about Kevin's behavior. Joyce acknowledged that the poisoning idea was "crazy." She was not willing, however, to see it as evidence that Kevin had a mental disorder. Joyce had known Kevin for 15 years. As far as she knew, he had never held any strange beliefs before this time, and he had never taken hallucinogenic drugs or smoked marijuana. Joyce said that Kevin had always been "a thoughtful and unusually sensitive guy." She claimed that other people liked his sensitivity too. When pressed for specifics, however, she admitted that Kevin had never had any really close friends of his own (other than their relationship). Joyce did not seem to attach a great deal of significance to Kevin's unusual belief. She was more preoccupied with the couple's present financial concerns and insisted that it was time for Kevin to "face reality." She was tired of babying him.

Kevin's condition deteriorated noticeably over the next few weeks. He became extremely withdrawn,

---

[†] Throughout this text we use fictitious names to protect the identities of the people involved.

frequently sitting alone in a darkened room after dinner, and going to bed much earlier than usual. On several occasions, he told her that he felt as if he had "lost pieces of his thinking." It wasn't that his memory was failing, but rather he felt a sensation as though parts of his brain were shut off.

Kevin's problems at work also grew worse. His supervisor informed Kevin that his contract would definitely not be renewed. Joyce exploded when Kevin indifferently told her the bad news. His apparent lack of concern was especially annoying. She called Kevin's supervisor, who confirmed the news. In fact, he told Joyce that Kevin's performance had become so erratic that continuation through the end of the year, when his original contract expired, could no longer be certain. Kevin was physically present at the library, but he was only completing a few hours of work each day. He sometimes spent long periods of time just sitting at his desk and staring off into space, and was sometimes heard mumbling softly to himself.

Kevin's speech was quite odd during the next therapy session. He would sometimes start to speak, drift off into silence for 5 or 10 seconds, then reestablish eye contact with a bewildered smile and a shrug of his shoulders. He had apparently lost his train of thought completely. His answers to questions were often off the point, and when he did string together several sentences, their meaning was sometimes obscure. For example, at one point during the session, the psychologist asked Kevin if he planned to appeal his supervisor's decision. Kevin said:

> I'm feeling pressured, like I'm lost and can't quite get here. But I need more time to explore the deeper side. Like in art. What you see on the surface is much richer when you look closely. I'm like that. An intuitive person. I can't relate in a linear way, and when people expect that from me, I get confused.

Joyce also explained that, despite her efforts to avoid the topic, Kevin's strange belief about poisoning had expanded. The Warners had recently received a letter from Kevin's mother, who lived in another city 200 miles away. She had become ill after going out for dinner one night, and mentioned that she must have eaten something that made her sick.

After reading the letter, Kevin told Joyce that he thought that his supervisor had tried to poison his mother too.

When questioned about this new incident, Kevin launched into a long, rambling story. He said that his supervisor was a Vietnam veteran, but he had refused to talk with Kevin about his years in the service. Kevin suspected that this was because the supervisor had been a member of army intelligence. Perhaps he still was a member of some secret organization. Kevin suggested that an operative from this organization had been sent by his supervisor to poison his mother. Kevin thought that he and Joyce also were in danger so he was guarding vigilantly against possible threats. He was particularly wary around men who were about his supervisor's age, because they too might be Vietnam veterans. Kevin said he also had some concerns about Asians, but would not specify these worries in more detail. He said that he knew many more things about "what was really going on," but he was not ready to share them.

Kevin's bizarre beliefs and his disorganized behavior convinced the psychologist that he needed to be hospitalized. Joyce reluctantly agreed that this was the most appropriate course of action. She had run out of alternatives. Arrangements were made to have Kevin admitted to a private psychiatric facility, where the psychiatrist prescribed haloperidol (Haldol), a type of antipsychotic medication. Kevin seemed to respond positively to the drug, because he soon stopped talking about plots and poisoning—but he remained withdrawn and uncommunicative. He said that he felt emotionally numb. After 3 weeks of treatment, Kevin's psychiatrist thought that he had improved significantly. Kevin was discharged from the hospital in time for the birth of their baby girl. Unfortunately, when the couple returned to consult with the psychologist, Kevin's adjustment was still a major concern. He did not talk with Joyce about the poisonings, but she noticed that he remained withdrawn and showed few emotions, even toward the baby.

When the psychologist questioned Kevin in detail, he admitted reluctantly that he still believed that he had been poisoned. Slowly, he revealed more of the plot. Immediately after admission to the hospital, Kevin had decided that his psychiatrist, who happened to be from Korea, could not be trusted.

Kevin was sure that he too was working for army intelligence, or perhaps for a counterintelligence operation. Kevin believed that he was being interrogated by this clever psychiatrist, so he had "played dumb." He did not discuss the suspected poisonings or the secret organization that had planned them. Whenever he could get away with it, Kevin simply pretended to take his medication. He thought that it was either poison or truth serum. When a nurse gave him a pill, he would hide it under his tongue, and would later flush it down a toilet.

Kevin was admitted to a different psychiatric hospital soon after it became apparent that his paranoid beliefs had expanded. This time, he was given intramuscular injections of antipsychotic medication in order to be sure that the medicine was actually taken. Kevin improved considerably after several weeks in the hospital. He acknowledged that he had experienced paranoid thoughts. Although he still felt suspicious from time to time, wondering whether the plot had actually been real, he recognized that it could not really have happened, and he spent less and less time thinking about it.

Kevin also described how he had been feeling between the two hospitalizations. He had believed that he was being tested. A part of the test was that many things were the opposite of what they seemed to be. For example, he had thought that his daughter's baptism was a ritual that could end in his excommunication from the church if he failed the test. Kevin did not know how to explain the test in more detail, except that it had something to do with his being "unworthy." Kevin could not say exactly how the poisoning and the testing fit together, but he knew that they were somehow related. As he spoke about his delusions, Kevin grew awkward and uncertain. He said that it frightened him that he had believed such things, and he feared that the beliefs might overwhelm him again. ■

Descriptive Psychopathology

The situation described in this case raises several fundamental questions about abnormal behavior. One of the most difficult issues in the field centers on the processes by which mental disorders are identified. Once Kevin's problems came to the attention of a mental health professional, could he have been tested in some way to confirm the presence or absence of a mental disorder?

At the present time, psychopathology is defined in terms of signs and symptoms rather than inferred causes. This approach is sometimes called *descriptive psychopathology*. Psychologists and psychiatrists do not have laboratory tests that can be used to confirm definitively the presence of psychopathology because the processes that are responsible for mental disorders have not yet been discovered. Unlike specialists in other areas of medicine where many specific disease mechanisms have been discovered by advances in the biological sciences, psychologists and psychiatrists cannot test for the presence of a viral infection or a brain lesion or a genetic defect to confirm a diagnosis of mental disorder. Clinical psychologists must still depend on their observations of the person's behavior and descriptions of personal experience.

Is it possible to move beyond our current dependence on descriptive definitions of psychopathology? Will we someday have valid tests that can be used to establish independently the presence of a mental disorder? If we do, what form might these tests take? The answers to these questions are being sought in many kinds of research studies that will be discussed throughout this book.

Given this focus, mental disorders are typically defined by a *set* of characteristic features. A group of symptoms that appear together and are assumed to represent a specific type of disorder is referred to as a **syndrome.** One problematic behavior is seldom necessary or sufficient to establish a diagnosis. The primary consideration in Kevin's case was his

▼ Clinical psychologists perform many roles. Some provide direct clinical services. Many are involved in research, teaching, and various administrative activities.

▲ In the movie *The Fisher King,* actor Robin Williams played a man with schizophrenia. To be diagnosed with a disorder such as schizophrenia, an individual must exhibit a set of symptoms, which are referred to as a syndrome.

paranoid delusion. Additional problems included his peculiar and occasionally difficult-to-understand patterns of speech, and his flat emotional responses. These are all symptoms of the disorder known as *schizophrenia*. Each symptom is taken to be a fallible, or imperfect, indicator of the presence of the disorder. The significance of any specific feature depends on whether the person also exhibits additional behaviors that are characteristic of a particular disorder. A person must usually exhibit more than one symptom to be diagnosed as having a particular disorder.

The duration of a person's symptoms is also important. Mental disorders are defined in terms of *persistent* maladaptive behaviors. Many unusual behaviors and inexplicable experiences are short-lived; if we ignore them, they go away. Unfortunately, some forms of problematic behavior are not transient, and they eventually interfere with the person's social and occupational functioning. In Kevin's case, he had become completely preoccupied with his suspicions about poison. Joyce tried for several weeks to ignore certain aspects of Kevin's behavior, especially his delusional beliefs. She didn't want to think about the possibility that his behavior was abnormal, and instead chose to explain his problems in terms of lack of maturity or lack of motivation. But as the problems accumulated, she finally decided to seek professional help. The magnitude of Kevin's problem was measured, in large part, by its persistence, and by the cumulative disruption it caused at work and in the family.

DEFINING ABNORMAL BEHAVIOR

Why do we consider Kevin's behavior to be abnormal? Many attempts have been made to define abnormal behavior, but none is entirely satisfactory. No one has been able to provide a consistent definition that easily accounts for all situations in which the concept is invoked (Gorenstein, 1992).

One approach to the definition of abnormal behavior places principal emphasis on the individual's experience of personal distress. We might say that abnormal behavior is defined in terms of subjective discomfort that leads the person to seek help from a mental health professional. This definition is fraught with problems, however. Kevin's case illustrates one of the major reasons that this approach does not work. Prior to his second hospitalization, Kevin was unable or unwilling to appreciate the extent of his problem or the impact his behavior had on other people. A psychologist would say that he did not have *insight* regarding his disorder (Markova & Berrios, 1992). The discomfort was primarily experienced by Joyce, and she had also attempted for many weeks to deny the nature of the problem. It would be useless to adopt a definition that only considered Kevin's behavior to be abnormal after he had been successfully treated.

Another approach is to define abnormal behavior in terms of statistical norms—the relative frequency of a specific condition in the general population. By this definition, people with unusually high levels of anxiety or depression would be considered abnormal because their experience deviates from the expected norm. Kevin's paranoid beliefs would be defined as pathological because they are idiosyncratic. Mental disorders are, in fact, defined in terms of experiences that most people do not have.

This approach, however, does not specify *how* unusual the behavior must be before it is considered abnormal. Some conditions that are typically considered to be forms of psychopathology are extremely rare. For example, *gender identity disorder*, the belief that one is a member of the opposite sex trapped in the wrong body, affects less than one person out of every 30,000. In contrast, other disorders are much more common. In the United States, major depression affects one out of every 20 women, and alcoholism affects at least one out of every 10 men (Robins, Locke, & Regier, 1991).

Another weakness of the statistical approach

to defining abnormal behavior is that it does not distinguish between deviations that are harmful and those that are not. Many rare behaviors are not pathological. Some "abnormal" qualities have relatively little impact on a person's adjustment. Examples are being extremely pragmatic or unusually talkative. Other abnormal characteristics, such as exceptional intellectual, artistic, or athletic abilities, may actually confer an advantage on the individual. For these reasons, the simple fact that a behavior is statistically rare cannot be used to define psychopathology.

The most important consideration in deciding whether a behavior is abnormal is its impact on the person's ability to function. Does the behavior produce a disadvantage? What kinds of disadvantages or harmful effects does it cause? British psychiatrist R.E. Kendell (1975) has argued that behaviors should be considered abnormal, or a form of mental illness, if they confer upon the individual a biological disadvantage—specifically, reduced fertility or increased mortality. By this definition, schizophrenia would be considered to be a mental disorder because research studies have shown that people with this condition are much less likely to have children than are other adults and because schizophrenic patients are much more likely to commit suicide.

Kendell's definition is relatively restrictive, however, because it would exclude many conditions, such as *phobias*, or extreme, circumscribed fears, that are typically considered to be forms of abnormal behavior but are not associated with a clear biological disadvantage. Therefore, in thinking about the harmful consequences of abnormal behaviors, most mental health professionals include personal discomfort as well as negative effects on the person's social functioning.

DSM IV DEFINITION
The definition of abnormal behavior presented in the official *Diagnostic and Statistical Manual of Mental Disorders* published by the American Psychiatric Association, currently in its fourth edition (DSM-IV, APA, 1994), incorporates many of the factors that we have discussed. This definition is summarized in Table 1–1. It places primary emphasis on the consequences of certain behavioral syndromes. According to this definition, mental disorders are defined by clusters of persistent, maladaptive behaviors that are associated with personal distress, such as anxiety or

depression, or with an impairment in social functioning, such as job performance or personal relationships. The official definition therefore recognizes the concept of disadvantage, but it does not confine this consideration solely to biological functions.

In an attempt to avoid becoming a vehicle for social regulation, the DSM-IV definition excludes voluntary behaviors, as well as beliefs and actions that are shared by religious, political, or sexual minority groups. In the 1930s, for example, participants in the Dada movement in the arts deliberately performed bizarre acts that were designed to provoke other members of society. In the 1960s, members of the Yippie Party intentionally engaged in disruptive behaviors such as throwing money off the balcony at a stock exchange. Their purpose was to challenge traditional values. These were certainly, by conventional standards, maladaptive behaviors that could result in social impairment if those involved had been legally prosecuted, but they were voluntary artistic and political gestures. Nothing would be gained by confusing this kind of behavior with psychopathology.

In actual practice, abnormal behavior is defined in terms of an official diagnostic system. Mental health, like medicine, is an applied rather than a theoretical field. It draws on knowledge from research in the psychological and biological sciences in an effort to help people whose behavior is disordered. Mental disorders are, in a real sense, those problems with which mental health professionals attempt to deal. As their activities and explanatory concepts expand, so does the list of abnormal behaviors. The practical boundaries of abnormal behavior are defined by the list of disorders that is included in the official *Diagnostic and Statistical Manual of Mental Disorders*. Table 1–2 lists the major categories in that manual. The DSM-IV thus provides another answer to our question as to why Kevin's behavior would be considered abnormal: He would be considered to be exhibiting abnormal behavior because his experiences fit the

▲ Abnormal behavior is not defined simply in terms of nonconforming behavior or appearance. A "punk appearance" is an example of social deviance flouting social norms—not a form of abnormal behavior.

TABLE 1-1

Summary of the DSM-IV Definition of Mental Disorders

Defining Characteristics

A behavioral or psychological syndrome (groups of associated features) that is associated with:
1. Present distress (painful symptoms), or
2. Disability (impairment in one or more important areas of functioning), or with
3. A significantly increased risk of suffering death, pain, disability, or an important loss of freedom

Conditions That Are Excluded from Consideration

This syndrome or pattern must not be merely:
1. An expectable and culturally sanctioned response to a particular event (such as the death of a loved one)
2. Deviant behavior (such as the actions of political, religious, or sexual minorities)
3. Conflicts that are between the individual and society (such as voluntary efforts to express individuality)

---

description of schizophrenia, which is one of the officially recognized forms of mental disorder.

The process by which the *Diagnostic and Statistical Manual* is constructed and revised is necessarily influenced by cultural and political considerations. The impact of particular behaviors and experiences on an individual's adjustment will, of course, depend on the culture in which the person lives. For example, a woman who grew up in a society that discouraged female sexuality might not be distressed or impaired by the absence of orgasmic responses. According to DSM-IV, she would not be considered to have a sexual problem. Therefore this definition of abnormal behavior is not culturally universal and might lead us to consider a particular pattern of behavior to be abnormal in one society and not in another.

There have been many instances in which political groups outside the scientific community have brought pressure to bear on decisions shaping the diagnostic manual. For example, feminist organizations have expressed great concern over the inclusion of *premenstrual dysphoric disorder* in DSM-IV, because they are concerned about the implications of labeling women who have these problems as mentally ill. In a compromise struck by APA's committee on DSM-IV, premenstrual dysphoric disorder appears in an appendix for disorders recommended for further study. These deliberations are a reflection of the practical nature of the manual and of the health-related professions. Value judgments

---

TABLE 1-2

Major Types of Mental Disorders Listed in DSM-IV

Anxiety disorders
Such as phobias and obsessive-compulsive disorder

Schizophrenic disorders

Mood disorders
Such as depression and mania

Sexual disorders
Such as inhibited orgasm and fetishism

Personality disorders
Such as paranoid, borderline, and antisocial types

Eating disorders
Such as bulimia nervosa

Dissociative disorders
Such as dissociative identity disorder (multiple personality)

Substance use disorders
Such as alcoholism

Disorders first evident during childhood and adolescence
Such as attention deficit/hyperactivity disorder and autistic disorder

are an inherent part of any attempt to define disease (Sedgwick, 1981).

Having introduced many of the issues that are involved in the definition of abnormal behavior, we now turn to another clinical example. The woman in our second case study, Mary Childress, suffered from a serious eating disorder known as *bulimia nervosa*. Her problems raise additional questions about the definition of abnormal behavior. Consider the defining characteristics of mental disorders that are listed in Table 1–1. As you are reading the next case, ask yourself about the impact of Mary's eating disorder on her subjective experience and social adjustment. In what ways are these consequences similar to those seen in Kevin Warner's case? How are they different? This case will also be used to introduce another important concept associated with the way that we think about abnormal behavior. How can we identify the boundary between normal and abnormal behavior? Is there an obvious distinction between eating patterns that are considered to be part of a mental disorder and those that are not? Or is there a gradual progression from one end of a continuum to the other, with each step fading gradually into the next?

CASE STUDY

Eating Disorder

Mary Childress was, in most respects, a typical 18-year-old sophomore at a large state university. She was popular with other students and a relatively good student, in spite of the fact that she spent relatively little time studying. She and her boyfriend had been dating for about 2 years. They got along well, cared about each other very much, and planned to get married after they finished college. Everything about Mary's life was relatively normal except for her bingeing and purging.

Mary's eating patterns were wildly erratic. She preferred to skip breakfast entirely, and often missed lunch as well. By the middle of the afternoon, she could no longer ignore the hunger pangs. At that point, on two or three days out of the week, Mary would drive her car to the drive-in window of a fast food restaurant. Her typical order included three or four double cheeseburgers, several orders of french fries, and a large milk shake (or maybe two). Then she binged, devouring all the food as she drove around town by herself. Later she would go to a private bathroom, where she wouldn't be seen by anyone else, and purge the food from her stomach by vomiting. Afterwards, she returned to her room feeling angry, frustrated, and ashamed.

Mary was 5'5" tall and weighed 110 pounds. She was neither fat nor thin, but she believed that her body was unattractive, especially her thighs and hips. She was extremely critical of herself and had worried about her weight for many years. Her weight fluctuated quite a bit, from a low of 97 pounds when she was a senior in high school to a high of 125 during her first year at the university. Her mother was a "full-figured" woman and bought most of her clothes at a special store. Mary swore to herself at an early age that she would never let herself gain as much weight as her mother had.

Purging had originally seemed like an ideal solution to the problem of weight control. You could eat whatever you wanted and quickly get rid of it so you wouldn't get fat. Unfortunately, the vomiting became a vicious trap. Disgusted by her own behavior, Mary often promised herself that she would never binge and purge again, but she couldn't stop the cycle.

For the past year, Mary had been vomiting at least once almost every day and occasionally as many as three or four times. The impulse to purge was very strong. Mary felt bloated after having only a bowl of cereal and a glass of orange juice. If she ate a sandwich and drank a diet soda, she began to ruminate about what she had eaten, thinking "I've got to get rid of that!" Before long, she usually found a bathroom and threw up. Her excessive binges were less frequent than the vomiting. Four or five times a week, she experienced an overwhelming urge to eat forbidden foods, especially fast food. Her initial reaction was usually a short-lived attempt to resist the impulse. Then she would space out or "go into a zone," becoming only vaguely aware of what she was doing and feeling. In the midst of a serious binge, Mary felt completely helpless and unable to control what she was doing. When she first started to binge and purge, Mary had to stick her fingers down her throat to make herself vomit. Now, 3 years after she began experimenting with this pattern of eating, she could vomit without using her fingers.

There weren't any obvious physical signs that would alert someone else to Mary's eating problems, but the vomiting had begun to wreak havoc with her body, especially her digestive system. She had suffered severe throat infections and frequent intense stomach pains. Her dentist had noticed problems beginning to develop with her teeth and gums, undoubtedly a consequence of constant exposure to strong stomach acids.

Mary's attitudes toward nutrition and health were irrational. Although she sometimes ate 10 or 12 double cheeseburgers a day, Mary insisted that she hated junk food, and she considered herself to be a vegetarian. The meat that she ate didn't count, she reasoned, because she seldom kept it down. For someone who could be described as totally preoccupied with food, she gave little thought to its consumption, never planning her meals. Mary was extremely concerned about the health consequences of obesity. She could cite detailed statistics regarding the increased risk for heart disease that are associated with every additional 5 pounds that a person gains over her ideal body weight. Of course, the physical consequences of repeated bingeing and purging are infinitely more severe than those associated with modest weight gain, but this irony was lost on Mary.

Her eating problem started to develop when Mary was 15. She had been seriously involved in gymnastics for several years but eventually developed a knee condition that forced her to give up the sport. She gained a few pounds in the next month or two and decided to lose weight by dieting. Buoyed by unrealistic expectations about the immediate, positive benefits of a diet that she had seen advertised on television, Mary initially adhered rigidly

to its recommended regimen. Six months later, after three of these fad diets had failed, she started throwing up as a way to control her intake of food.

Then her father got sick. He was diagnosed with bone cancer when she was a junior in high school (only a couple of months after she had starting purging), and he died the next year. Everyone in the family was devastated. Mary's mother became seriously depressed. Her brother dropped out of high school after his sophomore year and continued living at home. Mary's eating problems multiplied. Her grades suffered, but she managed to maintain an adequate record through the remainder of her senior year and graduate, gaining admission to the state university.

Mary looked forward to leaving home and starting over again at the university, but her problem followed her. She felt guilty and ashamed about her eating problems. She was much too embarrassed to let anyone else know what she was doing and would never eat more than a few mouthfuls of food in a public place like the dorm cafeteria. Her roommate, Julie, was from a small town on the other side of the state. They got along reasonably well, but Mary managed to conceal her bingeing and purging, thanks in large part to the fact that she was able to bring her own car to campus. The car allowed her to drive away from campus several times a week so that she could binge.

Mary's boyfriend, Tim, was a freshman at a community college in her home town. They saw each other one or two weekends each month, usually when she went home. Tim was completely unaware of Mary's eating problems, and she would do anything to keep him from finding out. Mary and Tim had been sexually active since shortly after they met, but they had only had intercourse five times, mostly because Mary had a difficult time enjoying sex. She was frightened by her sexual impulses, which often seemed difficult to control, and she worried about what might happen if she ever let herself go completely. Sexual experiences were a source of great conflict to her. She didn't like her own body, but it made her feel good to know that Tim found her desirable. ■

Boundaries of Abnormal Behavior

Mary's case illustrates many of the characteristic features of bulimia nervosa. As in Kevin's case, her behavior could be considered abnormal, not only because it fit the criteria for one of the categories in DSM-IV, but also because it resulted in obvious negative consequences. In this case, the impact of the disorder was greatest in terms of her physical health: Eating disorders can be fatal if they are not properly treated because they affect so many vital organs of the body, including the heart and kidneys. Mary's social functioning and her academic performance were not yet seriously impaired. There are many different ways in which to measure the harmful effects of abnormal behavior.

Mary's case also illustrates the subjective pain that is associated with many types of abnormal behavior. In contrast to the situation described in Kevin's case, Mary was acutely aware of the nature of her disorder. She was frustrated and unhappy. In an attempt to relieve this emotional distress, she entered psychological treatment. Unfortunately, painful emotions associated with mental disorders can also interfere with, or delay, the decision to look for professional help. Guilt, shame, and embarrassment often accompany psychological problems and sometimes make it difficult to confide in another person.

DIMENSIONS VERSUS CATEGORIES

If we accept the argument that Mary's behavior is abnormal, how can we identify the boundaries of this condition? Should we expect to find discrete boundaries? It is relatively easy to describe an obvious or prototypical case of bulimia, where there is no question that the behavior is causing serious problems. There are many borderline cases, however, and borderline cases may outnumber prototypical cases. What if Mary only purged once a month instead of several times each week? What if she binged but didn't purge, and when she binged she didn't eat such large quantities of food? If we assume that there is an eating disorder that Mary either has or does not have, we have adopted a *categorical approach* to classification. But it might be more useful to assume that there is a continuous distribution of uncontrolled eating, with the best description of Mary's behavior lying somewhere along that continuum from normal behavior to com-

plete loss of control. This is known as a *dimensional approach* to classification. The distinction between these approaches is one of the central issues involved in the way we think about abnormal behavior. It is always difficult to identify a clear boundary between normal patterns of behavior and psychopathology.

The choice between the categorical and dimensional approaches carries with it important assumptions about the best way to describe a trait or condition and about the mechanisms by which it might develop. Perhaps the behaviors associated with bulimia are simply an exaggeration of the ways in which most women respond to a culture that places such an incredible emphasis on having a slender figure. They may represent one extreme of a continuum of attitudes and behaviors that are present in most women who are exposed to these values (Yates, 1989). In that sense, the difference between Mary and other women in her dorm may be *quantitative*—one of degree. On the other hand, there may be something about Mary's behavior—her ability to perceive internal cues, including satiety and emotion, or some other mechanism that helps to control appetitive behaviors—that is specifically impaired. In that case, the distinction between Mary and other women may be *qualitative* in nature.

The dimensional and categorical approaches can be combined in the form of a **threshold model** (Gottesman, 1991). According to this approach, the various features of a disorder may be distributed as continuous dimensions. People can presumably exhibit these characteristics in different numbers and combinations and in varying levels of severity without experiencing any adverse impact on their adjustment *until they pass*

▲ This young dancer suffers from an eating disorder. Some experts maintain that the differences between abnormal and normal behavior are essentially differences in degree; that is, quantitative differences.

a critical threshold. Beyond that level, there is presumably a dramatic increase in the number of problems that they encounter. A diagnosis would be assigned only above the threshold, even though the features themselves are continuously distributed.

The DSM-IV follows the categorical approach to classification. Each disorder is defined in terms of specific diagnostic criteria, and the dividing line between normal and abnormal is clearly identified. The clinician's job, in assigning a diagnosis, is to make a dichotomous decision—to determine whether a particular individual fits the category, not to determine how much or to what degree the person possesses a particular characteristic. In establishing their diagnostic cutoff points, the committees that wrote DSM-IV have obviously made somewhat arbitrary decisions. We will discuss the relative merits of the categorical and dimensional approaches to classification in Chapter 4.

EPIDEMIOLOGY

Many important decisions about mental disorders are based on data regarding the frequency with which these disorders occur. With regard to bulimia nervosa, data obtained in surveys and community-based interview studies indicate that perhaps as many as 40 percent of normal-weight college women consider themselves to be fat. Approximately 80 percent report eating episodes that seem beyond their control, and 75 percent have tried dieting. At least 24 percent and perhaps as many as 90 percent, have engaged in binge eating, and 16 percent have purged (Strober, 1991). Only 4 percent, however, would meet the criteria for a diagnosis of bulimia nervosa. These data are the source of considerable concern, especially among those who are responsible for health services on college campuses.

Epidemiology is the scientific study of the frequency and distribution of disorders within a population. Epidemiologists are concerned with questions such as whether the frequency of a disorder has increased or decreased during a particular period of time, whether it is more common in one geographical area than in another, and whether certain types of people—based on factors such as gender, race, and socioeconomic status—are at greater risk for the development of the disorder. Health administrators often use this kind of information to make decisions about the allocation of resources for professional training programs, treatment facilities, and research projects.

Two terms are particularly important in epidemiological research. **Incidence** refers to the number of *new cases* of a disorder that appear in a population during a specific period of time. **Prevalence** refers to the total number of active cases, both old and new, that are present in a population during a specific period of time. The *lifetime prevalence* of a disorder is the total proportion of people in a given population who have been affected by the disorder at some point during their lives.

Epidemiological information can raise interesting questions regarding possible causal mechanisms. Consider the following example (from Gottesman, 1991). Prior to 1940, many people who were admitted to psychiatric hospitals in the southern United States exhibited unusual psychotic symptoms that resembled those seen in schizophrenia. The condition was especially common among poor African-American patients, accounting for 20 percent of black admissions to one mental hospital in North Carolina. Epidemiological research was able to determine that these people were suffering from *pellagra*, a disease that is caused by a vitamin deficiency in people whose diets included relatively large quantities of unprocessed corn. The disease has now been all but eliminated in developed countries through dietary improvements among economically disadvantaged populations.

Astounding breakthroughs like the pellagra example have not yet been made with regard to other types of psychopathology. Some interesting patterns have emerged, however, regarding the frequency of mental disorders. Some disorders, like schizophrenia, show important consistencies in cross-cultural comparisons (see Research Close-up). Others, like bulimia, are more specifically associated with certain demographic, cultural, and socioeconomic conditions.

There are, for example, dramatic differences between women and men in the frequency of eating disorders. Almost 85 to 90 percent of bulimic patients are women (Hsu, 1989). The incidence of bulimia is 5 times higher among university women than among working women, and it is more common among younger women than among older women. Bulimia is relatively rare among African-American women, although it may be increasing among more affluent African Americans who have adopted the attitudes of

Cross-cultural Study of Abnormal Behavior

Some severe forms of psychopathology have been found in virtually every culture that social scientists have studied. One classic paper that supports this conclusion was reported by Jane Murphy (1976), an anthropologist at Harvard University. Murphy studied two groups of non-Western people: the Inuit (or Eskimos) of northwest Alaska and the Yoruba of rural, tropical Nigeria. Murphy lived with each group for several months, talking with them about their lives and observing their everyday behaviors. She became intimately acquainted with their languages and the ways in which they think about problem behaviors. A key informant described for Murphy the life experiences of all 500 people in the Inuit village. Among the Yoruba, most of the data were provided by three native healers.

Murphy discovered that both cultures recognize certain forms of behavior as "being crazy." These behaviors center around aberrant beliefs, feelings, and actions: hearing voices when no one is talking; laughing when there is nothing to laugh at; believing things that are so strange that other people cannot imagine them to be true; talking in strange ways that do not make sense to other people; and behaving in erratic or unpredictable ways. These syndromes bear a striking resemblance to the disorder that is called schizophrenia in DSM-IV. The specific content of hallucinations and delusions varies from one culture to the next, but the underlying processes appear to be the same. Perhaps most important was the observation that the words that the Inuit and Yoruba use to describe "losing one's mind" refer to a set of problematic behaviors rather than to a single problem.

Murphy also noted that members of both groups viewed "crazy behavior" as being quite different from the behaviors associated with being a shaman or spiritual healer. At certain times, the shaman also behaved in unusual ways, such as responding to voices that other people could not hear or speaking in ways that other people did not understand. This distinction is apparently based primarily on the extent to which these behaviors are controlled (turned on and off voluntarily by the person) and utilized for a socially approved purpose, such as attempting to heal a sick person. One Yoruba villager explained, "When the shaman is healing, he is out of his mind, but he is not crazy." Murphy was able to identify 18 Inuit villagers who had served the group as shaman at some point during their lives. They appeared to be a random sample from the entire group of 500 people. None of them was considered to be mentally disturbed by their fellow villagers.

The Inuit and Yoruba have their own hypotheses concerning the origins of mental disorders, which often involve magic. They also have developed special treatment procedures, or native healing rituals, that they use to help people with these disorders. The prevailing attitudes in both groups appeared to be neither entirely positive nor entirely negative. These observations indicate that the ways in which societies respond to psychopathology can vary greatly, even if the basic forms of abnormal behavior with which they are confronted are quite similar.

Murphy's conclusions have been supported by a large-scale epidemiological study of schizophrenia, sponsored by the World Health Organization (WHO) (Jablensky et al., 1992). This study included 1,200 patients who were admitted to psychiatric hospitals in nine countries—Colombia, Czechoslovakia, Denmark, India, Nigeria, Taiwan, Russia, England, and the United States. In each setting, the investigators found patients who exhibited symptoms of schizophrenia. The frequency of this disorder was approximately the same in each location, in spite of obvious cultural contrasts between sites in developing (India, Nigeria) and developed (Denmark, England) countries. As in Murphy's report, the WHO study found some cross-cultural variations with regard to the specific subtypes of schizophrenic symptoms and with regard to the outcome of the disorder 5 years after treatment. Nevertheless, the data support the conclusion that severe forms of mental illness are not limited to Western cultures or developed countries. ■

the dominant culture toward slimness (Dolan, 1991; Hsu, 1989). This pattern suggests that immersion in a particular set of values related to eating and women's appearance is an important ingredient in establishing risk for development of an eating disorder.

TABLE 1–3

Prevalence Rates for Various Mental Disorders

	Women (%)		Men (%)	
	1-year	Lifetime	1-year	Lifetime
Phobic disorder	12.9	17.8	6.3	10.4
Alcohol abuse/dependence	2.2	4.6	11.9	23.8
Major depression	4.0	7.0	1.4	2.6
Antisocial personality	0.4	0.8	2.1	4.5
Obsessive-compulsive disorder	1.9	3.2	1.4	2.0
Panic disorder	1.2	2.1	0.6	1.0
Schizophrenia	1.1	1.7	0.9	1.2
Bipolar mood disorder	0.8	0.9	0.6	0.7

Source: Adapted from L.N. Robins, B.Z. Locke, and D.A. Regier, 1991. An overview of psychiatric disorders in America. Pp. 328-366 in L.N. Robins and D.A. Regier (Eds.), *Psychiatric disorders in America: The Epidemiological Catchment Area Study.* New York: Free Press.

What about the other disorders listed in Table 1–2? How common are these problems? One large-scale epidemiological study, known as the Epidemiologic Catchment Area Study (ECA), was conducted in the 1980s (Robins &

▲ Lee Robins, professor of sociology in psychiatry at Washington University, was the principal investigator in the ECA study, which is the most extensive base of information regarding the prevalence of mental disorders in the United States.

Regier, 1991). Approximately 20,000 people were interviewed in five large metropolitan areas in the United States. Questions were asked pertaining to 30 of the major disorders listed in the DSM. Table 1–3 lists some results from this study. Gender differences are found in many types of mental disorder. Anxiety disorders (phobias and panic) and depression are more common among women. Alcoholism and antisocial personality are more common among men. Other conditions, like schizophrenia and mania, appear with equal frequency in women and men. Patterns of this sort raise interesting questions regarding possible causal mechanisms. What conditions would make women more vulnerable to one kind of disorder and men more vulnerable to another? There are many possibilities, including factors such as hormones, patterns of learning, and social pressures.

Comparisons between *1-year prevalence rates*—the number of people with active symptoms during the 12 months prior to the interview—and lifetime prevalence rates are also interesting. In most cases, the lifetime rates are much higher. This discrepancy reflects the fact that mental disorders are not always chronic conditions. Most people experience periods of remission, in which their symptoms improve, in between active episodes of disorder. Many people recover completely. Therefore, although the relatively high lifetime prevalence rates in Table 1–3 are obviously a source of serious concern, the contrast with 1-year prevalence rates is also an indication that mental disorders are not always enduring.

Causes of Abnormal Behavior

The cases of Kevin Warner and Mary Childress illustrate why it is difficult to define abnormal behavior. They also raise questions about the causes of these problems. Some people may be born with a predisposition to disorder that will emerge later in their lives. Was Kevin genetically vulnerable to schizophrenia? Did Mary possess a genotype associated with obesity? Could it have increased the probability that she would develop an eating disorder?

Traumatic experiences may set the stage for emotional problems. Did the stress of Kevin's

job or Joyce's pregnancy cause Kevin's condition to deteriorate? Was the death of Mary's father responsible for a serious escalation of her eating problems? Finally, what is the role of society in creating psychological problems? Would Mary have begun her frantic efforts to control her weight if our culture didn't place such a high value on thin female figures? These are all questions about the **etiology,** or causes, of psychopathology. Keep these questions in mind as you read the next case study.

Substance Dependence (Alcoholism)

Will Gregory was a 34-year-old salesman who had been separated from his wife, Kathryn, for 1 year. His two children lived with their mother. By the time he finally admitted to himself that he had a drinking problem, Will had a long and painful story to tell. Will grew up in a middle-class family with three sisters. His father, a successful businessman in their small community, focused considerable attention on his son's athletic activities. Many people felt that he put too much pressure on Will, who could never live up to his father's expectations. Will was a gifted athlete, but no matter how successful he was, it was never enough for his father.

Alcohol had been a central part of Will's life for as long as he could remember. When he was a child, his parents had drinks before dinner every night, and their weekends revolved around alcohol. They started drinking cocktails at noon on Saturdays and Sundays. His parents ordinarily did not express affection to Will, but alcohol opened them up. Will remembered that at times his mother gushed over him, while being aloof much of the rest of the time. This confused him as a child. He now realized that she had been drunk. His father's behavior was much less predictable and was the source of considerable pain. When his father was sober, he was quite reserved in his comments to Will. The effects of drinking seemed to depend on the mood of the moment. If Will played well in his most recent game, his father bragged loudly about him. But if Will played poorly, his father had nothing but the harshest criticism after he had been drinking.

When Will started high school, his parents frequently asked him to be the bartender at their parties. Everyone knew that he also mixed drinks for himself, and no one objected. Will's initial response to alcohol was very positive. It made him feel good and eased the tension he felt around his family. After he got a "buzz," he would chat with his parents' friends, who were always eager to hear the local sports hero talk about his latest game. Most of Will's friends were also drinking by their sophomore year. Will drank a bit more than the others, but getting drunk was the norm for his group of friends on weekends.

When Will went to college, he experimented with other drugs, like marijuana and cocaine, but he quickly learned that he preferred alcohol. It was cheaper, it was legal, and, most importantly, it made him feel better than did the other drugs. Will played football his first year of college, but he dropped off the team when he failed to excel. Athletically, he had become a small fish in a much bigger pond. He joined a fraternity with a reputation as a party house, and he soon became one of its most active social members. If anyone wanted to party, Will was always ready. He was still outstanding at getting drunk.

Will and Kathryn met at one of her sorority's parties during their junior year. Although she was a more serious student than Will, Kathryn also enjoyed parties and drinking. They were soon spending all of their free time together, and were married shortly after graduating from college. They continued living in the city where they had attended college and socializing with old friends. Most of the people in this group were heavy weekend drinkers, but Will had become the heaviest. He constantly encouraged his wife and friends to drink, primarily because it made him feel better about his own drinking.

Kathryn quit her job when she became pregnant with their son, who was born when she and Will were both 26 years old. A girl was born 3 years later. By this point, Will's drinking was no longer confined to weekends. After the first baby was born, he had started having a beer regularly after work, saying that it helped him unwind. Within a few months, he was having two or three. As time passed, the beers became martinis. Dinners gradually began to be served at a later hour, as Kathryn waited for Will to unwind. Eventually, Will encouraged Kathryn to eat without him. He would fix a drink and retire to the living room to watch television, asking Kathryn to leave his dinner for later.

Kathryn resented this pattern of isolation, but it was easier to accept it than to argue with Will. He had developed a nasty streak. He sometimes was charming and gregarious when drinking, but he grew increasingly critical with his family and friends. Will's barbs often were delivered in the context of humor, but gradually his remarks became more pointed. They often provoked shocked silence instead of laughter. This distressed Will, who was not really aware of his own anger. He typically dealt with the embarrassment by fixing another drink for himself.

Kathryn eventually confronted Will about his drinking. Her doctor's warnings had persuaded her to stop drinking almost entirely when she was pregnant. She now drank occasionally at parties, but she never got drunk. She wanted to stay in control of herself for the children, and, increasingly, for Will. Kathryn pleaded with him to stop drinking. In order to get her off his back, Will eventually agreed to quit drinking for 2 weeks. Quitting was harder than he thought it would be, but he told Kathryn that this voluntary abstinence proved beyond doubt that he did not have a problem. He even persuaded himself.

After the 2-week layoff, Will immediately went back to drinking. He was actually drinking more than ever, but he started concealing some of it. When he arrived home from work, he would fix only one martini, but he now kept a second bottle hidden in the bathroom. He would have his second or third "very dry martini" there, by himself. This struck Will as a socially acceptable amount of alcohol, in spite of the need for deception. Many of his friends drank that much without complaint from their spouses. Sometimes, he would allow himself to have a private party, where he might drain the entire pint that he kept hidden. Restocking the bar was not too difficult. He would sneak a new pint home concealed in his briefcase every other day or so. The empty was smuggled out the same way.

Soon after his 2-week period of self-imposed abstinence, Will began drinking at lunch. He felt better about participating in meetings after a drink, thinking that it made him more enthusiastic and sociable. Will's physical appearance was beginning to show the effects of heavy drinking. He told himself that he was in good shape because he remained thin—primarily the result of drinking gin instead of beer and of missing evening meals. Still, many blood vessels in his eyes and nose had burst, and there were heavy bags under his eyes. Will was also having trouble sleeping and getting up in the

morning. Too often to be believed, Kathryn had to call his office to say that he had the flu or had strained his back working in the yard. His boss began to question his productivity and commitment to the job. A couple of close friends raised the issue with Will gently, but he became indignant, insisting that he did not have a problem with alcohol. A negative annual review was followed by a demotion from management to a field sales position. Will was angry when his boss broke the bad news, but he soon learned that the change had one important advantage: Being out of the office made it easier to have a quick drink almost anytime during the day.

Shortly after Will's demotion, Kathryn found his secret bottle. When she confronted him, Will exploded with anger. He remained angry and began to drink openly. He often got visibly drunk in the evenings, and fell asleep on the living room sofa. The children began to ask questions. After 6 months of shouting matches, Will agreed to a trial separation.

For several months after he moved into his own small apartment, Will's drinking improved. When he visited Kathryn and the children during the day on weekends, he was perfectly sober; then he would have several drinks after returning to his lonely apartment later in the evening. He also gave up drinking on weekdays for awhile, restricting himself to two martinis alone in his apartment on weeknights. Will was once again convinced that this proved that he could control his drinking. Things were improving with Kathryn and at work.

The incident that finally led Will to recognize the severity of his drinking problem occurred 1 year after he was separated from Kathryn. Her father died, and Will got so drunk that he missed the funeral. He loved his father-in-law more than his own father. He had missed his chance to share his grief with the rest of the family. For the first time in years, he was overcome with emotion and cried alone for hours. Once again, he had demonstrated that the bottle was more important to him than even his own family. Most painful of all was Will's sudden realization that he had missed more than the funeral. He had missed the last 3 years of his father-in-law's life because he had been drunk whenever they were together. Will finally acknowledged that he was an alcoholic and told Kathryn that he had decided to seek professional help. ■

Integrating Etiology

Will had resisted the label, but those who knew him best agreed that he had become an alcoholic. They did not agree, however, about the origin of his problems. Why did Will go on to develop serious drinking problems when many of his friends, who also drank heavily, did not? Was alcoholism a genetic condition that ran in Will's family? How important was the role played by his parents' behavior? They obviously introduced him to the drug and served as models of how you can incorporate alcohol into your lifestyle. Is it necessary both to have a genetic predisposition and to grow up in an environment that encourages the heavy use of alcohol? Was Will's drinking caused by his father's criticism and impossible expectations? Perhaps the alcohol helped dampen his responses to stress or reduced his self-awareness. He often felt more relaxed and confident after drinking. Was that because of the biological influence of the drug on his brain, or was it because he *expected* that the drug would have that effect? Why did he eventually need to drink more and more alcohol to achieve the same psychological effect? Was this transition affected by changes in his brain chemistry after he had been drinking for many years?

These are the types of questions asked by psychologists and other mental health professionals in their work both as scientists and as practitioners. Once a disorder has been carefully described, the next step for the scientist is to attempt to uncover its cause. Case studies of the sort that you are reading in this chapter do not provide definitive answers (see Research Methods). We can ponder questions about the cause of Will's alcoholism informally, but the scientist must shape each of these queries into a formal hypothesis—a highly specific and testable prediction about cause and effect.

RESEARCH METHODS

Case Studies as Research Tools

One of the oldest methods employed in clinical research is the **case study**, in which a clinician provides a detailed description and analysis of the problems experienced by one particular person. The four cases that appear in this chapter are brief examples of the ways in which this procedure can be employed. Elaborate case studies can provide an exhaustive catalogue of the symptoms that the person displayed, the manner in which these symptoms developed, the developmental and family history that preceded the onset of the disorder, as well as whatever response the person may have shown to treatment efforts. The clinician's theoretical interpretation of the case is supported by selective reference to various facets of the case. At their best, case studies can provide compelling descriptions of mental disorders.

Case studies can be useful in several respects. First, they can provide rich clinical descriptions of disorders. This is especially important for conditions that have not previously received much attention in the literature or for problems that are relatively unusual. Multiple personality disorder and transsexualism are examples of conditions that are so infrequent that it is difficult to find groups of patients for the purpose of research studies. Much of what we know about these problems is based on descriptions of individual patients.

Second, case studies can be used to generate hypotheses. For example, Freud developed his psychoanalytic theory on the basis of extended case studies (see Chapter 2). His compelling descriptions and insightful analyses of the circumstances under which his patients' problems developed helped make his point of view enormously popular during the first half of the twentieth century.

Third, case studies can provide important insights about the nature of mental disorders, especially when special circumstances happen to prevail in combination with the appearance of a disorder. Consider, for example, the case of the Genain quadruplets—four identical sisters who all had symptoms of schizophrenia (Rosenthal et al., 1963). Because the sisters were genetically identical, variations in the severity of their symptoms and the course of their disorders over time could be attributed to environmental factors. A study of triplets by McGuffin, Reveley, and Holland (1982) led to interesting speculation about the diagnostic boundaries between schizophrenia and mania (see Further Thoughts in Chapter 12). Two of the triplets obviously had schizophrenia, but the third had symptoms that were more clearly associated with mood disorders.

Case studies can be a useful tool, but they have several drawbacks and therefore provide only a starting point for scientific investigation. The most obvious limitation of case studies is that they can be viewed from many different perspectives. Will Gregory's problematic drinking, for example, could be interpreted in several ways. You could build a persuasive case to suggest that he drank to reduce awareness of his father's criticism. You could also argue that he drank because he believed that it made him more socially skilled. Another possibility is that his drinking was genetically determined. All these explanations are equally plausible.

The other main limitation of case studies is that it is risky to draw general conclusions about a disorder from a single example. How can we know that this individual is representative of the disorder as a whole? Are his or her experiences typical for people with this disorder? Again, hypotheses generated on the basis of the single case must be tested in research with larger, more representative samples of patients. ■

The etiology of most forms of abnormal behavior is poorly understood. This is true both at the level of the individual and at the level of the disorder as a whole. This textbook cannot provide many unequivocal answers about the causes of abnormal behavior. We hope that you will become intrigued rather than frustrated by this uncertainty. The origins of psychopathology represent a compelling mystery that motivates the search for future knowledge.

NATURE AND NURTURE

Of all of the questions about the cause of abnormal behavior, the **nature–nurture controversy** is perhaps the most longstanding. This debate pits genetic and biological factors against life experiences as causes of abnormal behavior. Those who argue for nature believe that psychopathology is caused by genes, by infectious diseases, by physical injuries, or by malfunctions of the brain or other parts of the nervous system. In all cases, the abnormality presumably resides in the person's physical makeup. Life experiences may shape the development of psychological disorders, but their ultimate cause is biological (McGuffin et al., 1994).

The nurture side of the controversy makes the opposite assumption: Experience is the central cause of abnormal behavior. Proponents of this view often focus on different types of life experiences at different times in development. Some proponents of this perspective emphasize how well or how poorly parents care for children during the first years of life. They suggest that these early experiences mold each individual's personality. Others point to the role of learning throughout life in shaping and maintaining abnormal behavior. Some argue that dysfunctional relationships and societal demands cause people to behave in abnormal ways.

Many scientists have come to believe that the nature–nurture controversy is based on a false distinction between the physical and the psychological worlds. We agree with this conclusion. Nature and nurture are not as different as they may seem at first glance (Plomin, 1990). The mind cannot be separated from the body. In the case of alcoholism, for example, the research evidence suggests that some type of genetic component is associated with the disorder (see Chapter 10). Therefore, nature clearly plays a role in determining who becomes an alcoholic—but no one becomes an alcoholic without drinking. At the very least, the experience of imbibing alcohol is necessary for someone to fulfill their potential to become an alcoholic. Even if genes completely determined who can and who cannot become an alcoholic (and genetic influences are not that powerful), it would be impossible to conceive of alcoholism apart from the combination of nature and nurture.

The dominant perspective on the cause of psychological disorders views abnormal behavior as resulting from a combination of nature and nurture. Typically, this combination is conceptualized so that physical factors form a predisposition or **diathesis.** Some people prefer the term **vulnerability.** A diathesis causes abnormal behavior only when it is combined with a psychological *stress* or challenging experience. This combination of factors is called the **diathesis–stress model.** In Will's case, perhaps he inherited a genetic vulnerability to the effects of alcohol. His inherited predisposition, however, resulted in a serious problem only when combined with parental models and difficult life experiences that pressured him to drink more and more.

The diathesis–stress approach to etiological models is quite flexible. Critics might call it vague. Many types of diathesis–stress models have been proposed for different kinds of abnormal behavior. A diathesis is not necessarily biological in origin, and a stress in not necessarily a psychological factor. For example, it is possible to consider Will's anger and hidden insecurity as a diathesis that caused him to drink heavily. The consumption of large amounts of alcohol, in turn, could be viewed as a physical stressor that eventually resulted in his addiction to the drug. The value of the diathesis-stress approach is that it allows for the integration of biological, psychological, and social factors in the etiology of psychopathology. The ongoing challenge is to identify the exact form of the diathesis and the stress and the specific ways in which they interact. These goals are being pursued actively on many fronts for all the disorders that we discuss throughout this book.

SYSTEMS OF INFLUENCE

The consideration of different levels or systems of influence is another way in which we focus on nature *and* nurture, not nature *or* nurture, in this textbook. Abnormal behavior can be studied on many different levels. Psychobiologists and neuroscientists sometimes study abnormal behavior in terms of the various chemicals in the brain. Clinical psychologists frequently focus on characteristics of the individual, such as the tendency to blame oneself or others for life's problems. Other clinical psychologists empha-

size social contributions to psychopathology, such as the role of social support or community resources in protecting people against the stresses of everyday life.

The study of biological, psychological, and social systems each offers a valuable perspective on understanding abnormal behavior. Will Gregory provides a good example of the contributions of these different levels of conceptualization. Genetic factors may well have predisposed Will toward alcoholism. From a psychological point of view, his parents certainly taught him that drinking was an acceptable way of coping with stress. Alcohol may have provided a welcome escape from his father's harsh criticism and, later in life, from the pressures of work and family responsibilities. From a social perspective, he may have derived crucial expectations about the effects of alcohol from the media and from prevailing community attitudes. Will's heavy drinking therefore cannot be explained by a single biological, psychological, or social factor. His alcoholism probably developed as the result of some combination of all three systems of influence.

In our view, too much time has been spent arguing about which approach to psychopathology is most valuable. Are most disorders psychological in nature? Are they ultimately biological? We believe that the task for scientists and for practitioners is not to decide whether mental disorders are caused by biological or psychological or societal influences. Rather, the task is to uncover how these different levels of influence interact to cause emotional suffering and psychological disorders. The analytic approach that combines these various levels of influence is called the **biopsychosocial model.**

▲ The Nobel Prize-winning author Ernest Hemingway was a chronic alcohol abuser who ended his own life with a shotgun. Uncovering the causes of behaviors such as substance abuse is one of the major challenges facing mental health professionals.

Treatment of Abnormal Behavior

We turn now to the final example of abnormal behavior that will be presented in this chapter. The woman in this case, Gina King, had been seriously depressed at various points in time over a period of several years. Gina's problems illustrate many important features of this common form of psychopathology. We also describe the ways in which the disorder had been treated by two different therapists, one psychiatrist and one psychologist. This case will help you understand the ways in which etiological hypotheses influence treatment decisions. It will also raise issues about the way in which a clinician's experience with different approaches to treatment becomes a source of ideas regarding etiology. As you read this case, ask yourself how the therapists' beliefs about the nature of depression influenced their plans for intervention.

CASE STUDY

Depression

Gina King was a 40-year-old mother of three children. Her 5-year-old daughter and 2-year-old son lived with Gina and her second husband, to whom she had been married for 7 years. She also had a 20-year-old daughter from an earlier marriage. Gina was employed as a secretary in a small insurance office, where she had worked for 18 years.

Although her problems had become more serious in recent years, Gina sometimes felt as though she had been born depressed. She had always lacked self-confidence, even though she had been relatively successful in school. During her first 3 years in high school, Gina was a better-than-average student. She was also a member of the band and a promising member of the track team. Her interest in these activities disappeared gradually prior to her senior year. Music and sports just didn't seem like fun any more, and she withdrew from everything. Her grades fell dramatically. It seemed to her friends and family that she was almost always feeling irritated or down about something. She spent almost all of her time with her boyfriend, whom she married shortly after graduation. This pattern of persistent, mild depression continued for the next few years.

Gina's first episode of severe depression occurred at the time of her divorce, when she was 26 years old. When she married her first husband, Gina loved him dearly. She became pregnant within a year after their marriage. Her husband held construction jobs off and on for the first couple of years of their mar-

riage, but he soon spent more time drinking and less time working. He was an alcoholic, like Gina's father. Gina tried to protect and help him, but her struggles were to no avail. She had not wanted to divorce him. She eventually realized, however, that her only other option was a life of total misery. It was not until after she left her husband that Gina fully realized how angry and unhappy she had been in the marriage.

The separation solved one set of problems, but it introduced another. Among them was Gina's depression, which became much more severe. Instead of being relieved, she felt guilty and miserable over leaving him. She cried constantly and felt more completely alone. During this period she believed that she was an incompetent mother and a terrible person. Gina still did not know how she pulled through that episode of depression. She relied heavily on the help of her mother, her church, and her friends at work.

Gina's mood eventually improved, but she did not recover completely. Lack of self-confidence and feelings of pessimism continued to plague her. She frequently found herself brooding about the failed marriage. Gina experienced additional periods of depression, some more serious than others, in the years prior to her current episode. These episodes did not seem to be tied to any major events in her life. She attributed these distressing times to the chaos of being a single mother, her mistrust of men, and eventually to the awkwardness of dating again.

Eventually, Gina became as depressed as she ever had been in her life. She felt miserable all the time. When she was really down, Gina ate. She gained 30 pounds. Her sleep was disturbed as well. She would wake up in the middle of the night, and typically could not fall back to sleep until daybreak. She spent most of her days feeling exhausted. When she was asked if she had ever contemplated suicide, she rolled her eyes and said that she didn't have time for that luxury. She added seriously that her life was not that bad, at least not yet, and suicide was against her religious beliefs.

Gina felt trapped in her current, miserable life. Her second marriage was nothing like what she had anticipated. Her husband was stable, and that was part of the reason she married him. He was a good provider, but there was little else to their marriage. He spent most evenings in front of the television or in his workshop in the basement. Gina complained that her husband rarely talked with her, they hardly ever went out, and they had no close friends. She often thought about getting divorced again. The only thing that held her back was her children. Her 20-year-old daughter was having chaotic relationships with men. More than once, her daughter accused Gina of having caused all of her problems by divorcing her father. Gina felt terribly guilty about this, and she vowed to herself that she would not make the same mistake twice.

Gina also loved her two younger children dearly, but she often felt overwhelmed by them. Her husband did not help with chores around the house, and Gina felt that she no longer had enough energy to devote to her children. She often screamed at them, although she knew that she needed to be more patient. Gina felt guilty about her loss of control, but she insisted that her ability to cope had reached its limits.

Gina finally decided to talk with her minister about her troubles. At his urging, she worked up the courage to ask her husband to come with her for marriage counseling. He adamantly refused, saying that he would not allow an outsider to pry into his life. Shortly thereafter, Gina read a magazine article about antidepressant medication. The article described a drug called fluoxetine—known commercially as Prozac—as a miracle cure for depression. Gina discussed the article with her minister. He agreed

that the medication seemed worth exploring and gave Gina the name of a psychiatrist.

Gina met with the psychiatrist twice before he prescribed Prozac. The psychiatrist explained to her that depression was caused by a chemical imbalance in the brain that could be corrected by the drug. Her mood should begin to lift after she had taken the drug for a few weeks. The idea that Gina's depression was caused by a chemical imbalance was new and encouraging to her. If that was true, maybe everything was not her fault after all. Gina took the Prozac exactly as prescribed and had a brief visit with the psychiatrist every other week to monitor her progress. During these 15-minute interviews, the psychiatrist asked Gina about her mood and about other symptoms of depression, such as sleeping difficulties and feelings of hopelessness. After a couple of weeks, she noticed that she was sleeping better.

Over the next few months, however, she made little additional progress. She still felt trapped and depressed. The psychiatrist tried two different medications with Gina, but nothing worked better than Prozac. After a few months, the psychiatrist referred her to a psychologist for psychotherapy, which would supplement the medication.

The psychologist agreed that Gina should continue to take her medication, and she should also plan to come for 10 to 20 weekly therapy sessions. For the first several meetings, Gina talked about her problems at great length, especially interpersonal relationships. When they were discussing her divorce, the therapist pointed out that Gina said that she did not want to make a second mistake. Did she believe her divorce was a mistake? This question led Gina to burst into tears. The divorce was not a mistake for her, she said, but it had been a tragedy for her former husband. She had heard from old friends that he was still drinking and was now in very poor health.

The psychologist said that he too was afraid that Gina was making the same mistake twice, but he was primarily concerned about Gina's exaggerated sense of responsibility for other people's feelings. She clung rigidly to the illogical belief that it was her job to make other people happy. This, in his view, was Gina's mistake. The psychologist told her that emotional problems are caused by the ways in which people interpret events in their lives and by the things that they say to themselves about those experiences.

Gina acknowledged that she felt responsible for her husband's happiness. She believed that it was, indeed, her job as a wife and as a Christian. The psychologist responded that it was irrational to insist that someone else must be happy. Ultimately, we can only be responsible for our own feelings.

Over the next several meetings, Gina and her psychologist also talked about her interpretations of daily events. The psychologist asked Gina to keep a diary in which she wrote down things that happened during the day as well as what she was saying to herself about these events. She focused a great deal of attention on events at home, blaming herself, for example, whenever anything negative happened with the children. Much of the discussion in therapy was devoted to helping her question these biased conclusions and developing more positive ways of interpreting her experiences. Gina also tended to think about herself in absolute, unchanging terms. During the course of therapy, she learned to recognize this pattern and to substitute more adaptive views.

Gina and her therapist repeatedly discussed her negatively biased view of the world, and the focus often returned to feelings of responsibility. She described her childhood at some length, noting that she believed it was her responsibility to keep her parents from fighting. She played the mediator, carrying apologies back and forth between her parents. She had a similar role in relation to her father's drinking, helping him keep his drinking a secret from her mother. Gina still felt guilty about that role, even though she was only a child when it happened.

Eventually, Gina began to distinguish her caring feelings from her responsible feelings. Caring feelings involved wanting another person to be happy. It was reasonable to try to help someone to be happy. Responsible feelings, on the other hand, involved insisting that someone else must happy. Since no one could necessarily make someone else happy, it was impossible and irrational to take on this responsibility.

Weekly therapy stopped after 15 sessions, although monthly follow-up sessions continued for a year. Under the psychiatrist's supervision, Gina decreased her Prozac gradually and stopped taking medication altogether after 8 months. By the end of therapy, Gina had lost 10 pounds and was sleeping well. She was still disappointed with her marriage, but she was no longer weighed down by her depression. She was finding ways to be happier with her children and with her friends at work. ∎

Treatment Methods

Gina's case has allowed us to introduce two of the most common forms of treatment for psychopathology: **psychopharmacology** (medication) and **psychotherapy.** It is not unusual for patients to receive medication at the same time that they are engaged in psychotherapy. There are many different approaches to psychotherapy (see Chapter 3). Gina's therapist employed one specific type, which is often referred to as *cognitive therapy*. Cognitive therapists help their patients identify and correct patterns of illogical thinking and maladaptive assumptions. They emphasize replacing self-defeating thoughts with more rational self-statements.

Unfortunately, we cannot assume that everyone who needs treatment gets it. At the beginning of this chapter, we noted that one out of every five Americans exhibited active symptoms of at least one mental disorder during a particular year (Robins & Regier, 1991). That same study also found that only about one out of five people with an active disorder had received treatment for their condition within the past few months. Similar findings have been reported in a more recent survey of 8,000 nationally representative young and middle-aged adults across the United States (Kessler et al., 1994). Many factors may account for this result. Some people who qualified for a formal diagnosis may not have been impaired to such an extent that they were willing to seek treatment. Others may not have recognized their disorder. In some cases, treatment may not have been available, the person may not have had the time or resources to obtain treatment, or the person may have tried treatments in the past that failed. For whatever reason, many people who experience mental disorders do not receive proper treatment.

Much of what we know about psychopathology has been learned in the attempt to help people who are suffering from mental disorders. The connection between etiological speculation and treatment procedures is a two-way street. Theories sometimes spawn new therapies, and successful therapies often spawn new theories.

One classic example of the latter case comes from Freud's experience at the turn of the century with the use of hypnosis, and later free association, to treat patients with a variety of physical and emotional complaints. Some of the patients showed remarkable improvements in their condition. To explain the success of this therapy, Freud developed what is now known as psychoanalytic theory. Another example comes from medication. The first antipsychotic drugs were discovered accidentally around 1950. Their dramatic success in relieving symptoms of schizophrenia led quickly to speculation regarding the neurochemical basis of psychotic disorders. Because of this close association between developments in etiological theories and treatment procedures, it is important for you to become familiar with some of the basic approaches to the treatment of abnormal behavior. For this reason, we devote Chapter 3 exclusively to an examination of major forms of treatment for psychological disorders.

BIOLOGICAL REDUCTIONISM

The development and progression of Gina's depression over time also illustrates the limitations associated with **biological reductionism,** the assumption that biological explanations are more useful than psychological explanations because they deal with smaller units. Consider the psychiatrist who explained to Gina that her depression was caused by a chemical imbalance in her brain. The psychiatrist was not necessarily wrong in offering this explanation. Gina may have had an imbalance of certain chemicals in her brain, although we do not yet have a reliable medical test to make this determination. The misconception in the explanation is the assumption that the chemical imbalance, if it exists, is the ultimate explanation of Gina's depression. This is the error of biological reductionism. Gina's alleged chemical imbalance may have been produced by her overriding feelings of responsibility, by her troubled marriage, or by the pressures associated with women's social roles in our society. Physical explanations of the causes of emotional disorders are not necessar-

ily better or more accurate than psychological explanations of causality. In fact, the two competing explanations are often complementary ways of talking about the same thing. Each focuses on a different system of influence.

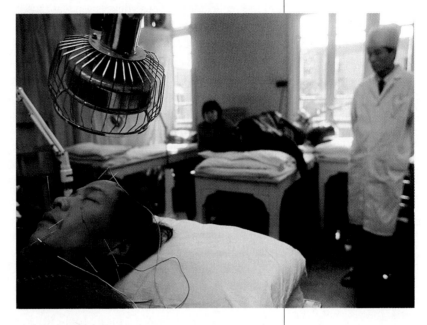

▲ The success of a treatment does not necessarily enlighten us as to the cause of the disorder. In China, for example, acupuncture has been used to treat depression. Regardless of how effective this procedure might be, it is not certain that the results of this therapeutic procedure can teach us much about the origins of depression.

To understand this point, consider the operation of a word-processing program on a computer. The workings of the program could be explained in terms of "biology"—the digital status of various switches in the computer hardware. They could also be explained in terms of "psychology"—the computer program or software. Neither explanation is better than the other. Ultimately, the word-processing program cannot operate without *both* hardware and software.

Explanation of the computer's operation purely in terms of either hardware or software is of interest, of course. In the terminology used in this chapter, both the hardware system and the software system are valuable to understand. Moreover, it is possible that a specific "bug"—an abnormality, in the present context—could reside either in the hardware or the software. Both systems need to be examined for malfunctions. Still, hardware and software, like biology and psychology, are inextricably interwoven. It makes little sense to suggest that either is the ultimate cause of the other, or, in fact, to suggest that either is independent of the other. Simply put, many conflicting biological and psychological accounts of causality are better seen as complementary ways of looking at the same phenomenon.

CAUSE AND CHANGE

Another very important point illustrated by the case of Gina King is that the success of a treatment does not prove the cause of a problem. After reading the case, for example, it is tempting to conclude that Gina's depression was caused by her excessive feelings of responsibility for others. These feelings apparently dated back to her childhood, and they appear to explain many of her reactions to different events in her life. Gina's successful treatment does not prove, however, that her feelings of responsibility caused her depression in the first place. Her depression may have been caused by these feelings, but it also may have been caused by a variety of other factors. The cause may have been an imbalance of chemicals in her brain, an unhappy marriage, or any number of factors not discussed in the case history. The solution to a problem by itself does not prove its cause.

Assuming the presence of a cause based on response to treatment represents an error in logic. Consider two analogies. Aspirin may cure headaches, but this does not mean that headaches are caused by a lack of aspirin. A filling is used to restore a cavity, but this does not mean that cavities are caused by a lack of fillings. The errors in reasoning are obvious in these examples, but logical fallacies are far less apparent when the cause of a disorder is unknown. When a psychological treatment solves a problem, we often assume that the disorder must have a psychological cause. Similarly, when biological treatments are successful, we often assume that this proves that the cause is biological. Even experienced scientists can fall victim to such errors in reasoning. You will therefore do well to remember that treatment does not prove cause.

The case of Gina King also illustrates that treatment can be successful even if the cause of an emotional problem remains unknown. Of course, understanding causality can be of great help in developing treatments. People who know how an automobile engine works are in a much better position to repair a breakdown than are people who are mystified by mechanical devices. This is one reason why psychological researchers devote so much effort to trying to discover the causes of various mental disorders.

Goals of This Book

The terms and concepts that have been introduced in this chapter provide a springboard to more detailed discussions of mental disorders. Most of the issues that we have raised are unresolved; many continue to be the focal points of heated controversies that will be considered later in this book. Before we leave this chapter, we want to highlight some additional questions that might be raised with regard to the cases that we have described.

The process of studying a mental disorder inevitably leads to careful consideration of the signs and symptoms by which it is defined. Were any of the symptoms that Kevin exhibited more useful than others in establishing his diagnosis? Definitions of all mental disorders are still being debated. Most clinical psychologists and psychiatrists agree that schizophrenia is a meaningful syndrome, but not everyone agrees on the most useful definition of the disorder. Delusions and hallucinations are included in almost all definitions of schizophrenia.

Disorganized speech is also widely accepted. There has been disagreement, however, regarding symptoms such as diminished emotional responsiveness. The boundaries of specific mental disorders have not been firmly established.

A syndrome such as schizophrenia must be evaluated using scientific evidence. Does the syndrome have any systematic meaning or importance? Does one diagnosis call for a different type of treatment than another diagnosis? Is it more useful for Kevin's psychiatrist to think in terms of treating the cluster of symptoms rather than treating each symptom separately? These are extremely important and difficult questions. Research in the field of abnormal behavior is concerned with providing answers.

This book will provide you with an introduction to the study of psychopathology, viewed from the perspective of psychological science. The application of science to questions regarding abnormal behavior carries with it the implicit assumption that these problems can be studied objectively. We believe that order can be found in the frequently chaotic and puzzling world of mental disorders. This order will eventually allow us to understand the processes by which abnormal behaviors are created and maintained. Clinical scientists adopt an attitude of open-minded skepticism, tempered by an appreciation for the research methods that are used to collect empirical data. They formulate specific hypotheses, test them, and then refine them based on the results of these tests. This book is, for the most part, an attempt to explain that process. In order to get the most from it, you may have to set aside—at least temporarily—personal beliefs that you have already acquired about mental disorders. Try to adopt an objective, skeptical attitude. We hope to pique your curiosity and share with you the satisfaction, as well as perhaps some of the frustration, of searching for answers to questions about complex behavioral problems.

This book has several goals that focus on developing your familiarity with specialized topics within the field of abnormal psychology. The most important are highlighted with headings and features that are consistent from chapter to chapter. These include:

1. To describe the experiences of a number of individuals who suffer from various types of psychopathology (*case studies*).
2. To describe more objectively the clinical problems that are associated with mental disorders (*typical symptoms*).

3. To explain the system that is used to classify these disorders, emphasizing how it has evolved and the criteria by which it is evaluated (*classification*).
4. To outline current knowledge regarding the frequency and distribution of these problems (*epidemiology*).
5. To highlight contemporary hypotheses regarding the causes of abnormal behaviors, focusing in particular on complementary relations among psychological, biological, and environmental systems (*etiology*).
6. To provide select examples of ways in which clinical scientists collect data to test these hypotheses (*research methods*).
7. To discuss psychological and biological interventions that are used to help people who experience various types of mental disorder (*treatment*).

We will consider these topics as they apply to each of the major categories of mental disorder listed in Table 1–2. Each chapter will include a summary of current knowledge regarding psychopathology. Keep in mind, however, the preliminary nature of our knowledge. Very little is actually known about the etiology of these problems. Therefore, we believe that it is more important for you to understand the principles that guide our ongoing search for knowledge than to digest whatever information is currently available.

Summary

Our primary goal in this chapter is to develop your familiarity with the symptoms of **psychopathology**. We have described four relatively common forms of mental disorder: schizophrenia, bulimia nervosa, alcoholism, and major depression. Schizophrenia is a form of **psychosis.** The symptoms of this disorder include **hallucinations, delusions,** and **disorganized speech.** Bulimia nervosa is an eating disorder that involves recurrent episodes in which the person cannot control what (or how much) he or she eats. These episodes of binge eating are followed by

KEY TERMS

- abnormal psychology
- biological reductionism
- biopsychosocial model
- case study
- classification
- clinical psychology
- diathesis
- diathesis-stress model
- epidemiology
- etiology
- incidence

efforts to prevent weight gain, such as self-induced vomiting. Alcoholism is also defined in terms of loss of control. In this case, the problem is a compulsive, self-destructive pattern of drinking that results in significant social and occupational impairment. Clinical depression is defined in terms of a set of symptoms that include depressed mood, loss of interest or pleasure, fatigue, and feelings of guilt or worthlessness. These and many other types of mental disorders are described in greater detail in the subsequent chapters of this book.

Mental disorders are defined in terms of typical signs and symptoms rather than indentifiable causal factors. A group of symptoms that appear together and are assumed to represent a specific type of disorder is called a **syndrome.** There are no definitive psychological or biological tests that can be used to confirm the presence of psychopathology. At the present time, the diagnosis of mental disorders depends upon observations of the person's behavior and descriptions of personal experience.

No one has been able to provide a universally accepted definition of abnormal behavior. Statistical infrequency and subjective distress cannot be used for this purpose because not all infrequent behaviors are pathological and because some people who exhibit abnormal behaviors do not have insight into their conditions. The most important consideration involves the consequences of the behavior. The official classification system, DSM-IV, defines mental disorders as a group of persistent maladaptive behaviors that result in personal distress or impaired functioning. On a practical level, mental disorders can be defined as those conditions that are included in the diagnostic manual.

Various forms of voluntary social deviance and efforts to express individuality are excluded from the DSM-IV definition of mental disorders. Political and religious actions, and the beliefs upon which they are based, are not considered to be forms of abnormal behavior, even when they seem unusual to many other people. We must recognize, however, that the process of defining psychopathology is still influenced by cultural and political values. The catagories described in DSM-IV have been appropriately subjected to public debate and criticism.

The boundaries of mental disorders are often difficult to define. They can be classified using either dimensional or categorical concepts. DSM-IV has adopted a categorical approach, but we do not have enough information to determine which is more appropriate.

The scientific study of the frequency and distribution of disorders within a population is known as **epidemiology**. Some severe forms of abnormal behavior—such as schizophrenia—have been observed in virtually every society that has been studied by social scientists. There are also forms of psychopathy—including eating disorders and alcoholism—for which substantial cross-cultural differences have been found. These epidemiological patterns may provide important clues that will help identify factors that influence the etiology of mental disorders.

Some of the best information that is currently available regarding the epidemiology of mental disorders in the United States was collected in the Epidemiologic Catchment Area (ECA) study. According to this study, the 12-month **prevalence** rate for at least one form of mental disorder was 20 percent. Lifetime prevalence was higher with 32 percent of adults reporting at least one mental disorder at some point in their lives. The ECA study found significant gender differences for several types of mental disorder, including anxiety disorders, mood disorders, and alcoholism.

Abnormal psychology represents the application of psychological science—its concepts and research tools—to the study of mental disorders. Various forms of professional training prepare people to work with those who suffer from mental disorders. These professions include **clinical psychology**, **psychiatry** and **social work**. People who study and treat mental disorders are best trained as **scientist-practitioners**. We want to introduce you to both sides of this process: learning more about the phenomenology of the disorders as well as the methodologies that are used to study them.

The **etiology** of mental disorders is not well understood. It is undoubtedly the product of an interaction among biological, psychological and societal factors. These are complementary systems. The interactive nature of these systems can be described as a **biopsychosocial model** of psychopathology. The resolution of the **nature–nurture controversy** hinges on the recognition that the artificial distinction between biological causes and environmental causes is not helpful in our search for further knowledge about mental disorders.

Several types of **psychopharmacology** and **psychotherapy** have been shown to be effective in the treatment of mental disorders. Many important hypotheses about the origins of mental disorders have been derived from efforts to treat these conditions. These hypotheses must then be tested in the context of carefully planned research programs. Individual cases do not provide definitve evidence for or against any hypothesis.

Critical Thinking

1. What does it mean for a behavior to be classified as "abnormal"? Why is it so difficult to produce an abstract definition of abnormal behavior? Some people argue that psychopathology is nothing more than the list of disorders presented in the *Diagnostic and Statistical Manual*. Do you agree? Can you provide a better definition?

2. Psychopathology is sometimes defined in terms of its consequences—maladaptive or harmful. What kinds of consequences do you think we should include in this debate? Should they be limited to increased mortality and reduced fertility? Should subjective pain or suffering play a role in our definition of abnormal behavior? Why or why not?

3. Do you think that it might be possible to completely eliminate social values from a definition of abnormal behavior? How would you accomplish that goal? Is there any way of defining mental disorders that would avoid value judgments about which behaviors are adaptive and which are not?

4. Case studies provide interesting descriptions of problems, but they don't help us choose among etiological theories. What kinds of limitations do you see with case studies? Why should we be careful about drawing general conclusions from them?

5. Why is it useful for clinical psychologists to be experts in understanding and conducting research? Does the scientist-practitioner model have any advantages for the training of clinical psychologists?

2

Causes of Abnormal Behavior: From Paradigms to Systems

You have probably heard or read a great deal of conflicting information about the causes of abnormal behavior. Magazine articles explain that depression is caused by a chemical imbalance in the brain, a problem that can be corrected with medication. Television advertisements tell us that alcoholism is a genetic disease that is best treated in a hospital. Books and films often portray emotional disturbances as dating back to traumatic childhood experiences that are relived in psychotherapy. Many manuals on parenting tell us that psychological problems are caused by parents who love their children too little and discipline them too much—or who love them too much and discipline them too little. Finally, television shows and newspaper headlines blame violence in our cities on everything from the breakdown of families to the breakdown of schools to the breakdown of society.

Overview

Scientists too have offered different, and often conflicting, explanations concerning the causes or *etiology* of psychopathology. Conflicting scientific explanations sometimes confuse the public—but such disagreements may actually be of benefit to science. Scientists pit theories against one another in a competition of research, and the "winner" is the more accurate explanation of psychopathology.

We favor the competition of theories in scientific enterprises. The rivalry encourages skepticism and challenges theorists to test their hypotheses. Unfortunately, the broad theories that have been proposed to explain psychopathology have many problems. One difficulty is that the traditional biological, psychoanalytic, behavioral, and humanistic approaches are more than alternative theories. They also are alternative *paradigms*. In other words, they conflict not only in their theories of abnormal behavior but also in what they view as acceptable scientific methods, as we discuss shortly.

The more substantial problem, however, is that most forms of psychopathology do not have a single cause or set of causes. Rather, abnormal behavior appears to be determined by **multifactorial causes**, the combination of a variety of different biological, psychological, and social factors. Thus, for example, the persistent *nature–nurture debate* is wrong in suggesting that psychopathology is caused either solely by nature or solely by nurture. In fact, abnormal behavior is caused by nature *and* nurture. Similarly, different forms of psychopathology are caused by a combination of the different factors highlighted by the traditional paradigms. Early childhood experience *and* current life events are important to abnormal behavior, as are troubled individuals *and* troubled relationships, or psychological difficulties *and* societal concerns.

The challenge for science, therefore, is not to identify a single theory that explains the causes of all forms of abnormal behavior. Rather, the challenge is to integrate evidence on the etiology of different disorders into a coherent whole, a system of contributing factors (Rutter & Rutter, 1993). In this chapter—and throughout the text—we adopt such a "systems" approach to understanding the etiology of psychopathology. Rather than arguing for or against one theoretical perspective, our systems approach integrates evidence across and among different biological, psychological, and social domains of behavior. Thus, the systems approach often is referred to as a *biopsychosocial* perspective. Biological contributions to abnormal behavior range from specific biochemical processes in the brain to broad genetic liabilities passed across generations. Psychological contributions range from unconscious cognitive processes to reinforcement for abnormal behavior. Social and cultural contributions range from conflict in relationships with family members to the broad influences of society and culture.

In adopting a systems approach, we must be clear about three issues. First, we do not mean to imply that all theories of the etiology of abnormal behavior are equally valid. Unlike the Dodo bird from *Alice in Wonderland*, we are *not* arguing that "Everyone has won and all must have prizes" (Luborsky, Singer, & Luborsky, 1975). The systems approach highlights biopsychosocial contributions to psychopathology, but clear hypotheses still must be supported by empirical evidence. Second, different types of abnormal behavior have very different causes, just as different physical diseases are caused by various underlying conditions. Differential etiology is another reason why we abandon the traditional approach of pitting one paradigm against another. Theoretical limitations become obvious when we apply the same etiological explanation to different disorders. Third, it is essential to acknowledge that the causes of almost all forms of abnormal behavior are unknown at present. Although we can provide insight into the origins of various disorders, anyone who claims to know the single, true explanation of the cause of psychopathology is wrong.

In this chapter, we explain the systems approach as a general method for understanding abnormal behavior. We also introduce a number of biological, psychological, and social concepts relevant to the etiology of psychopathology. We do not extensively evaluate these potential explanations of the causes of abnormal behavior. Instead, various concepts are critically evaluated in subsequent chapters where we review evidence on those specific biopsychosocial factors that are relevant to the etiology of a particular psychological problem.

Each chapter in this text includes a case history near the beginning. The case illustrates key topics from the practitioner side of the scientist-practitioner model. Most cases, including the following one, come from our own therapy files.

CASE STUDY

Possible Causes of Behavioral Problems

At the age of 14, Meghan B. attempted to end her life by taking approximately 20 Tylenol capsules. Meghan took the pills after an explosive fight with her mother over Meghan's grades and over a boy she was dating. Meghan was in her room when she impulsively took the pills, but shortly afterwards she told her mother what she had done. Her parents rushed Meghan to the emergency room, where her vital signs were closely monitored. As the crisis was coming to an end, Meghan's parents agreed that she should be hospitalized to make sure that she was safe and to begin to treat her problems.

Meghan talked freely about many of her problems during the 30 days she spent on the adolescent unit of a private psychiatric hospital. Most of her complaints focused on her mother. Meghan insisted that her mother was always "in her face," telling her what to do and when and how to do it. Her father was "great," but he was too busy with his job as a chemical engineer to spend much time with her.

Meghan also said she had long-standing problems in school. She barely maintained a C average despite considerable efforts to do better. Meghan said she didn't care about school, and her mother's insistence that she could do much better was a major source of conflict between them. Meghan also complained that she had few friends in school or outside of school. She described her classmates as "preppy" and "straight," and said she had no interest in them. Meghan was obviously angry as she described her family, school, and friends, but also showed sadness on a few occasions. She denounced herself as being "stupid" one time, and she cried about being a "reject" when discussing why no friends, including her boyfriend, contacted her while she was in the hospital.

Mrs. B. provided details on the history of Meghan's problems. When Meghan was 2 years old, she had been adopted by Mr. and Mrs. B., who could not have children of their own. According to the adoption agency, Meghan's birth mother was 16 years old when she had the baby. Meghan's biological mother was a drug user, and she haphazardly left the baby in the care of friends and relatives for weeks at a time. Little was known about Meghan's biological father except that he had had some trouble with the law, and Meghan's mother had known him only briefly. When Meghan was 14 months old, her pediatrician reported her mother to a child abuse agency after noting bruises on Meghan's thighs and hips. After a 6-month legal investigation, Meghan's mother decided to give her up for adoption. Meghan came to live with Mr. and Mrs. B. shortly thereafter.

Mrs. B. was eager to give Meghan all the love they both had missed in their lives to that point, and she happily doted on her daughter. Mr. B. also was very loving with Meghan, although Mrs. B, like Meghan, noted that he was rarely at home. Everything seemed fine with Meghan until first grade, when teachers began to complain about her. She disrupted the classroom with her restlessness, and she did not complete her schoolwork. In second grade, Meghan was diagnosed by a school psychologist as having hyperactivity and a learning disability,

and her pediatrician recommended medication. Mrs. B. was horrified by the thought of medication or of sending Meghan to a "resource room" for part of the school day. Instead, she decided to redouble her efforts at parenting.

According to Mrs. B., she and Meghan succeeded in getting Meghan through elementary school in reasonably good shape. Meghan's grades and classroom behavior remained acceptable as long as Mrs. B. consulted repeatedly with the school. Mrs. B. noted with bitterness, however, that the one problem that she could not solve was Meghan's relationships with other girls. The daughters of Mrs. B.'s friends and neighbors were well-behaved and were excellent students. Meghan did not fit in with them. They were polite when they saw her, but Meghan never got invited to play with other girls.

Mrs. B. was obviously sad when discussing Meghan's past, but she became agitated and angry when discussing the present. She was very concerned about Meghan, but she wondered out loud if the suicide attempt had been manipulative. Mrs. B. said that she had had major conflicts with Meghan ever since Meghan started middle school at the age of 12. Meghan would no longer work regularly with her mother on her homework for the usual 2 hours each night. In addition, her mother said that Meghan fought with her about everything from picking up her room to her boyfriend, an 18-year-old whom Mrs. B. abhorred. Mrs. B. complained that she did not understand what had happened to her daughter. She clearly stated, however, that whatever it was, she would fix it. ■

What was causing Meghan's problems? Her case history suggests many plausible alternatives. Some of her troubles seem to be a reaction to a mother whose attentiveness at age 8 seems more like intrusiveness at age 14. Maybe Mrs. B. became more concerned with her own needs for love than with Meghan's changing needs for parenting. Meghan's problems seem bigger than this, however. We could trace some of her troubles to anger over her failures in school or to rejection by her peers. We also can speculate about the effects of Meghan's early childhood experiences. Surely she was affected adversely by the physical abuse, inconsistent love, and chaotic living arrangements during the first, critical years of her life. Finally, we can wonder about possible biological contributions to Meghan's problems. Did Meghan's mother take drugs during pregnancy that affected the developing baby? Was Meghan a healthy, full-term newborn? Given her biological parents' history of troubled behavior, could Meghan's problems be caused by genetic factors?

These searching questions defy a ready answer in the case of Meghan or any individual. Abnormal psychology does not now have objective tools for pinpointing the specific causes of most types of abnormal behavior. Still, psychological theory and research does offer some good leads about etiology. We introduce current psychological approaches to understanding the causes of psychopathology by first considering them in historical perspective. In fact, we offer a brief historical perspective in every chapter of the text. We hope that you were able to understand the problems of Meghan B. better after you read the facts of her case and learned about her developmental history. Similarly, we hope that our brief historical perspectives will enable you to better understand current theory—and gain a sense for future developments in psychological research.

Brief Historical Perspective

The search for explanations of the causes of abnormal behavior dates to ancient times, as do conflicting opinions about the etiology of emotional disorders. References to abnormal behavior have been found in ancient accounts from Chinese, Hebrew, and Egyptian societies. Many of these records attribute abnormal behavior to the disfavor of the gods or the mischief of demons. In fact, abnormal behavior continues to be attributed to demons in some preliterate societies today.

Attempts to offer more earthly and systematic accounts of the etiology of psychopathology can be traced to the Greek physician Hippocrates (460–367 B.C.), who ridiculed *demonological* accounts of insanity (Deutsch, 1949). Instead, Hippocrates hypothesized that abnormal behavior had natural causes, specifically an imbalance of one of four body fluids—blood, phlegm, black bile, and yellow bile. Hippocrates argued that different personality styles resulted from an excess of each of the four respective fluids. He believed that a sanguine (cheerful) personality was caused by an excess of blood. A phlegmatic (sluggish) personality was thought to be due to too much phlegm. Excess black bile was assumed to be the cause of a melancholic (gloomy) style, and a choleric (ill-tempered) personality was said to result from too much yellow bile. The specifics of Hippocrates's theories obviously have little value today, but his systematic attempt to uncover natural, biological explanations for mental disorders is a lasting contribution.

Many of the traditions begun by Hippocrates

died away after the fall of the Roman Empire. Although systematic, naturalistic accounts of mental illness were kept alive in Arab cultures (Deutsch, 1949), the emphasis on objectivity and careful observation faded in Europe. In fact, some scholars have concluded that, in Europe during the Middle Ages, mental illness came to be blamed on witchcraft. Historical accounts indicate that fears of witches abounded during this period, and witch hunts were conducted with fervor under the formal sanctions of the Roman Catholic Church. More recent research, however, refutes the argument that witchcraft was the dominant explanation of mental illness. In examining records from British mental incompetency trials dating back to the thirteenth century, Neugebauer (1979) uncovered only one case where officials judged that insanity was caused by witches. Explanations in the medieval records that seem reasonable even today were much more frequent. Records directly attributed "lunacy" (a medieval synonym for mental illness) in various cases to "a blow received on the head," "a long and incurable infirmity," "her husband's death," and "fear of his father" (Neugebauer, 1979). Thus, medieval notions about the causes of abnormal behavior were not as far-fetched as suggested by some accounts of demonology and witchcraft.

The rudiments of the scientific method were not rediscovered in Europe until the Renaissance (approximately 1300 to 1600). The scientific method was not applied to the study of abnormal behavior until much later. In fact, advances in the scientific understanding of the etiology of psychopathology did not appear until the nineteenth and early twentieth centuries, when three major events occurred. One was the discovery of the cause of general paresis, a severe mental disorder that has a deteriorating course and eventually ends in death. The second was the writing of Sigmund Freud, a thinker who has had a profound influence not only on the field of abnormal psychology but also on Western society as a whole. The third was the creation of a new academic discipline called psychology.

GENERAL PARESIS AND THE BIOLOGICAL APPROACH
The **biological approach** to abnormal psychology can be traced back to the study of the condition we now know as **general paresis** (general paralysis). Prior to 1800, general pare-

sis was not recognized as a distinct disorder, and it therefore attracted no special attention. In 1798, John Haslam identified a set of symptoms that proved to be unique to this mental disorder. Some of the symptoms that distinguished general paresis from other forms of "lunacy" included delusions of grandeur, cognitive impairment (dementia), and progressive paralysis, all of which had an unremitting course that ended in death after many years. The diagnosis inspired a search for the cause of the new disorder. Many different etiological hypotheses were considered and evaluated, and most correctly focused on biological explanations. Still, it took over 100 years of investigation before the search was successful.

The etiological breakthrough began with the observation that people with general paresis had contracted the sexually transmitted disease *syphilis* earlier in their lives. Recognition of this essential correlation was not without missteps, however. One study conducted by Fournier in 1894, for example, concluded that only 65 percent of paretic patients reported having a history of syphilis. Thus, questions were raised about whether syphilis alone was a necessary cause of general paresis. Research conducted in 1897 by Kraft-Ebbing demonstrated that Fournier's statistic was wrong. Kraft-Ebbing attempted to inoculate paretic patients against syphilis, but none of them became infected when exposed to a mild form of the disease. There could be only one explanation for their body's failure to respond to the inoculation: All of the patients—not 65 percent of them—had been infected with syphilis previously.

After the turn of the twentieth century, the spirochete that causes syphilis was discovered. Post-mortem examination of the brains of paretic patients later proved that the infection had invaded and destroyed parts of the central nervous system. In 1910, Paul Ehrlich, a German microbiologist, developed *arsphenamine*, an arsenic-containing chemical that destroyed the spirochete and prevented general paresis. Unfortunately, the drug worked only if the patient was treated in the early stages of infection. Later, it was learned that syphilis could be cured by a new discovery, penicillin—the first antibiotic. As a result, general paresis was virtually eliminated when antibiotics became widely available after the end of World War II.

The slow but dramatic discoveries about general paresis gave great impetus to the search for biological causes for other mental disorders. For some problems, a purely biological approach has been successful in establishing etiology. This is most notable for the cognitive disorders (see Chapter 13) and for many forms of mental retardation (see Chapter 14). Unfortunately, the causes of most forms of mental illness do not appear to be as straightforward as for general paresis. Like heart disease and cancer, most mental disorders appear to be "lifestyle diseases," problems that have multifactorial causes including both biological and environmental contributions. These disorders may defy straightforward etiological explanations and dramatic, "magic bullet" treatments (as Ehrlich's treatment was called in a 1940 film about his discovery).

FREUD AND THE
PSYCHOANALYTIC APPROACH

Unlike the biological paradigm, which has been influenced by many notable people, the **psychoanalytic approach** owes its origins primarily to the writings of a single individual, Sigmund Freud (1856–1939). Freud introduced many influential ideas, but perhaps his most basic contribution was providing a counterpoint to the growing biological paradigm. Although he was trained as a neurologist and remained interested in biological influences throughout his lifetime, Freud argued that early childhood experiences played a central role in the development of mental illness, even in illnesses that had physical manifestations.

Freud was trained in Paris by Jean Charcot (1825–1893), a neurologist who successfully used hypnosis to treat what used to be called *hysteria*, an emotional problem that seems to demonstrate that there must be different levels of conscious awareness. One type of hysteria is characterized by the conversion of psychological conflicts into physical symptoms. (It is now called conversion disorder; see Chapter 8.) "Hysterical blindness," for example, is the inability to see. This dramatic symptom is not caused by a known organic impairment, and the afflicted individual sometimes recovers functioning after resolving an emotional problem. Both of these observations suggest that the problem may have a psychological origin.

Patients neither "fake" conversion symptoms, nor do they consciously associate them with emotional distress. Thus, it would seem

▲ **Sigmund Freud (1856–1939) founded the psychoanalytic approach to abnormal behavior. Freud's approach has been criticized as being unscientific, but the influence of his ideas is unquestionable.**

that psychological conflicts are somehow "converted" into physical symptoms outside of conscious awareness. The peculiar problem of hysteria thus led Freud to emphasize the importance of **the unconscious** in the etiology of emotional disorders. Freud argued that many memories, motivations, and protective psychological processes resided in the unconscious mind, thus explaining how problems like hysteria might be produced outside of conscious awareness.

Freud was derided by many of his contemporaries who favored biologically oriented explanations of abnormal behavior, but he proved to have an immense influence on psychiatry and psychology. He can be credited with calling attention to unconscious processes, formulating a stage theory of child development, creating the metaphorical division of the personality into the id, ego, and superego, and identifying numerous intrapsychic defenses (see Further Thoughts). However, Freud built his elaborate theory of the development of normal and abnormal behavior on introspection about himself and his past, as well as on several key case histories. His failure to offer more specific hypotheses, and to test them empirically, has been the source of many legitimate criticisms of Freudian theory, as we discuss at various points throughout the text.

FURTHER THOUGHTS

An Outline of Freudian Theory

Freud's direct influence on psychology is diminishing, but his ideas continue to have a tremendous influence on the intellectual culture of Western society. As one example of this, many of the terms he coined have become a part of everyday language. If for no other reason, Freud's influence on our culture is sufficient justification for introducing some of his basic concepts.

Freud divided the mind into three parts: the id, the ego, and the superego. He suggested that the **id** is present at birth and is the source of basic drives and motivations. The id houses biological drives such as hunger, as well as two key psychological drives: sex and aggression. (Freud's term *libido* can be viewed as a synonym for sexual or life energy.) In Freudian theory, the id operates according to the *pleasure principle*—the impulses of the id seek immediate gratification and create discomfort or unrest until they are satisfied. Thus, in Freud's view, sexual or aggressive urges are akin to biological urges like hunger.

The **ego** is the part of the personality that must deal with the realities of the world as it attempts to fulfill id impulses as well as perform other functions. Thus, the ego operates on the *reality principle*. The ego begins to develop in the first year of life, and it continues to evolve, particularly during the preschool years. Unlike id impulses, which are primarily unconscious, much of the ego resides in conscious awareness.

The third part of the personality is the **superego**, which is roughly equivalent to the conscience. The superego contains societal standards of behavior, particularly rules that children learn from trying to be like their parents in their later preschool years. In Freud's view, societal rules are attempts to govern id impulses. For the individual, this means that the three parts of the personality often are in conflict with one another. The ego must constantly mediate between the demands of the id and the prescriptions of the superego. According to Freud, conflict between the superego and the ego produces *moral anxiety*, while conflict between the id and the ego produces *neurotic anxiety*.

Freud suggested that the ego protects itself by utilizing various **defense mechanisms**, unconscious processes that reduce conscious anxiety by distorting anxiety-producing memories, emotions, and impulses. For example, the defense of *projection* turns the tables psychologically. When you use projection, you project your own feelings on to someone else: "I'm not mad at you. You're mad at me!" In this example, projection protects the ego from the conflict and anxiety produced by unacceptably aggressive id impulses. Other defense mechanisms serve similar functions. A list of some of the more important and familiar defenses can be found in Table 2–1.

One index of Freud's continuing influence is the fact that all of these defense mechanisms, and several additional ones, appear in an appendix in DSM-IV on issues requiring further study.

Freud also formulated a stage theory of child development, as we discuss briefly toward the end of this chapter (see Table 2–4). Freud highlighted sexual conflicts in his theory of *psychosexual development*. The most important psychosexual conflict is the **Oedipal conflict**. Freud reasoned that boys harbor forbidden sexual desires for their mothers. Because these impulses are both overwhelming and impossible to fulfill, boys typically resolve the dilemma between the ages of 4 and 6 by *identifying* with their fathers. In a sense, they fulfill their desire for their mother by adopting the actions and values of her spouse. In Freud's view, girls face a similar dilemma that he termed the **Electra complex**. Freud hypothesized that girls, unlike boys, do not desire their opposite-gender parent sexually as much as they yearn for something their fathers have and they are "missing"—a penis. This is the Freudian notion of "penis envy," which has been roundly criticized for being blatantly sexist.

It is not difficult to criticize other Freudian concepts as well. Many of these criticisms call the theory to task for being too vague, broad, and untestable. We certainly agree with these objections. We also recognize, however, that Freud offered a host of innovative and sometimes penetrating ideas. Some followers of psychoanalytic theory insist on interpreting Freud literally, a position Freud himself surely would have criticized given the changes he made in his own theories during the course of his life. In this spirit, we prefer to view Freud's ideas as broad metaphors. Freudian theory offers few answers, but it offers many challenging concepts, some of which are worthy of attempts at careful definition and research. ∎

▲ Psychologist B.F. Skinner (1904–1990) outlined the principles of operant conditioning. Skinner's determination to make psychology a science profoundly influenced the discipline in the twentieth century.

EXPERIMENTAL PSYCHOLOGY AND THE BEHAVIORAL APPROACH

The nineteenth century witnessed another critical development in approaches to understanding abnormal behavior. The science of psychology was born in 1879 at the University of Leipzig in the laboratory of Wilhelm Wundt (1842–1920). Wundt's ambitious goal was to understand the nature of human consciousness. He attempted to achieve this end by using a technique called **introspection**, in which his subjects reported systematically and in detail about their inner experiences. Wundt's introspective method proved to be inadequate, and he failed in his attempt to detail the components of human consciousness. Still, Wundt made a profound and lasting contribution by scientifically studying psychological phenomena.

The development of a scientific understanding of learning was a central goal for Wundt, and other early psychologists had similar ambitions. The two most prominent contributors to early learning theory and research were the Russian physiologist Ivan Pavlov (1849–1936) and the U.S. psychologist B.F. Skinner (1904–1990). These psychological scientists respectively articulated the principles of classical conditioning and operant conditioning—concepts that continue to be central to contemporary learning theory.

In his famous experiments, Pavlov (1928) rang a bell every time he fed meat powder to dogs. After repeated trials, the salivation that was produced by the sight of food came to be elicited by the sound of the bell alone. In formalizing his theory of **classical conditioning** based on these and related experiments, Pavlov developed many important concepts. He defined an **unconditioned stimulus** (the meat powder) as a stimulus that automatically produces a reaction, that is, an **unconditioned response** (salivation). A **conditioned stimulus** (the bell) is a neutral stimulus that, when repeatedly paired with an unconditioned stimulus, comes to produce a **conditioned response** (salivation).[†] Finally, **extinction** occurs once a conditioned stimulus no longer is presented together with an unconditioned stimulus. Eventually, the conditioned stimulus no longer elicits the conditioned response.

[†] Note that the unconditioned response and the conditioned response are very similar (both involve salivation in this example). One difference is that the conditioned responses generally are somewhat weaker than unconditioned responses.

Skinner's (1953) principle of **operant conditioning** asserts that behavior is a function of its consequences. Specifically, behavior increases if it is rewarded, and it decreases if it is punished. In his numerous studies of rats and pigeons in the famous "Skinner box," Skinner identified four different, crucial consequences of behavior. **Positive reinforcement** occurs when the onset of a stimulus increases the frequency of behavior (for example, you get paid for your work). **Negative reinforcement** occurs when the *cessation* of a stimulus increases the frequency of behavior (for example, when you give in to a nagging friend, thereby stopping the nagging). **Punishment** occurs when the introduction of a stimulus decreases the frequency of behavior (for example, you spend less money after your parents scold you), and **response cost** is when the removal of a stimulus decreases the frequency of behavior (for example, you no longer stay out late after your parents take away use of the car).[†] **Extinction** results from ending the *contingency* or association between a behavior and its consequences, similar to the concept of extinction in classical conditioning.

The person most responsible for applying learning theory to the study of abnormal behavior was the U.S. psychologist John B. Watson (1878–1958). Watson wanted to promote psychology as a science, and he founded the approach called **behaviorism,** arguing that observable behavior was the only appropriate subject matter for the science of psychology. Watson believed that thoughts and emotions could not be measured objectively; thus, he rejected the study of these "internal events." In contrast to Freud, Watson did not offer an elaborate theory of the etiology of abnormal behavior. He did make the very important assumption that abnormal behavior was learned in much the same manner as normal behavior. In his well-known experiment with Little Albert, Watson and Rosalie Rayner (1920) used classical conditioning to induce the fear of a rat in an 11-month-old boy. They paired the sight of the rat with a loud noise, thus demonstrating that fears could be learned through classical conditioning. Although this was his most famous experiment, Watson and his followers were less concerned with how people

TABLE 2–1
Some Examples of Common Defense Mechanisms

Denial	Insistence that an experience, memory, or internal need did not occur or does not exist. For example, you completely block a painful experience from memory as if it never occurred.
Displacement	Feelings or actions are transferred from one person or object to another that is less threatening. For example, you kick your dog when you are upset with your boss.
Projection	Attributing one's own feelings or thoughts to other people. For example, a husband argues that his wife is angry at him when, in fact, he is angry at her.
Rationalization	Intellectually justifying a feeling or especially a disappointment. For example, after not getting the offer, you decide that a job you applied for was not the one you really wanted.
Reaction formation	Converting a painful or unacceptable feeling into its opposite. For example, you "hate" a former lover, but underneath it all you still really love that person.
Repression	Suppressing threatening material from consciousness, although you do not deny the memory when reminded of it. For example, you "forget" about an embarrassing experience.
Sublimation	Diverting id impulses into constructive and acceptable outlets. For example, you study hard to get good grades rather than giving in to desires for immediate pleasure.

learn abnormal behavior than with how people learn new, more adaptive ways of behaving.

FREE WILL AND THE
HUMANISTIC APPROACH

Abraham Maslow (1908–1970), Fritz Perls (1893–1970), and Carl Rogers (1902–1987) were the major advocates of a fourth major approach to conceptualizing abnormal behavior, **humanistic psychology**. In many respects, humanistic psychology, which emerged in the 1950s and 1960s, was a reaction against biological, psychoanalytic, and behavioral theories of abnormal behavior. Humanistic psychologists objected to the *determinism* of these approaches —the assumption that human behavior is caused by predictable and potentially knowable internal and/or external events. To humanistic psychologists, the very essence of humanity is

---

[†] People frequently use the terms *negative reinforcement* and *punishment* interchangeably, but the two are quite different. With negative reinforcement, behavior becomes more frequent after a stimulus is removed. With punishment, behavior becomes less frequent after a stimulus is introduced.

free will, the assumption that human behavior is *not* determined but is a product of how people choose to act. Humanistic psychology also is distinguished by its explicitly positive view of human behavior. Human nature is assumed to be inherently good, and humanistic psychologists therefore blame dysfunctional, abnormal, or aggressive behavior on society instead of on the individual. (See Table 2–2, where the assumptions of the four major approaches are compared.)

The assumption of free will makes it impossible to conduct research on the causes of normal or abnormal behavior, because free will, by definition, is not predictably determined. For this reason, humanistic psychology perhaps is best considered to be an alternative philosophy of human behavior, not an alternative psychological theory. In this regard, we note that the term *humanistic* must be considered carefully. All attempts to understand the etiology of psychopathology are humanistic in the sense that the ultimate goal is to improve the human condition.

Paradigms and the Causes of Abnormal Behavior

As we have noted, the biological, psychoanalytic, behavioral, and humanistic approaches are more than alternative theories of abnormal behavior (see Table 2–2). They are also alternative paradigms. A **paradigm** includes both the substance of a theory and a set of assumptions about how scientists should collect data and test theoretical propositions. The term *paradigm* was applied to the progress of science by Thomas Kuhn (1962), an influential historian and philosopher who argued that paradigms can both direct and misdirect scientists. Paradigms tell the researcher or clinician where and how to look for answers to questions, but sometimes the apparent guidance can be a hindrance. The idea that a paradigm can be either enlightening or blinding can be illustrated by a brain teaser. As an example, you should pause and try to solve the following enigma, written by Lord Byron, before looking ahead for the answer:

> I'm not in earth, nor the sun,
>   nor the moon.
> You may search all the sky—
>   I'm not there.

> In the morning and evening—
>   though not at noon,
> You may plainly perceive me,
>   for like a balloon,
> I am suspended in air.
> Though disease may possess me,
>   and sickness and pain,
> I am never in sorrow nor gloom;
> Though in wit and wisdom
>   I equally reign
> I am the heart of all sin and have
>   long lived in vain;
> Yet I ne'er shall be found in the tomb.

What is this poem about? The topic of this rhyme is not the soul or ghosts. It is not life or shadows, or a dozen other possibilities that may have occurred to you. Rather, the topic is the letter i. (Suspended in a<u>i</u>r. The heart of all s<u>i</u>n.) Why is the puzzle so difficult to solve? Because most people approach it with the assumption that the solution lies in the *content* of the poem, not in its *form*. The misdirection of this brain teaser illustrates one of Kuhn's central points about paradigms. The assumptions made by a paradigm can act as blinders; they can lead an investigator to overlook what otherwise might be obvious. At the same time, however, sometimes paradigms open up new perspectives and avenues for research. For example, now that you have been able to adopt a new "paradigm"—to focus on the form, not the content of words—you can easily solve the following puzzle:

> The beginning of eternity, the end of
>   time and space,
> The beginning of every end, the end of
>   every place.

It is obvious that the answer is the letter e.

The four traditional paradigms of psychopathology make assumptions about the appropriate focus of abnormal psychology which, like your initial approach to the brain teaser, sometimes are too narrow. The biological paradigm can be criticized for overemphasizing the *medical model*, the analogy between physical and psychological illnesses and consistently locating emotional problems "within the skin" of the individual. Objections to the psychoanalytic paradigm highlight its unyielding focus on the unconscious, even in the face of current life difficulties. As noted, the approach also is

TABLE 2-2

Some Comparisons among the Biological, Psychodynamic, Behavioral, and Humanistic Paradigms

Topic	Biological	Psychodynamic	Behavioral	Humanistic
Inborn human nature	Competitive, but some altruism	Aggressive	Neutral— blank slate	Basic goodness
Cause of abnormality	Genes, infection, physical damage	Early childhood experiences	Social learning	Frustrations of society
Type of treatment	Medication, other somatic therapies	Psychodynamic therapy	Cognitive behavior therapy	Nondirective therapy
Paradigmatic focus	Bodily functions and structures	Unconscious mind	Observable behavior	Free will

criticized for failing to offer testable hypotheses and for relying on case histories instead of systematic research. The behavioral paradigm often is critiqued for being too literal in focusing on observable events, as well as for being devoid of theory about the development of normal or abnormal behavior. Finally, the humanistic approach is chided for being unscientific, for reasons we have already discussed.

We agree that each of these approaches has weaknesses—and strengths. The clash of paradigms has dominated abnormal psychology for half a century; however, our concern is not to determine which approach is "right." Rather, our goal is to highlight the scientific understanding of the multifactorial causes of specific emotional disorders. In attempting to understand psychological disorders, we find promise in elements of each of the four traditional paradigms. As with the examples of word puzzles, the trick is knowing when to use which strategy.

Systems Theory

Unlike the traditional paradigms, our approach to psychopathology is based on a theory that is not specific to psychopathology, or even to psychology. Rather, we begin with **system theory**, an innovation in understanding and conducting science. The Austrian biologist and philosopher of science Ludwig von Bertalanffy (1901–1972), who taught in universities in Austria, England, Canada, and the United States, has been called the "father of systems theory" (Davidson, 1982). Systems theory, however, has multiple origins; its roots lie not only in psychology, but also in engineering, computer science, biology, and philosophy. Systems theory has revolutionized scientific approaches within each of these disciplines and in other scientific fields as well (Davidson, 1982; Ford & Lerner, 1992; Gleick, 1987; Hinde, 1992; von Bertalanffy, 1968).

Holism

The central principle of systems theory is **holism,** the idea that the whole is more than the sum of its parts. This common statement can be illustrated with numerous familiar examples across many disciplines. A water molecule (H_2O) is much more than the sum of two hydrogen atoms and one oxygen atom. A human being is much more than the sum of a nervous system, an organ system, a circulatory system, and so on. Similarly, psychopathology is more than the sum of inborn temperament, early childhood experiences, and learning history. Psychopathology is more than the sum of nature and nurture.

REDUCTIONISM

We can better appreciate the importance of the principle of holism when we consider its scientific counterpoint, **reductionism**. According to reductionist views, the whole *is* the sum of its parts, and the task for scientists is to divide the world into its smaller and smaller components. To give a very general example, a reductionistic approach to understanding the cause of abnormal behavior would explain dysfunctional families in terms of disordered individuals, disordered individuals in terms of specific psychological disturbances, psychological disturbances in terms of disrupted brain functions, and disrupted brain functions in terms of specific chemical deviations. According to the principle of reductionism, ultimate explanations are found when problems are reduced to their smallest possible components.

The influence of reductionism is pervasive in everyday thinking about the causes of abnormal behavior (Cacioppo & Bernston, 1992). For example, when scientists discover that a depletion of certain chemicals in the brain accompanies depression (see Chapter 5), the public assumes that scientists have discovered the ultimate cause of depression. This is an example of *biological reductionism*, as we discussed in Chapter 1. The public, and many scientists, seem to overlook the fact that brain chemistry is affected by a negative view of the world or by difficult life experiences. These psychological and social experiences, in fact, may be the ultimate cause of depression, and the "chemical imbalance in the brain" may merely be a consequence of certain types of life events. Reductionists believe, however, that ultimate answers come in smaller and smaller packages, and they therefore prematurely conclude that depression is a chemical problem.

Subsystems and Levels of Analysis

The holistic principle of systems theory maintains that it is a mistake to view the smallest cause as "the" cause of something. Rather, smaller units are better conceived as *subsystems* within a larger system. The human circulatory system is an example of a subsystem of the human body, which is also made up of the skeletal, muscular, nervous, digestive, respiratory, and reproductive subsystems.

A far-out example can illustrate some implications of the concept of subsystems for reasoning about causality. Assume for a moment that three Martian scientists are sent to Earth to discover what causes those metallic vehicles to speed, sometimes recklessly and sometimes slowly, across the planet's landmass. One Martian, an ecologist by training, reports back that the vehicles (called automobiles, the scientist discovers) move at different speeds based on the width of the black paths on which they are set, whether the paths are straight or curved, and the presence of some unexplained phenomenon known as "radar traps." A second Martian, a psychologist, disagrees. This scientist notes that the speed of automobiles is determined by the age, gender, and mood of the individual who sits inside them. Together these factors cause automobiles to move at different speeds. The third scientist, a physicist, derides the other two for their simplistic thinking. This Martian notes that the speed of automobiles is caused by a chemical process that occurs inside an antiquated machine called an internal combustion engine. The process involves oxygen, fuel, and heat and results in mechanical energy.

In this example, it is obvious that the most reductionistic or *molecular* explanation is no more (or less) accurate than the most general or *molar* one. Reductionist traditions in science often lead us to believe that the most molecular account (biological or biochemical) is the ultimate explanation of causality (Alessi, 1992; Rachlin, 1992). The Martian example, however, demonstrates the potential fallacy of blind reductionism.

The Martian example also suggests an important way of integrating information about multiple influences on the development of psychopathology. Various subsystems can be conceptualized as different *levels of analysis* for conceptualizing causal factors (Hinde, 1992). As illustrated in Figure 2–1, the biological, psychological, and social approaches to psychopathology are potentially compatible explanations at different levels of analysis. Each approach uses a different lens to analyze a subject; one is a microscope, another a magnifying glass, and the third a telescope. In fact, the various academic disciplines also can be ordered according to levels of analysis (Schwartz, 1982; see Table 2–3). The use of a different "lens" by different academic disciplines does not make one approach right and the others wrong.

ABNORMALITIES AND CAUSALITY ACROSS SUBSYSTEMS

We want you to recognize that the biological, psychological, and social levels of analysis can simply be different ways of conceptualizing the same problem. It is also true, however, that an abnormality might occur within any one of these subsystems. In the Martian example, an engine might break down, a driver might be intoxicated, or a road could be washed out. Similarly, the causes of different types of abnormal behavior might be located primarily within biological, psychological, or social functioning. Scientists hope to identify such specific causes at one or another level of analysis for at least some psychological problems. Our caution, however, is that once a problem has been identified at one level of analysis, you cannot assume that other factors are unimportant. A chemical imbalance in the brain may be caused by a stressful life event. Similarly, a difficult family experience may be caused by a genetically determined personality trait (McGue & Lykken, 1992).

Our point is this: It is not enough to focus on one subsystem or level of analysis. Ultimately, we must understand the relations among biological, psychological, and social functioning. In fact, many emotional problems apparently are caused by a *combination* of biological, psychological, and social risk factors.

Common Processes within Different Levels of Analysis

The concepts of holism and multiple levels of analysis are two major contributions of systems theory. A third is the idea that the same or very similar processes operate within different subsystems (von Bertalanffy, 1968). Although the content differs, similar processes are hypothesized to operate within the biological, psychological, and social systems.

One of the most important of these common processes is **reciprocal causality**, the idea that causality is bidirectional. Reciprocal causality is most easily understood when contrasted with *linear causality*, a scientific corollary of reductionism. According to linear assumptions, causation operates in one direction only: Parents cause their children to behave in a certain way, for example. Both formal reviews of the literature (Bell, 1968; Maccoby, 1992) and informal observations by millions of parents indicate, however, that children also change their parents' behavior. Such mutual influences define reciprocal causality, a process that occurs in all types of natural interaction. Even the traditional oper-

ant conditioning experiment must be conceptualized in terms of reciprocal causality.

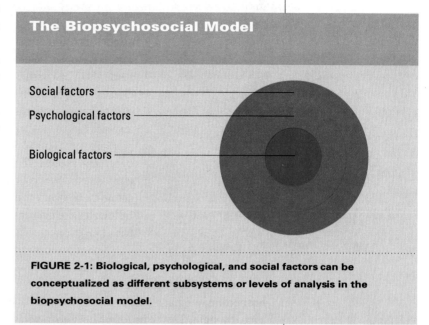

FIGURE 2-1: Biological, psychological, and social factors can be conceptualized as different subsystems or levels of analysis in the biopsychosocial model.

TABLE 2-3

Academic Disciplines at Different Levels of Analysis

Level of Analysis	Academic Discipline
Beyond Earth	Astronomy
Supranational	Ecology, economics
National	Government, political science
Organizations	Organizational science
Groups	Sociology
Organisms	Psychology, ethology, zoology
Organs	Cardiology, neurology
Cells	Cellular biology
Biochemicals	Biochemistry
Chemicals	Chemistry, physical chemistry
Atoms	Physics
Subatomic particles	Subatomic physics
Abstract systems	Mathematics, philosophy

Source: Based on G. E. Schwartz (1982). Testing the biopsychosocial model: The ultimate challenge facing behavioral medicine. *Journal of Consulting and Clinical Psychology*, 50, 1040–1053.

Psychologists cause rats to press the bar in a Skinner box, but rats also cause scientists to feed them, as the cartoon on page 44 illustrates.

Cybernetics is another critical systemic process. Cybernetics is a communication and control process that uses *feedback loops* to adjust progress toward a goal. The operation of a thermostat is a good example of a simple cybernetic process. Air temperature is monitored continuously to maintain room temperature within a constant range by either turning on or shutting off a heat source. Many social interactions also can be conceptualized as cybernetic processes. For example, instructors often direct questions toward silent students in discussion classes—a way of engaging quiet students and stifling overeager participants. This is a cybernetic process. The class contributions constitute the feedback that influences the instructor's behavior.

"Boy, have I got this guy conditioned! Every time I press the bar down he drops a piece of food."

The concept of cybernetics is essential to understanding another systemic process, **homeostasis**—that is, the tendency to maintain a steady state. The concept of homeostasis is familiar in biology, but it is also widely applicable in psychology. For example, people attempt to maintain a balance between too little stimulation and too much stress or anxiety. Some people are thrill seekers. They find that challenging activities like skydiving provide the right balance between the push of boredom and the pull of excitement. Other people are timid, and they find an equilibrium between the need for novelty and fear of the unknown in a limited and carefully controlled world. The setpoints for optimal levels of stimulation differ like the hotter and cooler settings on a thermostat, but all people engage in the homeostatic process of finding an individualized balance between too little and too much stimulation.

Development

Homeostasis serves to maintain equilibrium, but change is also essential in systems. *Development* is the most basic source of change among humans. Over time, people follow a fairly predictable trajectory of change. Children learn to crawl, walk, and run in an established sequence, and their cognitive skills also unfold in a predictable manner. Development is not limited to children or to the physical or intellectual domains. Development continues throughout adult life, and predictable changes occur in both psychological and social experiences. In fact, we devote an entire chapter of the text (Chapter 16)

to a discussion of the normal but psychologically trying changes that result from developmental transitions during adult life.

Because people develop and change over time, knowledge of normal development is essential to understanding psychopathology. **Developmental psychopathology** is a new approach to abnormal psychology that emphasizes the importance of changing *developmental norms*—age-graded averages—to determining what constitutes abnormal behavior (Cicchetti & Cohen, in press; Rutter & Garmezy, 1983). Developmental norms tell us that a full-blown temper tantrum is normal at 2 years of age, for example, but that kicking and screaming to get your way is abnormal at the age of 22. Similarly, we need to know the developmental norm for a difficult psychological experience like grieving in order to know when mourning should be considered pathological (too intense) or unresolved (too long-lasting).

For these reasons, we frequently consider questions about normal development in this textbook on abnormal psychology. We also discuss the development of abnormal behavior itself. Many psychological disorders follow unique developmental patterns. Sometimes there is a characteristic **premorbid history**, a pattern of behavior that precedes the onset of the disorder. People with schizophrenia, for example, often are withdrawn and awkward before the onset of their psychosis.

A disorder also may have a predictable course or **prognosis** for the future. When schizophrenia is untreated, the condition often deteriorates—psychotic symptoms may improve, but day-to-day coping becomes less adequate (see Chapter 12). By discussing the premorbid adjustment and the course of different psychological disorders, we hope to present abnormal behavior as a moving picture of development and not just as a diagnostic snapshot.

The remainder of this chapter is divided into sections on biological, psychological, and social factors relevant to the causes of psychopathology. In each of these three sections, we focus most of our discussion on normal development, although we highlight some implications for understanding the etiology of abnormal behavior. In subsequent chapters on specific disorders, we present more information on abnormal development in the context of biological, psychological, and social functioning.

Biological Factors

In considering biological influences on normal and abnormal behavior, it is helpful to note the distinction between the study of biological structures and of biological functions. The field of *anatomy* is concerned with the study of biological structures, and the field of *physiology* investigates biological functions. *Neuroanatomy* and *neurophysiology* are subspecialties within these broader fields that are of particular importance to abnormal psychology, because these disciplines focus specifically on the investigation of brain structures and brain functions.

We begin our discussion by considering the smallest anatomical unit within the nervous system, the neuron or nerve cell. An overview of the major brain structures, and current knowledge of their primary behavioral functions, is presented next. We then turn to discuss psychophysiology, the effect of psychological experience on the functioning of various body systems. Finally, we consider the broadest of all biological influences, the effect of genes on behavior.

The Neuron

Billions of tiny nerve cells or **neurons** form the basic building blocks of the brain. Each neuron has four major anatomical components; the soma or cell body, the dendrites, the axon, and the terminal buttons (see Figure 2–2). The **soma**—the cell body and largest part of the neuron—is where most of the neuron's metabolism and maintenance is controlled and performed. The **dendrites** branch out from the soma; they serve the primary function of receiving messages from other cells. The **axon** is the trunk of the neuron. Messages are transmitted down the axon toward other cells with which a given neuron communicates. Finally, the **terminal buttons** are "buds" found on the small branches at the end of the axon where messages are sent out to other neurons (Barondes, 1993).

Scientists have made great strides in deciphering the neurophysiological processes involved in communication within and between neurons. Within each neuron, information is transmitted as a change in electrical potential that moves from the dendrites and cell body, along the axon, toward the terminal buttons. The terminal buttons are separated from other cells by a **synapse**, a small gap filled with fluid. Neurons typically have synapses with thousands of other cells.

Unlike the electrical communication within a neuron, information is transmitted chemically across a synapse to other neurons. The terminal buttons release chemical substances called **neurotransmitters** into the synapse, which are received at the **receptors** on the dendrites or soma of another neuron. Dozens of different chemical compounds serve as neurotransmitters in the brain, and the functions of particular neurotransmitters vary. Moreover, different receptor sites are more or less responsive to particular neurotransmitters.

Not all neurotransmitters cross the synapse and reach the receptors on another neuron. The process of **reuptake** captures some neurotransmitters in the synapse and returns the chemical substances to the terminal button. The neurotransmitter then is reused in subsequent neural transmission.

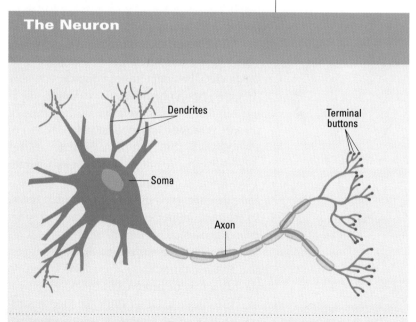

The Neuron

FIGURE 2-2: The anatomical structure of the neuron or nerve cell.

Source: John G. Seamon and Douglas T. Kenrick (1994). *Psychology* (2nd ed.), p.44. Englewood Cliffs, NJ: Prentice Hall.

In addition to the neurotransmitters, a second type of chemical affects communication in the brain. **Neuromodulators** are chemicals that may be released from neurons or from endocrine glands (which we will discuss shortly). Neuromodulators can influence communication among many neurons, and they often affect regions of the brain that are quite distant from where the neuromodulator was released. The most familiar neuromodulators are the *endorphins*—chemicals that have a structure similar to the drug opium (see Chapter 10). Thus, they are often referred to as *opioids*. The endorphins were discovered in the 1970s, but active research is being conducted on their possible role in a number of emotional disorders (Barondes, 1993; Nemeroff & Bissette, 1986).

NEUROTRANSMITTERS AND THE ETIOLOGY OF PSYCHOPATHOLOGY

Scientists have found that disrupted communication among neurons, particularly disruptions in the functioning of various neurotransmitters, plays a role in the etiology of several types of abnormal behavior. An oversupply of certain neurotransmitters is found in some mental disorders, an undersupply in other cases, and disturbances in reuptake in other psychological problems. In addition, the density and/or sensitivity of postsynaptic receptors has been implicated as playing a role in some forms of abnormal behavior.

Much research linking mental disorders with neurotransmitters has investigated how drugs affect the symptoms of a disorder and how they alter brain chemistry. For example, medications that are effective in alleviating some of the symptoms of schizophrenia are known to alter the availability of the neurotransmitter *dopamine* in the brains of animals (see Chapter 12). (Scientists cannot currently measure neurotransmitter levels in the living human brain, so neurotransmitter levels must be inferred either from animal studies or from indirect measures in humans.) These and related findings suggest that abnormalities in the dopamine system in the brain may be involved in the development of schizophrenia. Other evidence links neurotransmitters with different forms of abnormal behavior, as we discuss in relevant chapters throughout the text.

Investigations of neurophysiology have produced exciting findings, and several new medications have been developed that have remarkable benefits in treating certain mental disorders. Still, the technical and practical advances should not cloud reasoning about the etiology of psy-

chopathology. In particular, we must not equate a neurophysiological explanation of a psychological disorder with the identification of a biological abnormality. We have already discussed our concerns about biological reductionism in this regard. Another potential problem stems from **dualism**, the philosophical view that the mind and body are somehow separable.

Dualism dates to the writings of the philosopher René Descartes (1596–1650), who attempted to balance the dominant religious views of his times with emerging scientific reasoning. Descartes recognized the importance of studying human biology, but he wished to elevate human spirituality beyond that of other animals. In so doing, he argued that although many human functions have biological explanations, some human experiences have no somatic representation. Thus, he argued for a distinction—a dualism—between mind and body.

Similar attempts to separate the psyche and the soma have clouded thinking for centuries. One contemporary dualism is that biological explanations may account for psychological abnormalities, but normal psychological experience is somehow independent of biology. (For example, see the discussion of free will and determinism in Chapter 17). Because of this persistent dualism, biological explanations of psychological experience sometimes are erroneously equated with the identification of an abnormality. The psychological world cannot exist apart from the physical world, however. Just as a computer software program has an invisible electronic representation in the hardware of microchips, all psychological experience has an underlying representation in the brain Even love must have a biochemical explanation, as Calvin ponders in the cartoon on page 47. This fact does not mean that love is no more than a "chemical imbalance in the brain." The same logic applies to biochemical explanations of psychopathology.

Major Brain Structures

Neuroanatomists commonly divide the brain into three subdivisions: the hindbrain, the midbrain, and the forebrain (see Figure 2–3). Basic bodily functions are regulated by the structures of the *hindbrain*, which include the medulla, pons, and cerebellum. The *medulla* controls various body functions involved in sustaining life, including heart rate, blood pressure, and respiration. The *pons* serves various functions in regulating stages of sleep. The **cerebellum** serves as a control center in helping to coordinate physical movements. The cerebellum receives information on body movements and integrates this feedback with directives from higher brain structures about desired actions. Few forms of abnormal behavior are identified with disturbances in the hindbrain, because the hindbrain's primary role is limited to supervising these basic physical functions (Matthysse & Pope, 1986).

The *midbrain* also is involved in the control of some motor activities, especially those related to fighting and sex. Much of the **reticular activating system** is located in the midbrain, although it extends into the pons and medulla as well. The reticular activating system regulates sleeping and waking. Damage to areas of the midbrain can cause extreme disturbances in sexual behavior, aggressiveness, and sleep, but such abnormalities typically result from specific and unusual brain traumas or tumors (Matthysse & Pope, 1986).

Most of the human brain consists of the *forebrain*. The forebrain evolved more recently than the hindbrain and midbrain, and it therefore is the location of most sensory, emotional, and cognitive processes. These higher mental processes of the forebrain are linked with the midbrain and hindbrain by the limbic system. The *limbic system* is made up of a variety of different brain structures that are central to the regulation of emotion and basic learning processes. Two of the most important components of the limbic system are the thalamus and the hypothalamus. The **thalamus** is involved in receiving and integrating sensory information both from the sense organs and from higher brain structures. The **hypothalamus** also plays a role in sensation, but its more important functions are behavioral ones. The hypothalamus controls basic biological urges such as eating, drinking, and sexual activity. Much of the functioning of the autonomic nervous system (which we will discuss shortly) also is directed by the hypothalamus (Watson, Khachaturian, Lewis, & Akil, 1986).

CEREBRAL HEMISPHERES

Most of the forebrain is composed of the two **cerebral hemispheres**. Many brain functions are **lateralized**, so that one hemisphere serves a specialized role as the site of specific cognitive and emotional activities. In general, the left cerebral hemisphere is involved in language and related functions, and the right side is involved in spatial organization and analysis. The later-

alization and the localization of certain brain functions often make it possible to pinpoint brain damage based solely on behavioral difficulties.

The two cerebral hemispheres are connected by the *corpus callosum*, which is involved in coordinating the different functions that are performed by the left and the right hemispheres of the brain. When we view a cross-section of the forebrain, four connected chambers or **ventricles** become apparent (see the image on page 48). The ventricles are filled with cerebrospinal fluid, and they become enlarged in some psychological and neurological disorders.

The **cerebral cortex** is the uneven surface area of the brain that lies just underneath the skull. The cerebral cortex is the site of the control and integration of sophisticated memory, sensory, and motor functions. Details on the specific regions and functions of the cerebral cortex are discussed in later chapters.

MAJOR BRAIN STRUCTURES AND THE ETIOLOGY OF PSYCHOPATHOLOGY

The brain is incredibly complex, and scientists are only beginning to understand its anatomical

Basic Anatomy of the Brain

Forebrain
Midbrain

Cerebellum
Pons
Medulla

Hindbrain

Spinal cord

FIGURE 2-3: The major anatomical structures of the brain.

Source: John G. Seamon and Douglas T. Kenrick (1994). *Psychology* (2nd ed.), p.51. Englewood Cliffs, NJ: Prentice Hall.

structures and their functions. Because of the rudimentary state of knowledge about the brain, only the most severe mental disorders have clearly been linked with abnormalities in neuroanatomy. In most of these cases, brain damage is extensive and obvious. For example, the deterioration of brain structures is notable in many cases of dementia, but at present the gross abnormalities can only be identified conclusively during postmortem autopsies (see Chapter 13). The atrophy of the brain found during autopsy is widespread, however, and it is not of great value in helping to pinpoint the functions of specific brain structures.

Still, research on the brain holds great promise. Scientists have made breakthroughs in observing the anatomical structure of the living brain and in recording some of its global physiological processes. These various imaging procedures are now being used to study psychological disorders ranging from schizophrenia to learning disabilities; they are discussed in Chapter 4 along with several methods of psychological assessment.

At the present time, the new brain imaging measures are more exciting technically than practically in terms of their contributions to furthering our understanding of the etiology of psychopathology. Scientific advances frequently follow the development of new measures, however, and there is every reason to hope that advances in brain imaging will lead to improvements in understanding abnormalities in brain structure and function.

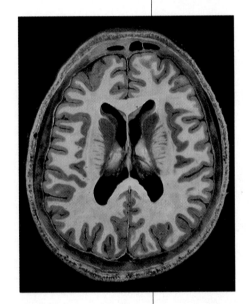

▲ **This cross-sectional image of the brain shows the ventricles, four connected chambers that are filled with cerebrospinal fluid.**

Psychophysiology

Psychophysiology is the study of changes in the functioning of the body that result from psychological experiences. Some of these physical reactions to environmental provocations are familiar. A pounding heart, a flushed face, tears, sexual excitement, and numerous other reactions are psychophysiological responses. These and other psychophysiological responses reflect a person's psychological state, particularly the degree and perhaps the type of the individual's emotional arousal.

ENDOCRINE SYSTEM

Psychophysiological arousal results from the activity of two different communication systems within the body, the endocrine system and the nervous system. The **endocrine system** is a collection of glands found at various locations throughout the body. Its major components include the ovaries or testes and the pituitary, thyroid, and adrenal glands (see Figure 2–4). Endocrine glands produce psychophysiological responses by releasing **hormones** into the bloodstream—chemical substances that affect the functioning of distant body systems and sometimes act as neuromodulators. The endocrine system regulates some aspects of normal development, particularly physical growth and sexual development. Parts of the endocrine system, particularly the adrenal glands, also are activated by stress and help prepare the body to respond to an emergency (see Chapter 7).

Certain abnormalities in the functioning of the endocrine system are known to cause psychological symptoms. For example, in *hyperthyroidism*, or *Graves' disease*, the thyroid gland secretes too much of the hormone thyroxin, causing restlessness, agitation, and anxiety. Recent research on depression also suggests that endocrine functioning may be involved in the etiology of this disorder (see Chapter 5).

NERVOUS SYSTEM

The more familiar and basic system of communication within the body is the nervous system. The human nervous system is divided into the *central nervous system*, which includes the brain and the spinal cord, and the peripheral nervous system. The *peripheral nervous system* includes all connections that stem out from the central nervous system and innervate the body's muscles, sensory systems, and organs.

The peripheral nervous system itself has two subdivisions. The voluntary or *somatic nervous system* governs muscular control, and the involuntary or **autonomic nervous system** regulates the functions of various body organs such as the heart and stomach. The somatic nervous system controls intentional or voluntary actions like scratching your nose. The autonomic nervous system is responsible for psychophysiological reactions—responses that occur with little or no conscious control.

The autonomic nervous system can be further divided into two branches, the sympathetic and parasympathetic nervous systems. In general, the **sympathetic nervous system** controls activities associated with increased arousal and energy expenditure, and the **parasympathetic nervous system** controls the slowing of arousal and energy conservation. The two branches thus work somewhat in opposition to one another as a means of maintaining homeostasis in the autonomic nervous system. In fact, optimal nervous system activity is described by an inverted U-shaped function, in which either too little or too much arousal is suboptimal (see Figure 2–5). At a behavioral level, this observation is supported by research on sensory deprivation in which people are found to hallucinate if they are deprived of sensory input for long periods of time. At the opposite extreme, chronic overstimulation leads to the shutting down of sensory awareness, as is demonstrated by comparing the reactions of out-of-town tourists and native New Yorkers on the streets of Manhattan. The tourists are overwhelmed by the stimulation; a New Yorker might ask "What stimulation?" Thus, maintaining homeostasis, a balance between unacceptable extremes, is the key to optimal psychophysiological arousal, as it is with the functioning of other biological, psychological, and social systems.

PSYCHOPHYSIOLOGY AND THE ETIOLOGY OF PSYCHOPATHOLOGY

Psychophysiological overarousal and underarousal have both been implicated in various theories of the causes of abnormal behavior. For example, autonomic overactivity is hypothesized to be responsible for excessive anxiety. In contrast, some theories suggest that chronic autonomic underarousal is responsible for the indifference to social rules and the failure to learn from punishment that characterize antisocial personality disorder (see Chapter 9).

Other theories of psychophysiology and abnormal behavior do not focus on dysfunctions in the autonomic nervous system. Instead, they emphasize psychophysiological assessment as a way of objectively measuring atypical reactions to psychological events. Scientists have developed numerous methods of measuring psychophysiological activity, ranging from assessments of sexual response to indices of muscle tension. We examine some of these psychophysiological measures in Chapter 4.

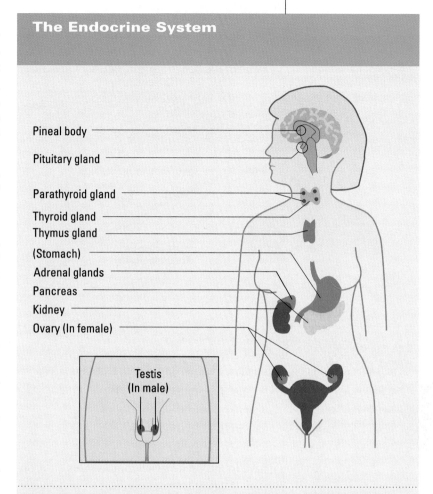

The Endocrine System

FIGURE 2-4: The glands that comprise the endocrine system, which affects physical and psychophysiological responses through the release of hormones.

Source: John G. Seamon and Douglas T. Kenrick (1994). *Psychology* (2nd ed.), p.67. Englewood Cliffs, NJ: Prentice Hall.

Behavior Genetics

The study of genetics is simultaneously the most molecular and the most molar approach to examining biological influences on behavior. **Genes** are ultramicroscopic units of DNA that carry information about heredity. Genes are located on **chromosomes**, chainlike structures found in the nucleus of cells. Humans normally have 23 pairs of chromosomes. The field of *genetics* identifies specific genes and their hereditary functions, often by literally focusing at the level of molecules. Geneticists typically have training in biochemistry, not psychology.

Behavior genetics is a much more molar approach that studies genetic influences on the evolution and development of normal and abnormal behavior (Goldsmith, 1988; McGuffin et al., 1994; Plomin & McClearn, 1990; Scarr,

1992). Behavior geneticists focus on behavior first and genes second. That is, they study behavior in an attempt to demonstrate that it has a more or less genetic origin. Behavior geneticists

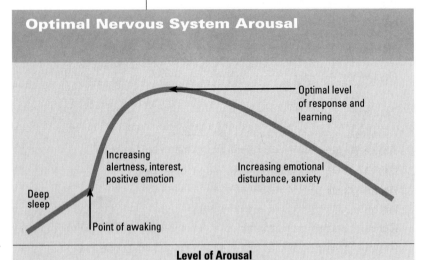

FIGURE 2-5: Donald Hebb's inverted U-shaped function indicates that a moderate level of arousal is optimal in the nervous system.

Adapted from D.O. Hebb. (1955). Drives and the CNS (conceptual nervous system). *Psychological Review, 62,* 243–254

have found broad genetic influences on problems ranging from alcoholism to schizophrenia—forms of psychopathology that once were thought to be determined solely by experience. Behavior geneticists seldom posit specific genetic causes of a disorder, however, and they rarely study individual genes.

SOME BASIC PRINCIPLES OF GENETICS
One of the most important principles of genetics is the distinction between genotype and phenotype. A **genotype** is an individual's actual genetic structure. Advances in biochemistry have allowed scientists to determine more and more aspects of genetic structure, but it still is impossible to observe much of an individual's genotype directly. Instead, what we observe is the **phenotype**, the expression of a given genotype. There is no one-to-one correspondence between phenotypes and genotypes. Different genotypes can produce similar phenotypes. And phenotypes, but not genotypes, are influenced by environmental experience. This means that it usually is impossible to infer a precise genotype from a given phenotype.

Differences between genotypes and phenotypes are evident in the simple mode of dom-

inant/recessive inheritance that was discovered by the Austrian monk Gregor Mendel (1822–1884) in his famous studies of garden peas. Mendel discovered that certain traits are dominant over other traits; for example, in peas, yellow color is dominant over green color. Today we know that inherited traits are controlled by genes, which have alternative forms known as *alleles.* Dominant/recessive inheritance occurs when a trait is caused by a gene that has only two alleles (for example, A and *a*) and only one *locus,* a specific location on a chromosome. In dominant/recessive inheritance, the phenotypic trait is either present or absent. In the case of Mendel's peas, for example, the gene for color has only two alleles, A (yellow, dominant) and *a* (green, recessive). Through cross-breeding, three genotypes are possible: AA, *a*A (or A*a*), and *aa.* Because A is dominant over *a,* however, both AA and *a*A plants will have yellow color. Thus, although three genotypes are possible, only two phenotypes are possible: yellow and green. The top panel in Figure 2–6 illustrates this concept.

Dominant/recessive inheritance causes some forms of mental retardation (Plomin, DeFries, & McClearn, 1990; Thapar et al., 1994; see Chapter 14). Most forms of abnormal behavior, however, are not caused by a single gene, if they have genetic causes at all. Instead, they are **polygenic,** that is, they are caused by more than one gene (Gottesman, 1991). Polygenic inheritance has an important effect on the distribution of traits. In contrast to the phenotypes produced by a single gene, polygenic inheritance produces continuous characteristics. In fact, the distribution of a phenotype in the population begins to resemble the normal curve as more genes are involved in determining the trait (see the bottom panel in Figure 2–6).

Polygenic inheritance greatly complicates the study of abnormal behavior. Single genes produce qualitatively different characteristics, such as color. In contrast, polygenic inheritance produces characteristics that differ quantitatively, such as height. Thus, the phenotype of most genetically influenced psychological disorders is on a continuum with normal behavior. As we mentioned in Chapter 1, the threshold of abnormal behavior can be difficult to determine when it differs from normal behavior only by a matter of degree. In addition to this diagnostic obstacle, polygenic inheritance obviously complicates the search for the specific genes involved in the etiology of psychopathology.

The complex reality of polygenic inheritance makes the study of genetic contributions to behavior difficult but not impossible. In fact, behavior geneticists have developed innovative methods for studying genetic contributions to behavior. The most important behavior genetic methods are twin studies, adoption studies, and family incidence studies.

TWIN STUDIES

Identical or **monozygotic (MZ)** twins are produced from a single fertilized egg. One egg is fertilized by one sperm; thus MZ twins have identical genotypes. Fraternal or **dizygotic (DZ)** twins are produced from separate fertilized eggs. There are two eggs and two sperm. Thus, like all siblings, DZ twins share an average of 50 percent of their genes, whereas MZ twins share 100 percent of their genes. Of course, most MZ and DZ twin pairs are raised in the same family. Thus, the two types of twins differ in their degree of genetic similarity, but they are alike in their environmental experiences.

Comparisons between MZ and DZ twin pairs therefore can shed light on the genetic and environmental contributions to a disorder. The key comparison involves determining whether MZ twins are more alike than DZ twins are alike. In the case of psychological disorders, the measure of interest is the degree of **concordance** in the twin pairs. A twin pair is concordant when both twins either have the same disorder or are free from the disorder. The twin pair is discordant when one twin has the disorder but the other does not.

If we can assume that the environmental effects on a disorder are the same for DZ twin pairs as they are for MZ twin pairs, then any differences between the concordance rates for MZ and DZ twins must be caused by genetics. To the extent that genetic inheritance contributes to a disorder, MZ twin pairs should be more alike than DZ twin pairs. If a disorder is purely genetic, for example, scientists should find a concordance rate of 100 percent for MZ twins (who are genetically identical) and 50 percent for DZ twins (who share half of the same genes on average). Any observed differences in concordance rates must be caused by genes, because we have assumed that the environmental effects are the same for both MZ and DZ twins.

In contrast, similar concordance rates for MZ and DZ twins rule out genetic contributions and instead implicate environmental causes of a disorder. Environmental causes are implicated regardless of whether the concordance rates

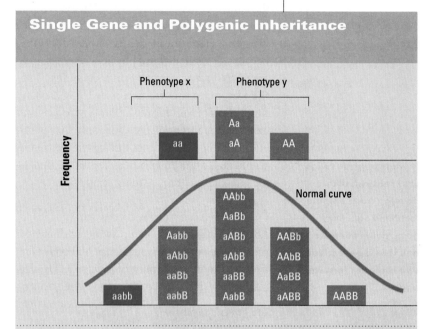

FIGURE 2-6: Single genes produce phenotypes that differ qualitatively, as illustrated in the top panel. Multiple genes produce phenotypes that differ quantitatively. As more genes are involved, the distribution of traits approximates the normal curve, as illustrated in the bottom panel.

for MZ and DZ twins are both 0 percent, both 100 percent, or both anywhere in between. Such differences in concordance rates can help scientists to understand the environmental contributions to a disorder, however. Higher concordance rates for both MZ and DZ twins point to the etiological role of *shared* environmental experiences. This is because both of the twins must have been affected by something that caused them both to develop a mental disorder. Since we know that the common cause is not their genes (because of the similar concordance rates for MZ and DZ pairs), the cause must be found in their shared environment. The experiences of a parental divorce or of living in poverty are examples of shared environmental experiences.

Lower concordance rates for both MZ and DZ pairs, on the other hand, point to the importance of different or *nonshared* environmental experiences in causing a disorder. In this case, genetic causes are again ruled out, and the importance of different experiences is indicated by the fact that only one twin has a psychological disorder. Being the favored child is an example of a nonshared environmental experience that can occur in the same family (Goldsmith, 1988).

All of this reasoning depends on the assumption that the environment affects DZ twins in the same way that it influences MZ twins. A number of critics have questioned this assumption. One important question is whether MZ twins, because of their striking physical resemblance, are treated more similarly than DZ twins. If so, then higher concordance rates for MZ twins might result from more similar environmental experiences and not from more similar genetic endowments. To address this criticism, many scientists have used another method of behavior genetic research, namely adoption studies.

ADOPTION STUDIES

Adoption studies also can provide evidence on the genetic versus the environmental contributions to the development of a disorder. In this research design, people who have been adopted as infants are compared with their biological versus their adoptive relatives (usually their parents) in terms of concordance for a disorder. If concordance is higher for biological than for adoptive relatives, then genetic factors are involved, because adopted children share their biological relatives' genes but not their environment. On the other hand, if children are more similar to their adoptive than to their biological relatives, then environment must influence the characteristic because adopted children share their adoptive relatives' environment but not their genes. Adoption studies also have some potential problems (for example, the fact that adoption placement is selective). Still, you can be confident in the findings of behavior genetic research when adoption and twin studies produce similar results (Goldsmith, 1988).

▼ Monozygotic twins are identical; they develop from a single fertilized egg. Dizygotic twins are fraternal; they develop from two different fertilized eggs.

FAMILY INCIDENCE STUDIES

The family incidence study is a final type of behavior genetic investigation that deserves brief mention, if only because findings from these studies are often misinterpreted. Family incidence studies ask whether diseases "run in families." Investigators identify normal and ill **probands**, or index cases, and tabulate the frequency with which other members of their families suffer from the same disorder. If a higher prevalence of illness is found in families where there is an ill proband, this is consistent with genetic causation. The finding also is consistent with environmental causation, however, because families share environments as well as genes. For this reason, no firm conclusions about the relative role of genes or the environment can be reached from family incidence studies alone.

MISINTERPRETING BEHAVIOR GENETICS FINDINGS

The methods of behavior genetics research are powerful, and mounting evidence indicates that genetics contributes to a wide variety of psychological disorders. Unfortunately, findings from behavior genetic research often are misinterpreted.

One serious misinterpretation is the conclusion that a psychological disorder will inevitably appear if it has a genetic component. This conclusion is wrong, in part, because genetics alone do not cause the vast majority of emotional disorders. Behavior genetics studies on mental illness typically find concordance rates for MZ twins that are well below 100 percent. Thus, the *diathesis–stress* model introduced in Chapter 1 is a more useful way to think about behavior genetics research. Genes can form a diathesis or predisposition for a psychological problem, but the disorder is produced only when the predisposition is combined with an environmental stress.

It also is wrong to think that genetic characteristics cannot be modified or controlled. For example, even in cases where mental retardation has a known genetic cause, certain environmental experiences such as diet or early stimulation have been demonstrated to lead to substantial increases—or decreases—in IQ (Turkheimer, 1991; see Chapter 14). The conclusion "It's genetic" does not provide an excuse for accepting the status quo. With rare exceptions, society remains responsible for helping people to maximize their genetic potential, and individuals remain personally responsible for their actions.

Finally, you should recognize that, when a genetic contribution to a disorder is found, it is not clear what mechanism or *mediating process* accounts for the findings. For example, researchers have found genetic contributions to adult criminality, but there obviously are no genes that predetermine assault, armed robbery, and so on. The critical question is: What partially inherited mediating process accounts for the behavior genetics finding? In the case of criminal behavior, one possible mediating process is the inheritance of a chronically underaroused autonomic nervous system. Thus, some people may be more likely to engage in criminal acts because they are less fearful and less likely to learn from experience (see Chapter 9).

GENETICS AND THE ETIOLOGY OF PSYCHOPATHOLOGY

There can be no doubt that genes have very broad effects on abnormal behavior, despite our cautions about interpreting behavior genetics research. Most influences appear to be polygenic; thus psychologists continue to be vexed by the question of where to draw the line between normal and abnormal behavior. Still, a relatively small number of genes may contribute to certain disorders, and the identification of specific genes could lead to breakthroughs in diagnosis and treatment.

Genes partially determine *individual differences*, or why people are different from one another. Genes also are basic to determining *species-typical characteristics*—characteristics that people have in common as a part of all human nature. Questions about inherent human nature are central to the understanding of abnormal behavior, because we must know what is normal in order to define what is abnormal. We consider species-typical characteristics—basic human nature—as part of our next topic, psychological contributions to abnormal behavior.

Psychological Factors

Proponents of the psychoanalytic, behavioral, and humanistic paradigms have clashed vehemently in theorizing about the etiology of psychopathology. Despite paradigmatic differences, however, common themes and issues are found across psychological approaches to understanding abnormal behavior. Psychology has not reached a consensus about its core contents and processes —the psychological equivalents of neuroanatomy and neurophysiology. Nevertheless, psychologists increasingly are struggling to define common ground. In this spirit, we highlight four key topics in the following discussion of psychological factors and the causes of abnormal behavior: (a) basic human motivations and temperamental styles; (b) learning and cognition (including distortions and defenses); (c) the sense of self; and (d) stages of psychological development.

Basic Motivations and Temperamental Styles

The foundation of any psychological theory is formed in its species-typical assumptions about human nature. In fact, we have already compared the traditional paradigms in terms of this essential starting assumption (see Table 2–2). What are the basic psychological motivations of humans—motivations that may or may not be shared with other animals?

HIERARCHY OF NEEDS

One influential ordering of human motivations is the **hierarchy of needs** developed by humanistic psychologist Abraham Maslow (1954). Maslow classified human needs according to more and less pressing priorities, giving precedence to biological needs over psychological ones (see Figure 2–7). According to Maslow, physical survival is the most basic human need, and it requires obtaining food, water, warmth, oxygen, and other necessities for human life. Safety needs come next, but these are of somewhat lesser priority. Humans will risk physical safety in order to maintain survival; for example, starving people will confront danger in order to obtain food.

In Maslow's theory the most basic psychological need is the need to belong to some social unit. The next psychological need is to be esteemed or valued by others. Just as psychological needs are sacrificed when biological needs are pressing, the need for esteem will be forsaken in order to meet the need to be a part of relationships. Finally, what distinguishes Maslow's theory as

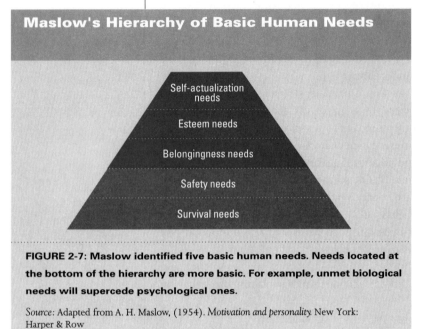

Maslow's Hierarchy of Basic Human Needs

- Self-actualization needs
- Esteem needs
- Belongingness needs
- Safety needs
- Survival needs

FIGURE 2-7: Maslow identified five basic human needs. Needs located at the bottom of the hierarchy are more basic. For example, unmet biological needs will supercede psychological ones.

Source: Adapted from A. H. Maslow, (1954). *Motivation and personality.* New York: Harper & Row

a humanistic approach is his identification of *self-actualization* as the fifth basic human need. Maslow believed that the need to fulfill one's human potential, to self-actualize, was an innate characteristic. The need for self-actualization clearly is a unique aspect of his theory, but when examined carefully, Maslow's hierarchy of human needs shares many broad assumptions with other approaches.

ATTACHMENT THEORY

The most basic psychological need in Maslow's hierarchy, the need to form close relationships, has been discussed in detail by the influential British psychiatrist and theorist John Bowlby (1907–1990). Bowlby was trained in psychoanalysis, but he explicitly rejected Freudian theory by placing the need to form close relationships at the core of his view of development (Bowlby, 1969/1982). The heart of Bowlby's theory is the observation that infants form **attachments** early in life—that is, they develop special and selective bonds with their caregivers. We discuss his approach, known as *attachment theory*, at various points throughout the text because it has stimulated considerable research.

Bowlby based attachment theory on findings from *ethology*, the study of animal behav-

ior. Ethologists have documented that close relationships develop between infants and caregivers in many species of animals. In some species, selective relationships develop in the first hours or days of life, a process called *imprinting*. Consistent with the ethological approach, Bowlby theorized that, like the far-less-flexible process of imprinting, the formation of attachments during the first year of life is a product of evolution. He noted that infants become distressed when separated from their caregivers, and their displays of distress—long and loud cries—keep caregivers in proximity. Proximity between human infants and their caregivers has survival value; thus, Bowlby theorized that attachment behavior developed as a result of natural selection.

DOMINANCE RELATIONS

The development of attachments, or more generally of *affiliation*, is only one of two basic social behaviors studied by ethologists. The second is the development of **dominance**, the hierarchical ordering of a social group into more and less powerful members (Sloman, Gardner, & Price, 1989). Dominance hierarchies are easily observed in human as well as animal social groups; thus it would seem that we also share this pattern of behavior with other animals. Note that the development of dominance relations in humans is not inconsistent with Maslow's theory that people need to be esteemed or valued by others.

Thus, we conclude that, in addition to more basic biological needs, humans have at least two sometimes competing psychological motivations: to form attachments and to compete for dominance. Our conclusion is consistent with the theories of U.S. psychiatrist Harry Stack Sullivan (1892–1949). As we discuss in Chapter 3, Sullivan developed an interpersonal theory of personality based on these two dimensions. In fact, some contemporary psychoanalytic theorists might agree with our conclusion. Some analytic theorists do not interpret Freud's basic drives of sex and aggression literally. They instead view Freud's ideas as metaphors that are not unlike the contemporary concepts of affiliation and dominance (Cameron & Rychlak, 1985).

EMOTIONS AND EMOTIONAL SYSTEMS

To this point, we have discussed basic psychological motivations at the level of social behavior—but how are they represented within the individual? Many contemporary theorists assert that key social interactions are motivated by *emotions* (much as searching for food is motivated by hunger). For example, attachment behaviors theoretically are motivated both by the fear experienced during separations and by the security felt by infant and caretaker during close contact.

Emotion is central to social motivation, but at present we highlight only two points about this important and controversial topic. First, emotion can be viewed as being more "primitive" than cognition, at least from the perspective of evolution. This suggestion is consistent with brain research indicating that emotions are controlled primarily by subcortical brain structures, whereas more abstract cognitive abilities are localized in the cerebral cortex, which is a more recent product of evolution. Our suggestion that humans share basic motivations with other species of animal also is consistent with the view that emotion is more primitive than cognition. Many aspects of human cognition—for example, our complex linguistic abilities—are unique, and distinguish us from other animals. These observations imply that cognition can shape or modify emotion, but feelings are more "basic": They are not wholly created by our intellectual interpretations of psychophysiological arousal (Panksepp, 1988).

Our second point is that it is useful to conceptualize emotions in terms of emotional *systems* instead of discrete emotions. That is, experiences may not activate a single isolated feeling, but instead they may elicit a constellation of emotions related to a particular social motivation (Panksepp, 1988). As an example of this, we have already described attachment in terms of a fear–security emotional system. In the attachment system, fear and security are not separate feelings. They are complementary emotions, and they motivate infants and caretakers to maintain proximity. Other emotional systems also appear to have been selected by evolution. These include the rage–fear emotional system associated with fight or flight (see Chapter 7) and the security–anger–sadness emotional constellation linked with grief (see Chapter 16).

The concept of emotional systems is consistent with evolutionary theory and with the biological realities of the brain (Panksepp, 1988). The focus on systems of emotion also holds important implications for understanding human

feelings. One example is that the same feeling may have a different meaning and a different opposing emotion depending on its social function or motivation. For example, anger in reaction to a physical threat clearly is different from anger in reaction to loss. In the first case, fear is the emotion opposing anger, but in the second case anger has two opposing emotions: security and sadness.

Understanding the experience of emotion clearly is central to understanding abnormal behavior. In fact, many psychological disorders are characterized primarily by emotional distress (for example, depression and anxiety disorders). Many theories of emotion have been proposed, and some hold contrasting implications for understanding psychopathology. For these reasons, we discuss emotion and theories of emotion frequently in subsequent chapters of the text.

▲ Characters from *Star Trek: The Next Generation* illustrate the central role of emotions in human personality. The android, Data (on the left), has superb cognitive capacities but lacks human emotion. In contrast, Troi comes from a race with extrahuman empathic abilities.

TEMPERAMENT

Recognition of common, species-typical needs, motivations, and emotions is basic to understanding abnormal behavior, but awareness of individual differences is equally critical. An important approach to research on individual differences is the study of **temperament**, characteristic styles of relating to the world. Some theorists assert that temperament is the expression of inborn characteristics (Goldsmith, 1988), while other psychologists equate temperament with the broader construct of personality (Zuckerman, 1991). In all cases, however, research on temperament focuses on the "how" of behavior, not the "what." Temperament theorists have attempted to identify consistencies in the process of relating to the world.

For decades psychologists have debated which elements comprise the basic *temperamental styles*, but recently a consensus on this topic has emerged (Goldberg, 1993; Zuckerman, 1991).

Based on extensive analysis of subjects' responses to structured questionnaires, a number of researchers have identified five bipolar dimensions of personality, sometimes called "the big five." These are: (1) *neuroticism*—nervous and moody versus calm and pleasant; (2) *extraversion*—active and talkative versus passive and reserved; (3) *openness to experience*—imaginative and curious versus shallow and imperceptive; (4) *agreeableness*—trusting and kind versus hostile and selfish; and (5) *conscientiousness*—organized and reliable versus careless and negligent.

Individual differences in temperamental styles have been hypothesized to play a role in the development of a number of different psychological disorders. Not surprisingly, these basic dimensions of personality have particularly influenced thinking about the development of personality disorders, as we discuss in Chapter 9. Temperament also holds a special place in research on the etiology of behavior problems among children, a topic we discuss in Chapter 15.

BASIC MOTIVATIONS, TEMPERAMENT, AND THE ETIOLOGY OF PSYCHOPATHOLOGY

Attachment theorists assert that the origins of psychopathology can be traced to the failure to meet a child's basic need to form a secure attachment. Of particular concern are the effects of *insecure* or *anxious attachments*—uncertain or ambivalent parent–child relationships that are a consequence of inconsistent and unresponsive parenting, particularly during the first year of life (Ainsworth et al., 1978). Anxious attachments are hypothesized to cause children to be mistrustful, dependent, and/or rejecting when ap-proaching subsequent relationships, a pattern that may continue into adult life. Attachment theorists also assert that similar uncertainties about relationships are created by parental separation and loss during childhood (Bowlby, 1973, 1980). Critics argue that early attachment difficulties are more easily overcome than attachment theory asserts, but they agree that close,

▼ **Robert Duvall portrayed a rigid and explosive father in** *The Great Santini.* **The character was a harsh disciplinarian who offered his children little love. Psychologists highlight the importance of the combination of parental love and discipline.**

supportive relationships promote mental health throughout the life span (Rutter & Rutter, 1993).

Little research has been conducted on the consequences of unfulfilled needs for social dominance or esteem. Much evidence does indicate, however, that children need to be "dominated"—disciplined is a much better word—if they are to learn to conform their behavior to social norms. It is worth noting, moreover, that according to a leading developmental theory, the most effective parents are those who are able to meet (or control) their children's needs in both of the two basic areas that we have highlighted. Specifically, children whose parents are loving *and* firm in their discipline are better adjusted in comparison to children whose parents are inadequate on one or both of these dimensions (Maccoby & Martin, 1983).

Finally, the role of temperament in the development of psychopathology generally is viewed in terms of the diathesis–stress model. Specifically, researchers have focused on the *goodness of fit* between children's temperament and their environment. A "difficult" temperament may increase the risk for the subsequent development of abnormal behavior, but experience determines whether or not problems emerge (Chess & Thomas, 1984).

Learning and Cognition

Emotions, motivations, and temperamental styles all can be modified, at least to some degree, by the higher processes of learning and cognition. In our historical review, we have already discussed two critical learning processes: classical and operant conditioning. These modes of learning are essential in normal development. As you will see in later chapters, classical and operant conditioning also play an important role in the etiology or maintenance of several psychological disorders.

MODELING

A third method of learning, known as modeling, was originally identified by U.S. psychologist Albert Bandura (Bandura & Walters, 1963). The concept of **modeling** suggests that people learn much of their behavior by imitating others, a process that you surely have observed many times.

A similar but more complex concept is the process of learning through identification. The concept of **identification** was introduced by Freud (1940/1969), who asserted that children identify strongly with one adult, normally the same-gender parent. The process of identification suggests that children not only imitate an adult's behavior, but they also adopt his or her values. Freud's emphasis on the need to identify with the parent of the same gender has been roundly criticized. However, the basic idea of identification—that children not only *act* like certain adults but want to *be* like them—suggests that modeling may involve more than mere imitation.

SOCIAL COGNITION

Cognitive psychologists commonly draw analogies between human thinking and the operation of computers in discussing additional, more complex processes of learning. Thus, the field highlights concepts such as information processing, memory systems, and retrieval processes. Social psychologists, in turn, have developed the parallel field of *social cognition*—the study of how humans process information about themselves and others.

The important concept of attribution illustrates the social cognition approach. **Attributions** are perceived causes—people's beliefs about cause-effect relations. In evaluating a friend's hostility toward you, for example, you rarely examine it scientifically. Instead, you attribute his or her actions to some reasonable cause, perhaps a tendency to overreact. Attribution theorists suggest that humans are "intuitive scientists" who routinely draw such conclusions about causality. We use shorthand calculations instead of more detailed methods in attributing causes because the quick assessments are efficient—they require little cognitive processing. Attributions can be inaccurate, however, in part because they are made intuitively rather than scientifically (Nisbett & Wilson, 1977). Moreover, errors in making attributions, and other cognitive biases, have increasingly been suggested to play a role in the development of abnormal behavior (Peterson & Seligman, 1984).

LEARNING, DISTORTED COGNITION, AND THE ETIOLOGY OF PSYCHOPATHOLOGY

As Watson suggested, at least some abnormal behavior apparently is learned. Fears can be classically conditioned, antisocial behavior often is rewarded, and some children imitate or identify with an alcoholic parent, to cite several examples. Abnormal behavior also may be learned

through more complex cognitive processes, particularly as a result of systematic errors or distortions in information processing. (Recall that Freud thought that distortions of reality—defense mechanisms—played a key role in the etiology of abnormal behavior.)

One important example of the cognitive approach suggests that errors in making attributions about the causes of life events play a role in the etiology of some psychological disorders. A topic that we discuss in Chapter 5, *learned helplessness theory*, suggests that depression is caused by wrongly attributing negative events to internal, global, and stable causes (Peterson & Seligman, 1984). For instance, you conclude that you got a bad grade on a calculus exam because "I'm stupid," not because the teacher was unfair, you are lousy at math, or you did not work hard enough. Your "stupid" attribution makes the grade more stressful and ultimately more depressing.

Another theory suggests that depression is caused by automatic and distorted perceptions of reality, particularly negative *cognitive errors* (Beck, 1979). For example, people prone to depression have been hypothesized to draw inaccurate, negative generalizations in processing information about themselves. They draw global conclusions about their inadequacies based on a single unpleasant experience. It is interesting to note that a treatment that was developed based on this theory encourages depressed people to be more scientific and less intuitive in evaluating their conclusions (see Chapter 5).

The Sense of Self

People share emotions and motivations with other animals, and we share some information-processing strategies with computers. Still, our sense of self seems to be a uniquely human quality. The exact definition of our sense of self is elusive. This often is true personally, and the definition of self clearly is elusive in the numerous psychological conceptualizations.

One important and influential conceptualization of self is Erikson's (1968) concept of **identity**. Erikson viewed identity as the product of the adolescent's struggle to answer the question "Who am I?" In his view, the conflict caused by this persistent question eventually produces an enduring identity, an integrated sense of individuality, wholeness, and continuity.

Some theorists have countered that identity is not a unitary construct. Instead, they argue that there are many "selves." Psychologist George Kelly (1905–1966), for example, emphasized the many different roles that people play in life. These include such obvious roles as being a daughter, a student, and a friend, and they also include less obvious roles like being a "caretaker," a "jock," or "the quiet one." Thus, rather than having a single identity, Kelly argued, people develop many different *role identities*, various senses of oneself that correspond with actual life roles.

Even more specific views on the individual's sense of self are found in cognitive conceptualizations that discuss specific **self-schema**—cognitions about oneself. Albert Ellis (1970), the visible and vocal advocate of rational emotive therapy (see Chapter 3), provides one example of this approach. He points to people's irrational beliefs as the source of much of their psychological distress. **Irrational beliefs** are impossible, absolute standards, such as "Everyone must love me all of the time." According to Ellis, failure and psychological distress are inevitable consequences of irrational beliefs, because nobody can live up to the impossible standards.

SELF SYSTEMS AND THE ETIOLOGY OF PSYCHOPATHOLOGY

There is no commonly accepted definition of self in psychology. Still, two ideas—self-control and self-esteem—are frequently found in theorizing and research on psychopathology.

The idea that children and adults must develop **self-control**—internal rules for guiding appropriate behavior—is commonly accepted in research on abnormal behavior. Self-control is learned through the process of *socialization,* wherein parents, teachers, and peers use discipline, praise, and their own good example to teach children prosocial behavior and set limits on their antisocial behavior. Over time, these standards are *internalized*—that is, the external rules become internal regulations. The result is self-control (Maccoby, 1992).

A sense of self-worth is a different aspect of the self. Various discussions of the importance of high self-esteem have been emphasized by psychoanalytic, behavioral, and humanistic theorists. Sigmund Freud (1940/1969) discussed the importance of a healthy ego, a strong and confident inner reserve (see Further Thoughts

earlier in this chapter). Carl Rogers (1959) highlighted a healthy *self-concept*—feeling worthy and capable—as the core structure of personality in his humanistic approach. Finally, social learning theorist Albert Bandura (1977) argued for the primacy of **self-efficacy**, the belief that one can achieve desired goals. Each theorist thus highlighted the importance of the individual's sense of self-worth for mental health. You should note, however, that low self-esteem could be a result rather than a cause of abnormal behavior. High self-esteem grows from success and fulfillment, while anxiety and depression—and low self-esteem—result from failure, loss, conflict, and rejection. In short, low self-esteem may only be an index of emotional problems, not a cause of them.

Stages of Development

Developmental change is a final topic that is especially relevant to psychological contributions to the etiology of psychopathology. Of particular importance are periods of very rapid developmental change, or what we can consider to be qualitative changes in development. Such shifts mark the end of one **stage of development**, a period of continuous and slow change focused on a particular set of psychological or social issues, and perhaps the beginning of a new developmental stage.

To illustrate the idea of stages of development, consider for a moment the schools you have attended. You have experienced at least four important "stages of development" in your schooling: elementary school, middle school, high school, and college. The shift from one "stage" to another (for example, going to college) required you to make rapid and perhaps challenging changes in your life. Moreover, once you entered a new "stage" you had to learn to master new tasks and perform according to a new set of expectations.

Stages of psychological development similarly challenge routine functioning and force the individual to learn new ways of thinking, feeling, and acting. Normal distress in response to such difficult transitions sometimes can be confused with abnormal behavior. Moreover, we have to be aware of the normal tasks of a particular stage of development in order to understand abnormal behavior.

Two prominent stage theories are especially relevant to abnormal psychology: Freud's theory of psycho*sexual* development and Erikson's theory of psycho*social* development. As is evident in the name given to his theory, Freud highlighted the child's internal struggles with sexuality as marking the various stages of development. In contrast, Erikson emphasized social tasks and focus, these ages seem to be key times of transition for children.

DEVELOPMENT AND THE ETIOLOGY OF PSYCHOPATHOLOGY

The idea of developmental stages suggests some new concepts for understanding the etiology of

---

TABLE 2-4

Freud and Erikson's Stage Theories of Development

Age[1]	0–1 1/2	1–3	2–6	5–12	11–20	18–30	25–70	65 on
Freud	**Oral** Oral gratification through breast feeding. Meeting one's own needs.	**Anal** Learning control over environment and inner needs through toilet training.	**Phallic** Recognition of sexuality and rivalry with opposite-gender parent. Oedipal conflicts, penis envy.	**Latency** Not a stage as psychosexual development is dormant during these ages.	**Genital** Mature sexuality and formation of mutual heterosexual relationships.			
Erikson	**Basic trust vs. basic mistrust** Developing basic trust in self and others through feeding and care taking.	**Autonomy vs. shame and doubt** Gaining a sense of competence and independence through sucess in toileting and mastering environment.	**Initiative vs. guilt** Gaining parental approval for initiative rather than guilt over rivalry and inadequacy.	**Industry vs. inferiority** Curiosity and eagerness to learn leads to a sense of competence or inadequacy.	**Identify vs. role confusion** Indentity crisis is a struggle to answer question, "Who am I?".	**Intimacy vs. self-absorption** Sense of aloneness of young adult resolved by forming close friendships and a lasting intimate relationship.	**Generativity vs. stagnation** Sucess in work but especially in raising the next generation or failure to be productive (even if children are born).	**Integrity vs. despair** A sense of satisfaction with the life one lived rather than despair over lost opportunities.

[1] Ages are approximate as indicated by overlap in age ranges.

---

the conflicts involved in meeting the demands of the external world. Importantly, Erikson also suggested that development does not end with adolescence; rather, he proposed that qualitative developmental changes continue throughout the lifespan. The key tasks, age ranges, and defining events of these two stage theories are summarized in Table 2–4. In considering differences between the theories, also note an interesting similarity. Both theorists use similar ages to denote the beginning and end of their developmental stages of childhood. Others also have suggested that key developmental transitions occur around the ages of 1½, 6, and 12. Included among this group is the noted Swiss psychologist Jean Piaget, who theorized about cognitive development. Irrespective of substantive

psychopathology. One key concept is the notion of a *developmental transition*, the idea that stressful and important changes occur during times of rapid biological, psychological, or social development. People often are stressed by normal developmental transitions, and frequently seek the help of a mental health professional as a result. For this reason, Chapter 16 is devoted exclusively to a discussion of difficult developmental transitions throughout the lifespan.

Two other concepts relevant to stage theories are the ideas of fixation and regression. *Fixation* occurs when psychological development is arrested at a particular stage. The person continues to grow physically but stops growing emotionally. *Regression* is characterized by the return to an earlier stage or style of coping or behaving. These concepts may be less useful as explanations of the etiology of psychopathology than they are as descriptions of the symp- toms of some psychological disorders, as we discuss in later chapters.

Social Factors

The broadest perspective for understanding the causes of abnormal behavior is at the level of the social system. Social factors incorporate an almost endless number of potential influences on psychopathology, including many aspects of interpersonal relationships, social roles, and cultural beliefs. It therefore is necessary to be selective in presenting an overview of social contributions to psychopathology. In this section, we begin with a focus on relationships, move on to consider gender roles, ethnicity, and poverty, and end with a brief mention of the influence of culture on abnormal behavior.

These social perspectives all emphasize that people's *social roles*, their characteristic styles of behaving according to the expectations of the social situation, influence the definition and development of psychopathology. Much the way an actor assumes a role in a play, people play roles in their families, in social relationships, and according to the very broad expectations associated with gender, race, social class, and culture. In fact, *labeling theory* views emotional disorders themselves in terms of role theory (Rosenhan, 1973). According to labeling theory, abnormal behavior is created by social expectations. Abnormality is only what a given group or society deems to be abnormal (see Chapter 4). Labeling theory also suggests that people's actions conform to the expectations created by the label, a process that has been termed the *self-fulfilling prophesy* (Rosenthal, 1966). For example, when an elementary school boy is labeled as "a troublemaker," both he and his teachers may act in ways that make the label come true.

There is little doubt that expectations affect behavior. Still, labeling alone cannot somehow cause the severe hallucinations, delusions, and life disruptions that characterize severe disorders like schizophrenia, for example. The roles people play in life help to shape who they become, but psychopathology is much more than the expectancies a label creates.

Relationships and Psychopathology

Much evidence links abnormal behavior with distressed or conflicted relationships. Obvious difficulties like anger and conflict in relationships are linked with a number of different emotional disorders ranging from schizophrenia to conduct problems among children (Emery, 1982; Fontana, 1966). Still, it often is impossible to determine if troubled relationships actually *cause* abnormal behavior. In many cases, it seems equally or more likely that relationship distress is the *effect* of individual problems (see Research Methods).

MARITAL STATUS AND PSYCHOPATHOLOGY

The relationship between marital status and psychopathology offers a good example of the cause–effect dilemma we have just discussed. The demographics of the U.S. family have changed greatly over the last few decades. Cohabitation before marriage is frequent, many children are born outside of marriage, and half of all marriages end in divorce (Cherlin, 1992). In part because of the uncertainty created by these rapid changes, researchers have frequently examined the psychological consequences of alternative family structures for children and for adults (Amato & Keith, 1991a, 1991b; Emery, 1988, 1994; Gotlib & McCabe, 1990).

The findings of this large body of research must be interpreted with caution and care. On the one hand, marital status and psychological problems clearly are *correlated*. Somewhat more emotional problems are found among children and adults from divorced or never-married families than among people living in always-married families. On the other hand, despite common assumptions to the contrary, it is not clear that marital status is a direct *cause* of the emotional problems. Alternative explanations of the correlation between marital status and psychopathology include suggestions that common genetic factors cause both emotional disorders and marital disruption (McGue & Lykken, 1992), as well as the likely possibility that marital status can be a consequence, not a cause, of some psycholog- ical problems, particularly among adults (Gotlib & McCabe, 1990). Thus, marital status may cause psychopathology, but abnormal behavior also can create dysfunctional families (see Research Close-up).

RESEARCH METHODS

The Correlational Method

In Chapter 1 we introduced the case study method. We noted its value for illustrating important or unusual problems and for helping the scientist- practitioner to develop hypotheses. As we dis- cussed, however, the case study has major weaknesses as a research method. Scientists have developed other more sophisticated methods for con- ducting research. These techniques are used to study psychological disorders systematically and objectively.

The correlational study is one of two major alter- natives to the case study. (The other is the experi- ment, as we discuss in Research Methods in Chapter 3.) In the **correlational method,** the relation between two factors (their co-relation) is studied in a sys- tematic fashion. For example, you might hypothe- size that psychology majors on your campus learn more about research methods than biology majors do. To support this hypothesis, you might simply argue your point, or you could rely on case studies. ("I know more about research than my roommate, and *she's* a biology major!")

If you were to conduct a correlational study on the question, however, you would collect a large sample of both psychology and biology majors and compare them on an objective measure of knowl- edge of research methods. You would then use sta- tistics to test whether or not research knowledge is *correlated* with academic major. (As we discuss in Research Methods in Chapters 9 and 15, the find- ings of correlational studies—and all scientific research—are influenced greatly by the sample that is recruited and the quality of measurement; for now, we will skip over these important issues.)

An important statistic for measuring how strong- ly two factors are related is the **correlation coeffi- cient**. The correlation coefficient is a number that always ranges between -1.00 and +1.00. When a cor- relation coefficient has a higher absolute value, regardless of whether it is positive or negative, then the two factors are more strongly correlated. If all psychology majors got 100 percent of the items cor- rect on your test of research methods and all biol- ogy majors got 0 percent correct, the absolute value of the correlation between academic major and research knowledge would be 1.00. That is, a per- fect relationship would exist between academic major and research knowledge. If all psychology and biology majors got 50 percent of the items correct, the correlation between major and knowledge would be zero; no correlation would exist between major and knowledge.

Positive correlations (from 0.00 to 1.00) indicate that, as one factor goes up, the other factor also goes up. For example, height and weight are positively correlated, as are years of education and employ- ment income. Taller people weigh more; educated people earn more money. *Negative correlations* (from -1.00 to 0.00) indicate that, as one number gets bigger, the other number gets smaller. For exam- ple, population and open space are negatively cor- related. As more people move into an area, the amount of open land diminishes.

In this chapter, we noted a number of factors that are correlated with psychological problems. Self-esteem is negatively correlated with emotion- al problems. The higher your self-esteem, the fewer problems you have. The levels of certain neuro- transmitters in the brain are positively correlated with some types of emotional problems (they are elevated in comparison to normal), and they are neg- atively correlated with other types of emotional prob- lems (they are depleted in comparison to normal). As we have suggested, however, a correlation between two factors must be interpreted cautious- ly. In particular, you should constantly remember that *correlation does not mean causation*.

In interpreting any correlation, there are always two alternative explanations to making a causal conclusion: reverse causality and third-variable alternative interpretations. We might want to conclude that *X* causes *Y*—that low self-esteem causes anxiety or that depleted neurotransmitters cause depression. However, the concept of **reverse causality** indicates that causation could be operating in the opposite direction: *Y* could be causing *X*. Anxiety could be causing low self-esteem, or depression could be causing the depletion of neurotransmitters.

The **third-variable** interpretation offers yet another alternative to causal conclusions. A correlation between any two variables could be explained by their joint relation with some unmeasured factor--a third variable. For example, both low self-esteem *and* anxiety could be products of a third variable, such as troubled family relationships. Similarly, stress might cause both depression *and* the depletion of neurotransmitters.

Let us return to the study of research knowledge and academic major to illustrate these issues further. Assume that you did find that psychology majors knew more about research methods. Based on this correlational finding, could you conclude that studying psychology *caused* students to learn more about research? No, you could not. A reverse causal-

ity interpretation of the correlation might suggest that people who knew more about research methods decided to become psychology majors. Knowledge about research caused them to choose this major, not vice versa. A third-variable interpretation of the correlation might suggest that more intelligent people choose to major in psychology, and more intelligent people also know more about the methods of scientific research. According to this interpretation, the correlation between academic major and research knowledge is *spurious*, an artifact of the relation of both of these variables with the third variable of intelligence.

As we discuss in Research Methods in Chapter 3, another method of research, the experiment, *does* allow scientists to determine cause and effect relations. As we note there, however, it often is impractical or unethical to conduct experiments on psychological problems. This is a particular problem for research on etiology. In contrast to the experiment, the correlational method poses far fewer practical or ethical problems. Thus, while the correlational method is characterized by the weakness that correlation does not mean causation, it also is characterized by the strength that it can be used to conduct research in many real-life circumstances. ■

SOCIAL RELATIONSHIPS

In addition to family relationships, key relationships outside the family also can affect mental health. For example, research indicates that a good relationship with an adult outside the family can buffer children from the effects of troubled family circumstances (Werner, 1993; Werner & Smith, 1982). The most important relationships outside the family are not with older adults, however, but with peers.

Research suggests that a few things are critical about **social support**—the emotional and practical assistance received from others. Close relationships sometimes provide protection against psychopathology (Cohen & Wills, 1985). Significantly, having one close relationship can provide as much support as being involved in many relationships. The greatest risk comes from having no social support. In addition, being actively rejected is much worse than simply being

neglected (Coie & Kupersmidt, 1983). Especially among children, it is far worse to be "liked least" than not to be "liked most" by your peers.

The association between abnormal behavior and the lack of supportive peer relationships may have several different causal explanations. In some circumstances, peer rejection may be the cause of emotional difficulties. Being made an outcast surely can cause much distress. In other cases, the lack of a close relationship may be a consequence of psychopathology, as when a disturbed individual is extremely awkward in social relationships. Finally, social support may help people to cope more successfully with emotional problems. The presence or absence of a close relationship might not affect the development of a psychological problem, but once the problem emerges, the availability of social support may be the difference between successful and failed coping.

Marriage and Mental Health

Psychologists and social policymakers often raise questions and concerns about a factor that is commonly found to be correlated with psychological well-being: marital status. Rates of divorce and childbirth outside of marriage have increased dramatically since the 1950s, and this has prompted particular concerns about children who grow up in alternative family forms. We discuss the consequences of divorce for children in some detail in Chapters 15 and 17. At present, we consider the correlation between adults' mental health and their marital status.

Valuable data on the relation between marriage and mental health are available from the Epidemiologic Catchment Area (ECA) study (Robins & Regier, 1991). The ECA is a large-scale study of the prevalence of mental disorders in the United States. We referred to the study briefly in Chapter 1, and we discuss it again at points throughout the book. Thousands of people were interviewed in this study in order to obtain state-of-the-art measurements of their mental health. The researchers also examined various life circumstances that were correlated with mental illness, including marital status.

The investigators found consistent correlations between marriage and mental health. As one example, 1.5 percent of people still in their first marriage were diagnosed as having experienced depression in the past year. For people who had never married, the 1-year prevalence of depression was 2.4 percent. Among those who had been divorced once, 4.1 percent had experienced depression in the past year. Finally, 5.8 percent of the people who had been divorced more than once had experienced an episode of depression in the previous 12 months. Thus, in comparison to people still in their first marriage, the never-married were about 1.5 times as likely to have been depressed; people who had been divorced once were almost 3 times as likely to be diagnosed with depression; and people divorced more than once were nearly 4 times as likely to be assigned the diagnosis.

Alcoholism also was found to be correlated with marital status. Among people in their first marriage, 8.9 percent met the diagnostic criteria for alcoholism at some time *in their life* (not the past year, which was the time frame for depression). For the never-married, the lifetime prevalence was 15 percent. Comparable figures were 16.2 percent for people divorced once and 24.2 percent for people divorced two or more times.

As a third and final illustration of the relation between marriage and mental illness, marital status was strongly related to a diagnosis of schizophrenia. (In fact, marital status was related to virtually every psychological disorder that was diagnosed in this study.) The lifetime prevalence of schizophrenia was 1.0 percent among the married, 2.1 percent among the never-married, and 2.9 percent among those who had ever separated or divorced.

How do we interpret the correlation between marriage and mental illness? The usual causal interpretation is that not being married causes emotional problems. According to this reasoning, the absence of a supportive mate makes unmarried people more susceptible to psychological problems, as do divorce and the conflict and loss of support that accompany it.

As we discussed in Research Methods in this chapter, however, reverse causality needs to be considered as an alternative explanation. Specifically, emotional problems may be the cause of marital status. Psychologically disturbed people may have more trouble dating and forming permanent relationships. If they do get married, their emotional struggles may make them or their spouses more unhappy with their marriages and more prone to divorce. Third-variable interpretations offer yet another possibility. Any number of third variables could create a spurious correlation between marital status and abnormal behavior. We know, for example, that poverty is correlated with an increased risk for remaining single or getting divorced, and we also know that poverty is correlated with an increased risk for developing psychological disorders. This suggests that poverty may be a third variable that creates an artificial relation between marriage and mental health.

These alternative explanations or alternative *models* of the relation between marriage and mental health hold important and vastly different implications for the treatment of psychological disorders and for social policy. If marital troubles are the cause of mental illness, our interventions should focus on improving or promoting marriage. For example, rather than treating individuals in therapy, psychologists may be more effective if they treat couples or families. Even more broadly, if marital status promotes mental health, then social policymakers might want to find ways to encourage marriage and discourage divorce.

Our perspective changes greatly, on the other hand, if mental illness causes marital troubles. Psychologists still may want to treat couples or families in addition to individual patients. These treatments would *not* attempt to improve relationships as a way of relieving psychological distress. Instead, the therapy might focus on helping family members to cope with the trying stressor of mental illness. Given the reverse causality scenario, social policymakers still may want to encourage marriage. At the same time they also may want to allow people to escape from at least some more troubling relationships—for example, when a woman is married to an abusive husband with alcohol problems.

We reach yet another set of conclusions if the correlation between marital status and psychopathology is caused by some third variable such as poverty. In this circumstance, it would be fruitless either to try to improve marriages in order to promote mental health or to treat psychological problems in order to ease the burden of mental illness on families. Rather, our interventions would focus on the third variable that presumably causes both of the other problems. In this case, that variable would be poverty, and the treatment and policy goal would be to try to eradicate it.

To this point, we have discussed marriage and mental health from a theoretical/methodological perspective. You may be wondering, more practically, what psychologists have concluded about the correlation between marriage and mental health. As we note in Research Methods throughout the text, scientists have developed various methods for attempting to determine causation from correlational methods. Despite these advances, we warn you that no one can definitively determine causation from correlation. With this caveat in mind, we can offer you three substantive conclusions about marriage and mental health.

First, the correlation between marriage and mental health may be partly explained by third variables like poverty, but much of it is "real." The correlation is still found even when we exclude the effects of poverty and related "third variables" (Gove, Hughes, & Styles, 1983). Second, for severe psychological disorders like schizophrenia, it seems clear that being single or getting divorced is a reaction to the emotional problem and is not a cause of it. Severe mental illness causes social difficulties that interfere with getting and staying married. Third, it does appear that being single, getting divorced, or having an unhappy marriage can cause some other, more common psychological problems such as depression (Beach, Sandeen, & O'Leary, 1990; Gotlib & McCabe, 1990). This conclusion is consistent with what many people say about their emotional struggles with divorce or with being single when "everyone else" is married.

These differing conclusions remind us of one reason why we follow the systems approach to etiology in this text rather than adopting a paradigms approach. The same life event can play a different role in the etiology of different psychological disorders. Our theory about the relation between marriage and mental illness must be adapted for different psychological disorders. ∎

Gender and Gender Roles

Gender and **gender roles** can dramatically affect social relationships and social interaction. Boys and girls, men and women, are different. One common distinction argues that women are more "relational," or oriented toward others, while men are more "instrumental," or oriented toward action and achievement (Gilligan, 1982). Whether such broad differences characterize the genders is a matter of debate, as are the causes of any differences that do exist. There is no doubt that some gender differences are determined by genetics and hormones, but there also is little doubt that socially prescribed gender roles exert a strong influence on our behavior (Maccoby, 1991).

Gender roles may influence the development, expression, or consequences of psychopathology. Some theorists have suggested, for example, that women's traditional roles foster dependency and helplessness, which accounts for the considerably higher rates of depression among women (Nolen-Hoeksema, 1990; see Chapter 5). Others have suggested that gender roles are not responsible for the etiology of abnormal behavior, but they do influence how psychopathology is expressed. According to this view, each gender may experience helplessness, but women are allowed to be depressed, whereas men's gender roles dictate that they "carry on" as if nothing were wrong. Instead of becoming depressed, men may express their inner turmoil as a psychosomatic disorder (see Chapter 7). In other cases, gender roles may shape the course and consequences of abnormal behavior. For example, women's but not men's gender roles may allow them to avoid feared circumstances following a panic attack, and this avoidance may help determine whether the difficulty develops into the generalized problem of agoraphobia (see Chapter 6).

Gender and gender roles are controversial and politically charged topics. To a lesser extent, so is the idea of **androgyny**—the possession of both "female" and "male" gender-role characteristics. Many people believe that androgyny is the answer to the problems associated with being either overly "feminine" or overly "masculine." Others reject this perspective and believe that traditional gender roles should be embraced, not criticized. We do not attempt to address such conflicting values in this text. We do, however, repeatedly consider evidence on epidemiological differences between men and women in the prevalence of psychological disorders. When appropriate, we interpret this evidence in terms of the roles played by men and women in U.S. society.

Race and Poverty

Race and poverty are broad social influences on psychological well-being in contemporary American culture. We consider these two factors together because they are so commonly linked in American life. In 1987, 12.5 percent

of white children were living below the poverty level, compared with 37.3 percent of black children and 32.1 percent of Latino children. Race and poverty also are closely linked to marital status. Among African-American children who lived with married parents, 13.6 percent lived in poverty, in comparison to 59.5 percent of children who lived with a single mother. Comparable figures among whites were 7 percent and 38.7 percent (Select Committee on Children, Youth and Families, 1989).

Evidence indicates that various psychological disorders are related to race and poverty, as we discuss in the epidemiology sections of subsequent chapters. In examining this evidence, one task is to disentangle the separate consequences of race and poverty. Poverty potentially may play several roles in the development of psychopathology. Children from poor inner-city neighborhoods witness and are victims of an incredible amount of violence in their communities. For example, one researcher found that 12 percent of school-aged children living in a Washington, D.C. neighborhood reported having seen a

▲ **Social isolation and especially active rejection by peers are linked with an increased prevalence of psychological disorders.**

▼ **Children's mental health can be undermined by extreme poverty and poor living conditions.**

dead body in the streets outside their home (Richters, 1993). Poverty also increases exposure to chemical toxins, such as to the lead found in old, chipping paint and automotive exhaust fumes. When ingested at toxic levels, lead can cause damage to the central nervous system.

The conditions of poverty are more likely to affect blacks, because more blacks live in poverty. The experiences of American blacks and whites differ in many more ways than their socioeconomic status, however. African Americans have endured a history of slavery and discrimination, and broad racial prejudices can undermine social opportunities and self-image. Moreover, distinctive aspects of African-American culture have too readily been labeled as deficits instead of differences. For example, the maternal grandmother often fulfills the role of a supportive second parent among African-American single-mother families, but these families are sometimes viewed by psychologists and policymakers as flawed nevertheless (Wilson, 1989). Some differences among ethnic groups are adaptive, some are maladaptive, and some are merely differences.

"Sick" Societies

Early in this century, anthropologists embraced the view known as **cultural relativity**. Cultural relativity held that the definition of normal and abnormal behavior is a product of culture, and therefore the definitions are relative rather than absolute. Thus, a sacrificial ritual could be viewed as normal, given the traditions and norms of the primitive culture in which it occurred. This culturally relative view held even though the ritual may seem abhorrent from the perspective of twentieth-century U.S. culture. In short, there were no "sick" societies from the perspective of cultural relativity.

There are limits to cultural relativity, however, as was proven by Hitler's genocide of European Jews during World War II. This period of German history gave the world the ultimate sick society. We must be cautious in labeling cultural differences as "wrong" or "sick." Still, there are absolutes; not everything is relative.

What constitutes a sick society clearly is a matter of debate. Some critics question the health of our own frenzied and competitive culture of materialism (Szasz, 1961). As humanistic psychologists have pointed out, in industrialized societies there often is conflict between societal demands and the requirements for healthy psychological development. Other people, however, find great value in the material, technological, and scientific gains that accompany industrialization. From this perspective, concerns about society's frustration of personal growth are, in fact, luxuries of the very success that commentators deride. Indeed, this is suggested by Maslow's (1970) hierarchy of needs. Higher needs for belongingness and for self-actualization can only be satisfied once the more basic needs for survival and safety are met.

Whether contemporary U.S. society is adaptive or maladaptive cannot be resolved in this textbook. However, the debate calls our attention to the broad influences of society and culture on the individual. Our personal lives, our education, and even our science are deeply embedded within contemporary U.S. culture. This makes it difficult, perhaps impossible, to gain perspective on which psychological processes or problems are universal and which are culture-bound. Nevertheless, it is essential to recognize that the practices and beliefs of society play a role in the definition and causes of abnormal behavior and in shaping the scientific enterprise that attempts to uncover the roots of psychopathology.

▼ **There are limits to cultural relativity. Nazi Germany clearly was a "sick"—abnormal—society.**

Summary

The **biological**, **psychoanalytic**, **behavioral**, and **humanistic** approaches to understanding the causes of abnormal behavior are alternative **paradigms**, and not just alternative theories. Biological approaches emphasize causes that occur "within the skin." Psychoanalytic theory highlights unconscious processes and detailed case histories. Behavioral viewpoints focus on observable, learned behavior. Finally, humanistic psychology argues that behavior is not determined but instead is a product of free will. In short, these approaches conflict not only in their explanations of abnormal behavior but also in what they view as acceptable scientific methods.

Although science benefits from competition, the conflict between these broad paradigms has outlived its usefulness, because none of these approaches offers the "right" explanation. Rather, abnormal behavior is determined by **multifactorial causes**, the combination of a variety of different biological, psychological, and social factors. The current challenge for scientists is to integrate evidence on the etiology of different psychological disorders into a coherent whole, a system of contributing factors.

Systems theory is an innovation in understanding and conducting science that offers assistance in this integration. Its central principle is **holism**, the idea that the whole is more than the sum of its parts—a scientific counterpoint to **reductionism**. In systems theory, smaller units are not "ultimate" causes but subsystems of the larger whole. Other important systems principles include **reciprocal causality**—the idea that causality is bidirectional; and **cybernetic** processes—the use of feedback loops to adjust progress toward a goal.

Biological factors relevant to abnormal behavior begin with the smallest anatomical unit within the nervous system, the **neuron** or nerve cell. Each neuron has four major anatomical components; the **soma** or cell body, the **dendrites**, the **axon**, and the **terminal buttons**. Communication between neurons occurs when the terminal buttons release chemical substances called **neurotransmitters** into the **synapse** between nerve cells. Disrupted communication among neurons, particularly disruptions in the functioning of various neurotransmitters, is implicated in the etiology of several types of abnormal behavior. We must not equate a neurophysiological explanation of a psychological disorder with a biological abnormality, however, since such a conclusion raises concerns about biological reductionism and mind–body **dualism**.

Neuroanatomists commonly divide the brain into three subdivisions: the hindbrain, the midbrain, and the forebrain. Basic bodily functions are regulated by the structures of the hindbrain, which is rarely implicated in abnormal behavior. The midbrain controls some motor activities, especially those related to fighting and sex. Damage to the midbrain can cause extreme disturbances, but such abnormalities typically result from specific and unusual brain traumas or tumors. The forebrain is the location of most sensory, emotional, and cognitive processes. Most of the forebrain is composed of the two **cerebral hemispheres**, and many brain functions are **lateralized**, so that each hemisphere is the site of specific cognitive and emotional activities. Finally, the **cerebral cortex** is the uneven surface area of the brain that lies just underneath the skull. It is the site of the control and integration of sophisticated memory, sensory, and motor functions. Because of the rudimentary state of our knowledge about the brain, only the most severe mental disorders have been

- modeling
- monozygotic (MZ)
- multifactorial causes
- negative reinforcement
- neuromodulators
- neurons
- neurotransmitters
- Oedipal conflict
- operant conditioning
- paradigm
- parasympathetic
  nervous system
- phenotype
- polygenic
- positive reinforcement
- premorbid history
- probands
- prognosis
- psychoanalytic
  approach
- psychophysiology
- punishment
- receptors
- reciprocal causality
- reductionism
- response cost
- reticular activating
  system
- reuptake
- reverse causality
- self-control
- self-efficacy
- self-schema
- social support
- soma
- state of development
- stimulus
- superego
- sympathetic nervous
  system
- synapse
- systems theory
- temperament
- terminal buttons
- thalamus
- third variable
- unconditioned
  response
- the unconscious
- ventricles

clearly linked with abnormalities in neuroanatomy. In most of these cases, brain damage is extensive and obvious.

Psychophysiology is the study of changes in the functioning of the body that result from psychological experiences. Psychophysiological arousal is caused by two different communication systems within the body; the **endocrine system** and the nervous system. Endocrine glands release **hormones** into the bloodstream, thus regulating some aspects of normal development as well as some responses to stress. The **autonomic nervous system** is the part of the central nervous system that is responsible for psychophysiological reactions. It has two branches, the **sympathetic** and **parasympathetic nervous systems**. In general, the sympathetic nervous system controls arousal, and the parasympathetic nervous system controls energy conservation. Psychophysiological overarousal and underarousal have both been implicated in theories of the causes of abnormal behavior.

Behavior genetics is the study of genetic influences on the development of behavior. Most forms of abnormal behavior are **polygenic**; they are caused by more than one **gene**. Polygenic inheritance makes the study of genetic contributions to behavior difficult but not impossible. Comparisons of **monozygotic (MZ)** and **dizygotic (DZ)** twins can yield information about polygenic contributions, as can adoption studies. It is important to understand that the fact that a psychological disorder has a polygenic component does not mean that the disorder will inevitably appear, and that genetically influenced behavior is influenced by the environment. Moreover, it is not clear what mechanism may account for behavior genetic findings. Few single genes directly affect abnormal behavior; thus, genetic effects probably occur at some more basic level—for example, by affecting psychophysiological arousal.

Psychology has not reached a consensus about its core constructs, but certain commonalities found across theories include issues of motivation and temperament, learning and

cognition, a sense of self, and stages of psychological development. In addition to biological needs, humans apparently have at least two basic psychological motivations: to form **attachments** and to compete for **dominance**. Emotion drives these basic motivations, and recent observations suggest that organized systems of emotion may be activated by certain social needs or challenges. **Temperament** is the individual's characteristic style of relating to the world. Researchers recently have agreed on consistencies in temperamental styles—the "how" of behavior.

Learning mechanisms include **classical conditioning**, **operant conditioning**, **modeling**, and information processing. At least some abnormal behavior is learned, and in the last two decades researchers have highlighted systematic cognitive biases that relate to some psychological disorders.

The sense of self is a uniquely human quality that would seem to play a role in causing emotional problems. It is possible, however, that self-esteem merely is another index of mental health. Finally, the idea of **developmental stages** not only charts the course of normal development, against which abnormal behavior must be compared, but it also highlights the important issue of developmental transitions.

Social roles influence the definition and development of psychopathology. Evidence links abnormal behavior with distressed or conflicted family relationships, and **social support** from people other than family members can be an important buffer against stress. **Gender roles** may influence the development, expression, or consequences of psychopathology. Some theorists suggest, for example, that women's traditional roles foster dependency and helplessness. Race and poverty, which are often related, also are broad social influences on psychological well-being in the United States today. Finally, humanistic psychologists have pointed out that there may be conflict between the demands of our competitive society and the requirements for healthy psychological development.

Critical Thinking

1. What were your beliefs about the causes of abnormal behavior before reading this chapter? Has the information here changed your beliefs? If so, in what ways? Do you adhere to one of the paradigms described here? Are your reasons for preferring a particular approach scientific or personal?

2. Think about social groups of which you are a member—your dormitory group, your family, or some small organization or club. Identify interactions in these groups based on concepts from systems theory—for example, reciprocal causality, cybernetics, homeostasis, subsystems.

3. Our review of psychological concepts in this chapter was selective, because psychologists do not yet agree about which concepts are basic to psychological functioning. Which concepts would you add to the list? Which ones would you subtract? What is the value of developing an "anatomy" of psychological concepts?

4. Think about the contributions of social roles to normal and abnormal behavior, including subtle roles (such as being "the smart one" in a group) and the more obvious roles and expectations associated with gender and ethnicity. Discuss these issues with other students.

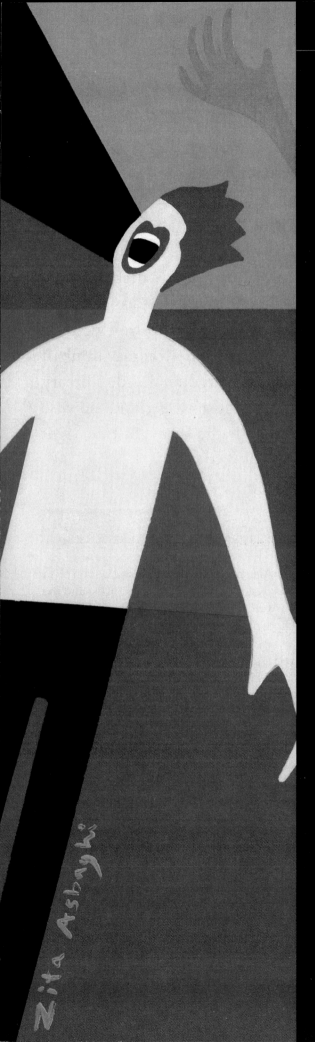

3

Treatment of Psychological Disorders

ow are psychological disorders treated? We examine this essential question in this chapter. First, though, pause to consider some stereotypes you may harbor about psychological treatment. Perhaps you imagine someone lying on a couch, talking at length about childhood memories. Suddenly, he remembers a long-forgotten trauma, and the memory frees him from his pain. Then again, perhaps you find such an approach silly—instead, you may envision a doctor sitting behind a desk and writing a prescription. The patient is relieved to learn that she has a biological problem that can be treated with medication. Perhaps you view the treatment of some mental disorders as inhumane—you may think of some unfortunate individual locked up and forgotten inside a dreary mental hospital. Or maybe you conceive of a therapist as a kind and wise elder: someone who listens, who cares, and who knows just the right things to say.

Overview

One reason for these conflicting images is our national ambivalence about the treatment of psychological disorders. Emotional problems are widely misunderstood, as are the professions of clinical psychology, psychiatry, and social work (see Chapter 1). Many severely disturbed people receive little or no treatment, while some people seek psychotherapy for personal growth or as a means of coping with life distress. Another reason for the conflicting images is the wide variety of approaches to treating psychological disorders. According to one review, over 240 different "schools" of psychotherapy can be identified (Corsini, 1981). If this seems baffling to you, imagine the possible range of consequences of picking different therapists out of the Yellow Pages.

We can greatly simplify the almost overwhelming array of psychological treatments by grouping them according to the four basic paradigms: the biological, psychodynamic, behavioral, and humanistic approaches. Very different treatments have been developed based on the principles of these four paradigms. "What is your theoretical orientation?" is a question often asked of mental health professionals, and the answer is supposed to be "biological," "psychodynamic," "behavioral," or "humanistic."

As we explained in Chapters 1 and 2, we reject this paradigmatic approach. Rather, our focus on scientific evidence emphasizes common elements across all the paradigms, and the need to use different treatments for different disorders. Nevertheless, the first section of this chapter elaborates on the contrasting biological, psychodynamic, social learning, and humanistic treatments of psychological disorders. These paradigms have had important historical influences on treatment, and they also have a continuing contemporary influence on therapy. Researchers have not yet identified the most promising treatment for many psychological disorders. This means that clinicians often must rely on a more general theory for guidance in planning treatments.

In the second section of the chapter, we emphasize the similarities rather than the differences across the four paradigms. One basic similarity is that three of the paradigms—the psychodynamic, behavioral, and humanistic approaches—all are forms of **psychotherapy**: Each approach uses psychological techniques in an attempt to produce change in the context of a special, helping relationship. We highlight this basic similarity in reviewing research on psychotherapy outcome and on psychotherapy process. *Psychotherapy outcome research* compares the effectiveness of alternative forms of treatment. One major finding from outcome research is that all three major schools of psychotherapy produce significantly more benefit than does no treatment at all. This finding suggests that there may be more similarities among alternative treatments in practice than is apparent in theory. *Psychotherapy process research* investigates similarities in practice by studying aspects of the therapist-client relationship. The process of psychotherapy has been demonstrated to contribute to successful treatment irrespective of the therapist's theoretical orientation. For example, all forms of psychological treatment have a very human side, and psychotherapy process research indicates that the special relationship between a therapist and a client is an essential part of what makes all treatments effective.

Although we discuss research and theory on traditional paradigms in order to introduce the range of treatments, the chapter also follows the biopsychosocial model. Our overview of biological treatments early in the chapter highlights efforts to produce psychological change through physiological means. The detailed discussion of psychotherapy process and outcome research highlights intervention at the psychological level. Toward the end of the chapter, we discuss treatments that focus on social relationships and societal institutions. Research increasingly supports the effectiveness of couples therapy, family therapy, and group therapy. Wider attempts at changing social institutions also have been advocated as promoting mental health and preventing mental illness.

At the end of the chapter, we highlight the most important finding about the treatment of psychological disorders: Different therapies are effective for treating different problems. The most promising recent advancements in therapy have come from the development and evaluation of specific treatments for specific disorders, not from theoretical debates among broad paradigms. In fact, the majority of therapists identify their approach as being **eclectic** (Garfield & Kurtz, 1976; Zook & Walton, 1989). Eclectic therapists do not adhere to any one paradigm; rather, they tailor their approach to individual disorders and clients. We are eclectic in our discussion of treatment in later chapters of this text. We do not reconsider the approach of each paradigm to treatment. Rather, consistent with our systems approach we focus only on specific treatments that—based on research evidence—appear to hold particular promise for treating specific disorders.

Paradigmatic Approaches to Psychotherapy

Obviously, we cannot attempt to review all 240 approaches to psychological treatment in this chapter, nor would we wish to do so. Rather, we divide the various approaches into biological, psychodynamic, behavioral, and humanistic therapies. Biological therapies understand mental illness by drawing an analogy to physical illness. Changing psychological experience through biological means is the goal of these treatments. Medication is by far the most common biomedical treatment for psychological disorders. Other biological techniques include convulsive therapy and psychosurgery.

Psychodynamic therapies are primarily outgrowths of Freudian psychoanalysis. These treatments begin with an exploration of the client's past, unconscious motivations, and defense mechanisms. The goal of psychodynamic therapy is to promote insight, the heightened awareness of unconscious conflicts and motivations. Conscious awareness of what was formerly unconscious—insight—is a sufficient means for promoting a cure, according to the psychodynamic tradition.

Behavior therapy emphasizes the application of basic psychological research to the treatment of psychological disorders. Behavior therapists believe that both normal and abnormal behavior are learned, and therapy is seen as a form of education. Promoting change, and not insight, is the major goal of behavior therapy, although the target for change may be behavior, cognition, or emotion. In fact, many professionals prefer to call themselves "cognitive behavior therapists" or simply "cognitive therapists." These terms underscore the increasing importance of cognition in psychological science and in therapy.

Humanistic therapies oppose the deterministic views of the biological, psychodynamic, and behavioral approaches (see Chapter 2). Humanistic therapists highlight free will, and clients in humanistic psychotherapy repeatedly are encouraged to take personal responsibility for their actions. Psychotherapy is viewed as a way of helping people to make their own life choices, not as a process in which an expert therapist diagnoses and solves problems. In order to help clients to make choices, humanistic therapists encourage increased awareness of current emotional experience as a major goal of therapy.

The following case history and discussion illustrates some of the contrasting ways in which biological, psychodynamic, social learning, and humanistic therapists conceptualize treatment.

CASE STUDY

Depression as Seen from the Four Paradigms

Frances was a 23-year-old woman who sought psychotherapy for depression. Frances reported having been depressed for almost 3 years, with intermittent periods of relative happiness or deeper despair. When she came into therapy, her depression was quite severe. She had little appetite, had lost 10 pounds over the previous 6 weeks, and her erratic sleeping patterns were worse than usual. She awoke around 2 or 3 A.M. every night, tossed in bed for several hours, and finally fell asleep again near dawn.

Frances reported feeling profoundly depressed about herself, her new marriage, and life in general. She freely admitted to frequent thoughts of suicide. She once sat in her bathroom holding a razor blade for over an hour, contemplating whether to slash her wrists. But she decided she could never commit the act. Now, she often wished she was dead, but she felt that she "lacked the courage" to take her own life.

Frances also noted that she found herself without motivation. She withdrew from her husband and the few friends she had, and she frequently called in sick at work when she felt blue. Frances's reports of depression were underscored by her careless dress, frequent bouts of crying, and slowed speech and body movements.

Frances reported that she had experienced a happy childhood. She had not known depression until the current episode began in her senior year in college. At first, she convinced herself that she was only suffering from "senior year syndrome." She wasn't sure what to do with her life. Secretly, she longed to move to New York and finally break out and do something exciting. But when she told her parents about her plans, her mother begged Frances to return home. She insisted the two of them needed to have fun together again after four long years with Frances away at college. After graduation, Frances returned home to live with her parents.

It was shortly after moving home that Frances realized that her difficulties were much more serious than she had thought. She found herself intermittently screaming at her anxious and doting mother and being "super-nice" to her after feeling guilty about losing her temper. Frances described her mother as "a saint." Frances thought that her erratic behavior toward her mother was all her fault. Her mother apparently agreed. In Frances's mind, she was a failure as a daughter.

Frances described both her mother and her father as loving and giving, but some of her comments about them were far from glowing. She said she was her mother's best friend. When asked if her mother was her best friend, Frances began to cry. She felt like her mother's infant, her parent, or even her husband, but not her friend and certainly not like her grown daughter. Frances had little to say about her father. She pictured him drinking beer, eating meals, and falling asleep in front of the television.

Throughout the time she lived at home, Frances's depression only seemed to deepen. After a year of living with her parents, she married her high school sweetheart. Frances felt pressured to get married. Both her future husband and her mother insisted that it was time for her to settle down and start a family. At the time, she had hoped that marriage would be the solution to her problems. The excitement of the wedding added to this hope. But after the marriage, Frances said that things were worse—if that were possible. Still, she insisted that her marriage problems were all her fault.

Frances's husband was a young accountant who she said reminded her more and more of her father. He didn't drink, but he spent most of his brief time at home working or reading in his study. She said they had little communication, and she felt no warmth in her marriage. Her husband often was angry and sullen, but Frances said she couldn't blame him for feeling that way. His problem was being married to her. She wanted to love him, but she never had. She was a failure as a wife. She was a failure in life.

The theme of self-blame pervaded Frances's descriptions of her family. She repeatedly noted that, despite their flaws, her parents and her husband were good and loving people. She was the one with the problem. She had everything that she could hope for, yet she was unhappy. One reason she wanted to die was to ease the burden on them. How could they be happy when they had to put up with her foul moods? When she talked about these things, however, Frances's tone of voice often made her sound more angry than depressed. ■

Biological, psychodynamic, behavioral, and humanistic therapists all would note Frances's depressed mood, her self-blame, and her troubled close relationships. Nevertheless, therapists working within these different theoretical frameworks would approach treatment with Frances in very different ways.

A therapist who was following a biological approach would focus first on making a diagnosis of Frances's problems over two or three appointments with her. This would not be difficult in Frances's case, because her problems paint a clear picture of depression. A biologically oriented therapist also would sympathize with Frances's interpersonal problems. However, the therapist likely would agree that Frances might be contributing to her troubled relationships. It is exhausting to deal with someone who is constantly agitated and depressed.

The biological therapist would not blame Frances for her depression or her family troubles. Rather, he or she would attach the blame to a problem that neither Frances nor her family members could control: depression. The therapist surely would take note of Frances's description of her father, who seems chronically depressed. Perhaps a genetic predisposition toward depression runs in her family. In the end, the therapist might explain that depression can be caused by a chemical imbalance in the brain. Medication would be recommended, and follow-up appointments would be scheduled to monitor the effects of the medication on Frances's mood and on her life.

In contrast, a psychodynamic therapist would take note of Frances's *defensive style*. Frances clearly was using the defense of rationalization to justify the behavior of her parents and husband, but she also used defenses that distorted reality more dramatically. She used denial in not admitting to her loved ones' imperfections and their apparent failure to fulfill her needs. In seeing herself as a burden on them, perhaps she also was projecting onto them her own sense of feeling burdened by them. Frances might resent the need to comfort her mother constantly and to work to get attention from her father and her husband. Admitting to her resentment might be too threatening to Frances. Instead, she may project her own feeling onto her loved ones.

Although a psychodynamic therapist would note these defensive styles, he or she would not discuss them with Frances early in therapy. Instead, the initial part of therapy would be more exploratory, focusing largely on Frances's past and her hopes, feelings, and frustrations throughout her life. The exploration would be directed minimally by the therapist, who would encourage Frances to talk about issues she wanted to discuss. This would allow the therapist to better understand Frances's unconscious motivations, intrapsychic conflicts, and style of defending herself against them. Gradually, a psychodynamic therapist would point out these patterns to Frances to help her achieve a new understanding of herself. Frances's hidden resentment toward her mother, her longing for a relationship with her father, and her unfulfilled fantasies about marriage are some of the unconscious issues that might be revealed. In order to gain insight into these motivations, Frances first would have to recognize her style of defending against them.

A cognitive behavior therapist would see many of the same issues in Frances's life but would approach therapy quite differently. Rather than focusing on intrapsychic defenses, a behavior therapist would note Frances's cognitive and behavioral styles. Frances's self-blame—her pattern of attributing all of her interpersonal difficulties to herself—would be seen as a cognitive error. Her withdrawal from pleasing activities and her apparent unassertiveness also would be seen as contributing to her depression. Although a behavior therapist would explore these topics with Frances, the therapist would direct the discussion much more than a psychodynamic therapist would. For example, a behavior therapist likely would tell Frances that she was thinking and acting like a depressed person. It therefore is not surprising that she was feeling depressed.

Learning new ways to think and act in the present would be the focus of behavior therapy. The therapist would want Frances to play an active role in this learning process. She would be encouraged to test whether she actually was the cause of all her family problems and to try out new ways of relating to her family. To do so, Frances would be expected to perform various *homework* activities designed to continue her treatment outside the therapy session. Homework might include careful monitoring of conflicts with her family to better understand the problems. The goal would be to help Frances learn that she was not the only one at fault. A more rational and realistic belief would be that her mother, father, and husband were causing many of the problems in the family. The behavior therapist also might teach Frances how to assert herself more with family members. Once she no longer blamed herself for everything and learned to assert her rights, Frances's mood should change. She should find greater

satisfaction in her relationships and more happiness in her life.

Like the biological, psychodynamic, and behavior therapists, a humanistic therapist would take note of Frances's depression, her self-blame, and her unsatisfactory relationships with loved ones. A more prominent focus, however, would be her lack of emotional *genuineness*—her inability to "be herself" with other people and within herself. Frances's tendencies to bury her true feelings would be explored as they related to the emotions she expressed in the therapy session. The humanistic therapist would want Frances to come to recognize her true feelings and would encourage Frances to make life choices based on her heightened emotional awareness.

In conducting therapy, the humanistic therapist would be nondirective in terms of the topic of discussion but would continually focus therapy on emotional issues. Initially, the therapist would simply empathize with the feelings of sadness, loneliness, and isolation that Frances expressed. Over time, the therapist would suggest that Frances was also feeling emotions that she did not express. These might include frustration and guilt over her mother's controlling yet dependent style, and anger at her husband's and her father's self-centeredness. The humanistic therapist would note that these are legitimate feelings and that Frances would feel better if she acknowledged that she felt them. Although the humanistic therapist would not directly encourage Frances to act in different ways, Frances would be expected to make some changes in her life as a result of her increased emotional awareness.

These four approaches to treating Frances are very different, but they may not be as different as they seem. All three approaches to psychotherapy focus on Frances's distorted thoughts and feelings, and each hones in on her troubled close relationships. Even a biological therapist who prescribed medication might also recommend psychotherapy for Frances. This might help her sort out to what extent her depression was causing her family problems versus the extent to which her family problems were causing her depression. We discuss such integrated approaches to treatment in more detail later in this chapter. First, we elaborate further on the differences among the four approaches. The contrasts among them can best be understood by examining the emergence of treatments from a historical perspective.

Brief Historical Perspective

The history of the treatment of psychological disorders is either very long or quite brief, depending on how we define treatment. If we use a broad definition, practices that date back to ancient times must be included. In searching back through history, we can trace the roots of psychotherapy to two broad traditions of healing: the spiritual/religious tradition and the naturalistic/scientific tradition (Frank, 1973).

The spiritual/religious tradition attributes both physical and mental ailments to supernatural forces. The tradition dates back through ancient times, and it continues today both inside and outside of formal religions. An ancient practice called *trephining* is one of the earliest examples of the spiritual/religious tradition. From skulls unearthed by archaeologists, researchers have concluded that tribal healers performed a primitive form of surgery as a treatment for mental disorders. Trephining involved chipping a hole through the unfortunate sufferer's skull with a crude stone tool. Presumably, the purpose of trephining was to allow evil spirits to escape.

There are numerous other examples throughout history and across cultures in which demons have been viewed as the cause of abnormal behavior and exorcism has been used as the treatment. Until the seventeenth century, in Europe and in the American colonies, at least some cases of mental disturbance were formally attributed to witchcraft (see Chapter 2). Those suspected of being witches were put through painful tests that they often could not pass. One examination was to dunk the suspected witch under water. The only way to pass the test—to be found *not* to be a witch—was to drown!

The spiritual/religious tradition certainly has produced bizarre explanations for and treatments of abnormal behavior. Still, the influence of spiritual beliefs and rituals on all forms of healing cannot be ignored. Believing is a powerful part of healing. Spiritual beliefs have essential influences on how people cope with all sorts of life difficulties in contemporary society. Ministers, priests, rabbis, and other religious figures provide both spiritual guidance and practical counseling to millions of people.

Just as the spiritual/religious tradition has a long history, naturalistic/scientific approaches to helping the mentally disturbed also have ancient roots. Hippocrates (460–377 B.C.) recommend-ed such treatments as rest, exercise, and a healthy diet. Witch hunting did occur during the Middle Ages, but naturalistic approaches similar to those outlined by Hippocrates were far more common during these times (Neugebauer, 1979). For example, "insane asylums" were developed as a new treatment for the mentally ill during the Middle Ages. One rationale for these institutions was to remove disturbed individuals from society, but another was the hope that rest and isolation would help their bizarre behavior. Unfortunately, asylums for the mentally ill too often were little more than human warehouses (see Chapter 17).

Although their beginnings can be traced to ancient times, contemporary biological, psychodynamic, behavioral, and humanistic treatments are tied much more directly to developments in the nineteenth and twentieth centuries. Some innovation has been due to improvements in theory. Other innovations are the result of the development of scientific research (see Research Methods for a discussion of the experimental method). We discuss these historically recent developments while reviewing the different approaches to the treatment of psychological disorders.

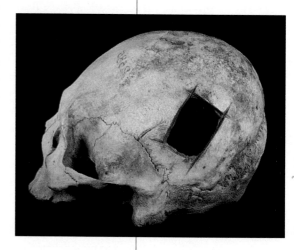

▲ **Trephining was an attempt to treat psychological problems by cracking a hole in the skull of the sufferer. Presumably, evil spirits could escape through the hole, thereby curing the problem.**

Biological Treatments

The scientific beginnings of the biological treatment of mental disorders can be traced to the nineteenth century and the discovery of the diagnosis, cause, and cure for general paresis (see Chapter 2). This remarkable achievement paralleled other medical advances in its course of discovery. As the first step in a scientific approach to treatment, an increasingly refined and accurate diagnosis is developed. Next, information pertaining to causal factors is put together like pieces of a puzzle to form a complete picture of the specific etiology of the disease. Finally, scientists develop treatments by experimenting with alternative methods for preventing or curing the disorder. These are far from simple tasks, of course, as is evident in the span of over a century between the diagnosis

The Experiment

Three basic methods are used in conducting psychological research. The case study was discussed in Research Methods in Chapter 1, and the correlational study was described in Research Methods in Chapter 2. The final essential method of scientific investigation is the **experiment**. The experiment is the most powerful of all scientific methods in one extremely important way: Researchers who use experimental methods can determine cause and effect relationships.

The experiment has four essential features. It begins with a **hypothesis**—the experimenter's specific prediction about cause and effect. For example, a researcher might predict that in comparison to no treatment at all, a particular type of medication will reduce certain symptoms of a given emotional disorder. The experimenter might further hypothesize that psychotherapy also will alleviate symptoms more than no treatment but psychotherapy will cause no more and no less symptom change than will medication.

The second feature of an experiment is the manipulation of an **independent variable**. Independent variables are controlled and deliberately manipulated by the experimenter. The independent variable in the hypothesis just outlined is whether the patients receive medication, psychotherapy, or no treatment. The experimenter controls the independent variable by deciding what specific type of medication or psychotherapy will be made available to the patients in the experiment, and by determining who will receive one of these treatments and who will receive no treatment at all.

The third feature of the experiment involves how subjects are assigned to receive different levels of the independent variable. In the present example, the issue is who will receive medication, psychotherapy, or no treatment. In an experiment, subjects must be **randomly assigned** to these alternative conditions. Random assignment ensures that each subject has a statistically equal chance of receiving any one of the different levels of the independent variable. Picking the number 1, 2, or 3 out of a hat is one of many possible ways of ensuring random assignment in the present example. Random assignment ensures that any differences among groups are caused by the independent variable and not by biased selection into groups.

The fourth feature of the experiment is the measurement of the **dependent variable**. The dependent variable is the outcome that is hypothesized to vary according to manipulations in the independent variable. The outcome depends on the experimental manipulation; thus the term *dependent variable*. In the present example, the various symptoms of the disorder comprise the dependent variables of the study. The symptoms are expected to change depending on whether the patients receive medication, psychotherapy, or no treatment at all.

Statistical tests typically are conducted to establish whether the independent variable has changed the dependent variable in a predictable manner or whether the outcome is a result of chance. According to current conventions, a finding is considered to be *statistically significant* if it would occur by chance in less than 1 out of every 20 experiments. That is, the probability of a chance outcome is less than 5 percent, a specification that is often written as $p < .05$. As is discussed in Research Methods in Chapter 6, however, a statistically significant result is not the same as a clinically significant finding. A treatment may produce a reliable change in symptoms, for example, but the change may be too small to produce a meaningful difference in the patient's life.

We can conclude that an independent variable *causes* changes in a dependent variable when the experimental method is used correctly and it produces statistically significant results. The ability to establish causation is a powerful strength of the experiment in comparison to the correlational study. The experimental method is limited, however, because many theoretically interesting independent variables cannot be manipulated practically or ethically in real life. We may hypothesize that abusive parenting causes psychological problems, for example, but we obviously cannot randomly assign children to grow up in abusive and nonabusive homes. In fact, practical and ethical limitations make it impossible to use the experiment to test most hypotheses about the causes of abnormal behavior. Thus, when studying the etiology of abnormal behavior we often must rely on correlational studies (see Chapter 2) or analogue studies (see Chapter 5).

The effectiveness of various forms of psychological treatment often can be studied using an experiment, because researchers can control whether or not someone receives a particular medication or form of psychotherapy. Still, it is not easy to control the independent variable in treatment outcome research. Some people may drop out of treatment, and others may seek additional help. Clinicians might not conduct psychotherapy according to the design of the experiment, or patients might not take their medication as prescribed.

These examples are only a few of the many ways in which the independent variable can be *confounded* with other factors in psychological research. Each of these examples is a threat to the **internal validity** of the experiment. An experiment has internal validity if changes in the dependent variable can be accurately attributed to changes in the independent variable. As we have noted, however, the independent variable can be manipulated poorly, or it can be confounded with other variables. For example, in our hypothetical study it obviously would be wrong to conclude that medication was ineffective if the patients failed to take it, or it would be difficult to draw conclusions about psychotherapy if many of the patients dropped out of the study. Later in this chapter we discuss a major threat to the internal validity of treatment outcome research: the placebo effect, in which the patients' expectations about the effectiveness of a treatment affect the outcome of a study.

Another set of questions can be raised about the **external validity** of an experiment—that is, whether the findings generalize to other circumstances. A number of questions typically can be raised about an experiment's external validity, because some artificiality needs to be introduced to give the experimenter control over the independent variable. In our hypothetical study, perhaps only a very narrow group of patients would be treated. Thus, the findings might not generalize to other people with other problems. Or perhaps psychotherapy might last for exactly ten sessions in the experiment in order to ensure control of the independent variable. Although this would help the study's internal validity, it might compromise the experiment's external validity. The findings might not apply in the real world, where the length of treatment is tailored to the individual client's needs.

There is no finite list of questions that can be raised about the internal and external validity of experiments. A common trade-off, however, is that the experimenter often must sacrifice one for the other. Recognizing this compromise is essential to conducting and evaluating science. We therefore raise questions throughout this book about the strengths and limitations of the experiment—and about case studies and correlational research. You now have a basic, abstract knowledge of these methods. In the pages that follow, we will help you apply these concepts to particular research findings. ■

of general paresis, the discovery of syphilis as its cause, and the development of antibiotics as a treatment for the disease.

A similar story cannot be told about the development of biological treatments for many other mental disorders. Uncovering specific etiologies for mental disorders has proved to be a vexing and perhaps impossible task, as indicated in our discussion of multifactorial etiology in Chapter 2. As a result, many efforts to develop biological treatments have attempted to skip the middle step in the process of discovery; that is, they fail to uncover a specific etiology.

These treatments focus on **symptom alleviation,** reducing the dysfunctional symptoms of a disorder but not eliminating its root cause.

Experimentation with developing biological treatments for symptom alleviation has produced mixed results in the treatment of emotional problems. Bleeding, forced hot baths, the use of various physical restraints, and the surgical removal of sexual organs are some of the unhappy experimental treatments that were used in the not-so-distant past. In contrast, the second half of the twentieth century has witnessed the discovery of numerous medications, many of which are remarkable in their effectiveness at symptom alleviation. Before presenting an overview of these new drugs, we briefly consider two controversial biological treatments.

ELECTROCONVULSIVE THERAPY

Electroconvulsive therapy (ECT) involves the deliberate induction of a seizure by passing electricity through the brain. The technique was originally developed in 1938 by Ugo Cerletti and Lucio Bini, two Italian physicians who were seeking a treatment for schizophrenia (see Chapter 12). At the time, schizophrenia was erroneously thought to be rare among people who had epilepsy. This led to speculation that epileptic seizures somehow prevented the disorder. Cerletti and Bini discovered their means of inducing seizures when visiting a slaughterhouse. There they observed electric current being passed through the brains of animals, which produced a convulsion and unconsciousness. Shortly thereafter, Cerletti and Bini began to use a modified electroconvulsive technique as an experimental treatment for schizophrenia.

Approximately 100 volts of electric current was passed through the patients' brains in what is now termed *bilateral ECT*: Electrodes are placed on the left and right temples, and the current passes through both brain hemispheres. In *unilateral ECT*, which is more common today, the electric current is passed through only one side of the brain. Both procedures induce brief unconsciousness and seizures, but unilateral ECT apparently produces less memory loss—a common side effect of ECT. The potentially dangerous, jerking body movements that occur during a convulsion are now controlled by restraints and the administration of a muscle relaxant. Typically, ECT involves a series of six or seven sessions scheduled over the course of a few weeks.

As you are probably aware, ECT is a controversial technique. It certainly was ineffective in achieving its original objective of curing schizophrenia. Moreover, as illustrated in popular movies like *One Flew Over the Cuckoo's Nest*, there is no doubt that ECT has been overused and abused. In addition, the side effects linked with ECT can be severe. These include long-term memory loss, fractures, and death in about 3 of every 10,000 patients (NIMH, 1985). Still, evidence indicates that ECT is quite effective in treating severe depressions that don't respond to other treatments (see Chapter 5). Even when other treatments for depression fail, however, ECT must be used cautiously given that it is invasive and has numerous potential side effects.

PSYCHOSURGERY

Psychosurgery is an even more controversial biological treatment, as it involves the surgical destruction of specific regions of the brain. Psychosurgery was introduced in 1935 by Egas Moniz (1874–1953), a Portuguese neurologist. *Prefrontal lobotomy* was the technique refined by Moniz—a procedure in which the frontal lobes of the brain are surgically and irrevocably severed. The technique was widely adopted throughout the world, and thousands of prefrontal lobotomies were performed throughout the middle of this century. In fact, Moniz won a Nobel Prize in 1949 for his discovery of this treatment.

Prefrontal lobotomy was subsequently discredited because of its frequent and severe side effects. These include a 25 percent mortality rate, excessive tranquility, and the absence of emotional responsiveness. Ironically, Moniz himself was shot and paralyzed by one of his lobotomized patients, a sad testament to the unpredictable outcome of the procedure.

Although prefrontal lobotomies are no longer performed, some forms of highly circumscribed psychosurgery are used today to treat severe disorders. Contemporary techniques are far more refined, as only small regions of the brain are selectively destroyed. Still, the complexity of the brain, limited knowledge of its functions, and the irreversibility of brain damage combine to make psychosurgery a procedure that is used very rarely today, as we discuss in Further Thoughts.

PSYCHOPHARMACOLOGY

Psychopharmacology, the study of the use of medications to treat psychological disturbances, has been the most promising avenue of biological treatment. Various drugs ranging from alcohol, tobacco, and caffeine to controlled substances have long been known to affect psychological states. These are the **psychoactive drugs.** In recent years, new psychoactive medications have been developed that have increasingly refined effects on emotional states and mental disorders.

You are no doubt familiar with the effects of some psychoactive drugs. Alcohol, for example, produces rapid and notable changes in thinking, mood, and behavior. Some medications produce similarly obvious changes. Many antianx-

Some Ethical Concerns in Psychological Treatment Research

Scientists often need to ask important ethical questions when they are conducting experiments on the treatment of psychological disorders. One essential question is whether a particular treatment poses a serious risk to the participants. Moniz's experiments with prefrontal lobotomy provide one extreme example of a seeming disregard for human life in the name of "science." Such a dangerous experimental treatment could not take place in the United States today unless there was substantial evidence supporting its effectiveness. Psychosurgery for mental disorders is performed very rarely today, and only for certain chronic conditions. Even in these cases, the procedure can be used only after extensive institutional review. In fact, every research institution in the United States has a specially designated panel that must review the ethics of proposed research with human subjects.

Human subjects committees often must consider controversial issues. One issue that typically receives considerable scrutiny is experimentation with biological treatments. Treatments like psychosurgery and ECT have dramatic and obvious side effects. Adverse consequences of medication are not always detected in the extensive animal research on the ingestion of drugs that must precede experimentation with human subjects. Similarly, research on psychotherapy often raises questions about the risk to research participants and the ethics of experimentation.

One set of ethical concerns involves coercive psychological treatments. The use of punishment as a treatment technique has been especially controversial, even when punishments are effective and involve relatively minor adverse consequences. Corporal punishment of children typically is prohibited, for example. Similarly, many people oppose the use of mild electric shocks as a treatment for the extreme self-injurious behavior that is found in the severe disorder called autism, even though this treatment has proved effective in many cases (see Chapter 14). Some readers may be familiar with the book

and film *A Clockwork Orange,* which raised these concerns in a dramatized manner. In this fictional portrayal, a violent young man was conditioned to find violence repulsive by having pain inflicted on him while he watched or imagined violent scenes. These are *not* the kinds of treatments that are taking place in clinics and hospitals, but the story perhaps reflects the public's fear of the coercive use of psychological treatments or brainwashing.

Some psychologists also believe that it is unethical to offer psychological treatments to the public in the absence of evidence supporting the effectiveness of the intervention. The treatment of sexual offenders is an example. There is little evidence that sex offenders can be treated effectively using psychological methods, but courts nevertheless routinely refer them to mental health professionals— and mental health professionals routinely accept them into treatment. The ethics of this practice can be questioned on several grounds, including the costs to the public, the consequences of perpetuating the myth that therapy works for this problem, and questions about the intellectual and professional honesty of practitioners who fail to acknowledge the limits of psychological treatments (McFall, 1991).

The opposite concern about offering treatments also has been raised in psychological research. Sometimes it may be unethical to withhold a treatment (O'Leary & Borkovec, 1978). Experimental treatments are commonly withheld when clients are randomly assigned to a no-treatment control group so that the outcome of a new treatment can be compared with the outcome of no treatment. One question that arises in this research is whether it is ethical to withhold a potentially effective treatment. Many researchers would respond that we do not know if a treatment is effective until it is studied.

The use of deception is a more controversial ethical problem with control groups. Because expectations about a treatment's success can have a substantial influence on its actual success, it may be necessary to have a *placebo control group*—a group of clients who think they are receiving a potentially effective treatment. For example, the clients might attend weekly appointments, but the therapists might offer only very general listening and support. When they are members of a placebo control group, the participants might be discouraged from seeking appropriate help or from noting important new symptoms, because they believe that they are getting treatment.

In addition to institutional review, ethical concerns are addressed in psychological research by the requirement that every human subject be able to give **informed consent** to participate in research. Participants in treatment research must be (a) informed about the potential risks and benefits of a study, (b) competent to understand them, and (c) able to agree to participate voluntarily (Carroll, Schneider, & Wesley, 1985). The first condition includes a detailed presentation of information, and it typically is made in writing. The second condition excludes both people whose understanding is impaired and minors, whose parents must give consent for their children

to participate. The third condition protects research subjects against excessive coercion. Coercion to participate in research is a particular worry in institutional settings like mental hospitals and prisons, where potential subjects may feel pressured into participating in research in order to gain privileges.

One more ethical consideration arises in treatment research. Investigators constantly must balance their ethical commitment to protect individuals from harm against their ethical obligation to increase knowledge and thereby better the human condition in general. The potential to create new knowledge that may benefit many people is, in fact, the ultimate justification for conducting research that may hold some risk or discomfort for the participants in a study. We revisit the tricky issue of the ethics of research periodically throughout the text. In the final chapter, we discuss mental health, ethics, and the law in some detail. ∎

▼ **Prozac is an effective antidepressant that is the best selling psychoactive medication. In fact, Prozac outsells all medications, including drugs used to treat all types of physical illnesses.**

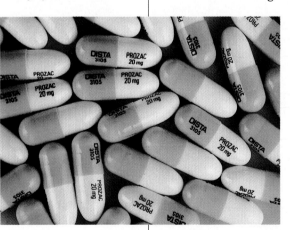

iety agents such as Xanax or Librium have effects that become apparent soon after the medication is taken (see Chapter 6). Other psychoactive medications have more subtle influences that build up gradually over time. The antidepressant medications are an example of this type of effect (see Chapter 5). Other psychoactive drugs affect people with mental disorders very differently from the way they affect someone who is functioning normally. Antipsychotic medications help to eliminate delusions and hallucinations among people suffering from schizophrenia (see Chapter 12), but the same medications would disorient most people and send them into a long, groggy sleep.

The success of psychopharmacology is evident in the proliferation of psychoactive medications in recent years. In fact, in the 1990s the antidepressant medication Prozac has outsold *every* prescrip-

tion medication—including all medications used to treat physical ailments. (In the 1970s, the antianxiety medication Valium held this distinction.) A listing of the major categories of psychoactive medications and their chemical, generic, and common trade names is found in Table 3–1. We review each of these categories of medication in more detail in the chapters that address the disorders these medications are designed to treat.

There are a few general points that you should note about psychopharmacology now. First, much evidence indicates that various medications are effective and safe treatments for particular mental disorders. Psychopharmacology lies well within the realm of modern medicine and far from the controversies of ECT and psychosurgery. A second point, however, is that psychoactive medications offer symptom relief, not a cure of underlying pathology. Symptom alleviation is extremely important. Where would we be without aspirin, another drug that treats symptoms but not causes? Still, it is valid to raise the question of whether treatments should directly address root causes rather than symptoms. In particular, we might wonder whether some psychological problems should be addressed by

TABLE 3–1

Major Psychotherapeutic Medications

Different medications used in the treatment of psychological disorders

Therapeutic Use	Chemical Structure or Psychopharmacologic Action	Generic Name	Trade Name
Antipsychotics (also called major tranquilizers or neuroleptics)	Phenothiazines		
	Aliphatic	Chlorpromazine	Thorazine
	Piperidine	Thioradazine	Mellaril
	Piperazine	Triflouperazine	Stelazine
	Thioxanthenes		
	Aliphatic	Chlorprothixene	Taractan
	Piperazine	Thiothixene	Navane
	Butyrophenones	Haloperidol	Haldol
	Dibenzoxazepines	Loxapine	Loxitane
	Dihydroindolines	Molindone	Moban
	Rauwolfia alkaloids	Reserpine	Sandril
	Benzoquinolines	Tetrabenazine	
	Atypical neuroleptics	Clozapine	Clozaril
Antidepressants	Tricyclic antidepressants (TCAs)		
	Tertiary amines	Amitriptyline	Elavil
		Imipramine	Tofranil
		Doxepin	Sinequan
	Secondary amines	Desipramine	Norpramin
		Nortriptyline	Pamelor
		Protriptyline	Vivactil
	Monoamine oxidase inhibitors (MAOIs)	Phenelzine	Nardil
		Tranylcypromine	Parnate
		Pargyline	Eutonyl
		Isocarboxazid	Marplan
	Atypical antidepressants	Trazodone	Desyrel
		Amoxapine	Asendin
	Selective Serotonin Reuptake Inhibitor	Bupropion	Wellbutrin
		Fluoxetine	Prozac
Psychomotor stimulants	Amphetamines	Amphetamine	Benzedrine
		Dextroamphetamine	Dexedrine
	Other	Methylphenidate	Ritalin
		Pemolline	Cylert
Antimanic		Lithium	Eskalith
		Carbamazepine	Tegretol
		Valproic acid	Depakene
Anxiolytic (also called antianxiety or minor tranquilizers)	Benzodiazepines	Chlordiazepoxide	Librium
		Diazepam	Valium
		Chlorazepate	Tranxene
		Oxazepam	Serax
		Lorazepam	Activan
	Triazolobenzodiazepine	Alprazolam	Xanax
	Propanediol carbamates	Meprobamate	Miltown
Sedative hypnotic	Barbiturates	Phenobarbital	
	Benzodiazepines	Triazolam	Halcion
Antipanic	Benzodiazepines	Alprazolam	Xanax
	MAOIs	Phenelzine	Nardil
	TCAs	Imipramine	Tofranil
Antiobsessional	TCA	Clomipramine	Anafranil
	SSRI	Fluoxetine	Prozac

Source: G.L. Klerman, M.M. Weissman, J.C. Markowitz, I Glick, P.J. Wilner, B. Mason, & M.K. Shear (1994). Medication and psychotherapy. In A.E. Bergin & S.L. Garfield (Eds.), *Handbook of psychotherapy and behavior change* (4th ed.) (pp. 734-782). New York: Wiley.

treatments aimed at psychological or social change. A third and related point is that psychoactive drugs typically are taken for long periods of time. Because the medications alleviate symptoms but do not produce a cure, it may be necessary to keep taking the drug—for months, years, or sometimes for a lifetime (Klerman et al., 1994).

Psychodynamic Psychotherapies

Psychodynamic approaches to psychological treatment were first developed during the nineteenth and early twentieth centuries. Joseph Breuer's (1842–1925) pioneering technique known as the "cathartic method" was one of the earliest influences. Breuer used hypnosis to induce his troubled patients to talk freely about problems in their lives. Upon awakening from the hypnotic trance, many patients reported relief from their symptoms, although they were unable to recall what they had said while hypnotized. Breuer used the principle of **catharsis** to explain the benefits of his hypnotic method. The concept suggests that psychological problems are caused by pent-up emotions, and that the release of previously unexpressed feelings—catharsis—reduces psychic strain. The sudden release of steam through the whistle of a boiling teapot is an appropriate visual metaphor for catharsis.

FREUDIAN PSYCHOANALYSIS

Breuer's contemporary and collaborator, Sigmund Freud (1856–1939), adopted the cathartic method for a time, but he soon concluded that hypnosis was not necessary to encourage open expression. Instead, Freud simply told his patients to speak freely about whatever thoughts crossed their mind. This method, called **free association**, became a cornerstone of Freud's famous treatment, **psychoanalysis.**

Unlike Breuer, Freud did not see the catharsis produced by discussing forbidden topics as an end in itself. The true benefit of free association, in Freud's view, was that it revealed aspects of the unconscious mind. Freud found clues about his patients' intrapsychic life in their unedited speech. Freud also believed that dreams (during which intrapsychic defenses presumably are weaker) and slips of the tongue (known commonly as "Freudian slips") provided especially revealing information about the unconscious.

Thus, according to Freud, free association, dreams, and slips of the tongue are all valuable because they serve as windows into the unconscious.

Freud viewed the task of psychoanalysis as uncovering the unconscious conflicts and motivations that he assumed to be the cause of psychological difficulties. According to Freudian theory, disorders will be cured when these unconscious conflicts are resolved. The psychoanalyst's discovery is only the beginning of resolving the unconscious conflicts. In order to overcome their dysfunction, patients must come to share the psychoanalyst's understanding of their intrapsychic life. The ultimate goal of psychoanalysis is to bring formerly unconscious material into conscious awareness. This is what Freud called **insight.**

The analyst's main tool for promoting insight is **interpretation.** In offering an interpretation, the analyst suggests hidden meanings to patients' accounts of their past and present life. Typically, interpretations relate to past experiences, especially experiences with loved ones. Recall from Chapter 2, however, that according to Freudian theory the ego defense mechanisms keep intrapsychic conflicts from conscious awareness. Thus, psychoanalysts must overcome defenses like repression and projection as patients resist their interpretations. Timing is everything in overcoming *resistance*. The patient must be on the verge of discovering the hidden meaning himself or herself; otherwise, the interpretation will be rejected. For example, consider the dilemma of convincing Frances that deep resentment lies beneath her unwavering love for her mother. Given her long history of subjugating her own needs to those of her mother, Frances would be unlikely to accept such an interpretation if it were made too early in her treatment.

In probing the unconscious mind and offering interpretations, *therapeutic neutrality* is viewed as essential in Freudian psychoanalysis. Psychoanalysts maintain a distant and uninvolved stance toward their patients in order to minimize their influence on free association. The therapist "sits behind the patient where the patient cannot see him, and avoids either telling the patient about his own private affairs or having social contacts with him. He tries to create, as far as possible, a controlled laboratory situation in which the individual peculiarities of the analyst shall play as little role as possible in stimulating the patient's reactions" (Alexander & French, 1947, p. 83).

The analyst's distant stance is thought to encourage **transference,** the process whereby patients transfer the feelings about some key figure in their life onto the shadowy figure of the analyst. For psychoanalysis to succeed, the analyst must not respond to transference in a manner that the patient views as critical or threatening. Psychoanalysts particularly must guard against *countertransference*, or letting their own feelings influence their responses to their patients. Analysts also must avoid reacting to their patients in the same way as the transference figure had reacted. Otherwise, the past will be repeated, and patients' fears will be confirmed. Instead, the analyst's job is to interpret the patient's actions and motivations in order to promote insight about the transference.

Insight into the transference relationship presumably helps patients to understand how and why they are treating the analyst in the same dysfunctional manner in which they treated a loved one. The awareness thus creates a new understanding both of past relationships and of unconscious motivations in present relationships. For example, consider a transference that might develop between Frances and a psychoanalyst. Frances might have difficulty accepting a therapeutic relationship in which she was receiving care instead of giving it. She might therefore try to get the analyst to reveal personal problems, or perhaps she would bring gifts to her therapist. The therapist's polite refusal of the gifts, and of Frances's attempts at caretaking, might cause her to feel hurt, rejected, and, eventually, angry. As therapy proceeded, these actions could be interpreted as reflecting Frances's style of relating to her mother and her tendency to deny her own needs.

A common misconception about psychoanalysis is that the ultimate goal of insight is to rid the patient of all defenses. This is not the case. According to Freud, defenses are essential for the functioning of a healthy personality. Thus, rather than ridding the patient of defenses, one goal of psychoanalysis is to replace them. Defenses such as denial and projection are confronted because they distort reality dramatically, whereas more "healthy" defenses such as rationalization and sublimation are left unchallenged. A second goal of psychoanalysis is to help the patient become more aware of basic needs or drives in order that the patient may find socially and psychologically appropriate outlets for

them (Maddi, 1980). A goal for Frances, for example, would be to admit that anger is a legitimate and acceptable part of her personality.

Current Status of Freudian Psychoanalysis

Freudian psychoanalysis involves several hour-long sessions each week, often lasting over the course of several years. Because psychoanalysis requires substantial time, expense, and self-exploration, it is accessible only to people who are relatively well functioning, introspective, and financially secure. In many respects, psychoanalysis now is construed more as a process of self-understanding than as a treatment for specific emotional disorders. This view is bolstered by the fact that very little therapy outcome research has been conducted on classical psychoanalysis. Freud believed that not every patient would benefit from the treatment—a belief shared by many contemporary practitioners. Those suffering from psychotic and personality disorders are thought to be especially unlikely to benefit, whereas people suffering from "neurotic" disorders, especially excessive anxiety, have been thought to benefit most.

Although it is still practiced, the expense and time involved, and the limited amount of data available on outcome, have caused a decline in the popularity of Freudian psychoanalysis. Variations on Freudian theory have led to the development of new forms of insight-oriented therapy, however. These revisionist approaches are termed **psychodynamic** rather than psychoanalytic. Psychodynamic psychotherapists often are more engaged and directive in therapy, and the process often is considerably less protracted than psychoanalysis.

EGO ANALYSIS

The development of **ego analysis** has been the most important innovation in Freudian theory and therapy. Ego analysis originated in the work of a number of different therapists who were trained in Freudian psychoanalysis but who independently developed innovations in theory and technique. Whereas Freud emphasized the paramount role of the id in personality and psychopathology, these new theorists focused much more on the ego. The major function of the ego, according to Freudian theory, is to mediate between the conflicting impulses of the id and the superego (see Chapter 2). Of equal importance to ego analysts, however, is the ego's role in dealing with reality (Hartmann, Kris, & Loewenstein, 1947). Ego analysts therefore are concerned with unconscious motivations, but they also consider the patient's dealings with the external world. They attend to the role of society and culture in producing emotional disturbance, as well to the effects of current life circumstances and the patient's reactions to them.

Of greatest importance in ego analysis are the patient's past and present interpersonal relationships. Ego analyst Harry Stack Sullivan (1892–1949) was extremely influential in highlighting this paramount role of relationships. He suggested that many characteristics of the personality could be conceptualized in interpersonal rather than intrapsychic terms. Like many interpersonal theorists, Sullivan saw two basic dimensions of interpersonal relationships. One dimension reflects interpersonal power, ranging from dominance to submission. A second dimension concerns interpersonal closeness, with affiliation on one end of the continuum and hostility at the opposite pole. Sullivan's followers, in fact, have developed a classification of personality based on these two dimensions (Leary, 1957).

Other especially influential ego analysts include Erik Erikson (1902–1994) and Karen Horney (1885–1952). Horney's (1939) most lasting contribution has been her suggestion that people have conflicting ego needs to move toward, against, and away from others. Essentially, Horney argued that there are competing human (ego) needs for closeness, for dominance, and for autonomy. She viewed people with interpersonal or intrapsychic conflicts as being too rigid in fulfilling only one of these needs. In her view, the key to a healthy personality is finding a balance among the three styles of relating to others. You might pause for a moment to reconsider the case of Frances to help you understand Horney's ideas. Frances's characteristic style and her conflicting needs should not be too difficult to discern.

Erikson's stage theory of development was introduced briefly in Chapter 2. As with other ego analysts, Erikson's critical departure from Freud focused on the interpersonal context. This can be seen in his emphasis on the externally oriented psycho*social* stages of development rather than the internally oriented psycho*sexual* stages. Erikson also introduced the argument that an individual's personality is not fixed by early experience but continues to develop as a result of predictable psychosocial conflicts throughout the lifespan (see Chapter 16). In contrast, Freud viewed personality patterns as being fixed by intrapsychic conflicts that occurred primarily during the first few years of life. He assumed that personality is difficult to change thereafter.

Attachment Theory   The work of British psychiatrist John Bowlby (1907–1991) perhaps has had the greatest effect on contemporary thought about interpersonal influences on personality and psychopathology. Bowlby's (1969; 1973; 1980) theorizing began with the assertion that humans, like other social animals, have a basic instinct to form close relationships with their caregivers early in life—an **attachment.** Bowlby maintained that studies of animal behavior and evolutionary theory both indicate that humans have a distinct, inborn need to form close relationships. In contrast, Freud viewed closeness in relationships only as an outgrowth of the reduction of primary drives such as hunger and sex. Thus, Bowlby elevated the need for close relationships from a secondary to a primary human characteristic.

According to attachment theory, much abnormal behavior can be traced back to difficulties in early relationships with key attachment figures, typically one's parents. The failure to form early attachments, the formation of insecure attachments (Ainsworth, 1979), or separation from or loss of attachment figures can all lead to psychopathology, according to Bowlby (1969; 1973; 1980). What makes Bowlby unique among ego analysts is that he, together with psychologist Mary Ainsworth (1979), have conducted and encouraged empirical research on attachment theory (Bretherton, 1992). We consider aspects of this body of research in subsequent chapters of the text.

PSYCHODYNAMIC PSYCHOTHERAPY

Many different approaches to psychotherapy have been developed based on the writings of Sullivan, Horney, Erikson, Bowlby, and other theorists who have been influenced by Freud. As with psychoanalysis, all of these approaches emphasize insight, but psychodynamic psychotherapists are much more actively involved with their patients. The psychodynamic psychotherapist is more ready to direct the patient's recollections, to focus on current life circumstances, and to offer inter-

▲ **Harry Stack Sullivan (1892–1949) was a U.S. psychiatrist and ego analyst. Sullivan suggested that personality could be conceptualized in interpersonal terms and not just in intrapsychic ones.**

pretations quickly and directly. Most psychodynamic psychotherapists are also much more "human" in conducting therapy. They may be distant and reflective at times, but they also are willing to offer appropriate emotional support (Garfield, 1989).

Short-term psychodynamic psychotherapy is a form of treatment that uses many psychoanalytic techniques. Therapeutic neutrality is typically maintained, and transference remains a central issue, but the short-term psychodynamic therapist actively focuses on a particular emotional issue rather than relying on free association (Garfield, 1989; Sifneos, 1988). The short-term approach is gaining increased attention because it typically is limited to 25 sessions or less and therefore is less expensive and more amenable to research (Garfield, 1989; Luborsky, 1984; Luborsky, Barber, & Beutler, 1993). Current research on psychodynamic psychotherapy generally supports Freud's observation that psychodynamic therapy is ineffective in treating more severe disorders, although it may be effective in treating milder anxiety (Luborsky et al., 1993). There still is a pressing need for further evidence on the technique, however.

Behavior Therapy

Behavior therapy focuses on behavior change in the present, not on insight about the past. The approach includes a diverse array of techniques, many of which were developed on the basis of psychological research findings. Despite the diversity of approaches, all behavior therapists adhere to the truism "Actions speak louder than words."

The beginnings of behavior therapy can be traced to John B. Watson's (1878–1958) writings in the early part of the twentieth century. Watson was the key figure in developing **behaviorism** in American psychology—the belief that observable behaviors, not unobservable cognitive or emotional states, are the appropriate focus of psychological study. Watson maintained that abnormal behavior was learned and could be unlearned, just like normal behavior. He viewed the behavior therapist's job as analogous to that of a teacher. The therapeutic goal is to provide new, more appropriate learning experiences. In developing treatments, Watson and his followers relied heavily on the findings of animal learning researchers, particularly Pavlov's theories of classical conditioning and Skinner's

theories of operant conditioning (see Chapter 2). More recently, behavior therapy has been powerfully influenced by the findings of cognitive psychologists (Mahoney, 1991).

Watson and his followers articulated some basic and continuing themes in behavior therapy. Unlike psychoanalysis, behavior therapy does not offer a substantive theoretical core concerning the composition of the human personality. Rather, it is an outcome-oriented approach. Perhaps the most important theme of behavior therapy is its reliance on empirical evaluation. This empirical emphasis is evident in the behavior therapist's application of psychological science to clinical problems, and in the hundreds of treatment outcome studies that have been conducted on behavior therapy. We will examine and raise some questions about research on behavior therapy later in this chapter and throughout the book. Regardless of how the evidence is interpreted, however, behavior therapists clearly have contributed greatly by constantly emphasizing the empirical evaluation of psychotherapy.

The behavior therapist's focus on present behavior, learning processes, and empirical evaluation can be seen in the diverse treatment techniques that are a part of the approach. Below we consider some of the most common techniques: classical conditioning, operant conditioning, and cognitive behavior therapy techniques.

CLASSICAL CONDITIONING TECHNIQUES

A number of behavior therapy techniques have been developed from Pavlov's theory of classical conditioning. All classical conditioning techniques use *counterconditioning* procedures. Counterconditioning involves altering existing responses by pairing new responses with old stimuli.

Joseph Wolpe (1958) developed the most influential counterconditioning technique. Wolpe is a South African psychiatrist whose initial work in classical conditioning involved experimental research on the development of neuroses in animals. This work convinced him that classical conditioning procedures could be applied to treat important human problems. He concentrated his efforts on eliminating phobias. Wolpe (1958) assumed that at least some phobias were learned through classical conditioning. Like other behavior therapists, however, he was much less concerned with the cause of a disorder than with its treatment. He reasoned that if fears could be learned, they could be unlearned. The key was to break the association between stimulus and response. The technique he developed to do so is called **systematic desensitization.**

▲ **Joseph Wolpe is a leading behavior therapist. Wolpe developed systematic desensitization, a pioneering technique that uses classical conditioning to eliminate fears.**

Systematic Desensitization Systematic desensitization has three key elements. The first is relaxation training. Wolpe believed that in order to replace anxiety in response to a feared stimulus, the new conditioned response, relaxation, must be easily elicited. He focused on the technique of *progressive muscle relaxation*, a method of inducing a calm state through the contraction and subsequent relaxation of all of the major muscle groups. The second component of systematic desensitization is the construction of a *hierarchy of fears* ranging from very mild to very frightening stimuli. Because anxiety initially is a stronger response to the feared stimulus than is relaxation, Wolpe thought that exposure to fears must be gradual, or the relaxation would be overwhelmed by the anxiety. The third part of systematic desensitization is the learning process, namely the pairing of the feared stimulus with the relaxation response. Wolpe had his clients carry out this pairing in their imagination. Thus, systematic desensitization involves imagining increasingly fearful events while simultaneously maintaining a state of relaxation.

Systematic desensitization has been the subject of volumes of research. In fact, the development of the technique can be credited with spurring psychotherapy outcome research in general. Overall, evidence supports the effectiveness of systematic desensitization as a treatment for fears and phobias (O'Leary & Wilson, 1987; Wolpe, 1990). It is not clear, however, that counterconditioning accounts for the change. Alternative interpretations suggest that the true mechanisms for change are the removal of reinforcement for avoidance, the extinction of the fear, an increased sense of self-efficacy that comes from confronting one's fears, or even the formation of a supportive therapeutic relationship (Kazdin & Wilcoxin, 1976; O'Leary & Wilson, 1987).

In Vivo Desensitization Although it is not yet clear exactly why systematic desensitization is an effective treatment, research has helped to pinpoint the crucial elements of the procedure. Most investigators agree that *exposure* is the key to fear reduction. This observation has led to the further development of new desensitization techniques, the most notable of which is **in vivo desensitization.** In vivo desensitization involves being gradually exposed to the feared stimulus in real life while simultaneously maintaining a state of relaxation. Research on in vivo desensitization indicates that the way to overcome fears is to confront them. Thus, behavior therapists follow another truism: If you fall off a horse, the best way to conquer the fear of riding is to get back in the saddle.

Flooding **Flooding** is another exposure technique. Unlike desensitization, exposure to the feared stimulus is not gradual in flooding, and there is no attempt to calm initial anxiety. Rather, flooding involves exposure at full intensity. The goal is to eliminate anxiety through extinction by repeatedly presenting the conditioned stimulus until it no longer produces the unconditioned response. Someone who was afraid of heights might be brought to the top of the CN tower in Toronto (the world's tallest structure). The intense anxiety initially produced by this experience should gradually be extinguished as the individual spends more time at the top of the building. The key to this treatment, and to flooding in general, is to prevent avoidance. Clients must not be allowed to retreat from the stimulus in fear, because the resulting reduction in anxiety would be negatively reinforcing (O'Leary & Wilson, 1987; Wolpe, 1990).

Aversion Therapy The counterconditioning in **aversion therapy** differs from that in systematic desensitization and flooding. The goal in aversion therapy is to create rather than eliminate an unpleasant response. As such, aversion therapy is used primarily in the treatment of substance use disorders such as alcoholism and cigarette smoking. Aversion therapy for these problems involves pairing an unpleasant response with the stimuli that elicit substance use. In working with alcoholism, the typical procedure is to pair the sight, smell, and taste of alcohol with severe nausea produced artificially by a drug. For cigarette smoking, the *rapid smoking technique* is the most common aversion therapy. In rapid smoking, the client engages in prolonged chain smoking in a poorly ventilated room until he or she becomes ill from the oppressive smoke.

Aversion therapies have the goal of reducing substance use by associating it with unpleasant consequences. Such treatments are controversial, however, precisely because of their aversive nature. Moreover, data on the effectiveness of aversion therapies are ambiguous (O'Leary & Wilson, 1987). Although these treatments often achieve short-term success, relapse rates are high. Everyday life offers the substance abuser the opportunity, and perhaps the motivation, to desensitize himself or herself to the classically conditioned responses learned in aversion therapy.

OPERANT CONDITIONING TECHNIQUES

A second set of behavior therapy techniques is based on Skinner's work on operant conditioning. The major assumption of these approaches is straightforward: Behaviors that are reinforced will increase, and those that are punished will diminish.

Contingency Management   One form of operant behavior therapy, **contingency management**, focuses on directly changing the rewards and punishments for various behaviors. A *contingency* is the relationship between a behavior and its consequences; thus, contingency management involves changing this relationship. Contingency management is generally used in circumstances where the therapist has considerable direct or indirect control over the client's environment, such as in institutional settings and group homes, or when children are brought for treatment by their parents. Such control is needed because the key to contingency management is for the therapist to reward desirable behavior systematically and to extinguish or punish undesirable behavior. To do this, the therapist must control relevant rewards and punishments.

The **token economy** is an example of contingency management that has been adopted in many institutional settings. In a token economy, desired and undesired behaviors are clearly identified, contingencies are defined, behavior is carefully monitored, and rewards or punishments are given according to the rules of the token economy. For example, in a group home for juvenile offenders, a token economy may specify that residents earn tokens for completing schoolwork and household chores, while they lose tokens for arguing or fighting. Each resident's behavior is monitored and recorded, and tokens are "paid" accordingly. The key to the success of the program is that tokens can be exchanged for rewards desired by the residents—for example, going out unescorted on a Saturday night.

Numerous studies have shown that contingency management works to change behavior among such diverse groups of clients as institutionalized schizophrenics (Paul & Lentz, 1977) and delinquents in group homes (Phillips, Wolf, & Fixsen, 1973). The evidence for success must be interpreted carefully, however. Many improvements occur in the setting where the operant program is in place, but they often do not generalize to real-life situations (Emery & Marholin, 1977). Rewards and punishments in controlled settings often differ from those in the natural environment. A psychologist can set up clear and consistent contingencies for a juvenile living in a group home, but it may be impossible to alter the rewards and punishments the teenager encounters when he or she returns to live with a chaotic family or delinquent peers. In the real world, contingencies are not clearly defined. Undesirable behavior often is rewarded, and punishments for inappropriate behavior—and rewards for appropriate behavior—often are inconsistent or delayed. Thus, token economies are assured of being effective only in environments that a therapist can easily control.

Social Skills Training   **Social skills training** is another behavior therapy technique based on operant conditioning principles. The goal is to teach clients new ways of behaving that are both desirable and likely to be rewarded in the everyday world (McFall, 1982). Two commonly taught skills are assertiveness (Lange & Jakubowski, 1976) and social problem solving (D'Zurrilla & Goldfried, 1971; Spivack & Shure, 1974).

The goal of *assertiveness training* is to teach clients to be direct about their feelings and wishes. The training can involve a variety of levels of detail in social skills, from learning to make eye contact to asking a boss for a raise. In teaching assertiveness, therapists frequently use **role-playing**, an improvisational acting technique that allows clients to rehearse new social skills. Clients try out new ways of acting, while the therapist assumes the role of some person in their life. Later, the therapist offers feedback and suggests different approaches to the clients. In addition to teaching new social skills, assertiveness training seeks to produce cognitive change in the client. Learning to recognize personal "rights" is one key change. All people have the right to make ordinary requests, for example, or to express their feelings. In contrast, no one necessarily has the right to get everything that he or she wants or to have his or her feelings understood. Thus, assertiveness is defined in terms of the individual's actions, not in terms of the consequences of those actions.

Social problem solving is a multistep process that has been used to teach children and adults ways to go about solving a variety of life's problems (D'Zurrilla & Goldfried, 1971; Spivack & Shure, 1974). The first step in social problem solving involves assessing and defining the problem in detail. This step is important, as we often see problems as being more manageable when they are defined specifically. "Brainstorming" is the second step in social problem solving. When individuals or groups brainstorm, they are asked to come up with as many creative alternative solutions as they can imagine—even wild and crazy options—without evaluating these alternatives. The third step in social problem solving involves carefully evaluating each of the options that has been generated. Finally, one alternative is chosen and implemented, and its success in solving the problem is evaluated objectively. If the solution is unsuccessful, the entire process can be repeated until an effective solution is found.

Clients can learn new social skills in therapy, but it is less clear whether they use these skills in real life or whether these skills help clients to obtain the rewards that they seek (Wilson & O'Leary, 1987). It is difficult to evaluate the overall effectiveness of the social skills training, because the technique has been applied to a wide variety of problems. We consider its effectiveness in treating particular problems in subsequent chapters of the text.

Cognitive Behavior Therapy

Many practitioners have expanded the scope of behavior therapy beyond the principles of classical and operant conditioning and into the cognitive realm of human information processing. **Cognitive behavior therapy,** as this approach is called, is a departure from Watson's exclusive focus on observable behavior. Psychological scientists have measured and documented the importance of many unobservable cognitive processes in human learning. In order to continue the commitment to applying basic research on learning to clinical problems, behavior therapists have had to incorporate cognition and to acknowledge that some very important psychological processes cannot be directly observed. Stanford University psychologist Albert Bandura, an advocate of modeling and social learning theory (see Chapter 2), has been a leader in encouraging the use of this broader approach.

Cognitive behavior therapy is a burgeoning field of treatment innovation. Some cognitive therapy treatments have been developed in working with clinical populations, as we discuss shortly. Other cognitive behavior therapy techniques involve direct attempts to apply basic research from cognitive psychology to clinical issues. Two examples of this latter approach are attribution therapy and self-instruction training.

ATTRIBUTION THERAPY

Attribution therapy is based on research on social cognition that defines humans as "intuitive scientists" who are constantly ascribing causes to various events in their lives. These perceived causes, which may or may not be objectively accurate, are called **attributions.** Attribution therapy involves trying to change attributions, often by asking clients to abandon intuitive strategies for determining causation. Instead, clients are instructed in more scientific methods, such as objectively testing hypotheses about themselves and others (Wilson & Linville, 1982).

Altering attributions may be especially relevant to the treatment of depression. Depressed people often attribute failures to themselves, whereas they attribute successes to other people (Peterson & Seligman, 1984; see Chapter 5). Frances's self-blame can be viewed as an example of this depressive attributional style, as she wrongly blamed herself for all of her family's problems. In order to change these erroneous attributions, a cognitive behavior therapist might ask Frances to be more objective in evaluating her life. In so doing, she could learn about her own biased attributions as well as about the problems of others in her family. Attribution therapy also has been used to treat other problems. Examples include helping new students realize that struggling in the first year of college is not a personal failure but a common problem (Wilson & Linville, 1982), and helping unhappily married partners to change the tendency to attribute negative interactions to a spouse's flawed personality (Fincham & Bradbury, 1990).

SELF-INSTRUCTION TRAINING

Self-instruction training draws on principles articulated by Luria (1961) and others about how children come to internalize rules over the course of their development. Meichenbaum (1977) has applied these theories in developing cognitive therapies for impulsive children. In Meichenbaum's **self-instruction training,** the adult first models an appropriate behavior while saying the self-instruction aloud. Next, the child is asked to repeat the action and also to say the self-instruction aloud. Following this, the child repeats the task while whispering the self-instructions. Finally, the child does the task while repeating the instructions silently. This procedure is designed to offer a structured way of helping children learn the internal controls that typically are acquired during the course of normal development.

In addition to specific applications of research from cognitive psychology, cognitive behavior therapy has been strongly influenced by the clinical work of Aaron Beck (1976) and Albert Ellis (1973). Both Beck and Ellis initially developed cognitive treatments outside the auspices of behavior therapy, but their approaches have since been adopted as a part of cognitive behavior therapy.

COGNITIVE THERAPY

Beck's **cognitive therapy** was developed specifically as a treatment for depression (Beck et al., 1979). Beck suggested that depression is caused by errors in thinking. These hypothesized distortions lead depressed people to draw incorrect, negative conclusions about themselves, thus creating and maintaining the depression. Simply put, Beck hypothesized that depressed people see the world through gray-colored glasses (as opposed to the rose-colored variety). According to Beck's analysis, this negative filter makes the world appear much bleaker than it really is.

Beck's cognitive therapy involves challenging these negative distortions through a technique he calls *collaborative empiricism*. Cognitive therapists gently confront their clients' cognitive fallacies in therapy, but the clients are asked to decide for themselves whether their thinking is distorted based on their analysis of their own life. Cognitive therapists later use the data that clients collect on themselves to challenge the negative distortions, thus presumably freeing them from the cognitive errors that cause depression (Beck et al., 1979). We discuss this important treatment in more detail in Chapter 5, where we also review the mounting research that it is an effective therapy.

RATIONAL–EMOTIVE THERAPY

Rational–emotive therapy (RET) also is designed to challenge cognitive distortions. According to Ellis (1962), emotional disorders are caused by *irrational beliefs*. Irrational beliefs are absolute, unrealistic views of the world, such as "Everyone must love me all of the time." The rational–emotive therapist searches for a client's irrational beliefs, points out the impossibility of fulfilling them, and uses any and every technique to persuade the client to adopt more realistic beliefs. Rational–emotive therapy shares concepts and techniques in common with Beck's approach. A major difference, however, is that rational–emotive therapists directly challenge the client's beliefs during therapy (Dryden & DiGuisseppe, 1990; Ellis, 1962).

TREATMENT EFFECTIVENESS

Psychotherapy outcome research on the effectiveness of cognitive behavior therapy indicates that it is generally equal to or superior to alternative forms of behavior therapy. The evidence supporting Beck's cognitive therapy for depression is particularly impressive. Evidence on rational–emotive therapy is less clear, in part because the treatment as not been studied as thoroughly (Hollon & Beck, 1986).

Clearly, behavior therapy is comprised of a diverse set of treatments. Unlike psychodynamic approaches, which are based on assumptions about the nature of psychopathology, behavior therapy is focused on treatment irrespective of its causes. What unites behavioral therapists is their emphasis on learning alternative ways of acting, thinking, and feeling. What unites them even more is a commitment to empiricism. Behavior therapists want to offer treatments that work, and they have been vigorous in conducting psychotherapy outcome research. Research indicates that behavior therapies are not the only effective treatments, but this finding does not distress empirically oriented behavior therapists. Rather, it challenges them to identify alternative approaches and to incorporate them into the ever-expanding realm of behavior therapy. In fact, we envision a blurring

▲ **Stanford University psychologist Albert Bandura is an advocate of social learning theory and a leading proponent of cognitive behavior therapy.**

of the lines between behavior therapy and other paradigms in the not-so-distant future, as empirical evidence and an integrated systems approach identify diverse but effective treatments for different disorders.

Humanistic Therapies

Humanistic psychotherapy originally was promoted as a "third force" to counteract what were seen as the overly mechanistic and deterministic views of both the psychodynamic and behavioral approaches to psychotherapy. Humanists argue that psychodynamic, behavioral, and biomedical therapists overlook the most essential of all human qualities: The individual's ability to make choices and freely determine his or her future.

Humanistic therapists believe that emotional distress results from the frustrations of human existence, particularly from alienation from the self and others. They also argue that each individual has the responsibility for finding meaning in her or his own life. Unlike the behavior therapist, the humanistic therapist does not believe that treatment can solve problems. Rather, treatment is seen only as a way of helping individuals to make their own life choices and to resolve their own dilemmas (Rogers, 1961).

To facilitate making choices, humanistic therapists strive to increase *emotional awareness*. They encourage their clients to recognize and experience their true feelings. Like psychodynamic approaches, this involves "uncovering" hidden emotions, and some psychologists therefore classify the two treatments together as insight therapies (London, 1964). However, humanistic therapists are more concerned with how their clients are feeling than with why they are feeling that way. They focus on experiencing life, not on the structure of the personality. Thus, like behavior therapy, humanistic therapy is much more oriented to the present than is psychodynamic treatment.

One of the major differences in technique between humanistic psychotherapy and both behavioral and psychodynamic approaches is the nature of the therapist–client relationship. Humanistic therapists view a genuine and reciprocal relationship between therapist and client as the central means of producing therapeutic change. Therapists from other schools also place importance on the therapist–client relationship,

▲ **Carl Rogers (1902–1987) was a U.S. psychologist who developed client-centered therapy. Rogers asserted that therapeutic warmth, empathy, and genuineness were the necessary and sufficient conditions for producing successful psychotherapy outcome.**

but the relationship is viewed primarily as a means of delivering the treatment. In humanistic therapy, the relationship *is* the treatment.

CLIENT-CENTERED THERAPY

Carl Rogers (1902–1987) and his **client-centered therapy** provide the clearest example of the humanistic focus on the therapeutic relationship. Rogers (1951) wrote extensively about the process of fostering a warm and genuine relationship between therapist and client. He particularly noted the importance of **empathy,** or emotional understanding. Empathy involves "putting yourself in someone else's shoes" as a way of understanding their unique feelings and perspectives. In order to demonstrate empathy, the therapist must communicate this emotional understanding. Empathy is conveyed by reflecting the client's feelings, and at a deeper level, by sharing an understanding of emotions that remain unexpressed.

In forming an empathic relationship, the client-centered therapist is not construed as an "expert" who knows more about the client than the client knows about himself or herself. Rather, the key to successful humanistic therapy is sharing in another human's experience. The ability to share another's perspective can come from many life experiences, not just from professional training; therefore Rogers felt that client-centered therapists could be *paraprofessionals* or people who had faced life difficulties similar to those of their clients. In fact, Rogers encouraged *self-disclosure* on the part of the therapist. In contrast to the psychoanalyst's distance, client-centered therapists may intentionally reveal aspects of their own feelings and experiences to their clients.

Rogers also felt that client-centered therapists must be able to demonstrate *unconditional positive regard* for their clients. This involves valuing the clients for who they are and refraining from judging them. Because of this basic respect for the client's humanity, client-centered therapists avoid directing the therapeutic process. According to Rogers, if clients are successful in experiencing and accepting themselves, they will achieve their own resolution to their difficulties. Thus, client-centered therapy is *nondirective*.

GESTALT THERAPY

Frederich (Fritz) Perls's (1893–1970) **Gestalt therapy** is another variation of the humanistic approach[†]. Perls (1969) shared many of Rogers's therapeutic goals, particularly the goal of helping clients to recognize and accept their emotional experiences. Perls especially underscored the importance of experiencing the moment—what he called living in the "here and now." He urged people to be genuine, and he accused many of being phony instead. Terms such as "here and now" and "phoniness" were part of the popular culture of the 1960s but may seem vague or even silly today. Perls might have countered that defining terms is a phony intellectual activity, not a genuine emotional one.

Gestalt techniques for increasing emotional awareness differ greatly from client-centered approaches. Rather than being supportive, the Gestalt therapist confronts the client's phoniness in the hope that the client's frustration will provoke genuine emotion. As long as the client is phony, the Gestalt therapist is confrontational. When genuine emotion is expressed, however, the therapist's confrontation switches to support and shared experience. The here and now is critical to this distinction. Talking about emotions is phony. Feeling them is genuine. To a Gestalt therapist, an engaged "I hate you!" is much more genuine than a detached "I'm feeling very angry with you right now."

Gestalt therapists also differ from Rogerians in that they are very directive. In fact, Perls developed a number of specific exercises designed to provoke emotion and thereby heighten awareness. One of the better-known strategies is the *empty chair technique*, in which the client has a dialogue with another part of himself or herself who is imagined to be sitting in an empty chair. For example, a woman who is trying to make a decision about a career change might argue in favor of the change—directing the argument to "herself" in the empty chair. Later, she might switch seats and make the case against the change. As with other Gestalt techniques, the goal of the empty chair exercise is to heighten emotional awareness and thereby increase genuineness.

EXISTENTIAL ANALYSIS

A third variation on humanistic therapy is *existential analysis*. Proponents of this approach include Ludwig Binswanger (1963), Medard Boss (1963), and Rollo May (1967), all of whom believed that authenticity is the key to successful living and to successful psychotherapy. They therefore rejected the notion that therapy was comprised of techniques. This makes existential analysis difficult to characterize. Existentialists want their clients to "be whatever they may be," and a core theme of the approach is helping clients to confront a huge dilemma: finding meaning in life.

It is impossible to provide an answer to the dilemma of finding meaning in life, and in many respects, that is the point of existential analysis. Each individual must find meaning in her or his own way. To support their clients' struggle to find meaning, existential analysts encourage emotional awareness, the experience of the present, and the process of living as opposed to the attainment of goals. Existential

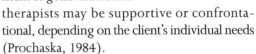

"*So, while extortion, racketeering, and murder may be bad acts, they don't make you a bad person.*"

therapists may be supportive or confrontational, depending on the client's individual needs (Prochaska, 1984).

Little research supports the effectiveness of client-centered, Gestalt, and existential therapy in treating abnormal behavior (Greenberg, Elliott, & Lietaer, 1994). One problem in evaluating effectiveness is that clients who seek humanistic treatments often are functioning rather well in their lives. They view therapy as a growth experience, not as a treatment for an emotional problem. Another problem is that the techniques have not been well studied in psychotherapy outcome research. Nevertheless, it should be noted that Rogers and his colleagues were strongly committed to psychotherapy *process* research. Empathy and other relationship factors have been empirically documented to predict successful outcome across different psychotherapies (Rogers, 1957; Truax & Carkhuff, 1967).

In many respects, process research is the lasting legacy of humanistic approaches to psychotherapy. As we discuss shortly, research on psychotherapy processes indicates that therapists who are humanistic in style are more effective when using virtually any treatment technique.

[†] A *Gestalt* is an organized whole. Gestalt psychology emphasizes wholeness, whether at the level of perception or the level of life experience.

The major task for psychotherapy research is to identify the most effective treatments for specific disorders, but psychologists must not lose sight of the fact that caring, concern, and respect

for the individual are essential components of the healing of emotional disorders—and of treating physical illnesses (see Chapter 7).

Research on Psychotherapy

A natural question to ask about the three major schools of psychotherapy is: Which treatment approach works best? This is a question posed in psychotherapy outcome research—a line of investigation in which alternative treatments are compared in terms of their effectiveness in alleviating emotional disturbances. Although the question is a straightforward one, outcome research does not offer a simple answer.

Psychotherapy Outcome Research

Before considering some of the complications involved in comparing the effectiveness of different schools of psychotherapy, an even more basic question must be asked: Does *any* form of psychotherapy work? Does psychotherapy produce more improvement than no treatment at all? Many people claim not to "believe" in psychotherapy. Is their skepticism founded?

Fortunately, there *is* a simple answer to this question. Psychotherapy does work—for many people with many problems. Researchers have conducted hundreds of studies comparing the outcome of various types of psychotherapy with the results of receiving no treatment at all. These investigations confirm the general effectiveness of therapy when compared with no treatment; but the topic is sufficiently complicated and sufficiently important to require a closer examination.

META-ANALYSIS

So many studies have been conducted on psychotherapy that psychologists increasingly have relied on a new method, called *meta-analysis*, to summarize findings across studies. Meta-analysis is a statistical technique that allows the results from different studies to be combined

in a standardized way. The findings of a meta-analysis are expressed in standard deviation units, a measure of deviation from the mean.[†]

In evaluating hundreds of studies of psychotherapy outcome, meta-analysis indicates that the average change produced is .85 standard deviations units (Smith, Glass, & Miller, 1980; see Figure 3–1). As one way of evaluating this finding, consider that 9 months of reading instruction leads to a .67 standard deviation unit increase in reading achievement among elementary school children (Lambert, Shapiro, & Bergin, 1986). Another useful comparison is that many well-accepted medical treatments have considerably smaller effect sizes (Lipsey & Wilson, 1993). A .85 standard deviation unit change also means that the average client who receives therapy is better off than 80 percent of untreated persons (Smith, Glass, & Miller, 1980).

Although meta–analysis is a useful way of summarizing information from a large number of studies, the meaning of standard deviation units can be difficult to grasp. One way to make the finding more readily understood is to translate it into improvement rates. A conversion of the .85 figure into improvement rates indicates that two-thirds of clients who undergo psychotherapy improve significantly, whereas about one-third of people who receive no treatment improve over time (Rosenthal, 1983).

IMPROVEMENT WITHOUT TREATMENT

Treatment outcome researchers widely accept the finding that about two-thirds of clients improve as a result of psychotherapy. Some skeptics have suggested, however, that far more than one-third of untreated emotional disorders have a *spontaneous remission*. That is, the problem may improve without any treatment at all. In fact, one of the earliest—and still among the most famous—

[†] The formula for computing the standard deviation is $S = \sqrt{\dfrac{\Sigma(X_i - M)^2}{N}}$

criticisms of psychotherapy concluded that treatment was totally ineffective for this very reason. Hans Eysenck (1952, 1992) agreed that evidence generally indicated that about two out of three people were helped by psychotherapy. Where he disagreed with other researchers was in his assertion that two-thirds of people with emotional problems improved *without* treatment. He thus concluded that psychotherapy offered little in the way of extra help (Eysenck, 1952, 1992).

Important controversies about defining a no-treatment group in psychotherapy outcome research contribute to debates about the rate of spontaneous remissions. Even if not all people with emotional problems pursue formal psychotherapy, most seek help by talking with family members, friends, or other helpers such as ministers. Such informal helping may be therapeutic, and some experts therefore argue that "untreated" cases do receive some form of "treatment." Based on this reasoning, the one-third figure could be said to overestimate the rate of spontaneous remission. On the other hand, improvement rates as high as one-half have been found to result simply from having unstructured conversations with a professional—which is not considered a form of psychotherapy (Lambert, Shapiro, & Bergin, 1986). Based on this evidence, the one-third figure might underestimate the true rate of spontaneous remission.

PREDICTORS OF TREATMENT OUTCOME

Together with most researchers, we agree that evidence indicates that about two-thirds of people improve as a result of psychotherapy. Based on available research, we also accept the estimate that one-third of cases improve without treatment. Thus, we agree with the conclusion that psychotherapy does, indeed, "work" (Lambert, Shapiro, & Bergin, 1986). This conclusion is a beginning, not an end, however. Different mental disorders have different rates of spontaneous remission, and different forms of treatment are more or less effective in treating different disorders. Psychotherapy can be and often is an effective treatment. The question is: What type of psychotherapy is most effective in treating which specific disorders? We do not attempt to answer this question in this chapter. Instead, we discuss research on various effective or promising treatments for specific disorders in later chapters on those disorders.

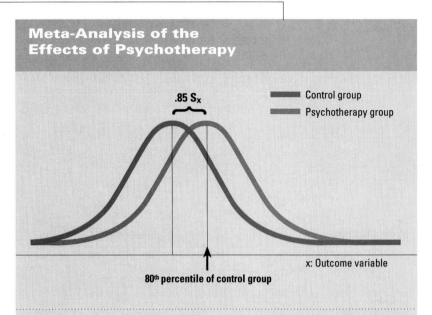

FIGURE 3-1: Average effect of psychotherapy based on a meta-analysis of 475 controlled studies.

Source: M.L. Smith, G.V. Glass, & T.I. Miller (1980). *The benefits of psychotherapy.* Baltimore: Johns Hopkins University Press.

Two other issues about the general effectiveness of psychotherapy should be noted. One concerns the length of treatment. Research indicates that if therapy is going to be effective, it will be effective rather quickly. As can be seen in Figure 3–2, most people who improve in psychotherapy do so in the first several months of treatment (Howard et al., 1986). This finding buttresses the growing trend toward providing relatively short-term psychotherapy. Another substantial influence on the effectiveness of psychotherapy is the background of the client. The acronym "YAVIS" was coined to indicate those people who are most likely to benefit from psychotherapy. Clients improve more in psychotherapy when they are *y*oung, *a*ttractive, *v*erbal, *i*ntelligent, and *s*uccessful. This finding has caused considerable concern, for it seems to indicate that psychotherapy works best for the most advantaged members of our society (Lorion & Felner, 1986).

OUTCOME RESEARCH ON DIFFERENT SCHOOLS OF PSYCHOTHERAPY

We can now address the question that we raised at the beginning of this section: Are psychodynamic, behavioral, or humanistic treatments more or less effective when compared with one another? Meta-analysis generally reveals few sizable differences among approaches (Smith,

Glass, & Miller, 1980), although behavior therapies may be somewhat more effective, especially in the treatment of anxiety (Shapiro & Shapiro, 1983). A recent major multisite comparison of medication and two forms of psychotherapy in the treatment of depression (see

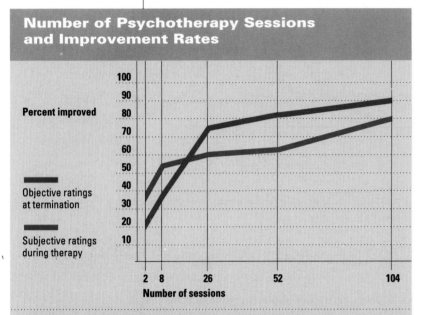

FIGURE 3-2: Relation between number of psychotherapy sessions and percentage of clients improved.

Source: K.I. Howard, S.M. Kopta, M.S. Krause, & D.E. Orlinsky (1986). The dose–effect relationship in psychotherapy. *American Psychologist, 41,* 159–164

Chapter 5) also highlighted the frequent finding that different treatments produce similar rates of improvement (Elkin et al., 1989). But these general findings mask important issues in comparing treatment approaches. Some of these issues can be illustrated by examining an exemplary investigation in which alternative forms of psychotherapy were compared.

Sloane and his colleagues (1975) conducted what remains a classic psychotherapy outcome study. These investigators compared the effectiveness of behavior therapy and psychodynamic psychotherapy in treating outpatients who were suffering from mild to moderate anxiety, depression, personality disorders, and similar problems. The investigators' procedures should be summarized briefly, because they point to some of the key methodological considerations in psychotherapy outcome research.

Clients with problems that were very mild (for example, job problems) or very severe (for example, suicide risk, serious substance abuse) were excluded from the study, and the remain-

ing 90 patients were assigned at random to receive either psychodynamic psychotherapy, behavior therapy, or no treatment. The different therapies were delivered by three psychodynamic and three behavior therapists, all of whom were highly experienced in their preferred form of treatment. Both treatments lasted for an average of 14 sessions. To ensure that the treatments were offered as planned, the differences between the two therapies were clearly defined (see Table 3–2), and tape recordings of the fifth therapy sessions were made and coded so that the actual treatments could be compared. Finally, an independent team of evaluators made detailed, objective assessments of the clients' functioning. Assessments were made before treatment, 4 months into therapy, and at 1 and 2 years after the original assessment. Assessments included ratings of symptom severity made by the evaluators; self-reports on objective measures including the MMPI, an objective measure of psychopathology (see Chapter 4); client and therapist ratings of therapeutic success and attainment of therapy goals; and ratings from a friend or relative who knew the client.

The study yielded many interesting results. All three groups, including the no-treatment group, improved over time, but the treated groups improved significantly more than the untreated groups. In general, behavior therapy and psychodynamic psychotherapy were equally effective. A few differences did favor behavior therapy. At 4 months, the assessors rated the behavior therapy clients as more improved in overall adjustment than the psychodynamic clients. At 1 year, the assessors found significantly more improvement in target symptoms for behavior therapy clients. On all the other measures listed above, however, there were no differences between the two treatment groups, indicating that the alternative treatments were similar in their effectiveness and superior to no treatment at all.

Another important set of findings concerned who was more likely to benefit from therapy. Psychodynamic psychotherapy was most effective with clients who had less severe problems. Behavior therapy was influenced less by client characteristics. In fact, there was a tendency for behavior therapy to be more effective with *more* severely disturbed clients.

These sets of findings are very important, but a third set of results seems most significant. Many expected differences between treatments were found in the tape recordings of the fifth session. Behavior therapists talked about as often as their clients talked, gave specific advice, and directed much of the course of therapy. In contrast, psychodynamic therapists talked only one-third as often as their clients, refused to answer specific questions, and followed their clients' lead during the session. Psychodynamic therapists also were more likely to focus on feelings, their underlying causes, and techniques such as free association, whereas behavior therapists focused on specific behaviors, ways of changing them, and techniques such as systematic desensitization.

Other differences between the two therapies were surprising. For example, behavior therapists and psychoanalysts offered the same number of interpretations, and according to both client report and objective ratings, the behavior therapists showed more empathy. Perhaps of most importance, the client's ratings of therapist warmth, empathy, and genuineness—the relationship factors Rogers emphasized—predicted successful outcome in *both* treatment groups. Clients also rated their personal relationship with their therapists as the single most important aspect of both behavior therapy and psychoanalytic psychotherapy (Sloane et al., 1975).

How can this be? Behavior therapy and psychodynamic psychotherapy clearly differ in theory. Even if the approaches are more similar in practice than in theory, substantial differences remain. Yet a number of studies have found that the two treatments produce similar results (Stiles, Shapiro, & Elliott, 1986). What do these very different treatments have in common? Perhaps the answer is more than is readily apparent. Part of the healing process might simply be engaging in psychotherapy of *any* form.

This suggestion may seem outlandish at first, but it is not an unfamiliar one. By way of analogy, consider children's sports. Baseball and soccer surely differ greatly, but they also share similarities at a higher level of abstraction. For children, participating in some sport—any sport—may be more important to physical and social development than whether they play basketball or football. Similarly, the fact of holding some belief in a higher power is an essential commonality across religions despite dramatic differences in dogma. Perhaps such similarities also are found among different approaches to

psychotherapy. This is an issue examined in psychotherapy process research.

		TABLE 3-2
Working Definitions of Psychotherapy and Behavior Therapy		
Technique	**Psychotherapy**	**Behavior Therapy**
Specific advice	Given infrequently	Given frequently
Transference interpretation	May be given	Avoided
Resistance interpretation	Used	Not used
Dreams	Interested and encouraged	Disinterested
Level of anxiety	Maintained when possible	Diminished when possible
Relaxation training	Only indirect	Directly undertaken
Desensitization	Only indirect	Directly undertaken
Assertion training	Indirectly encouraged	Directly encouraged
Report of symptoms	Discouraged	Encouraged
Childhood memories	Explored	Historical interest only

Source: Differences in technique in behavior therapy and psychotherapy as adapted from R.B. Sloane, F.R. Staples, A.H. Cristo, N.J. Yorkston, & K. Whipple (1975). *Psychotherapy versus behavior therapy* (pp. 237-240). Cambridge, MA: Harvard University Press.

Psychotherapy Process Research

Psychotherapy process researchers study qualities of the therapist–client relationship that predict successful outcome irrespective of the theoretical orientation of the therapist. This approach to research investigates whether different psychotherapies contain "common ingredients" that are responsible for therapeutic success (Goldfried, 1982). Much interest in the common ingredients in psychotherapy was prompted by Jerome Frank's (1961, 1973) incisive book on psychotherapy, *Persuasion and Healing*. Frank is an American trained both in psychology and psychiatry, who has spent most of his career at the Johns Hopkins Medical School. Frank's analysis begins with his very broad definition of psychotherapy as involving:

"(1)   a trained, socially sanctioned healer, whose healing powers are accepted by the sufferer and by his social group or an important segment of it

(2)   a sufferer who seeks relief from the healer

(3)   a circumscribed, more-or-less structured series of contacts between the

healer and the sufferer, through which the healer, often with the aid of a group, tries to produce certain changes in the sufferer's emotional state, attitudes, and behavior. All concerned believe these changes will help him. Although physical and chemical adjuncts may be used, the healing influence is primarily exercised by words, acts, and rituals in which sufferer, healer and—if there is one—group, participate jointly." (Frank, 1973, pp. 2–3)

Frank goes on to point out, "These three features are common not only to all forms of psychotherapy as the term is generally used, but also to methods of primitive healing" (p. 3).

It is easy to misunderstand Frank's argument. Is he saying that psychotherapy is little more than voodoo? No, Frank's point is just the opposite. He argues that psychotherapists should attempt to harness and use the powerful psychological tools used intuitively by both primitive and modern healers. He notes that rituals performed by healers in different cultures often provoke strong emotions that have been demonstrated to have powerful effects on physical health. He cites the "voodoo death" as one dramatic example. In some primitive cultures, actual deaths have been documented to result from elaborate death curses, even when no physical harm is inflicted (Frank, 1973).

Frank (1961, 1973) notes that like primitive healers, psychotherapists and other helping professionals are imbued with powers that stem from culturally sanctioned roles. The power comes from the mystery of the unconscious mind, incomprehensible medical treatments, or even from science itself. In the United States today, we strongly believe in the effectiveness of science, and we often treat science as if it were a mystical force. In short, even in modern societies part of the professional helper's healing power comes from the belief that doctors can heal.

THE PLACEBO EFFECT

One way in which the healing power of beliefs has been documented in medicine and in psychotherapy is through evidence on the **placebo effect.** In medicine, placebos are pills that are pharmacologically inert; that is, they have no medicinal value. More broadly, placebos are any type of treatment that contains no known "spe-

cific ingredients" for treating the condition being evaluated. The ultimate goal of treatment research is to identify therapies that do have specific ingredients that produce change above and beyond placebo effects. Thus, many investigations in medicine and psychotherapy include **placebo control groups**—that is, groups of patients who are given treatments that are intentionally designed to have no specific ingredients. If a treatment produces change beyond the placebo effect, then it contains one or more specific ingredients for treating a particular disorder.

The absence of specific ingredients does not prevent placebos from healing. Placebos have been found to have powerful influences on both physical and psychological ailments. In medicine, potent placebo effects have been demonstrated in dentistry, optometry, cancer treatment, and even surgery (Shapiro & Morris, 1978). Some psychiatric outpatients who are given placebo medications report greatly improved comfort that lasts over an extended period of time (Frank, 1973). The power of placebos also lies behind the common wisdom to "use new treatments quickly before they lose their power to heal." All helping professionals know that the latest treatment owes part of its effectiveness to its being the latest treatment (Shapiro & Morris, 1978).

Placebos apparently work because they create an *expectation* of change. They work because the patient expects them to work. Placebos also work because the healer expects them to work, thus making double-blind placebo control studies necessary. In a **double-blind study,** neither the physician nor the patient knows whether the prescribed pill is the real medication or a placebo. These double precautions are necessary because the expectations of both the patient and the physician repeatedly have been found to influence the success of all kinds of biomedical treatments (Rosenthal & Rosnow, 1969).

Some people view placebo effects as nuisances or even as hoaxes. This opinion is understandable, because a goal of research is to isolate the "active ingredients" in a treatment beyond placebo effects. But we can also view placebo effects as "treatments"—treatments that heal through psychological mechanisms. Psychological healing also is the goal of psychotherapy, of course. Thus, for the purposes of understanding and improving psychotherapy, placebo effects should be embraced and not dismissed (Critelli

▲ **Jerome Frank is trained in both psychology and psychiatry. Frank has analyzed psychotherapy as a process of persuasion and healing, drawing broad analogies between therapy and healing rituals in both industrialized and nonindustrialized cultures.**

& Neumann, 1984; Frank & Frank, 1991). Ironically, psychotherapy researchers need to identify the "active ingredients" in placebos.

In fact, health care providers attempt to maximize expectancies in many subtle ways. Consider your physician's office. An exclusive address, expensive furniture, and diplomas on the wall all help to heighten the expectancy that this is a powerful healer. (You might not be as hopeful if the office was in some beat-up basement, and there were no signs indicating the physician is a licensed professional.) Much more important to expectancies is the sense of confidence and competence that a helper instills. People seek professional help when they have been unable to solve their own problems, and assistance will not be accepted without some hope or reassurance (Frank & Frank, 1991). The helper also must be able to fulfill or reshape a client's expectations about particular forms of treatment. Someone who wants some direct advice is unlikely to return to see a therapist who offers nothing but reflection (Eisenthal, Emery, & Lazare, 1977).

Heightened expectancies surely are among the common ingredients found across different schools of psychotherapy, but there are more important common factors (Mahoney, 1991; see Table 3–3). Most of these involve aspects of the relationship formed between the therapist and the client. Different schools of therapy construe the therapist-client relationship in various ways, but they all recognize its importance. Some essential part of the therapeutic process is derived from forming a helping, human relationship (Strupp, 1986). We consider some essential components of this unique relationship in the two brief sections that follow.

PSYCHOTHERAPY AS SOCIAL SUPPORT

The importance of warmth in the therapist–client relationship has been emphasized by all major schools of psychotherapy. As noted earlier, Rogers and the client-centered therapists argued that warmth, empathy, and genuineness formed the center, and not the periphery, of the healing process. Freud (1912) also suggested that a client's positive feelings toward the psychoanalyst added to the success of the treatment, even though he clearly viewed this influence as secondary. Similarly, behavior therapists have emphasized warmth in the therapeutic relationship in practice even if it plays a minor role in theory. For example, consider Wolpe's (1958) comments about systematic desensitization: "All that the patient says is accepted without question or criticism. He is given the feeling that the therapist is unreservedly on his side. This happens not because the therapist is expressly trying to

TABLE 3-3
Common Characteristics of Effective Brief Psychotherapies

1. Treatment is offered soon after the problem is identified.
2. Assessment of the problem is rapid and occurs early in treatment.
3. A therapeutic alliance is established quickly, and it is used to encourage change in the client.
4. Therapy is designed to be time-limited, and the therapist uses this to encourage rapid progress.
5. The goals of therapy are limited to a few specified areas.
6. The therapist is directive in managing the treatment sessions.
7. Therapy is focused on a specific theme.
8. The client is encouraged to express strong emotions or troubling experiences.
9. A flexible approach is taken in the choice of treatment techniques.

Source: Adapted from M.P. Koss & J.M. Butcher (1986). Research on brief psychotherapy. In S.L. Garfield & A.E. Bergin (Eds.), *Handbook of psychotherapy and behavior change* (3rd ed.) (pp. 627-670). New York: Wiley.

appear sympathetic, but as a natural outcome of a completely nonmoralizing objective approach to the behavior of human organisms" (p. 106).

Research on psychotherapy process indicates that a therapist's supportiveness is related to positive outcomes across approaches to treatment (Parloff, Waskow, & Wolfe, 1978). Significantly, objective indicators of a therapist's support have been found to be less potent predictors of successful outcome than are a client's rating of the therapist. A supportive relationship is not defined simply by a therapist's behavior, but by a therapist's behavior in relation to a particular client. Some, perhaps most, people feel that they are understood by a therapist who makes empathic statements, but others may be more comfortable with a therapist who is somewhat detached (Beutler, Crago, & Arizmendi, 1986). Thus, different therapeutic stances may be perceived as supportive by clients who are more or less comfortable with particular types of relationships.

A supportive therapeutic relationship is important, but is therapy more than this? Rogers (1957) argued that warmth, empathy, and genuineness were *necessary and sufficient* conditions for therapeutic success. He clearly stated that a therapist must be warm, empathetic, and genuine in order to be successful, and further, that this supportiveness was all that was needed for therapy to be effective. However, research indicates that therapist supportiveness is neither necessary nor sufficient for therapeutic success, despite the fact that supportiveness predicts a more successful outcome (Beutler, Crago, & Arizmendi, 1986). Many other factors influence treatment effectiveness.

PSYCHOTHERAPY AS SOCIAL INFLUENCE

Psychotherapy can be viewed as a process of social influence as well as of social support. The three major schools of therapy clearly differ in terms of the degree to which therapists directly attempt to influence clients. Beyond the explic-

▲ **Warmth is a vital aspect of relationships with family and friends. Social support also is instrumental to therapeutic relationship.**

it theoretical stance, however, the therapeutic relationship influences clients in ways that are both obvious and subtle, intentional and unintentional.

One social influence is the nonjudgmental attitude found across all major approaches to psychotherapy. People often fear that their secret fears and failures will be met with criticism or ridicule, and the therapist's acceptance can come as a welcome relief. Whether construed as catharsis, extinction, or a corrective emotional experience, a common change process found in all psychotherapies is the provision of a safe forum for secret revelations (Pennebaker, 1990; Strong, 1978).

All therapists also influence their clients by pointing out discrepancies to them. That is, they offer interpretations. For example, a therapist may note inconsistencies between a client's professed beliefs and her or his actions: "You talk about being sad, but you sound angry." Such an interpretation can create *dissonance* or conflict in the client's self-system of beliefs. People resolve dissonance by altering their beliefs to be consistent, thus restoring equilibrium or homeostasis in the belief system. Inducing discrepancies is an important technique for changing beliefs, provided that the therapist is a credible source for offering interpretations (Strong, 1978). If a therapist is not credible, a client can resolve dissonance, not by challenging personal beliefs, but by discounting what the therapist has to say.

The social influence of psychotherapy clearly is demonstrated by evidence that, over time, clients adopt beliefs similar to those of their therapists. In fact, treatment is more effective when clients' beliefs become more similar to those of their therapists. This suggests that an initial discrepancy between the beliefs of the client and those of the therapist can help the process, provided that the discrepancy is not so large as to interfere in the relationship (Beutler, Crago, & Arizmendi, 1986; Kelly, 1990).

The idea that clients' beliefs become more similar to those of their therapists raises questions about values in psychotherapy. Psychotherapy is not value-free. There are values inherent in the nature of therapy itself—for example, the belief that expressing emotions is good. Moreover, the values of individual therapists about such topics as love, marriage, work, and religion necessarily exert an influence on clients. In general, clients improve more in treatment when they adopt therapists' beliefs about psychotherapy. Changes in broader social and religious values are both less common in therapy and less clearly related to a positive outcome (Beutler, Machado, & Neufeldt, 1994). Nevertheless, because it is impossible to transcend one's own values, psychotherapists must recognize their own biases and be direct about their values with their clients. This is another reason why we must understand therapy as a social influence process. Awareness of the social influences not only is a way of increasing the effectiveness of treatment, but also is a means of recognizing when values enter into therapy.

Changing Social Systems: Couples, Family, and Group Therapy

The systems approach indicates that biomedical treatments and psychotherapy are not the only interventions that hold the potential to improve psychological disorders. Treatments designed to change social systems, the third component of the biopsychosocial model, also may change the individual. Social interventions include treatments for couples and entire families, group therapy, and even broader efforts at preventing emotional disorders through improving society. These treatments offer a diverse array of approaches, and the goals of intervention can vary widely. For these reasons, our present overview of social approaches to treatment must be selective.

There is one perspective that these diverse approaches have in common. They all emphasize the reciprocal relation between individual functioning and the social context. To appreciate this perspective, recall the case of Frances. Treating her depression with medication or individual psychotherapy—treatments designed to help her function effectively as an individual—might improve her relationships with family members. Conversely, couples or family therapy, which are intended to improve her relationships with other people, might also alleviate the physical and psychological symptoms of her depression. Some theorists might argue, moreover, that Frances would be in less of a predicament if women were encouraged to assume more independent roles in society.

Ultimately, the goal of all interventions is to develop treatments based on the specific etiology of particular disorders. In the absence of knowledge of etiology, however, it is important to recognize that interventions directed toward social change can be beneficial even if a particular problem has a biological or psychological cause. Thus, our survey of interventions in social systems encompasses approaches aimed both at eliminating the social causes of abnormal behavior and at helping people to cope effectively with psychopathology that is clearly caused by biological or psychological abnormalities.

Couples Therapy

Couples therapy involves seeing partners together in psychotherapy who are involved in an inti-

mate relationship. This approach is sometimes called marital therapy or marriage counseling, but the reference to couples captures the range of partners who may seek treatment together. Dating pairs, prospective mates, live-in partners, and gay couples also may seek couples therapy.

The goal of couples therapy typically is to improve the relationship, and not to treat the individual. As we shall see shortly, however, couples treatment increasingly has been used to help both partners function more adequately when one member suffers from individual psychopathology. In treating relationships, all couples therapists focus on resolving conflicts and promoting mutual satisfaction. Couples therapists do not tell couples what compromises they should accept or how they should change their relationship. Instead, they typically help partners to improve their *communication* and *negotiation skills* (Baruth & Huber, 1984; Fincham & Bradbury, 1990; Margolin, 1987).

The goal of improving communication is best illustrated with an example. A couples therapist might suggest to Frances that she had a problem with "mind reading" in her marriage. Frances may have been hoping (or expecting) that her husband would somehow know her wishes without her telling him. She might have wanted more attention, for example, but perhaps she never told her husband that lack of attention was a problem for her. She may have wanted him to "figure it out for himself." Couples therapists point out that it is impossible to read another person's mind, and they encourage partners in close relationships to communicate such wishes directly (Gottman et al., 1976). This may sound like a simple task, but learning to be direct can be tricky for many people. Frances may have felt selfish when making requests, for example, or perhaps she wanted to be "surprised" with her husband's attention. That is, at first she might find that his attention seemed less meaningful because she had asked for it.

Negotiation or *conflict resolution* is another component of most approaches to couples therapy (Heitler, 1992). Negotiation is the imprecise art of give and take. Most approaches to negotiation emphasize the importance of clearly defining problems, considering a wide range of solutions, uncovering "hidden agendas" (unstated issues), and experimenting with alternative solutions. These strategies are similar to the social problem-solving model discussed earlier, and this approach has been effectively applied to work with couples (Emery, 1994). Polite communication also is an essential component of negotiation. Setting ground rules such as not raising your voice, speaking about your own feelings, and not interrupting the other person can be essential to effective negotiation (Gottman et al., 1976).

Research has documented that couples therapy can improve satisfaction in marriages (Baucom & Epstein, 1990; Holtzworth-Munroe & Jacobson, 1991). However, questions remain about the long-term effectiveness of couples therapy, the relative efficacy of alternative approaches to couples therapy, and the role of couples therapy in the broader societal context (Alexander, Holtzworth-Munroe, & Jameson, 1994). Couples therapy also has been used in the treatment of specific disorders including depression, anxiety, substance abuse, and child behavior problems. This typically is done either as a supplement or an alternative to individual therapy. When couples therapy is used in conjunction with individual treatment, the combined approach often has been found to have a more positive outcome in comparison to individual therapy alone (Barlow, O'Brien, & Last, 1984; Beach, Sandeen, & O'Leary, 1990; Dadds, Schwartz, & Sanders, 1987; Jacobson, Holtzworth-Monroe, & Schmaling, 1989). Research on treatment effectiveness is discussed in more detail in the relevant chapters on specific disorders.

▼ Family therapy includes at least two and perhaps many or all family members in treatment. Changing relationships is viewed as a way of improving individual mental health.

Family Therapy

Family therapy might include two, three, or more family members in the psychotherapy sessions. Family therapy shares many features in common with couples therapy, as improving communication and negotiation also are common goals. The inclusion of children in family therapy can add complexity to this treatment approach, however, as does the obvious fact that relationships and treatments get more complicated when more people are involved.

Like couples therapy, family therapy has the general goal of improving satisfaction with relationships. Some forms of family therapy also are designed to resolve specific conflicts, such as disputes between adolescents and their parents (Robin, Koepke, & Nayar, 1986). *Parent management training* is an approach that teaches parents new skills for rearing troubled children (Patterson, 1982; McMahon & Forehand, 1981). Finally, some important new approaches are designed to educate families about how best to cope with the serious psychopathology of one family member (Falloon, 1985).

As with individual and couples therapy, there are many different theoretical approaches to family therapy (Gurman & Kniskern, 1991). Many approaches to family therapy differ from other treatments, however, in their long-standing emphasis on the application of systems theory. In applying systems theory, family therapists emphasize interdependence between family members and the paramount importance of the family social system. For example, family systems therapists often call attention to the pattern of *alliances* or strategic loyalties among family members (P. Minuchin, 1985). In well-functioning families, the primary alliance is between the two parents, even when the parents do not live together. In contrast, dysfunctional families often have alliances that cross generations—that is, "teams" that include one parent and some or all of the children opposing the other parent. Like a poorly organized business, families function inadequately when their leaders fail to cooperate. Thus, a common goal in systems approaches to family therapy is to strengthen the alliance between the parents, to get parents to work together and not against each other (S. Minuchin, 1974).

Early family therapists overemphasized the role of the family in causing individual psychopathology, particularly severe psychological disorders. Many contemporary approaches to family therapy have a much broader view of etiology. Irrespective of etiology, however, troubled relationships often intensify individual psychopathology, and individual psychopathology commonly strains relationships. Thus, individual therapy can benefit the family, and family therapy can help the individual. Current evidence indicates that family therapy might serve as an alternative or adjunct to individual treatment (Alexander, Holtzworth-Munroe, & Jameson, 1994). Further research will determine whether this promise is fulfilled.

Group Therapy

Like couples therapy and family therapy, **group therapy** involves the treatment of more than one person at one time. Therapy groups may be as small as 3 or 4 people or as large as 20 or more. Group therapy has numerous variations in terms of paradigmatic approaches and targets for treatment (Yalom, 1985). These variations are far too numerous to discuss here, so we highlight only a few facets of the group approach.

Psychoeducational groups are designed to teach group members specific information or skills relevant to psychological well-being. The term *psychoeducational* aptly conveys the goals of this type of group, since teaching is the primary mode of treatment, but the content of the course focuses on psychological issues. For example, assertiveness might be taught in a group format. Other psychoeducational groups focus on teaching systematic desensitization or cognitive therapy. In still other circumstances, a common disorder, not a common treatment, is the reason for group membership. In fact, psychoeducational groups have been developed for virtually every disorder discussed in this textbook.

There are at least two basic reasons for offering therapy in a psychoeducational group instead of in individual psychotherapy. Lower expense is one obvious justification. A second rationale is the support, encouragement, and practice that group members can offer to one another. Many people who have psychological problems feel isolated, alone, and sometimes "weird." Thus, the simple act of coming to a group can be part of the therapeutic process (Bloch & Crouch, 1987). Learning that you are not alone with your problems can be a powerful experience that is one of the unique "active ingredients" in group therapy.

In contrast to psychoeducational groups, in *experiential group therapy* the relationships between group members form the primary, not a secondary, component of treatment. The experience of interacting with others in a unique setting is the rationale for experiential groups. Group members might be encouraged to look beyond each other's "facades," to reveal secrets about themselves, or otherwise to break down the barriers that we all erect in relationships (Bloch & Crouch, 1987; Yalom, 1985). Group members, in turn, can offer each other feedback and support. In an "encounter group," for example, group members may question the genuineness of some self-disclosures but support more honest appraisals of oneself. Experiential group leaders typically adhere to a humanistic approach to therapy, and the members often are well-functioning people who view the group as an opportunity for personal growth. Little research has been conducted on the effectiveness of this type of group.

▲ **Group therapy gives clients the opportunity to meet with and learn from other people who have similar problems.**

The *self-help group* is a third type of group therapy that has grown tremendously in popularity. Self-help groups bring together people who share a common problem. Self-help group members share information and experiences in an attempt to help themselves and one another. There are thousands of topics that bring people together, and you are no doubt familiar with at least a few self-help groups.

Technically, self-help groups are not therapy groups. They typically are not led by a professional. If there is a leader, it may be someone who already has faced the particular problem, perhaps a former group member. The popularity of self-help groups attests to their perceived benefits. Moreover, available evidence suggests that self-help groups and other treatments can be quite effective even when they are delivered by *paraprofessionals*—people who do not have professional training but who have personal experience with the problem (Christensen & Jacobson, 1994). However, the dearth of research on process and outcome is a notable shortcoming for self-help groups and for group therapy in general (Kaul & Bednar, 1986).

Community Psychology and Prevention

Social influences on psychopathology extend far beyond interpersonal relationships. Social institutions such as child care centers, schools, and work environments are important contributors to mental health, as are such broad societal concerns as poverty, racism, and sexism. The goal of improving society is hardly the exclusive domain of psychologists, of course. Still, **community psychology** is one approach within clinical psychology that attempts to improve individual well-being by promoting social change.

The concept of prevention is an important consideration in promoting social change. Community psychologists often distinguish among three levels of prevention (Kaplan, 1964). **Primary prevention** tries to improve the environment in order to prevent new cases of a mental disorder from developing. The goal of primary prevention is to promote health, not just treat illness. Efforts at primary prevention range from offering prenatal care to impoverished pregnant women to teaching schoolchildren about the dangers of drug abuse.

Secondary prevention focuses on the early detection of emotional problems in the hope of preventing them from becoming more serious and difficult to treat. The screening of "at-risk" schoolchildren is one example of an effort at secondary prevention. The development of crisis centers and hot lines are additional examples of efforts to detect and treat problems before they become more serious. Finally, **tertiary prevention** may involve any of the treatments discussed in this chapter, because the intervention occurs after the illness has been identified. In addition to providing treatment, however, tertiary prevention also attempts to address some of the adverse, indirect consequences of mental illness. Helping the chronically mentally ill to find adequate housing and employment is an example of a tertiary prevention effort.

No one can doubt the importance of prevention, whether prevention efforts are directed toward biological, psychological, or social causes of abnormal behavior. Unfortunately, many prevention efforts face an insurmountable obstacle: We simply do not know the specific cause of most psychological disorders. Prevention efforts directed at broader social change face another obstacle that also seems insurmountable at times. Poverty, racism, and sexism defy easy remedies. We do not wish to blame the victim of social injustice, but blaming the system can be equally problematic. Each individual must take personal responsibility for changing his or her own life, even as we collectively work to shape a world that promotes mental health.

Developing Specific Treatments for Specific Disorders

The field of psychotherapy began with the development of treatments based solely in theory and case histories. It progressed as researchers documented the superiority of some form of psychotherapy over no treatment at all. Contemporary psychotherapy researchers are advancing knowledge by recognizing and studying factors common to all therapies and by using these common ingredients to predict successful outcome across different approaches to therapy.

These efforts are important, and scientists can point with increasing pride to research on psychotherapy, which has grown both in volume and in quality. The ultimate goal of treatment research, however, is to discover more than the common ingredients across paradigmatic approaches to psychotherapy. Researchers must continue to work to identify different treatments that have specific ingredients for specific disor-

ders, as discussed in the Research Close-up study. Consistent with this goal, we examine various treatments that either are promising or have proved to be effective for alleviating the problems discussed in subsequent chapters of this text.

The treatment of psychological disorders has moved beyond the point where the therapist's theoretical orientation, rather than the client's individual problems, should determine the choice of treatment. For some emotional problems, sufficient scientific evidence exists to identify the treatment of choice or at least to rule out some forms of therapy. In these cases, we feel very strongly that mental health professionals should at the very least inform their clients about research evidence and treatment alternatives.

For other emotional problems, researchers have not yet identified a clear treatment of choice. This does not mean that "anything goes" in treat-

Identifying Common Factors and Isolating Specific Treatments

A recent study by Thomas Borkovec and Ellen Costello (1993) illustrates how psychotherapy outcome research can account for some common factors across treatments while also isolating specific effects. These psychologists at Pennsylvania State University wanted to identify the effectiveness of different approaches to behavior therapy in treating generalized anxiety disorder, an emotional problem characterized by excessive anxiety that is experienced in a variety of circumstances (see Chapter 6).

Borkovec and Costello compared two types of behavior therapy. *Applied relaxation* (AR) involved training the clients in the use of relaxation techniques to cope with thoughts, feelings, or situations that provoked anxiety. Most of the 12-session treatment involved discussions of how to anticipate and deal with stressful events, including practice at using relaxation techniques. *Cognitive behavior therapy* (CBT) began with the same types of discussions and relaxation training as AR did. Most of the sessions, however, involved elements of Beck's cognitive therapy as well as other cognitive techniques designed to alter anxiety-producing thoughts. Finally, a third group of clients received *nondirective therapy* (ND) in order to test and control for the contributions of common factors to treatment outcome. The 12 sessions of nondirective therapy consisted of offering support and empathy in response to issues the clients chose to explore in therapy.

Borkovec and Costello randomly assigned 55 clients carefully diagnosed as suffering from generalized anxiety disorder to one of the three treatments. All treatments were offered by the same therapists, thus ensuring that differences in outcome would not be due to differences in therapists. This raised a new problem, however. The therapists generally held a cognitive behavioral orientation, and their low expectations about ND might have affected the success of the treatment. To help control for this possibility, an expert nondirective therapist helped to supervise the ND cases. Finally, audio-

tapes of a portion of the sessions were coded to ensure that what was supposed to happen during the therapy sessions actually occurred.

A number of measures of the clients' anxiety were administered prior to treatment, immediately after treatment, and 6 months and 1 year after treatment. No differences were found among groups prior to treatment, but statistically significant differences were found immediately after treatment. The AR and CBT groups both were functioning significantly better than the ND clients at this time, but they were not significantly different from each other. Both the AR and CBT groups also improved significantly from the beginning to the end of treatment. The anxiety of the ND group did not change during this time. Analysis of audiotapes indicated that the ND group experienced deeper discussions about their emotions during psychotherapy, but this apparently had little positive effect on reducing their anxiety.

At the follow-up assessments, the AR, CBT, and ND groups no longer were significantly different from one another. This likely was due to further treatment received by members of the ND group. Approximately 60 percent of the ND clients received further psychotherapy, in comparison to about 15 percent of clients in the other two groups. (The need for increased therapy for the ND group was an important outcome in its own right.) Finally, evidence indicated that differences among groups were clinically significant—and they favored CBT. A year after treatment, 58 percent of the CBT group was functioning within a normal range, in comparison with 37 percent of the AR clients and 28 percent of ND participants.

These findings indicate that specific treatment effects can be obtained beyond the influence of common factors. In the treatment of generalized anxiety disorders, cognitive behavior therapy has specific benefits both in the short term and in the long run, and these benefits exceed the general improvement associated with seeking psychotherapy. Identifying such specific treatments for specific disorders is the major goal of future psychotherapy outcome research, as is further specification of the "active ingredients" in cognitive behavior therapy.

One additional finding from this study demonstrated the importance of common factors despite the specific benefits of cognitive behavior therapy. The best predictor of a successful outcome across all three groups was the clients' expectations for success, which were measured after the first therapy appointment. It is not clear what aspects of treatment raised or lowered expectations in this study. Nevertheless, this finding demonstrates once again that nonspecific factors like increasing expectancies are an important part of the process of psychotherapy. ■

ing these problems. Rather, this circumstance requires the development of carefully constructed therapies that follow some clear rationale as to why they may prove to be effective treatments for the particular disorder. In considering promising alternative treatments, we examine a range of approaches to psychopharmacology, psychotherapy, and couples, family, and group therapies in later chapters. Our coverage of alternative treatments is selective, however, as it is based on current knowledge about the particular disorder.

The identification of specific, effective treatments for specific disorders is necessary if clinical psychology is to fulfill its scientific promise.

Still, the importance of establishing a human, helping relationship must not be overlooked. Many people seek a therapist for help in coping with a difficult life transition. They do not seek or expect a standardized "cure" for their problems. More generally, we must remember that individual people, not diagnostic categories, seek treatment for psychological disorders. The challenge for mental health professionals is to approach treatment both as scientists and as practitioners. Awareness of diagnostic categories is essential for applying scientific knowledge, but sensitivity to the individual is also essential to maximizing the effectiveness of clinical practice.

Summary

A tremendous number of different treatments have been developed for psychological disorders, but the various forms of **psychotherapy** can be roughly classified into four broad groups. Biological approaches alter the functioning of the body, primarily by using medication to alter physiology. **Psychodynamic psychotherapies** encourage the exploration of the past in order to obtain insight into unconscious motivations. **Cognitive behavior therapy** focuses on present experience in helping their clients overcome maladaptive behaviors and learn adaptive ones. **Humanistic psychotherapists** offer their clients warmth, empathy, and unconditional positive regard in helping them to heighten emotional awareness and make life choices.

KEY TERMS

- attachment
- attribution
- aversion therapy
- behaviorism
- behavior therapy
- catharsis
- client-centered therapy
- cognitive behavior therapy
- cognitive therapy
- community psychology
- contingency management
- couples therapy
- dependent variable
- double-blind study
- eclectic
- ego analysis

Psychotherapy "works" in that research indicates that approximately two-thirds of outpatient clients benefit from treatment, whereas about one-third of the same population improves without treatment. However, psychotherapy outcome researchers have documented only small differences in the effectiveness of the alternative paradigmatic approaches to treatment. **Behavior therapy** is somewhat more effective in treating some disorders, but there is a clear need to establish the effectiveness of different treatments for different disorders. The rates of "spontaneous remission" of different psychological problems also need to be clearly identified.

A renewed interest in psychotherapy process research is one consequence of evidence that different approaches to psychotherapy produce similar outcomes (Goldfried & Castonguay, 1993). Dimensions of the therapist–client relationship that are related to improved outcome include increasing the client's expectations of help, forming a warm therapist–client relationship, encouraging the experience of emotions in therapy, offering new learning experiences, and persuading clients to accept new, more adaptive explanations for their problems.

Another area of innovation in psychotherapy is the development of effective treatments that extend into the social system. These interventions include **couples therapy**, **family therapy**, and **group therapy**. They also include efforts to change dysfunctional aspects of the broader society. Thus, consistent with the systems approach, intervention for psychological problems may be directed toward biological, psychological, or social systems.

The future of psychotherapy outcome research involves developing therapies that have effectiveness beyond the "common ingredients" found across different approaches to psychotherapy. The task is to identify specific therapies for specific disorders. In subsequent chapters of this text, we review progress toward this goal, as we highlight only those treatments that have demonstrated success or promise in alleviating the symptoms of a particular disorder.

Critical Thinking

1. The chapter opened with some conflicting images of treatments for psychological disorders. What are some of your personal thoughts about the treatment of psychological disorders? Were your previous beliefs changed by this chapter? Why or why not? What evidence would convince you that treatments for psychological disorders do (or do not) "work"?

2. Do you prefer one of the major theoretical orientations discussed in this chapter? If you were looking for a therapist for yourself, would you pick one based on her or his theoretical orientation? We argue that mental health professionals should offer treatments based on proven effectiveness rather than on the therapist's theoretical orientations. Do you agree?

3. What are your reactions to meta-analysis? Do you find the technique of collapsing results across many studies to be convincing? Are you more convinced by the findings of a few very carefully conducted reports?

4. Think about the "common factors" across treatments in deciding how psychotherapy is similar to and different from friendship.

5. What is the appropriate level for intervention with psychological disorders? Do you favor medication, psychotherapy, family treatment, or social change? In what ways do your views about the nature and causes of abnormal behavior influence your thoughts about treatment?

- electroconvulsive therapy (ECT)
- empathy
- experiment
- external validity
- family therapy
- flooding
- free association
- Gestalt therapy
- group therapy
- humanistic psychotherapy
- hypothesis
- independent variable
- informed consent
- insight
- internal validity
- in vivo desensitization
- interpretation
- placebo control group
- placebo effect
- primary prevention
- psychoactive drugs
- psychoanalysis
- psychodynamic
- psychopharmacology
- psychosurgery
- psychotherapy
- random assignment
- rational-emotive therapy
- role playing
- secondary prevention
- self-instruction training
- social skills training
- systematic desensitization
- symptom alleviation
- tertiary prevention
- token economy
- transference

Classification and Assessment

Psychologists have to collect a considerable amount of information before they can make decisions about the nature of a person's problems or formulate plans for treatment. They need to know about various psychological and biological aspects of the person as well as the social context in which the problem has appeared. The general process of information gathering is called **assessment**. Psychologists use many different assessment tools to generate information systematically. Interviews, observations, and tests are among the most frequently used procedures. These procedures are often supplemented by information from additional sources, including formal records from schools and clinics as well as informal reports from other people who are well acquainted with the person. After psychologists have collected information, they must organize and integrate it before it can be useful. Therefore, the assessment process also involves judgments and decisions.

Overview

One important part of the assessment process involves making a diagnostic decision based on the official classification system—the set of categories in DSM-IV that describe mental disorders. **Diagnosis** is the process of deciding that a person fits into a particular category, such as schizophrenia or major depressive disorder. In the field of psychopathology, assigning a diagnosis does not mean that we understand the etiology of the person's problem. It does mean that the person's behavior meets the specific criteria for a particular type of disorder. This decision enables the clinician to use the general base of knowledge for the disorder in question, including associated features, probable course, and treatments that are likely to be effective. Formulation of a treatment plan depends on the diagnosis plus many other types of information that we will discuss in this chapter.

Our consideration of the assessment enterprise and diagnostic issues will begin with an example from our own clinical experience. In the following pages, we will describe one person's problems and the social context in which they appeared. This case illustrates the kinds of decisions that psychologists have to make about ways to collect and interpret information.

CASE STUDY

Obsessions, Compulsions, and Other Unusual Behaviors

Michael was an only child who lived with his mother and father. He was 16 years old, a little younger than most of the other boys in the 11th grade, and he looked even younger. From an academic point of view, Michael was an average student, but he was not a typical teenager in terms of social behavior. He felt completely alienated from other boys, and he was extremely anxious when he talked to girls. He hated being at school; he despised everything about school. His life at home was not much more pleasant than his experience at school. Michael and his parents argued frequently. His relationship with his father was especially volatile. In fact, things had become so tense that the whole family had been in therapy for several months.

One awful incident seemed to sum up Michael's bitter feelings about school. As a sophomore, he decided to join the track team. Michael was awkward and somewhat clumsy, hardly an athlete; when he worked out with the other long-distance runners at practice, he soon became the brunt of their jokes. One day, a belligerent teammate forced Michael to take off his clothes and run naked from the bushes to a shelter in the park. When he got there, Michael found an old pair of shorts, which he put on and wore back to the locker room. The experience was humiliating. Later that night, Michael started to worry about those shorts. Who had left them in the park? Were they dirty? Had he been exposed to some horrible disease? Michael quit the track team the next day, but he couldn't put the experience out of his mind. Every time he saw the other boys in school, he became enraged. He said to himself, over and over again, "That team has ruined my life!"

Although he knew it was irrational, Michael began to fear that he would catch AIDS from those shorts. He couldn't get the thought out of his mind. He read everything he could find regarding early symptoms of the disease. These fears progressed to the point where every time he coughed, he thought he was getting a respiratory infection. If he lost his balance, he thought he had a neurological complication. The list of "symptoms" went on and on.

In the following year, Michael became more and more consumed by anxiety. He was constantly obsessed about "contamination," which he imagined to be spreading from his books and school clothes to the furniture and other objects in his house. When the clothes that he had worn to school rubbed against a chair or a wall at home, he felt as though that spot had become contaminated. He didn't believe this was literally true; it was more like a reminder by association. When he touched something that he had used at school, he was more likely to think of school. That triggered unpleasant thoughts and the negative emotions with which they were associated (anger, fear, depression).

Michael tried in various ways to minimize the spread of contamination. For example, he took a shower and changed his clothes every evening at 6 o'clock immediately after he finished his homework. After this "cleansing ritual" he was careful to avoid touching his books or dirty clothes as well as anything that they had touched. If he bumped into one of these contaminated objects by accident, he would go to the bathroom and wash his hands. Michael washed his hands 10 or 15 times in a typical evening. He also paced back and forth watching television without sitting down so that he would not touch contaminated furniture.

Whenever he was not in school, Michael preferred to be alone at home. Being with other people made him very uncomfortable. If he spent more than a few minutes with other people, he felt drained, and he had to recuperate by withdrawing to his room to play games on his computer. He did not enjoy sports, music, or outdoor activities. The only literature that interested him was fantasy and science fiction. Dungeons and Dragons was the only game that held his attention. It had, in fact, become an important escape for Michael. He read extensively about the magical powers of fantastic characters and spent hours dreaming up new variations on themes described in books about this imaginary realm. When Michael talked about the Dungeons and Dragons characters and their adventures, his speech would sometimes become vague and difficult to follow. He would begin to speak more rapidly and his thoughts would jump from one topic to the next in an excited and confused manner. Although other students at Michael's school shared his interest in Dungeons and Dragons, he didn't want to play the game with them. Michael said he was different from the other students. He was suspicious of their motives and afraid that they would reject him. He expressed disdain and contempt for other teenagers, as well as for the city in which he lived and for his own neighborhood.

Michael and his parents had been working with a family therapist for more than 2 years. Although the level of interpersonal conflict in the family had been reduced, Michael's anxiety seemed to be getting worse. He had become even more isolated from other boys his own age, and was actually quite suspicious about their motives. He said that he sometimes felt that they were talking about him, and that they were planning to do something else to him in order to humiliate him again.

His worries about contamination had become almost unbearable to his parents, who were deeply confused and frustrated by his behavior. They could obviously see that he had become socially isolated and extremely unhappy. They believed that he would never be able to resume a more normal pattern of development until he gave up these "silly" ideas. Michael's fears also disrupted his parents' own activities in several ways. They weren't allowed

to touch him or his things after being in certain rooms of the house. His peculiar movements and persistent washing were troublesome to them. Michael's father usually worked at home, and he and Michael frequently ended up quarreling with each other especially when Michael ran water in the bathroom next to his father's study. The conflict became so severe that Michael's father once asked his wife to make a choice: "Is it me or Michael? One of us has to go!"

Michael and his mother had always been very close. In fact, he was quite dependent on her, and she was devoted to him. They spent a lot of time together while his father was working. Although they still supported each other, his mother had begun to find it difficult to be close to Michael. He shunned physical contact. When she touched him, he sometimes cringed and withdrew. Once in a while he would shriek, reminding her that she was contaminated by her contact with chairs and other objects like his laundry. Recently, Michael had also become aloof intellectually. His mother felt that he was shutting her out as he seemed to withdraw further into his world of Dungeons and Dragons fantasy and obsessional thoughts about contamination.

Michael's parents eventually decided to seek individual treatment for him. They talked with their family therapist and asked her whether anything could be done to help Michael deal with his fear of contamination. Could he stop his repeated washing? Would he be able to develop normal friendships? ■

Issues and Choices

Michael's situation raises several fundamental issues with regard to assessment and classification. The first is the *level* of analysis at which a psychologist should think about the problem. Is this primarily Michael's problem, or should we consider this problem in terms of all members of the family? One possibility is that Michael has a psychological disorder that is disrupting the life of his family. It may be the other way around, however: Perhaps the family system as a whole is dysfunctional, and Michael's problems are only one symptom of this dysfunction.

Another set of choices involves the type of data that a psychologist will employ to describe

Michael's behavior. What kinds of information should be collected? We can consider several sources of data. One is Michael's own report. Another is the report of his parents. A psychologist may also decide to employ psychological tests. Although biological tests have not achieved definitive status in psychopathology, there are some intriguing suggestions that biochemical assays and images of the brain may shed important light on the distinctions among different forms of abnormal behavior.

In conducting an assessment and arriving at a diagnosis, one question we must face is whether Michael's abnormal behavior is similar to problems that have been exhibited by other people. Given the information that the psychologist has obtained, the two most likely diagnostic alternatives are obsessive–compulsive disorder and schizotypal personality disorder (see Chapters 6 and 9). These conditions can be difficult to tell apart. Because they respond to different forms of treatment, the distinctions are extremely impor-

tant. The process of making an individual diagnosis for Michael is guided by the general system of classification. These are issues that involve classification. In the next section we will review the development and modification of classification systems for abnormal behavior.

Basic Issues in Classification

A **classification system** is used to subdivide or organize a set of objects. The objects of classification can be inanimate things such as rocks or books, living organisms such as plants, insects, or primates, or abstract concepts such as numbers, religions, or historical periods. Formal classification systems are essential for the collection and communication of knowledge in all sciences and professions. For example, biologists depend on the classification system for living organisms that was introduced in 1758 by Carolus Linnaeus, who is typically considered the "father of taxonomy" (the theory of classification procedures and systems).

There are, of course, many ways to subdivide any given class of objects. Classification systems can be based on different principles. Some systems are based on descriptive similarities. For example, both a diamond and a ruby may be considered jewels because they are valuable stones. Other systems are based upon less obvious characteristics such as structural similarities. A diamond and a piece of coal, for example, may belong together because they are both made of carbon. They don't look or feel similar to each other, but they are created in similar ways. Other examples can be taken from the classification of living organisms. From a descriptive point of view, dolphins may appear to be more similar to sharks than to zebras. But dolphins and zebras breathe oxygen through their lungs, they are warm-blooded, and they share many other functional and structural similarities that serve to distinguish them (and other mammals) from fish.

The point is simple. Classification systems can be based on various principles, and their value will depend primarily on the purpose for which they were developed. Different classification systems are not necessarily right or wrong; they are simply more or less useful. In the fol-

lowing section, we will consider several fundamental principles that affect all attempts to develop a useful classification or typology of human behavior.

Categories versus Dimensions

Classification is often based on "yes or no" decisions (Hempel, 1961). After a category has been defined, any object is either a member of the category or it is not. A **categorical system** typically assumes that distinctions between members of different categories are qualitative in nature. In the classification of living organisms, for example, we usually consider species to be qualitatively distinct. Human beings are different from other primates; an organism is either human, or it is not. Many medical conditions are categorical in nature. Pregnancy is one clear example. A woman is either pregnant, or she is not. It doesn't make sense to talk about "how pregnant" a person might be.

Although categorically based classification systems have often been useful, they are not the only kind of system that can be used to organize information systematically. As an alternative to the use of categories, scientists often choose to employ a **dimensional system**—that is, to describe the objects of classification in terms of continuous dimensions. Rather than assuming that an object either has, or does not have, a particular property, it may be useful to focus on a

▲ Classification is an important part of all scientific endeavors. The objects of classification range from subatomic particles to living organisms to weather systems and solar systems. These skeletons came from three different types of primates: a human, a gorilla, and an orangutan.

specific characteristic and determine how much of that characteristic the object exhibits. This kind of system is based on an ordered sequence or on quantitative measurements rather than on qualitative judgments.

For example, in the case of intellectual ability, psychologists have developed sophisticated measurement procedures. Rather than asking whether or not a particular person is intelligent (a "yes or no" judgment), the psychologist sets out to determine *how much* intelligence the person exhibits on a particular set of tasks. This process offers some advantages over dependence on categorical distinctions. It allows scientists to record subtle distinctions that would be lost if they were forced to make all-or-none decisions. It also provides for more powerful quantitative measurements.

Monothetic versus Polythetic Classes

Some classification systems define categories in terms of a small number of singly necessary and jointly sufficient characteristics. Any object that possesses these characteristics is considered a member of the category, and objects that fail to possess exactly these characteristics are not members of the category. For example, within geometry, the category "square" is defined by four features: the number of sides (four), the number of angles (four), the length of the sides (equal), and the size of the angles (equal). Each feature is necessary, and taken together they are sufficient to identify a geometric figure as a square. This is an example of a **monothetic class.**

Contemporary numerical taxonomists have developed an alternative approach to classification that involves the use of polythetic categories (Corning, 1986). A **polythetic class** is defined in terms of a set of criteria that are neither necessary nor sufficient. Each member of the category must possess a certain minimal number of the defining features, but none of the features has to be found in each member of the category. The category "mammals" is an example of

a polythetic class; each member of the class possesses a significant number of the defining features, but there are mammals that do not possess certain features. For example, some mammals lay eggs, and some are not warm-blooded.

There are some important differences between monothetic and polythetic classification systems. In polythetic classes, not all members of a particular category are identical, even with regard to the defining features of the category. There is no central characteristic that they all share. Furthermore, some members of the class possess more of the defining features than other members of the class. This fact results in the observation that certain members are good examples of the category, whereas others are marginal. Scientists must determine at which point to establish a cutoff for group membership. How many criteria should an object possess before it is considered a member of the class? The number is determined by utility: Which definition allows scientists and clinicians to make the most useful predictions about members of the group?

Description versus Theory

The development of scientific classification systems typically proceeds in an orderly fashion from the initial stages, which primarily involve simple descriptions of observations, to more advanced theoretical stages, in which greater emphasis is placed on scientific concepts that explain causal relationships among objects. In the study of many medical disorders, this progression begins with an emphasis on the description of specific symptoms that seem to cluster together and that follow a predictable course over time. The systematic collection of further information regarding this syndrome may then lead to the discovery of etiological factors.

An example may help to illustrate the progression from descriptive to theoretically based classification. One form of mental retardation can be produced by an inherited metabolic disorder known as *phenylketonuria* (PKU). People with this disease are missing a liver enzyme that is required to break down a common amino acid, phenylalanine, that is present in protein foods (Pollitt, 1987) (see Chapter 14). If a child with PKU is allowed to eat a normal diet containing protein foods, incompletely metabolized products of phenylalanine will accumulate in the blood, cause damage to the developing

▲ Although a person's height clearly lies on a continuous dimension, it is sometimes convenient and useful to describe people in categorical terms. Basketball players are often described as inside players (like Manute Bol, who at 7'7" is the tallest player ever to play in the National Basketball Association) and perimeter players (like Mugsy Bogues, who at 5'3" is one of the shortest players ever to play in the NBA).

central nervous system, and eventually lead to mental retardation.

The etiology of PKU was discovered in 1934 when a woman in Norway brought her two young sons, who were both mentally retarded, to a physician. The woman reported that the boys often gave off a peculiar, musty odor. Using ordinary laboratory tests, the physician found high concentrations of phenylalanine in the children's blood and urine. Using the descriptive features of mental retardation and urinary tests to isolate further cases of the disorder, clinical scientists were able to identify the specific nature of the metabolic defect and establish that it is caused by a recessive gene (Bickel, 1980). Methods of early detection of PKU, using blood tests that are employed soon after birth, were developed in the 1950s. Treatment methods were introduced shortly thereafter. Infants who test

positive are placed on a special diet that is very low in phenylalanine, preventing the development of severe mental retardation.

Phenylketonuria is an example of a disorder that was originally identified on the basis of observable symptoms—intellectual deficiencies and a peculiar odor—and is now classified in terms of a specifically identified etiological pathway involving a recessive gene and a known metabolic defect. Mental disorders are currently classified on the basis of descriptive features because specific causal mechanisms have not yet been discovered.

▲ In polythetic classes, all members of a category are not identical. The animals in this picture (except for the man) all share certain features that place them in the category known as "dog."

Classification of Abnormal Behavior

We need a classification system for abnormal behavior for two primary reasons. First, the system will be used in making management and treatment decisions. A classification system is useful to clinicians who must match their clients' problems with the form of intervention that is most likely to be effective. Second, a classification system must be used in the search for new knowledge. The history of medicine is filled with examples of problems that were recognized long before they could be treated successfully. The definition of a specific set of symptoms has often laid the foundation for research that eventually identified a cure or a way of preventing the disorder.

Brief Historical Perspective

There have been many attempts to classify personality and psychopathology throughout history. The oldest written descriptions can be traced to the Egyptians, Greeks, and Romans, but these bear little resemblance to contemporary perspectives. Progress toward the adoption of a single, internationally accepted system began during the nineteenth century, when cities in Europe and the United States established large asylums for people with major mental disorders.

The physicians who presided over these institutions had an unprecedented opportunity to observe the behavior of many patients over an extended period of time. Many different classification systems were introduced during the ensuing years. In some areas, each hospital or university clinic developed and used its own unique system (Kendell, 1975).

Emil Kraepelin (1856–1926), a German psychiatrist, is generally regarded as the father of the categorical classification system that currently prevails in psychopathology. He believed that mental illness could be understood in terms of a finite number of specific disorders. Each disorder was presumed to have an identifiable set of symptoms and a unique course, and was the product of a yet-to-be-determined form of cerebral pathology (Berrios & Hauser, 1988). Kraepelin identified two primary forms of psychosis: *dementia praecox* (which we now call schizophrenia) and *manic-depressive psychosis* (which we now call bipolar mood disorder). His views were widely influential, but they did not lead directly to a formal, universally adopted classification system.

Two major diagnostic systems were developed shortly after World War II. In 1948, the World Health Organization published the sixth edition of the *International Classification of Diseases*

▲ **Robert Spitzer, professor of psychiatry at Columbia University, chaired the committee that produced DSM-III. Spitzer's vision and forceful leadership in this process was able to accomplish one of the most important changes in psychiatric classification of the twentieth century.**

(ICD). The ICD manual is used by physicians throughout the world to diagnose problems they treat. The sixth edition, known as ICD-6, was the first edition of this manual to include a section on mental illness. Its classification system for mental illness was used officially throughout the United Kingdom and in several other countries. Shortly after the publication of ICD-6, the American Psychiatric Association published its own classification system in the form of a *Diagnostic and Statistical Manual of Mental Disorders*, which came to be known as DSM-I. The second edition of the American manual, DSM-II, was published in 1968.

During the 1950s and 1960s, psychiatric classification systems were widely criticized. From an empirical point of view, principal concern was focused on the lack of consistency in diagnostic decisions (Spitzer & Fleiss, 1974). Independent clinicians frequently disagreed with one another regarding the use of diagnostic categories as they were listed in DSM-I and DSM-II. Objections were also raised from philosophical, sociological, and political points of view. Some critics charged that diagnostic categories in psychiatry would be more appropriately viewed as "problems in living" than as medical disorders (Szasz, 1960). Others were concerned about *self-fulfilling prophesies*. In other words, once a psychiatric label had been assigned, the person so labeled might be motivated to continue behaving in ways that were expected from someone who is mentally disturbed (see Further Thoughts). For all of these reasons, many mental health professionals paid less and less attention to the formal process of diagnosis during these years.

Renewed interest in the value of psychiatric classification grew steadily during the 1970s, culminating in the publication of the third edition of the DSM (APA, 1980). This version of the manual represented a dramatic departure from previous systems. It was clearly a major turning point in the history of psychiatric classification (Kendell, 1991; Sabshin, 1990). The committee that was responsible for developing DSM-III was chaired by Robert Spitzer, a psychiatrist at the New York State Psychiatric Institute. Spitzer and his colleagues made several bold changes in the manual. One broad consideration was their commitment to the production of a classification system that was based on clinical description rather than on theories of psychopathology that had not been empirically validated. This principal led to the elimination of some terms and categories that had been based on psychoanalytic concepts, like neurosis and hysteria (see Chapters 6 and 8). Other major changes included the introduction of a multiaxial system and the production of specific, detailed criterion sets for each disorder.

All of these changes have been retained in the latest version of the U.S. diagnostic system, which is known as DSM-IV (APA, 1994). They have also been incorporated into the current version of the World Health Organization's manual, which is known as ICD-10 (WHO, 1993). These features will be described in the following section. The two manuals are quite similar in most respects (Kendell, 1991). Deliberate attempts were made to coordinate the production of DSM-IV and ICD-10. Most of the categories listed in the manuals are identical, and the criteria for specific disorders are usually quite similar.[†]

The DSM-IV System

The DSM-IV employs a **multiaxial** classification system; that is, the person is rated with regard to five separate axes. Two are concerned with diagnostic categories, and the other three provide for the collection of additional relevant information. The rationale for this approach hinges on the recognition that the management of individual cases depends on a consideration of several important dimensions beyond specific symptoms. These supplementary factors include the environment in which the patient is living, aspects of the person's health that might affect psychological functions, and fluctuations in the overall level of the patient's adjustment. Table 4–1 lists the five specific axes from DSM-IV.

DIAGNOSTIC AXES

The first two axes are concerned with clinical disorders that are defined largely in terms of symptomatic behaviors. Most diagnoses appear on Axis I, which includes conditions such as

---

[†] There are some interesting differences between DSM-IV and ICD-10. There are, for example, differences in the ways in which they subdivide mood disorders and personality disorders. The U.S. system also devotes more attention to eating disorders and sexual disorders, which appear to be less prevalent in other cultures (Kendell, 1991).

Labeling Theory

Labeling theory is a perspective on mental disorders that is primarily concerned with the social context in which abnormal behavior occurs and the ways in which other people respond to this behavior. It assigns relatively little importance to specific behaviors as symptoms of a disorder that resides within the person. Labeling theory is more interested in social factors that determine whether a person will be given a psychiatric diagnosis than in psychological or biological reasons for the abnormal behaviors (Levine & Perkins, 1987). In other words, it is concerned with events that take place *after* a person has behaved in an unusual way rather than with factors that might explain the original appearance of the behavior itself.

Thomas Scheff, a sociologist at the University of California at Santa Barbara, is one of the leading figures in labeling theory (Scheff, 1966, 1984). According to Scheff, it is useful to think of mental disorders as maladaptive social roles, with the process of diagnostic labeling being the most important factor in establishing that role for a particular person. Scheff's theory is concerned with the violation of *residual rules,* which are implicit social expectations that are usually taken for granted. Scheff suggests that the symptoms of mental disorders are best viewed as violations of residual rules: showing too much emotion; not showing enough emotion; or talking too much or in strange ways. These behaviors create situations in which a person *might* be labeled as mentally disturbed.

Scheff maintains that people break residual rules frequently and for many different reasons. These behaviors are usually ignored or dismissed as unimportant. Scheff assumes that in such cases the behaviors will be transient. *Persistent* abnormal behaviors develop only after someone has been brought to the attention of the mental health system and assigned an official diagnostic label. That process sets in motion a number of other events that ensure that the person will accept the social role that is associated with the diagnosis and will continue to exhibit abnormal behaviors that are expected from people in that role. We all presumably learn the role of "mental patient" through cultural stereotypes, such as the negative images of people with mental disorders that are repeatedly displayed in the media (Signorielli, 1989). After a diagnosis has been assigned, patients are rewarded for accepting the role--behaving as if they are "crazy"--and are also punished if they attempt to return to normal social and occupational roles.

According to labeling theory, the probability that a person will receive a diagnosis is determined by several factors. These include the extent of the rule-breaking and its visibility, as well as the tolerance level of the community. The most important considerations are the social status of the person who breaks the rules and the social distance between that person and mental health professionals. People from disadvantaged groups, such as racial and sexual minorities and women, are presumably more likely to be labeled than are white males.

The merits and limitations of labeling theory have been hotly debated since the mid-1960s. The theory has inspired research on a number of important questions. Some studies have found that people from lower-status groups are indeed more likely to be assigned severe diagnoses (Holman & Caston, 1987). On the other hand, it would also be a great exaggeration to say that the social status of the patient is the most important factor influencing the diagnostic process. In fact, clinicians' diagnostic decisions are determined primarily by the form and severity of the patient's symptoms rather than by factors such as gender, race, and social class (Farmer & Griffiths, 1992; Gove, 1990).

Another focus of the debate regarding labeling theory is the issue of *stigma.* Is a diagnosis of mental disorder a sign of disgrace or discredit? Do people avoid those who have mental disorders? Labeling theory assumes that negative attitudes toward mental disorders prevent patients from obtaining jobs, finding housing, and forming new relationships. Negative attitudes are undoubtedly associated with many types of mental disorder, such as alcoholism, schizophrenia, and sexual disorders (Fabrega, 1991; Fink & Tasman, 1992).

Research studies have also found, however, that stigma is a complicated issue. Critics of labeling theory have argued that the effects of stigma are generally short-lived (Gove, 1970, 1990). Furthermore, some patients maintain positive attitudes about their own difficulties and about the mental health systems in which they are treated (Weinstein, 1983). The impact of stigma on a person's self-esteem is difficult to predict (Major & Crocker, 1993).

Although labeling theory has drawn needed attention to a number of important problems associated with the classification of mental disorders, it does not provide an adequate explanation for abnormal behavior. It is clearly an exaggeration to think of mental disorders as nothing more than social roles. Many factors other than the reactions of other people contribute to the development and maintenance of abnormal behavior. Furthermore, a diagnosis of mental illness can have positive consequences, such as encouraging access to proper treatment. Many patients and their family members are relieved to learn that their problems are similar to those experienced by other people and that help may be available. The effects of diagnostic labeling are not always harmful.

In addition to these reservations, several other questions about the theory should be mentioned. The analogy between residual rule-breaking and symptoms of mental disorders is strained at best. Many symptoms of psychopathology, such as anxiety and depression, are subjective in nature. People who endure these experiences often define themselves as suffering, regardless of the reactions of other people. Furthermore, there is no evidence to support the contention that abnormal behaviors are transient if they are ignored. In fact, data from the ECA and NCS studies indicate that many problems are long-lasting, even if they have not been treated (Robins & Regier, 1991; Kessler et al., 1994). ■

TABLE 4–1

Major Axes in DSM-IV

Axis I	Clinical Syndromes
Axis II	Personality Disorders and Mental Retardation
Axis III	General Medical Conditions
Axis IV	Psychosocial and Environmental Problems
Axis V	Global Assessment of Functioning

schizophrenia and mood disorders that form the topics of most chapters in this text. Many of the diagnoses that are described on Axis I are characterized by episodic periods of psychological turmoil. Axis II is concerned with more stable, long-standing problems, known as personality disorders. These disorders are usually less severe than those that are categorized on Axis I, and they are less likely to interfere with the person's functioning.

The separation of disorders on Axis I and Axis II is designed to draw attention to conditions such as personality disorders, which might be overlooked in the presence of a more dramatic symptomatic picture such as the hallucinations and delusions frequently found in schizophrenia. Clinicians are encouraged to list both types of problems when they are present. A person can be assigned more than one diagnosis on either Axis I or Axis II (or on both axes) if the person meets criteria for more than one disorder.

More than 200 specific diagnostic categories are described in DSM-IV. These are arranged under 18 primary headings, most of which were listed in Chapter 1, Table 1–2. The organization of the manual is based on descriptive similarities rather than on presumed causes, because the causes of abnormal behavior are not known. Numerous theories have been proposed to explain the origins of psychopathological conditions, but they have not been confirmed. In recognition of that state of affairs, the authors of DSM-IV have tried to avoid unnecessary theoretical assumptions. They adopted the descriptive approach in an effort to make the manual useful and acceptable to the widest possible range of mental health professionals. Disorders that present similar kinds of symptoms are grouped together. For example, conditions that include a prominent display of anxiety are listed together under "Anxiety Disorders," and conditions that involve a depressed mood are listed together under "Mood Disorders."

The manual lists specific criteria for each diagnostic category. Most of the categories are based on the polythetic approach to classification. We can illustrate the ways in which these criteria are used by examining the diagnostic decisions that would be considered in Michael's case. The criteria for obsessive–compulsive disorder, which is an Axis I disorder, and schizotypal personality disorder, which is an Axis II disorder, are listed in Table 4–2. First, let's consider obsessive–compulsive disorder, which is coded on Axis I. Michael would meet all of the criteria in "A" for both obsessions and compulsions. His repetitive hand-washing rituals were performed in response to obsessive thoughts regarding contamination. He also meets criterion "B" in that these rituals were time-consuming and interfered with his family's routine. His relationships with friends were severely limited because he refused to invite them to his house, fearing that they would spread contamination.

On Axis II, Michael would also be coded as meeting criteria for schizotypal personality disorder. He exhibited five of the nine symptoms listed under criterion "A": odd speech, suspiciousness, eccentric behavior, no close friends, and excessive social anxiety. This pattern illustrates an important feature of DSM-IV. For many disorders, a patient must exhibit a certain number of symptoms, but the specific pattern is not determined. Michael happened to exhibit symptoms 4, 5, 7, 8, and 9. Another person who happened to exhibit a different combination could also be classified as having schizotypal personality disorder. The specific items are not weighted in terms of their importance for making the diagnosis. These are, of course, somewhat arbitrary diagnostic standards. Little evidence suggests that four symptoms is a better cutoff point than three or five.

In addition to the **inclusion criteria,** symptoms that must be present, many disorders are also defined in terms of certain **exclusion**

criteria. In other words, the diagnosis can be ruled out if certain conditions prevail. For example, in the case of schizotypal personality disorder, the diagnosis would not be made if the symptoms occurred only during the course of a schizophrenic disorder.

You should also note that, in certain instances, the duration of a problem is considered as well as the clinical picture. Criterion B for obsessive–compulsive disorder specifies that the patient's compulsive rituals must take more than 1 hour each day to perform.

OTHER DOMAINS FOR ASSESSMENT

Axis III is concerned with general medical conditions that are outside the realm of psychopathology, but may be relevant to either the etiology of the patient's abnormal behavior or the patient's treatment program. Examples include thyroid conditions, which may lead to symptoms of psychosis; and diabetes in children, which is sometimes associated with conduct disorders. In Michael's case, there were no known physical disorders that were relevant to his psychological problems.

Axis IV is concerned with psychosocial and environmental problems that may affect the diagnosis or treatment of a mental disorder. The clinician is asked to indicate specific factors that are present in the person's life (see Chapter 7). The clinician is asked to record those problems that were present during the year prior to the current assessment. Problems that occurred prior to the previous year may be noted if the clinician is convinced that they made a significant contribution to the development of the person's current problems or if they have become a focus of treatment.

In Michael's case, the clinician noted three psychosocial problems: frequent arguments within the family, social isolation, and discord with classmates at school. Note that stressful circumstances may be the products as well as the causes of mental disorders. In Michael's case, for example, many of the family's arguments were precipitated by his washing rituals. In deciding whether to list social stresses on Axis IV, psychologists need not determine whether the stresses primarily arose from or contributed to the condition. They are all listed if they are relevant to treatment planning, and these were all important considerations in Michael's case.

Finally, Axis V provides for a global rating

TABLE 4–2

DSM-IV Criteria for Obsessive-Compulsive Disorder

A. Either obsessions or compulsions:

Obsessions as defined by (1), (2), (3), and (4):
1. Recurrent and persistent thoughts, impulses, or images that are experienced, at some time during the disturbance, as intrusive and inappropriate, and that cause marked anxiety or distress
2. The thoughts, impulses, or images are not simply excessive worries about real-life problems
3. The person attempts to ignore or suppress such thoughts, impulses, or images or to neutralize them with some other thought or action
4. The person recognizes that the obsessional thoughts, impulses, or images are a product of his or her own mind (not imposed from without as in thought insertion)

Compulsions as defined by (1) and (2):
1. Repetitive behaviors (such as hand washing, ordering, checking) or mental acts (such as praying, counting, repeating words silently) that the person feels driven to perform in response to an obsession, or according to rules that must be applied rigidly
2. The behaviors or mental acts are aimed at preventing or reducing distress or preventing some dreaded event or situation; however, these behaviors or mental acts either are not connected in a realistic way with what they are designed to neutralize or prevent, or are clearly excessive

B. At some point during the course of the disorder, the person has recognized that the obsessions or compulsions are excessive or unreasonable.

C. The obsessions or compulsions cause marked distress; are time-consuming (take more than one hour a day); or significantly interfere with the person's normal routine, occupational (or academic) functioning, or usual social activities or relationships with others.

D. If another Axis I disorder is present, the content of the obsessions or compulsions is not restricted to it (for example, preoccupation with food in the presence of an Eating Disorder; preoccupation with drugs in the presence of a Substance Use Disorder; or guilty ruminations in the presence of Major Depressive Disorder).

E. The disturbance is not due to the direct effects of a substance (such as drugs of abuse, medication) or a general medical condition.

DSM-IV Criteria for Schizotypal Personality Disorder

A. A pervasive pattern of social and interpersonal deficits marked by acute discomfort with, and reduced capacity for, close relationships as well as by cognitive or perceptual distortions and eccentricities of behavior, beginning by early adulthood and present in a variety of contexts, as indicated by five (or more) of the following:
1. Ideas of reference (excluding delusions of reference)
2. Odd beliefs or magical thinking that influence behavior and are inconsistent with subcultural norms—for example superstitiousness, belief in clairvoyance, telepathy, or "sixth sense"
3. Unusual perceptual experiences, including bodily illusions
4. Odd thinking and speech (for example, vague, circumstantial, metaphorical, overelaborate, or stereotyped)
5. Suspiciousness or paranoid ideation
6. Inappropriate or constricted affect
7. Behavior or appearance that is odd, eccentric, or peculiar
8. Lack of close friends or confidants other than first-degree relatives
9. Excessive social anxiety that does not diminish with familiarity and tends to be associated with paranoid fears rather than negative judgments about self

B. Does not occur exclusively during the course of Schizophrenia, a Mood Disorder with Psychotic Features, another Psychotic Disorder, or a Pervasive Developmental Disorder.

of adaptive functioning (Goldman, Skodol, & Lave, 1992). This rating is made on a scale that ranges from 1 to 100, with higher numbers representing better levels of adjustment. The scale applies only to psychological, social, and occupational functioning. Impairments that are due to physical or environmental limitations are excluded from consideration. Ratings are typically made for the person's current level of functioning. In some circumstances, the clinician might also consider the person's highest

level of functioning during the past year. This information is considered useful because it draws attention to recent changes in the patient's condition and because it provides a balanced view of the patient's strengths as well as his or her weaknesses.

In Michael's case, the psychologist assigned a rating of 50 for the current level of functioning. Michael was performing at an adequate level academically, but his social life was clearly impaired as a consequence of his rituals.

Evaluation of Classification Systems

It is important to remember that the *Diagnostic and Statistical Manual* is an evolving document. In fact, the pace of change has increased in recent years. Sixteen years elapsed between the initial publication of DSM-I and the appearance of DSM-II. The DSM-III (APA, 1980) was published 12 years after DSM-II, and it was formally revised (DSM-III-R) only 7 years later (APA, 1987). The DSM-IV appeared in 1994. Nothing is set in stone. Our attention should be focused on the identification of strengths and the revision of weaknesses as this process of development continues.

How can we evaluate a system like DSM-IV? Is it a useful classification system? Utility can be measured in terms of two principal criteria: reliability and validity.

Reliability

The term **reliability** refers to the consistency of measurements, including diagnostic decisions. If a diagnostic category is to be useful, it will have to be used consistently. One important form of reliability, known as inter-rater reliability, refers to agreement among clinicians. Suppose, for example, that two different psychologists interview the same patient and that each psychologist independently assigns a diagnosis using DSM-IV. If both psychologists decide that the patient fits the criteria for a major depressive disorder, they have used the definition of that category consistently. Of course, one or two cases would not provide a sufficient test of the reliability of a diagnostic category. The real question is whether the clinicians would agree with each other over a large series of patients.

Several formal procedures have been developed for use in the evaluation of diagnostic reliability. Most studies of psychiatric diagnosis in the past 20 years have employed a measure known as *kappa*. Instead of measuring the simple proportion of agreement between clinicians, **kappa** indicates the proportion of agreement that occurred *above and beyond that which would have occurred by chance*. Negative values of kappa indicate that the rate of agreement was less than that which would have been expected by chance in this particular sample of people. A kappa of zero indicates chance agreement, and a kappa of +1.0 would indicate perfect agreement between raters.

How should we interpret the kappa statistic? There is no easy answer to this question (Grove et al., 1981; Kirk & Kutchins, 1992). It would be unrealistic to expect perfect consistency, especially in view of the relatively modest reliability of other diagnostic decisions that are made in medical practice (Cameron & McGoogan, 1981; Koran, 1975). On the other hand, it isn't very encouraging if someone finds that the level of agreement among clinicians is significantly better than chance. We expect more than that from a diagnostic system that is used as a basis for treatment decisions. One convention suggests that kappa values of .70 or higher indicate relatively good agreement (Matarazzo, 1983; Spitzer, Foreman, & Nee, 1979). Values of kappa below .40 are often interpreted as an indication of poor agreement.

Most people who have published formal evaluations of DSM-III and DSM-III-R agree that the inclusion of more extensive descriptions of disorders and specific diagnostic criteria had a positive impact on the reliability of many categories. Most studies also indicate, however, that there is still considerable room for improvement in most categories. The reliability of some diagnostic categories is still well below acceptable standards. Consider, for example, evidence from one investigation that was concerned with the reliability of anxiety disorder categories (DiNardo et al., 1993).[†] Patients in the study were 267 people who sought treatment at a clinic for stress and anxiety disorders. Each person was interviewed separately by two clinicians who independently arrived at a diagnosis. Kappa values for some of the diagnostic categories are presented in Table 4–3.

Using the standard of .70 or higher, good agreement was found for some categories, including obsessive–compulsive disorder, social phobia, and panic disorder with agoraphobia. For

some other categories, such as major depression, diagnostic reliability was acceptable while clearly leaving room for improvement. Reliability for generalized anxiety disorder (GAD) was only fair. Further examination of disagreements for GAD indicated that the clinicians in this study frequently had difficulty deciding whether a person's worries were *excessive*, a judgment that is necessary in order to arrive at a diagnosis of GAD. Problems of this sort were taken into consideration in revising the criteria for GAD prior to publication of DSM-IV, which now provides a more explicit definition of the term "excessive." In this way, reliability studies contribute to making further refinements in the classification system.

You should note that the data presented in Table 4–3 probably represent the "best-case scenario" with regard to reliability of diagnostic decisions. These figures are only estimates of reliability based on one particular set of clinicians working with one specific sample of patients. The investigators who conducted this study are experienced, widely respected experts in psychiatric diagnosis and leaders in the area of anxiety disorders. If we expect agreement in any particular setting, it would seem most likely among those clinicians who are intimately familiar with the diagnostic system and especially careful in the application of diagnostic procedures. The reliability of diagnostic systems may be lower among clinicians who do not have time to employ standardized interview procedures and who may not scrutinize carefully the list of specific diagnostic criteria each time they make diagnoses. Therefore, we should not accept uncritically the assumption that DSM-IV can be used reliably (Kirk & Kutchins, 1992).

Validity

The ultimate issue in the evaluation of a diagnostic category is whether the category is useful. By knowing that a person fits into a particular group or class, do we learn anything *meaningful* about that person? For example, if a person fits the diagnostic criteria for schizophrenia, is that person likely to improve when he or she is given antipsychotic medication? Or is that person likely to have a less satisfactory level of social

TABLE 4–3

Reliability Data for Specific Types of Anxiety and Mood Disorders

Diagnostic Category	Kappa
Obsessive-compulsive disorder	.80
Generalized anxiety disorder	.57
Panic disorder with agoraphobia	.72
Social phobia	.79
Major depression	.65

Source: Diagnoses based on DSM-III-R criteria; from P.A. Di Nardo, et al. 1993. Reliability of DSM-III-R anxiety disorder categories: Using the Anxiety Disorders Interview Schedule-Revised (ADIS-R). *Archives of General Psychiatry, 50,* 251-256.

[†] We present data regarding the reliability of DSM-III-R criteria (APA, 1987) because the reliability data from field trials for DSM-IV are not yet available.

adjustment in 5 years than a person who meets diagnostic criteria for bipolar mood disorder? Does the diagnosis tell us anything about the factors or circumstances that might have contributed to the onset of this problem? These questions are concerned with the validity of the diagnostic category. The term **validity** refers to the meaning or importance of a measurement, in this case a diagnostic decision (Hempel, 1961; Kendell, 1989). Importance is not an all-or-none phenomenon; it is a quantitative issue. Diagnostic categories are more or less useful, and their validity (or utility) can be determined in several ways.

The process of discovery that surrounds the investigation of a diagnostic category represents an attempt to understand the nature of the problem. Validity is, in a sense, an index of the success that has been achieved in that search. Have important facts been discovered? Systematic studies aimed at establishing the validity of a disorder often proceed in a sequence of phases (Robins & Guze, 1989), which are listed in Table 4–4. After a clinical description has been established, these phases may occur in any order. Diagnostic categories are refined and validated through this process of scientific exploration.

Various types of information are associated with specific types of validity. It is helpful to think of these types of validity in terms of their relationship in time with the appearance of symptoms of the disorder. *Etiological validity* is concerned with factors that contribute to the onset of the disorder. These are things that have happened in the past. Was the disorder regularly triggered by a specific set of events or circumstances? Did it run in families? *Concurrent validity* is concerned with the present time and with correlations between the disorder and other test procedures. Is the disorder currently associated with any other types of behavior, such as performance on psychological tests? Do precise measures of biological variables, such as brain structure and function, distinguish reliably between people who have the disorder and those who do not? *Predictive validity* is concerned with the future, and with the stability of the problem over time. Will it be persistent? If it is transient, will it last for a predictable period of time? Will it have a predictable outcome? Do people with this problem typically improve if they are given a specific type of medication or a particular form of psychotherapy? The overall utility or validity of a diagnostic category depends on the body of the evidence that accumulates as scientists seek answers to these questions.

TABLE 4–4

Types of Studies Used to Validate Clinical Syndromes

Identification and description of the syndrome, either by clinical intuition or by statistical analyses.

Demonstration of boundaries or "points of rarity" between related syndromes.

Follow-up studies establishing a distinctive course or outcome.

Therapeutic trials establishing a distinctive treatment response.

Family studies establishing that the syndrome "breeds true."

Demonstration of association with some more fundamental abnormality—psychological, biochemical, or molecular.

Source: Adapted from R.E. Kendell (1989). Clinical validity. *Psychological Medicine, 19,* 45-55, p. 47.

You should not assume that every diagnostic category that is included in DSM-IV will eventually be found to be useful. Many thorny problems are involved in the process of validating a disorder. Important questions remain to be answered for all forms of mental disorder. The list of categories included in DSM-IV is based heavily on conventional clinical wisdom. Each time the manual is revised, new categories are added and old categories are dropped, presumably because they are not sufficiently useful. Up to the present time, clinicians have been more willing to include new categories than to drop old ones. It is difficult to know when we would decide that a particular diagnostic category is not valid. At what point in the accumulation of knowledge are clinical scientists willing to conclude that a category is of no use, and to recommend that the search for more information should be abandoned? This is a difficult question that the authors of DSM-IV have confronted, and it will become increasingly important in the production of future revisions.

Unresolved Questions

Several important issues will have to be addressed as more systematic information is collected about the diagnostic categories in DSM-IV. One set of questions is centered on the polythetic criteria that are employed for many disorders. In the current system, cutoff points for establishing a diagnosis were chosen arbitrarily. Future research should be able to determine optimal thresholds for each disorder. For example, in the case of schizotypal personality disorder, the present cutoff point is five out of nine features. Perhaps one of the features is unnecessary or redundant with another. In that case, the list could be shortened to eight criteria. Should one or more of the features be given special weight? Are they all equally important? These questions will have to be answered by investigators who explore the validity of each individual category.

Another set of questions is concerned with the use of specific time periods in the definition of various disorders. To what extent will the pattern of onset and the duration of symptoms be considered diagnostically important? The course of a disorder is often considered to be diagnostically important in medical disorders, and there are places in DSM-IV in which the course of the disorder is used to define that disorder. For example, in the case of schizophrenia, DSM-IV requires that the person exhibit symptoms for a period of at least 6 months. Again, the utility of these aspects of the diagnostic criteria are important topics for future empirical studies.

Finally, we should also mention the continuing discussion of ancillary axes. The three that have been included in DSM-IV could have been supplemented (or replaced) by other important considerations. In addition to psychosocial problems and a global assessment of functioning, it might be useful to record information regarding factors such as previous course of the disorder, quality of interpersonal relationships, work functioning, family functioning, and response to treatment. Although each of these factors might provide useful information that would help a clinician in planning a treatment program, it seems unlikely that they could all be included in a comprehensive classification system, because it would become too unwieldy and complicated.

Nonscientific Factors that Affect Diagnostic Systems

Scientific considerations are not the only factors that influence the development of a classification system. Treatment and research are practical activities that take place in the real world, and they are intimately tied to many impor-

tant pragmatic issues. As one example, consider the enormous increases in health care that have occurred during the past decade. Who will pay for these expenses, and which professional groups will be the primary beneficiaries? Attempts to curtail costs have had a dramatic effect on the services that are delivered and on the way that professionals and scientists think about medical problems. We will discuss briefly two important considerations that continue to influence the development of classification systems in abnormal psychology: professional issues, and laypeople and political organizations.

PROFESSIONAL ISSUES

Several different professions are involved in research and treatment within the broad field of mental health services. These professions include psychology, psychiatry, social work, and nursing, to name only a few. Each profession is concerned with its ability to provide quality services to patients, as well as its right to be reimbursed for these services. By virtue of tradition, physicians have controlled many of the central features of the mental health delivery system, including hospital admissions, medication, and the diagnostic system. The American Psychiatric Association has been responsible for the development of the various versions of DSM. This particular organization has gained substantial financial benefits from the publication and widespread adoption of its manual.

Some psychologists have argued against the use of this system, primarily because it is controlled by physicians, who are members of another profession (see Schacht & Nathan, 1979). Viewed from this perspective, a diagnostic system becomes an economic resource that can be used strategically in an effort to gain control of the mental health service delivery marketplace. We believe that this is an unnecessarily partisan view of an important issue. Nevertheless, it would be naive to ignore such influences.

LAYPEOPLE AND POLITICAL ORGANIZATIONS

In some cases, political organizations have also had an important influence on the diagnostic system (Spitzer, 1985). One of the best-known recent examples centered on the issue of homosexuality. In both DSM-I and DSM-II, homosexuality was listed as a form of mental illness. People who were actively engaged in sexual activities with members of their own gender were, by definition, considered to be psychologically disturbed. By the late 1960s, gay and lesbian rights organizations had begun to pressure the American Psychiatric Association to change this definition. Action was finally taken in December, 1973, when the Board of Trustees of the American Psychiatric Association voted to remove homosexuality from its official list of mental disorders. This was clearly a political decision. Although science was invoked by both sides of the debate, the board's action was based largely on an effort to avoid further social protest (see Chapter 11).

Various feminist organizations have been concerned with the possible introduction of a new type of personality disorder—*self-defeating personality disorder*—that would be used to describe some women who are involved in, and fail to abandon, abusive relationships. The objection, of course, is that introducing such a category would place the responsibility for abuse with

the woman who is victimized rather than with the violent male. Efforts to incorporate this category into DSM-III ultimately were defeated, and the category was relegated to an appendix for "diagnostic categories needing further study." It was dropped completely in DSM-IV.

▲ The construction and revision of the DSM has been influenced by political forces, as when lesbian and gay activists persuaded the APA to drop homosexuality from the manual during the 1970s.

Basic Issues in Assessment

Up to this point, we have discussed the development and use of classification systems. But we haven't talked about the way in which a psychologist might collect the information that is necessary to arrive at a diagnostic decision. Furthermore, we have looked at the problem only in relatively general terms. The diagnostic decision is one useful piece of information. It is not, however, a systematic picture of the specific person's situation. It is only a starting point. In the following section, we extend our discussion to consider methods of collecting information. In so doing, we discuss a broad range of data that may be useful in the understanding of psychopathological behavior.

The Purposes of Clinical Assessment

To appreciate the importance and complexity of assessment procedures, let's go back to the example of Michael. When Michael and his parents initially approached the psychologist, they were clearly upset. But the nature of the problem, in terms of Michael's behavior and the family as a whole, was not clearly defined. Before he could

attempt to help this family, the psychologist had to collect more information. He needed to know more about the range and frequency of Michael's obsessions and compulsions, including when they began, how often he experienced these problems, and the factors that made them better and worse. He also needed to know whether there were other problems, such as depression or psychotic thought processes, that might either explain these responses or interfere with their treatment. In addition, he had to learn how Michael got along with classmates, how he was doing in school, and how his parents responded when he behaved strangely. Was his behavior, at least in part, a response to environmental circumstances? How would the family support (or interfere with) the therapist's attempts to help him change? The psychologist needed to address Michael's current situation in terms of several different facets of his behavior, and at both the broad and specific levels of abstraction.

Psychological assessment is the process of collecting and interpreting information that will be used to understand another person. Numerous data-gathering techniques can be employed in this process. Several of these procedures are described in the following pages. We must remember, however, not to confuse the process of assessment with this list of specific techniques. Assessment procedures are tools that can be used in many ways. They cannot be used in an intellectual vacuum. Interviews can be used to collect all sorts of information for all sorts of reasons. Psychological tests can be interpreted in many different ways. The value of assessment procedures can be determined only in the context of a specific purpose (McFall & McDonel, 1986).

Three primary goals guide most assessment procedures: making predictions, planning interventions, and evaluating interventions. The practical importance of predictions should be obvious: Many crucial decisions are based on psychologists' attempts to determine the probability of future events. Will a person engage in violent behavior? Can a person make rational decisions? Is a parent able to care for his or her children? Assessment is also commonly used to evaluate the likelihood that a particular form of treatment will be helpful for a specific patient, and to provide guideposts by which the effectiveness of treatment programs can be measured (Hayes, Nelson, & Jarrett, 1987). Different assessment procedures are likely to be employed for different purposes. Those that are useful in one situation may not be helpful in another.

Assumptions about Behavior

Assessment is governed by several important concepts and assumptions regarding the nature of human behavior and the ability of psychological science to measure and explain these events (Goldfried & Kent, 1972; McFall & McDonel, 1986). We will examine a number of these, beginning with assumptions concerning the consistency of human behavior.

CONSISTENCY OF BEHAVIOR

Assessment involves the collection of specific samples of a person's behavior. These samples may include things that the person says during an interview, responses that the person makes on a psychological test, or things that the person does while being observed. None of these would be important if we assumed that they were isolated events. They are useful to the extent that they represent examples of the ways in which

the person will feel or behave in other situations. Psychologists must therefore be concerned about the consistency of behavior across time and situations. They want to know if they can *generalize*, or draw inferences about the person's behavior in the natural environment on the basis of the samples of behavior that are obtained in their assessment. If the client is depressed at this moment, how did she feel one week ago, and how will she feel tomorrow? In other words, is this a persistent phenomenon, or is it a transient state? If a child is anxious and unable to pay attention in the psychologist's office, will he also exhibit these problems in his classroom at school? And how will he behave on the playground?

Psychologists typically employ more than one source of information when conducting a formal assessment. Because we are trying to compose a broad, integrated picture of the person's adjustment, we must collect information from several sources and then attempt to integrate these data. Each piece of information may be considered to be one sample of the person's behavior. One way of evaluating the possible meaning or importance of this information is to consider the consistency across sources. Do the conclusions drawn on the basis of a diagnostic interview agree with those that are suggested by a psychological test? Do the psychologist's observations of the client's behavior and the client's self-report agree with observations that are reported by parents or teachers?

LEVELS OF ANALYSIS

The kind of information that is collected will depend on the way in which the clinician views the problem. Mental disorders are embedded in multiple, interacting systems that involve biological, psychological, and social factors (see Chapter 2). At one level, the clinician must decide whether to concentrate on the individual client or to focus more broadly on social systems. For example, a depressed married person might be treated as an individual or as part of a couple. In Michael's case, his problem might be viewed in terms of the family system, which also involves his parents. Michael's relatively poor relationships with his peers could also be considered relevant to understanding his problems.

At another level, the clinician has to decide whether to concentrate on psychological variables or biological factors that might also influence the etiology of the problem. In all cases, the clinician's choice of the level of analysis will determine in large part the sorts of instruments that will be employed in the assessment process. Because assessment is a finite process, the decision to use one set of procedures will inevitably lead to the omission of others.

Suppose we decide to focus primarily on psychological variables, as we have done in our description of Michael's case. We must then make decisions regarding the level of analysis within the psychological system. One relatively broad conceptual scheme involves the consideration of diagnostic categories. Does Michael meet the DSM-IV criteria for obsessive–compulsive disorder? If he does, then the clinician is likely to employ particular forms of intervention. But we also know that not all obsessive–compulsive clients are exactly the same. Their fears and worries may involve many different kinds of things, and the ways in which they attempt to cope with, or neutralize, these fears may also vary tremendously. Response to treatment will also be influenced by additional considerations, such as personality traits, cognitive abilities, social skills, and the presence or absence of co-morbid conditions, such as a seriously depressed mood. Therefore, the clinician will require a great deal of additional information in order to formulate a treatment plan.

No single assessment instrument can address all of these issues. There is simply too much ground to be covered, and each issue may require a different measurement approach. The clinician's approach to the problem will determine which unique features are measured with regard to the individual person and the relation between that person's problems and his or her social environment. These issues might include information about characteristic ways of interacting with other people (personality traits), current mood states, attitudes about oneself and others, and interpersonal skills, as well as the environmental resources and demands with which the person is currently confronted. The assessment must be planned to cover those features that are particularly relevant to the problem in question, using whatever reliable sources of information may be available.

Evaluating the Utility of Assessment Procedures

The same criteria that are used to evaluate diagnostic categories are used to evaluate the utility of assessment procedures: reliability and validity. We have already discussed inter-rater reliability with regard to diagnostic decisions. Will two clinicians agree with each other if they independently assign a diagnosis to the same person? In the case of assessment procedures, reliability can refer to various types of consistency. For example, the consistency of measurements over time is known as *test–retest reliability*. Will a person receive the same score if an assessment procedure is repeated at two different points in time? The internal consistency of items within a test is known as *split–half reliability*. If a test with multiple items measures a specific trait or ability, and if the items are divided in half, will the person's scores on the two halves agree with each other? Assessment procedures must be reliable if they are to be useful in either clinical practice or research.

The *validity* of an assessment procedure refers to its meaning or importance. Is the person's score on this test or procedure actually a reflection of the trait or ability that the test was designed to measure? And does the person's score tell us anything useful about the person's behavior in other situations? Knowing that the person has achieved a particular score on this evaluation, can we make meaningful predictions about the person's responses to other tests, or about the person's behavior in future situations? These are all questions about the validity of an assessment procedure. If a person's score on a psychological test indicates that he or she is depressed, we expect that the results of other assessment procedures, such as clinical interviews, will most often confirm that impression (see Research Methods). Convergence of information across sources of information provides support for the validity of the individual measurement procedures.

RESEARCH METHODS

Diagnostic Efficiency

Suppose someone has developed a test that is intended to be able to predict the future onset of schizophrenia. We want to know whether it is useful. The test is given to a sample of 1,000 college students, and their scores identify 60 students who will eventually develop the disorder. The students are then followed up 10 years later, after some of them have developed the disorder. Let's say 20 of these people have become schizophrenic and 15 of these are people who tested positive when they were in college. The test was right some of the time, and it also made some mistakes. It predicted incorrectly that 45 others would become schizophrenic. These people are called **false positives**: people who tested positive but didn't eventually develop the disorder. The test also missed 5 people--those who did not test positive but later developed the disorder. These people are called **false negatives**. Is this "hit rate" good enough? Can we get any more specific in our evaluation of the test?

Several specific quantitative procedures can be used to evaluate the utility of this assessment device (Kessel & Zimmerman, 1993; Sackett, 1992). The ways in which these measures are computed are illustrated in Table 4–5. **Sensitivity** refers to the ability of the test to identify correctly people who have the disorder in question. This is also called the *true positive rate*. Will the test "pick up" all of the cases in the sample? In Table 4–5, sensitivity is computed by dividing the number of people who test positive by the total number of people who actually have the disorder: $A/(A + C)$. In the hypothetical example that we have posed, the sensitivity of the test would be 75 percent: $15/(15 + 5)$. Sensitivity will be higher as the rate of false negatives decreases.

Specificity refers to the ability of the test to identify as being "negative" people who do not have the disorder. In other words, in the process of picking up those people who have the disorder, will the test also pick up a lot of people who do not have the disorder? In Table 4–5, specificity is computed by dividing the number of people who tested negative and

	TABLE 4–5

Procedures for Computing Sensitivity, Specificity, and Predictive Power

Disorder	Test Result	
	Positive	**Negative**
Present	A	C
Absent	B	D

Sensitivity:	$A/(A + C)$
Specificity:	$D/(B + D)$
Positive predictive power:	$A/(A + B)$
Negative predictive power:	$D/(C + D)$
False positive rate:	$B/(B + D)$
False negative rate:	$C/(A + C)$
Diagnostic efficiency:	$(A + D)/(A + B + C + D)$

did not have the disorder (D) by the total number of people who did not have the disorder (B + D). For our hypothetical example, the specificity of the test would be 95 percent: $935/(45 + 935)$. Specificity will be lower as the rate of false positives increases.

In actual practice, sensitivity and specificity don't produce the kind of information that we want to know about individual cases. We really want to know what the chances are that a particular person will get the disorder if he or she receives a particular test score. These questions are concerned with predictive power. **Positive predictive power** refers to the probability that a person who has a positive test response will actually have the disorder. In Table 4–5, positive predictive power is computed by dividing the number of people who tested positive and eventually developed the disorder (A) by the total number of people who tested positive (A + B). In our hypothetical example, positive predictive power would be only 25 percent: $15/(15 + 45)$.

These terms can be used to describe the **diagnostic efficiency** of an assessment procedure. This concept refers to the overall ability of a test to make correct and incorrect predictions (Gehlbach, 1988).

Efficiency can be computed by adding together the numbers of people who are correctly identified (true positives plus true negatives) and dividing that number by the total number of people who were evaluated. In our hypothetical example, the overall efficiency of the test is 95 percent: (15 + 935)/1,000.

There are clearly trade-offs among the different criteria that are used to evaluate diagnostic efficiency. No diagnostic test is perfect. Errors are going to be made, and a careful consideration of the relative importance of sensitivity, specificity, and predictive power can help the clinician decide which type of error is more acceptable in a particular situation. Which one we decide to emphasize will depend on the way in which we hope to use the test and the consequences of various outcomes. Is it more important to identify all true cases in the sample (high sensitivity), even if it is accomplished at the expense of increasing the rate of false positives (low positive predictive power)? Or are we especially concerned about maximizing positive predictive power, regardless of a possible reduction in the sensitivity of the test? For a specific example of this type of decision, applied to the case of identifying cases of depression, see the Research Close-up on identifying mood disorders. ∎

Assessment Procedures

The most useful assessment procedures are likely to vary from one problem to the next. Assessment procedures that are useful in evaluating the efficacy of a drug treatment program for hospitalized depressed patients may be quite different from those that might be used in an effort to predict the need for medication among hyperactive schoolchildren. Our purpose in the rest of this chapter is to outline a range of assessment procedures. This is a selective sampling of measures rather than an exhaustive review of assessment procedures.

An enormous array of assessment tools is available to clinicians who are interested in treating or studying abnormal behavior. Many of these procedures are commonly employed in clinical practice, and they are also used in the process of research. We consider several prominent alternatives in the following section, which is organized in accordance with our emphasis on systems that influence mental disorders. We begin our discussion with measures that are typically concerned with psychological variables—characteristic traits and behaviors that are associated with abnormal behavior. These include interviews, observations, and self-report instruments. From there, we move to a consideration of the assessment of social systems, such as families and institutional environments (schools and hospi-

tals). The last section of this chapter will be concerned with measures that are concerned with biological systems—the neurological and biochemical underpinnings of mental disorders. In many cases, the assessment of psychopathology is based on the combined use of measures that cover selective aspects of all of these systems.

At the end of each section, we have provided a quick summary of the advantages and limitations of each type of procedure. These are intended only as general guides and not as definitive critiques. Please keep in mind our earlier comment: Each procedure is a tool that can be used for different purposes. The true value of the tool can be determined only in light of the specific purpose for which it is employed.

Assessment of Psychological Systems

"Person variables" are typically the first thing that comes to mind when we think about the assessment of psychopathology. What did the person do or say? How does the person feel about his or her current situation? What skills and abilities does the person possess, and are there any important cognitive or social deficits that should be taken into consideration? These are all questions about the individual person, and they can be addressed through a number of procedures, including interviews, observations, and various types of self-report instruments and psychological tests.

INTERVIEWS

The best way to find out about someone else is often to talk with that person directly. The *clinical interview*, which has been described as "a conversation with a purpose" (Bingham & Moore, 1924), is the most commonly used procedure in psychological assessment. Most of the categories that are defined in DSM-IV are based on information that can be collected in an interview. These data are typically supplemented by information that is obtained from official records (previous hospital admissions, school reports, court files) and interviews with other informants (for example, family members), but the clients' own direct descriptions of their problems are the primary basis for diagnostic decisions. None of the diagnostic categories in DSM-IV is defined in terms of psychological or biological tests, with the exception of mental retardation.

Interviews provide an opportunity to ask patients for their own descriptions of their problems. Many of the symptoms of psychopathology are subjective in nature, and an interview can provide a detailed analysis of these problems. Consider, for example, Michael's problems with anxiety. The unrelenting fear and revulsion that he experienced at school was the central feature of his problem. His obsessive thoughts of contamination were private events that could only be known to the psychologist on the basis of Michael's self-report, which was quite compelling. His family could observe Michael's peculiar habits with regard to arranging his school books, changing his clothes, and washing his hands, but the significance of these behaviors to Michael was not immediately apparent without the knowledge that they were based on an attempt to control or neutralize his anxiety-provoking images of taunting classmates.

Interviews also allow clinicians to observe important features of a person's appearance and nonverbal behavior. In Michael's case, the psychologist noticed during their initial interview that the skin on Michael's hands and lower arms was red and chafed from excessive scrubbing. He was dressed neatly but seemed especially self-conscious about his hair and glasses, which he adjusted repeatedly. Michael was reluc-

tant to make eye contact, and his speech was soft and hesitant. His obvious discomfort in this social situation was consistent with his own descriptions of the anxiety that he felt during interactions with peers. It was also interesting to note that Michael became visibly agitated when discussing particular subjects, such as the incident with his track team. At these points in the interview, he would fidget restlessly in his seat and clasp his arms closely around his sides. His speech became more rapid, and he began to stutter a bit. On one occasion, he found it impossible to sit still, and he began to pace quickly back and forth across the psychologist's office. These nonverbal aspects of Michael's behavior provided useful information about the nature of his distress.

The psychologist asked Michael to describe the sequence of events in a typical day. How did he spend his time when he was at school? What were his interests outside of school? How did his rituals and obsessive thoughts interfere with these activities? Taken together, this information provides a broader context in which the specific symptoms can be understood. The relationship that was established between Michael and his psychologist became an essential factor in the subsequent efforts they made toward changing Michael's behavior.

Structured Interviews Assessment interviews vary with regard to the amount of structure that is imposed by the clinician. Some are relatively open-ended or nondirective. In this type of interview, the clinician follows the train of thought supplied by his or her client. One goal of nondirective interviews is to help people clarify their subjective feelings and to provide general empathic support for whatever they may decide to do about their problems. In contrast to this open-ended style, some interviews follow a more specific question-and-answer format. *Structured interviews*, in which the clinician must ask each patient a specific list of detailed questions, are frequently employed for collecting information that will be used to make diagnostic decisions and to rate the extent to which a person is impaired by psychopathology.

Several different structured interviews were developed for the purpose of making psychiatric diagnoses in large-scale epidemiological and cross-national studies in the late 1960s and early 1970s. Investigators reasoned that the reliability of their diagnostic decisions would improve if they could ensure that clinicians always made a consistent effort to ask the same questions when they interviewed patients. One currently popular example of this procedure is the Structured Clinical Interview for DSM (SCID), which was written by Robert Spitzer and his colleagues at the New York State Psychiatric Institute. The SCID includes modules that are designed to address all of the different disorders that are represented in DSM-IV. Other forms of structured diagnostic interviews have been designed for use in the diagnosis of specific types of problems, such as personality disorders (see Widiger & Francis, 1985), anxiety disorders (see DiNardo et al., 1988), and the behavior problems of children (see Edelbrock & Costello, 1984).

Structured interviews typically begin with an overview of the current episode of disturbance. The interviewer uses open-ended questions to elicit a description of these events in the patient's own words, rather than "yes" or "no" responses to questions about the presence of specific symptoms. Examples of open-ended questions are, "Why did you decide to ask for help?" and "What kinds of problems have you been having?" If the patient does not provide sufficient information, the interviewer might say, "Tell me more about that." After this opening section, the clinician follows leads that have been raised and begins to impose more structure as the interview progresses.

After open-ended questions have established an initial description of the person's problems, a structured interview schedule provides the clinician with a series of specific questions that are aimed at eliciting the information that will be necessary to arrive at a diagnosis or a more complete description of the presenting symptoms. As an example, consider the Yale-Brown Obsessive Compulsive Scale (Y-BOCS; Goodman et al., 1989), which might have been used in the assessment of Michael's disorder. A list of questions from the Y-BOCS is presented in Table 4–6. For each topic or set of questions, the interviewer is required to make a rating from 0 to 4, indicating the person's level of distress or impairment. The composite rating—the total across all the items in the scale—can be used as an index of the severity of the disorder. The Y-BOCS can also be used as the basis for diagnostic decisions, because the items included in the scale also cover all the criteria for OCD in DSM-IV.

Structured interview schedules provide a systematic framework for the collection of important diagnostic information, but they don't eliminate the need for an experienced clinician. If

---

TABLE 4–6

Sample Questions from the Yale-Brown Obsessive-Compulsive Scale

Time Occupied by Obsessive Thoughts
How much of your time is occupied by obsessive thoughts?
0 = None
1 = Mild, less than 1 hour per day
2 = Moderate, 1 to 3 hours per day
3 = Severe, greater than 3 and up to 8 hours per day
4 = Extreme, greater than 8 hours per day

Interference Due to Obsessive Thoughts
How much do your obsessive thoughts interfere with your social or work (or role) functioning? Is there anything that you don't do because of them?
0 = None
1 = Mild, slight interference, but overall performance not impaired
2 = Moderate, definite interference, but still manageable
3 = Severe, causes substantial impairment
4 = Extreme, incapacitating

Distress Associated with Obsessive Thoughts
How much distress do your obsessive thoughts cause you?
0 = None
1 = Mild, not too disturbing
2 = Moderate, disturbing, but still manageable
3 = Severe, very disturbing
4 = Extreme, near constant and disabling distress

Resistance Against Obsessions
How much of an effort do you make to resist the obsessive thoughts? How often do you try to disregard or turn your attention away from these thoughts as they enter your mind?
0 = None
1 = Mild, not too disturbing
2 = Moderate, disturbing, but still manageable
3 = Severe, very disturbing
4 = Extreme, near constant and disabling distress

Degree of Control Over Obsessive Thoughts
How much control do you have over your obsessive thoughts? How successful are you in stopping or diverting your obsessive thinking? Can you dismiss them?
0 = None
1 = Mild, not too disturbing
2 = Moderate, disturbing, but still manageable
3 = Severe, very disturbing
4 = Extreme, near constant and disabling distress

---

the interviewer is not able to establish a comfortable rapport with the client, then the interview might not elicit useful information. Furthermore, it is impossible to specify in advance all the questions that should be asked in a diagnostic interview. The client's initial responses to open-ended questions frequently require additional clarification. The interviewer must formulate specific follow-up questions and also determine when it is necessary to probe further, and in what ways to probe. Finally, clinical judgment is required in rating people's responses to questions. Consider the fourth Y-BOCS item in Table 4–6. The interviewer must determine whether the person's attempts to ignore or resist the repetitive thoughts are excessive or unreasonable. In many cases, that is a difficult judgment. Having lists of specific questions and clear definitions of diagnostic criteria will make the clinician's job easier, but clinical judgment remains a crucial ingredient in any diagnostic interview.

Advantages The clinical interview is the primary tool employed by clinical psychologists in the assessment of psychopathology. Several features of interviews account for this popularity, including the following issues:

 1. The interviewer can control the interaction and can probe further when necessary.

 2. By observing the patient's nonverbal behavior, the interviewer can detect areas of resistance. In that sense, the validity of the information may be enhanced.

 3. An interview can provide a lot of information in a short period of time. It can cover past events and many different settings.

Limitations There are also several limitations that must be kept in mind in the use of clinical interviews as part of the assessment process. These include the following considerations:

1. Some patients may be unable or unwilling to provide a rational account of their problems. This may be particularly true of young children, who have not developed verbal skills, as well as some psychotic and demented patients who are unable to speak coherently.

2. People may be reluctant to admit experiences that are embarrassing or frightening. They may feel that they should report to the interviewer only those feelings and behaviors that are socially desirable.

3. Subjective factors play an important role in the interpretation of information provided in an interview. The person's responses to questions are not scored objectively, and there is always some variation in the format. The situation is not entirely structured and depends heavily on the training and experience of the interviewer.

4. Information provided by the client is necessarily filtered through the client's eyes. It is a subjective account and may be influenced or distorted by errors in memory and by selective perception.

5. The interviewer may, in some circumstances, suggest symptoms and problems to the client. Interviewers can influence their clients' accounts by the ways in which they phrase their questions and respond to the clients' responses.

OBSERVATIONAL PROCEDURES

In addition to the information that we gain from what people are willing to tell us during interviews, we can also learn a lot by watching their behavior. Observational skills play an important part in most assessment procedures. Sometimes the things that we observe confirm the person's self-report, and at other times the person's overt behavior appears to be at odds with what he or she says. A juvenile delinquent might express in words his regret at having injured a classmate, but his smile and the twinkle in his eye may raise doubts about the sincerity of this statement. In situations such as this, we must reconcile information that is obtained from different sources. The picture that emerges of another person's adjustment is greatly enriched when data collected from interviews are supplemented by observations of the person's behavior.

Observational procedures may be either informal or formal in nature. *Informal observations* are primarily qualitative in nature. The clinician observes the person's behavior and the environment in which it occurs without attempting to record the frequency or intensity of specific responses. Michael's case illustrates the value of informal observations in the natural environment. When the therapist visited Michael and his parents at their home, he learned that his ritualistic behaviors were more extreme than Michael had originally described. This was useful but not particularly surprising, since patients with OCD are often reluctant to describe in an interview the full extent of their compulsive behavior. The therapist also learned that the parents themselves were quite concerned with rules and order. Everything in their home was highly polished and in its place. This observation helped the therapist understand the extent to which Michael's parents might contribute to, or reinforce, his rigid adherence to a strict set of rules.

Although observations are often conducted in the natural environment, there are times when it is useful to observe the person's behavior in a situation that the psychologist can arrange and control. Sometimes it isn't possible to observe the person's behavior in the natural environment because the behavior in question occurs infrequently or at times when an observer cannot be present; at other times the environment is inaccessible; and sometimes the behavior that is of interest is inherently a private or seclusive act. In these cases, the psychologist may arrange to observe the person's behavior in a situation that in some ways approximates the real environment. These artificial situations may also allow for more careful measurements of the person's problem than could be accomplished in a more complex situation.

In the case of obsessive–compulsive behavior, this approach might involve asking the person deliberately to touch an object that would ordinarily trigger ritualistic behaviors. The therapist might collect a set of objects that Michael would not want to touch, such as a school book, a pair of old track shorts, and the knob of a door leading to the laundry room. It would be useful to know specifically which objects he would touch, the degree of discomfort that he experienced when touching them, and the length of time that he was able to wait before washing his hands after touching these objects. This information could also be used as an index of change as treatment progressed.

Rating Scales Various types of procedures can be used to provide quantitative assessments of a person's behavior that are based on observations. One alternative is to use a **rating scale** in which the observer is asked to make judgments that place the person somewhere along a dimension. For example, a clinician might observe a person's behavior for an extended period of time and then complete a set of ratings that are concerned with dimensions such as the extent to which the person exhibits compulsive ritualistic behaviors.

Rating scales provide abstract descriptions of a person's behavior rather than a specific record of exactly what the person has done. They require social judgments on the part of the observer, who must compare this person's behavior with an ideal view of other people (Cairns & Green, 1979). How does this person compare to someone who has never experienced any difficulties in this particular area? How does the person compare to the most severely disturbed patients? The value of these judgments will depend, in large part, on the experience of the person who makes the ratings. They are useful to the extent that the observer is able to synthesize accurately the information that has been collected and then rate the frequency or severity of the problem relative to the behavior of other people.

Behavioral Coding Systems Another approach to the quantification of observational data depends on recording the person's actual activities. Rather than making judgments about where the person falls on a particular dimension, **behavioral coding systems**—also known as *formal observation schedules*—focus on the frequency of specific behavioral events (Foster & Cone, 1986). This type of observation therefore requires fewer inferences on the part of the observer. Coding systems can be used with observations that are made in the person's natural environment as well as with those that are performed in artificial, or contrived, situations that are specifically designed to elicit the problem behavior under circumstances in which it can be observed precisely. In some cases, the observations are made directly by a therapist, and at other times the information is provided by people who have a better opportunity to see the person's behavior in the natural environment, including teachers, parents, spouses, and peers.

▲ Direct observations can provide one of the most useful sources of information about a person's behavior. In this case, the children are being observed from behind a one-way mirror in order to minimize the effect that the observer's presence might have on their behavior.

Systematic observations are intended to provide a detailed record of the frequency of particular behaviors. This information is based on selective observations that are made during a given time interval. The formal record includes only those specific behaviors that have been identified as relevant. Efforts are also made to describe, as specifically as possible, the situation in which the behaviors are observed. These descriptions may include information regarding other people who are present and any events that happened just prior to or following the target behaviors.

Some approaches to systematic observation can be relatively simple. Consider, once again, the case of Michael. After the psychologist had conducted several interviews with Michael and his family, he asked Michael's mother to participate in the assessment process by making detailed observations of his hand-washing over a period of several nights. The mother was given a set of forms—one for each day—that could be used to record each incident, the time at which it occurred, and the circumstances that preceded the washing. The day was divided into 30-minute intervals starting at 6:30 A.M., when Michael got out of bed, and ending at 10:30, when he usually went to sleep. On each line (one for each time interval), his mother indicated whether he had washed his hands, what had been going on just prior to washing, and how anxious (on a scale from 1 to 100) Michael felt at the time that he washed.

Some adult clients are able to complete this kind of record by keeping track of their own behavior—a procedure known as *self-monitoring*. In this case, Michael's mother was asked to help because she was considered a more accurate observer and because Michael did not want to touch the form that would be used to record these observations. He believed that it was contaminated because it had touched his school clothes, which he wore to the therapy session.

Two weeks of observations were examined prior to the start of Michael's treatment. They indicated several things, including the times of the day when Michael was most active with his washing rituals (between 6 and 9 o'clock at night) and those specific objects and areas in the house that were most likely to trigger a washing incident. This information helped the therapist to plan the treatment procedure, which would depend on approaching his problem at the level that could most easily be handled and moving toward those situations that were the most difficult for him. The observations provided by Michael's mother were also used to mark his progress after treatment began.

More formal observational procedures are used in research studies. Detailed behavioral coding systems are typically employed in circumstances that lend themselves to the presence of observers, such as schools and hospitals. One excellent example of a sophisticated observational system is the Time-Sample Behavioral Checklist (TSBC), which was developed for use with severely disturbed patients in psychiatric hospitals (Paul & Lentz, 1977; Power, 1979). The TSBC provides for the observation of 69 specific behaviors, including both appropriate and inappropriate behaviors (such as bizarre behaviors, incoherent speech, verbal aggression). For each behavior, the observer notes contextual factors such as the patient's physical location, posture, and facial expression. The system allows an observer to monitor sequentially all of the patients on a particular hospital ward, with each patient being observed for a 2-second interval. It takes about 30 seconds to record that person's behavior and the context in which it occurred, and then the observer moves on to the next patient.

Some research projects have used this system to record patients' behavior on an hourly basis throughout the day, 7 days a week (Paul & Lentz, 1977). A system like the TSBC can provide an enormous amount of very detailed information that can be used as individual scores or compiled to produce overall indices of disturbance (Spaulding, 1986).

Advantages Observational measures, including rating scales and more detailed behavioral coding systems, can provide an extremely useful supplement to information that is typically collected in an interview format. Their advantage lies primarily in the fact that they can provide a more direct source of information than interviews can, because clinicians observe behavior directly rather than relying on patients' self-reports (Foster & Cone, 1986; Gottman, 1985). Specific types of observational measures have distinct advantages.

1. Rating scales are primarily useful as an overall index of symptom severity or

functional impairment.

2. Behavioral coding systems provide detailed information about the person's behavior in a particular situation.

Limitations Observations are sometimes considered to be analogous to photographs: They provide a more direct or realistic view of behavior than do people's recollections of their actions and feelings. But just as the quality of a photograph is influenced by the quality of the camera, the film, and the process that is used to develop it, the value of observational data depends on the procedures that are used to collect them (Nietzel, Bernstein, & Milich, 1994).

1. Observational procedures can be time-consuming and therefore expensive. Raters usually require extensive training before they can use a detailed behavioral coding system.
2. Observers can make errors. Their perception may be biased, just as the inferences of an interviewer may be biased. The reliability of ratings as well as behavioral coding must be monitored.
3. People may alter their behavior, either intentionally or unintentionally, when they know that they are being observed. This phenomenon is known as **reactivity.** In other words, the way in which the person reacts to the presence of an observer may cause a change such that the observation is not a meaningful sample of the person's behavior in the absence of an observer. For example, a person who is asked to count the number of times that he washes his hands may wash less frequently than he does when he is not keeping track.
4. Observational measures tell us only about the particular situation that was selected to be observed. We don't know if the person will behave in a similar way elsewhere or at a different time, unless we extend the scope of our observations.
5. There are some aspects of psychopathology that cannot be observed by anyone other than the person who has the problem (Jacobson, 1985). This is especially true for subjective experiences such as guilt or low self-esteem.

PERSONALITY TESTS AND SELF-REPORT INVENTORIES

Personality tests represent another important source of information about an individual's adjustment. Tests provide an opportunity to collect *samples* of a person's behavior in a *standardized* situation. These samples of behavior presumably reflect underlying abilities or personality traits. In any psychological test, the person who is being tested is presented with some kind of standard stimuli. The stimuli may be specific questions that can be answered "true" or "false." They might be problems that require solutions, or they can be completely ambiguous inkblots. Exactly the same stimuli are used every time that the test is given. In that way, we can be sure that differences in performance can be interpreted as differences in abilities or traits rather than differences in the testing situation.

The psychologist observes peoples' responses in the test situation and draws inferences or makes predictions about how they will behave in other situations. For example, achievement tests present students with a series of mathematical and verbal problems. Performance on these standardized problems is taken as a reflection of the amount of learning that has taken place and is also used to predict how well the student will do in future academic situations. Performance on the test itself is not important for its own sake, but only as a reflection of the amount of knowledge that the student has acquired.

Personality Inventories Because of their structure, **personality inventories** are sometimes referred to as "objective tests." They consist of a series of straightforward statements; the person being tested is typically required to indicate whether each statement is true or false in relation to himself or herself. Several types of personality inventories are used widely. Some are designed to identify personality traits in a normal population, and others focus more specifically on psychopathological problems. We have chosen to focus on the most extensively used personality inventory—the Minnesota Multiphasic Personality Inventory (MMPI)—to illustrate the characteristics of these tests as assessment devices.

The original version of the MMPI was developed in the 1940s at the University of Minnesota by Starke Hathaway (1903–1984) and his colleagues. For the past 30 or 40 years, it has been the most widely used psychological test. Thousands of research articles have been published on the MMPI (Archer, 1992). A revised version of the MMPI, known as the MMPI-2, has also been developed (Graham, 1990; Greene, 1991). Some psychologists still prefer to use the original version of the MMPI because the extensive body of research evidence that has accumulated over the past 50 years is based on that version. It may take several years before people are able to untangle all of the similarities and differences between the two versions (Helmes & Reddon, 1993).

The MMPI and the MMPI-2 are based on a series of more than 500 statements that cover topics ranging from physical complaints and psychological states to occupational preferences and social attitudes. Examples are statements such as "I sometimes keep on at a thing until others lose their patience with me"; "My feelings are easily hurt"; and "There are persons who are trying to steal my thoughts and ideas." After reading each statement, the person is instructed to indicate whether it is true or false.

Scoring of the MMPI is objective. After totaling the responses to all questions, the person receives a numerical score on each of ten clinical scales as well as four validity scales. These scores are plotted as a profile with lines connecting the scores obtained for each particular scale. We will return to a consideration of the profile's interpretation after describing a few important features of the MMPI items and scales.

Items were selected for inclusion in the MMPI on the basis of extensive preliminary testing. The responses of normal subjects were compared to those of various groups of psychiatric patients. For example, the criterion group that was used in the original selection of items for Scale 2 (Depression) was composed of 50 hospitalized depressed patients. The frequency of "true" and "false" responses was tabulated for normal and depressed people. Items were retained for inclusion in Scale 2 if there was a significant difference in frequency of response between the criterion group and the normal reference group. Further scale refinement was based on comparisons with additional samples of normal subjects as well as a consideration of overlap with other scales. During the recent revision of the MMPI, some items were deleted or changed if their content had become archa-

ic or obsolete. New norms were established on the basis of testing normal subjects who were more representative of the general population than were those who had participated in the original testing.

Before considering the possible clinical significance of a person's MMPI profile, the psychologist will examine a number of *validity scales*, which reflect the patient's attitude toward the test and as well as the openness and consistency with which the questions were answered. The L (Lie) Scale is sensitive to unsophisticated attempts to avoid answering in a frank and honest manner. For example, one statement on this scale says, "At times I feel like swearing." Although this is perhaps not an admirable trait, virtually all normal subjects indicate that the item is true. Subjects who indicate that the item is false (does not apply to them) receive one point on the L scale. Several responses of this sort would result in an elevated score on the scale and would indicate that the person's overall test results should not be interpreted as a true reflection of his or her feelings. Other validity scales reflect tendencies to exaggerate problems, carelessness in completing the questions, and unusual defensiveness.

If the profile is considered valid, the process of interpretation will be directed toward the ten clinical scales, which are described in Table 4–7. Some of these scales carry rather obvious meaning, whereas others are associated with a more general or mixed pattern of symptoms. For example, Scale 2 (Depression) is a relatively straightforward index of degree of depression. Scale 7 (psychasthenia), in contrast, is more complex and is based on items that measure anxiety, insecurity, and excessive doubt. There are many different ways to obtain an elevated score on any of the clinical scales, because each scale is composed of many items. The schizophrenia scale, for example, is based on 78 items, and a person who endorses any 20 of these statements in a deviant direction will receive an elevated score. Therefore, even the more obvious scales can indicate several different types of problems, and the pattern of scale scores is more important than the elevation of any particular scale.

Many clinicians interpret MMPI profiles using an **actuarial** procedure. Rather than depending on only their own experience and clinical judgment, which may be subject to various sorts of bias and inconsistency, clinicians

▲ Starke Hathaway, professor of psychology at the University of Minnesota, created the Minnesota Multiphasic Personality Inventory (MMPI), which has become the most widely employed objective test of personality.

analyze the results of a specific test on the basis of an explicit set of rules that are derived from empirical research. We can illustrate this process using Michael's profile. The profile is first described in terms of the pattern of scale scores, beginning with the highest and proceeding to the lowest. Those that are elevated above a scale score of 70 are most important, and interpretations are sometimes based on the "high-point pair." Following this procedure, Michael's profile could be coded as a 2–0; that is, his highest scores were on scales 2 and 0. The clinician then looks up this specific configuration of scores in a kind of MMPI "cookbook" to see what kinds of descriptive characteristics apply. One cookbook offers the following statement about adolescents (mostly 14 and 15 years old) who fit the 2-0/0-2 code type:

> Eighty-seven percent of the 2–0/0–2s express feelings of inferiority to their therapists. They say that they are not good-looking, that they are afraid to speak up in class, and that they feel awkward when they meet people or try to make a date (91% of high 2–0/0–2s). Their therapists see the 2–0/0–2s as anxious, fearful, timid, withdrawn, and inhibited. They are depressed, and very vulnerable to threat. The 2–0/0–2 adolescents are over-controlled; they cannot let go, even when it would be appropriate for them to do so. They are afraid of emotional involvement with others and, in fact, seem to have little need for such affiliation. These adolescents are viewed by their psychotherapists as schizoid; they think and associate in unusual ways and spend a good deal of time in personal fantasy and daydreaming. They are serious young people who tend to anticipate problems and difficulties. Indeed, they are prone toward obsessional thinking and are compulsively meticulous. (Marks, Seeman, & Haller, 1974, p. 201)

Several comments must be made about this statement. First, nothing is certain. Actuarial descriptions are probability statements. They indicate that a certain proportion of the people who produce this pattern of scores will be associated with a certain characteristic or behavior. If 87 percent of the adolescents who produce this code type express feelings of inferiority, 13 percent do not. Many aspects of this description apply to Michael's current adjustment, but they

TABLE 4–7

Clinical Scales for the MMPI

Scale Number	Scale Name	Interpretation of High Scores
1	Hypochondriasis	Excessive bodily concern; somatic symptoms
2	Depression	Depressed; pessimistic; irritable; demanding
3	Hysteria	Physical symptoms of functional origin; self-centered; demands attention
4	Psychopathic Deviate	Asocial or antisocial; rebellious; impulsive, poor judgment
5	Masculinity-Femininity	Male: aesthetic interests Female: assertive; competitive; self-confident
6	Paranoia	Suspicious; sensitive; resentful; rigid; may be frankly psychotic
7	Psychasthenia	Anxious; worried; obsessive; lacks self-confidence; problems in decision-making
8	Schizophrenia	May have thinking disturbance, withdrawn; feels alienated and unaccepted
9	Hypomania	Excessive activity; lacks direction; low frustration tolerance; friendly
0	Social Introversion	Socially introverted; shy; sensitive; overcontrolled; conforming

don't all fit. Second, the 2–0/0–2 code type represents only one aspect of the test results. In Michael's case, the elevation on scales 8 and 5 was also prominent. Unfortunately, cookbooks often don't include code types that are that detailed, and the clinician must attempt to piece together descriptions from close approximations. Third, any profile can be interpreted in several ways (Greene, 1991).

The MMPI must be used in conjunction with other assessment procedures. The accuracy of actuarial statements can be verified through interviews with the person or through direct observations of his or her behavior.

Advantages The MMPI has several advantages in comparison to interviews and observational procedures. In clinical practice, it is seldom used by itself, but, for the following reasons, it can serve as a useful supplement to other methods of collecting information.

1. The MMPI provides information about the person's test-taking attitude, which alerts the clinician to the possibility that clients are careless, defensive, or exaggerating their problems.
2. The MMPI covers a wide range of problems in a direct and efficient manner. It would take a clinician several hours to go over all of these topics using an interview format.
3. Because the MMPI is scored objectively, the initial description of the person's adjustment is not influenced by the clinician's subjective impression of the client.
4. The MMPI can be interpreted in an actuarial fashion, using extensive banks of information regarding people who respond to items in a particular way.

Limitations The MMPI also has a number of limitations. Some of its problems derive from the fact that it has been used for many years. When the MMPI-2 was developed in the late 1980s, its authors decided to maintain the same clinical scales (see Table 4-7). New standardization data were obtained, and some old-fashioned items were replaced, but the underlying structure of the MMPI-2 is still based on diagnostic concepts and dimensions of psychopathology that were used 40 years ago (Helmes & Reddon, 1993). More specific limitations of the MMPI are listed below.

1. The test is not particularly sensitive to certain forms of psychopathology, especially those that have been added with the publication of DSM-III and DSM-IV. These include certain types of anxiety disorders, personality disorders, and subtypes of mood disorders.
2. The test depends on the person's ability to read and respond to written statements. Some people cannot complete the rather extensive list of questions.

These include many people who are acutely psychotic, intellectually impaired, or poorly educated.
3. Specific data are not always available for a particular profile. Many patients' test results do not meet criteria for a particular code type with which extensive data are associated. Therefore, actuarial interpretation is not really possible for these profiles.
4. Some studies have found that profile types are not stable over time. It is not clear whether this instability should be interpreted as lack of reliability or as sensitivity to change in the person's level of adjustment.

Other Self-Report Inventories Sophisticated personality inventories like the MMPI are not the only approach to the measurement of subjective psychological states. Many other questionnaires and checklists have been developed to collect information about adjustment problems including subjective mood states such as depression and anxiety; patterns of obsessive thinking; and attitudes about drinking alcohol, eating, and sexual behavior. One example is the Beck Depression Inventory (BDI), which is used extensively in both clinical and research settings as an index of severity of depression. Sample items from the BDI are presented in Table 4–8.

The format of most *self-report inventories* is similar to that employed with objective personality tests like the MMPI. The primary difference is the range of topics covered by the instrument. Tests like the MMPI are designed to measure several dimensions that are related to abnormal behavior, while a self-report inventory is aimed more specifically at a focal topic or at one aspect of the person's adjustment. Self-report inventories usually don't include validity scales, and they may be based on less extensive research evidence. In other words, they may not be standardized on large samples of normal subjects prior to their use in a clinical setting.

Self-report inventories offer many advantages as supplements to information that is collected during clinical interviews. They are an extremely efficient way to gather specific data regarding a wide range of topics. They can also be scored objectively and, therefore, provide a specific index that is frequently useful in measuring change from one period of time to the next—for example, before and after treatment.

Despite their many advantages, self-report inventories can lead to serious problems if they are used carelessly. One striking example centers around the use of checklists for diagnostic purposes. The BDI and the Hopkins Symptom Checklist (SCL-90) were both designed as indices of change. Unfortunately, many investigators and clinicians have erroneously decided to use them for diagnostic purposes. The problems that can arise as a result of this practice are described in the Research Close-up.

Projective Personality Tests In **projective tests**, the person is presented with a series of ambiguous stimuli. The best-known projective test, introduced in 1921 by Hermann Rorschach (1884–1922), a Swiss psychiatrist, is based on the use of inkblots. The *Rorschach test* consists of a series of ten inkblots. Five contain various shades of gray on a white background, and five others contain elements of color. The person is asked to look at each card and indicate what it looks like or what it appears to be. There are, of course, no correct answers. The instructions are intentionally vague in order to avoid influencing the person's responses through subtle suggestions.

Projective techniques such as the Rorschach test were originally based on psychodynamic assumptions about the nature of personality and psychopathology. Considerable emphasis was placed on the importance of unconscious motivations—conflicts and impulses of which the person is largely unaware. In other words, people being tested presumably *project* hidden desires and conflicts when they try to describe or explain the cards. In so doing, they may reveal things about themselves of which they are not consciously aware or that they might not be willing to admit if they were asked directly. The cards are not designed or chosen to be realistic or representational; they presumably look like whatever the person wants them to look like.

Michael did not actually complete any projective personality tests. We can illustrate the way in which these tests might have been used in his case, however, by considering another man, who had been given a diagnosis of obsessive–compulsive disorder on Axis I as well as showing evidence of two types of personality disorder, dependent and schizotypal features. This patient

was 22 years old, unemployed, and living with his mother. His father had died in an accident 4 years earlier. Like Michael, this man was bothered by intrusive thoughts of contamination, and

TABLE 4–8

Sample Items from the Beck Depression Inventory

A. Sadness
0 I do not feel sad
1 I feel sad
2 I am sad all the time and I can't snap out of it
3 I am so sad or unhappy that I can't stand it

B. Pessimism
0 I am not particularly discouraged about the future
1 I feel discouraged about the future
2 I feel I have nothing to look forward to
3 I feel that the future is hopeless and that things cannot improve

C. Sense of Failure
0 I do not feel like a failure
1 I feel I have failed more than the average person
2 As I look back on my life, all I can see is a lot of failures
3 I feel I am a complete failure as a person

D. Dissatisfaction
0 I get as much satisfaction out of things as I used to
1 I don't enjoy things the way I used to
2 I don't get real satisfaction out of anything any more
3 I am dissatisfied or bored with everything

he frequently engaged in compulsive washing (Hurt, Reznikoff, & Clarkin, 1991). His responses to the cards on the Rorschach frequently mentioned emotional distress ("a man screaming"), interpersonal conflict ("two women fighting over something"), and war ("two mushrooms of a nuclear bomb cloud"). He did not incorporate color into any of his responses to the cards.

The original procedures for scoring the Rorschach were largely impressionistic and placed considerable emphasis on the content of the person's response. Responses given in the example above might be taken to suggest a number of important themes. Aggression and violence are obvious possibilities. Perhaps the man was repressing feelings of hostility, as indicated by his frequent references to war and conflict. These themes were coupled with a guarded approach to emotional reactions, which is presumably reflected by his avoidance of color. The psychologist might have wondered whether the man felt guilty about something, such as his father's death. This kind

Identifying Mood Disorders:
Clinical Interviews versus Self-Report Inventories

How should we identify cases of depression? The answer to this question is crucial to several areas of research. Consider, for example, epidemiological surveys in which the investigators hope to identify those individuals within a given population who suffer from mood disorders. This is also a fundamental problem in laboratory research. Anyone hoping to examine psychological or biological correlates of a depressed mood must be able to distinguish people who are depressed from those who are not.

In treatment settings, the most widely accepted procedure for identifying cases of depression depends on the use of structured interviews in combination with specific diagnostic criteria. A trained and experienced professional asks the person about his or her recent experiences. Based on the person's answers and on observations of his or her behavior during the interview, the clinician decides whether the person fits within a particular diagnostic category, using specific criteria such as those listed in DSM-IV. This approach is very widely accepted, but it is also expensive and time-consuming.

As an alternative to traditional interviews, many investigators have chosen to rely on the person's subjective rating of symptoms on a self-report scale such as the Beck Depression Inventory (BDI). Originally designed as an index of severity, the BDI consists of 21 items, covering cognitive, affective, motivational, and somatic symptoms of depression (see Table 4-8). The more items to which a person answers "yes," the higher the person's BDI score, and therefore the more severe the depression.

Several studies have raised serious questions about the validity of self-report scales when they are used for diagnostic purposes. Self-report scales sometimes fail to identify patients who are considered depressed on the basis of a clinical interview. One investigation found that more than one-third of all subjects who were considered "not depressed" on the basis of the self-report scale were diagnosed

TABLE 4-9

Number of People Identified as Being Depressed on the Basis of DSM-III Criteria and the Beck Depression Inventory (BDI)

DSM-III Diagnosis	Low BDI Cutoff Score	
	Depressed ($\geq$10)	Not Depressed (0–9)
Depressed	21	0
Not Depressed	38	239

DSM-III Diagnosis	High BDI Cutoff Score	
	Depressed ($\geq$22)	Not Depressed (<22)
Depressed	10	11
Not Depressed	4	273

Adapted from J.M. Oliver and M.E. Simmons. 1984. Depression as measured by the DSM-III and the Beck Depression Inventory in an unselected adult population. *Journal of Consulting and Clinical Psychology, 52,* 892–898.

as being depressed after a mental status interview (Myers & Weissman, 1980).

In fact, the relationship between the BDI and diagnoses based on interviews and clinical ratings depends on the cutoff score that is used with the BDI. Oliver and Simmons (1984) administered a standard diagnostic interview as well as the BDI to a random sample of 298 adults. Their results are presented in Table 4-9. When Oliver and Simmons used-DSM-III criteria with information provided during the interview, they diagnosed 21 people (7 percent of the sample) as being depressed. In contrast, when they used a relatively low cutoff score of 10 or greater on the BDI, 59 people were identified as being depressed (20 percent of the sample). This group included all of the people who were considered depressed on the basis of DSM-III. The sensitivity of the BDI was

100 percent when using a relatively low cutoff score. Specificity was also relatively high at 86 percent. Unfortunately, because the BDI included 38 people who *did not* meet DSM-III criteria for a depressive disorder (false positives), the positive predictive power of the test was only 36 percent.

What if a higher cutoff score were used? Would that eliminate the false positives and leave only the more serious cases? Unfortunately, it would not. Using a higher cutoff score of 22 or greater on the BDI, Oliver and Simmons identified 14 people as being depressed. Of these 14 people, 10 also met DSM-III criteria; 4 were false positives. Positive predictive power was improved to 71 percent, but the sensitivity of the test fell off to only 48 percent. This cutoff score missed 11 of the 21 people who were considered depressed by DSM-III criteria. Higher cutoff scores clearly don't solve the problem.

How should we interpret these data? Do they mean that self-report inventories are not useful? Obviously not. In the Oliver and Simmons study, the diagnostic efficiency of the BDI was 89 percent at the low cutoff scores and 95 percent at the high cutoff scores. The evidence also indicates, however, that self-report measures do not always agree with clinicians' ratings based on diagnostic interviews. One reason for this discrepancy is the fact that some depressed patients consider themselves to be less depressed than they appear to a clinician when they are interviewed (Sayer et al., 1993).

The BDI can provide a useful index of *severity* among patients who have been diagnosed as being depressed. It can also be used (particularly with relatively low cutoff scores) to screen large samples of subjects to identify those most likely to be considered depressed on the basis of a clinical interview. On the other hand, it is a serious mistake to assume that anyone who appears to be depressed on the basis of a self-report inventory would necessarily be diagnosed as being depressed after a clinical interview. ■

of interpretation, which depends heavily on symbolism and clinical inference, provides intriguing material for the clinician to puzzle over. Unfortunately, the reliability and validity of this intuitive type of scoring procedure is very low (Shontz & Green, 1992).

When we ponder the utility of these interpretations, we should also keep in mind the relative efficiency of projective testing procedures. Did the test tell us anything that we didn't already know or that we couldn't have learned in a more straightforward manner? Consider the following story, told by Robyn Dawes, a psychologist at Carnegie Mellon University:

I once tested a very depressed man who responded to the first blot that "it looks like a bat that has been squashed on the pavement under the heel of a giant's boot." Wow! A confabulated response indicative of extreme depression and feelings of being overwhelmed and crushed by forces beyond one's control. What response could possibly have been more "one-down"? The fact that the man was obviously depressed led me to believe in the validity of the Rorschach at that point. I realized only later that I already knew that he was depressed and hence that the response provided me with no new information whatsoever." (Dawes, 1994, p. 149)

In this young man's case, the clinician might have become aware of his feelings of anger or guilt through clinical interviews, which would be a more direct and efficient way of collecting information.

More recent approaches to the use of projective tests view the person's descriptions of the cards as a sample of his or her perceptual and cognitive styles. Psychologist John Exner has developed an objective scoring procedure for the Rorschach that is based primarily on the form rather than the content of the subject's responses (Exner, 1986; Kleiger, 1992). According to Exner's system, interpretation of the test depends on the way in which the descriptions take into account the shapes and colors on the

▼ Projective tests require a person to respond to ambiguous stimuli. Here, a woman is taking the Thematic Apperception Test (TAT), in which she will be asked to make up a story about a series of drawings of people.

cards. Does the person see movement in the card? Does she focus on tiny details, or does she base her descriptions on global impressions of the entire form of the inkblot? These and many other considerations contribute to the overall interpretation of the Rorschach test. The reliability of this scoring system is better than would be achieved by informal, impressionistic procedures. The validity of the scores, however, remains open to question (Davis, 1978; Shontz & Green, 1992).

There are many different types of projective tests. Some employ stimuli that are somewhat less ambiguous than the inkblots in the Rorschach. The Thematic Apperception Test (TAT), for example, consists of a series of drawings that depict human figures in various ambiguous situations. Most of the cards portray more than one person. The figures and their poses tend to elicit stories with themes of sadness and violence. The person is asked to describe the identities of the people in the cards and to make up a story about what is happening. These stories presumably reflect the person's own ways of perceiving reality.

To illustrate the way in which the TAT is used, consider once again the man whose Rorschach responses were described above. His TAT stories reflected a preoccupation with death as well as the disruptive consequences for those who tried, usually unsuccessfully, to cope with such a loss. For example, the following was his response to a picture in which a young man is seen standing next to an older woman who appears to be looking out of a window.

A mother and son are really, really close, especially since her husband died. His father. And he lives right near her now that he's grown up, and takes care of her. And one day he finds out that because of his job he has to move away. He decides—and when he tells her here, he's really saddened, and she's shocked and depressed and confused, and doesn't know what she's gonna do. He finally moves away and she seems to adjust, but he doesn't like being away from his home

and he really misses his mother. So eventually he moves back to—home—quits his job, and moves back home. And even though he can't make as much money and things like that, he's a lot happier being home. (Hurt, Reznikoff, & Clarkin, 1991, p. 293)

The clinicians inferred from this and his other responses to the TAT as well as the results of the Rorschach that this man was afraid that he would not be able to cope with the difficulties associated with moving out of his mother's home. They recommended that treatment would need to address the considerable anger that he felt toward his parents. Again, it seems reasonable to ask whether this conclusion might also have been reached on the basis of interviews with the man and his mother, without the use of projective tests.

Advantages The advantages of projective tests center on the fact that the tests are interesting to give and interpret and they sometimes provide a way to talk to people who are otherwise reluctant or unable to discuss their problems. Projective tests are more appealing to psychologists who adopt a psychodynamic view of personality and psychopathology. Some specific advantages are listed below.

1. Some people may feel more comfortable talking in an unstructured situation than they would if they were required to participate in a structured interview or to complete the lengthy MMPI.
2. Projective tests can provide an interesting source of information regarding the person's unique view of the world.
3. To whatever extent a person's relationships with other people are governed by *unconscious* cognitive and emotional events, projective tests may provide information that cannot be obtained through direct interviewing methods or observational procedures (Stricker & Healey, 1990).

Limitations There are many serious problems with the use of projective tests. The popularity of projective tests has declined considerably since the 1970s, even in clinical settings, primarily because research studies have found little evidence to support their reliability and validity (Dawes, 1994; Wierzbicki, 1993).

1. Lack of standardization in administration and scoring are serious problems, even though Exner's system for the Rorschach has made some improvements in that regard.

2. Little information is available to use as norms for either adults or children.

3. Some projective procedures, such as the Rorschach, can be very time-consuming, particularly if the person's responses are scored with a standardized procedure such as Exner's system.

4. The reliability of scoring and interpretation tends to be low.

5. Information regarding the validity of projective tests is primarily negative (see Dawes, 1994).

Assessment of Social Systems

The same range of procedures that we have discussed for the assessment of person variables (psychological systems) can also be used to examine situation variables (social systems). For example, clinical interviews can be used to describe the client's family and social environment, both past and present. In Michael's case, the psychologist was interested in Michael's social relationships with classmates as well as his interactions with his parents. His father indicated that he was quite concerned about Michael's problems and that he was willing to help as they planned a treatment procedure that would allow Michael to learn to cope more effectively with his obsessive thoughts about contamination. Michael's mother also told the psychologist that arguments between Michael and his father often seemed to trigger an increase in the frequency of his compulsive washing rituals. This information convinced the psychologist that Michael's treatment should focus on improving his relationship with his father and not just on his compulsive washing.

Clinicians have developed structured as well as informal interviews to assess the social and emotional climate within families. One example is the Camberwell Family Interview (CFI), a measure of expressed emotion or EE (see Chapter 12) that has been used extensively in studying families in which one of the members has a serious mental disorder, especially schizophrenia or depression (Hooley, 1986). Questions in the CFI are designed to elicit comments from the patient's parents or spouse that reflect their own attitudes and feelings about the patient's behavior. It is therefore an index of the emotional climate of the home that is based primarily on whether the person expresses a significant level of criticism or hostility toward the patient. Patients who return to high-EE homes after being discharged from a psychiatric hospital are much more likely to experience another episode of disorder within the next few months than are patients who live in a more tolerant family environment.

Many self-report inventories, rating scales, and behavioral coding systems have been designed for the assessment of marital relationships and family systems. One popular self-report inventory is the Family Environment Scale (FES), which is composed of 90 true–false items and was designed to measure the social characteristics of families (Moos, 1974, 1981). The scale is composed of 10 subscales that are aimed at three dimensions of the family: *relationships* (cohesion, expressiveness, and conflicts); *personal growth* (independence, achievement orientation, intellectual–cultural orientation, active–recreational orientation, and moral–religious emphasis); and *system maintenance* (organization and control). Extensive testing with large numbers of families has been used to establish norms on the FES for distressed and nondistressed families. The FES has been used widely in clinical settings and in research studies. Unfortunately, evidence regarding test–retest reliability and the validity of the subscales is not impressive (L'Abate & Bagarozzi, 1993).

Direct observations can also be used to assess the social climate within a family. The Family Interaction Coding System (FICS) was developed by Gerald Patterson and John Reid, clinical psychologists at the Oregon Research Institute, for the purpose of observing interactions between parents and children in their homes (Jones, Reid, & Patterson, 1975; Reid, 1978). A trained observer visits the family's home and collects information for at least 70 minutes just prior to lunch or dinner. Everyone in the family must be present during this time period, and they must stay in a two-room area. For each 5-minute block of time, the observer focuses on two members of the family and describes their behavior, using the coding system. The observer rotates his or her attention from one "target" to the next throughout the observation period.

The FICS code includes 29 non-mutually-exclusive categories that are used to describe a single interaction between two members of the family. These include behaviors such as: approval; attention; command; compliance; cry; disapproval; destructiveness; humiliate; ignore; laugh; play; physical negative; physical positive; talk; tease; touch; whine; and yell. Standards have been published for normal boys and girls as well as for children who have been treated for conduct disorders and aggression.

Trained raters can achieve high levels of reliability with the FICS. In addition, a number of research studies have demonstrated that it is a valid measure of aggressive behaviors in children as well as a useful way to assess the family context in which these behaviors occur. It can distinguish between the families of children with antisocial behavior or conduct disorders and nondisturbed families. The FICS is also a useful clinical tool that is sensitive to changes that occur during the course of family treatment (Grotevant & Carlson, 1989). The main disadvantage of this coding system is that the process of training observers is expensive and the collection of data is time-consuming. Remember also that a number of other limitations, such as reactivity and generalizability, are generally associated with direct observational measures.

Assessment of Biological Systems

In addition to psychological and social factors, biological factors affect human behavior. Clinicians have developed a number of techniques for measuring the behavioral effects of biological systems. These techniques are seldom used in clinical practice (at least for the diagnosis of psychopathology), but they have been used extensively in research settings, and it seems possible that they will one day become an important source of information regarding individual patients.

PSYCHOPHYSIOLOGICAL ASSESSMENT

Changes in physiological response systems, such as heart rate, respiration rate, and skin conductance, provide another important source of information regarding a person's psychological adjustment. The basic components of the human nervous system have already been reviewed in Chapter 2. They include the central nervous system (CNS) and the peripheral nervous system (PNS). The PNS is subdivided into two parts: the somatic nervous system and the autonomic nervous system. The *somatic nervous system* is responsible for communicating back and forth between the brain and external sense receptors as well as regulating voluntary muscle movements. The *autonomic nervous system* is responsible for body processes that occur without conscious awareness, such as heart rate. It maintains equilibrium in the internal environment.

The autonomic nervous system is highly reactive to environmental events and can provide useful information about a person's internal states, such as emotion (Kozak & Miller, 1992). Recording procedures have been developed to measure variables such as respiration rate, heart rate, and skin conductance. Table 4–10 summarizes some of the most important psychophysiological responses. As the person becomes aroused, the activity of these systems changes. Psychophysiological measures can therefore provide sensitive indices of the person's internal state.

It must be emphasized, however, that all of these measures do not act together. The concept of general arousal was abandoned many years ago (for example, Lacey, 1967; Lang, 1971). If several physiological responses are measured at the same time, they may not all demonstrate the same strength, or even direction, of response. Moreover, physiological measures frequently disagree with the person's own subjective report. Therefore, as with other assessment procedures, physiological recordings should be used in conjunction with other measures. They represent supplements to, rather than substitutes for, the other types of measures that we have already considered (Iacono, 1991).

Anxiety disorders represent one type of problem in which psychophysiological measurements have been employed (Turpin, 1991). Let's consider Michael's case again. He was afraid to touch contaminated objects in his house. If he had been forced to do so, it is likely that his heart rate would have increased dramatically. Psychophysiological events of this sort can be monitored precisely. To the extent that the clinician might be in need of information that would confirm data from other sources (observation, self-report) or that could be used to measure changes in the person's response to particular stimuli in the environment, physiological measurements may be quite useful.

Physiological measurements have been employed extensively in the study of sexual arousal and in the treatment of sexual disorders (Freund & Watson, 1991; see Chapter 11). In both men and women, sexual arousal is associated with the engorgement of genital tissue with blood, which

as the *vaginal plethysmograph*, is used to measure sexual arousal in women. This device, which is shaped like a tampon, is inserted into the vagina and records changes in blood flow using a tiny photocell.

In the case of several types of abnormal behavior, physiological assessment procedures are being used in the search for meaningful sub-

TABLE 4–10

Characteristics of Biological Response Systems and Psychophysiological Measurement Procedures

Response System	Psychophysiological Response	Basis of Response
Cardiovascular	Electrocardiogram (EKG)	Action potential of cardiac muscle during contraction
	Blood Pressure (BP)	Systolic: Force of blood leaving the heart Diastolic: Residual pressure in the vascular system
Electrodermal	Skin Resistance Level (SRL) and Response (SRR); Skin Conductance Level (SCL) and Response (SCR)	Source of signal is uncertain; current theories favor sweat gland activity
Central Nervous System	Electroencephalogram (EEG)	Electrical activity of cortical neurons
	Average Evoked Response (AER) & Event-Related Potential (ERP)	Same as EEG in response to specific stimulus
	Contingent Negative Variation (CNV)	Same as EEG, appears during preparatory responses
Specialized Responses	Sexual (plethysmograph)	Engorgement of genital tissue with blood
	Respiration rate	Inhalation and exhalation of air
	Rapid Eye Movements (REM) sleep latency	Latency to onset of pattern associated with dreaming
	Smooth Pursuit Eye Movements (SPEM)	Visual tracking of an oscillating, pendulum-like stimulus

Source: Adapted from W.M. Kallman, & M.J. Feuerstein (1986), p. 329.

causes erection in the male and lubrication in the female. Scientists have developed electronic recording devices that can measure these responses precisely. The *penile plethysmograph*, an index of male sexual arousal, is used to measure changes in the circumference of the penis. A thin rubber tube, filled with mercury, is placed over the penis and connected to an electronic device known as a polygraph. As the man becomes sexually aroused, the tube stretches and the electrical resistance inside the tube changes. A similar device, known

types of mental disorders. One example is the use of EEG recordings to assess the latency between sleep onset and onset of rapid eye-movement (REM) sleep among people who are depressed (Kupfer & Thase, 1989). Many depressed people show a relatively rapid onset of REM sleep, and this pattern may be associated with poor response to treatment. Another area in which physiological recordings have produced promising results is in the investigation of smooth-pursuit eye movements (SPEM) of schizophrenic patients and their relatives (Iacono, 1991). Considerable speculation currently surrounds the notion that impaired eye tracking may be associated with a predisposition or genetically determined vulnerability to schizophrenia (see Chapter 12).

Physiological assessments have also been used in studies concerned with patterns of marital interaction and divorce. These measures provide an interesting perspective on the emotional responses of both marital partners. Husbands and wives who are dissatisfied with their marriages experience higher levels of negative emotion. In assessments conducted during interactions that are contrived in the laboratory, husbands often exhibit physiological responses such as changes in heart rate and skin conductance that indicate intense arousal, but these feelings are not expressed in their verbal behavior. Men who show this response are more likely to be dissatisfied with their marriages, and their relationships are more likely to end in divorce (Gottman & Levenson, 1986, 1992). These data suggest that psychophysiological measures represent an important addition to the assessment of marital interactions.

Advantages Physiological procedures are not used frequently in clinical settings, but they are employed extensively in research on psychopathology. One clinical situation in which they are employed is in the assessment of sexual arousal, which is difficult or awkward to measure using direct observations and in which self-report measures are often questionable. These tools have several advantages in comparison to other assessment procedures.

1. Psychophysiological recording procedures do not depend on self-report and therefore may be less subject to voluntary control. People may be less likely to make the assessment show what they want it to show.
2. Some of these measures can be obtained while the subject is sleeping or while the subject is actively engaged in some other activity.

Limitations In addition to the fact that they require relatively sophisticated equipment and a technician who is trained in their use, physiological measures have a number of drawbacks.

1. The recording equipment and electrodes may be frightening or intimidating to some people.
2. There are generally low correlations between different autonomic response systems. It is not wise to arbitrarily select one specific physiological measure, such as heart rate, and assume that it is a direct index of arousal.
3. Physiological reactivity and the stability of physiological response systems vary from person to person. The measures may be informative for some people but not for others.
4. Physiological responses can be influenced by many other factors. Some are *person variables*, such as age and medication, as well as psychological factors such as being self-conscious or fearing loss of control (Anderson & McNeilly, 1991). Other important considerations are *situational variables*, such as extraneous noise and electrical activity.

BRAIN IMAGING TECHNIQUES

The past several decades have seen a tremendous explosion of information and technology in the neurosciences. We now understand in considerable detail how neurons in the central nervous system communicate with one another, and scientists have invented sophisticated methods to create images of the living human brain (see Andreasen, 1984). Some of these procedures provide static pictures of various brain structures at rest, just as an X-ray provides a photographic image of a bone or some other organ of the body. More recently, sophisticated methods have made it possible to create dynamic images of the brain while a person is performing different tasks.

Static Brain Imaging Many investigations of brain structure in people with various forms of psychopathology have employed an imaging technique known as *computerized tomographic (CT) scanning*. In CT scanning, X-ray beams are passed through the brain to a series of detectors that measure the density of the tissues through which the beams have passed. A series of two-dimensional images are created at sequential slices or planes of the brain by rotating the scanner around the body for the full 360 degrees. The amount of detail in the picture, or the quality of its resolution, depends on the thickness of the slices and the number of units in the grid. A more precise measure of brain structure can be obtained using a technique known as *magnetic resonance imaging (MRI)*. Both CT scanning and MRI provide a static image of specific brain structures.

Dynamic Brain Imaging In addition to CT-scan and MRI procedures, which provide a static view of brain structures, revolutionary advances in the neurosciences have also produced techniques that create images of brain functions. Unlike CT scanning, which is now available at most hospitals, the newer procedures are considered highly experimental, and they are quite expensive. Therefore, they are currently available only to a small number of investigators.

One of these procedures involves the measurement of *regional cerebral blood flow (rCBF)*. The subject inhales a radioactive tracer element that is taken up into the brain and then emits small particles of energy called *photons*. These photons can be collected and used to create an image of brain activity. Those regions of the brain that are active and in which metabolism is very high emit more photons and are assigned brighter colors in the image (for example, red). Less active areas emit fewer photons and are assigned cooler colors, such as blues and greens. Images can be generated while the subject is at rest or during the performance of a specific task. Visual stimulation will produce increased cerebral blood flow in the visual cortex; subjects performing a simple motor task exhibit increased flow in the motor cortex.

Another dynamic brain imaging technique is known as *positron emission tomography (PET) scanning*. This procedure is much more expensive than the other imaging techniques because it requires a nuclear cyclotron to produce special radioactive elements. PET scans are capable of providing very detailed images of the brain. In addition, like rCBF, they can reflect changes in brain activity as the person responds to the demands of various tasks.

Advantages Brain-imaging techniques provide detailed information regarding the structure of brain areas and activity levels in the brain that are associated with the performance of particular tasks.

Limitations Brain-imaging procedures are used extensively in the study and treatment of neurological disorders. In the field of psychopathology, they may lead to important discoveries in the near future. Nevertheless, at the present time, they are primarily research tools and have little clinical importance outside the assessment and treatment of disorders such as Alzheimer's disease (see Chapter 13). Some of the major limitations are listed below.

1. Norms have not been established for any of these measures. It is not possible to use brain-imaging procedures for diagnostic purposes.
2. These procedures are relatively expensive—especially PET scans—and some procedures must be used cautiously because the patient is exposed to radioactive substances.

▲ **Positron emission topography (PET scan) can provide useful images of dynamic brain functions. Areas that appear red or yellow indicate areas of the brain that are active (consuming the labeled glucose molecules), whereas those that are blue or green are relatively inactive. Different areas of the brain become active depending on whether the person is at rest or engaged in particular activities when the image is created.**

Summary

Formal **classification** systems for mental disorders have been developed in order to facilitate communication, research, and treatment planning. The current official system published by the American Psychiatric Association is the fourth edition of the *Diagnostic and Statistical Manual of Mental Disorders*, or DSM-IV. It is based on a categorical approach to mental disorders and typically employs **polythetic** criterion sets to define specific types of disorder. The categories that are defined in DSM-IV are based primarily on descriptive principles rather than on theoretical knowledge regarding the etiology of the disorders. Five axes are included in this system. Axes I and II are employed for describing mental disorders (personality disorders on Axis II). The remaining three axes are concerned with supplementary information that may also be useful in treatment planning.

KEY TERMS

- actuarial
- assessment
- behavioral coding systems
- categorical systems
- classification system
- diagnosis
- diagnostic efficiency
- dimensional systems
- exclusion criterion
- false negative
- false positive
- inclusion criterion
- kappa
- labeling theory
- monothetic class
- multiaxial
- personality inventories
- polythetic class
- positive predictive power
- projective tests
- rating scale
- reactivity
- reliability
- sensitivity
- specificity
- validity

The utility of a classification system depends on several criteria, including **reliability**, **validity**, and **coverage**. The reliability of many categories in DSM seems to have improved with the introduction of specific **inclusion criteria** and **exclusion criteria** in DSM-III. Nevertheless, serious questions remain about this issue. The reliability of some categories, such as the personality disorders, is still found to be marginal in many studies. Reliability is also likely to be diminished in clinical settings where clinicians are not experts in a particular disorder and reliability is not being monitored. The validity, or systematic meaning, of most categories is still under active investigation.

The general process of collecting and interpreting information is called **assessment**. Many different assessment tools can be used to generate information systematically. Interviews, observations, and tests are among the most frequently used procedures. These tools can be used for many purposes. Assessments can be directed toward biological, psychological, and social systems. In many cases, information is collected and integrated across more than one system, but it is never possible to learn everything about a particular person. Choices have to be made, and some information must be excluded from the analysis.

The utility of assessment procedures depends on their reliability and validity. One way to evaluate the validity of a test is to consider its **diagnostic efficiency**: Does the test allow a clinician to predict accurately whether the person has a particular characteristic or mental disorder? Precise answers to this question depend on the computation of the test's **sensitivity, specificity**, and **predictive power**.

Psychological systems are typically assessed using interviews, observations, or self-report inventories. Structured diagnostic interviews are used extensively in conjunction with the DSM-IV classification system. They can also form the basis for ratings of the person's adjustment on a number of dimensions. Interviews can also be used to collect additional information that is relevant to planning treatment. Their main advantage is their flexibility. Their primary limitation lies in the inability or unwillingness of some clients to provide a rational description of their own problems as well as the subjective factors that influence the clinician's interpretation of data collected in an interview.

Objective personality tests, like the MMPI, offer several advantages as supplements to interviews and observations. They can be scored objectively, they often contain validity scales that reflect the person's attitude and test-taking set, and they can be interpreted in reference to well-established standards for people with and without specific types of adjustment problems. The assessment of psychological systems typically involves collection and integration of data using all three types of procedures.

Social systems, including marital relationships and families, can be evaluated using interviews, observations, and self-report inventories.

Although the instruments that are used for this purpose have not been developed as extensively as those that are used to address psychological systems, they represent an important consideration in thinking about mental disorders and their treatment.

Many different tools are available for assessing biological systems related to mental disorders. These include psychophysiological recording procedures as well as brain-imaging techniques, such as CT scans, MRI, PET scans, and measurements of rCBF. Biological assessment procedures are used more extensively in research studies than in clinical settings.

Critical Thinking

1. Do we need a classification system in the field of psychopathology? If so, how should it be evaluated? What are the characteristics of a useful classification system? Should we expect that it will be based solely on scientific considerations?

2. What are some of the inherent limitations of a classification system? What are the trade-offs (advantages and disadvantages) associated with the process of psychiatric diagnosis? If there are problems, how can they be solved, or at least minimized?

3. How will your choice of an assessment procedure be influenced by the conceptual frame of reference that you adopt in thinking about a clinical problem? How will it be influenced by the nature of the specific problem that you are trying to address? Why isn't it possible to have a universal assessment battery that could be used consistently for all clinical problems?

LEAVE ME LEAVE ME LEAVE ME . .

ME LEAVE...

Mood Disorders

S ome of the simplest emotions require little description. We all know how it feels to be angry and how it feels to be sad. Most of our feelings are momentary—like the apprehension that grips us while watching a frightening movie, or the amusement we experience when listening to a comedian. Others can be relatively enduring, like the grief we may suffer when a close friend moves away. Most emotional fluctuations, including many that are unpleasant, represent part of normal experience. Unfortunately, some people experience extreme fluctuations in emotion that become persistent and severely debilitating.

Overview

Psychopathologists use several terms to describe problems that are associated with emotional response systems. **Emotion** refers to a state of arousal that is defined by subjective feeling states, such as sadness, anger, and disgust. Emotions are often accompanied by physiological changes, such as changes in heart rate and respiration rate. **Affect** refers to the pattern of observable behaviors that are associated with these subjective feelings. People express affect through changes in their facial expressions, the pitch of their voices, and their hand and body movements. **Mood** refers to a pervasive and sustained emotional response that, in its extreme form, can color the person's perception of the world (APA, 1994). The disorders that are discussed in this chapter are primarily associated with two specific moods: depression and elation.

Depression can refer either to a mood or to a clinical syndrome—a combination of emotional, cognitive, and behavioral symptoms. The feelings associated with a *depressed mood* often include disappointment and despair. Although sadness is a universal experience, profound depression is not. People who are in a severely depressed mood describe the feeling as overwhelming, suffocating, or numbing. In the syndrome of depression, which is also called *clinical depression*, a depressed mood is accompanied by several additional symptoms such as fatigue, loss of energy, sleeping difficulties, and appetite changes. Clinical depression also involves a variety of changes in thinking and overt behavior. The person may experience cognitive symptoms such as extreme guilt, feelings of worthlessness, concentration problems, and thoughts of suicide. Behavioral symptoms may range from constant pacing and fidgeting to extreme inactivity. Throughout the rest of this chapter, we will use the term *depression* to refer to the clinical syndrome rather than the mood.

Mania, the flip side of depression, also involves a disturbance in mood that is accompanied by additional symptoms. Euphoria or elated mood defines the opposite emotional state from a depressed mood. This condition is characterized by an exaggerated feeling of physical and emotional well-being (APA, 1994). Manic symptoms that frequently accompany an elated mood include inflated self-esteem, decreased need for sleep, distractibility, pressure to keep talking, and the subjective feeling of thoughts racing through the person's head faster than they can be spoken. Mania is therefore a syndrome in the same sense that clinical depression is a syndrome.

Mood disorders are defined in terms of episodes—discrete periods of time, in which the person's behavior is dominated by either clinical depression or mania. Unfortunately, many people with a mood disorder experience more than one episode. The following cases illustrate the way that numerous symptoms combine to form the syndromes that define mood disorders. They also provide examples of the two primary types of mood disorders: (1) those in which the person experiences only episodes of depression, known as **unipolar mood disorder**, and (2) those in which the person experiences episodes of mania as well as episodes of depression, known as **bipolar mood disorder**.[†] You should review the case of Gina King from Chapter 1, which illustrates the way in which episodes of severe depression can occur during a chronic state of mild depression. This combination is called *double depression*.

CASE STUDY

Unipolar Mood Disorder: Major Depressive Episode

Cathy was a 31-year-old attorney who had been promoted to the rank of partner the previous year and was considered one of the brightest, most promising young members of her firm. In spite of her apparent success, she was plagued by doubts about her own abilities and was convinced that she was unworthy of her promotion. Cathy decided to seek treatment because she was profoundly miserable. Beyond feeling depressed, she felt numb. She had been feeling unusually fatigued and irritable for a period of several months, but her mood took a serious swing for the worse after one of the firm's clients, for whom Cathy was primarily responsible, decided to switch to another firm. Although the decision was clearly based on factors that were beyond her control, Cathy blamed herself. She interpreted this event as a reflection of her professional incompetence, in spite of the fact that virtually all of her other clients had praised her work and the senior partners in her firm had given her consistently positive reviews.

Cathy had always looked forward to going to the office, and she truly enjoyed her work. After she lost this client, however, going to work had seemed like an overwhelming burden. She found it impossible to concentrate on her work and spent her time brooding about her own incompetence. Soon she started calling in sick. She began to spend her time sitting in bed staring at the television screen, without paying attention to any program, and she never left her apartment. She felt lethargic all the time, but she wasn't sleeping well. Her appetite disappeared. Her best friend tried repeatedly to get in touch with her, but Cathy wouldn't return her calls. She listened passively as her friend left messages on the answering machine. She just didn't feel like doing anything or talking to anyone.

Her social life was, in Cathy's view, a disaster, and it didn't seem to be getting any better. She had been separated from her husband for 5 years, and her most recent boyfriend started dating another woman. She had tried desperately for several weeks to force herself to be active. Eventually she stopped caring. The situation seemed completely hopeless. Although she had often gone to parties with other members of her law firm, she usually felt as though she didn't fit in. Everyone else seemed to be part of a couple, and Cathy was usually on her own. Other people didn't appreciate the depth of her loneliness. Sometimes it seemed to Cathy that she would be better off dead. She spent a good deal of time brooding about suicide, but she feared that if she tried to harm herself she might make things worse than they already were. ■

[†] A small number of patients have only manic episodes with no evidence of depression, and they are included in the bipolar category.

CASE STUDY

Bipolar Mood Disorder: Manic Episode

Debbie, a 21-year-old single woman, was admitted to a psychiatric hospital in the midst of a manic episode. She had been in psychotherapy for depression for a period of several months while she was in high school but had not received any type of psychological treatment since that time. After she completed two semesters at a community college, Debbie found a well-paying job in the advertising office of a local newspaper for 2 years.

The manic episode could be traced to events that began several weeks prior to her admission to the hospital. Debbie quit her job suddenly so that she could go visit her boyfriend, who lived in a distant city. Giving up her job without careful consideration and with no prospect for alternative employment was the first indication that Debbie's judgment was becoming impaired. Although she left home with only enough money to pay for her airplane ticket, she stayed for several weeks, mostly engaged in idle leisure activities. It was during this time that she began to have trouble sleeping. Her mood was frequently irritable.

On one occasion she had a loud and heated argument with her boyfriend in the parking lot of his apartment complex. She took off her blouse and angrily refused to put it on again in spite of his demands and the presence of several interested bystanders. Shortly after the fight, she packed her clothes and hitchhiked back home.

After returning to her parents' home, Debbie argued with them almost continuously for several days. She phoned an exclusive tennis club to arrange for private lessons, which she obviously could not afford, especially now that she was unemployed. Her mother interrupted the call and canceled the lessons. Debbie left the house in a rage and set off to hitch a ride to the tennis club. She was picked up by two unknown men, who persuaded her to accompany them to a party rather than go to the club. She stayed at the party all night and had intercourse with three men whom she had never met before.

The following day, she borrowed some money from a friend and took a train home. Another argument ensued upon her arrival at home. Debbie struck her father and took the family car. Angry and frightened by her apparently irrational behavior, her parents phoned the police, who found her and brought her home. When another argument broke out, even more hostile than the first, the police took Debbie to their precinct office, where she was interviewed by a psychiatrist. Her attitude was flippant, and her language was abusive and obscene. On the basis of her clearly irrational and violent mood as well as her marked impairment in judgment, the psychiatrist arranged for her to be committed to a psychiatric hospital.

Her behavior on the ward was belligerent, provocative, and demanding. Although she hadn't slept a total of more than 4 hours in the previous 3 days, she claimed to be bursting with energy. Her affect vacillated quickly and frequently. The slightest provocation could change an elated, expansive mood into a furious burst of anger. She behaved seductively toward some of the male patients, sitting on their laps, kissing them, and occasionally unfastening her clothing. Although her speech was coherent, it was rapid and pressured. She expressed several grandiose ideas, including the boast that she was an Olympic swimmer and skier and that she was a premed student in college. She had no insight into the severity of her mental condition. Failing to recognize that her judgment was impaired, she insisted that she had been brought to the ward so that she could help the other patients ("I am a psychic therapist"). ∎

Typical Symptoms and Associated Features

The cases of Cathy, Debbie, and Gina illustrate many of the most important symptoms and signs of mood disorders, which can be divided into three general areas: emotional symptoms, cognitive symptoms, and somatic symptoms. Each area is typically involved in episodes of major depression and mania.

Emotional Symptoms

Depressed or **dysphoric** (unpleasant) mood is the most common and obvious symptom of depression. Most people who are depressed describe themselves as feeling utterly gloomy, dejected, or despondent. There is not a clearcut line dividing normal sadness from a depressed mood that is associated with clinical depression. Clinicians use several features to help guide this diagnostic distinction, including the severity, the quality, and the pervasive impact of the depressed mood.

The severity of a depressed mood can reach painful and overwhelming proportions. William Styron, a Pulitzer Prize-winning author, has described the feeling as "despair beyond despair." Styron's account of his own experience with profound depression, which took him to the brink of suicide, provides a compelling description of the disorder. He says that the sensation most closely resembled drowning or suffocation. Styron pointed out that the word *depression*, which can also be used to describe an economic decline or a rut in the ground, is somehow inadequate to describe the catastrophic depths to which a person's mood can descend. He argued that clinicians should employ a more eloquent term to describe this dreadful experience:

> As one who has suffered from the malady in extremis yet returned to tell the tale, I would lobby for a truly arresting designation. "Brainstorm," for instance, has unfortunately been preempted to describe, somewhat jocularly, intellectual inspiration. But something along these lines is needed. Told that someone's mood disorder has evolved into a storm—a veritable howling tempest in the brain, which is indeed what a clinical depression resembles like

nothing else—even the uninformed layman might display sympathy rather than the standard reaction that "depression" evokes, something akin to "So what?" or "You'll pull out of it" or "We all have bad days." (Styron, 1990, pp. 37–38)

The suffocating gloom and despair associated with clinical depression often has a somewhat different character than normal sadness. William Styron (1990) also wrote about the unique quality of his depressed mood:

> What I had begun to discover is that, mysteriously and in ways that are totally remote from normal experience, the gray drizzle of horror induced by depression takes on the quality of physical pain. But it is not an immediately identifiable pain, like that of a broken limb. It may be more accurate to say that despair, owing to some evil trick played upon the sick brain by the inhabiting psyche, comes to resemble the diabolical discomfort of being imprisoned in a fiercely overheated room. And because no breeze stirs this caldron, because there is no escape from this smothering confinement, it is entirely natural that the victim begins to think ceaselessly of oblivion. (p. 50)

In contrast to the unpleasant feelings associated with clinical depression, manic patients like Debbie experience periods of inexplicable and unbounded joy known as **euphoria**. Debbie felt extremely optimistic and cheerful—"on top of the world"—in spite of the fact that her inappropriate behavior had made a shambles of her current life circumstances. Bursting with energy, she exhibited boundless enthusiasm, even

▲ The quality of a depressed mood is often different from the sadness that might arise from an event such as the loss of a loved one. Some depressed people say that they feel like they are drowning or suffocating.

▲ **William Styron, a Pulitzer Prize-winning author, described his own agonizing experience with depression in *Darkness Visible*. He referred to depression as "despair beyond despair."**

after she was admitted to the psychiatric hospital. In bipolar mood disorders, periods of elated mood tend to alternate with phases of depression. The duration of each episode and the frequency of the cycle vary from one patient to the next.

Many depressed and manic patients are also irritable. Their anger can be directed either at themselves or at others—frequently both. Gina, for example, often felt hostile and resentful. Even when they are cheerful, people in a manic episode, like Debbie, are easily provoked to anger. She became extremely argumentative and abusive, particularly when her grandiose statements about herself and her inappropriate judgment were challenged.

Anxiety is also common among people with mood disorders, just as depression is a common feature of some anxiety disorders (see Chapter 6). Two out of every three depressed patients also report feeling anxious (Kendall & Watson, 1989). People who are depressed are sometimes apprehensive, fearing that matters will become even worse than they already are, or that others will discover their inadequacy. They may report that they are chronically tense and unable to relax.

Cognitive Symptoms

In addition to changes in the way people feel, mood disorders also involve changes in the way they think about themselves and their surroundings. People who are clinically depressed frequently note that their thinking is slowed down, that they have trouble concentrating, and that they are easily distracted. Cathy's ability to concentrate was so disturbed that she became unable to work. She had extreme difficulty making even the simplest decisions. After she started staying home, she sat in front of the television set but was unable to pay attention to the content of even the simplest programs. Her thought processes were almost completely shut down.

Guilt and worthlessness are common preoccupations. Depressed patients blame themselves for things that have gone wrong, regardless of whether they are in fact responsible. They focus considerable attention on the most negative features of themselves, their environments, and the future—a combination that Beck (1967) has labeled the "depressive triad." Cathy exhibited this pattern. She saw herself as an incompetent person, both professionally and personally. She viewed her occupational and social worlds as being lonely and overwhelming. Her future looked gloomy and threatening.

In contrast to the cognitive slowness associated with depression, manic patients commonly report that their thoughts are speeded up. Ideas flash through their minds faster than they can articulate their thoughts. Manic patients can also be easily distracted, responding to seemingly random stimuli in a completely uninterpretable and incoherent fashion. Grandiosity and inflated self-esteem are also characteristic features of mania.

SUICIDAL IDEAS

Some people experience self-destructive ideas and impulses when they are depressed. Interest in suicide usually develops gradually and may begin with the vague sense that life is not worth living (Hamilton, 1982). Such feelings may follow directly from a loss of pleasure and overwhelming fatigue that typically accompany a seriously depressed mood. In addition, feelings of guilt and failure can lead depressed people to consider killing themselves. Over a period of time, depressed people may come to believe that they would be better off dead or that their family would function more successfully and happily without them. Preoccupation with such thoughts then leads to specific plans and may culminate in a suicide attempt.

Not all depressed people think of harming themselves, and many people who commit suicide do not appear to be depressed. There are no definitive data on this subject, in part because many intentional deaths are not recognized as suicides. Cultural and legal sanctions against suicide cause others to go unreported. Even if a death is determined to be the result of suicide, it may be very difficult to determine whether the person had been depressed.

The available evidence suggests that between 50 and 67 percent of all suicides occur as a result of, or in the context of, a primary mood disorder (Whybrow, Akiskal, & McKinney, 1984). Follow-up studies consistently indicate that 15 percent of all patients with mood disorders will eventually kill themselves (Sainsbury, 1982). Although psychopathology doesn't explain all suicidal behavior, there is undoubtedly a strong relationship between depression and self-destructive acts. (see Further Thoughts)

Somatic Symptoms

The **somatic symptoms** of mood disorders are related to basic physiological or bodily functions. They include fatigue, aches and pains, and serious changes in appetite and sleep patterns. People like Cathy who are clinically depressed often report feeling tired all the time. The simplest tasks, which she had previously taken for granted, seemed to require an overwhelming effort. Taking a shower, brushing her teeth, and getting dressed in the morning became virtually impossible.

Sleeping problems are also common, particularly trouble getting to sleep. This disturbance frequently goes hand in hand with cognitive difficulties mentioned earlier. Worried about her endless problems and unable to relax, Cathy found that she would toss and turn for hours before finally falling asleep. Some people also report having difficulty staying asleep throughout the night, and awaken 2 or more hours before the usual time. Early morning waking is often associated with particularly severe depression. A less common symptom is for a depressed individual to spend more time sleeping than usual.

Depressed people frequently experience a change in appetite. Some report that they eat more than usual. Most patients reduce the amount that they eat; some may eat next to nothing. Food just doesn't taste good any more. Depressed people can also lose a great deal of weight, even without trying to diet.

People who are severely depressed commonly lose their interest in various types of activities that are otherwise a source of pleasure and fulfillment. One common example is a loss of sexual desire. Depressed people are less likely to initiate sexual activity, and they are less likely to enjoy sex if their partners can persuade them to participate. Gina exhibited a distinct loss of interest in several activities while she was still in high school. She dropped out of the band and quit the track team, even though music and sports had previously been among her most important sources of pleasure and fulfillment.

Psychomotor retardation includes several features of behavior that may accompany the onset of serious depression. The most obvious behavioral symptom of depression is slowed movement. Patients may walk and talk as if they are in slow motion. Others become completely immobile and may stop speaking altogether. Some depressed patients pause for very extended periods—perhaps several minutes—before answering a question.

Various ill-defined somatic complaints can also accompany mood disorders. Some patients complain of frequent headaches and muscular aches and pains. These concerns may develop into a preoccupation with bodily functions and fear of disease. Styron (1990) described these physical sensations in the following way:

> I felt a kind of numbness, an enervation, but more particularly an odd fragility—as if my body had actually become frail, hypersensitive and somehow disjointed and clumsy, lacking normal coordination. And soon I was in the throes of a pervasive hypochondria. Nothing felt quite right with my corporeal self; there were twitches and pains, sometimes intermittent, often seemingly constant, that seemed to presage all sorts of dire infirmities. (p. 43)

In marked contrast to periods when they are depressed, manic patients are typically quite gregarious and energetic. Debbie's behavior provided many examples, even after her admission to the psychiatric hospital. Her flirtatious and provocative behavior on the ward was clearly inappropriate. She found it impossible to sit still for more than a moment or two. Virtually everything was interesting to her, and she was easily distracted, flitting from one idea or project to the next. Like other manic patients, Debbie was full of plans that were pursued in a rather indiscriminate fashion. She quit her job without warning in order to visit a friend. She tried to arrange expensive tennis lessons that she could not afford. When she tried to hitch a ride to the club, she was easily persuaded to change these plans and accompany two men to a party. Her impulsive sexual relationships with these men provided another example of her poor judgment.

Common Elements of Suicide

Most people who kill themselves are suffering from some form of mental disorder, such as depression, substance dependence, or schizophrenia (Caldwell & Gottssman, 1992). No single explanation can account for all self-destructive behavior. Edwin Shneidman (1966), a clinical psychologist who is a leading authority on suicide, described ten characteristics that are commonly associated with completed suicide. Schneidman's list includes features that occur most frequently and may help us understand many cases of suicide:

1. The common purpose of suicide is to seek a solution. Suicide is not a pointless or random act. To people who think about ending their own lives, suicide represents an answer to an otherwise insoluble problem or a way out of some unbearable dilemma. It is a choice that is somehow preferable to another set of dreaded circumstances, emotional distress, or disability, which the person fears more than death.

Attraction to suicide as a potential solution may be increased by a family history of similar behavior. If someone else whom the person admired or cared for has committed suicide, then the person is more likely to do so.

2. The common goal of suicide is cessation of consciousness. People who commit suicide seek the end of conscious experience, which to them has become an endless stream of distressing thoughts with which they are preoccupied. Suicide offers oblivion.

3. The common stimulus (or information input) in suicide is intolerable psychological pain. Excruciating negative emotions—including shame, guilt, anger, fear, and sadness—frequently serve as the foundation for self-destructive behavior. These emotions may arise from any number of sources.

▲ Jack Kevorkian has helped terminally ill people end their own lives. His persistent efforts have sparked a national debate on the ethics of physician-assisted suicide. Is suicide ever a rational act? Do people have a "right" to end their own lives?

4. The common stressor in suicide is frustrated psychological needs. People with high standards and expectations are especially vulnerable to ideas of suicide when progress toward these goals is suddenly frustrated. People who attribute failure or disappointment to their own shortcomings may come to view themselves as worthless, incompetent, or unlovable. Family turmoil is an especially important source of frustration to adolescents. Occupational and interpersonal difficulties frequently precipitate suicide among adults. For example, rates of suicide increase during periods of high unemployment (Yang et al., 1992).

5. The common emotion in suicide is hopelessness-helplessness. A pervasive sense of hopelessness, defined in terms of pessimistic expectations about the future, is even more important than other forms of negative emotion, such as anger and depression, in predicting suicidal behavior (Weishaar & Beck, 1992). The suicidal person is convinced that absolutely nothing can be done to improve his or her situation; no one else can help.

6. The common internal attitude in suicide is ambivalence. Most people who contemplate suicide, including those who eventually kill themselves, have ambivalent feelings about this decision. They are sincere in their desire to die, but they simultaneously wish that they could find another way out of their dilemma.

7. The common cognitive state in suicide is constriction. Suicidal thoughts and plans are frequently associated with a rigid and narrow pattern of cognitive activity that is analogous to tunnel vision. The suicidal person is temporarily unable or unwilling to engage in effective problem-solving behaviors and may see his or her options in extreme, all-or-nothing terms. As Shneidman points out, slogans such as "death before dishonor" may have a certain emotional appeal, but they do not provide a sensible basis for making decisions about how to lead your life.

8. The common action in suicide is escape. Suicide provides a definitive way to escape from intolerable circumstances, which include painful self-awareness (Baumeister, 1990).

9. The common interpersonal act in suicide is communication of intention. One of the most harmful myths about suicide is the notion that people who really want to kill themselves don't talk about it. Most people who commit suicide have told other people about their plans. Many have made previous suicidal gestures. Schneidman estimates that in at least 80 percent of committed suicides, the people provide verbal or behavioral clues that indicate clearly their lethal intentions.

10. The common consistency in suicide is with life-long coping patterns. During crises that precipitate suicidal thoughts, people generally employ the same response patterns that they have used throughout their lives. For example, people who have refused to ask for help in the past are likely to persist in that pattern, increasing their sense of isolation. ■

Other Problems Commonly Associated with Depression

Many people with mood disorders suffer from additional clinical problems that are not typically considered symptoms of depression. Within the field of psychopathology, the simultaneous manifestation of a mood disorder and other syndromes is referred to as **co-morbidity**, suggesting that the person exhibits symptoms of more than one underlying disorder.

Alcoholism and depression are clearly related phenomena. Many people who are depressed also drink heavily, and many people who are dependent on alcohol—between 33 and 59 percent—eventually become depressed (Merikangas & Gelernter, 1990; Schuckit & Monteiro, 1988). There is also an association between these disorders within families. Alcohol abuse is quite common among the immediate families of patients with mood disorders. Eating disorders and anxiety disorders are also more common among first-degree relatives of depressed patients than among people in the general population.

Classification

Psychopathologists have proposed hundreds of systems for the description and classification of mood disorders (Grove & Andreasen, 1992). In the following pages, we will describe briefly some of the historical figures who played a prominent role in the development of classification systems (Berrios, 1992). This discussion should help place our description of the current diagnostic system, DSM-IV, in perspective.

Brief Historical Perspective

Although written descriptions of clinical depression can be traced to ancient times, the first

TABLE 5–1

Important Considerations in Distinguishing Clinical Depression from Normal Sadness

Intensity	The mood change pervades all aspects of the person and impairs social and occupational functions.
Absence of precipitants	The mood may arise in the absence of any discernible precipitant or may be grossly out of proportion to those precipitants.
Quality	The mood change is different from that experienced in normal sadness.
Associated Features	The change in mood is accompanied by a cluster of signs and symptoms, including cognitive and somatic features.
History	The mood change may be preceded by a history of past episodes of elation and hyperactivity.

Source: P.C. Whybrow, H.S. Akiskal, and W.T. McKinney, Jr. (1984). *Mood Disorders: Toward a new psychobiology,* New York: Plenum.

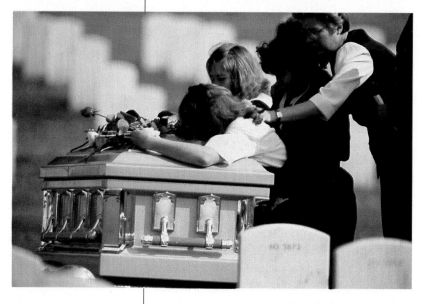

▲ **Freud's view of depression was built upon a consideration of the relation between grief and clinical depression. His observations were concerned particularly with psychological mechanisms in response to loss.**

widely accepted classification system was proposed by German physician Emil Kraepelin (1921). Kraepelin divided the major forms of mental disorder into two categories: *dementia praecox,* which we now know as schizophrenia (see Chapter 12), and *manic-depressive psychosis.* The distinction was based on age of onset, clinical symptoms, and the course of the disorder (its progress over time). The manic-depressive category included all depressive syndromes, regardless of whether the patients exhibited

manic and depressive episodes or simply depression. In comparison to dementia praecox, manic-depressive patients typically showed an episodic, recurrent course with a relatively good prognosis. Kraepelin observed that most patients returned to a normal level of functioning between episodes of depression or mania. His classification system recognized several specific subtypes of manic-depressive psychosis, including dysthymia and melancholia. All were presumably forms of illness; some could be attributed to brain dysfunction, whereas others might be a response to life events.

Despite the widespread acceptance and influence of Kraepelin's diagnostic system, other psychiatrists, most notably Adolf Meyer (1866–1950) and Sigmund Freud, proposed alternative approaches. These individuals included milder forms of disorder in their definitions of depression and placed greater emphasis on the role played by environmental events. Meyer, an American psychiatrist, preferred to talk about *depressive reactions* rather than illness. His writings stressed the important roles played by both biological and psychological functions in the process of adapting to environmental circumstances. Freud's view of depression (see the later section on etiology) was built upon a consideration of the relation between grief and clinical depression. His observations were concerned particularly with psychological mechanisms in response to loss. Subsequent interest in *neurotic depression* can be traced directly to his influence.

Two primary issues have been central in the debate regarding definitions of mood disorders. First, should these disorders be defined in a broad or narrow fashion? Table 5-1 presents a list of considerations that can be used to distinguish clinical depression from normal sadness. Definitions of depression that incorporate all these criteria tend to be more narrow than those that include only some of them. Some clinicians prefer to exclude unhappiness and grief from the more severe mood disorders. Others believe that this distinction is artificial and leads us to overlook large numbers of people who are also depressed but may not seek help for their problems.

The second issue concerns heterogeneity. All depressed patients do not have exactly the same set of symptoms, the same pattern of onset, or the same course over time. Some patients have manic episodes, whereas others experience only depression. Some exhibit psychotic symptoms, such as delusions and hallucinations, in addition to their symptoms of mood disorder; others do not. In some cases, the person's depression is apparently a reaction to specific life events, whereas in others the mood disorder seems to come out of nowhere. Are these qualitatively distinct forms of mood disorder, or are they different expressions of the same underlying problem? Is the distinction among the different types simply one of severity?

Experts have taken different positions on this issue. For example, British psychiatrists Aubrey Lewis (1938) and R. E. Kendell (1968) have argued that depression should be viewed as a unitary phenomenon, with various cases being distributed along a continuum from less to more severe. According to this point of view, the more severe cases are those in which the quality of the mood tends to be different from typical sadness and in which additional features — such as somatic symptoms, psychotic symptoms, and manic episodes— are likely to be seen. In contrast to the unitary position, many clinicians believe that it is more useful to think in terms of discrete subtypes of depression, each of which might have distinct causes.

One approach to the formation of subtypes has come to be widely accepted. Considerable evidence points to the conclusion that the unipolar/bipolar distinction is meaningful. For example, the average age of onset is considerably younger for patients with bipolar disorders than for patients with unipolar disorders (Depue & Monroe, 1978). Also, some studies indicate that genetic factors may be more influential in the etiology of bipolar disorders than in unipolar disorders (for example, Bertelson, Harvald, & Hauge, 1977). Bipolar patients are also more likely to benefit from certain forms of drug treatment, such as lithium carbonate.

Contemporary Diagnostic Systems

The DSM-IV (APA, 1994) approach to classifying mood disorders recognizes several subtypes of depression, placing special emphasis on the distinction between unipolar and bipolar disorders. The overall scheme is outlined in Table 5-2. It includes two types of unipolar

mood disorder and three types of bipolar mood disorder.

UNIPOLAR DISORDERS

The unipolar disorders include two specific types: major depressive disorder and dysthymia. In order to meet the criteria for major

---

TABLE 5-2

DSM-IV System for Classifying Mood Disorders

Unipolar Disorders

Major Depressive Disorders
- One or more major depressive episode
- No manic or unequivocal hypomanic episodes

Dysthymic Disorders
- Depressed mood for at least 2 years
- Never without these symptoms for more than 2 months during this period
- No major depressive episode during first 2 years

Bipolar Disorders

Bipolar I Disorder
- One or more manic episode

Bipolar II Disorder
- One or more major depressive episode
- At least one hypomanic episode
- No manic episodes

Cyclothymic Disorder
- Numerous periods with hypomanic symptoms and numerous periods with depressed mood for at least 2 years
- Never without thest symptoms for more than 2 months during 2-year period
- No major depressive episodes
- No manic episode during first 2 years

---

depressive disorder, a person must experience at least one major depressive episode in the absence of any history of manic episodes. Table 5-3 lists the DSM-IV criteria for a major depressive episode. Although some people experience a single, isolated episode of major depression followed by complete recovery, most cases of unipolar depression follow an intermittent course with repeated episodes.

Dysthymia differs from major depression in terms of both severity and duration. Dysthymia represents a chronic mild depressive condition that has been present for many years.[†] In order to fulfill DSM-IV criteria for this disorder, the

---

[†] Dysthymia, as it is presently defined in DSM-IV, closely resembles the subtype that others have called neurotic depression.

person must, over a period of at least 2 years, exhibit a depressed mood for most of the day on more days than not. Two or more of the following symptoms must also be present:

1. Poor appetite or overeating
2. Insomnia or hypersomnia
3. Low energy or fatigue
4. Low self-esteem
5. Poor concentration or difficulty making decisions
6. Feelings of hopelessness

These symptoms must not be absent for more than 2 months at a time during the 2-year period. If, at any time during the initial 2-year period, the person met criteria for a major depressive episode, the diagnosis would be major depression rather than dysthymia. As in the case of major depressive disorder, the presence of a manic episode would rule out a diagnosis of dysthymia.

BIPOLAR DISORDERS

All three types of bipolar disorders involve manic or hypomanic episodes. Table 5-4 lists the DSM-IV criteria for a manic episode. The mood dis-

turbance must be sufficiently severe to cause marked interference with occupational or social functioning. A person who has experienced at least one manic episode would be assigned a diagnosis of bipolar I disorder. The vast majority of patients with this disorder experience episodes of major depression in addition to manic episodes.

Some patients experience episodes of increased energy that are not sufficiently severe to qualify as full-blown manic episodes. These episodes are called **hypomania**. A person who has experienced at least one major depressive episode, at least one hypomanic episode, and no full-blown manic episodes would be assigned a diagnosis of bipolar II disorder. The symptoms that are used in DSM-IV to identify a hypomanic episode are the same as those for manic episode (at least 3 out of the 7 symptoms listed in Table 5-4). The differences between manic and hypomanic episodes involve duration and severity. The symptoms need to be present only for a minimum of 4 days to meet the threshold for a hypomanic episode (as opposed to 1 week for a manic episode). The mood change in a hypomanic episode must be noticeable to others, but the disturbance must not be severe enough to cause

---

TABLE 5–3

Symptoms Listed in DSM-IV for Major Depressive Episode

A. Five or more of the following symptoms have been present during the same 2-week period and represent a change from previous functioning; at least one of the symptoms is either (1) depressed mood, or (2) loss of interest or pleasure.

1. Depressed mood most of the day, nearly every day, as indicated either by subjective report (for example, feels sad or empty) or observation made by others (for example, appears tearful). Note: in children and adolescents, can be irritable mood.
2. Markedly diminished interest or pleasure in all, or almost all, activities most of the day, nearly every day (as indicated either by subjective account or observation by others).
3. Significant weight loss when not dieting or weight gain (for example, a change of more than 5 percent of body weight in a month), or decrease or increase in appetite nearly every day. Note: in children, consider failure to make expected weight gains.
4. Insomnia or hypersomnia nearly every day.
5. Psychomotor agitation or retardation nearly every day (observable by others, not merely subjective feelings of restlessness or being slowed down).
6. Fatigue or loss of energy nearly every day.
7. Feelings of worthlessness or excessive or inappropriate guilt (which may be delusional) nearly every day (not merely self-reproach or guilt about being sick).
8. Diminished ability to think or concentrate, or indecisiveness, nearly every day (either by subjective account or as observed by others).
9. Recurrent thoughts of death (not just fear of dying), recurrent suicidal ideation without a specific plan, or a suicide attempt or a specific plan for committing suicide.

TABLE 5-4

Symptoms Listed in DSM–IV for Manic Episode

A. A distinct period of abnormally and persistently elevated, expansive, or irritable mood, lasting at least 1 week (or any duration if hospitalization is necessary).

B. During the period of mood disturbance, three or more of the following symptoms have persisted (four if the mood is only irritable) and have been present to a significant degree:

   1. Inflated self-esteem or grandiosity.
   2. Decreased need for sleep—for example, feels rested after only 3 hours of sleep.
   3. More talkative than usual, or pressure to keep talking.
   4. Flight of ideas or subjective experience that thoughts are racing.
   5. Distractibility—that is, attention too easily drawn to unimportant or irrelevant external stimuli.
   6. Increase in goal-directed activity (either socially, at work or school, or sexually) or psychomotor agitation.
   7. Excessive involvement in pleasurable activities that have a high potential for painful consequences— for example, the person engages in unrestrained buying sprees, sexual indiscretions, or foolish business investments.

impairment in social or occupational functioning or to require hospitalization.

Cyclothymia is considered by DSM-IV to be a chronic but less severe form of bipolar disorder. It is therefore the bipolar equivalent of dysthymia. In order to meet criteria for cyclothymia, the person must experience numerous hypomanic episodes and numerous periods of depression (or loss of interest or pleasure) during a period of 2 years. There must be no history of major depressive episodes and no clear evidence of a manic episode during the first 2 years of the disturbance.

DSM-IV also provides for several ways of qualifying and describing subtypes of the five primary mood disorders. For example, the clinician may describe a major depressive episode as having melancholic features. **Melancholia** is a term that has been used to describe a particularly severe type of depression. Some experts believe that melancholia represents a subtype of depression that is caused by different factors than those that are responsible for other forms of depression (Zimmerman & Spitzer, 1989). In order to meet the DSM-IV criteria for melancholic features, a depressed patient must either: (1) lose the feeling of pleasure associated with all, or almost all, activities, or (2) lose the capacity to feel better—even temporarily—when something good happens. The person must also exhibit at least three of the following: (1) the person's depressed mood feels distinctly different from the depression a person would feel after

the death of a loved one; (2) the depression is most often worst in the morning; (3) the person awakens early, at least 2 hours before usual; (4) marked psychomotor retardation or agitation; (5) significant loss of appetite or weight loss; and (6) excessive or inappropriate guilt.

DSM-IV also provides a list of "course specifiers" that allow the clinician to describe further the pattern and sequence of episodes as well as the person's adjustment between episodes. For example, a mood disorder (either unipolar or bipolar) is described as following a seasonal pattern if, over a period of time, there is a regular relationship between the onset of a person's episodes and particular times of the year. The most typical seasonal pattern is one in which the person becomes depressed in the fall or winter, followed by a full recovery in the following spring or summer. The course of a bipolar disorder can be specified as rapid cycling if the person experiences at least four episodes of major depression, mania, or hypomania within a 12-month period. The final course specifier applies to women who become depressed or manic following pregnancy. A major depressive or manic episode can be specified as having a *postpartum onset* if it begins within 4 weeks after childbirth.

Seasonal affective disorder is a term used by researchers to refer to a mood disorder in which the onset of episodes is regularly associated with changes in seasons. The episodes most commonly occur in winter, presumably in response to fewer hours of sunlight. Seasonal disorders have attracted considerable interest among mental health professionals since the 1980s (Blehar & Rosenthal, 1989). This type of depression is usually characterized by somatic symptoms such as overeating, carbohydrate craving, weight gain, fatigue, and sleeping more than usual. One study found that, among outpatients who had a history of at least three major depressive episodes, 16 percent met criteria for the seasonal pattern (Thase, 1989). Most patients with seasonal affective disorder have a unipolar disorder, but many would meet criteria for bipolar II disorder. The latter group typically become depressed in the winter followed by a mood reversal to hypomania in the spring. Relatively few have bipolar I disorder (Oren & Rosenthal, 1992).

Course and Outcome

To consider the typical course and outcome of mood disorders, it is useful to study unipolar and bipolar disorders separately. Most studies point to clear-cut differences between these two conditions in terms of age of onset and in terms of prognosis (Perris, 1992).

BIPOLAR DISORDERS

Numerous studies of bipolar disorders have established a general picture of their typical onset and course. The onset of bipolar mood disorders usually occurs between the ages of 28 and 33 years, with the first episode being as likely to be manic as depressive in nature (Coryell & Winokur, 1992). The average duration of a manic episode seems to run between 2 and 3 months, and depressive episodes last somewhat longer (Keller, 1987). By contrast, bipolar II patients tend to have shorter and less severe episodes (Coryell et al., 1985).

The long-term course of bipolar disorders is most often episodic, and the prognosis is mixed. Most patients have more than one episode, and bipolar patients tend to have more episodes than unipolar patients. The length of intervals between episodes is difficult to predict.

The long-term prognosis is mixed for patients with bipolar mood disorder. Although some patients recover and function quite well, oth-

ers experience continued impairment. Several studies that have followed bipolar patients over periods of up to 10 years have found that 40 to 50 percent of patients are able to achieve a sustained recovery from the disorder (Coryell & Winokur, 1992). Many patients remain chronically disabled. Rapid cycling patients are less likely to recover from an episode and are more likely to relapse after they do recover (Keller et al., 1993). In comparison to patients with a diagnosis of schizophrenia, bipolar patients have a better average outcome in terms of marital, residential, occupational, and symptomatic status (Tsuang et al., 1979).

UNIPOLAR DEPRESSION

Data regarding the onset and course of unipolar mood disorders must be viewed with some caution because virtually all studies have focused exclusively on the people who have sought treatment for their depression. Very little is known about untreated depressions, but it seems reasonable to assume that they are likely to remit spontaneously in a short period of time.

The average age of onset for unipolar mood disorders is significantly older than that for bipolar disorders, with most studies suggesting first episodes in the mid-forties. Episodes of unipolar depression also tend to be somewhat longer in duration. A slightly higher proportion of unipolar than bipolar patients experience only a single episode, but somewhere between 50 and 85 percent of unipolar patients will have at least one more depressive episode. The mean number of lifetime episodes is five or six.

Although some studies have reported relatively better rates of long-term recovery among unipolar than bipolar patients, several others report equivalent rates (Coryell & Winokur, 1992). Data collected as part of the NIMH Collaborative Program on Depression indicate that approximately 65 percent of unipolar patients recover within 6 months of the beginning of an episode. Between 10 and 20 percent have not recovered after 5 years (Keller et al., 1986). Among those who do recover, 40 percent relapse within 1 year. Older patients tend to relapse more quickly than younger patients, and females relapse more quickly than males.

Epidemiology

Questions about the frequency and distribution of mood disorders are difficult to answer precisely. One problem, of course, is associated with widespread variations in the definition of clinical depression. Some investigators have adopted a rather broad approach to diagnosis, whereas others have focused on a narrow range of severely disturbed patients. The procedure used to identify potential cases is also important. Many of the early epidemiological studies focused on patients treated at hospitals and mental health centers. Unfortunately, there are large numbers people who experience serious depression without wanting, or being able to seek, professional help. Formal statistics must therefore be considered with caution.

Several large epidemiological studies have been completed in recent years, and they provide relatively consistent data regarding mood disorders. Most notable among these has been the Epidemiologic Catchment Area (ECA) study, in which nearly 20,000 residents of five American communities were interviewed (Robins & Regier, 1991).

Incidence, Prevalence, and Morbid Risk

Depression is one of the most common forms of psychopathology. During the 1970s, several community surveys using self-report checklists found that the *point prevalence* of depressive symptoms—that is, the percentage of the population that reports certain experiences at any given point in time—was between 13 and 20 percent (Smith & Weissman, 1992). These alarming figures suggested that, at any given point in time, depression might affect as many as one out of every five people. On the other hand, self-report scales may exaggerate the apparent frequency of depression (see Chapter 4, Research Close-up).

Epidemiological studies, such as the ECA program, that have relied upon clinical interviews for the assessment of symptoms have consistently reported lower rates for mood disorders. Among those people interviewed in New Haven, Baltimore, and St. Louis as part of the ECA program, approximately 3 percent met DSM-

III criteria for major depressive episode within a given 6-month period. An additional 3 percent met criteria for dysthymia in the same period, and slightly less than 1 percent met criteria for a manic episode (Weissman et al., 1991). Thus, slightly more than 6 percent of the population in this sample was suffering from a diagnosable mood disorder during a period of 6 months. The ECA data are also consistent with other studies in suggesting that unipolar disorders are much more common than bipolar disorders. The ratio of unipolar to bipolar disorders is at least 5:1 (Smith & Weissman, 1992).

Lifetime risk for major depressive disorder was approximately 5 percent, averaged across sites in the ECA program (Weissman et al., 1991). The lifetime risk for dysthymia was approximately 3 percent, and the lifetime risk for bipolar I disorder was close to 1 percent. Almost half of the people who met diagnostic criteria for dysthymia had also experienced an episode of major depression at some point in their lives. At each of the sites examined by Robins and her colleagues, the lifetime prevalence of mood disorders ranked third behind substance use disorders (about 17 percent) and anxiety disorders (about 12 percent).

Because the ECA study identified a representative sample of community residents rather than patients already in treatment, it also allows some insight regarding the proportion of depressed people who seek professional help for their problems. Slightly more than 30 percent of those people who met DSM-III criteria for a mood disorder made contact with a mental health professional during the 6 months prior to their interview (Shapiro et al., 1984). These data indicate that a substantial proportion of people who are clinically depressed do not receive professional treatment for their disorders. Finding ways to help these people represents an important challenge for psychologists and psychiatrists who treat mood disorders.

Gender Differences

Women are 2 or 3 times more vulnerable to depression than men are. This pattern has been reported in study after study, using samples of

▲ **Myrna Weissman, professor of psychiatry at Columbia University, is one of the leading investigators in the study of the epidemiology of depression.**

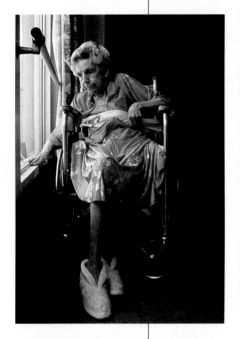

▲ **Contrary to popular views, older people are actually less likely to be depressed than are younger people. Some subgroups of elderly people, however, are at high risk for depression. For example, among the 5 percent of elderly people who live in nursing homes, rates of depression can be as high as 50 percent.**

treated patients as well as community surveys, and regardless of the assessment procedures employed. The increased prevalence of depression among women is particularly marked in the case of unipolar disorders (Nolen-Hoeksema, 1990). In the ECA program, for example, 4 percent of women but only 1.7 percent of men were diagnosed with a major depressive disorder, based on DSM-III criteria. Studies based on self-reports also indicate higher rates of depression among women (see, for example, Eaton & Kessler, 1981).

Some observers have suggested that the higher reported rates for women actually reflect shortcomings in the data-collection process. Women might simply be more likely than men to seek treatment or to be labeled as depressive. Another argument holds that culturally determined sanctions make it more difficult for men to admit to subjective feelings of distress such as hopelessness and despair. None of these alternatives has been substantiated by empirical evidence (Nolen-Hoeksema, 1990). Research studies clearly indicate that the higher prevalence of depression among women is genuine.

Cross-Cultural Differences

Questions about the relation between culture and mood disorders were raised early in the twentieth century, when Kraepelin (1921) visited the island of Java (now part of Indonesia). It was his impression, based on visits to psy-

chiatric hospitals in that country, that the disorder that he called "manic-depressive insanity" was just as common in Java as it was in Europe. He also noted, however, that patients in Java suffered "almost exclusively states of excitement and often confusion" (Leff, 1992). Manic episodes were apparently much more common in this culture than were episodes of major depression.

Comparisons of emotional expression and emotional disorder across cultural boundaries encounter a number of methodological problems. One problem involves vocabulary. Each culture has its own ways of interpreting reality, including different styles of expressing or communicating symptoms of physical and emotional disorder (Good & Kleinman, 1985; Katschnig & Amering, 1990). Words and concepts that are used to describe illness behaviors in one culture might not exist in other cultures. For example, some African cultures have only one word for both anger and sadness. Interesting adaptations are therefore required to translate questions that are supposed to tap experiences such as anxiety and depression. One investigation, which employed a British interview schedule that had been translated into Yoruba— a language spoken in Nigeria—used the phrase "the heart goes weak" to represent depression (Leff, 1988).

We must remember that our own diagnostic categories have been developed within a specific cultural setting; they are not culture-free and are not necessarily any more reasonable than the ways in which other cultures have come to describe and categorize their own behavioral and emotional disorders. One illustration of this principle comes from the study of neurasthenia, which is a relatively common problem in China but is rarely diagnosed in Western societies. Although the diagnostic term was not introduced to Chinese physicians until the twentieth century, the concept fits closely with ancient traditions in Chinese folk medicine. Neurasthenic patients present many different complaints that focus primarily on physical symptoms: headaches, insomnia, dizziness, pain, weakness, loss of energy, poor appetite, tingling in the head, and so on. Related psychological symptoms include memory problems, anxiety, disturbing dreams, and poor concentration.

Arthur Kleinman, a psychiatrist and anthropologist at Harvard University, and a group of Chinese psychiatrists studied 100 neurasthenic patients at an outpatient clinic associated with a Chinese medical school (Kleinman, 1982). Interviews were conducted using a translation of an American diagnostic interview schedule, and diagnoses were assigned using DSM-III criteria. In all, 87 of the 100 patients received a diagnosis of major depressive disorder, and 69 received a diagnosis of anxiety disorder. Thus, most of the patients fit the criteria for both depression and anxiety.

What does this study tell us about mood disorders in cross-cultural perspective? Does it mean that the DSM categories are truly universal and that Chinese psychiatrists inappropriately tend to diagnose their patients as suffering from neurasthenia? No. The Chinese psychiatrists could just as easily argue that the Americans had misdiagnosed neurasthenia as depression or anxiety. The results suggest that depression, anxiety, and associated somatic complaints are universal psychological phenomena. Each culture, however, has its own way to interpret and organize these phenomena. The officially recognized language of the culture—in this case the diagnostic system employed by mental health professionals—provides members of the society with an acceptable way to communicate the experience of personal distress. The nature of the disorder is interpreted in its social context.

The cross-cultural differences suggested by Kleinman's study have been confirmed by a number of large-scale research projects, including the World Health Organization's Collaborative Study on Depression (WHO, 1983), which examined cultural variations in symptomatology among depressed patients in Canada, India, Iran, Japan, and Switzerland. Trained clinicians conducted standardized interviews with more than 500 patients and based their diagnostic decisions on a common set of criteria. They found comparable overall frequencies of mood disorders across all five countries, but the specific symptoms expressed by the patients varied considerably from one culture to the next. Some of these differences are illustrated in Figure 5-1.

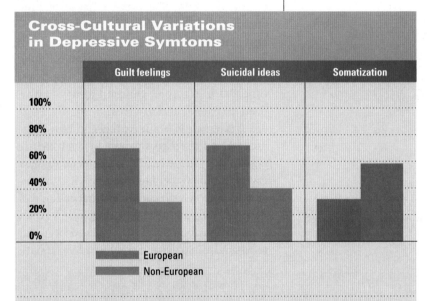

FIGURE 5-1: The cross-cultural differences suggested by Kleinman's study have been confirmed by a number of large-scale research projects, including the World Health Organization's Collaborative Study on Depression (WHO, 1983), which examined cultural variations in symptomatology among depressed patients in Canada, India, Iran, Japan, and Switzerland.

Source: A.J. Marsella, N. Sartorius, A. Jablensky, and F.R. Fenton (1985). Cross-cultural studies of depressive disorders: An overview. In A. Kleinman and B. Good (Eds.), *Culture and Depression.* Berkeley: University of California Press, p.305.

These cross-cultural comparisons suggest that, at its most basic level, clinical depression is a universal phenomenon that is not limited to Western or urban societies. They also indicate that a person's cultural experiences, including linguistic, educational, and social factors, may play an important role in shaping the manner in which different people express and cope with the anguish of depression. Cross-cultural variations should also be kept in mind when clinicians attempt to identify central or defining features of depression. We will return to this point later in the chapter when we discuss the rationale behind studies that rely on animal models of depression.

Risk for Depression Across the Life Span

Age is another important consideration in the epidemiology of mood disorders. Several studies indicate that the prevalence of depressive symptoms (as measured by self-report checklists) is particularly high among the elderly (Gurland, 1976). This pattern may reflect the fact that many older people experience brief episodic states of acute unhappiness, often precipitated by changes in status (for example, retirement, relocation) and loss of significant others (for example, children moving away, death of friends and relatives).

It is less clear, however, that clinically diagnosed mood disorders are more frequent among people over the age of 65. The incidence of new cases is much higher in middle age. It is unusual for a person to experience a first episode of depression or mania after the age of 65 (Post, 1982). The symptoms of mood disorders appear to be similar in older and younger adult patients,

of whether they are depressed (Allen & Blazer, 1991). It should be noted, of course, that the frequency of depression among elderly people varies substantially from one population to the next. The prevalence of depression is likely to be much higher among those who are about to enter residential care facilities than among a random sample of elderly people living in the community. One study found that approximately one out of three elderly applicants for community social services would meet criteria for a clinical depressive disorder (Goldberg, 1970).

Although many people mistakenly identify depression with the elderly, data from the ECA project actually suggest that mood disorders are most frequent among young and middle-aged adults. Six-month point prevalence rates for major depressive episodes and dysthymia were significantly lowest for people over the age of 65. Several possible explanations have been offered for this result, including the possibility that the ECA investigators misdiagnosed mood disorders as cognitive impairment or other problems common among the elderly. Also, because mood disorders are associated with increased mortality (for example, suicide), many depressed patients might not have survived into old age. Another possibility is that the frequency of depression has actually increased in recent years (Lavori et al., 1987). People born after World War II seem to be more likely to develop mood disorders than were people from previous generations. The average age of onset also appears to be earlier in the former group (Smith & Weissman, 1992).

Epidemiology of Suicide

In the United States the rate of completed suicide across all age groups has averaged 12 per 100,000 people during the twentieth century. The rate among adolescents has increased since the 1960s, while rates among other age groups have either fallen or remained steady (see Figure 5-2). Suicide has become the third leading cause of death for people between the ages of 15 and 24, and it is the eighth leading cause of death in the general population (Ryland & Kruesi, 1992). Thoughts about suicide are not uncommon among adolescents. In one study, 27 percent of high school students indicated that they had "seriously thought about attempting suicide" in the past year (CDC, 1991).

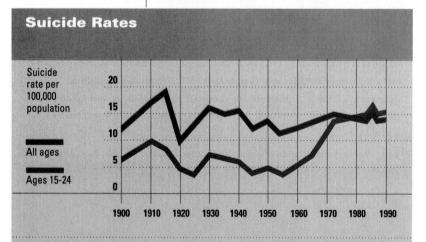

Suicide Rates

Suicide rate per 100,000 population

All ages

Ages 15-24

FIGURE 5-2: Suicide rates for the general population and for people 15-24 years old in the United States, 1900 to 1990. Note the dramatic increase in the rates for young people since the 1960s.

Source: Adapted from M.T. Tsuang, J.C. Simpson, & J.A. Fleming, (1992), Epidemiology of suicide. *International Review of Psychiatry, 4,* 119.

especially when we take into account that elderly people are more likely to experience physical illnesses and cognitive impairment, regardless

Fortunately, relatively few of these students acted on these ideas.

There are important gender differences in rates of attempted suicide versus rates of completed suicide. Females aged 15 to 19 years make three times as many suicide attempts as males. Completion rates, however, are four times higher among males (Tsuang, Simpson, & Fleming, 1993). The difference in fatalities may be due, in part, to the methods that are employed. Females tend to use less lethal methods. Males are more likely to use violent methods such as firearms and hanging, whereas females are more likely to use a drug overdose, which may allow time for discovery and interventions by another person. The risk of fatal

suicide does increase with age. Although attempts are most common among younger people, with most being made by those younger than 30, the proportion of suicide attempts that end in death is particularly high among the elderly. It is not clear whether this pattern should be attributed to a difference in method or decreased physical resilience. In either case, people over the age of 65 account for 25 percent of all suicidal deaths (Post, 1982). In European countries and the United States, older men are at particularly high risk. The pattern for women is somewhat different. Their risk for suicide increases steadily with age up until the period of menopause and then tends to level off (Hankoff, 1982).

Etiological Considerations and Research

In the next few pages, we turn our attention to current speculation and knowledge concerning possible causes of mood disorders. Several of these hypotheses are based on careful consideration of the specific symptoms of mood disorders—what depressed people say, ways in which they behave, and the effects they have on other people. Other hypotheses grow out of an attempt to explain epidemiological data. Why are women at greater risk for depression than men? Why is depression expressed somewhat differently in Western countries than in the Middle East? Why do bipolar mood disorders seem to run in families? A truly useful etiological theory must address these questions.

Throughout much of this century, two principal views dominated discussions regarding the causes of mood disorders. The first, exemplified by Kraepelin's writings, held that depression is largely biological in origin. According to this point of view, some people are predisposed to the development of serious mood disorders because of a genetically determined imbalance or impairment in brain function. The second approach, which was popularized by psychodynamic theorists, focused on the influence of personality factors and the effects of loss, such as the death of a parent or a close friend. In fact, these views are not incompatible. Various psychological, biological, and social factors undoubtedly combine, or interact, to

produce mood disorders (Kendler, Kessler, Neale, Heath, & Eaves, 1993; Whybrow, Akiskal, & McKinney, 1984).

In the following pages, we will outline some of the central ideas that have guided research efforts to examine the etiology of mood disorders. We will demonstrate that the empirical evidence, generated within social, psychological, and biological perspectives, suggests that the system's perspective may best account for the development of depression.

Social Factors

It should not be surprising that much of the literature regarding depression has focused on the issues of interpersonal loss and separation. From birth to death, our lives are intertwined with those of other people. We are fundamentally social organisms, and we feel sad when someone close to us dies. Similar feelings occasionally follow major disappointments, such as failure to win acceptance to a prestigious university or being fired from a job. In these cases, rather than losing other people, some clinicians have suggested that we may be losing "social roles" or ways in which we think about ourselves.

Various theories of depression have been built around a consideration of the impact of stressful life events. Beginning around the turn of the century, psychodynamic theories emphasized the central role played by interpersonal relationships and loss of significant others in setting the stage for depression as well as in bringing about a depressive episode.

FREUD'S THEORY OF DEPRESSION

Freud's classic paper on the etiology of depression focused on a comparison of clinical depression with the normal process of grieving (Freud, 1917). Among the various symptoms of depression, Freud was particularly interested in self-reproach and guilt. The fundamental assumption of Freud's view of depression was that depressed people are, in fact, not so much complaining about themselves as they are angry with someone else. The other person is presumably someone with whom the patient has had a very close relationship and who has either died or been lost in some other way—either in reality or in the patient's imagination. Instead of recognizing and dealing with this anger consciously, depressed people identify with the other person and direct their anger toward themselves.

Freud argued further that the distinction between people who mourn the loss of another and those who become clinically depressed is reflected in the types of interpersonal relationships they formed. People predisposed to depression tend to form "narcissistic" relationships in which they depend on the other person to maintain their self-esteem. This dependence invariably leads to negative as well as positive emotions, resulting in an *intense ambivalence*. The depressed individual cannot express this ambivalence openly, however, for fear of alienating and perhaps losing the other person. When the other person is no longer available, the anger is turned inward and directed toward the self; this expression of inwardly directed anger is presumably depression.

Freud's theory laid the intellectual foundation for many subsequent studies of psychological and social factors in the development and maintenance of depression. He focused interest on the possibility that stressful life events may precipitate the onset of mood disorders. We will consider contemporary research on this issue in the next section. Freud's notion of narcissistic relationships also anticipated subsequent studies of social skills in depression and the importance of interpersonal relationships over the course of mood disorders. We will review these considerations in our later section on psychological factors.

THE IMPACT OF LOSS AND STRESSFUL LIFE EVENTS

Several investigations have carefully explored the relationships between stressful life events and the development of unipolar and bipolar mood disorders. Do people who become clinically depressed actually experience an increased number of stressful life events? The answer is yes. Several research studies have shown that the experience of stressful life events is associated with an increased probability that a person will become depressed. This correlation has been demonstrated many times (Paykel & Dowlatshahi, 1988). Most of the research literature on stressful life events has been concerned with unipolar depression. Considerably less attention has been paid to bipolar mood disorders, but some evidence suggests that the period of several weeks preceding the onset of a manic episode is marked by an increased frequency of stressful life events (Kennedy et al., 1983).

Once the relatively strong relationship between stressful life events and depression was found, difficult methodological issues had to be faced before it could be interpreted. One is the use of retrospective self-reports to identify the occurrence of life events. Most studies have asked subjects, including some who are depressed and others who are not, to indicate how many negative events occurred in their lives during the preceding several months. The subjects' memories may be faulty, and some evidence suggests that depressed people have a distorted perception that overemphasizes negative experiences. To compensate for this, investigators focus their interview on specific events and collect as much detailed information as possible about the context in which these events occurred (Brewin, Andrews, & Gotlib, 1993).

Stress as a Cause of Depression Another problem centers around the independence of life events and mood disorders. For example, being fired from a job might lead a person to become depressed. On the other hand, the onset of a depressive episode, with its associated difficulties in energy and concentration, could easily affect the person's job performance and lead to being fired. Therefore, if depressed people experience more stressful events, what is the direction of effect? Does failure lead to depression, or does depression lead to failure?

Several procedures have been used to resolve questions about the direction of the relationship between stressful life events and depression. The use of prospective research designs, in which subjects are followed over time, has allowed investigators to avoid problems associated with retrospective reports. Prospective studies, like retrospective studies, have found that stressful life events were useful in predicting the subsequent onset of unipolar depression (Lewinsohn, Hoberman, & Rosenbaum, 1988). All of this evidence supports the argument that stressful life events contribute to the onset of mood disorders.

Another approach to determining the direction of effect is to consider only events that are clearly not consequences of mental disorder. Bruce Dohrenwend, an epidemiologist at Columbia University, has focused on "fateful" events, defined as adverse events that are outside the person's control and cause significant negative disruption in the person's life. These include experiences such as the death of a relative or close friend and being laid off from work. Extensive interviews explored the circumstances surrounding each event reported by a subject. Some were reclassified as being "nonfateful" or not beyond the person's control. One "death of a friend" event, for example, was rated as nonfateful because the friend shot himself while he and the research subject were playing with a loaded gun. Patients with a diagnosis of major depression were more than 3 times as likely to have experienced a fateful, disruptive event than were nondepressed community residents (Shrout et al., 1989).

Although many kinds of negative events are associated with depression, a special class of circumstances—those involving major *losses* of important people or roles—seems to play a crucial role in precipitating unipolar depression (Monroe & Simons, 1991). This conclusion is based, in large part, on a series of studies reported by George Brown and his colleagues. Their studies have compared the living circumstances and life experiences of depressed and nondepressed women living in the community, regardless of whether they are receiving treatment for their problems.

Brown and Harris (1978) found that "severe" events—those that are particularly threatening and have long-term consequences for the woman's adjustment—increased the probability that a woman would become depressed. The frequency of nonsevere events was roughly equivalent for depressed and nondepressed women. Only 16 percent of the events that were reported by all of the women in the study were considered severe by these standards. Most cases of depression appeared after a single severe event. (The Research Close-up provides further details regarding the nature of these events.) Brown's data suggest that depression is not caused by an accumulation of ordinary hassles and difficulties to which most of us are exposed on a daily basis (Monroe & Simons, 1991).

Depression as a Cause of Stress The relationship between stressful life events and depression is not entirely one-way; it runs in both directions. In comparison to women who are not depressed and women with other medical disorders, unipolar depressed women have also been found to generate higher levels of stress, especially with regard to interpersonal circumstances such as marital conflict (Hammen, 1991). This pattern suggests a dynamic process that may lead to an escalation of stress. Independent stressors, which are not caused by the person's own behavior, contribute to the onset of depression. The depressed person then behaves in a maladaptive fashion, leading to even higher levels of stress and perhaps a further deterioration in his or her mood. We will return to our consideration of interpersonal behaviors later in the section on psychological factors.

▲ **Stressful life events and depression are clearly correlated, but the direction of this relationship is not always clear. For example, does the loss of a job lead a person to become depressed? Or does the onset of depression interfere with the person's ability to perform the job, thereby increasing the risk of losing it?**

RESEARCH CLOSE-UP

Social Origins of Depression in Women

Some of the most influential studies regarding the link between depression and stressful life events have been conducted by George Brown, a sociologist, and Tirril Harris, a clinical psychologist, both at the Royal Holloway and New Bedford College (University of London in England). One of their investigations focused on 400 working-class women between the ages of 18 and 50 with children living at home (Brown, Bifulco, & Harris, 1987). This sample was chosen because previous research had demonstrated that women with children living at home are particularly vulnerable to depression (Brown & Harris, 1978).

The study was completed in two phases, separated by approximately a year. During the first phase, the investigators asked each woman an extensive series of questions about her psychological adjustment (including symptoms of mental disorders as well as self-esteem) and her living circumstances (including personal relationships and social support). During the second phase, the investigators collected information regarding life events and difficulties that had occurred during the follow-up year. They also inquired, once again, about symptoms of depression and other mental disorders. They identified cases of depression using specific diagnostic criteria that assured that the symptoms were comparable to those found among patients being treated for mood disorders.

The investigators made a concerted effort to describe each life event and to consider the circumstances in which it occurred. Each interviewer recorded detailed descriptions that they later provided to a panel of judges. The judges in turn rated how threatening each event would be to an average woman under the same living circumstances. Brown and his colleagues were particularly interested in the meaning that the events held for the woman. Judges were allowed to consider all information except the woman's mental status and the actual manner in which she responded to the event.

Results were reported only for the 303 women

TABLE 5–5

Onset of Depression Among 130 Women Who Experienced a Severe Event

Description of Life Event	Number of Women	Percent Depressed
Event matches prior difficulty	35	46%
Event does not match prior difficulty	95	14%
Event matches prior commitment	40	40%
Event does not match prior commitment	90	14%

Source: G.W. Brown, A. Bifulco, & T.O. Harris. (1987). Life events, vulnerability, and onset of depression: Some refinements. *British Journal of Psychiatry, 150,* 30-42.

who were not depressed at the time of the first assesment and who completed the second phase of assessment. Within this sample, 130 women experienced a severe event during the follow-up year. Of these women, 29 (22 percent) became depressed. Among the 173 women who did not experience a severe event, only 3 (2 percent) became depressed. In other words, 29 out of 32 (90 percent) women who became depressed had experienced a severe event in the 6 months prior to onset. This pattern is consistent with other reports that indicate a close association between stressful life events and depression.

Severe events did increase the probability of depression, but 78 percent of the 130 women who experienced a severe event in the follow-up year did *not* become depressed. What is the difference between the circumstances of women who become depressed after a severe event and those who do not? The investigators decided to examine the relationship between severe events and several other aspects of each woman's situation. One consideration involved ongoing difficulties that had been identified at the time of the first interview. Some severe events matched prior difficulties. For example, if a woman's pregnancy was rated as a severe event because she lived in poor housing, the event would have been rated as matching, or linked to, the difficulty. Another consideration involved areas of the woman's commitment, such as children, marriage, and employment, which had also been identified during the first phase of assessment.

The results of these analyses are illustrated in Table 5-5. Remember that all of the women in this table had experienced a severe event during the follow-up period. Prior difficulties and prior commitments were both significantly associated with risk for onset of depression after a severe event. In those situations where the severe event matched an ongoing area of difficulty, almost half of the women (16 out of 35) became depressed. An example would be if the woman's husband left home following a history of marital conflict. Only 14 percent of the women became depressed (13 out of 95) if their severe event did not match a prior difficulty. Similarly, women who experienced a severe event that matched an area to which they had previously demonstrated marked commitment were almost three times more likely to become depressed than those women whose severe events did not match an area of commitment. Eleven women experienced severe events that matched both a prior difficulty and an area of major commitment; 8 of them became depressed during the 1-year follow-up.

This study is important for two primary reasons. First, the use of a prospective design minimizes questions about the direction of effect. For these women, depression clearly followed their stressful experiences. Second, the data point to a particularly powerful relationship between the onset of depression and certain kinds of stressful life events. The likelihood that a woman will become depressed is especially high if she experiences a severe event in an area of her life that represents a serious commitment and in which she has experienced on-going difficulties. ■

Psychological Factors

Severe events are clearly related to the onset of depression, but they do not provide a complete account of who will become depressed. Many women who do not become depressed also experience severe events. In the study reported by Brown and Harris (1978), only one out of every five women who reported a severe event in the preceding year became depressed. Therefore, the investigators looked for characteristics that might identify women who were more likely than others to become depressed if they experienced a severe event. They found four such features, which they called "vulnerability factors." These included: (1) absence of an intimate, confiding relationship, (2) having several young children at home, (3) lacking employment away from home, and (4) loss of her mother at an early age. Vulnerability factors of this sort presumably reduce the woman's self-esteem and her sense that she will be able to cope successfully in the face of adversity (Brown, Bifulco, & Andrews, 1990). If a threatening event occurs at a time when a woman is less able to be hopeful and to persevere, the probability of serious depression is increased.

Several psychological factors may contribute to a person's vulnerability to stressful life events. In the following pages, we will consider two principal areas that have received attention in the research literature: cognitive factors and social skills.

COGNITIVE RESPONSES TO FAILURE AND DISAPPOINTMENT

Cognitive theories concerning the origins of depression have become extremely influential in recent years. These theories are based on the recognition that humans are not only social organisms; they are also thinking organisms. Cognitive therapists assume that the ways in which people think about and perceive their world have an important influence on the way that they feel. Two people may react very differently to the same event, in large part because they may interpret the event differently.

Beck's Cognitive Model Aaron Beck, a psychiatrist at the University of Pennsylvania, has been one of the most influential proponents of a cognitive view of depression (for example, Beck, 1967, 1974, 1984). Like Freud, Beck began with a primary interest in the things that depressed people say, particularly their self-critical thoughts and their extremely pessimistic views of their environment. He has defined the "depressive triad"—negative, demeaning views of the self, the world, and the future—as being central to our understanding of mood disorders. In contrast to the psychodynamic position, however, Beck has not chosen to view depressed peoples' critical self-statements as a reflection of their anger toward others. He argues instead that the negative things that depressed people say represent direct manifestations of fundamental cognitive distortions or erroneous ways of thinking about themselves. "The depressed person is overly sensitive to obstacles to goal-directed activity, interprets trivial impediments as substantial, reads disparagement into innocuous statements by others, and, at the same time, devalues himself or herself (Kovacs & Beck, 1978, p. 242)." According to Beck's theory, these pervasive and persistent negative cognitions play a central role in the onset of depression.

Beck has described various types of distortions, errors, and biases that characterize the thinking of depressed people. These include tendencies to assign global, personal meaning to experiences of failure; to overgeneralize conclusions about the self based on negative experiences; to draw arbitrary inferences about the self in the absence of supporting evidence (often in spite of contradictory evidence); to selectively recall events with negative consequences; and to exaggerate the importance of negative events while simultaneously discounting the significance of positive events.

Several research studies have demonstrated that these types of cognitive distortions are indeed more common among depressed people than among normal subjects when they are measured with self-report checklists and on laboratory tasks. Most of the evidence suggests, however, that cognitive errors are present during episodes of depression, but they are not readily apparent prior to the onset of an episode or after its resolution (for example, Barnett & Gotlib, 1988; Rhode, Lewinsohn, & Seeley, 1990).

How might these self-defeating biases eventually lead to the onset of depression? Why aren't they evident prior to the onset of an episode? According to Beck's theory, cognitive distortions and "depressogenic premises" (for example, "I should be able to endure any hardship with grace," "I should be smart and capable all the time") combine to form a general pattern or cognitive **schema** that guides the ways in which people perceive and interpret events in their environment. Schemas are described as enduring and highly organized cognitive structures—representations of prior experience. Although schemas may be latent—that is, not prominently represented in the person's conscious awareness at any given point in time—they are presumably reactivated when the person experiences a similar event. Depressive schemas increase the probability that the person will overreact to similar stressful events in the future.

The schemas that are most clearly related to depression are those that are concerned with self-evaluation and relationships with other people. They are presumably based on various unfavorable life experiences such as loss of a parent or chronic rejection by peers.

Beck's theory offers one perspective on the relations that may operate among various factors related to the development of depression. Negative cognitions are assigned a central role, but they are not seen as being the sole cause of depression. Rather, they represent "an important link in the sequence from remote causes (such as hereditary factors and developmental experience) and precipitating causes (such as traumatic events and depressogenic drugs) to the observable signs and symptoms of depression (Beck, 1984, p. 1113)."

Hopelessness Theory Another, related view of the role played by cognitive events has been proposed by Lynn Abramson, a clinical psychologist at the University of Wisconsin, and Lauren Alloy, a clinical psychologist at Temple University. This perspective has evolved out of "learned helplessness theory" (Seligman, 1974, 1975). The original version of learned helplessness theory as proposed by Martin Seligman suggested that depression was similar to the passive behavior shown by animals who had been exposed to inescapable shock in laboratory experiments. The theory argued that people who are depressed do not recognize a contingency between their behavior and outcomes in their environments. In other words, they believe that they are helpless in the sense that they cannot control events in their lives. The theory was revised (Abramson, Seligman, & Teasdale, 1978) to account for various problems that had been noted with the original version. For example, most people do not become depressed when they experience a negative event that is beyond their control.

This perspective has most recently been described in terms of **hopelessness** (Abramson, Metalsky, & Alloy, 1989).[†] According to this view, depression may be associated with the expectation that very desirable events probably will not occur or that aversive events probably will occur *regardless of what the person does*. Hopelessness refers to the person's negative expectations about future events and the associated belief that these events cannot be controlled. After a negative life event has occurred, the probability that the person will become depressed is a function of the explanations and importance that the person ascribes to these events. These explanations are known as causal attributions.

Abramson, Alloy, and their colleagues argue that some people exhibit a general "depresssogenic" attributional style that is characterized by a tendency to explain negative events in terms of internal, stable, global factors. For example, after failing an important exam, the person who possesses a depressogenic attributional style would be likely to think that her poor performance was the result of her own inadequacies (internal), which she has recognized for a long time and which will persist into the future (stable), and which are also responsible for her failure in many other important tasks, both academic and otherwise (global). As in Beck's description of negative schemas, attributional style is not seen as a sufficient cause of depression. It does represent an important predisposition to depression, however, to the extent that people with a generalized depressogenic attributional style will be more likely to develop hopelessness if they experience a negative life event.

The literature regarding cognitive factors in depression is filled with controversy as well as with interesting speculation (Brewin, 1985; Segal & Dobson, 1992). Research studies have provided some support for the argument that attributional style is useful in predicting people's responses to negative events (Metalsky et al., 1993). On the other hand, some reviewers have concluded that, although depressed people may present themselves in a negative light on various questionnaires, differences between groups are inconsistent and are smaller than the theories would seem to predict, and cognitive distortions are generally not unique to depressed patients (Coyne, 1992). Although cognitive factors may play an important role in mood disorders, they are only one piece of the etiological puzzle.

INTERPERSONAL FACTORS AND SOCIAL SKILLS

If cognitive factors alone cannot account for the relation between stressful life events and the onset of depression, what other considerations might be important? Several investigators have suggested that, in addition to the ways in which we think about negative or stressful experiences, the ways in which we actually respond to these events may also influence the probability that we will become depressed. In other words, it's not just how you think about an event or circumstance, but the things that you actually do that will determine its eventual outcome. This focus on overt behavior has been stimulated, in part, by the application of learning theory to the study of depression.

Lewinsohn's Behavioral Model Behavioral psychologists who have studied depression have traditionally focused on the absence of certain behaviors—on reduced activity levels and a withdrawal from social interactions. Peter Lewinsohn (1974), a psychologist at the University of Oregon, proposed an influential behavioral model in which depression is seen as the eventual product of a reduction in response-contingent positive reinforcement. Depressed people presumably become less active because their behavior is not followed by positive reinforcement. The decrease in adaptive behavior, which is produced by this prolonged "extinction schedule," presumably has a negative impact on the person's mood. Thus, a vicious cycle is set in motion: Reduced rate of response-contingent positive reinforcement leads to reduced activity, which is followed by a further reduction in reinforcement, and so on.

The behavioral model suggests that the initial reduction in response-contingent positive

---

[†] Hopelessness theory is proposed as an explanation for a subtype of mood disorder that Abramson calls "negative cognition depression." At the present time, on the basis of clinical symptoms, it is not possible to distinguish these cases from others in which cognitive factors are presumably less involved.

reinforcement may be the result of several factors, including the range of events that the person finds pleasant, the availability of these events within the person's present environment, and the extent to which the person is able to elicit reinforcement from his or her environment. Lewinsohn has paid considerable attention to the latter category, including the social skills with which people form friendships.

The role of interpersonal relationships is perhaps the most important aspect of this model. According to Lewinsohn, some "depressed behaviors," such as crying, complaining, and criticizing oneself, may be initially reinforced by other people in their attempts to provide comfort and support. By making these social contacts contingent upon the expression of a depressed mood, significant others may unintentionally increase the frequency and stability of their friend's depression. Lewinsohn proposed further that the continued manifestation of depressed behaviors has an aversive impact on other people. Thus, the depressed person's few remaining sources of social support will eventually be driven away.

The behavioral model has stimulated interest in the role played by social skills and interpersonal relationships in mood disorders. How does the depressed person cope with stressful events and respond to other people? What types of responses does the patient elicit from others? What are the extent and form of social resources that are available to help support the person during a crisis? Notice that in many ways these questions also bring us back to the issue of intimacy, which Brown and Harris identified as one vulnerability factor in their model of depression, as well as the notion of interpersonal dependency, which has been an important consideration in psychodynamic views of depression.

Research on Interpersonal Factors James Coyne, a psychologist at the University of Michigan, has studied the ways in which depressed people interact with those around them (Coyne, 1976; Coyne, Downey, & Boergers, 1993). This interpersonal perspective, which emphasizes the active, reciprocal nature of our social environments, has produced some interesting findings regarding factors that contribute to the development and maintenance of depression. The assumptions behind this model are quite different from those incorporated in more cog-

nitively oriented theories. For example, Beck might argue that faulty processing of information from their environment leads those who are depressed to believe (erroneously) that their relationships with other people are inadequate. Coyne suggested that depressed people may actually behave in ways that have a genuinely negative effect on other people, thus alienating themselves from friends and family members. When this occurs, depressed people may come to see their self-critical comments as an *accurate perception* of the fact that they are not well liked by others.

Several research studies have demonstrated that depressed people do indeed have a negative impact on other people's moods and on their nonverbal behavior (Gotlib & Meltzer, 1987; Hokanson et al., 1989). In addition, depressed people have smaller and less supportive social networks than do people who are not depressed. They know fewer people, interact with them less often, and consider them to be less supportive (Gotlib & Lee, 1989). Family interactions are generally more negative and argumentative. Perhaps most importantly, these maladaptive patterns of interpersonal relationships are ongoing characteristics of the individual's behavior that persist into periods of symptomatic remission. They are not evident only during active episodes of major depression (Gotlib & Hammen, 1992).

Response Styles and Gender A slightly different aspect of coping behavior may help to explain gender differences in the frequency of depression. Susan Nolen-Hoeksema (1990), a psychologist at Stanford University, has proposed that the manner in which a person responds to the onset of a depressed mood will influence the duration and the severity of the mood. The model emphasizes two different response styles. Some people respond to feelings of depression by turning their attention inward, contemplating the causes and implications of their sadness. Nolen-Hoeksema refers to this as a *ruminative style*. Writing in a diary or talking extensively with a friend about how you feel are indications of a ruminative style. Other people employ a *distracting style* to divert themselves from their unpleasant mood. They work on hobbies, play sports, or otherwise become involved in activities that draw their attention away from symptoms of depression.

▲ Peter Lewinsohn, whose behavorial model of depression inspired much of the research on interpersonal factors in depression. His longitudinal studies have contributed important information regarding the role of cognitive factors and social skills in the development of depression.

The first hypothesis of Nolen-Hoeksema's model is that people who engage in ruminative responses have longer and more severe episodes of depression than do people who engage in distracting responses. Her second hypothesis is that women are more likely to employ a ruminative style in response to depression, whereas men are more likely to employ a distracting style. Because the ruminative style leads to episodes of greater duration and intensity, women are more susceptible to depression than men are.

Research evidence provides some support for both of Nolen-Hoeksema's hypotheses. A ruminative response style does tend to be associated with longer and more severely depressed moods, and women are more likely than men to exhibit a ruminative style in response to depressed mood (Nolen-Hoeksema, Morrow, & Frederickson, 1993). The model has been tested most extensively with analogue subjects, normal subjects who are experiencing a dysphoric mood. Relatively little information is available regarding its applicability with clinically depressed subjects.

INTEGRATION OF COGNITIVE AND INTERPERSONAL FACTORS

Ian Gotlib, a clinical psychologist at Northwestern University, and Constance Hammen, a clinical psychologist at UCLA, have proposed a conceptual framework for understanding unipolar disorders that emphasizes the interaction of cognitive factors and interpersonal skills (Gotlib & Hammen, 1992). Their model is especially interesting because it considers depression in terms of several stages: vulnerability, onset, and maintenance. Both cognitive factors and interpersonal skills play an important role within each stage. At each point in the model, Gotlib and Hammen emphasize the importance of ongoing transactions between the person and his or her environment. Adverse events influence a person's mood, but people also play an active role in selecting and shaping their own environments. Gotlib and Hammen provide the following summary of cognitive and interpersonal factors.

Vulnerability to depression is influenced by experiences during childhood, including events such as the loss of a parent, which was one of the vulnerability factors identified by Brown and Harris (1978). Negative schemas, or ways of thinking about the world, and dysfunctional

interpersonal skills are presumably learned early in life. Gotlib and Hammen argue that the combination of cognitive schemas and deficits in interpersonal skills affects the person's social environment in several ways. It increases the likelihood that the person will enter problematic relationships; it diminishes the person's ability to resolve conflict after it occurs; and it minimizes the person's ability to solicit support and assistance from other people.

The *onset* of depression is most often triggered by life events and circumstances. The stressful life events that precipitate an episode frequently grow out of difficult personal and family relationships. Gotlib and Hammen note, at this point, another factor that may make women more likely than men to develop depression. Women are more likely to respond empathically to life events that happen to friends and family members. Men, in contrast, are affected only by things that happen directly to them (Kessler & McLeod, 1984). It is important to remember that most people do not become clinically depressed in response to such events. The impact of these experiences depends upon the meanings that people assign to them. People

▼ Stressful life events that lead to the onset of depression often involve interpersonal relationships. Women may be more vulnerable to depression than men are because they are likely to respond empathically when something bad happens to their friends or family members.

become depressed when they interpret events in a way that diminishes their sense of self-worth. Their depressed mood can become worse if they respond to the early symptoms by focusing attention on their feelings and ruminating about their problems.

Depression is *maintained* over an extended period of time, and it escalates to clinical proportions, as a result of persistent interpersonal and cognitive problems. Depressed people behave in ways that elicit negative reactions and rejection from others. Their conversational style may be negative, hostile, or inappropriately self-disclosing. Deficits in problem solving and conflict resolution also contribute to these problems. Depressed people are also more likely to notice and dwell on negative events in their environments. Negative cognitive schemas remain activated, accentuating the impact of stressful circumstances. They are more likely to be acutely aware of criticism and rejection, which, in many cases, they have elicited with their own aversive interpersonal style.

Biological Factors

We have already considered a number of social and psychological factors that contribute to the etiology of mood disorders. Biological factors also play an influential role in the regulation of mood. Research conducted since the 1970s has established that certain biological factors are associated with both unipolar and bipolar mood disorders. Various studies suggest that genetic factors are somehow involved, that the process of neural transmission in the brain is dysfunctional in some patients, and that hormonal abnormalities are regularly associated with depression.

GENETICS

In Kraepelin's early writings on manic-depressive psychoses, he noted the presence of a "hereditary taint" in the majority of cases. This inference was based on his observation that many of the patients' relatives exhibited symptoms of the same disorder. Subsequent studies have confirmed his impression that genetic factors are involved in the transmission of mood disorders. They have also provided useful insights regarding the utility of the unipolar/bipolar distinction.

Family Studies If the development of mood disorders is influenced by genetic factors, these disorders should show a *familial* pattern of transmission. In other words, they should be more common among the biological relatives of people who are depressed than they are among the general population. First-degree relatives (siblings, parents, and children) of patients with mood disorders should be more vulnerable to the disorder because they share 50 percent of

their genes with an affected individual. Several carefully controlled studies have confirmed this hypothesis. Family studies begin with the identification of an individual who has been diagnosed as having a mood disorder, who is known as the *proband*. Researchers obtain as much information as possible about the proband's relatives, either through personal interviews, family informants, or mental health records. They use this information to decide whether each relative fits criteria for mood disorders. They can then compare the lifetime morbid risk among patients' relatives with those figures already established for the general population.

Table 5-6 presents a summary of data from several family studies of mood disorder. An interesting pattern distinguishes unipolar and bipolar mood disorders. Remember that the lifetime risk for major depressive disorder was approximately 5 percent in the ECA study, whereas the lifetime risk for bipolar disorder was approximately 1 percent. With these figures in mind, consider the frequency of disorder among the relatives of unipolar probands. The risk for bipolar disorder among their relatives is close to that seen in the general population, but the risk for unipolar disorder is almost doubled. Among the relatives of bipolar probands, the risk for both bipolar and unipolar disorder is much higher than that seen in the general population. The combined risk for both types of mood disorder is about 19 percent, almost double the combined risk of 10 percent found among the relatives of unipolar probands. Both types of mood disorder are therefore markedly familial.

Twin Studies The comparison of monozygotic (MZ) and dizygotic (DZ) twin pairs provides a more stringent test of the possible influence of genetic factors (see Chapter 2). Several twin studies of mood disorders have reported higher concordance rates among MZ than among DZ twins (Katz & McGuffin, 1993; Moldin, Reich, & Rice, 1991).

One classic study was reported by Axel Bertelson, a Danish psychiatrist, and his colleagues (1977). They used national twin and psychiatric registers in Denmark to identify 110 pairs of same-sexed twins in which at least one member was diagnosed as having a mood disorder. The concordance rates for bipolar disorders in MZ and DZ twins were .69 and .19, respectively. For unipolar disorders, concordance rates for MZ and DZ twins were .54 and .24, respectively. The fact that the concordance rates were significantly higher for MZ than for DZ twins indicates that genetic factors are involved in the transmission of both bipolar and unipolar mood disorders. The fact that the difference between the MZ and DZ rate was somewhat higher for bipolar than for unipolar disorders may suggest that the effects of genes are more important in the case of bipolar disorders. Similar patterns of MZ and DZ concordance rates have subsequently been reported from twin studies of mood disorders conducted in Sweden (Torgersen, 1986) and in England (McGuffin, Katz, & Rutherford, 1991).

Twin studies also indicate that environmental factors mediate the expression of a genetically determined vulnerability to depression. The best evidence for the influence of nongenetic factors is the concordance rates in MZ twins, which consistently fall short of 100 percent. If genes told the whole story, MZ twins would always be concordant. Mathematical analyses have been used to estimate the relative contributions of genetic and environmental events to the etiology of mood disorders (Katz & McGuffin, 1993). They indicate that genetic factors are particularly influential in bipolar mood disorders, accounting for more than 80 percent of the variance in vulnerability. Genes contribute about half (52 percent) of the variance in the case of major depressive disorder. The genetic contribution may be relatively minor for dysthymia or neurotic depression, where environmental factors seem to account for more than 90 percent of the variance.

Combined Studies of Life Stress and Genetic Factors

The relative contributions of genetic and environmental factors can be evaluated by combining mathematical procedures with the traditional twin design. The first study to follow this procedure employed 680 pairs of female same-sexed twins from the Virginia Twin Registry (Kendler et al., 1993). At three points in time, each separated from the next by approximately 1 year, the investigators collected information regarding symptoms of major depression, lifetime traumas, recent stressful life events, social support, and personality characteristics. Sixteen percent of the women reported at least one episode of major depression during the 2-year follow-up period.

Among all the variables included in the analyses from Kendler's Virginia Twin Study, genetic background was the second-best predictor of clinical depression. It was exceeded only by recent stressful events, which had the strongest influence on the development of depression in this particular sample. Fateful events (random traumatic experiences) seemed to play the most important role, but the investigators also found that genetic risk factors for depression also predicted lifetime traumas and recent stressful events. Genes may contribute to the development of

	TABLE 5–6

Average Morbid Risk for Mood Disorders in First-Degree Relatives of Unipolar and Bipolar Patients

	Relatives' Disorder (% with disorder)	
Type of proband	Unipolar	Bipolar
Unipolar	9.1%	0.6%
Bipolar	11.4%	7.8%

Based on 7 studies of relatives of unipolar probands and 12 studies of relatives of bipolar probands.

Source: R. Katz and P. McGuffin. (1993). The genetics of affective disorders. In L.J. Chapman, J.P. Chapman, and D. Fowles (Eds.), *Progress in experimental personality and psychopathology research.* New York: Springer.

depression by influencing some people to select or create a personal environment that puts them at high risk for a mood disorder. The overall results of this study indicate that both genetic factors and stressful life events play a substantial role in the etiology of major depressive disorder.

Mode of Transmission and Linkage Studies

The family and twin studies indicate that genetic factors play an important role in the development of mood disorders. They have not, however, established the operation of a particular mode of inheritance. Most investigators view mood disorders as being polygenic—they are influenced by several different genes.

Some investigators favor the single-locus model of inheritance, which holds that one gene at a particular location, or *locus*, on a particular chromosome is responsible for mood disorders. To support their arguments they have searched for evidence of chromosomal linkage between the locus of a known gene and the locus for a gene that is responsible for mood disorders. Two loci are said to be *linked* when they occupy positions that are close together on the same chromosome. Linkage is usually detected by examining the degree of association between two or more traits within specific families (see Research Methods, Chapter 13).

Linkage studies of mood disorders have focused on bipolar patients because the effects of genetic factors appear to be more salient in bipolar than in unipolar disorders, and because transmission within specific families follows the pattern expected in a simple Mendelian dominant trait. With the introduction of new gene-mapping techniques, our knowledge in this area is expanding dramatically. Thus far, the results are mixed (Craddock & McGuffin, 1993). One group has reported the detection of linkage with markers on chromosome 11 among Amish people living in Pennsylvania (Egeland et al., 1987). Another found evidence for linkage between bipolar mood disorder and markers on the X (female sex) chromosome such as colorblindness (Risch, Baron, & Mendlewicz et al., 1986). Unfortunately, several other laboratories have been unable to duplicate these results (Heberbrand, 1992; Mitchell et al., 1991).

The possibility of detecting linkage to known traits is very exciting. This knowledge would enable health professionals to identify those individuals who are vulnerable to a disorder before the onset of overt symptoms. At the same time, however, two important cautions should be kept in mind with regard to genetic linkage studies. One problem involves genetic *heterogeneity*. Within the general population, there may be more than one locus that is capable of producing the trait in question. Mood disorders may be linked to one marker within a certain pedigree and to an entirely different marker in another pedigree. Second, it will not be possible to establish linkage unless a single gene of main effect is responsible for the development of a particular disorder. In the case of mood disorders, several genes might be responsible.

NEUROTRANSMITTERS AND DEPRESSION

Chemical activity in the brain is another important biological factor that is undoubtedly involved in the etiology of mood disorders. Over the past several decades, scientists have gathered a great deal of information concerning the neural underpinnings of depression and mania (Delgado, Price, Heninger, & Charney, 1992).

This information comes from two principal areas: psychopharmacology and neuroscience. Our knowledge in this area initially was based on the accidental discovery of several drugs that have the ability to alter people's moods. Some of the most crucial discoveries occurred within a fairly short period of time during the late 1940s and the 1950s.

- Iproniazid was being used to treat people suffering from tuberculosis. Clinicians observed that some patients who took this drug experienced inappropriate mood elevation. Neuroscientists soon determined that iproniazid inhibits the action of monoamine oxidase (MAO), one of the enzymes that breakdown monoamines, such as norepinephrine and serotonin, in the nerve terminal. Psychiatrists found that this general class of drugs, known as monoamine oxidase (MAO) inhibitors, could be used successfully to treat depressed patients.

- A related discovery was made by scientists working for a pharmaceutical company. They were looking for a variant of the phenothiazines, a class of drugs shown to have beneficial effects for people with schizophrenia (see Chapter 12). Imipramine was tested with a variety of psychiatric patients, and although it did not prove useful with schizophrenia, it did appear to have mood-elevating properties and was subsequently shown to be effective with depressed patients. One pharmacological action of imipramine is to block the reuptake of catecholamines (norepinephrine and dopamine) into the nerve terminal. Imipramine and several related compounds form the group of drugs known as tricyclic antidepressants (TCAs).

- Another drug, reserpine, was identified in 1952 and was soon used widely in the treatment of hypertension. Physicians noticed that approximately 15 percent of hypertensive patients being treated with reserpine developed a major depressive disorder. Scientists subsequently discovered that reserpine depletes the store of norepinephrine in the nerve terminal by pushing it out of the vesicles into the cell, where it is broken down.

Based on this evidence, Schildkraut (1965) and Bunney and Davis (1965) proposed a simple biochemical theory—the *catecholamine hypothesis*—to explain the etiology of depression.[†] According to this theory, depression was associated with a decrease in the levels of brain catecholamines, especially norepinephrine. Mania, on the other hand, was presumably associated with an excess of norepinephrine. Shortly thereafter, and based largely on the same pharmacological data, Glassman (1969) suggested that serotonin, another neurotransmitter in the central nervous system, might also be related to depression because MAO inhibitors and TCAs affect this neurotransmitter in the same way that they affect norepinephrine. This second theory came to be known as the *indolamine hypothesis*.

Two important considerations have recently led to a somewhat different perspective on neurochemistry and mood disorders. First, several new drugs—known as second-generation or "atypical" antidepressants—have been discovered. These drugs are effective in the treatment of depressed patients, but they have different physiological effects than the classic antidepressant drugs. More specifically, they do not affect the reuptake of monoamines (norepinephrine or serotonin), and they do not inhibit MAO. The second consideration involves the distinction between short-term and long-term drug effects. Antidepressants typically must be taken for 1 to 3 weeks before they have a clinical effect. The catecholamine and indolamine hypotheses were based on evidence regarding the immediate effects of these drugs on cell functioning. If depression is associated with a low level of norepinephrine in certain brain areas, and if TCA antidepressants block the uptake of norepinephrine right away, why don't these antidepressants have *immediate* beneficial effects on the patient's mood?

Studies of the *long-term* effects of antidepressants on membrane receptors have cast a new light on the neurochemistry of mood disorders. These studies suggest that the original notions presented in the catecholamine and indolamine hypotheses—that depression was produced by a simple reduction in the amount of norepinephrine or serotonin—were much too simple. Current theories tend to place a greater emphasis on the interactive effects of several neurotransmitter systems, including dopamine (Depue & Iacono, 1989; Kapur & Mann, 1992) as well as serotonin, norepinephrine, and neuropeptides—short chains of amino acids that exist in the brain and appear to modulate the activity of the classical neurotransmitters. These theories focus more on the role of postsynaptic receptor sensitivity and density rather than on a simple deficiency in the amount of neurotransmitter substances that are available (Charney et al., 1991; Siever & Davis, 1985). In essence, they propose that postsynaptic receptors are both more sensitive and more dense in depressed patients. These theories are based in part on animal studies that have demonstrated that treatment with antidepressants decreases the sensitivity and density of these receptors (McNeal & Cimbolic, 1986).

THE NEUROENDOCRINE SYSTEM

The endocrine system plays an important role in regulating a person's response to stress. As we saw in Chapter 2, endocrine glands, such as the pituitary, thyroid, and adrenal glands, are located at various sites throughout the body. In response to signals from the brain, these glands secrete hormones into the bloodstream. One important pathway in the endocrine system that may be closely related to the etiology of mood disorders is called the hypothalamic–pituitary–adrenal (HPA) axis. Signals from the hypothalamus cause the pituitary gland to secrete a hormone called ACTH, which in turn modulates secretion of hormones by the adrenal glands.

Interest in the relation between mood disorders and the endocrine system was stimulated in part by descriptions of Cushing's syndrome, a disease associated with the adrenal glands that results in abnormally high concentrations of the hormone cortisol in the bloodstream. Approximately half of all patients with Cushing's syndrome are also clinically depressed. After Cushing's

---

[†] One general class of neurotransmitters in the central nervous system is known as the monoamines, which are organic compounds containing nitrogen in one amino group. The monoamine neurotransmitters contain two important subtypes: catecholamines, which have a catechol portion (such as norepinephrine and dopamine) and indolamines, which have an indole portion (such as serotonin and tryptamine).

syndrome is corrected, most patients also recover from their depression. This pattern suggests that abnormally high levels of cortisol may lead to the onset of depression (Checkley, 1992).

An association between the HPA axis and depression is also indicated by evidence regarding the dexamethasone suppression test (DST), which has been used extensively to study endocrine dysfunction in patients with mood disorders (Friedman, Clark, & Gershon, 1992). Dexamethasone is a potent synthetic hormone. People who have taken a test dose of dexamethasone normally show a *suppression* of cortisol secretion because the hypothalamus is fooled into thinking that there is already enough cortisol circulating in the system (Whybrow, Akiskal, & McKinney, 1984). Approximately half of depressed patients show a failure of suppression in response to the DST. Most of these patients exhibit a normal response on the DST after their clinical condition improves. This pattern is consistent with the hypothesis that a dysfunction of the HPA axis may be involved in the development or maintenance of clinical depression, at least for some people. Relatively high rates of nonsuppression have also been found among patients with anxiety disorders and substance abuse disorders.

In what ways might endocrine problems be related to other etiological factors we have already discussed? Several possibilities exist. In terms of the specific link between the endocrine system and the central nervous system, overproduction of cortisol may lead to a reduced density of serotonin receptors (Roy et al., 1987). At a more general level, hormone regulation may provide a process through which stressful life events interact with a genetically determined predisposition to mood disorder. Stress causes the release of adrenal steroids, such as cortisol, and steroid hormones play an active role in regulating the expression of genes (Checkley, 1992).

The Interaction of Social, Psychological, and Biological Factors

In the preceding sections of this chapter, we have considered a variety of social, psychological, and biological factors that appear to be related to the etiology of mood disorders. How can all of these factors be combined or integrated? Do we need to choose among them, advocating either a radical biological or psychological perspective? Some clinicians have argued that certain kinds of mood disorder are caused by biological factors and others are psychological in nature. We favor the systems view, which holds that mood disorders and other forms of psychopathology are typically produced by a combination of interacting biopsychosocial systems.

One interesting line of investigation that illustrates this type of interaction has been pursued using an animal model of depression based on Seligman's helplessness theory (see Research Methods). When laboratory animals are exposed to uncontrollable electric shock, they frequently exhibit behavioral deficits that are *similar to* (yet obviously not the same as) those seen in depressed humans. The animals develop deficits in motor activity, sleep, and eating behaviors. Furthermore, the administration of antidepressant drugs to these animals has been shown to reverse or prevent the behavioral effects of uncontrollable shock.

Jay Weiss, a clinical psychologist who has spent most of his career studying animal models of stress, and his colleagues have studied these effects in great detail, emphasizing in particular the neurochemical basis of "stress-induced depression" in laboratory rats (Weiss & Simson, 1985). They demonstrated that the experience of stress sometimes causes a large decrease in the concentration of norepinephrine within the locus coeruleus region of the brain. Following exposure to uncontrollable shock, rats that showed this neurochemical effect also exhibited signs of depression. If the neurotransmitter was not depleted, the rats did not appear to be depressed.

Weiss's research program illustrates the need to consider the interaction between biological and psychological phenomena. His data suggest that various neurochemical processes may be reactions to environmental events, such as uncontrollable shock in rats or major stressful events in people. Some psychological and biological explanations of depression may be compatible views that differ in terms of their level of analysis.

Analogue Studies of Psychopathology

Many questions about the etiology of psychopathology cannot be addressed using highly controlled laboratory studies with human subjects. Does prolonged exposure to uncontrollable stress cause anxiety disorders? Can the destruction of specific neurotransmitter pathways produce clinical depression? These issues have been addressed using correlational studies with people who have the disorders in question, but experiments on these issues cannot be done with human subjects (see Research Methods, Chapter 3). For obvious ethical reasons, investigators cannot randomly assign people to endure conditions that are hypothesized to produce full-blown disorders like clinical depression, schizophrenia, and alcoholism. The best alternative is often to study a condition that is similar, or analogous, to the clinical disorder in question. Investigations of this type are called **analogue studies** because they focus on behaviors that resemble mental disorders—or isolated features of mental disorders—that appear in the natural environment.

Many analogue studies depend on the use of animal models of psychopathology, which have provided important insights regarding the etiology of conditions such as anxiety, depression, and schizophrenia (Mineka & Zinbarg, 1991). The first influential animal models of psychopathology were developed in Pavlov's laboratory during the 1920s and 1930s. They were concerned with the role of classical conditioning in the etiology of anxiety disorders. In the 1960s, Harry Harlow's research demonstrated that rhesus monkey infants develop despair responses after being separated from their mothers. The somatic symptoms exhibited by these monkeys—facial and vocal displays of sadness and dismay, social withdrawal, changes in appetite, sleep, and psychomotor retardation—were remarkably similar to many symptoms of clinical depression in humans.

This social separation model of depression has been used to explore several important social variables that may be involved in mood disorders. For example, infant monkeys who have extensive experience with peers and other adults are less likely to become depressed following separation from their mothers. The skills that they learn through social exploration apparently allow them to cope more successfully with stress. The social separation model has also been used to explore neurochemical underpinnings of mood disorders. For example, drug companies have tested potential antidepressant drugs on monkeys that were separated from their mothers (Mineka & Zinbarg, 1991).

Some clinicians have argued that mental disorders like depression cannot be modeled in a laboratory setting, especially using animals as subjects. Cognitive symptoms, such as Beck's depressive triad (negative view of the self, the world, and the future), cannot be measured with animals. Do monkeys feel guilty? Can rats experience hopelessness or suicidal ideas? These symptoms are not necessarily the most central features of mood disorders, however. Cross-cultural studies have shown that somatic symptoms are the most prominent symptoms of depression in some non-Western societies. Many of these aspects of mood disorder are seen in animals. The value of any analogue study hinges, in large part, on the extent of the similarity between the analogue condition and the actual clinical disorder. Some models are more compelling than others.

Another type of analogue study uses human subjects whose behaviors resemble psychopathology. For example, many investigators have studied college students who produce high scores on paper-and-pencil measures of depression. The rationale for these studies is that these students experience problems that are similar to mood disorders. In most cases, these students would not be classified as clinically depressed, despite their high scores.

Analogue studies have one important advantage over other types of research design in psychopathology: They can employ an experimental procedure. Therefore, the investigator can draw strong inferences about cause and effect. The main disadvantage of analogue studies involves the extent to which the results of a particular investigation can be generalized to situations outside the laboratory. If a particular set of circumstances produced a set of maladaptive behaviors in the laboratory, is it reasonable to assume that similar mechanisms produce the actual clinical disorder in the natural environment?

In actual practice, questions about the etiology of disorders like depression will probably depend upon converging evidence generated from the use of many different research designs. Theories should be tested using correlational designs with samples of clinical patients as well as experimental designs based on analogue conditions. The combination of results from these complementary research methods has provided important information regarding several disorders that are discussed elsewhere in this book. ∎

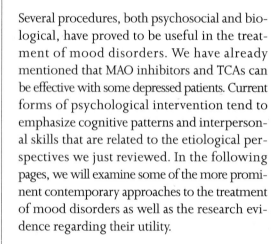

Treatment

Several procedures, both psychosocial and biological, have proved to be useful in the treatment of mood disorders. We have already mentioned that MAO inhibitors and TCAs can be effective with some depressed patients. Current forms of psychological intervention tend to emphasize cognitive patterns and interpersonal skills that are related to the etiological perspectives we just reviewed. In the following pages, we will examine some of the more prominent contemporary approaches to the treatment of mood disorders as well as the research evidence regarding their utility.

Psychological Interventions

Most psychological approaches to the treatment of depression owe some debt to psychodynamic procedures and Freud's emphasis on the importance of anger and interpersonal dynamics. According to his view, the primary goal of therapy should be to help the patient understand and express the hostility and frustration that are being directed against the self. These negative emotions are presumably rooted in dysfunctional relationships with other people. Freud also placed considerable emphasis on the apparently irrational beliefs that depressed people hold about themselves and their world. These cognitive factors are also emphasized by cognitive therapists.

▲ **Aaron Beck has developed an influential cognitive theory of depression, emphasizing the importance of distorted ways of thinking about the self. He has pioneered the use of cognitive therapy for the treatment of depression.**

COGNITIVE THERAPY

Cognitive therapy has been developed and promoted by Aaron Beck and his colleagues (for example, Beck et al., 1979). It is based on his cognitive model, which assumes that emotional dysfunction is influenced by the ways in which people interpret events in their environments and the things that they say to themselves about those experiences. Unlike Freud and other proponents of the psychodynamic perspective, Beck did not believe that patients' irrational statements about themselves are actually complaints about other people. He argued instead that these statements are reflections of negative schemas that guide the patient's interpretation of life events.

Cognitive treatments are based on the assumption that the patient's depression will be relieved if these irrational beliefs are changed. Therefore, instead of probing delicately for the unconscious roots of anger, Beck has encouraged a more directive, rational approach to changing these dysfunctional attitudes. Cognitive therapists focus on helping their patients replace self-defeating cognitions with more rational self-statements.

A specific example may help illustrate this process. Consider the case of Cathy, the depressed attorney whom we introduced at the beginning of the chapter. Cathy focused a great deal of attention on relatively minor negative events at work, blaming herself for anything other than a perfect performance. Her therapist helped her to recognize that she was engaging in a pattern of cognitive distortion that Beck has labeled "selective abstraction." Taking a detail out of context, she would invariably ignore those aspects of her performance that refuted the conclusion that she was professionally incompetent. Her therapist helped her overcome these tendencies by teaching her to question her conclusions and to develop more objective ways of evaluating her experiences.

Cathy also tended to think about herself in absolute and unvarying terms. During the course of therapy, she learned to recognize this pattern and to substitute more flexible self-statements. Instead of saying to herself "I am a hopeless introvert and will never be able to change," she learned to substitute "I am less comfortable in social situations than some other people, but I can learn to be more confident."

Although Beck's approach to treatment emphasizes the importance of cognitive events, it shares many features with behavioral approaches to intervention. Cognitive therapists are active and directive in their interactions with clients, and they focus most of their attention on their clients' current experience. They also assume that people have conscious access to cognitive events: Our thinking may not always be rational, but we can discuss private thoughts and feelings. Another important aspect of Beck's approach to treatment, and a characteristic that it shares with the behavioral perspective, is a serious commitment to the empirical evaluation of the efficacy of treatment programs. Several studies have found that cognitive therapy is quite effective in the treatment of nonpsychotic, unipolar depression (Hollon, Shelton, & Davis, 1993). Two direct comparisons of cognitive therapy and behavioral therapy in the treatment of major depressive disorder have found that both types of treatment were effective, with neither being superior to the other (Hollon et al., 1993; Murphy et al., 1984).

INTERPERSONAL THERAPY

Interpersonal therapy is another contemporary approach to the psychological treatment of depression (Klerman et al., 1984). Based originally on traditional psychodynamic notions regarding dependent personality traits and depression, interpersonal therapy focuses primarily on current relationships, especially those involving family members. The therapist helps the patient develop a better understanding of the interpersonal problems that presumably give rise to depression (Gotlib & Hammen, 1992) and attempts to improve the patient's relationships with other people by building communication and problem-solving skills. Therapy sessions often include nondirective discussions of social difficulties and unexpressed or unacknowledged negative emotions as well as role-playing to practice specific social skills.

The Treatment of Depression Collaborative Research Program was a large-scale study that compared the effectiveness of two types of psychotherapy—cognitive and interpersonal therapy—with the use of antidepressant medication (Elkin et al., 1989). It was sponsored by the National Institute of Mental Health (NIMH) and was conducted at three different sites. Unipolar depressed outpatients were assigned to one of four treatment groups: cognitive therapy, interpersonal therapy, antidepressant medication (imipramine or Tofranil, a standard TCA), or placebo plus clinical management. Patients in the latter group met regularly with a therapist to receive pills that they believed to be antidepressants and also received rather extensive support and encouragement. Treatment lasted approximately 16 weeks in all conditions.

The results of the Collaborative Research Program are extensive and complex, given the large number of measures that were collected on all patients, differences across the three treatment sites, and variability in dropout rates in the different types of treatment. A few major findings stand out. First, all three types of active treatment were superior to the placebo plus clinical management condition in terms of their ability to reduce depression and improve overall levels of functioning. Second, there were no significant differences between cognitive and interpersonal therapy, and both were generally as effective as antidepressant medication. Third, patients improved somewhat more rapidly if they were receiving imipramine, but the rate of improvement in both psychotherapy groups caught up to the drug condition by the end of treatment. Fourth, contrary to expectations, patients who received different forms of psychotherapy did not exhibit improvements in specific psychological domains that were addressed in therapy. In other words, patients who received interpersonal therapy showed as much improvement on measures of cognitive distortion as the patients who received cognitive therapy.

The results of this study were quite positive over the short run. Unfortunately, follow-up evaluations conducted 18 months after the completion of treatment were less encouraging. By that point, patients in the three active treatment groups were no longer functioning at a higher level than those who received only the placebo and clinical management. Less than 30 percent of the patients who were considered markedly improved at the end of treatment were still nondepressed at follow-up. This aspect of the study's results points to the need for continued efforts to improve currently available treatment methods.

Biological Interventions

Somatic methods of intervention grew out of a different tradition. Kraepelin and many other psychiatrists at the end of the nineteenth century believed that mental illnesses such as manic-depressive psychosis would eventually be understood in terms of biological factors. Their observations tended to focus on institutionalized patients who were severely disturbed and for whom there was little hope of recovery. During the early years of the twentieth century, treatments in mental hospitals relied on procedures such as hot and cold baths and the use of physical restraints. The 1930s witnessed the introduction of psychosurgery (see our discussion of this topic in Chapter 3) and shock treatments, which were all initially hailed as major advances in the treatment of psychoses. Within 20 years, brain surgery and the chemical induction of comas and convulsions had been largely abandoned in favor of newly discovered forms of medication. Electroconvulsive therapy (ECT), a more precise manner of inducing electrical seizure activity in the brain, evolved out of the more primitive chemical procedures and continues to be used as an effective form of treatment for depression.

ELECTROCONVULSIVE THERAPY

The procedure known as *electroconvulsive therapy* (or *ECT*) has proved beneficial for many depressed patients. Electroconvulsive therapy is typically administered in an inpatient setting and consists of a series of treatments (Fink,

1992). Treatments are given two or three times a week. Many patients show a dramatic improvement after six to eight sessions, but some require more. In current clinical practice, muscle relaxants are always administered before a patient receives ECT. This procedure has eliminated bone fractures and dislocations that were unfortunate side effects of earlier techniques. The electrodes can be placed either bilaterally (on both sides of the head) or unilaterally (at the front and back of the skull on one side of the patient's head). Unilateral placement on the nondominant hemisphere (the right side of the head for right-handed people) may minimize the amount of postseizure memory impairment, but it may also be less effective in terms of antidepressant results (Royal College of Psychiatrists, 1989).

Although the mode of action in ECT remains largely a mystery (Sackheim, 1989), several empirical studies have demonstrated that it is an effective form of treatment for patients who are severely depressed (Consensus Conference, 1985). It is certainly more effective than no treatment at all, and in many studies it has been found to be superior to antidepressant medication. One early study (Greenblatt et al., 1964) compared the effects of ECT, tricyclic drugs, and placebo in the treatment of more than 200 hospitalized depressed patients. The investigators found that 76 percent of the patients who received ECT were considered markedly improved at the end of treatment, compared with only 50 percent for the patients who received medication. Furthermore, the patients who received ECT improved more quickly than those on medication.

Convulsive therapy remains controversial, perhaps in part because it has been widely misrepresented in the popular media. Commercial films such as *One Flew Over the Cuckoo's Nest* (released in 1975) have suggested erroneously that it is used primarily as a form of punishment. More legitimate reservations regarding the use of ECT center around widely publicized, although apparently infrequent, cases of pervasive and persistent memory loss.

No one denies that ECT is an invasive procedure that should usually be reserved for patients who have been resistant to other forms of intervention such as medication and cognitive therapy. Nevertheless, it remains a viable and legitimate alternative for some severely depressed patients, especially those who may otherwise be in danger of harming themselves. Rapid cycling bipolar patients and depressed patients with psychotic symptoms may also be more responsive to ECT than to medication. As always, the risks of treatment must be carefully weighed against those associated with allowing the disorder to follow its natural course.

ANTIDEPRESSANT MEDICATIONS

Pharmacological treatments for mood disorders have been in relatively widespread use since the 1950s. They have had a dramatic impact on clinical practice and have also been responsible for important developments in neurochemical theories regarding the causes of depression. New compounds are introduced on a fairly regular basis, and the list of antidepressant drugs has become rather extensive and complicated. The most commonly used forms of medication fall into four general categories: tricyclics, monoamine oxidase inhibitors, selective serotonin reuptake inhibitors, and lithium carbonate.

Tricyclics **Tricyclic** drugs such as imipramine and amitriptyline affect brain functions by blocking the uptake of neurotransmitters (for example, norepinephrine and dopamine) from the synapse. Several controlled double-blind studies indicate that tricyclics provide beneficial effects for many depressed patients (Goodwin, 1992), although improvements might not be evident until 2 or 3 weeks after the beginning of treatment. There are several different kinds of tricyclic medication that vary in potency and side effects, but they are generally equal in terms of effectiveness.

Because some depressed patients do not improve after receiving tricyclic medication, considerable research efforts have been devoted to identifying those patients who will show a positive therapeutic response (Joyce, 1992). Although many clinicians believe that a family history of depression and various premorbid personality characteristics are associated with drug response, the empirical evidence has failed to establish any reliable relations among these variables. Alternative assessment methods that focus on biological variables, such as the dexamethasone suppression test (Peselow et al., 1989) and EEG patterns during sleep (Rush et al., 1989), have been more encouraging, but their results have not been consistent. At the pre-

sent time, the utility of tricyclic medication must still be determined on an individual basis.

Monoamine Oxidase Inhibitors The antidepressant effects of **monoamine oxidase (MAO) inhibitors** were discovered at about the same time as those of the tricyclic drugs. These drugs have not been used as extensively as tricyclics, however, primarily for two reasons. First, patients who used MAO inhibitors and also consumed foods containing large amounts of the compound tyramine, such as cheese and chocolate, often developed very high blood pressure. Second, some early empirical evaluations of antidepressant medications suggested that MAO inhibitors were not as effective as tricyclics (for example, British Medical Research Council, 1965).

More recent studies have shown that MAO inhibitors are indeed useful in the treatment of depressed patients (Larsen, 1991). They can be used safely when proper caution is used regarding the patient's diet. In addition, MAO inhibitors

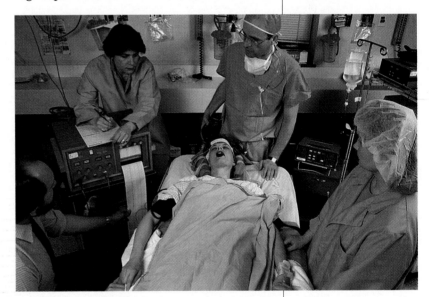

are now widely used in the treatment of certain anxiety disorders, especially agoraphobia and panic attacks (see Chapter 6).

Selective Serotonin Reuptake Inhibitors A relatively new class of antidepressant medication known as **selective serotonin reuptake inhibitors (SSRIs)** was developed in the early 1980s (Silverstone, 1992). Unlike the original forms of antidepressant medication, which were discovered by accident, SSRIs were synthesized in the laboratories of pharmaceutical companies on the basis of theoretical speculation regard-

▼ In 1938, two Italian psychiatrists introduced a technique for inducing convulsions through electrical, rather than chemical, methods. In this procedure, electrodes were placed on either side of the patient's head, and an alternating current of 110 volts was passed through the brain for approximately half a second.

ing the role of serotonin in the etiology of mood disorders. The SSRIs inhibit the reuptake of serotonin into the presynaptic nerve ending and

"...IS IT MY IMAGINATION OR DOES IT SEEM LIKE EVERYONE IS TAKING PROZAC?..."

therefore promote neurotransmission in serotonin pathways by increasing the amount of serotonin in the synaptic cleft. They are called "selective" because they seem to have little if any effect on the uptake of other neurotransmitters. The TCAs, in contrast, are far less specific to a particular neurotransmitter system, blocking the uptake of both norepinephrine and serotonin and affecting many types of postsynaptic receptors.

The SSRIs now account for more than half of all prescriptions written for antidepressant medications. These drugs have fewer side effects (such as weight gain, constipation, and drowsiness) than TCAs or MAO inhibitors, they are easier to take (one pill a day instead of experimenting for weeks to find the proper dosage), and they are less dangerous if the patient takes an overdose. This does not mean, of course, that they are completely without side effects. Some patients experience nausea, headaches, fatigue, and restlessness, although these symptoms are usually mild and transient.

The best known of the SSRIs is Prozac (fluoxetine). Shortly after its introduction (Byerley et al., 1988), Prozac was featured on the cover of national magazines such as Newsweek and was inappropriately hailed as a miracle cure for depression. Within several months, a backlash occurred in the media, and Prozac became a

focus of controversy. A few individual case studies suggested that the drug might reduce inhibitions for violent behavior or increase preoccupation with suicidal ideas (Teicher, Glod, & Cole, 1990). Controlled investigations have subsequently disproved these fears, and Prozac is now a well-established form of treatment that is prescribed by psychiatrists more than twice as often as the next most common type of antidepressant drug (Brink, 1993; Thompson, 1993). The popularity of Prozac can be attributed largely to the minimal side effects.

Controlled outcome studies indicate that Prozac and other SSRIs are at least as effective as traditional forms of antidepressant medication (Stokes, 1993). There are also preliminary indications (Boyer, 1992) that the SSRIs may also be effective in use with other forms of mental disorder, such as obsessive-compulsive disorder, panic disorder, and personality disorders (see chapters 6 and 9).

Lithium Carbonate In 1949 the Australian psychiatrist J. Cade discovered that the salt lithium carbonate was effective in treating bipolar mood disorders. Although lithium was soon used widely throughout Europe, it was temporarily banned by the Food and Drug Administration in the United States before being introduced into clinical practice in the mid-1970s.

An extensive literature indicates that lithium carbonate is an effective form of treatment in the alleviation of manic episodes (Abou-Saleh, 1992). It is also useful in the treatment of bipolar patients who are experiencing a depressive episode. Perhaps most importantly, bipolar patients who continue to take lithium between episodes are significantly less likely to experience a subsequent relapse.

LIGHT THERAPY FOR
SEASONAL MOOD DISORDERS

The observation that fluctuations in seasons can help bring on episodes of mood disorder leads to the relatively obvious implication that patients might respond to manipulations of the natural environment. For centuries, physicians have prescribed changes in climate for their depressed clients (Wehr, 1989). The prominent French psychiatrist Jean Esquirol (1772–1840) reportedly advised a patient whose depression appeared when the days grew shorter to move from Belgium to Italy during the winter.

Modern light therapy was introduced in the 1980s (Rosenthal et al., 1984; Oren & Rosenthal, 1992). Typical treatment involves exposure to bright (2,500 LUX) broad-spectrum light for a period of 1 to 2 hours every day. Some patients respond positively to shorter periods (30 minutes) of high intensity (10,000 LUX) light (Hill, 1992). The light source—most often a rectangular box containing fluorescent ceiling fixtures—must be placed close (90 cm) to the patient at eye level. Improvement in the person's mood is often seen within 2 to 5 days.

Outcome studies have found that light therapy is an effective form of treatment for seasonal affective disorder (Terman et al., 1989). The most difficult issue in evaluating this type of treatment has been to control for placebo effects. It is not possible to conduct a true double-blind study because patients know that they are being exposed to light and they often believe that light will be helpful. The general conclusion is that light therapy is not simply a placebo effect. It is not clear, however, how or why it works (Hill, 1992).

Clinical Practice Guidelines

National guidelines for clinical practice in the treatment of depression have been developed and published by a panel of experts who have extensive experience in treating depressed patients (Rush, 1993).[†] These guidelines are intended for use by primary care providers, such as physicians in general practice, who often provide the first point of professional contact for people who are suffering from mood disorders. Recommended treatments are those that have been documented to be effective in carefully controlled studies.

The Clinical Practice Guidelines indicate four major types of treatment for depression:

- Antidepressant medication
- Psychotherapy (specifically cognitive therapy, behavior therapy, or interpersonal therapy)
- Antidepressant medication combined with psychotherapy
- Other treatments (including ECT and light therapy)

Several effective forms of treatment are available for patients suffering from mood disorders. Considerably more research is needed, however, to identify better predictors of response to current treatment methods and to develop more and better treatments for depression (Rush, 1993).

Summary

Mood disorders are defined in terms of emotional, cognitive, and **somatic symptoms**. In addition to a feeling of pervasive despair or gloom, people experiencing an episode of major **depression** are likely to show a variety of symptoms such as diminished interest in their normal activities, changes in appetite and sleep, fatigue, and problems in concentration. A person in a manic episode, on the other hand, feels elated and energetic. Manic patients also exhibit related symptoms such as inflated self-esteem, rapid and pressured speech, and poor judgment in activities that can have painful consequences.

KEY TERMS

- affect
- analogue study
- bipolar mood disorder
- comorbidity
- cyclothymia
- depression
- dysphoria
- dysthymia
- emotion
- euphoria
- hopelessness
- hypomania
- learned helplessness
- mania
- melancholia

[†] Free copies of the guidelines can be obtained from the Agency for Health Care Policy and Research (AHCPR) Clearinghouse by writing to P.O. Box 8547, Silver Spring, MD 20907.

DSM-IV lists two major categories of **mood disorders**. People with **unipolar mood disorders** experience only episodes of **depression**. People with **bipolar mood disorders** experience episodes of **mania**, which are most often interspersed with episodes of depression. There are two specific types of unipolar mood disorder in DSM-IV. Major depressive disorder is diagnosed if the person has experienced at least one episode of major depression without any periods of mania. **Dysthymia** is a less severe, chronic form of depression in which the person has been depressed for at least 2 years without a major depressive episode.

A person who has experienced at least one manic episode would receive a diagnosis of bipolar I disorder, regardless of whether he or she has ever had an episode of depression. One episode of major depression combined with evidence of at least one period of **hypomania** would qualify for a diagnosis of bipolar II disorder. **Cyclothymia** is a less severe, chronic form of bipolar mood disorder in which the person has experienced numerous periods of hypomania interspersed with periods of depressed mood.

The validity of the distinction between unipolar and bipolar mood disorders is supported by several types of information. Bipolar disorders tend to have an earlier age of onset and a worse prognosis than unipolar disorders.

Mood disorders are among the most common forms of psychopathology. Epidemiological studies have found that the lifetime risk for major depressive disorder is approximately 5 percent and the lifetime risk for dysthymic disorder is approximately 3 percent. Rates for both of these disorders are two or three times higher among women than among men. The lifetime risk for bipolar I disorder is close to 1 percent. Women and men are equally likely to develop bipolar mood disorder. The prevalence of depression appears to be increasing, with people born after World War II being more likely to become clinically depressed than people born in earlier generations.

The etiology of mood disorders can be traced to the combined effects of social, psychological, and biological factors. Social factors include primarily the influence of stressful life events, especially severe losses that are associated with significant people or significant roles. Fateful events, those beyond the individual's control, contribute to the onset of depression

and may be more influential than stressful circumstances that are consequences of the development of a mood disorder. Nevertheless, some studies show that people who are clinically depressed help to create some of the stressful events that they experience, especially those involving interpersonal relationships.

Two types of psychological factors play an important role in the development of mood disorders: cognitive responses to disappointment and failure, and interpersonal skills. Cognitive theories are primarily concerned with the way in which depressed people experience a severe event. Beck's **schema** model places principal emphasis on cognitive distortions or the erroneous ways in which some people think about themselves and their environments. Abramson and Alloy's **hopelessness** model holds that depression is associated with the expectation that desirable events will not occur or that aversive events will occur regardless of what the person does. Furthermore, people will be more likely to become depressed if they attribute negative events to internal, stable, global factors.

Interpersonal theories focus on the ways in which individuals respond to people and events in their environment. Lewinsohn and Coyne proposed that depressed people behave in ways that have a negative impact on other people. In this way, they contribute to the stressful nature of their social environment. Coping behaviors may help to explain gender differences in the prevalence of unipolar depression. A ruminative style, in which the person's attention is turned inward, may be associated with longer and more severe episodes of depression. Women may be more likely than men to employ a ruminative style of response to the onset of a depressed mood.

Family and twin studies indicate that genetic factors play an important role in the etiology of both unipolar and bipolar mood disorders. They also indicate that stressful events are more common among the first-degree relatives of mood disorder patients. Genes may contribute to the development of depression directly through an effect on the central nervous system and indirectly by influencing some people to select or create a personal environment that puts them at elevated risk for a mood disorder. The mode of genetic transmission in mood disorders has not been identified. Linkage studies may help locate these pathways and could allow clinical scientists to identify individuals who are genetically predisposed to depression.

Neurochemical messengers in the brain also play a role in the regulation of mood and the etiology of mood disorders. Current thinking is focused on serotonin, norepinephrine, and dopamine, although many other neurotransmitters may be involved. Evidence regarding the long-term effects of antidepressant medications points to the importance of sensitivity and density of postsynaptic receptors as well as to the interactive effects of multiple neurotransmitter systems.

Several types of psychological and biological treatment have been shown to be effective for mood disorders. Two types of psychotherapy, cognitive therapy and interpersonal therapy, are beneficial for unipolar and dysthymic patients. Three types of antidepressant medication are also useful in the treatment of major depressive disorder: **tricyclics**, **mono-**

amine oxidase inhibitors, and **selective serotonin reuptake inhibitors**. Medication and psychotherapy are frequently used in combined treatment. Outcomes studies do not consistently favor either psychological or psychopharmacologic treatment. Clinical practice guidelines established by the U.S. Department of Health and Human Services recommend a trial-and-error strategy to find the most beneficial treatment for individual patients.

Three other types of biological treatment are beneficial for specific types of mood disorder. Lithium carbonate is useful for patients with bipolar mood disorders. Electroconvulsive therapy has been shown to be effective in the treatment of certain depressed patients, and may be especially useful for patients who are severely suicidal or have failed to respond to other types of treatment. Light therapy seems to be effective for managing seasonal affective disorders.

Critical Thinking

1. Women are more likely to become depressed at some point during their lives than men are. Can you think of any possible explanations for this difference? Some data from epidemiological studies suggest that depression is more prevalent among young adults than among elderly persons. Can you explain this fact?

2. Imagine that you're talking to a psychiatrist. She tells you that depression is nothing more than a biochemical imbalance in the brain because certain medications are effective with depressed people. Is she right? What else do we know about the etiology of depression? Suppose a drug changes a neurotransmitter. Does taking that drug eliminate the cause of depression? How do biological factors (neurotransmitters and neurohormones) interact with stress to cause depression? What is the connection?

3. Contemporary psychological views of depression focus on cognitive reactions to negative experiences as well as interpersonal behaviors. Do these theories owe any debts to Freud's view? How are they similar to Freudian theory? How are they different?

4. What are the relative risks and benefits of (a) medication and (b) cognitive therapy in the treatment of depression? If you were going to be treated, which would seem more useful to you? Imagine that somebody close to you is severely depressed and is threatening suicide. Medication doesn't work. The psychiatrist recommends ECT but wants your consent. What would you decide? Why?

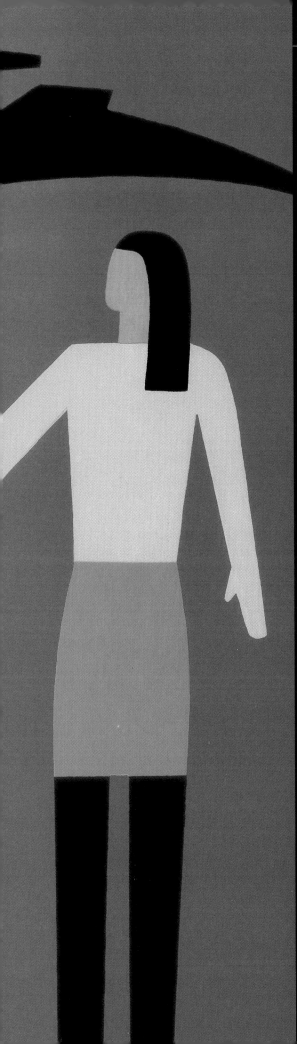

6

Anxiety Disorders

Anxiety disorders play an important role in the study of abnormal behavior for several reasons. One is the magnitude of the problem. Taken together, the various forms of anxiety disorders—including phobias, obsessions, compulsions, and extreme worry—represent the most common type of abnormal behavior. One national study found that 17 percent of adults in the U.S. population have at least one type of anxiety disorder in any given year (Kessler et al., 1994). This figure was higher than the 1-year prevalence rates that were observed for mood disorders (11 percent) and substance-use disorders (11 percent). A second reason for the importance of studying anxiety disorders involves history. The anxiety disorders have played a crucial role in the history of psychopathology research and treatment that cuts across theoretical perspectives.

Overview

Anxiety disorders share several important similarities with mood disorders. From a descriptive point of view, both categories are defined in terms of negative emotional responses. Guilt, worry, and anger are examples of feelings that frequently accompany both anxiety and depression. There is also considerable overlap between anxiety disorders and major mood disorders such as depression. Many patients who are anxious are also depressed, and similarly many patients who are depressed are also anxious.

The close relationship between symptoms of anxiety and those for depression suggests that these disorders may share common etiological features. In fact, clinicians and researchers have focused on similar considerations when investigating these disorders. Stressful life events seem to play a role in the onset of both depression and anxiety. Cognitive factors are also important in both types of problems. From a biological point of view, certain neurotransmitters such as serotonin are involved in the etiology of various types of anxiety disorder as well as mood disorders. This chapter employs many of the concepts that you studied in our discussion of mood disorders in an effort to understand the onset and maintenance of anxiety disorders.

We address questions such as: Why do some stressful life events lead to mood disorders while others seem to cause chronic anxiety? What is the difference between cognitive factors that contribute to depression and those that are involved in anxiety disorders?

The following cases illustrate the kinds of problems that are currently included under the heading of anxiety disorders. One feature that should become obvious is the overlap among different features of anxiety disorders, including worry, panic, avoidance, and obsessions and compulsions. After you read these cases, you should also review the case of Michael in Chapter 4, which also illustrates problems associated with anxiety and avoidance, especially obsessive thoughts.

The first narrative was written by Johanna Schneller (1988), a freelance writer who has been treated for panic disorder. Her vivid description of her own problems highlights the remarkable clarity of insight that is typical of people with anxiety disorders. *Agoraphobia* refers to an exaggerated fear of being in situations from which escape might be difficult, such as being caught in a traffic jam on a bridge or in a tunnel.

Panic Disorder with Agoraphobia

"Three years have passed since my first panic attack struck, but even now I can close my eyes and see the small supermarket where it happened. I can feel the shoppers in their heavy coats jostling me with their plastic baskets, and once again my stomach starts to drop away.

"It was November. I had just moved to New York City and completed a long search for a job and an apartment. The air felt close in that checkout line, and black fuzz crept into the corners of my vision. Afraid of fainting, I began to count the number of shoppers ahead of me, then the number of purchases they had. The overhead lights seemed to grow brighter. The cash register made pinging sounds that hurt my ears. Even the edges of the checkout counter looked cold and sharp. Suddenly I became nauseated, dizzy. My vertigo intensified, separating me from everyone else in the store, as if I were looking up from underwater. And then I got hot, the kind of hot you feel when the blood seems to rush to your cheeks and drain from your head at the same time.

"My heart was really pounding now, and I felt short of breath, as if wheels were rolling across my chest. I was terrified of what was happening to me. Would I be able to get home? I tried to talk myself down, to convince myself that if I could just stay in line and act as if nothing was happening, these symptoms would go away. Then I decided I wasn't going to faint—I was going to start screaming. The distance to the door looked vast and the seconds were crawling by, but somehow I managed to stay in the checkout line, pay for my bag of groceries and get outside, where I sat on a bench, gulping air. The whole episode had taken ten minutes. I was exhausted.

"At home, I tried to analyze what had happened to me. The experience had been terrifying, but because I felt safe in my kitchen, I tried to laugh the whole thing off—really, it seemed ridiculous, freaking out in a supermarket. I decided it was an isolated incident; I was all right, and I was going to forget it ever happened.

"Two weeks later, as I sat in a movie theater, the uncomfortable buzz began to envelop me again. But the symptoms set in faster this time. I mumbled something to my friends about feeling sick as I clambered over them. It was minutes before I caught my breath, hours before I calmed down completely.

"A month full of scattered attacks passed before they started rolling in like Sunday evenings, at least once a week. I tried to find a pattern: They always hit in crowded places, places difficult to escape. My whole body felt threatened, primed to run during an attack. Ironically, my attacks were invisible to anyone near me unless they knew what to look for—clenched neck muscles, restless eyes, a shifting from foot to foot—and I was afraid to talk to anyone about them, to perhaps hear something I wouldn't want to hear. What if I had a brain tumor? And I was embarrassed, as if it were my fault that I felt out of control. But then one night I had an attack alone in my bed—the only place I had felt safe. I gave in and called a doctor.

"As the weeks passed and the attacks wore on, I began to think maybe I was crazy. I was having attacks in public so often I became afraid to leave my house. I had one on the subway while traveling to work almost every morning—but, luckily, never panicked on the job. Instead, I usually lost control in situations where I most wanted to relax: on weekend trips, or while visiting friends. I felt responsible for ruining other people's good time. One attack occurred while I was in a tiny boat deep-sea fishing with my family; another hit when I was on a weekend canoe trip with my boyfriend. I also suffered a terrifying attack while on my way to see friends, stuck in traffic, merging into a tunnel near Boston's Logan Airport, with no exit ramp or emergency lane in sight.

"I began declining offers I wanted to accept: all I could think was, 'What if I panic in the middle of nowhere?' The times I did force myself to go out, I sat near the doors of restaurants, in aisle seats at movie theaters, near the bathroom at parties. For some reason, I always felt safe in bathrooms, as if whatever happened to me there would at least be easy to clean up.

"On days when I didn't have an actual attack,

I could feel one looming like a shadow over my shoulder; this impending panic was almost worse than the real thing. By remembering old episodes, I brought on new ones, and each seemed to pull me closer to a vision I had of my mind snapping cleanly in half, like a stalk of celery." (Schneller, 1988). ■

This case illustrates many of the most important features of a panic attack, as well as the manner in which agoraphobia sometimes develops. The author's first attack came suddenly and without warning, while she waited in a grocery line. The attack was characterized by various somatic sensations, including breathing difficulties, a pounding heart, nausea, and dizziness. This overwhelming and terrifying experience was over almost as quickly as it had begun. Subsequent attacks caused the author to restrict her social activities, avoiding situations in which she might have another attack. She became fearful of crowded situations from which she might not easily escape.

Johanna's description of her problems also raises a number of interesting questions, to which we will return later in the chapter. Was it just a coincidence that her first attack occurred shortly after the difficult experience of moving to a new city, starting a new job, and finding a new apartment? Could the stress of those experiences have contributed to the onset of her disorder? Was there a pattern to her attacks? Why did she feel safe in some situations and not in others? She mentions feeling out of control, as if she were responsible for her attacks. Could she really bring on another attack by remembering one from the past? These questions are related to research studies in the literature on anxiety disorders.

CASE STUDY

Obsessive-Compulsive Disorder

Ed, a 38-year-old lawyer, lived with his wife, Phyllis. Most aspects of Ed's life were going well, except for the fears and obsessions that lurked beneath his relatively easygoing exterior—problems that had plagued him since adolescence. One focus of Ed's anxiety was handwriting. The fear and tension had become so great that his eyes hurt whenever he was forced to write. Feeling drained by this anxiety, Ed avoided writing whenever possible. The problem seemed utterly crazy to Ed, but he couldn't rid himself of his obsessive thoughts.

Several years earlier, sinister meanings had somehow become linked in Ed's imagination to the way in which letters and numbers were formed. The worst letters were "P" and "T" (the first letters in "Phyllis" and in "Tim," his younger brother's name). "Improperly" formed letters reminded Ed of violent acts, especially decapitation and strangulation. If the parts of a letter, such as the two lines in the letter "T," were not connected, an image of a head that was not attached to its body might pop into his mind. Closed loops reminded him of suffocation, like a person whose throat had been clamped shut. These images were tied to people whose names began with the malformed letter. As a result of these concerns, Ed had developed an awkward style of handwriting that was often difficult to read.

These writing problems had their greatest impact at work, especially when he was under time pressure. In one particularly upsetting incident, Ed was responsible for completing an important official form that had to be in the mail that day. He came to a section in which he needed to write a capital "P" and became concerned that he hadn't done it right. The loop seemed to be closed, which meant that Phyllis might be strangled! He tore up the first copy and filled it out again. When it was finally done to his satisfaction, Ed sealed the form in an envelope and put it in the box for outgoing mail. After returning to his desk, he was suddenly overwhelmed by the feeling that he had indeed made a mistake with that "P." If he allowed the form to be mailed, the evil image would be associated forever with his wife. Consumed by fear, Ed rushed back to the mailbox, tore up the envelope, and started a new form. Twenty minutes later, he had the form filled out and back in the mailbox. Then the cycle repeated itself. Each time, Ed became more distraught and frustrated, until he eventually felt that he was going to lose his mind.

In addition to his problems with writing, Ed was also afraid of axes. He would not touch one, or even get close to one. Any situation in which he could possibly encounter an ax made him extremely uncomfortable. He refused to shop in hardware stores because they sell axes, and he would not visit museums because their exhibits often contain artifacts such as medieval armor. His fear of axes was quite specific. Ed wasn't afraid of knives, guns, or swords. He couldn't remember when he had first become afraid of axes, and he didn't recall whether this fear had appeared before or after his problems with writing.

One crucial incident seemed to have triggered the pervasive anxiety that had plagued Ed for 20 years. When he was 17 years old, some friends persuaded Ed to try smoking marijuana. They told him that it would make him feel high—relaxed, sociable, and perhaps a bit giddy. Unfortunately, Ed didn't react to the drug in the same way that the others had. The physical effects seemed to be the same, but his psychological reaction was entirely different. After sharing two joints with his friends, Ed began to feel light-headed. Then things around him began to seem unreal, as though he were watching himself and his friends in a movie. The intensity of these feelings escalated rapidly, and panic took over. Frightening thoughts raced through his head. Was he losing his mind? When would it stop? This frightening experience lasted about 2 hours.

The marijuana incident had an immediate and lasting impact. Ed became preoccupied with a fear of accidentally ingesting any kind of mind-altering drug, especially LSD. Every spot on his skin or clothing seemed as though it might be a microscopic quantity of this hallucinogen. He felt compelled to clean his hands and clothes repeatedly to avoid contamination. Intellectually, Ed knew that these concerns were silly. How could a tiny spot on his hand be LSD? It didn't make any sense, but he couldn't keep the thought out of his mind.

The most horrifying aspect of the drug experience was the sensation of being totally out of control of his actions and emotions. The fear of returning to that state haunted Ed. He struggled to resist impulses that he had never noticed before, such as the temptation to shout obscenities out loud in church. He also began to worry that he might hurt his younger brother. He resisted the impulses with all his might. He never acted on them, but they pervaded his consciousness and absorbed his mental energy. The irrevocable consequences of his violent impulses were especially troublesome. He thought, "If I killed Tim, I couldn't undo it. If I let my guard down for a minute, I would never be able to correct what I might do."

The thoughts were so persistent and unshakable that Ed began to wonder if he might, in fact, be a pathological killer. Could he be as deranged and evil as Richard Speck, who had brutally murdered eight nurses in a Chicago apartment building in 1966? Ed became obsessed with reading articles about Speck and other mass murderers. The number "8" came to have special meaning to him because of the number of Speck's victims. Over time, Ed's fears and worries became focused on numbers and letters. The violent images and impulses became a less prominent part of his everyday life, but the writing difficulties escalated proportionately. ■

Typical Symptoms and Associated Features

People with anxiety disorders share a preoccupation with, or persistent avoidance of, thoughts or situations that provoke fear or anxiety. In some cases, the direct experience of fear or anxiety is characteristic of the disorder. Johanna's panic attacks and her dread of crowded theaters and long bridges provide one set of examples. Ed's compulsive pattern of forming letters was designed to minimize the frequency of intrusive, violent images that he found quite upsetting. His fear of axes could be avoided altogether if he stayed away from places where they were found.

▲ Anxiety is not associated with an immediate threat from the environment. People with anxiety disorders anticipate future negative events, even in situations that are not actually dangerous.

Anxiety disorders frequently have a negative impact on various aspects of a person's life. Both Johanna and Ed found that their anxiety and associated problems constrained their ability to work and their social relationships. In spite of these problems, most people who knew them probably did not know that they suffered from a mental disorder. In spite of the private terrors that they both endured, they were able to carry on most aspects of their lives.

One hallmark of anxiety disorders is the paradoxical nature of the person's behavior. If people understand that they are harming themselves with their irrational actions, why do they persist in them? This question hinges on the fact that insight is rarely impaired in anxiety disorders. Ed was acutely aware of the nature of his disorder. He knew that his writing compulsions were interfering with his ability to work, but he was helpless to control them. He clung desperately to a pattern of behavior that he recognized to be maladaptive. Patients with anxiety disorders recognize this dilemma. They are going through excruciating discomfort, but they understand that their emotional responses are completely incongruent with reality.

In addition to these general considerations, the diagnosis of anxiety disorders depends upon a consideration of several specific types of symptoms, which are described in the following pages. We will begin by discussing the nature of anxiety, which should be distinguished from more discrete emotional responses like fear and panic.

Anxiety

Like depression, the term *anxiety* can refer to either a mood or a syndrome. We will use the term to refer to a mood. Specific syndromes associated with anxiety disorders are discussed later in the chapter.

Anxious mood is often defined in contrast to the specific emotion of fear, which is more easily understood. **Fear** is experienced in the face of real, immediate danger. It usually builds quickly in intensity and helps to organize the person's behavioral responses to threats from the environment (escaping or fighting back). Classic studies of fear among normal adults have often focused on people in combat situations, such as air crews during bombing missions over Germany in World War II (Rachman, 1991). **Anxiety**, on the other hand, involves a more general or diffuse emotional reaction—beyond simple fear—that is out of proportion to threats from the environment (Roth & Argyle, 1988). Rather than being directed toward the person's present circumstances, anxiety is typically associated with the anticipation of future problems.

Anxiety can be adaptive at low levels, because it serves as a signal that the person must prepare for an upcoming event (Costello, 1976). When you think about final exams, for example, you may become somewhat anxious. That emotional response may help to initiate and sustain your efforts to study. In contrast, high levels of anxiety become incapacitating as concentration and performance are disrupted.

A pervasive anxious mood is typically associated with pessimistic thoughts and feelings ("If something bad happens, I probably won't be able to control it"). The person's attention may also turn inward, focusing on negative emotions and self-evaluation ("Now I'm so upset that I'll never be able to concentrate during the exam!") rather than on the organization or rehearsal of adaptive responses that might be useful in coping with negative events. Taken together, these factors can be used to define maladaptive anxiety, or what David Barlow, a psychologist at the State University of New York at Albany, has called *anxious apprehension*, which consists of: (1) high levels of diffuse negative emotion, (2) a sense of uncontrollability, and (3) a shift in attention to a primary self-focus or a state of self-preoccupation (Barlow, 1991).

Perhaps because we all experience brief periods of anxiety, patients who suffer from anxiety disorders often find it difficult to describe the terrifying intensity of their experiences. More than 40 years ago, a physician wrote the following anonymous account:

It is as difficult to describe to others what an acute anxiety state feels like as to convey to the inexperienced the feeling of falling in love. Perhaps the most characteristic impression is the constant state of causeless and apparently meaningless alarm. You feel as if you were on the battlefield or had stumbled against a wild animal in the dark, and all the time you are conversing with your fellows in normal peaceful surroundings and performing duties you have done for years. (*Lancet*, 1952, pp. 83–84)

Worrying is one specific cognitive activity that is associated with anxiety. In recent years psychologists have studied this phenomenon carefully because they consider it to be critical in the subclassification of anxiety disorders (DSM-IV).

Worry can be defined as a relatively uncontrollable sequence of negative, emotional thoughts and images that are concerned with possible future threats or danger (Pruzinsky & Borkovec, 1990). When excessive worriers are asked to describe their thoughts, they emphasize the predominance of verbal, linguistic material rather than images (Borkovec & Inz, 1990). In other words, worriers appear to be preoccupied with "self-talk" rather than unpleasant visual images.

Because everyone worries at least a little bit, you might wonder whether it is possible to distinguish between pathological and normal worry. The answer is yes. Excessive worriers are more likely than other subjects to report that the content of their thoughts is negative, that they feel that they have less control over the content and direction of their thoughts, and that in comparison to other adults, they believe that their worries are less realistic (Craske et al., 1989). This evidence suggests that the crucial features of pathological worrying may be lack of control and negative affect rather than simply the anticipation of future events.

Panic Attacks

A **panic attack** is a sudden, overwhelming experience of terror or fright, like the attack that was experienced by Johanna as she waited in the checkout line. Whereas anxiety involves a blend of several negative emotions, panic is more focused. Some clinicians think of panic as a normal fear response that is triggered at an inappropriate time (Barlow, 1991). In that sense, panic is a "false alarm." Descriptively, panic can be distinguished from anxiety in two other respects: It is more intense, and it has a sudden onset.

Panic attacks are defined largely in terms of a list of somatic or physical sensations, ranging from heart palpitations, sweating, and trembling to nausea, dizziness, and chills. Table 6–1 lists the complete set of DSM-IV criteria for a panic attack; the person must experience at least 4 of these 13 symptoms in order for the experience to qualify as a full-blown panic attack. The actual numbers and combinations of these symptoms vary from one person to the next, and they may also change over time within the same person.

People undergoing a panic attack also report a number of cognitive symptoms. They may feel as though they are about to die, lose control, or go crazy. Some clinicians believe that the misinterpretation of bodily sensations lies at the core of panic disorder. Patients may interpret heart palpitations as evidence of an impending heart attack, or they may interpret racing thoughts as evidence that they are about to lose their minds.

TABLE 6–1

Diagnostic Criteria for Panic Attack in DSM-IV

A discrete period of intense fear or discomfort, in which four (or more) of the following symptoms developed abruptly and reached a peak within 10 minutes:

1. Palpitations, pounding heart, or accelerated heart rate
2. Sweating
3. Trembling or shaking
4. Sensations of shortness of breath or smothering
5. Feeling of choking
6. Chest pain or discomfort
7. Nausea or abdominal distress
8. Feeling dizzy, unsteady, lightheaded, or faint
9. Derealization (feelings of unreality) or depersonalization (being detached from oneself)
10. Fear of losing control or going crazy
11. Fear of dying
12. Paresthesias (numbness or tingling sensations)
13. Chills or hot flushes

Johanna said that she eventually felt as though her mind was going to snap in half.

Panic attacks are further described in terms of the situations in which they occur as well as the person's expectations about their occurrence (Barlow & Craske, 1988). An attack is said to be situationally *cued* if it occurs only in the presence of a particular stimulus. Ed might have a panic attack, for example, if he was suddenly confronted by an ax. Other panic attacks, like Johanna's experience in the grocery checkout line, appear without any warning or expectation, as if "out of the blue."

Is there a typical pattern for panic attacks in the natural environment? In one descriptive study, panic disorder patients kept daily diaries describing panic experiences, and they also wore an ambulatory heart rate/physical activity recorder (Margraf et al., 1987). The average (mean) number of panic attacks among these patients was slightly less than one per day, but the number varied considerably across patients. Expected and unexpected panic attacks were experienced in roughly equivalent proportions. Unexpected attacks occurred most frequently at home, whereas situational attacks occurred most frequently in the car, usually while driving on freeways. The timing of unexpected attacks was evenly distributed across the day and night hours, with some occurring while the patient was asleep or trying to fall asleep. The results of this study and several others indicate that the symptoms and timing of panic attacks can vary quite a bit from one patient to the next (Dukman-Caes, Kraan, & deVries, 1993).

Phobias

In contrast to both diffuse anxiety, which represents a blend of negative emotions, and panic attacks, which are frequently uncued, **phobias** are persistent and irrational narrowly defined fears that are associated with a specific object or situation. Ed, for example, was intensely afraid of axes and went out of his way to avoid them. Avoidance is an important component of the definition of phobias. A fear is not considered phobic unless the person either avoids contact with the source of her or his fear or experiences intense anxiety while in the presence of the stimulus. Phobias are also irrational or unreasonable. Avoiding only snakes that

THE FAR SIDE   By GARY LARSON

© 1990 FarWorks, Inc./Dist. by Universal Press Syndicate

"Okay, now listen up. Nobody gets in here without answering the following question: A train leaves Philadelphia at 1:00 p.m. It's traveling at 65 miles per hour. Another train leaves Denver at 4:00.... Say, you need some paper?"

Math phobic's nightmare

are poisonous, or only guns that are loaded, would not be considered phobic.

The most straightforward type of phobia involves fear of specific objects or situations. Different types of specific phobias have traditionally been named according to the Greek words for these objects. Examples of typical specific phobias include fear of heights (acrophobia); fear of enclosed spaces (claustrophobia); fear of small animals, especially cats, dogs, snakes, and mice (zoophobia); fear of blood or injury; and fear of traveling on airplanes.

Some people also experience marked fear when they are forced to engage in certain activities, such as public speaking, initiating a conversation, eating in restaurants, and using public restrooms, which might involve being observed or evaluated by other people (Liebowitz et al., 1985). Attempts to avoid these feared situations cause serious impairment in the person's social and occupational activities. For example, one young man who was treated by one of the authors of this text was afraid of urinating in public restrooms. He planned his daily schedule with great care so that he would always be near a restroom with a locking door in which he could be alone. Consequently, he was unable to attend movies or eat in public restaurants unless they happened to have single-person restrooms that he could lock from the inside.

AGORAPHOBIA

The most complex and incapacitating form of phobic disorder is known as **agoraphobia,** which literally means "fear of the marketplace (or places of assembly)" and is usually described as fear of public spaces. The case of Johanna, presented at the beginning of the chapter, provides a brief description of the types of problems experienced by a person suffering from agoraphobia. The fear usually becomes more intense as the distance between the person and his or her familiar surroundings increases, or as avenues of escape are closed off. In that sense, agoraphobia is somewhat different from the other phobias because it is not so much a fear of being *close to* one specific object or situation (for example, heights, animals, public speaking) as it is fear of being *separated from* signals associated with safety.

Typical situations that cause problems include crowded streets and shops, enclosed places like theaters and churches, traveling on public forms of transportation, and driving an automobile on bridges, in tunnels, or on crowded expressways. In any of these situations, the presence of another person may help the agoraphobic feel more comfortable. In the most extreme form of the disorder, agoraphobic patients are unable to venture away from their own homes. Some agoraphobics are able to visit public places (for example, shopping malls, theaters, crowded classrooms), but may remain near exits or aisles so that their escape cannot be easily blocked.

The uncomfortable sensations experienced by agoraphobics are similar to those that have already been described for other anxiety disorders. They range from vague feelings of apprehension to specific physical sensations and full-blown panic attacks. Agoraphobics are frequently afraid that they will experience an "attack" of these symptoms that will be either incapacitating or embarrassing, and that help will not be available to them. Many patients report that they are afraid of becoming dizzy, fainting, losing bladder or bowel control, or having heart problems. In some cases, previous experiences of this sort may have triggered persistent fear of repeated episodes.

Some clinicians have suggested that "fear of fear" is the central feature of agoraphobia (for example, Goldstein & Chambless, 1978; Klein, 1981). The crucial event that triggers subsequent fears is often a terrifying, unexpected, or uncued panic attack. Following such an experience, the person may become acutely aware of all internal bodily sensations that may signal the onset of another attack.

▲ **People with agoraphobia are afraid of crowded places from which they might not be able to escape. They also frequently experience panic attacks that are not cued by particular environmental circumstances.**

Obsessions and Compulsions

Obsessions are repetitive, unwanted, intrusive cognitive events that may take the form of thoughts or images or impulses. They intrude suddenly into consciousness and lead to an increase in subjective anxiety. The violent images that frequently popped into Ed's mind provide one example of this phenomenon.

It is not just the intrusive quality of the thought but rather the unwanted nature of the thought that makes it an obsession. Some scientists and artists, for example, have reported experiencing intrusive thoughts or inspirational ideas that appear in an unexpected, involuntary way, but these thoughts are not unwanted. Obsessions are unwelcome thoughts, and they are also nonsensical; they may seem silly or "crazy." But in spite of the recognition that these thoughts do not make sense, the person with full-blown obsessions is unable to ignore or dismiss them.

The following are examples of typical obsessive thoughts (taken from Rachman & Hodgson, 1980): "Did I kill the old lady?" "Christ was a bastard!" "Am I a sexual pervert?" Examples of obsessive impulses include "I might expose my genitals in public," "I am about to shout obscenities in public," "I feel I might strangle a child." Obsessional images might include mutilated corpses, decomposing fetuses, or a family member being involved in a serious car accident. Although obsessive impulses are accompanied by a compelling sense of reality, obsessive people seldom act upon these impulses (with the possible exceptions of impulses to steal and impulses to molest children; see Rachman & Hodgson, 1980).

Most normal people experience obsessions in one form or another. Eighty to 90 percent of normal subjects report experiencing intrusive, unacceptable thoughts or impulses that are similar in many ways to those experienced by patients being treated for obsessive-compulsive disorder (Rachman & deSilva, 1978; Salkovskis & Harrison, 1984). These include impulses to hurt other people, impulses to do something dangerous, and thoughts of accidents or disease. In contrast to the obsessions described by people who are not in treatment, those experienced by clinical patients occur more frequently, last longer, and are associated with higher levels of discomfort than normal obsessions. Clinical obsessions are also resisted more strongly, and patients report more difficulty dismissing their unwanted thoughts and impulses. Research evidence suggests that obsessions are relatively common, and that clinical obsessions differ from normal obsessions in degree rather than in nature.

Compulsions are repetitive behaviors that are considered by the person who performs them to be senseless or irrational. The person attempts to resist but cannot. Ed's inability to resist his compulsive style of writing is one example. His concern about someone being strangled or decapitated if the letters were not properly formed was not delusional, because he readily acknowledged that this was a "silly" idea. Nevertheless, he couldn't shake the obsessive idea that some dreadful event would occur if he was not excruciatingly careful about his writing. He felt as though he had to act, even though he knew that his obsessive thought was irrational. This paradox is extremely frustrating to obsessive-compulsive patients, and it is one of the most common and interesting aspects of the disorder.

Compulsions reduce anxiety, but they do not produce pleasure. Thus, some behaviors such as gambling and drug use that people often regard as compulsive are not considered true compulsions according to this definition.

Although some clinicians have argued that compulsive rituals are associated with a complete loss of voluntary control, it is more accurate to view the problem in terms of *diminished control* (Rachman & Hodgson, 1980). For example, Ed could occasionally manage to resist the urge to write in his compulsive style. The behavior was not totally automatic. But whenever he did not engage in this ritualistic behavior, his subjective level of distress increased dramatically, and within a short period of time he returned to the compulsive writing style.

The two most common forms of compulsive behavior are cleaning and checking. Compulsive cleaning is often associated with an irrational fear of contamination, and in that respect it bears a strong resemblance to certain phobias (Rachman & Hodgson, 1980). There are passive as well as active features of compulsive cleaning. Compulsive cleaners go out of their way to avoid contact with dirt, germs, and other sources of contamination. Then, when they believe that they have come into contact with a source of contamination, they engage in ritualistic cleaning behavior, such as washing their hands, taking showers, cleaning kitchen counters, and so on. These rituals typically involve a large number of repetitions. Some people may wash their hands 50 times a day, taking several minutes to scrub their hands up to the elbow with industrial-strength cleanser. Others take showers that last 2 or 3 hours in which they wash each part of their body in a fixed order, needing to repeat the scrubbing motion an exact number of times.

Compulsive checking frequently represents an attempt to ensure the person's safety or the safety and health of a friend or family member. The person checks things over and over again in an attempt to prevent the occurrence of an imagined, unpleasant, or disastrous event (for example, accidents or sickness). Rachman and Hodgson (1980) provide the following examples of checking rituals:

A 34-year old married woman had checking rituals precipitated by contact with other people. Looking at or talking to people, or giving them food, led to checking behavior in order to ensure that no harm came to them.

A 36-year-old man had checking rituals focused on excrement; he engaged in prolonged and meticulous inspections of any speck of brown, particularly on his clothes and shoes.

A 40-year-old nursery school teacher checked that all rugs and carpets were absolutely flat lest someone trip over them, and spent long periods looking for needles and pins on the floor and in furniture. She repeatedly checked to ensure that all cigarettes and matches were extinguished.

Co-morbidity: Disorders Commonly Associated with Anxiety

The various symptoms of anxiety disorders overlap considerably. Many people who experience panic attacks develop phobic avoidance, and many people with obsessive thoughts would also be considered chronic worriers. One study found that 50 percent of people who met the criteria for at least one anxiety disorder also met the criteria for at least one other form of anxiety disorder or mood disorder (Brown & Barlow, 1992). For this reason, it is sometimes difficult to establish the frequency of anxiety disorders.

Given the emotional bases of anxiety disorders, it is not surprising that considerable overlap exists between anxiety and depression (see Further Thoughts). People with a diagnosis of major depressive episode are 19 times more likely to experience a panic disorder and 15 times more likely to develop agoraphobia than are nondepressed people (Weissman, 1988). Brown and Barlow (1992) reported that 40 percent of patients with obsessive-compulsive disorder and 55 percent of patients who experienced panic disorder with agoraphobia also suffered from a mood disorder. Studies that have considered the temporal order in which these disorders appeared have generally found that anxiety disorders are more likely to develop before depression, rather than the other way around.

Substance dependence is another common complication associated with anxiety disorders. In one sample of alcoholic patients, Chambless and her colleagues found that 40 percent would have met diagnostic criteria for at least one anxiety disorder at some point during their lives (Chambless et al., 1987). Within samples of patients with agoraphobia, investigators typically find that between 10 and 20 percent have serious alcohol problems. In situations such as these, of course, questions of cause and effect are not clear. Did the person use alcohol in an attempt to control abnormal anxiety, or did the alcoholic become anxious after drinking excessively? It can work both ways. Chambless concluded that, in most cases, anxiety was the more long-standing problem. This is especially true for phobic disorders and panic disorder with agoraphobia (Kushner, Sher, & Beitman, 1990).

A Model of Anxiety and Depression

Anxiety and depression are closely related concepts. Both are defined primarily in terms of negative emotional responses. In actual clinical practice, they often appear together: People who are anxious are also likely to be depressed, and people who are depressed are frequently anxious. What does this overlapping pattern mean? Some clinicians have argued that anxiety and depression are different manifestations of the same underlying problem. Others hold that they are distinctly different disorders, while recognizing that they can appear together. The relationship between the symptoms of anxiety and those of depression has been the focus of many interesting debates.

Lee Anna Clark and David Watson, both psychologists at the University of Iowa, have proposed a model of anxiety and depression that helps to explain the distinction between these conditions (Clark & Watson, 1991). Their proposal is based, in part, on the distinction between two dimensions of mood: positive and negative affect[†] (Tellegen, 1985). A person who is experiencing a high level of **negative affect** would be described as being upset, whereas someone whose level of negative affect is low would be considered calm or relaxed. Adjectives that describe negative affect include *angry, guilty, afraid, sad, scornful, disgusted,* and *worried.* A person who is experiencing high levels of **positive affect** would be described as energetic or having a zest for life, whereas someone whose level of positive affect is low would be considered tired or sluggish. Adjectives that describe positive affect include *active, delighted, interested, enthusiastic,* and *proud.* These dimensions are largely independent. In other words, a person who is high on one is not necessarily low on the other. Some people are high on both dimensions.

Using this conception of emotional responses as a guide, Clark and Watson carefully examined evidence from several studies that tried to distinguish between anxiety and depression in psychiatric patients as well as in nonclinical subjects. They concluded that the data are best explained in terms of three separate elements: (1) *general distress* (high negative affect), which is common to both anxiety and depression; (2) *physiological hyperarousal,* which is specific to anxiety; and (3) *absence of positive affect,* which is specific to depression. All three elements must be considered in order to describe completely the symptoms of anxiety and depression.

General distress is a diffuse combination of several negative emotional responses, including guilt, anger, fear, sadness, and disgust. These may be accompanied by related symptoms such as mild disturbances of sleep and appetite, distractibility, and vague somatic complaints. According to Clark and Watson's model, elevated levels of this nonspecific component indicate that the person may be suffering from either a mood disorder or an anxiety disorder. The distinction between these alternatives then hinges on a consideration of the other two elements in their model.

Physiological hyperarousal is presumably associated with anxiety rather than depression. This element of the model is defined in terms of symptoms such as heart palpitations, feeling short of breath, excessive sweating, muscular tension and restlessness, shakiness or trembling, and abdominal distress. People with anxiety disorders would presumably exhibit symptoms of physiological hyperarousal as well as high levels of general distress or negative affect.

Absence of positive affect is presumably associated with depression rather than with anxiety. This element of the model is defined in terms of symptoms such as loss of interest in usual activities, inability to experience pleasure (anhedonia), fatigue, and feelings of hopelessness. A patient with a major depressive disorder would be expected to show high levels of negative affect (general distress) in combination with low levels of positive affect.

[†] Clark and Watson use the term "affect" to refer generally to "emotionality," rather than specifically to the observable behaviors associated with emotional responses (see our definition in Chapter 5). Their self-report measure of positive and negative affect, the Positive and Negative Affect Schedule—Expanded Form, includes items tapping subjective feelings as well as interests and behaviors (Watson & Clark, 1990).

This model clarifies the phenomenology of anxiety and also explains epidemiological evidence regarding the frequent comorbidity of anxiety and mood disorders. It also provides an interesting and important guide to efforts aimed at the assessment and classification of anxiety disorders and mood disorders. The assessment of anxiety disorders depends heavily on the consideration of physiological symptoms.

The assessment of depression would benefit from a consideration of the absence of positive affect to complement information regarding the presence of negative affect. With regard to classification, Clark and Watson favor the creation of a diagnostic category that would include mixed symptoms of anxiety and depression. ■

Classification

To understand the way in which anxiety disorders are currently classified, we must briefly consider the history of these concepts. This general set of problems has been the topic of considerable diagnostic controversy throughout the course of the twentieth century.

Brief Historical Perspective

Anxiety and abnormal fears did not play a prominent role in the psychiatric classification systems that began to emerge in Europe during the second half of the nineteenth century (see Chapter 4). Anxiety disorders were probably left out of these descriptions because the authors were primarily superintendents of large asylums whose patients were psychotic or were so disorganized that they could no longer reside in the larger community (Jablensky, 1985; Klerman, 1990). Patients with anxiety problems seldom came to the attention of nineteenth-century psychiatrists because very few cases of anxiety disorder require institutionalization.

Freud and his followers were responsible for some of the first extensive clinical descriptions of pathological anxiety states. Working primarily with patients who were not hospitalized, Freud had an opportunity to treat and study a variety of anxiety-related problems. He described cases of phobia, generalized anxiety, and obsessive-compulsive behavior. His approach emphasized etiological similarities among the various manifestations of anxiety disorders. The form of specific symptoms (a phobia as compared to a compulsion) was considered to be

less important than the underlying causes, which were presumably similar.

A different approach to anxiety disorders was proposed by an influential French psychiatrist, Pierre Janet (1859–1947). In 1903, Janet published a book that provided rich clinical descriptions of his patients' problems (see Pitman, 1984, for an English translation). Based on longitudinal observations of more than 300 patients, Janet proposed a category of mental disorder that he called "psychasthenia." This broad diagnostic category, which was to be distinguished from "hysterical neuroses" (discussed later in this chapter), included people with many different symptoms associated with anxiety. Psychasthenia was described in terms of a series of clinical stages, beginning with a preliminary phase that includes several cognitive (indecision, forgetfulness), emotional (anhedonia), and behavioral (rigidity) problems. According to Janet, the disorder eventually progresses to an advanced stage that is characterized by full-blown obsessions and compulsions.

The concept of psychasthenia is not included in DSM-IV or ICD-10. Nevertheless, Janet's descriptions of obsessions and compulsions have influenced current definitions of obsessive-compulsive disorder or OCD (Berrios, 1989; Pitman, 1987), and his portrayal of the early stages of psychasthenia bear a striking resemblance to current conceptions of obsessive-compulsive personality disorder (see Chapter 9).

Both DSM-I and DSM-II grouped anxiety disorders together under the general heading of "neuroses." According to DSM-II, "Anxiety is

▼ Specific phobias are irrational fears associated with specific situations that the person avoids. Acrophobia is the name given to fear of heights.

▲ Donald Klein, psychiatrist at Columbia University, suggested that panic disorder should be classified separately from generalized anxiety disorder on the basis of his clinical experience, which indicated that panic attacks could be treated successfully with medication.

the chief characteristic of the neuroses. It may be felt and expressed directly, or it may be controlled unconsciously and automatically by conversion, displacement[†] and various other psychological mechanisms (p. 39)." In other words, a person did not have to exhibit obvious signs of anxiety to be considered neurotic.

The authors of DSM-III (APA, 1980) decided to employ a more descriptive approach to classification (see Chapter 4). One of their most significant and controversial changes was to drop the use of the concept *neurosis* as a general organizing principle. Individual forms of neurosis were regrouped into new diagnostic categories based on essential descriptive features. Most were subsumed under a new class known as anxiety disorders. The hysterical neuroses were moved out of this general heading to new categories known as somatoform and dissociative disorders (see Chapter 8).

Subclassification

Changes that were made formal with the publication of DSM-III highlight a trend toward greater specificity in the diagnosis of anxiety disorders. Experts who classify mental disorders usually belong to one of two general groups, the "lumpers" and the "splitters." Lumpers argue that anxiety is a generalized condition or set of symptoms without any special subdivisions. The splitters distinguish among a number of conditions, each of which is presumed to have its own etiology. Until recently, European psychiatry has tended to adopt a more generalized position with regard to anxiety disorders. Janet's broad definition of psychasthenia is one example.

In contrast, American psychiatrists tend to support the idea of many subtypes (see Jablensky, 1985). Both DSM-I and DSM-II included a category of anxiety neurosis that encompassed all disorders characterized by "free-floating anxiety." The validity of this classification was later

challenged, in part by the work of Donald Klein, a psychiatrist at Columbia University. Klein argued that some people who suffered from anxiety neurosis experienced uncued panic attacks leading to agoraphobia, whereas others did not. Klein's results were reflected in DSM-III, which divided the category of anxiety neurosis into two specific groups: **generalized anxiety disorder (GAD)** and panic disorder, with or without agoraphobia. People with panic disorder experienced panic attacks; those with GAD did not. Another important piece of evidence that supported the separation of panic disorder from GAD came from the use of medication to treat anxiety disorders. Patients with panic disorder responded well to certain drugs that were not effective for patients with GAD.

Although it is not currently a popular position, an argument might still be made in favor of a more unified approach to the classification of anxiety disorders. Consider, for example, the cases of Ed in this chapter and Michael in Chapter 4. Both exhibited a relatively wide range of anxiety symptoms. The high rate of comorbidity among anxiety disorders suggests that these cases are not atypical. Should Ed be considered to have both a phobic disorder (fear of axes) and obsessive-compulsive disorder? Or are these diverse symptoms best viewed as manifestations of the same anxiety disorder? These are questions about the *validity* of diagnostic categories (see Chapter 4). Decisions regarding the breadth or specificity of anxiety disorders will ultimately depend on evidence from many different areas. Do phobias and OCD show distinct and separate patterns in family studies? Do they respond to different types of treatment? Can we distinguish between them in terms of typical patterns of onset and course? Definitive answers are not yet available. Future research efforts are needed to address these issues.

Contemporary Diagnostic Systems (DSM-IV)

The DSM-IV (APA, 1994) approach to classifying anxiety disorders recognizes several specific subtypes. The overall scheme is outlined

---

[†] Conversion and displacement are, according to psychoanalytic theory, defense mechanisms employed by the ego to combat anxiety. *Conversion* is the symbolic representation of psychic conflict in terms of motor or sensory symptoms (see the discussion of somatoform disorders in Chapter 8). *Displacement* is the process by which emotions are transferred from one object or idea to another or impulses are shifted from one pathway to another.

in Table 6–2. It includes panic disorder, phobic disorder, obsessive-compulsive disorder, and generalized anxiety disorder as well as post-traumatic stress disorder (PTSD) and acute stress disorder. The latter conditions are discussed in Chapter 7.

To meet the diagnostic criteria for panic disorder, a person must experience recurrent *unexpected* panic attacks. At least one of the attacks must have been followed by a period of 1 month or more in which the person has either persistent concern about having additional attacks, worry about the implications of the attack or its consequences, or a significant change in behavior related to the attacks. Panic disorders are divided into two subtypes, depending upon the presence or absence of agoraphobia.

or unreasonable, and the person must avoid the phobic situation. DSM-IV also provides a severity threshold that holds that the avoidance or distress associated with the phobia must interfere significantly with the person's normal activities or relationships with others.

The DSM-IV definition of *social phobia* is almost identical to that for specific phobia, but it includes the additional element of performance. A person with a social phobia is unable to do something in front of other people. Fear of being humiliated or embarrassed presumably lies at the heart of the person's discomfort.

Generalized anxiety disorder (GAD) is defined in terms of excessive anxiety and worry that the person finds difficult to control and that lead to significant distress or impairment in occupa-

---

TABLE 6–2

Categories Listed as Anxiety Disorders in DSM-IV

Panic Disorder
    without Agoraphobia
    with Agoraphobia
	Obsessive-compulsive Disorder

Agoraphobia (without history of panic disorder) **Specific Phobia** **Social Phobia**	**Posttraumatic Stress Disorder** **Acute Stress Disorder** **Generalized Anxiety Disorder**

DSM-IV defines agoraphobia in terms of anxiety about being in situations from which escape might be either difficult or embarrassing. Avoidance and distress are important elements of the definition. In order to meet the DSM-IV criteria, the person must either avoid agoraphobic situations, such as traveling away from his or her own home; endure the experience with great distress; or insist on being accompanied by another person who can provide some comfort or security. People who fit this description of agoraphobia without meeting the criteria for panic disorder would be assigned a diagnosis of agoraphobia without history of panic disorder.

A *specific phobia* is defined in DSM-IV as "a marked and persistent fear that is excessive or unreasonable, cued by the presence or anticipation of a specific object or situation." Exposure to this stimulus must be followed by an immediate fear response. Furthermore, the person must appreciate the fact that the fear is excessive

tional or social functioning. The worry must occur more days than not for a period of at least 6 months, and it must be about a number of different events or activities. In order to distinguish GAD from other forms of anxiety disorder, DSM-IV notes that the person's worries should not be focused on having a panic attack (as in panic disorder), being embarrassed in public (as in social phobia), or being contaminated (as in obsessive compulsive disorder). Finally, the person's worries and "free floating anxiety" must be accompanied by at least three of the following symptoms: (1) restlessness or feeling keyed up or on edge, (2) being easily fatigued, (3) difficulty concentrating or mind going blank, (4) irritability, (5) muscle tension, and (6) sleep disturbance.

▼ Social phobias involve a performance element. The person is afraid of being embarrassed in front of other people. Singer Carly Simon has suffered from performance anxiety throughout her successful career.

DSM-IV defines obsessive-compulsive disorder in terms of the presence of either obsessions or compulsions. Most people who meet the criteria for this disorder actually exhibit both of these symptoms. The person must recognize that the obsessions or compulsions are excessive or unreasonable. Obsessions are described as "recurrent and persistent thoughts, impulses, or images that are experienced, at some time during the disturbance, as intrusive and inappropriate, and cause marked anxiety or distress." The diagnostic manual specifies further that these thoughts must not be simply excessive worries about real problems. Intrusive thoughts about overdue bills, for example, would not qualify as obsessions. The DSM-IV definition also requires that the person must attempt to ignore, suppress, or neutralize the unwanted thoughts or impulses. Compulsions are defined as "repetitive behaviors or mental acts that the person feels driven to perform in response to an obsession, or according to rules that must be applied rigidly." These behaviors or mental acts must be aimed at reducing or avoiding distress or anxiety.

The line of demarcation between compulsive rituals and normal behavior is often difficult to define. How many times should a person wash her hands in a day? How long should a shower last? Is it reasonable to check more than one time to be sure that the door is locked or the alarm clock is set? DSM-IV has established an arbitrary threshold that holds that rituals become compulsive if they cause marked distress, take more than an hour per day to perform, or interfere with normal occupational and social functioning.

Epidemiology

Some epidemiological studies focus exclusively on treated cases of a disorder, but that strategy can provide a distorted view of the distribution of the disorder within the general population. Many factors can influence a person's decision as to whether or not to obtain treatment. For example, some cases are less severe than others, some people treat themselves, some people are suspicious of medical facilities, and so on. This issue has been a special problem in epidemiological studies of anxiety disorders. Recent evidence indicates that only about 25 percent of people who qualify for a diagnosis of anxiety disorder ever seek psychological treatment. Therefore, our estimates of the frequency and severity of these problems must be based on community surveys.

The results of an epidemiological study also reflect the definition of the disorder that is employed in the survey. Until recently, clinicians did not distinguish between the various subtypes of anxiety disorders that are represented in DSM-IV. Data that were collected prior to 1980, when DSM-III was published, are therefore somewhat difficult to interpret in the light of contemporary diagnostic criteria.

Prevalence

Based on epidemiological studies conducted during the 1960s and 1970s, researchers concluded that between 2 and 5 percent of the general population experienced "anxiety states" broadly defined. More recent studies suggest that these figures are a bit low, and Weissman (1988) argues that 4 to 8 percent is a good general estimate for the percentage of people who are affected by at least one type of anxiety disorder.

The Epidemiologic Catchment Area (ECA) study examined the frequency of specific types of anxiety disorders (Robins & Regier, 1991) and found that anxiety disorders are more common than any other form of mental disorder (see Table 1–3). Phobias are the most common type of anxiety disorder, with a 1-year prevalence of about 9 percent of the adult population. Generalized anxiety disorder affects approximately 4 percent of the adult population, which is roughly equivalent to the rate for major depressive episodes. Obsessive-compulsive disorder affects another 2 percent of the population, and 1 percent of the population experiences panic disorder in any given year.

Further evidence regarding the prevalence of anxiety disorders comes from the National

Comorbidity Study (NCS), which included approximately 8,000 people aged 15 to 54 throughout the United States (Kessler et al., 1994). The most common types of anxiety disorder were specific phobias, which had a 1-year prevalence rate of 9 percent, and social phobias, which had a 1-year rate of 8 percent. Other specific disorders include generalized anxiety disorder (3 percent), agoraphobia without panic disorder (3 percent), and panic disorder (2 percent). The 1-year prevalence rate for people reporting any type of anxiety disorder was 17 percent.

Why are the prevalence rates reported by the ECA and NCS studies considerably higher than those reported in previous studies? One possible explanation holds that the assessment procedures employed in the ECA and NCS studies, which depended upon laypersons as interviewers, may have resulted in an excessively broad definition of some disorders. Another study, which was conducted in Canada at about the same time as the ECA data were being collected in the United States, may help us understand the relatively high rates presented for phobias. Costello (1982) interviewed more than 400 women selected at random from the community. Each woman was asked how she felt in situations such as crowds, going out alone, enclosed places, bridges, traveling, and heights. Additional questions were asked about animals, insects, blood, thunderstorms, and darkness. For each item, the interviewer rated the woman's answer on a scale from 0 (no fear), 1 (mild fear), or 2 (intense fear). Avoidance was also rated on a scale from 0 to 2.

Costello found that prevalence rates were greatly influenced by the severity and avoidance criteria. If he ignored avoidance, 68 percent of the women reported at least one mild fear. This figure dropped to 24 percent if he counted only cases who rated their fear as "intense." When the avoidance criterion was included and made rather stringent (that is, a rating of "2"), only three women in the entire sample reported an *incapacitating* phobia. Costello's results for specific animal phobias and social phobias are summarized in Figure 6–1.

The data from Costello's study suggest that the prevalence rates for simple phobias in the ECA study may be somewhat inflated. Nevertheless, they are still the best data available. And even if the prevalence rates are high, comparisons involving factors such as gender, age,

and race still probably reflect the relative proportions of these disorders.

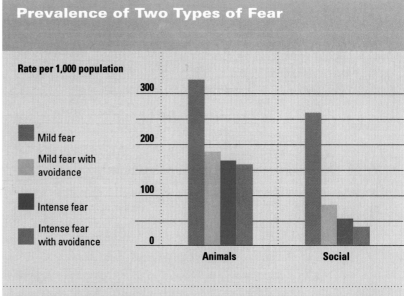

FIGURE 6-1: Prevalence of two types of fear–fear of animals and social fear–as a function of intensity of fear and presence or absence of avoidance.

From C.G. Costello. 1982. Fears and phobias in women: A community study. *Journal of Abnormal Psychology*, 91, 283.

It is also worthwhile to consider the difference between symptoms of a disorder and the prevalence of the full-blown syndrome. Consider the example of panic attacks. In the ECA study, 1 out of every 10 people answered "yes" to the following question: "Have you ever had a spell when all of a sudden you felt frightened, anxious, very uneasy in situations when most people wouldn't be afraid?" Although panic symptoms are relatively common, only 1 in 100 people in the study qualified for the full *diagnosis* of panic disorder using DSM-III criteria.

Gender Differences

The ECA study confirmed the existence of gender differences in several types of anxiety disorders, which had also been reported in many earlier studies (Cameron & Hill, 1989). Pertinent data are summarized in Table 6–3. Women are about twice as likely as men to experience specific phobias, agoraphobia, and panic disorder. A similar result was found for generalized anxiety disorder, in which the one-year prevalence rate for men was 0.9 percent, and the corresponding rate for women was 2.4 percent.[†] In contrast to this pattern, significant gender differences were not found for social phobias. The rates of obsessive-

TABLE 6-3

Gender Differences in the Frequency of Anxiety Disorders

Disorder	Lifetime Risk (%)	
	Women	Men
Specific phobia	14.45	7.75
Agoraphobia	7.86	3.18
Social phobia	2.91	2.53
Obsessive-compulsive disorder	3.04	2.03
Panic disorder	2.10	.99

Source: Adapted from L.N. Robins and D.A. Regier (1991). *Psychiatric Disorders in America: The Epidemiologic Catchment Area Study.* New York: Free Press.

▼ In Western societies, anxiety disorders often arise from work-related issues. In contrast, in non-Western societies anxiety may be more frequently associated with family or religious concerns.

compulsive disorder were also similar in men and women after factors such as marital status, socioeconomic status, and age were taken into account (Karno & Golding, 1991).

The significant gender differences in panic disorder, generalized anxiety disorder, and specific phobias must be interpreted in the light of etiological theories, which will be considered in the next section of this chapter. Several explanations remain plausible. Psychological speculation has focused on factors such as gender differences in child-rearing practices or differences in the way in which men and women respond to stressful life events (Cameron & Hill, 1989). Gender differences in hormone functions or neurotransmitter activities in the brain may also be responsible (Arato et al., 1991).

Cross-cultural Comparisons

Peoples in many kinds of cultures experience anxiety disorders. Population surveys suggest that between 1 and 4 people out of 100 experience various types of anxiety disorders in different cultures (Good & Kleinman, 1985). The focus of typical anxiety complaints can vary dramatically across cultural boundaries, however. People in Western societies often experience anxiety in relation to their work performance, whereas people in other societies may be more concerned with family issues or religious experiences. In the Yoruba culture of Nigeria, for example, anxiety is frequently associated with fertility and the health of family members.

Anxiety disorders have been observed in preliterate as well as Westernized cultures. Of course, the same descriptive and diagnostic terms are not used in every culture, but the basic psychological phenomena appear to be similar. Cultural anthropologists have recognized many different culture-bound syndromes that, in some cases, bear striking resemblance to anxiety disorders listed in DSM-IV. Consider the following example of "kayak angst" in an Inuit (Eskimo) hunter. The problem sounds a lot like panic disorder.

> Isak H., aged 34, (was a) hunter fisherman of mixed race from Nugatsiak. He had been quite well before. In 1939 he saw a kayak man drowned and was very much upset. In the summer of 1946, when he was paddling along in his kayak on a calm day with a soft backwash and bright sunshine he suddenly became terrified when looking down to the bottom of the sea. He seemed to feel the kayak filling with water, the point of the kayak being very distant and dim. His head felt queer and he took off his cap. His heart started beating rapidly and he trembled so violently that the kayak shook. Perspiration ran down his face, his heart seemed to turn over and his arms were heavy and numb. He made an effort to reach shore, he vomited, his bowels were loose and he had a strong desire to pass water. Next time he set out in his kayak the same symptoms occurred. He felt more and more terrified of crouching down in his kayak, and he finally gave up all attempts and stopped fishing by kayak. (From Katschnig & Amering, 1990, pp. 77–78)

Very few epidemiological studies have attempted to collect cross-cultural data using standardized interviews and specific diagnostic criteria.

One such study recently was conducted to evaluate specific drugs for the treatment of panic attacks (Cross-National Collaborative Panic Study, 1992). More than 1,000 patients were treated in 14 different countries across North America, Latin America, and Europe.

Several interesting findings emerged from this study. Panic disorder occurred in all the countries that were included in the study. Nevertheless, some important differences were found among panic patients from different regions. Choking or smothering and fear of dying were more common among patients from southern countries in both the Americas and in Europe. Phobic avoidance was much more common among panic patients seen at clinics in the United States and Canada—9 out of every 10—compared to patients seen at clinics in Latin American countries.

Etiological Considerations and Research

Now that we have discussed the various symptoms associated with anxiety disorders and their distribution within the population, we can consider the origins of these disorders. How do these problems develop? Going back to the cases that were presented at the beginning of the chapter, what might account for the onset of Johanna's panic attacks? Why would Ed find himself plagued by violent images and compelled to form letters in a meticulous fashion?

In the following pages, we summarize some of the most important information that has been collected regarding the origins of problems such as panic, fears, and obsessions. In many cases, especially in the case of psychological factors, we point out ways in which specific etiological mechanisms relate to specific types of anxiety disorders. The person's perception of control, for example, is discussed in terms of its influence on the precipitation of panic attacks. These discussions will help you understand the ways in which clinical scientists are currently thinking about the etiology of these disorders. They should not be taken to imply, however, that there is an exclusive relationship between a particular psychological or biological mechanism and only one subtype of anxiety disorder. Factors such as stressful life events, perception of control and neurochemical activities may play an important role in many forms of anxiety disorder.

Social Factors

We begin with a consideration of social factors, which have played a prominent role in theories concerned with anxiety disorders throughout the twentieth century. We include in this section theoretical perspectives that have focused on parent–child relationships and their potential role in laying the foundation for the later development of anxiety disorders.

PSYCHOANALYTIC THEORY

Freud was responsible for defining the anxiety neuroses as a diagnostic category, and his psychological explanations for their origins have played an extremely influential role in the literature on this topic (Eagle & Wolitzky, 1988). His views focused primarily on the importance of mental conflicts and innate biological impulses (primarily sexual and aggressive instincts) in the etiology of anxiety (see Chapter 2).

The basic outline of Freud's theory of signal anxiety hinges on the notion that the person's ego can experience a small amount of anxiety as a signal indicating that an instinctual impulse that has previously been associated with punishment and disapproval is about to be acted upon. Usually this would mean that the person is about to do something aggressive or sexual that is considered inappropriate. The signal anxiety triggers the engagement of ego defenses—primarily repression—that prevent conscious recognition of the forbidden impulse, inhibit its expression, and thereby reduce the person's anxiety. When the system works as it should, anxiety is adaptive, and the person's behavior is regulated to conform with social expectations.

Unfortunately, people can still experience pathological levels of anxiety if the system is overwhelmed. Traumatic events or circumstances can lead to extreme levels of free-floating anxiety. The ego is then forced to resort to additional defensive maneuvers that can produce symptoms such as phobias and compulsions. The specific form of overt symptoms is determined by the defense mechanisms that are employed by the ego. Different types of anxiety disorders could be distinguished in terms of such factors as the developmental stage at which the person experiences problems, the dangers and instinctual drives that are associated with each developmental stage, and the primary defenses that are associated with the ego's efforts to cope with signal anxiety.

Consider, for example, a Freudian explanation for the etiology of Ed's obsessive-compulsive disorder. According to this model, the instinctual drive that is most problematic in OCD is aggression. Problems that Ed encountered during early childhood must have left him with serious difficulties in dealing with aggressive impulses, which are coupled with resentment harbored toward his younger brother, Tim. Violent aggressive impulses are unacceptable to the ego, and they have to be dealt with using reaction formation, which is presumably the primary defense in obsessive-compulsive disorder. Rather than attempting to harm his brother (decapitating him or strangling him, as in his violent images), Ed was obliged to spend his time correcting printing errors in order to "protect" Tim or ensure that Tim's name is not forever associated with the image of a violent act. The compulsive rituals are viewed as the product of the defense mechanism that was unconsciously employed to fend off anxiety associated with aggression.

Freud's conceptual model for the anxiety neuroses incorporated several important features, including the importance of biologically based impulses, learning experiences based on interactions with other people, and cognitive (or intrapsychic) events that played an important role in mediating between current and past experience. It was firmly grounded in Freud's observations of his own patients' experiences. Although it served as a useful stimulus to future clinicians and identified many important factors in the etiology of anxiety disorders, it suffered from a number of weaknesses. Perhaps the major problem was that of measurement. Because Freud's concepts were not linked directly to observable behaviors, his theory of anxiety could not be tested empirically (outside of case studies).

DEVELOPMENTAL PRECURSORS: SEPARATION ANXIETY

Mary Ainsworth (1984) and John Bowlby (1973) have proposed an explanation for anxiety disorders that centers on an infant's relationship with caretakers. Attachment theory integrates the psychodynamic perspective with field observations of primate behavior and with laboratory research with human infants (Bretherton, 1992). Within Ainsworth and Bowlby's theory, anxiety is an innate response to separation, or the threat of separation, from the caretaker. (See Chapter 2.)

Ainsworth developed a procedure, which she called the "strange situation," to observe infants' reactions when they are separated from their mothers. Research with the strange situation led Ainsworth and her colleagues to identify three types of reactions. The largest group, perhaps two-thirds of all infants, protested and cried when their mothers left the room in which they had been playing. When their mothers returned, however, these infants greeted them with pleasure and affection. Infants in this group were considered "securely attached" (Ainsworth et al., 1978).

In contrast to this normal pattern, some other infants were considered to be "insecurely" or "anxiously" attached. These infants fell into two groups. "Ambivalent/resistant" infants were clingy and afraid to explore the laboratory room, even when their mother was present. Like the securely attached babies, they reacted with strong protests when the mother left the room. When the mother returned, they sought comfort with her, but they remained upset and were not easily consoled. The second group of insecurely attached infants were considered "avoidant" by Ainsworth and her colleagues. These infants explored the laboratory space independently, even when the mother was present, with little apparent concern for her presence. When she left, they did not react with typical protests or anxiety, and they seemed indifferent upon her return. According to attachment theory, the avoidant infants are presumed to be upset by their mothers' departure, but they somehow manage to inhibit overt manifestations of this distress.

Individual differences in attachment styles, presumably rooted in early social relationships, may set the stage for the development of future anxiety reactions, especially childhood fears and agoraphobia among adults (Bowlby, 1973, 1980). The recent literature on this topic reports mixed results. Some studies have found that agoraphobics are more likely to report problems associated with insecure attachment as children (for example, Silove et al., 1993; Tearnan & Telch, 1988), whereas other studies have failed to find this pattern (for example, Van der Molen et al., 1989). Zitrin and Ross (1988) found that childhood separation anxiety was associated with increased risk for development of agoraphobia in women but not in men. Overall, the evidence for a causal relationship between childhood attachments and adult anxiety disorders is not strong. To test these hypotheses further, psychologists must conduct more studies based on direct observations of parent–child relationships rather than on retrospective accounts of childhood behaviors, which are highly subjective and not always accurate or reliable.

STRESSFUL LIFE EVENTS

The relationship between stress and anxiety seems intuitively obvious. Common sense might suggest that people who experience high stress levels are likely to develop negative emotional reactions, which can range from feeling "on edge" to the onset of full-blown panic attacks. In Chapter 5 we reviewed the literature concerning stressful life events and depression. As we have seen, the measurement of stressful events is a complex matter, and it is difficult to establish causal relations between stress and psychological disorders.

Several investigations suggest that stressful life events can also influence the *onset* of anxiety disorders (Blazer, Hughes, & George, 1987; Monroe & Wade, 1988). Patients with anxiety disorders are more likely than control subjects to report having experienced a negative event in the months preceding the initial development of their symptoms.

Perhaps more interesting than this global finding is the suggestion that certain kinds of stresses may be differentially associated with particular types of emotional disorder. Consider, for example, the results reported by Goldstein and Chambless (1978). Their sample included agoraphobic patients and patients with specific phobias. Goldstein and Chambless used clinic records and therapists' descriptions to examine the circumstances surrounding the onset of each patient's symptoms. Interpersonal conflict—for

example, marital distress—was evident in 63 percent of the patients with agoraphobia compared with only 3 percent of those with specific phobias. Patients with specific phobias were much more likely to have experienced a *conditioning event*, such as a sudden painful injury or unexpected confrontation with a dangerous animal, than were the patients with agoraphobia (47 percent compared with 13 percent).

The possibility that the onset of agoraphobia may be associated with interpersonal conflict provides a conceptual link to the literature on attachment theory (see Monroe & Wade, 1988). Some studies have found that agoraphobic patients report an increased rate of separation anxiety as children. Anxious attachment as infants may make these individuals more vulnerable, once they are adults, to the threats that are contained in interpersonal conflict—for example, loss of a loved one if a marriage dissolves.

The quality or nature of the stressful event may also be important in influencing the type of problem that develops. One interesting demonstration of this possibility was reported by Finlay-Jones and Brown (1981), who interviewed women attending a general medical clinic. This group included women who were depressed, women with anxiety disorders, and women who qualified for a dual diagnosis of anxiety and depression. For the 1-year period immediately preceding the onset of their symptoms, 82 percent of the depressed women, 85 percent of the anxious women, and 93 percent of the anxious/depressed women reported at least one severe event. Only 34 percent of the control group reported a similar event.

The investigators then examined the nature of the severe events. The women with anxiety symptoms were much more likely to have experienced a severe event involving danger, where-

▲ **Conditioning events, such as an automobile accident, often give rise to specific phobias. In contrast, agoraphobia is more often associated with interpersonal conflicts.**

as the women who were depressed were more likely to have experienced a severe loss. Mixed cases frequently reported both types of events. These data suggest that the form of the environmental stress may influence the type of symptoms exhibited by the patient.

Psychological Factors

Up to this point, we have considered two theoretical perspectives, psychoanalysis and attachment theory, both of which emphasize the importance of parent–child relationships in the etiology of anxiety disorders. Behaviorism is a third traditional paradigm that has been applied extensively to the study of anxiety disorders, especially to specific phobias. Beginning in the 1920s, the same decade in which Freud proposed his theory of signal anxiety, experimental psychologists working in laboratory settings became interested in the possibility that fears might be learned through classical (or Pavlovian) conditioning (see Eysenck, 1979; Mineka, 1985). One early pioneer in these efforts was John Watson (see Chapter 2).

LEARNING PROCESSES: SPECIFIC PHOBIAS

The central mechanism in the classical conditioning process is the association between an unconditioned stimulus (UCS) and a conditioned stimulus (CS). The UCS is able to elicit a strong unconditioned emotional response (UR)—such as fear. Examples of potential UCSs might be painfully loud and unexpected noises, the sight of dangerous animals, or sudden, intense pain. According to the original version of the conditioning model, the CS could be any neutral stimulus that happened to be present when an intense fear reaction was provoked. Through the process of association, the CS would subsequently elicit a conditioned response (CR), which was similar in quality to the original UCR. (See Chapter 2.)

The original conditioning model offered several advantages over psychoanalytic theory (Wolpe & Rachman, 1960). It fits easily with common sense as well as with clinical experience. Some intense, persistent, irrational fears seem to develop after the person has experienced a traumatic event (Öst & Hugdahl, 1981). Most importantly, the conditioning model employed concepts and procedures that could

be subjected to empirical tests. An enormous body of evidence has now been accumulated with regard to the process of fear acquisition and extinction in laboratory animals and in humans (Davey, 1989; Eysenck, 1979; Merckelbach et al., 1989). The evidence from these studies has led to several revisions of the original conditioning theory, which will be reviewed in the next few pages.

Seligman's Preparedness Model   Martin Seligman, a psychologist at the University of Pennsylvania, identified several problems with the original conditioning model of phobias. These included the following (Seligman, 1971):

1. Conditioned fear responses that are learned in a laboratory situation are typically easy to extinguish. Phobic responses, on the other hand, are extremely persistent and difficult to change.
2. Phobias that develop after traumatic experiences are typically learned in one trial, but very few laboratory studies have been able to demonstrate one-trial conditioning with fear responses.
3. The original conditioning model held that *any* neutral stimulus could be used as the CS. If that model is correct, why are phobias associated only with certain types of objects and situations, such as animals, heights, and small enclosed spaces?

In order to account for these difficulties, Seligman proposed a modified conditioning view known as **preparedness theory.** This theory is based on the notion that organisms are biologically "prepared," on the basis of neural pathways in their central nervous systems, to learn certain types of associations. According to this model, it is not possible to use simply *any* neutral stimulus as the CS in a classical conditioning paradigm. There are biological constraints on the kinds of associations that members of a particular species are able to make, and these constraints have presumably developed throughout the long process of evolution. Rats, for example, can learn to associate the sensation of nausea (UCS) with the taste of food (CS). They can learn this association in one trial, and once they have developed an aversion to a particular taste, that aversion is highly resistant to extinction.

Seligman argued that human fears that reach phobic proportions may be similar to the taste aversion phenomenon. We may be prepared to develop intense, persistent fears only to a select set of objects or situations. Fear of these stimuli may have conferred a selective advantage upon those people—hundreds of thousands of years ago—who were able to maintain their fear and consequently avoid certain kinds of dangerous stimuli, such as heights and animals.

In Chapter 2 we argued that most disorders arise from the interaction of biological and psychological factors. The preparedness model of phobias offers another example of the way in which these factors may combine and interact in the production of specific phobias. The key biological factor is the neurological system, which is prepared to associate certain types of stimuli with intense fear responses. The psychological and social factors in this model involve the nature of the person's developmental history and environmental experience, through which he or she actually learns to associate fear with specific stimuli.

Many investigations have been conducted to test various facets of Seligman's preparedness conditioning model (McNally, 1987). The results of these studies support certain features of the model. For example, Öhman found that conditioned responses to fear-relevant stimuli are more resistant to extinction than are those to fear-irrelevant stimuli. In addition, they are not affected by verbal instructions; that is, they are more like irrational phobias. Öhman also found that it was possible to develop conditioned fear responses after only one trial of learning.

Vicarious Learning and Preparedness The original version of the conditioning model of phobias also did not provide for *vicarious learning* (Rachman, 1978). Children can learn many behaviors through imitation. Bandura's early work on modeling, for example, demonstrated that children who observe a model hitting a doll are more likely to behave aggressively themselves when given the opportunity. Similar processes may also affect the etiology of intense fear, because some phobias develop in the absence of any direct experience with the feared object. People can apparently learn to avoid certain stimuli if they observe other people showing a strong fear response to those stimuli.

Susan Mineka, a psychologist at Northwestern University, and her students have conducted a series of intriguing experiments that combine vicarious learning and the preparedness formulation. Their studies have focused on an animal model of phobias—fear reactions among rhesus monkeys (see Research Methods in Chapter 5). Rhesus monkeys that were raised in their natural environment are markedly afraid of certain kinds of stimuli such as snakes. Most monkeys reared in the laboratory do not initially react fearfully when they are presented with a toy snake. They quickly acquire this fear, however, after watching a monkey reared in the wild exhibit intense fear in the presence of snakes. The greater the fear exhibited by the wild monkey, the more intense the fears developed by the observer monkey. Live observation is not necessary: Monkeys can learn to fear snakes by watching videotapes of other monkeys exhibiting fear reactions.

Fear of snakes is clearly adaptive, because snakes represent a threat to rhesus monkeys in their natural environment. In Seligman's terms, this could be seen as a prepared association. Will monkeys also learn to avoid nonthreatening stimuli if they observe a model reacting with intense fear? Is the association between fear and particular stimuli random—as the original conditioning model had presumed—or is it selective? Mineka conducted a series of investigations that proved that the relationship is in fact selective: Monkeys are prepared to learn to avoid fear-relevant stimuli but are not prepared to learn to avoid fear-irrelevant stimuli.

The contemporary version of the conditioning model of phobias maintains that learning experiences are clearly important but that they must include consideration of prepared associations between stimuli and fear as well as the role of vicarious learning. The importance of the latter factor can be illustrated by considering the development of children's fears during the bombing of London in World War II. When civilian areas were subjected to prolonged and terrifying attacks, families sought safety in underground shelters. The original conditioning model would predict that most of the people subjected to this traumatic experience would develop specific phobic responses in association with whatever stimuli happened to be present during the worst moments of a raid (fear of tunnels, fear of the dark).

In fact, it didn't work that way. Although people showed transient emotional reactions, very few developed persistent, irrational phobic responses as a result of these terrifying experiences. Anecdotal evidence suggested that children were more likely to become fearful if they had observed their parents exhibiting strong emotional responses during the raids (Rachman, 1978). Social phobias are less likely than specific phobias to develop through vicarious learning (Barlow, 1988; Öhman; 1986).

In summary, specific phobias are best understood in terms of learning experiences, especially prepared conditioning and vicarious learning. Certain objects and situations are fear-relevant, and phobic responses can develop through several pathways. The association between the object and intense fear can evolve either through direct experience (for example, being bitten by a snake), observational learning (for example, seeing someone else being bitten by a snake), or exposure to warnings and instructions about dangerous situations that should be avoided (for example, being told repeatedly by your parents that snakes are extremely dangerous and must be avoided at all costs).

▲ **Vicarious learning can influence the development of strong fear responses. Children who observe adults demonstrating strong emotional responses, like this child in the aftermath of the California earthquakes in 1994, may be more likely to develop phobias.**

COGNITIVE FACTORS

Up to this point, we have talked about the importance of life events and specific learning experiences. These variables can all be measured outside the organism. But cognitive events also play an important role as mediators between experience and response. Perceptions, memory, and attention all influence the ways that we react to events in our environments. It is now widely accepted that these cognitive factors play an especially crucial role in the etiology and maintenance of anxiety disorders. We will focus on four aspects of this literature: (1) perception of controllability and predictability, (2) catastrophic misinterpretation (panic attacks), (3) self-focused, narrowed attention (worry), and (4) thought suppression.

Perception of Control: Panic Attacks Cognitive theories of emotion have, for many years, empha-

sized the important relationship between anxiety and the perception of control (for example, Mandler, 1966). People who believe that they are able to control events in their environment are less likely to show symptoms of anxiety than are people who believe that they are helpless.

The importance of this factor can be seen in laboratory studies that have focused on animal models of anxious behavior, sometimes known as "experimental neurosis." Beginning with Pavlov's research on classical conditioning with dogs in the 1920s (see Chapter 2), experimental psychologists have shown that procedures such as extremely difficult discrimination learning tasks (in which an animal is required to make choices between two almost identical stimuli, such as a circle and an ellipse) can produce neurotic behaviors that resemble disorders seen in adult humans. Examples include generalized anxiety and agitation, increased startle responses, and the disruption of purposeful behaviors (such as feeding and harm avoidance). The common feature running through all of these procedures involves repeated exposure to uncontrollable or unpredictable environmental events (Mineka & Kihlstrom, 1978). Laboratory research with panic disorder patients indicates that feelings of lack of control contribute to the onset of panic attacks (see Research Close-up).

Catastrophic Misinterpretation: Panic Attacks
A somewhat different approach to cognitive factors and panic has been proposed by David Clark, a psychologist at Oxford University in England. According to this model, panic disorder may be caused by the catastrophic misinterpretation of bodily sensations or perceived threat (Clark, 1986b). This model is illustrated in Figure 6–2. Although panic attacks can be precipitated by external stimuli, they are usually triggered by internal stimuli, such as bodily sensations, thoughts, or images. On the basis of past experience, these stimuli initiate an anxious mood, which leads to a variety of physiological sensations that typically accompany negative emotional reactions (changes in heart rate, respiration rate, dizziness, and so on). Anxious mood is accompanied by a narrowing of the person's attentional focus and increased awareness of bodily sensations.

The crucial stage comes next, when the person misinterprets the bodily sensation as a catastrophic event. For example, a person who believes that there is something wrong with his or her heart might misinterpret a slight acceleration in heart rate as being a sign that he or she is about to have a heart attack. This reaction ensures the continued operation of this feedback loop, with the misinterpretation enhancing the person's sense of threat, and so on until the process spirals out of control. Thus, cognitive misinterpretation and biological reactions associated with the perception of threat are *both* necessary for a panic attack to occur.

Cognitive theories of panic disorder have stimulated several research studies. Many of these studies have found that the subjective experience of body sensations is closely associated with maladaptive self-statements among patients with panic disorder (McNally, 1990). Critics have pointed out, however, that this evidence provides relatively weak support for the cognitive theories (Costello, 1992). There are several methodological problems associated with this research. For example, the measures of body sensations and cognitive concepts that were used in most studies were not clearly distinguished. (They relied on self-report checklists that overlapped in content).

In addition to these methodological issues, Clark's cognitive theory of panic also has problems explaining some clinical observations regarding panic disorder (Klein & Klein, 1989). For example, patients with panic disorder sometimes experience panic attacks in their sleep. How could that happen if the escalation to panic requires catastrophic misinterpretation of physical sensations?

Worrying: Generalized Anxiety Disorder The negative emotions associated with perception of lack of control can also trigger a related cognitive process that most of us call worrying. **Worry** can be defined as "a special state of the cognitive system, adapted to anticipate possible future danger" (Mathews, 1990). When we are worried, we are preoccupied with potentially harmful or otherwise aversive future events. Various scenarios run through our minds as we attempt to anticipate what might happen and how we might avoid disastrous outcomes.

Several lines of research have converged in recent years to clarify the basic cognitive mechanisms involved in worry. Experts now believe that attention plays a crucial role in the onset of

this process. People who are prone to excessive worrying are unusually sensitive to cues that

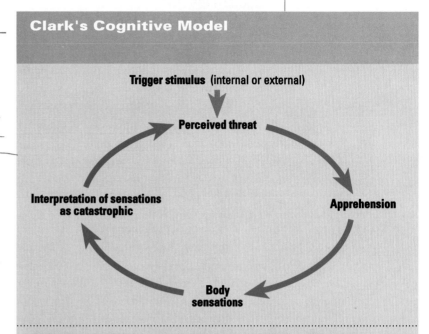

Clark's Cognitive Model

FIGURE 6-2: Diagram of Clark's cognitive model of panic attacks.

From D.M Clark. (1986). A cognitive approach to panic. *Behaviour Research and Therapy, 24,* 461–470.

signal the existence of future threats (Mathews, 1990; Rapee, 1991). They attend vigilantly to even fleeting signs of danger, and this propensity becomes exaggerated when they are under stress. At such times, the recognition of danger cues triggers a maladaptive, self-perpetuating cycle of cognitive processes that can quickly spin out of control.

The threatening information that is generated in this process is presumably encoded in memory in the form of elaborate *schemas* (see Chapter 5), which are easily reactivated. In comparison with the depressed person, who is convinced that failure will *definitely* occur, the anxious person is afraid of failure that *may* occur as a future event; the outcome remains uncertain (Beck & Emery, 1985). The threat schemas of anxious people contain a high proportion of "What if?" questions, such as "What am I going to do if I don't do well in school this semester?" (Kendall & Ingram, 1987; Vasey & Borkovec, 1992).

Once attention has been drawn to threatening cues, the performance of adaptive, problem-solving behaviors is disrupted, and the worrying cycle launches into a repetitive sequence in which the person rehearses anticipated events

RESEARCH CLOSE-UP

Panic and Perception of Control

For many years, psychopathologists have experimented with conditions that are able to produce panic attacks in laboratory situations. If researchers can induce an attack in a lab situation, they might be able to show that the variables that were used to induce panic in the lab are also responsible for its induction in the real world. Several different procedures have been used to induce artificial panic attacks, including the injection of chemical substances and the inhalation of air enriched with carbon dioxide.

Using laboratory panic-induction procedures, research studies have confirmed the importance of the perception of uncontrollability in the precipitation of panic attacks. One procedure that has been shown to induce panic attacks in patients with anxiety disorders involves the inhalation of air that has been enriched with carbon dioxide (CO_2). Sanderson, Rapee, and Barlow (1989) utilized this technique, and they manipulated the subjects' impressions of whether they were in control of the air mixture that they were breathing.

The subjects in the study all met DSM-III-R criteria for panic disorder. During the experimental procedure, each subject was seated alone in a quiet room. He or she simply breathed the air mixture through a gas mask and provided subjective ratings of his or her anxiety level. The instructions indicated that, while they were breathing the CO_2-enriched air, subjects might experience various emotions, ranging from relaxation to anxiety, and that they might experience some physical sensations. They were also told that they might be able to control the gas mixture:

> "During the assessment you will be undergoing, a box in the room *may* light up. When this box is lit, you will be able to adjust the mixture of CO_2 by using the dial which will be on your lap. You will be able to do this only if the box lights up. We ask that you adjust the mixture *only* if you find it *necessary,* as the assessment would be most useful if the CO_2 remains unchanged."

In fact, the dial that the subjects held in their hands did not have any effect on the mixture of gas. All the patients received 5 minutes of compressed air followed by 15 minutes of CO_2-enriched air. For 10 of the 20 patients (selected at random), the light went on just as the CO_2-enriched air began, and it remained on for the remainder of the session. For the other 10 patients, the light did not go on at all.

Immediately after this procedure, each patient was interviewed to determine whether he or she had experienced a panic attack during the inhalation procedure. The results indicated that the illusion of control had a dramatic impact on the probability that patients would panic. Eight of the 10 patients in the "no illusion" group—those for whom the light did not go on—experienced a panic attack. Most of the people in this group who did panic said that the experience was similar to their naturally occurring panics. Among the "illusion of control group" (patients for whom the light had been illuminated), in contrast, only 2 out of the 10 patients experienced a panic attack. Patients in the no illusion group reported significantly more symptoms of panic than did patients in the illusion of control group (an average of 9.2 and 4.3 symptoms for each group, respectively). Patients in both groups reported high levels of breathlessness and smothering sensations, dizziness, light-headedness, and pounding or racing heart, but the patients in the illusion of control group were less likely than the no illusion patients to report almost every other type of panic symptom.

The results of this study highlight the interactive nature of biological and psychological events that combine to produce the experience of panic. The biological foundations of the experience—whether precipitated by an "alarm" response to stressful events, the direct administration of lactate, or CO_2 inhalation—are undoubtedly important but by themselves are not sufficient. Also important are the person's perceptions of the situation. ■

and searches for ways to avoid them. The readily accessed network of threat-related schemas then activates a series of additional "What if?" questions that quickly lead to a dramatic increase in negative affect.

If worriers are preoccupied with the perception of threat cues and the rehearsal of dangerous scenarios but are unable to reach satisfactory solutions to their problems, why do they continue to engage in this vicious, maladaptive cycle?

Thomas Borkovec, a clinical psychologist at Penn State University, and his students have studied the uncontrollable nature of the worry process. Two of Borkovec's conclusions are particularly important in explaining the self-perpetuating nature of worry: (1) worry is primarily a verbal-linguistic event (as opposed to visual images), and (2) worry serves the function of avoiding unpleasant somatic activation through the suppression of imagery (Borkovec & Inz, 1990; Roemer & Borkovec, 1993). In other words, some people apparently continue to worry, even though it is not productive, because worrying is reinforced by an immediate (though temporary) reduction in uncomfortable physiological sensations.

Thought Suppression: Obsessive-Compulsive Disorder The model of worry or anxious apprehension that has been developed by Borkovec, Mathews, and others places primary emphasis on the role of attentional processes. Worrying is unproductive and self-defeating in large part because it is associated with a focus on self-evaluation (fear of failure) and negative emotional responses rather than on external aspects of the problem and active coping behaviors. We may be consciously aware of these processes and simultaneously be unable to inhibit them. The struggle to control our thoughts often leads to a process known as **thought suppression,** an active attempt to stop thinking about something.

It seems simple to say "Stop worrying," but it is virtually impossible for some people to do so. In fact, recent evidence suggests that efforts that are directed toward the control or suppression of unwanted thoughts can frequently have ironic consequences. For example, research by Daniel Wegner (1989), a psychologist at the University of Virginia, has demonstrated that trying to rid your mind of a distressing or unwanted thought can have the unintended effect of

making the thought more intrusive. Subsequent research (Wegner et al., 1990) further suggested that thought suppression might actually increase, rather then decrease, the strong emotions associated with those thoughts. Recently, Wegner and his colleagues have also found that thought suppression results in a strong connection between suppressed thoughts and their associated moods, and vice versa (Wenzlaff, Wegner, & Klein, 1991). This bond between a thought and its associated emotion allows activation of one to result in the reinstatement of the other, a kind of dual pathway.

Obsessive-compulsive disorder may be related, in part, to the maladaptive consequences of attempts to suppress unwanted or threatening thoughts which the person has learned to see as being dangerous or forbidden (Barlow, 1988). Remember that obsessive thoughts are a common experience in the general population. They resemble "abnormal" obsessions in form and content (Rachman & DeSilva, 1978). However, the obsessions of those in treatment for OCD are more intense and, perhaps most importantly, are more often strongly resisted and more difficult to dismiss. This resistance may be a key component in the association between emotional sensitivity and the development of troublesome obsessive thoughts. It may be that certain individuals react strongly to events that trigger an emotional response. These individuals become aware of their exaggerated reactivity and find it unpleasant. In an effort to control their reaction, they attempt to resist or suppress the emotion.

As a result of an individual's attempt to suppress strong emotion, a rebound effect occurs, culminating in a vicious cycle. Thoughts that are present during the instigation of such a cycle become robustly associated with the emotion and may become the content of an obsessive thought. This model may help to explain the episodic nature of obsessive-compulsive symptoms; relapse may be triggered by intense emotional episodes. Indeed, Wenzlaff et al. (1991) found that suppressed thoughts are reencountered when the associated mood returns.

INTERPERSONAL FACTORS: SOCIAL PHOBIAS

Social phobias may be produced through a process that combines direct prepared conditioning with anxious apprehension. The prepared stimulus in social phobias may involve other people's faces. Öhman (1986) has noted that we are prepared to fear faces that appear angry, critical, or rejecting if they are directed toward us. When a performer makes eye contact with his or her audience, an association may develop between fear and these facial expressions.

TABLE 6-4

Frequency of Anxiety Disorders in First-Degree Relatives of Three Types of Subjects

	Percent of Relatives with		
Proband with:	Panic disorder	GAD	Specific phobia
Panic disorder	14.9	5.4	1.7
Generalized anxiety disorder	4.1	19.5	1.6
No psychiatric diagnosis	3.5	3.5	1.8

Source: Adapted from R. Noyes, Jr., et al. (1987). A family study of generalized anxiety disorder. *American Journal of Psychiatry, 144,* 1019-1024.

Another important difference between social phobias and specific phobias is that social phobias involve an element of performance—a social behavior that must be performed in the presence of others. In that sense, performance deficits may also play an important role in social phobias, but they are less likely to be involved in the etiology of specific phobias. People who are less able to perform the requisite behaviors, such as public speaking, may be more likely to become apprehensive or worried as they approach the situation.

In many cases, people who are clearly capable of performing the necessary tasks will develop intense fear responses in social situations. They can perform when they are alone (in practice), but they cannot perform in front of an audience. Barlow (1988) has argued that this deterioration in skill is caused by anxious apprehension, which is similar to Borkovec's description of the process of worrying. An increase in negative affect presumably triggers a shift toward self-focused attention ("Oh no, I'm getting really upset") and activates threat schemas ("What if I make a mistake?"). The person becomes distracted by these thoughts, and performance deteriorates. In a sense, the person's fearful expectations become a self-fulfilling prophesy.

Biological Factors

Several pieces of evidence indicate that biological events play an important role in the development and maintenance of the anxiety disorders. In the following pages, we review the role of genetic factors and the use of chemicals to induce symptoms of panic. These factors undoubtedly interact with the social and psychological variables that we have considered in the preceding sections.

GENETIC FACTORS: FAMILY STUDIES

Family studies support the hypothesis that genetic factors are involved in the transmission of anxiety disorders. Early studies did not make subdivisions among specific types of anxiety disorders; instead, they referred broadly to the "anxiety neuroses." Most investigators found that anxiety states were roughly twice as common among the first-degree relatives of patients with anxiety disorders as they were among relatives of normal control subjects (Torgerson, 1988).

Some family studies conducted after the introduction of DSM-III have focused specifically on the risk for panic disorder among relatives of panic patients. All of these studies have found a relatively high rate of panic disorder—between 16 percent and 31 percent—among the patients' relatives (Crowe, 1990). These results support the argument that some people inherit a genetic predisposition to developing a panic disorder. But what about the relatives' risk for generalized anxiety disorder? Family studies also provide an opportunity to evaluate the validity of the split between GAD and panic disorder, which was introduced in DSM-III. Data from one study are summarized in Table 6–4. They indicate that the relatives of people with panic disorder show an elevated risk of panic disorder themselves, but not an elevated risk of generalized anxiety disorder. The same pattern holds for the relatives of people with generalized anxiety disorder: The relatives exhibit a high rate of GAD but not a high rate of panic disorder (Noyes et al., 1987). These patterns are consistent with the proposition that panic disorder and GAD are etiologically separate disorders.

Family history data regarding obsessive-compulsive disorder suggest that a general vulnerability to anxiety disorders is genetically transmitted in these families, but the predisposition can apparently be expressed in different ways. One study examined the frequency of mental disorders among 120 relatives of 32 patients with OCD and 129 relatives of 33 normal subjects (Black et al., 1992). The lifetime prevalence of OCD was roughly 2 percent in both groups, no higher than would be expected in the general population. There were significant differences between groups, however, with regard to other types of anxiety disorder. Thirty percent of the patients' relatives met the diagnostic criteria for at least one anxiety disorder, most often GAD. In comparison, only 17 percent of the relatives of the control subjects qualified for a diagnosis of at least one type of anxiety disorder. This evidence suggests that the relatives of the OCD probands did not inherit a specific predisposition to this disorder, but they did inherit a more global tendency toward anxiety disorders. The expression of that tendency is presumably influenced by subsequent experience.

The results of the family studies all point toward some form of genetic influence. They are inconsistent with regard to their implications for the classification of anxiety disorders. Comparisons of panic and GAD support the movement toward splitting these disorders apart in the diagnostic manual. Data regarding relatives of OCD probands, in contrast, are more consistent with the older European preference for lumping anxiety disorders together.

TWIN STUDIES

Family studies do not prove the involvement of genes, because family members also share environmental factors (for example, diet, culture, and so on). Twin studies provide a more stringent test of the genetic hypothesis (see Chapter 2). Table 6–5 summarizes the results of various twin studies on anxiety disorders. Torgerson (1983) studied 13 MZ twin pairs and 16 DZ twin pairs in which the proband had been diagnosed as suffering from panic disorder. The concordance rate was 31 percent in the MZ pairs and 0 percent in the DZ pairs. Torgerson also noted that the MZ concordance rate did not appear to be influenced by factors such as whether the twins had spent a lot of time together or whether they had been treated in a similar way by their parents. The conclusion is, once again, that genetic factors are involved in the development of panic disorder.

An inconsistent picture has emerged from twin studies concerned with generalized anxiety disorder. A few studies have been conducted since GAD was listed as a diagnostic category separate from the other anxiety disorders. Some of these studies suggest that the co-twins of GAD patients are not at increased risk for the disorder. Torgerson (1983) examined concordance rates among 12 MZ twin pairs and 20 DZ twin pairs in which the proband had a diagnosis of GAD. None of the 12 MZ co-twins qualified for a diagnosis of GAD, and only one of the DZ co-twins met the criteria for GAD (see Table 6–5). It is interesting to note, however, that approximately 25 percent of the co-twins in both groups did have some other kind of psychiatric diagnosis. This evidence suggests that, although GAD may not be influenced by genetic factors, some type of nonspecific environmental circumstance may be associated with psychological disturbance in these families.

Kenneth Kendler, a psychiatrist at the Medical College of Virginia, and his colleagues have studied generalized anxiety disorder in a sample of more than 2,000 female–female twin pairs (Kendler et al., 1992a). The subjects in this study were not psychiatric patients. Diagnoses were assigned following structured diagnostic interviews conducted by the research team. Concordance rates for MZ and DZ twin pairs were 28 percent and 17 percent, respectively (excluding cases in which the person only met criteria for GAD while also experiencing an episode of panic disorder or major depression).

TABLE 6-5

Twin Concordance Rates for Specific Anxiety Disorders

		Percent Concordance (# twins)	
Disorder	**Study**	**MZ**	**DZ**
Panic	Torgerson (1983)	.31	.00
GAD	Torgerson (1983)	.00	.05*
GAD	Kendler et al. (1992a)	.28	.17
Agoraphobia	Kendler et al. (1992b)	.23	.15
Social phobia	Kendler et al. (1992b)	.24	.15
Animal phobia	Kendler et al. (1992b)	.26	.11
Phobias (all)	Carey & Gottesman (1981)	.88**	.31
OCD	Carey & Gottesman (1981)	.87**	.47

Although concordance rates for GAD were very low, about 25 percent of the co-twins in both groups had some other type of psychiatric diagnosis.

** *Concordance, in this study, was phobic symptoms or features and OCD symptoms or features. In other words, the co-twin did not have to receive a diagnosis of OCD in order to be considered concordant.*

This comparison, as well as additional analyses of the data, supported the conclusion that genetic factors are involved in the etiology of GAD. Statistical estimates indicated that the disorder is modestly heritable, with genetic factors accounting for somewhere between 20 and 30 percent of the variance in the transmission of GAD. (See Research Methods in Chapter 16 for a discussion of heritability.)

Twin studies of other anxiety disorders are consistent with the pattern seen for panic disorder and suggest the influence of genetic factors. Carey and Gottesman (1981), for example, studied eight MZ twin pairs in which the proband carried a diagnosis of phobic disorder. Seven of the co-twins exhibited phobic symptoms or features (that is, not necessarily a diagnosable phobia) that were similar to those of the proband. This evidence is also summarized in Table 6–5. The same report found much higher concordance rates for obsessive-compulsive disorder among MZ than DZ twin pairs.

Interviews with women in the Virginia Twin Registry have also been used to examine concordance rates for specific types of phobias (Kendler et al., 1992b). These data are summarized in Table 6–5. Although all types of phobias appear to be influenced by genetic factors in this study, the greatest genetic influence was found for agoraphobia. The etiology of specific phobias was relatively more influenced by specific environmental factors. Social phobias lay between the other types.

What does this evidence tell us? The twin and family studies clearly suggest that genetic factors are involved in the transmission of most forms of anxiety disorders. They also indicate that the picture may be somewhat different for generalized anxiety disorders. More information is needed on that topic. It seems reasonable to conclude that some people inherit a predisposition that makes them especially vulnerable to the development of an anxiety disorder. The specific form of this predisposition is currently unknown. Considerable speculation has focused on the role of neurochemical factors in

this regard. One area of study that has played an increasingly important role in exploring these variables with regard to panic disorder involves the use of chemicals to induce panic attacks.

PHARMACOLOGICAL PROVOCATION OF PANIC

One laboratory procedure that is capable of inducing panic attacks in those people who suffer from panic disorder involves the infusion of lactate.[†] The discovery of this effect was inspired by a few clinical studies, reported in the 1940s and 1950s, that noted that patients with "anxiety neurosis"[††] sometimes experienced an increase in subjective anxiety following vigorous physical exercise. This change in subjective symptoms appeared to be associated with an extremely rapid and excessive increase in lactic acid in the blood.

In order to examine this phenomenon more closely, two psychiatrists at Washington University in St. Louis decided to infuse lactate directly into anxiety disorder patients and a control group of normal subjects (Pitts & McClure, 1967). Each subject was also given a placebo injection on a separate occasion. Subjects in both groups reported few symptoms after the placebo injections. Shortly after the lactate infusion began, however, 13 out of 14 of the anxiety patients experienced an anxiety attack, which they described as being similar to their typical symptoms. In contrast, only 2 of the 10 normal subjects reported an anxiety attack during lactate infusion. Pitts and McClure concluded that a marked increase in lactate production might trigger anxiety symptoms in anyone, but that anxiety patients were especially vulnerable to this effect because of some as-yet-unspecified neurochemical or metabolic difference.

Since the Pitts and McClure experiment, a large number of studies have demonstrated that lactate infusions can provoke panic attacks in anywhere from 50 to 90 percent of patients with anxiety or panic disorders, as compared to only between 0 and 25 percent of normal control subjects (Barlow, 1988). Several other procedures can also be used to induce panic in the

---

[†] Lactic acid is formed during anaerobic respiration, the phase of cellular respiration that occurs in the absence of oxygen. The respiratory and circulatory systems are usually able to support aerobic respiration when a person is resting. These systems become overloaded when skeletal muscles are used strenuously. Muscle fibers then need to depend on anaerobic respiration to generate energy (Hole, 1984). This process converts glucose to pyruvic acid. As the oxygen supply becomes depleted, pyruvic acid is converted to lactic acid, which accumulates in the bloodstream and is later converted back to glucose by the liver.

[††] Remember that panic disorder was not listed as a separate diagnostic category when this experiment was conducted. Anxiety neurosis was a general category in DSM-I that included what we now call panic disorder as well as generalized anxiety disorder.

laboratory. These include the infusion of other chemicals, such as caffeine, as well as the inhalation of air that has been enriched with carbon dioxide (CO_2). Some investigators discovered that the administration of certain types of medication, such as MAO inhibitors, could prevent the experience of lactate-induced panic attacks.

Panic induction procedures allow investigators to monitor brain activities that occur during a panic attack. For example, positron emission tomography, or PET scans, have been used to compare blood flow to various areas of the brain before and after anxiety disorder patients experienced lactate-induced panic attacks. One study found that panic is associated with increased blood flow in the temporal lobes (Reiman et al., 1989), an area that is generally considered to be associated with fear and other emotions (Gray, 1990). As the power of brain-imaging procedures improves, enhancing our ability to isolate anatomical regions, this type of experimental procedure may lead to the localization of specific areas of the brain that mediate symptoms of anxiety. These are, of course, exciting possibilities. Information of this sort would tell us *where* neurological underpinnings of panic are located in the brain. That knowledge, coupled with data regarding social and psychological factors, will help us understand *why* people experience panic attacks.

False Suffocation Alarm Theory Over a period of 30 years, Donald Klein has developed an integrated model of panic attacks and agoraphobia that incorporates biological and psychological factors (see Klein, 1981). Klein's interest in these phenomena began in 1959, when he was experimenting with the effects of a newly discovered antidepressant drug, imipramine (Tofranil). Some of his hospitalized patients were seriously impaired agoraphobics who had responded poorly to all previous attempts at treatment, including psychotherapy, sedative drugs, and ECT. Three weeks after they began taking imipramine, the patients suddenly improved. In contrast to their anxious and clinging behavior prior to this treatment, they began to venture out on their own, away from the ward, especially if they were prompted and encouraged by the hospital staff.

What had happened to these patients? Why, after months and years of fearful confinement, were they suddenly willing to move about in the open environment? To answer these questions, we must recognize that the patients' problems could be divided into two categories: (1) the occasional, ongoing experience of uncued panic attacks, and (2) the fear of having an attack. Careful observations led Klein to conclude that imipramine had a relatively specific effect. It prevented the occurrence of panic attacks. It did not, however, reduce the patients' anticipatory anxiety about possibly having an attack until they left the security of the hospital ward and directly confronted situations that they had learned to fear.

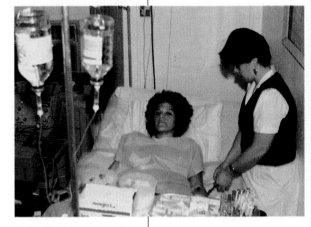

Klein spent the next 30 years developing and revising a theory about the process by which the attacks develop and the ways in which they can be treated. Evidence in support of his theory is drawn primarily from studies regarding both the pharmacological treatment of panic disorder and the provocation of panic in laboratory settings.

Klein (1993) has most recently proposed that the human brain contains a suffocation monitor, an adaptive mechanism that increases a person's chances of survival and has evolved with our species. When it detects a threat of suffocation, this monitor triggers distressing feelings associated with breathlessness that in turn provoke urgent efforts to escape to open surroundings. The monitor is sensitive to several different variables, including increased levels of CO_2, that might signal that the person is trapped and being forced to breathe his or her own exhalations (as might happen in a cave-in). An increased level of lactate can also set off the alarm because it acts like CO_2 by inducing dilation of cerebral arteries. According to Klein's model, unexpected panic attacks represent a misfire of this system, or a false suffocation alarm, which may be triggered by hypersensitivity to carbon dioxide.

The threshold for a person's suffocation alarm can presumably be influenced by a number of biological, social, and psychological factors. Biological factors include hormone levels, which change during pregnancy and may explain reductions in panic among pregnant women. Social and psychological factors include stress-

▲ Clinical scientists have studied factors that influence the onset of panic attacks by using lactate infusion, which can elicit a full-blown panic attack among people who have panic disorder.

ful life events (such as maternal loss) and the development of separation anxiety during childhood, which seem to increase the rate of panic disorder when these children become adults.

In contrast to current cognitive conceptions of panic (Clark, 1986b), Klein views panic and fear as different types of emotional response. Both are accompanied by general physiological arousal and distress, but Klein believes that certain symptoms can distinguish between these reactions. He argues that respiratory distress (shortness of breath, smothering sensations) is the most important feature of unexpected panic attacks. Heart palpitations occur in both fear and panic, but shortness of breath is specifically associated with panic.

According to this perspective, agoraphobic avoidance—anticipatory fear of having a panic attack—most often appears after a person has experienced a number of unexpected, uncued panic attacks. The probability of developing agoraphobia is a function of the number and severity of these attacks. It is probably also influenced by the person's tendency toward worrying or anxious apprehension. This is the point, in Klein's model, at which psychological variables may play their most important role. The suffocation alarm itself is presumably a primitive (from an evolutionary point of view) biological mechanism that is not affected by cognitive processes.

The model suggests that panic and fear are mediated by different biological pathways. Fear is accompanied by activation of the hypothalamic-pituitary-adrenal (HPA) axis (see the section in Chapter 5 on the neuroendocrine system), including the release of increased levels of certain hormones such as free cortisol. Panic is not associated with activation of the HPA axis. Relatively little is known about the biological underpinnings of the suffocation alarm, but speculation is focused on specific areas in the brain in which serotonin is the primary neurotransmitter (Klein, 1993).

Treatment

In the following pages, we review some of the treatment procedures that have been demonstrated to be useful with anxiety disorders. This is one of the areas of psychopathology in which clinical psychologists and psychiatrists are best prepared to improve the level of their clients' functioning. We begin our discussion by describing procedures that were used in an effort to help Ed, the person with obsessive-compulsive disorder whose problems were described at the beginning of this chapter.

Ed had been in and out of various forms of psychotherapy since he was 18 years old. Most recently, he had been in psychoanalytic therapy with a psychiatrist for almost 5 years. His therapist focused on Ed's relationship with his parents when he was a child, usually steering him away from discussion of the present situation. The writing problems and fear of axes were, according to the psychiatrist, overt signs of deeply rooted mental conflicts that had been festering for many years. These conflicts had to be resolved before the overt symptoms of anxiety would disappear. Considerable emphasis was placed on the anger that Ed still harbored toward his bio-

logical father, who had abandoned him and his mother. The resentment that he felt at the arrival of his younger brother also seemed important. Ed found these sessions interesting, because they helped him understand his emotions, but progress was slow. This form of psychotherapy did not have an impact on his writing problems or other overt symptoms of anxiety.

Ed's psychiatrist eventually gave him a prescription for clomipramine (Anafranil), an antidepressant drug that is also used to treat people with severe obsessions. Weekly psychotherapy sessions continued as the dose was gradually increased. The medication had a beneficial impact after 4 weeks. Ed said that he had begun to feel as though he was trapped at the bottom of a well. After the medication, he no longer felt buried. His situation still wasn't great, but it no longer seemed hopeless or unbearable. He was also less intensely preoccupied by his obsessive violent images. They were still there, but they weren't as pressing. The drug had several annoying, though tolerable, side effects. His mouth felt dry, and he was occasionally a bit dizzy. He also noticed that he became tired more easily. Although Ed was no longer feeling seriously depressed, and the intensity of his obsessions was diminished, they had not disappeared, and he was now avoiding writing altogether.

Because the obsessions were still a problem, Ed's psychiatrist referred him to a psychologist who specialized in behavior therapy for anxiety disorders. He continued seeing the psychiatrist every other week for checks on his medication, which he continued to take. The new therapist told Ed that his fears of particular letters and numbers would be maintained as long as he avoided writing. Ed agreed to begin writing short essays every day, for a period of at least 30 minutes. The content could vary from day to day—anything that Ed felt like writing about—but he was encouraged to include the names of his wife and brother as often as possible. Furthermore, he was instructed to avoid his compulsive writing style, intentionally allowing the parts of letters to be separated or loops to be closed. At the beginning and end of each essay, Ed was required to record his anxiety level so that the therapist could monitor changes in his subjective discomfort. Over a period of 8 or 10 weeks, Ed's handwriting began to change. It was less of a struggle to get himself to write, and his handwriting became more easily legible.

The final aspect of behavioral treatment was concerned with his fear of axes. Ed and his therapist drew up a list of objects and situations related to axes, arranging them from those that were the least anxiety-provoking through those that were most frightening. They began with the least frightening. In their first exposure session, Ed agreed to meet with the psychologist while a relatively dull, wood-splitting maul was located in the adjoining room. Ed was initially quite anxious and distracted, but his anxiety diminished considerably before the end of their 2-hour meeting. Once that had been accomplished, the therapist helped him to confront progressively more difficult situations. These sessions were challenging and uncomfortable for Ed, but they allowed him to master his fears in an orderly fashion. By the end of the twelfth session of exposure, he was able to hold a sharp axe without fear.

Psychological Interventions

Psychoanalytic psychotherapy has been used to treat patients with anxiety disorders since Freud published his seminal papers at the turn of the century. The emphasis in this type of treatment is on fostering insight regarding the unconscious motives that presumably lie at the heart of the patient's symptoms. Ed's experience illustrates this process. Although many therapists continue to employ this general strategy, it has not been shown to be effective in controlled outcome studies.

EXPOSURE: DESENSITIZATION AND FLOODING

Like psychoanalysis, behavior therapy was initially developed for the purpose of treating anxiety disorders, especially specific phobias. The first widely adopted procedure was known as *desensitization* (Wolpe, 1958). In desensitization, the client is first taught progressive muscle relaxation. Then the therapist constructs a hierarchy of feared stimuli, beginning with those items that provoke only small amounts of fear and progressing through items that are most frightening. Then, while the client is in a relaxed state, he or she imagines the lowest item on the hierarchy. The item is presented repeatedly until the person no longer experiences an increase in anxiety when thinking about the object or situation. This process is repeated several times as the client moves systematically up the hierarchy, sequentially confronting images of stimuli that were originally rated as being more frightening.

In the years since Wolpe introduced desensitization, many different variations on this procedure have been employed. The crucial feature of the treatment involves systematic maintained exposure to the feared stimulus (Marks, 1987; Rachman, 1990). Positive outcomes have been reported, regardless of the specific manner in which exposure is accomplished. Some evidence indicates that direct ("in vivo") exposure works better than imaginal exposure. A few prolonged exposures can be as effective as a larger sequence of brief exposures. Another variation on exposure procedures, known as *flooding*, begins with the most frightening stimuli rather than working up gradually

▼ Exposure treatments can be administered in imagination or in the person's natural environment. In this photograph, a patient with acrophobia is accompanied to the top of a tall building by a therapist who is conducting exposure therapy.

from the bottom of the hierarchy. All of these variations on the basic procedure have been shown to be effective in the treatment of phobic disorders. Several research studies have demonstrated that exposure therapy leads to *clinically meaningful* improvement when compared to placebo treatments (see Research Methods). Positive results are typically maintained several months after the end of treatment (O'Sullivan & Marks, 1991). Exposure is often accomplished in the presence of the therapist, but the treatment can be just as effective when the client directs his or her own systematic exposure in the natural environment (Al-Kubaisy et al., 1992).

PROLONGED EXPOSURE AND RESPONSE PREVENTION

The most effective form of psychological treatment for obsessive-compulsive disorder combines prolonged exposure to the situation that increases the person's anxiety with prevention of the person's typical compulsive response (Steketee & Foa, 1986; Turner & Beidel, 1988). Neither component is effective by itself. The combination of exposure and response prevention is necessary because of the way in which people with obsessive-compulsive disorder use their compulsive rituals to reduce anxiety that is typically stimulated by the sudden appearance of an obsession. If the compulsive behavior is performed, exposure is effectively cut short.

Consider, for example, the treatment program employed with Ed. His obsessive thoughts and images, which centered around violence, were associated with handwriting. They were likely to pop into his mind when he noticed letters that were poorly formed. In an effort to control these thoughts, Ed wrote very carefully, and he corrected any letter that seemed a bit irregular. By the time he entered behavior therapy, Ed had avoided writing altogether for several months. The therapist arranged for him to begin writing short essays on a daily basis to be sure that he was exposed, for at least 30 minutes each day, to the situation that was most anxiety-provoking. He encouraged Ed to deliberately write letters that did not conform to his compulsive style. In their sessions, for example, Ed was also required to write long sequences of the letter "T" in which he deliberately failed to connect the two lines. He was not allowed to go back and correct this "mistake." The combination represents prolonged exposure to an anxiety-provoking stimulus and response prevention.

Controlled-outcome studies indicate that this approach is effective with OCD patients (Rachman & Hodgson, 1980). One review of 18 outcome studies found that 51 percent of the OCD patients who had been treated with prolonged exposure and response prevention were either free of symptoms or much improved at the end of treatment; another 39 percent were considered moderately improved. Only 10 percent did not benefit at all (Foa, Steketee, & Ozarow, 1985).

There are some limits associated with the utility of exposure and response prevention. It is most effective with patients who have compulsive rituals. Pure obsessions are less responsive to treatment. The outcome of behavior therapy is correlated with the severity of the patient's symptoms. The most seriously disturbed patients are less likely to respond positively to treatment (Basoglu et al., 1988).

APPLIED RELAXATION

Behavior therapists have used relaxation procedures for many years. Progressive muscle relaxation was originally developed and studied by Jacobson (1938) and was incorporated into desensitization when that procedure was developed by Wolpe (1958). Relaxation training usually involves teaching the client alternately to tense and relax specific muscle groups while breathing slowly and deeply (Bernstein & Borkovec, 1973). This process is usually described to the client as an active coping skill that can be learned through consistent practice and used to control anxiety and worry.

Outcome studies indicate that relaxation is a useful form of treatment for generalized anxiety disorder (Durham & Allan, 1993; Öst, 1987). Borkovec and Costello (1993) compared applied relaxation and cognitive behavior therapy to nondirective psychotherapy for the treatment of patients with generalized anxiety disorder (see Research Close-up in Chapter 3). Patients who received relaxation training and those who received cognitive therapy were more improved at the end of treatment than those who received only nondirective therapy.

One risk associated with the use of applied relaxation methods is that some patients with panic disorder experience unexpected panic attacks during the induction of deep muscle relaxation (Barlow & Cerny, 1988). This is especially likely to happen when they practice relaxation at home. The risk of relaxation-induced panic can be minimized in several ways, including the provision of detailed instructions that alert the client to physical sensations that are likely to be experienced during this procedure, thus reducing the chance that the client will cat-

astrophically misinterpret these sensations as signaling the onset of a panic attack.

COGNITIVE THERAPY

Cognitive therapy is used extensively in the treatment of anxiety disorders. Cognitive treatment procedures for anxiety disorders have been developed by Aaron Beck (Beck & Emery, 1985)

RESEARCH METHODS

Statistical Significance and Clinical Importance

The fact that someone has observed a statistically significant effect in a treatment outcome study does not necessarily mean that this effect is clinically important. We can explain this point by using a hypothetical example. Imagine that you want to know whether exposure-based treatment is effective in the treatment of social phobias. You could conduct a study, using an experimental design, in which 50 patients with this disorder are randomly assigned to receive exposure therapy and another 50 patients—the control group—are not. The latter group might receive a placebo pill or nondirective supportive psychotherapy for purposes of comparison. Measures of anxiety and avoidance are collected before and after treatment for patients in both groups. Your hypothesis is that exposure treatment will lead to more improvement than will placebo or nondirective therapy. The *null hypothesis,* on the other hand, holds that the two forms of treatment are not truly different. To conclude that exposure therapy is effective, you must reject the null hypothesis.

After collecting your data, you can use statistical tests to help you decide whether you can reject the null hypothesis. These tests assign a probability to that result, indicating how often we would find that result if there are not really differences between the two treatments. Psychologists have adopted the .05 level, meaning that if a difference occurs only by chance, you would find this difference less than 5 times out of every 100 times you repeated this experiment. Differences that exceed the .05 level therefore are assumed to reflect real differences between the variables rather than mere chance. Such results are said to be *statistically significant.*

Statistical significance should not be equated with clinical importance (Jacobson & Truax, 1991). It is possible for an investigator to find statistically significant differences between groups (and therefore reject the null hypothesis) on the basis of relatively trivial changes in the patients' adjustment. Consider the hypothetical example outlined above and suppose that you measured outcome in terms of a rating scale for anxiety whose scores could range from 0 (no symptoms of anxiety) to 100 (highest ratings on all items). Let's also assume that a rating of 50 or higher is typically considered to indicate the presence of important anxiety problems that are often associated with a disruption of the person's social and occupational functioning. Both groups have a mean rating of 85 on the scale prior to treatment. At the end of treatment, the mean rating for the exposure group has dropped to 65 and the mean for the control group is now 75. If you have included enough subjects, and depending upon the amount of variation among scores within each group, this difference might reach statistical significance. But is it clinically important? Probably not. The average patient in the exposure group still has a score above the cutoff for identifying meaningful levels of psychopathology.

The investigator must therefore consider carefully not only whether there are statistically significant differences between groups, but also the relative amount of change that is observed and the consistency of change across patients within each group. It is also important to employ assessment procedures that measure aspects of behavior that are clinically important (Beidel, Turner, & Cooley, 1993). ∎

and Albert Ellis (1962). They are similar to those employed in the treatment of depression. Therapists help clients identify cognitions that are relevant to their problem; recognize the relation between these cognitions and maladaptive emotional responses (such as prolonged anxiety); examine the evidence that supports or contradicts these beliefs; and teach more useful ways of interpreting events in their environments (Schuyler, 1991).

In the case of anxiety disorders, cognitive therapy is usually accompanied by additional behavior therapy procedures. Barlow's approach to the treatment of panic disorder, for example, includes a cognitive component in addition to applied relaxation and exposure (Barlow & Cerny, 1988). One aspect of the cognitive component involves an analysis of errors in the ways in which people think about situations in their lives. Typical examples of faulty logic include jumping to conclusions before considering all of the evidence, overgeneralizing (basing negative predictions about future performance on a very limited set of previous experiences), all-or-none thinking (assuming that one mistake means total failure), and so on.

A second aspect of Barlow's cognitive component for panic patients is called "decatastrophisizing." In this procedure, the therapist asks the client to imagine what would happen *if* his or her worst-case scenario actually happened. The same principles that are used in examining faulty logic are then applied to the consideration of this situation. The therapist might say, "I don't think that you will fail the exam. But what would happen if you did fail the exam?" The client's initial reaction might be catastrophic ("I would die." "My parents would kill me." "I would flunk out of school."). Upon more careful analysis, however, the client might agree that these negative predictions actually represent gross exaggerations that are based on cognitive errors. Discussions in the therapy session are followed by extensive practice and homework assignments during the week. Clients are encouraged to write down predictions that they make about specific situations and then keep track of the actual outcomes as one way of evaluating the accuracy of their own hypotheses.

Several controlled outcome studies attest to the efficacy of cognitive therapy in the treatment of various types of anxiety disorder, including panic disorder, agoraphobia, social phobia, generalized anxiety disorder, and obsessive-compulsive disorder (Chambless & Gillis, 1993; Durham & Allan, 1993; Emmelkamp & Beens, 1991; Margraf et al., 1993; Zinbarg et al., 1992).

Biological Interventions

Medication is the most effective and most commonly used biological approach to the treatment of anxiety disorders. Several types of drugs have been discovered to be useful. They are often used in conjunction with psychological treatment.

ANTIANXIETY MEDICATIONS

The most frequently used types of minor tranquilizers are from the class of drugs known as benzodiazepines, which includes diazepam (Valium) and alprazolam (Xanax). These drugs reduce many symptoms of anxiety, especially vigilance and subjective somatic sensations such as increased muscle tension, palpitations, increased perspiration, and gastrointestinal distress. They have relatively less effect on a person's tendency toward worry and rumination (Hoehn-Saric & McLeod, 1991). The benzodiazepines were the most widely prescribed form of psychotropic medication until the 1990s.

The benzodiazepines bind to specific receptor sites in the brain that are ordinarily associated with a neurotransmitter known as gamma-aminobutyric acid (GABA). Benzodiazepines, which inhibit the activity of GABA neurons, fall into two types, based on their rate of absorption and elimination from the body. Some, such as alprazolam and lorazepam (Ativan), are absorbed and eliminated quickly, whereas others, such as diazepam, are absorbed and eliminated slowly.

Benzodiazepines have been shown to be effective in the treatment of generalized anxiety disorders. Drug effects are most consistently evident early in treatment. The long-term effects of benzodiazepines (beyond six months of treatment) are not well established (Hoehn-Saric & McLeod, 1991). They are not typically beneficial for patients with phobic disorders or obsessive-compulsive disorder.

Certain high-potency benzodiazepines are also useful for treating panic disorder (Rosenberg, 1993). Alprazolam (Xanax) is considered by some psychiatrists to be the drug of choice for patients with this condition because it produces clinical improvement more quickly than the antidepressants (within 1 to 3 weeks instead of the 8 to 12 weeks that may be required for a full therapeutic response to tricyclic antidepressants) and because it has fewer side effects than antidepressants.

The results of most placebo-controlled outcome studies have been positive. The Cross-National Collaborative Panic Study (CNCPS), which was conducted in two phases, provides some of the best evidence in this regard. The first phase compared alprazolam to a placebo in 500 patients (Ballenger et al., 1988). Among the patients who received alprazolam, 30 percent were markedly improved after 8 weeks of treatment, and another 52 percent were moderately improved. Only 10 percent of the patients who received the placebo were markedly improved after treatment, and another 43 percent in this group were moderately improved.

The second phase of the CNCPS compared alprazolam, imipramine, and placebo treatment in a sample of 1,100 panic disorder patients. The investigators found that alprazolam and imipramine were equally effective in comparison to a placebo. Fewer patients dropped out of the alprazolam group, because the drug had fewer side effects than imipramine. Patients improved faster on alprazolam, but there were no differences between the two drugs after 6 to 8 weeks of treatment.

There are some important inconsistencies in the literature regarding alprazolam and panic disorder with agoraphobia. One recent study compared four types of treatment over a period of 8 weeks: alprazolam plus exposure; alprazolam plus relaxation;[†] placebo plus exposure; and placebo plus relaxation (Marks et al., 1993). Medication was gradually withdrawn during weeks 8 through 16. Patients were followed up 6 months after the end of treatment. All four groups, including those receiving placebos, showed a significant improvement in terms of diminished number of panic attacks by the end of treatment (8 weeks). On the other measures of anxiety and phobic avoidance, both alprazolam and exposure were effective, but the exposure group exhibited larger gains. The alprazolam group lost therapeutic gains after the medication was withdrawn, whereas patients who received exposure treatment maintained their improvement throughout the follow-up period. The authors concluded that exposure is a preferable form of treatment for patients with a diagnosis of panic disorder with agoraphobia, because of the high relapse rate that was observed after alprazolam was withdrawn.

Common side effects of the benzodiazepines include sedation accompanied by mild psychomotor and cognitive impairments. These drugs can, for example, increase the risk of automobile accidents, because they interfere with motor skills. They can also lead to problems in attention and memory, especially among elderly patients.

The most serious adverse effects of benzodiazepines is their potential for addiction. Approximately 40 percent of people who use benzodiazepines for 6 months or more will exhibit symptoms of withdrawal if the medication is discontinued (Sussman & Chou, 1988). Withdrawal reactions include the reappearance of anxiety, somatic complaints, concentration problems, and sleep difficulties. They are most severe among patients who abruptly discontinue the use of benzodiazepines that are cleared quickly from the system, such as alprazolam. The risk for becoming dependent on benzodiazepines is greatest among people who have a history of abusing other substances, like alcohol.

ANTIDEPRESSANT MEDICATIONS

In the early 1960s, Donald Klein and his research group discovered that tricyclic antidepressant drugs, especially imipramine, can be effective in treating panic attacks in patients with agoraphobia. They recommended that psychological intervention be used to eliminate anticipatory anxiety and avoidant behavior after the medication eliminated the threat of further panic attacks. Some psychiatrists still consider imipramine to be the preferred medication for panic disorder (Agras, 1993; Noyes, 1991) because patients are less likely to become dependent on the drug than they are to high-potency benzodiazepines like alprazolam. In addition, patients experience fewer problems when imipramine is withdrawn. The usual duration of treatment is 6 months. Relapse may occur after medication is withdrawn.

The tricyclic antidepressants produce several unpleasant side effects, including weight gain, dry mouth, and overstimulation (sometimes

---

[†] The investigators considered relaxation to be a psychological placebo with regard to the treatment of panic disorder.

referred to as an "amphetamine-like" response). Some of the side effects, like palpitations, sweating, and light-headedness, are upsetting to patients because they resemble symptoms of anxiety. Side effects often lead patients to discontinue treatment prematurely. In one study of patients who received long-term treatment with imipramine, 50 percent experienced distressing side effects, including 17 percent who found the effects intolerable (Noyes et al., 1989).

Clomipramine (Anafranil), another tricyclic antidepressant, has been used extensively in treating obsessive-compulsive disorder since being approved for use in 1989 by the U.S. Food and Drug Administration. Several placebo-controlled studies have shown clomipramine to be effective in treating OCD (deVeaugh-Geiss, 1993). One study found that more than 50 percent of the patients who received clomipramine improved to a level of normal functioning over a period of 10 weeks, compared to only 5 percent of the patients in a placebo group (Katz, deVeaugh-Geiss, & Landau, 1990). Patients who continue to take the drug maintain the improvement, but relapse is common if medication is discontinued (Pato et al., 1988).

Monoamine oxidase (MAO) inhibitors, another type of antidepressant medication (see Chapter 5), are also used in the treatment of panic disorder. One double-blind, placebo-controlled outcome study demonstrated that the MAO inhibitor phenelzine (Nardil) was effective with panic disorder patients (Tyrer, Candy, & Kelly, 1973). Overall, however, MAO inhibitors are used less frequently than imipramine and alprazolam because the patient must observe dietary restrictions while taking them and because they are associated with a risk of serious side effects, such as hypertensive crises. Phenelzine is also used in the treatment of social phobias, especially those in which the person's avoidance is generalized to most types of social interaction (Liebowitz, 1991).

The selective serotonin reuptake inhibitors (SSRIs) have also been employed with anxiety disorders, but they have not been evaluated extensively in double-blind, placebo-controlled studies. Panic disorder and OCD have been treated with SSRIs such as fluvoxamine (Boyer, 1992).

In actual practice, anxiety disorders are often treated with a combination of psychological and biological procedures. The selection of specific treatment components depends upon the specific group of symptoms that the person exhibits. Table 6–6 presents a summary of various types of psychological treatment and specific types of medication that are effective with anxiety disorders. These are, of course, not the only types of treatment that are available, but they include those that have been subjected to empirical validation.

TABLE 6–6

Treatments of Choice for Anxiety Disorders

Disorder	Drug Treatment		Psychological Treatment
	Generic Name	Trade Name	
Panic disorder	Imipramine	Tofranil	Cognitive therapy
	Alprazolam	Xanax	
Agoraphobia	Imipramine	Tofranil	Exposure in vivo
			Cognitive therapy
Generalized anxiety disorder	Alprazolam	Xanax	Applied relaxation
	Diazepam	Valium	Cognitive therapy
Specific phobias	Medication not typically recommended		Exposure in vivo
Social phobia	Propranolol	Inderal	Cognitive therapy
			Social skills training
Obsessive-compulsive disorder	Clomipramine	Anafranil	Exposure plus Response
	Fluoxetine	Prozac	Prevention

Source: Adapted from R. Noyes, Jr. (1991) Treatments of choice for anxiety disorders. In W. Coryell and G. Winokur (eds.), *The clinical management of anxiety disorders*. New York: Oxford University Press.

Summary

Anxiety disorders are defined in terms of a preoccupation with, or persistent avoidance of, thoughts or situations that provoke fear or anxiety. Anxiety involves a diffuse emotional reaction that is associated with the anticipation of future problems and is out of proportion to threats from the environment. A pervasive anxious mood is typically associated with pessimistic thoughts and feelings. The person's attention may also turn inward, focusing on negative emotions and self-evaluation rather than on the organization or rehearsal of adaptive responses that might be useful in coping with negative events.

KEY TERMS

- agoraphobia
- anxiety
- compulsion
- fear
- generalized anxiety disorder (GAD)
- lactate
- mixed anxiety-depressive disorder
- negative affect
- neurosis
- obsessions
- panic attack
- phobia
- positive affect
- preparedness theory
- thought suppression
- worry

A panic attack is a sudden, overwhelming experience of terror or fright. Panic attacks are defined largely in terms of a list of somatic sensations, ranging from heart palpitations, sweating and trembling, to nausea, dizziness, and chills.

Phobias are persistent and irrational narrowly defined fears that are associated with avoidance of a specific object or situation. The most complex and incapacitating form of phobic disorder is known as agoraphobia, which is usually described as fear of public spaces. It is not so much a fear of being close to one specific object or situation as it is fear of being separated from signals associated with safety.

Obsessions are repetitive, unwanted, intrusive cognitive events that may take the form of thoughts or images or impulses. They intrude suddenly into consciousness and lead to an increase in subjective anxiety. Compulsions are repetitive behaviors, considered by the person to be senseless or irrational, that reduce the anxiety associated with obsessions. The person attempts to resist but cannot. The two most common forms of compulsive behavior are cleaning and checking.

DSM-IV recognizes several specific subtypes of anxiety disorders: panic disorders (with and without agoraphobia), phobic disorders (specific phobia, social phobia, and agoraphobia without panic attacks), obsessive-compulsive disorder, and generalized anxiety disorder, as well as post-traumatic stress disorder and acute stress disorder.

The ECA study found that anxiety disorders are more common than any other form of mental disorder. Phobias are the most common type of anxiety disorder, with a 1-year prevalence of about 9 percent of the adult population, followed by generalized anxiety disorder (4 percent), obsessive-compulsive disorder (2 percent), and panic disorder (1 percent). Women are about twice as likely as men to experience specific phobias, agoraphobia, panic disorder, and generalized anxiety disorder. Gender differences are less marked in social phobias and obsessive-compulsive disorder.

Stressful life events can influence the onset of anxiety disorders. Certain kinds of stresses may be differentially associated with particular types of emotional disorders: Severe events involving danger are most often associated with anxiety symptoms, while severe events involving loss are more often associated with depression. Among those people who have developed an anxiety disorder, interpersonal conflict is more characteristic of people with agoraphobia, and conditioning events are found with specific phobias.

The conditioning model explained the development of phobic disorders in terms of classical conditioning, or the pairing of fear with originally neutral stimuli which happen to be present during a traumatic experience. A modified conditioning view, known as preparedness theory, is based on a recognition that there are biological constraints on the kinds of associations that members of a particular species are able to make. We may be prepared to develop intense, persistent fears only to a select set of objects or situations. People can apparently learn to avoid certain stimuli if they observe other people showing a strong fear response to those stimuli. Studies with infant monkeys support the preparedness model.

Cognitive theorists have argued that panic disorder is caused by the catastrophic misinterpretation of bodily sensations or perceived threat. This theory has the support of several research studies, but there are methodological problems associated with some of the studies. The cognitive theory of panic also has problems explaining some clinical observations regarding panic disorder, such as the fact that some patients experience panic attacks in their sleep.

People who are prone to excessive worrying are unusually sensitive to cues that signal the existence of future threats. The recognition of danger cues triggers a maladaptive, self-perpetuating cycle of cognitive processes that can quickly spin out of control. The threatening information that is generated in this process is presumably encoded in memory in the form of elaborate schemas that are easily reactivated. In comparison to the depressed person, who is convinced that failure will definitely occur, the anxious person is afraid of failure that may occur as a future event. Some people apparently continue to worry, even though it is not productive, because worrying is reinforced by an immediate (though temporary) reduction in uncomfortable physiological sensations.

Family studies support the separate classification of panic disorder and generalized anxiety disorders. An increased prevalence of panic disorder is found among the relatives of patients with panic disorder. Similarly, an increased prevalence of generalized anxiety is found among the relatives of patients with generalized anxiety disorder. In other words, the two disorders "breed true." This does not seem to be the case for obsessive-compulsive disorder, where patients' relatives show an increased risk for several types of anxiety disorder rather than a specific risk for OCD.

Twin studies indicate that genetic factors are involved in the etiology of several types of anxiety disorder, especially panic disorder. The evidence is inconsistent for generalized anxiety disorder. There appears to be a modest genetic influence on the development of phobic disorders. The influence of environmental events seems to be greatest in specific phobias.

The false suffocation alarm theory explains the etiology of panic disorder in terms of a brain monitor that has evolved specifically for the purpose of detecting threat of suffocation. Unexpected panic attacks presumably represent a misfire of this system. The alarm's threshold can be influenced by a number of biological and psychological factors. Support for this theory comes from studies that provoke panic in a laboratory setting, using procedures such as the infusion of lactate or the inhalation of air that has been enriched with carbon dioxide.

Several psychological approaches to the treatment of anxiety disorders have been shown to be effective. These include the use of exposure and flooding in the treatment of phobic disorders and prolonged exposure and response prevention in the treatment of obsessive-compulsive disorders. Various types of medication are also effective treatments for anxiety disorders. These include benzodiazepines for generalized anxiety disorder, selective serotonin reuptake inhibitors for obsessive-compulsive disorder, and antidepressants for panic disorder.

Critical Thinking

1. What is the difference between being afraid and being anxious? If low levels of anxiety can enhance a person's performance, why and how do high levels of anxiety interfere with that same person's ability to function? What role does worry play in this process?

2. Anxiety and depression frequently appear together. Someone with a diagnosis of clinical depression is also likely to exhibit symptoms of anxiety disorders, and vice versa. In what ways are these maladaptive emotions alike, and how are they different?

3. Why did the ECA study find such a high rate of anxiety disorders in the general population? Can these figures be reconciled with reports from earlier studies? Is it useful to define mental disorders in such broad terms?

4. Stressful life events are correlated with the appearance of both depression and anxiety disorders. Can you think of any ways in which this relationship is different in anxiety than it is in depression? What determines whether a person will become anxious or depressed in response to a serious negative event?

5. How do social, psychological, and biological factors interact in the production of various types of anxiety disorder? Consider the preparedness model of phobias, the suffocation alarm model of panic, and the cognitive model of generalized anxiety.

7

Maladaptive
Responses
to Stress

The U.S. public is regularly warned in newspaper stories and magazine articles about the dangers associated with stress. We are cautioned that stress not only can cause tension, anxiety, and unhappiness, but also can lead to physical illnesses ranging from the common cold to heart attacks. Stress is bad, something to be avoided. So many dangers are attributed to stress that it becomes stressful to read about them. Scientific studies support many of the popular concerns about the role of stress in both physical and psychological disorders. As we will see in this chapter, however, scientific evidence is not nearly as clear-cut as is popular belief. In fact, evidence suggests that, under the right conditions, stress can promote "toughness" rather than disorder. A certain amount of stress is adaptive. The key is maintaining a balance between being challenged and being overloaded by stress.

Overview

Stress can be defined as an event that creates physiological or psychological strain for the individual. Stressors may include minor, daily events like the frustration of being trapped in a traffic jam, as well as major events such as experiencing the death of a loved one. **Traumatic stress** involves exposure to some catastrophic event that involves actual or threatened death or serious injury to self or others and creates intense fear, helplessness, or horror. Rape, military combat, and exposure to natural or man-made disasters all are examples of traumatic stressors.

Stress plays a role in many different psychological disorders. For this reason, we discuss the relation between stress and the onset of specific psychological disorders in the chapters on each disorder, as we already have done for depression and anxiety. In this chapter, we discuss the relation between stress and only one psychological problem, **posttraumatic stress disorder (PTSD)**. As the term aptly conveys, PTSD is a set of prolonged reactions to experiencing a traumatic stressor. It often is found among rape victims, combat veterans, and other people who are exposed to overwhelming stressors. Other factors must contribute to the etiology of the disorder, however,

because not everyone who experiences traumatic stress develops PTSD.

Stress plays a role in causing or exacerbating physical diseases as well as emotional disorders. The causes of physical (or somatic) illnesses once were thought to reside solely "within the skin." In particular, physical illness was thought to be caused either by invasions of microorganisms or by alterations in the structure or function of internal organ systems. Later, it was recognized that psychological distress contributed to some physical illnesses, but it was assumed that the influence was limited to certain diseases such as asthma, ulcers, and heart disease. Contemporary theories recognize stress as being a factor in all physical illnesses ranging from the common cold to AIDS. In short, theories of the etiology of physical illnesses have adopted the biopsychosocial model.

This systemic or "holistic" view of disease and health has brought about major changes both in psychology and in medicine. The changes are evident in the emergence of the new disciplines of behavioral medicine and health psychology. **Behavioral medicine** is a multidisciplinary field that includes both health-care professionals and mental health experts. The field is concerned with studying and altering the behavioral components of coping with and treating physical illness. Examples of behavioral medicine interventions include providing education and support to parents with a chronically ill child, helping people cope with chronic pain, and increasing patients' adherence to taking medication as prescribed.

Health psychology is a broader field than behavioral medicine, since it incorporates a concern with maintaining health and not just combating physical illness. Health psychologists define disease as "dis-ease," indicating that illness is a departure not only from adaptive biological functioning but also from adaptive social and psychological functioning. In turn, health is viewed as successful adaptation to the environment, not merely the absence of somatic illness (Weiner & Fawzy, 1989). From the health psychology perspective, stress is basic to all forms of illness, because ill health incorporates behavior and not just biology. Health psychologists therefore study and encourage stress management and such healthy behaviors as proper eat-

ing, regular exercise, and avoiding tobacco use.

In this chapter, we examine the fields of behavioral medicine and health psychology and the new views of disease that have promoted the development of these disciplines. While acknowledging that stress plays a role in *all* physical and psychological disorders, we focus on hypertension and coronary heart disease as examples of how stress and physical illness are intertwined. We also consider posttraumatic stress disorder, both as an important emotional problem and as an illustration of how stress can affect psychological well-being. Throughout the chapter, we devote considerable attention to scientific controversies about the general construct of stress and the physiological, emotional, cognitive, and behavioral symptoms that characterize it. When friends tell us they are "stressed," we may assume that we know what they mean. Scientists cannot make such assumptions, however. Scientists must define stress precisely, and this has proven to be a difficult task.

Before addressing these topics, we turn to a case history from our files.

CASE STUDY

Stress, Lifestyle, and Coronary Heart Disease

One Thursday afternoon, Bob Carter, a salesman for a beer and liquor wholesaler, was completing his regular route, calling on customers. Throughout the morning, he had felt a familiar discomfort in his chest and left arm. As had been happening on occasion for at least a year, that morning he experienced a few fleeting but sharp pains in the center and left side of his chest. This was followed by a dull ache in his chest and left shoulder and a feeling of congestion in the same areas. Breathing deeply made the pain feel worse, but Bob could manage it as long as he took shallow breaths. The discomfort was not bad enough to interfere with Bob's work, although this time the pain lasted longer than usual. Still, he continued on his route, alternately vowing to see a doctor soon and cursing his aging body for not performing up to his expectations.

After grabbing a hamburger and a beer for lunch, Bob called on a customer who was behind in his

payments to the wholesaler. At first, Bob shared a cigarette with the customer and chatted with him in a friendly way. He was a salesman after all. Soon it was time to pressure him about the bill. As Bob was raising his voice in anger, a crushing pain returned to his chest and radiated down his left arm. This was much worse than anything he had experienced before. The pain was so intense that Bob was unable to continue speaking. He slumped forward against the table, but with his right arm he waved away any attempts to help him. After sitting still for about 10 minutes, Bob was able to drag himself to his car and drive to his home 30 miles away. When his wife saw him shuffle into the house looking haggard and in obvious pain, she called for an ambulance. The Carters soon discovered that Bob had suffered a myocardial infarction (a heart attack).

Bob was 49 years old at the time. He was married and the father of three children. Bob's home life was normal and happy, but it also put a lot of pressures on him. His 24-year-old daughter was living at home while her husband was serving in combat duty overseas. Naturally, the entire family was anxious about the son-in-law's well-being. More stress came from Bob's 21-year-old daughter, who had just graduated from college and was getting married in 3 weeks. Finally, Bob's 19-year-old son was home from his first year of college full of rebellion and ideas that challenged Bob's authority. There was no shortage of family stress.

Bob also put plenty of stress on himself. A former high school athlete, he had always been competitive and hard-driving. He wanted to be the best at whatever he did, and right now his goal was to be the best salesman in his company. Bob worked hard selling beer and liquor. He used his charm, humor, and some not-so-gentle pressure to sell his products, and it worked. But once he had become the best salesman in his wholesaling company, Bob wanted to be the best salesman for the producers whose products he sold. No matter what he accomplished, Bob drove himself hard to meet a new goal.

Bob maintained his drive and competitiveness from his youthful days as a star athlete, but he had not maintained his physical condition. The only exercise he got was playing golf, and he usually rode in a cart instead of walking the course. He was at least 30 pounds overweight, smoked a pack and a half of cigarettes a day, ate a lot of fatty red meat, and drank heavily. If he had seen a physician earlier, Bob would have been told that he was a good candidate for a heart attack. As it was, he heard this from a cardiologist only after his heart attack.

Bob recuperated quickly in the hospital. He was tired and in considerable pain for a couple of days, but he was telling jokes before the end of a week. His cardiologist explained what had happened to him and gave Bob a stern lecture about how he needed to change his lifestyle. He wanted Bob to quit smoking, lose weight, cut down on his drinking, and gradually work himself back into shape with a careful program of exercise. He urged Bob to "slow

down" at work and told him to quit worrying about his children—they were old enough to take care of themselves.

To underscore these messages, the cardiologist asked a psychologist from the hospital's behavioral medicine unit to consult with Bob. The psychologist reviewed information on coronary risk with Bob and gave him several pamphlets to read on risk factors. The psychologist also explained that the hospital ran several programs that might interest Bob after discharge. These included workshops on stress management, weight reduction groups, and exercise classes. The fees for these programs were minimal, because the hospital ran them primarily as a community service. The psychologist asked Bob if he had other concerns that he wanted to discuss, but Bob said there were none. The psychologist suggested that some issues might come up in the future, and Bob should feel free to raise them with the psychologist or with his cardiologist. The psychologist noted that cardiac patients and their families sometimes had trouble adjusting to the illness and the sudden reminder of the patient's mortality. Bob thanked the psychologist for the information but waved off the professional's offer of assistance much as he had waved off help in the middle of his heart attack.

Bob was discharged from the hospital 10 days after being admitted. Against his doctor's advice, he walked his daughter down the aisle at her wedding the following weekend, and he was back to work within a month. At his 6-week checkup, Bob admitted to his cardiologist that he was smoking again. His weight was unchanged, and his exercise and drinking were only a "little better," according to Bob. When the cardiologist chastised Bob for not following medical advice, Bob promised to renew his efforts. He belied his assertion of commitment, however, by commenting that giving up these small pleasures might or might not make him live any longer, but life surely would seem longer without any indulgences. Clearly, one heart attack was not going to get Bob Carter to slow down. ■

The case of Bob Carter illustrates a number of critical issues and questions about the potential link between stress and physical illness. Most basically, the case strongly suggests that life stress is a factor in the onset of coronary heart disease. Bob's life was full of familiar but stressful pressures that may have increased his risk for myocardial infarction. In addition to these chronic

stressors, the episode of getting angry with his customer appears to have been the "straw that broke the camel's back." In fact, a relation between stress and coronary heart disease has been documented in numerous research studies, as we shall see later in the chapter.

The case of Bob Carter also raises a number of questions about the link between stress and coronary heart disease. What is the physiological mechanism that transforms psychological stress into coronary risk? Is stress the problem, or is the real culprit the unhealthy behaviors that result from stress–smoking, drinking, and overeating? What is more important to the experience of stress–a single major life change such as the marriage of Bob's daughter, or ongoing hassles like Bob's fighting with his son? What is the role of personality in stress? Bob constantly put pressure on himself, whereas another person might have been more likely to "roll with the punches" on the job and at home. Can someone like Bob be helped to change his lifestyle, and if so, does this lower the risk for future heart attacks? We consider these and related questions in this chapter. First, we need to consider more carefully exactly what we mean by "stress."

Defining Stress, Stressors, Distress, and Stress Responses

In the introduction to this chapter, we briefly defined stress as a life event that causes a physical or psychological reaction in the individual. Questions arise when we examine this definition closely. Is stress the event itself, or must we define stress in terms of certain reactions to an event? Some people would relax after becom-

ing the top salesman, but for Bob this achievement only produced another, more difficult challenge. It would therefore seem that stress must be defined in terms of the individual's reactions to the event. Our theories, however, suggest that stress causes adverse reactions. Thus, defining stress in terms of these reactions runs the risk of becoming an exercise in circular logic.

Some clarity comes from carefully defining some terms. A *stressor* is a trying event or stimulus irrespective of its effect on the individual. Subjective *distress* is the individual's unique cognitive appraisal of a stressor as being stressful. A *stress response* is the set of psychophysiological reactions that occur in response to stressors. Different scientists have defined stress as a stressor, distress, or a stress response; thus, these distinctions are essential to understanding research on stress and illness, as we discuss in the following sections.

STRESS AS A STIMULUS

The emphasis on defining stress in terms of stressors has been reflected in various attempts to quantify particular life events in terms of the amount of stress they produce. The work of Holmes and Rahe (1967) has been particularly influential. Holmes and Rahe developed the Social Readjustment Rating Scale (SRRS), a list of various troublesome life events. They assigned stress values to life events, basing these ratings on the judgments of a large group of normal adults who participated in their research. Their approach resulted in a provocative and controversial categorization of the amount of stress caused by a number of different life events. These researchers concluded that different stressors cause more or less stress, as indexed by what

▲ **Stress is a part of everyday life. Stress cannot be avoided, but some ways of coping with life's challenges are more effective than others.**

The Social Readjustment Rating Scale

Life Event	Life Change Units
Death of one's spouse	100
Divorse	73
Marital Separation	65
Jail term	63
Death of a close family member	63
Personal injury or illness	53
Marriage	50
Being fired at work	47
Marital reconciliation	45
Retirement	45
Change in the health of a family member	44
Pregnancy	40
Sex difficulties	39
Gain of a new family member	39
Business readjustment	39
Change in one's financial state	38
Death of a close friend	37
Change to a different line of work	36
Change in number of arguements with one's spouse	35
Mortgage over $10,000	31
Foreclosure of a mortgage or loan	30
Change in responsibilities at work	29
Son or daughter leaving home	29
Trouble with in-laws	29
Outstanding personal achievement	28
Wife beginning or stopping work	26
Beginning or ending school	26
Change in living conditions	25
Revision of personal habits	24
Trouble with one's boss	23
Change in work hours or conditions	20
Change in residence	20
Change in schools	20
Change in recreation	19
Change in church activities	19
Change in social activities	18
Mortgage or loan of less than $10,000	17
Change in sleeping habits	16
Change in number of family get-togethers	15
Change in eating habits	15
Vacation	13
Christmas	12
Minor violations of the law	11

*The SRRS rates different stressors as causing more or less life change for people. More difficult stressors have a higher number of "life change units."

Reprinted with permission from Holmes and Rahe, "The social adjustment rating scale," *Journal of Psychosomatic Research*, 11, 1967. ©1967, Pergamon Press

they called *life change units* (see Table 7–1). Thus, an individual's total stress is the sum of the life change units for each item that is checked on the scale.

The Social Readjustment Rating Scale and similar instruments have been used frequently in research (Miller, 1989). Not surprisingly, investigators have repeatedly found that more life stress as measured by life change units is associated with a wide variety of physical and psychological disorders. This method of defining stress has been subjected to several criticisms, however. Some critics have raised the possibility that people who experience physical or psychological disorders are simply more likely to recall difficult life events than are people who are doing well. Another concern is the limited number of life stressors that are compiled on such scales and the appropriateness of these limited listings for subjects of different ages and ethnicities. For example, the SRRS includes many life events that are irrelevant to most college students—getting divorced, receiving a jail term, obtaining a mortgage. At the same time, the measure omits many of the most relevant stressors that might be experienced by this age group, such as moving away from home, considering abortion, or changing career plans.

Another objection to the SRRS is the inclusion of both positive and negative events as stressors. People may rate getting married and getting fired from a job as being similar in terms of life change units, but the (presumably) positive event of getting married would seem to differ in many important ways from the negative event of being dismissed from a job. Still another objection is the failure to distinguish between transient and chronic life events. Most of the items on the SRRS are not isolated events. Rather, as we shall see in Chapter 16, events such as marital separation or beginning college are major *life transitions* that have consequences extending into many realms of life and lasting over long periods of time.

The most important objection to instruments like the Social Readjustment Rating Scale is that a given stressor does not always produce the same number of life change units for all individuals in all situations. Different life events have different consequences and different meanings for different people at different points in their lives. For example, getting pregnant has a very different meaning for an unwed teenager who failed to use birth control than it has for a married couple in their thirties who are eager to conceive a baby.

A study by Dohrenwend and colleagues (1990) provides an excellent illustration of the need to consider individual differences in response to a stressor. Table 7–2 lists the percentage of people who reported that an event (for example, losing one's job) produced either a large, moderate, small, or no amount of change in their lives. Note that the same event clearly had very different effects on different participants in the study. For example, the death of a family member other than a spouse or child caused a large change for almost 10 percent of the respondents, but it caused no change for over half of them (Dohrenwend et al., 1990). Clearly, there are individual differences in the meaning and consequences of similar types of life events.

TABLE 7–2

Variability Across People in the Amount of Change Caused by the Same Life Event

Type of Event	Percentage of Subjects Reporting Each Amount of Change			
	Large	Moderate	Little	None
Serious physical illness	47.2%	27.8%	8.3%	16.7%
Relations with mate got worse	41.2	47.1	0.0	11.8
Relative died (not child/spouse)	8.3	8.3	29.2	54.2
Close friend died	5.3	15.8	29.8	49.1
Financial loss (not work related)	16.3	44.2	18.6	20.9
Assaulted	18.5	22.2	40.7	18.5
Broke up with a friend	0.0	26.1	37.0	37.0
Laid off	13.3	63.3	13.3	10.0
Had trouble with a boss	17.5	35.0	32.5	15.0
Got involved in a court case	9.5	9.5	28.6	52.4

Adapted from B.P. Dohrenwend et al. (1990). Measuring life events: The problem of variability within event categories. *Stress Medicine*, 6, p.182.

STRESS AS A STIMULUS AND A RESPONSE

Richard Lazarus (1966) has been perhaps the most effective proponent of the need to consider such individual differences in response to stressors. He has argued that stress arises not from life events themselves but from the individual's cognitive appraisal of these events. A life event is a stressor only when it is perceived as being distressing–specifically, when it taxes or overwhelms the individual's ability to cope with it. Lazarus thus defines stress as the combination of a difficult event and an adverse appraisal of it. This is what we have called distress.

Hans Selye (1907–1982) was an American physiologist and an extremely influential stress researcher who also defined stress in terms of a combination of a trying event and a reaction to the event. In Selye's case, however, the defining reaction is a physiological response, not a psychological one. This is what we have called a stress response.

We will discuss the details of Selye's and Lazarus's approaches shortly. For now, we note that there is a potential problem with defining stress as a combination of an event and a reaction to the event. Such a definition runs the risk of being *tautological*, or circular. What causes the reaction? Stress. What is stress? An event that causes the reaction. We stand by our definition of stress as an event that causes physiological or psychological strain. Because of the potential circularity, however, we note that great cau-

tion must be exercised in distinguishing independent variables (stressors) from dependent variables (illnesses) in research on stress. The hypothesis that stress causes illness obviously is meaningless if stress is defined in terms of the illness it is hypothesized to cause.

With this issue in mind, we now turn to consider some of the immediate physiological, emotional, cognitive, and behavioral components of stress. We distinguish these short-term reactions from the much longer-term physical and psychological disorders that are hypothesized to be caused by intense or prolonged stress.

Typical Symptoms and Associated Features of Stress

PHYSIOLOGICAL RESPONSES TO STRESS

American physiologist Walter Cannon (1871–1945) was one of the first researchers to conduct systematic studies of stress, and his profound influence on the field continues to the present day. Cannon (1935) was primarily interested in what he called the *emergency response*, the mobilization of the body in reaction to a perceived threat. According to Cannon, physical or psychological threats produce generalized emotional reactions accompanied by psychophysiological responses, specifically the general arousal of the sympathetic nervous system (see Figure

7–1). When the sympathetic nervous system is aroused, heart and respiration rates increase; blood pressure rises; the pupils dilate; blood sugar levels elevate; and blood flow is redirected in preparation for muscular activity (Baum et al., 1987; Koranyi, 1989).

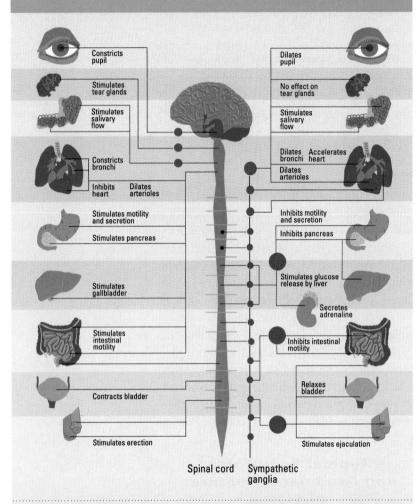

Sympathetic and Parasympathetic Divisions of the Autonomic Nervous System

Constricts pupil
Stimulates tear glands
Stimulates salivary flow
Constricts bronchi
Inhibits heart   Dilates arterioles
Stimulates motility and secretion
Stimulates pancreas
Stimulates gallbladder
Stimulates intestinal motility
Contracts bladder
Stimulates erection

Dilates pupil
No effect on tear glands
Stimulates salivary flow
Dilates bronchi   Accelerates heart
Dilates arterioles
Inhibits motility and secretion
Inhibits pancreas
Stimulates glucose release by liver
Secretes adrenaline
Inhibits intestinal motility
Relaxes bladder
Stimulates ejaculation

Spinal cord   Sympathetic ganglia

FIGURE 7-1: The sympathetic nervous system is activated by stress and generally increases arousal. The parasympathetic nervous system typically calms the individual and returns the body to homeostasis.

Source: From *Biology*, 4th ed., by Willis H. Johnson, Louis E. Delanney, Thomas A. Cole, and Austin E. Brooks, copyright © 1972 by Holt, Rinehart and Winston, Inc.

Cannon argued that these reactions prepared humans (and many other animals) for **fight or flight** in response to the threat. This is the reaction you witness when a cat is surprised by a barking dog. At the behavioral level of analysis, the cat can either flee to safety or turn to fight the dog. Physiologically, the cat's body becomes prepared for either action. Attention is height-

ened, energy is provided for sudden action, and its body prepares for the possibility of injury (Sapolsky, 1992).

The fight or flight response has obvious survival value when we are confronted with a physically dangerous threat. Many theorists have suggested, however, that the human environment may have outpaced our physiological reactions to it. Fight or flight seems to be a maladaptive response to the common psychological threats that characterize the modern world. The fight or flight response may be evoked by such stressors as a reprimand from the boss, giving a speech before a large audience, or remembering a traumatic stressor. Behavioral fight or flight is inappropriate in such circumstances, and the physiology of the response is similarly maladaptive.

In fact, physiological reactions may be prolonged precisely because we cannot respond to such threats with fight or flight. The load on the heart has been found to be greater, for example, when a stressed individual cannot respond to stressors with physical activity than when the same person can respond physically (Charvat et al., 1964). Herein lies Cannon's (1935) theory of the link between stress and physical disorders. He hypothesized that some stress is so intense or chronic that it overwhelms the body's homeostatic mechanisms. (Cannon, in fact, coined the term *homeostasis*.) In Cannon's view, prolonged arousal of the sympathetic nervous system can cause physical damage to the body.

General Adaptation Syndrome   Like Cannon, Hans Selye devoted much of his career to the study of psychophysiological reactions to stressors. Selye's (1956) concept of the **general adaptation syndrome (GAS)** has been particularly influential. The GAS consists of three stages: alarm, resistance, and exhaustion. The *stage of alarm* is similar to Cannon's concept of the emergency response. The *stage of resistance* is a period of replenishment during which the body becomes physiologically prepared to deal with new threats. *Exhaustion* is a final stage that occurs if the body's resources are depleted by chronic stress, making further adaptation impossible.

Selye identified the stage of exhaustion as the mechanism through which stress causes physical illness. In his view, if stress is sufficiently intense or prolonged, the body can no longer respond appropriately to it and is subsequently damaged. An analogy for Cannon's theory is a car in which the engine continues to race instead of idling down after running fast. In contrast, an analogy for Selye's theory is a car that has run out of gas and is damaged because stress keeps turning the key, trying repeatedly and unsuccessfully to restart the engine. Contemporary researchers suggest that stress can create physical illness through both mechanisms, but a third explanation may be even more important. According to this viewpoint, the problem is that the body cannot perform routine functions such as storing energy or repairing injuries because the stress response demands too much energy and uses the energy inefficiently (Sapolsky, 1992). The result is greater susceptibility to illness. The automotive analogy for the demands of stress in this third model is constantly running a car at high speeds, thus increasing the risk of a breakdown.

Immune Function Scientists have begun to study immune functioning as a specific mechanism through which stress might cause physical illness. In fact, research in this area has spawned a new field of study called **psychoneuroimmunology**, research on the effects of stress on the functioning of the immune system. Beginning with Selye's (1956) work and continuing into a diverse field of contemporary research, numerous studies have found that stress impairs immune functioning. In particular, scientists have documented that adrenal hormones called *glucocorticoids* inhibit and may even destroy various immune agents, particularly *T cells*, one of the major types of *lymphocytes*, a category of white blood cells that fight off *mitogens*, foreign substances such as bacteria that invade the body.

Experts hypothesize that *immunosuppression*, the decreased production of T cells and other immune agents, makes the body more susceptible to infectious diseases. For example, researchers have found that T-cell activity diminishes and the rates of various infectious diseases increase among medical students during exam periods (Glaser et al., 1987). Immunosuppression also has been documented among people who are depressed (Herbert & Cohen, 1993). Empirical evidence linking stress and infectious disease remains cloudy (Sapolsky, 1992), but some researchers hypothesize that immunosuppression is an important mechanism linking stress and physical illnesses (Rogers, 1989). It is essential to conduct further research on the effects of

stress on immunity, because immune system functioning is critical to many diseases, including infectious diseases, cancers, allergies, and autoimmune disorders.

Researchers have also raised the possibility that stress affects immune response indirectly, by affecting health behaviors, rather than directly (Cohen & Williamson, 1991). Stress can lead people to sleep less, to eat poorly, and to exercise infrequently. These poor health habits, and not stress per se, may be responsible for immunosuppression. Untangling the direct and the indirect effects of stress on immune functioning is an exciting challenge for future researchers. Another critical question is why stress would inhibit immunity, when increasing the functioning of the immune system would seem to be adaptive in the face of threat.

Neurophysiology and Physiological Toughness
In addition to studying the arousal of the sympathetic nervous system, researchers have documented numerous details of the neurophysiology of the stress response. Two major processes have been identified, and both involve the adrenal gland, a part of the endocrine system (see Chapter 2). One process is the release of *adrenaline* (also known as *epinephrine*) directly into the bloodstream from the adrenal medulla and other body sites. This was a major focus of Cannon's research. Selye identified a second process, the release of glucocorticoids (Baum et al., 1987; Sapolsky, 1992). Epinephrine and the glucocorticoids both stimulate the regulatory systems associated with fight or flight, and they act to inhibit other bodily functions including reproduction, growth, and the storage of sugar.

A recent theory suggests that the release of epinephrine may have very different meanings for the stress response than does release of the glucocorticoids. Dienstbier (1989) has suggested that when production of epinephrine increases as a result of stress, the result is not a weakening of the organism but a beneficial effect that he calls *physiological toughness*. Research indicates that exposure to intermittent stressors of mild or moderate intensity promotes resilience rather than weakness, and Dienstbier theorizes that such exposure increases the availability of epinephrine in both the central and the peripheral nervous systems. He hypothesizes that this protects against the depletion of epinephrine during times of more intense or chronic stress,

▲ **Walter Cannon (1871–1945) was one of the first scientists to conduct systematic research on stress. Cannon focused on the emergency response, the body's physiological preparation for fight or flight.**

▲ **Hans Selye (1907–1982) was a physiologist and prolific stress researcher. Selye's concept of the general adaptation syndrome continues to influence contemporary research on the stress response.**

much as moderate exercise prepares us for intense physical exertion. Dienstbier sees no such toughness benefit associated with the release of the glucocorticoids, however. Thus, he views glucocorticoid release as an index of physiological stress, whereas the release of epinephrine is seen as indicating physiological toughness.

Different Physiological Responses to Different Stressors? Selye and many other stress researchers assumed that *all* stressors cause the same psychophysiological response. Whatever its nature, Selye believed a stressor would cause the GAS, as long as it was sufficiently intense or prolonged (see Figure 7–2). Because responses to stress were assumed to be uniform, he also assumed that all stressors could be grouped together into the single category of stress.

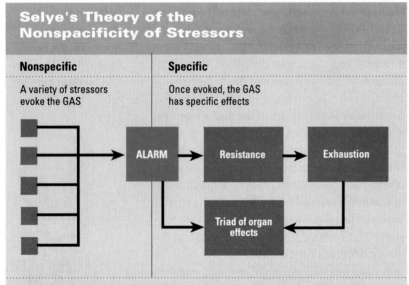

Selye's Theory of the Nonspacificity of Stressors

Nonspecific	Specific
A variety of stressors evoke the GAS	Once evoked, the GAS has specific effects

ALARM → Resistance → Exhaustion

Triad of organ effects

FIGURE 7-2: Multiple stressors producing a single stress response. Hans Selye's theory of nonspecificity assumes that the GAS is activated in the same way by different stressors.

Adapted from A. Baum, L.M. Davidson, J.E. Singer, & S.W. Street (1987). Stress as a psychophysiological response. In A. Baum & J.E. Singer (Eds.), *Handbook of psychology and health. Stress*, (Vol. 5, pp. 1–24). Hillsdale, NJ: Erlbaum, p. 4.

Researchers since Selye have questioned this assumption of *nonspecificity*. For example, Mason (1975) documented that unpredictable stressors produce different patterns of hormonal reactions than do predictable stressors. Thus, although all stressors tend to trigger the release of epinephrine and glucocorticoids and to impair immune functioning, different categories of stressors appear to cause somewhat different physiological responses.

EMOTIONAL RESPONSES TO STRESS

Changes in the functioning of the immune system occur outside of conscious awareness, but many physiological reactions to stress are very much a part of conscious awareness. You are familiar with the psychic experience that accompanies a "rush of adrenaline," for example. Consistent with the systems perspective, such psychophysiological responses can be understood at the physiological level, but the same responses also can be conceptualized at broader levels of analysis. Fight or flight can be analyzed as a physiological process, but it can also be studied as a psychological state with emotional, cognitive, and behavioral components.

Psychophysiological activity is an indicator of emotional arousal (see Chapter 4), and the emotions aroused by stress generally are negative ones (Baum et al., 1987). Anxiety, depression, and anger are the primary affective responses to stressors, although different individuals may experience these emotions as tension, sadness, frustration, numbness, or simply as a somatic symptom like an upset stomach. Similar but far more intense emotional reactions are found among victims of such traumatic stressors as natural disasters and physical assault. Emotional reactions to traumatic stress include terror, a sense of helplessness, rage, or sometimes complete emotional numbness.

Consideration of psychological responses to stress introduces the vital topic of *coping*. An important distinction that is often made in differentiating coping styles is between problem-focused and emotion-focused coping (Lazarus & Folkman, 1984). **Problem-focused coping** is externally oriented and involves attempts to change a stressor. If your job is too stressful, you can look for a new one. If conflict with a friend is causing problems, you can end the friendship. In contrast, **emotion-focused coping** is an attempt to alter internal distress, perhaps because it is impossible to control the stressor itself. Emotion-focused coping may involve a deliberate effort to relax or to reevaluate a stressor. When a romance ends, you may tell yourself that you really don't care. Similarly, before taking a big exam you can sit quietly and breathe deeply for several minutes.

Other forms of emotion-focused coping involve unconscious methods for dampening emotional experience. The activation of various intrapsychic defense mechanisms, for example, is widely considered to influence emotional responses to stress. Repression is one defense mechanism that may be commonly involved in emotional coping—sometimes with maladaptive consequences. Many experts speculate that repression protects people from consciously experiencing unpleasant emotions, but "repressors" thereby place themselves at greater risk for developing stress-related physical illnesses.

The repression hypothesis is difficult to test empirically. Some evidence suggests that people who do not acknowledge their experience of anxiety show exaggerated psychophysiological reactions to stressors (Schwartz, 1989). Similar findings have been reported for "defensive-deniers"—subjects who report positive mental health but whom clinicians judge to have emotional problems (Shedler, Mayman, & Manis, 1993). Other research indicates that when people are encouraged to recount very stressful experiences, they show reductions in various psychophysiological indicators of the stress response (Pennebaker, 1990; see Research Close-up). Repression as defined in psychoanalytic theory is perhaps an unnecessarily complex explanation for such findings, but at the very least, this evidence does support the common wisdom that it is helpful to "talk about your feelings."

COGNITIVE RESPONSES TO STRESS

Findings from animal research indicate that cognition can dramatically alter the stress response. Two critical issues are the *predictability* of the onset of stressors and *control* over them. A rat that is given a signal of an impending shock will have a smaller stress response than a rat given an unsignalled shock of the same magnitude (Sapolsky, 1992). This predictability allows the rat to anticipate the stressor. Anticipation elicits a response that is similar to, but weaker than, the response to the actual stressor. Although anticipation is stressful in its own right, it decreases negative responding to the actual stressor (Baum et al., 1987). Thus, anticipation can be viewed as a way of coping with stress before the stressor even begins.

Control is another important cognitive component of responding to and coping with stress, as has been documented in research with animals and humans. Rats who are able to stop a shock by pressing a bar have a smaller stress response than rats exposed to exactly the same shock but who have no opportunity of stopping

it through their own actions (Sapolsky, 1992). Even the illusion of control can help to alleviate stress (Mineka & Kihlstrom, 1978), but the perception of being able to control a stressor is not always a good thing. The perception of control can *increase* stress when people believe they can exercise control but find they are unable to do so. Distress also is greater when control over a formerly controllable stressor is lost (Mineka & Kihlstrom, 1978). Thus, control alleviates stress when it can be exercised or even when it is illusory, but failed attempts at control intensify stress.

Appraisal is a third cognitive component of stress, at least among humans. Lazarus and Folkman (1984) have suggested that stress occurs only when the individual appraises a stressor as exceeding his or her ability to cope with it. An exam causes stress when students feel unprepared for it, but not when they feel confident about the subject matter. When a stressor is perceived as overwhelming coping abilities, the individual experiences distress, as we defined the term earlier.

These cognitive components of stress are evident in the extreme reactions that people experience in response to a traumatic stressor. Traumatic stressors like major motor vehicle accidents are unpredictable, uncontrollable, and overwhelming. Such experiences can lead to yet another cognitive symptom of stress: the intrusive reliving of traumatic experiences that can recur months, or even years, after the trauma. This symptom of posttraumatic stress disorder is discussed later in this chapter.

BEHAVIORAL RESPONSES TO STRESS

There are a wide range of possible behavioral responses to stress. The fight or flight response obviously includes a behavioral component, for example. In fact, research indicates that being able to respond behaviorally to stress can help to lessen the stress response. The behavioral response need not be fight or flight, but may include other *outlets for frustration*. For example, rats have been found to secrete fewer glucocorticoids if they can attack another rat or run on a running wheel following an electric shock (Sapolsky, 1992).

Some behavioral responses are attempts to cope with stress. It is often unclear, however, which behavioral response will be effective, or even whether a stressor can be changed by a behavioral response. A difficult class may be caus-

Disclosure of Trauma and Immunity

We have briefly discussed the exciting new field of psychoneuroimmunology, in which scientists study the effects of stress on the functioning of the immune system. We also have mentioned the hypothesis that the risk for stress-related illness is increased by repressing feelings, an observation that implies a dramatic idea: People may be able to lower the risk for physical disease somewhat by talking openly about their troubles. Could the open discussion of feelings actually improve the functioning of the immune system? This was the question asked in an intriguing study conducted by James Pennebaker, Janice Kiecolt-Glaser, and Ronald Glaser (1988).

Subjects in the experimental group in this study were asked to do something fairly simple: write about traumatic events in their lives for 4 consecutive days, preferably about stressors that they had not previously discussed with others. A control group of subjects was told to write about trivial topics for the same time period. All writing took place in the laboratory. Twenty-five psychology undergraduates were randomly assigned to each of these two levels of the independent variable. Dependent variables in the study included self-reported mood before and after writing, measures of autonomic arousal including blood pressure and heart rate, and immunological assays of the subject's blood before the study, immediately afterwards, and 6 weeks later.

The students handed in their writing to the experimenters, and evaluations of the reports indicated that the students in the experimental group had indeed written about very upsetting experiences, including difficulties they had coming to college,

serious family conflicts, and problems with the opposite sex. Writing did not produce an immediate benefit, however, as students who wrote about their troubles reported being more upset immediately after writing than did students who wrote about trivial matters.

Remarkable longer-term benefits were noted even from this brief intervention, however. Students who wrote about personal distress had significantly fewer subsequent medical visits to the student health center and better immune responses than did students in the control group. No differences were found for the measures of autonomic arousal. Further support for the repression hypothesis came from evidence that subjects in the personal writing condition improved more on blood pressure and immunological measures when they wrote about previously undisclosed events rather than events they had discussed with others.

These findings need to be viewed with some caution. Several questions have been raised about aspects of the study's methods (Neale et al., 1988). Clearly, it would be a mistake to draw simplistic conclusions about the complex processes involved in psychoneuroimmunology. Nevertheless, the study offers an example of two exciting areas of research. First, the effects of psychological experience on immune functioning suggest that immunocompetence may be one mechanism linking stress with illness. Second, although talking about your feelings surely will not cure a cold, this research provides basic support for the long-debated idea that repression may contribute to somatic illness. ■

ing you great stress because you cannot maintain your usual grades. Should you redouble your efforts, drop the course, or accept that this is not your best subject? Problem-focused (behavioral) coping is the appropriate way to conquer or avoid many actual stressors, but the success of problem-focused coping depends greatly on

the nature of a stressor and the resources of the individual. Sometimes attempts to change a stressor are doomed to failure. In this circumstance, efforts at problem-focused coping will increase, not reduce, distress. The only alternative is to accept the stressor for what it is and to use emotion-focused coping to alter your response to it. There is truth to Reinhold Niebuhr's (1951) "Serenity Prayer":

> God, give us the serenity to accept what cannot be changed;
> Give us the courage to change what should be changed;
> Give us the wisdom to distinguish one from the other.

Health Behavoir Not all behavioral responses to stress are aimed at changing stressors directly. Health behavior is an example of a behavioral response to stress that can have extremely important implications for physical well-being. The expression **health behavior** encompasses a wide range of activities that are essential to promoting good health. In fact, health behaviors like attending to personal hygiene, maintaining sanitation, and eating an adequate diet are more responsible for the vast increases in life expectancy over the last two centuries than are even dramatic scientific advances like the discovery of penicillin (Starr, 1982). Today, important health behaviors include positive actions like proper diet, sleep, and exercise. Health behavior also includes the avoidance of negative activities such as cigarette smoking, excessive alcohol consumption, and drug use. Stress is related to health behavior in that people may ignore routine positive health practices during times of stress or may use negative health behavior as a means of coping with it. For example, a business executive might cope with a stressful day by drinking a few martinis in the evening instead of exercising, which only seems like "more work." Such unhealthy behaviors may account for much of the relation between stress and illness (Cohen & Williamson, 1991).

Stress also may be related to the very important health behavior of compliance with a prescribed treatment regimen. Evidence indicates that as many as 93 percent of all patients fail to follow all of the medical advice that would aid in the treatment of their illnesses (Taylor, 1990). Many medical patients fail to take their medications as prescribed by their physicians, for example. This is a particular problem in illnesses like hypertension, where the medication treats a dangerous underlying disorder that has no noticeable symptoms. Stressors like conflict with family members can interfere with adherence to treat-

ment regimens, as an ill person may "punish" the family member by not taking care of himself or herself.

Illness behavior—behaving as if you are sick—also appears to be stress-related. Considerable research indicates that increased stress is correlated with such illness behaviors as making more frequent office visits to physicians or having chronic pain interfere with everyday activities (Taylor, 1990). Such illness behaviors may be caused by emotional motivations, perhaps an attempt to gain sympathy. Stress can contribute to such motivations, and many of the concerns of medical patients have been documented to be psychological, not physical, in nature (Taylor, 1990). A happier, less stressful life also can motivate

people to cope successfully with chronic physical problems. Effective coping with chronic illnesses sometimes involves ignoring high levels of physical discomfort and living life as normally as possible.

The fact that many people consult physicians for psychological rather than physical concerns underscores the value of **social support**—the aid and understanding received from friends and family as well as from professionals. Social support is of help in encouraging adaptive coping with illness, but research involving humans and other primates suggests that social support also has direct, physical benefits. For example, in a recent investigation, stressed monkeys exhibited less immunosuppression when they interacted more with other monkeys (Cohen et al., 1992).

ILLNESS AS A CAUSE OF STRESS

Although this chapter is concerned with how stress can help to cause disorders, the reverse can also be true: Disorders can cause stress. The stresses caused by illness may involve minor aggravations like those that accompany a common cold, but some diseases can lead to major changes in a person's life. For example, consider the effects of the diagnosis of insulin-dependent diabetes on a 10-year old boy and his family. In order to maintain a normal range of blood sugars, the child with diabetes and his parents must frequently test his blood sugars, adjust to giving and receiving one, two, or three injections of insulin daily, and carefully monitor exercise and diet because of their profound effect on blood sugars. In addition, the child and his family must somehow cope with the stigma of being "different" that often accompanies a chronic disease like diabetes, as well as with the possibility of profound, long-term side effects of hyperglycemia (high blood sugars) such as kidney dysfunction or blindness. Surely the chronic disease of diabetes is a cause of much stress, particularly when it is first diagnosed.

As with other physical and psychological disorders, however, the link between diabetes and stress involves reciprocal causality. That is, the disease causes stress, but evidence also indicates that stress affects the course of diabetes. The influence has been hypothesized to be both direct and indirect. Emotional experiences may alter blood sugars directly. However, stress in the form of parent–child conflicts has clearly been documented to affect the management of diabetes indirectly by influencing the health behaviors of monitoring blood sugars, giving regular insulin injections, and maintaining appropriate diet and exercise (Miller et al., 1994). Such reciprocal linkages between stress and illness clearly operate for other disorders ranging from physical illnesses like coronary heart disease to psychological problems such as posttraumatic stress disorder.

Classification of Maladaptive Responses to Stress

Now that we have discussed short-term responses to stress, we can consider the relation between stress and more general physical and psychological health. We will begin with an overview of classification of maladaptive responses to stress. First, however, we need to correct a common misconception concerning the term **psychosomatic disorder**. The term indicates that a given physical disease is a product both of the psyche (mind) and the soma (body). The term often has been misunderstood, however. "Her problems are all psychosomatic" is a commonly heard phrase that in everyday usage means "Her problems are all in her head." This usage suggests that psychosomatic illnesses are somehow imaginary or feigned. They are not. Psychosomatic illnesses are very real physical disorders that involve demonstrable damage to the body's structure or function. The *somatoform disorders* are physical symptoms that are purely psychological–they involve no damage to the body. These are discussed in Chapter 8.

BRIEF HISTORICAL PERSPECTIVE

Modern medicine in Western cultures traditionally has viewed disease as a purely physical problem, but many non-Western cultures have never made such a formal distinction between mind and body. In these cultures, physical and mental disorders have been attributed to both the physical being and to life experience. Even within Western culture, many professionals and laypeople have suggested that life stress can be a cause of physical and mental illnesses. For example, Hippocrates (460–377 B.C.), the father of modern medicine, argued that emotional states could affect physical well-being.

In addition to mind–body dualism (see Chapter 2), much of the Western emphasis on illness as physical abnormality is attributable to the success of a purely biological approach. Louis Pasteur's discovery of the causes of infectious disease and the subsequent development of antibiotics and immunization produced great advances in medicine in the nineteenth and twentieth centuries. The successes of the *germ theory* of physical illness encouraged generations of researchers to conceptualize diseases purely in terms of the body's biological functions and structures (Weiner & Fawzy, 1989). Views of mental disorders similarly were influenced by some successes of the germ theory, particularly the identification of the cause of general paresis (see Chapter 2).

Scientific interest in the link between life experience and physical illnesses was first pursued with vigor by those involved in the field of psychosomatic medicine. The term *psychosomatic* was coined by Heinroth in 1818 as a way of emphasizing that both mind and body are important in the development of disease (Granville-Grossman, 1983). However the field of psychosomatic medicine did not develop into a medical subspecialty until the middle of the twentieth century, when it was dominated by psychoanalytically oriented psychiatrists. One of the major undertakings of that generation of theorists was the development of a classification of psychosomatic illnesses, based on what has become known as the *specificity hypothesis*. According to the specificity hypothesis, specific personality types cause specific psychosomatic diseases. Consistent with the theory, attempts were made to classify physical illnesses according to personality type. Franz Alexander (1950) was one of the most influential of these analytically oriented theorists. His formulation of the psychodynamics of peptic ulcers illustrates the specificity hypothesis:

> The crucial finding in ulcer patients is the frustration (external or internal) of passive, dependent, and love-demanding desires that cannot be gratified in normal relationships . . . . Onset of illness occurs when the intensity of the patient's unsatisfied dependent cravings increases either because of external deprivation or because the patient defends against his cravings by assuming increased responsibilities. The external deprivation often consists in the loss of a person upon whom the patient has been dependent, in leaving home, or in losing money or a position that had given the patient a sense of security. The increased responsibility may take the form of marriage or the birth of a child or the assumption of a more responsible job. (Alexander, French, & Pollock, 1968, p. 16)

CONTEMPORARY APPROACHES

Few contemporary researchers believe the specificity hypothesis, as a more generalized view of stress now dominates modern science. Contemporary approaches also reject the psychosomatic medicine view that only certain physical illnesses have psychological causes. The Diagnostic and Statistical Manual II (DSM-II, 1968) contained a list of ten "psychophysiologic disorders" (APA, 1968). No such list was found in the DSM-III (1980), however, and none is contained in the DSM-IV. Psyche and soma are now considered to play a role in all physical illnesses; thus, a list of "psychosomatic disorders" would contain every known physical illness (see Table 7–3).

The essential integration of mind and body is highlighted in DSM-IV by the inclusion of a separate diagnostic axis. Physical illnesses that are judged to be relevant to the understanding or treatment of an emotional disorder are coded on Axis III, *general medical conditions*. The only criteria for coding a physical illness on this axis are that the disorder involves organic pathology (that is, it is not a somatoform disorder) and that the physical illness is related to the Axis I diagnosis in a meaningful way. It also should be noted that the DSM-IV explicitly acknowledges that the distinction between physical and mental illness is a useful, but false dichotomy. Introductory material notes that psychological experiences are critical to "physical" illnesses and that biological processes are essential in "mental" disorders.

▲ A Biami tribesman willing himself to death. Such "taboo deaths" illustrate the powerful influence of psychological experience on physical well being.

TABLE 7–3
Major Components of the Stress Response and Common Pathological Consequences of Prolonged Stress

Stress Response	Its Pathological Consequences
Mobilization of energy; little storage	Fatigue
Increased cardiovascular activity	Hypertension
Suppressed digestion	Ulceration
Suppressed growth	Psychogenic dwarfism
Suppressed reproduction	Impotence, loss of sexual interest
Lowered immunity and inflammatory response	Impaired resistance to disease
Neural responses	Accelerated neuronal degeneration

Based on R.M. Sapolsky (1992). Neuroendocrinology of the stress response. In J.B. Becker, S.M. Breedlove, & D. Crews (Eds.), *Behavioral endocrinology* (pp. 288–324). Cambridge, MA: MIT Press.

STRESS AND PSYCHOLOGICAL DISORDERS

A historical review of theories about the role of stress in psychological problems would encompass all of abnormal psychology. However, there is a more circumscribed history of thought that focuses specifically on the relationship between traumatic stress and emotional problems.

TABLE 7-4

Categories of Psychosocial and Environmental Problems in DSM-IV

Category	Examples
Problems with primary support group	Death of a family member, family health problems, divorce, sexual abuse, inadequate discipline, family discord, birth of a sibling
Problems related to the social environment	Death or loss of a friend, social isolation, discrimination, adjustment to life cycle transition
Educational problems	Illiteracy, academic problems, discord with teacher, inadequate school environment
Occupational problems	Unemployment, stressful work schedule, job change, discord with boss
Housing problems	Homelessness, unsafe neighborhood, discord with neighbors
Economic problems	Extreme poverty, inadequate finances
Problems with access to health-care services	Inadequate health-care services, inadequate health insurance
Problems related to interaction with the legal system/crime	Arrest, litigation, incarceration, victim of crime
Other psychosocial problems	Exposure to disasters, war, discord with non-family caregivers

Traumatic stress was and continues to be of major interest to the military, who obviously are interested in maintaining "normal" performance in the face of the trauma of combat. In World War I, the term "shell shock" was commonly applied to those who "broke" in the face of combat. Shell shock was attributed to direct damage to the brain as a result of changes in air pressure produced by exploding artillery shells. Today, experts identify psychological causes of such reactions, with current debates focusing on the threshold and illness models. Threshold models assert that "everyone has a breaking point." Illness models instead suggest that battle dropout is caused by individual maladjustment that preceded the trauma (Figley, 1978).

During the Vietnam War, battle dropout was less frequent than in earlier wars, but delayed reactions to traumatic stress were much more frequent (Figley, 1978). This prompted much research on posttraumatic stress disorder. In the DSM-IV, posttraumatic stress disorder is classified as one of the anxiety disorders (see Chapter 6), but we consider it in this chapter as an example of maladaptive responses to stress.

Adjustment disorders are another DSM-IV diagnosis that is defined by maladaptive psychological responses to stress. The symptoms of adjustment disorder include anxiety, depression, and withdrawal from work or relationships, as well as impairment in adaptive life functioning. In contrast to PTSD, adjustment disorders are caused by stressors that are a part of normal experience, and the distress that characterizes these disorders is much milder. In addition, the symptoms of an adjustment disorder usually disappear after the stressor is resolved or removed.

Finally, the DSM-IV contains a classification that reflects a general acknowledgement of the importance of stress in all mental disorders. This is Axis IV, *psychosocial and environmental problems*. The DSM makes no attempt to offer an exhaustive listing of potential life stressors for Axis IV. Instead, it simply includes categories of stressors with specific examples under each heading. These categories can be found in Table 7–4.

In the DSM-III and DSM-III-R, clinicians were instructed to rate the amount of stress caused by various life stressors. A listing of a few stressors of differing intensities was the only guidance for making these judgments. Not surprisingly, research on this scheme found that it was not very reliable for rating either the presence or the severity of stressors (Skodol et al., 1990). As a result, the DSM-IV makes no attempt to rate the severity of stressors. As indicated by our earlier discussions, scientists have not resolved the numerous conceptual problems in defining stress. The direction for the immediate future is toward developing categories of life stress, but the only certainty is that the DSM definition of stress will change as researchers continue to refine methods of categorizing and quantifying stress and stressors.

Cardiovascular Disease

Much promising research focuses on the role of stress in the development of many different physical illnesses. Active research in this area includes the study of the role of stress in both chronic illnesses like diabetes, cancer, and hypertension and in acute disorders such as the onset or recurrence of infectious diseases like colds and eruptions of the herpes virus. Because this literature is so vast, we will focus on one disorder, cardiovascular disease, as an illustration of the link between stress and physical illness.

Cardiovascular disease (CVD) is a group of disorders that affect the heart and circulatory system. The most important of these illnesses are **hypertension** (high blood pressure) and **coronary heart disease (CHD)**. Hypertension increases the risk for CHD, as well as for other serious disorders such as stroke. The most deadly and well-known form of coronary heart disease is *myocardial infarction* (MI), commonly known as a heart attack.

Cardiovascular disorders are the leading cause of mortality in most industrialized countries, including the United States, where they account for almost half of all deaths. About two-thirds of the deaths due to cardiovascular disorders are caused by coronary heart disease (Jenkins, 1988). Mortality due to CHD is a particular concern because victims of the disease tend to be relatively young. About half of all Americans with CHD and about a quarter of all stroke victims are under the age of 65.

An individual's risk for developing CVD, and particularly CHD, is associated with a number of health behaviors including weight, diet, exercise, and cigarette smoking, as we saw in the case of Bob Carter. This link between CVD and lifestyle is one reason why health psychology is so important in preventing and treating these disorders. Psychology also is important in under-standing hypertension and heart disease, because behavioral and physical risk indicators account for only about half of all cases of CHD (Jenkins, 1988). Psychological factors are important in explaining some of the additional risk. Certain personality styles, behavior patterns, and forms of emotional expression appear to contribute to the development of CVD regardless of how they influence health behavior.

Typical Symptoms and Associated Features of Hypertension and CHD

Hypertension often is referred to as the "silent killer" because it produces no obvious symptoms. For this reason, high blood pressure often goes undetected, and routine blood pressure monitoring is extremely important. The measurement of blood pressure includes two readings. *Systolic* blood pressure is the highest pressure that the blood exerts against the arteries. This occurs when the heart is pumping blood. *Diastolic* blood pressure is the lowest amount of pressure that the blood creates against the arteries. This occurs between heartbeats. Generally, hypertension is defined by a systolic reading above 140 and/or a diastolic reading above 90 when measured while the patient is in a relaxed state.

The most notable symptom of CHD is chest pain. The pain typically is centralized in the middle of the chest, and it often extends through the left shoulder and down the left arm. In less severe forms of the disorder, the pain that accompanies CHD is mild, or it may be sharp but brief. The pain during more severe forms of CHD such as myocardial infarction typically is so intense that it is crippling. In fact, MI often results in sudden death. Two-thirds of all deaths from CHD occur within 24 hours of a coronary event

(Kamarck & Jennings, 1991). In over half of these sudden deaths, the victim received no previous treatment for CHD, an indication that either there were no warning symptoms or the symptoms were mild enough to have been ignored. Research using portable electrocardiogram monitoring indicates that many episodes of inadequate oxygen supply to the heart occur outside of the patient's awareness (Schneiderman, Chesney, & Krantz, 1989).

Classification of CVD

Myocardial infarction and *angina pectoris* are the two major forms of coronary heart disease. Angina involves intermittent chest pains that are usually brought on by some form of exertion. Attacks of angina do not damage the heart, but the chest pain can be a sign of underlying pathology that puts the patient at risk for a myocardial infarction. MI (heart attack) does involve damage to the heart, and as noted, it often causes *sudden cardiac death*, which is usually defined as death within 24 hours of a coronary episode.

Hypertension can be primary or secondary. *Secondary hypertension* results from a known problem such as a diagnosed kidney or endocrine disorder. It is called secondary hypertension because the high blood pressure is secondary to (a consequence of) the principal physical disorder. Primary or *essential hypertension* is the major concern of behavioral medicine and health psychology. In the case of essential hypertension, the high blood pressure is the principal disorder. There is no single, identifiable cause of essential hypertension, which accounts for approximately 85 percent of all cases of high blood pressure. Instead, multiple physical and behavioral risk factors are thought to contribute to the primary disorder, elevated blood pressure.

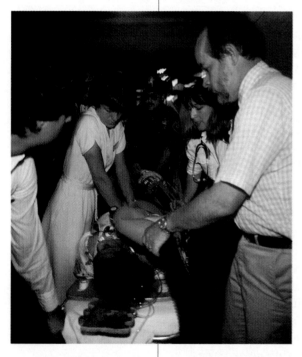

▲ Cardiovascular disease is the leading cause of death in the United States. It is a lifestyle illness that is related to poor health behavior, stress, and anger.

Epidemiology of CVD

Infectious diseases were the leading cause of death in the United States for the first two decades of the twentieth century, but since the 1920s cardiovascular disease has been the nation's leading killer. Cardiovascular disease also is the major cause of death in most other industrialized countries, but some important differences among nations have emerged in recent years. The rate of death due to CVD has declined by 25 percent or more in the United States, Japan, and many Western European countries, while mortality rates attributed to CVD have increased in many Eastern European countries. Some of these differences in recent trends seem attributable to changes in diet, cigarette smoking, and blood pressure, but improved health behavior does not fully account for the recent epidemiological differences (Jenkins, 1988). Such differences provide a fascinating challenge for researchers to explain. The increased awareness of the negative effects of stress in the West–and the increased experience of stress in the East–may be part of the explanation.

Risk Factors for CHD Epidemiological studies have identified several risk indicators for CHD. Men are twice as likely to suffer from CHD as are women; these sex differences are even greater with more severe forms of the disorder. Age is another major risk factor. For men, risk for CHD increases in a linear fashion with increasing age after 40, whereas for women it accelerates more slowly until they reach menopause and increases sharply afterwards. Rates of CHD also are higher among low-income groups, a finding that likely accounts for the higher rates of CHD among black than among white Americans (Jenkins, 1988).

In addition to these background factors, several health behaviors have been linked to CHD. Hypertension increases the risk for CHD by a factor of 2 to 4. The risk for CHD also is 2 to 3 times greater among those who smoke a pack or more of cigarettes a day. Obesity, a fatty diet, elevated serum cholesterol levels, heavy alcohol consumption, and lack of exercise also are related to an increased risk for CHD. Specific risk ratios are difficult to identify for each of these factors, however, because weight, diet, cholesterol, alcohol consumption, and exercise all are closely interrelated (Jenkins, 1988).

The specific risk for CHD associated with psychological characteristics other than health behaviors also is difficult to calculate. This is because of difficulties in measuring some relevant behavioral styles and because of conflicting findings in epidemiological research. A great deal of research on the psychological contributions to CHD has focused on what is known as the Type A behavior pattern, which is a highly driven, competitive personality type. In 1981, the National Heart, Lung, and Blood Institute officially concluded that Type A behavior increased the risk for CHD independently of other health behaviors. However, recent research has challenged this conclusion, as we discuss shortly.

Risk Factors for Hypertension About 30 percent of all U.S. adults suffer from hypertension, and many of the same risk factors that predict CHD also predict high blood pressure. Hypertension is more common in industrialized countries, for example. In the United States, high blood pressure is found with greater frequency among men, African Americans, low-income groups, and people exposed to high levels of chronic life stress. Although many of these risk factors are interrelated, they appear to have independent effects in increasing the prevalence of hypertension. For example, one study found that twice as many blacks as whites suffer from hypertension, but among black men who lived in high-stress neighborhoods, the risk was four times as great (Roberts & Rowland, 1981).

Etiological Considerations and Research on CVD

BIOLOGICAL FACTORS IN CVD
The most important, immediate cause of essential hypertension is *atherosclerosis*, the thickening of the coronary artery wall that occurs over age as a result of the accumulation of blood lipids (fats). The restriction of blood flow due to atherosclerosis increases the pressure on the arterial walls, much the way the pressure increases on a balloon when it is squeezed. A number of biological conditions are related to the development of atherosclerosis, including genetic factors, blood saline levels (from salty diets), and increased blood flow from the heart caused by physical exertion or psychological stress.

The immediate cause of CHD is the deprivation of oxygen to the heart muscle. Oxygen deprivation can be caused by increased oxygen demands on the heart of the kind that occur as a result of exercise, for example. More problematic is when atherosclerosis causes the gradual deprivation of the flow of blood (and the oxygen it carries) to the heart. The most dangerous circumstance is when the deprivation is sudden, as occurs in a *coronary occlusion*. Coronary occlusions result either from arteries that are completely blocked by fatty deposits or from blood clots that make their way to the heart muscle.

No permanent damage to the heart is caused by the temporary oxygen deprivation (*myocardial ischemia*) that accompanies angina pectoris, although the disorder may indicate a risk of more serious heart disease. In the case of myocardial infarction, damage to the heart muscle results from the oxygen deprivation, as part of the heart muscle dies.

The immediate biological causes of hypertension and CHD are well recognized, but the more distant biological causes are far less clear. It has been well established that a positive family history is a risk factor for both hypertension and CHD. Most experts interpret this association as indicating a genetic contribution to CVD, but the specific mediating mechanism has yet to be identified. Moreover, research on animal models of CVD suggests that heritable risk interacts with environmental risk. For example, rats prone to develop hypertension do so only when exposed to salty diets or environmental stress (Schneiderman, Chesney, & Krantz, 1989). Other biological risk factors for CVD, such as obesity and elevated serum cholesterol, involve health behaviors, and we therefore consider them as a part of psychological contributions to the disease.

Psychological factors can be thought of as contributing in two general ways to the physical conditions that cause CVD. First, poor health behaviors or long-lasting stress can contribute to the gradual buildup of chronic conditions like atherosclerosis. In addition, a current stressor can tax the cardiovascular system and thereby create immediate symptoms or broader episodes of disease. As in the case of Bob Carter, many people report that episodes of stress precede more minor events like the symptoms of angina pectoris or major ones like a myocardial infarction.

PSYCHOLOGICAL FACTORS IN CVD

The most important known psychological contributions to CVD are straightforward. They involve a variety of health behaviors that have a well-documented association with heart disease, that decrease the risk for CVD when they are modified, and that often are frustratingly difficult to change. As is the case with many of the other major causes of death in industrialized societies, CVD is a *lifestyle disease.* Coronary heart disease is one of the clearest examples of the inextricable link between behavior and physical health. Poor maintenance of the body is the most important behavioral contributor to heart disease. Regular monitoring of blood pressure, taking antihypertensive medication as prescribed, avoiding or quitting smoking, maintaining a proper weight, following a low-cholesterol diet, and frequent exercise all can reduce the risk of heart disease. Our bodies need routine maintenance, much as our cars do.

In addition to poor care of the body, stress is another contributing factor to CVD. Increased blood pressure and heart rate are among the direct consequences of stress, as we saw at the beginning of the chapter. Some theories suggest that, like a car that is abused by its driver, the heart can be simply worn out by constant stress—especially when routine maintenance is ignored. Although research on cardiovascular disease provides some support for this analogy, the linkage between the short-term effects of stress on the cardiovascular system and the much longer-term link between stress and cardiovascular disease is not a simple one. We consider attempts to establish this linkage on three levels: (1) physiologic reactivity to stress, (2) actual exposure to life stress, and (3) characteristic styles of responding to stress (Krantz et al., 1988).

Physiological Reactivity to Stress If increases in blood pressure and heart rate are normal reactions to stress, an important issue to address is whether individual differences in reactivity account for long-term differences in the risk for cardiovascular disease. Researchers have long observed that different people exhibit greater or lesser stress responses when exposed to controlled stressors in the laboratory. *Physiological reactivity* is a measure of these reactions, as increases in blood pressure and heart rate in response to stress are measured, rather than simple resting rates. Are people who show greater physiological reactivity to stress more likely to develop CVD?

The hypothesis that physiological reactivity is related to CVD has received at least limited support from research on humans and animals (Krantz et al., 1988). Some research on patients with coronary disease indicates that they show greater physiological reactivity (Corse et al. 1982), and one study found that diastolic blood pressure reactivity predicted the subsequent development of CHD (Keys et al., 1971). Such research is complicated, however. Research on physiological reactivity assumes that responses in the laboratory mimic physiological responses to stress in everyday life. Even if this is a completely accurate assumption, which is unlikely, not everyone is exposed to the same degree of life stress. It is obvious, for example, that having a high degree of physiological reactivity will have little effect on an individual if he or she experiences little stress. Thus, actual life stress must also be considered in the prediction of cardiovascular disease.

Life Stressors and Cardiovascular Disease
Considerable evidence indicates that exposure to chronic stressors increases risk for cardiovascular disease (Krantz et al., 1988). For example, some research in this area has linked increased rates of coronary heart disease with high-stress occupations. A stressful job is more than just a demanding one. What appears to be most important is *job strain*, a situation that pairs high psychological demands with a low degree of decisional control (Karasek et al., 1982). A waitress has relatively high demands and low control, for instance, whereas a forest ranger has relatively few demands and a high degree of control. Figure 7–3 portrays a number of occupations and how they vary in terms of psychological demands and decisional control.

A handful of studies have found a relationship between job strain and CHD (Krantz et al., 1988). For example, among women who participated in the Framingham Heart Study—a study of the development of coronary heart disease—the risk for CHD was 1 ½ times higher among those who were rated as having high job strain based on objective evaluations of their occupations. It was 3 times higher among women whose self-reports indicated high job strain (LaCroix & Haynes, 1987).

Such strains are not limited to employment,

but include work that is performed in other life roles. In an earlier analysis of women in the Framingham Study, women who were employed for more than half of their adult lives were no more likely to develop CHD than were homemakers. However, working women with children were more likely to suffer from heart disease. In fact, the risk for CHD increased with the number of children for working women but not for homemakers (Haynes & Feinleib, 1980). This finding echoes the dilemma of contemporary women who feel strains not only within their occupation but also among the various roles they are expected to fulfill.

Type A Behavior and Styles of Responding to Stressors Scientists have identified another instance in which psychological stress affects the cardiovascular system: the **Type A behavior pattern**. The Type A behavior pattern, originally identified by cardiologists Meyer Friedman and Ray Rosenman (1959), refers to a characterological response to challenge that is competitive, hostile, urgent, impatient, and achievement-striving. The Type A individual is a "superachiever" who knows no obstacle to success and who may sacrifice everything for the sake of achievement (Jenkins, 1988). (*Type B* individuals, in contrast, are more calm and content.) You have already encountered a clear instance of Type A behavior in the case of Bob Carter. You may want to glance back at the case and note Bob's Type A characteristics.

Friedman and Rosenman believed that people with Type A personalities were at higher risk for developing CHD. To identify Type A personalities, Friedman and Rosenman developed a structured interview that not only assesses subjects' reports about their achievement striving, urgency, and related characteristics but also attempts to provoke these very behaviors in the context of the interview. This is important, because the investigators believed that Type A behavior is most evident when the individual is challenged.

Friedman and Rosenman's interview has been found to have adequate reliability and concurrent validity (Glass, 1977). The validity of the interview in predicting CHD also has been supported in several prospective, longitudinal investigations (see Research Methods), most notably the Western Collaborative Group Study conducted by Rosenman, Friedman, and colleagues (Booth-Kewley & Friedman, 1987). The culmination of this research occurred in 1981 when the National Blood, Heart, and Lung Institute concluded that Type A was an independent risk factor for CHD. This official sanc-

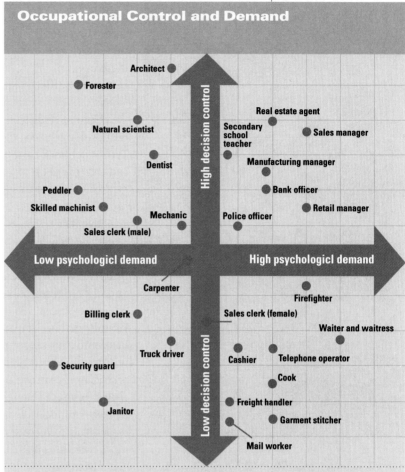

FIGURE 7-3: Occupations classified according to the degree of demand and control that are associated with them. Jobs with low control and high demands are associated with increased cardiovascular risk.

From Karasek as appeared in D.S. Krantz, R.J. Contrada, D.R. Hill, & E. Friedler (1988). Environmental stress and biobehavioral antecedents of coronary heart disease. *Journal of Consulting and Clinical Psychology, 56,* 334.

tion stimulated a great deal of additional research, but much of the research conducted since 1980 has failed to support earlier findings. A quantitative review of a number of large, prospective studies concluded that Type A was unrelated to CHD when all studies were examined, although exceptions were found for a few, specific types of research (Matthews, 1988). Thus, there are far more questions about the Type A construct today than there were 10 years ago. Nevertheless, results across studies document Type A behavior among 70 percent of middle-aged men with heart disease, while only 46 percent of men without heart disease exhibit Type A behavior. This conclusion is heavily dependent upon the research methods used, however, including the use of Friedman and Rosenman's structured interview technique instead of self-report measures of Type A behavior (Miller et al., 1991).

Although the precise relationship between the Type A behavior pattern and CVD continues to be debated, certain elements of the Type A pattern consistently predict heart disease; these include hostile or competitive behavior patterns, work overload, and chronic, negative emotions (Jenkins, 1988). Hostility, in particular, has a more consistent relationship to heart disease than do other elements of the behavior pattern, or indeed, than does the Type A pattern as a whole (Booth-Kewley & Friedman, 1987; Matthews, 1988; Schneiderman, Chesney, & Krantz, 1989). The central role of hostility is evident both in older studies, including some that failed to support the Type A construct, and in some more recent research (Schneiderman, Chesney, & Krantz, 1989). For example, a Finnish investigation found that three items reliably predicted death among men who had a history of CHD or hypertension: ease with which anger was aroused, argumentativeness, and irritability (Koskenvuo et al., 1988).

▲ These stock traders illustrate the Type A behaviour pattern. Type A is a personality style characterized by competitiveness, hostility, urgency, impatience, and achievement-striving in response to challenge.

SOCIAL FACTORS IN CVD

The research we already have reviewed makes it clear that CVD is affected by both interpersonal relations and broader societal influences. As you no doubt recognize from your own life, social support from friends and family members, as well as from professionals, can encourage a healthy—or an unhealthy—lifestyle (Rook & Dooley, 1985). Interpersonal conflict obvi-

ously is a source of much of the anger and hostility that can increase the risk for coronary heart disease. Finally, the cross-cultural differences in the epidemiology of CVD surely are influenced by a range of societal values, such as attitudes about health behaviors like smoking and cultural norms about competition in the workplace.

Experts recognize the importance of interpersonal and societal influences on CVD and on physical health in general. A multitude of efforts have been directed toward structuring the *social ecology*—the interrelations between the individual and the social world—in such a way as to promote health (Stokols, 1992). As a child, you were exposed to many of these efforts, such as the awards given in school for physical fitness or antismoking campaigns. Many employers also encourage health maintenance, and health promotion is a common message in the media. Do these broad-scale efforts work? We examine this question and other issues in treating CVD, after briefly discussing the integration of risk factors.

INTEGRATING BIOLOGICAL, PSYCHOLOGICAL, AND SOCIAL RISK FACTORS

Much progress has been made in identifying biological, psychological, and social risk factors for CVD. An important goal for future research is to integrate knowledge across risk factors. Numerous questions need to be addressed. For example, how do physiological reactivity and the experience of life stress interact in producing risk? How do we distinguish the effects of stress as an immediate, precipitating cause of CHD from its cumulative effects on health over long periods of time (Matthews, 1988)? To what extent are the risks associated with stress caused by poor health behavior and not by stress itself? What protects those individuals who do not become ill even when they are exposed to multiple risk factors?

In considering these questions, the analogy raised earlier between the functioning of the cardiovascular system and an automobile remains a useful one. Some cars are built for high performance, some for economy. Some are defective when they leave the factory. Whatever the condition of the new automobile, its state of repair is affected by how it is maintained and how it is driven. Like the wear and tear on different automobiles used under different conditions, the etiology of CVD appears to combine

Longitudinal Research Designs

We have already reviewed problems with attempting to infer causation from correlation in Research Methods in Chapter 2. Analogue experiments, which were considered in Research Methods in Chapter 5, are one alternative to correlational designs. Analogue experiments are frequently used in stress research. One example that you have already encountered is the analogue experiment with laboratory animals. Two particular advantages of the animal analogue in stress research is the systematic control of exposure to stressors and the ability to obtain direct measures of physiological and anatomical outcomes. Still, many important questions about stress and illness can only be answered with research on humans; however, ethical and practical constraints often prohibit the use of the experimental method with humans.

The **longitudinal study** is one innovative research design that can allow researchers to draw stronger conclusions about causation. Subjects are studied over time in a longitudinal study, an approach that contrasts with the more common **cross-sectional** approach of studying subjects only at one point in time. The basic goal of a longitudinal study is to determine whether hypothesized causes come before their assumed effects. We know that causes must precede effects in time. The bat must be swung before the ball can be hit over the fence. If we can demonstrate that stress comes before heart disease in longitudinal research, this helps scientists to rule out the alternative interpretation (reverse causality) that the illness caused the stress.

As you can easily recognize, a major liability of a longitudinal study is higher cost. It is much less expensive to study both stress and heart disease at one point in time than it is to assess the stress now and CHD as it develops over the next 10 years. One way around this problem is to use the *retro-spective* or follow-back study. In this research design, scientists look backwards in time either by asking subjects to recall past events or by examining records from the past. The retrospective method is relatively inexpensive, but it is of limited value because of distorted memories and limited records.

The **prospective** or follow-up design is a more effective and more expensive alternative to the follow-back method. In prospective research, supposed causes are assessed in the present, and subjects are then followed into the future to see if the hypothesized effects develop over time. Using the follow-up method, scientists can assess a range of possible predictors more thoroughly and more objectively than in follow-back studies. For example, scientists can use standardized tests to measure a wide variety of personality characteristics like Type A behavior in their subjects over time.

Researchers have used both retrospective and prospective methods fairly often in studying health and illness. Therefore, you will encounter both methods in discussions of a variety of mental health issues throughout this text. When you learn that a finding was supported in prospective longitudinal research, you can have greater confidence in the investigator's hypothesis about causality than if the research was only cross-sectional. Remember, however, that correlation does not mean causation even in a longitudinal study. It remains possible that the supposed "cause" and the "effect" both result from some third variable. For example, a researcher might find that Type A behavior measured at one point in time predicts CHD several years later. But chronic job stress may cause both the Type A behavior and the heart disease. Scientists need many studies utilizing many different types of research methods to establish causation. In order to be a good consumer of scientific information, you need to understand the methods of research and not just the results of a single study. ∎

genetic makeup, an occasional structural defect, maintenance in the form of health behavior, and how hard the heart is driven by stress, coping, and societal standards. Even though some cars and some hearts operate well after being abused, routine maintenance is prudent. We should attend to each risk factor associated with CVD. Still, as is the case with a new automobile, avoidance of life's challenges is not the way to avoid heart disease. A moderate amount of use is healthy for a car, and a moderate amount of stress is healthy for the heart.

▲ Cigarette smoking, obesity, lack of exercise, and a fatty diet are some of the poor health behaviors associated with an increased incidence of cardiovascular disease.

Prevention and Treatment of Cardiovascular Disease

Several medications known as *antihypertensives* have demonstrated effectiveness as treatments for reducing high blood pressure. Other drugs, called *beta blockers*, reduce the risk of myocardial infarction or sudden coronary death following a cardiac episode (Johnston, 1989). Other biomedical interventions reduce the risk factors associated with CVD. For example, serum cholesterol can be reduced with medication.

Because most of the risk factors for CVD are linked with health behavior, however, it may be possible to reduce or prevent heart disease using psychological interventions. Below, we consider efforts to alter lifestyle and lower the risk for heart disease in terms of the three levels introduced in Chapter 3: primary, secondary, and tertiary prevention.

PRIMARY PREVENTION

Attempts at the primary prevention of CVD include public advertising campaigns designed to encourage people to quit smoking, to eat well, exercise, monitor their blood pressure, and otherwise improve their health behavior. Most of these familiar efforts have not been evaluated systematically, although a handful of careful studies have been conducted. One of the most important studies took place in three small California communities near Stanford University (Farquhar et al., 1977). Media campaigns designed to improve knowledge and change the behavior that makes up CHD risk factors were offered in two towns that formed the experimental groups, whereas no intervention was given in one town that was used as a control group. The media campaigns were supplemented with face-to-face interviews in one of the two towns receiving the intervention. Findings indicated that the media campaigns increased the public's knowledge about CHD and resulted in improved diet and lower serum cholesterol. Knowledge of CHD risk factors was greater in the community where face-to-face interviews took place, but smoking behaviors changed little in either of the experimental communities (Farquhar et al., 1977). Whether the interventions helped reduce the incidence of heart disease could not be determined in this study, but several related investigations currently are ongoing (Johnston, 1989). Still, it is worth reiterating the epidemiological finding noted earlier in the chapter. Rates of CVD have declined in Western countries as health behavior has improved (Jenkins, 1988).

SECONDARY PREVENTION

The treatment of essential hypertension is one of the most important attempts at the secondary prevention of CHD, because hypertension is one of the risk factors for heart disease. Health psychology's treatments of hypertension fall into two categories. One focuses on improving health behavior, and the other emphasizes **stress management**, attempts to teach more effective coping skills.

Improvements in health behavior clearly can lead to lowered blood pressure. This includes weight reduction, decreased alcohol consumption, and perhaps reduced intake of dietary salt. For many patients these behavioral changes eliminate the need for taking antihypertensive medication (Johnston, 1989). What is less clear is the extent to which psychological interventions with hypertensives bring about improvements in health behavior. Available evidence suggests that psychological intervention is minimally effective at best. This overall lack of success is attributable in part to the poorly constructed interventions that typically are offered. Many efforts to alter health behavior among hypertensives take the form of simply encouraging patients to lose weight or of giving patients educational pamphlets to read. More encouraging findings come from research on more intensive weight reduction and alcohol consumption programs, but more research on their effectiveness is needed (Johnston, 1989). Given that improved health behavior has a demonstrated effect on reducing blood pressure, the development of more thorough psychosocial interventions, and research on their effectiveness, is of considerable importance.

The use of stress management with hypertensives has been dominated by behavior therapy. Two specific behavioral techniques that have commonly been used in treating hypertension are relaxation training (see Chapter 3) and biofeedback. **Biofeedback** uses laboratory equipment to monitor physiological processes that generally occur outside of conscious awareness and to provide the patient with conscious feedback about them. Blood pressure may be continuously displayed on a video screen, for example, so that increases or decreases are readily apparent.

The theory is that biofeedback can help individuals learn how to control their autonomic nervous system functions voluntarily. This is an innovation conceptually and practically, because the functions of the autonomic nervous system traditionally have been viewed as uncontrollable, as conveyed by the term *autonomic*. During biofeedback, the patient can experiment with various coping strategies and observe whether the techniques are successful in lowering blood pressure or whatever autonomic response is being monitored.

Both relaxation training and biofeedback produce reliable, short-term reductions in blood pressure. Unfortunately, the reductions are small, often temporary, and are considerably less than those produced by antihypertensive medications (Andrews et al., 1984). Although these stress management treatments occasionally may be a useful adjunct to medication, they are not an alternative at this point in time. In particular, the viability of biofeedback has not been supported by empirical evidence, and some well-respected investigators have suggested that this technique should be abandoned altogether as a treatment for hypertension (Johnston, 1989).

In addition to treating hypertension, other attempts at the secondary prevention of CHD have targeted subjects who are at risk and attempted to alter their health behavior. The Multiple Risk Factor Intervention Trial (MRFIT) is perhaps the most important of these efforts. In this study, over 12,000 men with a high risk for developing CHD were assigned at random to intervention and control groups, and the effectiveness of intervention was evaluated. Carefully developed intervention programs, including education and social support for improving health behavior, were found to produce such improvements in health behavior as reduced smoking and lower serum cholesterol. However, the men randomly assigned to the treatment groups did not have a lower incidence of heart disease during the 7 years following intervention (MRFIT, 1982). An encouraging interpretation of this discouraging outcome is that the failure to find a treatment effect may have been due to the improved health behavior of the men in the control group. The control group had a lower disease rate than was expected based on their risk indicators, and the study was conducted during a time when the public's concern with health increased dramatically.

TERTIARY PREVENTION OR TREATMENT

Tertiary prevention of CHD targets patients who have already had a cardiac event, typically a myocardial infarction. The hope is to reduce the incidence of recurrence of the illness. Exercise programs are probably the most common treatment recommended for cardiac patients, but evidence on their effectiveness is limited (Johnston, 1989). Some recent evidence suggests that carefully implemented exercise training programs can reduce the risk for cardiovascular death for up to 3 years (O'Connor et al., 1989). Other researchers have found that treatment programs may lead to a dramatic reduction in death rates if they are individualized and target multiple health behaviors (Frasure-Smith & Prince, 1985). One patient may benefit from entering a smoking reduction program, a second may be helped by a stress reduction workshop, and a third may be assisted by exercise classes. Together, the findings on successful programs underscore the need to offer behavioral medicine programs that are both highly structured and carefully tailored to the individual (see Blanchard, 1992). Handing out educational pamphlets or delivering stern lectures in the physician's office does little to alter health behavior, as you saw in the case of Bob Carter.

Some of the most optimistic evidence on the treatment of CHD comes from studies of interventions designed to alter the Type A behavior pattern (Friedman et al., 1986). This is somewhat surprising given the uncertainty about the extent to which the Type A pattern actually contributes to CHD. Intervention with Type A individuals following myocardial infarction is multifaceted. It includes efforts to teach patients how to respond to stressful interactions with reduced hostility. This approach makes use of modeling techniques (see Chapter 3) and **role playing**, the improvisational play acting of alternative ways of handling frustrating situations. In role playing, cardiac patients act out their usual responses to such situations as dealing with a bothersome subordinate, and the therapist models alternative, less hostile means of responding to the frustration. In subsequent role plays, the patients try out the new way of coping. Cognitive therapy designed to alter faulty thought patterns also is a part of the intervention with Type A cardiac patients (Thoresen & Powell, 1992). For example, patients' beliefs about their self-worth and professional goals may be examined and challenged as being irrational using the techniques of rational-emotive therapy (see Chapter 3). At some level, Bob Carter probably believed that he had to be the best at everything he did in life. Such a belief obviously is irrational, and one goal of cognitive therapy is to help patients like Bob to develop beliefs and goals that are realistic—and healthy.

One study of nearly 600 patients receiving these and related instructions in stress management found that the annual incidence of cardiac events was reduced by almost 50 percent in comparison with 300 patients who received standard medical care (Friedman et al., 1986). Importantly, subjects who showed the greatest reduction in Type A behavior were 4 times less likely to experience a myocardial infarction during the following 2 years. Although evidence is not definitive, studies suggest that Type A behavior can be modified, and this may reduce the subsequent risk for CHD (Nunes, Frank, & Kornfeld, 1987; Thoresen & Powell, 1992).

As a final note, it should be mentioned that some important psychological treatments focus on the effects of heart disease on life stress rather than the other way around. Several investigators have helped cardiac patients cope more successfully with the anxiety and depression that often result from having a heart attack, as well as with the effects of a myocardial infarction on their everyday life. Coronary patients frequently report difficulties with sexuality, marriage and family relationships, and accepting the necessary restrictions on normal activities, and psychological treatment can help them adjust to the illness (Johnston, 1985). In addition to the obvious value for heart patients and their families, these treatments serve as a reminder of the reciprocal linkages between stress and physical health.

Posttraumatic Stress Disorder

Stress is an inevitable, and in some cases a desirable, fact of everyday life. Some stressors, however, are so catastrophic and horrifying that they can cause serious psychological harm to those who experience them. Examples of these traumatic stressors include rapes, bombings, airline crashes, earthquakes, major fires, and devastating automobile wrecks. Both the survivors of and witnesses to traumatic stressors are expected to be greatly distressed as a part of their normal response. For some victims, the trauma continues long after the event itself has ended. The horrifying experience leads to general increases in anxiety and arousal, avoidance of emotionally charged situations, and the frequent reliving of the traumatic event. When these symptoms persist for more than a month, this condition is referred to as posttraumatic stress disorder (PTSD).

Typical Symptoms and Associated Features of PTSD

Posttraumatic stress disorder is characterized by three broad clusters of symptoms: (1) reexperienced trauma; (2) numbed responsiveness and avoidance of stimuli associated with the trauma; and (3) persistent symptoms of increased autonomic and emotional arousal.

The traumatic event may be reexperienced in a number of ways. Some people with PTSD have repeated and intrusive **flashbacks** or memories of the trauma. Others relive it in horrifying dreams. In rare cases, the reexperience occurs as a *dissociative state*, in which the person relives the trauma in the moment. A combat veteran in a dissociative state might act as if he believes he is back in battle, and he may even take dangerous actions like gathering weapons or barricading himself in his residence. Dissociative states typically are of short duration, but in unusual cases they can last for days.

The alteration in memory and consciousness that characterizes dissociative states resembles the symptoms of dissociative disorder (see Chapter 8). In fact, some investigators believe that PTSD should be classified as one of the dissociative disorders rather than as an anxiety disorder. This is because the reliving of trauma, even when it is less dramatic than a dissociative state, resembles some aspects of dissociative disorders (Brett, Spitzer, & Williams, 1988). Our consideration of PTSD in this chapter reflects a third classification alternative: classifying PTSD based on its etiology as a maladaptive response to stress (Davidson & Foa, 1991).

The diminished responsiveness that characterizes PTSD has been referred to as "psychic numbing" or "emotional anesthesia." People suffering from PTSD often complain that their feelings are dampened or even nonexistent, and they frequently withdraw from others, particularly from close relationships. In addition to this avoidance of emotion, those with PTSD also will avoid situations that evoke memories of the traumatic event.

Despite their general withdrawal from feelings, people, and painful situations, individuals with PTSD also experience symptoms that indicate increased arousal in comparison to what they felt before the trauma. Excessive fear, anxiety, irritability, and general physiological arousal are among the most common complaints.

▲ The record-breaking flooding of the Mississippi River in the summer of 1993 was a traumatic stressor for the families who lived in the flood's path.

Table 7–5 lists the specific DSM-IV diagnostic criteria for the three symptom clusters of reexperiencing, numbing and avoidance, and increased arousal.

Classification of PTSD

The major issue in the classification of PTSD concerns the nature of the traumatic stressor that is responsible for the onset of the disorder. Delayed stress reactions to combat experience, particularly among Vietnam War veterans, have been the most common focus of research on PTSD. Valuable recent efforts have extended this focus to such events as rape (Kilpatrick et al., 1989), child sex abuse (Deblinger et al., 1989), and witnessing disasters (Rubonis & Bickman, 1991). Each of these traumas may result in PTSD, but it is obvious that diagnosis and treatment must be extremely sensitive to the unique consequences of different traumatic events.

A particular concern is the experience of **victimization**. Victims of violent crimes, particularly rape, have been found to suffer from a number of emotional difficulties, including fear, guilt, self-blame, powerlessness, and lowered self-esteem (see Further Thoughts). Crime victims also have an increased risk for developing affective and anxiety disorders, and as many as one-quarter may develop PTSD. Among

TABLE 7-5

DSM IV Diagnostic Criteria for Posttraumatic Stress Disorder (PTSD)

A. The person has been exposed to a traumatic event in which both of the following were present:
1. The person experienced, witnessed, or was confronted with an event or events that involved actual or threatened death or serious injury, or a threat to the physical integrity of self or others.
2. The person's response involved intense fear, helplessness, or horror.

B. The traumatic event is persistently reexperienced in one (or more) of the following ways:
1. Recurrent and intrusive distressing recollections of the event including images, thoughts, or perceptions
2. Recurrent distressing dreams of the event
3. Acting or feeling as if the traumatic event were recurring
4. Intense psychological distress at exposure to internal or external cues that symbolize or resemble an aspect of the traumatic event
5. Physiologic reactivity upon exposure to internal or external cues that symbolize or resemble an aspect of the traumatic event

C. Persistent avoidance of stimuli associated with the trauma and numbing of general responsiveness, as indicated by three (or more) of the following:
1. Efforts to avoid thoughts, feelings, or conversations associated with the trauma
2. Efforts to avoid activities, places, or people that arouse recollections of the trauma
3. Inability to recall an important aspect of the trauma
4. Markedly diminished interest or participation in significant activities
5. Feeling of detachment or estrangement from others
6. Restricted range of affect
7. Sense of a foreshortened future

D. Persistent symptoms of increased arousal, as indicated by two (or more) of the following:
1. Difficulty falling or staying asleep
2. Irritability or outbursts of anger
3. Difficulty concentrating
4. Hypervigilance
5. Exaggerated startle response

E. Duration of the disturbance is more than 1 month

rape victims, the rate of PTSD may climb to half or more (Kilpatrick et al., 1989).

The psychological effects of exposure to natural disasters such as the extensive flooding of the Mississippi River or man-made disasters like the Three Mile Island nuclear accident are also of concern both to scientists and to public policy makers. A recent review of 50 studies on disasters and psychological problems concluded that a small but significant relation between the two exists (Rubonis & Bickman, 1991). Specifically, the risk for a number of different psychological problems was found to be 17 percent higher among those exposed to a disaster. Anxiety or alcohol use were the most common problems, although PTSD was not included as a possible outcome in this review. The highest rates of psychological problems were linked with natural (as opposed to man-made) disas-

ters that caused the greatest loss of life (Rubonis & Bickman, 1991).

Other than the essential issue of the nature of the traumatic stressor, differential diagnosis is the major concern in the subclassification of PTSD. PTSD is distinguished from **acute stress disorder**, a similar but somewhat less intense reaction to trauma that lasts for more than 2 days and less than 4 weeks. PTSD is distinguished from the diagnosis of *adjustment disorder* both by the nature of the stressor experienced and by the type and severity of the symptoms it causes. Adjustment disorders are not considered to be mental disorders. They are caused by normal stress, and they involve normal (if distressing) emotional, cognitive, and behavioral reactions. Co-morbidity is another issue in differential diagnosis. Many people suffering from PTSD also meet the diagnostic criteria for another mental disorder, particularly depression and substance abuse (Breslau et al., 1991). In such cases, the co-occurring disorders must be diagnosed, and it often is important to treat these problems separately from the PTSD.

Epidemiology of PTSD

Only in recent years have experts begun to study the epidemiology of PTSD. One study of a representative sample of 3,000 individuals living in the St. Louis area found that 1 percent of the subjects had experienced PTSD at some point in their lives, and approximately 15 percent had experienced at least one symptom of the disorder (Helzer, Robins, & McEvoy, 1987). The most common cause of PTSD among men was participation in the Vietnam War, with 20 percent of wounded veterans having experienced the disorder. Other estimates suggest that between 19 percent and 30 percent of Vietnam veterans have suffered from PTSD (Oei, Lim, & Hennessy, 1990). For women, physical attack was the most common cause of PTSD, as 4.5 percent of victims experienced the disorder. These figures must be interpreted with caution due to small sample sizes, however. The small number of PTSD cases in the population sample also may be the reason why the researchers found no differences in the prevalence of PTSD among subjects of different ages, races, or sexes (Helzer et al., 1987).

These are useful data on the prevalence of PTSD, but the issue of how many people are exposed to traumatic stress–and how many develop PTSD–is an epidemiological question of even greater importance. This question was addressed recently in a random sample of 1,200 adults living in the Detroit area (Breslau et al., 1991). A high number of adults–39 percent–reported that they had experienced a traumatic stressor. About 25 percent of those exposed to such a stressor later developed PTSD. The disorder was more likely following rape in comparison to other traumas and was less likely following a sudden injury or serious accident. Figure 7–4 illustrates the results of this study.

This important study also documented factors that increased the risk for experiencing trauma and conditions that made PTSD more likely among the trauma victims. Trauma was more likely to be experienced by men; by those with less education; and by people who were

more neurotic or extroverted, had a history of conduct problems during childhood, and had a family history of mental disorder. Among victims of traumatic stress, PTSD was more likely to be found among women, the more neurotic, those with a family history of mental disorder, and people who themselves previously suffered from an emotional problem (Breslau et al., 1991). Thus, people with a history of emotional problems are more likely both to experience trauma and to suffer PTSD as a consequence.

Prevalence of Experienced Trauma and Risk for PTSD with Different Traumatic Events

	A. Experience trauma	B. Has had PTSD
Sudden injury or accident	9.4	11.6
Physical assault	8.3	22.6
See someone hurt or killed	7.1	23.6
Death or injury of loved one	5.7	21.1
Threat to life	2.5	24
Rape*	1.6	80
Other	3.7	

FIGURE 7-4: These bar graphs highlight the prevalence of trauma and the risk for posttraumatic stress disorder. Part (A) illustrates the percentage of the overall population that had experienced a particular trauma (based on a study of 1,200 adults in Detroit between the ages of 21 and 30). Part (B) shows the pecentage of people exposed to those traumas who developed PTSD. Note that the rape victems were by far the most likely to experience a stress disorder.

*The prevalence of rape as reported in this study was much lower than that reported in other studies. We assume that this statistic reflects only stranger rape and does not include acquaintance rape, which is far more common. It also might reflect the limited age group (21–30) studied.

Source: Adapted from N. Breslau, G.C. Davis, P. Andreski, and E. Peterson (1991). Traumatic events and posttraumatic stress disorder in the urban population of young adults. *Archives of general psychiatry, 48,* 216–22

These findings, and those from other research, raise questions about the role of premorbid personality in experiencing trauma and PTSD. In the St. Louis study, childhood behavior problems predicted an increased risk of subsequently experiencing a traumatic stressor. In comparison to subjects with few childhood difficulties, people who retrospectively reported having four or more behavior problems before the age of 15 were about twice as likely to have served in Vietnam or to have been beaten or mugged. The St. Louis study further concluded that people with a history of behavior problems were more

PTSD and the Sexual Assault of Women

Posttraumatic stress disorder is a useful way of conceptualizing the similarities in the reactions of victims to different types of traumatic events. Still, we have noted the importance of also recognizing victims' unique reactions to particular forms of trauma. This concern is shared by psychologists who are studying the consequences of the sexual assault of women (Goodman, Koss, & Russo, 1993b). The PTSD diagnosis is helpful, because it captures many of women's reactions to sexual assault. Moreover, it calls attention to the fact that extreme distress is a normal response to being a victim of abnormal events. But the PTSD diagnosis fails to capture many details of women's experience of sexual assault.

One problem is that, unlike many traumatic stressors, sexual assault is not outside the realm of normal human experience, at least in the United States today. Several surveys have found that approximately 20 percent of U.S. women have been victims of rape. More than 80 percent of these rapes are *acquaintance rapes*–assaults committed by people known to the victim, rather than by strangers (Goodman, Koss, & Russo, 1993a).

Neither should the physical consequences of rape be ignored. Thirty-nine percent of rape victims are physically injured on parts of their bodies other than the genitals. A significant proportion of rape victims are infected with a sexually transmitted disease, and about 5 percent of rapes result in pregnancy. Finally, many victims of sexual assault suffer from subsequent gastrointestinal problems such as nausea (Goodman et al., 1993a).

Most victims of sexual assault show the symptoms of PTSD. Victims may reexperience the horrors of the assault; they may feel numbed in reacting to others, particularly sexual partners; they may avoid any potentially threatening situation; and they may maintain both autonomic hyperarousal and hypervigilance against possible victimization. At the same time, victims of sexual assault also may experience profound relief and fears about simply being alive. They are grateful to be alive, yet fearful that their life could be so threatened. Depression is also common among victims of sexual assault. Sadness, crying, and withdrawal from others often are coupled with sleep and appetite disturbances. Loss of interest in sex, insecurities about sexual identity, sexual dysfunction, and negative feelings toward men also are common.

Another frequent psychological problem is that many victims of sexual assault blame themselves despite the fact that they are the victims. Women may wonder if they unwittingly encouraged their assailant, or they may chastise themselves for not being more cautious in avoiding dangerous circumstances. This irrational self-blame is abetted by cultural myths that women provoke rape, they enjoy it, or they are now "damaged goods." These myths also may explain why as many as two-thirds of stranger rapes and 80 percent of acquaintance rapes are not reported to authorities. In fact, many women feel that they cannot discuss the sexual assault with anyone, which surely impedes recovery of more normal functioning.

Because sexual assault is difficult to discuss, Goodman, Koss, and Russo (1993a) recommend that all mental and physical health-care providers routinely ask their patients whether they have been victims of physical or sexual violence. This is critical information for making a diagnosis of both physical and mental conditions, and questions may encourage some victims to open up about their experiences. There also is the hope that the prevalence of sexual assault can be reduced by increasing awareness of its frequency and devastating consequences. ∎

likely to respond to trauma with PTSD. In fact, the prevalence of PTSD symptoms was about 50 percent higher among those Vietnam veterans or victims of attack who had experienced earlier behavior problems than it was among veterans or victims who were better adjusted during childhood (Helzer, Robins, & McEvoy, 1987). These findings suggest that premorbid maladjustment is not necessary for the development of PTSD, but preexisting psychological problems may increase the risk for the disorder in two ways. They increase the likelihood of experiencing traumatic stress, and they decrease the individual's ability to cope with trauma.

Etiological Considerations and Research on PTSD

Although a traumatic experience is, by definition, the cause of PTSD, the fact that not everyone who experiences trauma suffers from the disorder indicates that the etiology of the disorder is more complex. Trauma is a necessary but not a sufficient cause of PTSD. As with etiological considerations for other mental disorders, a complete understanding of the causes of PTSD requires a systems approach that examines biological, psychological, and social factors.

BIOLOGICAL FACTORS IN PTSD

One important way in which biological factors contribute to PTSD may be by contributing to the development of premorbid personality. Although it is an issue of continuing debate (Jones & Barlow, 1990), some data indicate that people who had psychological difficulties before they were exposed to trauma are at greater risk for developing PTSD than are people without such problems. Premorbid personality therefore may constitute a diathesis that creates PTSD when combined with the stress of trauma.

Several different psychological characteristics have been suggested to form a diathesis for PTSD. These include antisocial behavior (Helzer, Robins, & McEvoy, 1987), depression (Frank et al., 1981), and neuroticism (McFarlane, 1989). One finding of particular interest is that premorbid personality (specifically, a positive family history of psychopathology) has been related to PTSD among veterans with low exposure to combat, but it is unrelated to PTSD when combat exposure is high (Foy et al., 1987).

It therefore appears that people subjected to intense levels of stress can develop PTSD even in the absence of premorbid personality.

Biological Effects of Exposure to Trauma In addition to examining how biology can contribute to a premorbid personality, some recent research focuses on the biological consequences of exposure to trauma and how these consequences may play a role in the development of PTSD (Watson, Hoffman, & Wilson, 1988). One group of investigators has suggested that trauma alters the activity of particular neurotransmitters in the brain (Van der Kolk et al., 1984). According to this theory, trauma increases the production of the neurotransmitter norepinephrine. This excess production of norepinephrine in turn causes the increased arousal and aggression that are symptoms of the disorder. (Recall our earlier discussion of norepinephrine and the stress response). This hypothesis further suggests that excess norepinephrine causes the stress response to be activated more intensely and by milder stressors.

Another hypothesis suggests that exposure to traumatic stress increases the production of endogenous (internally produced) *opiods*, chemicals manufactured by the body that have similar effects to exogenous (produced outside of the body) opiods like morphine (see Chapter 9). According to this hypothesis, the increase in internally produced opiods causes the numbing that characterizes PTSD (Van der Kolk et al., 1984). One interesting study of the hypothesis found that Vietnam veterans with PTSD showed *decreased* pain sensitivity following exposure to a film of combat. No change in pain threshold was found when they were administered naloxone, a chemical that blocks the effects of the opiods, and no changes in pain tolerance were found among veterans without PTSD either with or without naloxone (Pitman et al., 1990). The findings of the study are open to several alternative interpretations, but they provide justification for further study of this intriguing hypothesis.

Yet another biological model focuses on neuroanatomy rather than on neurophysiology. It suggests that trauma creates new neural pathways while altering or destroying old ones (Kolb, 1987). This and other biological models of PTSD are supported only by limited research, however. Some evidence supports the suggestion that neurotransmitter levels are higher among those with PTSD, at least as measured in sites peripheral to the brain (Krystal et al., 1989). Moreover, psychophysiological assessment of PTSD veterans indicates higher resting levels of arousal, and particularly greater increases in arousal when presented with the sights and sounds of combat (Gerardi, Blanchard, & Kolb, 1989). Still, research on the neurobiological correlates of PTSD is just beginning, and these tentative findings are only initial leads on the trail to discover the biological contributions to PTSD.

We also must remember that such biological explanations can be perfectly consistent with psychological and social hypotheses about the development of the disorder. Because every psychological experience has an underlying biological counterpart, PTSD must be accompanied by changes in brain structure or function. The task for psychobiologists and biochemists who wish to understand the effects of psychological trauma is to identify specific brain sites and biochemical actions that are linked with PTSD.

PSYCHOLOGICAL FACTORS IN PTSD

In addition to the role of premorbid personality, several hypotheses have been offered about how psychological reactions to trauma may play a role in the development of PTSD. Psychodynamic formulations emphasize the role of the defenses in protecting the individual against the anxiety created by trauma. Massive repression is suggested to play a role in numbing and withdrawal, a result of the need for strong intrapsychic defenses to cope with intense trauma. Conversely, reexperiencing is thought to result from a breakdown of repression (Oei, Lim, & Hennessy, 1990). Thus, the essential difficulty according to the psychodynamic formulation is achieving a homeostatic balance between anxiety and defense.

Learning theories of PTSD emphasize the importance of **two-factor theory** in the development of the disorder. Two-factor theory involves a combination of classical conditioning and operant conditioning. The pairing of the terror inherent in trauma with a variety of cues that are associated with the traumatic event is hypothesized to create a number of fears as a result of classical conditioning. The avoidance of fear-producing situations is argued to maintain these fears as a result of operant condition-

ing, specifically the negative reinforcement associated with the reduction of aversive anxiety (Keane, Zimering, & Caddell, 1985). Psychologist Edna Foa, a leading researcher on the cause and treatment of PTSD, has used two-factor theory to explain the development of symptoms of PTSD following a number of traumas (Foa, Steketee, & Rothbaum, 1989). For example, a woman who had been attacked while walking alone at night quite understandably would be afraid of similar circumstances. Her fears could extend far beyond this instance, however, as she might avoid being alone in many less threatening situations.

Cognitive-behavioral models suggest that higher cognitive processes like self-blame, expectancies of further trauma, and the development of fear structures are important in the etiology of PTSD (Foa, Steketee, & Rothbaum, 1989; Jones & Barlow, 1990). A recent cognitive-behavioral model draws an analogy between PTSD and panic disorder. Of particular interest is the suggestion that panic may be a cause and not a consequence of the symptom of reexperiencing. Although panic generally is considered to be a result of flashbacks, it may be that the onset of a panic attack activates emotions and memories of the trauma, thus causing the event to be relived. The suggestion is speculative, but it is supported by several research studies, including evidence that flashbacks can be brought on by lactate infusions—a procedure that, as we saw in Chapter 6, also can bring about panic attacks (Jones & Barlow, 1990).

SOCIAL FACTORS IN PTSD

As is the case with biological models, theorizing about the psychological causes of PTSD is well ahead of evidence on the issue. More research has been conducted on social and situational correlates of the disorder. Not surprisingly, researchers have found that more intense and life-threatening traumatic events are more likely to result in PTSD. For example, the disorder is more prevalent among Vietnam veterans who were wounded, were involved in the deaths of noncombatants, or witnessed atrocities (Oei, Lim, & Hennessy, 1990). Similarly, victims of attempted rape are more likely to develop PTSD if the rape is completed, if they are physically injured during the assault, and if they perceive the sexual assault as life-threatening (Kilpatrick et al., 1989).

▲ Edna Foa is a psychologist at the Eastern Pennsylvania Psychiatric Institute in Philadelphia. Foa has done extensive research on the etiology and the treatment of PTSD.

As with less severe stressors, the availability of social support after the occurrence of the trauma appears to play a crucial role in alleviating long-term psychological damage. Such evidence serves as one rationale for attempts to help the victims of rape become less secretive about their victimization. Many victims of rape mistakenly feel guilty and somehow responsible for being attacked. *Rape crisis centers* and rape support groups offer social support that helps women to recognize that they are victims of a heinous crime. Lack of social support also is thought to have contributed to the high prevalence of PTSD found among Vietnam veterans (Oei, Lim, & Hennessy, 1990). Rather than being praised as heros, returning veterans often were treated with disdain and even disgust. This absence of support made it difficult for many veterans to justify the trauma that they had suffered, and it likely increased the number of cases of PTSD as a result.

The combination of evidence suggests that although trauma is a necessary cause of PTSD, the specific etiology of PTSD is more complex. Factors that are present before the trauma, during the trauma, and after its occurrence all contribute to the development of the disorder. Future research should clarify what preexisting personality characteristics and forms of posttraumatic social support influence the risk for PTSD following exposure to traumas of different forms and intensities.

Prevention and Treatment of PTSD

The symptoms of PTSD can begin months or years following the experience of trauma, but in most cases the difficulties start immediately or shortly afterwards. Whether the onset is immediate or delayed, the reexperiencing of the trauma can continue for long periods of time. In addition to situations that are reminiscent of the trauma, reminders such as anniversary dates often cause the horror to be relived. For these reasons, it is important to distinguish emergency attempts to help trauma victims from longer-term treatment efforts.

EMERGENCY TREATMENT OF TRAUMA VICTIMS

Trauma is a known cause of PTSD, and this knowledge makes prevention the first consideration in the treatment of the disorder. Early intervention with trauma victims holds the hope of both easing the pain of coping with a horrific event and of preventing the subsequent development of PTSD. The potential for secondary prevention is so important that the Federal Emergency Management Agency, the government agency designated to deal with natural or man-made disasters, is required to provide community mental health centers with special funding during times of local or regional disaster.

Psychologists and other mental health professionals frequently offer emergency assistance to individual victims of trauma or to groups of people who have experienced a disaster. These emergency treatments range from intensive, individual counseling with rape victims to group discussions with children whose school has been destroyed by a tornado. There are many differences in the therapeutic approaches used across such prevention efforts, but offering immediate social support to trauma victims is a common goal of all early interventions.

Little systematic research has been conducted on the effectiveness of most emergency interventions with the victims of trauma. The treatment of soldiers in combat is one of the few exceptions where empirical evidence recently has become available. Since World War I, the treatment of soldiers who experience combat stress has been based on the three principles of offering (a) immediate treatment in the (b) proximity of the battlefield with the (c) expectation of return to the front lines upon recovery. The effectiveness of these treatment principles has been long assumed, but they were not studied systematically until 1982, when the Israeli army implemented the practices during the Lebanon War. Evaluation of the emergency services indicated that 60 percent of soldiers who were treated near the front recovered suf-

▼ Rape crisis centers offer women support in dealing with sexual assault.

ficiently to return to battle within 72 hours. Soldiers who expected to return to the front experienced lower rates of PTSD than did those who did not expect to return to battle. In addition, those soldiers who were treated on the front lines were less likely to develop PTSD subsequently when compared to soldiers who were treated in civilian facilities away from the battlefield (Oei, Lim, & Hennessy, 1990).

It seems reasonable to generalize these principles to the treatment of victims of many, but not all, forms of trauma. For example, we would expect that victims of a natural disaster would benefit from immediate treatment near their communities with the expectation of a rapid return to normal life. Perhaps the key to this intervention strategy is the creation of the expectation that extreme distress in the face of trauma is normal, as is recovery from the trauma. This expectation may become a reality when combined with successful, subsequent coping.

TREATMENT OF PTSD

Psychotropic medication frequently is used in the treatment of PTSD, but there is no single medication that has specific effects on the disorder. Rather, various antidepressant and antianxiety medications sometimes are used to treat particular symptoms associated with PTSD (Krystal et al., 1989). For example, one group of investigators found that the antidepressant medication amitriptyline led to improvements in self-reported depression ratings among veterans with PTSD. However, 64 percent of the treated patients continued to meet the diagnostic criteria for PTSD, compared with 72 percent of a control group that was given a placebo (Davidson et al., 1990).

Psychotherapists who specialize in PTSD have suggested some general principles for the psychological treatment of the disorder. In the order in which they are likely to be addressed in therapy, these include: (a) establishing a trusting therapeutic relationship, (b) providing education about the process of coping with trauma, (c) stress-management training, (d) encouraging the reexperience of the trauma, and (e) integrating the traumatic event into the individual's experience (Scurfield, 1985). Reexposure to the traumatic event is perhaps the least obvious but most important of these strategies. Perhaps because the terrifying and uncontrollable reliving of trauma is one

of the most distressing symptoms of PTSD, reexperiencing in a controlled treatment setting becomes basic to the therapeutic process. Therapeutic approaches different widely in how this reexperience is encouraged, yet all treatments encourage the recounting of trauma in some form. The most direct method is **trauma desensitization**. Trauma desensitization is a theoretical and practical variation of the well-researched treatment for phobias, systematic desensitization (see Chapter 6). Initially, the client is taught a basic relaxation technique. Once the client masters a relaxation procedure, he or she relives the traumatic event through discussions with the therapist or through fantasies of the experience. Exposure to the trauma is gradual, so that the client can maintain a state of relaxation. Increasingly distressing details are confronted only after the client can relive less upsetting events while remaining calm.

As is the case with emergency interventions with trauma victims, little research has been conducted on the effectiveness of trauma desensitization or other treatments for PTSD. A study conducted in the Netherlands compared the effectiveness of trauma desensitization, hypnotherapy, and psychodynamic therapy in the treatment of people suffering from the effects of a variety of traumatic experiences (Brom, Kleber, & Defares, 1989). Trauma desensitization followed the procedures described above. Hypnotherapy was similar to trauma desensitization, except that hypnosis was used to facilitate the reliving of the traumatic experience. Psychodynamic therapy focused on the intrapsychic conflicts caused by the trauma rather than on the trauma itself.

All treatments produced significantly more positive outcomes in comparison with an untreated control group. Approximately 4 months after an initial assessment, clinically significant improvements in trauma symptoms were found among 60 percent of treated subjects in comparison with 26 percent of untreated controls. The most notable improvements were a decreased avoidance of difficult situations and lesser frequency of intrusive thoughts. Psychodynamic therapy tended to produce the most benefits on intrusive thinking, while desensitization and hypnotherapy were more effective with avoidance. There were no statistically significant differences among the three alternative treatments, however (Brom, Kleber, & Defares, 1989).

The similarities in treatment effectiveness may be another indication of the common factors found across different types of psychotherapy (see Chapter 3). In this study, the common factor may have been the reliving of the trauma, whether through desensitization, hypnosis, or discussion of its effect on intrapsychic life. This conclusion is supported by a recent treatment outcome study of rape victims (Foa et al., 1991). Prolonged exposure involving repeated reliving of the trauma over nine therapy sessions produced more long-term reductions in PTSD symptoms than did three alternatives: (a) stress inoculation training (focusing on relaxation and stress management), (b) supportive counseling (which explicitly omitted exposure procedures), and (c) a wait list control group. Also of interest was the finding that stress inoculation training produced more short-term benefits, while prolonged exposure was more effective in the long run. Reliving traumatic events is painful initially, and it may appear to impede progress. This painful reexperiencing may be exactly the right therapy, however (Foa et al., 1991). An important therapeutic ingredient is reliving the experience in memory, in discussions, or, if practical, in returning to the scene of the trauma.

COURSE AND OUTCOME

Very little is known about the long-term course of PTSD. Some evidence indicates that the problem can be chronic and can interfere with functioning in other areas of life. One study of World War II prisoners of war who suffered from PTSD (as diagnosed by retrospective report) found that only about 30 percent were fully recovered, while 60 percent continued to have mild to moderate symptoms of the disorder. Another 10 percent had no recovery or had a deteriorating course (Kluznik et al., 1986). Given that the follow-up study was conducted 40 years after the imprisonment, these data suggest a poor prognosis, at least for those subjected to the extreme and prolonged trauma of being a prisoner of war. Clearly, more research is needed on the eventual outcome of PTSD and on the factors that predict whether an individual can make a successful long-term adjustment.

Summary

Different scientists have emphasized different aspects of the definition of **stress**. Some focus on stressors, the trying events themselves. Others highlight distress, the individual's unique cognitive appraisal of a stressor. Still other scientists emphasize the stress response or physiological reactions to stressors.

Each approach has strengths and weaknesses. Defining stress in terms of stressors enables scientists to measure stress independent of its hypothesized effects. A problem, however, is that different people have different reactions to the same event. This shortcoming can be corrected by defining stress as a combination of an event and a reaction to it (distress, stress response), but this approach runs the risk of being tautological or circular. Thus, there is no simple definition of stress.

Despite this basic problem, much is known about people's reactions to stressful events. Fight or flight is a response to threat that is activated by stress and is characterized by intense arousal of the sympathetic nervous system. The **general adaptation syndrome** (**GAS**) is a more global

KEY TERMS

- acute stress disorder
- behavioral medicine
- biofeedback
- cardiovascular disease
- coronary heart disease
- cross-sectional study
- emotion-focused coping
- flashback
- fight or flight
- general adaptation syndrome
- health behavior
- health psychology
- hypertension
- longitudinal study
- posttraumatic stress disorder
- problem-focused coping

response to stress. The GAS includes the stage of alarm (similar to the emergency response), the stage of resistance (a period of replenishment), and exhaustion (which occurs when the body's resources are depleted by chronic stress). Recent research on **psychoneuroimmunology** has identified yet another physiological consequence of stress, less adequate functioning of the immune system.

Emotional responses to stress are especially likely to include increased anxiety, depression, and anger. Coping with these reactions may involve **problem-focused coping**, which is an attempt to change the stressor, or **emotion-focused coping**, which is an attempt to alter distress internally. In general, predictability and control over stressors can greatly facilitate coping.

Behavioral responses to stress include not only attempts to avoid or alter a stressor but also the search for other outlets for frustration. Poor health behavior can be another behavioral consequence of stress, one that clearly can have negative affects on physical well-being. **Health behaviors** include positive actions such as maintaining good hygiene, exercise, and diet, as well as the avoidance of unhealthy activities such as cigarette smoking, excessive alcohol consumption, and drug use. Illness behavior, behaving as if you are sick, also is stress-related. For example, people visit their physicians more often during times of stress, suggesting that illness behavior may have emotional motivations.

Psychosomatic disorders are real physical illnesses that involve demonstrable damage to the body and are thought to be caused, in part, by stress. In the past, only certain illnesses were thought to be psychosomatic disorders; however, the DSM-IV contains no such listing. Stress now is recognized as playing a role in all physical illnesses.

The role of stress in physical illness is illustrated by research on cardiovascular disease (CVD), disorders that affect the heart and circulatory system. Cardiovascular diseases include **hypertension** (high blood pressure) and **coronary heart disease** (**CHD**), particularly myocardial infarction, or heart attacks. Several health behaviors have been linked to CHD, including cigarette smoking, obesity, a fatty diet, heavy alcohol consumption, and lack of exercise.

In addition to poor health behavior, several psychological factors may contribute to CVD. People's physiological reactivity, their greater or lesser responses to stressors presented in a laboratory, may be one contributing factor. Evidence also links exposure to chronic stressors in real life (for example, job strain) with an increased risk for CVD. Another psychological risk factor is the **Type A behavior pattern**, a characterological response to challenge that involves competitive, hostile, urgent, impatient, and achievement-striving behaviors. Of all of these Type A behaviors, recent evidence suggests that hostility may be the central characteristic related to CHD.

The primary prevention of CHD includes attempts to encourage people to quit smoking, eat well, exercise, monitor their blood pressure, and otherwise improve their health behaviors. The treatment of hypertension through improved health behaviors or through stress management is one of the most important attempts at the secondary prevention of CHD. Tertiary prevention of CHD targets patients who have already had a cardiac event. The hope is to reduce the rate of recurrence of the illness through exercise and other health programs. Studies also suggest that Type A behavior can be modified, and this may reduce the subsequent risk for CHD.

Sources of **traumatic stress** include rapes, bombings, airline crashes, earthquakes, major fires, and devastating automobile wrecks. For some individuals, the normal and devastating reactions to trauma continue long after the event has ended. These people suffer from **post-traumatic stress disorder** (**PTSD**).

PTSD is characterized by the three symptoms of reexperiencing, numbed responsiveness or avoidance, and increased autonomic arousal. Trauma may be reexperienced as a flashback, or as a dissociative state in which the person relives the trauma in the moment. The diminished responsiveness has been referred to as psychic numbing or emotional anesthesia. The increased arousal in PTSD may include excessive fear, anxiety, or irritability, as well as general psychophysiological arousal.

Scientists have only begun to study the epidemiology of PTSD. Current evidence points to the surprisingly high frequency with which people experience some traumatic experiences. Epidemiology also calls attention to the particularly devastating consequences of rape for women and combat exposure for men.

By definition, the experience of trauma is the central cause of PTSD, but other factors appear to be important in its etiology. For example, premorbid personality may be a diathesis that creates PTSD when combined with the stress of trauma. Learning theories also emphasize the importance of **two-factor theory** in the development of PTSD. A number of adverse reactions may be produced by classical conditioning during the experience of trauma, and the reactions can be maintained by operant conditioning as people continue to avoid stressful circumstances. Finally, **social support** after the occurrence of the trauma appears to be crucial to facilitating long-term adjustment.

Early intervention with trauma victims can contribute to easing the pain of coping with a horrific event and to preventing the subsequent development of PTSD. Reliving the traumatic event is perhaps the least obvious but most important strategy for subsequent treatment. According to research that is being conducted on therapy outcome, recounting and reexperiencing the trauma in a controlled treatment setting appears to be basic to the therapeutic process.

Critical Thinking

1. Scientists struggle with defining the construct of stress. How do *you* define stress in your own life? How does your definition fit with the definition of terms like stressors, stress response, and distress? If you were conducting research on stress, what dimensions (or types) of stress would you hypothesize are critical for physical and mental health? What about coping? How do you cope with life's struggles? What are your theories about effective and ineffective coping?

2. Are you Type A? Do you know people who are Type A? Pause to think about your lifestyle. How has research on stress and health behavior affected your life? Are pressures to live a healthier lifestyle stressful? Are they coercive?

3. National health care has become a widely debated issue. Assuming that the United States adopts some form of national health system, how should the treatment of stress be handled within this system? Should stress-related therapies be included among the benefits to which Americans would be entitled? Why or why not?

8

Dissociative and Somatoform Disorders

Case histories of dissociative and somatoform disorders have long fascinated both professionals and the public, because these unusual problems challenge many ordinary assumptions about the psyche. **Dissociative disorders** are characterized by persistent, maladaptive disruptions in the integration of memory, consciousness, or identity. You may be familiar with the actual case histories of multiple personality (now called dissociative identity disorder) explored in the book *Sybil* and in the movie *The Three Faces of Eve*. Sometimes dissociative disorders are used as plot elements, as was done with amnesia in the movie *Desperately Seeking Susan*.

Overview

Equally fascinating are **somatoform disorders**—problems characterized by unusual physical symptoms that occur in the absence of a known physical illness. The sudden onset of paralysis or blindness without a clear biological cause is a dramatic example of a somatoform disorder. Unlike the real, organic pathology that underlies psychosomatic illnesses (see Chapter 7), somatoform disorders are, in a sense, "all in your head." There is no demonstrable physical cause for the physical symptoms of somatoform disorders. They are somatic in form only—thus their name.

Although other psychological problems may or may not be traceable to unconscious processes, dissociative and somatoform disorders involve unconscious processes by definition. Memories become inaccessible in dissociative disorders; psychological distress is converted into physical symptoms in somatoform disorders. These transformations occur without intention and often without awareness—an indication that the mind possesses different levels of consciousness.

We have already discussed numerous problems involved in objectively measuring people's reports about their conscious experience. Imagine, then, the difficulties involved in developing objective, scientific measures of unconscious processes. Our inability to adequately assess unconscious experiences challenges clinicians as well as research scientists. For skeptical clinicians, the most pressing diagnostic question is one of *malingering:* Could the patient be pretending to have a dissociative or somatoform disorder in order to achieve some gain?

Because of the limited assessment and research on dissociative and somatoform disorders, we must be cautious in attempting to explain these problems. At the same time, we cannot help but be captivated and challenged by unusual case histories of the disorders. Below we examine in some detail one case history with which we are familiar. Throughout the chapter we consider briefer cases, as well as the difficult scientific and clinical questions raised by these intriguing problems.

▼ **Joanne Woodward played the role of Eve in the film** *The Three Faces of Eve*. **Lee J. Cobb played the role of the therapist who treated Eve White, Eve Black, and, eventually, Jane.**

Dissociative Fugue

Dallae disappeared mysteriously during final exams in December of her junior year at a California university. She was reported missing by her roommate, who had last seen Dallae when she was supposed to be studying for her organic chemistry exam. Dallae had been agitated that night. She left her room several times and kept interrupting her roommate, who was cramming for the same exam. Dallae did not take the exam the next day, and she still had not reappeared 2 days later. She had missed two more final exams before her roommate contacted the authorities.

At first, the police suspected foul play. It did not seem likely that Dallae had left college on her own. None of her personal possessions were missing from her room; even her eyeglasses were still sitting on her desk. However, bank records indicated that Dallae had withdrawn all of her money from her bank account the day before the exam. It also was discovered that Dallae had been lying to her parents. She had told them that she had an "A" average in organic chemistry. In fact, she was failing the course, and she had not attended her laboratory section for almost 2 months.

Dallae's roommate and another friend indicated that they had noted changes in her behavior in recent weeks. She had been irritable and unpredictable, and was spending less and less time in classes and in her room. She was also complaining constantly about her physical ailments. Dallae's medical records indicated that she had made four visits to the student health center during this time, complaining of stomach pains, headaches, and fatigue. No illness was diagnosed, and the center prescribed a tranquilizer for anxiety. The pills were not found in her room.

When the police failed to locate Dallae, they contacted the FBI. After a futile 4-week investigation, Dallae was located in a college town on the East Coast, where she was identified from a missing persons report. She had been brought to a hospital emergency room after she was found wandering on the streets. At the time, she appeared confused and disoriented. She told the emergency room physician that her name was Dawn and that she had been living on the streets and sleeping in dormitory lounges. She said that she had just moved from the West Coast and had come here because she hoped eventually to attend the university. She gave a vague and sketchy account about other details of her life. For example, she could not say how she got to the East Coast.

Dallae allowed herself to be voluntarily admitted to the hospital's psychiatric unit. On the ward, she talked little and spent most of her time watching television. She told a bit more about herself—she said that she was Vietnamese and had been adopted by American parents, but her stories continued to be vague and inconsistent. She said that she didn't remember other things, but she did not seem greatly distressed by her memory impairment. A CAT scan and neuropsychological tests detected no physical abnormalities or deficits in short-term memory or motor functioning.

A hospital social worker contacted the local police about the disoriented young patient, and the police were able to identify Dallae from an FBI report. The social worker contacted Dallae's parents shortly thereafter, and her mother immediately flew east to see her. When her mother appeared at the hospital a week after Dallae had been admitted, Dallae did not recognize her. Her mother was greatly distressed by Dallae's indifference, and she noted other puzzling oddities and inconsistencies. For one thing, Dallae was not Vietnamese, and she was not adopted. She had grown up with her married parents, who were Korean immigrants. Her mother also noted that although Dallae was right-handed, she used her left hand to write a note on the ward. Dallae's consistent use of her left hand was confirmed by the staff and by the neuropsychologist who had tested her.

Two nights after her mother arrived, Dallae's memories apparently returned. That night, she attempted suicide by slashing her wrists, but she was discovered by a hospital staff member, who quickly stopped the bleeding. Dallae was intermittently depressed and extremely agitated for the next several days, especially after seeing her mother. Although she would not talk at length, her conversation indicated that much of her memory was now intact, and she began writing with her right hand again.

During the next 2 weeks, Dallae gradually related details about her life to the psychologist who was treating her. Dallae had been a quiet and obedient girl all through her childhood. Dallae's parents worked very hard, and they had high ambitions for their three children. Dallae's older brother had an MBA and was a very successful young executive. Her older sister currently was editor of the law review at a prestigious law school. Ever since she was a young child, Dallae's parents had planned for her to become a doctor. In fact, all her life her parents had told friends and relatives that Dallae would be a doctor one day.

Dallae worked extremely hard throughout high school and gained admission to a highly regarded public university in her home state despite her mediocre SAT scores. Through continued effort, Dallae had maintained a 3.0 grade point average as a premedical student during her first 2 years of college. Her course work was becoming overwhelming in her third year, however, and her motivation was evaporating. Dallae now admitted, in fact, that she had personally never been interested in medicine. She also noted that she had wanted to attend the college in the town where she was found. She was drawn there during her episode for reasons she could not explain, and she still did not recall exactly how she had arrived at her destination. Dallae did note, however, that she felt comforted and somewhat relieved after she had made her way east.

Dallae remained sullen and agitated for several weeks after her mother's arrival, and she continued to talk about wanting to die. During discussions with her therapist, Dallae began to talk more freely about her past. She frequently discussed her poor grades in organic chemistry and other courses, and she said she remembered everything that happened after her suicide attempt. She noted that she had been terrified to tell her parents about her grades and her feelings about studying medicine. In part, she was concerned about disappointing her mother. Her father was a much bigger worry, however. He put endless pressure on her to fulfill what she saw as his dream. She cried at length when relating how he had struck her across the face during the previous Thanksgiving break, when she tried to tell him about her lack of interest in studying medicine.

After spending 6 weeks in the hospital, Dallae was released, and she returned to California with her parents. Her memory was intact at the time of the discharge, except that she continued to have no recollection of her trip across the country or of many of her days living on the streets. She remained uncertain why she thought her name was Dawn, although she did mention being influenced by a television show she had seen about a Vietnamese child who had been adopted. She could not recall the name of the character in the story, but she did remember concluding that she too was Vietnamese and adopted. At the time of Dallae's discharge, her depression had abated somewhat, and she was no longer actively suicidal. She reported being relieved at having told her mother about her feelings about medical school, but she remained very anxious about facing her father once she returned to the West Coast. ■

Dallae suffered from **dissociative fugue**, a rare and unusual disorder characterized by sudden, unplanned travel, the inability to remember details about the past, and confusion about identity or the assumption of a new identity. Dissociative fugue typically follows a traumatic event. It is sometimes observed among soldiers following a particularly gruesome battle, for example. For Dallae, perhaps her poor grades could be considered to be a trauma, given her father's intense and constant pressure to succeed.

The travel in dissociative fugue is purposeful, despite the memory impairments. Dallae knew where she was going, and she could provide at least a vague explanation about why she was going there. Purposeful travel is the distinguishing symptom, but the core questions about fugue—and about all dissociative and somatoform disorders—concern the split between conscious and unconscious psychological experience. How could Dallae be aware of the present but still be unaware of her past? Why didn't all her memories return after she saw her mother? Several key figures in the history of abnormal psychology have attempted to answer such perplexing questions. In fact, attempts to explain these puzzling disorders led to the development of some of the first theories about unconscious psychological processes.

Brief Historical Perspective: Hysteria and Unconscious Processes

Scientific interest in somatoform and dissociative disorders began with attempts to treat **hysteria,** a diagnostic category that included both somatoform and dissociative disorders. The origins of the term hysteria date to ancient Greece. In Greek, *hystera* literally means "uterus." The name *hysteria* reflects ancient speculation that these unusual disorders were restricted to women and were caused by frustrated sexual desires, particularly the desire to have a baby. According to the theory, the uterus becomes detached from its normal location and moves about the body, causing a problem in the location where it eventually lodges. Variants of this fantastic view of hysteria continued throughout Western history, and as late as the nineteenth century many physicians erroneously believed that hysteria occurred only among women (van der Hart & Friedman, 1989).

New speculation about the etiology of hysteria emerged toward the end of the nineteenth century. The work of Jean Charcot, who used hypnosis both to treat and to induce hysteria, was particularly important (see Chapter 2). Charcot greatly influenced the thinking of Freud, who observed Charcot's hypnotic treatments early in his training. Charcot also had a strong influence on the work of Freud's contemporary and rival, Pierre Janet (1859–1947). Janet was a French philosophy professor who conducted psychological experiments on dissociation and who later trained as a physician in Charcot's clinic (see Chapter 6).

Janet and Freud were both eager to explain and treat hysteria, and the problem led both of them to develop theories about unconscious mental processes. The two competitors differed in the specifics of their views about dissociation and the unconscious mind. Janet viewed dissociation as an abnormal process. To him, detachment from conscious awareness occurred only as a part of psychopathology. Thus, Janet defined unconscious processes narrowly, con-

sistent with what he observed in dissociative and somatoform disorders. In contrast, Freud viewed dissociation as a normal process, a routine means through which the ego defended itself against unacceptable unconscious thoughts. Freud saw dissociation and repression as similar processes, and, in fact, he often used the two terms interchangeably (Erdelyi, 1990; Perry & Laurence, 1984). Thus, Freud considered dissociative and somatoform disorders to be merely one of many expressions of unconscious conflict.

▼ French neurologist Jean Charcot (1825–1893) demonstrating a case of hysteria at the Salpetriere, a famous hospital in Paris. Charcot's work with hysteria and hypnosis greatly influenced the thinking of both Sigmund Freud and Pierre Janet.

The two theorists criticized each other frequently. Janet thought Freud greatly overstated the importance of the unconscious; Freud thought that Janet greatly underestimated it. One culmination of their debate was Janet's (1914/1915) famous critique of psychoanalysis in the *Journal of Abnormal Psychology*, one of the leading sources of research on psychopathology in the early—and the late—twentieth century. In this article, Janet raised doubts about the originality of many of Freud's ideas. In referring to the famous studies of Joseph Breuer and Freud (see Chapter 3), Janet stated, "At most, these writers only changed some terms in their psychological descriptions; what I called psychological analysis, they called psychoanalysis; where I used 'psychological system,' they used complex.... The names were different but all essential conceptions... were accepted without modification" (p. 10).

Janet's work influenced a number of investigators, including U.S. psychologist Morton Prince (1854–1929), who founded the journal in which Janet published his critique and who wrote several case histories of patients with multiple personalities (Prince, 1906). Janet's work

▲ Pierre Janet (1859–1947) conducted psychological experiments as a professor in Paris, and he later trained as a physician in Jean Charcot's clinic. Janet's views on dissociation were much more circumscribed than those of his rival, Sigmund Freud.

became increasingly obscure, however, as Freudian theory dominated the mental health professions throughout much of the twentieth century.

UNCONSCIOUS PROCESSES AND CONTEMPORARY COGNITIVE SCIENCE

Contemporary psychologists continue to raise important and controversial questions about dissociation and unconscious processes, but they generally agree about two things. First, unconscious processes do exist, and they play a role in both normal and abnormal emotion and cognition (Wegner, 1994). Second, contemporary cognitive scientists carefully distinguish their more restricted view of unconscious processes from Freud's elaborate view of *the* unconscious.

Freud postulated a global unconscious mind, comprised of an intricate set of processes (for example, the defenses) and contents (for example, id impulses). Contemporary cognitive scientists also recognize unconscious contents (for example, inaccessible memories) and processes (for example, memory search strategies). In contrast to Freud, however, contemporary scientists view unconscious events as being much less influential in shaping both normal and abnormal behavior (Bowers & Meichenbaum, 1984; Singer, 1990). In the words of one evaluation by cognitive scientists, the contemporary view is

that the unconscious mind is "dumb," not "smart"; that is, it has a limited influence on human behavior (Loftus & Klinger, 1992).

HYSTERIA AND CONTEMPORARY DIAGNOSIS

As a result of Freudian influences, hysteria eventually came to be classified as a type of *neurosis*—a diagnostic category that also included anxiety and depressive disorders. This categorization reflected the Freudian view that unconscious conflict was the common cause of each of these apparently different disorders. Still, the historical link between somatoform and dissociative disorders was preserved in many classification systems. The two disorders were listed together as subtypes of "hysterical neurosis" in DSM-II (1968), for example.

The descriptive approach to classification introduced in DSM-III (1980) led to the separation of dissociative and somatoform disorders into discrete diagnostic categories. The distinction is preserved in DSM-IV (1994), as the two disorders clearly differ greatly in appearance. Consistent with DSM-IV, we review the two problems separately. We nevertheless discuss both problems in a single chapter because of their historical relationship and because both apparently involve unconscious processes.

Dissociative Disorders

Until recent years, the dissociative disorders have been of more interest to theorists—and novelists—than to empirically oriented mental health professionals. There has been an explosion of interest in dissociative disorders since the late 1980s, however. This bodes well for future research, but current empirical evidence remains sharply limited, as you will soon discover.

Typical Symptoms and Associated Features

The defining symptom of the dissociative disorders is **dissociation,** the disruption of mental processes involved in memory or consciousness that normally are integrated (Spiegel & Cardena, 1991). Some experiences of dissociation are normal. Examples include fleeting feelings of unre-

ality and *deja vu* experiences—the odd and short-lived feeling that an event has happened before. Table 8–1 lists other examples from a commonly used measure of dissociation, the Dissociative Experiences Questionnaire (Bernstein & Putnam, 1986). Some scientists also believe that hypnosis involves dissociation—a theme we explore in the Research Close-Up "Hypnosis."

The dissociation found in dissociative disorders is much more dramatic. Extreme cases of dissociation involve a split in the functioning of the individual's entire sense of self. In dissociative identity disorder, two or more personalities may coexist within a single individual. *Depersonalization* is another form of dissociation wherein people feel detached from themselves or their social or physical environment. Examples of depersonalization include feeling like a stranger or a "robot" in social interactions, and out-of-body experiences—feelings of detachment from one's physical being.

A dramatic dissociation in memory is termed *amnesia*—the partial or complete loss of memory for particular events or for a particular period of time. Brain injury or disease can cause amnesia (see Chapter 13), but *psychogenic amnesia* results from traumatic stress or other sources of emotional distress. Psychogenic amnesia may occur alone or in conjunction with other dissociative experiences. For example, in dissociative identity disorder one personality may not remember the actions—or even the existence—of another (Spiegel & Cardena, 1991).

Trauma often plays a role in dissociation and dissociative disorders. Fugue and amnesia typically are precipitated by a traumatic event, for example. In other cases, the onset of dissociation is more gradual and is not clearly linked with a present trauma, although problems like dissociative identity disorder often appear to be tied with a trauma from the past. Recovery of functioning typically is rapid when amnesia or fugue immediately follows a traumatic event. Psychological functioning returns to normal in these cases, and recurrence is unlikely. The reintegration of cognitive or emotional functioning is less certain or sudden when the trauma is distant or ambiguous. These more severe cases of dissociation may also be accompanied by substantial impairment in life functioning, and by a risk of violence toward oneself or others.

Classification

The DSM-IV distinguishes four major subtypes of dissociative disorders: fugue, amnesia, depersonalization disorder, and dissociative identity disorder. Dissociative fugue is characterized by sudden and unexpected travel away from home, an inability to recall the past, and confusion about identity or the assumption of a new identity. The case of Dallae is an example of dissociative fugue.

Dissociative amnesia involves a sudden inability to recall extensive and important personal information that exceeds normal forgetfulness. The memory loss in dissociative amnesia is not attributable to substance abuse, head trauma, or a cognitive disorder such as Alzheimer's disease. As with fugue, dissociative amnesia typically is characterized by a sudden onset in response

TABLE 8–1

Sample Items from the Dissociative Experiences Questionnaire

- Some people find that sometimes they are listening to someone talk and they suddenly realize that they did not hear part or all of what was said.

- Some people have the experience of being in a familiar place but finding it strange and unfamiliar.

- Some people have the experience of finding themselves dressed in clothes that they don't remember putting on.

- Some people are told that they sometimes do not recognize friends or family members.

- Some people have the experience of feeling that their body does not seem to belong to them.

- Some people find that in one situation they may act so differently compared with another situation that they feel almost as if they were two different people.

Source: E.M. Bernstein & F.W. Putnam. (1986). Development, reliability, and validity of a dissociation scale. *Journal of Nervous & Mental Disease, 174,* 727–735.

to trauma or extreme stress, and by an equally sudden recovery of memory. Amnesia may take many forms, including *retrograde amnesia*—loss of memory for events before the trauma; *posttraumatic amnesia*—loss of memory for events after the trauma; and *anterograde amnesia*—impairment in learning new material (see also Chapter 13). The most common form in dissociative disorders is *selective amnesia*, in which patients don't lose their memory completely but instead are unable to remember only selected personal events and information. In one study of 25 patients in

▲ Soldiers sometimes experience dissociative fugue in response to the trauma of combat.

Hypnosis: Altered State or the Power of Suggestion?

The nature of **hypnosis** is a matter of continuing debate and uncertainty. On the one hand, there are impressive demonstrations of the power of hypnotic suggestion. For example, in laboratory studies, hypnotized subjects have been shown to have an increased threshold for pain when given various suggestions, such as that a particular body part is numb and insensate. One particularly interesting aspect of this work has been the identification of what is called the "hidden observer." At some level of consciousness, many hypnotized individuals recognize and can report on their experience of pain, even as they indicate insensitivity to the pain at another level of consciousness (Kihlstrom, 1984).

Not everyone can be hypnotized. People who are most hypnotizable are the same ones who are most powerfully influenced by suggestion. For example, one indicator of hypnotizability is an individual's response to the suggestion to close his or her eyes and imagine a helium balloon being tied to his or her wrist. Subjects whose arm rises with the imagined balloon tend to be more easily hypnotized. This observation has led some researchers to suggest that hypnosis is not an altered state of consciousness. Instead, hypnosis is explained in social–psychological terms as a response to suggestion and expectation (Spanos, 1986).

Miller and Bowers (1986) conducted a study that is difficult to explain in terms of suggestibility alone, however. They identified subjects who were categorized as being either low or high in terms of hypnotizability. Next, they exposed the subjects to three experimental manipulations designed to increase tolerance for pain. Hypnosis was the first condition, and this involved the suggestion that sensitivity to pain would be reduced. The second condition was a cognitive behavioral procedure in which subjects were trained in strategies for coping with pain. The third condition was identical to the second, but the subjects were told that the cognitive coping would involve hypnotic reduction of pain.

▲ **A person undergoing a hypnotic induction.**

Subjects were pretested for pain tolerance using the cold pressor test, which involves immersing one's hands in ice water. No differences among groups were found. The cold pressor test was repeated again after the subjects were taught (and had used) one of the three coping strategies. In fact, all three strategies significantly increased pain tolerance. Members of the cognitive behavioral groups reported using the strategies they had learned, but members of the hypnotic group did not report using similar coping strategies on their own. Importantly, hypnotizability was correlated with increased pain tolerance among the subjects who were hypnotized. The more hypnotizable the subjects were, the more pain they tolerated. Hypnotizability was not related to pain tolerance in the other conditions. These findings suggest that hypnosis, and not susceptibility to suggestion, can lead to increased pain tolerance.

This study does not unequivocally demonstrate that hypnosis is "real," but it makes hypnosis difficult to dismiss out of hand. We are right to remain skeptical about hypnosis, dissociation, and related topics, given the current state of evidence. Our skepticism does not mean, however, that we should dismiss these unusual phenomena. Rather, skepticism should encourage us to devise increasingly sophisticated ways of testing these intriguing ideas. ■

a dissociative disorders clinic, 76 percent had selective amnesia (Coons & Milstein, 1988, cited in Spiegel & Cardena, 1991).

Depersonalization disorder is a less dramatic problem that is characterized by severe and persistent feelings of being detached from oneself. Depersonalization experiences include such sensations as feeling as though you are in a dream, or the sensation of floating above your body and observing yourself act. Occasional depersonalization experiences are normal, and are reported by about half the population. In depersonalization disorder, however, such experiences are persistent or recurrent, and they cause marked personal distress. The onset of the disorder commonly follows a new or disturbing event such as drug use. All depersonalization experiences are "as if" feelings, not rigid, delusional beliefs. In fact, some experts question whether depersonalization should be considered a type of dissociative disorder. Unlike other dissociative disorders, depersonalization disorder involves only limited splitting between conscious and unconscious mental processes, and no memory loss occurs (Spiegel & Cardena, 1991).

To many people, the most fascinating subtype of dissociative disorder is **dissociative identity disorder**, a condition that has also been known as **multiple personality disorder** prior to the introduction of DSM-IV. This unusual mental disorder is characterized by the existence of two or more distinct personalities in a single individual. At least two of these personalities repeatedly take control over the person's behavior, and some personalities have limited or no memory of the others. The original personality especially is likely to have amnesia for subsequent personalities, which may or may not be aware of the "alternates" (Aldridge-Morris, 1989).

THE THREE FACES OF EVE: THE CASE OF CHRIS SIZEMORE

Perhaps the best-known case history of multiple personality disorder was detailed in Thigpen and Cleckley's (1957) book, *The Three Faces of Eve*, which subsequently was made into a motion picture. Thigpen and Cleckley described the case of Eve White, a young mother with a troubled marriage who sought psychotherapy for severe headaches, feelings of inertia, and "blackouts." Eve White was seen for several therapy sessions and was hypnotized during this time as a treatment for her amnesia. Then, during what proved to be a remarkable session, Eve White became agitated and complained of hearing an imaginary voice. As Thigpen and Cleckley wrote, "after a tense moment of silence, her hands dropped. There was a quick, reckless smile and, in a bright voice that sparkled, she said, 'Hi there, Doc!' " (p. 137). Eve Black had emerged—a carefree and flirtatious personality who insisted upon being called "Miss" and who scorned Eve White, the wife and mother.

Therapy with Eve White, Eve Black, and a third, more calm and mature personality, Jane, lasted over a period of 2½ years. Thigpen used hypnosis to bring out the different personalities in an attempt to understand and reconcile them with one another. He eventually adopted the goal of fading out the two Eves and allowing Jane to take control. Therapy appeared to be successful. According to the psychiatrists' account, treatment ended with one integrated personality in control. This personality was much like Jane, but she decided to call herself "Mrs. Evelyn White."

The end of therapy with Thigpen and Cleckley was not the end of therapy for "Eve." Eve, whose real name is Chris Sizemore, claims to have had a total of 22 different personalities, some of which developed before her treatment with Thigpen and Cleckley and some of which developed afterwards. The personalities always occurred in groups of three, and they always included a wife/mother image, a party girl, and a more normal, intellectual personality (Sizemore & Pittillo, 1977). Sizemore has written several books about her life, and as a well-functioning, unified personality, she has become a spokesperson for mental health concerns. In her book *A Mind of My Own*, she offers the following observations on her personalities:

Among these twenty-two alters, ten were poets, seven were artists, and one had taught tailoring. Today, I paint and write, but I cannot sew. Yet these alters were not moods or the result of role-playing. They were entities that were totally separate from the personality I was born to be, and am today. They were so different that their tones of voice changed. What's more, their facial expressions, appetites, tastes in clothes, handwritings, skills, and IQs were all different, too. (Sizemore, 1989, p. 9)

The case of Chris Sizemore dramatically illustrates the characteristics of dissociative identity disorder. Sizemore's words also foreshadow controversies about the condition. Some professionals argue that dissociative identity disorder is nothing more than role-playing; others assert that multiple personalities are very real and very common.

Epidemiology

The prevalence of dissociative disorders is difficult to establish. The conditions generally have been considered to be extremely rare. For example, only about 200 case histories of dissociative identity disorder were reported in the entire world literature prior to 1980 (Greaves, 1980). A number of clinicians have diagnosed dissociative identity disorder with much greater frequency in recent years, however. This increase in diagnosis has occurred in conjunction with

▼ **This work of art captures one experience of depersonalization: the feeling of being outside your body and watching your actions.**

the recognition of the distressingly high prevalence of child sexual abuse, a traumatic experience that is hypothesized to play a role in the etiology of many dissociative disorders (Kluft, 1987). Thus, in comparison to the 1980 survey, a 1986 report suggested that approximately 6,000 cases of dissociative identity disorder had been diagnosed in North America (Coons, 1986).

Obviously, these more recent figures constitute a dramatic increase in the diagnosis of dissociative identity disorder. In fact, a study of a random, nonclinical sample in Manitoba, Canada went even further and suggested an unbelievably high prevalence rate. According to diagnoses obtained through a structured, diagnostic interview, over 10 percent of the adult population was designated as suffering from a dissociative disorder! This figure included 7 percent of the population with dissociative amnesia, 3 percent with dissociative identity disorder, 2 percent with depersonalization disorder, and 0.2 percent with dissociative fugue (Ross, 1991).

Clearly, either some investigators have been overzealous in defining dissociative disorders,

or diagnosticians have been highly inaccurate for years. In fact, a small but apparently growing group of professionals has argued that most clinicians commonly overlook dissociative disorders. According to this analysis, many patients who are truly suffering from dissociative disorders are misdiagnosed as having schizophrenia, borderline personality disorder, depression, panic disorder, and substance abuse (Ross, Norton, & Wozney, 1989).

DISORDER OR ROLE ENACTMENT?

Despite such claims, the majority of mental health professionals remain skeptical about the prevalence of dissociative disorders. The diagnosis remains extremely rare in Europe and Japan, perhaps reflecting a North American diagnostic "fad" (Mersky, 1992). Some professionals have even raised doubts about the very existence of dissociative identity disorder, arguing that this phenomenon was created by the power of suggestion (Mersky, 1992). Canadian psychologist Nicholas Spanos has been a particularly outspoken critic, who has argued that multiple personalties are caused by role-playing. Spanos asserts that patients are influenced by their own and their therapists' goals and expectations about dissociative identity disorder, and, like an actor who loses all perspective, eventually they may come to believe that the role is real.

In support of his theorizing, Spanos and his colleagues have conducted analogue experiments on role-playing and the "symptoms" of dissociative identity disorder. These studies were inspired by the case of Kenneth Bianchi, the infamous "Hillside Strangler." In 1979, Bianchi was charged with murdering two college women and was implicated in several other rape–murder cases where victims were left naked on the hillsides of Los Angeles. Considerable evidence supported Bianchi's guilt, but he reported frequent episodes of "blanking out," including an inability to remember events from the night that the murders were committed. At the request of his attorney, Bianchi was seen by a mental health expert, who hypnotized Bianchi and suggested to him, "I've talked a bit to Ken, but I think that perhaps there might be another part of Ken that I haven't talked to, another part that maybe feels somewhat differently from the part I've talked to. And I would like to communicate with that other part" (Watkins, 1984).

Bianchi responded that he was not Ken but Steve. Steve knew of Ken, and he hated him. Steve also confessed to strangling "all of these girls."

Numerous experts who interviewed Bianchi disagreed about whether his apparent dissociative identity disorder was real or feigned. In fact, the conflicting expert opinion reveals the unreliability of the diagnosis (Aldridge-Morris, 1989). One of the experts was psychologist and psychiatrist Martin Orne, an internationally recognized authority on hypnosis. Orne tested Bianchi by suggesting new symptoms to him. If Bianchi was faking dissociative identity disorder, he might further the deception by developing the new symptoms. Orne suggested, for example, that if Bianchi really had dissociative identity disorder, he should have a third personality. Sure enough, a third personality, Billy, "emerged" when Bianchi was subsequently hypnotized (Orne, Dinges, & Orne, 1984). While hypnotized, Bianchi also followed Orne's suggestion to hallucinate that his attorney was in the room. Bianchi actually shook hands with the supposed hallucination—a very unusual behavior because tactile hallucinations are rare for someone under hypnosis. Orne concluded from this and other evidence that Bianchi was indeed faking, and that Bianchi actually suffered from antisocial personality disorder (see Chapter 9). Bianchi's insanity defense failed, and he was found guilty of murder.

In testing his role theory, Spanos simulated procedures from the Bianchi case. In one study, undergraduate students played the role of accused murderer and were randomly assigned to one of three conditions. In the "Bianchi" condition, the subjects were hypnotized, and the interviewer asked to communicate with their other part—just as Bianchi's interviewer had asked. Subjects assigned to the second, "hidden part" condition also were hypnotized, but this time it was suggested that hypnosis could get behind the "wall" that hid inner thoughts and feelings from awareness. In the final condition, there was no hypnosis, and subjects simply were told that personality included "walls" between hidden thoughts and feelings.

When subsequently asked "Who are you?" by the interviewer in the mock murder case, 81 percent of the subjects in the Bianchi condition gave a name different from the one assigned to them in the role play, as did 70 percent of the subjects in the hidden part condition. In con-

trast, only 31 percent of the subjects in the no-hypnosis condition gave a new name. Increases in amnesia also were found for the two hypnosis conditions in comparison to the control group (Spanos, Weekes, & Bertrand, 1985). These results were replicated in a subsequent study. In this later experiment, hypnotized subjects also provided more "information" on exactly when in the past their alternate personalities had first emerged (Spanos et al., 1986).

These findings certainly raise the caution that the "symptoms" of dissociative identity disorder can be induced through role-playing and hypnosis. However, analogue studies cannot prove that role-playing causes real cases of multiple personality. Given the current status of research, we reach a cautious conclusion about the epidemiology of dissociative disorders. True dissociative disorders appear to be rare, and although some cases no doubt are misdiagnosed, a much greater problem is the creation of the diagnosis in the minds of clinicians and clients (Mersky, 1992). At the same time, we do not doubt the existence of the dissociative disorders. These real but apparently rare psychological problems raise probing questions not only about the disorders themselves, but about the very nature of the human psyche.

Etiological Considerations and Research

Little systematic research has been conducted on the etiology of dissociative disorders. Thus, theory and outright speculation dominate discussions of the etiology of the disorder. One exception is the widely held view that the disorders often are precipitated by trauma, a view that is beginning to find some research support. In fact, some researchers have argued that post-traumatic stress disorder (see Chapter 7) and dissociative disorders should be classified together because of some similarity in symptoms and because of the role of trauma in the etiology of both problems (Spiegel & Cardena, 1991).

Trauma may contribute to dissociative disorders, but it clearly is not a sufficient cause. Many people experience trauma without developing a dissociative disorder. Thus, consistent with the systems perspective, other biological, psychological, and social factors must contribute to the etiology of these disorders, as we consider in the following sections.

BIOLOGICAL FACTORS

Virtually no evidence and little speculation has been offered about the role of biological factors in the etiology of dissociative disorders. Some researchers have theorized that disturbances of the temporal lobe of the brain, including seizure disorders, play a role in dissociative identity disorder (Mesulam, 1981), but this possibility has not been systemically investigated. Still, it is known that dissociative states or permanent dissociation can result from biological causes. Examples include the dramatic personality changes that sometimes accompany substance use or abuse (see Chapter 10) and the amnesia that is found in various cognitive disorders associated with aging (see Chapter 13).

Biological contributions to dissociation are dramatically suggested by investigations of unusual perceptual disturbances. For example, *prosopagnosia* is an impairment of face recognition that sometimes follows specific forms of brain damage. Patients with prosopagnosia report that they are unable to recognize faces, but indirect testing indicates that recognition occurs at some

tion between conscious and unconscious cognitive processes, since recognition must be occurring at some preconscious level.

Such findings have limited direct implications for understanding the etiology of dissociative disorders. In DSM-IV, a diagnosis of dissociative disorders is explicitly excluded if the dissociation occurs in conjunction with substance abuse or organic pathology. Evidence that biological factors can produce dissociative symptoms does have two important implications, however. First, these findings offer further evidence of the existence of dissociation in cognitive processing. The challenge of explaining unconscious processes is a real one in contemporary science, not merely a remnant of Freudian theory. Second, research on prosopagnosia suggests avenues and methods for future research.

PSYCHOLOGICAL FACTORS

As noted earlier, there is little controversy about the idea that trauma can produce dissociative amnesia and fugue, because the onset of the dissociation often can be traced to a specific traumatic experience. A more controversial question is the extent to which trauma plays a role in the etiology of dissociative identity disorder. Many case histories suggest that multiple personalities develop in response to trauma, particularly the trauma of child abuse.

In support of this observation, some recent research has compiled large numbers of case histories from surveys of practitioners. As Table 8–2 indicates, a history of childhood sexual abuse was indicated in 79 percent of 236 cases of dissociative identity disorder, according to the results of one survey. Physical abuse was reported in 75 percent of the same cases. Other surveys of clinicians have reported similar results (Kluft, 1987; Putnam, Guroff, et al., 1986; see Table 8–2). When interpreting these findings, however, be aware that they are case observations based on patients' memories and clinicians' evaluations. They are not objective assessments of the past.

Researchers have raised many concerns about the validity of such **retrospective reports**—evaluations of the past from the vantage point of the present (see Research Methods later in the chapter). A particular concern is that memories may be selectively recalled, may be distorted, or may even be created to conform with subsequent experiences. This possibility has become a pressing and controversial issue in relation to

---

TABLE 8–2

Features of Dissociative Identity Disorder in Two Large-Scale Surveys of Clinicians' Case Histories

Item	Ross[1] N = 236	Putnam[2] N = 100
Average age	30.8	35.8
Percentage of females	87.7%	92.0%
Average years of treatment before diagnosis	6.7	6.8
Average number of personalities	15.7	13.3
Opposite-sex personality present	62.6%	53.0%
Amnesia between personalities	94.9%	98.0%
Past suicide attempt	72.0%	71.0%
History of child physical abuse	74.9%	75.0%
History of child sexual abuse	79.2%	83.0%

[1] Based on data from C.A. Ross, G.R. Norton, & K. Wozney (1989). Multiple personality disorder: An analysis of 236 cases. *Canadian Journal of Psychiatry, 34,* 413–418.

[2] Based on data from F.W. Putnam, J.J. Curoff, et al. (1986). The clinical phenomenology of multiple personality disorder: Review of 100 recent cases. *Journal of Clinical Psychiatry, 47,* 285–293.

---

lower level of perception or consciousness. In particular, patients with prosopagnosia demonstrate the normal preference for viewing faces that are familiar, even though they claim that the face is not familiar to them (Farah, O'Reilly, & Vecera, 1993). This finding implies a dissocia-

Recovered Memories?

In 1990, George Franklin was convicted of the brutal murder of an 8-year-old girl. The crime had occurred over 20 years earlier, and the major evidence was the "recovered memory" of Franklin's daughter Eileen. Eileen claimed to have witnessed the rape and murder of her friend by her father, but dissociation pushed the memory of the horrid experience into her unconscious. Twenty years later, according to the daughter, the memory returned. In fact, Eileen provided both verifiable and inconsistent accounts of the horrifying event. She recalled a smashed ring on her friend's finger as she raised her hand to protect herself from a blow with a rock. Case records corroborated the memory. On the other hand, Eileen changed her story about the presence of her sister in the van she was riding in that day, and she changed the time of day from morning to afternoon. George Franklin was convicted of murder, but the question remains; Was Eileen's memory accurate?

Recovered memories have become an important and controversial issue. Popular books and earnest therapists urge people to unearth past traumas, particularly remembrances of physical and sexual abuse, and an increasing number of people have claimed that they have recovered horrible memories from the past. Many parents faced with accusations about the past suggest, however, that they are being caused to suffer unnecessary pain. They suggest that false memories are being created by misguided, overeager therapists. Are recovered memories examples of dissociation, or are they merely examples of the power of suggestion?

This question was recently examined in detail by psychologist Elizabeth Loftus (1993), a specialist in memories of painful events who has served as an expert witness in numerous trials. Although it is impossible to verify—or disprove—many memories from the distant past, Loftus suggests numerous reasons for skepticism, or at least caution. One area of recovered memories that Loftus clearly disputes are recollections that date to very early childhood. A number of people have claimed to recall trauma dating from infancy or toddlerhood, but such mem-

ories are inconsistent with current knowledge of memory in early childhood. Most memories prior to school age are forgotten, and few people can report memories dating back before age 3 or 4. One study found, for example, that few subjects who were under the age of 3 at the time could recall where they were when President Kennedy was assassinated. In contrast, most subjects who had been at least 8 years old at the time of the assassination reported at least some memory of being told about the tragedy (Winograd & Killinger, 1983).

More suspicions emerge from an examination of some case histories of recovered memories. Studies indicate that therapists rarely doubt their clients' recovered memories of the past (Loftus, 1993), but the concern embraces much more than a lack of skepticism. Many therapists and popular books encourage people to search for (create?) memories that they do not recall. Symptoms as common and mild as low self-esteem are sometimes interpreted as indications of past, forgotten trauma. Gaps in memory are also interpreted as a sign of dissociated memories. One example of this approach is noted in the popular book *The Courage to Heal.* The authors state:

> You may think you don't have memories, but often as you begin to talk about what you do remember, there emerges a constellation of feelings, reactions and recollections that add up to substantial information. To say, 'I was abused,' you don't need the kind of recall that would stand up in a court of law.

> Often the knowledge that you were abused starts with a tiny feeling, an intuition. It's important to trust that inner voice and work from there. Assume your feelings are valid. So far, no one we've talked to thought she might have been abused, and then later discovered that she hadn't been. (Bass & Davis, 1988, p. 22)

Could such suggestions lead some people to create memories about events that never happened? We think the answer is "yes." Determining the truth in any one case is difficult, sometimes impossible. Nevertheless, there is considerable evidence that memories, even of highly dramatic events, can be inaccurate (Loftus, 1993). In one study, subjects were interviewed the day after the explosion of the space shuttle *Challenger,* and described the circumstances of how they learned of the memorable tragedy on the previous day. Three years later, the same subjects were reinterviewed. They were again asked how they had learned about the *Challenger* tragedy. It was found that about one-third of the subjects reported vivid—and grossly inaccurate—memories of what they were doing and how they learned about the *Challenger* (Neisser & Harsch, 1992).

These observations do not prove that recovered memories are false, but they do suggest grounds for skepticism. A therapist's unwillingness to believe a patient can damage the therapeutic relationship, but false memories also can produce great harm to anyone who is falsely accused. Skepticism and clinical sensitivity are not incompatible. There is dramatic and apparently accurate evidence to suggest that traumatic memories sometimes are repressed. Dissociation should not be dismissed merely because it is difficult to demonstrate. On the other hand, psychologists must not be overzealous in assuming certain knowledge about topics that inherently involve much uncertainty. ■

▲ **Eileen Franklin at the murder trial of her father, George. Ms. Franklin testified about her "recovered memories" of witnessing her father's rape and murder of an 8-year-old girl. George Franklin was tried and convicted of murder more than 20 years after the girl's death.**

"recovered memories"—recollections of long-forgotten traumatic experiences that supposedly occurred during childhood. Some professionals and lay enthusiasts have searched so hard to recover their own or others' unconscious memories that psychologists recently have become concerned that many "memories" may have been created by the power of suggestion (see Further Thoughts).

An adequate test of the hypothesized relation between child abuse and dissociative disorders requires prospective research using objective assessments of dissociation. Assuming for the moment that this relation is real, however, how might child abuse lead to the development of multiple personalities? One theory suggests that the trauma overwhelms children's usual intrapsychic defenses, and dissociation is used as a more dramatic alternative. According to this perspective, over time dissociation increasingly is used as a means of coping with distress. If the memory of the trauma is not resolved or if the traumatic experience is repeated (as in many cases of child abuse), the recurrent use of dissociation can lead to the development of full, alternative personalities during adolescence (Kluft, 1987).

A similar model of the psychological etiology of multiple personality disorders invokes the concept of **state-dependent learning**. Laboratory research has demonstrated that learning that occurs in one state of affect or consciousness is best recalled in the same state of affect or consciousness (Bower, 1990). For example, memories that are acquired when you are sad are more easily recalled during future times when you are sad rather than happy. By extension, some people have hypothesized that experiences that occur during a dissociated state are most easily recalled within the same state of consciousness. Through the repeated experience of trauma, dissociation, and state-dependent learning, more complete and autonomous memories develop over time. Ultimately, this process results in the development of independent personality states that dominate during different states of consciousness (Braun, 1989).

Other speculation has focused on hypnosis as both a cause of, and a treatment for, dissociative disorders. Janet and Freud both were impressed by the similarity in the dissociation experienced during hypnotic states and in hysteria, and at least one contemporary writer has suggested that multiple personality disorder is caused by self-hypnosis (Bliss, 1986). The same questions that have been raised about dissociation can be asked about hypnosis, however. In particular, there is debate about whether hypnosis represents an independent state of consciousness or whether different individuals merely are more or less susceptible to suggestion and only appear to be "hypnotized" (Frankel, 1990; see Research Close-up). Obviously, the possible etiological role of hypnosis in the development of dissociation depends on accurate answers to this question.

SOCIAL FACTORS

Few interpersonal or societal factors have been suggested to play a role in the development of dissociative disorders. One exception is that some clinicians have pointed to the risk posed by relationships that are simultaneously abusive and loving. For example, dissociation has been hypothesized to be more common when children are abused by parents. In this circumstance, the child obviously cannot seek parental support in coping with the trauma. Instead, she or he must rely on internal coping mechanisms. According to this speculation, if the conflict between the terror of the abuse and the need for love is great, the child may cope by dissociating these two experiences (Braun, 1989).

A sociological view offers a very different perspective on the etiology of dissociative disorders. At least one theorist has suggested that dissociative disorders are produced by **iatrogenesis,** the manufacture of the dissociative disorders by their treatment. Mersky (1992) reviewed classic case histories of dissociative identity disorder and concluded that many "cases" were created by the expectations of therapists. Mersky does not doubt the pain experienced by the patients in these cases. He argues, however, that they developed multiple personalities in response to leading questions asked by their therapists, not as a result of their own defense mechanisms. Thus, consistent with Spanos's theorizing discussed earlier, Mersky asserts that dissociative identity disorder is little more than a social role. A recent twist on this reasoning is that perhaps highly hypnotizable people are convinced that they have a dissociative disorder because of their susceptibility to suggestion (Kihlstrom, Glisky, & Angiulo, 1994).

Treatment of Dissociative Disorders

Dating from the time of Janet and Freud, perhaps the central aspect of the treatment of dis-

sociative disorders has been uncovering and recounting past traumatic events. A basic assumption of this approach is that dissociation occurs as a response to unacceptable and overwhelming trauma. Thus, it is presumed that if the trauma can be expressed and accepted, then the need for dissociation will disappear.

As we have already noted, many clinicians use hypnosis to help patients explore and relive traumatic events. The painful experience is assumed to be more easily recalled while the patient is under hypnosis. These recollections, in turn, are thought to facilitate the integration of the trauma into conscious experience. Unfortunately, no research is available either on *abreaction*, the emotional reliving of a past traumatic experience, or on hypnosis as a treatment for dissociative disorders.

In addition to helping patients reexperience trauma, clinical experts emphasize the need to win the trust of the dissociative patient (Braun, 1989; Kluft, 1987). In particular, therapists underscore the importance of establishing rapport with each of the personalities of patients who suffer from dissociative identity disorder. The difficulty of this task can be readily recognized if you recall that, in theory, each personality has developed as a protection against the others.

Clinicians also note that the goal of treatment is not to have one personality triumph over the others. Rather, the objective is to reintegrate the different personalities into a whole. This is not unlike the far-less-difficult task faced by all of us as we struggle to integrate the different life roles we play into a coherent sense of self.

Antianxiety, antidepressant, and antipsychotic medications also may play a role in the treatment of dissociative disorders. The objective in prescribing these medications is to reduce distress, not to cure the disorder. The ultimate goal of reintegrating the dissociated states, memories, or personalities is considered to be more of a psychological than a pharmaceutical task.

At this time, little research has been conducted on the effectiveness of any treatment for dissociative disorders, let alone on the comparison of alternative treatments. Advances in therapy await a more accurate description of the disorder and, more generally, a better understanding of the split between conscious and unconscious cognitive processes.

Somatoform Disorders

In addition to dissociative disorders, the old diagnostic category *hysteria* included what we now know as somatoform disorders—somatic symptoms in the absence of a physical illness. Indeed, somatoform disorders are synonymous with hysteria in the eyes of many people, because Janet and Freud frequently wrote case histories about patients with unusual and unexplained physical symptoms.

Typical Symptoms and Associated Features

All somatoform disorders involve complaints about physical symptoms. In contrast to psychosomatic disorders (see Chapter 7), the symptoms of somatoform disorders cannot be explained by an underlying organic impairment. There is nothing physically wrong with the patient. The symptoms are not feigned, however, as the physical problem is very real in the mind of the person with a somatoform disorder.

The physical symptoms can take a number of different forms. In some dramatic cases, the symptom involves substantial impairment of a somatic system, particularly a sensory or muscular system. The patient will be unable to see, for example, or will report a paralysis in one arm. In other types of somatoform disorder, patients experience multiple physical symptoms rather than a single, substantial impairment. In these cases, patients usually have numerous, constantly evolving complaints about such problems as chronic pain, upset stomach, and dizziness. Finally, some types of somatoform disorder are defined by a preoccupation with a particular part of the body or with fears about a particular illness. The patient may constantly worry that he or she has contracted some deadly disease, for example, and the anxiety persists despite negative medical tests and clear reassurance by a physician.

The following brief case history illustrates an unusual type of somatoform disorder called *body dysmorphic disorder*. People with body dysmorphic disorder are constantly preoccupied with some imagined defect in their physical appearance.

> **BRIEF CASE STUDY**
>
> **Body Dysmorphic Disorder**
> A 28-year-old single white man became preoccupied at the age of 18 with his minimally thinning hair. Despite reassurance from others that his hair loss was not noticeable, he worried about it for hours a day, becoming "deeply depressed," socially withdrawn, and unable to attend classes or do his schoolwork. Although he could acknowledge the excessiveness of his preoccupation, he was unable to stop it. He saw four dermatologists but was not comforted by their reassurances that his hair loss was minor and that treatment was unnecessary. The patient's preoccupation and subsequent depression have persisted for 10 years and have continued to interfere with his social life and work, to the extent that he avoids most social events and has been able to work only part-time as a baker. He only recently sought psychiatric referral, at the insistence of his girlfriend, who said his symptoms were ruining their relationship. (Phillips, 1991, pp. 1138–39) ■

Unnecessary Medical Treatment

As this case illustrates, people with somatoform disorders typically do not bring their problems to the attention of a mental health professional. Instead, they repeatedly consult their physicians about their "physical" problems (National Institute of Mental Health, 1990). This often leads to unnecessary medical treatment. In the Epidemiologic Catchment Area study of the prevalence of mental illness in the general population, patients who met the diagnostic criteria for *somatization disorder* (another subtype of somatoform disorder) had seen a health care provider for an average of more than 6 visits during the previous 6 months (Swartz et al., 1987).

In addition, 25 percent of people diagnosed with somatization disorder had been hospitalized in the past year, compared with 12 percent of the general population (Swartz et al., 1990).

Unlike the young man who was preoccupied with hair loss, patients with somatoform disorders often complain about realistic physical symptoms that are difficult to evaluate objectively. Thus, physicians frequently do not recognize the psychological nature of the patient's problems, and they sometimes perform unnecessary medical procedures. For example, patients with somatoform disorders have surgery twice as often as people in the general population (Zoccolillo & Cloninger, 1986). In fact, some common surgical procedures are performed with startling frequency on patients with somatoform disorders. One research group concluded that, after discounting cancer surgeries, 27 percent of women undergoing a hysterectomy suffered from somatization disorder (Martin et al., 1980).

Such data are distressing, not only because of the risk to the patient, but also because of the costs of unnecessary medical treatment. Estimates indicate that anywhere from 20 to 84 percent of patients who consult physicians do so for problems for which no organic cause can be found (Swartz et al., 1990). Such visits may account for as much as *half* of all ambulatory health-care costs (Kellner, 1985). A variety of emotional problems can motivate people to consult their physicians, but much excessive health-care utilization is specific to somatoform disorders. Patients with somatization disorder are 3 times more likely to consult physicians than are depressed patients, for example (Morrison & Herbstein, 1988; Zoccolillo & Cloninger, 1986). In fact, health-care expenditures for patients with somatization disorder are 9 times the average annual per capita cost of medical treatment (Smith et al., 1986).

Classification

The DSM-IV lists five major subcategories of somatoform disorders: (1) body dysmorphic disorder, (2) hypochondriasis, (3) somatization disorder, (4) pain disorder, and (5) conversion disorder.

BODY DYSMORPHIC DISORDER

In **body dysmorphic disorder** the patient is preoccupied with some imagined defect in appearance, as illustrated in the case of the man with thinning hair. The preoccupation typically focuses on some facial feature such as the nose or mouth, and in some cases may lead to repeated visits to a plastic surgeon. Preoccupation with the body part far exceeds normal worries about physical imperfections. The endless worry causes significant distress, and in extreme cases, it may interfere with work or social relationships.

Little research has been conducted on body dysmorphic disorder. The problem has received more attention among European and Asian mental health professionals than in the United States, but systematic research has not been conducted anywhere. One controversy is whether the diagnosis should be grouped with other somatoform disorders. In Japan and Korea, body dysmorphic disorder is classified as a type of social phobia (Phillips, 1991).

▲ Body dysmorphic disorder is characterized by a preoccupation with some imagined defect in appearance.

HYPOCHONDRIASIS

A more typical subtype of somatoform disorder is **hypochondriasis,** a problem characterized by a fear or belief that the individual is suffering from a physical illness. Aspects of this mental disorder surely are familiar to you. The pejorative term *hypochondriac* is a part of everyday language. We all worry about our health, and even unrealistic worries sometimes are normal. Medical students often fear that they have contracted each new disease they encounter in their studies. Many students in abnormal psychology worry that each problem they read about is a perfect description of themselves!

Hypochondriasis is much more serious than these normal and fleeting worries. The preoccupation with fears of disease extends over long periods of time. The worries must last for at least 6 months according to DSM-IV criteria. In addition, in hypochondriasis, a thorough medical evaluation or examination does not alleviate the fear of the disease. The person still worries that the illness may be emerging or that a test was overlooked. Still, the anxiety of hypochondriasis falls short of being delusional. For example, a person may worry excessively about contracting AIDS and therefore may repeatedly go for blood tests. When faced with negative results, however, the person does not delusionally believe that he or she actually has contracted the illness. Nevertheless, the persistent worries that characterize hypochondriasis are severe and preoccupying, and often result in substantial impairment in life functioning.

SOMATIZATION DISORDER

Somatization disorder is a type of somatoform disorder that is characterized by a history of multiple, somatic complaints in the absence of organic impairments. The extent of the health concerns in somatization disorder is apparent from a cursory examination of the DSM-IV diagnostic criteria. In order to be diagnosed with somatization disorder, the patient must complain of at least eight physical symptoms as listed in Table 8–3. The complaints must involve multiple somatic systems, moreover, including symptoms of pain, gastrointestinal symptoms (for example, nausea and diarrhea), sexual symptoms (sexual dysfunction, menstrual difficulties), and pseudoneurologic symptoms. *Pseudoneurologic symptoms* are complaints that mimic neurological diseases—for example, double vision, numbness, seizures, and amnesia (see Table 8–3).

Patients with somatization disorders sometimes present their symptoms in a *histrionic* manner—a vague but dramatic, self-centered, and seductive style (see Chapter 9). Patients also occasionally exhibit **la belle indifference** ("beautiful indifference"), a flippant lack of concern about the physical symptoms. A patient may list a long series of somatic complaints in an offhanded and cheerful manner, for example. Although some clinicians have viewed either or both of these styles as defining characteristics of somatization disorders, research indicates that they are found in only a minority of cases (Lipowski, 1988).

In contrast to some stereotypes, somatization disorder is not more common among the aged, who consult health-care professionals frequently because of chronic and real physical

▲ **Felix Unger, a character from** *The Odd Couple* **played here by Jack Lemmon, had numerous hypochondriacal complaints—much to the annoyance of his roommate, Oscar (portrayed by Walter Matthau).**

illnesses (National Institute of Mental Health, 1990). In fact, somatization disorder often begins in adolescence, and it must have an onset prior to the age of 30 according to DSM-IV criteria. The problem is sometimes referred to as *Briquet's syndrome*, in recognition of French physician Pierre Briquet, who was among the first to call attention to the multiple somatic complaints found in some "hysterias" (Goodwin & Guze, 1979; National Institute of Mental Health, 1990).

PAIN DISORDER

As its name implies, **pain disorder** is a subtype of somatoform disorder that is characterized by preoccupation with pain. Although there is no objective way to evaluate pain, psychological factors are judged to be significant in creating or intensifying the chronic pain in pain disorder. Complaints seem excessive and apparently are motivated at least in part by psychological factors. Some pain disorder patients may seem to relish the attention their illness brings to them. The DSM-IV distinguishes between pain disorder that occurs with associated problems in general medical conditions and pain disorder that appears in the absence of such problems. For example, low back pain that begins following a physical injury would be differentiated from back pain that cannot be traced to any physical cause.

As with hypochondriasis and somatization disorder, pain disorder can lead to the repeated, unnecessary use of medical treatments. People who experience chronic pain are at a particular risk for developing a dependence on minor tranquilizers or painkillers. The disorder also frequently disrupts social and occupational functioning.

CONVERSION DISORDER

In many respects, the classic type of somatoform disorder is **conversion disorder**. The symptoms of conversion disorder often mimic those found in neurological diseases, and they can be dramatic. "Hysterical" blindness or "hysterical" paralysis are examples of conversion symptoms. Although conversion disorders often resemble neurological impairments, some can be distinguished from these disorders because they make no anatomical sense. The patient may complain about anesthesia (or pain) in a way that does not correspond with the innervation of the body part. In some facial anesthesias, for exam-

TABLE 8–3

DSM-IV Diagnostic Criteria for Somatization Disorder

A. A history of many physical complaints beginning before age 30 that occur over a period of several years and result in treatment being sought or significant impairment in social, occupational, or other important areas of functioning.

B. Each of the following criteria must have been met, with individual symptoms occurring at any time during the course of the disturbance.

1. Four pain symptoms: A history of pain related to at least four different sites or functions (for example, head, abdomen, back, joints, extremities, chest, rectum, during sexual intercourse, during menstruation, or during urination)

2. Two gastrointestinal symptoms: A history of at least two gastrointestinal symptoms other than pain (for example, nausea, diarrhea, bloating, vomiting other than during pregnancy, or intolerance of several different foods)

3. One sexual symptom: A history of at least one sexual or reproductive symptom other than pain (for example, sexual indifference, erectile or ejaculatory dysfunction, irregular menses, excessive menstrual bleeding, vomiting throughout pregnancy)

4. One pseudoneurologic symptom: A history of at least one symptom or deficit suggesting a neurological disorder not limited to pain (conversion symptoms such as blindness, double vision, deafness, loss of touch or pain sensation, hallucinations, aphonia, impaired coordination or balance, paralysis or localized weakness, difficulty swallowing or lump in throat, difficulty breathing, urinary retention, seizures; disso-

---

ple, numbness begins at the middle of the face; but the nerves involved in sensation do not divide the face into equal halves (see Figure 8–1).

The term *conversion disorder* accurately conveys the central assumption of the diagnosis—the idea that psychological conflicts are converted into physical symptoms. Conversion disorders were the problems that particularly captivated the attention of Charcot, Freud, and Janet and that led them to develop theories about unconscious mental processes. The following case is from Janet's writings, and it illustrates his view of hysteria.

BRIEF CASE STUDY

A Case Study from Janet

A girl of nineteen years of age suffered, at the time of her monthly period, convulsive and delirious attacks which lasted several days. Menstruation began normally, but a few hours after the commencement of the flow the patient complained of feeling very cold and had a characteristic shivering; menstruation was immediately arrested and delirium ensued. In the interval of these attacks the patient had paroxysms of terror with

the hallucination of blood spreading out before her, and also showed various permanent stigmata, among others anesthesia of the left side of the face with amaurosis of the left eye.

During a careful study of this patient's history, and particularly of the memories she had conserved of various experiences of her life, certain pertinent facts were ascertained. At the age of thirteen years she had attempted to arrest menstruation by plunging into a tub of cold water with resulting shivering and delirium; menstruation was immediately arrested and did not recur for several years; when it did reappear the disturbance I have just cited took place. Later on she had been terrified by seeing an old woman fall on the stairs and deluge the steps with her blood. At another time, when she was about nine years old, she had been obliged to sleep with a child whose face, on the left side, was covered with scabs, and during the whole night she had experienced a feeling of intense disgust and horror. (Janet, 1914/1915, pp. 3–4) ■

This case describes symptoms that are consistent with conversion disorder. The numbness on the left side of the face of Janet's young patient is a clear example of a conversion symptom. At the same time, we wonder about other aspects of this classic case. The frightening hallucinations of blood might suggest another diagnosis, perhaps psychotic depression (see Chapter 5) or schizophrenia (see Chapter 12), with the conversion symptom as a secondary aspect of the case. Many alternative diagnoses were not available during the time of Charcot, Janet, and Freud, and this might explain why conversion disorders once were thought to be quite prevalent but are uncommon today.

Anesthesia Responses

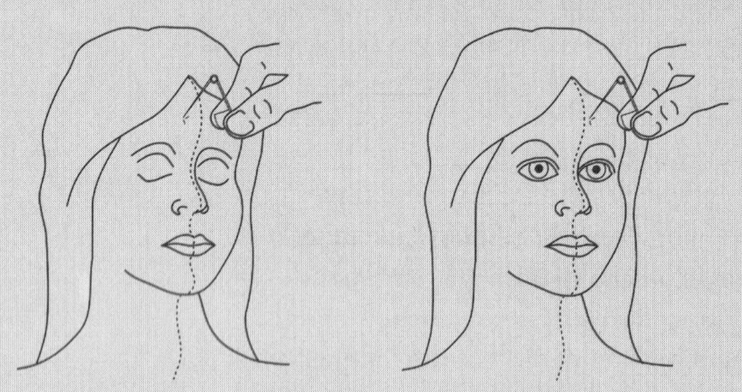

FIGURE 8-1: In certain types of anesthesia, a person does not seem to feel a pinprick on one side of the face. This response, however, is not consistent with the patterns of innervation in the facial area. That is, the nerves involved in sensation do not divide the face in half. This suggests that the problem is psychological, not neurological, in origin.

Adapted from D.M. Kaufman. (1985). *Clinical neurology for psychiatrists*, 2nd ed. Orlando, Fl: Grune and Stratton, p. 28.

Epidemiology

No one knows how prevalent conversion disorders were during the time of Charcot, Janet, and Freud, but the literature of the period suggests that they were common (Shorter, 1992). Today, conversion disorders are rare. For example, one investigation found only a 0.4 percent prevalence of conversion symptoms in an urban community sample (Weissman et al., 1978), a figure which probably overestimates the prevalence in the general population. Ironically, the unusual disorders treated by Freud and Janet

appear to have been less enduring than the theories they developed to explain them. This change in prevalence across time may be a result of improved diagnostic practices, as we have suggested, or it may reflect the role of society in the etiology of conversion disorder, a theory that we discuss shortly.

Other somatoform disorders appear to be equally rare, although sound epidemiological research has not been conducted on hypochondriasis, body dysmorphic disorder, and pain disorder. According to the Epidemiologic Catchment Area study, the lifetime prevalence of somatization disorder within the 50 states is only 0.13 percent (Swartz et al., 1990). On the other hand, physical complaints that do not meet all of the diagnostic criteria for somatization disorder are very common. In the same study, 11.6 percent of people were found to suffer from four to six physical symptoms with no identifiable organic cause (fewer than the eight required for the diagnosis of somatization disorder; see Table 8–3) (Swartz et al., 1990).

Hypochondriasis is equally common among men and women, but all other forms of somatoform disorder are more common among women. This is particularly true of somatization disorder, which is 10 times more common among females than among males (Swartz et al., 1990). The disproportionate number of women is consistent with early observations about "hysteria."

Somatization disorder also is more common among lower socioeconomic groups and among people who have less than a high school education. It is 4 times as common among African Americans as among Americans of European heritage, and a considerably higher rate of somatization disorder (0.7 percent) has been reported for Puerto Rico than for the U.S. mainland (Canino, Bird, et al., 1987). Finally, more somatic symptoms are found among people who have lost a spouse through divorce, separation, or death. Never-married adults actually have lower rates than the married population, suggesting that loss may play a role in the etiology of the disorder (Swartz et al., 1990).

CO-MORBIDITY

An important epidemiological issue is the overlap between somatoform disorders and other psychological problems. People who suffer from somatoform disorders, particularly somatization disorder and hypochondriasis, also frequently suffer from depression (Bridges & Goldberg, 1985; Prestige & Lake, 1987; Swartz et al., 1990). The link between depression and somatoform disorders has several possible explanations. Either condition may cause the other, or both could be caused by a third variable such as life stress. One possibility that primary care physicians should consider is that some patients may express depression indirectly through their somatic complaints (Lipowski, 1988). This possibility is particularly important to consider. Evidence indicates that the majority of depressed people approach their primary care physician first about their problems, but less than half of them are appropriately diagnosed and treated (Prestige & Lake, 1987).

Increased anxiety also is associated with hypochondriasis and somatization disorder (National Institute of Mental Health, 1990; Swartz et al., 1990). As with depression, there are several possible explanations for this co-morbidity, including some similarities in the defining symptoms of hypochondriasis or somatization disorder and generalized anxiety disorder. A particular concern is the accurate, differential diagnosis of panic disorder (see Chapter 6). Some symptoms of panic such as dizziness, numbness, and fears about dying may be dismissed by physicians, or they may be misdiagnosed as either hypochondriasis or somatization disorder (Lipowski, 1988).

Finally, somatization disorder has frequently been linked with antisocial personality disorder, a lifelong pattern of irresponsible behavior that involves habitual violations of social rules (see Chapter 9). The two disorders do not typically co-occur in the same individual, but they often are found in different members of the same family (Lilienfeld, 1992). The problems share other similarities as well. Both begin early in life, have a chronic course, are more common among lower socioeconomic groups, and are associated with marital troubles, substance abuse, and suicide attempts. Because antisocial personality disorder is far more common among men, while somatization disorder has the opposite pattern, some have speculated that the two problems are flip sides of the same coin. Antisocial personality disorder is seen as the male expression of high negative emotion and the absence of inhibition, whereas somatization disorder is viewed as the female expression of the same underlying characteristics (Lilienfeld, 1992).

Etiological Considerations and Research

Little systematic research has been conducted on the etiology of somatoform disorders. Few contemporary hypotheses have been offered about these problems, moreover, despite their historical significance in Janet's and Freud's theories about unconscious psychological processes. We consider perspectives on the etiology of somatoform disorders in the context of the biopsychosocial model. However, the limited evidence prohibits us from offering a complete, systemic model of contributing factors.

BIOLOGICAL FACTORS

An obvious—and potentially critical—biological consideration in somatoform disorders is the possibility of misdiagnosis. A patient may be incorrectly diagnosed as suffering from a somatoform disorder when, in fact, he or she actually has a real physical illness that is undetected or is perhaps unknown. The diagnosis of a somatoform disorder requires that no organic cause of the symptom can be identified. This is very different from the positive identification of a psychological cause of the symptom.

Diagnosis by Exclusion Because mental health professionals currently cannot demonstrate psychological causes of physical symptoms objectively and unequivocally, the identification of somatoform disorders involves a process called *diagnosis by exclusion*. The physical complaint is assumed to be a part of a somatoform disorder only when various known physical causes are excluded or ruled out. The possibility always remains, however, that an incipient somatic disease has been overlooked. Some of the problems with diagnosis by exclusion can be appreciated by way of analogy. Consider the difference in certainty between two police line-ups, one in which a victim positively identifies a criminal—"That's him!"—versus a second in which an identification is made by ruling out alternatives; "It isn't him or him or him, so it must be that one."

The possibility of misdiagnosis is more than a theoretical concern. Follow-up studies of patients diagnosed as suffering from conversion disorders indicate that somatic illnesses are later detected in some cases (Shalev & Munitz, 1986). Typically, a neurological disease such as epilepsy or multiple sclerosis is the eventual diagnosis. In one classic study, about a quarter of patients diagnosed as having a conversion symptom later were found to develop a neurological disease (Slater, 1965). Thus, a significant number of cases of "somatoform disorder" eventually may prove to be real, neurological diseases. This possibility poses a dilemma for diagnosticians. They must weigh the consequences of an incorrect diagnosis of somatoform disorder against the consequences of incorrectly diagnosing a psychological problem as a physical illness.

Perhaps because somatoform disorders are diagnosed only after ruling out numerous potential biological illnesses, few theorists have speculated about biological contributions to somatoform disorders themselves. This is unfortunate, because biological factors may increase the risk for certain somatoform disorders. Even if no biological abnormalities are involved, somatoform disorders pose a challenge for neuroscientists. Brain researchers must explain how neuroanatomy or neurophysiology can account for the dramatic dissociation between psychological and somatic experience found in some of these puzzling problems.

PSYCHOLOGICAL FACTORS

Both Janet and Freud developed psychological theories in an attempt to explain the dissociation between emotional conflicts and physical symptoms. Both theorists initially assumed that a traumatic experience was the starting point for conversion disorder. According to their reasoning, the trauma overwhelmed normal coping efforts, and unconscious coping processes were called into action as a result. Janet viewed this dissociation of experience as an abnormal process. His explanation of conversion disorder followed his account of dissociative disorders, as we discussed earlier in this chapter.

In contrast, Freud came to view dissociation—a term that he used synonymously with repression—as a normal psychological process. He initially viewed traumatic stress as a necessary precondition for conversion disorders (see Research Methods). Later, however, Freud suggested that normal id impulses (particularly sexual urges) were unacceptable to the conscious mind and therefore required unconscious coping efforts—that is, the use of intrapsychic defenses.

Primary and Secondary Gain   Freud came to believe, therefore, that "normal" unconscious processes could lead to the development of hysteria. He assumed that the unacceptable impulse or intolerable memory was unconsciously converted into a physical symptom by intrapsychic defenses (Freud, 1924/1962). The symptom thus served the function of protecting the conscious mind by expressing the psychological conflict unconsciously. In psychoanalytic terminology, this is referred to as the **primary gain** of the symptom. Freud thought that clues about the nature of the primary gain might be found in the symbolism of the specific physical symptom that was expressed. Hysterical blindness might result from witnessing some horrifying event, for example.

Freud also recognized that hysterical symptoms could help a patient to avoid work or responsibility or to gain attention and sympathy. He referred to this as the **secondary gain** of the symptom. Cognitive behavioral theorists agree that secondary gain contributes to somatoform disorders, but they use a more direct term to describe the process: reinforcement. More generally, cognitive behaviorists suggest that *learning the sick role* is a part of the etiology of somatoform disorders. In addition to positive reinforcement (extra attention) or negative reinforcement (avoidance of work), social learning theorists suggest that modeling may be involved in learning the sick role (Lipowski, 1988).

The sick-role account may partially explain the etiology of pain disorder, hypochondriasis, and somatization disorder. However, it fails to account for conversion disorder and the fascinating question of how psychological distress may be converted into physical symptoms. Although the specifics of Freud's or Janet's accounts can be readily criticized, the etiology of conversion disorder seems to require theorizing about unconscious processes. Thus, these disorders pose a theoretical challenge for cognitive scientists as well as for neuroscientists.

SOCIAL FACTORS

Social and cultural theorists offer a more straightforward explanation of the physical symptoms of somatization disorder, hypochondriasis, and pain disorder. Theorists assume that patients with these disorders are experiencing some sort of underlying psychological distress. However,

Retrospective Reports

Researchers have raised probing questions about the validity of recovered memories—memories that allegedly are recalled only after being blocked from consciousness for a long period of time. The topic of recovered memories has created great controversy in recent years, but scientists have long been skeptical about the accuracy of people's *ongoing* memories of the past, even memories that people report readily and confidently. In terms of research methods, particular questions have been raised about the reliability and validity of **retrospective reports**—current recollections of past experiences. Thus, for example, when trying to demonstrate a relationship between current psychopathology and childhood experiences, psychological researchers have called into question the accuracy of the patient's reports of past difficulties. In fact, these concerns about retrospective reports are one of several reasons why investigators prefer prospective, longitudinal studies over retrospective research designs (see Research Methods in Chapter 7).

Concerns about the use of retrospective reports focus on three particular issues that are relevant to abnormal psychology (Brewin, Andrews, & Gotlib, 1993). The first concern addresses normal limitations in memory. As we have noted, scientists doubt the reliability and validity of everyone's memory, particularly memory for events that occurred long ago and early in life. The second objection about retrospective reports is specific to abnormal psychology: Some methodologists have suggested that the memories of people with emotional problems are particularly unreliable. Finally, a third concern is that psychopathology systematically biases people's memories. Investigators have speculated that memory processes are "mood congruent," in that depressed people remember sad experiences better, anxious people tend to recall fearful events, and so on. Thus, reported experiences of negative events from the past may reflect a memory bias rather than an actual etiological process.

Brewin, Andrews, and Gotlib (1993) revisited these concerns about retrospective memory in a recent review of the literature. Their evaluation acknowledges several sound reasons for concern about retrospective reports. They argue, however, that retrospective memories may be less flawed than some methodologists have suggested.

With respect to the reliability and validity of memory in general, Brewin, Andrews, and Gotlib agree that retrospective reports are often inaccurate. They note, for example, that only moderate correlations are found between children's and parents' reports about their past relationships with each other. Moreover, on average, children report more negative memories about the past than do parents, raising the question of whose report is biased. At the same time, the reviewers note that reliability increases to an acceptable level for reports of specific, factual aspects of the past such as the events that occurred around the time of the birth of a sibling. Evidence also supports the validity of many of these specific memories. Thus, memory for specific, important events appears to be acceptably reliable and valid, but people may "rewrite" their histories with regard to more global experiences.

Brewin, Andrews, and Gotlib also question the blanket assumption that psychopathology impedes memory. They assert that many flaws are found in research that supposedly documents memory impairments associated with various psychological problems. They conclude that there is no evidence for memory impairments associated with anxiety or depression. They also conclude that research does not support the conclusion that memories are mood congruent. In particular, depressed people do not erroneously recall more than their share of negative events about the past. Thus, with the exception of severe psychopathology, emotional problems do not appear to impair or systematically distort memories.

Evidence that memories are both accurate and inaccurate creates a dilemma in assessing patients' retrospective reports. The quandary was encountered by Sigmund Freud in interpreting his work with "hysterical" patients. Freud initially believed his female patients' reports about their past experience of trauma, particularly sexual abuse. As a result, he concluded that these traumatic experiences caused their conversion symptoms. Freud's patients recounted episodes of childhood sexual abuse with such frequency, however, that he later assumed that the "memories" could not be real. He concluded that his patients were discussing fantasies rather than real memories, and this conclusion led him to develop his theory of childhood sexuality (Freud, 1924/1962). Contemporary researchers, who have found a startlingly high prevalence of childhood sexual abuse in the general population, now assert that Freud's initial position was

the accurate one. Perhaps the "fantasies" of Freud's patients were memories after all.

For current research methods, the implication of Brewin, Andrews, and Gotlib's analysis is that retrospective reports should not be dismissed. Serious consideration must be given to studies that link current emotional problems with accounts of past difficulties. Uncertain memories create enough doubt, however, that researchers continue to prefer prospective, longitudinal research designs over retrospective methods. Still, memories of specific past events are sufficiently reliable and valid to justify using retrospective reports as a first, less expensive research method before investing limited resources in prospective research on life events and the development of abnormal behavior. ■

the patients describe their problems as physical symptoms, and to some extent experience them that way, because of limited insight into their emotional distress and/or the lack of social tolerance of psychological complaints. Thus, sociocultural theorists assume that people with somatoform disorders really are fearful, sad, or uncertain about their life, but they experience, or at least express, these emotional concerns in terms of physical complaints. A simple analogy for this theorizing is a child who complains about an upset stomach, not about fear of failure, before giving a piano recital.

Prevalence data form the basis for sociocultural theories of somatoform disorders. Somatoform disorders are more common in nonindustrialized countries, and they are more frequent among less-educated people in the United States (Kirmayer, 1984; Mechanic, 1986). The hypothesized explanation for this is that people with less education or financial security do not have the opportunity to learn to describe their inner turmoil in detailed psychological terms (Lipowski, 1988). As Maslow argued, people have time for introspection only after meeting more basic needs for safety and survival (see Chapter 2). Similarly, it has been suggested that the apparent reduction in the prevalence of conversion disorders today as compared with 100 years ago is a result of the increased social acceptance of inner feelings (Shorter, 1992).

Treatment of Somatoform Disorders

The sociocultural view of the etiology of somatoform disorders is consistent with the approaches to treatment developed by Charcot, Janet, and Freud. These therapists encouraged their patients to recall and recount psychologically painful events as a way of treating the disorder.

The exploration and uncovering of past or present traumas may free some patients of conversion symptoms, as it apparently did in some classic cases. Nevertheless, virtually no systematic research has been conducted on any treatment for somatoform disorders. The one exception is behavior therapy for chronic pain, which may involve both operant and cognitive behavioral treatments. Operant approaches to chronic pain attempt to alter contingencies that reward "pain behavior" and the sick role. The goal is to reward successful coping and life adaptation instead (Fordyce, 1976). Cognitive behavior therapy typically incorporates operant techniques but also uses cognitive restructuring to address the emotional and cognitive components of pain. Research demonstrates the effectiveness of both variations on behavior therapy in treating chronic lower back pain (Blanchard, 1994).

One reason for the limited research on the psychological treatment of somatoform disorders is that primary care physicians treat most of these patients. Patients with somatoform disorders typically consult physicians about their ailments, and they often insist that their problems are physical even after extensive testing. They are likely to refuse a referral to a mental health professional. Thus, primary care physicians often must learn how to manage hypochondriasis, somatization disorder, and related problems in the medical setting.

This can be a difficult task for primary care physicians. They may become frustrated by their failure to identify a clear physical problem or may be unsympathetic toward "hypochondriacs" when they have so many patients with "real" problems. Not surprisingly, such reactions can weaken the physician–patient relationship, a consequence that can intensify the problem. In fact, the major recommendation for the medical management of patients with somatization disorder is to establish a strong and consistent physician–patient relationship. Physicians are urged to schedule routine appointments with these patients every month or two, and to conduct brief medical exams during this time (National Institute of Mental Health, 1990). In addition to offering consistent emotional support and medical reassurance, one goal of this approach is to eliminate the iatrogenic effects of the somatization disorder by reducing unnecessary medical procedures. A physician who is familiar with a patient with somatization disorder is more likely to recognize the psychological origin of the physical complaints, and is less likely to order unnecessary medical tests or treatment procedures. In fact, the effectiveness of this management approach has been documented in at least one study (Smith, Monson, & Ray, 1986).

Whatever the approach to treatment, it is essential for the physician to convey a sense of concern about patients' complaints. There is a place for reassurance and optimism about the patient's good health, but the evaluation is likely to be rejected unless it is coupled with some expression of concern. Patients who do not receive this empathy are likely to ignore the physician's advice and simply recruit a new, more understanding physician (National Institute of Mental Health, 1990).

Referrals to a mental health professional must be made with care by primary health-care providers. Patients may believe that the recommendation belittles their problems and may reject it out of hand. When a referral is made successfully, the mental health professional might need to coordinate treatment with the referring physician. Behavior therapy with chronic pain patients typically is offered in medical settings. This location surely contributes to the treatment's success. Other, new approaches to somatoform disorders may be best situated in behavioral medicine programs.

Summary

Dissociative disorders are characterized by persistent, maladaptive disruptions in the integration of memory, consciousness, or identity. **Somatoform disorders** are identified by unusual physical symptoms that occur in the absence of a known physical illness. Memories become inaccessible in dissociative disorders; psychological distress is converted into physical symptoms in somatoform disorders. Thus, these unusual emotional problems involve unconscious processes by definition, and they challenge psychological theorists to explain these psychological events that occur outside of awareness. In fact, both Freud and Janet developed their influential theories about unconscious processes when attempting to explain these disorders.

KEY TERMS

- body dysmorphic disorder
- conversion disorder
- depersonalization disorder
- dissociation
- dissociative amnesia
- dissociative disorders
- dissociative fugue
- dissociative identity disorder
- hypnosis
- hypochondriasis
- hysteria
- iatrogenesis

The DSM-IV distinguishes four major subtypes of dissociative disorders: fugue, amnesia, depersonalization disorder, and dissociative identity disorder. **Dissociative fugue** is characterized by sudden and unexpected travel away from home, an inability to recall the past, and confusion about identity or the assumption of a new identity. **Dissociative amnesia** involves a sudden inability to recall extensive and important personal information that exceeds normal forgetfulness. As with fugue, dissociative amnesia typically is characterized by a sudden onset in response to trauma or extreme stress and an equally sudden recovery of memory.

Depersonalization disorder is a less-dramatic problem that is characterized by severe and persistent feelings of being detached from oneself—such sensations as feeling as if you are in a dream, or as though you are floating above your body and observing yourself act. Occasional depersonalization experiences are normal, and are reported by about half the population. In depersonalization disorder, however, depersonalization experiences are persistent or recurrent, and they cause marked personal distress. Finally, **dissociative identity disorder**, also known as multiple personality disorder, is characterized by the existence of two or more distinct personalities in a single individual. At least two of these personalities repeatedly take control over the person's behavior, and some of the personalities have limited or no memory of the others.

Although some investigators suggest that the conditions are pervasive, dissociative disorders appear to be quite rare. A growing body of evidence links the conditions with traumatic experiences, particularly with child abuse. Childhood trauma is thought to be critical in the etiology of the conditions. Evidence is weak or nonexistent on other factors that may contribute to the development of the disorder. Similarly, there is no systematic research on the treatment of dissociative disorders, although clinical tradition emphasizes reliving trauma as a way of reintegrating experience.

In contrast to psychosomatic disorders, somatoform disorders cannot be explained by an underlying organic impairment. Still, many patients with these purely psychological problems seek a physician's care and receive unnecessary medical treatment.

The DSM-IV lists five major subcategories of somatoform disorders: body dysmorphic disorder, hypochondriasis, somatization disorder, pain disorder, and conversion disorder. In **body dysmorphic disorder** the patient is preoccupied with some imagined defect in appearance—a preoccupation that typically focuses on some facial feature such as the nose or mouth. **Hypochondriasis** is characterized by a fear or belief that the individual is suffering from a physical illness. The persistent worries that characterize hypochondriasis are severe and preoccupying, and often result in substantial impairment in life functioning.

Somatization disorder is characterized by a history of multiple, somatic complaints in the absence of organic impairments. The complaints involve multiple somatic systems, including symptoms of pain, gastrointestinal symptoms, sexual symptoms, and pseudoneurologic symptoms. **Pain disorder** is characterized by preoccupation with pain. Although there is no objective way to evaluate pain, psychological factors are judged to be significant in creating or exacerbating the chronic pain in pain disorder.

In many respects, the classic type of somatoform disorder is conversion disorder. "Hysterical" blindness or "hysterical" paralysis are examples of conversion symptoms. The term **conversion disorder** accurately conveys the central assumption of the diagnosis—the idea that psychological conflicts are converted into physical symptoms. Conversion disorders were the problems that particularly captivated the attention of Charcot, Freud, and Janet, and that led them to develop theories about unconscious mental processes.

Like dissociative disorders, true somatoform disorders are rare, although complaints about somatic symptoms that do not have an organic cause are common and represent a significant proportion of medical care. The etiology of somatoform disorders has not been the subject of much research. Etiological concerns include the misdiagnosis of incipient neurological diseases as somatoform disorders, **secondary gain** or reinforcement for the sick role, and the role of culture in creating the conditions. Perhaps the most interesting and unanswered etiological question, however, concerns the role of unconscious processes in the development of somatoform disorders.

Treatment research on somatoform disorders is sorely lacking. Some evidence indicates that behavior therapy is effective in the treatment of chronic pain. Investigators also are beginning to identify aspects of effective medical management of somatoform disorders. Still, in many ways, these disorders continue to pose as much of a challenge now as they did at the turn of the twentieth century when they attracted the attention of leading figures in the history of abnormal psychology.

Critical Thinking

1. There is much controversy about several of the topics in this chapter, including such issues as hypnosis, multiple personality disorder, recovered memories, and conversion reactions. These elusive ideas are difficult to demonstrate empirically, and at present require a certain amount of "believing" as opposed to "knowing." If you believe in the existence of these phenomena, how could you prove your beliefs to skeptics? If you are a skeptic, what evidence would convince you that the psychic phenomena are "real"?

2. Some theorists such as Freud and Janet emphasize the importance of a single traumatic event in the development of psychopathology. Others assert that ongoing relationships and life circumstances are much more important. Based on what you have learned so far about abnormal psychology, what is your opinion on this matter? How do you justify your position based on theory and research?

3. Do you know people who seem to express their psychological concerns through somatic complaints? How do you explain this? Did you express your feelings in this way as a child? Do you still experience or express your emotions in terms of physical sensations or symptoms?

Personality Disorders

ersonality is an elusive concept that is based largely on our observations of interpersonal behaviors. Most of us find it useful to distinguish between people who are aggressive and those who are not; people who are friendly and outgoing and those who are not; people who are fearful and those who are not. The combination of traits or characteristics that, taken as a whole, describe a person's behavior are considered to be his or her **personality**. In DSM-IV, personality is defined as "enduring patterns of perceiving, relating to, and thinking about the environment and oneself, which are exhibited in a wide range of important social and personal contexts" (APA, 1994). Without these presumed consistencies in others' behaviors, we would find it difficult to think about and organize our social worlds.

Overview

When these traits bring a person into repeated conflict with others, an individual's personality may be considered disordered. The DSM-IV employs two primary criteria to define **personality disorder**: The person's behavior must be rigid and inflexible, and it must result in either social or occupational problems or distress to the individual. The impairment associated with most forms of personality disorder causes less personal distress than that found in other types of mental disorder. Most disorders that are discussed in this book tend to result in referral for treatment by a mental health professional. Personality disorders usually do not. In fact, some studies estimate that as many as 80 percent of people with personality disorders have never sought professional help for these problems (Drake & Vaillant, 1983).

The personality disorders are among the most controversial categories in the diagnostic system for mental disorders. They are difficult to identify reliably, their etiology is poorly understood, and there is relatively little evidence to indicate that they can be treated successfully. There are, for example, important discrepancies between DSM-IV and ICD-10, its European counterpart, in their descriptions of these prob-

lems. Two types of personality disorder in the U.S. system—borderline and schizotypal—are not even included in ICD-10. For all of these reasons, you should think critically about the validity of these categories.

Personality disorders are considered separately from other primary forms of psychopathology in DSM-IV. Most clinical disorders are listed on Axis I, whereas the personality disorders are listed on Axis II. The authors of DSM-IV have organized ten specific forms of personality disorders into three clusters on the basis of broadly defined characteristics. The specific disorders in each cluster are listed in Table 9–1. The first cluster includes *asocial* people—those who tend to be odd or eccentric. The second cluster includes *flamboyant* people, who appear to be excessively dramatic, emotional, or erratic. The third cluster includes *anxious* people—those who appear fearful. All of the personality disorders are based on exaggerated personality traits that are frequently annoying or disturbing to other people.

The following cases illustrate several of the most important features of personality disorders. Our first case is an example of *antisocial personality disorder*, which is defined in terms of a

TABLE 9–1

Personality Disorders Listed in DSM-IV

Cluster A	Characteristic Features
Paranoid	Distrust and suspiciousness of others
Schizoid	Detachment from social relationships and restricted range of expression of emotions
Schizotypal	Discomfort with close relationships; cognitive and perceptual distortions; eccentricities of behavior
Cluster B	
Antisocial	Disregard for and frequent violation of the rights of others
Borderline	Instability of interpersonal relationships, self-image, emotions, and control over impulses
Histrionic	Excessive emotionality and attention seeking
Narcissistic	Grandiosity, need for admiration, and lack of empathy
Cluster C	
Avoidant	Social inhibition, feelings of inadequacy, and hypersensitivity to negative evaluation
Dependent	Excessive need to be taken care of, leading to submissive and clinging behavior
Obsessive-compulsive	Preoccupation with orderliness and perfectionism at the expense of flexibility

pervasive and persistent disregard for, and frequent violation of, the rights of other people. In the nineteenth century, British psychiatrist James Pritchard (1785–1850) referred to this condition as "moral insanity."

The following description of a 21-year-old man was written by Hervey Cleckley in his classic treatise on this topic (Cleckley, 1976). The man had been referred to Cleckley by his parents and his lawyer after his most recent arrest for stealing. The parents hoped that their son might avoid a long prison sentence if Cleckley decided that he was suffering from a mental disorder. Notice that the fundamental features of this man's problems were clearly evident by early adolescence, and they were exhibited consistently over an extended period of time. The stable, long-standing nature of personality disorders is one of their most characteristic features. In this way, they are distinguished from many other forms of abnormal behavior, which are episodic in nature (Hirschfeld, 1993).

CASE STUDY

Antisocial Personality Disorder

Tom looks and is in robust physical health. His manner and appearance are pleasing. In his face a prospective employer would be likely to see strong indications of character as well as high incentive and ability. He is well informed, alert, and entirely at ease, exhibiting a confidence in himself that the observer is likely to consider amply justified. This does not look like the sort of man who will fail or flounder about in the tasks of life but like someone incompatible with all such thoughts.

Evidence of (Tom's) maladjustment became distinct in childhood. He appeared to be a reliable and manly fellow but could never be counted upon to keep at any task or to give a straight account of any situation. He was frequently truant from school. No advice or persuasion influenced him in his acts, despite his excellent response in all discussions. Though he was generously provided for, he stole some of his father's chickens from time to time, selling them at stores downtown. Pieces of table silver would be missed. These were sometimes recovered from those to whom he had sold them for a pittance or swapped them for odds and ends which seemed to hold no particular interest or value for him. He resented and seemed eager to avoid punishment, but no modification in his behavior resulted from it. He did not seem wild or particularly impulsive, a victim of high temper or uncontrollable drives. There was nothing to indicate he was subject to unusually strong temptations, lured by definite plans for high adventure and exciting revolt.

He lied so plausibly and with such utter equanimity, devised such ingenious alibis or simply denied all responsibility with such convincing appearances of candor that for many years his real career was poorly estimated. Among typical exploits with which he is credited stand these: prankish defecation into the stringed intricacies of the school piano, the removal from his uncle's automobile of a carburetor for which he got 75 cents, and the selling of his father's overcoat to a passing buyer of scrap materials.

At 14 or 15 years of age, having learned to drive, Tom began to steal automobiles with some regularity. Often his intention seemed less that of theft than of heedless misappropriation. A neighbor or friend of the family, going to the garage or to where the car was parked outside an office building, would find it missing. Sometimes the patient would leave the stolen vehicle within a few blocks or miles of the owner, sometimes out on the road where the gasoline had given out. After he had tried to sell a stolen car, his father consulted advisers and, on the theory that he might have some specific craving for automobiles, bought one for him as a therapeutic measure. On one occasion while out driving, he deliberately parked his own car and, leaving it, stole an inferior model which he left slightly damaged on the outskirts of a village some miles away.

Private physicians, scoutmasters, and social workers were consulted. They talked and worked with him, but to no avail. Listing the deeds for which he became ever more notable does not give an adequate picture of the situation. He did not every day or every week bring attention to himself by major acts of mischief or destructiveness. He was usually polite, often considerate in small, appealing ways, and always seemed to have learned his lesson after detection and punishment. He was clever and learned easily. During intervals in which his attendance was regular, he impressed his teachers as outstanding in ability. Some charm and apparent modesty, as well as his very convincing way of seeming sincere and to have taken resolutions that would count, kept not only the parents but all who encountered him clinging to hope. Teachers, scoutmasters, the school principal, and others, recognized that in some very important respects he differed from the ordinary bad or wayward youth. (They) made special efforts to help him and to give him new opportunities to reform or readjust.

When he drove a stolen automobile across a state line, he came in contact with federal authorities. In view of his youth and the wonderful impression he made, he was put on probation. Soon afterward he took another automobile and again left it in the adjoining state. It was a very obvious situation. The consequences could not have been entirely overlooked by a person of his excellent shrewdness. He admitted that the considerable risks of getting caught had occurred to him but felt he had a chance to avoid detection and would take it. No unusual and powerful motive or any special aim could be brought out as an explanation.

Tom was sent to a federal institution in a distant state where a well-organized program of rehabilitation and guidance was available. He soon impressed authorities at this place with his attitude and in the way he discussed his past mistakes and plans for a different future. He seemed to merit parole status precociously and this was awarded him. It was not long before he began stealing again and thereby lost his freedom. (Cleckley, 1976, pp. 64–67) ∎

This case provides an excellent example of the senseless nature of the illegal and immoral acts committed by people who meet the diagnostic criteria for antisocial personality disorder. Another puzzling feature of this disorder is the apparent lack of remorse and the inability to learn from experience that accompany such a history of delinquent behavior. It is difficult to understand why someone would behave in this manner. Psychopathologists appeal to the notion of personality disorder to help them understand these irrational behaviors.

The case of Tom also illustrates some other important features of personality disorders.

Most other forms of mental disorder, such as anxiety disorders and mood disorders, are *ego-dystonic*; that is, people with these disorders are distressed by their symptoms and uncomfortable with their situations. Personality disorders are usually *ego-syntonic*—the ideas or impulses with which they are associated are acceptable to the person. People with personality disorders frequently do not see themselves as being disturbed. We might also say that they do not have insight into the nature of their own problems. Tom did not believe that his repeated antisocial behavior represented a problem. The other people for whom he created problems were suffering, but he was not. Many forms of personality disorder are defined primarily in terms of the problems that these people create for others rather than in terms of their own subjective distress.

We turn now to another example of personality disorder. The person described in the next case illustrates one of the most important characteristics of personality disorders as they are defined in DSM-IV: overlap among categories. Most people who meet the criteria for one type of personality disorder will also meet the criteria for at least one more. The person in this case met the diagnostic criteria for narcissistic personality disorder and also exhibited some features of *histrionic personality disorder*. According to DSM-IV, the former is characterized by "grandiosity, lack of empathy, and hypersensitivity to the evaluation of others." The latter is associated with attention seeking and excessive emotionality.

CASE STUDY

Narcissistic Personality Disorder

Lawrence was a 34-year-old professor of English literature at an exclusive private university. He was clever, engaging, and ambitious. The chairperson of the English department and the university administration considered him to be one of their brightest academic stars, even though he was much younger than most other distinguished faculty members. They treated him with considerable deference, but their efforts were never sufficient to fulfill Lawrence's own expectations for the special consideration that he felt he deserved.

Not surprisingly, Lawrence's colleagues came to view him as pompous and unbearably self-centered. He had a successful record of scholarship for a person of his age, but most of his colleagues in the English department were similarly productive, and were highly regarded by their peers at other universities. Lawrence refused to acknowledge the accomplishments of his colleagues, and behaved as though he were the only eminent professor in the entire university. Instead of being grateful for the special position he had attained after a series of rapid promotions, Lawrence complained constantly that the university did not know how to treat someone as famous as he. He argued that he was entitled to special privileges. For example, he adamantly refused to teach undergraduate students after he was granted tenure, arguing that undergraduates were not intelligent enough to benefit from the things that he could teach them.

Although Lawrence held an inflated opinion of himself, he also appeared at times to be remarkably insecure. He bombarded colleagues with copies of everything he wrote. His critical reviews and short stories were distributed widely shortly after their publication. His intent was clearly to seek the approval and praise of his peers, who had learned that it was not wise to engage Lawrence by attempting to offer constructive criticism.

Lawrence's personal appearance was also distinctive. Most of his colleagues dressed casually when they were teaching or working in their offices, but Lawrence always insisted on wearing expensive tailored suits. His shirts were carefully pressed and starched, and he wore expensive ties and shoes. His hair was always carefully trimmed and blown dry in a contemporary style that also minimized the effect of his slightly receding hairline and the barely visible thinning patch at the crown of his head. Lawrence was exceedingly sensitive, and responded with surprisingly intense anger if he was teased about these hints that he might be going bald at an early age. He was completely unable to laugh at himself. At the same time, however, he frequently chastised colleagues for the casual way in which they dressed.

Lawrence was married for 10 years before being separated from his wife, Kathleen, and their two young children. The separation had seemed inevitable to everyone who knew the family. Kathleen had always been responsible for all the household chores and for caring for the children, because Lawrence worked at least 12 hours a day, every day of the week. He maintained that this was an eminently fair arrangement because it was Kathleen who had wanted to have children. Given the importance of his academic work, and his unique intellectual talents, he did not believe that his time should be wasted on pedestrian tasks, such as raising his children, that could be accomplished by anyone. He also

noted that Kathleen should be happy to have married as handsome and successful a person as he, and that she should be fulfilled simply in being the mother of his children.

One of Lawrence's most annoying characteristics was his complete insensitivity to the feelings of other people. He could be charming and witty, particularly when he was trying to impress someone whom he considered to be (almost) as important as he, but he was also known for his sharp remarks that seemed designed to put other people down. He was particularly likely to say rude things when someone else had become the center of attention and he felt he was being ignored. Parties and celebrations that were called in someone else's honor were particularly difficult for him to handle, especially if the recipient was being honored for an academic achievement. ■

Typical Symptoms and Associated Features

Many specific traits and symptoms are used to define the ten types of personality disorder that are included in DSM-IV. These descriptors vary from one disorder to the next and will be identified in more detail later in this chapter. In this section, we outline broad dimensions of adjustment that are typically affected or disrupted in individuals suffering from personality disorders.

Temperament and Personality

By definition, personality disorders are enduring patterns of interacting with one's environment, especially other people. The foundations of these characteristics are presumably evident during childhood. It therefore seems reasonable that our discussion of personality disorders should begin with a brief consideration of interpersonal behaviors during childhood. A critical concept in this consideration is **temperament**, which refers to individual differences in several behavioral tendencies, especially those that are evident during the first year of life (Campos et al., 1983; Goldsmith et al., 1987). Definitions of temperament typically include

response dimensions such as irritability, activity level, and fearfulness. These factors vary considerably in level or degree from one infant to the next and have important implications for later development, such as social and academic adjustment when the child eventually enters school (Rutter, 1987).

Personality is a broader concept than temperament. Both terms are concerned with consistency in styles of behavior. Unlike temperament, however, personality includes a consideration of cognitive and motivational factors. According to British psychiatrist Michael Rutter (1987), personality is the pattern of behavior that each person develops as a way of coping with her or his traits and abilities, the social environment in which she or he lives, and the events that she or he has experienced. According to this view, we are active participants in the construction of our unique patterns of behavior. In their healthy or adaptive form, the patterns that we construct are used in a flexible way to cope with the challenges and demands presented by our environments.

Two important qualifications must be made with regard to the development and persistence of individual differences in temperament and personality (Rutter, 1987). First, these differences may not be evident in all situations. Some important personality features may be expressed only under certain challenging circumstances that require or facilitate a particular response. Emotional reactivity is one example. Observations of social development in rhesus monkeys indicate that individual differences in reactivity are relatively stable during a period extending from infancy to adolescence, but they become apparent only when measurements are made in stressful situations (Suomi, 1983). The same principle applies in humans.

Some traits are exhibited only when the person is confronted with particular environmental circumstances. Note, for example, that Tom did not always appear to be impulsive. Similarly, Lawrence was not always pompous and overbearing. He could be charming and unpretentious at times, especially when in the presence of an older, distinguished person whom he was trying to impress. His sharp, hostile remarks were most often triggered by situations in which his self-esteem seemed threatened. It was under these circumstances that his narcissistic tendencies could be regularly observed.

The second qualification involves the consequences of exhibiting particular traits. Social circumstances frequently determine whether a specific pattern of behavior will be assigned a positive or negative meaning by other people. Difficult temperament, for example, may serve an adaptive function when it is beneficial for an infant to be demanding and highly visible—for example, during a famine or in a large institution. On the other hand, in some circumstances, difficult temperament can be associated with an increased risk for certain psychiatric and learning disorders. The long-term effects of stylistic patterns of behavior are therefore dependent on the interaction between the child's temperament and the social environment in which the behavior is observed and interpreted by other people.

Consider the traits that Tom exhibited, especially impulsivity and lack of fear. These characteristics might be maladaptive under normal circumstances, but they could be useful—indeed admirable—in certain extraordinary settings. War is one extreme example. People in combat situations are frequently called upon to act quickly and decisively, often at great risk to their own physical health. A casual disregard for personal safety might be adaptive under these circumstances. Tom's ability to lie in a calm and convincing fashion was another interesting trait. Again, this might have been a valuable adaptive skill if Tom had been an espionage agent. The meanings that are assigned to particular traits depend on the environment in which they are observed.

One fundamental assumption of most personality theories is the notion that a person's behavior is stable over time and across situations. People who interact aggressively with colleagues at work presumably will also behave aggressively in leisure athletic activities or while playing with their children. Social learning theorists have questioned this assumption, arguing that human behavior is often determined primarily by the specific context in which it occurs rather than by the person's internal personality traits (Mischel, 1968). The controversy over this distinction, frequently known as the *person–situation debate*, has resulted in the development of improved methods for measuring cross-situational consistencies in behavior (see Research Methods). It has also spawned an *interactional* view of personality, which holds that behavior is the product of both situations and personality traits (Magnusson, 1981). There is general agreement that some types of behavior are more consistent than others (Funder & Colvin, 1991).

▲ **Characteristic styles of behavior in childhood may become enduring patterns of behavior.**

Dimensions of Personality

Granted that there are cross-situational consistencies in some types of behavior, how should these characteristics be described? Experts disagree regarding the basic dimensions of personality (Wiggins & Pincus, 1992). Some theories of normal personality are relatively simple, using only 3 or 4 dimensions. Others are more complicated, and consider as many as 30 or 40 traits.

One widely accepted position is known as the five-factor model of personality (Costa & McCrea, 1992; Goldberg, 1990). The basic traits included in this model are outlined in

Measuring Stable Personality Traits

Psychologists have struggled for many years to find tools for measuring personality traits in ways that are consistent over time and across situations. This is a difficult task, because people often behave quite differently from one situation to the next. Several methods have been employed to improve the procedures used to identify stable traits, including: (1) *rating general response styles* rather than counting the frequency of specific behaviors, and (2) *aggregating assessments* over time rather than observing a person's behavior at one or two isolated moments. The rationale behind these procedures can be illustrated using a concrete example from a study of normal personality (Funder & Colvin, 1991).

Imagine that a man and a woman are participating in a psychology experiment. They have never met before and find themselves sitting together in a room. Their instructions are simply to spend 5 minutes getting acquainted with each other while their interaction is recorded by a videocamera. What will they do? Some people fall easily into a friendly conversation. Others are hesitant and awkward, sitting in relative silence until the experimenter returns. A third type of response is more theatrical, with the subjects clowning in front of the camera, directing comments to the experimenter rather than to each other. Individual differences in this situation are interesting. We do not yet know whether they reflect personality traits, however, because we have observed the subjects' behavior in only one situation and at one point in time.

To examine the stability of behavior, each subject is called back several weeks later and invited to participate in another study, this time with a new partner. Each pair of subjects goes through the "get-acquainted" procedure. Then they are asked to engage in a debate about capital punishment. This second set of assessments allows the experimenter to examine several simple questions. Will people's behaviors in the first "get-acquainted" situation predict what they will be like in the second

"get-acquainted" situation? Will their behavior in these unstructured situations be consistent with the way they perform in the debate? Finally, will ratings of the subjects' performance in these laboratory situations bear any relationship to observations of their behavior in the natural environment?

One methodological issue that will influence the consistency of measurements involves the level at which behavior is examined. Greater consistency will often be found using *ratings* of general response styles rather than concrete behavioral coding procedures. Consider the laboratory example described above. Observers watched the videotapes of each interaction and rated each person's behavior on a number of dimensions, such as the degree to which the subject "exhibited an awkward interpersonal style." The correlation between ratings at Time 1 and Time 2 was .66 on awkwardness, which indicates a relatively high level of consistency across time. Less consistency would have been achieved if the investigators had counted the frequency of specific behaviors, such as instances of mumbling or the number of irrelevant questions that the person asked. The main point is that personality traits, such as fearfulness, awkwardness, or cheerfulness, can be exhibited in many specific ways. These concrete acts may not be consistent over time or across situations, but composite ratings that are aimed at a more general level of behavior are likely to show more consistency (Funder & Colvin, 1991).

A second methodological issue involves the number of times that the person's behavior is observed. A useful or valid measure of "awkwardness" in the laboratory—one that might accurately predict the extent to which each subject would be rated as being awkward by his or her friends—must be reliable. Classical test theory provides one important clue in this regard: The number of items in a test has a direct influence on reliability. Suppose your instructor wants to know whether you understand the material in this chapter. He or she might create a test that has only one question, but it would probably have low reliability, and reliability sets a limit on validity. If the test has 50 questions, it will be more reliable, and it is more likely to be a meaningful reflection of your true knowledge of the material.

Seymour Epstein, a psychologist at the University of Massachusetts, developed this line of reasoning and pointed out that some behavioral measures of personality traits have been designed like one-item tests (Epstein, 1979, 1980). A more reliable procedure would employ observations at several points in time. In the laboratory situation described above, the most reliable measure of awkwardness would be constructed by the *aggregation* of awkwardness ratings across all three observations (the two "get-acquainted" situations plus the debate). This composite rating was, in fact, significantly correlated with ratings of awkwardness that were made by the subjects' friends. ■

Table 9–2. **Neuroticism** is generally concerned with emotional stability, especially the expression of negative emotions such as anxiety, depression, and anger. This trait has also been called "negative affectivity" (Watson & Clark, 1984). **Extraversion** describes the person's activity level, especially interest in interacting with other people and the ease with which the person expresses positive emotions. **Openness to experience** involves the person's willingness to consider and explore unfamiliar ideas, feelings, and activities. **Agreeableness** describes the willingness to cooperate and empathize with other people. **Conscientiousness** is a reflection of the person's persistence in the pursuit of goals, ability to organize activities, and dependability in completing expected duties. Taken as a whole, these five dimensions can provide a relatively comprehensive description of any person's behavior.

Many personality disorders are defined in terms of maladaptive variations on the kinds of traits listed in Table 9–2 (Widiger & Costa, 1994). Problems may arise in association with extreme variations in either direction. Consider the following examples. Although most forms of personality disorder are associated with high levels of neuroticism, people with antisocial personality disorder frequently exhibit unusually low levels of anxiety. Similarly, low levels of openness to experience may be associated with rigidity and lack of spontaneity, and high levels of openness may lead to daydreaming, thrill seeking, or preoccupation with bizarre ideas and perceptual illusions. We will return to these dimensions later in this chapter, after we have outlined the specific types of personality disorder listed in DSM-IV.

TABLE 9–2

Brief Description of the Five-Factor Model of Personality

Global Traits	Characteristics of the High Scorer	Characteristics of the Low Scorer
Neuroticism Identifies individuals prone to psychological distress, unrealistic ideas, excessive cravings or urges, and maladaptive coping responses.	Worrying, nervous, emotional, insecure, inadequate, hypochondriacal	Calm, relaxed, unemotional, hardy, secure, self-satisfied
Extraversion Assesses quantity and intensity of interpersonal interaction; activity level; need for stimulation; and capacity for joy.	Sociable, active, talkative, person-oriented, optimistic, fun-loving, affectionate	Reserved, sober, unexuberant, aloof, task-oriented, retiring, quiet
Openness to Experience Assesses proactive seeking and appreciation of experience for its own sake; toleration for and exploration of the unfamiliar.	Curious, broad interests, creative, original, imaginative, untraditional	Conventional, down-to-earth, narrow interests, unartistic, unanalytical
Agreeableness Assesses the quality of one's interpersonal orientation along a continuum from compassion to antagonism in thoughts, feelings, and actions.	Soft-hearted, good-natured, trusting, helpful, forgiving, gullible, straightforward	Cynical, rude, suspicious, uncooperative, vengeful, ruthless, irritable, manipulative
Conscientiousness Assesses the individual's degree of organization. Contrasts dependable, fastidious people with those who are lackadaisical and sloppy.	Organized, reliable, hard-working, self-disciplined, punctual, scrupulous, neat, ambitious, persevering	Aimless, unreliable, lazy, careless, lax, negligent, weak-willed, hedonistic

Source: Reproduced by special permission of the publisher, Psychological Assessment Resources, Inc., 16204 North Florida Avenue, Lutz, Florida 33549, from the NEO Personality Inventory–Revised by Paul Costa and Robert McCrae, Copyright ® 1978, 1989, 1992 by PAR, Inc. Further reproduction is prohibited without permission of PAR, Inc.

Classification

In the following pages, we provide descriptions for all of the personality disorder subtypes that are included in DSM-IV, as well as brief cases that illustrate some subtypes. We have chosen cases that are prototypes for each disorder. In other words, these are people who exhibit most, if not all, of the features of the disorder. You should not infer from these descriptions that everyone who meets the criteria for these disorders would represent this type of prototypical case. Remember also that many people simultaneously meet the criteria for more than one personality disorder; these cases are relatively simple examples. Later in the chapter we describe in more detail three disorders that have been studied extensively: schizotypal, borderline, and antisocial personality disorders.

THE FAR SIDE   By GARY LARSON

The four basic personality types

Axis II: Specific Subtypes in DSM-IV

The specific types of personality disorders are arranged in three clusters, which were formed on an intuitive basis. The disorders in each cluster were put together because they seem to be similar. Little empirical evidence exists to support these groupings (Frances, 1985). Serious questions have been raised, for example, about the extent of similarity between antisocial personality disorder and the other subtypes in Cluster B, which is intended to include people who are dramatic, emotional, or erratic (Widiger & Costa, 1994).

CLUSTER A

Cluster A includes three disorders: paranoid, schizoid, and schizotypal forms of personality disorder. The behavior of people who fit the subtypes in this cluster is typically odd, eccentric, or asocial. All three of these types share similarity with the symptoms of schizophrenia (see Chapter 12). One implicit assumption in the DSM-IV system is that these types of personality disorder may represent behavioral traits or interpersonal styles that precede the onset of full-blown psychosis.

Paranoid personality disorder is characterized by the pervasive tendency to be inappropriately suspicious of other people's motives and behaviors. People who fit the description for this disorder are constantly on guard. They expect that other people are trying to harm them, and they take extraordinary precautions to avoid being exploited or injured. Relationships with friends and family members are difficult to maintain because these people don't trust anyone. They frequently overreact in response to minor or ambiguous events to which they attribute hidden meaning.

Schizoid personality disorder is defined in terms of a pervasive pattern of indifference to other people, coupled with a diminished range of emotional experience and expression. These people are loners; they prefer social isolation to interactions with friends or family. Other people see them as being cold and aloof. By their own report, they do not experience strong subjective emotions, such as sadness, anger, or happiness.

Schizotypal personality disorders center around peculiar patterns of behavior rather than on the emotional restriction and social withdrawal that are associated with schizoid personality disorder. Many of these peculiar behaviors take the form of perceptual and cognitive disturbance. People with this disorder may report bizarre fantasies and unusual perceptual experiences. Their speech may be slightly difficult to follow because they use words in an odd way or because they express themselves in a vague or disjointed manner. Their affective expressions may be constricted in range, as in schizoid personality disorder, or they may be silly and inappropriate.

In spite of their odd or unusual behaviors, people with schizotypal personality disorder are not psychotic or out of touch with reality. Their bizarre fantasies do not reach delusional proportions, and their unusual perceptual experiences are not sufficiently real or compelling to be considered hallucinations. The description of the following case, taken from Walsh (1990), illustrates some of these features:

BRIEF CASE STUDY

Schizotypal Personality Disorder
Leslie was a 43-year-old unemployed widow fighting to retain custody of her two adolescent children. Shortly after her husband's death from cancer eight years ago, her parents-in-law accused her of being an unfit mother and successfully acquired temporary custody of the children through the county children's service bureau. Leslie wanted her children with her, and after many appeals the children's bureau was preparing to return them to her. At this time a casual friend suggested to Leslie that getting counseling for herself would further impress the bureau, and this is why she set up her initial appointment. For some unclear reason, however, Leslie chose to keep her counseling experience a secret.

During her early sessions Leslie was quiet, suspicious, and ill at ease. She had no particular agenda for her counseling, only noting in vague terms that she wanted to "get out to the pool." Her affect was constricted, her communications terse and obscure, and her vocabulary rather primitive. Her grooming was haphazard; on some summer days she came dressed in a fur coat, shorts, and hiking boots. Most sessions lasted only 15 to 20 minutes. Leslie would abruptly announce that she had to leave, sometimes to get to work, and quickly walk out, although she always made a point of rescheduling for the following week. Eventually I learned that her work involved collecting tin cans for recycling. Otherwise she spent her time taking long walks in her small town of residence.

Despite her presentation, it eventually became clear that Leslie was not psychotic, and in fact was a college graduate with an impressive athletic background. She had married shortly after college when she became pregnant, but had done little since then aside from raising her children as best she could and tolerating an irresponsible husband. Leslie actually felt relieved when he died, saying "being married never did me any good." She had functioned marginally ever since leaving college. (Walsh, 1990) ∎

Dramatic CLUSTER B

The second cluster includes four specific types: antisocial, borderline, histrionic, and narcissistic personality disorders. According to DSM-IV, these disorders are characterized by dramatic, emotional, or erratic behavior, and all are associated with marked difficulty in sustaining interpersonal relationships. The rationale for grouping these disorders together is less compelling than that provided for Cluster A. In particular, antisocial personality disorder clearly involves something more than just a dramatic style or erratic behavior.

▲ In *The Treasure of the Sierra Madre*, Humphrey Bogart played a prospector whose pervasive paranoia culminated in his murdering his partners and stealing their gold.

Antisocial personality disorder is defined in terms of a persistent pattern of irresponsible and antisocial behavior that begins during childhood or adolescence and continues into the adult years. The case study of Tom, with which we opened this chapter, illustrates this pattern of behavior. The DSM-IV definition is based on features that—beginning in childhood—indicate a pervasive pattern of disregard for, and violation of, the rights of others. Once the person has become an adult, these difficulties include persistent failure to perform responsibilities that are associated with occupational and family roles. Conflicts with others, including physical fights, are also common. These people are irritable and aggressive with their spouses and children as well as with people outside the home. They are impulsive, reckless, and irresponsible.

We have all read newspaper accounts of famous examples of antisocial personality disorder. These often include people who have committed horrendous crimes against other people, including serial murders. One such person who attracted considerable attention in the national media was Wesley Allan Dodd, who was executed after being found guilty of raping, torturing, and killing three young boys. His apparent indifference to the boys' suffering, and his insistence that he would commit similar crimes if he were ever released from prison, led many observers to believe that he fit the criteria for antisocial personality disorder. You should not be misled, however, into thinking that only serious criminals meet the criteria for this disorder. Many other forms of persistently callous and exploitative behavior could lead to this diagnosis.

Borderline personality disorder is a rather diffuse category whose essential feature is a pervasive pattern of instability in mood and interpersonal relationships. People with this disorder find it very difficult to be alone. They form intense, unstable relationships with other people and are often seen by others as being manipulative. Their opinions of significant others frequently vacillate between unrealistically positive and negative extremes. They also exhibit emotional instability. Their mood may shift rapidly and inexplicably from depression to anger to anxiety over a pattern of several hours. Intense anger is common, and may be accompanied by temper tantrums, physical assault, or suicidal threats and gestures.

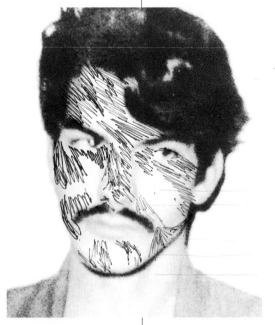

▼ **Wesley Allen Dodd was hanged in 1991 in the state of Washington for the sadistic rape and murder of three small boys.**

Many clinicians consider identity disturbance to be the diagnostic hallmark of borderline personality disorder. People with this disturbance presumably have great difficulty maintaining an integrated image of themselves that incorporates their positive and negative features. They frequently express uncertainty about issues such as personal values, sexual preferences, and career alternatives. Chronic feelings of emptiness and boredom may also be present. The following case, written by Krohn (1980), illustrates many of the features associated with borderline personality disorder.

BRIEF CASE STUDY

Borderline Personality Disorder

Miss L. was a 21-year-old, reasonably attractive, slightly overweight woman of medium height who walked with a brusque gait, held herself very erect, seemed aloof, and appeared to know just where she was going. She had a high, loud, and shaky voice that was experienced by many as grating and demanding. Though she did not deliberately behave dramatically, her body movements and speech habits seemed a bit larger than life, like postures or poses, and tended to draw attention to herself.

Following puberty, the patient had developed interests in music and writing that quickly became all-consuming preoccupations. She began to ruminate interminably about her future, became preoccupied with what others thought of her, and became extremely sensitive to the most subtle slights, real or imagined. A fantasy of herself as a great artist alternated with an image of herself as completely worthless. Disgusted by the prospect of a drab, workaday life, she dreamed of living on an exalted plane, continuously achieving and creating—fantasizing inside herself founts of dazzling creativity that would permit her to write, sing, and perform effortlessly.

People often initially experienced the patient as pushy and obnoxious. Her manner made others feel that she was blaming them for her difficulties, that she felt she had been treated unfairly and that she deserved and needed more. What came through in her manner was a gnawing hunger, a sense of being deprived, a demand for recompense, and a haughty demand to be looked up to and respected. The patient initially felt that she was shy, modest, and unnoticed. In consciously trying to compensate for this, she often struck others as trying to impress and boast.

Though she had some friends, she had very few who felt capable of gratifying her intense and continuous needs for support, reassurance, and maternal comfort. She grew enraged even at those who befriended her, because they could not do enough. At moments when she felt people were actually depriving her, she felt a "white-hot rage," involving impulses to murder, smash windows, or throw herself out a window. These rageful episodes frightened her greatly and would make her feel she should kill herself. Alternately, she deprecated herself, feeling like a loathsome, ugly, fat person who contributed nothing to the world, who was a parasite and therefore deserved to be hated. She would develop clinging, dependent relationships characterized by intense wishes to *have* the qualities of the other (person), often including intense envy of the (person). (Krohn, 1980 pp. 344–345) ■

Histrionic personality disorder is characterized by a pervasive pattern of excessive emotionality and attention-seeking behavior. People with this disorder thrive on being the center of attention. They are self-centered, vain, and demanding, and they constantly seek approval from other people. Their emotions tend to be shallow and may vacillate erratically. They frequently react to situations with inappropriate exaggeration.

The essential feature of **narcissistic personality disorder** is a pervasive pattern of grandiosity. The case of Lawrence, described at the beginning of this chapter, illustrates this type of personality disorder. Narcissistic peo-

ple have a greatly exaggerated sense of their own importance. They are preoccupied with their own achievements and abilities. Because they consider themselves to be very special, they cannot empathize with the feelings of other people.

anxious
CLUSTER C

Cluster C includes three subtypes: avoidant, dependent, and obsessive-compulsive personality disorders. The common element in all these disorders is presumably anxiety or fearfulness. This description fits most easily with the avoidant and dependent types. In contrast, obsessive-compulsive personality disorder is more accurately described in terms of preoccupation with rules and with lack of emotional warmth than in terms of anxiety.

Avoidant personality disorder is characterized by a pervasive pattern of social discomfort, fear of negative evaluation, and timidity. People with this disorder tend to be socially isolated when outside their own family circles because they are afraid of criticism. Unlike people with schizoid personality disorder, they want to be liked by others, but they are easily hurt by even minimal signs of disapproval from other people. Thus, they avoid social and occupational activities that require significant contact with other people.

The essential feature of **dependent personality disorder** is a pervasive pattern of dependent and submissive behavior. These people are exceedingly dependent on other people for advice and reassurance. Often unable to make everyday decisions on their own, they feel anxious and helpless when they are alone. Like people with avoidant personality disorder, they are easily hurt by criticism and are extremely sensitive to disapproval, as illustrated by the following brief case from Turkat and Carlson (1984).

▲ Singer Little Richard is known for his flamboyant style. Attention-seeking styles of dress and behavior are typically not considered abnormal when they are part of the entertainment industry.

BRIEF CASE STUDY

Dependent Personality Disorder

The patient, Mrs. S, was a 48-year-old married, Caucasian female. (She) reported numerous decision making situations which provoke anxiety and attempts to seek reassurance. For example, buying food in the supermarket, deciding what to make for dinner, and buying furniture all provoked anxiety and attempts to seek reassurance from her husband. Further, she reported feeling anxious when the availability of her husband's reassurance was denied (such as Mr. S. being away and Mrs. S. being responsible for the style of trimming the garden bushes and lawn). Finally the patient related numerous anxiety-provoking instances in which decisions she made were initially approved of by an authority figure (such as her husband or physician) and then criticized by an important other (such as after following the instructions of her physician, she was criticized for doing so by a friend).

During school years, she always wanted to be part of the "group" but felt uncomfortable because no one would explicitly point out that she did in fact "fit in." In line with the above, her high school advisor noted on Mrs. S's record that she "lacked initiative."

When the patient went to college, she studied nursing because "a lot of people my age went into nursing." When the time came to choose between a university based or hospital based program, this was decided largely from the advice of another.

The patient's first job as a nurse went rather smoothly because she had readily available supervisors. Unfortunately, her second position did not fare well. Apparently, Mrs. S. had trouble adjusting because she did not have "supportive" supervisors. She left this position after a short time.

Mrs. S. did not have much of a dating history. Her husband was her first and only lover. She was greatly attracted to him because he was "very forceful" and an "independent decision maker." (Turkat & Carlson, 1984) ∎

Obsessive-compulsive personality disorder is defined by perfectionism and inflexibility. People with this disorder set ambitious standards for their own performance that frequently are so high as to be unattainable. They are preoccupied with rules and efficiency. Intellectual activities are favored over feelings and emotional experience. These people also procrastinate. They are excessively conscientious, moralistic, and judgmental, and they tend to be intolerant of affective behavior in other people. Obsessive-compulsive personality disorder should be distinguished from obsessive-compulsive disorder, which is a type of anxiety disorder (see Chapter 6). The latter is characterized by intrusive, unwanted thoughts and ritualistic behaviors, which are not part of the definition of obsessive-compulsive personality disorder.

A Dimensional Perspective on Classification

DSM-IV treats personality disorders in the same way that it handles other disorders—as discrete categories. Specific criteria are listed for each type of personality disorder. If a person exhibits a sufficient number of the criteria, the disorder is considered to be present. Otherwise it is considered to be absent. This approach assumes that

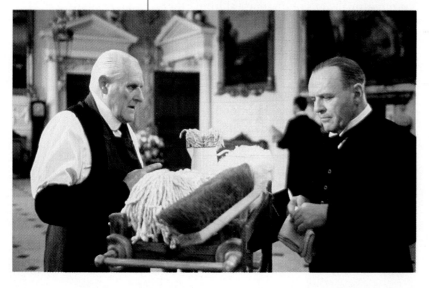

▼ In *The Remains of the Day,* Anthony Hopkins played a butler who exhibited obsessive-compulsive personality disorder. Hopkins's character was so consumed by devotion to duty that he was unable to spend time with his father (the character on the left) as he was dying.

there are sharp boundaries between normal and abnormal personalities and is designed for all-or-nothing decisions. For example, people either fit the criteria for borderline personality disorder, or they do not; it is not possible, using this system, to indicate that a person exhibits *some* borderline traits.

Some clinicians have argued that a dimensional system would be preferable to the categorical approach (Livesley et al., 1994; Widiger, 1993). For example, one of the frequent complaints about the description of personality disorders has been that there is considerable overlap between categories. Many patients meet the criteria for more than one type. It is cumbersome to list multiple diagnoses, especially when the clinician is already asked to list problems on both Axis I and Axis II. In fact, many clinicians are reluctant to make more than one diagnosis on Axis II; consequently, much information is frequently lost. A dimensional system would provide a more complete description of each person, and it would be more useful with patients who fall on the boundaries between different types of personality disorder.

The considerable overlap among categories in the DSM-IV system suggests that these cat-egories are not the most useful or meaningful dimensions on which people might be rated. A more streamlined set of dimensions would be preferable. Thomas Widiger, a clinical psychologist at the University of Kentucky, has been one of the leading proponents of such a change (Widiger & Costa, 1994). The relationship between the normal personality traits listed in the five-factor model and the specific categories of personality disorders in DSM-IV is outlined in Table 9–3. Notice that this approach helps to clarify the extent of overlap between DSM-IV categories. The trait descriptions of borderline and histrionic personality disorder are very similar. It is therefore not surprising that studies have found very high rates of co-morbidity among these categories. Obsessive-compulsive personality disorder, on the other hand, is relatively unique, being one of only two categories that are defined in terms of a high score on the dimension of conscientiousness. This disorder shows much less overlap with the other personality disorders.

If personality disorders are described most accurately and efficiently using a dimensional model, it follows that assessment procedures should perhaps be aimed at identifying where

TABLE 9-3

Relationship Between the Five-Factor Model of Personality and DSM-IV Personality Disorders

DSM-IV Category	Neuroticism negative affect	Extraversion positive affect	Openness	Agreeableness	Conscientiousness
Paranoid		low	low	**low**	
Schizoid		**low**			
Schizotypal	**high**	**low**	high		
Borderline	**high**	high		low	low
Narcissistic	high	high		**low**	high
Histrionic	high	high	high		low
Antisocial	low			**low**	**low**
Dependent	**high**	high		**high**	
Avoidant	**high**	**low**			
Obsessive-compulsive	high	low	low		**high**

Boldface letters indicate features that are strongly associated with the definition of the disorder (defining features). Letters in regular typeface indicate "associated features" that are frequently associated with the disorder, sometimes based on clinical experience. Blank spaces indicate that the trait is not relevent to this DSM-IV category.

Source: Adapted from T.A. Widiger (1993). The DSM-III-R categorical personality disorder diagnoses: A critique and an alternative. *Psychological Inquiry, 4,* 83.

a person stands on each relevant trait. Dimensional measures of maladaptive personality traits have been developed as an alternative to the exclusive use of DSM-IV personality disorder categories to describe these problems. The *Schedule for Nonadaptive and Adaptive Personality* (SNAP) is one useful example (Clark et al., 1993). The SNAP is a self-report inventory that includes 375 true–false items. The person's answers are used to generate scores on 12 primary trait dimensions that form the core of the specific categories listed in DSM-IV: mistrust, manipulativeness, aggression, self-harm, eccentric perceptions, dependency, exhibitionism, entitlement, detachment, impulsivity, propriety, and workaholism. The SNAP also produces scores on three temperament dimensions: negative temperament, positive temperament, and disinhibition. Taken together, these scales provide a relatively simple and comprehensive description of adaptive and maladaptive personality traits that may be more useful and efficient than the set of 87 specific symptoms that are needed to complete formal diagnoses for all of the DSM-IV categories of personality disorder.

Epidemiology

Personality disorders are generally considered to be one of the most common forms of psychopathology, but it is difficult to provide empirical support for that claim (Maier et al., 1992; Weissman, 1993). With the exception of antisocial personality, these disorders did not receive close scrutiny until after the publication of DSM-III.

The results of existing studies are mixed. Several factors may account for the inconsistency in prevalence rates reported by different studies. First, the rates should be expected to vary across settings. They will be higher among patients who are being treated at psychiatric hospitals or outpatient clinics, and they will presumably be lower in the general population.

Second, prevalence rates differ as a function of the method that is used to diagnose personality disorders. Self-report measures produce lower estimates of antisocial personality disorder than are found on the basis of structured interviews. This may be attributable to the fact that people are reluctant to admit antisocial traits on a questionnaire, whereas an interviewer can probe for this information. Conversely, prevalence rates for dependent and compulsive personality disorders tend to be higher when based on questionnaires than on interviews. People are willing to admit the presence of these traits on paper-and-pencil inventories, but interviewers do not consider the traits sufficiently severe that the person meets the threshold for a diagnosis.

Prevalence among Adults in Community Samples

How many people in the general population will meet the criteria for at least one personality disorder? In studies that have examined community samples of adults, the overall lifetime prevalence of Axis II disorders varies between 10 percent and 14 percent (Weissman, 1993). Considerable overlap exists among specific categories.

Evidence regarding the prevalence of specific types of personality disorder in community samples is summarized in Table 9–4. This table presents evidence from two community-based studies that employed structured interviews to arrive at diagnoses of personality disorders. The results of these studies agree that borderline, dependent, and obsessive-compulsive personality disorders are found in 1 to 2 percent of people in the general population. The schizotypal, antisocial, and histrionic types actually had the highest lifetime prevalence in the U.S. sample, but rates in Germany were much lower. This was especially true for antisocial personality disorder. Two types of personality disorder appear to be relatively rare in an adult community sample: schizoid and narcissistic. Both types were found in less than 1 percent of the general population in both studies.

There is considerable overlap among categories in the personality disorders. Most people who meet the diagnostic criteria for one personality disorder in DSM-IV also meet the criteria for another disorder (Widiger & Rogers, 1989). Some patterns are striking. For example, almost half of the people who meet criteria for histrionic personality disorder also meet the criteria for borderline personality disorder. Obsessive-compulsive personality disorder, on the other hand, tends to have little overlap with any of the other categories.

Prevalence among Patients

The prevalence of personality disorders is much higher among people who are being treated for another mental disorder listed on Axis I of DSM-IV. Borderline personality disorder appears to be the most common disorder in both inpatient and outpatient settings. Averaged across studies, the evidence suggests that this disorder is found among 8 percent of all psychiatric outpatients and 15 percent of all patients hospitalized for psychological disorders (Widiger & Rogers, 1989). Approximately 10 to 15 percent of patients seeking outpatient treatment meet diagnostic criteria for schizotypal personality disorder (Bornstein et al., 1988). Rates are even higher among those who have been hospitalized, although the specific figures vary considerably from one study to the next. Several studies of inpatients reported figures between 20 percent and 30 percent for schizotypal personality disorder, and one study reported a prevalence rate of 64 percent among psychiatric inpatients (Widiger & Rogers, 1989).

Rates of antisocial personality disorder are also high among people who are being treated for mental disorders on an outpatient basis (approximately 5 percent) and among hospitalized psychiatric patients (12 to 37 percent, depending on the particular study; Widiger & Rogers, 1989). As we might expect, the prevalence of antisocial personality disorder is particularly high in prison populations, with estimates ranging from 30 percent to 70 percent depending on the sample and the diagnostic criteria employed.

Stability over Time

Temporal stability is one of the most important assumptions about the personality disorders. Evidence for the assumption that personality disorders appear during adolescence and persist

TABLE 9–4

Summary of Epidemiological Data on Personality Disorders (Community Samples Using Structured Interviews)

Subtype	Lifetime Prevalence (percent)	
	German Sample	U.S. Sample
Paranoid	1.8	0.4
Schizoid	0.4	0.7
Schizotypal	0.7	3.0
Antisocial	0.2	3.0
Borderline	1.1	1.7
Histrionic	1.3	3.0
Narcissistic	0.0	0.0
Avoidant	1.1	1.3
Dependent	1.5	1.7
Obsessive-compulsive	2.2	1.7

Sources: The data from the German sample were reported by Maier et al. (1992). Prevalence of personality disorders (DSM-II-R)in the community. *Journal of Personality Disorders, 6,* 187–196. The U.S. data are from M. Zimmerman and W.H. Coryell (1990). Diagnosing personality disorders in the community:A comparison of self-report and interview measures. *Archives of General Psychiatry, 47,* 527–531.

into adulthood has, until recently, been limited primarily to antisocial personality disorder. A classic follow-up study by Lee Robins (1966) began with a large set of records describing young children treated for adjustment problems at a clinic during the 1920s. Robins was able to locate and interview almost all of these people, who by then were adults. The best predictor of an adult diagnosis of antisocial personality was conduct disorder in childhood. The people who were most likely to be considered antisocial as adults were boys who had been referred to the clinic on the basis of serious theft or aggressive behavior; who exhibited such behaviors across a variety of situations; and whose antisocial behaviors created conflict with adults outside their own homes. More than half of the boys in Robins's study who exhibited these characteristics were given a diagnosis of antisocial personality disorder as adults.

Another longitudinal study has collected information regarding the prevalence and stability of personality disorders among adolescents (Bernstein et al., 1993). This investigation is particularly important because it did not depend solely upon subjects who had been referred for psychological treatment and because it was concerned with the full range of personality disor-

▲ **Vivien Leigh won Academy Awards for her performances as Scarlett O'Hara in** *Gone with the Wind* **(1940) and Blanche DuBois in** *A Streetcar Named Desire* **(1952). Both characters exhibit blends of histrionic and narcissistic features that fit stereotyped views of female personality traits.**

ders. The rate of personality disorders was relatively high in this sample: 17 percent of the adolescents received a diagnosis of at least one personality disorder. While many of these people continued to exhibit the same problems over time, fewer than half of the adolescents who were originally considered to have a personality disorder qualified for that same diagnosis 2 years later. This evidence suggests that maladaptive personality traits are frequently transient phenomena among adolescents. Further details regarding the methods and results of this study are presented in our Research Close-up.

Several studies have examined the stability of personality disorders among people who have received professional treatment for their problems, especially those who have been hospitalized for schizotypal or borderline disorders. Many patients who have been treated for these problems are still significantly impaired several years later, but the disorders are not uniformly stable (Perry, 1993). Recovery rates are relatively high among patients with a diagnosis of borderline personality disorder. If patients who were initially treat-

ed during their early twenties are followed up when they are in their forties and fifties, only about one person in four would still qualify for a diagnosis of borderline personality disorder (Stone, 1993). The long-term prognosis is less optimistic for schizotypal and schizoid personality disorders. People with these diagnoses are likely to remain socially isolated and occupationally impaired (McGlashan, 1986, 1992).

Gender Bias

One of the controversies that has surrounded the diagnosis of personality disorders involves the issue of gender. Some of the categories, such as histrionic and dependent, were originally assumed to be more common among women than among men (Chodoff, 1982). Such claims led to concern that the definitions of some personality disorders are inherently sexist. Critics contend that these definitions reflect sex-role stereotypes that arbitrarily assign responsibility for interpersonal difficulties to the women themselves. In this way, these definitions minimize the extent to which women diagnosed with personality disorders may simply be trying to cope with unreasonable or oppressive environmental circumstances, including discrimination and sexual abuse (Brown, 1992).

Epidemiological evidence contradicts the view that histrionic personality disorder is more common among women. Researchers have examined data from the ECA study to determine the prevalence of histrionic personality disorder in a community sample of more than 3,400 adults (Nestadt et al., 1990). The estimated

RESEARCH CLOSE-UP

Stability of Personality Disorders in Adolescents

The first large-scale study of the prevalence and stability of personality disorders among adolescents was conducted by psychologists David Bernstein, Patricia Cohen, and their colleagues at the New York State Psychiatric Institute (Bernstein et al., 1993).

Subjects in this study were identified from a random sample of more than 700 families in upstate New York who had at least one child between the ages of 11 and 21. In families with more than one child in that age range, one child was randomly chosen to become the subject in this study.

The children and their families were broadly representative of people living in the northeastern United States in terms of socioeconomic status. Half the adolescents were male, with an average age of 16 years at the time of the first assessment. Sixty-one percent were from intact families, and 76 percent lived in urban areas. They were less representative with regard to race (91 percent were white) and religious background (56 percent were Catholic).

Each adolescent was assessed at two points in time, separated by 2 years. The investigators collected information about the children's behavior using both structured interviews (conducted independently with both the adolescents and their mothers) and self-report questionnaires (completed only by the adolescents). These data were combined to identify individuals with various types of personality disorder. These individuals were then further classified as having either a moderate or severe form of the disorder.

A total of 31 percent of the adolescents met the criteria for at least one moderate personality disorder, and 17 percent met the criteria for at least one severe personality disorder. The most prevalent form of moderate disorder was obsessive-compulsive disorder, which was found in 13 percent of the adolescents. The most prevalent form of severe disorder was narcissistic personality disorder; 6 percent of the adolescents met these criteria. The least common form of personality disorder in this sample was schizotypal, judging by both the moderate and severe diagnostic thresholds.

Only one significant difference was found between boys and girls: Boys were more than twice as likely as girls to qualify for a diagnosis of dependent personality disorder. This result was somewhat surprising in light of the expectation that, in adults, dependent personality disorder is more common among women than among men.

The prevalence of both moderate and severe personality disorders peaked at the age of 12 or 13 years for both boys and girls and then declined. By the time these subjects reached 18 to 21 years of age, the prevalence of severe personality disorder fell to 9 percent for males and 11 percent for females, approximately the same rates found in other epidemiological studies with adult populations.

Less than half of the adolescents who received an Axis II diagnosis at the time of the first assessment qualified for a diagnosis at the second assessment. The most persistent forms of personality disorder were the paranoid, narcissistic, obsessive-compulsive, and borderline types. In these categories, 25 to 32 of the cases identified at the first assessment continued to meet diagnostic criteria 2 years later. This pattern indicates that symptoms of personality disorder are frequently unstable during adolescence. They also indicate, however, that a fairly large minority of the adolescents in this study continued to qualify for a diagnosis of personality disorder 2 years after the problem was originally identified.

The results of this study indicate that personality disorders are relatively common among adolescents in the general population. The conclusions with regard to temporal stability are mixed. On the one hand, symptoms of personality disorder usually are not stable over time. On the other hand, adolescents who exhibit a severe personality disorder at one point in time are much more likely than their peers to have similar problems over the next few years. Some of the subjects followed a stable pattern that is consistent with the image of these disorders presented in DSM-IV. Further studies will be needed to determine how many of the adolescents whose problems were stable over this initial 2-year period continue to exhibit stable difficulties in subsequent years. ■

prevalence of histrionic personality disorder in the general population was found to be 2.2 percent in *both* men and women.

Why would some clinicians believe that histrionic disorder is predominantly a female disorder? There are several possible explanations. One is that the previous impression was based on evidence from clinics and hospitals. Women with the disorder may seek treatment more frequently than men. Another possibility involves diagnostic practices. In the ECA study, 76 percent of the men with histrionic personality disorder also had substance abuse disorders. If these men enter clinics, they may be diagnosed as having an alcohol or drug addiction problem rather than histrionic personality disorder.

The overall prevalence of personality disorders is approximately equal in men and women (Weissman, 1993). There are, however, consistent gender differences with regard to some specific disorders, especially antisocial personality, which is much more common among men than among women. The ECA study reported a male-to-female sex ratio of 6 to 1 for lifetime prevalence (Robins, Tipp, & Przybeck, 1991).

Schizotypal Personality Disorder (SPD)

Now that we have reviewed some of the important general issues that involve the entire set of personality disorders, we consider three specific types of disorder in greater detail. We have decided to focus on schizotypal, borderline, and antisocial types because they have been the subject of extended research and debate in the scientific literature.

These three disorders illustrate different ways in which the personality disorders have been conceptualized (Blashfield & McElroy, 1988; Rutter, 1987). Each of these views has been associated with a somewhat different approach to thinking about, and studying, the etiology of the disorder. One approach has been to think in terms of a personality style that is closely associated with a specific form of adult psychopathology. This is the tradition out of which the concept of schizotypal personality disorder has grown. In this view, the etiology of the personality disorder is closely linked to the etiology of the Axis I disorder with which it is associated. The maladaptive personality traits are considered early manifestations of the predisposition to develop the full-blown disorder.

A second approach to the issue has been based on psychodynamic theories regarding the origins of personality traits and interpersonal styles (see Chapter 2). The concept of borderline personality disorder has been heavily influenced by this tradition. Finally, a third approach to etiology has been to think in terms of specific psychological deficits, especially as they are evident in performance on laboratory tasks. That is the tradition that influenced the development of antisocial personality disorder. Investigators have attempted to identify factors that might account for these people's inability to learn from experience.

As in the case of other forms of psychopathology, the etiology of personality disorders is most likely the product of an interaction among biological, psychological, and social systems (Paris, 1993). Although relatively little information is available regarding the etiology of schizotypal and borderline personality disorders, we summarize some of the most useful data that have been collected. In the case of antisocial personality disorder, which has been studied more extensively, we present a more thorough discussion of etiology.

Brief Historical Perspective

The concept of schizotypal personality disorder is closely tied to the history of schizophrenia as a diagnostic entity (Gottesman, 1987). As we will see in Chapter 12, the term *schizophrenia* originally was applied to a number of related conditions, all of which were characterized by unusual behaviors. One of these conditions, called "latent schizophrenia," included people who were socially withdrawn and intellectually dull but were not actively psychotic.

It has been recognized for many years that a fairly large proportion of the family members of schizophrenic patients exhibit strange or unusual behaviors that are similar to, but milder in form than, the disturbance shown by the patient. Research studies have described first-degree relatives who are not psychotic but who nevertheless exhibit symptoms that resemble those of schizophrenia, such as disordered thinking and a lack of deep interpersonal relationships (Kendler, 1985). Clinicians often referred to these individuals as *schizoid*.

By the 1960s, the concept of schizoid personality had become widely accepted and broadly defined. The term was used interchangeably with *simple schizophrenia*, and in DSM-II it was listed as a form of schizophrenia. The concept was applied so indiscriminately that it conveyed little meaning. The authors of DSM-III (1980) decided to move this concept out of the schizophrenic disorders, in part because they wanted to "clean up" and narrow the use of that concept. They moved the nonpsychotic conditions whose symptoms resembled those of schizophrenia into the personality disorders and divided them into three categories: schizoid, schizotypal, and avoidant personality disorders.[†] The former two categories were then grouped together with paranoid personality disorder, which had always been listed as a separate category, to form Cluster A. Avoidant personality disorder was placed in Cluster C because of the manifest anxiety exhibited by these people.

This approach has been maintained in DSM-IV. The value of these distinctions is still open to debate. Some critics have argued that there is too much overlap among categories for these different categories to be meaningful (for example, Gottesman, 1987; Livesley & West, 1986).

Clinical Features and Co-morbidity

The DSM-IV criteria for schizotypal personality disorder are listed in Table 9–5. These criteria represent a blend of those characteristics that have been reported among the relatives of schizophrenic patients and those symptoms that seem to characterize nonpsychotic patients with schizophrenic-like disorders (Kendler, 1985; Siever, Bernstein, & Silverman, 1991). In addition to social detachment, emphasis is placed on eccentricity and cognitive or perceptual distortions.

People who meet the criteria for schizotypal personality disorder frequently meet the criteria for additional Axis II disorders. The relationship between schizotypal personality disorder and the other specific types of personality disorder is illustrated in Figure 9–1. The data in this figure were taken from a study of case records describing approximately 300 patients whose therapists identified them as manifesting at least one personality disorder (Morey, 1988). There is a considerable amount of overlap between schizotypal personality disorder and other personality disorders in Cluster A (paranoid and schizoid) as well as with avoidant personality disorder. This finding is not particularly surprising given the conceptual origins of the schizo-

typal category. There is also quite a bit of overlap between schizotypal personality disorder and borderline personality disorder. In this study, 33 percent of the patients with schizotypal personality disorder also met the criteria for borderline personality disorder.

Etiological Considerations

Most of the interest in the etiology of schizotypal personality disorder has focused on the importance of genetic factors. Family studies have demonstrated that the first-degree relatives of schizophrenic patients are considerably more likely than people in the general population to exhibit schizotypal personality disorder, but the range of estimates is very broad. The prevalence of schizotypal personality disorder among first-degree relatives of schizophrenic patients varies from 5 to 34 percent (Kendler, 1988). Some studies have reported, however, that schizotypal personality disorder is also found with increased frequency among the children of parents with mood disorders (Squires-Wheeler et al., 1989).

The relationship among schizotypal personality disorder, schizophrenia, and major depression can be better understood through an

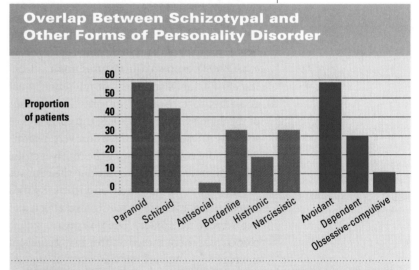

Overlap Between Schizotypal and Other Forms of Personality Disorder

FIGURE 9-1: The proportion of patients meeting the DSM–III–R criteria for schizotypal personality disorder who also met the diagnostic criteria for each of the other types of personality disorder.

Source: From L.C. Morey (1988). Personality disorders in DSM-III and DSM-III-R: Convergence, coverage, and internal consistency. *American Journal of Psychiatry, 145,* 576.

[†] The authors of DSM-III were inconsistent in this decision (Francis, 1980). At the same time that they moved schizophrenia spectrum disorders to the personality section of the manual, they also moved the affective spectrum disorders away from personality (for example, depressive personality disorder) and directly into the section on mood disorders (for example, cyclothymic and dysthymic disorder).

TABLE 9-5

DSM-IV Criteria for Schizotypal Personality Disorder

A. A pervasive pattern of social and interpersonal deficits marked by acute discomfort with, and reduced capacity for, close relationships as well as by cognitive or perceptual distortions and eccentricities of behavior, beginning by early adulthood and present in a variety of contexts, as indicated by five (or more) of the following:

1. Ideas of reference (excluding delusions of reference)
2. Odd beliefs or magical thinking that influences behavior and is inconsistent with subcultural norms (such as superstitiousness, belief in clairvoyance, or telepathy)
3. Unusual perceptual experiences, including bodily illusions
4. Odd thinking and speech (vague, circumstantial, metaphorical, overelaborate, or stereotyped)
5. Suspiciousness or paranoid ideation
6. Inappropriate or constricted affect*
7. Behavior or appearance that is odd, eccentric, or peculiar
8. Lack of close friends or confidants other than first-degree relatives
9. Excessive social anxiety that does not diminish with familiarity and tends to be associated with paranoid fears rather than with negative judgments about self

B. Does not occur exclusively during the course of Schizophrenia, a Mood Disorder with Psychotic Features, another Psychotic Disorder, or a Pervasive Developmental Disorder.

*Inappropriate affect refers to emotional responses that appear to be inconsistent with the social context—for example, uncontrollable giggling at a wake or funeral. Constricted affect refers to the absence of emotional responsiveness, such as lack of facial expressions. See Chapter 12 for a more detailed discussion.

---

examination of the specific criteria that are used to define schizotypal personality. One study compared the nonpsychotic first-degree relatives of schizophrenic patients with the first-degree relatives of depressed patients (Torgersen et al., 1993). Some of the features, such as lacking close friends and ideas of reference, were actually more common among the relatives of the depressed patients. Only three features of schizotypal personality disorder were significantly more common among the relatives of the schizophrenic patients than among the relatives of the depressed patients: odd thinking and speech, inappropriate or constricted affect, and excessive social anxiety. The investigators concluded that these three features may represent the core of "true" schizotypal personality disorder, if that disorder is viewed as a form of personality that is genetically related to schizophrenia.

Several investigators have looked to the literature on schizophrenia to provide clues to the biological correlates of schizotypal personality disorder. This interest should be expected because schizotypal disorder is presumed to be a preliminary or subclinical form of full-blown schizophrenia. If schizophrenic patients have been shown to have a specific type of biological or

psychological abnormality, it stands to reason that it might also be evident among those people who exhibit features of schizotypal personality disorder.

One example of a biological variable that has been extended from the schizophrenia literature to schizotypal personality disorder is the accuracy of smooth-pursuit eye movements. (See Chapter 12 for a discussion of this literature in relation to schizophrenia.) *Smooth-pursuit eye movements* (SPEM) allow the eyes to track a moving target such as a pendulum. Many studies have demonstrated that schizophrenic patients are frequently impaired in their ability to perform smooth-pursuit eye movements (for example, Iacono, 1987; Holzman, 1988). These abnormalities have also been observed among approximately 50 percent of the first-degree relatives of schizophrenic patients.

Psychiatrist Larry Siever and his colleagues have studied schizotypal personality disorder and SPEM abnormalities in a college-student population (Siever et al., 1985; Zemishlany, Siever, & Coccaro, 1988). They found that students who were low-accuracy trackers were significantly more likely than high-accuracy trackers to exhibit features of schizotypal personality disorder. A related study found that subjects who met criteria for schizotypal personality disorder were more likely than normal subjects to exhibit impaired eye tracking. Taken together, these results suggest that similar deficits may be found in subjects with schizotypal personality disorder and schizophrenic patients. They do not prove that the two types of disorder are linked from an etiological perspective, but they are consistent with that hypothesis.

Treatment

Two important considerations complicate the treatment of people with personality disorders. They also make it difficult to evaluate the effectiveness of various forms of intervention (Gorton & Akhtar, 1990). The first consideration involves the ego-syntonic nature of many personality disorders. Many of these people do not seek treatment for their problems because they do not see their own behavior as being the source of distress or interpersonal difficulties. A related difficulty involves premature termination: A relatively high proportion of personality disorder patients drop out of treatment before it is completed.

When people with personality disorders do appear at hospitals or clinics, it is often because they are also suffering from another type of mental disorder, such as depression or substance abuse. This co-morbidity is the second consideration that complicates treatment. "Pure forms" of personality disorder are relatively rare. There is tremendous overlap between specific personality disorder categories and other forms of abnormal behavior, including disorders that would be listed on both Axis I and Axis II. Treatment is seldom aimed at problem behaviors that are associated with only one type of personality disorder, and the efficacy of treatment is therefore difficult to evaluate.

The literature regarding treatment of schizotypal personality disorder, like that dealing with its causes, mirrors efforts aimed at schizophrenia. A few studies have focused on the possible treatment value of antipsychotic drugs, which are effective with many schizophrenic patients. Some studies have found that low doses of antipsychotic medication are beneficial in alleviating cognitive problems and social anxiety in patients who have received a diagnosis of schizotypal personality disorder (for example, Goldberg et al., 1986). There is also some indication that patients with schizotypal personality disorder may respond positively to antidepressant medication (Markovitz et al., 1991). In general, the therapeutic effects of medication are positive, but they tend to be modest (Gitlin, 1993).

Clinical experience seems to suggest that these patients do not respond well to insight-oriented psychotherapy, in part because they do not see themselves as having psychological problems and also because they are so uncomfortable with close personal relationships (Hoch & Polatin, 1949). Some clinicians have suggested that a supportive, educational approach that is focused on fostering basic social skills may be beneficial if the goals of treatment are modest (Stone, 1985; Walsh, 1990). Unfortunately, controlled studies of psychological forms of treatment with schizotypal personality disorder have not been reported.

Borderline Personality Disorder

The intellectual heritage of borderline personality disorder is quite diverse, and is more difficult to trace than is the case with schizotypal personality disorder. It is, in fact, rather confusing. Several traditions are important, and in some cases they represent conflicting points of view (Leichtman, 1989).

Brief Historical Perspective

Otto Kernberg (1967, 1975), a psychiatrist at Cornell University, has developed an explanation of borderline personality disorder that is based on psychodynamic theory. According to Kernberg, borderline disorder is not a specific syndrome. Rather, it refers to a set of personality features or deficiencies that can be found in individuals with various disorders.

In Kernberg's model, the common characteristic of people diagnosed with borderline disorder is faulty development of ego structure. People with this ego weakness frequently try to achieve satisfaction or pleasure through behaviors that normally are associated with infants rather than adults. Especially common are *primary process thinking*, in which the id relieves tensions by imagining the things it desires; and lack of impulse control. Another common feature of people with borderline disorder is *splitting*—the tendency to see people and events alternately as entirely good or entirely bad. Thus, a man with borderline disorder might perceive his wife as almost perfect at some times and as highly flawed at other times. The tendency toward splitting helps explain the broad mood swings and unstable relationships associated with borderline personalities.

Kernberg's emphasis on a broadly defined level of pathology, rather than on discrete clinical symptoms, expanded the boundaries of the concept of borderline personality disorder. Viewed from this perspective, borderline disorder can include a great many types of abnormal behavior, including paranoid, schizoid, and cyclothymic personality disorders, impulse control disorders, substance use disorders, and various types of mood disorder. It should not be surprising, therefore, that the DSM-IV category of borderline personality disorder has been shown to overlap extensively with other forms of personality disorder and with a number of Axis I disorders.

In an effort to foster research on borderline disorders, these psychodynamic views regarding personality organization were translated into more reliable, descriptive terms by several prominent clinicians. John Gunderson, a psychiatrist at Harvard University (1975, 1984), identified a number of descriptive characteristics that are commonly associated with Kernberg's concept of borderline personality. Gunderson and his colleagues developed a structured interview that would allow clinicians to diagnose the condition reliably. Their definition of the concept depends heavily on the presence of intense, unstable interpersonal relationships, manipulative suicide attempts, unstable sense of the self, negative affect, and impulsivity.

Psychiatrist Hagop Akiskal (for example, Akiskal, 1981; Davis & Akiskal, 1986) has proposed another model of borderline personality disorder. Akiskal contends that the borderline personality concept includes a heterogeneous collection of symptoms that are associated with mild forms of brain dysfunction (for example, epilepsy, attention deficit disorder, pregnancy and birth complications), schizophrenic-like conditions, and typical as well as subclinical mood disorders. The title of one classic paper written by Akiskal is particularly revealing: "Borderline: An Adjective in Search of a Noun." In other words, he does not believe that borderline personality disorder is a valid or meaningful diagnostic concept. Akiskal favors the separation of these various conditions into more homogeneous categories. After brain dysfunctions, mood disorders, and schizophrenic spectrum disorders have been excluded, he notes that there remains a "residual" borderline group that is difficult to distinguish from many of the other types of personality disorder.

Clinical Features and Co-morbidity

The DSM-IV criteria for borderline personality disorder are presented in Table 9–6. Their relation to Gunderson's descriptive translation of Kernberg's theoretical perspective should be obvious. The overriding characteristic of borderline personality disorder is a pervasive pattern of instability in self-image, in interpersonal relationships, and in mood. Identity disturbance may be manifested by indecision in areas such as career goals, sexual orientation, and personal values. Chaotic interpersonal relationships are also common. People with borderline personality disorder have a great deal of trouble being alone. Their opinions of significant other people may vacillate from one extreme (overidealization) to the other (devaluation) and back again. Finally, their moods may also shift rapidly and unpredictably from anger to depression and anxiety.

Borderline personality disorder overlaps with several other categories on Axis II, including the histrionic, narcissistic, paranoid, dependent, and avoidant types. Co-morbidity rates from one study (Morey, 1988) are presented in Figure 9–2. This figure actually provides a relatively low estimate of the overlap between schizotypal and borderline personality disorders in comparison to some other studies. Widiger and his colleagues (1986) studied the relations among specific symptoms of borderline personality disorder and schizotypal personality disorder in a sample of hospitalized psychiatric patients. Within their sample, there was a 40 percent overlap of these diagnoses.

▲ **John Gunderson, a psychiatrist at Harvard University, has played a central role in the development of diagnostic criteria for borderline personality disorder.**

There is also a significant amount of overlap between borderline personality disorder and Axis I disorders, especially depression. Several studies have reported rates of major depression ranging from 24 percent to 74 percent among borderline personality disorder patients. Many patients with other types of impulse control problems, such as substance dependence and eating disorders, also qualify for a diagnosis of borderline personality disorder.

Follow-up studies suggest many similarities between borderline personality disorder and mood disorders. Akiskal and his colleagues studied a group of 100 outpatients with a diagnosis of borderline personality disorder. Forty percent were subsequently diagnosed as suffering from a depressed or manic episode. During follow-up, 29 percent of the sample developed severe depression. A longitudinal study of patients who were discharged from a private psychiatric hospital is also interesting in this regard. Of the patients with a pure diagnosis of borderline personality disorder (that is, those who did not receive any other diagnosis on Axis I or II), 23 percent developed major depressive episodes in the course of the 15-year follow-up (McGlashan, 1986). The social and treatment outcome data also suggested that the borderline patients experienced a better outcome than schizophrenic and schizotypal patients, and in that respect they are more similar to patients with mood disorders.

Etiological Considerations

The theoretical perspective of object relations theory and self-psychology has provided the primary view of the origins of borderline personality disorder. Although these arguments are intuitively appealing and based on a rich base of clinical experience, they have been difficult to test empirically.

Akiskal elaborated on Kernberg's psychodynamic theory and proposed a similar model for the development of "residual" borderline conditions, those that remain after the exclusion of brain disorders, mood disorders, and schizotypal disorders. He argued that these people suffer from the negative consequences of parental loss during childhood (Davis & Akiskal, 1986). The model is supported by studies of the families of borderline patients and by comparisons with the literature on social development in monkeys, which has examined the effects of separating infants from their mothers.

The **primate separation model** was proposed by other investigators as an analogue for mood disorders in humans. After young monkeys have been separated from their mothers or peers, they experience persistent problems in the area of attachment behavior (see Chapter 2) and negative affect. Their relationships with peers are disrupted—for example, they have difficulty in establishing and maintaining social hierarchies—and they may exhibit self-destructive behaviors.

TABLE 9–6

DSM-IV Criteria for Borderline Personality Disorder

A pervasive pattern of instability of interpersonal relationships, self-image, and affects, and marked impulsivity beginning by early adulthood and present in a variety of contexts, as indicated by five (or more) of the following:

1. Frantic efforts to avoid real or imagined abandonment
2. A pattern of unstable and intense interpersonal relationships characterized by alternating between extremes of idealization and devaluation
3. Identity disturbance: markedly and persistently unstable self-image or sense of self
4. Impulsiveness in at least two areas that are potentially self-damaging (for example, spending, sex, substance abuse, reckless driving, binge eating)
5. Recurrent suicidal behavior, gestures, or threats, or self-mutilating behavior
6. Affective instability due to a marked reactivity of mood (such as intense episodic dysphoria, irritability, or anxiety usually lasting a few hours and only rarely more than a few days)
7. Chronic feelings of emptiness
8. Inappropriate, intense anger or difficulty controlling anger (for example, frequent displays of temper, constant anger, recurrent physical fights)
9. Transient, stress-related paranoid ideation or severe dissociative symptoms

Many of these problems are reminiscent of the interpersonal difficulties of borderline patients.

Studies of patients with borderline personality disorder point toward the influence of widespread problematic relationships with their parents (Crowell et al., 1993). Separation appears to be only one aspect of this complicated picture. Adolescent girls with borderline personality disorder report pervasive lack of supervision, frequent witnessing of domestic violence, and being subjected to inappropriate behavior by their parents and other adults, including verbal, physical, and sexual abuse (Ludolph et al., 1990; Weston et al., 1990). The extent and severity of abuse varies widely across individuals. Many patients describe multiple forms of abuse by more than a single individual.

We must be careful, however, when we interpret the evidence regarding the relationship between borderline personality disorder and environmental factors such as separation and abuse. With the exception of the data from primate models, all the evidence is correlational. It is therefore risky to draw causal inferences.

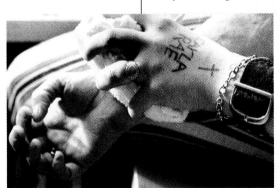
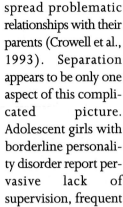

▲ Some people with borderline personality disorders engage in recurrent suicidal gestures or self-mutilating behaviors.

What is the direction of effect? It seems likely that this type of family conflict represents the result of a dynamic, transactional process in which children and parents influence each other over an extended period of time (Crowell et al., 1993). Although traumatic experiences are reported frequently by borderline subjects, they are relatively low in severity, and the overall prevalence of this type of environmental event is also relatively high among people with other types of mental disorder (Paris, 1992). A model that attempts to account for the etiology of borderline personality disorder in particular, rather than mental disorder in general, will need to explain why some people develop these specific types of symptoms in response to experiences such as neglect, separation, and abuse while many others do not.

Treatment

Given that the concept of borderline personality disorder is rooted in psychodynamic theory, it should not be surprising that many leading clinicians have advocated the use of psychotherapy for the treatment of these conditions (Freeman & Gunderson, 1989; Shea, 1991). In psychodynamically based treatment, the *transference relationship*, defined as the way in which the patient behaves toward the therapist, is used to increase patients' ability to experience themselves and other people in a more realistic and integrated way.

Personality disorders have traditionally been considered to be hard to treat from a psychological perspective, and borderline conditions are among the most difficult. Close personal relationships form the foundation of psychological intervention, and it is specifically in the area of establishing and maintaining such relationships that borderline patients experience their greatest difficulty. Their persistent alternation between overidealization and devaluation leads to frequent rage toward the therapist, and can become a significant deterrent to progress in therapy. Not surprisingly, between one-half and two-thirds of all patients with borderline personality disorder discontinue treatment, against their therapists' advice, within the first several weeks of treatment (Kelly et al., 1992).

One promising approach to psychotherapy with borderline patients is called *dialectical behavior therapy* (DBT) (Linehan, 1987; Linehan et al.,

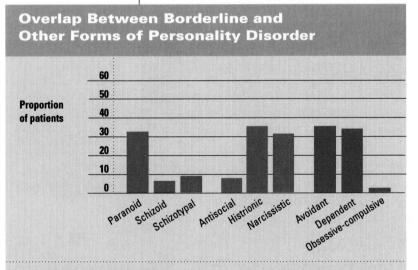

Overlap Between Borderline and Other Forms of Personality Disorder

Proportion of patients

60
50
40
30
20
10
0

Paranoid · Schizoid · Schizotypal · Antisocial · Histrionic · Narcissistic · Avoidant · Dependent · Obsessive-compulsive

FIGURE 9-2: The proportion of patients meeting the DSM–III–R criteria for borderline personality disorder who also met the diagnostic criteria for each of the other types of personality disorder.

Source: From L.C. Morey (1988). Personality disorders in DSM-III and DSM-III-R: Convergence, coverage, and internal consistency. *American Journal of Psychiatry, 145,* 576.

1991). This procedure combines the use of broadly based behavioral strategies with the more general principles of supportive psychotherapy. Traditional behavioral and cognitive techniques, such as skill training, exposure, and problem solving, are employed to help the patient improve interpersonal relationships, tolerate distress, and regulate emotional respon-ses. Considerable emphasis is also placed on the therapist's acceptance of patients, including their frequently demanding, manipulative, and contradictory behaviors. This factor is important, because borderline patients are extremely sensitive to even the most subtle signs of criticism or rejection by other people.

A controlled study of dialectical behavior therapy produced encouraging results with regard to some aspects of the patients' behavior (Linehan et al., 1991). Patients were randomly assigned to receive either DBT or treatment as usual, which was essentially any form of treatment that was available within the community. The adjustment of patients in both groups was measured after 1 year of treatment and over a 1-year period following termination. One of the most important results involved the dropout rate. Almost 60 percent of the patients in the treatment-as-usual group terminated prematurely, whereas the rate in the DBT group was only 17 percent. The patients who received DBT also showed a significant reduction in the frequency and severity of suicide attempts, and they spent fewer days in psychiatric hospitals over the course of the study. The groups did not differ, however, on other important measures such as level of depression and hopelessness. In general, the study suggests that DBT is a promising form of treatment for people with borderline personality disorder.

Psychotropic medication is also used frequently in the treatment of borderline patients. Unfortunately, no disorder-specific drug has been found. Psychiatrists employ the entire spectrum of psychoactive medication with borderline patients, from antipsychotics and antidepressants to lithium and anticonvulsants. Different types of drugs are recommended to treat individual symptoms, but there is no systematic proof that a specific drug is effective for any of the borderline features (Davis & Akiskal, 1986).

Antisocial Personality Disorder

The final type of personality disorder that we will consider in detail is antisocial personality disorder. It is the oldest and most thoroughly studied form of personality disorder. Unlike schizotypal personality disorder, it is not generally considered to be a precursor to a more severe form of Axis I disorder, with the possible exception of substance dependence problems. Unlike borderline personality disorder, the recognition of this disorder did not grow out of psychodynamic theory or experience with psychotherapy.

Brief Historical Perspective

The history of the concept can be traced to Pritchard's concept of moral insanity, which was originally proposed in 1830 (Blashfield & McElroy, 1989). The terms *moral insanity* and *psychopathic insanity* were used throughout the nineteenth century to refer to persistent patterns of immoral and criminal behavior, including thievery, swindling, and drug abuse.

The current American view of antisocial personality disorder was heavily influenced by two specific books. The first, *The Mask of Sanity*, was written by Hervey Cleckley, a psychiatrist at the University of Georgia, and was originally published in 1941. It included numerous case examples of impulsive, self-centered, pleasure-seeking people who seemed to be completely lacking in certain primary emotions such as anxiety, shame, and guilt. Cleckley used the term **psychopathy** to describe this disorder. According to Cleckley's definition, the psychopath is a person who is intelligent and superficially charming, but also chronically deceitful, unreliable, and incapable of learning from experience.

The second book that influenced the concept of antisocial personality disorder was a report by Lee Robins of her follow-up study of children who had been treated many years earlier at a child guidance clinic. The book, titled *Deviant Children Grown Up* (Robins, 1966), demonstrated that certain forms of conduct disorder that were evident during childhood, especially among boys, were reliable predictors of other forms of antisocial behavior when these same people became adults.

Clinical Features and Co-morbidity

The DSM-III definition of antisocial personality disorder departed from Cleckley's concept by emphasizing the importance of specific antisocial behaviors rather than more general traits such as lack of empathy or disregard for the truth. Cleckley's definition was difficult to use reliably because it relied on such elusive categories as "incapacity for love" and "failure to learn from experience." Therefore, the authors of DSM-III focused their definition on more tangible consequences of these personality traits, such as failure to sustain consistent work behavior, failure to function as a responsible parent, and failure to conform to social norms with respect to lawful behavior.

This shift in emphasis became one of the more controversial features of the personality disorder section in DSM-III. Critics argued that DSM-III had blurred the distinction between antisocial personality behavior and criminality. Research studies indicated that 50 percent of prison inmates would meet the DSM-III criteria for antisocial personality disorder, whereas only 35 percent of these same prisoners would fit Cleckley's definition of the psychopath (Hare, 1991). It seemed that the true meaning of the concept might have been sacrificed for the sake of improved reliability.

Table 9–7 lists the DSM-IV criteria for antisocial personality disorder. One prominent feature in this definition is the required presence of symptoms of conduct disorder (see Chapter 15) prior to the age of 15, which reflects the impact of Robins's work. The definition also requires the presence of at least three out of seven signs of irresponsible and antisocial behavior after the age of 15. One of these criteria, "lack of remorse," did not appear in DSM-III but was one of Cleckley's original criteria. Its inclusion

▲ **The best predictor of adult antisocial personality disorder in Lee Robins's study was conduct disorder that is characterized by physical aggression and other rule violations.**

in DSM-IV clearly signals an attempt to move the definition back toward the original concept.

The relationship between antisocial personality disorder and other types of personality disorder is illustrated in Figure 9–3, again using data from the study reported by Morey (1988). The greatest overlap is between antisocial personality disorder and the narcissistic, borderline, and histrionic categories. Conversely, there is relatively little overlap between antisocial personality disorder and the three categories that fall in the so-called anxious cluster: avoidant, dependent, and obsessive-compulsive personality disorders.

Overlap between antisocial personality disorder and Axis I disorders involves primarily substance dependence. This topic will be discussed more fully in Chapter 10. Contrary to Cleckley's original formation, recent evidence suggests that antisocial personality disorder is not incompatible with the presence of anxiety disorders or depression.

Some clinicians believe that antisocial behavior dissipates with age. Follow-up studies suggest that psychopaths tend to "burn out" when they reach middle age. For example, Hare, McPherson, and Forth (1988) conducted a longitudinal study with a sample of men who were in prison. They divided the sample into men who were considered psychopaths and those who were not. They then collected various pieces of information regarding the criminal histories of both groups of men from the ages of 16 to 45. Differences between these two groups were greatest between the ages of 30 and 40, when the psychopaths' criminal activities were particularly marked. After age 40, the differences gradually disappeared. The psychopathic men continued to engage in a relatively high rate of criminal activity, even after the age of 50, but their antisocial behavior was less exaggerated than in previous years.

Several explanations might account for this *relative* decrease in criminal behavior. One is that psychopaths may mature more slowly than control subjects with regard to social behavior, and this developmental lag may eventually be outgrown. Another possibility is that the psychopaths become more adept at avoiding being caught or convicted. A third possibility is that the psychopaths shift their antisocial behaviors away from the kinds of activities that lead to criminal convictions and incarceration. (We exam-

TABLE 9-7

DSM-IV Criteria for Antisocial Personality Disorder

A. There is a pervasive pattern of disregard for and violation of the rights of others occurring since age 15, as indicated by three (or more) of the following:

1. Failure to conform to social norms with respect to lawful behaviors as indicated by repeatedly performing acts that are grounds for arrest
2. Deceitfulness, as indicated by repeated lying, use of aliases, or conning others for personal profit or pleasure
3. Impulsivity or failure to plan ahead
4. Irritability and aggressiveness, as indicated by repeated physical fights or assaults
5. Reckless disregard for safety of self or others
6. Consistent irresponsibility, as indicated by repeated failure to sustain consistent work behavior or honor financial obligations
7. Lack of remorse, as indicated by being indifferent to or rationalizing having hurt, mistreated, or stolen from another

B. The individual is at least 18 years old

C. Evidence of Conduct Disorder with onset before age 15

ine this issue in greater detail in Further Thoughts in this chapter.)

Etiological Considerations

Psychologists have studied etiological factors for antisocial personality disorder more extensively than for any of the other personality disorders. Research studies on this topic fall into three general areas. One is concerned with biological underpinnings of the disorder, especially the possible influence of genetic factors. The second focus of investigation has been the relationship between familial conflict and the development of antisocial behavior in children. A third group of studies has addressed the nature of the psychological deficit that might explain the apparent inability of people with antisocial personality disorder to learn from experience. This research has typically focused on the ability of psychopathic subjects to perform avoidance learning tasks in a laboratory setting.

BIOLOGICAL FACTORS

Several investigators have employed adoption methods to evaluate the relative contributions of genetic and environmental factors to the development of antisocial personality disorder, and of criminal behavior more generally (Crowe, 1983; DiLalla & Gottesman, 1991). This strategy is based on the study of *adoptees*—people who

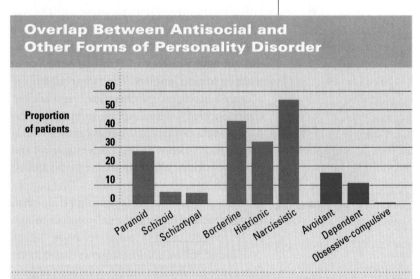

Overlap Between Antisocial and Other Forms of Personality Disorder

Proportion of patients

FIGURE 9-3: The proportion of patients meeting the DSM–III–R criteria for antisocial personality disorder who also met the diagnostic criteria for each of the other types of personality disorder.

Source: From L.C. Morey (1988). Personality disorders in DSM-III and DSM-III-R: Convergence, coverage, and internal consistency. *American Journal of Psychiatry*, 145, 576.

were separated from their biological parents at an early age and raised by adoptive families. Adoptees share a large proportion of their genes with their biological relatives, but the environments in which they were raised were presumably not especially similar to those of their biological relatives. They have, on the other hand, shared the same environment with their adoptive families. The extent to which the adoptees' behavior resembles that of their biological relatives is taken to be evidence for the influence of genetic factors, and the extent to which their behavior is similar to that of their adoptive relatives presumably reflects the influence of environmental factors.

Adoption studies have focused more on criminal behavior, as measured by the subjects' arrest records, than on personality traits associated with psychopathy. The implicit assumption is that there is a close association between antisocial personality disorder and criminal behavior. The results of these studies indicate that both genetic and environmental factors contribute to the etiology of criminal behavior (Cloninger & Gottesman, 1987).

Consider, for example, one large-scale study of adopted men in Sweden, the results of which are presented in Table 9–8. The prevalence of petty criminal behavior among adoptees who did not have a history of criminal behavior in either their biological or adoptive families was 3 percent. The rate doubled among men whose adoptive families included criminals but who did not have a history of criminal behavior in their biological families. The rate tripled if the adoptee's biological parents were criminals but their adoptive families were not criminal. The highest rate of criminal behavior was found among those men who had both biological and adoptive parents with criminal records; almost half of these men were criminals. This pattern of results provides strong support for the notion that genetic and environmental events combine in the production of criminal behavior.

The adoption studies suggest that genetic factors are involved in the development of criminal behavior, but what about specific personality traits that are associated with antisocial personality disorder? Twin studies have addressed this issue using dimensional measures of personality, similar to the traits identified in the five-factor model (see Table 9–2). Like the adoption studies, these investigations indicate that personality traits are influenced by a combined effect of genetic and environmental factors. The relative contributions of these factors varies from one trait to the next. Relatively substantial contributions of genetic factors are found for traits that are considered to be associated with antisocial personality disorder, such as callousness, oppositionality, and stimulus seeking (Livesley et al., 1993).

SOCIAL FACTORS: THE ROLE OF THE FAMILY

Adoption studies and twin studies indicate that genetic factors interact with environmental events to produce patterns of antisocial and criminal behavior. What kinds of environmental events might be involved in this process? One obvious candidate is family conflict. Robins (1966) found that inconsistent discipline or the complete absence of discipline in a family was associated with an increased probability that children would receive a diagnosis of antisocial personality disorder when they reached adulthood. She also found that subjects who received a diagnosis of antisocial personality disorder as adults were likely to have had fathers who exhibited antisocial behavior themselves. The general picture that emerged from Robins's study suggests that parental behaviors can have an important influence on the development of antisocial behavior in their children.

How can the interaction between genetic factors and family processes be explained? One possibility involves the concept of children's temperament and the effect that their characteristic response styles may have on parental behavior. Children with a "difficult" temperament—whose response style is characterized by high levels of negative emotion or excessive activity—may be especially irritating to their parents and caretakers. Their resistance to disciplinary efforts may discourage adults from maintaining persistent strategies in this regard (Lee & Bates, 1985; Maccoby & Jacklin, 1983). This type of child may be most likely to evoke maladaptive reactions from parents who are poorly equipped to deal with the challenges presented by this kind of

TABLE 9–8

Rates of Criminal Behavior Among Male Adoptees

Criminal History in Biological Relatives	Criminal History in Adoptive Relatives	
	NO	YES
NO	3%	7%
YES	12%	40%

Source: From C.R. Cloninger, et al. (1982). Predisposition to petty criminality in Swedish adoptees. II: Cross-fostering analysis of gene-environment interaction. *Archives of General Psychiatry, 39,* 1242-1249.

behavior. Parents who are disadvantaged themselves, by being psychologically disturbed or poorly educated, may respond in maladaptive ways and thus increase the antisocial behaviors exhibited by their children. One theory that has incorporated this type of interactional sequence is outlined in Further Thoughts.

PSYCHOLOGICAL FACTORS: AVOIDANCE LEARNING AND DISINHIBITION

Adoption, twin, and family studies provide clues to the types of etiological factors that may cause antisocial personality disorder. Another series of studies, beginning in the 1950s and extending to the present, has been concerned with the psychological mechanisms that may mediate this type of behavior. These investigations have attempted to explain several characteristic features of psychopathy, such as lack of anxiety, impulsivity, and failure to learn from experience, using various types of laboratory tasks. Subjects in these tasks are typically asked to learn a sequence of responses in order to either receive a reward or avoid an aversive consequence, such as electric shock or loss of money. Although the overall accuracy of psychopaths' performance on these tasks is generally equivalent to that of nonpsychopathic subjects, their behavior sometimes appears to be unaffected by the anticipation of punishment (Lykken, 1957; Kosson & Newman, 1986). Two primary hypotheses have been advanced to explain the poor performance of psychopaths on these tasks.

One point of view holds that psychopaths are relatively insensitive to, or able to ignore, the effects of punishment. Evidence for this hypothesis is based in large part on an examination of physiological responses while subjects are performing laboratory tasks. When they are at rest, the average skin conductance level (SCL) of psychopaths is lower than that of normal subjects. Psychopaths' SCLs are also lower than normals' when subjects are presented with, or anticipating, an aversive event such as electric shock. A different pattern is found using heart rate as the dependent measure. When psychopaths are anticipating unpleasant or stressful stimuli, their heart rate is *elevated* in comparison to normal subjects. Increased heart rate has been interpreted as a reflection of "gating out" sensory input. This effect may indicate that psychopaths are able to easily ignore aversive events that might

be contingent on their behaviors (Hare, 1978; Harpur & Hare, 1990).

The other hypothesis holds that psychopaths have difficulty shifting or reallocating their attention to consider the possible negative consequences of their behavior after a response pattern has been well established. Evidence for this explanation is based in large part on the observation that psychopaths respond normally to punishment in some situations but not in others. This is especially evident in mixed-incentive situations, in which the person's behavior might be either rewarded or punished. The behavior of psychopaths appears to be disinhibited because they are less able than other people to suspend activities that may be rewarded in order to reflect upon the meaning of important, but less salient, cues that indicate that their behavior might lead to punishment (Newman, Kosson, & Patterson, 1992; Patterson & Newman, 1993).

Critics of this line of research have noted that there are problems with existing psychological explanations for the psychopath's behavior. One limitation is the implicit assumption that most people conform to social regulations and ethical principles because of anxiety or fear of punishment. The heart of this criticism seems to lie in a disagreement regarding the relative importance of Cleckley's criteria for psychopathy. It might be argued that the most crucial features are not low anxiety and failure to learn from experience, but lack of shame and pathological egocentricity. According to this perspective, the psychopath is simply a person who has chosen, for whatever reason, to behave in a persistently selfish manner that ignores the feelings and rights of other people. "Rather than moral judgment being driven by anxiety, anxiety is driven by moral judgment" (Levenson, 1992).

Treatment

People with antisocial personalities seldom seek professional mental health services unless they are forced into treatment by the legal system. When they do seek treatment, the general consensus among clinicians is that it is seldom effective (Quality Assurance Project, 1991). This widely held impression is based, in part, on the traits that are used to define the disorder; like people with borderline personality disorder, people with antisocial personality disorder are

A Systems View of Life-Course-Persistent Antisocial Behavior

Terrie Moffitt, a clinical psychologist at the University of Wisconsin, has proposed that there are two primary forms of antisocial behavior: transient and nontransient. Moffitt considers *adolescence-limited antisocial behavior* to be a common form of social behavior that is often adaptive and disappears by the time the person reaches adulthood. This type presumably accounts for most antisocial behavior, and it is unrelated to antisocial personality disorder.

A small proportion of antisocial individuals—mostly males—engage in antisocial behavior at all ages. Moffitt calls this type *life-course-persistent antisocial behavior*. The specific form of these problems may vary from one age level to the next.

> Biting and hitting at age 4, shoplifting and truancy at age 10, selling drugs and stealing cars at age 16, robbery and rape at age 22, and fraud and child abuse at age 30, the underlying disposition remains the same, but its expression changes form as new social opportunities arise at different points in development. (Moffitt, 1993, p. 679)

This argument suggests an interpretation of the criminal histories of psychopaths reported by Hare et al. (1988). Rather than "burning out" as they grow older, psychopaths may find new outlets for their aggression, their impulsive behavior, and their callous disregard for others. For example, they might resort to fraud or child abuse, for which they are less likely to get caught. The variability of expression of antisocial behavior across time and situations also brings to mind the methodological issues involved in measuring stable personality traits. There is a clear need to make composite ratings of antisocial traits rather than counting specific behaviors, and to aggregate measures of antisocial behavior over time (see Research Methods).

Moffitt's explanation for the etiology of life-course-persistent antisocial behavior depends on the influence of multiple, interacting systems. Several studies have found that children and adolescents who engage in persistently antisocial behavior exhibit two subtle kinds of deficits on neuropsychological tests: problems with language and impaired "executive" functions. The verbal deficits interfere with reading, listening, remembering, and problem-solving abilities. Impaired executive functions become evident in the child's impulsive behavior, lack of attention, and poor self-control.

These subtle neuropsychological problems, which may well be genetically determined, are initially expressed in the form of "difficult" temperament. The child may be clumsy, overactive, inattentive, irritable, or impulsive. These characteristics presumably elicit maladaptive responses from parents and other adults, who may be driven to the use of unusually harsh punishments or the eventual abandonment of any attempt at discipline. This interaction between the child and the social environment fosters the development of poorly controlled behavior. Antisocial behavior is perpetuated when the person selects friends who share similar antisocial interests and problems.

After a pattern of antisocial behavior has been established during childhood, many factors lock the person into further antisocial activities, narrowing his or her options and increasing the likelihood that he or she will continue to behave the same way. Moffitt emphasizes two sources of continuity. The first is a limited range of behavioral skills. The person does not learn social skills that would allow him or her to pursue more appropriate responses than behaviors such as lying, cheating, and stealing. Once the opportunity to develop these skills is lost during childhood, they may never be learned. The second source of continuity involves the results of antisocial behavior during childhood and adolescence. The person becomes progressively ensnared by the aftermath of earlier choices. Many possible consequences of antisocial behavior, including being addicted to drugs, becoming a teenaged parent, dropping out of school, and having a criminal record, can narrow the person's options. ■

typically unable to establish intimate, trusting relationships, which obviously form the basis for any treatment program.

The research literature regarding the treatment of antisocial personality disorder is actually rather sparse (Blackburn, 1990; Perry, 1990). Very few studies have identified cases using official diagnostic criteria for antisocial personality disorder. Most of the programs that have been evaluated have focused on juvenile delinquents, adults who have been imprisoned, or people otherwise referred by the criminal justice system. Outcome is often measured in terms of the frequency of repeated criminal offenses rather than in terms of changes in behaviors more directly linked to the personality traits that define the core of antisocial personality. The high rate of alcoholism and other forms of substance dependence in this population is another problem that complicates planning and evaluating treatment programs aimed specifically at the personality disorder itself.

Although no form of intervention has proved to be effective for antisocial personality disorder, psychological interventions that are directed toward specific features of the disorder might be useful. Examples are behavioral procedures that were originally designed for anger man-

agement and deviant sexual behaviors. Behavioral treatments can apparently produce temporary changes in behavior while the person is closely supervised, but they may not generalize to other settings (Freeman & Gunderson, 1989).

In spite of this generally pessimistic conclusion, there are some hints in the literature that suggest that some people who meet the criteria for antisocial personality disorder may benefit from psychological treatment. One such study was concerned with the use of psychotherapy for the treatment of former opiate addicts who were attending a methadone maintenance clinic (Gerstley et al., 1989; Woody et al., 1985). The overall result was consistent with negative expectations based on the rest of the literature. Patients who had a diagnosis of antisocial personality disorder were less improved at the end of 6 months of treatment than were patients without a diagnosis of antisocial personality disorder. The investigators also found, however, that the patients with antisocial personality disorder who were *also depressed* at the start of treatment improved as much as the patients who did not have antisocial personality disorder. They concluded that the presence of depression in people with antisocial personality disorder may be associated with a better prognosis for treatment.

Summary

Personality disorders are defined in terms of rigid, inflexible, maladaptive ways of perceiving and responding to oneself and one's environment that lead to social or occupational problems or subjective distress. Major problems in interpersonal relationships are among the hallmark features of personality disorders. Many of the traits and symptoms that are associated with these problems are ego-syntonic. In other words, many people with personality disorders do not see themselves as being disturbed. Most people in the general population who would qualify for a diagnosis of personality disorder do not seek treatment for these problems.

Personality disorders are controversial for a number of reasons, including their low diagnostic reliability, the tremendous overlap among specific personality disorder categories, and the relative absence of effective forms of treatment.

Individual differences in **temperament** are

KEY TERMS

- agreeableness
- antisocial personality disorder
- avoidant personality disorder
- borderline personality disorder
- conscientiousness
- dependent personality disorder
- extraversion
- histrionic personality disorder
- narcissistic personality disorder
- neuroticism

evident early in infancy and childhood. These characteristic response styles are not invariably present in all situations, but they do have an important effect on the way in which children interact with their social environments. The responses that children elicit from other people in turn influence the development of more elaborate **personality** traits, which include consideration of cognitive and motivational factors. Human behavior is obviously determined by a dynamic, ongoing interaction between personality traits and situational variables.

Many systems have been proposed to describe the fundamental dimensions of human personality. One that has become quite popular is known as the five-factor model, which includes basic traits known as **neuroticism**, **extraversion**, **openness to experience**, **agreeableness**, and **conscientiousness**. Extreme variations in any of these traits—being either pathologically high or low—can be associated with personality disorders. Lack of flexibility in adapting to challenges and demands presented by a person's environment is an extremely important consideration in deciding whether or not the person's location on these dimensions warrants possible consideration as a personality disorder.

DSM-IV lists ten types of personality disorder, arranged in three clusters. There is considerable overlap among and between these types. Cluster A includes the **paranoid**, **schizoid**, and **schizotypal** forms of personality disorder. These are generally people who are seen as being odd or eccentric. Cluster B includes the **antisocial**, **borderline**, **histrionic**, and **narcissistic** forms of personality disorder. People who fit into this cluster are generally seen as being dramatic, unpredictable, and overly emotional. Cluster C includes the **avoidant**, **dependent**, and **obsessive-compulsive** types. The common element in these disorders is presumably anxiety or fearfulness.

Dimensional approaches to the description of personality disorder provide an interesting alternative to this categorical system. These procedures provide for rating a person on a number of traits, such as those included in the five-factor model. Dimensional classification systems have the advantage of being better able to account for similarities and differences between people with various combinations of personality traits.

The lifetime prevalence of personality disorders among adults in the general population is between 10 and 14 percent. Rates are much higher during adolescence. They peak at age 13 or 14 and decline steadily until early adulthood, when they seem to stabilize. Evidence regarding the prevalence of specific subtypes varies considerably from one study to the next and is influenced in part by the choice of assessment method. Borderline, dependent, and obsessive-compulsive personality disorders seem to affect 1 to 2 percent of adults in community samples. Schizotypal, antisocial, and histrionic types are relatively common in U.S. samples, but they are found less frequently in studies conducted in other countries. Schizoid and narcissistic personality disorders appear to be relatively rare.

The history of the concepts behind specific types of personality disorder can take several different forms. The disorders listed in Cluster A, especially schizoid and schizotypal personality disorder, have been viewed as possible antecedents or subclinical forms of schizophrenia. They are defined largely in terms of minor symptoms that resemble the hallucinations and delusions seen in the full-blown disorder, as well as peculiar behaviors that have been observed among the first-degree relatives of schizophrenic patients. Research on the etiology of schizotypal personality disorder has focused primarily on studies of its genetic relationship to schizophrenia and on the comparison of people with schizotypal personality disorder to patients with schizophrenia on a variety of laboratory measures.

The origins of the concept of borderline personality disorder are somewhat difficult to explain, because it is based on more than one theoretical perspective. One primary source is object relations theory, which is a modern branch of psychoanalytic theory. The DSM-IV definition of borderline personality disorder grew out of an attempt to translate speculation regarding personality structure and defense mechanisms into more reliable, descriptive terms. Some investigators believe that borderline personality disorder is still an extremely heterogeneous category that should be further subdivided.

Research regarding the etiology of borderline personality disorder has focused on two primary areas. One involves the impact of chaotic and abusive families. The other is concerned with the premature separation of children from their parents. Both sets of factors can presumably lead to problems in emotional regulation.

Treatment procedures for people with personality disorders are especially difficult to design and evaluate, for three principal reasons. First, people with these disorders frequently don't have insight into the nature of their problems. They are therefore unlikely to seek treatment, and if they do, they frequently terminate prematurely. Second, pure forms of personality disorder are relatively rare. Most people with a personality disorder who are in treatment also exhibit co-morbid forms of personality disorder and/or co-morbid Axis I disorders, such as depression or drug addiction. Third, people with personality disorder have difficulty establishing and maintaining meaningful, stable interpersonal relationships of the sort that are required for psychotherapy.

Treatment for schizotypal and borderline personality disorders often involves the use of antipsychotic medication or antidepressant medication. A few controlled studies indicate that these drugs can be beneficial for patients with these problems. Long-term outcome tends to be better for patients with borderline than schizotypal personality disorder. Various types of psychological intervention, including psychodynamic procedures as well as dialectical behavior therapy, have frequently been employed with borderline patients.

Critical Thinking

1. The DSM-IV lists the personality disorders on a separate axis from the other types of mental disorder. In what ways are these problems different from disorders like depression, schizophrenia, and alcoholism? How are they similar?

2. Imagine that you are a clinical psychologist who is treating a client who is depressed. How would your treatment plan change if you knew that, in addition to a diagnosis of unipolar mood disorder on Axis I, the person also met the DSM-IV criteria for borderline personality disorder? What if the Axis II diagnosis was dependent personality disorder?

3. Think of a prototypical case of borderline personality disorder, as defined by DSM-IV. How would you describe that person's behavior in terms of the dimensions of the five-factor model? Can you think of any advantages to thinking about the person's behavior in terms of these dimensions rather than using the DSM-IV category?

4. Imagine that you are a judge who must decide the fate of a 17-year-old male juvenile delinquent who has just been convicted of his first felony offense (theft). You know that he has a long history of truancy from school and of running away from home. His attorney asks you to place him on probation contingent upon his entering into psychological treatment, on the grounds that he is suffering from a mental disorder. What would you do? Does that seem like a plausible alternative to jail? Would you respond differently if the man were 40 years old?

10

Alcoholism and Substance Use Disorders

The abuse of alcohol and other drugs is one of the most serious problems facing our society. The costs of substance abuse are astronomical; the price is paid in the form of lost productivity, as well as higher costs for health care, aid to families, and law enforcement. Alcohol and drug problems receive a great deal of attention in the popular media, as illustrated by former baseball player Mickey Mantle's struggle with alcoholism and the drug-related suicide of Kurt Cobain, leader of the rock group Nirvana. Research efforts, treatment priorities, and national publicity have all helped transform national attitudes toward the abuse of chemical substances. The picture of the drug addict as a homeless derelict whose personality defects and lack of motivation are largely responsible for the problem is being replaced by a new view in which substance abuse is seen to affect people from all walks of life. Experts now locate the causes of alcoholism and substance abuse within a comprehensive biopsychosocial model, and treatment is increasingly included within mainstream health-care programs and health insurance (Roman & Blum, 1987).

▼ Addicts will abandon other important responsibilities and risk losing everything just to take the drug. According to the photographer who took this picture, the woman used her food stamps to purchase crack cocaine, which she is smoking while children (her own and her sister's) stand nearby.

Overview

The habitual use of various kinds of drugs or chemical substances can create problems that interfere with a person's social and occupational functioning. The DSM-IV uses two terms to describe substance use disorders, which reflect two different levels of severity. **Substance dependence**, the more severe of the two forms, refers to a pattern of repeated self-administration that often results in *tolerance*, the need for increased amounts of the drug to achieve intoxication; *withdrawal*, unpleasant physical and psychological effects that the person experiences when he or she tries to stop taking the drug; or compulsive drug-taking behavior. **Substance abuse** describes a more broadly conceived, less severe pattern of drug use that is defined in terms of interference with the person's ability to fulfill major role obligations at work or at home, the recurrent use of a drug in dangerous situations, or the experience of repeated legal difficulties that are associated with drug use. People with a substance use disorder frequently abuse several types of drugs; this condition is known as **polysubstance abuse**.

Addiction is another, older term that is often used to describe problems such as alcoholism. The term has been replaced in official terminology by the term *substance dependence*, with which it is synonymous, but it is still used informally by many lay people. Most people have two principal things in mind when they use the word *addiction*: craving and lack of control. A person who is addicted to something presumably has a compelling need for it and also experiences considerable difficulty regulating behaviors that are associated with it.

When used in this fashion, the notion of addiction can be applied to many forms of behavior that extend well beyond the use of drugs. Many people feel that they are addicted to food. Others have difficulty with "compulsive" behaviors, such as gambling and sex. In fact, the list could probably be expanded to include things like watching television, shopping, working, and running. Because of the similarities across these various types of problems, some experts have chosen to view them all as "excessive appetites" (Orford, 1985). These problems have also been called "central activities," which are defined in terms of (1) a puzzling inability to manage the problem behavior, and (2) a self-destructive component (Fingarette, 1988). This is a legitimate and interesting approach to the problems of addiction. For the sake of this chapter, however, we will focus on problems that center on the abuse of chemical substances.

A **drug of abuse**—sometimes called a *psychoactive substance*—is a chemical substance that alters a person's mood, level of perception, or brain functioning (Schuckit, 1989). All drugs of abuse can be used to increase a person's psychological comfort level (make you feel "high") or to alter levels of consciousness. The list of chemicals on which people can become dependent is long, and seems to be growing longer. It includes drugs that are legally available in our society, whether over the counter or by prescription only, as well as many that are illegal (see Table 10–1).

The *central nervous system (CNS) depressants* include alcohol as well as types of medication that are used for helping people sleep, called *hypnotics*, and those for relieving anxiety, known as *sedatives* or *anxiolytics*. The *CNS stimulants* include illegal drugs like amphetamine and cocaine, as well as nicotine and caffeine. The *opiates*, also called *narcotic analgesics*, can be used clinically to decrease pain. The *cannabinoids*, such as marijuana, produce euphoria and an altered sense of time. At higher doses, they may produce hallucinations.

One basic question we must address is whether we should view each type of addiction as a unique problem. Experts who answer "yes" to this question point out that each class of abused substance seems to affect the body in distinct ways. For example, the long-term use of opiates such as heroin does not seem to cause

many chronic physical health problems (Brecher, 1972; Room, 1987), whereas alcohol and tobacco can have a devastating impact on a person's physical health.

TABLE 10-1

Classification of Psychoactive Drugs

Class	Examples
CNS depressants	Alcohol Hypnotics (barbiturates) Anxiolytics (antianxiety drugs)
CNS stimulants	Amphetamine ("speed") Cocaine Caffeine Nicotine Methylphenidate (Ritalin) Weight-loss products
Opiates	Heroin Morphine Methadone Prescription painkillers (almost all)
Cannabinoids	Marijuana Hashish
Hallucinogens	Lysergic acid diethylamide (LSD) Mescaline Psilocybin
Solvents	Aerosol sprays Glues Paint thinner
Over-the-counter drugs	Sedatives (sleep aids) Weak stimulants
Others	Phencyclidine (PCP)

Source: Adapted from M.A. Schuckit (1989). *Drug and alcohol abuse: A clinical guide to diagnosis and treatment* (3rd ed.). New York: Plenum.

Despite these differences, the various forms of substance abuse share many common elements. The psychological and biochemical effects on the user are often similar, as are the negative consequences for both social and occupational behaviors. At the most fundamental level, all forms of abuse represent the inherent conflict between immediate pleasure and longer-term harmful consequences (Lang, 1983). The reasons for initial experimentation with a drug, the factors that influence the transition to dependence, and the processes that lead to relapse after initial efforts to change are all similar in many respects. For these reasons, many clinicians and researchers have moved toward a view of substance abuse that emphasizes common causes, behaviors, and consequences (Marlatt et al., 1988; Miller, 1987). In fact, DSM-IV employs a single set of diagnostic criteria that defines dependence for all types of drugs.

In this chapter, we employ a commonalities approach rather than deal with each substance in isolation. We use alcohol dependence and abuse to illustrate various diagnostic and etiological issues, with occasional reference to other drugs. We have chosen this approach because more is known about alcohol and its abuse than about any of the other drugs.

Alcoholism affects an enormous number of people in especially devastating ways. It also wreaks havoc with the lives of those around them.

No other habit or culturally determined behavior pattern creates more medical problems than does alcohol abuse; no other social "deviance" leads to more somatic pathology. But at the same time, there is no other so-called disease in which both etiology and cure are more profoundly dependent upon social, economic, and cultural variables. (Vaillant, 1983, p. 15)

It is difficult to exaggerate the severity of health problems associated with alcohol use and abuse. The most obvious effects are cirrhosis of the liver and the irreversible memory deficits associated with dementia (see Chapter 13). In addition, alcohol plays an important role in many suicides, homicides, and accidents. When all of these problems are taken together, alcohol is the fourth leading cause of death in the United States (Merikangas, 1990).

Ernest Hemingway (1899–1961), a Nobel Prize-winning writer, was a chronic alcohol abuser (Goodwin, 1988). The following paragraphs, quoted from an article by Paul Johnson (1989), describe the progression of Hemingway's drinking and the problems that it created. They illustrate many typical features of alcohol dependence as well as the devastating impact that alcohol can eventually have on various organs of the body. These paragraphs also raise a number of interesting questions about the etiology of this disorder. Most men and women consume alcoholic beverages at some point during their lives. Why do some people become dependent on alcohol while others do not? What factors influence the transition from social drinking to abuse?

CASE STUDY

Ernest Hemingway's Alcohol Dependence

Hemingway began to drink as a teenager, the local blacksmith, Jim Dilworth, secretly supplying him with strong cider. His mother noted his habit and always feared he would become an alcoholic. In Italy he progressed to wine, then had his first hard liquor at the officers' club in Milan. His wound [from World War I] and an unhappy love affair provoked heavy drinking: in the hospital, his wardrobe was found to be full of empty cognac bottles, an ominous sign. In Paris in the 1920s, he bought Beaune by the gallon at a wine cooperative, and would and did drink five or six bottles of red at a meal. He taught Scott Fitzgerald to drink wine direct from the bottle, which, he said, was like "a girl going swimming without her swimming suit." In New York he was "cock-

eyed," he said, for "several days" after signing his contract for *The Sun Also Rises*, probably his first prolonged bout.

Hemingway particularly liked to drink with women, as this seemed to him, vicariously, to signify his mother's approval. Hadley [the first of his four wives] drank a lot with him, and wrote: "I still cherish, you know, the remark you made that you almost worshipped me as a drinker." The same disastrous role was played by his pretty 1930s companion in Havana, Jane Mason, with whom he drank gin followed by champagne chasers and huge jars of iced daiquiris; it was indeed in Cuba in this decade that his drinking first got completely out of hand. One bartender there said he could "drink more martinis than any man I have ever seen." On safari, he was seen sneaking out of his tent at 5 A.M. to get a drink. His brother Leicester said that, by the end of the 1930s, at Key West, he was drinking seventeen Scotch-and-sodas a day, and often taking a bottle of champagne to bed with him at night.

At this period, his liver for the first time began to cause him acute pain. He was told by his doctor to give up alcohol completely, and indeed tried to limit his consumption to three whiskeys before dinner. But that did not last. During World War II his drinking mounted steadily and by the mid-1940s he was reportedly pouring gin into his tea at breakfast. A. E. Hotchner, interviewing him for *Cosmopolitan* in 1948, said he dispatched seven double-size Papa Doubles (the Havana drink named after him, a mixture of rum, grapefruit and maraschino), and when he left for dinner took an eighth with him for the drive. And on top of all, there was constant whiskey: His son Patrick said his father got through a quart of whiskey a day for the last 20 years of his life.

Hemingway's ability to hold his liquor was remarkable. Lillian Ross, who wrote his profile for the *New Yorker*, does not seem to have noticed he was drunk a lot of the time he talked to her. Denis Zaphior said of his last safari: "I suppose he was drunk the whole time but seldom showed it." He also demonstrated an unusual ability to cut down his drinking or even to eliminate it altogether for brief periods, and this, in addition to his strong physique, enabled him to survive.

But despite his physique, his alcoholism had a direct impact on his health beginning with his damaged liver in the late 1930s. By 1959, following his last big drinking bout in Spain, he was experiencing both kidney and liver trouble and possibly hemochromatosis (cirrhosis, bronzed skin, diabetes), edema of the ankles, cramps, chronic insomnia, blood-clotting and high blood uremia, as well as his skin complaints. He was impotent and prematurely aged. Even so, he was still on his feet, still alive; and the thought had become unbearable to him. His father had committed suicide because of his fear of mortal illness. Hemingway feared that his illnesses were not mortal: On July 2, 1961, after various unsuccessful treatments for depression and paranoia, he got hold of his best English double-barreled shotgun, put two canisters in it, and blew away his entire cranial vault.

Why did Hemingway long for death [and why did he drink]? . . . He felt he was failing his art. Hemingway had many grievous faults, but there was one thing he did not lack: artistic integrity. It shines like a beacon through his whole life. He set himself the task of creating a new way of writing English, and fiction, and he succeeded. It was one of the salient events in the history of our language and is now an inescapable part of it. He devoted to this task immense resources of creative skill, energy, and patience. That in itself was difficult. But far more difficult, as he discovered, was to maintain the high creative standards he had set himself. This became apparent to him in the mid-1930s, and added to his habitual depression. From then on his few successful stories were aberrations in a long downward slide.

If Hemingway had been less of an artist, it might not have mattered to him as a man: He would simply have written and published inferior novels, as many writers do. But he knew when he wrote below his best, and the knowledge was intolerable to him. He sought the help of alcohol, even in working hours. He was first observed with a drink, a "Rum St. James," in front of him while writing in the 1920s. This custom, rare at first, became intermittent, then invariable. By the 1940s, he was said to wake at 4:30 A.M. [He] "usually starts drinking right away and writes standing up, with a pencil in one hand and a drink in another." The effect on his work was exactly as might be expected, disastrous. Hemingway began to produce large quantities of unpublishable material, or material he felt did not reach the minimum standard he set himself. Some was published nonetheless, and was seen to be inferior, even a parody of his earlier work. There were one or two exceptions, notably *The Old Man and the Sea* (1952), which won him the Nobel Prize, though there was an element of self-parody in that, too. But the general level was low, and falling, and Hemingway's awareness of his inability to recapture his genius, let alone develop it, accelerated the spinning circle of depression and drink. (Johnson, 1989, pp. 58–59) ■

Typical Symptoms and Associated Features

Hemingway's life, and the devastating problems that resulted from his drinking, illustrate many of the most important features of alcohol abuse. The case of Will Gregory, described in Chapter 1, provides a description of related problems. The fact that the behavior of these men was observed carefully for many years highlights one very important issue: Substance dependence in general, and alcoholism in particular, can be viewed in terms of a series of phases or stages. These phases are not always experienced in the same order, and one phase does not inevitably lead to the next.

Short-term Effects of Alcohol

Alcohol affects virtually every organ and system in the body (Yi, 1991). After alcohol has been ingested, it is absorbed through membranes in the stomach, small intestine, and colon. The rate at which it is absorbed is influenced by many variables, including the concentration of alcohol in the beverage (for example, distilled spirits are absorbed more rapidly than beer or wine), the volume and rate of consumption, and the presence of food in the digestive system. After it is absorbed, alcohol is distributed to all the body's organ systems, with the greatest accumulation being in those organs with the largest blood supply and tissue fluid volume. Almost all the alcohol that a person consumes is eventually broken down or metabolized in the liver. The rate at which alcohol is metabolized varies from person to person, but the average person can metabolize about 1 ounce of 90-proof liquor or 12 ounces of beer per hour (Nathan, 1993). If the person's consumption rate exceeds this metabolic limit, then blood alcohol levels will rise.

Blood alcohol levels are measured in terms of the amount of alcohol per unit of blood. The average 160-pound man who consumes 5 drinks in 1 hour will have a blood alcohol level of 100 milligrams (mg) per 100 milliliters (ml) of blood, or 100 mg percent. There is a relatively strong correlation between blood alcohol levels and CNS intoxicating effects (Verebey, 1991). According to DSM-IV, the symptoms of *alcohol intoxication* include slurred speech, incoordination, an unsteady gait, nystagmus (involuntary to-and-fro movement of the eyeballs induced when the person looks upward or to the side), impaired attention or memory, and stupor or coma.

Some people become intoxicated after drinking relatively small quantities of alcohol, with blood levels less than 10 to 30 mg percent. In most states, the current legal limit of alcohol concentration for driving is 100 mg percent. Some state legislatures are considering lowering this limit, because slowed reaction times and interference with other driving skills may be found at lower blood alcohol levels. People with levels of 150 to 300 mg percent will almost always act intoxicated. Neurological and respiration complications begin to appear at higher levels. There is an extreme risk of coma leading to toxic death when blood alcohol levels go above 400 mg percent (Slaby & Martin, 1991).

Patterns of Consumption

Alcoholism is associated with a host of problems—many of which are illustrated in the life of Ernest Hemingway. Nevertheless, the disorder itself is difficult to define. George Vaillant (1983), a psychiatrist at Dartmouth Medical School and the author of an important longitudinal study of alcoholic men, notes that it is difficult to say that one specific problem or set of problems represents the core features of the disorder:

> Not only is there no single symptom that defines alcoholism, but often it is not who is drinking but who is watching that defines a symptom. A drinker may worry that he has an alcohol problem because of his impotence. His wife may drag him to an alcohol clinic because he slapped her during a blackout. Once he is at the clinic, the doctor calls him an alcoholic because of his abnormal liver-function tests. Later society labels him a drunk because of a second episode of driving while intoxicated." (Vaillant, 1983, p. 22)

The *number* of problems that a person encounters seems to provide the most useful distinction

need drug to prepare to function

between people who are dependent on alcohol and those who are not. These problems can be sorted loosely into two general areas: (1) patterns of pathological consumption, including psychological and physiological dependence, and (2) consequences that follow upon a prolonged pattern of abuse, including social and occupational impairment, legal and financial difficulties, and deteriorating medical condition.

It might seem that the actual amount of alcohol that a person consumes would be the most useful index of an alcohol problem. Hemingway, for example, clearly consumed enormous quantities of alcohol over a period of many years. In fact, this measure turns out to be of little use in defining alcoholism, because people vary significantly in the amount of alcohol they can consume. Factors such as age, gender, activity level, and overall physical health have a great impact on a person's ability to metabolize alcohol. Some people can drink a lot without developing problems; others drink very little and encounter difficulties.

Although the amount that a person consumes is difficult to interpret, the pattern of a person's drinking and the behaviors that are associated with drinking are useful from a diagnostic standpoint. Several considerations are important in this regard, including whether the person engages in frequent *binges*, which are defined as episodes of prolonged, uninterrupted drinking and intoxication. People who engage in drinking binges are most likely to encounter additional problems with alcohol. Another pathological pattern of consumption involves *concealed drinking*. Some people become self-conscious about the amount of alcohol that they drink. They begin to drink when they are alone, or they quickly consume extra drinks when they think they are not being observed. This pattern also signals an increased risk for additional drinking problems.

CRAVING

Many psychological features or problems are associated with the abuse of alcohol. One such feature involves craving. People who are dependent on alcohol often say that they drink to control how they are feeling. They need the drug to relieve negative mood states or to avoid hangovers from previous episodes of drinking. They may feel compelled to drink as a way to prepare for certain activities, such as public speaking, writing, and sex. Some clinicians refer to this condition as **psychological dependence**. One useful index of this craving is the amount of time that the person spends planning to drink. Is access to alcohol a constant preoccupation? If the person is invited to a party or planning to eat at a restaurant, does he or she always inquire about the availability of alcoholic drinks? If the person is going to spend a few days at the beach in a neighboring state, will he or she worry more about whether liquor stores will be closed on weekends or holidays than about having enough food, clothes, or recreational equipment?

DIMINISHED CONTROL

As the problem progresses, it is not unusual for the drinker to try to stop. It is possible for even heavy drinkers to abstain for at least short periods of time (Fingarette, 1988). Most clinicians and researchers agree that diminished control over drinking is one of the crucial features of the disorder. Some experts have described this issue as "freedom of choice." When a person initially experiments with the use of alcohol, his or her behavior is clearly voluntary; he or she is not compelled to drink. After drinking heavily for a long period of time, most people with a drinking disorder try to stop. Unfortunately, efforts at self-control are typically short-lived and usually end in failure.

Tolerance and Withdrawal

Two particularly important features of substance dependence are the phenomena known as

▲ **Mickey Rourke played an alcoholic writer in the film *Barfly*. The screenplay was written by Charles Bukowski and is based on the author's own struggles with alcoholism.**

tolerance and withdrawal. **Tolerance** refers to the process through which the nervous system becomes less sensitive to the effects of alcohol or any other substance. A person who has been regularly exposed to alcohol will need to drink increased quantities to achieve the same subjective effect ("buzz," "high," or level of intoxication). The specific mechanisms that are responsible for the development of tolerance are unknown.

Some drugs are much more likely than others to produce a buildup of tolerance (APA, 1994). The most substantial tolerance effects are found among people who are heavy users of opioids, such as heroin, and CNS stimulants, such as amphetamine and cocaine. Pronounced tolerance is also found among people who use alcohol and nicotine. The evidence is unclear regarding tolerance effects and prolonged use of marijuana and hashish. Most people who use cannabinoids are not aware of tolerance effects, but these effects have been demonstrated in animal studies. Hallucinogens (LSD) and phencyclidine (PCP) may not lead to the development of tolerance.

Withdrawal refers to the symptoms that are experienced when a person stops using a drug. They can go on for several days. For example, alcohol is a CNS depressant, and the heavy drinker's system becomes accustomed to functioning in a chronically depressed state. When the person stops drinking, the system begins to rebound within several hours, producing many unpleasant side effects. These include hand tremors, sweating, nausea, anxiety, and insomnia. The most serious forms of withdrawal may include convulsions and visual, tactile, or auditory hallucinations. Some people develop *delirium*, a sudden disturbance of consciousness that is accompanied by changes in cognitive processes such as lack of awareness of the environment or inability to sustain attention (see Chapter 13). This syndrome is called *delirium tremens* if it is induced by withdrawal from alcohol.

The symptoms of withdrawal vary considerably for different kinds of substances. Table 10–2 provides a comparison of various drugs of abuse in terms of withdrawal and other related characteristics. Unpleasant reactions are most evident during withdrawal from alcohol, opioids, and the general class of sedatives, hypnotics, and anxiolytics (such as Valium). Withdrawal symptoms are also associated with stimulants, such as amphetamine, cocaine, and nicotine, though they are sometimes less pronounced than those associated with alcohol and opioids. Withdrawal symptoms are not often seen after repeated use of cannabis or hallucinogens, and they have not been demonstrated with phencyclidine.

All these problems serve to emphasize the continuous nature of symptoms of substance use disorders. It is convenient to talk about each of these problems in terms of qualitative distinctions: people who can control their drinking and those who cannot; people who crave alcohol and those who do not; people who have developed a tolerance to the drug and those who have not; and so on. The simple fact is that there are no clear dividing lines on any of these dimensions. The ambiguity that results from this fact causes considerable difficulty for those who have attempted to define the nature of the substance dependence disorders, such as alcoholism.

Consequences of Prolonged Abuse

We must also consider the longer-term consequences of substance dependence, a problem we illustrate by focusing on alcohol. Addiction can have a devastating impact on many areas of a person's life. The disruption of relationships

TABLE 10–2

Comparison of Various Types of Substances

Name	Can Produce Intoxication	Associated Withdrawal	Can Produce Dementia
Alcohol	yes	yes	yes
Amphetamines	yes	yes	no
Caffeine	no	no	no
Marijuana/Hashish	yes	no	no
Cocaine	yes	yes	no
Hallucinogens	yes	no	no
Inhalants (solvents)	yes	no	yes
Nicotine	no	yes	no
Opioids	yes	yes	no
Phencyclidine (PCP)	yes	no	no
Sedatives, hypnotics, and anxiolytics	yes	yes	yes

Source: American Psychiatric Association, *Diagnostic and Statistical Manual of Mental Disorders* (DSM-IV) (4th ed.) (p. 177). Washington, D.C.: American Psychiatric Association.

with family and friends can be especially painful. The impact of Hemingway's drinking on his writing career and his family life is clearly evident. Most critics agree that his literary accomplishments were confined primarily to the early stages of his career, before his alcoholism began to interfere with his ability to write. Drinking also took its toll on his marriages, which were characterized by frequent and occasionally furious conflict in public and by repeated episodes of verbal and physical abuse in private (Johnson, 1989).

Many people who abuse alcohol experience *blackouts.* In some cases, abusers may continue to function without passing out, but they will later be unable to remember their previous behavior. An example is the person who drives home drunk from a party and in the morning finds a dent in the car bumper but can't remember how it got there. Sometimes problem drinkers will be told by a friend about how they behaved at the previous night's party even though they cannot remember what they did.

Regular heavy use of alcohol is also likely to interfere with job performance. Co-workers and supervisors may complain. Attendance at work may become sporadic. Eventually the heavy drinker may be suspended or fired. Related to job performance is the problem of financial difficulties. Losing one's job is clearly detrimental to one's financial stability, as are the costs of divorce, health care, liquor, and so on.

Many heavy drinkers encounter problems with legal authorities. These problems may include arrests for drunken driving and public intoxication, as well as charges of spouse and child abuse. Many forms of violent behavior are more likely to be committed when a person has been drinking. The association between crime and alcohol is rather strong. In Vaillant's longitudinal study, 61 percent of the men who were dependent on alcohol had been arrested more than twice for alcohol-related offenses (Vaillant, 1983).

On a biological level, prolonged exposure to high levels of alcohol can disrupt the functions of several important organ systems, especially the liver, pancreas, gastrointestinal system, cardiovascular system, and endocrine system.

The symptoms of alcoholism include many secondary health problems, such as cirrhosis of the liver, heart problems (in part the result of being overweight), various forms of cancer, as well as severe and persistent forms of dementia and memory impairment, or *amnestic disorders*, such as Korsakoff's syndrome (see Chapter 13). Alcoholism is also associated with nutritional disturbances of many types, because chronic abusers often drink instead of eating balanced meals. Alcohol can suppress a person's appetite, and it can also interfere with normal eating patterns as a result of its effects on the gastrointestinal system. In fact, over an extended period of time, alcohol dependence has more negative health consequences than does abuse of almost any other drug.

Some experts have argued that the consequences of drinking are inevitable and are therefore a useful indicator of alcohol abuse. In fact, some clinicians would argue that people who drink heavily for many years without developing these problems should not be considered alcohol abusers. We must recognize, however, that the presence or absence of these problems can reflect social and cultural factors as well as drinking patterns. Financial resources determine how vulnerable a person may be to impaired health or lack of job security. People who are well off financially are more likely to be buffered, at least for a longer period of time. The legal consequences of addiction are directly influenced by social policies. The sale of alcoholic beverages was made illegal in the United States during Prohibition, between 1919 and 1933. During these years, a criminal underworld developed around the sale and consumption of alcohol.

The legal consequences of using drugs such as marijuana and cocaine are currently serious issues. Much criminal activity occurs in relation to the distribution and use of these drugs. In fact, some commentators argue that many illicit drugs should be legalized in order to discourage illegal activity and establish governmental control over these substances. Others fear that legalization would only bring about increased abuse of psychoactive drugs.

Classification

The problems that we have reviewed in the preceding pages indicate that alcoholism and heavy drinking represent an extremely diverse set of problems. Everyone—clinicians and researchers as well as problem drinkers and their families—seems to recognize the existence of a serious psychological disorder. But does it have a core? What is the best way to define it? In the following pages, we briefly review some of the ways in which alcoholism has been defined, beginning with the recognition that it has not always been viewed as a medical condition that requires treatment.

Brief History of Legal and Illegal Substances

One of the most widely recognized facts about alcohol consumption is that drinking patterns vary tremendously from one culture to the next and, within the same culture, from one point in time to another. Public attitudes toward the consumption of alcohol have changed dramatically during the course of U.S. history. For example, heavy drinking was not generally considered to be a serious problem in Colonial times (Levine, 1978). In fact, it seemed to be an integral part of daily life. The average amount of alcohol consumed per person each year was much higher in those days than it is today. A typical American in the eighteenth century drank approximately 4 gallons of alcohol a year; the corresponding figure for our own society is about 2.5 gallons (Fingarette, 1988). Drunkenness was not considered to be either socially deviant or symptomatic of medical illness.

Public attitudes toward alcohol changed dramatically in the United States during the first half of the nineteenth century. Members of the temperance movement preached against the consumption of alcohol in any form. Temperance workers ardently believed that *anyone* who drank alcohol would become a drunkard. Their arguments were largely moral and religious rather than medical or scientific, and many of their publications included essays on the personality weaknesses that were associated with such morally reprehensible behaviors (Levine, 1978). As a result of their activities, many people who acknowledged problems with drinking made public confessions and took pledges of abstinence. The temperance movement was, in fact, able to persuade many thousands of people to abandon the consumption of alcohol.

The movement finally succeeded in banning the manufacture and sale of alcoholic beverages when Congress approved the Eighteenth Amendment to the Constitution in 1919. In the following years, known as the Prohibition era, the average consumption of alcohol fell substantially, and the incidence of associated medical illnesses, such as cirrhosis of the liver, also declined. Nevertheless, these laws were extremely difficult to enforce, and Prohibition was repealed in 1933.

JELLINEK'S PHASES OF ALCOHOLISM

Scientific interest in the study of alcoholism expanded considerably during the 1940s and 1950s, in large part through the research activities and publications of E. M. Jellinek (1890–1963), founding director of the Center of Alcohol Studies at Yale University. Perhaps more than any other person, Jellinek was responsible for organizing and promoting large-scale, interdisciplinary research programs aimed at the scientific understanding of alcoholism (Keller, 1970; Page, 1988).

Jellinek's own publications described alcoholism as a progressive disorder whose central feature is the person's inability to control drinking. His classic article, titled *Phases of Alcohol Addiction* (1952), was based on an examination of the responses of 2,000 members of Alcoholics Anonymous (AA) to a questionnaire regarding their drinking histories. He concluded that alcoholic men progress through a predictable and inflexible series of four phases, which end in either total abstinence or death. In the *prealcoholic phase*, the person drinks socially. He may drink heavily on some occasions to relieve tension. The *prodromal phase* is characterized by the onset of concealed drinking and occasional blackouts. When the person enters the *crucial phase* of alcoholism, he has started to drink during the day, and the drinking has started to affect his social and occupational adjustment. The person can still choose to abstain from drinking for weeks or months at a time, but if he has even one drink,

is they stop for a while

he will not be able to stop until he is totally intoxicated and loses consciousness. In the *chronic phase*, the person lives only to drink. Severe withdrawal symptoms are evident whenever he tries to stop. By the time this model was expanded in Jellinek's book, *The Disease Concept of Alcoholism* (1960), it had become the predominant way of thinking about alcohol dependence.

EARLY CLASSIFICATION SYSTEMS

When DSM-I was published in 1952, alcoholism was listed under the general heading of personality disorders, and it was specifically associated with antisocial personality disorder (see also Chapter 9). This heading also included other forms of behavior that were considered socially deviant, such as sexual deviations. The decision to lump alcoholism together with personality disorders apparently hinged on the assumption that people who drink excessively are motivated in large part by a deficiency in character or willpower. The moral implications of this classification system are reminiscent of the teachings of the temperance movement.

Contemporary Diagnostic Systems (DSM-IV)

The authors of DSM-III (1980) moved the addictions to their own separate category of the manual, removing all assumptions about their association with personality disorders. The DSM-III divided these disorders into two separate categories: substance abuse and substance dependence, with the latter being the more severe and advanced form of disorder. This distinction arose, in part, because several studies had shown that many people who suffer serious impairment from substance abuse do not progress to the dependence stage. To be considered dependent, an individual had to experience either tolerance or withdrawal, or both.

The concept of substance dependence is defined more broadly in DSM-IV than it was in DSM-III. Tolerance and withdrawal are no longer necessary for a diagnosis of substance dependence. Instead, they are now listed along with five other criteria that describe a pattern of compulsive use. The person has to exhibit at least three of the seven criteria for a diagnosis of substance dependence (see Table 10–3). This approach recognizes the heterogeneous nature of substance use disorders such as alcoholism.

Proposed Subtypes of Alcoholism

Given the wide range of variability in terms of symptoms, age of onset, and associated problems, many clinicians and researchers have suggested subdividing alcohol-related problems into more homogeneous groups than the very broad categories of abuse and dependence. These subtyping procedures have been proposed on the basis of many different procedures. Some are the product of extensive clinical experience. Others have

grown out of family history and adoption studies. Jellinek's system allowed for five different kinds of alcoholism, which were distinguished by considerations such as the presence of tolerance and withdrawal, the loss of control of drinking, and the onset of damage to various organ systems such as the liver (Jellinek, 1960).

Although DSM-IV does not recognize any systems for subtyping alcoholism, such groupings have been employed extensively in research studies (Sher, 1991). One system that is currently influential was proposed by Robert Cloninger (1987), a psychiatrist at Washington University in St. Louis. Cloninger proposed that there are two prototypical varieties of alcoholism. According to this system, Type 1 alcoholism is characterized by a somewhat later onset, prominent psychological dependence (loss-of-control drinking), and the absence of antisocial personality traits. It is found in both men and women. Type 2 alcoholism, which is found almost exclusively among men, typically has an earlier onset and is associated with the co-occurrence of persistent antisocial behaviors. We return to a discussion of

▼ This photograph, taken in 1923, shows the destruction of 18,000 bottles of illegal beer during Prohibition. Despite control efforts, alcohol was still available from illegal sources throughout the Prohibition years.

▲ E.M. Jellinek argued that male alcoholics progress through a predictable series of four phases, which end in either total abstinence or death.

TABLE 10–3

DSM-IV Criteria for Substance Dependence

A. A maladaptive pattern of substance use, leading to clinically significant impairment or distress, as manifested by three (or more) of the following, occurring at any time in the same 12-month period:

1. Tolerance, as defined by either of the following:
   a. A need for markedly increased amounts of the substance to achieve intoxication or desired effect.
   b. Markedly diminished effect with continued use of the same amount of the substance.
2. Withdrawal, as manifested by either of the following:
   a. The characteristic withdrawal syndrome for the substance (criteria sets for withdrawal are listed separately for specific substances).
   b. The same (or a closely related) substance is taken to relieve or avoid withdrawal symptoms.
3. The substance is often taken in larger amounts or over a longer period than was intended.
4. There is a persistent desire or unsuccessful efforts to cut down or control substance use.
5. A great deal of time is spent in activities necessary to obtain the substance (for example, visiting multiple doctors or driving long distances), use the substance (for example, chain-smoking), or recover from its effects.
6. Important social, occupational, or recreational activities are given up or reduced because of substance use.
7. The substance use is continued despite knowledge of having a persistent or recurrent physical or psychological problem that is likely to have been caused or exacerbated by the substance (for example, current cocaine use despite recognition of cocaine-induced depression, or continued drinking despite recognition that an ulcer was made worse by alcohol consumption).

these two types when we consider the influence of genetic factors on the etiology of alcoholism.

Course and Outcome

Despite the widespread popular acceptance of Jellinek's phases of alcoholism, it is actually impossible to specify a typical course for substance dependence, especially alcoholism. Age of onset varies tremendously, ranging from childhood and early adolescence all the way through the life span. Although we can roughly identify stages that intervene between initial exposure to a drug and the eventual onset of tolerance and dependence, the timing with which a person moves through these phases can vary enormously. Jellinek's stages do not represent an inevitable sequence or progression.

Even when alcoholism has become well established, the specific course of the problem varies from one person to the next. The only thing that seems to be certain is that periods of heavy use alternate with periods of relative abstinence, however short-lived they may be. In an effort to examine the natural history of alcoholism, Vaillant (1992) studied the lives of 83 men and 17 women who were hospitalized in 1971 for the treatment of severe alcoholism. Their average age at the time

of hospitalization was 45 years, and most had been abusing alcohol for at least 10 years. Of the 100 patients, 80 had previously been through at least one detoxification program.

Vaillant conducted follow-up studies of the patients every 18 months for a period of 10 to 12 years after discharge. He gathered information from interviews with the patients and their relatives and from hospital records. Most of the alcoholic subjects went through repeated cycles of abstinence followed by relapse. The average subject in this study went through detoxification treatment 15 times in 8 years. At the end of the study, 37 percent of the patients had died, most before the age of 65. At the time of last contact with the investigators (including at the time of death), 38 percent of the sample had been abstinent. The proportion of patients who were completely abstinent went up slowly but consistently during the follow-up period, whereas the proportion of patients who were still dependent on alcohol went down over time. Table 10–4 summarizes the outcome information over this follow-up period. The results indicate that the typical pattern of the disorder—at least among those who have been hospitalized for treatment—represents a cycle among periods of drug consumption, cessation, and relapse.

The relapse process is an important problem for all types of substance dependence. Some evidence suggests that this process may include certain common elements across various types of drugs (Brownell et al., 1986). Most people who have quit using drugs like alcohol or tobacco describe a sequence of circumstances, beginning with cognitive events (contemplating change, making a commitment to change) leading to behavioral outcomes (initial cessation, long-term maintenance).

Many important questions remain to be answered about the relapse process. Is there a "safe point" that separates a period of high risk for relapse from a period of more stable change? Do relapse rates stabilize over time? Is an addicted person more likely to succeed on a later attempt to quit than on an early attempt? Answers to these questions will be useful in the development of more effective treatment programs.

Other Disorders Commonly Associated with Addictions

People who abuse alcohol often exhibit other forms of mental disorder as well. Most prominent among these are antisocial personality disorder, mood disorders, and anxiety disorders (Kushner, Sher, & Beitman, 1990; Merikangas & Gelernter, 1990; Weissman, 1988). The complexity of the association among these problems makes them difficult to untangle. In some cases, prolonged heavy drinking can result in feelings of depression and anxiety. The more the person drinks, the more guilty the person feels about his or her inability to control the drinking. In addition, increased drinking often leads to greater conflict with family members, co-workers, and other people. Sometimes the depression and anxiety precede the onset of drinking. In fact, some people seem to use alcohol initially in a futile attempt to self-medicate for these other conditions. The alcohol ultimately makes things worse.

	Time after Index Hospitalization		
TABLE 10-4 Outcome of 100 Alcohol-dependent Patients at Three Points in Time after Index Hospital Discharge	4 years	8 years	12 years
Stable abstinence	24%	32%	25%[†]
Uncertain status (or institutionalized)	3%	17%	21%
Dead	12%	27%	37%
Alcohol dependence	61%	27%	17%

[†] 38 percent were stably abstinent at time of death or last contact.

Source: G.E. Vaillant (1992). Is there a natural history of addiction? In C.P. O'Brien and J.H. Jaffe (eds.), *Addictive states.* New York: Raven Press.

▲ George Vaillant's longitudinal study of alcoholic men and women indicated that the disorder follows an unpredictable, episodic course in which periods of abstinence are often followed by relapse.

Epidemiology

The distribution of alcohol abuse and dependence varies widely as a function of several demographic factors, including gender as well as social and cultural background. Some occupations are associated with higher rates of alcoholism, perhaps because they provide for regular exposure to alcohol throughout the day or because they lack structured hours, which preclude excessive drinking for other people. For example, the rate of alcoholism among professional writers—especially males—may be higher than that in other professions (Goodwin, 1988). Of the six American men who have been awarded the Nobel Prize in literature, five have struggled with serious drinking problems (Goodwin, 1991). In addition to Hemingway, the others are Eugene O'Neill, William Faulkner, Sinclair Lewis, and John Steinbeck; the only exception was Saul Bellow. Neither of the American women who have been awarded the Nobel Prize in literature (Pearl Buck and Toni Morrison) had a drinking problem.

Several methodological problems make it difficult to collect epidemiological information on substance abuse and dependence. One major obstacle has been the lack of a consistent and uniform definition of substance dependence and abuse. Another problem, which is especially marked in alcoholism, is the large variability in behavior across the life span. There is great diversity in terms of age of onset and the pattern of problems. Any single individual can change dramatically over a relatively short period of time. Co-morbidity with other forms of mental disorder is another problem. Finally, the illegal status of many drugs discourages many subjects from providing accurate reports of their drug use (Kozel & Adams, 1986; Merikangas, 1990).

Prevalence of Alcohol Use, Abuse, and Dependence

Approximately 67 percent of males in Western countries drink alcohol regularly, at least on a social basis; less than 25 percent abstain from drinking completely. Several studies suggest that somewhere between 12 and 33 percent of men in the United States could be considered "heavy drinkers," defined in the ECA study as those who report consumption of seven or more drinks at least one evening a week for several months. At least 10 percent of men in the United States develop problems at some point during their lives as a consequence of prolonged alcohol consumption (Helzer, 1987). These statistics seem fairly straightforward, but they hide many difficult issues.

The Epidemiologic Catchment Area (ECA) study provides one detailed picture of the prevalence of alcoholism. Table 10–5 presents the study's findings regarding lifetime prevalence rates for men and women. Alcohol abuse plus dependence were the most common diagnoses assigned to men before the age of 65 in the study. These problems most often went untreated; only 15 percent of the men and women who were assigned a diagnosis of alcohol abuse or dependence had ever mentioned their symptoms to a doctor. More than half (54 percent) of these people had not experienced symptoms of alcoholism in the past year. This finding is consistent with the episodic cycle of consumption and abstinence observed by Vaillant in his longitudinal study.

The ECA data are difficult to interpret, for several reasons. First, people who had stopped drinking before participating in the study might have been reluctant to report their earlier problems. Another issue involves the way that the diagnoses were assigned. The investigators considered subjects to have met the criteria if they had experienced any of the problems at any point during their lives. Someone who met one criterion 10 years ago and another criterion 6 months ago would qualify for a diagnosis on the basis of exhibiting two criteria, even though the criteria appeared years apart. Given these methodological drawbacks, it is difficult to determine whether this study overestimated or underestimated the prevalence of alcoholism.

The samples studied by Vaillant and his colleagues provide one of the most comprehensive and detailed examinations of alcohol problems among men. By virtue of their longitudinal nature, they avoid many of the limitations associated with the ECA study. Vaillant's study has one major limitation of its own, however: All the subjects were male. Alcohol abuse was defined in terms of the presence of four or more problems in areas such as employer complaints, marital and family difficulties, medical problems, and legal problems. Dependence was defined using DSM-III criteria (that is, either tolerance or withdrawal was required). The study included two groups of men: 450 who were chosen from Boston inner-city schools when they were between the ages of 11 and 16, and 200 upper-middle-class men who entered the study while they were sophomores at an elite college. In his sample of inner-city men, Vaillant found a lifetime prevalence of 28 percent for alcohol abuse and 18 percent for alcohol dependence by the age of 47. In comparison, among the college men, Vaillant found a lifetime prevalence of 13 percent for alcohol abuse and 5 percent for alcohol dependence by age 55.

OTHER DRUGS

The ECA study found that the lifetime prevalence of other types of drug abuse and dependence was 6 percent (Anthony & Helzer, 1991). The substance that was most frequently abused was cannabis, with a lifetime prevalence of 4 percent of the people in this study. Lifetime prevalence figures for the other drugs were: stimu-

---

TABLE 10–5

Lifetime Prevalence of Alcohol Abuse and Dependence in the United States (All Ages and Races)

Diagnosis (DSM-III Criteria)	Men	Women
Abuse only	10.3%	1.8%
Dependence only	2.7%	0.5%
Both abuse and dependence	10.8%	2.3%

Source: J.E. Helzer, A Burnam, & L.T. McEvoy, (1991). Alcohol abuse and dependence. In L.N. Robins and D.A. Regier (Eds.), *Psychiatric disorders in America: The Epidemiologic Catchment Area study* (pp. 81–115) New York: Free Press.

lants (2 percent), sedatives (1 percent), opioids (0.7 percent), hallucinogens (0.4 percent), and cocaine (0.2 percent).

In the ECA study, 22 percent of the people who qualified for a diagnosis of alcohol abuse or dependence also met the criteria for some other type of drug abuse or dependence. The rate of alcoholism among people who abuse other drugs was also very high. For example, 67 percent of those who abused opioids also received a diagnosis of alcohol abuse or dependence (Helzer, Burnam, & McEvoy, 1991).

Gender Differences

Drinking patterns differ between men and women in virtually all societies. Women are most likely to drink alcohol when they are young adults. Increased rates of drinking are found among those women who are better educated, employed, and earn a higher income. Women tend to reduce their consumption of alcohol after marrying and becoming parents (Blume, 1991; Gomberg, 1993).

Data from all sources indicate that substance abuse disorders are much more common among men than among women. Among people who chronically abuse alcohol, men outnumber women by a ratio of approximately 5 to 1 (Robins & Regier, 1991). Recent information suggests that this disparity may be narrower today than it was 20 years ago, especially among younger people. The National Comorbidity Survey (NCS) found a 12-month prevalence rate for alcohol dependence of 11 percent for men and 4 percent for women (Kessler et al., 1994). Although the rate of alcoholism among younger women appears to be increasing, prevalence is still much higher in men, and the rates do not seem likely to converge. Persistent differences can probably be attributed to a number of factors, including physiological variables related to the metabolism of alcohol, as well as social factors such as negative attitudes toward intoxication in women (see Further Thoughts).

Gender differences are also found for the prevalence of other forms of substance dependence and abuse, although they are not as marked as in the case of alcoholism. The ECA study found that the lifetime prevalence rate for dependence on drugs other than alcohol was 2.1 percent in men and 1.2 percent in women (Anthony & Helzer, 1991). Much higher rates

have been reported by the authors of the NCS: 9.2 percent for men and 5.9 percent for women (Kessler et al., 1994). The increase in prevalence in the more recent study can be attributed, in part, to the switch to DSM-III-R criteria for substance dependence, which no longer required the presence of either tolerance or withdrawal for a diagnosis.

Risk for Addiction across the Life Span

Older people do not drink as much alcohol as younger people. The proportion of people who abstain from drinking alcohol is only 22 percent for people in their thirties, goes up to 47 percent for people in their sixties, and is approximately 80 percent for people over 80 years of age (Ticehurst, 1990). This decrease in alcohol consumption is most evident in heavy drinkers and in men. Although most people drink less alcohol when they are older, 7 percent of men and 11 percent of women report that they began drinking more in old age (Busby et al., 1988).

Prevalence rates for alcohol dependence are highest among young adults and lowest among the elderly (Caracci & Miller, 1991). In the ECA study, for example, the lifetime prevalence for alcohol dependence was 27 percent among men between 18 and 44 years of age, 21 percent among men between the ages of 45 and 64 years of age, and 14 percent among men over the age of 65 years. The corresponding prevalence rates among women in the same age groups were 7 percent, 3 percent, and 1.5 percent. Most elderly alcohol abusers are people who have had drinking problems for many years, but for some

▲ **The problems of female alcoholics are illustrated in the film *When a Man Loves a Woman*, starring Meg Ryan.**

alcoholic men and women—perhaps one-third of those who enter treatment—the disorder has an onset late in life (Rosin & Glatt, 1988).

The use of illegal drugs is relatively infrequent among the elderly (Anthony & Helzer, 1991), but there is a problem associated with their abuse of, and dependence on, prescription drugs and over-the-counter medications, espe-cially hypnotics, sedatives, anxiolytics, and painkillers. The elderly use more legal drugs than do people in any other age group. One esti-mate suggested that 25 percent of all people over the age of 55 use psychoactive drugs of one kind or another (Koch & Knapp, 1987). The risk for substance dependence among the elderly is increased by frequent use of multiple psychoactive

---

FURTHER THOUGHTS

Gender Differences in Drinking and Alcoholism

About 60 percent of women in the United States drink alcohol at least occasional-ly (Fillmore, 1987; Wilsnack & Wilsnack, 1991). The comparable figure for men is higher—approximately 75 percent. This discrepancy is not large enough to account for the fact that men are five times more likely than women to develop alcoholism. Most women drink, but—in comparison to men—relatively few develop alcoholism. Gender differences in the prevalence of alcoholism are undoubtedly the result of a combi-nation of social, psychological, and biological fac-tors. These include the social stigma that is associated with excessive drinking by women and the fact that women are, on average, less physically tolerant of alcohol (Helzer, Bucholz, & Robins, 1992).

Our society has traditionally held a rather neg-ative view of intoxication among women. This pervasive attitude is reflected in opinions voiced by both men and women, including those who are dependent on alcohol (Gomberg, 1988). Social disapproval probably explains why women are more likely than men to drink in the privacy of their own homes, either alone or with another person. Women may be less likely than men to drink heavily because the range of situations in which they are expected to drink, or in which they can drink without eliciting social disapproval, is more narrow.

There are also important gender differences in alcohol metabolism. A single standard dose of alco-hol, measured in proportion to total body weight, will produce a higher peak blood alcohol level in women than in men (Jones & Jones, 1976). One explanation for this difference lies in the fact that men have a higher average content of body water

than women. A standard dose of alcohol will be less diluted in women because alcohol is distributed in total body water.

When women do develop alcohol dependence, is the disorder similar to the problems seen among men who abuse alcohol? Definitive answers are not available because relatively little research has been conducted on female alcoholics. Some studies sug-gest that there are gender differences in the symp-toms of the disorder—the physiological and social consequences of prolonged drinking—as well as in its course (Blume, 1991; Gomberg, 1993). The fol-lowing list summarizes many of these differences.

1. The average age of onset for alcoholism is older among women than among men. Women tend to seek treatment after a shorter history of alcohol abuse, however, so the average age of men and women who present for treatment at clinics and hos-pitals is about the same (Ross, 1989).

2. Women who are dependent on alcohol consume less alcohol, on a daily basis, than men who are dependent on alcohol, but they experience the same number of alcohol-related problems and similar lev-els of social and occupational impairment.

3. The drinking patterns of alcoholic women are more closely tied to the drinking patterns of their partners (Wilsnack, Wilsnack, & Klassen, 1984). Women who are in treatment frequently have a spouse or a lover who is also a heavy drinker.

4. Alcoholic women are more likely to report that they began drinking heavily after a particular traumatic

or stressful event, most often some type of loss like divorce or the death of a child or other loved one.

5. Alcoholic women are more likely to exhibit co-morbid symptoms of depression and anxiety. Alcoholic men, on the other hand, are more likely to display antisocial personality traits.

6. Women who drink heavily for many years are more vulnerable to liver disorders.

7. Contrary to some previous clinical impressions, the research literature indicates that treatment is equally effective for men and women who abuse alcohol (Jarvis, 1992). ■

drugs combined with enhanced sensitivity to drug toxicity (caused by slowed metabolic breakdown of alcohol and other drugs).

The following case illustrates several issues that are associated with substance use disorders among the elderly, including the abuse of alcohol together with abuse of prescription medications, the presence of prominent symptoms of anxiety and depression, and the tendency to deny the extent of their use or abuse of drugs.

BRIEF CASE STUDY

Ms. E is an 80-year-old woman who was brought in for an evaluation by her daughters because they noticed depressive symptoms, appetite disturbance, and memory deficits. She denied all problems related to her daughters' concerns. She had a depressed affect, mild psychomotor agitation, and decrements of recent and remote memory. She was disoriented to time. She verbalized statements of guilt and self-deprecation. She denied ever drinking alcohol, which was corroborated by the daughter with whom she lived but was refuted by her other daughter, who stated that Ms. E drank one or two glasses of brandy almost every day. She had been taking various barbiturates for "nerves" for over 30 years. The dosage she ingested gradually increased over the years, and she frequently took more medications than were prescribed. Because it was unclear if her symptoms were related to her barbiturate use, she reluctantly agreed to be slowly and gradually detoxified. She refused a dementia work-up. Once detoxification was complete, her affect and appetite were improved, but her cognitive deficits were unchanged. Several months later, she and her family dropped out of treatment. She was reportedly drinking brandy, wine, and "hard liquor" every afternoon and evening, with her hired caregiver mixing the drinks. (Solomon et al., 1993). ■

Diagnostic criteria for substance dependence and abuse are sometimes difficult to apply to the elderly, primarily because drug use has somewhat different consequences in their lives. Tolerance to many drugs is reduced in the elderly, and the symptoms of withdrawal may be more severe and prolonged. On the other hand, they are less likely to suffer occupational impairment because they are less likely to be employed than younger people. The probability of social impairment may be reduced because elderly people are more likely to live apart from their families.

Etiological Considerations and Research

The etiology of substance abuse and dependence represents a clear example of the need for a multifactorial model of etiology. Most contemporary investigators approach the development of alcoholism in terms of the systems (for example, Cloninger, 1987; Kissin & Hanson, 1982). Biological factors obviously play an important role. The addicting properties of certain drugs are crucial; people become addicted to drugs like heroin, nicotine, and alcohol, but they do not become addicted to drugs like the antidepressants or to food additives like Nutrasweet. We must therefore understand how addicting drugs affect the brain in order to understand the process of dependence. On the other hand, most adults in our society drink alcohol on a regular basis without becoming addicted to it. Only 1 out of 10 drinkers develops serious problems. Why? What is the difference between people who drink socially without problems and those who develop alcoholism? The complexity of causal networks mirrors the wide-ranging nature of the clinical problems that we have already considered in this chapter.

It is also important to remember that the etiology of alcoholism must be viewed within a developmental framework, emphasizing the importance of various stages of the problem (Lettieri, 1987; Marlatt & Baer, 1988; Vaillant, 1992). Some investigators view alcoholism in terms of a sequence of stages: (1) initiation and continuation; (2) escalation and transition to abuse; and (3) development of tolerance and withdrawal.

Various social, psychological, and biological factors influence the person's behavior at each stage in this cycle. The process seems to progress in the following way: drinking alcohol leads to short-term positive effects that reinforce continued consumption; drinking becomes heavier and more frequent; the person gradually becomes tolerant to the effects of alcohol and must therefore drink larger quantities to achieve the same reinforcing effects; after the person becomes addicted to alcohol, attempts to quit drinking are accompanied by painful withdrawal symptoms. In the following pages, we review some of the factors that might explain why people begin to drink, how their drinking behaviors are reinforced, and how they develop tolerance after prolonged exposure.

Early Stages: Initiation and Continuation

People who don't drink obviously won't develop alcoholism. Therefore, one important link in the chain of causal events is the process of initiation. Which people will expose themselves to addictive substances, and why? Among those young people who choose to drink alcohol (or smoke cigarettes, or consume other addictive substances), which ones will eventually develop problems? The development of drug dependence requires continued use, and it is influenced by the manner in which the drug is consumed. In other words, with regard to alcohol, will the person's initial reaction to the drug be pleasant, or will the person become sick and avoid alcoholic beverages in the future? If the person continues drinking, will he or she choose strong or weak drinks, with or without food, with others or alone, and so on?

Several studies have examined factors that predict substance use among adolescents. Initial experimentation with drugs is most likely to occur among those individuals who are rebellious and extroverted and whose parents and peers model or encourage use (Chassin, 1984). The relative influence of parents and friends varies according to the gender and age of the adolescent as well as the drug in question. For example, parents may have a greater influence over their children's decision to drink alcohol, whereas peers seem to play a more important role in the initial exposure to marijuana.

The specific processes by which parents influence their children's drinking take many forms. Parents may serve as models for the use of drugs as a coping response during stressful circumstances. They may also influence the development of attitudes and expectations regarding the positive benefits of drug consumption, and they may simply provide access to licit or illicit drugs (Hesselbrock & Hesselbrock, 1987). Adolescents with alcoholic parents are more likely to drink alcohol than those whose parents do not abuse alcohol. This increased risk seems to be due to several factors, including the fact that alcoholic parents monitor their children's behavior less closely, thereby providing more opportunities for illicit drinking. The level of negative affect is also relatively high in the families of alcoholic parents. This unpleasant emotional climate, coupled with reduced parental monitoring, increases the probability that an adolescent will affiliate with peers who use drugs (Chassin et al., 1993). Taken together, these considerations indicate that parents' drinking has a definite influence on their children's use of alcohol and that the mechanisms involved in this relationship are quite complex.

Initial physiological reactions to alcohol can have a dramatic negative influence on a person's early drinking experiences. For example, millions of people are unable to tolerate even small amounts of alcohol. These people develop flushed skin, sometimes after only a single drink; they may also feel nauseated, and some experience an abnormal heartbeat. This phenomenon is most common among people of Asian ancestry and may affect 30 to 50 percent of this population. Not coincidentally, the prevalence of alcoholism is unusually low among Asian populations. Research studies indicate that there is a link between these two phenomena. For example, Japanese Americans who experience the fast-flushing response do, indeed, tend to drink less than those who do not flush (Nakawatase et al., 1993). The specific mechanisms involved in this sensitivity reaction to alcohol have not been determined (Newlin, 1989; Wall et al., 1991). The basic evidence suggests that in addition to looking for factors that make some individuals especially vulnerable to the addicting effects of alcohol, it may also be important to identify protective factors that reduce the probability of substance dependence.

Once people begin to drink, why do they continue? Studies that examine the short-term consequences of drinking in normal subjects can help address this question. The effects of acute intoxication vary, but laboratory investigations have found that nonalcoholic drinkers experience several effects that are potentially rewarding or beneficial, including reduced self-awareness, improved mood, and dampened cardiovascular responses to stress (Hull & Bond, 1986; Levenson, 1987). These immediate, positive reactions may encourage some people to continue their use of this drug, in spite of the fact that drinking can lead to dire long-term outcomes.

Middle Stages: Escalation and Transition to Abuse

A person's initial use of addictive drugs is obviously an important step toward the development of substance dependence, but the fact remains that most people who drink alcohol do not develop alcoholism. What accounts for the next important phase of the disorder? Why do some people abuse the drug while others do not? In the next section, we outline several important considerations. We begin by examining genetic factors, and we then consider the neurochemical effects of the drugs themselves and the psychological characteristics of drug users.

GENETICS OF ALCOHOLISM

An extensive literature attests to the fact that patterns of alcohol consumption, as well as psychological and social problems associated with alcohol abuse, tend to run in families. The lifetime prevalence of alcoholism among the parents, siblings, and children of people with alcoholism is at least 3 to 5 times higher than the rate in the general population (Merikangas, 1990; Schuckit, 1987). Of course, this elevated risk among first-degree relatives could reflect the influence of either genetic or environmental factors, because families share both types of influence. Therefore, we must look to the results of twin and adoption studies in an effort to disentangle these variables.

Twin Studies Several twin studies have examined patterns of alcohol consumption in nonalcoholic twins. The evidence indicates that both genetic factors and shared environmental factors influence the quantity and frequency of social drinking in normal men and women (Heath, Jardine, & Martin, 1989; Merikangas, 1990; Prescott et al., 1994a).

▲ **The circumstances in which an adolescent is initially exposed to alcohol can influence the person's pattern of drinking as well as the person's response to the drug. Drinking small amounts of wine with meals on a regular basis may be less likely to lead to alcohol dependence than the sporadic consumption of hard liquor for the purpose of becoming intoxicated.**

Additional studies have examined twin concordance rates for alcoholism when the proband is identified through a treatment program. Here the focus is on severely disabling drinking problems rather than simply the consumption of alcohol. Several studies have found that concordance rates are higher among MZ than among DZ twin pairs, but in some studies this finding is limited to male subjects. For example, psychologist Matt McGue and his colleagues at the University of Minnesota found concordance rates for DSM-III diagnoses of alcohol abuse or dependence of 77 percent in male MZ twins and 54 percent in male DZ twins (McGue, Pickins, & Svikis, 1992). The corresponding figures for MZ and DZ female twin pairs were 39 percent and 42 percent. This result suggests that different etiological pathways may be responsible for alcoholism in men and women. The possibility is particularly interesting in light of the marked gender differences in the prevalence of alcohol abuse and dependence.

The implications of this disparity between the twin study results for males and females are not entirely clear. They may suggest that genetic factors are more important in the development of alcoholism among men. As Merikangas (1990) points out, however, other factors could account for these results. Fewer studies have examined alcoholism in female twins; the sample sizes for female twin pairs tend to be small; and women may be less likely to enter treatment programs through which probands are typically identified. Two studies have examined concordance rates for alcohol abuse in large samples of men and women living in a community. Both found equally strong levels of familial resemblance in male and female twins (Kendler et al., 1992; Prescott et al., 1994b). Thus, we cannot conclude definitively on the basis of twin studies that alcoholism among males has a larger genetic element than does alcoholism among females.

Adoption Studies The strategy that is followed in an adoption study allows the investigator to separate relatively clearly the influence of genetic and environmental factors. The probands in this type of study are individuals who meet two criteria: (1) they had a biological parent who was alcoholic, and (2) they were adopted away from their biological parents at an early age and raised by adoptive parents.

Two major adoption studies have examined the possible role of genetic factors in the etiology of alcoholism. One investigation was conducted in Denmark by psychiatrist Donald Goodwin of the University of Kansas and his colleagues. This study revealed that by the age of 30, 18 percent of the male offspring of alcoholic biological parents had developed alcoholism, compared to only 5 percent of the control adoptees. The results were quite different for the daughters of alcoholic parents; the risk for alcoholism among female offspring was only 4 percent among both the index cases and the control sample. These data are consistent with the results of McGue's twin study. Genetic factors apparently influence the development of alcoholism among men, but their influence is more ambiguous among women.

A second adoption study was conducted in Sweden by Robert Cloninger and his colleagues (see Research Close-up). The results of this investigation are consistent with Goodwin's adoption study in pointing toward the influence of genetic factors in the etiology of alcohol abuse and dependence. They also indicate, however, that the manner in which genetic and environmental events combine probably differs from one type of alcoholism to another. Cloninger's adoption study also suggests an explanation for the ambiguous pattern of evidence regarding female alcoholism. Using Cloninger's subtyping system, genetic factors may play a role in the etiology of Type 1 alcoholism in women. The daughters of people with Type 2 alcoholism, on the other hand, are at risk for the development of certain types of anxiety disorders, but they are not more likely to develop alcoholism themselves. Studies that lump together these different types of drinking problems are therefore likely to produce less consistent results for women than for men.

What can we conclude from the adoption studies? There are obviously some differences in both methods and results from one study to the next, but there are also consistent indications that genetic factors play some role in the etiology of alcohol abuse and dependence. McGue (1993) conducted a comprehensive review of the adoption study evidence and reached the following general conclusions:

- The offspring of alcoholic parents who are reared by nonalcoholic adoptive parents are more likely than people in the general population to develop drinking problems of their own. Thus, the familial nature of alcoholism is at least partially determined by genes.

- Being reared by an alcoholic parent, in the absence of other etiological factors, does not appear to be a critical consideration in the development of the disorder.
- The etiology of alcoholism is probably heterogeneous in nature; that is, there are several pathways to the disorder.
- There is an association between antisocial personality traits, or "behavioral undercontrol," and alcohol abuse or dependence. The exact nature of this relation and the direction of effect have not been determined.

NEUROCHEMICAL MODES OF ACTION

Assuming that some people are genetically more vulnerable to the addicting effects of alcohol than others, what genetic mechanisms are involved, and how do they function? Considerable speculation has focused on brain mechanisms, especially those involving neural transmission (Schuckit, 1994). All of the addicting psychoactive drugs produce changes in the chemical processes by which messages are transmitted in the brain.

Endogenous Opioid Receptors One promising research area in the neurosciences involves the discovery of the endogenous opioids known as **endorphins**. These relatively short chains of amino acids, or *neuropeptides*, are naturally synthesized in the brain and are closely related to morphine (an opioid) in terms of their pharmacological properties. Endorphins possess a chemical affinity for specific receptor sites, in the same way that a key fits into a specific lock. More than a dozen endorphins are distributed widely throughout the brain. They appear to be especially important in the activities associated with systems that control pain, emotion, stress, and reward as well as biological functions such as feeding and growth (Cohen, 1988).

Research studies have demonstrated many interesting features of the endorphins. Laboratory animals can develop tolerance to injections of endorphins, just as they develop tolerance to addicting drugs like morphine, and they also exhibit symptoms of withdrawal if the injections are suddenly discontinued. These studies confirm the pharmacological similarity between endogenous and exogenous opioids, but one crucial difference remains: We don't become addicted to endorphins in normal brain functioning.

The discovery of endorphins has led scientists to propose neurochemical explanations for many different phenomena (Dalayeun, Nores, & Bergal, 1993). For example, individual differences in naturally occurring levels of endorphins may account for varying levels of pain sensitivity: People with higher levels of endorphins or more opioid receptors may be less sensitive to pain than those with lower levels or fewer receptors. Some investigators have reported that people who respond positively to placebos experience an increased production of endorphins. Others have found an association between endorphin production and activities such as long-distance running and hypnosis. These are obviously intriguing results, but they are tentative at best and are seriously in need of replication.

Some theorists associate alcoholism with excessive production of endogenous opioids (Blum & Payne, 1991; Gianoulakis, 1993). This hypothesis suggests that common neurochemical mechanisms might account for addiction to alcohol and to opioids such as heroin and morphine. It is based on several observations that indicate that the behavioral and pharmacological effects of alcohol are similar to those of the opioids. For example, laboratory animals that have received injections of small amounts of morphine will increase their consumption of alcohol. Although the relationship between endorphins and alcoholism is intriguing, the hypothesis is also inconsistent with some other facts. The experiences of alcoholics during withdrawal differ markedly from those of heroin addicts (APA, 1994). The endorphin hypothesis would predict that the reactions should be similar because they are caused by common neurochemical processes (Cohen, 1988).

The Serotonin Hypothesis Addicting drugs probably have widespread effects on the process of neural transmission in the brain, including systems that involve catecholamines (for example, dopamine, norepinephrine, and serotonin) as well as the neuropeptides. Although alcohol does not bind directly to any receptor sites in the brain, it does alter the permeability of neuronal membranes (Yi, 1991). Channels for potassium and chlorine ions are opened, and

The Swedish Adoption Study

An adoption study conducted in Sweden by Robert Cloninger, a psychiatrist at Washington University, and Michael Bohman, a Swedish psychiatrist, suggests that genetic and environmental factors may interact in different ways for different forms of alcohol abuse (Cloninger, 1987). The investigators began with a list of all male children who were born out of wedlock in Stockholm between 1930 and 1949 and who were also adopted away from their biological parents at an early age. At the time of the study, these men were between the ages of 23 and 43. The investigators collected information about the men's adjustment by using official records of local Temperance Boards, hospital and insurance records, and the national criminal register. They expected this procedure to identify about 70 percent of all people in this population who had a serious drinking problem.

The adoptees were divided into two groups on the basis of the type of alcohol abuse exhibited by their biological parents, using Cloninger's system of Type 1 and Type 2 alcoholism. The subject was considered to have a Type 1 genetic background if the biological father or mother had an adult (later) onset of drinking problems and had not engaged in severe criminal behavior. The subject was classified as having a Type 2 genetic background if the biological father had undergone extensive treatment for alcoholism as well as showing evidence of serious criminal behavior beginning in adolescence or early adulthood.[†]

The top panel of Table 10–6 summarizes the results for adoptees with a Type 1 genetic background. Preliminary analyses indicated that, by itself, the presence of treated alcoholism in the adoptive parents did not increase the risk for alcoholism in the adoptees. The results were different, however, when the investigators combined the effects of an alcoholic parent with family income and social class. The investigators assumed that, in Sweden during that particular time, children who were raised by adoptive fathers with unskilled occupations would be exposed to a pattern of heavy recreational drinking. When the groups were subdivided in this way, Cloninger and his colleagues found that both a genetic predisposition and environmental factors were necessary to increase the risk for severe alcohol abuse in the offspring of people with Type 1 alcoholism. The presence of either a genetic background for the disorder or a lower social-class background did not significantly increase the adoptees' risk for alcoholism. But when an individual experienced both of these vulnerability factors, the risk for alcoholism was significantly increased—approximately double that expected in the general population.

TABLE 10–6

Analysis of Severe Alcohol Abuse in the Swedish Adoption Study

		Male Adoptees Observed	
Type 1 Genetic Background	Environmental Background	Total Sample Size	Severe Abuse (%)
No	No	376	4.3
No	Yes	72	4.2
Yes	No	328	6.7
Yes	Yes	86	11.6
		Male Adoptees Observed	
Type 2 Genetic Background	Environmental Background	Total Sample Size	Type 2 Abuse (%)
No	No	567	1.9
No	Yes	196	4.1
Yes	No	71	16.9
Yes	Yes	28	17.9

A different pattern emerged among the adoptees with a genetic background associated with Type 2 alcoholism (see the bottom panel of Table 10–6). Here the genetic component was more pronounced. Regardless of the environment provided by the adop-

---

[†] They could not find enough mothers with a Type 2 form of alcoholism to include these subjects in the study.

tive family, the male offspring in this group were much more likely to abuse alcohol.

Cloninger also examined rates of alcohol abuse among the daughters of biological parents with both types of alcoholism. Female adoptees with a genetic predisposition to Type 1 alcoholism (where either the father or the mother may have abused alcohol) were three times more likely to abuse alcohol than were women in the control group. It therefore appears that genetic factors influence the development of this form of alcoholism in both men and women. A completely different pattern emerged in daughters of Type 2 alcoholic fathers. They were *not* more likely than the control subjects to abuse alcohol (although they did show an increased risk for somatic anxiety). On the basis of this result, Cloninger and

his colleagues have argued that Type 2 alcoholism may be "male-limited."

The distinction between people with Type 1 and Type 2 alcoholism has been incorporated into many other studies. On the other hand, some aspects of the study have been criticized (Searles, 1988, 1990; McGue, 1993). For example, the examination of environmental circumstances in the adoptive homes was quite limited in scope. The interesting interaction of genes and environment in the Type 1 families was based primarily on socioeconomic status, which is a rather crude measure. The investigators were not able to measure specific drinking patterns or attitudes toward alcohol among the adoptive parents. Still, the Swedish adoption study has generated enormous interest and has served as a catalyst for many other investigations. ∎

corresponding channels for sodium and calcium are closed, thus producing a depression of the central nervous system. Concentrations of neurotransmitters, such as serotonin and dopamine, are initially increased. If the person continues to drink heavily over an extended period of time, the drinking produces many effects that are opposite to those of short-term intoxication: The central nervous system becomes excited rather than depressed, and the ion channel events are reversed.

The serotonin theory of the etiology of alcoholism assumes that alcohol dependence is caused by a genetically determined deficiency in serotonin activity in certain areas of the limbic system of the brain (Ferreira & Soares da Silva, 1991; Wallis, Rezazadeh, & Lal, 1993). Some studies have reported that acute intoxication is accompanied by an increase in serotonin activity. When the person sobers up, serotonin activity is reduced to subnormal levels. The serotonin theory suggests that some people begin with a deficiency in serotonin, and the consumption of alcohol initially helps to correct for this deficiency. Unfortunately, prolonged consumption further depletes the system. Therefore, the person initially drinks to feel good—alcohol stimulates activity in the reward systems of the brain—but after a while he or she must drink more to avoid feeling worse

when serotonin levels are reduced below their initial point.

Evidence supporting this theory comes from several kinds of investigation. First, animals that are bred to exhibit high and low preferences for alcohol exhibit differences in serotonin levels. Those with a high preference for alcohol have lower levels of serotonin in areas of the brain that regulate emotional responses (McBride et al., 1993). Second, serotonin activity differs between two groups of people with alcohol use disorders. Those with an early onset and a family history for the disorder have lower serotonin activity than those with a later onset and no family history for the disorder (Buydens-Branchey et al., 1989). Third, drugs that enhance serotonin transmission (such as selective serotonin reuptake inhibitors or SSRIs—see Chapter 5) can decrease voluntary alcohol consumption in human subjects. The fact that these types of medication are also effective in treating mood disorders, as well as panic and obsessive-compulsive disorder, suggests an etiological link between alcoholism and these disorders (Tollefson, 1991).

PSYCHOLOGICAL FACTORS

Pharmacological effects undoubtedly account for many of the problems associated with addicting drugs, but as the systems perspective indicates, biological explanations are not incompatible with psychological ones. In fact, extensive research over the past several decades has found that the progression of substance dependence depends on an interaction between environmental and biological events. One time-honored perspective on the development of alcoholism is the *tension-reduction hypothesis*. At its most general level, this viewpoint holds that people drink alcohol in an effort to reduce the impact of a stressful environment. The tension-reduction hypothesis became the focal point for scientific investigation when Conger (1956) adapted formal learning theory to the problem and proposed that alcohol consumption is reinforced by its ability to relieve unpleasant emotional states, especially fear and anxiety. As we will see in the following pages, the relation between stress and alcohol has turned out to be more complex than this theory suggested.

The influence of additional psychological variables is also important. Drug effects interact with the person's beliefs and attitudes as well as with the social context in which the drugs are taken. In this section, we review a few of the most influential ideas about some of these etiological mechanisms.

Expectations about the Effects of Alcohol

Placebo effects demonstrate that expectations are an important factor in any study of drug effects (see Chapter 3). During the 1970s, several research studies sought to evaluate the influence of alcohol on various facets of behavior using the **balanced placebo design** (see Research Methods). This procedure allows the investigator to separate the direct, biological effects of the drug from the subjects' expectations about how the drug should affect their behavior. The results indicated that expectations can account for many effects that have often been attributed to the drug itself. For example, subjects who believed that they had ingested alcohol but who had actually consumed only tonic water displayed exaggerated aggression and reported enhanced feelings of sexual arousal (Goldman, Brown, & Christiansen, 1987, Goldman, Brown, Christiansen, & Smith, 1991; Hull & Bond, 1986). Much less is known about expectancies for drugs other than alcohol, but there is good reason to believe that these cognitive factors also influence the ways in which people respond to cannabinoids, stimulants, anxiolytics, and sedatives (Brown, 1993).

RESEARCH METHODS

The Balanced Placebo Design

Most people have formed beliefs about the ways in which the consumption of alcohol will affect their behavior. These beliefs have an important influence on drinking patterns as well as on the ways in which people actually react to alcohol. For example, the expectation that you may feel happy or act silly after having a few beers may actually increase the probability of that response pattern. Investigators who want to demonstrate the effect of alcohol on human behaviors must somehow control for the role that these beliefs may play. They must separate the direct effects of alcohol from those that are mediated by expectations.

A placebo group is typically used in drug studies to control the influence of subjects' expectations regarding the effects of the drug. For example, all subjects are told that they will drink an alcoholic beverage when, in fact, half of the subjects are randomly assigned to receive a placebo—a drink that tastes like alcohol but does not actually contain alcohol. For ethical reasons (in order to minimize the extent of deception), investigators usually inform potential subjects that they may, or may not, receive an alcoholic beverage.

One important issue is not addressed by the placebo-controlled design. All the subjects expect to drink alcohol. What would happen to subjects—how would they behave or feel—if they received alcohol when they did not expect it? This condition has been called an *antiplacebo* group.

The *balanced placebo design* represents a combination of the placebo and antiplacebo methods. Initially used in studies of alcohol during the early 1970s, it can be used to assess the effects of alcohol, the effects of alcohol expectations, and the interaction of alcohol by expectation. The balanced placebo design includes four conditions (Martin & Sayette, 1993):

- Expect alcohol/receive alcohol (the "alcohol" condition)
- Expect alcohol/receive nonalcohol (the "placebo" condition)
- Expect nonalcohol/receive nonalcohol (the "nonalcohol" condition)
- Expect nonalcohol/receive alcohol (the "antiplacebo" condition)

This design has been employed extensively in studies of the effect of alcohol on behaviors ranging from drinking to aggression and sexual arousal (Hull & Bond, 1986; Marlatt & Rohsenow, 1980). The data indicate that some responses to alcohol are determined primarily by beliefs about its effects rather than by its actual pharmacologic effects. For example, Lang and Marlatt (1975) found that subjects were more likely to behave aggressively if they *thought* that they had consumed alcohol, regardless of whether they drank vodka and tonic water or only tonic water.

The balanced placebo design has been useful, but it also has some weaknesses. The value of the placebo and antiplacebo conditions depends on the extent to which subjects are actually deceived into thinking that they did drink alcohol when they actually did not (the placebo condition) or that they did not drink alcohol when they actually did (the antiplacebo condition). The most serious limitations have been found in the antiplacebo condition. Investigators have asked subjects in this condition whether they believed that they had actually consumed a nonalcoholic beverage. The success of this manipulation decreases as the dose of alcohol increases. At higher doses, most subjects are able to discern that they have consumed alcohol.

Questions regarding the validity of the antiplacebo condition have caused some investigators to abandon this aspect of the balanced placebo design—relying instead on three cells: alcohol, placebo, and nonalcohol. Of course, the specific design will depend on the nature of the questions that are being asked in the experiment. ■

The results of experiments using the balanced placebo design stimulated considerable thought about the role that alcohol expectancies may play in the etiology of drinking problems. These studies do not manipulate expectancies directly, however. They only lead subjects to believe that they have consumed alcohol when, in fact, they have not. The investigators infer that the subjects believed that alcohol would make them aggressive.

But is that really the case? Subsequent investigations began to examine alcohol expectancies directly (Brown et al., 1980). Investigators asked people directly, Why do you drink? What do you expect to happen after you have consumed a few beers or a couple of glasses of wine? Answers that subjects provided to these questions fit into six primary categories:

1. Alcohol transforms experiences in a positive way (for example: Drinking makes the future seem brighter).

2. Alcohol enhances social and physical pleasure (for example: Having a few drinks is a nice way to celebrate special occasions).

3. Alcohol enhances sexual performance and experience (for example: After a few drinks, I am more sexually responsive).

4. Alcohol increases power and aggression (for example: After a few drinks it is easier to pick a fight).

5. Alcohol increases social assertiveness (for example: Having a few drinks makes it easier to talk to people).

6. Alcohol reduces tension (for example: Alcohol enables me to fall asleep more easily).

Many people believe that alcohol can enhance arousal and improve their mood. These expectations may constitute one of the primary reasons for continued and increasingly heavy consumption of alcoholic beverages. In fact, expectancy patterns can help predict drinking behaviors: People who have the most positive expectations about the effects of alcohol consume greater amounts of alcoholic beverages. This association holds across all stages of the drinking spectrum, including chronic heavy drinkers as well as adolescents who are just beginning to experiment with alcohol (Goldman, Brown, & Christiansen, 1987; Goldman et al., 1991).

Where do these expectations come from, and when do they develop? In some cases they may arise from personal experiences with alcohol, but they can also be learned indirectly. Many adolescents hold strong beliefs about the effects of alcohol long before they take their first drink. These expectations may be influenced by parental and peer attitudes and by the portrayal of alcohol in the mass media. Follow-up studies have demonstrated that adolescents' expectations about the effects of alcohol are useful in predicting which individuals will later develop drinking problems (Christiansen et al., 1989; Stacy, Newcomb, & Bentler, 1991). Positive expectancies about alcohol—which are likely to encourage people to drink—are especially influential. Negative expectancies are associated with diminished use, but seem to be less powerful (Leigh & Stacy, 1993; Stacy, Widaman, & Marlatt, 1990).

Attention Allocation Scientists have studied the behavioral effects of alcohol extensively, especially its influence on anxiety, aggression, sexual responsiveness, and mood. One of the puzzling results of this research is the inconsistency that has emerged from one study to the next. Some papers report that alcohol reduces tension, whereas others have found that it increases anxiety. Some investigators have found that drinking alcohol can increase self-esteem, whereas others have concluded that it can increase depression. Claude Steele, a psychologist at Stanford University, and Robert Josephs, a psychologist at the University of Texas, have proposed an *attention-allocation model* of alcohol effects that provides an explanation for these apparent inconsistencies (Steele & Josephs, 1988, 1990).

Steele and Josephs's theory is based on two general factors. First, when alcohol reaches the brain, it interferes with the capacity for controlled and effortful cognitive activities. Intoxicated peo-

ple focus their attention, by necessity, on immediate internal and external cues. they are less able to consider subtle or complex aspects of a problem. Steele and Josephs (1990) call this process *alcohol myopia*—a marked tendency to engage in short-sighted information processing. The second component of the attention-allocation model involves the nature of the immediate environment. The impact of drinking on behavior will depend on the specific situation with which the intoxicated person is confronted.

Steele and Josephs have used this model to study the effects of alcohol on several aspects of human behavior, including *drunken excess*, the tendency for social behavior to become more extreme under the influence of alcohol. The attention-allocation model predicts that alcohol myopia will lead to drunken excess only in specific types of situations: those in which there are strong cues pulling for a particular response, but in which that response is also inhibited by higher-level cognitive processing. Suppose, for example, that somebody insults you. If you are sober, you might be tempted to respond by punching or slapping the person, but you would also anticipate several negative consequences that might be associated with this choice of action. If you are intoxicated, however, you will be cognitively impaired and therefore less able to invoke these inhibitory cues. Therefore, you are more likely to respond in an excessively aggressive fashion.

Josephs and Steele (1990) have shown that inconsistencies regarding the effect of alcohol on responses to stress can also be explained by alcohol myopia. The influence of alcohol on one type of stress—anxiety associated with worry—depends, in large measure, on what the person is doing while intoxicated. Alcohol reduces the person's capacity to think about several things at one time. A simple activity, like watching television, might engage the person's full capacity after a few drinks. No resources are left over to allow the person simultaneously to ruminate about his or her own difficulties, and as a result, his or her anxiety may diminish. On the other hand, if the same person drinks alcohol while preoccupied with troubling thoughts and does *not* engage in distracting activities, his or her worries might become more salient as the full focus of narrowed attention is directed toward them. Anxiety might actually increase in this situation. Laboratory studies support these predictions (Josephs & Steele, 1990b).

The attention-allocation theory is an intriguing explanation for the short-term effects of alcohol on human behavior. Of course, like all theoretical models of psychopathology, some facts are inconsistent with the theory. For example, it cannot explain why some studies have found that alcohol reduces stress in the absence of distraction. The most important point to be emphasized in considering this approach is that the short-term effects of alcohol on the behavior of nonalcoholic subjects is determined, at least in part, by the disruptive effects of alcohol consumption on the cognitive processes (Sayette, 1993).

Advanced Stages: Development of Tolerance and Withdrawal

Tolerance typically appears after extensive exposure to alcohol and therefore represents a more advanced stage in the development of alcoholism, although some aspects of tolerance to alcohol can appear after only a few exposures. Tolerance and withdrawal have frequently been considered to be complementary processes. Mechanisms responsible for the development and maintenance of tolerance and withdrawal are currently the topic of considerable research.

For many years, scientists assumed that the development of tolerance was an exclusively biological phenomenon that was dependent entirely on the dose of the drug, the number of times that it was administered, the amount of time between administrations, and so on. Speculation regarding the mechanisms that were responsible for tolerance focused on a variety of factors associated with the way in which drugs are absorbed, distributed, and metabolized by the body. Prolonged exposure to a drug may have long-term effects on neural transmission by altering the permeability of nerve cell membranes or the sensitivity of receptor sites (Tiffany & Baker, 1986). There is little question that these pharmacological events play an important role, but they don't explain the whole story.

Several psychological models have been proposed to explain drug tolerance (Baker, Morse, & Sherman, 1986; Poulos & Cappell, 1991). One influential theory, advocated by Shepard Siegel (1988), a psychologist at McMaster University in Canada, views the development of tolerance in terms of Pavlovian conditioning. Siegel's the-

ory starts with the recognition that for many drugs the conditioned response is anticipatory compensation. In other words, drug-associated environmental cues—those that are regularly paired with use of the drug—begin to elicit a *drug compensatory response*. It is called a compensatory response because it is opposite in direction to the drug's original pharmacologic effect. Compensatory responses can be viewed as homeostatic mechanisms that serve to maintain the equilibrium of physiological systems. Compensatory responses may develop simultaneously in more than one system (heart rate, respiration rate, body temperature, and so on). The person eventually needs larger doses of the drug to achieve its original effect because the drug has to overcome these compensatory responses.

▲ **Attitudes and expectations about the effects of drugs are shaped, in part, by the beliefs of peers. Many people believe that alcohol makes them more sociable.**

Consider, for example, the effects of morphine, which is an analgesic. The acute administration of morphine normally causes a *reduction* in pain sensitivity. After repeated administrations, stimuli that signal the imminent injection of morphine begin to evoke an *increase* in pain sensitivity. This effect can be measured if animals that are accustomed to receiving morphine injections are tested for pain sensitivity shortly after being given an injection of placebo in the presence of cues that have previously signaled morphine administration. Increasingly larger doses of morphine are required to produce reduction in pain sensitivity because the drug must override this paradoxical compensatory response.

If tolerance develops because cues that regularly signal drug use eventually trigger compensatory responses, it follows that tolerance effects may be found only in a specific environment. Various kinds of research support this prediction. For example, people who are addicted to opioids show a *release from tolerance*—defined as the failure to experience drug-opposite physiological responses in temperature, skin resistance, and heart rate—if they receive opioids in the absence of rituals that typically signal the injection of the drug (Ehrman et al., 1992).[†]

Perhaps the most dramatic demonstration of release from tolerance was provided in a study of heroin overdose deaths in laboratory rats (Siegel et al., 1982). Rats in the "prior exposure" groups were injected with heroin on alternating days for a period of 2 weeks. The first injection contained 1 milligram of heroin for every kilogram of body weight (1 mg/kg). Subsequent injections contained increased doses of heroin until the fifteenth injection contained 8 mg/kg. Rats in the control group received a sequence of placebo injections on the same schedule. At the end of this sequence, each rat was given one large dose of heroin (15 mg/kg).

▲ **Drinking increases the risk for aggression and violence. This may be due to expectancies or attention allocation in addition to direct effects of alcohol.**

The most important variable in Siegel's study was the location in which the rats in the prior exposure groups received the final large dose of heroin. *Similarly tested* rats received this injection in the presence of the same contextual cues—the same lab room and cage—that had previously been associated with heroin injections. *Differently tested* rats received the last injection in the context of cues that had never been previously associated with the drug.

Siegel's theory predicts that the differently tested rats should experience a release from tolerance because, in the absence of stimuli that ordinarily trigger drug compensatory responses, their bodies would react more strongly to the heroin. A simple biological explanation of tolerance would not take into account the influence of environmental cues. I would predict that the mortality rate should be the same in both prior exposure groups. The mortality rate in the control group, which included rats who had never received heroin, was 96 percent. This relatively large dose of heroin overwhelmed their

systems, and they died from a massive drop in heart rate and respiration rate. In the similarly tested group, only 32 percent of the rats died. They had developed tolerance and were presumably protected by compensatory increases in heart rate and respiration rate that were conditioned to the drug cues. The mortality rate in the differently tested rats was 64 percent, midway between the other two groups. The higher proportion of deaths in comparison to the similarly tested rats must be attributed to the absence of environmental cues that ordinarily signaled heroin injections.

Siegel's theory can also explain the onset of withdrawal, which is presumably the manifestation of compensatory responses in the absence of the expected drug effects (Siegel, 1988). Suppose that an addict is in an environment where he or she has used drugs on many occasions, but the drug is not available. Drug-compensatory conditioned responses will still occur. They are not countered by the effects of the drug and may be expressed in physiological reactions, such as sweating, watery eyes, runny nose, or other related symptoms that are frequently associated with drug withdrawal reactions.

Siegel's work has stimulated a considerable number of studies, many of which support his conclusions. There are, however, some findings that the model cannot explain easily. For example, it cannot account for tolerance that develops in the *absence* of environmental cues that consistently predict administration of the drug (Baker et al., 1987; Goudie, 1990; Tiffany & Baker, 1986).

Learning models of tolerance are not incompatible with the existence of more straightforward biological drug effects. It is entirely possible that neuroscientists will discover such mechanisms in the next few years. Psychological research has simply demonstrated that there are important, environmentally determined effects that complement whatever pharmacological processes are involved in the development of tolerance. Once again, multiple overlapping systems are required to explain this particular aspect of substance dependence.

[†] The unexpected delivery of opioids was accomplished in this study by unsignaled intravenous infusion.

Treatment

The treatment of alcoholism and other types of substance use disorders is an especially difficult task. Many people with these problems do not acknowlege their difficulties, and only a relatively small number seek professional help. When they do enter treatment, it is typically with reluctance or on the insistence of friends, family members, or legal authorities. Compliance with treatment recommendations is often low, and dropout rates are high. The high rate of co-morbidity with other forms of mental disorder presents an additional challenge, complicating the formulation of a treatment plan. Treatment outcome is likely to be least successful with those people who have co-morbid conditions.

The goals of treatment for substance use disorders are a matter of controversy. Some clinicians believe that the only acceptable goal is total abstinence from drinking or drug use. Others have argued that, for some people, it is preferable to aim for a return to the use of legal drugs in moderation. Important questions have also been raised about the scope of improvements that might be expected from a successful treatment program. Is the goal simply to eliminate, or minimize, drug use? Or should we expect that treatment will also address the social, occupational, and medical problems that are typically associated with drug problems? If these associated problems are the result of the person's prolonged abuse of alcohol or other drugs, they may improve on their own if the person becomes abstinent. On the other hand, to the extent that family problems or interpersonal difficulties contribute to the person's use of drugs, it may be necessary to address these difficulties before the drug problem can be resolved (McLellan et al., 1992).

Detoxification and Pharmacotherapy

Treatment of alcoholism and related forms of drug abuse is often accomplished in a sequence of stages, beginning with a brief period of **detoxification**—the removal of a drug on which a person has become dependent—lasting between 3 and 6 weeks (Dackis & Gold, 1991). This process is often extremely difficult, as the person experiences marked symptoms of withdrawal and gradually accommodates to the absence of the drug. Detoxification is accomplished gradually for many types of CNS depressants, such as alcohol, hypnotics, and sedatives. Stimulant drugs, on the other hand, can be stopped abruptly (Cohen, 1988). The patient's vital signs are monitored closely by medical staff during the detoxification period to prevent seizures and delirium. Although hospitalization is used frequently, there is evidence to indicate that detoxification can be accomplished with close supervision on an outpatient basis.

Various types of medication, including anxiolytics, are sometimes given to people who are going through alcohol detoxification, primarily as a way of minimizing withdrawal symptoms (Weddington, 1992). This practice is controversial, in part because many people believe that it is illogical to use one form of drug—especially one that can be abused itself—to help someone recover from dependence on another drug.

Psychiatrists have also used SSRIs, such as Prozac, for the long-term treatment of alcoholic patients. Their use is based, in part, on evidence from animal studies indicating that consumption of alcohol is suppressed by the increased availability of serotonin in the brain. The effectiveness of this type of pharmacotherapy has not been evaluated extensively (Litten & Allen, 1991).

DISULFIRAM (ANTABUSE)

Disulfiram (Antabuse) is a drug that can block the chemical breakdown of alcohol. It was introduced as a treatment for alcoholism in Europe in 1948 and is still used fairly extensively. If a person who is taking Antabuse consumes even a small amount of alcohol, he or she will become violently ill. The symptoms include nausea, vomiting, profuse sweating, and an increase in heart rate and respiration rate. People who are taking Antabuse will stop drinking alcohol in order to avoid this extremely unpleasant reaction.

Unfortunately, voluntary compliance with this form of treatment is rather poor. Many patients discontinue taking Antabuse, usually because they want to resume drinking or because they believe that they can manage their problems without this form of treatment (Børup, Kaiser,

& Jensen, 1992). People can drink alcohol without experiencing an unpleasant reaction about 2 or 3 days after they stop taking Antabuse. Treatment therefore requires close medical supervision and careful observation of ingestion of the drug (Brewer, 1992).

Antabuse is used frequently, especially with patients who are older and highly motivated to stop drinking, but the research evidence regarding its effectiveness is unclear (Kristenson, 1992; Larson et al., 1992). Studies that have employed placebo control groups have found that patients who receive Antabuse are no more likely to remain sober than are those receiving a placebo (Fuller & Roth, 1979). Although most patients eventually relapse, those who are taking Antabuse may be able to stay sober for longer periods of time.

Self-help Groups: Alcoholics Anonymous

One of the most widely accepted forms of treatment for alcoholism is Alcoholics Anonymous (AA). Organized in 1935, this self-help program is maintained by alcohol abusers for the sole purpose of helping other people who abuse alcohol become and remain sober. Because it is established and active in virtually all communities in North America and Europe as well as many other parts of the world, AA is generally considered to be "the first line of attack against alcoholism" (Nathan, 1993). Surveys conducted by AA indicate that its membership increased considerably during the 1970s and 1980s. In 1989, there were approximately 1 million members of AA in the United States and Canada (Chappel, 1993). Many members of AA are also involved in other forms of treatment offered by various types of mental health professionals, but AA is not officially associated with any other forms of treatment or professional organizations. Similar self-help programs have been developed for people who are dependent on other drugs, such as opioids (Narcotics Anonymous) and cocaine (Cocaine Anonymous).

The viewpoint espoused by AA is funda-

▼ Group therapy, like this session from the movie *Clean and Sober*, is an important part of most inpatient treatment programs. It offers an opportunity for patients to acknowledge and confront openly the severity of their problems.

mentally spiritual in nature. AA is the original "12-step program." In the first step, the person must acknowledge that he or she is powerless over alcohol and unable to manage his or her drinking. The remaining steps involve spiritual and interpersonal matters such as accepting "a Power greater than ourselves" that can provide the person with direction; recognizing and accepting personal weaknesses; and making amends for previous errors, especially instances in which the person's drinking caused hardships for other people. One principal assumption is that people cannot recover on their own (Bean, 1975; Chappel, 1992).

The process of working through the 12 steps to recovery is facilitated by regular attendance at AA meetings, as often as every day during in the first 90 days after the person stops drinking (Chappel, 1992). Most people choose to attend less frequently if they are able to remain sober throughout this initial period of time. Meetings provide chronic alcohol abusers with an opportunity to meet and talk with other people who have similar problems. New members are encouraged to call older members for help at any time if they experience an urge to drink. There is enormous variability in the format and membership of local AA meetings (Montgomery, Miller, & Tonigan, 1993).

It is difficult to evaluate the effectiveness of AA, for a number of reasons. Long-term follow-up is difficult, and it is generally impossible to employ some of the traditional methods of outcome research, such as random assignment to groups and placebo controls. Early dropout rates are relatively high: About half of all the people who initially join AA drop out in less than 3 months. On the other hand, survival rates (defined in terms of continued sobriety) are much higher for those people who remain in AA. About 80 percent of AA members who have remained sober for between 2 and 5 years will remain sober in the next year (Mäkelä, 1994).

Although the format of AA presents several obstacles to research, some studies indicate that AA does provide important help to many people. In his longitudinal study of alcoholic men, Vaillant (1983) found that attendance at AA meetings was an important predictor of positive outcomes. More recent outcome studies that have examined the effects of AA in combination with other forms of treatment indicate that participation in AA makes a significant positive contribution to treatment outcome (Pisani et al., 1993; Walsh et al., 1991).

Although AA does seem to help people, it is not clear how it helps, or why. Several mechanisms are possible. One explanation centers on the personal growth process that is described in the 12-step program, but the active ingredient may be more social than spiritual. Membership in AA provides members with a stable social network that discourages rather than encourages the use of drugs. Another possible explanation involves personality traits that are present before the person enters treatment. Those people with traits that are compatible with continued membership in a group like AA may be most likely to recover (Pisani et al., 1993). People who exhibit antisocial traits of the type associated with Cloninger's Type 2 alcoholism, who also presumably have an earlier onset and more difficulty abstaining from drinking, may be least likely to benefit from AA.

Controlled Drinking

One psychological approach to the treatment of alcoholism, known as Individualized Behavior Therapy for Alcoholics (IBTA), was developed by psychologists Mark and Linda Sobell (Sobell & Sobell, 1973, 1976). It employed a wide range of therapeutic procedures in an effort to address abusive drinking patterns as well as other types of maladaptive behavior that are associated with alcohol dependence. The latter included training in the use of social skills, which might be used to resist pressures to drink heavily, and problem-solving procedures, which might help the person both to identify situations that lead to heavy drinking and to formulate alternative courses of action.

The most controversial aspect of IBTA was its consideration of **controlled drinking** as a potential goal for alcoholics. This concept refers to the moderate consumption of alcohol in a pattern that avoids drinking to the point of intoxication. Most forms of intervention, including AA, hold firmly to the belief that the only acceptable outcome of treatment is total abstinence. The assumption of this approach is that, for people with alcoholism, a single drink will lead inevitably to complete loss of control. The Sobells set out to teach chronic alcohol abusers to drink in more appropriate ways. Their procedures encouraged patients to choose mixed drinks rather than straight liquor and to take small, intermittent sips rather than gulping drinks quickly. Results suggested that patients who were trained to drink in a controlled fashion had a better outcome, on average, than those in a control group for whom the goal was total abstinence.

The results of the Sobells' IBTA study were subjected to close scrutiny, and they ignited an intense controversy that has lasted for several years (Cook, 1985; Maltzman, 1989; Peele, 1992a, 1992b; Pendery, Maltzman, & West, 1982; Sobell & Sobell, 1989). Their critics claimed, based on their own subsequent follow-up assessments, that the patients who had received IBTA did not return successfully to controlled drinking. The general consensus seems to be that methodological problems with the IBTA study preclude definitive conclusions.

Relatively few mental health professionals currently consider controlled drinking to be a realistic goal for people who are dependent on alcohol. On the other hand, a substantial minority of alcoholics do apparently return to the use of alcohol on a *moderate* basis. For example, one follow-up study found that approximately 20 percent of a group of people with alcohol use disorders had returned to nonproblem drinking 10 years after receiving inpatient treatment (Finney & Moos, 1991). Therefore, treatment aimed at reduced levels of drinking rather than total abstinence may be successful for some people with drinking problems. This approach is perhaps most reasonable with patients who have only recently begun to experience problems associated with alcohol consumption, especially young adults (Kivlahan et al., 1990).

Relapse Prevention

Most people who have been addicted to a drug will say that quitting is the easy part of treatment. The most difficult challenge is to maintain this change after it has been accomplished. Unfortunately, most people will "slip up" and return to drinking soon after they stop. The same thing can be said for people who stop smoking or using any other drug of abuse. These slips often precipitate a full-scale return to excessive and uncontrolled use of the drug. Successful treatment therefore depends on making preparations for such incidents.

Psychologist Alan Marlatt of the University of Washington and his colleagues have proposed a cognitive behavioral view of the process of relapse (Brownell et al., 1986; Marlatt, 1985). This process applies to all forms of substance dependence, ranging from alcoholism to nicotine dependence. It has also been applied to other disorders associated with compulsive behavior, such as obesity and inappropriate sexual behaviors (see Chapter 11). It places principal emphasis on events that take place after detoxification and the initial efforts at intensive treatment.

The relapse prevention model addresses several important issues that confront the addict in trying to deal with the challenges of life without drugs. These include craving as well as occasional returns to the old habit. Emphasis is placed on increasing people's self-efficacy—the belief that they will be able to control their own behavior and events in their lives. The therapist also helps patients learn more adaptive coping responses, such as applied relaxation and social skills, that can be used in situations that might formerly have triggered drug use.

Another important feature of the relapse prevention model is concerned with the **abstinence violation effect**, which refers to the guilt and perceived loss of control that the person feels whenever he or she slips and finds himself or herself having a drink (or a cigarette or whatever drug is involved) after an extended period of abstinence. People typically blame themselves for failing to live up to their promise to quit. They also interpret the first drink as a signal that further efforts to control their drinking will be useless, saying to themselves, "Well, that's it. I might as well get drunk." Marlatt's approach to relapse prevention teaches patients to expect that they may slip occasionally and to interpret these behaviors as a temporary "lapse" rather than a total "relapse." This procedure will presumably minimize the negative affect associated with a slip and increase the probability that the person will be able to cope effectively rather than lose control completely.

General Conclusions Regarding Treatment

In spite of the difficult challenges presented by these disorders, concerted efforts on the part of addicts who have organized self-help groups, and on the part of clinical scientists, have created some promising alternatives that offer hope to people with substance use disorders as well

as their families. Comprehensive reviews of the research literature regarding treatment of alcoholism and drug abuse point to several general conclusions (McLellan et al., 1992):

- People who enter treatment for various types of substance abuse and dependence typically show improvement in terms of reduced drug use that is likely to persist for several months following the end of treatment. Unfortunately, relapse is also relatively common.
- There is little if any evidence to suggest that one form of treatment (inpatient or outpatient, professional or self-help, individual or group) is more effective than another.
- Among those people who are able to reduce their consumption of drugs, or abstain altogether, improvements following treatment are usually not limited to drug use alone, but extend to the person's health in general as well as to the person's social and occupational functioning.

Long-term outcome for the treatment of alcoholism is best predicted by the person's coping resources (social skills and problem-solving abilities), the availability of social support, and the level of stress in the environment. These considerations appear to be more important than the specific type of intervention that people receive or the severity of their problems at the beginning of treatment (Finney & Moos, 1992). Those individuals who are in less stressful life situations, whose families are more cohesive, and who are themselves better equipped with active coping skills are most likely to sustain their improvement for a period of several years.

We must also remember that the vast majority of people with substance use disorders do not receive treatment from either professionals or self-help organizations (Kessler et al., 1994). Nevertheless, many of these people manage to recover on their own. By studying the process of "natural recovery," clinicians may find clues that can be used to develop more effective forms of treatment. For example, the Sobells have compared people who were able to recover from alcohol dependence without the aid of treatment or AA to untreated drinkers who had not recovered (Sobell et al., 1993). More than half of all recoveries were initiated by cognitive events, primarily a reappraisal of the benefits and problems associated with continued drug use. They were not triggered by negative life events, which were frequent in the lives of both groups. These observations suggest that the process of appraising the perceived costs and benefits of continued drinking may play a crucial role in the natural path to recovery.

Summary

The DSM-IV recognizes two types of substance use disorder. **Substance dependence** is defined in terms of a pattern of repeated self-administration of a drug that results in **tolerance**, **withdrawal**, or compulsive drug-taking behaviors. **Substance abuse** represents a less severe pattern of drug use that is defined in terms of interference with the person's ability to fulfill major role obligations, recurrent use of a drug in dangerous situations, or the experience of repeated legal difficulties that are associated with drug use.

Drugs of abuse are chemicals that alter a person's mood, level of perception, or brain functioning. They include central nervous system depressants, stimulants, opiates, cannabinoids, and hallucinogens. There are many differences among these drugs in terms of their behavioral and pharmacological effects. Some are more likely than others to lead to the development of tolerance and withdrawal. Some have more serious long-term health consequences than others—alcohol and nicotine are particularly harmful in terms of their negative impact on body organs. Social policy in the United States treats these drugs in different ways; some are legal and others are not. This has an important impact on the lives of people who are dependent on these drugs.

There are many common features of substance use disorders. All represent an inherent conflict between immediate pleasure and longer-term harmful consequences. Factors that account for initial experimentation with drugs, influence the transition to dependence, and lead to relapse are similar in many respects from one type of substance to another. Furthermore, many people are simultaneously addicted to more than one substance—a phenomenon known as **polysubstance abuse**. Therefore, this chapter employs a commonalities approach rather than dealing with each type of substance separately. We have examined alcoholism as an example of substance dependence and abuse because it is the most common and the most debilitating form of substance use disorder, and because it has been studied more extensively than other drugs.

The DSM-IV system does not recognize subtypes of alcohol dependence. Nevertheless, alcoholism can take many forms, and several systems have been proposed to identify meaningful subtypes. Cloninger's Type 1 and Type 2 system is one method of classification that has proven useful in some research studies. People with Type 1 alcoholism have a later onset and are more likely to experience frequent loss-of-control drinking as well as guilt and anxiety about their drinking. People with Type 2 alcoholism, who are almost always men, have an earlier onset and also exhibit traits that are associated with antisocial personality disorder.

In spite of a widespread popular belief in the progressive nature of alcoholism, it is actually impossible to describe a typical course for the disorder. Age of onset varies considerably. Although we can identify stages of the development of the disorder—beginning with early experimentation, followed by a transition to abuse, and later by the development of tolerance and withdraw-

KEY TERMS

- abstinence violation effect
- addiction
- balanced placebo design
- controlled drinking
- delirium tremens
- detoxification
- drug of abuse
- endorphins
- polysubstance abuse
- psychological dependence
- substance abuse
- substance dependence
- tolerance
- withdrawal

al—the timing with which a person moves through these stages can vary enormously. There is no regular or inevitable progression from one phase to the next. The only thing that seems certain is that periods of heavy use alternate with periods of relative abstinence.

Alcohol dependence and abuse are the most common forms of mental disorder among men, with a lifetime prevalence of 14 percent in the ECA study. Among people with alcohol use disorders, men outnumber women by a ratio of approximately 5 to 1. Prevalence rates for alcohol dependence are highest among young adults and lowest among the elderly.

The etiology of alcoholism is best conceived in terms of a sequence of stages. At each stage, biological, psychological, and social factors influence the probability that a person will drink heavily. During the initial stage, in which people first expose themselves to alcohol, the influence of peers and family members is especially important. These groups influence an adolescent's attitudes and expectations about the positive effects of alcohol, serve as models for its use, and provide access to the drug. Initial phys-

iological reactions can also influence the probability that a person will continue to drink. Some people experience an unpleasant flushing response to the ingestion of alcohol.

The middle stages of substance dependence—sometimes referred to as the transition to abuse—are probably influenced by genetic factors and neurochemical responses as well as by psychological factors, such as cognitive expectancies.

The later stages are also influenced by a combination of biological and psychological factors. Tolerance and withdrawal are determined, in part, by the development of conditioned compensatory responses.

Treatment of substance use disorders is an especially challenging and difficult task in light of the fact that many people with these problems do not recognize or acknowledge their own difficulties. Recovery begins with a process of **detoxification**, which can take place on either an inpatient or outpatient basis. Self-help programs, such as Alcoholics Anonymous, are the most widely used and probably one of the most beneficial forms of treatment.

Critical Thinking

1. What is the difference between the rituals characteristic of obsessive-compulsive disorders and the compulsive drug-taking behaviors associated with substance dependence? Are there any similarities? Do you think that these disorders should be classified together?

2. Some drugs of abuse are illegal in the United States, whereas others are legally available. What impact does this legal policy have on the definition of substance dependence as well as the probability that a person will receive a DSM-IV diagnosis?

3. Most adults in Western countries drink alcohol on a fairly regular basis, yet relatively few develop alcoholism. Why? There are gender differences and age differences in the prevalence of alcohol dependence. Why would women be less likely than men to become dependent on alcohol?

4. Although most people believe that alcohol makes them feel more relaxed, experimental studies indicate that it sometimes makes people more anxious or more aggressive. Why?

Sexual and Gender Identity Disorders

Sex is often a perplexing area of our lives. When something interferes with our ability to function sexually, it can be devastating both to the person who is affected and to the person's partner. Sexual behavior is considered abnormal when it results in personal distress or when it involves nonconsenting partners. Inhibitions of sexual desire and interference with the physiological responses leading to orgasm are called **sexual dysfunctions**. These experiences often lead to anxiety and depression, and they are frequently associated with interpersonal problems, especially marital distress. Another group of sexual disorders is known as the **paraphilias**; the term applies to people who are sexually aroused by unusual objects and situations, such as inanimate objects, sexual contacts with children, exhibiting their genitals to strangers, and inflicting pain on another person.

A person's sense of being either male or female, known as *gender identity*, is almost always consistent with his or her physical anatomy. In some rare cases, a person develops a strong and persistent identification with the other gender as well as a discomfort with his or her own assigned gender. For example, a person with a penis might insist that, in spite of his genitalia, he is more like a woman than a man. This phenomenon is called **gender identity disorder**.

Overview

The discussion of sexual disorders requires some frank consideration of normal sexuality. Such openness has been encouraged and promoted by mental health professionals who specialize in the study and treatment of sexual behavior.

William Masters, a physician, and Virginia Johnson, a psychologist, have undoubtedly been the best-known sex therapists and researchers in the United States since the late 1960s. Their first book, *Human Sexual Response*, published in 1966, was based on their studies of nearly 700 normal men and women. Observations and physiological recordings were made in a laboratory setting while these individuals engaged in sexual activities, including masturbation and intercourse. Their research received widespread attention in the popular media and helped make laboratory studies of sexual behavior acceptable.

On the basis of their data, Masters and Johnson described the human sexual response cycle in terms of a sequence of overlapping phases: excitement, orgasm, and resolution. Analogous processes occur in both men and women, but the timing may differ. There are of course individual differences in virtually all aspects of this cycle. Variations from the most common pattern may not indicate a problem unless the person is concerned about the response.

Sexual *excitement* increases continuously from initial stimulation up to the point of orgasm. It may last anywhere from a few minutes to several hours. Among the most dramatic physiological changes during sexual excite-

The Reproductive System

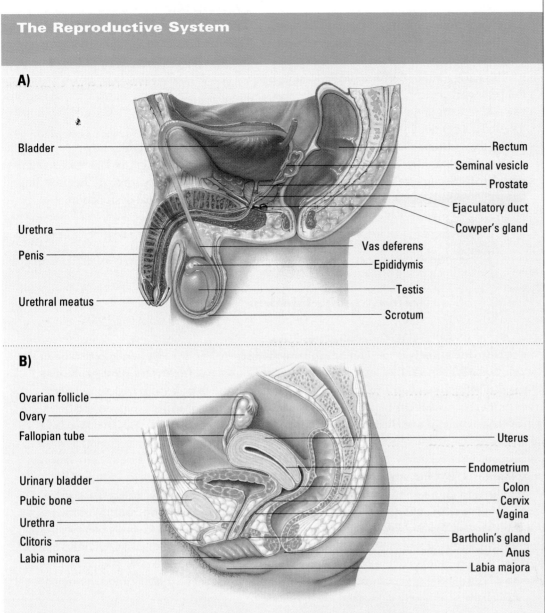

A)

Bladder — Rectum
— Seminal vesicle
— Prostate
— Ejaculatory duct
— Cowper's gland
Urethra —
Penis — — Vas deferens
— Epididymis
— Testis
Urethral meatus — — Scrotum

B)

Ovarian follicle —
Ovary —
Fallopian tube — — Uterus
— Endometrium
Urinary bladder — — Colon
Pubic bone — — Cervix
— Vagina
Urethra —
Clitoris — — Bartholin's gland
Labia minora — — Anus
— Labia majora

FIGURE 11-1: (A) Male reproductive system. (B) Female reproductive system.

Source: Adapted from Frederic Martini, *Fundamentals of Anatomy and Physiology*, 2nd ed. Englewood Cliffs, NJ: Prentice Hall, 1992. Drawing (A) by Craig Luce. Drawing (B) by William C. Ober M.D., and Claire W. Garrison, R.N.

▲ **William Masters and Virginia Johnson conducted groundbreaking research on the human sexual response cycle. They have also been pioneers in the field of treatment for sexual dysfunction.**

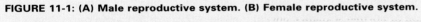

ment are those associated with vasocongestion—engorgement of the blood vessels of various organs, especially the genitals. The male and female genitalia (illustrated in the prearousal state in Figure 11–1) become swollen, reddened, and warmed. Sexual excitement also produces an increase in muscular tension, heart rate, and respiration rate. These physiological responses are accompanied by subjective feelings of arousal, especially at more advanced stages of excitement.

The experience of orgasm is usually quite distinct from the gradual build-up of sexual excitement that precedes it. This sudden release of tension is almost always experienced as being intensely pleasurable, but the specific nature of the experience varies from one individual to the next (Geer, Heiman, & Leitenberg, 1984). The female orgasm occurs in three stages, beginning with a "sensation of suspension or stoppage," which is associated with strong genital sensations. The second stage involves a feeling of warmth spreading throughout the pelvic area. The third stage is characterized by sensations of throbbing or pulsating, which are tied to rhythmic contractions of the vagina.

The male orgasm occurs in two stages, beginning with a sensation of ejaculatory inevitability. This is triggered by the movement of seminal fluid toward the urethra. In the second stage, regular contractions propel semen through the urethra, and it is expelled through the urinary opening. During the *resolution* or "aftereffects" phase, which may last 30 minutes or longer, the person's body returns to its resting state. Men are typically unresponsive to further sexual stimulation for a variable period of time after reaching orgasm. This is known as the *refractory period*. Women, on the other hand, may be able to respond to further stimulation almost immediately.

Sexual dysfunctions can involve a disruption of any stage of the human sexual response cycle. The following case study, which was described by McCarthy (1989), is concerned with a man who had difficulty controlling the rate at which he progressed from excitement to orgasm. It illustrates some of the most important features of sexual dysfunction.

CASE STUDY

Premature Ejaculation

Margaret and Bill, both in their late twenties, had been married for 2 years, and they had intercourse frequently. Margaret seldom reached orgasm during these experiences, but she was orgasmic during masturbation. The central feature of their problem was the fact that Bill was unable to delay ejaculation for more than a few seconds after insertion.

Unbeknownst to Margaret, Bill had attempted a "do-it-yourself" technique to gain better control [of ejaculation]. He had bought a desensitizing cream he'd read about in a men's magazine and applied it to the glans of his penis 20 minutes before initiating sex. He also masturbated the day before couple sex. During intercourse he tried to keep his leg muscles tense and think about sports as a way of keeping his arousal in check. Bill was unaware that Margaret felt emotionally shut out during the sex. Bill was becoming more sensitized to his arousal cycle and was worrying about erection. He was not achieving better ejaculatory control, and he was enjoying sex less. The sexual relationship was heading downhill, and miscommunication and frustration were growing.

Margaret had two secrets that she had never shared with Bill. Although she found it easier to be orgasmic with manual stimulation, she had been orgasmic during intercourse with a married man she'd had an affair with a year before meeting Bill. Margaret expressed ambivalent feelings about that relationship. She felt that the man was a very sophisticated lover, and she had been highly aroused and orgasmic with him. Yet, the relationship had been a manipulative one. He'd been emotionally abusive to Margaret, and the relationship had ended when he accused Margaret of giving him herpes and berated her. In fact, it was probably he who gave Margaret the herpes. Margaret was only experiencing herpes outbreaks two or three times a year, but when they did occur, she was flooded with negative feelings about herself, sexuality, and relationships. She initially saw Bill as a loving, stable man who would help rid her of negative feelings concerning sexuality. Instead, he continually disappointed her with the early ejaculation. Bill knew about the herpes but not about her sexual history and strong negative feelings.

Bill was terribly embarrassed about his secret concerning masturbation, which he engaged in on a twice-daily basis. From adolescence on, Bill had used masturbation as his primary means of stress reduction. For him, masturbation was a humiliating secret (he believed married men should not masturbate). The manner in which he masturbated undoubtedly contributed to the early ejaculation pattern. Bill focused only on his penis, using rapid strokes with the goal of ejaculating as quickly as he could. This was both to prevent himself from being discovered (he usually masturbated in the bedroom or bathroom—sometimes with Margaret in the house—and he would also masturbate while sitting in the stall at the men's room at work) and from a desire to "get it over with" as soon as he could and forget about it. Bill's view of his masturbation was very negative, and he strove to keep it a brief, isolated part of his life.

When it came to his personal and sexual life, Bill was inhibited, unsure of himself, and had particularly low sexual self-esteem. As an adolescent, Bill remembered being very interested sexually, but very unsure around girls. Bill's first intercourse at 19 was perceived as a failure because he ejaculated before he could insert his penis in the woman's vagina. He then tried desperately to insert because the young woman urged him to, but he was in the refractory period (a phenomenon Bill did not understand), and so he did not get a firm erection and felt doubly humiliated. (from McCarthy [1989, pp. 151–159] in Lieblum & Rosen) ■

The case of Bill and Margaret illustrates several important points. First, sexual problems are best defined in terms of the couple rather than the individuals involved. Classification systems tend to ascribe psychological impairments to one person, but in the case of sexual dysfunction, this decision is usually arbitrary. Bill would be assigned a diagnosis of premature ejaculation, but he and Margaret were both distressed, and both had important concerns about sex.

Second, although problems in sexual behavior clearly involve basic physiological responses and behavioral skills, mental scripts regarding the meaning of sexual behavior are also extremely important. Sexual behavior usually takes place in the context of a close, personal relationship. The partners need to talk to each other about the things that they enjoy as well as about their worries. Failure to communicate is often motivated by feelings of guilt and frustration, which can easily escalate over time.

Classification of Sexual Disorders

The classification of sexual disorders has changed dramatically during the twentieth century. Before describing the current system that is included in DSM-IV, we outline briefly some of the clinical and scientific views on sexuality that laid the foundation for the current system.

Brief Historical Perspective

Early medical and scientific approaches to sexual behavior were heavily influenced by religious doctrines and by prevailing cultural values. The exclusive purpose of sexual behavior was assumed to be biological reproduction; anything that varied from that narrow goal was considered to be a form of psychopathology and was usually subject to severe moral and legal sanctions. For example, throughout the eighteenth and nineteenth centuries, masturbation was widely condemned and was generally considered to be responsible for causing various physical and mental disorders (Bullough, 1976). Medical authorities were more worried about excessive sexuality and inappropriate or unusual sexual activities than they were about a person's subjective dissatisfaction or impaired sexual performance. This was especially true with regard to the sexual experiences of women, who were, in Victorian society, supposed to remain "pure" and asexual (Heiman & Grafton-Becker, 1989).

Early efforts to develop a classification system for sexual problems were primarily concerned with the definition of "normal" behavior and with a description of *sexual perversions*. The most influential system was proposed by Richard von Krafft-Ebing (1840–1902), who was professor of psychiatry and neurology at the University of Vienna and a contemporary of Freud. Krafft-Ebing's classification of what he called the "sexual neuroses" made only brief mention of sexual dysfunctions, in particular erectile impairment and ejaculatory control. The vast majority of the manual was devoted to the so-called perversions, especially sadism, masochism, fetishism, and homosexuality.

The period between 1890 and 1930 saw many crucial changes in the ways in which society viewed sexual behavior (D'Emilio & Freedman, 1988). A significant number of people were beginning to think of sex as something other than a simple procreative function. If the purpose of sexual behavior was to foster marital intimacy or to provide pleasure, then interference with that goal might become a legitimate topic of psychological inquiry. Changes in prevailing social attitudes led to a change in the focus of systems for the classification of sexual problems. Over the course of the twentieth century, there has been a trend toward greater tolerance of sexual variation among consenting adult partners and toward increased concern about impairments in sexual performance and experience.

INFLUENTIAL CLINICIANS AND SCIENTISTS

Several leading intellectuals influenced public and professional opinions regarding sexual behavior during the first half of the twentieth century (Hogan, 1990). Freud's groundbreaking contribution regarding sexual disorders, *Three Essays on the Theory of Sexuality*, appeared in 1905. Freud stimulated public discussion of such controversial topics as children's sexual interests and sexual conflict within the family (D'Emilio & Freedman, 1988). He argued that sexual impulses were among the most salient motivational factors throughout childhood and adolescence. Perhaps most important was the recognition that, in both men and women, psychological problems can result from attempts to deny or repress sexual urges. This perspective stood in direct contrast to the notion contained in Krafft-Ebing's textbook, that sexual impulses had to be severely restricted.

Havelock Ellis (1859–1939) was the leading figure in the study of sexual behavior at the turn of the twentieth century. The author of a series of influential monographs titled *Studies in the Psychology of Sex* between the years 1897 and 1910, Ellis has been called the first sexual modernist (Robinson, 1976). His papers advocated a much broader interpretation of behaviors that could be considered acceptable and even desirable human sexuality. He approved of masturbation and argued against the stigma that many of his contemporaries associated with homosexuality. Above all else, Ellis became a leading advocate for the open discussion and expression of sexual desires.

The tolerant attitudes espoused by Ellis were extended and given scientific support in the work of Alfred Kinsey (1894–1956), a biologist at Indiana University. Kinsey was chosen in 1938 to coordinate a university course on marriage. The absence of scientific information regarding human sexual behavior led him to begin collecting comprehensive personal histories from people regarding their own sexual experiences. In keeping with his conscious adherence to scientific methods, Kinsey adopted a behavioral stance, focusing specifically on those experiences that resulted in orgasm. His research largely ignored subjective experience. In their efforts to describe human sexual behavior, Kinsey and his colleagues interviewed 18,000 men and women between 1938 and 1956. The results of this groundbreaking investigation were published in two seminal volumes, one concerned with men (1948) and the other with women (1953).

The incredible diversity of experiences reported by his subjects led Kinsey to reject the distinction between normal and abnormal sexual behavior (Robinson, 1976). He argued that differences among people are quantitative rather than qualitative in nature. For example, Kinsey argued that the distinction between heterosexual and homosexual persons was essentially arbitrary and fundamentally meaningless. His comments regarding sexual dysfunction reflected a similar view. Kinsey believed that low sexual desire was simply a reflection of individual differences in erotic capacity rather than a reflection of psychopathology (Kinsey et al., 1948).

EARLY VERSIONS OF DSM

The descriptions of sexual disorders in the first and second editions of the *DSM* (APA, 1952, 1968) were more influenced by psychodynamic theory than by scientific data, Kinsey's views, or Masters and Johnson's early work. In DSM-I, sexual deviations were listed together with antisocial personality disorder. In DSM-II, sexual deviations were listed along with alcoholism and drug dependence under the general heading "Personality Disorders and Certain Other Non-psychotic Mental Disorders." Sexual dysfunctions were given only superficial mention, under "Psychophysiologic Genito-Urinary Disorders."

Ereud

▲ On the basis of his extensive interviews, Alfred Kinsey argued that the distinction between normal and abnormal sexual behavior was not useful.

Cultural and political considerations have also influenced the development and revision of official classification in the area of sexual problems. Revisions of the DSM reflect several important changes in society's attitudes toward sexual behavior, including the following major factors (Bullough, 1976):

- Growing acceptance by women of their own sexuality
- Increased recognition that the main purpose of sexual behavior need not be reproduction
- Tolerance for greater variety in human sexuality
- The influence of organized groups, representing specific forms of sexual orientation and expression

Homosexuality: A Case of Politics and Diagnosis

The influence of politics on psychiatric classification is perhaps nowhere better illustrated than in the case of homosexuality. The psychiatric community had maintained in DSM-I and DSM-II that homosexuality was, by definition, a form of mental disorder. This position reflected, in large part, the views of psychodynamic therapists and was adopted in spite of the attitudes expressed by scientists such as Kinsey and many others (such as Ford & Beach, 1951). Toward the end of the 1960s, the gay and lesbian rights movement became more forceful and outspoken. Some of its leaders began to challenge the assumption that homosexuality was pathological, and to oppose the inclusion of homosexuality in the official nomenclature.

Between the years 1970 and 1974, a dramatic series of events led to important changes in the American Psychiatric Association's classification of sexual disorders, especially homosexuality (Bayer, 1981). The first incident took place at a meeting in 1970, where gay activists disrupted presentations concerned with psychodynamic theories of sexual deviations. Among the demands presented by gay leaders was a call for the removal of homosexuality from the DSM-II.

Direct discussions between members of the gay community and members of the APA Committee on Nomenclature (which is responsible for producing the diagnostic manual) began in 1972 and continued throughout the following year. A compromise position, drafted by Robert Spitzer, was eventually presented to the board of trustees of APA at the end of 1973. The trustees voted unanimously to remove homosexuality from DSM-II. In the spring of 1974, the entire membership of APA participated in a referendum on the board's decision. Approximately 60 percent of the 10,000 votes were cast in favor of the board's decision, thus affirming the removal of homosexuality as a form of mental illness.

One important consequence of this debate was a shift in the basis on which sexual disorders are classified. Spitzer and his allies on the committee came to believe that the classification system should be concerned primarily with subjective distress. They were impressed by the numerous indications, in both personal appeals and in the research literature, that homosexuality per se was not invariably associated with impaired functioning. They decided that, in order to be considered a form of mental disorder, a condition ought to be associated with subjective distress or seriously impaired social or occupational functioning. This emphasis opened the door to a more detailed consideration of sexual dysfunction and relatively less concern with the choice of sexual partners or preferred activities, as long as the participants were mutually consenting adults.

When Spitzer chaired the committee that created DSM-III, there was a rather drastic change, with increased emphasis placed on sexual dysfunction. Sexual disorders were moved to their own separate section of the manual. Specific types of sexual dysfunction were listed in terms of interruptions of the response cycle that had been described by Masters and Johnson and another prominent sex therapist, Helen Singer Kaplan (1979).

DSM-IV includes three principal forms of sexual disorder: sexual dysfunctions, the paraphilias, and gender identity disorders. We discuss the typical symptoms, etiology, and treatment of these disorders separately in the following sections of this chapter.

Sexual Dysfunction

Sexuality represents a complex behavioral process that can easily be upset. Sexual dysfunction can arise anywhere from the earliest stages of interest and desire through the climactic release of orgasm. In some cases, these problems take the form of inhibitions of sexual response or diminished pleasure. Some people also experience pain in association with sexual intercourse. The following sections describe the DSM-IV system for classifying various types of sexual dysfunction.

Typical Symptoms and Associated Features

Sexual dysfunctions are subdivided into several types in DSM-IV (see Table 11–1). In order to meet diagnostic criteria, all categories of sexual dysfunction require that (1) the disturbance causes marked distress or interpersonal difficulty, and (2) the sexual dysfunction is not better accounted for by another Axis I disorder (such as major depression) and is not due to the direct physiological effects of a chemical substance (such as alcohol) or a general medical condition. For many types of disorder, the clinician must decide whether the person has engaged in sexual activities that would normally be expected to produce sexual arousal or orgasm. Diagnostic judgments must frequently take into consideration the person's age as well as the circumstances in which the person is living, such as the presence of a partner, access to privacy, and so on.

Each of the specific types of sexual dysfunction can be characterized in terms of its pattern of onset and context of occurrence. With regard to pattern of onset, the problem can be either *lifelong*, meaning that the problem has been present since the person's first sexual activities, or it can be *acquired*, meaning that the problem developed only after a period of normal functioning. With regard to context of occurrence, the problem can either be *generalized*, meaning that the dysfunction is not limited to certain situations or partners, or *situational*, meaning that the dysfunction is limited to certain situations or partners.

TABLE 11–1

Sexual Dysfunctions Listed in DSM-IV

Hypoactive Sexual Desire Disorder: Persistently or recurrently deficient (or absent) sexual fantasies and desire for sexual activity.

Sexual Aversion Disorder: Persistent or recurrent extreme aversion to, and avoidance of, all (or almost all) genital sexual contact with a sexual partner.

Female Sexual Arousal Disorder: Persistent or recurrent inability to attain, or to maintain until completion of the sexual activity, an adequate lubrication-swelling response of sexual excitement.

Male Erectile Disorder: Persistent or recurrent inability to attain or maintain until completion of the sexual activity, an adequate erection.

Female Orgasmic Disorder: Persistent or recurrent delay in, or absence of, orgasm following a normal sexual excitement phase.

Male Orgasmic Disorder: Persistent or recurrent delay in, or absence of, orgasm following a normal sexual excitement phase during sexual activity.

Premature Ejaculation: Persistent or recurrent ejaculation with minimal sexual stimulation before, on, or shortly after penetration and before the person wishes it.

Dyspareunia: Recurrent or persistent genital pain associated with sexual intercourse in either a male or a female.

Vaginismus: Recurrent or persistent involuntary spasm of the musculature of the outer third of the vagina that interferes with sexual intercourse.

HYPOACTIVE SEXUAL DESIRE DISORDER

One difficulty that was originally recognized as a type of sexual dysfunction by sex therapist Helen Singer Kaplan (1979) and is becoming an increasingly common reason for referral to a sex clinic is lack of sexual desire; a condition known as **hypoactive sexual desire**. Sexual desire sets the stage for sexual arousal and precedes the phases of the sexual response cycle outlined by Masters and Johnson. Some clinicians refer to sexual desire as the person's willingness to approach or engage in those experiences that will lead to sexual arousal. Inhibited sexual desire is defined in terms of subjective experiences, such as lack of sexual fantasies and lack of interest in sexual experiences. The absence of interest in sex must be both persistent and pervasive to be considered a clinical problem.

How often should a person be interested in sex? There isn't a definite answer to this question. Although the notion of lack of sexual desire makes intuitive sense, the concept is difficult to define clinically (Letourneau & O'Donohue, 1993). The absolute frequency with which a person engages in sex cannot be used as a measure of inhibited sexual desire because the central issue is interest—actively seeking out sexual experiences—rather than participation. For example, some people acquiesce to their partners' demands, even though they would not choose to engage in sexual activities if it were left up to them. It is difficult to say how often a person should experience sexual fantasies or impulses. Kinsey and others have observed tremendous variability from one person to the next in this regard.

In the absence of any specific standard, the identification of hypoactive sexual desire must depend upon a clinician's subjective evaluation of the level of desire that is expected given the person's age, gender, marital status, and many other relevant considerations. Because sexual desire is so difficult to define, it remains a controversial topic.

SEXUAL AVERSION DISORDER

Kaplan (1988) also noted that some people develop an active *aversion* to sexual stimuli and begin to avoid these situations altogether. Some people avoid only certain aspects of sexual behavior, such as kissing, intercourse, or oral sex. This reaction is stronger than simple lack of interest.

Fear of sexual encounters can occasionally reach intense proportions. This problem might be viewed as a form of panic disorder because it extends well beyond anxiety regarding sexual performance.

In clinical practice, the distinction between hypoactive sexual desire and **sexual aversion disorder** is not always easy to make. Consider, for example, the following case from our files. The couple sought help at a psychological clinic in the hope that they might improve their sexual relationship.

BRIEF CASE STUDY

Sexual Aversion Disorder

Doug and Jennifer were both 32 years old. They had been married for 5 years, but they had never had sexual intercourse. They cared for each other very much and described themselves as being like brother and sister. Their inability to have intercourse was upsetting to them both for many reasons. Most important was their mutual desire to have children. Doug also felt that their marriage would be stronger and more enjoyable if they were sexually intimate. Jennifer wasn't interested in sexual activity; she never experienced sexual fantasies or erotic thoughts. She did view sex as her duty, however, and she felt guilty about not fulfilling that part of her "marital obligation." Jennifer's primary concern about the relationship involved a different kind of intimacy; she wished that Doug would spend more time with her—talking, taking walks, and doing things together that did not involve sex.

Neither Doug nor Jennifer had been experienced sexually at the time of their marriage. Jennifer was clearly anxious in the presence of stimuli that were sexual in nature, such as movies or books with a sexual theme, but she did not avoid these situations or sexual interactions altogether. She and Doug had engaged in kissing and gentle touching early in their marriage. Jennifer masturbated Doug to orgasm several times, but she felt disgusted at the sight of semen when he ejaculated. Doug had persuaded her to engage in oral sex on a few occasions. She found it unpleasant and was unable to continue long enough for Doug to reach orgasm. They attempted intercourse once, but Jennifer was unable to become aroused and insertion had been impossible.

Doug and Jennifer gradually lost interest in sexual activities. He was extremely busy with his work and said that he no longer thought about sex very often, although he continued to masturbate. Since their failed attempt at intercourse, Doug had also begun to feel less sexually attracted to Jennifer. They eventually entered treatment in order to explore their feelings for each other and to see if they could do anything to salvage their sexual relationship, primarily in the hope that they would be able to have children.

Several weeks after entering therapy, Jennifer reluctantly confided in her therapist that she had been sexually abused by an uncle with whom she had lived for two years as a child. He had forced her to perform oral sex several times when she was about 9 years old. She had never told anyone about the abuse—her parents, her aunt, or Doug—for many reasons. She was ashamed of the experience and frightened of what her uncle might do to her. The memories of this experience were still vivid, especially when she attempted to have sex with her husband. ∎

Jennifer's aversion to sexual activity was easily understandable in the context of previous abuse. In terms of diagnostic criteria, however, her symptoms were initially difficult to distinguish from hypoactive sexual desire. She originally reported that she was not interested in sex, and she had not avoided all sexual contact with Doug. The symptoms of sexual aversion disorder are often more pronounced than those that were exhibited by Jennifer. In some people, full-blown symptoms of panic attack may be triggered by exposure to sexual stimuli.

MALE ERECTILE DISORDER

Many men experience difficulties either obtaining an erection that is sufficient to accomplish intercourse or maintaining an erection long enough to satisfy themselves and their partners during intercourse. Both problems are examples of **erectile dysfunction**. Men with this problem may report feeling subjectively aroused, but the vascular reflex mechanism fails, and sufficient blood is not pumped to the penis to make it erect. These difficulties can appear at any time prior to orgasm. Some men have trouble achieving an erection during sexual foreplay, whereas others lose their erection around the time of insertion or during intercourse. This phenomenon used to be called *impotence*, but the term has been dropped because of its negative implications.

Erectile dysfunctions can be relatively transient, or they can be more chronic. Some information suggests that, at some point, around half of the adult male population has experienced problems achieving an erection. Occasional experiences of this type are not considered unusual (Kaplan, 1974). When they persist and become a serious source of distress to the couple, however, erectile difficulties can lead to serious problems.

FEMALE SEXUAL AROUSAL DISORDER

Sexual arousal can also be impaired in women, but it is somewhat more difficult to describe and identify than is erectile dysfunction in men. Put simply, a woman is said to experience **inhibited sexual arousal** if she cannot either achieve or maintain genital responses, such as lubrication and swelling, that are necessary to complete sexual intercourse. The desire is there, but the physiological responses that characterize sexual excitement are inhibited.

The capacity for intercourse is somewhat less obvious and more difficult to measure for a woman than for a man, whose erect penis usually serves as a signal of readiness (see Research Methods). Investigators who have studied sexual responses in normal women have reported low correlations between self-reports of subjective arousal and physiological measures such as the amount of vaginal lubrication or vasocongestion (Morokoff, 1989). Among women who experience sexual difficulties, the problem may more often be decreased subjective arousal rather than impaired physiological responses

Hypothetical Constructs and Construct Validity: Physiological Measures of Sexual Arousal

The term *sexual arousal* refers to the state that precedes orgasm. It is defined in terms of two factors: (1) physiological responses, such as vascular engorgement of the genitals; and (2) subjective feelings of pleasure and excitement. Psychologists refer to sexual arousal as a hypothetical **construct**. Many of the concepts that we have discussed in this book are hypothetical constructs: anxiety, depression, psychopathy, and schizophrenia. Hypothetical constructs are theoretical devices. In the field of psychopathology, they refer to events or states that reside within the person and are proposed to help us understand or explain a person's behavior.

Constructs cannot be observed directly, but in order to be scientifically meaningful they must be defined in terms of observable referents (Cronbach & Meehl, 1955; Kimble, 1989). These referents are all associated with the construct, but they are not perfectly related, and the construct is not exhaustively defined by them. For example, an erect penis is not always accompanied by subjective feelings of sexual excitement, and subjective feelings of arousal are not always associated with physiological responses. In other words, the construct of sexual arousal is anchored by feelings and responses that can be measured directly, but it is more than the sum of these parts.

An **operational definition** is a procedure that is used to measure a theoretical construct. For men, one obvious component of sexual arousal is penile erection. The most widely accepted procedure for measuring male sexual arousal uses a device called a **penile plethysmograph** (Barker & Howell, 1992; Harris et al., 1992). In this procedure, the man places a thin elastic *strain gauge* around his penis, underneath his clothing. The rubber loop is filled with a column of mercury that changes in its electrical conductance as the circumference of the penis changes. The wire extending from the strain gauge is connected to a plethysmograph, which amplifies the electrical signal passing through the strain gauge and produces a record reflecting changes in penile tumescence.

The *vaginal photometer*, a device shaped like a tampon and inserted into the vagina, is used to measure female sexual arousal. Like the penile strain gauge, the photometer can be placed in position in private and worn underneath clothing during the assessment procedure. As the woman becomes sexually aroused, the walls of the vagina become congested with blood. Vasocongestion causes changes in the amount of red light that can be transmitted through the tissue. The photometer is sensitive to subtle changes in vaginal tissue and is probably most useful in measuring moderate to low levels of sexual arousal (Geer, Heiman, & Leitenberg, 1984).

Clinical scientists must always think carefully about the meaning of their operational definitions. Although the penile strain gauge and the vaginal photometer measure physiological events that are directly related to sexual arousal, the responses that they measure are not the same thing as sexual arousal. They are reflections of the construct, which has many dimensions (McAnulty & Adams, 1992; McConaghy, 1989). One important goal of scientific studies is to determine more specifically how (and when) these physiological measures are related to the other observable referents of sexual arousal. This process will determine the **construct validity** of the penile strain gauge and the vaginal photometer, that is, the extent to which these specific measures produce results that are consistent with the theoretical construct. ∎

(Morokoff & Heiman, 1980). Therefore, inhibitions in sexual arousal must be defined in terms of this self-report dimension as well as in terms of specific genital responses.

PREMATURE EJACULATION

Some men experience problems with the control of ejaculation. They are unable to prolong voluntarily the period of sexual excitement for a period of time that is sufficient to complete intercourse. Once they become intensely sexually aroused, they reach orgasm very quickly. How quickly? As we have noted previously, the human sexual response cycle is quite variable in duration. Some couples are able to prolong sexual intercourse for hours; others are satisfied with relatively brief encounters of several minutes' duration.

There have been many attempts to establish specific, quantitative criteria for this condition, known as **premature ejaculation**, but none has been widely adopted. One approach has emphasized temporal limits. Some clinicians have suggested that the threshold for premature ejaculation be set at 1 or 2 minutes following insertion of the penis in the vagina. None of these has been entirely satisfactory. Nevertheless, certain boundaries might serve to identify conditions that signal the possibility of a problem. If the man ejaculates before or immediately upon insertion, or after only three or four thrusts, almost all couples will identify his response as premature ejaculation (McCarthy, 1989).

Another way to think about premature ejaculation places emphasis on the couple's satisfaction rather than on the amount of time required to reach orgasm. Masters and Johnson (1970) suggested that premature ejaculation might be present if the man was unable to delay ejaculation until his partner reached orgasm at least 50 percent of the time. Kaplan (1974) placed primary emphasis on the subjective perception of control. She argued that prematurity should be defined in terms of the reflexive nature of the man's orgasm. If progression to orgasm is beyond the man's voluntary control once he reaches an intense level of sexual arousal, Kaplan would conclude that he has a problem with premature ejaculation.

FEMALE ORGASMIC DISORDER

Some women are unable to reach orgasm even though they apparently experience uninhibited sexual arousal. Women who experience orgasmic difficulties may have a strong desire to engage in sexual relations, they may find great pleasure in sexual foreplay, and they may show all the signs of sexual arousal. Nevertheless, they cannot reach the peak erotic experience of orgasm. Women whose orgasmic impairment is generalized have never experienced orgasm by

any means. Situational orgasmic difficulties occur when the woman is able to reach orgasm in some situations but not in others. That might mean that she is orgasmic during masturbation but not during intercourse, or perhaps she is orgasmic with one partner but not with another.

Orgasmic disorder is somewhat difficult to define in relation to inhibited sexual arousal because the various components of female sexual response are more difficult to measure than are erection and ejaculation in the male. One experienced researcher has described this issue in the following way:

> In my experience, many women who have never reached orgasm present the following set of symptoms: They report that when engaging in intercourse they do not have difficulty lubricating and experience no pain. However, they report no genital sensations (hence the term genital anesthesia) and do not appear to know what sexual arousal is. Typically they do not masturbate and often have never masturbated. They do not experience the phenomenon that a sexually functional woman would call sexual desire. . . . Most of these women seek therapy because they have heard from others or have read that they are missing something, rather than because they themselves feel frustrated. (Morokoff, 1989, p. 74)

PAIN DURING SEX

Some people experience persistent genital pain during or after sexual intercourse, which is known as **dyspareunia**. The problem can occur in either men or women, though it is considered to be much more common in women (Quevillon, 1993). The severity of the discomfort can range from mild irritation following sexual activities to searing pain during insertion of the penis or intercourse (Lazarus, 1989). The pains may be sharp and intense, or they make take the form of a dull, aching sensation; they may be experienced as coming from a superficial area near the barrel of the vagina or as being located deep in the lower abdominal area; they may be intermittent or persistent.

The experience of severe genital pain is often associated with other forms of sexual dysfunction. Not surprisingly, many women with dyspareunia develop a lack of interest in, or an aversion toward sexual activity.

Access to the vagina is controlled by the muscles surrounding its entrance. Some women find that whenever penetration of the vagina is attempted, these muscles snap tightly shut, preventing insertion of any object. This involuntary muscular spasm, known as **vaginismus,** prevents sexual intercourse as well as other activities such as vaginal examinations and the insertion of tampons. Women with vaginismus may be completely sexually responsive in other respects, fully capable of arousal and orgasm through manual stimulation of the clitoris. Women who seek therapy for this condition often report that they are afraid of intercourse and vaginal penetration (Beck, 1993). The problem can be severe or partial in nature. Some couples report that a mild form of vaginismus occurs from time to time, making intercourse difficult and sometimes painful.

Interpersonal Factors and Social Relationships

The DSM-IV system places primary emphasis on physiological responses and sexual performance in its classification of sexual dysfunction. Disruptions of the sexual response cycle, which involve the genital aspects of sexuality, are not the only kinds of subjective discomfort associated with sexual experience. Disturbed relationships with other people, and other forms of psychopathology, such as depression and anxiety, are also frequently associated with sexual problems.

Many people's complaints about their sexual experiences focus primarily on a lack of tenderness, intimacy, and affection. This may be especially true of women. Remember, for example, the case of Bill and Margaret described at the beginning of this chapter. Margaret said that she felt emotionally shut out when they were having sex. This complaint is similar to the following observations, which were made in response to a national survey of women's sexual experiences and attitudes (Hite, 1976):

- I would like more love and gentleness instead of bare sexual stimulation, more emotion and communication.
- More kisses, more time, more tenderness. Why don't men like to be touched in other parts of their bodies?
- I have viewed married love as a grow-

ing together in the ability to express love and pleasure. . . . My husband doesn't seem to enjoy anything besides intercourse. . . . I don't feel my husband is emotionally involved during sex.

These quotations provide eloquent testimony to the existence of problems with sexuality that extend beyond the mechanical boundaries of intercourse. Some clinicians have argued that the emphasis on orgasm, and on those conditions that set the stage for that experience, reflects a male perspective on sexuality (Tiefer, 1988). Whether or not that is the case, it seems safe to say that problems in interpersonal relationships and subjective feelings of intimacy represent important problems for both men and women (see Research Close-up).

ANXIETY AND DEPRESSION

Strong negative emotions such as anger, fear, and resentment are often associated with sexual problems. In some cases, these emotional states appear before the onset of the sexual problem, and sometimes they develop later. Given the connection that many cultures make between virile sexual performance and "manhood," it is not surprising that men with erectile difficulties are often embarrassed and ashamed. Their humiliation can lead to secondary problems such as anxiety and depression. Similar feelings frequently accompany premature ejaculation and the recognition that a partner's sexual impulses have not been fulfilled. Women who have trouble becoming aroused or reaching orgasm also frequently experience profound frustration and disappointment. The emotional consequences of sexual problems can be devastating for both members of a couple.

▲ **Intimacy and communication are important components of sexuality. Although problems in these areas are not part of the official classification system, they can be a source of great concern for many couples.**

Epidemiology

Evidence regarding the frequency of various types of conventional and unconventional sexual behavior is scanty, at best. People are understandably reluctant to describe such intimate aspects of their lives. Prevalence data are great-

Sexual Dissatisfactions

Ellen Frank, a clinical psychologist at Western Psychiatric Institute and the University of Pittsburgh School of Medicine, and her colleagues conducted a study with 100 married couples that provides interesting evidence regarding the nature of people's complaints about their sexual relationships (Frank, Anderson, & Rubenstein, 1978). These men and women were not a random sample of married couples. In fact, they were recruited because they identified themselves as being part of a happy marriage. Each person completed a checklist that described two types of sexual problems: those that involved sexual arousal and orgasm, which the investigators called *dysfunctions*, and those that were more concerned with the emotional tone of the relationship, which the investigators called *dissatisfactions*. Their results are summarized in Table 11–2.

You should notice several important findings in this table. One is that the frequency of both types of sexual problems is relatively high, in spite of the fact that the couples were selected on the basis of their having described themselves as being happily married. Second, women were more likely than their husbands to report almost every type of sexual problem, except reaching orgasm too quickly. Finally, both women and men reported more dissatisfaction resulting from emotional aspects of sexuality than from interference with arousal and orgasm.

Evidence of this sort indicates that people experience problems with sexuality that cannot be defined fully in terms of a disruption of the sexual response cycle. The DSM-IV emphasizes performance in its definition of sexual dysfunction. In the context of

helping a couple become more satisfied with their relationship, clinicians also need to address related issues, especially physical intimacy and communication, rather than focusing exclusively on genital stimulation (Tiefer, 1988) ∎

TABLE 11–2

Sexual Problems Reported by "Happily Married" Couples

The Dysfunction Type of Sexual Problems	Women (%)	Men (%)
Difficulty getting excited† (an erection)	48	7
Difficulty maintaining excitement (erection)	33	9
Reach orgasm (ejaculate) too quickly	11	36
Difficulty reaching orgasm (ejaculating)	46	0
Inability to have an orgasm (ejaculate)	15	0
Total (one or more listed)	63	40

The Emotional Type of Sexual Problems	Women (%)	Men (%)
Partner chooses inconvenient time	31	16
Inability to relax	47	12
Attraction to person other than mate	14	21
Disinterest	35	16
"Turned off"	28	10
Too little foreplay before intercourse	38	21
Too little tenderness after intercourse	25	17
Total (one or more listed)	77	50

† The wording in the questions on dysfunction-type problems was slightly different for husbands than for wives. The women were asked about getting excited and reaching orgasm; the men were asked about getting an erection and ejaculation.

Source: E. Frank, C. Anderson, & D. Rubenstein (1978). Frequency of sexual dysfunction in normal couples. *New England Journal of Medicine, 299,* 111–115.

ly influenced by the methods that are used to collect information. Studies of people living in various communities suggest that, in comparison to interview data, their responses to questionnaires provide an underestimate of the prevalence of sexual dysfunction (Solstad & Hertoft, 1993). Evidence from mental health clinics is useful, but it probably does not reflect the true prevalence of these problems in the general population, because most people who experience sexual difficulties do not seek treatment.

Surveys conducted among people in the general population indicate that various forms of sexual dysfunction are relatively common. Table 11–3 summarizes some of these data. Premature ejaculation may be the most frequent form of sexual dysfunction, affecting nearly 1 in every 3 adult men. We have to be careful when interpreting these figures, however, because the definition of this condition has varied considerably from one study to the next. Difficulties with arousal are probably the most common form of sexual dysfunction among women, but, once again, the evidence is incomplete.

Research studies have revealed several trends pertaining to the prevalence of specific types of sexual dysfunction among those people who seek professional treatment for these problems (Spector & Carey, 1990):

- Orgasmic and erectile dysfunction have become more frequent complaints among people seeking treatment.
- Clinics have witnessed a decrease in premature ejaculation as the presenting problem among people seeking treatment for sexual dysfunction.
- There has been an increase in the frequency of desire disorders as presenting problems in sex clinics.
- Recently, males have outnumbered females as the person with the presenting problem when couples seek treatment.

GENDER DIFFERENCES

Orgasm disorders, arousal disorders, and inhibited sexual desire are more common among women (Nathan, 1986). The reasons remain uncertain. One study that compared men and women who sought treatment for low sexual desire found an interesting age difference. Men with this condition were significantly older than women (Donahey & Carroll, 1993).

SEXUAL BEHAVIOR
ACROSS THE LIFE SPAN

Sexual behavior changes with age. Masters and Johnson devoted considerable attention to this topic. Their data challenged the myth that older adults are not interested in, or capable of performing, sexual behaviors. Differences between younger and older people are mostly a matter of degree. As men get older, they tend to achieve erections more slowly in response to erotic stimuli, but they can often maintain erections for longer periods of time. Older men find it more difficult to regain an erection if it is lost before orgasm. As women get older, vaginal lubrication may occur at a slower rate, but the response of

TABLE 11–3

Epidemiology of Sexual Dysfunction in Community Samples

	Males	Females
Desire disorder	1–15%[b]	1–35%[b]
Arousal disorder	4–9%[a]	11–48%
Orgasmic disorder	3–4%[b]	5–10%[a]
Premature ejaculation	36–38%[a]	

[a] *Source:* Data from I.P. Spector & M.P. Carey (1990). Incidence and prevalence of the sexual dysfunctions: A critical review of the empirical literature. *Archives of Sexual Behavior, 19,* 389–408.

[b] *Source:* Data from S.G. Nathan (1986). The epidemiology of the DSM-III psychosexual dysfunctions. *Journal of Sex and Marital Therapy, 12,* 267–281.

the clitoris remains essentially unchanged. The intensity of the subjective experience of orgasm is decreased for older men and women. For both men and women, healthy sexual responsiveness is most likely to be maintained among those who have been sexually active as younger adults.

The prevalence of sexual dysfunction increases among the elderly. In Kinsey's classic study, approximately 2 percent of the entire sample of men reported that they had "reached more or less permanent erectile impotence." The frequency of this problem increased with age, so that by the age of 70, 27 percent of the men reported serious erectile disorder. Another survey of men over the age of 75 found that 50 percent reported experiencing erectile dysfunction, but the decline in sexual performance appeared to be caused more by poor physical health than by aging alone (Mulligan et al., 1988).

Etiology

At each stage of the sexual response cycle, a person's behavior is determined by the interaction of many biological and psychological factors, ranging from vasocongestion in the genitals to complex cognitive events involving the perception of sexual stimuli and the interpretation of sexual meanings. Interference with this system at any point can result in serious problems. In the following pages, we review some of the factors that frequently contribute to the etiology of various types of sexual dysfunction.

SEXUAL DESIRE

A person's appetite for sexual experience is based

on many ingredients. These include the spontaneous appearance of sexual thoughts and feelings, the inclination to seek out sexually arousing stimuli, and the capacity to respond positively to sexual advances from a partner. Almost everyone recognizes that sexual desire fluctuates in intensity over time, sometimes dramatically and frequently, for reasons that we do not understand (Levine, 1987). The fact that hypoactive sexual desire is listed in DSM-IV as a type of disorder should not lead us to believe that it is a unitary condition with a simple explanation. It is, in fact, a collection of many different kinds of problems. Reduced interest in sexual activity can be associated with many other problems, including medical illnesses, other mental disorders, and interpersonal difficulties.

There is some evidence to suggest that biological factors are involved in the experience of sexual desire. Among males, sexual desire is influenced by sex hormones, especially testosterone (Davidson, 1990). Men with inadequate levels of sex hormones show an inhibited response to sexual fantasies, but they are still able to have erections in response to viewing explicit erotic films (Bancroft & Wu, 1983). The influence of male sex hormones on sexual behavior is therefore thought to be on sexual appetite rather than on sexual performance. This process probably involves a threshold level of circulating testosterone (Bancroft, 1989). In other words, sexual appetite is impaired if the level of testosterone falls below a particular level (close to the bottom of the laboratory normal range), but above that threshold, fluctuations in testosterone levels will not be associated with changes in sexual desire. The reduction of male sex hormones over the life span probably explains, at least in part, the apparent decline in sexual desire among elderly males.

Although sexual desire is rooted in a strong biological foundation, psychological and social variables also play an important role in the determination of which stimuli a person will find arousing. John Gagnon and William Simon (1973) have argued that sexual desire and arousal are determined by *mental scripts* that we learn throughout childhood and adolescence. According to this view, the social meaning of an event is of paramount importance in releasing the biological process of sexual arousal. Both members of the potential couple must recognize similar cues, defining the situation as potentially sexual in nature, before anything is likely to happen.

Beliefs and attitudes toward sexuality, as well as the quality of interpersonal relationships, have an important influence on the development of low sexual desire, especially among women. Women seeking treatment for hypoactive sexual desire report negative perceptions of their parents' attitudes regarding sexual behavior and the demonstration of affection. In comparison to a group of normal women, they also indicate that they feel less close to their husbands, they have fewer romantic feelings, and they are less attracted to their husbands. The quality of the relationship is an important factor to consider with regard to low sexual desire (Stuart, Hammond, & Pett, 1987).

People who suffer from low levels of sexual desire frequently experience other forms of mental disorder. Perhaps as many as 85 percent of males and 75 percent of females seeking treatment for hypoactive sexual desire report other forms of sexual dysfunction (Donahey & Carroll, 1993). Men and women with low sexual desire also have high rates of mood disorders (Schreiner-Engel & Schiavi, 1986). The mood disorder typically appears before the onset of low sexual desire. It therefore appears likely that many cases of low sexual desire develop after the person has experienced other forms of psychological distress.

SEXUAL AROUSAL IN MEN

Men's erectile difficulties have been studied more extensively than any other form of sexual dysfunction. Masters and Johnson (1970) claimed, on the basis of their clinical experience, that 95 percent of erectile dysfunctions were caused by psychological, rather than biological, factors. More recent evidence indicates that erectile dysfunction is more often biologically based than any other type of sexual problem. Therapists at one clinic for sexual disorders reported that more than half of the cases they treated could be attributed to vascular, neurologic, or hormonal impairment (Melman, Tiefer, & Pederson, 1988).

Erection is the direct result of a threefold increase in blood flow to the penis. It is therefore not surprising that vascular diseases, which may affect the amount of blood reaching the penis, are likely to result in erectile difficulties. Neurological disease, such as epilepsy and multiple sclerosis, can also produce erectile difficulties, because erection depends on spinal reflexes. Diabetes may be the most common neurologically based cause of impaired erectile responsiveness (Wincze & Carey, 1991). We must remember, however, that the distinction between psychological and biological causes is often arbitrary. It is not clear that this simple dichotomy is useful, and in many cases the etiology involves some combination or interaction of many factors (LoPiccolo, 1985).

Many other factors can influence a man's erectile response, including various drugs. One interesting set of results indicates that men who smoke cigarettes are more likely to experience erectile difficulties than are men in the general population (see Mohr & Beutler, 1990). Many other drugs, including alcohol and marijuana, may have negative effects on sexual arousal. Medication used to treat hypertension can impair erectile responsiveness, and so can various types of antipsychotic and antidepressant drugs.

Among the psychological factors contributing to impaired sexual arousal, Masters and Johnson (1970) gave primary emphasis to *performance anxiety,* or fear of failure. People who have experienced inhibited sexual arousal on one or two occasions may be likely to have further problems to the degree that these difficulties make them more self-conscious or apprehensive regarding their ability to become aroused in future sexual encounters. Several prominent and experienced sex therapists (for example, Kaplan, 1974) have assumed that anxiety and sexual arousal are incompatible emotional states. People who are afraid will presumably be less responsive to sexual stimuli.

David Barlow and his colleagues have conducted a series of studies comparing sexually dysfunctional men with control subjects in laboratory settings (for example, Cranston-Cuebas et al., 1993). Subjects in these studies viewed explicit, erotic films while wearing a penile strain gauge. The experimenters manipulated several variables, such as the subjects' anxiety levels and the extent to which they were distracted by non-sexual stimuli. A number of factors have been shown to have different effects for functional in comparison to dysfunctional subjects. For example, men who experience erectile failure are less responsive when they are confronted with demands to become sexually aroused, but sexually functional men show the opposite effect. Dysfunctional men also tend to be less aware of their level of sexual arousal, and they are more likely to experience negative affect in the presence of erotic stimuli. The results of these studies suggest that sexual arousal problems may be mediated by a negative feedback loop in which unpleasant feelings lead to self-distraction and avoidance of erotic stimuli (Barlow, 1986; Cranston-Cuebas & Barlow, 1990).

SEXUAL AROUSAL IN WOMEN

Relatively less research has been conducted on problems of sexual arousal in women. Many biological factors and physiological diseases can impair a woman's ability to become sexually aroused. Various types of neurological disorder, pelvic disease, and hormonal dysfunction can interfere with the process of vaginal swelling and lubrication. As we have already discussed in the case of Jennifer, a previous history of sexual abuse can lead to sexual aversion, and it can interfere with a woman's ability to become sexually aroused (Becker, 1989). Failure to engage in effective behaviors during foreplay—inadequate stimulation, poor timing, and poor communication—are also important contributing factors (Kaplan, 1974; Wincze & Carey, 1991).

Culturally determined values can have a dramatic impact on women's attitudes toward sexual feelings and behaviors (Heiman, 1983). Some societies openly encourage female sexuality; others foster a more repressive atmosphere. Within U.S. culture, there are tremendous variations with regard to women's ability to experience and express their sexuality, and some studies have found that different attitudes are associated with different levels of sexual responsiveness. For example, many women feel guilty about having sexual fantasies, in spite of the fact that such fantasies are extremely common. Women who feel guilty about fantasizing while they are having intercourse are more likely to be sexually dissatisfied and to encounter sexual problems, including arousal difficulties (Cado & Leitenberg, 1990).

PREMATURE EJACULATION

Several factors contribute to the development of premature ejaculation. We must remember, in this regard, that Kinsey and others have argued that premature ejaculation is not necessarily a form of dysfunction when viewed from a biological perspective. Some men simply reach orgasm more quickly than others. From an evolutionary point of view, there is nothing inherently disadvantageous about premature ejaculation. Nevertheless, premature ejaculation can bring about relationship difficulties and personal distress, and until recently, it was the most frequent complaint for which men sought help at clinics for sexual problems.

Premature ejaculation may be a normal, early stage in male sexual development (McCarthy, 1989). Almost all males experience orgasm for the first time through masturbation or nocturnal emission. Adolescent males typically masturbate in an intense manner that is focused specifically on stimulating the rigid penis to the point of orgasm as quickly as possible. In Bill's case, he continued this practice as an adult. This process is inconsistent with learning ejaculatory control.

INHIBITED ORGASM

Inhibited orgasm, in both men and women, is sometimes caused by the abuse of alcohol and other drugs. It can also be associated with the use of prescribed forms of medication (Segraves, 1988; Zajecka et al., 1991).

One of the most interesting factors associated with rates of female orgasm is that women who were born in more recent decades are more likely to reach orgasm successfully than are women born longer ago (Morokoff, 1978). This information suggests that cultural values play an important role in sexual experience. Public attitudes toward female sexuality, and especially the expectation that women can and should experience orgasms as an important part of a sexual relationship, have changed progressively over the past several decades. These attitudes and expectations have become more positive, and as people have communicated more openly about those forms of stimulation that women find most arousing, there has been an associated increase in the probability that women will share equally in the pleasures of sexual intercourse.

Evidence that is consistent with this general hypothesis has been reported by a study that compared patterns of sexual arousal in *anorgasmic* women—those who experience inhibited orgasm—and orgasmic women while they viewed erotic films in a laboratory (Kelly, Strassberg, & Kircher, 1990). The women also completed a set of questionnaires regarding their attitudes and beliefs about sexuality as well as their patterns of sexual behavior with their partners. The subjects were all involved in a relationship with a sexually functional man at the time of the study. The anorgasmic women reported that, although

they were interested in sex and actively engaged in sexual activity at least once each week, less than 5 percent of their sexual activities with their partners resulted in orgasm. In comparison to the control subjects, the anorgasmic women reported that they (1) were more uncomfortable talking to their partner about sexual activities involving direct stimulation of the clitoris; (2) held more negative attitudes toward masturbation; and (3) felt greater guilt about sex. Equally interesting was the fact that the two groups of women did *not* differ in their levels of arousal while viewing explicit videotapes of various heterosexual activities. The most important factors contributing to failure to reach orgasm involved negative attitudes, feelings of guilt, and failure to communicate effectively, rather than the simple practice of engaging in particular types of stimulation.

Treatment

Publication of the book *Human Sexual Inadequacy* by Masters and Johnson in 1970 represented a major turning point in the treatment of sexual dysfunctions. Previously, psychological interventions aimed at these problems had focused on long-term therapies directed toward helping couples understand the intrapsychic factors that presumably caused their problems. Masters and Johnson were pioneers in developing and popularizing a short-term, skills-based approach. Hundreds of couples who visited their clinic in St. Louis went through a 2-week course of assessment and therapy in which they became more familiar with their bodies, learned to communicate more effectively with their partners, and received training in procedures designed to help them diminish their fears about sexuality. The results of this treatment program were very positive and quickly spawned a burgeoning industry of psychosocial treatment for sexual dysfunction.

Psychological treatments for sexual dysfunction address several of the etiological factors discussed in the previous section, especially negative attitudes toward sexuality, failure to engage in effective sexual behaviors, and deficits in communication skills. Sex therapy centers around three primary types of activity: (1) sensate focus and scheduling, (2) education and cognitive restructuring, and (3) communication training (Wincze & Carey, 1991).

SENSATE FOCUS AND SCHEDULING

The cornerstone of sex therapy is known as **sensate focus,** a procedure developed by Masters and Johnson. Sensate focus involves a series of simple exercises in which the couple spends time in a quiet, relaxed setting, learning to touch each other. They may start with tasks as simple as holding hands or giving each other back rubs. The rationale for sensate focus hinges on the recognition that people with sexual problems must learn to focus on erotic sensations rather than on performance demands. The goal is to help them become more comfortable with this kind of physical sharing and intimacy, to learn to relax and enjoy it, and to talk to each other about what feels good to them and what does not.

The related facet of psychological approaches to treating sexual dysfunction is *scheduling.* This is, in fact, closely related to sensate focus because the technique of sensate focus requires that people schedule time for sex. Couples need a quiet, relaxed, and private environment in order to engage in pleasurable and satisfying sexual behavior.

EDUCATION AND COGNITIVE RESTRUCTURING

The second major aspect of sex therapy involves education and *cognitive restructuring*—changing the way in which people think about sex. In many cases, the therapist needs to help the couple correct mistaken beliefs and attitudes about sexual behavior. Examples are the belief that intercourse is the only true form of sex, that foreplay is an adolescent interest that most adults can ignore, and that simultaneous orgasm is the ultimate goal of intercourse. Providing information about sexual behaviors in the general population can often help alleviate people's guilt and anxiety surrounding their own experiences. Some people are relieved to know that they are not the only ones who fantasize about various kinds of sexual experiences, or that the fact that they fantasize about these things does not mean that they are going to be compelled to behave in deviant ways.

Education can address many commonly held mistaken beliefs about sexuality. Zilbergeld (1978) has described several myths about men and sexual behavior. These stereotypes, which are often promoted in the popular media, include notions such as the following:

- In sex, it's performance that counts.
- The man must take charge of and initiate sex.
- A man always wants and is ready to have sex.

Sexually dysfunctional men are more likely than nondysfunctional men to believe these statements (Baker & DeSilva, 1988). It is, of course, difficult to determine whether these beliefs were present before the onset of the men's sexual problems or whether they might be consequences of having experienced problems in sexual behavior. Nevertheless, it seems likely that these beliefs are detrimental to achieving a satisfactory level of sexual adjustment.

In some cases, deeply ingrained, maladaptive attitudes do not change just because clients receive new information. Sometimes therapists have to work more directly on modifying irrational cognitions. This process involves cognitive restructuring, similar to the cognitive techniques that we have already discussed with regard to the treatment of depression and anxiety disorders. In the first step of this process, the therapist helps the client recognize the presence of irrational or illogical beliefs about sexuality. The therapist then challenges these beliefs directly and teaches the client to substitute more adaptive self-statements and to interpret events in a more positive light.

COMMUNICATION TRAINING

The final element of treatment for sexual dysfunction is *communication training*. This is another technique that was emphasized by Masters and Johnson in their early work with sexually dysfunctional couples. Many different studies have indicated that people with sexual dysfunction often have deficits in communication skills (for example, Kelly et al., 1990). They find it difficult to talk to their partners about matters involving sex, and they are especially impaired in the ability to tell their partners what kinds of things they find sexually arousing and what kinds of things turn them off. Therefore, sex therapists often employ structured training procedures aimed at improving the ways in which couples talk to each other.

The outcome results of psychosexual treatment programs for sexual disorders have been quite positive. Initial reports from Masters and Johnson's clinic were especially glowing. One summary of their results reported an overall success rate of 85 percent for male patients and 78 percent for female patients. These positive findings offered hope to many couples who had experienced serious difficulties, as well as inspiration to other therapists who became interested in this area of service.

This initial optimism has subsequently been tempered by other studies that have reported less positive results (such as Bancroft et al., 1986). Important questions have also been raised about the adequacy of the research methods employed in Masters and Johnson's outcome studies (Cole, 1985; Warner & Bancroft, 1986).

The overall conclusion is still that psychological treatments for sexual dysfunction are frequently successful (see Leiblum & Rosen, 1989; LoPiccolo & Stock, 1986; O'Donohue & Geer, 1993).

The past 25 years have seen many changes in sex therapy, which have been summarized by Leiblum and Rosen (1989). One important consideration involves an increased emphasis on the treatment of desire disorders. There has also been a shift toward the use of psychological treatments that emphasize interpersonal relationships and family systems in addition to the more directive, short-term behavioral procedures described earlier in this section.

Paraphilias

▼ **Some gay men who dress in women's clothes refer to themselves as "drag queens." This is different from transvestic fetishism, which applies only to heterosexual men whose cross-dressing is associated with intense, sexually arousing fantasies or urges.**

In certain extreme forms of unusual sexual behavior, called *paraphilias*, sexual arousal is associated with atypical stimuli, and the person is preoccupied with, or consumed by, these activities. Literally translated, paraphilia means "love" (*philia*) "beyond the usual" (*para*). This term refers to conditions that were formerly called perversions or sexual deviations. According to DSM-IV, the central features of all paraphilias are persistent sexual urges and fantasies that are associated with (1) nonhuman objects, (2) suffering or humiliation of oneself or one's partner, or (3) children or other nonconsenting persons. In the following pages, we summarize

a few of the most common types of paraphilias, and we consider some of the factors that might influence the development of unusual sexual preferences.

Typical Symptoms and Associated Features

People are capable of associating sexual arousal with a wide range of stimuli and activities. Some are quite common, while others are unusual and perhaps startling. For some people, unusual erotic intentions remain limited to fantasies. Others act on them. One hundred years ago, many psychiatrists considered any type of sexual behavior other than heterosexual intercourse to be pathological. Contemporary researchers and clinicians recognize a much broader range of sexual behavior as falling within the boundaries of normal behavior. Today's more open-minded attitudes are due, in part, to the recognition that a large proportion of men and women engage in sexual fantasies and mutually consenting behaviors such as oral sex, and that these experiences enhance their relationships without causing problems (Kinsey et al., 1948, 1953).

Problems with sexual appetites arise when a pattern develops involving a long-standing, unusual erotic preoccupation that is highly arousing, coupled with a pressure to act on the erotic fantasy. The diagnosis of paraphilia is made only if the person has acted on the urges or is distressed by them. Some people are able to

become sexually aroused only by using para-philic fantasies or stimuli. Others find that they are usually able to respond sexually to "normal" stimuli, and their paraphilic preferences emerge only intermittently, such as during periods of stress. The DSM-IV requires that the erotic preoccupation must have lasted at least 6 months before the person would meet diagnostic criteria for a paraphilia.

It is actually somewhat misleading, or imprecise, to say that paraphilias are defined in terms of reactions to unusual stimuli. The central problem is that sexual arousal is dependent on images that are detached from reciprocal, loving relationships with another adult (Levine, Risen, & Althof, 1990). Themes of aggression, violence, hostility, and revenge are common in paraphilic fantasies, as are impulses involving strangers or unwilling partners. For example, a man might become sexually aroused by images of displaying his erect penis to unsuspecting women, making obscene phone calls, rubbing his genitals against women in a crowded bus, or fondling small children. In other more benign instances, the arousing stimuli are inanimate, such as touching or wearing women's undergarments. Rather than focusing on whether the stimuli are common or uncommon, some investigators have placed principal emphasis on the lack of human intimacy that is associated with many forms of paraphilias (Marshall, 1989).

Compulsion and lack of flexibility are also important features of paraphilic behaviors. Paraphilias may occupy large amounts of time and consume much of the person's energy. In that sense, they are similar to the addictions. People with paraphilic disorders are not simply aroused by unusual images or fantasies. Their choice of sexual behaviors does not appear to be voluntary. They feel *compelled* to engage in certain acts that may be personally degrading or harmful to others, in spite of the fact that these actions are often repulsive to others and are sometimes illegal. The following case describes some of the central features of paraphilias:

BRIEF CASE STUDY

Paraphilia

For the past 40 years, Jon has masturbated to images of barely clad women

---

violently wrestling each other. Periodically throughout his marriage, he has tried to involve his wife in wrestling matches with her friends and, eventually, with their adolescent daughter. When Jon was drunk, he occasionally embarrassed his wife by trying to pick fights between her and other women. On summer vacations, he sometimes jokingly suggested the women wrestle. During much of his sober life, however, his daydreams of women wrestling were private experiences that preoccupied only him. He amassed a collection of magazines and videotapes depicting women wrestling, to which he would resort when driven by the need for excitement.

Jon presented for help with his inability to maintain his erection with his wife for intercourse. With the exception of procreational sex, he was not able to consummate his long marriage. He was able to (become) erect if his wife described herself wrestling other women while he stimulated his penis in front of her, but he always lost his erection when intercourse was attempted. (Levine, Risen, & Althof, 1990) ■

This case illustrates the way in which paraphilias can interfere with a person's life, especially relationships with other people. Jon's preoccupation with fantasies of women wrestling led him to say and do things that disrupted his marriage and his friendships with other people.

Many people with paraphilias experience sexual dysfunction involving desire, arousal, or orgasm during conventional sexual behavior with a partner (Levine, Risen, & Althof, 1990). This feature is not always present, and it is not included as part of the official diagnostic criteria for paraphilias in DSM-IV. It is, nevertheless, an important consequence of the disorder. The wives of men with paraphilias frequently protest that their husbands are not interested in their sexual relationship. In fact, the husband may be actively engaged in frequent masturbation to paraphilic fantasies. Cases of this sort present an interesting diagnostic challenge to

TABLE 11–4

Paraphilias Listed in DSM-IV

Type	Focus of Sexual Urges and Fantasies
Exhibitionism	The exposure of one's genitals to an unsuspecting stranger
Fetishism	The use of nonliving objects (such as female undergarments)
Frotteurism	Touching and rubbing against a nonconsenting person
Pedophilia	Sexual activity with a prepubescent child or children (generally age 13 or younger)
Sexual masochism	The act (real, not simulated) of being humiliated, beaten, bound, or otherwise made to suffer
Sexual sadism	Acts (real, not simulated) in which the psychological or physical suffering (including humiliation) of the victim is sexually exciting to the person
Transvestic fetishism	Cross-dressing (only in heterosexual males)
Voyeurism	The act of observing an unsuspecting person who is naked, in the process of disrobing, or engaging in sexual activity

the clinician, who must distinguish a paraphilia from what might otherwise appear to be low sexual desire.

Several researchers have noted that men with paraphilias can typically be described as timid, low in self-esteem, and lacking in social skills (Blair & Lanyon, 1981). It is, of course, difficult to know whether these characteristics are traits that set the stage for the development of paraphilias or whether they are consequences associated with the performance of sexual behaviors that are considered repugnant by society.

Classification of Paraphilias

The range of objects, situations, and behaviors that can become a source of sexual arousal is virtually infinite (Stoller, 1975). Money (1984) suggested that there are at least 30 different types of paraphilias, including sexual arousal associated with stimuli ranging from animals, enemas, diapers, and tattoos to self-strangulation, and having sex with children, amputees, and

people old enough to be your parents or grandparents. In actual practice, a few prominent forms of paraphilias appear in DSM-IV. These types, which are described in Table 11–4, are the ones that are seen most often in clinics that specialize in the treatment of sexual disorders. Not surprisingly, they are also the ones that frequently lead to the person's being arrested.

RAPE AND SEXUAL ASSAULT

The legal definition of **rape** includes "acts involving nonconsensual sexual penetration obtained by physical force, by threat of bodily harm, or when the victim is incapable of giving consent by virtue of mental illness, mental retardation, or intoxication" (Goodman et al., 1993). One conservative estimate of rape prevalence based on a national survey indicated that 14 percent of adult women had been raped (National Victims Center, 1992). The actual rate is probably higher—perhaps in the vicinity of 20 or 25 percent (Koss, 1992, 1993).[†] Some rapes are committed by strangers, but many others—known as *acquaintance rapes*—are committed by men who know their victims. Most female victims know the person who raped them (Russell, 1984).

Rapes are committed by many different kinds of people for many different reasons (Newcomb, 1993). The feministic perspective on rape emphasizes male aggression and violence. The traditional clinical perspective has been concerned with sexual deviance. The authors of DSM-IV considered including rape as a type of paraphilia. This proposal was rejected, primarily because it might imply that rape is always motivated by sexual arousal, and it is not. Nevertheless, the behavior of some rapists does include essential features of paraphilias: recurrent, intense sexually arousing fantasies and urges that involve the suffering of nonconsenting persons. Half of the convicted rapists in one study report a history of other types of paraphilia: pedophilia (24 percent), exhibitionism (19 percent), and voyeurism (17 percent) (Abel, 1990). Current efforts to classify sexual offenders attempt to distinguish between those for whom deviant sexual arousal contributes to the act and those whose behavior is motivated primarily by anger or violent impulses (see Further Thoughts).

[†] The impact of sexual assault on the victim is described in Chapter 7 (Further Thoughts).

The Classification of Rapists

Raymond Knight, a psychologist at Brandeis University, and Robert Prentky have studied convicted rapists who were imprisoned at the Massachusetts Treatment Center (MTC) for sexually dangerous persons (Knight & Prentky, 1990; Knight, Prentky, & Cerce, 1994). Their research indicates that rape is motivated by both aggressive and sexual components, in varying mixtures. Knight and Prentky developed a classification system for rapists, known as the MTC-R3, that includes four main categories, which are reproduced in Table 11–5.

TABLE 11–5

Basic Structure of the MTC Typology for Rapists

Primary Motivation	General Category	Description of Rapists
Aggressive	Vindictive	Actions intended to degrade and humiliate the victim
	Opportunistic	Impulsive, unplanned actions; seeking immediate gratification; indifferent to the victim's plight
Sexual	Sadistic	Preoccupation with sadistic sexual fantasies; actions typically brutal and violent
	Nonsadistic	Distorted views of sexuality and women; feelings of inferiority; poor social skills

Source: Adapted from R.A. Knight & R. A. Prentky (1990). Classifying sexual offenders. In W. Marshall, D.R. Laws, and H.E. Barbaree (Eds), *Handbook of sexual assault: Issues, theories, and treatment of the offender,* p. 43. New York: Plenum.

Two of the categories include men whose motivation for sexual assault is primarily sexual in nature. *Sadistic* rapists exhibit features that are close to the DSM-IV definition of a paraphilia. Their behavior is determined by a combination of sexual and aggressive impulses. The *nonsadistic* category also includes men who are preoccupied with sexual fantasies, but these fantasies are not blended with images of violence and aggression. The sexual aggression of these men may result, in part, from serious deficits in the ability to process social cues, such as the intentions of women (Lipton, McDonel, & McFall, 1987; McFall, 1990).

The other two categories in Knight and Prentky's system describe men whose primary motivation for rape is not sexual. *Vindictive* rapists seem intent on violence directed exclusively toward women. Their aggression is not erotically motivated, as with sadistic rapists. *Opportunistic* rapists are men with an extensive history of impulsive behavior in many kinds of settings, who might be considered psychopaths (see Chapter 9). Their sexual behavior is governed largely by immediate environmental cues. They will use whatever force is necessary to ensure compliance, but they express anger only in response to the victim's resistance.

The utility of the MTC-R3 typology has been examined in a study of rapists who were being treated at a sexual behavior clinic (Barbaree et al., 1994). Most of these men could be placed reliably into one of Knight and Prentky's main categories. Overall, 22 of the men fit the description of the opportunistic rapist, 14 exhibited features of the vindictive type, 15 were described as nonsadistic rapists, and 8 fell into the sadistic category.

The investigators compared rapists in the four major categories on several laboratory measures. Deviant sexual arousal was measured using a penile strain gauge (see Research Methods) while each subject listened to a series of audiotapes describing scenes of mutually consenting sex and of rape. Sadistic and nonsadistic rapists showed greater sexual arousal in response to the rape scenes than the vindictive and opportunistic rapists. This pattern of results supports the validity of Knight and Prentky's classification system. It indicates that deviant patterns of sexual arousal may play a more important role in the sexual aggression displayed by the sadistic and nonsadistic rapists.

These studies help explain some of the factors that contribute to the disturbing rate of sexual aggression that is found in our society. They may lay the foundation for efforts aimed at the prevention of this form of violence as well as the treatment of rapists. We must keep in mind, however, that this type of research has been based almost exclusively on a small subset of rapists—those who have been con-

victed of their offenses. It would be naive to generalize from this group to all rapists, for several reasons. Most instances of acquaintance rape are not reported. Among those rapes that are reported to the police, less than 10 percent ever lead to conviction. Therefore, studies of convicted rapists must be interpreted with caution. We should not conclude that the motivations of all—or even most—rapists are accurately portrayed in these studies. ∎

Overlap in Three Major Types of Paraphilias

- Fetishism
- Sexual sadism and sexual masochism
- Fetishistic transvestism

FIGURE 11-2: The extent of overlap in the interests of three major types of paraphilias. Note that only 37 percent of men who practice fetishistic transvestism, 32 percent of men who practice sexual sadism and masochism, and 12 percent of those who practice fetishism exhibited those interests exclusively.

Source: G.D. Wilson (1987). An ethological approach to sexual deviation. In G.D. Wilson (Ed.), *Variant sexuality: research and theory* (p. 92). London: Croom Helm.

ple who engage in them will readily divulge their secret urges and fantasies.

With the exception of masochism, paraphilias are almost always male behaviors. Some 95 percent of the people who seek treatment for paraphilic disorders are men (Levine, Risen, & Althof, 1990; Kaplan, 1989). Chalkley and Powell (1983) described 48 cases of fetishism admitted for treatment at a clinic for sexual disorders, and only 1 was female.

We do know that paraphilias are usually not isolated phenomena. People who exhibit one type of paraphilia often exhibit others. Gosselin and Wilson (1980) surveyed men who belonged to private clubs that cater to fetishists, sadomasochists, and transvestites, and they found that the members of different clubs often shared the same interests. This overlap is illustrated in Figure 11–2.

This pattern has been called *crossing* of paraphilic behaviors. Another study categorized a group of approximately 500 sexual offenders on the basis of many different features: whether or not they touched their victims, whether their victims were relatives, whether their victims were male or female, and whether their victims were children or adults. The data indicated a considerable amount of crossover. Of the offenders who had carried out paraphilic acts against male victims, 63 percent had previously engaged in similar behaviors against female victims; 49 percent of those who had committed acts against adults had previously committed acts against children; 64 percent of those who committed acts that did not involve touching their victims had previously committed acts that involved touching (Abel & Osborn, 1992).

Epidemiology

There is very little evidence regarding the frequency of various types of unconventional sexual behavior. This is especially true for victimless or noncoercive forms of paraphilia, such as fetishism, sexual masochism, and transvestic fetishism, because most of these people do not seek treatment or come to the attention of law enforcement officials. Furthermore, the fact that these forms of behavior are considered deviant or perverse makes it unlikely that peo-

Etiology

When we attempt to explain the origins of paraphilias, it is useful to remember that they are, in some ways, similar to substance dependence disorders. In Chapter 10, we emphasized the need to think about the development of addiction in terms of a sequence of stages: initiation, transition to abuse, and the development of tolerance. Similar stages may be involved in the paraphilias. We have to consider why the person might originally experiment with atypical forms of sexual stimulation, how repeated experiences with these stimuli might develop into a strong preference, and finally, through which mechanisms these behaviors might become ingrained and extremely resistant to change.

The high rate of overlap among paraphilias indicates that the etiology of these behaviors might be most appropriately viewed in terms of common factors rather than in terms of distinct pathways that lead exclusively to one form of paraphilia or another. Those experiences and conditions that predispose an individual to one form of paraphilia are apparently also likely to lead to another. In the following pages, we review a number of proposals regarding the etiology of paraphilias. Some of these have been associated with specific types of paraphilia. For the most part, however, they are concerned more generally with many forms of paraphilias.

The epidemiological evidence suggests another important pattern that must be explained by any theory of paraphilias: They are more prevalent among men than among women. The exception to this rule seems to be masochism, which may be equally common in both genders. We might conclude, therefore, that the development of masochism may be governed by different factors than those that account for the etiology of other types of paraphilias. Nevertheless, theoretical accounts of most paraphilias must explain why they are more common among men than women.

IMPRINTING AND FETISHES

Genital responses associated with sexual arousal are evident at a very early age in both boys and girls. Gender differences are evident in childhood, especially with regard to masturbation and sexual fantasies (Geer, Heiman, & Leitenberg, 1984). These behavioral factors, in combination with gender differences in neural organization

and hormonal development, are undoubtedly involved in the etiology of paraphilias.

Glenn Wilson (1987), a British ethologist, has explained the development of fetishes in terms of biologically prepared learning. According to Wilson's model, the male brain is biologically programmed to associate certain visual features with sexual arousal. Men are presumably more attracted by the physical features of their partners, whereas women are more concerned about their partner's social skills and the emotional aspects of the relationship (Buss, 1992). The range of stimuli that male infants are capable of associating with sexual arousal may be very narrow. These associations are built early in life, during critical periods that resemble the *imprinting process* that has been observed in other species.

Given the opportunity to view a nude female body, male infants may quickly learn to associate sexual arousal with the expected stimuli, such as female genitals, buttocks, and breasts. In the absence of such experience, however, the toddler's associations may become misprogrammed. Sexual arousal may become paired with objects that are related, through visual or other sensory cues, to the mother's body. In other words, the system may be susceptible to errors, which result in the production of unusual associations that become highly resistant to extinction (Wilson, 1987).

COURTSHIP DISORDERS

Some types of paraphilias seem to be distortions of the normal mating process when viewed in a broad, evolutionary context. For male primates, sexual behavior involves a sequence of steps: location and appraisal of potential partners; exchange of signals in which partners communicate mutual interest; and tactile interactions that set the stage for sexual intercourse. Voyeurism, exhibitionism, and frotteurism may represent aberrant versions of these social processes. Kurt Freund and Ray Blanchard, both at the University of Toronto, have described the paraphilias as "courtship disorders" (Freund & Blanchard, 1986). Something has apparently gone wrong, disrupting whatever mechanisms facilitate the

▲ Wilson's imprinting theory begins with the assumption that the male brain is programmed to associate particular types of visual stimuli with sexual arousal. These associations are typically developed early in life.

identification of a sexual partner and govern behaviors used for attracting a partner.

If people with paraphilias have somehow failed to learn more adaptive forms of courtship behavior, what sort of childhood experiences might have produced such unexpected results? Several background factors have been observed repeatedly among people who engage in atypical sexual behaviors (Wincze, 1989). These include:

- Early crossing of normative sexual boundaries through a direct experience (for example, sexual abuse by an adult) or an indirect experience (hearing about a father's atypical sexual behavior).
- Lack of a consistent parental environment in which normative sexual behavior and values were modeled
- Lack of self-esteem
- Lack of confidence and ability in social interactions
- Ignorance and poor understanding of human sexuality

All these factors may increase the probability that a person might experiment with unusual types of sexual stimulation or employ maladaptive sexual behaviors.

INTIMACY DEFICITS

The most salient feature of paraphilias is sexual arousal, but the paraphilias are ultimately problems in social relationships. Interpersonal skills may therefore play as important a role as sexual arousal. William Marshall (1989), a psychologist at Queen's University in Canada, has argued that the core feature of unusual sexual behavior is a failure to achieve intimacy in relationships with other adults. According to his perspective, people with paraphilias are lonely, insecure, and isolated, and have significant deficits in social skills. Offensive sexual behaviors, such as those observed in pedophilia, are maladaptive attempts to achieve intimacy through sex. These efforts are invariably unsuccessful and self-defeating in the sense that they serve to further isolate the person from the rest of the community. Paradoxically, the pattern may become deeply ingrained because it results in the momentary pleasure associated with orgasm and because it offers the illusory hope of eventually achieving intimacy with another person.

DISTORTED LOVEMAPS

John Money (1984), a psychologist at Johns Hopkins University, has described the development of paraphilias in somewhat different terms, using a geographical metaphor that he calls a *lovemap*. A lovemap is a mental picture representing the person's ideal sexual relationship. It might also be viewed as the software that encodes his or her sexual fantasies and preferred sexual practices. These "programs" are written early in life, and they are quite persistent. Children learn their lovemaps during sexual play, by imitation of their parents and other adults, and through messages that they digest from the popular media. According to Money, when optimal conditions prevail, the child develops a lovemap that includes intercourse as a preferred form of sexual expression. The child learns that love—romantic attachment to another adult—and lust—erotic attraction—can be directed toward the same person.

The lovemap can be distorted, according to Money's metaphor, if the child learns that romantic attachment and sexual desire are incompatible—that these feelings cannot be directed toward the same person. The inability to integrate these aspects of the lovemap lies at the heart of Money's explanation of paraphilias. One solution to this dilemma would be to avoid or deny sexual expression altogether. That might explain the development of lack of sexual desire. Sexual impulses are powerful, however, and they are not easily denied. In some cases, they are rerouted rather than being shut off completely. Various types of paraphilias represent alternative strategies through which the person finds it possible to express sexual feelings outside of an intimate, loving relationship with another adult. Exhibitionism, voyeurism, and fetishism are therefore partial solutions to the perceived incompatibility of love and lust.

OPPONENT PROCESSES AND MASOCHISM

The etiological mechanisms that we have considered thus far seem most applicable to paraphilias that are found predominantly among men, such as fetishes, voyeurism, and exhibitionism. A different story may be necessary to explain masochism, the association of sexual arousal with pain and suffering, because this condition is equally common among women and men.

One intriguing clue regarding the origins of masochism has been reported by Robert Stoller (1991), a psychoanalyst at UCLA who wrote extensively about unusual erotic behaviors. Stoller spent several months conducting detailed interviews with people who were seriously involved in sadomasochistic behaviors with consenting partners. Those who were most committed to physical sadism and masochism had, as children, experienced traumatic physical disease followed by frightening forms of medical treatment. These people described to Stoller how they had "consciously forced themselves to master what at first, in infancy and childhood, was uncontrollable physical agony and terror by taking the pain and working with it in their heads, eventually via daydreams, altered states of consciousness, or genital masturbation, until it was converted into pain-that-is-pleasure (Stoller, 1991, p. 25)." In other words, a strong positive emotion like sexual arousal can be actively employed to control intolerable physical pain. The unfortunate consequence is the development of a persistent association between pain and arousal.

Money (1987) has also speculated about the role of conditioned anticipatory responses in the development of masochism. He points out that this effect is undoubtedly mediated by neurochemical effects that have not yet been identified. If the analogy to addictions holds true, the process may have something to do with the conditioned release of endorphins (see Chapter 10).

Treatment

The treatment of paraphilias is different from the treatment of sexual dysfunctions in several ways. Perhaps most important is the fact that most people with paraphilias do not enter treatment on a voluntary basis. They are often referred to a therapist by the criminal justice system after they have been arrested for exposing themselves, peeping through windows, or engaging in sexual behaviors with children. Their motivation to change is therefore open to question (Wincze, 1989). Participation in treatment may help them receive reduced sentences or perhaps avoid other legal penalties. In many cases, they are being asked to abandon highly reinforcing behaviors in which they have engaged for many years. Their families and other members of society may be much more concerned about change than they

are. We mention this issue at the beginning of our discussion because the results of outcome studies in this area are typically less positive than are those concerning the treatment of sexual dysfunction (Furby, Weinrott, & Blackshaw, 1989; McConaghy, 1990).

AVERSION THERAPY

For the past several decades, the most commonly used form of treatment for paraphilias has been **aversion therapy**. In this procedure, the therapist repeatedly presents the stimulus that elicits inappropriate sexual arousal—such as slides of nude children—in association with an aversive stimulus, such as repulsive smells, electric shock, or chemically induced nausea. Revolting cognitive images are sometimes used instead of tangible aversive stimuli. Whatever the exact procedure, the rationale is to create a new association with the inappropriate stimulus so that the stimulus will no longer elicit sexual arousal. Several research studies have suggested that aversion therapy does produce some positive effects (Kilmann et al., 1982). It has more recently fallen into disfavor, however, because the studies that were used to evaluate it suffered from design flaws. Moreover, the mechanism by which aversion therapy presumably works, classical conditioning, is open to serious question.

COGNITIVE-BEHAVIORAL TREATMENT

Alternative treatment programs for paraphilic behaviors reflect a broader view of the etiology of these conditions. There is considerable reason to believe that paraphilias are based on a variety of cognitive and social deficits (Marshall, 1989; McFall, 1990). Marshall, Eccles, and Barbaree (1991) compared two different approaches to the treatment of exhibitionists. The first was based on aversion therapy, and the second employed cognitive restructuring, social skills training, and stress management procedures. The men who received the second type of treatment were much less likely to return to their deviant forms of sexual behavior than

▲ This photo shows the staff at a bondage club in Hollywood. Robert Stoller's study of staff members and clients of S & M parlors led him to believe that the development of masochism is often associated with physically painful experiences as a child.

were the men who received aversion therapy. Treatment with aversion therapy was no more effective than was treatment with a placebo. These data suggest that broad-based cognitive and social treatment procedures may ultimately be most useful in the treatment of paraphilias and sexual disorders (Marshall & Pithers, 1994).

Encouraging results have been reported from the Sex Offender Treatment and Evaluation Project (Marques et al., 1993), which was designed for men convicted of either rape or child molestation. Men selected for the treatment program are transferred to a special hospital unit, where they remain for several months. They receive education in human sexuality as well as cognitive behavior therapy, including applied relaxation and social skills training as well as stress and anger management. Treatment also includes a relapse prevention component that is based on procedures used in the treatment of alcoholism (see Chapter 10). Relapse prevention procedures help the men confront personal, social, and sexual difficulties that may increase their risk of relapse after they are released from prison.

The men in the treatment group are compared to those in two control groups. Outcome is measured in several ways, but the most important consideration is being arrested again for similar crimes. Men in the treatment group were significantly less likely than were men in the control groups to commit new sex offenses during their first 5 years after release (Marques et al., 1994). Results were somewhat more encouraging with men convicted of rape than with those who had molested children. The number of people who had been treated by the time of these reports was still relatively small, so the results should be interpreted with caution. Nevertheless, the data from this program indicate that broadly based behavioral programs that focus on education, social skills, and relapse prevention procedures may be more promising than more traditional forms of therapy.

HORMONES AND MEDICATION

Another approach to the treatment of paraphilias involves the use of drugs that reduce levels of testosterone, on the assumption that male hormones control the sexual appetite. One study has reported that this type of treatment can selectively reduce the responses of people with pedophilia to sexual stimuli, with a greater reduction for images of children than for images of sex between consenting adults (Bradford & Pawlak, 1993).

Several different types of medication, primarily antidepressants and antianxiety drugs, have also been used to treat paraphilias. One study (Perilstein, Lipper, & Friedman, 1991) found that three patients with paraphilias responded positively to Prozac. The process by which these drugs manage to alter sexual behavior is open to question. For example, medication may reduce social anxiety, which interferes with the ability to enjoy an intimate sexual relationship with another adult (Golwyn & Sevlie, 1992). This hypothesis is consistent with the approach taken by Marshall and his colleagues, whose psychological treatment program is aimed at similar types of social deficits.

Gender Identity Disorders

Our sense of ourselves as being either male or female is known as **gender identity**. Gender identity almost always reflects the child's physical anatomy: Toddlers who possess a penis learn that they are boys, and those with a vagina learn that they are girls. Gender identity is usually fixed by the time a child reaches 2 or 3 years of age (Serbin & Sprafkin, 1987).

Gender identity must be distinguished from **sex roles**, which are characteristics, behaviors, and skills that are defined within a specific culture as being either masculine or feminine. For example, certain aspects of appearance and behavior are more often associated with men than with women. These are considered to be masculine. Those behaviors and appearances that are more often associated with women are considered feminine. In our own culture, masculine and feminine sex roles have changed considerably in recent years, and there is overlap between them.

Typical Symptoms and Associated Features

Some people are firmly convinced that they are living in the wrong kind of body. In males, this means that they feel strongly that they are women trapped in a man's body. For females, the opposite pattern holds. This sense of discomfort with one's anatomic sex is called **gender identity disorder** in DSM-IV. It has also been known as **transsexualism** (Satterfield, 1988) or gender dysphoria (Blanchard, 1989). People with gender identity disturbances are not delusional. In other words, they do not literally believe that they are members of the opposite gender. Rather, they feel that, with the exception of their physical anatomy, they are more like the opposite gender.

Most transsexuals report that they were aware of these feelings very early in childhood. Many report that they dressed in clothing and adopted sex role behaviors of the opposite gender during childhood and adolescence. The intensity of the person's discomfort varies from one individual to the next. It almost invariably becomes more intense during adolescence, when the person develops *secondary sexual characteristics*, such as breasts and wider hips for girls; facial hair, voice changes, and increased muscle mass for boys. These characteristics make it more difficult for a person to pass for the opposite gender. Many transsexuals become preoccupied with the desire to change their anatomic sex through surgical procedures.

Gender identity disorders should be distinguished from *transvestic fetishism*, which is a form of paraphilia in which a heterosexual man dresses in the clothing of the opposite gender in order to achieve sexual arousal. These are, in fact, very different conditions. Transvestic fetishists do not consider themselves to be women, and transsexuals are not sexually aroused by cross-dressing.

The relation between gender identity disorder and sexual orientation has also been a matter of some controversy. Some clinicians have suggested that transsexuals are homosexuals who claim to be members of the opposite gender as a way to avoid cultural and moral sanctions that discourage engaging in sexual relationships with members of their own sex. This proposal doesn't make sense for two reasons. First, lesbians and gay men are not uncomfortable with their own gender identity. This observation suggests that transsexuals are not simply escaping the stigma of homosexuality. Second, laboratory studies suggest that transsexual and homosexual subjects exhibit different patterns of sexual arousal in response to erotic stimuli (Barr, 1973).

Epidemiology

Gender identity disorders are quite rare in comparison to most of the other disorders that we have considered in this book. Male-to-female transsexuals are apparently more common than female-to-male transsexuals, at least based on the numbers of people who seek treatment at clinics. One study estimated the prevalence figures to be 1 person with gender identity disorder for every 18,000 males and 54,000 females (Eklund, Gooren, & Bezemer, 1988).

Deeply ingrained cross-gender behaviors and attitudes among children occur infrequently in the general population (Zucker, 1985). Mild forms of cross-gender behavior, such as dressing up in the clothes of the opposite gender or expressing a desire to be a member of the opposite sex, are relatively common during the preschool years. Extreme forms of these behaviors are relatively rare, however, especially among boys (Achenbach & Edelbrock, 1981).

Etiology

Very little is known about the origins of gender identity in normal men and women, so it is not surprising that the etiology of gender identity disorders is also poorly understood.

There is some reason to believe that gender identity is strongly influenced by sex hormones, especially during the prenatal period (Hoenig, 1985). Much of the research in this area has been done with animals, but an interesting set of data comes from studies of people with a condition that is sometimes called *pseudohermaphroditism.* Individuals with this condition are genetically male, but they are unable to produce a hormone that is responsible for shaping the penis and scrotum in the fetus. Therefore, the child is born with external genitalia that are ambiguous in appearance; thus the term *pseudohermaphrodites.*[†]

[†] A hermaphrodite has both male and female reproductive organs.

▲ **Transsexual Christine Jorgenson (right) in 1952 and the former George Jorgenson (left), an Army veteran from New York. Jorgenson's sex-reassignment surgery, performed in Denmark, attracted worldwide attention.**

Many of these children are raised as girls by their families. When they reach the age of puberty, a sudden increase in testosterone leads to dramatic changes in the appearance of the adolescent's genitals. The organ that had previously looked more like a clitoris becomes enlarged and turns into a penis, and testicles descend into a scrotum. The child's voice becomes deeper, muscle mass increases, and the child quickly begins to consider himself to be a man (Imperato-McGinley et al., 1974). The speed and apparent ease with which people with these conditions adopt a masculine gender identity suggest that their brains had been prenatally programmed for this alternative (Hoenig, 1985).

Treatment

There are two obvious solutions to problems of gender identity: change the person's identity to match his or her anatomy, or change the anatomy to match the person's gender identity. Various forms of psychotherapy have been used in an effort to alter gender identity, but the results have been fairly negative.

SEX-REASSIGNMENT SURGERY

One alternative to psychological treatment is *sex-reassignment surgery*, in which the person's genitals are changed to match the gender identity. Medical science can construct artificial male and female genitalia. The artificial penis is not capable of becoming erect in response to sexual stimulation, but structural implants can be used to obtain rigidity. These surgical procedures have been used with thousands of patients over the past 50 or 60 years. Clinics that perform these operations employ stringent selection procedures, and patients are typically required to live for several months as a member of the opposite gender before they can undergo the surgical procedure.

The results of sex-reassignment surgery have generally been positive. Interviews with patients who have undergone surgery indicate that most are satisfied with the results, and the vast majority believe that they do not have any trouble passing as a member of their newly assumed gender (Kuiper & Cohen-Kettenis, 1988). Psychological tests obtained from patients who have completed surgery indicate reduced levels of anxiety and depression (Mate-Kole, Freschi, & Robin, 1988).

not always the case

KEY TERMS

- aversion therapy
- construct
- construct validity
- dyspareunia
- erectile dysfunction
- gender identity
- gender identity disorder
- hypoactive sexual desire
- inhibited sexual arousal
- operational definition
- orgasmic disorder
- paraphilia

Summary

The DSM-IV recognizes two major forms of sexual disorders. **Sexual dysfunctions** involve an inhibition of sexual desire or disruption of the physiological responses leading to orgasm. **Paraphilias** are defined in terms of extreme forms of unusual sexual behavior, in which sexual arousal is associated with atypical stimuli. The central problem in paraphilias is that sexual arousal has become detached from a reciprocal, loving relationship with another adult.

Sexual dysfunctions are divided into several types, based on the stages of the sexual response cycle.

These include problems related to sexual desire, sexual arousal, and orgasm. Related difficulties include sexual aversion disorder and **premature ejaculation**. **Dyspareunia** is defined in terms of persistent genital pain during or after sexual intercourse. **Vaginismus** is an involuntary spasm of the muscles surrounding the entrance to the vagina. All forms of sexual dysfunction can lead to personal distress, including anxiety and depression, as well as interpersonal and marital difficulties.

Sexual behavior is dependent on a complex interaction among biological, psychological, and social factors. These factors include cognitive events related to the perception of sexual stimuli, social factors that influence sexual meanings or intentions, and physiological responses that cause vasocongestion of the genitals during sexual arousal.

Biological factors that contribute to sexual dysfunction include inadequate levels of sex hormones, which can contribute to diminished sexual desire, and a variety of medical disorders. Vascular and neurological diseases are important factors in many cases of erectile disorder. The effects of alcohol, illicit drugs, and some forms of medication can also contribute to erectile disorder in men and to **orgasmic disorder** in men and women.

Several psychological factors are involved in the etiology of sexual dysfunction. Prominent among these are performance anxiety and guilt. Communication deficits also can contribute to sexual dysfunction. Previous experiences, including sexual abuse, play an important role in some cases of sexual dysfunction.

Psychological treatments for sexual dysfunction are quite successful. They focus primarily on negative attitudes toward sexuality, failure to engage in effective sexual behaviors, and deficits in communication skills.

Common characteristics of paraphilias include lack of human intimacy and urges toward sexual behaviors which the person feels compelled to perform. Many people with paraphilias experience sexual dysfunctions during conventional sexual behavior with an adult partner. The diversity and range of paraphilic behavior is enormous. DSM-IV describes a few of the most prominent forms, such as exhibitionism, fetishism, frotteurism, pedophilia, sexual masochism, sexual sadism, transvestic fetishism, and voyeurism. These are not typically isolated preferences or patterns of behavior; people who exhibit one form of paraphilia often exhibit others.

Treatment outcome is generally less successful with paraphilias than with sexual dysfunction. The most promising approaches to the treatment of paraphilias currently use a combination of cognitive and behavioral procedures to address a broad range of etiological factors, including deficits in social skills and stress and anger management as well as knowledge and attitudes regarding sexuality.

Gender identity disorder represents a disturbance in the person's sense of being either a man or a woman. People with this problem, which is also known as **transsexualism**, have developed a **gender identity** that is inconsistent with their physical anatomy. These disorders are extremely rare. Very little is known about their etiology. Gender identity seems to be strongly influenced by sex hormones, perhaps during the process of fetal development. Treatment of gender identity disorders may involve sex-reassignment surgery.

- premature ejaculation
- rape
- sensate focus
- sex roles
- sexual aversion disorder
- sexual dysfunction
- transsexualism
- transvestic fetishism
- vaginismus

Critical Thinking

1. Suppose that you are a therapist who has been contacted by a couple who are concerned that the woman is unable to reach orgasm. What are the first things that you would want to know? Would you want to see each partner alone?

2. Drag queens are gay men who dress up in women's clothing. Their masquerade balls are typically a source of pride and enjoyment. Why wouldn't this type of behavior be considered a sexual disorder? How is their behavior different from transvestic fetishism?

3. Do you think that rape—or some specific subtype of rape—should have been included in DSM-IV under paraphilias? Why or why not?

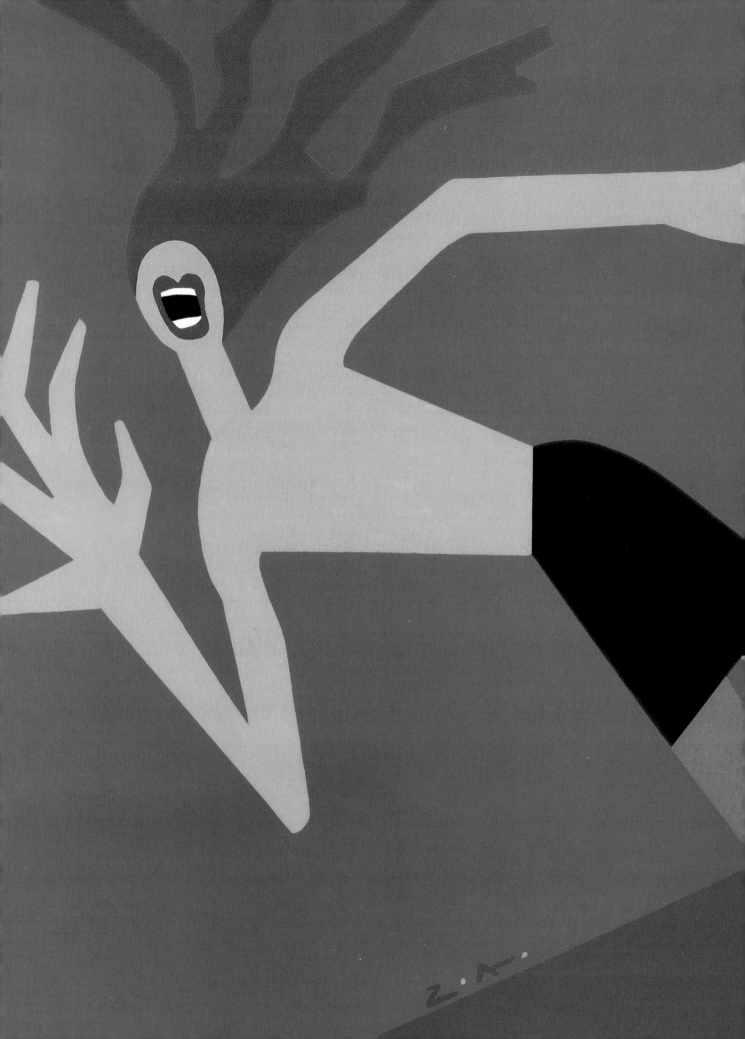

Schizophrenic Disorders

S chizophrenia is a pervasive and sometimes chronic form of abnormal behavior that encompasses what most of us have come to know as "madness." People with schizophrenia exhibit many different symptoms. They may hear voices that aren't there, express absurd ideas and beliefs, or make comments that are difficult, if not impossible, to understand. Their symptoms follow different patterns over time. Some recover fairly quickly, whereas others deteriorate progressively after the initial onset of symptoms. In the face of this marked diversity, many clinicians believe that schizophrenia, or "the group of schizophrenias," may actually include several forms of disorder that have different causes. On the other hand, variations from one patient to the next in symptoms and course of the disorder could also reflect differences in the expression or severity of a single pathological process.

Overview

The most common symptoms of schizophrenia include changes in the way the person thinks, feels, and relates to other people and the outside environment. It is a disorder of "multiple handicaps" (Bellack & Mueser, 1993). No single symptom or specific set of symptoms is characteristic of all schizophrenic patients. All of the individual symptoms of schizophrenia can also be associated with other psychological and medical conditions. Schizophrenia is defined by various combinations of psychotic symptoms *in the absence of other forms of disturbance*, such as mood disorders (especially manic episodes), substance dependence, delirium, or dementia (see Chapter 13).

The symptoms of schizophrenia are sometimes divided into two types: **negative symptoms** and **positive symptoms** (Strauss et al., 1974; Andreasen 1985; Andreasen et al., 1990). Negative symptoms are those that presumably reflect the absence of normal functioning—symptoms such as deficits in emotional responding, lack of initiative, and social withdrawal. Positive symptoms, on the other hand, are assumed to indicate the presence of abnormal functioning. Hallucinations, delusions, and disorganized speech are typically considered positive symptoms of schizophrenia.

In the following pages, we describe the experiences of three people who exhibited symptoms of schizophrenia. You should also review the case of Kevin, which was described in Chapter 1. The DSM-IV divides schizophrenic disorders into several subtypes, based primarily on the type of symptoms that the patient exhibits. Our first case illustrates the paranoid subtype of schizophrenia, which is characterized by a preoccupation with one or more delusions or by frequent auditory hallucinations, most often persecutory in nature.

CASE STUDY

Paranoid Schizophrenia

Ann was 21 years old the first time that she was admitted to a psychiatric hospital. She had completed business college and had worked as a receptionist until she became pregnant with her son, who was born 6 months prior to her admission. She and her husband lived in a small apartment with his 5-year-old daughter from a previous marriage. This was her first psychotic episode.

The first signs of Ann's disturbance appeared during her pregnancy, when she accused her husband of having an affair with her sister. The accusation was based on a conversation that Ann had overheard on a bus. Two women (who were neighbors in Ann's apartment building) had been discussing an affair that some woman's husband was having. Ann believed that this might have been their way of telling her about her husband's infidelity. Although her husband and her sister denied any romantic interest in each other, Ann clung to her suspicions and began to monitor her husband's activities closely. She also avoided talking with her neighbors and friends.

Before this period of time, Ann had been an outgoing and energetic person. Now she seemed listless and apathetic, and would often spend days without leaving their apartment. Her husband at first attributed this change in her behavior to the pregnancy, believing that she would "snap out of it" after the baby was born. Unfortunately, Ann became even more socially isolated following the birth of her son. She seldom left her bedroom and would spend hours alone, mumbling softly to herself.

Ann's behavior deteriorated markedly 2 weeks prior to her hospital admission, when she noticed that some photographs of herself and her baby were missing. She told her husband that they had been stolen and were being used to cast a voodoo spell on her. Ann became increasingly preoccupied with this belief in subsequent days. She called her mother repeatedly, insisting that something would have to be done to recover the missing photographs. Her friends and family tried to reassure Ann that the photographs had probably been misplaced or accidentally discarded, but she was totally unwilling to consider alternative explanations.

Ann finally announced to everyone who would listen that someone was trying to kill her and the children. Believing that all the food in the house had been poisoned, she refused to eat and would not feed the children. She became increasingly suspicious, hostile, and combative. Her husband and parents found it impossible to reason with her. She was no longer able to care for herself or the children. The family sought advice from their family physician, who recommended that they contact a psychiatrist. After meeting with Ann briefly, the psychiatrist recommended that she be hospitalized for a short period of time.

After admission, Ann argued heatedly with the hospital staff, denying that she was mentally disturbed and insisting that she must be released so that she could protect her children from the conspiracy. She had no insight into the nature of her problems. ■

The onset of schizophrenia typically occurs during adolescence or early adulthood. The period of risk for the development of a first episode is considered to be between the ages of 15 and 35. The number of new cases drops off slowly after that, with very few people experiencing an initial episode after the age of 55 (Gottesman, 1991).

The subsequent course of the disorder can follow many different patterns. The problems of most patients can be divided into three phases of variable and unpredictable duration: prodromal, active, and residual. Symptoms such as hallucinations, delusions, and disorganized speech are characteristic of the active phase of the disorder. The **prodromal phase** precedes the active phase and is marked by an obvious deterioration in role functioning as a student, employee, or homemaker. The person's friends and relatives often view the beginning of the prodromal phase as a change in the person's personality. Prodromal signs and symptoms are quite similar to those associated with schizotypal personality disorder (see Chapter 9). They include peculiar behaviors (such as talking to one's self in public), blunted affect, unusual patterns of speech, and unusual perceptual experiences. Social withdrawal and avolition are often seen during the prodromal phase.

The **residual phase** follows the active phase of the disorder and is defined by the same signs and symptoms as the prodromal phase. At this point, the psychotic symptoms have improved, but the person continues to be impaired in various ways. Negative symptoms, such as affective flattening, may be more pronounced during the residual phase.

After the onset of schizophrenia, many people do not return to expected levels of social and occupational adjustment. The man in our next case illustrates this pattern. He is also an example of the disorganized type of schizophrenia. Patients who fit criteria for this category exhibit disorganized speech, disorganized behavior, and flat or inappropriate affect.

CASE STUDY

Disorganized Schizophrenia

Edward was 39 years old and had lived at home with his parents since dropping out of school after the 10th grade. Edward worked on and off as a helper in his father's roofing business prior to his first psychotic episode at the age of 26. After that time, he was socially isolated and unable to hold any kind of job. He was hospitalized in psychiatric facilities 10 times in the next 14 years. When he was not in the hospital, most of his time at home was spent watching television or sitting alone in his room.

The tenth episode of psychosis became evident when Edward told his mother that he had seen people arguing violently on the sidewalk in front of their house. He believed that this incident was the beginning of World War II. His mother tried to persuade him that he had witnessed an ordinary, though perhaps heated, disagreement between two neighbors, but Edward could not be convinced. He continued to mumble about the fight and became increasingly agitated over the next few days. When he wasn't pacing back and forth from his bedroom to the living room, he could usually be found staring out the front window. Several days after witnessing the argument, he took curtains from several windows in the house and burned them in the street at 2 A.M. A neighbor happened to see what Edward was doing and called the police. When they arrived, they found Edward wandering in a snow-covered vacant lot, talking incoherently to himself. Recognizing that Edward was psychotic, the police took him to the psychiatric hospital.

Although his appearance was somewhat disheveled, Edward was alert and cooperative. He knew the current date and recognized that he was in a psychiatric hospital. Some of his speech was incoherent, and his answers to questions posed by the hospital staff were frequently irrelevant. His expressive gestures were severely restricted. Although he said that he was frightened by the recent events that he reported to his mother, his face did not betray any signs of emotion. He mumbled slowly in a monotonous tone of voice that was difficult to understand. He said that he could hear God's voice telling him that his father was "the Master of the universe" and he claimed that he had "seen the shadow of the Master." Other voices seem to argue with one another about Edward's special calling and whether he was worthy of this divine power. The voices told him to prepare for God's return to earth. At times Edward said that he was a Nazi soldier and that he was born in Germany in 1886. He also spoke incoherently about corpses frozen in Greenland and maintained that he was "only half a person." ■

Schizophrenia is not a transient disorder. The definition of schizophrenia that is presented in DSM-IV requires that the person exhibit symptoms of the disorder for a period of at least 6 months before the person is considered to meet the diagnostic criteria. If the person displays psychotic symptoms for at least 1 month but less than 6 months, the diagnosis would be schizophreniform disorder. The diagnosis would be changed to schizophrenic disorder if the person's problems persist beyond the 6-month limit. The following case illustrates this early phase of schizophreniform disorder.

CASE STUDY

Schizophreniform Disorder

Marsha was a 32-year-old graduate student in political science. She had never been treated for psychological problems. Marsha called Dr. Higgins, a clinical psychologist who teaches at the university, to ask if she could speak with him about her twin sister's experience with schizophrenia. When she arrived at his office, she was neatly dressed and had a Bible tucked tightly under her arm. The next 3 hours were filled with a rambling discussion of Marsha's experiences during the past 10 years. She talked about her education, her experience as a high school teacher before returning to graduate school, her relationships with her parents, and—most of all—her concern for her identical twin sister, Alice, who had spent 6 of the last 10 years in psychiatric hospitals.

Marsha's emotional expression vacillated dramatically throughout the course of this conversation, which was punctuated by silly giggles and heavy sighs. Her voice would be loud and emphatic one moment as she talked about her stimulating ideas and special talents. At other moments, she would whisper in a barely audible voice or sob quietly as she described the desperation, fear, and frustration that she had experienced watching the progression of her sister's disorder. She said that she had been feeling very uptight in recent months, afraid that she might be "going crazy" like her sister. She had been scared to death to go home because her parents might sense that something was wrong with her. Her behavior was frequently inconsistent with the content of her speech. As she described her intense fears, for example, Marsha occasionally giggled uncontrollably.

Dr. Higgins also found Marsha's train of thought difficult to follow. Her speech rambled illogically from one topic to the next, and her answers to his questions were frequently tangential. For example, when Dr. Higgins asked what she meant by her repeated use of the phrase "the ideal can become real," Marsha replied, "Well, after serving the Word of Christ in California for 3 years, making a public spectacle of myself, someone apparently called my parents and said I had a problem. I said I can't take this anymore and went home. I perceived that Mom was just unbelievably nice to me. I began to think that my face was changing. Something about my forehead resembled the pain of Christ. I served Christ, but my power was not lasting."

At the end of this 3-hour interview, Dr. Higgins was convinced that Marsha should be referred to the mental health center for outpatient treatment. He explained his concerns to Marsha, but she refused to follow his advice, insisting that she did not want to receive the medication with which her sister had been treated. She agreed to return to Dr. Higgins's office in 3 days for another interview, but she did not keep that appointment.

Two weeks later, Marsha called Dr. Higgins to ask if he would talk with her immediately. It was very difficult to understand what she was saying, but she seemed to be repeating in a shrill voice "I'm losing my mind." The door to his office was closed when she arrived, but he could hear her shuffling awkwardly down the hallway, breathing heavily. He opened his door and found Marsha standing in a rigid posture, arms stiffly at her sides. Her eyes were opened wide, and she was staring vacantly at the nameplate on his door. In contrast to her prim and neat appearance at their first meeting, Marsha's hair and clothes were now in disarray. She walked stiffly into the office without bending her knees and sat, with some difficulty, in the chair next to Dr. Higgins's desk. Her facial expression was rigidly fixed. Although her eyes were open and she appeared to hear his voice, Marsha did not respond to any of Dr. Higgins's questions. Recognizing that Marsha was experiencing an acute psychotic episode, Dr. Higgins and one of the secretaries took her to the emergency room at the local hospital. ■

Typical Symptoms and Associated Features

In the following pages, we describe in greater detail various types of positive and negative symptoms that are commonly observed among schizophrenic patients and that are currently emphasized by official diagnostic systems, such as DSM-IV. When you are reading these descriptions, remember that all of these symptoms can fluctuate in severity over time. Some patients exhibit persistent psychotic symptoms. Others experience symptoms during acute episodes and are relatively better adjusted between episodes.

▲ This woman was acutely psychotic at the time that this photograph was taken. She was admitted to a psychiatric hospital the following day.

Hallucinations

Our senses provide us with fundamental information about ourselves and the world in which we live—information that is vital to our notions of who we are, what we are doing, and what others think of us. Many people with schizophrenia experience perplexing and often frightening changes in perception. The most obvious perceptual symptoms are **hallucinations**, or sensory experiences that are not caused by actual external stimuli. Although hallucinations can occur in any of the senses, those experienced by schizophrenic patients are most often auditory in nature. Many patients hear voices that comment on their behavior or give them instructions. Others hear voices that seem to argue with one another. Edward heard the voice of God talking to him. Although Edward's voices were frightening, in some cases hallucinations can be comforting or pleasing to the patient.

Hallucinations should be distinguished from the transient mistaken perceptions that most people experience from time to time (Heilbrun, 1993; Slade & Bentall, 1988). Have you ever turned around after thinking you heard someone call your name, to find that no one was really there? You probably dismissed the experience as "just your imagination." Hallucinations, in contrast, strike the person as being quite real, in spite of the fact that they have no basis in reality. They are also persistent over time. Patients who experience auditory hallucinations often hear the voice (or voices) speaking to them throughout the day and for many days at a time.

Hallucinations are typically associated with other symptoms, particularly delusional beliefs. This relation makes considerable intuitive sense. Because hallucinations are vivid perceptual experiences, people who experience them need to explain their origin. These "explanations" often involve delusional beliefs. A patient, like Edward, who hears the voice of God telling him that he has been given divine powers may conclude that he is an important religious figure; this conclusion would be considered a delusion.

Delusional Beliefs

Many schizophrenic patients express **delusions**, or idiosyncratic beliefs that are rigidly held in spite of their preposterous nature. Delusions have sometimes been defined as false beliefs based on incorrect inferences about reality. This definition has a number of problems, including the difficulty of establishing the ultimate truth of many situations. Ann's accusation that her husband was having an affair, for example, could easily become a choice between her word and his. This suspicion would not, on its own, be considered a delusion. The judgment that her beliefs were delusional depended to a large extent on their expansion to more absurd concerns about stolen photographs, voodoo spells, and alleged plots to kill her children.

Several additional characteristics are important in identifying delusions (Harrow & Rattenbury, 1988). In the most obvious cases, delusional patients express and defend their beliefs with utmost *conviction*, even when presented with contradictory evidence. For example, Ann's belief that the stolen photographs were being used to cast a spell on her was totally fixed and resistant to contradiction or reconsideration. *Preoccupation* is another defining characteristic of delusional beliefs. During periods of acute psychosis, many patients like Ann find it difficult, if not completely impossible, to avoid thinking or talking about these beliefs. Finally, delusional patients are typically unable to consider the *perspective* that other people hold with regard to their beliefs. Ann, for example, was unable to appreciate the fact that other people considered her paranoid beliefs to be ridiculous.

Although delusional beliefs can take many forms, they are typically personal in nature. They are not shared by other members of the person's family or cultural group. Common delusions include the belief that thoughts are being inserted into the patient's head, that other people are reading the patient's thoughts, or that the patient is being controlled by mysterious, external forces. Many delusions focus upon grandiose or paranoid content. For example, Edward expressed the grandiose belief that his father was the Master of the universe. Kevin (in Chapter 1) clung persistently to the paranoid belief that his supervisor at work was trying to poison him as well as other members of his family.

In actual clinical practice, delusions are complex and difficult to define (Maher & Spitzer, 1993; Oltmanns, 1988). Their content is some-times bizarre and confusing, as in the case of Edward's insistence that he had witnessed the beginning of World War II. Delusions are often fragmented, especially among severely disturbed patients. In other words, delusions are not always coherent belief systems that are consistently expressed by the patient. At various times, for example, Edward talked about being a Nazi soldier, the son of God, and half a person. Connections among these fragmented ideas are difficult to understand.

Disorganized Speech

Another set of schizophrenic symptoms, known as **disorganized speech**, involves the tendency of some patients to say things that don't make sense. Signs of disorganized speech include making irrelevant responses to questions, expressing disconnected ideas, and using words in peculiar ways (Marengo & Harrow, 1993). This symptom is sometimes called *thought disorder* because clinicians have assumed that the failure to communicate successfully reflects a disturbance in the thought patterns that govern verbal discourse. Marsha's speech provides one typical example of this phenomenon. She was not entirely incoherent, but parts of her speech were difficult to follow. Connections between sentences were sometimes arbitrary, and her answers to the interviewer's questions were occasionally irrelevant.

The following excerpt from an interview with another patient illustrates a more extreme form of disorganized speech.

▲ Many of the symptoms of schizophrenia, including hallucinations and delusions, can be extremely distressing.

Interviewer: Have you been nervous or tense lately?

Patient: No, I got a head of lettuce.

Interviewer: You got a head of lettuce? I don't understand.

Patient: Well, it's just a head of lettuce.

Interviewer: Tell me about lettuce. What do you mean?

Patient: Well, . . . lettuce is a transformation of a dead cougar that suffered a relapse on the lion's toe. And he swallowed the lion and something happened. The . . . see, the . . . Gloria and Tommy, they're two heads and they're not whales. But they escaped with herds of vomit, and things like that. (Neale & Oltmanns, 1980, p. 102)

When speech becomes this disrupted, it is considered *incoherent*. Notice that this patient did not string words together in a random fashion. His speech followed grammatical rules. He was placing nouns and verbs together in an appropriate order, but they didn't make any sense. His speech conveyed little, if any, meaning, and that is the hallmark of disorganized speech.

Several types of verbal communication disruption contribute to clinical judgments about disorganized speech (Andreasen, 1979). Common features of disorganized speech in schizophrenia include shifting topics too abruptly, called *loose associations* or *derailment;* replying to a question with an irrelevant response, called *tangentiality;* or persistently repeating the same word or phrase over and over again, called *perseveration*. We all say things from time to time that fit these descriptions. It is not the occasional presence of a single feature but rather the accumulation of a large number of such features that defines the presence of disorganized speech.

Another type of speech disturbance is called **alogia**, which literally means speechlessness. In one form of alogia, known as *poverty of speech,* patients show remarkable reductions in the amount of speech. In another form, referred to as *poverty of content of speech,* patients speak without conveying any meaningful information.

Motor Disturbances

Schizophrenic patients may also exhibit various forms of unusual motor behavior, such as the rigidity displayed by Marsha when she appeared for her second interview with Dr.

Higgins. **Catatonia** most often refers to immobility and marked muscular rigidity, but it can also refer to excitement and overactivity. For example, some patients engage in apparently purposeless pacing or repetitious movements, such as rubbing their hands over each other in a special pattern for hours at a time. Many catatonic patients exhibit reduced or awkward spontaneous movements. In more extreme forms, patients may assume unusual postures or remain in rigid standing or sitting positions for long periods of time. For example, some patients will lie flat on their backs in a stiff position with their heads raised slightly off the floor as though they were resting on a pillow. Catatonic patients typically resist attempts to alter their position even though the maintenance of their awkward postures would normally result in extreme discomfort or pain.

Catatonic posturing is often associated with a *stuporous state* or generally reduced responsiveness. The person seems to be unaware of his or her surroundings. For example, during her acute psychotic episode, Marsha refused to answer questions or to make eye contact with others. Unlike people with other stuporous conditions, however, catatonic patients seem to maintain a clear state of consciousness, and it is likely that Marsha could hear and understand everything that Dr. Higgins said to her. Many patients report, after the end of a catatonic episode, that they were perfectly aware of events that were taking place around them, in spite of their failure to respond appropriately.

Affective and Emotional Disturbances

Schizophrenic patients demonstrate emotional changes of various kinds. Ann, Edward, and Marsha all displayed emotional symptoms. One of the most characteristic phenomena involves a flattening or restriction of the person's nonverbal display of emotional responses that has sometimes been called **blunted affect**. This symptom was clearly present in Edward's case. Blunted patients fail to exhibit signs of emotion or feeling. They are neither happy nor sad, and they appear to be completely indifferent to their surroundings. The faces of blunted patients are apathetic and expressionless. Their voices lack the typical fluctuations in volume and pitch that others use to signal changes in their mood. Events in their environment hold little consequence for them. They may demonstrate a complete lack of concern for themselves and for others.

Another type of emotional deficit is called **anhedonia**, which refers to the inability to experience pleasure. Whereas blunted affect refers to the lack of outward expression, anhedonia is a lack of positive subjective feelings. People who experience anhedonia typically lose interest in recreational activities and social relationships, which they do not find enjoyable.

Although many schizophrenic patients appear to be emotionally blunted, others exhibit affective responses that are obviously inconsistent with their situation. This symptom is particularly difficult to describe in words. The most remarkable features of **inappropriate affect** are incongruity and lack of adaptability in emotional expression. For example, when Marsha described the private terror that she felt in the presence of her family, she giggled in a silly fashion. The content of Marsha's speech was inconsistent with her facial expression, her gestures, and her voice quality.

Social Withdrawal and Avolition

One of the most important and seriously debilitating aspects of schizophrenia is a malfunction of interpersonal relationships (Meehl, 1993). Many people with schizophrenia withdraw from social relationships. This is, of course, not surprising in light of the extensive cognitive and emotional difficulties that we have considered in the preceding pages. In many cases, however, social isolation develops before the onset of symptoms such as hallucinations, delusions, and disorganized speech. It can be one of the earliest signs that something is wrong. This was certainly true in Ann's case. She became socially isolated from her family and friends many weeks before she started to talk openly about the stolen pictures and the plot to kill her children. Social withdrawal appears to be both a symptom of the disorder and a strategy that is actively employed by some patients to deal with their other symptoms. They may, for example, attempt to minimize interactions with other people in order to reduce levels of stimulation that can exacerbate perceptual and cognitive disorganization (Walker, Davis, & Baum, 1993).

The withdrawal seen among many schizophrenic patients is accompanied by indecisiveness, ambivalence, and a loss of willpower. This symptom is known as **avolition** (lack of volition or will). A person who suffers from avolition becomes apathetic and ceases to engage in purposeful actions.

Classification

The broad array of symptoms outlined in the previous section have all been described as being part of schizophrenia. The specific organization of symptoms has been a matter of some controversy for many years. Schizophrenia has been defined in many different ways. In the following pages, we briefly review some of the more prominent trends that led up to the DSM-IV description of this disorder.

Brief Historical Perspective

Descriptions of schizophrenic symptoms can be traced far back in history, but they were not considered to be symptoms of a single disorder until late in the nineteenth century (Gottesman, 1991).

At that time, Emil Kraepelin suggested that several types of problems that previously had been classified as distinct forms of disorder should be grouped together under a single diagnostic category called **dementia praecox**. This term referred to psychoses that ended in severe intellectual deterioration (dementia) and that had an early or premature (praecox) onset, usually during adolescence. Kraepelin argued that these patients could be distinguished from those suffering from other disorders (most notably manic-depressive psychosis) largely on the basis of changes that occurred as the disorder progressed over time, primarily those changes involving the integrity of mental functions.

In 1911, Eugen Bleuler (1857–1939), a Swiss

▲ These dementia praecox patients, treated by Emil Kraepelin near the turn of the century, display "waxy flexibility," a feature of catatonic motor behavior. "They were put without difficulty in the peculiar positions and kept them, some with a sly laugh, others with rigid seriousness."

▲ Swiss psychiatrist Eugen Bleuler coined the term "schizophrenia" in his 1911 monograph on the disorder.

psychiatrist and a contemporary of Kraepelin, published an extremely influential monograph in which he agreed with most of Kraepelin's suggestions about this disorder. He did not believe, however, that the disorder always ended in profound deterioration or that it always began in late adolescence. Kraepelin's term *dementia praecox* was therefore unacceptable to him. Bleuler suggested a new name for the disorder—**schizophrenia.** This term referred to the *splitting of mental associations*, which Bleuler believed to be the fundamental disturbance in schizophrenia. One unfortunate consequence of this choice of terms has been the confusion among laypeople of schizophrenia with multiple personality, a severe form of dissociative disorder that sometimes has been called "split personality" (see Chapter 8). The two disorders actually have very little in common.

Many additional suggestions have been made in subsequent years regarding the description and diagnosis of schizophrenia (Neale & Oltmanns, 1980). Some clinicians have favored a broader definition, whereas others have argued for a more narrow approach. These differences of opinion have focused on a number of issues.

One such issue has been the relative importance of specific types of symptoms in establishing a diagnosis of schizophrenia. Are some symptoms more useful than others in predicting the course of the disorder or the patient's response to treatment? Many clinicians have dis-

agreed with Bleuler's choice of fundamental symptoms. One prominent alternative opinion was offered by Kurt Schneider (1959), a German psychiatrist, whose diagnostic system for schizophrenia placed primary emphasis on a set of specific types of hallucinations, delusions, and perceptual distortions that he considered to be "first-rank symptoms." Examples include *thought broadcasting*, in which the person believes that his or her thoughts are being transmitted so that others know what he or she is thinking; *voices commenting*, in which the person hears someone else's voice provide a running commentary that describes or criticizes his or her behavior; and *somatic passivity*, in which the person believes that he or she is a passive, unwilling recipient of physical sensations imposed by some outside force.

Several other issues have also been involved in the debate surrounding the diagnosis of schizophrenia. One critical question is whether the label of schizophrenia should be limited to patients who show a chronic deteriorating course, as Kraepelin had originally proposed. Many European psychiatrists maintain a separate diagnostic category, **brief reactive psychosis,** for those patients who exhibit transient symptoms of schizophrenia followed by a complete recovery. Another question is whether patients should be considered schizophrenic if they experience hallucinations and delusions in conjunction with the symptoms of a major mood disorder (depression or mania).

The first two editions of the DSM (APA, 1952; APA, 1968) presented a broad definition of schizophrenia. Very little was provided in the way of specific diagnostic guidelines for the clinician to follow in diagnosing this disorder.

The diagnostic criteria for schizophrenia in DSM-III departed significantly from those presented in previous editions of the manual. DSM-III eliminated certain conditions from the schizophrenia category. Borderline conditions and simple schizophrenia[†], which do not feature overt psychotic features, were listed with the personality disorders (now called schizotypal and schizoid personality disorders; see Chapter 9). Patients who exhibit schizophrenic symptoms for a period less than 6 months were diagnosed as having **schizophreniform disorders,** and those whose psychotic symptoms last

---

[†] Bleuler described a subtype, simple schizophrenia, which was presumably characterized by a gradual and cumulative decline in intellectual and social adjustment as well as an absence of other symptoms such as hallucinations and delusions.

less than 2 weeks were considered to have brief reactive psychoses. The overall impact of the changes introduced in DSM-III was to narrow considerably the definition of schizophrenia.

DSM-III adopted a middle ground on the issue of chronicity. Kraepelin's definition of dementia praecox held that dementia praecox was a progressive disorder that followed a chronic, deteriorating course. Bleuler's description included a broader range of patients and held that a larger percentage of patients improved after periods of acute psychosis. By requiring 6 months' duration, DSM-III favored the notion that schizophrenia is a disorder that tends to be chronic in nature, but it does not rule out the possibility of recovery.

Contemporary Diagnostic Systems

The DSM-IV lists several specific criteria for diagnosing a patient as schizophrenic (see Table 12–1). The first criterion is that the patient must exhibit two (or more) psychotic symptoms for at least 1 month. In comparison to DSM-III, DSM-IV gives less emphasis to Schneider's first-rank symptoms. This change has occurred because research studies have demonstrated that first-rank symptoms are not unique to schizophrenia (O'Grady,

1990), do not identify an etiologically homogeneous group of patients, and are not predictive of treatment response or short-term outcome (McGuffin et al., 1984; Mellor, 1982).

Negative symptoms, such as blunted affect, avolition, and social withdrawal, assume a more prominent role in the DSM-IV definition of schizophrenia. These symptoms were largely ignored in DSM-III because of concern about their reliability. The work group that developed DSM-IV considered these symptoms very important and therefore vital both to determining the causes of the disorder and to treating it successfully (Andreasen & Carpenter, 1993).

The DSM-IV definition, like that in DSM-III, takes into account interpersonal relationships and the duration of the disorder. The DSM-IV definition of schizophrenia requires evidence of a decline in the person's social or occupational functioning as well as the presence of disturbed behavior over a continuous period of at least 6 months.

Subtypes

Schizophrenia is a heterogeneous disorder with many different clinical manifestations and levels of severity. The title of Bleuler's classic text referred to "the group of schizophrenias" in an

---

TABLE 12–1

DSM-IV Diagnostic Criteria for Schizophrenia

A. Characteristic Symptoms: Two (or more) of the following, each present for a significant portion of time during a one month period (or less if successfully treated):
1. delusions
2. hallucinations
3. disorganized speech (such as frequent derailment or incoherence)
4. grossly disorganized or catatonic behavior
5. negative symptoms, such as affective flattening, alogia, or avolition

   [Note: only one A symptom is required if delusions are bizarre or hallucinations consist of a voice keeping up a running commentary on the person's behavior or thoughts, or two or more voices conversing with each other].

B. Social/Occupational Dysfunction: For a significant portion of the time since the onset of the disturbance, one or more major areas of functioning such as work, interpersonal relations, or self-care is markedly below the level achieved prior to the onset.

C. Duration: Continuous signs of the disturbance persist for at least six months. This six-month period must include at least one month of symptoms that meet criterion A (active phase symptoms), and may include periods of prodromal or residual symptoms. During these prodromal or residual periods, the signs of the disturbance may be manifested by only negative symptoms or two or more symptoms listed in Criterion A present in an attenuated form (such as odd beliefs, unusual perceptual experiences).

effort to draw attention to the varied presentations of the disorder. It is not clear, however, how best to think about the different forms of schizophrenia. Many clinicians and investigators believe that schizophrenia is a general term for a group of disorders, each of which may be caused by a completely different set of factors. Other clinicians believe that the numerous symptoms of schizophrenia are most likely varying manifestations of the same underlying condition (Gottesman, 1991). Given the current state of evidence, it is not possible to choose between these conceptual options. Nevertheless, most investigators agree that we should at least consider the possibility that there are distinct forms.

DSM-IV SUBCATEGORIES

Kraepelin's definition of dementia praecox was based on an integration of three patterns of symptoms that had previously been considered separate syndromes: hebephrenia, catatonia, and dementia paranoides. He argued that they were all manifestations of a single disorder, and since that time they have been considered symptomatic subtypes of schizophrenia. They represent three of the five subtypes that are recognized in DSM-IV.

▼ **People with schizophrenia sometimes exhibit disorganized behavior, like this hospitalized woman.**

Disorganized Type Hebephrenia is now known as the **disorganized type** of schizophrenia because it is characterized by disorganized speech, disorganized behavior, and flat or inappropriate affect. Social impairment is usually quite marked in these patients. The patient's speech is frequently incoherent, and, if delusions or hallucinations are present, their content is not well organized. Consider, for example, the delusions expressed by Edward. At various times, he talked about Nazi soldiers and World War II, frozen corpses in Greenland, being "half a person," and having special powers because he was the son of God. These fragmented and bizarre ideas were clearly delusional, but they were not woven into a coherent framework.

Catatonic Type The **catatonic type** is characterized by symptoms of motor immobility (including

rigidity and posturing) or excessive and purposeless motor activity. Catatonic patients may also be stuporous. If her disorder lasted more than 6 months, Marsha would probably have received a diagnosis of schizophrenic disorder, catatonic type on the basis of her prominent motor symptoms and stuporous behavior.

Paranoid Type The most prominent symptoms in the **paranoid type** are systematic delusions with persecutory or grandiose content. Preoccupation with frequent auditory hallucinations can also be associated with the paranoid type. Ann would have received a diagnosis of schizophrenic disorder, paranoid type because of her preoccupation with the systematic delusion about the photographs that had been stolen and the attempt to harm her children. Patients who exhibit disorganized speech, disorganized behavior, flat or inappropriate affect, or catatonic behavior are excluded from a diagnosis of paranoid schizophrenia and would fall into one of the other subtypes.

Undifferentiated Type Two additional subtypes are described in DSM-IV, presumably to cover those patients who do not fit one of the traditional types. The **undifferentiated type** of schizophrenia includes schizophrenic patients who display prominent psychotic symptoms and either meet the criteria for several subtypes or otherwise do not meet the criteria for the catatonic, paranoid, or disorganized types.

Residual Type The **residual type** includes patients who no longer meet the criteria for active-phase symptoms but nevertheless demonstrate continued signs of negative symptoms or attenuated forms of delusions, hallucinations, or disorganized speech.

The utility of the traditional subtypes has been seriously questioned for a variety of reasons. Although some patients fit traditional descriptions of schizophrenic types, many others do not. Subtype diagnoses are used less consistently than the global diagnosis of schizophrenia (Carpenter & Stephens, 1979). It is not unusual for schizophrenic patients to exhibit a mixed set of symptoms that are simultaneously characteristic of more than one subtype. Patients who fit a single traditional category during one psychotic episode may satisfy criteria for a different subtype diagnosis during a subsequent period of disturbance (Kendler, Gruenberg, & Tsuang, 1985). Over time, patients who initially exhibit symptoms of the paranoid and disorganized subtypes are likely to fit the criteria for less specific types such as undifferentiated or residual schizophrenia. Traditional subtypes do not appear to predict either the course of the disorder or response to treatment.

Manfred Bleuler (1978), a Swiss psychiatrist and the son of Eugen Bleuler, has treated and observed more than 200 schizophrenic patients over a long period of time. His experience suggests that the distinctions between subtypes become blurred over time. Bleuler's follow-up data and much of the other research evidence supports the hypothesis that symptomatic subtypes are a reflection of varying stages of a single disorder or varying levels of severity of the disorder (Gottesman, 1991; Sorensen, Paul, & Mariotto, 1988).

Related Disorders

Since the publication of DSM-III, the American concept of schizophrenia has become more narrow. This change has been accomplished by excluding patients with certain types of psychotic symptoms from a diagnosis of schizophrenic disorder. The DSM-IV lists three disorders other than schizophrenia that are characterized by prominent psychotic symptoms.

Schizoaffective disorder represents a combination of schizophrenia and mood disorder. It is defined by a period of disturbance during which the symptoms of schizophrenia partially overlap with a major depressive episode or a manic episode. The key to making this diagnosis is the presence of delusions or hallucinations for at least 2 weeks *in the absence of prominent mood symptoms*. If the delusions and hallucinations are present only during a depressive episode, for example, the diagnosis would be major depressive episode with psychotic features.

People with **delusional disorder** do not meet the full symptomatic criteria for schizophrenia but they are preoccupied for at least 1 month with delusions that are not bizarre. These are beliefs about situations that could occur in real life, such as being followed or poisoned. Ann's delusion, for example, might have fit this description. She believed that someone was trying to kill her and her children and that someone was trying to cast a voodoo spell on them.

Ann would not be assigned a diagnosis of delusional disorder, however, because she also displayed negative symptoms, such as avolition. The presence of hallucinations, disorganized speech, catatonic behavior, or negative symptoms rules out a diagnosis of delusional disorder. The definition of delusional disorder also holds that the person's behavior is not bizarre, and that social and occupational functioning are not impaired except for those areas that are directly affected by the delusional belief.

Brief psychotic disorder is a category that includes those people who exhibit psychotic symptoms—delusions, hallucinations, disorganized speech, or grossly disorganized or catatonic behavior—for at least 1 day but no more than 1 month. After the symptoms are resolved, the person returns to the same level of functioning that had been achieved prior to the psychotic episode. This diagnosis is not assigned if the symptoms are better explained by a mood disorder, schizophrenia, or substance abuse.

Course and Outcome

Schizophrenia has traditionally been considered a severe, progressive disorder with a typically poor outcome. In fact, Kraepelin considered the deteriorating course to be one of the principal defining features of the disorder. Recent evidence suggests that this view may be unnecessarily pessimistic: Many patients in fact experience a good outcome (Harding, Zubin, & Strauss, 1992). For example, Manfred Bleuler (1978) studied a sample of 208 schizophrenic patients who had been admitted to his hospital in Switzerland during the years 1942 and 1943. After a follow-up period of 23 years, 53 percent of the patients were either recovered or significantly improved. The evidence from several studies indicates that at least 30 percent of all schizophrenic patients recover fairly well after their initial serious episode (Cutting, 1986). Another 30 percent follow the path of deterioration originally defined by Kraepelin. The remaining patients continue to experience intermittent episodes that may require hospitalization.

Clearly the choice of diagnostic criteria will, in many ways, influence the results of outcome studies. For example, DSM-IV requires that a patient exhibit signs of disturbance for a period of at least 6 months before a diagnosis of schizophrenia can be made. This criterion excludes those patients who recover very rapidly. Consequently, follow-up studies based on this criterion will focus on patients with more persistent symptoms, and it would not be surprising if they reported more poor outcomes than studies that do not require the 6-month duration.

Follow-up studies of schizophrenic patients have found that the description of outcome can be a complicated process. Many factors must be taken into consideration other than whether the person is still in the hospital. Is the person still exhibiting symptoms of the disorder? Does he or she have any other problems, such as depression or anxiety? Is the person employed? Does he have any friends? How does he get along with other people? The evidence indicates that different dimensions of outcome, such as social adjustment, occupational functioning, and symptom severity, are only loosely correlated. As in most situations where psychologists attempt to predict future behavior, the outcome data regarding schizophrenia suggest that the best predictor of future social adjustment is previous social adjustment. Similarly, the best predictor of symptom severity at follow-up is severity of psychotic symptoms at initial assessment (Carpenter & Strauss, 1978; 1991).

Epidemiology

One of the most informative ways of examining the frequency of schizophrenia is to consider the *lifetime morbid risk*, or the proportion of a specific population that will be affected by the disorder at some time during their lives. Most studies in Europe and the United States have reported lifetime morbid risk figures of approximately 1 percent (Jablensky, 1986). In other words, approximately 1 out of every 100 people will experience or express schizophrenic symptoms at some time during their lives. Of course, these figures depend upon the diagnostic criteria that are used to define schizophrenia in any particular study, as well as the methods that are used to identify cases in the general population. Those investigators who have used more narrow or restrictive criteria for the disorder, for example, typically report lower morbid risk figures.

Data from the Epidemiologic Catchment Area (ECA) study are consistent with these earlier figures, and confirm previous impressions regarding age of onset and course (Keith, Regier, & Rae, 1991). Using DSM-III criteria for the disorder, the investigators found a lifetime prevalence of 1.3 percent for schizophrenia and 0.2 percent for schizophreniform disorder. The mean age of onset was 20 years, and 71 percent of the people who met criteria for schizophrenia had experienced their first symptoms by the age of 25. For those persons who no longer exhibited active symptoms at the time of the interview, the mean duration of the disorder was 15 years.

Gender Differences in Onset and Course

Epidemiological studies have found that, across the lifespan, men and women are equally likely to be affected by schizophrenia (Keith, Regier, & Rae, 1991). There are, however, some interesting differences between the genders with regard to patterns of onset and course. For example, the average age at which schizophrenic males begin to exhibit overt signs of the disorder is younger by about 4 or 5 years than the average age at which schizophrenic women first experience problems (Riecher et al., 1991). A summary of proposed gender differences in schizophrenia is presented in Table 12–2.

Gender differences in the age of onset and symptomatic expression of schizophrenia might be interpreted in several ways. Lewine (1981, 1988) has proposed two hypotheses. One is based on the assumption that schizophrenia is a single disorder and that its expression varies in men and women. A common, genetically determined vulnerability to schizophrenia might be expressed differently in men than in women. Mediating factors that might account for this difference could be biological differences between men and women— perhaps involving certain hormones—or different environmental demands— such as the timing and form of stresses associated with typical male and female sex roles. An alternative hypothesis suggests that there are two qualitatively distinct subtypes of schizophrenia:

one with an early onset that affects men more often than women, and another with a later age of onset that affects women more often than men. Both hypotheses fit the general diathesis-stress model. The available evidence does not allow us to favor one of these explanations over the other.

Cross-Cultural Comparisons

Schizophrenia has been observed in virtually every culture that has been subjected to careful scrutiny. Of course, the formal term *schizophrenia* is not used in societies that have not adopted modern medical practices, but the symptoms of the disorder are nevertheless present (see Research Close-up in Chapter 1).

Two large-scale epidemiological studies, conducted by teams of scientists working for the World Health Organization (WHO), indicate that the incidence of schizophrenia is relatively constant across different cultural settings. The International Pilot Study of Schizophrenia (IPSS) began in the 1960s and was conducted in nine countries across Europe, North America, South America, Africa, and Asia. It included 1,200 patients who were followed for a period of 5 years after their initial hospitalization. The Collaborative Study on the Determinants of Outcome of Severe Mental Disorders (DOS) was conducted a few years later in six of the same countries that had participated in the IPSS, plus four others. The DOS study included more than 1,500 patients. Both the IPSS and DOS projects examined rural and urban areas in both Western and non-Western countries. For purposes of cultural comparison, the countries were divided into those that were "developing" and those that were already "developed" on the basis of prevailing socioeconomic conditions. The interviewers were all trained in the use of a single, standardized interview schedule, and all employed the same sets of diagnostic criteria.

The IPSS results indicated that patients who exhibited characteristic signs and symptoms of schizophrenia were found in all of the study sites. Comparisons of patients across research centers revealed more similarities than differences in clinical symptoms at the time of entry into the study, which was always an active phase of disorder that required psychiatric treatment. Using a relatively narrow set of diagnostic cri-

TABLE 12-2

Prototypical Gender Differences in Schizophrenia

Variable	Men	Women
Onset Age	Earlier (20s)	Later (30s)
First Hospital Admission	Early	Late
Symptoms	Typical Withdrawn, passive Negative	Atypical Affective, active Positive
Premorbid Social Competence	Poor	Good
Course	More often chronic	Less often chronic

Based on R.J. Lewine, 1981. Sex differences in schizophrenia: Timing or subtypes? *Psychological Bulletin, 90,* 432-444; and Lewine, 1988. Gender and schizophrenia. In H.A. Nasvallah (ed.), *Handbook of schizophrenia,* vol. 3 (pp. 379-397). Amsterdam: Elsevier.

teria, scientists found that the incidence of schizophrenia did not differ significantly among the research centers. One interesting difference emerged with regard to symptom patterns: The proportion of patients who fit the catatonic subtype was significantly larger among patients in developing countries (India, Colombia, and Nigeria). The IPSS investigators also found that clinical and social outcomes at 2-and 5-year follow-up were significantly better for schizophrenic patients in developing countries than in developed countries, such as the United States, England, and Russia (Leff et al., 1992). The DOS study confirmed these results (Jablensky et al., 1992).

Taken together, the WHO studies provide compelling support for the conclusion that schizophrenia occurs with similar frequency and presents with similar symptoms in different cultures. The more favorable clinical outcome that was observed in India and Nigeria has been interpreted as being a product of the greater tolerance and acceptance that is extended to people with psychotic symptoms in developing countries. This conclusion is consistent with evidence regarding the relationship between frequency of relapse and patterns of family communication, which we consider later in this chapter in the section on expressed emotion.

Etiological Considerations

Having considered the defining characteristics of schizophrenia, ways in which it has been classified, and some basic information regarding its distribution within the general population, we can now review the evidence regarding factors that might contribute to the development of the disorder as well as its course and outcome.

Biological Factors

Many of the early investigators who originally defined schizophrenia at the beginning of the twentieth century believed that the disorder was the product of a biological dysfunction. At that time, very little was known about human genetics or the biochemistry of the brain. Gregor Mendel's pioneering work with pea plants—in which he identified basic patterns of inheritance for simple characteristics such as the color of their flowers—had been completed, but its implications were not widely recognized in the scientific community. The chemical nature of neural transmission was not validated experimentally until the 1920s. Research in the areas of molecular genetics and the neurosciences has progressed at an explosive rate in the past decade. Much of what we know today about the biological substrates of schizophrenia has emerged from advances that have taken place in other sciences.

GENETICS

The role of genetic factors has been studied more extensively with regard to schizophrenia than with any other type of mental disorder. The existing data are based on sophisticated methods that have been refined over many years. The cumulative weight of this evidence points clearly toward some type of genetic influence in the transmission of this disorder.

Family Studies Clinicians have often noted that schizophrenia seems to run in families. This observation has been confirmed by several empirical studies of the families of schizophrenic patients. These studies begin with the identification of a schizophrenic patient, who is termed the proband. Evidence is then collected regarding the proband's relatives. In the earliest family studies, this information was usually gleaned from hospital records. Contemporary researchers usually arrange to conduct personal interviews with the relatives. The latter procedure is preferable because it allows the investigator to use specific criteria for the diagnosis of schizophrenia, which makes the diagnosis more reliable.

Figure 12–1 illustrates the lifetime risk for schizophrenia for various types of relatives of a person with schizophrenia. Irving Gottesman, a psychologist at the University of Virginia, created this figure by pooling data from 40 European studies that were published between 1920 and 1987 (Gottesman, 1991). All of the studies employed conservative diagnostic criteria for the disorder.

Consider the data for first-degree relatives and second-degree relatives. On average, siblings and children share 50 percent of their genes with the schizophrenic proband; nieces, nephews, and cousins share only 25 percent. The lifetime morbid risk for schizophrenia is much greater among first-degree relatives than it is among second-degree relatives. The risk in the second-degree relatives is greater than the 1 percent figure that is typically reported for people in the general population. As the degree of genetic similarity increases between an individual and a schizophrenic patient, the risk to that person increases. The family history data are consistent with the hypothesis that the transmission of schizophrenia is influenced by genetic factors. They do not prove the point, however, because family studies do not separate genetic and environmental events. Family members share not only genes but also an environment, which may shape their behavior through modeling and other learning processes. We therefore must consider other sources of information before concluding that genetic factors contribute to the development of schizophrenia.

Twin Studies Several twin studies have examined concordance rates for schizophrenia. The results of these studies are also summarized in Figure 12–1. The average concordance rate for MZ twins is 48 percent, whereas the comparable figure for DZ twins is 17 percent. One study from Norway, published after Gottesman computed average rates for his figure, found a concordance rate of 48 percent among MZ twins and only 4 percent among DZ twins (Onstad et al., 1991). Although the specific rates vary somewhat from study to study, all of the published reports have found that MZ twins are significantly more likely than DZ twins to be concordant for schizophrenia. This pattern suggests strongly that genetic factors play an important role in the development of the disorder.

It should also be pointed out, however, that none of the twin studies of schizophrenia has found a concordance rate that even approaches 100 percent, which would be expected if genetic factors were *entirely* responsible for schizophrenia. Thus, the twin studies also provide compelling evidence for the importance of environmental events. Some people apparently inherit a predisposition to the development of schizophrenia. Among that select group of vulnerable individuals, certain environmental events must determine whether a given person will eventually exhibit the full-blown symptoms of the disorder.

Although the twin studies provide persuasive evidence for the role of genetic factors, they have been criticized on a number of grounds. One inherent difficulty centers around the assumption that the twin method is able to hold the influence of environmental factors constant across MZ and DZ pairs. Some critics have pointed out that MZ twins, by virtue of their striking physical resemblance, are much more likely than DZ twins to be treated in exactly the same way by their parents. If that were the case, the greater concordance rates for a disorder such as schizophrenia might be attributed to the greater similarity in their environmental experiences rather than to their greater genetic similarity. It would therefore be helpful to find a research method that would provide a more convincing separation of the influence of genetic and environmental events.

Adoption Studies Studies of children who were adopted away from their biological parents and reared by foster families provide this type of clear distinction between genetic and environmental influence. The first adoption study of schizophrenia was reported by Leonard Heston (1966), a psychiatrist at the University of Washington. He began by identifying records for a group of 49 children who were born

between 1915 and 1945 while their mothers were hospitalized for schizophrenia. All the children were apparently normal at birth and were separated from their mothers within 3 days of birth. To rule out possible exposure to the environment associated with the mother's psychosis, any child who had been in contact with maternal relatives was excluded from the study. A control group of children was selected using the admission records of foundling homes where many of the target children had originally been placed. These children were matched to the patients' children on a number of variables, including age, sex, type of eventual placement, and length of institutionalization.

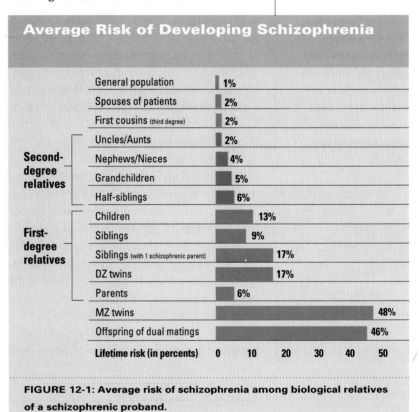

FIGURE 12-1: Average risk of schizophrenia among biological relatives of a schizophrenic proband.

From I.I. Gottesman. 1991. *Schizophrenia genesis: The origins of madness,* p. 96. New York: Freeman.

Heston was able to locate and interview most of the offspring, the majority of whom were then in their mid-thirties. Five of the adult offspring of schizophrenic mothers received a diagnosis of schizophrenia. Correcting for the fact that most of the subjects were still within the period of risk for the disorder, this resulted in a lifetime morbidity risk for schizophrenia of 16.6 percent in the target group, which is almost exactly the rate observed among children of schizophrenic parents who were raised by their biological parents (see Figure 12–1). In contrast, none of the adult offspring in the control group received a diagnosis of schizophrenia. Because the only difference between the two groups was the genetic relationship between the target offspring and their schizophrenic biological mothers, Heston's data indicate that genetic factors play a role in the development of the disorder.

Several other adoption studies have been concerned with schizophrenia, and all reach the same conclusion as Heston's original report (see Gottesman, 1991, and Kendler & Diehl, 1993 for reviews of this literature). One especially important study was conducted in Denmark, using national adoption records as well as the national psychiatric register to identify subjects. Psychiatrist Seymour Kety and his colleagues identified people, known as the index adoptees, who had been adopted away from their biological parents at an early age and who had subsequently developed schizophrenia after reaching adulthood. The investigators also found a group of people, known as the control adoptees, who had also been adopted away from their biological parents at an early age, but who had not shown any signs of mental disorder as adults. The investigators then compared these groups with regard to the prevalence of schizophrenia among their biological and adoptive relatives. They found a significantly higher rate of schizophrenia among the biological relatives of the index adoptees than among the biological relatives of the control adoptees (Kety, 1987; Kety et al., 1975). They also found low rates of schizophrenia among the adoptive relatives of both groups. This pattern is consistent with the results of Heston's adoption study and, once again, supports the conclusion that genetic factors are involved in the development of schizophrenia.

The Spectrum of Schizophrenic Disorders
Results from adoption and twin studies have also provided interesting clues regarding the boundaries of the schizophrenia concept. Several types of psychotic disorders and personality disorders resemble schizophrenia in one way or another. These include schizoaffective disorder, delusional disorder, and schizotypal personality

disorder. Are these conditions a reflection of the same genetically determined predisposition as schizophrenia, or are they etiologically distinct disorders? If they are genetically related, then investigators should find that the biological relatives of schizophrenic adoptees are more likely to exhibit these conditions as well as schizophrenia. Twin studies should also find an increased prevalence of these disorders among the MZ co-twins of schizophrenic probands (see Further Thoughts). The results of such analyses have been inconsistent from one study to the next, which prevents us from reaching firm conclusions. Nevertheless, the overall pattern of results from both adoption and twin studies suggests that vulnerability to schizophrenia is sometimes expressed as schizophrenia-like personality traits and other types of psychosis that are not specifically included in the DSM-IV definition of schizophrenia (Kendler & Diehl, 1993).

Linkage Studies The combined results from twin and adoption studies indicate that genetic factors are involved in the transmission of schizophrenia (Gottesman, 1991; Kendler & Diehl, 1993). This conclusion does not imply, however, that the manner in which schizophrenia develops is well understood. We really know little beyond the fact that genetic factors are involved in some way. They do not explain the whole story. Some individuals apparently inherit a predisposition to schizophrenia, but the mode of transmission has not been identified. Some clinical scientists believe that a single dominant gene is involved.[†] Others believe that schizophrenia is a *polygenic* characteristic, which means that it is the product of a reasonably large number of genes rather than a single gene.

One of the most exciting areas of research on genetics and schizophrenia is now focused on the search for genetic linkage (see Research Methods in Chapter 13 for an explanation of this process). Studies of this type are designed to identify the location of a specific gene that is responsible for the disorder (or some large component of the disorder). In 1988, Hugh Gurling, Robin Sherrington, and a large group of colleagues reported the results of linkage analyses in seven large families. Each of these families

▲ Irving Gottesman, Sherrell J. Aston Professor of Psychology at the University of Virginia, is one of the world's leading experts on genetic factors and schizophrenia.

[†] The pattern of inheritance for schizophrenia clearly does not follow the classic Mendelian ratios that are expected for a single dominant gene, in which 50 percent of the offspring of a parent with the trait would also be affected. Advocates of the single major locus position explain this deviation from expected patterns in terms of reduced penetrance. Reduced penetrance means that the person possesses the genotype for the disorder, but for some reason it is not expressed; that is, the person does not develop the full-blown clinical disorder.

FURTHER THOUGHTS

Identical Triplets with Different Types of Psychosis?

Sets of two or more individuals who share exactly the same genes provide fascinating opportunities to examine the nature of specific human problems. Data from studies of MZ and DZ twins represent some of the most compelling evidence for the role of genetic factors in the etiology of schizophrenia. They can also be used to examine the boundaries of the disorder and the value of various approaches to subclassification. One fascinating case study involves a set of monozygotic triplets living in England (McGuffin, Reveley, & Holland, 1982). The varying symptomatic pictures presented by these brothers raise important questions about the distinction between schizophrenia and manic-depressive psychosis. Since Kraepelin's original monograph on dementia praecox, most clinicians have taken these to be qualitatively distinct disorders.

The brothers, R., M., and G., were 28 years old at the time of the original report. Their development during infancy and early childhood was generally unremarkable. R.'s first episode, at the age of 16, was characterized by social withdrawal coupled with complaints of diffuse anxiety and difficulty concentrating. His first extended hospitalization (followed by three others) occurred after he became markedly paranoid. He was arrested at a U.S. Air Force base after he had attempted to break in, claiming to be a CIA agent "under direct orders from Nixon and Hoover." In addition to hearing accusatory voices that told him to do things against his will, R. exhibited signs of disorganized speech and blunted affect. His adjustment between recurrent psychotic episodes has never returned to normal levels of occupational or social functioning.

M. was also treated for the first time at the age of 16. Like his brother R., M. reported persistent feelings of anxiety and had difficulty concentrating. He was admitted to a psychiatric hospital 2 years later because he had become increasingly withdrawn and apathetic. He was discharged after 8 months in the hospital, even though he had not responded positively to antipsychotic medication.

When he was next admitted to the hospital, M. was in an excited state. He spoke rapidly and jumped quickly from one topic to the next, often with little connection between ideas. Auditory hallucinations and delusions, which were similar to those experienced by R., became evident over the next 4 years, most of which were spent in the hospital. One of the voices that he reported was presumably that of his deceased uncle, who was heard commenting on M.'s behavior and giving him instructions, such as to throw himself on the railroad tracks. At times, M. believed that he was completely taken over by his uncle, who would, for example, "make me think I was a married man with a wife and three children (M. had never dated women)."

Both R. and M. exhibited typical symptoms of schizophrenia, although some of M.'s behaviors were also characteristic of patients with mood disorders. The latter included maniclike patterns of speech, such as flight of ideas, occasionally boasting of exceptional talent, and moods that cycled back and forth between lethargy and periods of cheerful, restless activity. Both brothers were assigned a diagnosis of schizophrenia.

The third brother, G., exhibited many of the same symptoms, but the composite picture was somewhat different. In fact, G. was considered to have a bipolar mood disorder by his hospital diagnosis. His first signs of disturbance appeared at the age of 14 when he suddenly became withdrawn and anxious, refusing to leave his room at home. He improved gradually, but he became paranoid the following year. His first inpatient admission followed a violent attack on a stranger, which stemmed from his belief that cars were following him on the streets. Hospital notes indicated that he was excited and friendly, that he claimed to feel "on top of the world," and that he spoke rapidly and without stopping. He also expressed grandiose delusions, including claims that his ability in mathematics was comparable to Einstein's and that he was Jesus Christ, endowed with miraculous healing powers.

During three subsequent relapses that required

inpatient treatment, G. exhibited sleeplessness, restlessness, pressured speech, and poor judgment in handling money. In addition to these symptoms, which are all characteristic of manic episodes, G. reported hearing voices that told him to do things. He also believed that outside forces were making him feel certain things, similar to the somatic passivity reported by M.

The three brothers are genetically identical, but they exhibit different types of psychosis. Two have a diagnosis of schizophrenia, and the third has a diagnosis of bipolar mood disorder. What should we make of this pattern? McGuffin, Reveley, and Holland (1982) suggested that the triplets illustrate the broad range of behavioral manifestations that may be associated with a single genotype. R., M., and G. may have different forms of the same condition. In this case, the symptoms of the condition straddle the boundaries of schizophrenia and mood disorder. Does that mean that people inherit a general predisposition to psychosis rather than one that is specifically associated with schizophrenia? Or does it mean that there are several discrete forms of psychosis, including some that represent a mixture of schizophrenic and mood symptoms (schizoaffective disorder)? This case of identical triplets helps to raise and clarify the key questions, which can be answered only by further research. ■

included an unusually high proportion of members with schizophrenia. These investigators found strong evidence indicating linkage between schizophrenia and DNA markers in a section of chromosome 5 (Sherrington et al., 1988). Unfortunately, other laboratories have not been able to replicate this dramatic result (Kennedy et al., 1988; McGuffin et al., 1990). Furthermore, the original group of investigators later reported additional data from a new set of families that contradict their initial conclusions (Mankoo et al., 1991).

Linkage analysis has not yet produced any firm conclusions or replicable findings. Kendler and Diehl (1993) reviewed more than 30 genetic linkage studies of schizophrenia that were published in the 5 years following the report by Gurling, Sherrington, and their colleagues. None of the subsequent studies has found strong support for linkage to chromosome 5 or to any other genetic locus. Supporters of linkage analysis contend that the absence of definitive discoveries is not necessarily surprising when we consider that there are probably tens of thousands of genes that influence activities in the brain. They feel that the search for a particular gene that causes schizophrenia will take more time. Critics respond that schizophrenia is a polygenic disorder and therefore we will never trace its etiology to a single gene. There is good reason to believe that polygenic models provide the best explanation for the distribution of the disorder within families (Vogler et al., 1990).

General Conclusions: A Diathesis-Stress Model

The combined results of many twin and adoption studies point strongly toward the influence of genetic factors in the etiology of schizophrenia. It is also clear, however, that these genetic factors do not provide a complete explanation for the disorder, because MZ twins are not always concordant for schizophrenia. In fact, the concordance rate for MZ twins is approximately 50 percent. A useful etiological model must therefore provide for the interaction of genetic factors and environmental events.

Paul Meehl has proposed a theory of schizophrenia that provides a useful guide to investigators who are trying to understand this complex disorder. According to Meehl (1962, 1990, 1993), all individuals who are predisposed to schizophrenia inherit a subtle neurological defect of unknown form. Meehl referred to this condition as **schizotaxia**. As a result of the interaction between this defect and inevitable learning experiences, schizotaxic individuals develop odd or eccentric behaviors, which he

▲ The Genain quadruplets, shown here as young children, all developed schizophrenia as adults.

called *schizotypic signs*.[†] Most prominent among these behaviors are "associative loosening," which is similar to the cognitive symptoms emphasized by Bleuler, and "aversive drift," in which the individual withdraws from interpersonal relationships because they are associated with negative affect. These are relatively subtle behaviors in comparison to the full-blown symptoms of psychosis. Only a small proportion of schizotypic persons will eventually become overtly schizophrenic.

NEUROPATHOLOGY

Meehl's model suggests that an important step toward understanding the etiology of schizophrenia would be to identify its neurological underpinnings. If schizophrenics suffer from a form of neurological dysfunction, shouldn't it be possible to observe differences between the structure of their brains and those of other people? The answer was certainly no in 1962 when Meehl originally proposed the schizotaxia concept. Until recent years, brain structures could be studied only at autopsy, after the person died, or through the use of invasive procedures. Gross observations could be made of various parts of the brain, but numerous problems complicated the interpretation of differences that might be obtained between the brains of deceased schizophrenics and those of other people.

Since the mid-1970s there has been a tremendous growth of information and technology in the neurosciences. We now understand in considerable detail how neurons communicate with one another, and scientists have invented sophisticated methods to create images of the living human brain. Some of these procedures provide static pictures of various brain structures at rest, just as an X-ray provides a photographic image of a bone or some other organ of the body. More recently, sophisticated methods have enabled us to create dynamic images of the brain while a person is performing different tasks. Studies using these techniques have produced evidence indicating that a number of brain areas are involved in schizophrenia (Gur & Pearlson, 1993; Sharif, Gewirtz, & Iqbal, 1993). You may want to review the description of brain structures in Chapter 2

and consult Figure 12–2 as well as Figure 13–3 before reading the next sections of this chapter.

Static Brain Imaging Many investigations of brain structure in people with schizophrenia have employed computerized tomographic (CT) scanning, which produces a series of two-dimensional images at sequential slices or planes of the brain (see Chapter 4 for an explanation of this process). The most consistent result across a large number of CT scan studies has been the finding that some people with schizophrenia have mildly to moderately enlarged *lateral ventricles*, the cavities on each side of the brain that are filled with cerebrospinal fluid (Raz & Raz, 1990; Seidman, 1983). These differences seem to reflect a natural part of the disorder, rather than a side effect of treatment with antipsychotic medication. In fact, some studies have found enlarged ventricles in young schizophrenic patients before they have been exposed to any form of treatment. One important study has also found enlarged ventricles prior to the onset of symptoms (see Research Close-up). Significantly, these differences do not appear to become more marked as time goes on. The structural changes seem to occur early in the development of the disorder and therefore may play a role in the onset of symptoms.

Many questions remain to be answered regarding the relation between enlarged ventricles and schizophrenia. Does the pattern reflect a generalized deterioration of the brain, or is it the result of a defect in specific brain sites? We don't know. Is the presence of enlarged ventricles consistently found in some subset of schizophrenic patients? Some investigators have reported an association between this type of neuropathology and other factors such as negative symptoms, poor response to medication, and absence of family history of the disorder. These are all interesting possibilities, but none has been firmly established (Torrey et al., 1994).

With magnetic resonance imaging (MRI), investigators are able to identify clearly many specific smaller structures within the brain that were not clearly visible using CT scans. The temporal lobes have been studied rather exten-

▲ **Paul Meehl, Regents Professor Emeritus of Psychology at the University of Minnesota, is the only clinical psychologist ever elected to the National Academy of Science. His theory of schizophrenia has guided research efforts to discover signs of vulnerability to the disorder.**

[†] Meehl (1990) notes that his assumption regarding the inevitable nature of the path from schizotaxia to schizotypy is based on current environmental circumstances and our lack of knowledge about the disorder. It is conceivable that, at some future point in time, it may be possible to design a special, protective environment that would prevent the appearance of schizotypy in at least some persons with a schizotaxic brain.

sively using MRI scans. Several studies have reported decreased size of the hippocampus and the amygdala, parts of the limbic system (Gur & Pearlson, 1993). These areas of the brain (located in the temporal lobes—see Figure 12–2) play a crucial role in the regulation of emotion as well as the integration of cognition and emotion. Decreased size of these structures in the limbic area of the temporal lobes may be especially noticeable on the left side of the brain, which plays an important role in the control of language. One interesting study found that schizophrenic patients who exhibited the greatest degree of disorganized speech were most likely to show a decrease in the size of left temporal lobe structures (Shenton et al., 1992).

Areas of the Brain Implicated in Schizophrenia

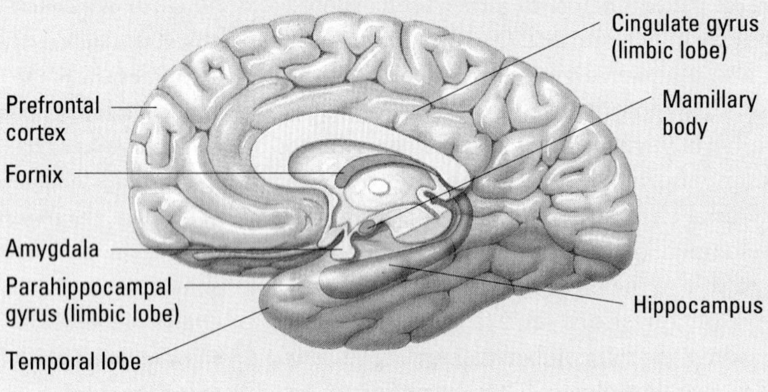

FIGURE 12-2: Brain-imaging studies have suggested that specific components of the limbic system, including the hippocampus and the amygdala, may be dysfunctional in schizophrenia.

Source: Adapted from F. Martini and M. Timmons (1995). *Human anatomy*, p. 381. Englewood Cliffs, NJ: Prentice Hall.

Results for several other brain areas have been less consistent than the data regarding ventricles, the hippocampus, and the amygdala. Some studies have reported significant differences between people with schizophrenia and comparison groups with regard to areas of the frontal cortex and the basal ganglia. Others report a general reduction in the overall size of the brain in some schizophrenic patients (Sharif, Gewirtz, & Iqbal, 1993).

Dynamic Brain Imaging In addition to CT- and MRI-scan procedures, which provide static pictures of brain structures, revolutionary devel-

opments in the neurosciences have also produced techniques that provide images of dynamic brain functions. One of these procedures involves the measurement of regional cerebral blood flow (rCBF). Images can be generated while the subject is at rest or during the performance of a specific task. Visual stimulation will produce increased cerebral blood flow in the visual cortex; subjects performing a simple motor task exhibit increased flow in the motor cortex.

Studies using the measurement of rCBF have found differences between people with schizophrenia and others, particularly in the frontal regions of the brain (Gur & Pearlson, 1993). Daniel Weinberger, a psychiatrist at the National Institute of Mental Health, and his colleagues have measured rCBF in the prefrontal cortex while subjects perform an abstract problem-solving task that presumably requires abilities that are mediated in the frontal lobes. Normal subjects show an increase in blood flow to the frontal regions of the brain when they are engaged in this task. Many schizophrenic patients, on the other hand, do not show this same increase (Weinberger et al., 1986). Studies of brain metabolism and blood flow have also identified functional changes in the temporal lobes and basal ganglia in many persons with schizophrenia.

Another dynamic brain imaging technique is known as *positron emission tomography* (PET) scanning. Although it is much more expensive than the other imaging techniques, it is capable of providing very detailed images of the brain. In addition, like rCBF, it can reflect changes in brain activity as the person responds to various task demands. The results of PET-scan studies are consistent with rCBF results and suggest dysfunction in the frontal cortex as well as the temporal lobes (Gur & Pearlson, 1993). These problems are also observed among patients with major mood disorders.

The role of neurological abnormalities in schizophrenia has been highlighted by a study of identical twins conducted by a group of investigators at the National Institute of Mental Health (NIMH). Subjects included 27 pairs of twins discordant for schizophrenia and 13 pairs that were concordant for the disorder. Changes in brain structure, measured by MRI, and changes in brain function, measured by cerebral blood flow, were prominent in the twins who had developed schizophrenia. Their well co-twins also exhibited more neurological impairment

The Danish High-Risk Project

Our ability to understand the etiology of schizophrenia has been limited by a lack of reliable and valid information regarding patients' developmental histories. Once a person has begun to exhibit symptoms of serious psychopathology, it is difficult to reconstruct events that took place in prior years. Furthermore, comparisons of schizophrenic patients and other groups are difficult to interpret because the patients have already been exposed to treatment. If differences are found with regard to brain structure, for example, they could be the consequences of antipsychotic drugs rather than contributing factors that were involved in the etiology of the disorder. For these reasons, it would be extremely useful if systematic information could be collected from individuals prior to the onset of the disorder.

In 1962, Sarnoff Mednick, now a psychologist at the University of Southern California, and Fini Schulsinger, a Danish psychiatrist, began in Denmark a longitudinal study of biological children of parents with schizophrenia (Mednick & Schulsinger, 1968). These subjects were selected because, in comparison to members of the general population, they are at **high risk** for schizophrenia. Roughly 13 percent of the high-risk group would be expected to develop the disorder as adults (see Figure 12–1). The project included 207 high-risk children whose biological mothers had been diagnosed as schizophrenic and 104 low-risk children who would serve as a comparison group. The families of the low-risk children had been free of mental illness for at least three generations. When the study was begun, none of the children had exhibited any overt signs of psychological disorder. The ages of the children in both groups ranged from 9 to 20 years. The family environments (for example, social class, rural or urban residence, length of time spent in children's homes) were similar in both groups.

Mednick and his colleagues have collected an enormous amount of information in order to describe the developmental histories of children in both groups, from birth to adulthood. The investigators had access to Danish public health records. They especially relied on hospital records to determine the frequency of pregnancy and delivery complications associated with each subject's birth. As the study progressed, they monitored national records of psychiatric facilities to detect evidence that any of the children had developed psychological problems. The investigators conducted follow-up assessments, including structured diagnostic interviews, with the subjects at two principal times: in the early 1970s and again in the late 1980s, when the subjects' average age was 42 years. The latter assessment included the use of CT scans to detect structural brain pathology.

It has been more than 30 years since the Danish study began, and 31 of the high-risk offspring have developed schizophrenia (Parnas et al., 1993). Age-corrected morbid risk rates for schizophrenia in the high- and low-risk groups are 17 percent and 3 percent[†] The high-risk offspring were also more likely than the low-risk subjects to develop disorders that are considered to be in the schizophrenia spectrum. The most obvious difference involved schizotypal personality disorder. This diagnosis was assigned to 36 offspring (18 percent) in the high-risk group, compared to only 5 offspring (5 percent) in the low-risk group. Rates of mood disorders were similar in both groups, suggesting that high-risk subjects were predisposed to schizophrenia in particular rather than to serious mental disorders in general.

The most important data in this project involve factors that may precede the onset of schizophrenic symptoms. Several intriguing findings have been reported. For example, researchers noted a correlation between delivery complications and enlarged ventricles among people in the high-risk group but not among people in the low-risk group (Cannon et al., 1993). In addition, an earlier report indicated that, in comparison to high-risk subjects who did not become schizophrenic, those high-risk individuals

---

[†] Two of the low-risk subjects have developed schizophrenia. One of these people had a mother who developed a paranoid psychosis after the study began. That person would have been excluded from the low-risk group if the mother's condition had been diagnosed earlier.

who did develop schizophrenia had experienced more pregnancy and birth complications (Cannon, Mednick, & Parnas, 1990). This was especially true for people who developed negative symptoms of the disorder. Thus far, the overall pattern of results suggests that vulnerability to schizophrenia may be associated with a pattern of fetal brain development that is especially sensitive to disruptions caused by delivery complications. The *combination* of genetic risk and problems in delivery seems to be especially relevant. Data from the Danish high-risk project are also consistent with the hypothesis that neurodevelopmental problems in schizophrenia are antecedents rather than consequences of the disorder. ■

than a group of normal control subjects, but these abnormalities were less marked than those found in the probands. Among discordant MZ pairs, the schizophrenic twin typically had the

▲ PET scanning procedures are being used extensively in an effort to identify neurological correlates of schizophrenia.

smaller hippocampus and smaller amygdala. The schizophrenic twins always showed reduced frontal lobe rCBF activity compared with their unaffected co-twins. Results for enlarged ventricles were less consistent. In general, neurological dysfunction seemed to be associated with the overall severity of the disorder rather than being indicative of an etiologically distinct subgroup of patients (Torrey et al., 1994).

General Conclusions The primary conclusion that can be drawn from existing brain imaging studies is that schizophrenia is associated with diffuse patterns of neuropathology. A specific brain lesion has not been identified, and it is unlikely that one will be found. As Meehl (1990) has argued, it is unlikely that a disorder as complex as schizophrenia will be traced to a single site in the brain. The various symptoms and cognitive deficits that have been observed in schizophrenic patients may be linked to a host of subtle disruptions in neurological functions (M. Strauss, 1993).

Evidence of neuropathology does not seem to be unique to schizophrenic patients. Many patients with other psychiatric and neurological disorders show similar changes in brain structure in function (Raz & Raz, 1990).

In the light of all the research findings, it should also be emphasized that brain imaging procedures are not diagnostically meaningful tests for mental disorders. For example, a CT scan showing enlarged ventricles does not prove that a patient is schizophrenic. Brain imaging procedures have identified interesting *group* differences, but they do not predict the presence of schizophrenia for *individuals*. The group differences that have been observed are quite subtle in comparison to the levels of neuropathology found in disorders such as Alzheimer's disease and Huntington's disease (see Chapter 13). Some schizophrenic patients do not show abnormalities in brain structure or function.

A dramatic example of this point was found in the NIMH study of discordant MZ twins. In one pair, the well twin was a successful businessman who had never had any problems with mental disorder. His twin brother had been severely impaired with schizophrenia for 20 years. The well twin had ventricles that were five times larger than those of the schizophrenic twin. Thus, we should approach all these hypotheses with caution and skepticism.

NEUROCHEMISTRY

The neurological underpinnings of schizophrenia may not take the form of changes in the size or organization of brain structures. They may be even more subtle, involving alterations in the functioning of particular parts of the brain. As we saw in Chapter 2, the process of chemical transmission in the brain is an active, dynamic system. Neurons regulate the synthesis and release of neurotransmitters as they monitor levels of these chemicals in the system. Too much dopamine in the synapse can result in decreased synthesis in the cell body. Similarly, insufficient amounts of dopamine can result in the synthesis of extra postsynaptic receptors. The significance of these dynamic properties is important to understanding the way in which antipsychotic drugs affect abnormal behavior.

The Dopamine Hypothesis of Schizophrenia
Various neurochemical theories have been proposed to account for the etiology of schizophrenia (Meltzer, 1987). The most influential theory, known as the *dopamine hypothesis*, focuses on the function of specific dopamine pathways in the limbic area of the brain. The dopamine hypothesis grew out of attempts to understand how antipsychotic drugs, also known as *neuroleptics*, improve the adjustment of many schizophrenic patients. Neuroscientists discovered that animals who received doses of neuroleptic drugs showed a marked increase in the production of dopamine. In 1963, Arvid Carlsson, a Swedish pharmacologist, suggested that neuroleptics block postsynaptic dopamine receptors. The presynaptic neuron recognizes the presence of this blockade and increases its release of dopamine in a futile attempt to override it.

Further support for the dopamine hypothesis came from two additional observations. First, patients who receive neuroleptic medication for an extended period of time often develop motor side effects that resemble the symptoms of Parkinson's disease, which is produced by the destruction of dopamine in certain brain pathways (see Chapter 13). It therefore seemed likely that schizophrenia was associated with an initially overactive dopamine system and that treatment with antipsychotic medication corrected this problem, sometimes to the point that Parkinsonlike symptoms were induced.

The second observation involves the effect of chronic amphetamine use. Amphetamine is a dopamine agonist. In other words, it is able to stimulate firing by dopamine neurons. People who take amphetamines for an extended period of time often develop a form of paranoid psychosis that is very similar to schizophrenia. This suggests that the natural form of schizophrenia may also be associated with overactivity in these neural pathways. All these observations are consistent with the general premise of the dopamine hypothesis.

If the dopamine system is dysfunctional in schizophrenic patients, what is the specific form of this problem? One possibility that has received a great deal of attention in the past few years is concerned with the number of postsynaptic dopamine receptors. Studies have established that the potency of various types of antipsychotic drugs is specifically related to their ability to block one type of dopamine receptor, known as D_2 receptors (Creese, Burt, & Snyder, 1978). Autopsy studies of schizophrenics' brains have found that some patients have an excessive number of D_2 receptors in the striatum, while the number of D_1 receptors is apparently normal (Kornhuber et al., 1989).

With regard to etiology, the most important question is whether an increased number of D_2 receptors is present before schizophrenic patients are treated with neuroleptic medication. Treatment with antipsychotic drugs produces an increase in the number of D_2 receptors. Two laboratories are currently studying this problem using PET to examine the brains of schizophrenic patients who have never received antipsychotic drugs. These studies are obviously very difficult to do because untreated patients are extremely rare, and PET is available only at a small number of research facilities. Investigators at Johns Hopkins Medical School found that schizophrenic patients had significantly more D_2 receptors than a group of normal volunteers (Wong et al., 1986). Another research team at the Karolinska Institute in Sweden, however, found no difference in D_2 receptor density between patients and controls (Farde et al., 1990).

This discrepancy may be due to differences in the details of the PET procedures employed by the two labs. Differences between the patient samples in the two studies may also be important. In comparison with the Swedish patients, those in the study at Johns Hopkins had shown signs of schizophrenia for a longer period of time prior to being tested. This is extremely important research, but the issue remains unresolved (Sharif, Gewirtz, & Iqbal, 1993).

Current Neurochemical Models The original dopamine hypothesis stimulated an enormous amount of research, and it has been an extremely useful model from that point of view. At least for some patients, a dysfunction of certain dopamine tracts in the brain is somehow involved in the disorder. On the other hand, biologically minded investigators now generally agree that this model was too simple. It failed to account for many different aspects of the disorder, including the following: Some patients do not respond positively to drugs that block dopamine receptors; the effects of antipsychotic drugs require several days to become effective, but dopamine blockage begins immediately; research studies that examined the byproducts of dopamine in cerebrospinal fluid were inconclusive at best.

One way to explain some of the inconsistencies regarding the dopamine hypothesis is to assume that a dopamine abnormality is present only in a certain subset of schizophrenic patients. According to one hypothesis, an increased density of D_2 receptors is involved in the development of a form of schizophrenia in which positive symptoms predominate (Crow, 1980; 1985). This hypothesis was based, in large part, on evidence that neuroleptic medication has a more beneficial effect on positive symptoms than on negative symptoms. Another form of schizophrenia, which is characterized by negative symptoms, is presumably caused by cell loss and structural damage in the brain. This proposal has inspired several research programs, but most of the results have been inconsistent with its predictions. Some studies have found, for example, that problems associated with dopaminergic pathways in the brain are found among patients with negative symptoms as well as in those with positive symptoms (Meltzer, 1992). The bulk of the evidence indicates that these are not independent syndromes.

Current neurochemical hypotheses regarding schizophrenia focus on a broad array of neurotransmitters, including GABA, acetylcholine, serotonin, and neuropeptides. Special interest has been focused on serotonin pathways since the introduction of a new class of antipsychotic drugs such as clozapine (Clozaril) that have beneficial effects on both positive and negative symptoms and are useful in treating patients who were resistant to traditional neuroleptic drugs. (See our later section on treatment.) These "atypical" antipsychotics apparently work by producing a strong blockade of serotonin receptors and only a weak blockade of D_2 receptors (Meltzer, 1993). This pattern leads to speculation that the neurochemical substrates of schizophrenia may involve a complex interaction between serotonin and dopamine pathways in the brain.

Social Factors

There is little question that biological factors play an important role in the etiology of schizophrenia, but twin studies also provide compelling evidence for the importance of environmental events. The disorder is expressed in its full-blown form only when vulnerable individuals experience some type of environmental event, which might include anything from nutritional variables to stressful life events (Fowles, 1992). What sorts of nongenetic events interact with genetic factors to produce schizophrenia? Specific answers are not available at the present time. We can, however, review some of the hypotheses that have been proposed and studied in previous investigations.

SOCIAL CLASS

One general indicator of a person's status within a community's hierarchy of prestige and influence is social class. People from different social classes are presumably exposed to different levels of environmental stress, with those people in the lowest class being subjected to the most hardships. More than 50 years ago, social scientists working in Chicago found that the highest prevalence of schizophrenia was found in neighborhoods of the lowest socioeconomic status (Faris & Dunham, 1939). Many additional research studies have subsequently confirmed this finding in several other geographic areas (Neale & Oltmanns, 1980). The evidence supporting an inverse relationship between social class and schizophrenia is rather substantial.

There are two ways to interpret the relationship between social class and schizophrenia. One holds that harmful events associated with membership in the lowest social classes, which might include many factors ranging from stress and social isolation to poor nutrition, play a causal role in the development of the disorder. This is often called the *social causation hypothesis*. It is also possible, however, that low social class is an outcome rather than a cause of schizophrenia. Those people who become schizophrenic may be less able than others to complete a higher-level education or hold a well-paying job. Their cognitive and social impairments may cause downward social mobility. In other words, regardless of the social class of their family of origin, many schizophrenic patients may gradually drift into the lowest social classes. This view is sometimes called the *social selection hypothesis*.

Research studies that have compared these alternative views have found evidence supporting both types of influence. The social selection hypothesis is supported by studies that have compared the occupational roles of male schizophrenic patients with those of their fathers. The patients are frequently less successful than their fathers, whereas the opposite pattern is typical of men who do not have schizophrenia (Goldberg & Morrison, 1963). It is also true, however, that a disproportionately high percentage of the fathers of schizophrenic patients were from the lowest social class (Turner & Wagonfeld, 1967). The latter finding is consistent with the social causation hypothesis.

Another research strategy that has been used to address the social causation and social selection hypotheses involves the simultaneous consideration of both social class and ethnic background. One study examined the relationship between social class and schizophrenia in two different ethnic groups in Israel: people with a European background and recent immigrants from North Africa and the Middle East (Dohrenwend et al., 1992). People in the latter category are subject to higher levels of prejudice and discrimination, *regardless of their social class*. The social causation hypothesis would therefore predict that the ethnic minority group would have higher rates of schizophrenia at all social class levels. Contrary to this prediction, rates of schizophrenia were actually found to be higher in the advantaged ethnic group. These results support the social selection model.

Support for the social causation hypothesis has been found using different research strategies. For example, one unique study considered the relation between economic conditions (employment rates) and rates of psychiatric hospitalization in the state of New York between 1852 and 1967 (Brenner, 1973). Throughout this extended period of time, increases in the rate of unemployment were followed closely, usually within a year, by sharp increases in the number of patients admitted to mental hospitals. The strongest relationship was found for schizophrenia and bipolar mood disorders. If we assume that the rate of hospitalization is a reflection of the incidence of these problems in the community, then these data support the social causation hypothesis.

In general, the evidence regarding socioeconomic status and schizophrenia indicates that the disorder is, to a certain extent, influenced by social factors. Adverse social and economic circumstances may increase the probability that persons who are genetically predisposed to the disorder will develop its clinical symptoms. The literature on social class has identified this relationship in very general terms. Some of the specific details have been examined in studies that are considered in the next section of this chapter.

Psychological Factors

Psychodynamic views of psychopathology encouraged the consideration of family interactions and patterns of interpersonal communication in the etiology of schizophrenia. Several clinicians proposed that schizophrenia was caused by deviant patterns of interaction between patients and their parents, typically while the patient was still a small child. These hypotheses were particularly popular in the United States during the 1950s and 1960s. Variations on this general theme were widely cited and became the subject of numerous empirical investigations (Jacob, 1975; Goldstein, 1988).

FAMILY INTERACTION

One particularly influential hypothesis was advanced by Lyman Wynne and Margaret Singer (1963), who were concerned with the relationship between thought disorder in young schizophrenic patients and communication problems exhibited by their parents. Wynne and Singer proposed that the parents of schizophrenics are often unable to communicate clearly. This deficiency results in disrupted conversations and confusion on the part of their intended listener, most often the child. Wynne and Singer argued that the child is caught between parents who are locked in conflict, and subsequently fails to develop either a secure identity or conventional forms of thinking and speaking. These problems eventually result in the onset of schizophrenic symptoms.

Wynne and Singer's hypothesis and related ideas were tested extensively during the 1960s and 1970s. Some investigators approached the problem by bringing young schizophrenic patients and their parents into a laboratory and directly observing the manner in which they communicated with one another (Mishler & Waxler, 1968). Results typically indicated that schizophrenics' families communicated less effectively than did the families of control subjects.

Wynne and Singer used a somewhat different method. Rather than observing parent–child interactions directly, they studied the parents' cognitive and linguistic abilities by examining their responses to standard psychological tests, most often the Rorschach test and the Thematic Apperception Test (TAT; see Chapter 4). Wynne and Singer asked the parents to interpret ambiguous stimuli such as ink blots. They then scored the responses for various forms of *communication deviance* (CD), such as peculiar statements, difficulty completing answers, and other types of disruptive verbal behavior during the test.

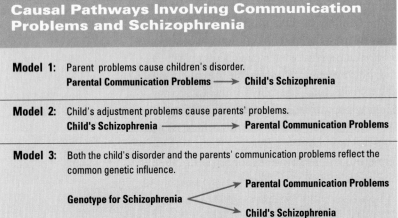

Causal Pathways Involving Communication Problems and Schizophrenia

Model 1: Parent problems cause children's disorder.
Parental Communication Problems ⟶ Child's Schizophrenia

Model 2: Child's adjustment problems cause parents' problems.
Child's Schizophrenia ⟶ Parental Communication Problems

Model 3: Both the child's disorder and the parents' communication problems reflect the common genetic influence.
Genotype for Schizophrenia ⟶ Parental Communication Problems
Genotype for Schizophrenia ⟶ Child's Schizophrenia

FIGURE 12-3: Research has indicated that communication problems between parents are related to schizophrenia among their children, but the nature of this relationship remains unclear. This figure illustrates three possible explanations for this relationship.

Consistent with their hypothesis, Singer and Wynne (1965) found that the parents of offspring with schizophrenia produced more instances of CD than did the parents of adolescents without mental disorders or the parents of offspring with other forms of psychological disturbance, such as borderline personality or anxiety disorders.

Family communication problems appear to be related to schizophrenia, but do these difficulties play a causal role in the onset of the disorder? Most of the data are correlational in nature: Schizophrenic patients tend to have parents who perform in an unusual way on psychological tasks, and vice versa. The direction of this relationship is unclear: Figure 12–3 illustrates several possible explanations. Singer and Wynne's data might indicate that subtle communication impairment among the parents may eventually cause their children to develop schizophrenia (Model 1 in Figure 12–3). Later studies also found, however, that parents of schizophrenic patients do not communicate in an unusual way when they are observed interacting with their offspring who did not become schizophrenic. Furthermore, parents whose offspring are all normal will also begin to exhibit communication problems if they interact with a schizophrenic patient in a laboratory setting (Liem, 1974). This pattern suggests that the children influence their parents, rather than the other way around (Model 2 in Figure 12–3).

A third explanation suggests that problems in verbal communication are symptoms of the genetically transmitted predisposition to schizophrenia, as Meehl's theory would suggest (Meehl, 1962, 1990). If that is the case, many of the patients' parents would speak in a disorganized or confusing way because they are predisposed to schizophrenia, even though they have not developed the full-blown disorder (Model 3 in Figure 12–3). According to this interpretation, the parents' communication problems may not directly influence the development of their children's disorder.

More complex research strategies are required to distinguish among the pathways illustrated in Figure 12–3. For example, the first and third models could be compared using families like the ones in Heston's adoption study. If schizophrenia is produced by exposure to deviant parental communication, then the adoptive parents of people who develop schizophrenia should exhibit problems similar to those that Singer and Wynne observed among the biological parents of schizophrenic patients. On the other hand, if high levels of CD reflect a genetically determined vulnerability to the disorder, then the speech of the adoptive parents should not differ from that of parents of normal offspring; communication problems would be most common among the biological parents of the adoptees.

A large adoption study that is being conducted in Finland is concerned with issues of this sort. Pekka Tienari (1991), Lyman Wynne, and their colleagues have identified 144 people, called *index cases*, who were adopted away at an early age from parents with schizophrenia. All were born between the years 1960 and 1979. Their comparison group is composed of 178 people, called *control cases*, who were adopted away from parents who never had a psychotic disorder. The investigators used Singer and Wynne's assessment procedure to examine levels of communication deviance among the adoptive parents of these individuals. They combined that information with data collected in interviews with the adoptive parents to produce global ratings of each family's level of functioning. This study offers a unique opportunity to examine the possible interaction of genetic factors and environmental events. All the index cases are genetically vulnerable to the disorder. The probability that these people will develop schizophrenia can be evaluated as a function of the presence of communication problems in the adoptive parents.

Preliminary reports from the Finnish Adoptive Family Study indicate that 15 of the adoptees have some type of psychosis: 13 of these people are the offspring of mothers with schizophrenia, and 2 were in the control group[†] (Tienari, 1991; Tienari et al., 1987). This pattern is consistent with earlier adoption studies, reflecting a genetically determined predisposition to the disorder. Tienari also found that, among those who were genetically predisposed, the people who became psychotic were most often those whose adoptive families were also rated as being disturbed. Very few cases of severe psychopathology were found among the people who were raised by healthy adoptive families, regardless of whether their biological mothers had schizophrenia. In other words, the *combination* of genetic and environmental factors seems to be especially harmful.

These results must be viewed with caution. By the time the investigators conducted their initial assessments of the adoptive families, some of the index cases had already become psychotic. In these cases, either of the first two models in Figure 12–3 provides a plausible explanation

of the relation between family disturbance and mental disorders in their offspring. Tienari's data cannot be explained in terms of the third model in the figure because the adoptive parents were no more genetically predisposed to the disorder than were people in the general population. The most important part of the Finnish Adoptive Family Study remains to be completed. The youngest adoptees had not entered the primary age of risk for schizophrenia when the family assessments were completed. These subjects are now being followed prospectively. The longitudinal data from this part of the study will address the distinction between models 1 and 2 in Figure 12–3 because the investigators will be able to determine whether the parents' communication problems appeared *before* the onset of psychopathology in their adoptive children.

EXPRESSED EMOTION

A considerable body of research indicates that the family environment has a significant impact on the course (as opposed to the etiology) of schizophrenia. These studies do not address the original onset of symptoms. Instead, they are concerned with the posttreatment adjustment of patients who have already exhibited schizophrenic symptoms.

The original observations in this area were reported by George Brown, John Wing, and their colleagues at the University of London. Their early studies, conducted during the 1950s, were concerned with the adjustment of schizophrenic patients who were discharged after being treated in a psychiatric hospital for at least 2 years. The investigators found that men with schizophrenia were much more likely to return to the hospital within the next 9 months if they went to live with their wives or parents than if they went to live in other lodgings or with their siblings. Furthermore, patients who returned to live with their mothers were particularly likely to relapse if both they and their mothers were unemployed. Although these results could be interpreted in a number of ways, the investigators chose to focus on the effects of interpersonal interactions. More specifically, they hypothesized that many of the patients who relapsed were reacting negatively to some feature of their close relationship with their wives

---

[†] Within the group of 13 index cases who had become psychotic, 7 were diagnosed with schizophrenia, 2 with schizophreniform disorder, 2 with delusional disorder, and 2 with bipolar mood disorder with psychotic features.

or mothers. The data suggested that the family environment had an effect on the course of the patient's disorder.

Subsequent research by the same group confirmed this initial impression (Brown, Birley, & Wing, 1972; Vaughn & Leff, 1976). These studies were particularly important because they assessed the emotional characteristics of the family directly and followed the patients' adjustment prospectively for a period of several months. The investigators interviewed relatives of schizophrenic patients prior to the patient's discharge from the hospital. Many of the relatives expressed hostility toward the patient or repeatedly criticized the patient's behavior. Others appeared to be overprotective or too closely identified with the patient. This general collection of negative or intrusive attitudes was referred to as **expressed emotion** (EE). If at least one of a patient's relatives was hostile, critical, or emotionally overinvolved, the family environment was considered *high in expressed emotion.* Patients who returned to live in a home with at least one member who was high in EE had a 51 percent relapse rate in

the first 9 months after discharge. Only 13 percent of the patients from low EE homes relapsed during the same period of time.

This result has been replicated many times as investigators have gradually expanded our understanding of this phenomenon. More than 20 studies have been conducted in several different countries. Average relapse rates—defined primarily in terms of the proportion of patients who show a marked exacerbation of positive symptoms in the first 9 to 12 months following hospital discharge—are 48 percent for patients in high EE families and 21 percent for patients in low EE families (Kavanagh, 1992). Among the various types of comments that can contribute to a high EE rating, criticism is usually most strongly related to patients' relapse. Observations of family interaction have shown that relatives who express hostility or criticism during an assessment interview with the research team also make more critical comments directly to the patient (Miklowitz et al., 1984).

The influence of expressed emotion is not unique to schizophrenia. Patients with unipolar

---

RESEARCH METHODS

Comparison Groups in Psychopathology Research

Research studies in the field of psychopathology typically involve comparisons among two or more groups of subjects. One group, sometimes called "cases," includes people who already meet the diagnostic criteria for a particular mental disorder, such as schizophrenia. Comparison groups are composed of people who do not have the disorder in question.[†] If the investigators find a significant difference between groups, they have demonstrated that the dependent variable is *correlated* with the disorder (see Research Methods in Chapter 2). They often hope to conclude that they have identified a variable that is relevant to understanding the etiology of this condition. Causal inferences are risky, however, in correlational research. Our willingness to accept these conclusions hinges

in large part on whether the investigators selected an appropriate comparison group.

The goal, in principle, is to identify and test a group of people who are just like the cases *except* that they do not have the disorder in question (Gehlbach, 1988). This typically means that the people in both groups should be similar with regard to such obvious factors as age, gender, and socioeconomic background. If the investigators find differences between people who have the disorder and those who do not, they want to attribute them to the disorder itself. Two main types of comparison groups are used in psychopathology research: people with no history of mental disorder, sometimes called "normal subjects," and people who have some other form of mental disorder, sometimes called "patient controls."

[†] This procedure is sometimes called the *case-control design* because it depends on a contrast between cases (people who already have the disorder) and control subjects.

Several interesting problems may arise in the selection of normal people for psychopathology research. Who are the so-called normal subjects? For example, brain-imaging studies of neuropathology in schizophrenia have sometimes used medical patients as normal subjects because it is difficult to justify exposing others to radiation simply for the purposes of comparison. The medical patients may include people who have been referred for a neurological assessment because of frequent headaches. Despite their somatic complaints, the medical patients have no history of schizophrenic symptoms or other psychopathology. Suppose the investigators find that schizophrenic patients have enlarged lateral ventricles in comparison to these medical patients? Does that mean that the ventricles of the schizophrenic patients are indeed enlarged relative to some absolute normal standard? Or does it mean that the ventricles of the medical patients are smaller than expected in the general population (Smith et al., 1988)?

Considerable attention is usually devoted to the criteria that are used for identifying patient groups in psychopathology research, but close scrutiny must also be given to the rationale for selecting normal comparison groups (Kendler, 1990). Does normal mean that the person has never had the disorder in question? Or does it mean a complete absence of any type of psychopathology? Should people be included as normal control subjects if they have a family history of the disorder, even though they do not have the disorder themselves?

The second research strategy involves the comparison of patients with one type of disorder to those who have another form of psychopathology. Investigators usually employ this design to determine whether the variable in question is specifically related to the disorder that they are studying. Are enlarged lateral ventricles or family communication problems unique to people with schizophrenia? Lack of specificity may raise questions about whether this variable is related to the cause of the disorder. It might suggest that this particular variable is, instead, a general consequence of factors such as hospitalization, which the patient control group has also experienced. Lack of specificity also raises questions about the role of the dependent variable in the etiology of the disorder in question.

In the case of schizophrenia research, many of the etiological variables that we have already discussed are not uniquely related to the disorder. Expressed emotion predicts relapse among patients with mood disorders as well as in those with schizophrenia. Should this result be taken to mean that EE does not play an important role in the etiology of schizophrenia? Not necessarily. The answer to this question depends upon the specific causal model that is being considered (Garber & Hollon, 1991). All forms of psychopathology depend on the interaction of multiple factors spanning biological, social, and psychological systems. Some of these may be specific, and others may be general. The development of schizophrenia may depend upon a specific genetically determined predisposition. The environmental events that are responsible for eventually causing vulnerable people to express this disorder might be nonspecific. The course of schizophrenia is clearly influenced by the social context in which the patient lives. The fact that similar factors influence people with mood disorders should not be taken to mean that EE is not an important factor in the complex chain of events that explain the etiology and maintenance of schizophrenia.

Another thing to keep in mind is the overlap of symptoms among different categories of mental disorder. For example, people in a manic episode often exhibit forms of disorganized speech that are similar to those seen in schizophrenia. If patients from these two groups are found to have similar problems on a laboratory task of attentional processing, that task may be studied measuring a cognitive factor that is related to this specific symptom. For this reason, several investigators have advocated a research strategy that places greater emphasis on specific symptoms rather than heterogeneous diagnostic categories (Costello, 1993; Persons, 1986; Strauss, 1993).

For all of these reasons, the selection of meaningful comparison groups can be a complex and difficult process. There are no perfect solutions to these issues. The research strategy selected in any particular study will depend on the specific questions that the investigators are trying to answer. ■

and bipolar mood disorders are also more likely to relapse following discharge if they are living with a high EE relative (Hooley, 1986; Hooley & Teasdale, 1989; Miklowitz et al., 1988). The extension of this phenomenon to other disorders should not be taken to mean that it is unimportant or that the social context of the family is irrelevant to our understanding of the maintenance of schizophrenia (see Research Methods). It may indicate, however, that this aspect of the etiological model is shared with other forms of psychopathology. The specific shape of the person's symptoms may hinge on the genetic diathesis.

High EE seems to be related, at least in part, to relatives' knowledge and beliefs about their family member's problems. Relatives find it easier to accept positive symptoms as being the product of a mental disorder (Brewin et al., 1991). They show less tolerance toward negative symptoms, such as avolition and social withdrawal, perhaps because the patient may appear to be simply lazy or unmotivated. Fortunately, relatives' negative attitudes can change. Ratings of relatives' EE can fluctuate over time and are often highest while the patient is hospitalized. Six months after the patient's discharge, roughly half of the people who were originally rated as being high EE are considered to be low EE (Leff et al., 1990).

Cross-cultural studies suggest that high EE may be more common in Western or developed countries than in non-Western or developing countries. This observation might help explain why the long-term course of schizophrenia is typically less severe in developing countries (Jablensky et al., 1992). Speculation has focused on the possibility that people in developing countries may be more tolerant of eccentric behavior among their extended family members (Kuipers & Bebbington, 1988; Lefley, 1992). These attitudes may create environments similar to those found in low EE homes in the West.

We must be cautious to avoid a narrow view of this phenomenon. The EE studies raise extremely sensitive issues for family members, who have too frequently been blamed for the problems of people with schizophrenia. Expressed emotion is not the only factor that can influence the course of a schizophrenic disorder. Some patients relapse in spite of an understanding, tolerant family environment. Furthermore, research studies have shown that the relationship between patients' behavior and relatives' expressed emotion is a

transactional or reciprocal process. In other words, patients influence their relatives' attitudes at the same time that relatives' attitudes influence the patient's adjustment. Persistent negative attitudes on the part of patient's relatives appear to be perpetuated by a negative cycle of interactions in which the patient plays an active role (Cook et al., 1989; Miklowitz et al., 1989).

The EE concept has stimulated a great deal of research on the family and schizophrenia (Hooley, 1985; Kuipers, 1992). Interest in EE has inspired innovative psychosocial treatment programs aimed at the family context in which schizophrenia is treated (see later section on treatment). Although the emotional climate of the family may not have an important effect on the original development of schizophrenia, it is clearly one factor that can influence the course of the disorder. EE has been a broadly defined concept that includes many different attitudes and behaviors, ranging from hostility and criticism to emotional overinvolvement. One goal of current and future research is to employ measures that will help us to understand more specific components of family dynamics and the pathways by which they combine with other factors to influence the patient's adjustment (Halford, 1991; Nuechterlein et al., 1992).

The Search for Markers of Vulnerability

Research evidence regarding the etiology of schizophrenia indicates that the disorder is most likely produced by a combination of events and circumstances. Some people apparently inherit a predisposition to the disorder. It would obviously be useful to be able to identify those people. Genetic linkage studies may provide the answer, if one gene (or a small set of genes) is found to be responsible for the disorder. But that possibility is open to question. If we are looking for observable signs of vulnerability that can be detected among individuals who are genetically predisposed to schizophrenia, where should we look? What form will these signs take? This issue has attracted considerable attention, but we don't have any firm answers to these questions.

According to Meehl's theoretical model, people who are vulnerable to schizophrenia might be detected by developing measures that could detect the underlying biological dysfunction (schizotaxia) or by developing sensitive measures of their subtle eccentricities of behavior (schizotypy). The range of possible markers is therefore quite large.

Assume that we have selected a specific measure, such as a biochemical assay or a psychological test, and we are interested in knowing whether it might be useful in identifying people who are vulnerable to schizophrenia. What criteria should a **vulnerability marker** fulfill? First, the proposed marker must distinguish between people who are already schizophrenic and those who are not. Second, it should be a stable characteristic over time. The more dramatic, psychotic symptoms of schizophrenia may come and go over the person's lifetime, but vulnerability is presumably a persistent trait that is present on a continuous basis. Third, the proposed measure of vulnerability should identify more people among the biological relatives of schizophrenic patients than among people in the general population. For example, it should be found among the discordant MZ twins of schizophrenic patients, even if they don't exhibit any symptoms of schizophrenia. Fourth, the trait measured by the test should be transmitted genetically. Finally, the proposed measure of vulnerability should be able to predict the future development of schizophrenia among those who have not yet experienced a psychotic episode (Iacono & Clementz, 1993; Meehl, 1990; Zubin & Spring, 1977).

Although reliable measures of vulnerability have not been identified, they are being actively pursued by many investigators with a wide variety of measurement procedures. In the following pages, we will outline some of the psychological procedures that have been shown to be among the most promising possibilities.

Attention and Cognition

Many investigators have pursued the search for signs of vulnerability by looking at measures of performance in which schizophrenics differ from other people. Some of these studies have focused on cognitive tasks that evaluate information-processing abilities and selective attention. The assumption that cognitive factors are central to this disorder can be traced to Bleuler's original suggestion that the disorder should be defined in terms of a splitting of mental functions.

One important set of results regarding attentional dysfunction is based on use of the Continuous Performance Task (CPT). In one version of this task, the subject is required to pick out a letter or sequence of letters from among a larger sequence of letters that is presented very briefly (less than 1 second per letter) on a computer screen. Whenever the subject notices the target, he or she is supposed to press a button. Several dependent measures can be collected using this procedure, including the number of correct button presses, the number of times the button was pressed when the target was not present, and the number of times the button was not pressed when the target was present.

Numerous studies have demonstrated that schizophrenic patients are less accurate than normal subjects and other psychiatric patients in their performance on the CPT (Nuechterlein, 1991). This seems to be a stable characteristic that does not fluctuate over time. Furthermore, the attentional deficits tapped by the CPT are found with increased prevalence among the unaffected first-degree relatives of schizophrenic persons (Grove et al., 1991, Lenzenweger et al., 1991).

Especially intriguing are the results of studies that have examined the performance of children with a biological parent who is schizophrenic. Many offspring of schizophrenic parents exhibit problems on the CPT that are similar to those seen in adult patients (Erlenmeyer-Kimling & Cornblatt, 1992). There is also some reason to believe that this problem may be specific to schizophrenia, because it is not as common among the offspring of mothers with mood disorders or among hyperactive children (Nuechterlein, 1984). Finally, within a group of children of schizophrenic parents, those who exhibited attentional deficits at approximately 10 years of age were more likely to develop maladaptive personality traits, such as social insensitivity and social indifference, in early adulthood (Cornblatt, Lenzenweger, Dworkin, & Erlenmeyer-Kimling, 1992). The CPT measure appears to fulfill several of the criteria for an index of vulnerability. The research results support the possibility that measures of attentional problems may be useful signs of vulnerability to schizophrenia.

Eye-Tracking Dysfunction

Another promising line of exploration involves impairments in eye movements—specifically, difficulty in tracking the motion of a pendulum or a similarly oscillating stimulus. The original

▼ This woman is attached to equipment used to record smooth pursuit eye movements. Sensors inside the helmet are positioned in front of her right eye. Eye movements are recorded while she watches a dot of light move back and forth on a computer screen. The electronic equipment behind her is used to record and amplify the ocular signals.

observations of this phenomenon were reported shortly after the turn of the century (Diefendorf & Dodge, 1908) and were mentioned by Kraepelin in his influential textbook on psychiatry. The finding soon fell into obscurity, however, until it was rediscovered in the early 1970s by Philip Holzman, who is now a psychologist at Harvard University.

When people with schizophrenia are asked to track a moving target, like an oscillating pendulum, with their eyes, a substantial number of them show dysfunctions in smooth-pursuit eye movement (Holzman, 1985; Levy, Holzman, Matthysse, & Mendell, 1993). Instead of reproducing the motion of the pendulum in a series of smooth waves, their tracking records show frequent interruptions of smooth-pursuit movements by numerous rapid movements. Examples of normal tracking records and those of schizo-

phrenic patients are presented in Figure 12–4. Only about 8 percent of normal people exhibit the eye-tracking dysfunctions illustrated in part (c) of Figure 12–4, although some studies have reported higher figures (Scarone et al., 1987).

The fascinating part of the eye-tracking story involves the performance of family members of people with schizophrenia. Approximately 50 percent of the first-degree relatives of schizophrenic persons show similar smooth-pursuit impairments (Holzman et al., 1984). Although the same eye movement problems are seen in many patients with bipolar affective disorder, only 10 percent of their parents exhibit eye-tracking dysfunctions, and the eye-tracking problems of the patients themselves appear to be side effects of treatment with lithium carbonate. The overall pattern of results seen in people with schizophrenia and their families suggests that poor tracking performance may be associated with the predisposition to schizophrenia. That conclusion becomes even more interesting in light of evidence from additional studies suggesting that tracking ability is influenced by genetic factors and is apparently a stable trait (Iacono & Clementz, 1993).

Several other interesting patterns have emerged from an extended program of eye-tracking research conducted by University of Minnesota psychologists William Iacono, William Grove, and Brett Clementz (Clementz et al., 1992; Iacono et al., 1992). Eye-tracking dysfunction is not found in all individuals with schizophrenia. Rather, it is present in 50 percent to 60 percent of all families in which at least one person has the disorder. Among those families in which eye-tracking problems have been identified, smooth-pursuit impairments tend to be found among those relatives who also exhibit schizotypic signs, such as odd interpersonal behaviors, and who perform deviantly on the CPT (Grove et al., 1991). These findings led Iacono and Grove (1993) to suggest that eye-tracking problems and attentional impairment are markers for one form of schizophrenia, which accounts for approximately half of all cases of this disorder. According to this model, in patients whose families do not exhibit eye-tracking anomalies, schizophrenia is caused by a different etiological mechanism.

How are abnormalities in smooth-pursuit eye movements related to the symptoms of schizophrenia? The answer is not clear. Current spec-

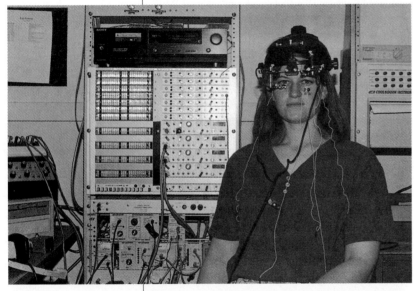

Eye-Tracking Patterns

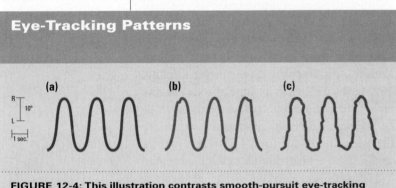

FIGURE 12-4: This illustration contrasts smooth-pursuit eye-tracking patterns of normal subjects with those of schizophrenic patients. Part (a) shows the actual target. Part (b) illustrates the pattern of normal subjects, and part (c) shows the pattern for people with schizophrenia.

From D.L. Levy, et al. 1993. Eye-tracking dysfunction and schizophrenia: A critical perspective. *Schizophrenia Bulletin, 19,* 462.

ulation suggests that they may be manifestations of neurological problems located in the frontal lobes of the cerebral cortex (Katsanis & Iacono, 1991; Levin, 1984).

It is not yet possible to identify people who are specifically predisposed to the development of schizophrenia, but research studies have identified potential vulnerability markers. The real test, of course, will center around predictive validity. Can any of these measures, such as smooth-pursuit eye-tracking impairment or attentional dysfunction, predict the later appearance of schizophrenia in people whose scores indicate possible vulnerability? High-risk stud-

ies will be useful in providing this type of evidence (see Research Close-up).

If valid vulnerability markers can be found, clinical scientists may be able to design early treatment programs that prevent the eventual onset of full-blown schizophrenic symptoms. Until that time, treatment efforts must be directed toward the resolution of acute episodes of the disorder, reducing the frequency and severity of relapse, and improving the level of functioning among patients in the residual phase of schizophrenia. We review these possibilities in the next section.

Treatment

Schizophrenia is a complex disorder that must often be treated over an extended period of time. Clinicians must be concerned about the treatment of acute psychotic episodes as well as the prevention of future episodes. A multifaceted approach to treatment is typically required. Neuroleptic medication is the primary mode of treatment for this disorder. Because many patients remain impaired between episodes, long-term care must often involve the provision of housing and social support. People with impaired occupational and social skills need special types of training. The treatment of schizophrenia requires attention on all of these fronts and is necessarily concerned with the cooperative efforts of many types of professionals.

Neuroleptic Medication

The antipsychotic properties of a class of drugs known as the *phenothiazines* were discovered quite accidentally in the early 1950s by a French neurosurgeon who was using them as a supplement to anesthesia. They were not effective for the purpose he intended, but they did have a calming effect on the patients. This experience prompted psychiatrists to try using the same drugs with their patients. Early reports of success treating

chronic psychotic patients quickly led to the widespread use of phenothiazines, such as chlorpromazine (Thorazine), in psychiatric hospitals throughout Europe and the United States. The discovery of these drugs quickly changed the way in which schizophrenia was treated. Large number of patients who had previously been institutionalized could be discharged to community care (but see Chapter 17 on the effects of deinstutionalization).

Several related types of drugs have been developed in subsequent years. They are called *antipsychotic drugs* because they have a relatively specific effect—to reduce the severity of, and sometimes eliminate, psychotic symptoms. Antipsychotics are also known as **neuroleptic** drugs[†] because they also induce side effects that resemble the motor symptoms of Parkinson's disease. Traditional forms of neuroleptic medication act by blocking D_2 dopamine receptors in the cortical and limbic areas of the brain (Marder et al., 1993). The antipsychotic efficacy of various types of neuroleptic drugs is directly proportional to their ability to block D_2 receptors. Animal studies demonstrating this effect provided the primary inspiration and best supporting evidence for the dopamine hypothesis of schizophrenia.

[†] The word neuroleptic is derived from the Greek, meaning "that takes hold of the nerves." It is defined operationally as drugs that produce a syndrome of side effects similar to those associated with chlorpromazine (Ellenbroek, 1993). The terms antipsychotic and neuroleptic are used interchangeably, but they do not have exactly the same meaning. Many newer forms of antipsychotic medication (usually called atypical neuroleptics) might not be neuroleptics from a technical standpoint because they do not produce motor side effects. We have decided to follow convention and use the term neuroleptic because it is most often used in the literature.

Beneficial effects are sometimes noticed within a week after the patient begins taking neuroleptics, but it often takes several weeks before improvement is seen. Among the traditional or standard types of neuroleptic medication, there is no convincing evidence to indicate that one is more effective than another (Kane & Marder, 1993). The possible exception to this conclusion involves clozapine (Clozaril), an atypical form of antipsychotic medication, to which we will return after a brief review of the traditional neuroleptics.

The enthusiasm that followed the introduction of neuroleptics was soon confirmed by double-blind, placebo-controlled studies that evaluated the effectiveness of antipsychotic drugs in the treatment of patients who are acutely psychotic. Literally thousands of studies have addressed this issue over a period of almost 40 years (Ellenbroek, 1993; Marder et al., 1993). One early study conducted by investigators at the National Institute of Mental Health still provides a good illustration of these outcome studies (Cole, 1964). More than 450 young, acutely disturbed schizophrenic patients participated in the study. Following hospital admission, they were randomly assigned to receive either neuroleptic medication or placebo. Treatment was continued for 6 weeks. Among the patients who received medication, 75 percent were rated as being either much improved or very much improved at the end of treatment. Only 35 percent of the placebo patients were improved to this same degree. These data and many subsequent studies provide compelling support for the effectiveness of neuroleptic medication.

Neuroleptic drugs may be more useful for certain types of symptoms than for others. Positive symptoms, such as hallucinations and disorganized speech, seem to respond better to medication than negative symptoms, such as alogia and blunted affect (Stahl & Wets, 1988). This differential effect is not entirely clear-cut, however. For example, some patients who are socially withdrawn become less isolated while they are taking neuroleptics (Meltzer, 1984).

▲ Lionel Aldridge was a defensive lineman for the Green Bay Packers when they won the first Super Bowl in 1965. He later developed schizophrenia. With the help of antipsychotic medication, his disorder is now in remission. Aldridge is a spokesman for the needs of people who suffer from schizophrenia.

Unfortunately, a substantial minority of schizophrenic patients—perhaps 25 percent—do not improve on neuroleptic medication (Davis & Casper, 1977; Lewander, 1992). Another 30 to 40 percent might be considered partial responders. These are people whose conditions improve but who do not show a full remission of symptoms. Investigators have been unable to identify reliable differences between patients who improve on medication and those who do not. Some people have suggested that the more severe the symptoms, the less the improvement brought about by medication (Farmer & Blewett, 1993).

SIDE EFFECTS

Several unpleasant side effects are associated with the use of most neuroleptic drugs. Many patients dislike taking medication because of these problems, and some discontinue pharmacologic treatment against their psychiatrist's advice. Side effects come in varying degrees and affect different patients in different ways. The most obvious and troublesome are called *extrapyramidal symptoms* (EPS) because they are mediated by the extrapyramidal neural pathways that connect the brain to the motor neurons in the spinal cord. These symptoms include an assortment of neurologic disturbances such as muscular rigidity, tremors, restless agitation, peculiar involuntary postures, and motor inertia. Some potent neuroleptics, such as haloperidol (Haldol) and fluphenazine (Prolixin), regularly produce more marked EPS than other neuroleptics, such as thioridazine (Mellaril). EPS may diminish spontaneously after 3 or 4 months of continuous treatment. Anticholinergic drugs can also be used to minimize the severity of EPS during the first few months of treatment. Unfortunately, some patients exhibit persistent signs of EPS in spite of these efforts.

Prolonged treatment with neuroleptic drugs frequently leads to the development of **tardive dyskinesia (TD)**. This syndrome consists of abnormal involuntary movements of the mouth and face, such as tongue protrusion, chewing, and lip-puckering, as well as spasmodic movements of the limbs and trunk of the body. The latter include writhing movements of the fingers and toes and leg jiggling as well as jerking movements of the head and pelvis. Taken as a whole, this problem is quite distressing to patients and their families. The TD syndrome is clearly induced by neuroleptic treatment, and it is irreversible in some patients, even after neuroleptics have been discontinued. In fact, some patients experience an exacerbation of TD if neuroleptic medication is withdrawn.

The incidence of TD increases steadily with continued use of neuroleptic medication. Roughly 5 percent of patients will develop TD during the first year of neuroleptic treatment. Another 5 percent of patients who continue to take neuroleptics on a continuous basis will develop the syndrome in each of the next few years. Approximately 25 percent of patients develop TD by the end of 6 years of treatment (Kane, Woerner, & Lieberman, 1988). Several studies have attempted to identify factors that increase a patient's risk of developing TD. Age is one important variable. Patients who are older than 40 are 3 times more likely to develop TD than are those under 40. There also appear to be gender differences in TD, with the prevalence being higher among women than among men (Jeste & Caligiuri, 1993).

MAINTENANCE MEDICATION

After patients recover from acute psychotic episodes, the probability that they will have another episode is still relatively high. The relapse rate may be as high as 65 to 70 percent in the first year after hospital discharge if patients discontinue medication. Continued neuroleptic treatment cannot prevent future episodes, but relapse rates can be reduced to approximately 40 percent with maintenance medication (Hogarty, 1993). Therefore, in spite of the increased risk of developing TD and the other unpleasant side effects of neuroleptics, the vast majority of schizophrenic patients continue to take medication after recovering from psychotic episodes. The need for maintenance medication is less clearly defined among patients who have had only one episode of schizophrenia. The relapse rate for these patients is lower than among those who have had multiple episodes.

Some patients who have had more than one psychotic episode can also avoid relapse without taking medication on a maintenance basis. Approximately 20 percent of chronic schizophrenic patients can avoid rehospitalization without taking neuroleptics and can function at least as well as they would on medication (Johnson, 1988). Unfortunately, we do not know how to distinguish these patients from those who do

need continued pharmacologic treatment, other than through trial and error.

Many psychiatrists recommend continuous maintenance treatment with low doses of neuroleptics. Research studies indicate that there are advantages and disadvantages associated with this approach. Patients on low-dose treatment programs have higher relapse rates than do patients receiving higher doses, but the low-dose patients also achieve better ratings on some measures of psychosocial adjustment, and they are also less impaired than high-dose patients in terms of ratings of blunted affect and motor retardation (Kane & Marder, 1993). The latter set of symptoms probably reflects increased levels of EPS among high-dose patients rather than lower levels of negative symptoms among low-dose patients. These trade-offs between high- and low-dose treatments obviously present difficult choices for patients and their psychiatrists.

ATYPICAL ANTIPSYCHOTICS

Some relatively new forms of antipsychotic medication are known as **atypical antipsychotics** because they do not produce EPS and may not be associated with increased risk of TD. In addition, at least 30 percent of schizophrenic patients who do not respond positively to classic neuroleptics improve after taking atypical antipsychotic drugs. Some studies have found that 50 to 60 percent of patients who were previously resistant to neuroleptic treatment improve in response to atypical antipsychotics (Breier et al., 1993; Farmer & Blewett, 1993). *Treatment resistance* is usually defined as failure to improve on at least three different types of classic neuroleptic medication after 6 weeks on moderate-to-high doses.

The best known of the atypical drugs, clozapine (Clozaril), was discovered in the 1970s and has been used extensively throughout Europe. Use of clozapine was delayed for several years in the United States because it can produce a lethal blood condition known as agranulocytosis in about 1 percent of patients (Lindenmayer, 1993). It was approved for use with treatment-resistant schizophrenic patients by the U.S. Food and Drug Administration in 1990, with the requirement that patients receive weekly monitoring of their white-blood-cell levels. Controlled-outcome studies indicate that clozapine has beneficial effects on positive symptoms of schizophrenia without inducing unpleasant motor side effects (Meltzer et al., 1990). Some reports have also noted improvements in negative symptoms among previously treatment-resistant patients, but this effect has not been found in other studies (Breier et al., 1993). Nevertheless, clozapine would probably be the treatment of choice for all schizophrenic patients if it were not for the risk of agranulocytosis (Kane & Marder, 1993).

Clozapine produces different neurochemical actions in the brain than do the classic neuroleptic drugs. It produces a relatively strong blockade of serotonin receptors and a relatively weak blockade of D_2 dopamine receptors (Meltzer, 1993). Its reduced affinity for dopamine receptors is presumably the reason for its failure to produce significant EPS. The fact that clozapine has well-documented beneficial effects for schizophrenic patients and that its site of action in the brain involves serotonin pathways has required important revisions to the original dopamine hypothesis.

GENERAL CONCLUSIONS

Classic and atypical forms of antipsychotic medication are perhaps the most important tools in the treatment of schizophrenia. The discovery of these drugs, and continued refinements in pharmacological treatment, have enabled many patients who formerly would have required hospitalization to be treated on an outpatient basis. In addition, these procedures and medications have raised the levels of functioning of many schizophrenic patients. The beneficial effects of medication, however, must be measured in the light of several limitations, including the production of unpleasant and occasionally incapacitating motor side effects by traditional forms of neuroleptics. The failure of many patients to respond to medication, either completely or at all, points to the need for additional forms of intervention.

Psychosocial Treatment

Several forms of psychological treatment have proved effective for schizophrenic patients. These procedures address a wide range of problems that are associated with the disorder. In contrast to pharmacological approaches, psychological approaches place relatively little emphasis on the treatment of acute psychotic episodes. Instead they concentrate on long-term strategies (Bellack & Mueser, 1993).

FAMILY-ORIENTED AFTERCARE

Studies of expressed emotion have inspired the development of innovative family-based treatment programs. Family treatment programs attempt to improve the coping skills of family members, recognizing the burdens that people often endure while caring for a family member with a chronic mental disorder. Patients are maintained on antipsychotic medication on an outpatient basis throughout this process. There are several different approaches to this type of family intervention. Most include an educational component that is designed to help family members understand and accept the nature of the disorder. One goal of this procedure is to eliminate unrealistic expectations for the patient, which may lead to harsh criticism. Behavioral family management also places considerable emphasis on the improvement of communication and problem-solving skills, which may enhance the family members' ability to work together and thereby minimize levels of conflict.

Several empirical studies have evaluated the effects of family interventions. Most have found dramatic reductions in relapse rates for people receiving family treatment. In the first year of treatment, relapse rates for patients who receive family treatment plus medication are typically below 20 percent, compared with 40 percent or 50 percent for those receiving medication alone (Hogarty, 1993; Lam, 1991). Relapse rates increase in the next year for both groups, with rates ranging from 17 percent to 44 percent for family interventions and 59 percent to 83 percent for control patients. Family-based treatment programs can delay relapse, but they do not necessarily prevent relapse in the long run. The beneficial effects of treatment may be lost shortly after treatment ends (Hogarty, 1993). In the case of a disorder such as schizophrenia, which is often chronic, treatment programs must be available to patients and their family members on a continuous basis.

SOCIAL SKILLS TRAINING

Many patients who avoid relapse and are able to remain in the community continue to be impaired in terms of residual symptoms. They also experience problems in social and occupational functioning. For these patients, drug therapy must be supplemented by psychosocial programs that address residual aspects of the disorder. The need to address these problems directly is supported by evidence that shows that deficits in social skills are relatively stable in schizophrenic patients and relatively independent of other aspects of the disorder, including both positive and negative symptoms (Mueser et al., 1991).

Social skills training (SST) is a structured, educational approach to these problems that involves modeling, role playing, and the provision of social reinforcement for appropriate behaviors (Liberman, DeRisi, & Mueser, 1989). Controlled-outcome studies indicate that, in combination with neuroleptic medication, SST leads to improved performance on measures of social adjustment. It is not clear, however, that SST has any beneficial effects on relapse rates (Bellack & Mueser, 1993). This may not be surprising in light of evidence regarding the course of this disorder, which suggests that various aspects of outcome, including symptom severity and social adjustment, tend to be relatively independent. Thus, this form of treatment should be provided to patients if it can address one dimension of their disorder.

INSTITUTIONAL PROGRAMS

Although schizophrenic persons can be treated with medication on an outpatient basis, various types of institutional care continue to be important. Most patients experience recurrent phases of active psychosis (Eaton et al., 1992). Brief periods of hospitalization (usually 2 or 3 weeks) are often beneficial during these times.

Some patients are chronically disturbed and require long-term institutional treatment. Social learning programs, sometimes called *token economies*, can be useful for these patients. In these programs, specific behavioral contingencies are put into place for all of the patients on a hospital ward. The goal is to increase the frequency of desired behaviors, such as appropriate grooming and participation in social activities, and to decrease the frequency of undesirable behaviors, such as violence or incoherent speech. Staff members monitor patients' behavior throughout the day. Each occurrence of a desired behavior is praised and reinforced by the presentation of a token, which can be exchanged for food or privileges, such as time to watch television. Inappropriate behaviors are typically ignored, but occasional punishment, such as loss of privileges, is used if necessary.

Psychologist Gordon Paul, now at the University of Houston, and his colleagues con-

ducted an extensive evaluation of behavioral treatment with chronic schizophrenic patients (Paul & Lentz, 1977). They compared two inpatient programs in the treatment of severely disturbed patients who had been continuously hospitalized for many years. One program followed a carefully designed and closely supervised social learning model, and the other followed a more traditional approach. These experimental treatments were compared to a group of similar patients who continued to reside in their original hospital wards. The patients' adjustment was evaluated at 6-month intervals over a period of approximately 6 years.

Both groups of patients who received treatment showed significant improvement, especially during the first 6 months of the study. This finding highlights the possibility for improvement, even among chronically disturbed patients. Patients in the social learning program showed even more improvement than those in the traditional group, especially with regard to social functioning and self-care. These benefits were maintained throughout the duration of the treatment program. Perhaps most impressive was the fact that, by the end of the first 4 years of active treatment, 11 percent of the patients in the social learning program were discharged to independent living in the community without being readmitted to the hospital. In contrast, none of the patients in the standard hospital comparison group were released to independent living. This study indicates that carefully structured inpatient programs, especially those that follow behavioral principles, can have important positive effects for chronic schizophrenic patients.

GENERAL CONCLUSION: A CONTINUUM OF CARE

Schizophrenia is a disorder that affects many areas of a person's life and therefore requires many levels of management and care. Treatment must provide for the resolution of acute episodes, the delay and perhaps prevention of relapse, and the remediation of chronic social impairments. Some patients require only brief periods of hospitalization followed by maintenance medication. Others need long-term support in the form of family and community-based treatment programs that foster the development of social skills and improve patterns of communication within families (Test et al., 1991).

Summary

People with schizophrenia exhibit many types of symptoms that represent impairments across a broad array of cognitive, perceptual, and interpersonal functions. These symptoms can be roughly divided into two types. Positive symptoms include hallucinations, delusions, and disorganized speech. Negative symptoms include blunted affect, alogia, avolition, and social withdrawal. The onset of schizophrenia is typically during adolescence or early adulthood. The disorder can follow different patterns over time. Some people recover fairly quickly from schizophrenia, whereas others deteriorate progressively after the initial onset of symptoms.

KEY TERMS

- alogia
- anhedonia
- atypical antipsychotics
- avolition
- blunted affect
- brief reactive psychosis
- catatonia
- catatonic type
- delusional disorder
- dementia praecox
- disorganized speech
- disorganized type
- expressed emotion
- high risk research
- inappropriate affect
- negative symptoms
- neuroleptic
- paranoid type
- positive symptoms
- prodromal phase
- residual phase
- residual type
- schizoaffective disorder
- schizophrenia
- schizophreniform disorder
- schizotaxia
- tardive dyskinesia (TD)
- undifferentiated type
- vulnerability marker

The disorder was originally defined by Emil Kraepelin, who emphasized the progressive course of the disorder in distinguishing it from manic-depressive psychosis. Eugen Bleuler coined the term *schizophrenia*, proposing that disturbances in speech and emotion are the fundamental symptoms of the disorder. The scope of the clinical definition has fluctuated over the course of the twentieth century.

The negative symptoms of schizophrenia have been given increased emphasis in DSM-IV. The manual requires evidence of a decline in the person's social or occupational functioning as well as the presence of disturbed behavior over a continuous period of at least 6 months. The DSM-IV recognizes several subtypes of schizophrenia, such as paranoid, catatonic, and disorganized types, that are based on prominent symptoms.

The lifetime prevalence of schizophrenia is approximately 1 or 2 percent in virtually all areas of the world. Men and women are equally likely to be affected, although the onset of the disorder appears at an earlier age in males. Two large cross-cultural studies found patients who exhibited characteristic signs and symptoms of schizophrenia in all of the study sites. Comparisons of patients across centers revealed more similarities than differences in clinical symptoms.

Genetic factors clearly play a role in the development of schizophrenia. Risk for developing the disorder is between 10 and 15 percent among first-degree relatives of schizophrenic patients.

Concordance rates are approximately 50 percent in MZ twins compared to only 15 percent in DZ pairs. Adoption studies have found that approximately 15 percent of the offspring of a schizophrenic parent will eventually develop the disorder themselves, even if they are separated from their biological parent at an early age and are raised by adoptive families. Twin and adoption studies also indicate that the disorder has variable expressions, sometimes called the schizophrenia spectrum. Related disorders include schizotypal personality disorder and schizoaffective disorder. Linkage studies have not found consistent evidence for a specific gene of major influence.

Advances in brain-imaging technology have allowed extensive study of structural and functional brain abnormalities in schizophrenia. A specific brain lesion has not been identified, and it is unlikely that a disorder as complex as schizophrenia will be traced to a single site in the brain. Structural images of schizophrenic patients' brains reveal enlarged ventricles as well as decreased size for parts of the limbic system. Studies of brain metabolism and blood flow have identified functional changes in the frontal lobes, temporal lobes, and basal ganglia in many persons with schizophrenia. Current evidence points toward a subtle and diffuse type of neuropathology in schizophrenia.

The discovery of antipsychotic medication stimulated interest in the role of neurochemical factors in the etiology of schizophrenia. The dopamine hypothesis provided the major unifying theme in this area for many years, but it is now considered too simple to account for the existing evidence. Current neurochemical hypotheses regarding schizophrenia focus on a broad array of neurotransmitters, with special emphasis on serotonin.

The importance of environmental events in the etiology of schizophrenia is evident in the results of twin studies, which show that concordance rates in MZ twins do not approach 100 percent. Several social and psychological factors have been shown to be related to the disorder. Social class is inversely related to the prevalence of schizophrenia. In some cases, low levels of socioeconomic achievement represent a consequence of the disorder. Several kinds of research studies have also found, however, that social factors appear to make a causal contribution to the disorder.

Disturbed patterns of family communication have been presumed to be related to the etiology of schizophrenia for many years. There is no evidence to indicate that the behavior of family members contributes to the original onset of schizophrenic symptoms. Recent efforts on this topic have examined the relation between the social context of the family and the long-term course of the disorder. Patients from families that are high in expressed emotion are more likely to relapse than those from low EE families. Expressed emotion is the product of an ongoing interaction between patients and their families, with patterns of influence flowing in both directions.

The evidence regarding etiology supports a diathesis-stress model. It should be possible to develop vulnerability markers that can identify individuals who possess the genetic predisposition to the disorder. Promising research on this topic is currently concerned with a broad range of possibilities, including smooth-pursuit eye-tracking movements and laboratory measures of sustained attention.

The central aspect of treatment for schizophrenia is antipsychotic medication. These drugs help to resolve acute psychotic episodes. They can also delay relapse and improve the level of patients' functioning between episodes. Unfortunately, they often produce troublesome side effects, and a substantial minority of schizophrenic patients are resistant to classic types of antipsychotic medication. The atypical antipsychotics are able to help some patients who do not respond to other drugs, and they are associated with fewer motor side effects.

Various types of psychosocial treatment also provide important benefits to schizophrenic patients and their families. Prominent among these are family-based treatment for patients who have been stabilized on medication following discharge from the hospital. Social skills training can also be useful in improving the level of patients' role functioning.

Critical Thinking

1. The typical course of schizophrenia may be less chronic in developing countries than in developed countries. How would you explain these differences? Why would the disorder tend to be more long-lasting among people living in the United States than in people living in rural India, for example?

2. Clinical scientists have been unable to identify a specific type of environmental event that is responsible for triggering the original onset of symptoms of schizophrenia. Where would you look if you were conducting research on the "stress" end of the diathesis–stress model?

3. How can we identify people who are vulnerable for schizophrenia? Would you place greater emphasis on studying behavioral markers or biological markers?

4. Imagine that you are the director of a large mental health center that provides services for all types of disorders. If you have limited resources, which aspects of schizophrenia would receive highest priority in your programs? Medication for the resolution of acute psychotic episodes? Support to family members? Alternative housing? Social skills training?

13

Dementia, Delirium, and Amnestic Disorders

Most of us can be absent-minded from time to time. We may forget to make a phone call, run an errand, or complete an assignment. Occasional lapses of this sort are part of normal experience. Unfortunately, some people develop severe and persistent memory problems that disrupt their everyday activities and their interactions with other people. Imagine that you have lived in the same house for many years. You go for a short walk, and then you can't remember how to get home. Suppose you are shown a photograph of your own parents, and you don't recognize them. These are the types of fundamental cognitive problems experienced by people with **dementia**, a gradually worsening loss of memory and related cognitive functions, including the use of language, as well as reasoning and decision making.

Overview

Delirium is a confusional state that develops over a short period of time and is often associated with agitation and hyperactivity. The primary symptom of delirium is clouding of consciousness, which might also be described as a person's reduced awareness of his or her surroundings. Memory problems may occur in association with impaired consciousness. This disturbance of consciousness typically fluctuates throughout the day and is usually worse at night. Daytime drowsiness and lapses in concentration are among the milder symptoms of delirium. If the condition is allowed to progress, the person may become stuporous and eventually lapse into a coma. The delirious person is also likely to be disoriented with relation to time ("What day, month, or season is it?") or place ("Where are we? What is the name of this place?").

People with **amnestic disorders** experience memory impairments that are more limited or circumscribed than those seen in dementia or delirium. The person loses the ability to learn new information or becomes unable to recall previously learned information, but other higher-level cognitive abilities—including the use of language—are unaffected.

Dementia, delirium, and amnestic disorders are listed as Cognitive Disorders in DSM-IV. Cognitive processes, including perception and attention, are related to many types of mental disorders that we have already discussed, such as depression, anxiety, and schizophrenia. In most forms of psychopathology, however, the cognitive problems are relatively subtle—mediating factors that help us understand the process by which clinical symptoms are produced. They are not considered to be the central, defining features of the disorder. In dementia, memory and other cognitive functions are the most obvious manifestations of the problem. The person's attention, concentration, judgment, planning, and decision making become severely disturbed as dementia progresses.

Dementia and amnestic disorders are often associated with specific identifiable changes in brain tissue. Many times these changes can be observed only at autopsy, after the patient's death. For example, in Alzheimer's disease—which is one form of dementia—microscopic examination of the brain reveals the presence of an unusual amount of debris left from dead neurons, called plaque, and neurofibrillary tangles indicating that the connections between nerve cells had become disorganized. We describe the neuropathology of Alzheimer's disease later in this chapter.

Because of the close link between cognitive disorders and brain disease, patients with these problems are often diagnosed and treated by neurologists—physicians who deal primarily with diseases of the brain and the nervous system. Multidisciplinary clinical teams are concerned with studying and providing care for people with dementia and amnestic disorders. Direct care to patients and their families is usually provided by nurses and social workers. *Neuropsychologists* have particular expertise in the assessment of specific types of cognitive impairment. This is true for clinical assessments as well as for more detailed laboratory studies for research purposes.

In the following pages, we describe two brief cases that illustrate the variety of symptoms and problems that are included in the general category of dementia. The first case describes the early stages of dementia.

CASE STUDY

Dementia

Jonathan was a 61-year-old physician who had been practicing family medicine for the past 30 years. His wife, Alice, worked as his office manager. A registered nurse, Kathryn, had worked with them for several years. Four months earlier, Alice and Kathryn both noticed that Jonathan was beginning to make obvious errors at work. On one occasion, Kathryn observed Jonathan prescribe the wrong medication for a patient's condition. At about the same time, Alice became concerned when she asked Jonathan about a patient whom he had seen the day before. Much to her surprise, he did not remember having seen the patient, in spite of the fact that he spent almost half an hour with her, and she was a patient whom he had treated for several years.

Jonathan's personality also seemed to change in small but noticeable ways. For example, Jonathan had always been a gentle and easygoing man. He had a special fondness and tolerance for small children. One day, one of his patients was accompanied to the office by her 2-year-old son. As Jonathan was talking with the mother, the little boy accidentally pushed some bottles of pills off a counter. No harm was done, but Jonathan screamed loudly at the boy, chastising him for being so clumsy and careless. The mother was quite embarrassed. So were Kathryn and Alice, who witnessed Jonathan's sudden and uncharacteristic display of temper.

Although Alice tried to convince herself that these were isolated incidents, she finally decided to discuss them with Kathryn. Kathryn agreed that Jonathan's memory was failing. He had trouble recognizing patients whom he had known for many years, and he had unusual difficulty making treatment decisions. These problems had not appeared suddenly. Over the past year or two, both women had been doing more things for Jonathan than they had ever done in the past. They needed to remind him about things that were routine parts of his practice. As they pieced together various incidents, the pattern of gradual cognitive decline became obvious.

Alice talked seriously with Jonathan about the problems that she and Kathryn had observed. He said that he felt fine, but he reluctantly allowed her to make an appointment for him to be examined by a neurologist, who also happened to be a friend. Jonathan admitted to the neurologist that he had been having difficulty remembering things. He believed that he had been able to avoid most problems, however, by writing notes to himself—directions, procedures, and so on. The results of psychological testing and brain-imaging procedures, coupled with Jonathan's own description of his experiences and Alice's account of his impaired performance at work, led the neurologist to conclude that Jonathan was exhibiting early signs of dementia, perhaps Alzheimer's disease. He spoke directly with Jonathan regarding his diagnosis and recommended firmly that Jonathan retire immediately. A malpractice suit would be devastating to his medical practice. Jonathan agreed to retire.

Although Jonathan was no longer able to cope with his demanding work environment, his adjustment at home was not severely impaired. The changes in his behavior remained relatively subtle for many months. In short conversations, his cognitive problems were not apparent to his friends, who still did not know the real reason for his retirement. His speech was fluent, and his memory for recent events was largely intact, but his comprehension was diminished. Alice noticed that Jonathan's emotional responses were occasionally flat or restricted. At other times, he would laugh at inappropriate times when they watched television programs together. If Alice asked him about his reaction, it was sometimes apparent that Jonathan did not understand the plot of even the simplest television programs.

Jonathan had become increasingly literal-minded. If Alice asked him to do something for her, she had to spell out every last detail. For example, he began to have trouble selecting his clothes, which had been a source of pride before the onset of his cognitive problems. Alice found that she had to sew labels into Jonathan's collars to distinguish for him the clothes that he wore to work in the yard from those that he wore if they were going shopping or out to eat. His judgment about what was appropriate to wear in different situations had disappeared altogether.

It had also become difficult for Jonathan to do things that required a regular sequence of actions or decisions, even if they were quite simple and familiar. Routine tasks took longer than before, usually because he got stuck part of the way through an activity. He had, for example, always enjoyed making breakfast for Alice on weekends. After his retirement, Alice once found him standing in the kitchen with a blank expression on his face. He had made a pot of coffee and some toast for both of them, but he ran into trouble when he couldn't find coffee cups. That disrupted his plan, and he was stymied. ∎

▲ **People with dementia can remain active longer by using signs to prompt their behavior. This man is reminded to lock the door when he leaves his apartment.**

Jonathan's case illustrates many of the early symptoms of dementia, as well as the ways in which the beginnings of memory problems can severely disrupt a person's life. The onset of the disorder is often difficult to identify precisely because forgetfulness increases gradually. Problems are most evident in challenging situations, as in Jonathan's medical practice, and least noticeable in familiar surroundings.

Changes in emotional responsiveness and personality typically accompany the onset of memory impairment in dementia. These changes may be consequences of the cognitive problems. Jonathan's irritability might easily have been exacerbated by his own frustration with himself for being forgetful and indecisive. His emotional responses may have seemed unusual sometimes because he failed to comprehend aspects of the environment that were obvious to his wife and other people.

Our next case illustrates more advanced stages of dementia, in which the person can become extremely disorganized. Memory impairment progresses to the point where the person no longer recognizes his or her family and closest friends. People in this condition are unable to care for themselves, and they become so disoriented that the burden on others is frequently overwhelming.

The second case also provides an example of delirium superimposed on dementia. It isn't always easy to distinguish dementia from delirium, especially when they appear in the same patient. One important consideration involves the period of time over which the symptoms appear. Delirium usually has a rapid onset, whereas dementia is more likely to follow a slow, progressive course. In dementia, the person usually remains alert and responsive to the environment. Speech is most often coherent in demented patients, at least until the end stages of the disorder, but it is typically confused in delirious patients. Finally, delirium can be resolved while dementia cannot.

Dementia (and Delirium)

Mary was an 84-year-old retired schoolteacher who had grown up in the same small, rural community in which she still lived. Never married, she lived with her parents most of her life, except for the years when she was in college. Her parents had died when Mary was in her early sixties. After her retirement at age 65, Mary continued living in her parents' farmhouse. She felt comfortable there, in spite of its relative isolation, and liked the fact that it had plenty of space for animals, including her dog, which she called "my baby," several cats, and a few cows that were kept in the pasture behind the house. Mary's niece, Nancy, who was 45 years old and lived an hour's drive away, stopped to visit her once every 2 or 3 months.

Over the past year, Nancy had noticed that Mary was becoming forgetful as well as more insistent that her routines remain unchanged. Bills went unpaid—in fact the telephone had been disconnected for lack of payment—and the mail wasn't brought in from the roadside box. Nancy had suggested to Mary that she might be better off in a nursing home, but Mary was opposed to that idea.

At her most recent visit, Nancy was shocked to find that conditions at Mary's home had become intolerable. Most distressing was the fact that some of her animals had died because Mary forgot to feed them. The dog's decomposed body was tied to its house, where it had starved. Conditions inside the house were disgusting. Almost 30 cats lived inside the house, and the smell was unbearable. Mary's own appearance was quite disheveled. She hadn't bathed or changed her clothes for weeks. Nancy contacted people at a social service agency, who arranged for Mary's admission to a nursing home. Mary became furious, refusing to go and denying that there was anything wrong with her own home. Nancy was soon declared her legal guardian because Mary was clearly not competent to make decisions for herself.

Mary grew progressively more agitated and belligerent during the few weeks that she lived at the nursing home. She was occasionally disoriented, not knowing where she was or what day it was. She shouted and sometimes struck people with her cane. She had trouble walking, a problem that was compounded by visual and spatial difficulties. After she fell and broke her hip, Mary was transferred to a general hospital.

Mary became delirious in the hospital, apparently as a result of medication she was given for her injury. She appeared to be having visual hallucinations, and often said things that did not make sense. These periods of incoherence fluctuated in severity throughout the course of the day. During her worst moments, Mary did not respond to her name being spoken, and her speech was reduced primarily to groans and nonsense words. This clouding of consciousness cleared up a few days after her medication was changed. She became less distractible and was once again able to carry on brief conversations. Unfortunately, her disorientation became more severe while she was immobilized in the hospital. When her hip eventually healed, she was moved to a psychiatric hospital and admitted to the geriatric ward.

Although Mary was no longer aware of the date or even the season of the year, she insisted that she did not have any problems with her mind. For the first 6 weeks at the psychiatric hospital, she would be surprised that she was not in her own home when she woke up each morning. After that time, she acknowledged that she was in a hospital, but she did not know why she was there, and she did not understand that the other patients on the unit were also demented. She didn't recognize hospital staff members from one day to the next. She was completely unable to remember anything that had happened recently. Nevertheless, her memory for events that had happened many years earlier was quite good. Mary repeated stories about her childhood over and over again.

Nurses on the unit were bombarded continuously with her complaints about being removed from her home. Every 20 minutes or so, Mary would approach the nurses' station, waving her cane and shouting, "Nurse, I need to go home. I have to get out of here. I have to go home and take care of my dog." The hospital staff would explain to her that she would have to stay at the hospital, at least for a while longer, and that her dog had died several months earlier. This news would usually provoke sadness, but she seemed unable to remember it long enough to complete the grieving process. Several minutes later, the whole scene would be repeated. Mary also became paranoid, claiming to anyone who would listen that people were trying to steal her things. The most common focus of her concern was her purse. If it was out of her sight, she would announce loudly that someone had stolen it.

In the midst of these obvious problems, Mary retained many other intellectual abilities. She was a well-educated and intelligent woman. Her attention span was reduced, but she was still able to do crossword puzzles and enjoyed reading short stories. Poetry had always been one of her special interests, and she was still able to recite many of her favorite poems beautifully from memory. In a quiet room, it was often possible to talk with her and pursue a meaningful conversation. Unfortunately, these lucid periods were interspersed with times of restless pacing and shouting. Her agitation would escalate rapidly unless staff members distracted her, taking her to a quiet room, talking to her, and getting her to read or recite something out loud. ■

Dementia: Typical Symptoms and Associated Features

These cases illustrate the changing patterns that emerge as dementia unfolds. Jonathan's cognitive symptoms were recognized at a relatively early stage of development, in part because of his occupational situation and because of his close relationships with other people. Mary's situation was much different, because she lived in a relatively isolated setting without close neighbors or friends. By the time Nancy recognized the full severity of Mary's problems, the cognitive impairment had progressed so far that Mary no longer was able to appreciate the nature of her own difficulties. In the following pages, we describe in more detail the types of symptoms that are associated with dementia.

Cognitive Symptoms

Dementia is an *acquired* disorder. In other words, it appears in people whose intellectual abilities have previously been unimpaired. Both of the people in our case studies were bright, well educated, and occupationally successful prior to the onset of their symptoms. The earliest signs of dementia are often quite vague. They include difficulty remembering recent events as well as the names of people and familiar objects. These are all problems that are associated with normal aging but differ from that process in order of magnitude (see Further Thoughts). The distinguishing features of dementia include cognitive problems in a number of areas, ranging from memory and learning to language and abstract thinking. By the final stages of dementia, intellectual and motor functions may disappear almost completely (Cummings, 1992).

MEMORY AND LEARNING

Memory loss is the diagnostic hallmark of dementia. In order to describe the various facets of memory impairment, it is useful to distinguish between old memories and the ability to learn new things. **Retrograde amnesia** refers to the loss of memory for events prior to the onset of an illness or the experience of a traumatic event. **Anterograde amnesia**, on the other hand, refers to the inability to learn or remember new material after a particular point in time.

Anterograde amnesia is usually the most obvious problem during the beginning stages of dementia. Consider, for example, the case of Jonathan. Alice eventually noticed that he sometimes could not remember things that he had done the previous day. Mary, the more severely impaired person, could not remember for more than a few minutes that her dog had died. Long-term memories are usually not affected until much later in the course of the disorder. Even

Memory Changes in Normal Aging

Changes in cognitive abilities are part of the normal aging process. Most elderly adults complain more frequently about memory problems than younger adults do, and they typically perform less efficiently than younger adults on laboratory tests of memory (Light, 1991). There are, of course, individual differences in the age at which cognitive abilities begin to decline, as well as in the rate at which these losses take place (Berkman et al., 1993). Nevertheless, some types of memory impairment are an inevitable consequence of aging.

In order to understand more clearly the cognitive changes associated with aging, it is useful to distinguish between two aspects of mental functioning. Paul Baltes, a cognitive psychologist at the Max Planck Institute in Germany, divides intellectual abilities into *mechanics* (also known as fluid intelligence) and *pragmatics* (sometimes called crystallized intelligence). Baltes uses the computer as a metaphor to explain this distinction. Cognitive mechanics are "the hardware of the mind." These functions are concerned with the speed and accuracy of basic processes such as perception, attention, and memory. The proficiency of mechanics is dependent on neurophysiological processes and on the structural integrity of the person's brain.

Cognitive pragmatics represent the "culture-based software of the mind." Reading and writing skills as well as knowledge about the self and ways of coping with environmental challenges are all examples of pragmatics. They represent information about the world that is acquired continually throughout the person's lifetime. Wisdom is a reflection of cognitive pragmatics.

According to Baltes (1993), mechanics and pragmatics follow different trajectories over the normal human lifespan. Both develop continuously during childhood and adolescence, reaching a point of optimal efficiency during young adulthood. After that point, mechanics follow a gradual pattern of decline. Pragmatics, on the other hand, remain unimpaired as the person reaches old age. The erosion

of cognitive mechanics over time is presumably due to subtle atrophy of brain regions such as the hippocampus that take place during normal aging (Golomb et al., 1993).

Several research studies support this general conclusion. One laboratory task designed to measure cognitive mechanics requires subjects to remember long lists of words in their correct order. Even after many training and practice sessions, most adults in their sixties and seventies are unable to achieve the level of performance shown by young adults after a small number of practice sessions (Baltes & Kliegl, 1992). Age-related deficits are found even among those normal elderly persons who are selected for study because of their experience with and talent for similar cognitive tasks.

▲ **Eubie Blake was an influential jazz pianist who performed well into his nineties.**

Different measurement procedures have been used to explore the relationship between aging and cognitive pragmatics. In one procedure, subjects are presented with a life dilemma, such as "A 15-year-old girl wants to get married right away. What should she consider and do?" The subjects' task is to think aloud about each dilemma. Responses are scored in terms of the amount of knowledge that the person displays with regard to facts, values, and procedures that must be considered in each circumstance. In contrast to the results of research on mechanics, studies of pragmatics have found no change in performance between the ages of 30 and 70. Elderly people are just as likely as younger adults to produce the best scores on this type of task.

Baltes (1993) suggested that "the aging mind" depends on the coordination of gains and losses. The elderly person strikes a balance through a process that Baltes calls *selective optimization with compensation.* Arthur Rubinstein, the brilliant pianist who performed concerts well into his eighties, provides an example of this process. Rubinstein described three strategies that he employed in his old age: (1) he was *selective,* performing fewer pieces, (2) he *optimized* his performance by practicing each piece more frequently, and (3) he *compensated* for a loss of motor speed by utilizing pieces that emphasized contrast between fast and slow segments so

that his playing seemed faster than it really was. Successful aging is based on this dynamic process. The person compensates for losses in cognitive mechanics by taking advantage of pragmatics— increased knowledge and information.

The fact that an older person begins to experience subtle memory problems does not necessarily indicate that he or she is becoming demented. Where can we find the line between normal aging and dementia? Is this distinction simply a matter of degree, or is there a qualitative difference between the expected decline in cognitive mechanics and the onset of cognitive pathology? These issues present an important challenge for future research. ∎

in advanced stages of dementia, a person may retain some recollections of the past. Mary was able to remember, and frequently described, stories from her childhood.

VERBAL COMMUNICATION

Language functions can also be affected in dementia. **Aphasia** is a term that describes various types of loss or impairment in language that are caused by brain damage (Benson, 1992). Language disturbance in dementia is sometimes relatively subtle, but it can include many different kinds of problems. Patients often remain verbally fluent, at least until the disorder is relatively advanced. They retain their vocabulary skills and are able to construct grammatical sentences. They may have trouble finding words, naming objects, and comprehending instructions.

In addition to problems understanding and forming meaningful sentences, the demented person may also have difficulty performing purposeful movements in response to verbal commands, a problem known as **apraxia**. The person possesses the normal strength and coordination to carry out the action, and is able to understand the other person's speech, but is nevertheless unable to translate the various components into a meaningful action.

Some aspects of the communication problems associated with dementia are captured in the following passage from a novel titled *Out*

of Mind, which provides an insightful and poignant description of the subjective experiences of a man from Holland, named Maarten, who is becoming demented (Bernlef, 1988). In this passage, Maarten is listening to his wife, Vera, as she discusses his situation with their physician.

Peace and quiet, keep indoors, familiar surroundings, carry on with the therapy. I hear a man's voice say. And Vera's timid voice in reply: "Sometimes he's like a stranger to me. I can't reach him. It's a terrible, helpless feeling. He hears me but at such times I don't think he understands me. He behaves as if he were on his own."

I know exactly what she means. Like it was just then, when it all went wrong. All of a sudden I had to translate everything into English first, before I could say it. Only the forms of sentences came out, fragments, the contents had completely slipped away.

Furiously I glare into the front room. I seem to lose words like another person loses blood. And then suddenly I feel terribly frightened again. The presence of everything! Every object seems to be heavier and more solid than it should be (perhaps because for a fraction of a second I no longer know its name). I quickly lie down on the settee and close my eyes. A kind of seasickness in my mind, it seems. Under this life stirs another life in which all times, names and places whirl about topsy-turvy and in which I no longer exist as a person.

"Curious," I say to Vera as she enters the room. "Sometimes I just have to lie down for a moment. I never used to."

"It doesn't matter. Have some time to yourself." She sits down, picks up a book.

"Have some time to yourself." I repeat the phrase because it appears strange to me.

She turns the pages but she isn't reading. I can tell from the look in her eyes that she doesn't understand me.

"It should be: have some time in yourself. That describes the situation better."

"Is that how you feel?"

"Less and less so."

"What do you mean?"

"Like a ship," I say, "A ship, a sailing vessel that is becalmed. And then suddenly there is a breeze, I am sailing again. Then the world has a hold on me again and I can move along with it."

"I find it so hard to imagine it, Maarten. I can't see anything wrong with you at all. It is as if you were looking at something, at something that I can't see. Are you afraid at those moments? What exactly happens to you then?"

I don't know. I can't remember. Only that feeling of a sudden heaviness, as if I am sinking through everything and there is nothing to hold on to." (Bernlef, 1988, pp. 54-55)

Some of the things that Maarten says in this passage reflect subtle problems in verbal communication. His description of the sailing ship, however, is a remarkable analogy that captures the intermittent quality of the cognitive impairment.

PERCEPTION

Some patients with dementia have problems identifying stimuli in their environments. The technical term for this phenomenon is **agnosia**, which means "perception without meaning." The person's sensory functions are unimpaired, but he or she is unable to recognize the source of stimulation. Agnosia can be associated with visual, auditory or tactile sensations, and it can be relatively specific or more

generalized. For example, visual agnosia is the inability to recognize certain objects or faces. Some people with visual agnosia are able to identify inanimate stimuli but unable to recognize human faces. Agnosia is often associated with brain dysfunction, of the kind that may occur in the aftermath of a stroke. The site of the brain lesion seems to determine the specific type of agnosia (Cutting & McClelland, 1991).

It is sometimes difficult to distinguish between aphasia and agnosia. Imagine, for example, that a clinician shows a patient a toothbrush and asks, "What is this object?" The patient may look at the object and be unable to name it. Does that mean that the person cannot think of the word "toothbrush"? Or does it mean that the person cannot recognize the object at all? In this case, the distinction could be made by saying to the person, "Show me what you do with this object." A person suffering from aphasia would take the toothbrush in his hand and make brushing movements in front of his mouth, thereby demonstrating that he recognizes the object but cannot remember its name. A person with agnosia would be unable to indicate how the toothbrush is used.

ABSTRACT THINKING

Another manifestation of cognitive impairment in dementia is loss of the ability to think in abstract ways. The person may be bound to concrete interpretations of things that other people say. It may also be difficult for the person to interpret words that have more than one meaning (for example, "pen") or to explain why two objects are alike ("Why are a basketball and a football helmet alike?" Because they are both types of sporting equipment.)

In our opening case, Jonathan became increasingly literal-minded in his conversations with other people. After he retired, he had much more time to become involved in routine tasks around the home. Alice found that she had to give him very explicit instructions if she wanted him to do anything. For example, if she asked him to mow the grass, he would do exactly that—nothing more. This was unusual for Jonathan, because he had always enjoyed taking care of their lawn and took great pride in their bushes and flower gardens. "Mowing the grass" would have previously been taken to include trimming, pulling weeds, raking leaves out from under bushes, and all sorts of related details. Now Jonathan interpreted this instruction in concrete terms.

JUDGMENT AND SOCIAL BEHAVIOR

Related to deficits in abstract reasoning is the failure of social judgment and problem-solving skills. In the course of everyday life, we must acquire information from the environment, organize and process it, and then formulate and perform appropriate responses by considering these new data in the light of past experiences. The disruption of short-term memory, perceptual skills, and higher-level cognitive abilities obviously causes disruptions of judgment. Examples from Jonathan's case include problems deciding which clothes to wear for working around his home as opposed to going out in public, as well as his inability to understand the humor in some television programs. Impulsive and careless behaviors are often the product of the demented person's poor judgment. Activities such as shopping, driving, and using tools can create serious problems.

Assessment of Cognitive Impairment

There are many ways to measure the level of cognitive impairment that a person displays. One is the Mini-Mental State Exam, which is outlined in Table 13–1. We include it here to give you a better feeling for the types of questions that a clinician might ask in order to elicit the cognitive problems of dementia. Some are directed at the person's orientation to time and place. Others are concerned with anterograde amnesia, such as the ability to remember the names of objects for a short period of time (items 3 and 5). Agnosia, aphasia, and apraxia are addressed by items 6, 7, and 8, respectively. Perceptual difficulties are tapped by the last item.

Neuropsychological assessment can be used as a more precise index of cognitive impairment. This process involves the examination of performance on psychological tests to indicate whether a person has a brain disorder. Neuropsychological tests can sometimes be used to infer the location of a brain lesion. The best-known neuropsychological assessment procedure is the Halstead-Reitan Neuropsychological Test Battery, which includes an extensive series of tests that tap sensorimotor, perceptual, and speech functions. For example, in the tactile performance test, the person is blindfolded and then required to fit differently shaped blocks into spaces in a form board. The time needed to perform this test reflects one specific aspect of the person's motor skills.

Some neuropsychological tasks require the person to copy simple objects or drawings. The drawings illustrated in Figure 13–1 demonstrate this process and the type of impairment typically seen in a patient during the relatively early stages of Alzheimer's disease. The patient was asked to reproduce a drawing. This was done initially while the original figure was still in sight, and then repeated after it had been covered up. The performance of the patient in this figure indicates two problems associated with the disorder. First, inconsistencies between panel (1) and panel (2) reflect perceptual difficulties. Second, the drastic deterioration from panel (2) to panel (3) indicates that the patient had a great deal of difficulty remembering the shape of the figure for even a few brief moments.

Associated Features

Personality changes, emotional difficulties, and motivational problems are frequently associated with dementia. Some patients also exhibit symptoms of psychosis, such as hallucinations and delusions. These problems may not contribute to the diagnosis of the disorder, but they do have an impact on the person's adjustment. They can also create additional burdens for people who care for demented patients.

EMOTION

The emotional consequences of dementia are quite varied. Some demented patients appear to be apathetic or emotionally flat. Their faces are less expressive, and they appear to be indifferent to their surroundings. Alice noticed, for example, that something seemed a bit vacant in Jonathan's eyes. At the same time, emotional reactions may become exaggerated and less predictable. The person may become fearful or angry in situations that would not have aroused strong emotion in the past. Jonathan's sudden rage at

▼ One of the tests in the Halstead Reitan Neuropsychological Test Battery is the Tactual Performance Task, in which the person must place differently shaped blocks of wood into holes without seeing the pieces or the board in which they are placed.

the boy who pushed bottles off the counter in his office provides one example. Changes like this often lead others to believe that the person's personality has changed.

Depression is another problem that is frequently found in association with dementia. In many ways, feelings of depression are understandable. The realization that your most crucial cognitive abilities are beginning to fail, that you can no longer perform simple tasks or care for yourself, would obviously lead to sadness and depression. Mary's case illustrates one way in which cognitive impairment can complicate depression: Her inability to remember from one day to the next that her dog had died seemed to interfere with her ability to grieve for the loss of her pet. Each time that she was reminded of his death was like the first time that she had heard the news.

MOTOR BEHAVIOR

Motor behavior may become agitated in demented persons, who may pace restlessly or wander away from familiar surroundings. In the later stages of the disorder, patients may develop problems in the control of the muscles by the central nervous system. Some patients develop muscular rigidity, which can be accompanied by painful cramping. Others experience epileptic seizures, which consist of involuntary, rapidly alternating movements of the arms and legs.

Some specific types of dementia are associated with involuntary movements or **dyskinesia**—tics, chorea, tremors. These motor symptoms help to distinguish among different types of dementia. We return to this point later in the chapter when we discuss the classification of differentiated and undifferentiated dementias. *Chorea* is a type of motor dysfunction that involves jerky, semipurposeful movements of the person's face and limbs (Cutting & McClelland, 1991).

PSYCHOTIC SYMPTOMS

Hallucinations and delusions are seen in about 20 percent of dementia cases (Bolger, Carpenter, & Strauss, 1994). The delusional beliefs are typically understandable consequences of the person's disorientation or anterograde amnesia. They are most often simple in nature and relatively short-lived. Mary's frequent insistence that someone had stolen her purse is an example.

A more dramatic example is described in the novel *Out of Mind*. In this incident, Maarten

wanders away from his house without a coat in freezing winter weather. When he is found on the beach, by a young man driving a jeep, Maarten

TABLE 13-1
Mini-Mental State Examination

1. What is the (year, season, date, day, month)?
2. Where are we (state, city, hospital)?
3. Name three objects (pen, sky, dog), then ask patient to repeat them.
4. Spell "world" backwards.
5. Ask for names of three objects given in question #3.
6. Point to a pencil and a watch. Ask the patient to name each as you point.
7. Ask the patient to repeat, "No ifs, ands, or buts."
8. Three-stage command: "Take this paper in your right hand. Fold the paper in half. Put the paper on the floor."
9. Ask the patient to read and obey the following (write on card in large letters): "CLOSE YOUR EYES."
10. Have the patient write a sentence of his or her choice.
11. Have the patient copy two intersecting pentagons.

Source: M.F. Folstein, S.E. Folstein, and P.R. McHugh. (1975). Mini-mental state: A practical method for grading the cognitive state of patients for the clinician. *Journal of Psychiatric Research, 2,* 189–198.

Neuropsychological Test Performances

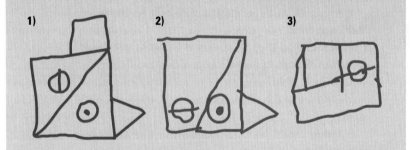

1) 2) 3)

FIGURE 13-1: These drawings represent part of the neuropsychological test performance of a 59-year-old woman with a diagnosis of Alzheimer's disease. The figure at the left (1) was drawn by the psychologist, who then handed the piece of paper to the patient and asked her to make an exact copy of the figure next to the original. After the patient had completed her replica (2), the piece of paper was turned over and she was asked to draw the figure again, this time from memory. The figure that she drew based on memory is presented at the right (3).

mistakenly believes that he is once again back in Holland at the end of World War II and that this man was an American soldier who has arrived to liberate their village. When a physician arrives to help, Maarten mistakes the doctor for an American officer. The ensuing conversation is puzzling to many of those present because Maarten continuously misinterprets the actions of other people based on his belief that they are all in Europe at the end of the war. For example, when he is given an injection of medication to calm him down, he assumes that he is being taken prisoner for collaborating with the Nazis during their occupation of Holland.

Amnestic Disorder: Typical Symptoms and Associated Features

Some cognitive disorders involve more circumscribed forms of memory impairment than those seen in dementia. In amnestic disorders, a person exhibits a severe impairment of memory while other higher-level cognitive abilities are unaffected. The memory disturbance interferes with social and occupational functioning and represents a significant decline from a previous level of adjustment. Subtypes of amnestic disorder are diagnosed on the basis of evidence, acquired from the patient's history, from a physical examination, or from laboratory tests, regarding medical conditions or substance use that is considered to be related to the onset of the memory impairment.

The following case, written by Oliver Sacks (1985), illustrates a form of amnestic disorder, involving severe anterograde amnesia, that developed after the patient had been dependent on alcohol for several years.

CASE STUDY

Alcohol-Induced Persisting Amnestic Disorder

Jimmie G. was admitted to our Home for the Aged near New York City early in 1975, with a cryptic transfer note saying, "Helpless, demented, confused and disoriented." Jimmie was a fine-looking man, with a curly bush of grey hair, a healthy and handsome 49-year-old. He was cheerful, friendly, and warm.

"Hiya, Doc!" he said. "Nice morning! Do I take this chair here?" He was a genial soul, very ready to talk and to answer any questions I asked him. He told me his name and birth date, and the name of the little town in Connecticut where he was born. He described it in affectionate detail, even drew me a map. He spoke of the houses where his family had lived—he remembered their phone numbers still. He spoke of school and school days, the friends he'd had, and his special fondness for mathematics and science. He talked with enthusiasm of his days in the navy—he was 17, had just graduated from high school when he was drafted in 1943. With his good engineering mind he was a "natural" for radio and electronics, and after a crash course in Texas found himself assistant radio operator on a sub-

marine. He remembered the names of various submarines on which he had served, their missions, where they were stationed, the names of his shipmates. He remembered Morse code, and was still fluent in Morse tapping and touch-typing.

A full and interesting early life, remembered vividly, in detail, with affection. But there, for some reason, his reminiscences stopped. He recalled, and almost relived, his war days and service, the end of the war, and his thoughts for the future. He had come to love the navy, thought he might stay in it. But with the GI Bill, and support, he felt he might do best to go to college.

With recalling, reliving, Jimmie was full of animation; he did not seem to be speaking of the past but of the present, and I was very struck by the change of tense in his recollections as he passed from his school days to his days in the navy. He had been using the past tense, but now used the present—and (it seemed to me) not just the formal or fictitious present tense of recall, but the actual present tense of immediate experience.

A sudden, improbable suspicion seized me.

"What year is this, Mr. G.?" I asked, concealing my perplexity under a casual manner.

"Forty-five, man. What do you mean?" He went on, "We've won the war, FDR's dead, Truman's at the helm. There are great times ahead."

"And you, Jimmie, how old would you be?"

Oddly, uncertainly, he hesitated a moment, as if engaged in calculation. "Why, I guess I'm 19, Doc. I'll be 20 next birthday."

Looking at the grey-haired man before me, I had an impulse for which I have never forgiven myself—it was, or would have been, the height of cruelty had there been any possibility of Jimmie's remembering it.

"Here," I said, and thrust a mirror toward him. "Look in the mirror and tell me what you see. Is that a 19-year-old looking out from the mirror?"

He suddenly turned ashen and gripped the sides of the chair. "Jesus Christ," he whispered. "Christ, what's going on? What's happened to me? Is this a nightmare? Am I crazy? Is this a joke?"—and he became frantic, panicked.

"It's okay, Jimmie," I said soothingly. "It's just a mistake. Nothing to worry about. Hey!" I took him to the window. "Isn't this a lovely spring day. See the kids there playing baseball?" He regained his color and started to smile, and I stole away, taking the hateful mirror with me.

Two minutes later I re-entered the room. Jimmie was still standing by the window, gazing with pleasure at the kids playing baseball below. He wheeled around as I opened the door, and his face assumed a cheery expression.

"Hiya, Doc!" he said. "Nice morning! You want to talk to me—do I take this chair here?" There was no sign of recognition on his frank, open face.

"Haven't we met before, Mr. G.?" I asked casually.

"No, I can't say we have. Quite a beard you got there. I wouldn't forget *you*, Doc!"

"Why do you call me 'Doc'?"

"Well, you are a doc, ain't you?"

"Yes, but if you haven't met me, how do you know what I am?"

"You *talk* like a doc. I can *see* you're a doc."

"Well, you're right, I am. I'm the neurologist here."

"Neurologist? Hey, there's something wrong with my nerves? And 'here'—where's 'here'? What is this place anyhow?"

"I was just going to ask you—where do you think you are?"

"I see these beds, and these patients everywhere. Looks like a sort of hospital to me. But hell, what would I be doing in a hospital—and with all these old people, years older than me. I feel good, I'm strong as a bull. Maybe I *work* here. . . . Do I work? What's my job? . . . No, you're shaking your head, I see in your eyes I don't work here. If I don't work here, I've been put here. Am I a patient, am I sick and don't know it, Doc? It's crazy, it's scary. . . . Is it some sort of joke?" (Sacks, 1985, pp. 22–25) ∎

The preceding case illustrates the most common type of amnestic disorder, alcohol-induced persisting amnestic disorder, also known as *Korsakoff's syndrome*. In this disorder, which is caused by chronic alcoholism, memory is impaired, but other cognitive functions are not. More detailed examination of the patients' cognitive abilities, using neuropsychological tests, have found evidence of more widespread cognitive deficits, especially those related to visuo-perceptual skills and abstract thinking (Jacobson, Acker, & Lishman, 1990). One theory regarding this condition holds that lack of vitamin B[1] (thiamin) leads to atrophy of the medial thalamus, a subcortical structure of the brain, and mammillary bodies, which are illustrated in Figure 12–2 (see Chapter 12) (Kolb & Whishaw, 1990). There is also some evidence that prolonged exposure to alcohol may have direct toxic effects on cortical tissue that are independent of vitamin deficiencies. Alcohol apparently can cause brain damage regardless of the person's nutritional habits (Lishman, 1987).

Classification

Cognitive disorders have been classified by a somewhat different process than most other forms of psychopathology because of their close link to specific types of neuropathology. Description of specific cognitive and behavioral symptoms has not always been the primary consideration. In the following pages, we describe the ways in which these disorders have been defined and some of the considerations that influence the way in which they are classified.

Brief Historical Perspective

During the early part of the 1800s, the influential French psychiatrist Phillip Pinel provided the first modern descriptions of dementia. Speculation from prominent European psychiatrists throughout the nineteenth century centered on the widely held belief that all mental disorders were associated with specific types of brain lesion (Horvath et al., 1991). Several important discoveries in the latter part of that century provided support for that position. In 1861, Paul Broca (1824–80), a French surgeon, demonstrated that a specific type of aphasia is associated with lesions in the left frontal lobe. In 1874, German neurologist Carl Wernicke (1848–1905) identified a different form of aphasia seen in patients with damage to the posterior cortex. In addition, Syergey Korsakoff (1854-1900), a Russian neurologist, showed that localized types of memory impairment were associated with lesions of the medial thalamus that are produced by nutritional defects associated with chronic alcoholism.

Alois Alzheimer (1864–1915) was a German psychiatrist who worked closely in Munich with Emil Kraepelin, who is often considered responsible for modern psychiatric classification (see Chapters 4, 5, and 12). Alzheimer's most famous case involved a 51-year-old woman who had become delusional and also experienced a severe form of recent memory impairment, accompanied by apraxia and agnosia. This woman died 4 years after the onset of her dementia. Following her death, Alzheimer conducted a microscopic examina-

tion of her brain and made a startling discovery: bundles of neurofibrillary tangles and senile plaques. Alzheimer presented the case at a meeting of psychiatrists in 1906 and published a three-page paper in 1907.

Emil Kraepelin began to refer to this condition as Alzheimer's disease in the eighth edition of his famous textbook on psychiatry, published in 1910. He distinguished between this form of dementia, which was characterized by an early onset, and senile dementia, which presumably has an onset after the age of 65. For many years, there was an argument about the distinction between senile and pre-senile dementia. As more and more evidence accumulated regarding these conditions, questions were raised about the value of the distinction. For example, several cases were reported in which two siblings developed dementia, but one had the presenile form and the other had the senile form. Clinical symptoms and brain pathology in the siblings were often the same. Katzman (1976) proposed that both types are forms of Alzheimer's disease, which may have either an early or a late onset, and that they are distinctly different from normal aging. Age of onset may be a reflection of the severity of the disorder. Most clinicians and researchers still believe that Alzheimer's disease is a heterogeneous category, and the genetic literature supports that contention.

DSM-IV

Until recently, the diagnostic manual classified the various forms of dementia as Organic Mental Disorders because of their association with known brain diseases. That concept has fallen into disfavor because it is founded on an artificial dichotomy between biological and psychological processes. If we call dementia an organic mental disorder, does that imply that other types of psychopathology are not organically based (Spitzer et al., 1992)? Obviously not. Therefore, in order to be consistent with the rest of the diagnostic manual, and so as to avoid falling into the trap of simplistic mind/body dualism, dementia and related clinical phenomena are now classified as Cognitive Disorders

▼ Aloise Alzheimer (left) on a pleasure cruise with his friend Emil Kraepelin. The form of dementia that Alzheimer described in his famous case was named after him, in part, because of the influence of Kraepelin's textbook.

in DSM-IV. These disorders are divided into three major headings: deliria, dementias, and amnestic disorders (see Table 13–2).

Many specific disorders are associated with dementia. They are distinguished primarily on the basis of known neuropathology—specific brain lesions that have been discovered throughout this century. These disorders can be subclassified into primary and secondary forms of dementia (Heston & White, 1991). A *primary dementia* is one in which the cognitive impairment is produced by the direct effect of a disease on brain tissue. A *secondary dementia* is one in which the cognitive impairment is a byproduct or side effect of some other type of biological or psychological dysfunction. Secondary dementias include those associated with vascular disease, infections, and substance abuse (such as chronic alcoholism). The distinction between primary and secondary dementias is important, in large part because the treatment outlook may be more positive for some forms of secondary dementias.

The primary dementias are further subdivided into *undifferentiated* and *differentiated* types. In the differentiated dementias, such as Huntington's disease and Parkinson's disease, cognitive deficits are most often accompanied by disturbances of muscular control. These types of dementia are much less common than the undifferentiated dementias. The undifferentiated dementias, such as Alzheimer's disease and Pick's disease, cannot be distinguished from one another on the basis of manifest symptoms (thus the term "undifferentiated"). Microscopic examination of brain tissue upon autopsy is necessary. Neuropsychological tests also suggest some important differences.

The DSM-IV lists several different categories of dementia: Dementia of the Alzheimer's Type (primary undifferentiated dementia); Vascular Dementia; Dementia due to Other General Medical Conditions; Substance-Induced Persisting Dementia (such as Korsakoff's syndrome); and Dementia due to Multiple Etiologies. The criteria for cognitive deficits of dementia are the same for each type, and they are listed in Table 13–3. In order to qualify for a diagnosis of dementia, the person must exhibit memory impairment (either anterograde or retrograde amnesia) and at least one other type of cognitive disturbance, such as aphasia, apraxia, agnosia, or problems in abstract thinking. There must also be evidence that the person's cognitive impairment interferes with his or her social or occupational functioning. Finally, for all forms of dementia, DSM-IV notes that the cognitive problems must be above and beyond anything that could be attributed solely to delirium.

TABLE 13–2

Cognitive Disorders listed in DSM-IV

Delirium	Delirium due to a general medical condition
	Substance-induced delirium
	Delirium due to multiple etiologies
Dementia	Dementia of the Alzheimer's type
	Vascular dementia
	Dementia due to other general medical conditions
	HIV disease
	Head trauma
	Parkinson's disease
	Huntington's disease
	Pick's disease
	Creutzfeldt-Jakob disease
	Substance-induced persisting dementia
	Dementia due to multiple etiologies
Amnestic Disorders	Amnestic disorder due to a general medical condition
	Substance-induced persisting amnestic disorder

Specific Disorders

DEMENTIA OF THE ALZHEIMER'S TYPE

Alzheimer's disease is distinguished from the other types of dementia listed in DSM-IV on the basis of speed of onset. In this disorder, the cognitive impairment appears gradually, and the person's cognitive deterioration is progressive. If the person meets these criteria, the diagnosis is then made on the basis of excluding other conditions such as vascular disease, Huntington's disease, Parkinson's disease, and chronic substance abuse.

A definite diagnosis of Alzheimer's disease requires the observation of two specific types of brain lesions: neurofibrillary tangles and senile plaques. The brain is composed of millions of neurons. Part of the internal structure of each neuron is composed of *neurofibrils*, which provide structural support for the cell and help transport chemicals that are used in the production of neurotransmitters (Kolb & Whishaw, 1990). In the normal cell, neurofibrils are organized symmetrically. In Alzheimer's disease, the struc-

Memory Differences in Alzheimer's Disease and Huntington's Disease

The cognitive deficits that are displayed by patients with dementia represent an important challenge as well as a unique opportunity for psychologists (Butters, 1992; Poon, Kaszniak, & Dudley, 1992). The challenge is to define more specifically the nature of the cognitive impairments associated with different types of dementia. If scientists can develop laboratory tests that identify specific types of cognitive impairment, these tests might be useful for several purposes: as early signs of the onset of dementia; as diagnostic tools to help clinicians distinguish among various types of dementia; and as measures of adjustment to mark the progression of the disorder or the response to treatment.

The opportunity is to find clues to the brain mechanisms that are responsible for different aspects of memory and information processing by studying individuals who have naturally occurring neurological dysfunctions. Carefully studied individual cases have given psychologists some insight regarding neurological underpinnings regarding the organization of memory in the brain. For example, one 52-year-old man, called R.B., developed severe amnesia in 1978 after the blood supply to his brain was temporarily interrupted during open-heart surgery. For the next 5 years, R.B.'s memory problems were studied extensively. His other cognitive functions were well preserved. After R.B.'s death in 1983, examination of his brain revealed extensive bilateral damage to the hippocampus (see Figure 12–2 in Chapter 12) (Zola-Morgan, Squire, & Amaral, 1986).

This case, together with many other types of data, sup-

ports the hypothesis that the hippocampus is essential to a specific kind of memory, which is sometimes called *declarative* or *explicit memory* (Squire, 1992). In tasks that require explicit memory, subjects are asked to remember and later retrieve or recognize target information, such as words, letters, and symbols. In an *implicit memory* task, the subject's performance may be enhanced by prior experience with target information, even though the subject was not explicitly asked to remember it.

Comparisons between the cognitive performance of patients with specific types of dementia and normal people of the same age may provide us with insights that are similar to those gleaned from case studies like R.B.'s. One especially intriguing study involved a comparison among patients with dementia of the Alzheimer's type, patients with Huntington's disease, and elderly normal control subjects. Each subject performed two implicit memory tasks. In the

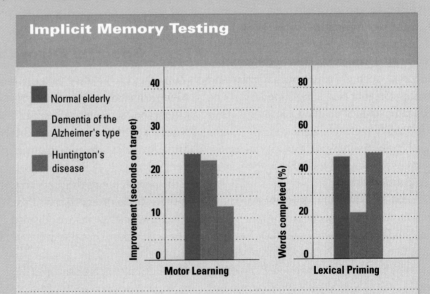

FIGURE 13-2: Comparison of patients with dementia and normal subjects on two tests of implicit memory: a pursuit-rotor learning task and a lexical priming task.

Source: Adapted from W.C. Heindel, et al. (1989). Neuropsychological evidence for multiple implicit memory systems. A comparison of Alzheimer's, Huntington's, and Parkinson's disease patients. *Journal of Neuroscience, 9,* 586.

motor learning task, they were seated in front of a rotating turntable upon which a small metallic disk was located. They were asked to maintain contact between a stylus, which they held in their preferred hand, and the rotating disk. The investigators kept track of "time on target," and improvement was measured over three series of eight trials.

In the lexical priming task, the subjects were shown a sequence of 10 words (for example, MOTEL, ABSTAIN). Each word was printed on a small card, and the subjects were asked to rate how much they liked each word. These ratings were completed twice in order to increase the subjects' exposure to the target words. They were not asked to remember the words. When the second set of ratings was completed, the subjects were asked to complete one final task. They were presented with a sequence of three-letter stems (for example, MOT, ABS) and asked to complete each stem with the first word that came

to mind. The index of implicit memory was the percentage of word stems completed with words that they had been asked to rate previously.

The results of this study are illustrated in Figure 13–2. The Alzheimer's patients were impaired on the lexical priming task, but their performance on the motor learning task was indistinguishable from that of the normal control subjects. The opposite pattern was found for patients with Huntington's disease. These data led to some interesting conclusions. First, although the cognitive symptoms associated with different forms of dementia may be difficult to distinguish on a clinical basis, laboratory tasks indicate that they may be associated with more specific types of cognitive impairment. Second, different types of implicit memory may be dependent on distinct brain mechanisms. Further, different mechanisms might be affected in varying ways by different disorders. ■

tural network of some neurofibrils becomes highly disorganized. Because these areas look like a tangled mass under the microscope, they are known as **neurofibrillary tangles**. They are found in both the cerebral cortex and the hippocampus. Cells with this appearance cannot function properly and are probably dead (Heston & White, 1991). Neurofibrillary tangles have also been found in adults with Down syndrome and patients with Parkinson's disease.

The other type of lesion in Alzheimer's disease is known as **senile plaques**, which consist of a central core of homogeneous protein material known as *amyloid* surrounded by clumps of debris left over from destroyed neurons. These plaques are located primarily in the cerebral cortex. They are found in large numbers in the brains of patients with Alzheimer's disease, but they are not unique to that condition. The brains of normal elderly people, especially after the age of 75, often contain some neurofibrillary tangles and senile plaques. A few widely scat-

TABLE 13–3

DSM-IV Criteria for Dementia of the Alzheimer's Type

A. The development of multiple cognitive deficits manifested by both:
  1. Memory impairment (impaired ability to learn new information or to recall previously learned information)
  2. One (or more) of the following cognitive disturbances:
     a. Aphasia (language disturbance)
     b. Apraxia (impaired ability to carry out motor activities despite intact motor function)
     c. Agnosia (failure to recognize or identify objects despite intact sensory function)
     d. Disturbance in executive functioning (that is, planning, organizing, sequencing, abstracting)

B. The cognitive deficits each cause significant impairment in social or occupational functioning and represent a significant decline from a previous level of functioning.

C. The course is characterized by gradual onset and continuing cognitive decline.

tered cells of this type do not interfere with normal cognitive functioning.

PICK'S DISEASE

Pick's disease is a form of primary dementia that is associated with atrophy of the frontal and temporal lobes of the brain. It is very similar to Alzheimer's disease in terms of both behavioral symptoms and cognitive impairment. Patients with both disorders display problems in memory and language. Early personality changes that precede the onset of cognitive impairment are more common among Pick patients. In comparison to Alzheimer patients, Pick patients are also more likely to engage in impulsive sexual actions, roaming and aimless exploration, and other types of disinhibited behavior (Mendez et al., 1993).

A detailed examination of brain tissue from patients with Pick's disease reveals the presence of *Pick's bodies*, a distinctive ballooning of nerve cells. The neurofibrillary tangles and senile plaques found in Alzheimer's disease are no more common in patients with Pick's disease than in normal people of the same age.

HUNTINGTON'S DISEASE

Huntington's disease is distinguished from the undifferentiated types of dementia by the presence of unusual involuntary muscle movements known as **chorea** (from the Greek word meaning "dance"). These movements are relatively subtle at first, with the person appearing to be restless or fidgety. As the disorder progresses, sustained muscle contractions become difficult. Movements of the face, trunk, and limbs eventually become uncontrolled, leaving the person to writhe and grimace. A large proportion of Huntington's patients also exhibit a variety of personality changes and symptoms of mental disorders, including primarily depression and anxiety. Between 5 percent and 10 percent develop psychotic symptoms (Shoulson, 1990). The symptoms of mental disorder may be evident before the appearance of motor or cognitive impairment. The movement disorder and the cognitive deficits are produced by progressive neuronal degeneration in the basal ganglia. This

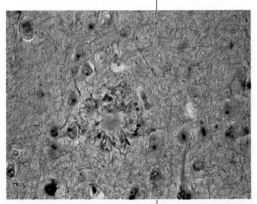

▲ **This microscopic photograph illustrates senile plaques, which are found throughout the cortex and hippocampus of patients with Alzheimer's disease.**

is a group of nuclei, including the caudate nucleus, the putamen, and the globus pallidus, that form a collaborative system of connections between the cerebral cortex and the thalamus (see Figure 13–3).

Dementia appears in all Huntington's disease patients, although the extent of the cognitive impairment and the rate of its progression are quite variable. Impairments in recent memory and learning are the most obvious cognitive problems. Patients have trouble encoding new information. Higher-level cognitive functions are typically well preserved, and insight is usually intact. Unlike the pattern of dementia seen in Alzheimer's disease, patients with Huntington's do not develop aphasia, apraxias, or agnosias (Kolb & Whishaw, 1991).

The diagnosis of Huntington's disease depends on the presence of a positive family history for the disorder. It is one of the few disorders that are transmitted in an autosomal dominant pattern with complete penetrance. In other words, the person must only inherit one gene—from either parent—to be vulnerable, and an individual who inherits the problematic gene will always develop the disorder.

PARKINSON'S DISEASE

Parkinson's disease is primarily a disorder of the motor system that is caused by a degeneration of a specific area of the brain stem known as the *substantia nigra* and loss of the neurotransmitter dopamine, which is produced by cells in this area. Typical symptoms include tremors, rigidity, postural abnormalities, and reduction in voluntary movements (Lishman, 1987). Unlike people with Huntington's disease, most patients with Parkinson's disease do not become demented. One prospective longitudinal study found that only 20 percent developed symptoms of dementia over a period of 4.5 years (Biggins et al., 1992).

VASCULAR DEMENTIA

Many conditions other than those that attack brain tissue directly can also produce symptoms of dementia. These are known as secondary dementias. The central agent in these problems can be either medical conditions or other types of mental disorder. Diseases that affect the heart and lungs, for example, can interfere with the circulation of oxygen to the brain. Substance abuse can also interfere with brain functions.

One of the leading causes of secondary dementia is vascular or blood vessel disease, which affects the arteries responsible for bringing oxygen and sugar to the brain. A *stroke*, the severe interruption of blood flow to the brain, can produce various types of brain damage, depending on the size of the blood vessel that is affected and the area of the brain that it supplies. The area of dead tissue produced by the stroke is known as an **infarct**. The behavioral effects of a stroke are usually obvious and can be distinguished from dementia on several grounds: (1) they appear suddenly rather than gradually; (2) they affect voluntary movements of the limbs and gross speech patterns as well as more subtle intellectual abilities; and (3) they often result in unilateral rather than bilateral impairment, such as paralysis of only one side of the body. There are instances, however, in which the stroke affects only a very small artery and may not have any observable effect on the person's behavior. If several of these small strokes occur over a period of time, and if their sites are scattered in different areas of the brain, they may gradually produce cognitive impairment.

The DSM-IV refers to this condition as **vascular dementia**. Another commonly used term for this condition is *multi-infarct dementia*. The cognitive symptoms of vascular dementia that are listed in the diagnostic manual are the same as those for Alzheimer's disease, but DSM-IV does not require a gradual onset for vascular dementia, as it does for dementia of the Alzheimer's type. In addition, the diagnosis of vascular dementia depends on the presence of either focal neurologic signs and symptoms associated with the experience of stroke, such as gait abnormalities or weakness in the extremities, or laboratory evidence of blood vessel disease. More stringent criteria for vascular dementia have been proposed for use in research studies (Roman et al., 1993). The research criteria would require that the presence of cerebrovascular disease be confirmed by brain imaging.

DEMENTIA VERSUS DEPRESSION

Depression is another condition that can be associated with symptoms of dementia, especially among the elderly (Lishman, 1987). There are, indeed, many areas of overlap between these disorders. Approximately 20 percent of patients with a diagnosis of dementia also exhibit symptoms of major depressive disorder (Allen &

Blazer, 1991). The symptoms of depression include a lack of interest in, and withdrawal of attention from, the environment. People who are depressed often have trouble concentrating, they appear preoccupied, and their thinking

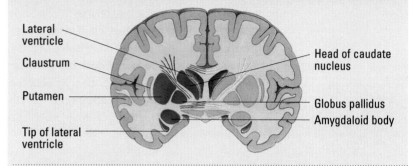

Areas of the Brain Implicated in Huntington's Disease

FIGURE 13-3: Huntington's disease involves deterioration of the basal ganglia (also known as the cerebral nuclie). The primary units of this system are the caudate nucleus, putamen, globus pallidus, and the claustrum.

Source: Adapted from F. Martini and M. Timmons (1995). *Human anatomy*, p. 378. Englewood Cliffs, NJ: Prentice Hall.

is labored. These cognitive problems closely resemble some symptoms of dementia. Some depressed patients exhibit poverty of speech and restricted or unchanging facial expression. A disheveled appearance, due to self-neglect and loss of weight, in an elderly patient may contribute to the impression that the person is suffering from dementia.

Despite the many similarities, there are important differences between depression and dementia. These are summarized in Table 13–4. Experienced clinicians can usually distinguish

	TABLE 13-4

Signs and Symptoms Distinguishing Depression from Dementia

Depression	Dementia
Uneven progression over weeks	Even progression over months or years
Complains of memory loss	Attempts to hide memory loss
Often worse in morning, better as day goes on	Worse later in day or when fatigued
Aware of, exaggerates disability	Unaware of or minimizes disability
May abuse alcohol or other drugs	Rarely abuses drugs

Source: Adapted from L.L. Heston and J.A. White. (1991). *The vanishing mind: A practical guide to Alzheimer's disease and other dementias.* New York: Freeman.

between depression and dementia by considering the pattern of onset and associated features (Allen & Blazer, 1991). In those cases where the distinction cannot be made on the basis of these characteristics, response to treatment may be the only way to establish a differential diagnosis. If the person's condition, including cognitive impairments, improves following treatment with antidepressant medication or electroconvulsive therapy, it seems reasonable to conclude that the person was depressed. These procedures can also be somewhat dangerous, because the cognitive symptoms of patients who are actually suffering from dementia may become exaggerated in response to medication (Horvath et al., 1991).

The relationship between depression and dementia has been the topic of considerable debate (Wertheimer, 1991). Is depression a consequence of dementia, or are the symptoms of dementia a consequence of depression? Some clinicians have used the term *pseudodementia* to describe the condition of patients with symptoms of dementia whose cognitive impairment is actually produced by a major depressive disorder. There is no doubt that cases of this sort exist (Bulbena & Berrios, 1991). In fact, depression and dementia are not necessarily mutually exclusive disorders. We know that these conditions coexist more often than would be expected by chance, but we do not know why (Teri & Wagner, 1992).

Epidemiology

Cognitive disorders represent one of the most pressing health problems in our society. Dementia is an especially important problem among elderly people. Although it can appear in people as young as 40 to 45, the average age of onset is much later. The incidence of dementia will be much greater in the near future, because the average age of the population is increasing steadily (see Chapter 16). People over the age of 80 represent one of the fastest growing segments of our population. By the year 2040, more than 9 million people in the United States will be affected by Alzheimer's disease (Max, 1993). The personal and economic impact of dementia on patients, their families, and our society clearly warrants serious attention from health-care professionals, policymakers concerned with health-care reform, and clinical scientists seeking more effective forms of treatment.

Epidemiologic studies must be interpreted with caution, of course, because of the problems associated with establishing a diagnosis of dementia. Mild cases are difficult to identify reliably. At the earliest stages of the disorder, symptoms are difficult to distinguish from forgetfulness, which can increase in normal aging (see Further Thoughts). Definitive diagnoses depend on information collected over an extended period of time so that the progressive nature of the cognitive impairment, and deterioration from an earlier, higher level of functioning, can be documented. Unfortunately, this kind of information is often not available in a large-scale epidemiologic study.

You should also bear in mind the fact that the diagnosis of specific subtypes of dementia, such as dementia of the Alzheimer's type and dementia due to Pick's disease, requires microscopic examination of brain tissue after the person's death. Again, these data are not typically available to epidemiologists. With these limitations in mind, we now consider what is known about the frequency of dementia in the general population.

Incidence and Prevalence by Age Groups

The incidence and prevalence of dementia increase dramatically with age. Longitudinal studies of community samples indicate that the annual incidence of dementia is 1.4 percent in people over the age of 65 and 3.4 percent for people over the age of 75 (Brayne, 1993). Because dementia is most often a progressive disorder from which patients do not recover, we would expect that prevalence rates would be much higher than incidence rates. Most studies have reported a prevalence rate of about 5 percent for moderate or severe dementia among all people over the age of 65 years (Hafner, 1990). Beginning with a rate of approximately 1 percent in the age group

60 to 64 years, the rate doubles approximately every 5 years. Almost 40 percent of people over 90 years of age exhibit symptoms of moderate or severe dementia.

Survival rates are reduced among demented patients. In Alzheimer's disease, for example, the average time between onset of the disorder and the person's death is approximately 8 years. Those with an earlier age of onset tend to live for a shorter period of time; the average survival period is only 4.5 years for those with an onset before age 45 (Heston & White, 1991). There is considerable variability in these figures. Some patients have survived more than 20 years after the first appearance of obvious symptoms.

There are no obvious differences between men and women with regard to the overall prevalence of dementia, broadly defined (Kokmen et al., 1993). It seems, however, that dementia in men is more likely to be associated with vascular disease or to be secondary to other medical conditions or to alcohol abuse (Brayne, 1993).

PREVALENCE BY SUBTYPES

The studies we have already reviewed refer to cross-sectional examinations of populations, which do not allow diagnosis of specific subtypes of dementia. Some clinical studies, based on hospital populations, have allowed investigators to look at the frequency of specific sub-

types of dementia. These data are summarized in Figure 13–4. Dementia of the Alzheimer's type appears to be the most common form of dementia, followed by dementia produced by vascular disease. Pick's disease is much less common. Huntington's disease, which is not included in this figure, is quite rare by comparison. It affects only 1 person in every 20,000 (O'Shea & Falvey, 1988; Shoulson, 1990).

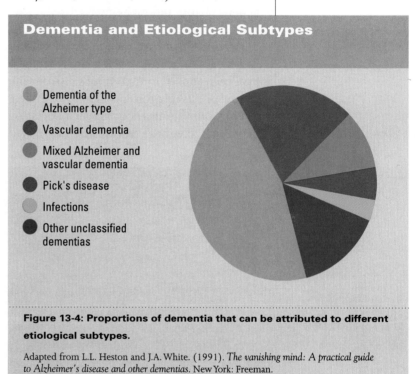

Figure 13-4: Proportions of dementia that can be attributed to different etiological subtypes.

Adapted from L.L. Heston and J.A. White. (1991). *The vanishing mind: A practical guide to Alzheimer's disease and other dementias.* New York: Freeman.

Etiological Considerations and Research

In discussing the classification of dementia and other cognitive disorders, we have already touched on many of the factors that contribute to the etiology of these problems. Most of the other disorders listed in DSM-IV are classified on the basis of symptoms alone. The classification of dementia is sometimes determined by specific knowledge of etiological factors, even though these may be determined only after the patient's death, as in Alzheimer's disease. In the following pages, we consider in greater detail a few of the specific pathways that are known to lead to dementia.

Genetic Factors

Neurologists who treat demented patients have recognized for many years that the disorder often runs in families. Until recently, twin studies have not been used extensively to evaluate the influence of genetic factors in dementia because of the comparatively late age of onset of these disorders. By the time a proband develops symptoms of dementia, his or her co-twin may be deceased. A few recent studies have capitalized on national samples to find an adequate number of twin pairs. They confirm the impression, based on family studies, that genetic factors play an important role in the development of dementia. One Swedish study, for example, found that the concordance rate in MZ twins was over 50 percent, more than double the DZ rate (Pedersen & Gatz, 1991). A U.S. study, based on a registry of aging twin veterans of World War II and the Korean War, found an MZ concordance rate of 35 percent in 24 male pairs. None of the 16 DZ pairs was concordant at the time of the report (Breitner et al., 1993).

Most of the research efforts concerned with genetic factors and Alzheimer's disease have focused on genetic linkage strategies. The astounding advances that have been made in molecular genetics since 1980 (see Research Methods) have been applied to Alzheimer's disease with fruitful results (Heston & White, 1991; Pollen, 1993). Some studies confirm an association between Alzheimer's disease and Down syn-

drome (see Chapter 14). It has been known for many years that senile plaques and neurofibrillary tangles are also found in the brains of all people who have Down syndrome. This similarity led investigators to search for a link between the gene for Alzheimer's disease and known markers on chromosome 21, because people with Down syndrome possess three copies of chromosome 21 in every cell instead of the normal two. Several research groups have independently confirmed this association. Within some families, the gene for Alzheimer's disease is located on chromosome 21. It has also been established that the gene responsible for producing proteins that serve as precursors to amyloid, found in the core of senile plaques, is also located on chromosome 21.

RESEARCH METHODS

Genetic Linkage Analysis

It is one thing to say that genetic factors "are involved" in the transmission of a disorder, and quite another to identify the specific mode of inheritance. Discovery of the gene that is responsible for a disorder would obviously represent an exciting step toward explaining the etiology of the disorder. It would also have crucial implications for people who are known to be at increased risk for the disorder. Exciting developments in the field of molecular genetics have allowed scientists to begin the search for such genes and, in some cases, to find them. The dementias, especially Huntington's disease, are one area in which important advances have been made in this regard.

The mode of inheritance in Huntington's disease has been relatively clear for many years because it follows an obvious Mendelian pattern: Almost exactly 50 percent of an affected person's first-degree relatives will also have the disorder. It is therefore considered to be an *autosomal dominant trait*. The term *autosomal* means that the gene is not located on one of the sex chromosomes. The knowledge that one gene, or a single locus on a particular chromosome, is apparently responsible for Huntington's disease made it an obvious candidate for genetic linkage analysis.

A gene is a strand of DNA, composed of a vast sequence of pairs of nucleic acid bases. These are the rods that lend a stairlike appearance to the familiar double helix structure of DNA, described by James D. Watson and Francis Crick in 1953. We all possess 46 chromosomes (23 pairs), which, taken together, contain 3 billion of these base-pairs. Locating a gene on a chromosome can be accomplished by demonstrating **genetic linkage** between the genetic locus associated with the disorder and the locus for a known gene, a *chromosome marker*. Two loci are said to be linked when they are sufficiently close together on the same chromosome. Because of this physical association, the alleles at the two loci do not segregate independently during meiosis, the cell division process that results in the formation of sperm and egg cells.

In order to identify linkage, an investigator must study a large extended family in which several members have been affected by the disorder in question. Samples of cells are collected from everyone in the family. If all (or almost all) of the members of the family who have the disorder also have the marker in question, and if all (or almost all) of the unaffected members do not have the marker, then genetic linkage has been established (Heston & White, 1991).

The concept of genetic linkage was introduced early in the twentieth century by Thomas Hunt Morgan. Progress toward establishing genetic linkage in human disorders was extremely limited, however, because very few markers were available. In the late 1970s, recombinant DNA procedures led to the discovery of *restriction fragment-length polymorphisms* (RFLPs), fragments of DNA that are not associated with any recognized phenotypic trait but nevertheless provide useful landmarks for DNA segments. RFLPs are scattered across all of the chromosomes. A number of scientists are currently involved in the Human Genome Project, which hopes to map the entire human genome—all 46 chromosomes—by the next decade.

In 1983, a group of scientists reported that the gene responsible for Huntington's disease was located on the short arm of chromosome 4 (Gusella et al., 1983). The data for their investigation came from a large extended family living in several remote villages on the northern coast of Venezuela. An unusually large number of the people in this family are victims of Huntington's disease. This is exactly the kind of pedigree required for genetic linkage analysis. Using blood samples collected from affected and unaffected members of the Venezuelan family, the investigators began looking for linkage with approximately a dozen RFLP markers. They were extremely lucky. The third marker that they tested produced a score indicating that the odds in favor of linkage between the Huntington's disease gene and this probe were over 200 million to 1. The probe was obviously located in very close proximity to the gene for which they were searching. Ten years later, the Huntington's Disease Collaborative Research Group (1993) announced that it had found the specific gene. ■

The link to chromosome 21 is tentative, however. Other labs have failed to find an association between Alzheimer's disease and chromosome 21, and some have reported linkage with other chromosomes. In some families, an unidentified gene on chromosome 14 appears to be responsible for an early-onset form of the disorder (Schellenberg et al., 1992). Experts now assume that Alzheimer's disease is genetically heterogeneous. In other words, there are several forms of the disorder, and each may be associated with a different gene or set of genes.

Neurotransmitters

In patients suffering from dementia, the process of chemical transmission of messages within the brain is probably disrupted, but the specific mechanisms that are involved have not been identified. We know that Parkinson's disease, which is sometimes associated with dementia, is caused by a degeneration of the dopamine pathways in the brainstem. This dysfunction is responsible for the motor symptoms seen in patients with that disorder. It is not entirely clear, however, that the intellectual problems experienced by patients with Parkinson's disease are directly related to dopamine deficiencies.

Other types of dementia have also been linked to problems with specific neurotransmitters. Huntington's disease may be associated with deficiencies in gamma amino butyric acid (GABA), and a decrease in the availability of acetylcholine, another type of neurotransmitter, has been implicated in Alzheimer's disease (Heston & White, 1991).

Viral Infections

Some forms of primary dementia are known to be the products of "slow" viruses—infections that develop over a much more extended period of time than do most viral infections. *Creutzfeldt-Jakob disease* is one example. Susceptibility to infection by a specific virus can be influenced by genetic factors. The demonstration that a condition is transmitted in a familial fashion does not rule out the involvement of viral infection. In fact, familial transmission has been demonstrated for the forms of dementia that are known to be associated with a specific virus.

Immune System Dysfunction

The immune system is the body's first line of defense against infection. It employs antibodies to break down foreign materials, such as bacteria and viruses, that enter the body. The regulation of this system allows it to distinguish between foreign bodies that should be destroyed and normal body tissues that should be preserved. The production of these antibodies may be dysfunctional in some forms of dementia, such as Alzheimer's disease. In other words, the destruction of brain tissue may be caused by a breakdown in the system that regulates the immune system.

The presence of amyloid at the core of senile plaques provides one important clue to the possible involvement of immune system dysfunction. In many known forms of immune system dysfunction, amyloid is present in dead tissues. Antibodies that destroy brain tissue are known to increase in normal aging, but they are found in even larger amounts among patients with dementia (Heston & White, 1991).

Environmental Factors

Epidemiologic investigations have discovered several interesting patterns that suggest that some types of dementia, especially Alzheimer's disease, may be related to environmental factors. One example is exposure to aluminum, a chemical that is abundant in the natural environment. Experimental studies with animals have demonstrated that exposure to aluminum can induce brain lesions that resemble the neurofibrillary tangles found in Alzheimer's disease. Excess levels of aluminum have also been found at autopsy in the brains of some victims of Alzheimer's

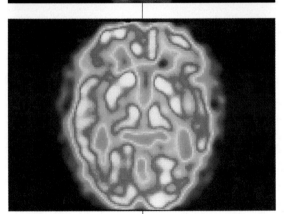

▲ PET scans of the brain of a normal subject (bottom) and a patient with Alzheimer's disease (top). The top image shows degeneration of brain tissue and lower brain activity, both of which are characteristic of the disease.

disease (Heston & White, 1991). Some epidemiological evidence indicates a correlation between levels of aluminum in the water supply and rates of dementia and cognitive impairment in the local population. Other studies have failed to replicate this result (Brayne, 1993; Jacqmin et al., 1994). The possible link between aluminum and dementia is both questionable and controversial, but it is still a topic of serious research efforts (Copestake, 1993; Zatta, 1993).

In addition to the aluminum connection, other studies have reported significant relationships between Alzheimer's disease and two other variables that seem to operate as protective factors: (1) cigarette smoking, and (2) levels of educational experience. Some reports indicate, for example, that people who have smoked cigarettes actually have a lower risk for developing Alzheimer's disease (Brenner et al., 1993). These data are interesting in light of the fact that autopsies of Alzheimer's victims have found a reduced density of nicotinic receptors in the brain. Some investigators have speculated that the experience of smoking cigarettes may reduce the risk for dementia of the Alzheimer's type by increasing the density or sensitivity of nicotinic receptors.

The final correlation we will consider is between dementia of the Alzheimer's type and educational attainment. Several investigators have found that people who have achieved high levels of education are less likely to develop Alzheimer's disease than are people with less education (Friedland, 1993). Snowdon et al. (1990), for example, found that among elderly Catholic nuns, those who had graduated from college were much less likely to be cognitively impaired than were those who had less than a college education. There are several ways to interpret this relationship. One suggests that increased "brain work" leads to a facilitation of neuronal activation, increased cerebral blood flow, and higher levels of glucose and oxygen consumption in the brain. This experience may reduce the person's risk for later neuronal deterioration in much the same way that higher levels of environmental stimulation can facilitate neural growth during early development in young animals (Greenough, 1986).

Although these findings are thought-provoking, a strong word of caution is in order. It is not clear whether these *correlations* indicate a *causal* relationship between these variables and dementia (Heston & White, 1991; Katzman, 1993). The correlations could easily be due to any number of third variables. Directionality is also a problem. For example, aluminum might become concentrated in brain tissue *after* the death of nerve cells, which is caused by some other factor. It is certainly the case that many people who have been exposed to comparatively high levels of aluminum—metal workers, people who take certain medications, and people who drink large quantities of tea, which is high in aluminum—have not become demented.

Treatment and Management

The most obvious consideration with regard to treatment of the cognitive disorders is accurate diagnosis (Cutting & McClelland, 1991). The distinction between delirium and dementia is important because many conditions that cause delirium can be treated. Delirium must be recognized as early as possible so that the source of the problem, such as an infection or some other medical condition, can be treated. Some types of secondary dementia can also be treated successfully. For example, if the patient's cognitive symptoms are the products of depression, there is a relatively good chance that he or she will respond positively to antidepressant medication or electroconvulsive therapy.

When the person clearly suffers from a primary type of dementia, such as dementia of the Alzheimer's type, a return to previous levels of functioning is extremely unlikely. No form of treatment is presently capable of improving cognitive functioning in dementia of the Alzheimer's type (Growdon, 1992). Realistic goals include helping the person to maintain his or her level of functioning for as long as possible in spite of cognitive impairment and minimizing the level of distress experienced by the person and the person's family. Several treatment options are typically used in conjunction, including medication, management of the patient's environment, behavioral strategies, and providing support to caregivers (Horvath et al., 1991).

Medication

We do not yet have specific drugs that can reverse the process of cell loss in the brain that is responsible for dementia. There are, however, a number of clues available regarding the nature of the neurochemical abnormalities involved in dementia of the Alzheimer's type. For the past decade, these clues have stimulated attempts to treat Alzheimer's patients with experimental types of medication. It has been demonstrated, for example, that levels of a transmitter known as *acetylcholine* (Ach) may be reduced in this disorder. The production of Ach in the brain is controlled by an enzyme known as *choline acetyl transferase*, and some studies have found that activity levels of this enzyme are reduced in the brains of people suffering from dementia of the Alzheimer's type.

Evidence regarding Ach and choline acetyl transferase generated a variety of efforts to stimulate increased production of Ach in the hope that it would lead to an improvement in cognitive functioning. Unfortunately, the earliest treatment studies of this sort were largely unsuccessful (Davis & Haroutunian, 1993). A few individual patients showed modest improvement, but most did not, and the side effects of the drugs were quite unpleasant. More recently, investigators have continued to pursue new types of medication that are intended primarily to increase levels of Ach in the brain. One specific drug, tetrahydroaminoacridine (THA), has shown promising results in terms of its ability to improve the immediate signs and symptoms of dementia of the Alzheimer's type, although it does not seem to prevent the long-term progression of the disorder.

Although the cognitive deficits associated with primary dementia cannot be reversed with medication, the severity of the motor dysfunctions associated with primary differentiated forms of dementia, such as Huntington's disease, can be reduced through the use of neuroleptic medications (Heston & White, 1991). These are the same drugs that are used to treat schizophrenia. Their pharmacological action is focused on blocking postsynaptic dopamine receptors.

Environmental and Behavioral Management

Severely impaired patients often reside in nursing homes and hospitals. The most effective residential treatment programs combine the use of medication and behavioral interventions with an environment that is specifically designed to maximize the level of functioning and minimize the emotional distress of patients who are cognitively impaired. Several goals guide the design of such an environment (Lawton, 1989). These include considerations that enhance the following aspects of the patient's life.

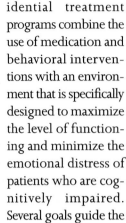

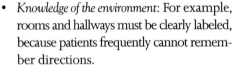

▲ **Residential programs attempt to keep patients with dementia as active as possible.**

- *Knowledge of the environment*: For example, rooms and hallways must be clearly labeled, because patients frequently cannot remember directions.
- *Negotiability*: In the case of dementia, psychological accessibility is at least as important as physical accessibility. For example, spaces that the person would use (a commons area or the dining room) should be visible from the patient's room if they cannot be remembered.
- *Safety and health*: For example, access to the setting must be secured so that patients who would otherwise wander away can remain as active as possible.

One important issue related to patient management involves the level of activity expected of the patient. It is useful to help the person remain active and interested in everyday events. Patients who are physically active are less likely to have problems with agitation, and they may sleep better. Engaging in pleasant activities may also minimize the frequency and severity of depression among patients with dementia (Teri & Gallagher-Thompson, 1991). Nevertheless, expectations regarding the patient's activity level may have to be reduced in proportion to the progression of cognitive impairment. Efforts should be made to preserve familiar routines and surroundings in light of the inevitable difficulties that are associated with learning new information and recalling past events. Helping the person to cope with these issues may minimize the emotional turmoil associated with the increasing loss of cognitive abilities.

Social interactions are often troublesome for patients with dementia. An example of this type of problem was described in the case of Mary at the beginning of this chapter. After Mary had been admitted to the hospital, she frequently approached the nurses insisting that she had to go home to take care of her dog, which had in fact died. Creative problem-solving strategies that accommodate the patient's distorted view of reality are sometimes useful in this type of situation. Imagine, for example, a patient who continually insists that he must go to his former place of employment. It might be more effective to inform him each morning that his office called to say that he was not needed until the next day, rather than engaging in futile and upsetting arguments about whether he had, in fact, retired for medical reasons—a fact that he is incapable of remembering (Zarit et al., 1990).

Support for Caregivers

A final area of concern is the provision of support to people who serve as caregivers for demented patients. In the United States, spouses and other family members provide primary care for more than 80 percent of people who have dementia of the Alzheimer's type (Mangone et al., 1993). Their burdens are often overwhelming, both physically and emotionally. Consider, for example, the situation described by Bernlef (1988) in *Out of Mind*. In the following passage, Maarten describes the experience of listening to his wife, Vera, describe to a young woman (whom Vera has hired to help care for Maarten) how she has felt while attempting to cope with his progressive cognitive deterioration:

> I hear Vera. "More than 40 years I have been married to him. And then suddenly this. Usually these things happen more slowly, gradually. But with him it came all at once. I feel it has been sprung on me. It's cruel and unfair. Sometimes I get so angry and rebellious when I see him looking at me as if from another world. And then again I feel only sad and I would so much like to

understand him. Or I just talk along with him and then I feel ashamed afterwards. I'm glad you're here because it really gets on top of me at times, when I just can't bear watching it any more. At least now I'll be able to get out occasionally."

There is a moment of silence. I feel the tears running under my eyelids and down my cheeks.

"And sometimes, sometimes his face radiates perfect peace. As if he's happy. Like a child can be. Those moments are so brief I sometimes think I imagine them. But I know only too well what I see at such moments: someone who looks exactly like my husband of long ago. At your age it's difficult to understand that. But people like us live by their memories. If they no longer have those there's nothing left. I am afraid he is in the process of forgetting his whole life. And to live alone with those memories while he sits there beside me . . . empty." (Bernlef, 1988, pp. 80–81)

In addition to the profound loneliness and sadness that caregivers endure, they must also learn to cope with more tangible stressors, such as the patient's incontinence, functional deficits, and disruptive behavior. Relationships among other family members and the psychological adjustment of the principal caregiver are more disturbed by caring for a demented person than by caring for someone who is physically disabled (Brody, 1989). Guilt, frustration, and depression are common reactions among the family members of patients.

Respite programs provide caregivers with tem-

porary periods of relief away from the patient. One model program was designed and evaluated by M. Powell Lawton and his colleagues at the Philadelphia Geriatric Center (Brody, Saperstein, & Lawton, 1989). They either would send someone to the patient's home to relieve the caregiver or, in more severe cases, would temporarily institutionalize the patient if the caregiver needed to be away from home for an extended period. In some cases, these services were planned in

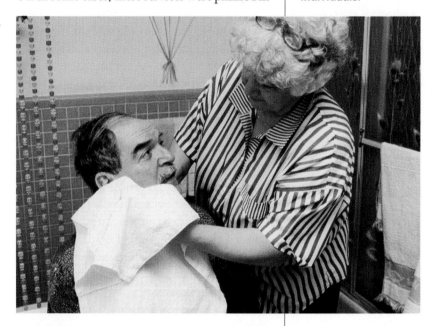

advance so that the caregiver could take a short vacation, attend special events, or make his or her own medical appointments. Respite care was also available in response to unexpected circumstances, such as the illness of the caregiver. This type of flexible, comprehensive program is clearly needed to relieve the enormous burden that is faced by people who care for demented patients.

▼ **Individuals who care for people with dementia assume an enormous burden. Respite programs attempt to provide assistance to these individuals.**

Summary

Dementia, delirium, and amnestic disorders are listed as Cognitive Disorders in DSM-IV. Disruptions of memory and other cognitive functions are the most obvious symptoms of these disorders. Dementia and amnestic disorders are often associated with specific forms of neuropathology. These changes in brain tissue can often be observed only at autopsy, after the person's death. Until recently, the DSM referred to the Cognitive Disorders

KEY TERMS

- agnosia
- Alzheimer's disease
- amnestic disorder
- amyloid
- anterograde amnesia
- aphasia
- apraxia
- chorea

as Organic Mental Disorders because of their association with known brain diseases. That expression has been abandoned because it implies an artificial dichotomy between biological and psychological processes.

Dementia is defined as a gradually worsening loss of memory and related cognitive functions, including the use of language as well as reasoning and decision making. **Aphasia** and **apraxia** are among the most obvious problems in verbal communication. Perceptual difficulties, such as **agnosia**, are also common.

In **amnestic disorder**, the memory impairment is more circumscribed. The person may experience severe **anterograde amnesia**, but other higher-level cognitive abilities remain unimpaired.

Delirium is a confusional state that develops over a short period of time and is often associated with agitation and hyperactivity.

Dementia can be associated with many different kinds of neuropathology. The most common form of dementia is associated with Alzheimer's disease. It accounts for approximately half of all diagnosed cases of dementia. Another 20 percent of cases are produced by vascular disease. Several small strokes over a period of time can produce **infarcts** scattered in different areas of the brain and can lead to the gradual onset of cognitive impairment. Less common forms of dementia are associated with *Pick's disease*, *Huntington's disease*, and *Parkinson's disease*.

A definitive diagnosis of Alzheimer's disease can be made only after the patient's death. It requires the observation of two specific types of brain lesions: **neurofibrillary tangles** and **senile plaques**, which are found throughout the cerebral cortex. Neurofibrillary tangles are also found in the hippocampus, an area of the brain that is crucial for memory.

The incidence and prevalence of dementia increase dramatically with age. The annual incidence of dementia is 1.4 percent in people over the age of 65 and 3.4 percent for people over the age of 75. Almost 40 percent of people over 90 years of age exhibit symptoms of moderate or severe dementia. Men and women are equally vulnerable to these disorders.

The etiology of dementia is dependent on many different factors. Some types of dementia are produced by viral infections and immune system dysfunction. Environmental toxins also may contribute to the onset of cognitive impairment.

Genetic factors clearly play a role in the etiology of some forms of dementia. Considerable research efforts have been devoted to the study of **genetic linkage** in Alzheimer's disease. Chromosome 21 has been examined closely because people with Down syndrome, who possess three copies of chromosome 21 in every cell, also have senile plaques and neurofibrillary tangles like those found in the brains of Alzheimer's patients. Within some families, the gene for Alzheimer's disease is located on chromosome 21. This pattern of linkage is not found for all families, however. Experts now assume that there are several forms of Alzheimer's disease, and each may be associated with a different gene or set of genes.

Delirium can often be resolved successfully by treating the infection or some other medical condition. In some types of secondary depression, the person can be restored to his or her original level of cognitive functioning. The intellectual deficits in primary forms of dementia are progressive and irreversible. The treatment goals in these disorders are more limited. They include maintaining the person's level of functioning for as long as possible while minimizing the level of distress experienced by the patient and the family, especially caregivers. Medication can produce modest cognitive benefits for some patients with dementia, but not all patients respond to such treatment, and the clinical significance of these changes is extremely limited. Drugs can be used to control motor dysfunctions associated with primary differentiated forms of dementia, such as Huntington's disease and Parkinson's disease.

Behavioral and environmental management are important aspects of any treatment program for demented patients. They allow patients to reside in the least restrictive and safest possible settings. Respite programs provide much-needed support to caregivers, usually spouses and other family members, who can easily be overwhelmed by the demands of caring for a person with dementia.

Critical Thinking

1. Suppose you know an elderly person who is beginning to show memory problems. Does that necessarily mean that he or she is becoming demented? What sort of measures might be used to distinguish normal aging from dementia?

2. Dementia and amnestic disorders are classified as cognitive disorders in DSM–IV. Many clinicians also talk about the role of cognitive factors in the development of disorders such as anxiety and depression. What is the difference between cognitive impairments seen in dementia and those seen in other forms of psychopathology?

3. Why has the etiology of Alzheimer's disease received increased attention in recent years? Why do clinical scientists consider this disorder to be one of the most pressing health problems in our society?

4. If dementia is an irreversible process, how can it be treated? To which considerations would you give the highest priority in addressing the needs of patients and their families?

14

Mental Retardation and Pervasive Developmental Disorders

ental retardation is a familiar and common problem characterized by significantly subaverage general intellectual functioning and deficits in adaptive life skills. By definition, mental retardation begins before the age of 18 years. Pervasive developmental disorders are much less familiar or common problems. These disorders are distinguished by their unusual behavioral symptoms, which include severe and pervasive impairments in communication, reciprocal social interaction, and stereotyped behavior, interests, and activities. The symptoms are severe in autistic disorder, a widely studied form of pervasive developmental disorder.

Overview

▼ Benny from the television show *L.A. Law* offered a realistic and positive portrayal about how mentally retarded people can fulfill valuable roles in work and in life.

Both mental retardation and pervasive developmental disorders typically either are present at birth or begin early in life. Both types of disorder are characterized by serious disruptions in many areas of functioning, often including an inability to care for oneself independently. Moreover, the majority of people who suffer from pervasive developmental disorder are also mentally retarded. For these reasons, we consider the two conditions together in a single chapter.

Approaches to the two problems have differed widely, however. Pervasive developmental disorders typically have been studied and treated from a mental health perspective. Scientists have considered pervasive developmental disorders as emotional problems. For example, a number of theorists have suggested that the intellectual impairments associated with pervasive developmental disorders are merely a consequence of disturbed behavior, emotions, or communication prob-

lems. Current evidence does not support this speculation, but pervasive developmental disorders continue to be viewed as mental health problems.

In contrast, mental retardation commonly has been approached from the perspective of the educational system. Mental retardation has been the domain of special educators more than of mental health professionals. One result of this focus on subaverage intellectual functioning is that practitioners often have overlooked the emotional problems found among mentally retarded people.

As an indication of these differing approaches in DSM-IV, mental retardation is coded on Axis II (see Chapter 4). This is one way of ensuring that adequate attention is paid to the Axis I mental disorders that may be found among mentally retarded people. In contrast, pervasive developmental disorders are coded as Axis I mental disorders. In this chapter, we discuss mental retardation before reviewing the pervasive developmental disorders, particularly autistic disorder. Our overview of mental retardation should increase your understanding of the pervasive developmental disorders, because most people with pervasive developmental disorders also are mentally retarded.

Mental Retardation

Mental retardation is a diverse diagnostic category. All mentally retarded people have impaired intellectual abilities, but they vary widely in academic ability and functioning. Mentally retarded people also differ substantially in their ability to communicate, to master social situations, and to participate in their own care. Some profoundly retarded people require total care and live their entire lives in institutions. However, the vast majority of the mentally retarded learn the self-care and vocational skills needed to allow them to live in the community. Both Benny, the engaging character from *L.A. Law*, and the char-

acter played by Tom Hanks in *Forrest Gump* are hopeful examples of the freedom, independence, and happiness that retarded people can achieve.

Although there are limits to what can be achieved, intensive intervention can bring about substantial improvements in the lives of retarded people. Unfortunately, mental retardation is not an especially fashionable topic for research or treatment. This is unfortunate, because much can be done, and much more needs to be learned, about the prevention and treatment of this very common problem. We begin our consideration of mental retardation with a case from our files.

CASE STUDY

A Mildly Mentally Retarded Mother

Karen Cross was a 41-year-old woman with three children when child protective services referred her and her husband, Mark, for a family evaluation. Two months earlier, the Crosses' 16-year-old daughter, Lucy, had called the police following a family fight. Lucy and her mother had been arguing about Lucy's excessive use of the telephone, and when Mr. Cross entered the dispute, he cuffed Lucy across her mouth in anger. Lucy was not seriously hurt, and the social workers who visited with the Cross family following the incident found no history of physical abuse. They were concerned about the adequacy of the Crosses' parenting, however, and the agency strongly recommended an evaluation for the family.

At the time of the referral, Mr. Cross was employed as a custodian at an elementary school where he had been working for 15 years. Testing indicated that he had an IQ of 88, and there was no sign of serious psychopathology based on a diagnostic interview or an MMPI. Both Mr. Cross and his wife admitted that he had exhibited increasingly frequent, angry outbursts, but they both denied any history of violence toward the children or Mrs. Cross.

Mrs. Cross was a homemaker who cared for Lucy and a 12-year-old daughter, Sue. The Crosses' 19-year-old son was serving in the Army. Mrs. Cross

had a tested IQ of 67, and she reported that she had attended special education classes throughout her schooling. She married at the age of 19 and lived a normal life with her husband and children, but their low income barely kept the family out of poverty. Although Mrs. Cross demonstrated many adaptive skills in caring for her family, her coping currently was impaired by a severe depression. During the interview, Mrs. Cross's speech and body movements were slowed, and she reported feeling constantly tired. She did not describe herself as "depressed," but she felt unhappy and unable to cope with her children. She was not sure what had caused her troubles, but Mr. Cross traced the onset of her problems to her mother's death a year earlier.

Mrs. Cross cried repeatedly when recalling the loss of her mother. She described her mother as her best friend. They had lived in the same trailer park, and mother and daughter spent most of their days together. Mrs. Cross's mother offered her much practical support, especially in raising the children. Now the children ignored their mother's directions, and Mr. Cross was of little help. Mrs. Cross felt that her husband was too harsh, and she often contradicted him when he tried to punish the girls.

A family interview with the parents and the two

teenagers together confirmed the impressions given by the parents. Lucy looked distracted and bored throughout the interview, and Sue frequently looked toward and imitated her older sister. The girls paid more attention briefly when their father got angry, but this ended when Mr. and Mrs. Cross started fighting over his tone of voice.

School records indicated that the girls were obtaining mostly C grades. Standardized test scores from the school indicated that the girls' academic abilities were in the normal range, although their scores were below average. Telephone calls with each of their homeroom teachers indicated that Sue was not much of a behavior problem in school, but Lucy had lately become very disruptive.

The data obtained from multiple sources led to several recommendations being made to the fam-ily and to child protective services. The psychologist suggested an evaluation for antidepressant medication for Mrs. Cross, a referral to the school counselor for Lucy, and a brief course of family therapy that would always include Mr. Cross and Mrs. Cross, as well as the girls on some occasions. The family therapy was designed to help the parents agree on a set of rules for the girls and enforce discipline with a clear system of rewards and punishments that would focus on the loss of privileges. Therapy also would be used to evaluate Mr. Cross's anger further and to monitor Mrs. Cross's depression. One possibility for the future for Mr. Cross was individual therapy focused on controlling his anger. Finally, an attempt would be made to identify services in the community for Mrs. Cross with the goal of helping her build a new system of support. ■

Typical Symptoms and Associated Features

The case of Karen Cross and her family illustrates some important features of mental retardation. One important issue is the adequacy of her functioning. Despite her recent struggles, Karen Cross had succeeded in living a productive life. Many people in her community would not consider her to be mentally retarded. In fact, she does not meet all of the criteria for the diagnosis because of her adaptive functioning. Another important feature of this case is Karen Cross's depression. Many mentally retarded people suffer from emotional difficulties, a fact that is overlooked all too often. Finally, the case of Karen Cross raises concerns about children reared in disadvantaged environments and questions about how society can be supportive but not intrusive in family life.

The American Association on Mental Retardation (AAMR), the leading organization for professionals concerned with mental retardation, offers the following definition of **mental retardation**:

Mental retardation refers to substantial limitations in present functioning. It is characterized by significantly subaverage intellectual functioning, existing concurrently with related limitations in two or more of the following applicable adaptive skill areas: communication, self-care, home living, social skills, community use, self-direction, health and safety, functional academics, leisure, and work. Mental retardation manifests before age 18. (AAMR, 1992, p. 1)

This definition has three major parts. "Significantly subaverage intellectual functioning" refers to an IQ below 70 to 75 as measured by an individually administered intelligence test. The range of 70 to 75 allows for the normal measurement error in assessing IQ, as well as for some clinical judgment in determining mental retardation. "With related limitations in two or more . . . adaptive skill areas" refers to deficits in life skills that are a consequence of the intellectual impairment. People like Karen Cross who have an IQ below 75 but who function well in life would not be considered mentally retarded according to the AAMR definition. The criterion "Mental retardation manifests before age 18" excludes people whose deficits begin during adult life. When factors such as injury or degenerative brain disease produce significantly subaverage IQ after the age of 18, dementia, and not mental retardation, may be the appropriate diagnosis (see Chapter 13).

This definition of mental retardation differs somewhat from the one found in DSM-IV (see

Table 14–1). DSM has not incorporated all of the AAMR's new definition, which was introduced in 1992, and instead adheres to some prior AAMR criteria. Because of the AAMR's preeminence in the field, we follow their new definition throughout most of this chapter. We also highlight some of the controversies that distinguish the AAMR's definition from the definition found in DSM-IV.

relative to the norms for his or her age group. Narrow age ranges are used in creating norms for children, because of their changing cognitive abilities and rapid acquisition of knowledge. In contrast, all adults are treated as a part of the same age group.

Intelligence tests are standardized to have a mean IQ score of 100 and a standard deviation of 15. Thus, about two-thirds of the population

TABLE 14–1
DSM-IV Diagnostic Criteria for Mental Retardation

A. Significantly subaverage intellectual functioning: an IQ of approximately 70 or below on an individually administered IQ test (for infants, a clinical judgment of significantly subaverage intellectual functioning).

B. Concurrent deficits or impairments in present adaptive functioning (i.e., the person's effectiveness in meeting the standards expected for his or her age by his or her cultural group) in at least two of the following skill areas: communication, self-care, home living, social/interpersonal skills, use of community resources, self-direction, functional academic skills, work, leisure, health and safety.

C. Onset is before age 18 years.

SIGNIFICANTLY SUBAVERAGE IQ

The AAMR (1992) defines subaverage intellectual functioning in terms of a score on an individualized *intelligence test* such as the Wechsler Intelligence Scale for Children—Revised (WISC-R) or the Wechsler Adult Intelligence Scale—Revised (WAIS-R). Intelligence tests yield a score called the **intelligence quotient** or **IQ**, a measure of an individual's intellectual ability.

Earlier versions of intelligence tests derived an IQ by dividing the individual's "mental age" by his or her chronological age. Mental age was determined by comparing test results with the average for various age groups. For example, someone who answered the same number of items correctly as did the average 10-year-old would be given a mental age of 10. Mental age next was divided by chronological age, and the ratio was multiplied by 100 to yield an IQ score.

Contemporary intelligence tests have abandoned the concept of mental age and instead are constructed according to the theory that intellectual ability is normally distributed in the population (see Figure 14–1). Most people are assumed to be near average in intelligence, while a few people are thought to be exceptionally low or exceptionally high in their intellectual abilities. The individual's IQ is determined based on how the person scores on an intelligence test

has an IQ within one standard deviation of the mean—between 85 and 115. The cutoff score for mental retardation is approximately two standard deviations below the average, which theoretically would include 2 to 3 percent of the population (see Figure 14–1).

IQ tests are widely used, and they have demonstrated value for predicting performance in school. Moreover, IQ is a trait that is stable over time. Preschool measures of intelligence tend to be unstable, but the IQ scores of school-age children are good predictors of IQ scores later in life. This is true for the mentally retarded as well as for those with IQs in the normal range (Baroff, 1986). A school-age child who has a significantly subaverage IQ is likely to continue to score below the cutoff point for mental retardation throughout life.

Despite the value of IQ tests in predicting academic performance, a number of important questions have been raised about them. One of the most controversial questions is whether intelligence tests are "culture fair." In the United States, African Americans and Latinos have average IQ scores that are lower than those obtained by Caucasians and Asians, and more members of these groups are classified as mentally retarded. Some of these differences among groups have been attributed to bias in the composition of intelligence tests; some test items seem geared toward the language and the experience of majority groups. Because of the possibility of cultural bias, the AAMR explicitly notes that the valid assessment of intelligence considers cultural and linguistic diversity (AAMR, 1992).

Another controversy about intelligence tests is how well intelligence is measured among the mentally retarded. Many mentally retarded children have sensory or physical handicaps that impede their performance on standard IQ tests;

TABLE 14–2

Sample Items from the Vineland Adaptive Behavior Scales

Daily Living Skills
Age 1:   Drinks from a cup.
Age 5:   Bathes or showers without assistance.
Age 10: Uses a stove for cooking.
Age 15: Looks after own health.

Socialization
Age 1:   Imitates simple adult movements like clapping.
Age 5:   Has a group of friends.
Age 10: Watches television about particular interests.
Age 15: Responds to hints or indirect cues in conversation.

From S.S. Sparrow, D.A. Balla, and D.V Cicchetti (1984). *Vineland Adaptive Behavior Scales.* Circle Pines, MN: American Guidance Service.

---

thus, they must take tests that are not influenced by their particular handicap. Despite the difficulties involved in assessment, evidence indicates that, if anything, the IQ test scores of the mentally retarded are more reliable and more valid than IQ scores in the normal range (Baroff, 1986).

The most basic concern about intelligence tests is the most important one: What is intelligence? IQ tests measure precisely what their original developer, Alfred Binet, intended them to measure: potential for school achievement. And IQ tests predict school achievement fairly well. IQ scores correlate 0.4 to 0.7 with school achievement (Baroff, 1986). School achievement is not the same as "intelligence," however. Common sense, social sensitivity, and so-called "street smarts" are also part of what most of us would consider to be intelligence, and they are not measured by IQ tests. There would be less controversy if IQ tests were labeled appropriately as measures of academic aptitude.

LIMITATIONS IN ADAPTIVE SKILLS

The AAMR recognizes that intelligence is more than an IQ score by including *adaptive skills* in its definition of mental retardation. The concept of adaptive skills obviously is a very general one. The AAMR (1992) suggests that adaptive skills include both practical intelligence and social intelligence. *Practical intelligence* refers to the ability to manage the ordinary activities of daily living, while *social intelligence* indicates the ability to understand how to conduct yourself in social situations. Specifically, the AAMR identifies ten adaptive skills that must be considered in defining mental retardation: communication, self-care, home living, social skills, community use, self-direction, health and safety, functional academics, leisure, and work.

As with academic aptitude, adaptive skills must be judged within the context of age. Among preschoolers, adaptive skills include the acquisition of motor abilities, language, and self-control. Key skills during the school-age years include adequate academic performance and developing social relationships with peers. In adult life, adaptive skills include the ability to manage oneself, live independently, and assume adult interpersonal roles. Such skills are difficult to quantify, but some standardized instruments such as the Vineland Social Maturity Scale—Revised are very useful measures (see Table 14–2).

An argument can be made for defining retardation solely on the basis of intelligence testing. The intellectual limitations of mental retardation imply that adaptive skills will necessarily be limited (Zigler & Hodapp, 1986). Since 1959, however, deficits in adaptive behavior have been an essential part of the AAMR's definition of mental retardation (Heber, 1959). The adaptive skills criterion highlights the importance of assessing life functioning in borderline cases, as well as the need for services for all of the mentally retarded (AAMR, 1992). Moreover, some people with significantly subaverage IQs lead quite normal lives, and deficits in adaptive behavior are less stable over time than are IQ limitations. In particular, a number of retarded people, like Karen Cross, successfully achieve independence during their adult years as practical and social demands change from school to work. Thus, mental retardation can be "cured" in the sense that deficits in adaptive skills can be eliminated. Academic achievement or IQ is not the only measure of a successful life.

The third criterion for defining mental retardation is an onset before 18 years of age. This excludes people whose deficits in intellect and adaptive skills begin later in life as a result of brain injury or disease. Besides obvious differences in etiology, the most important aspect of this criterion is the experience of normal development. The cognitive development, social relationships, and life experiences of people who have lived normal lives into adulthood differentiates them from mentally retarded people in numerous important ways. Mentally retarded people have not lost skills they once had mastered, nor have they experienced a notable change in their condition. Unfortunately, this means that their retardation may be perceived as "who they are" and not as something that has "happened to them."

Classification

Many people whom we view today as being mildly retarded would not have been seen as having notable problems at earlier times in history. Academic aptitude was less necessary to successful living in earlier, agrarian societies than it is in our modern, technological world. Even today, mental retardation is defined differently in more industrialized countries than in less industrialized ones (Scheerenberger, 1983).

BRIEF HISTORICAL PERSPECTIVE

Severe mental retardation has been recognized as an abnormality throughout history, but few special efforts were directed toward helping the seriously mentally retarded. Until late in the Middle Ages, no distinction was made between mental illness and mental retardation in terms of treatment. Both "lunatics" and "idiots," as the mentally ill and mentally retarded were called from the Middle Ages through the nineteenth century, were either abandoned to roam the streets, sheltered inadequately in poorhouses, or warehoused in institutions (see Chapter 17). Socially, the retarded often were derided because of their disabilities. Such pejorative terms as "idiot," "fool," "moron," and "imbecile" actually were used in formal diagnostic or legal terminology well into the twentieth century (Grossman, 1983).

The work of French physician Jean Marc Itard (1774–1838) was instrumental in spurring efforts to develop special education programs for the mentally retarded. Itard worked extensively with a feral child, whom he named "Victor," found living in the woods near Aveyron, France, in 1799. Itard worked with the "wild boy of Aveyron" for 5 years in an attempt to educate and socialize him. In the end, Itard felt that he had failed in his efforts, but his work nevertheless encouraged others to develop special programs for educating mentally retarded people (Patton, Beirne-Smith, & Payne, 1990).

The beginnings of contemporary classifications of mental retardation can be traced to the second half of the nineteenth century. In 1866, British physician Langdon Down first described a subgroup of mentally retarded children who had a characteristic appearance. Their faces reminded Down of the appearance of Mongolians, and he used the term "mongolism" to describe them. Despite this offensive terminology, Down's classification helped subsequent scientists to establish a specific etiology for what we now know as Down syndrome.

The creation of IQ tests in the early twentieth century also greatly furthered the classification of mental retardation. French psychologists Alfred Binet (1856–1911) and Theophile Simon developed the first successful intelligence test in 1905 in response to a French government effort to identify children in need of special educational services. The Binet scale was refined further by psychologist Lewis Terman of Stanford University, and these efforts resulted in the Stanford-Binet intelligence tests. The first Wechsler intelligence test was developed by David Wechsler in 1939, and revisions of Wechsler's individualized intelligence tests continue to dominate contemporary intellectual assessment.

As intelligence tests developed into reliable and valid measures, controversy grew about what IQ score cutoff should define mental retardation. This debate reached a climax in 1959 when the AAMR greatly expanded the definition of retardation. In an attempt to help more people in need of services, the IQ cutoff was shifted from two standard deviations below the mean to one standard deviation below the mean. Anyone who scored 85 or lower was considered to be retarded, a criterion that included almost 15 percent of the U.S. population. This well-intentioned change included far too many well-functioning individuals, and it distracted attention from those most in need of help. Thus, the AAMR returned to the two-standard-deviation cutoff of 70 in 1973 (Grossman, 1983). In 1983, the range of 70 to 75 was first introduced as a way of accommodating measurement error and of acknowledging the fact that IQ scores are continuous rather than categorical differences. A child with an IQ score of 71 is not notably different from a child with an IQ of 69.

CONTEMPORARY CLASSIFICATION

Today, mental retardation can be classified according to two different criteria, an excellent illustration of the idea that the value of a classification system depends upon its purposes (see Chapter 4). One way to classify mental retardation is based on IQ scores, while an alternative approach is to make classifications based on known or presumed etiology. Both approaches are reliable, and each is valid for different purposes.

The value of both approaches is seen in some conflicts between the AAMR and the DSM-IV definitions of mental retardation. The AAMR (1992) now uses a multiaxial diagnosis of mental retardation in which etiology is rated on a separate dimension from the primary diagnosis of mental retardation. This is an important step, since many specific causes of mental retardation have been identified. (Additional axes in the new AAMR definition also rate emotional problems, physical health, and environmental characteristics.) These multidimensional ratings are not included in DSM-IV. Instead, DSM-IV follows an earlier AAMR scheme and divides mental retardation into four levels based primarily on IQ scores: mild, moderate, severe, and profound mental retardation.

As an alternative to these categories, the new AAMR subclassification defines four levels of *intensity of needed support* (see Table 14–3). Unlike levels of retardation, support intensities are not assumed to be global. Instead, needed supports are rated separately for different areas of functioning. This focus is intended to convey the diversity of skills and needs among the mentally retarded. Although this is an important concern, we highlight the subclassification from DSM-IV because it has been the topic of considerable research.

Mild mental retardation is the designation for those with IQ scores between 50–55 and 70. This category accounts for about 85 percent of the mentally retarded. People with mild mental retardation typically have few, if any, physical impairments, generally reach the sixth-grade level in academic functioning, acquire vocational skills, and typically live in the community with or without special supports.

People with *moderate mental retardation* have IQs between 35–40 and 50–55; they make up about 10 percent of the mentally retarded. They may have obvious physical abnormalities such as the features of Down syndrome. Academic achievement generally reaches to the second-grade level, work activities require close training and supervision, and special supervision in families or group homes is needed for living in the community.

Severe mental retardation is defined by IQ scores between 20–25 and 35–40. This category accounts for 3 to 4 percent of the retarded. At this severity level, motor development typically is abnormal, communicative speech is sharply limited, and close supervision is needed for community living.

About 1 to 2 percent of the mentally retarded have *profound mental retardation*. This severity level is characterized by an IQ below 20–25. Motor

---

TABLE 14–3

AAMR's Definitions of Intensities of Needed Support

Intermittent
Supports on an "as needed basis." Characterized by episodic nature, person not always needing the support(s), or short-term supports needed during life-span transitions (e.g., job loss or acute medical crisis). Intermittent supports may be high or low intensity when provided.

Limited
An intensity of supports characterized by consistency over time, time-limited but not of an intermittent nature, may require fewer staff members and less cost than more intense levels of support (e.g., time-limited employment training or transitional supports during the school to adult provided period).

Extensive
Supports characterized by regular involvement (e.g., daily) in at least some environments (such as work or home) and not time-limited (e.g., long-term support and long-term home living support).

Pervasive
Supports characterized by their constancy, high intensity; provided across environments; potential life-sustaining nature. Pervasive supports typically involve more staff members and intrusiveness than do extensive or time-limited supports.

From American Association on Mental Retardation (1992). *Mental retardation: Definition, classification, and systems of supports* (9th ed.) (p. 26). Washington, D.C.: AAMR.

skills, communication, and self-care are severely limited, and constant supervision typically is required in the community or in institutions.

Epidemiology

Because IQ theoretically is distributed according to the normal curve, 2 to 3 percent of the population should have IQs of 70 or below. In reality, however, more than the expected number of people are below the 70 cutoff. Departures from the normal distribution are particularly large for lower IQ scores, a result of the various biological conditions that produce mental retardation (Grossman, 1983). It therefore is useful to think of two IQ distributions. One distribution includes the normal range of IQ within the population. The second is based on the IQs of people with biological disorders known to cause mental retardation (Zigler, 1967). These two theoretical distributions are portrayed in Figure 14–1.

IQ distributions overestimate the observed prevalence rates of mental retardation. The most widely accepted estimate is that approximately 1 percent of the population in the United States—not 2 or 3 percent—is mentally retarded at any given point in time. This lower figure is a result of several factors. For one, IQs cannot be adequately assessed among very young children, who therefore are omitted from prevalence figures. Also, many adults with low IQs are not designated as retarded because they do not have deficits in the adaptive skills needed for work and community living. As an indication of these influences, studies indicate that twice as many school-age children as preschoolers are retarded, but the prevalence rates drop again among adults (Grossman, 1983).

Mental retardation in the United States is more common among the poor and, as a result, among certain ethnic groups. The increased prevalence is not found for all subtypes of retardation. Mental retardation with a specific, known organic cause (for example, Down syndrome) generally has an equal prevalence among all social classes, whereas retardation of nonspecific etiology is more common among families living in poverty (Patton, Beirne-Smith, & Payne, 1990). This epidemiological fact is the source of much controversy, as we discuss in the following sections.

Etiological Considerations and Research

As we have noted, the etiology of mental retardation can be grouped into two broad categories: cases caused by known biological abnormalities, and cases resulting from normal variations in IQ. We review known biological causes before considering the debate about the cause of the largest category of mental retardation, those cases at the extreme end of the normal IQ distribution.

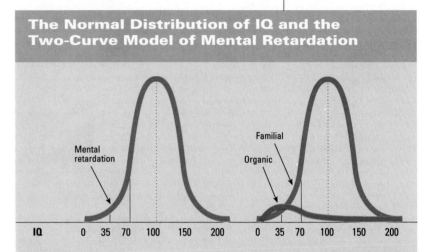

The Normal Distribution of IQ and the Two-Curve Model of Mental Retardation

FIGURE 14-1: Theoretically, IQ distributions follow the normal curve. This places 2 to 3 percent of the population below the 70 cutoff as illustrated on the left side of this figure. In reality, there are two IQ distributions, as portrayed on the right: the normal distribution and the IQ distribution for known biological causes of mental retardation.

Source: E. Zigler. Familial mental retardation: a continuing dilemma. *Science* (1967), *155*, 292–98. Copyright 1967 by the American Association for the Advancement of Science.

BIOLOGICAL FACTORS

About one-quarter of all cases of mental retardation are caused by known biological abnormalities (Grossman, 1983). In contrast to cases of unknown origin, known biological causes more often lead to retardation of moderate to profound severity and are associated with physical handicaps. Of the over 250 known biological causes (AAMR, 1992), we focus only on several major ones here.

Chromosomal Disorders The most common known biological cause of mental retardation is the chromosomal disorder **Down syndrome**. People with Down syndrome have a distinctively abnormal physical appearance. They have slanting eyes with an extra fold of skin in the inner corner, a small head and stature, a protruding tongue, and a variety of organ, muscle, and skeletal abnormalities. They also have physical handicaps and limited speech.

The cause of Down syndrome is the presence of an extra chromosome. Children with Down syndrome have 47 chromosomes instead of the normal 46. The extra chromosome is attached to the 21st pair (Donnell et al., 1975); thus, the disorder often is referred to as *trisomy 21*.

▲ **This girl with Down syndrome shows that mentally retarded children can join in many normal childhood activities.**

The incidence of Down syndrome is related to maternal age. For women under the age of 30, about 1 in 1,000 births are Down syndrome infants. The incidence rises to 1 in 750 births for mothers between ages 30–34, 1 in 300 between 35–39, and over 1 in 100 after age 40. Increasing paternal age also is associated with Down syndrome and is thought to cause about 25 percent of the cases (Magenis et al., 1977). Down syndrome can be detected by testing during pregnancy, raising the extremely difficult question of selective abortion.

In general, children and adults with Down syndrome function within the moderately to severely retarded range. They exhibit substantial variation in their intellectual level, however, and research suggests that intensive intervention can lead to higher achievement and greater independence. Institutionalization once was commonly recommended, but home or community care is now the rule. In fact, many experts who have worked with people with Down syndrome report that they are especially sociable

and eager to help, although research findings on their distinctive personality traits are not conclusive (Cicchetti & Beegly, 1990).

A potentially important recent discovery is that, by their thirties, the majority of adults with Down syndrome develop brain pathology similar to that found in Alzheimer's disease. About one-third also exhibit the symptoms of dementia (Thase, 1988). Death in mid-adult life is common, although some adults with Down syndrome live into their fifties and sixties.

Another chromosomal abnormality, **fragile-X syndrome** (Lubs, 1969) is now known to be the second most common identified biological cause of mental retardation. Fragile-X syndrome is indicated by a weakening or break on one arm of the X sex chromosome, and it is transmitted genetically. The disorder occurs in 1 out of every 1,000 to 2,000 male births (Bregman et al., 1987). Inconsistent evidence has been found on the prevalence of fragile-X among girls, in part because girls with the syndrome are considerably less likely to be mentally retarded than are boys.

Not all boys or girls with the fragile-X abnormality are mentally retarded, and the clinical picture varies considerably among those who are. Intellectual functioning ranges from moderately mentally retarded to the normal range. Among those with normal intelligence, learning disabilities are common. Most of those who display intellectual abnormalities have a characteristic facial appearance that includes an elongated face, high forehead, large jaw, and large, underdeveloped ears (Bregman et al., 1987). Although most fragile-X children behave fairly normally, some display the symptoms of autism. Recent advances make it possible to detect fragile-X in the fetus during pregnancy.

Several other chromosomal abnormalities have been linked to mental retardation. As in fragile-X syndrome, abnormalities of the sex chromosomes are particularly notable. *Klinefelter syndrome*, found in about 1 in 600 live male births, is characterized by the presence of one or more extra X chromosomes in males. The most common chromosome configuration is XXY. With Klinefelter syndrome, IQ functioning typically is in the low normal to mildly mentally retarded range. Another chromosomal abnormality, *XYY syndrome*, once was thought to increase criminality (see Chapter 9), but the syndrome is now recognized to be linked with a mean IQ about 10 points lower than average. The syndrome occurs in about 1 in 700 male births. *Turner syndrome*, the XO configuration in females, is characterized by a missing X chromosome. Girls with Turner syndrome are small, fail to develop sexually, and generally have intelligence near or within the normal range. The disorder occurs in about 1 in every 2,200 live female births.

Genetic disorders Few cases of mental retardation result from dominant genetic inheritance, because such a mutation is unlikely to remain in the gene pool. Mental retardation is known to be caused by several recessive gene pairings, however. **Phenylketonuria**, or **PKU**, is one of these. Geneticists estimate that about 1 in every 54 normal people carries a recessive gene for PKU, but the two genes are paired only in 1 of every 11,500 births.

PKU is caused by abnormally high levels of the amino acid *phenylalanine*, usually due to the absence of *phenylalanine hydroxylase*, an enzyme that metabolizes phenylalanine. Children with PKU are of normal intelligence at birth. The ingestion of foods containing phenylalanine early in life causes a buildup of the amino acid, however. This *phenylketonuria* produces the brain damage that eventually results in mental retardation. Retardation typically progresses to the severe to profound range. PKU sometimes results in the behavioral symptoms of autism, as does the extremely rare dominant-gene disorder *tuberous sclerosis*, a disorder characterized by white growths in the ventricles of the brain that appear tuberous.

Fortunately, PKU can be detected by blood testing in the first several days after birth. (The musty odor of the infant's urine is a much less exact but notable clinical indicator of PKU.) Early detection is very important, because intellectual and behavioral impairments are diminished dramatically if the child maintains a diet low in phenylalanine. In such cases the child is likely to have normal to mildly impaired intelligence. For this reason, all state laws now require routine screening of newborns for PKU. In order to maximize the benefits of the diet, the child should maintain it until he or she is at least 12 years old, a very difficult task for the family because of the extensive effort involved in maintaining a diet free of phenylalanine, a natural protein found in most foods (Baroff, 1986).

As it solved one problem, the prevention of mental retardation in PKU has created another one. Pregnant women with PKU who developed normally because of a phenylalanine-free diet may expose their fetuses to phenylketonuria. A low-phenylalanine diet during pregnancy can help avoid this threat (Vogel & Motulsky, 1986).

Other relatively rare recessive-gene disorders also can cause mental retardation. *Tay-Sachs disease* is a particularly severe disorder that eventually results in death during the infant or preschool years. The recessive gene that causes Tay-Sachs is particularly common among Jews of Eastern European heritage. *Hurler syndrome*, or *gargoylism*, results in gross physical abnormalities including dwarfism, humpback, a bulging head, and clawlike hands. Children with this disorder usually do not live past the age of 10. *Lesch-Nyhan syndrome* is most notable for the self-mutilation that accompanies the mental retardation. Children with this recessive gene disorder bite their own lips and fingers, often resulting in tissue loss. As with Down syndrome, many of these genetic abnormalities can be detected during pregnancy. Thus, selective abortion is a possibility.

Infectious Diseases Mental retardation can also be caused by various infectious diseases. Damaging infections may be contracted during pregnancy, at birth, or in infancy to early childhood.

Much progress has been made in preventing mental retardation caused by diseases passed from mother to fetus during pregnancy. No well-accepted treatments are available for *cytomegalovirus*, the most common fetal infection (and one that is usually innocuous), or for *toxoplasmosis*, a protozoan infection contracted from ingestion of infected raw meats or from contact with infected cat feces. Treatments are available for other infectious diseases.

Rubella (German measles) is a viral infection that may produce few symptoms in the mother. It can cause severe mental retardation and even death in the developing fetus, however, especially if it is contracted in the first 3 months of pregnancy. Fortunately, rubella can be completely prevented by vaccination of prospective mothers before pregnancy. Vaccination against rubella is now a part of routine health care.

Syphilis is a bacterial disease that is transmitted through sexual contact. Infected mothers can pass the disease to the fetus. If untreated, syphilis results in a number of physical and sensory handicaps to the fetus, including mental retardation. The adverse consequences are avoided by testing the mother and administering antibiotics when an infection has been detected. Because penicillin crosses the placental barrier, treatment of the mother also will cure the disease in the fetus.

Another sexually transmitted disease, *genital herpes*, can be transmitted to the infant during birth. Herpes is a viral infection that produces small lesions on the genitals immediately following the initial infection and intermittently thereafter. Generally, the disease can be transmitted only when the lesions are present. If there is an outbreak of genital lesions near or at the time of delivery, a cesarean section can be performed, thus preventing infection of the newborn. About half of all infants delivered genitally in the presence of active lesions are infected, resulting in a number of very serious problems including mental retardation, blindness, and possible death.

Two infectious diseases that occur after birth, primarily during infancy, can cause mental retardation. *Encephalitis* is an infection of the brain that produces inflammation and permanent damage in about 20 percent of all cases. *Meningitis* is an infection of the meninges, the three membranes that line the brain. The inflammation creates intracranial pressure that can irreversibly damage brain tissues. Encephalitis and meningitis can be caused by a variety of infectious diseases. Cases resulting from bacterial infections usually can be successfully treated with antibiotics. In other cases, the outcome of both encephalitis and meningitis is unpredictable. Neuromuscular problems, sensory impairments, and mental retardation are possible.

Toxins Exposure to a variety of environmental toxins also can cause mental retardation. Like infectious diseases, toxic chemicals can produce mental retardation when exposure occurs either before or after birth, but exposure during pregnancy creates the greatest risk.

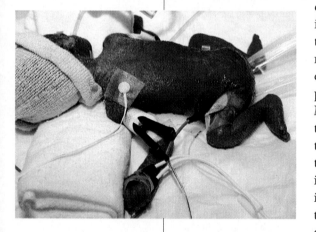

▼ A newborn of a mother who used crack cocaine. Crack babies often are premature and have low birth weights, and they are typically irritable and difficult to soothe.

Both licit and illicit drugs pose a risk to the developing fetus. Because of its frequent use, alcohol presents the greatest threat. One or two of every 1,000 births is a baby with **fetal alcohol syndrome**. This disorder is characterized by retarded physical development, a small head, narrow eyes, cardiac defects, and cognitive impairments. Intellectual functioning ranges from mild mental retardation to normal intelligence accompanied by learning disabilities.

Women who drink heavily during pregnancy (an average of 5 ounces of alcohol per day) are twice as likely to have a child with the syndrome as are women who average 1 ounce of alcohol per day or less (Baroff, 1986). Controversy continues about the risk for difficulties associated with drinking in the intermediate range. Because of possible adverse effects of even low or moderate consumption, many experts recommend that pregnant women abstain from alcohol altogether.

Illicit drugs also are a cause of considerable concern. Although heroin and methadone addiction have not been directly linked with mental retardation, they do result in the serious problems of low birth weight and drug addiction for the newborn. Particular concern has been raised recently about the effects of the drug crack cocaine when it is used during pregnancy. *Crack babies* are more likely to be born prematurely, to have a lower-than-normal birth weight, and to have a smaller-than-normal head circumference. These adverse conditions have been linked in other research to an increased risk for mental retardation, but the long-term intellectual and psychological outcomes for crack babies have yet to be adequately documented (Hawley & Disney, 1992).

Toxins also present a potential hazard to intellectual development after birth. *Mercury poisoning* is known to produce severe physical, emotional, and intellectual impairments, but it does not present a major public health problem because few children are exposed to mercury. Much more threatening to the public health is **lead poisoning**. Until banned by federal legislation, the lead commonly used in paint and produced by automobile emissions exposed hundreds of thousands of children to a potentially serious risk. Although controversy continues about the effects of exposure to low levels of lead, at toxic levels lead poisoning can produce a number of adverse behavioral and cognitive impairments, including mental retardation. Despite federal bans on lead-based paints and leaded gasoline, lead poisoning continues to pose a particular risk to children reared in dilapidated housing where old, peeling, lead-based paint chips may be ingested.

Other Biological Abnormalities A variety of pregnancy and birth complications also can cause mental retardation. One major complication is known as *Rh incompatibility*. The Rh factor is a protein found on the surface of red blood cells, and it is a dominant hereditary trait. People who possess this protein are known as Rh-positive; people who don't are Rh-negative. Rh incompatibility can occur when the mother is Rh-negative and the father is Rh-positive. In such cases the mother can develop antibodies that attack the blood cells of her Rh-positive fetus. The antibodies destroy oxygen-carrying red blood cells in the developing fetus, with a number of adverse consequences including possible mental retardation.

Rh-negative women develop antibodies only after exposure to their infant's Rh-positive blood. If this exposure occurs at all, it usually does not happen until delivery. Thus, the risk of Rh incompatibility in first births is minimal; the greatest risk is for subsequent pregnancies. This risk can be largely prevented, however, by the administration of the antibiotic RhoGAM to the mother within 72 hours after birth of the first child. RhoGAM prevents the mother's body from developing internal antibodies against the Rh-positive factors. This eliminates most of the risk for a future pregnancy. In the event that an Rh-negative mother develops antibodies against Rh-positive factors during pregnancy, a fetal blood transfusion must be carried out to replace the destroyed red blood cells.

Another pregnancy and birth complication that can cause intellectual deficits is premature birth. *Premature birth* is defined either as birth before 38 weeks of gestation or a birth weight of less than 5½ pounds. There are many potential causes of prematurity, including the hereditary, infectious, and toxic factors already discussed. Other risk factors include poor maternal nutrition, maternal age of less than 18 years or more than 35 years, maternal hypertension or diabetes, and damage to the placenta. The effects of prematurity on the infant are variable, ranging from few or no deficits to sensory impairments, poor physical development, and mental retardation. More serious consequences occur at lower birth weights, and infant

mortality is common at very low weights.

Other known biological causes of mental retardation include extreme difficulties in delivery, particularly *asphyxia*, or oxygen deprivation; severe *malnutrition* (which is rare in the United States but a major problem in less developed countries); and the seizure disorder *epilepsy*. The intellectual difficulties associated with each of these causes vary but are potentially significant.

Normal Genetic Variation All of the biological causes of mental retardation discussed so far are clear abnormalities in development. The last biological factor we consider, however, focuses on the tail of the normal IQ distribution (see Figure 14–1). These are the cases of mental retardation of unknown etiology—what is often referred to as **cultural-familial retardation**. As the term suggests, cultural-familial retardation tends to run in families and is linked with poverty. A controversial issue is whether this typically mild form of mental retardation is caused primarily by genes or by psychosocial disadvantage.

Normal genetic variation clearly contributes to individual differences in intelligence. As summarized in Table 14–4, numerous family, twin, and adoption studies have been conducted on IQ. All of this research points to a substantial genetic contribution to intelligence. For example, the IQs of adopted children are more highly correlated to the IQs of their biological parents than to those of their adoptive ones (Horn, Loehlin, & Willerman, 1979; Plomin & Daniels, 1987).

How much of intelligence is inherited? Behavior geneticists have calculated indices to measure the extent of genetic contribution to a

TABLE 14–4

Correlations Between the IQ Scores of Pairs of Relatives Reared Together or Apart

Type of Relative	Reared Together Correlation	(N)	Reared Apart Correlation	(N)
Monozygotic twins	.86	(4,672)	.72	(65)
Dizygotic twins	.60	(5,546)	—	
Biological siblings	.47	(26,473)	.24	(203)
Adoptive siblings	.34	(369)	—	
Parent–child	.42	(8,633)	.22	(814)
Adoptive parent–child	.19	(1,397)	—	

Adapted from T.J. Bouchard, Jr., and M. McGue (1981). Familial studies of intelligence: A review. *Science, 212,* 1055–1059. Coppyright ® 1981 by the American Association for the Advancement of Science.

characteristic, called *heritability ratios*. Estimates of the genetic contribution to intelligence generally range from 30 percent to 70 percent, but as we will discuss in Research Methods in Chapter 16, heritability ratios can be misleading. For present purposes, we note that the basic problem with heritability ratios is that they suggest a false dichotomy between genes and environment. The concept of reaction range better conveys how genes and environment interact together to determine IQ (Gottesman, 1963). The **reaction range** concept proposes that heredity determines the upper and lower limits of IQ, and experience determines the extent to which people fulfill their genetic potential. Figure 14–2 portrays some theoretical reaction ranges for children with Down syndrome, cultural-familial retardation, normal intelligence, and superior intelligence. This figure illustrates the key point that genetics and environment determine intelligence together, not independently (Turkheimer, 1991).

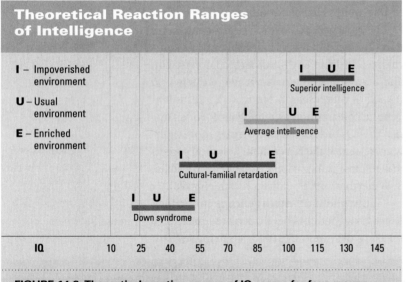

Theoretical Reaction Ranges of Intelligence

I – Impoverished environment

U – Usual environment

E – Enriched environment

FIGURE 14-2: Theoretical reaction ranges of IQ scores for four groups of people. Note that the usual environmental contributions to intelligence differ among the four groups.

From G.S. Baroff (1986). *Mental retardation: Nature, cause, and management.* p. 151. Washington D.C.: Hemisphere.

PSYCHOLOGICAL FACTORS

Genetic models of cultural-familial retardation are polygenic. The assumption that many genes are involved in determining normal intelligence differs markedly from the single-gene models for disorders like PKU. Single-gene disorders fit a categorical model of mental retardation: The abnormality either is present or absent. In contrast, polygenic viewpoints hold to a continu-ous model of intelligence in which many genes contribute to normal variations in intellectual ability. Thus, cases of polygenically determined low intelligence appropriately are viewed as variations in the normal distribution of intelligence.

Scientists similarly hold a continuous view of psychological contributions to intelligence. Nevertheless, it is important to note that grossly abnormal environments can produce gross abnormalities in intelligence. This apparently is what happened with Itard's "wild boy," and environmentally caused mental retardation has been documented in some horrific case histories.

One such case is Koluchova's (1972) documentation of the effects of the abuse and deprivation experienced by two identical twin boys. Until they were discovered at the age of 6, the twins lived in a closet in almost total isolation. Apparently, they were beaten regularly throughout their early life. When discovered, the twins could barely walk, had extremely limited speech, and showed no understanding of abstractions like photographs. Over several years of intervention, however, their measured intelligence moved from moderately retarded when first discovered to the normal range by the age of 11.

Fortunately, cases of such torturous abuse are rare. They illustrate the theoretical contribution of experience to intelligence more than the actual contribution. Awareness of this theoretical contribution is important, however, because contemporary research on intelligence necessarily reflects the effects of a limited range of environments. As a social ideal, Americans hope to provide all citizens with an equally advantaged environment. In working toward this laudable goal, we can overlook the fact that heritability increases as environmental variation decreases. In fact, the heritability of intelligence would be 1.0 if everyone had exactly the same environmental advantages. Such a circumstance would *not* mean that environment does not contribute to intelligence, and consideration of the potentially devastating consequences of abnormal environments reminds us of that fact.

SOCIAL FACTORS

The range of "normal" environments in the United States includes many undesirable circumstances for children. Millions of children are reared in psychosocial disadvantage in our cities and in the equally unstimulating environments found among the rural poor. In fact, children are the most impoverished age group in this country: Over 21 percent of U.S. children are reared in poverty (Select Committee on Children, Youth and Families, 1989).

Cultural-familial retardation is found far more frequently among the poor. Part of this association certainly is due to the fact that lower intelligence can cause lower social status. People with below-average IQ will make less money in our society; thus, they will remain in, or move into, lower socioeconomic classes. However, part of the link between poverty and cultural-familial retardation is caused by the effects of psychosocial disadvantage in lowering IQ scores.

Impoverished environments lack the *stimulation* and *responsiveness* required to promote children's intellectual development. A stimulating environment is one that challenges children's developing intellectual skills; a responsive environment offers encouragement for their pursuits. Parents or siblings mimic the infant's first sounds and words. Toys and other playthings make the toddler's environment interesting to explore. The developing creative interests of the preschooler are encouraged with crayons and drawing paper, building blocks, and the like.

Studies of adopted children demonstrate the positive effects of stimulating and responsive environments (Turkheimer, 1991). A famous early study by Skodak and Skeels (1949) demonstrated that children who were adopted away from unfortunate circumstances early in life achieved IQ scores at least 12 points higher on average than those of their biological mothers. More recent studies have found similarly dramatic increases (Capron & Duyme, 1989; Schiff et al., 1982). The potential for increasing IQ by 10 to 15 points obviously holds important implications for prevention and intervention. Many people with cultural-familial retardation could function normally if stimulating and responsive environments helped them to achieve their potential to function near the upper end of their reaction range.

Treatment: Primary, Secondary, and Tertiary Prevention and Normalization

Three major categories of intervention are essential in the treatment of mental retardation. First, many cases of both organic and cultural-familial mental retardation can be prevented through adequate maternal and child health care, as well as through early psychoeducational programs. Second, educational, psychological, and biomedical treatments can help mentally retarded individuals raise their achievement levels. Third, the lives of the mentally retarded can be normalized through mainstreaming in public schools and promoting care in the community.

PRIMARY PREVENTION

The availability and use of good maternal and child health care is one major step toward the primary prevention of many biological causes of mental retardation. Health care measures include specific actions such as vaccinations for rubella and the detection and treatment of infectious diseases like syphilis. In addition, an adequate diet and abstinence from alcohol, cigarettes, and other drugs are essential to the health of pregnant women and the welfare of the developing fetus.

Planning for childbearing also can help prevent mental retardation. Pregnancy and birth complications are notably more common among mothers younger than 18 and older than 35. Although most babies born to women outside of this age range are healthy and normal, many women are aware of the statistical risks and attempt to time their pregnancies accordingly. Children of teenaged mothers also face a much greater threat of a life of poverty—a pressing issue, since almost 8 percent of all children in the United States are born to adolescent mothers (Select Committee on Children, Youth, and Families, 1989).

A more controversial means of preventing retardation is through diagnostic testing and selective abortion. One diagnostic procedure is **amniocentesis**, in which fluid is extracted from

▲ The conditions associated with extreme poverty may cause cultural-familial retardation.

▼ During amnio-
centesis, amniotic
fluid is extracted from
the sac protecting
the fetus. Tests of the
amniotic fluid can
detect some genetic
and chromosomal
defects that cause
mental retardation.

the sac that protects the fetus during pregnancy. Some chromosomal and genetic defects in the fetus can be determined from testing of the amniotic fluid, leaving parents with the difficult decision of whether to terminate the pregnancy if an abnormality is found. Despite the emotional turmoil that such a decision can provoke, many parents opt for amniocentesis. The procedure is particularly common among older women, whose infants are at a greatly increased risk for having an infant with Down syndrome.

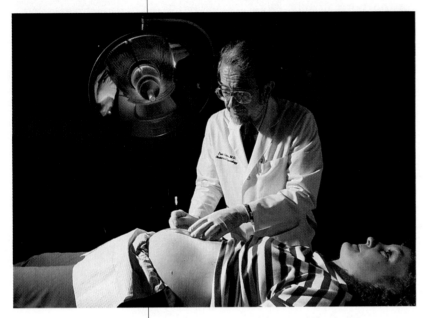

SECONDARY PREVENTION

In addition to medical and health care measures, early social and educational interventions can lead to the secondary prevention of cultural-familial retardation. The most important current secondary prevention effort is Head Start, a federal intervention program begun in 1964. The goals of Head Start include providing early educational experiences, nutrition, and health care monitoring for preschool children living in poverty. Evidence indicates that Head Start produces short-term increases in IQ (5 to 10 points) and achievement. The academic advantages diminish or disappear within a few years after intervention ends, but some data indicate that children who participate in Head Start are less likely to repeat a grade or to be placed in special education classes. They also are more likely to graduate from high school (McKey et al., 1985; Zigler & Styfco, 1993). These data indicate that Head Start undoubtedly reduces the prevalence of cultural-familial retardation through its influence on adaptive behavior if not on IQ itself.

More specific evidence on preventing mental retardation through early intervention comes from two research programs—the Carolina Abcedarian Project (Ramey & Bryant, 1982) and the Milwaukee Project (Garber, 1988). Both interventions offered a variety of services to children of mothers with below-average IQs, and both used control groups to assess the effectiveness of intervention. Gains of 20 or more points in IQ have been reported for experimental versus control children in the Milwaukee Project (Garber, 1988), but questions about the methods of this study suggest that they be interpreted with caution (Baroff, 1986). More modest gains of 5 to 10 IQ points have been reported for the Abcedarian Project (Ramey & Bryant, 1982). Regardless of the magnitude of change, these projects, together with adoption studies and findings from Head Start, indicate that at least some cases of familial retardation can be prevented through increasing environmental stimulation and responsiveness.

TERTIARY PREVENTION

A huge array of services has been developed for the tertiary prevention and treatment of the various cognitive, socioemotional, and medical difficulties faced by mentally retarded people from birth through adult life. Given the volumes of work devoted to the subject, we can only touch on a few treatments here.

One of the most important aspects of tertiary prevention is careful assessment early in life. Medical screening is essential for certain conditions such as PKU, as is the early detection of mental retardation through cognitive tests. Unfortunately, many cases of mental retardation are not detected early, as the doubling in prevalence during the school years indicates. Public screening of children's academic potential typically is not conducted until school age, and the intelligence tests available for infants and preschoolers are of questionable reliability and validity.

Accurate detection is important, because early interventions can benefit children diagnosed as mentally retarded. Intervention with mentally retarded infants typically takes place in the home and focuses on stimulating the infant, educating parents, and promoting good parent–infant relationships (Shearer & Shearer, 1976). During the preschool years, special instruction may take place in child development centers, which also offer *respite care* for the parents who need relief from the added demands of rearing a mentally retarded child.

Treatment of the social and emotional needs of the mentally retarded is an essential component of their care. This treatment includes teaching basic self-care skills such as feeding, toileting, and dressing during the younger ages, and various "life-survival" skills at later ages. Mentally retarded children also may need treatment for unusual behaviors such as self-stimulation or aggressiveness. In general, research indicates that operant behavior therapy is the most effective treatment approach (Matson & Frame, 1986). Still, the effectiveness of behavioral approaches in absolute terms has been questioned, since problem behavior may remain despite some improvements (Scotti et al., 1991).

Medical care for physical and sensory handicaps is critical in the treatment of certain types of mental retardation. In addition, medications are helpful in treating disorders such as epilepsy that may co-occur with mental retardation. Medication is not especially helpful in treating the intellectual or socioemotional problems of the mentally retarded. Nevertheless, estimates indicate that 30 to 50 percent of institutionalized mentally retarded people are prescribed medication to control their behavior problems (Singh, Guernsey, & Ellis, 1992).

Neuroleptics (discussed in Chapter 12) are used with particular frequency to treat aggressiveness or other uncontrolled behavior among the retarded (Grossman, 1983). In some institutional settings, these drugs have been used primarily to sedate patients, and various public exposés have raised broad questions about their misuse (Scheerenberger, 1983). The use of neuroleptics with the mentally retarded is especially questionable because behavior therapy provides a safe alternative (Matson & Frame, 1986).

NORMALIZATION

Normalization is a major focus of the treatment of the mentally retarded. **Normalization** means that the mentally retarded are entitled to live as much as possible like other members of society. Mainstreaming mentally retarded children into public schools and promoting a role in the community for the mentally retarded have been the major goals of normalization.

Schooling is of great importance to the mentally retarded, as it is to all children. Prior to 1975, however, only about half of all mentally retarded children received an education at public expense. That year Congress passed the Education for All Handicapped Children Act, also known as Public Law 94-142. According to Public Law 94-142, all handicapped children have a right to a free and appropriate education in the "least restrictive environment" (see Chapter 17). Within the limits set by the handicapping condition, services are to be provided in a setting that restricts personal liberty as little as possible.

For many mentally retarded children, particularly those with mild retardation, providing the least restrictive environment means **mainstreaming** them into regular classrooms. Rather than being taught in "special" classes, mentally retarded children enter the mainstream and receive as much of their education as possible in normal classrooms. Unfortunately, there are broad inconsistencies in the extent of mainstreaming and in the quality of support services provided to the mentally retarded across school districts and across states. The lack of consistent quality is a matter of concern, because some evidence indicates that mentally retarded children who are mainstreamed into regular classrooms learn as much as or more than they do in "special" classes. A broader concern is that there are philosophical justifications for integrating classrooms, such as the right to education in the least restrictive environment, irrespective of the academic outcome of mainstreaming (Baroff, 1986).

The *deinstitutionalization* movement that began in mental hospitals in the 1960s (see Chapter 17) also has greatly helped to normalize the lives of the mentally retarded. Between 1970 and 1981, the number of mentally retarded people living in institutions dropped from 190,000 to 126,000. Deinstitutionalization has been particularly rapid for those with milder forms of mental retardation. Of those now living in institutions, 7.1 percent have mild, 13.0 percent have moderate, 24.4 percent have severe, and 55.5 percent have profound levels of retardation (Baroff, 1986). Evidence indicates that mentally retarded people who move from institutions to the community receive better care and function at a higher level. Despite some continued fear and prejudice, it is clear that mentally retarded people living in our communities can contribute through their work and their play, and through relationships between themselves and all of us.

Autistic Disorder and Pervasive Developmental Disorders

The **pervasive developmental disorders** are unusual problems that begin early in life and involve severe impairments in a number of areas of functioning. The majority of people with pervasive developmental disorders also are mentally retarded. In addition, however, they exhibit profound disturbances in relationships, engage in repetitive, stereotyped activities, and typically have substantial communication difficulties. These difficulties are most severe in **autistic disorder** (also known as *autism*), the most carefully researched form of pervasive developmental disorder. Autistic disorder was brought to the public's awareness by Dustin Hoffman's stirring portrayal of Raymond in the movie *Rain Man*. Most of our discussion of pervasive developmental disorders focuses on autistic disorder, although we also note some other problems that involve less severe impairments and that have a more optimistic prognosis. We begin with a case history.

CASE STUDY

A Child with Autistic Disorder

John was 3½ years old when he was first seen at a treatment center that specialized in autism. He spoke very little, and most of what he said wasn't meaningful. He used no names for himself or for others. If asked "What is your name?" he repeated "Name?" rather than answering "John." John would sometimes respond "you, you" as an affirmative answer to the question "Do you want something to eat?" This odd response was one of his few verbalizations that conveyed any meaning.

John's relationships were equally troubling. He literally showed no interest in other people. His parents reported that he never did such everyday things as seeking them out for play or sitting in their laps just to cuddle. In fact, John sometimes would throw a violent tantrum when touched. His mother said that when she tried to hug him, John frequently screamed in apparent pain and twirled away from her. She touched him rarely because of these horrible reactions. John was equally uninterested in his 6-year-old sister, who was functioning normally. He didn't tease her or follow her around like most little brothers. In fact, he didn't even seem to know she existed. John also was terrified of the gentle family dog. The dog was kept tied up when John was awake, because its attempts to play with John provoked fearful tantrums.

According to his parents, John was most content when he was by himself in the family room at home. He liked to have the television set turned on, although his parents felt that he didn't really watch or understand the shows. He would sit on the floor near the set and rock back and forth for hours. He spent several hours like this every day.

John's parents could remember no particular incident that marked the beginning of his problems. They became aware of them very gradually. They recalled that John had been an easy baby, but they now felt that his meager need for attention may have been an early sign of his problems. His parents were concerned by his very limited speech and odd behavior as a toddler, but they were reassured by the fact that he had learned to walk at the appropriate age and otherwise seemed normal physically. John's pediatrician also had been reassuring about the boy's apparently delayed development until his annual checkup at age 3. That was when the pediatrician suggested that John might be mentally retarded. After subsequent visits to several mental health professionals in their community, John's parents were referred to a treatment center that specialized in autism.

John was diagnosed as suffering from autistic disorder by members of the center staff. Although the center had an inpatient program for autistic children that used intensive behavior modification, John's parents wanted him to remain with them. They were given extensive information about autism and about behavior modification programs, and John was referred to a child development center in his community. The child development center offered preschool programs for mentally retarded children, and the staff would help the parents attempt to teach

John language and self-care skills. The center also would give John's parents a break from the demands of caring for him. His parents were warned, however, that without intensive inpatient treatment or truly heroic efforts on their part, John would continue to have severe difficulties with language, social relationships, and age-appropriate activities. ■

Typical Symptoms and Associated Features

The case of John illustrates several of the central characteristics of autistic disorder and its diagnosis. Like John, most autistic children are normal in physical appearance. Some observers have even suggested that they are especially attractive youngsters. Although they sometimes have unusual actions and postures (Wing, 1988), their body movements are not grossly uncoordinated, and their physical growth and development is generally normal. Judging from physical appearance alone, one would not expect autistic children to have severe psychological impairments.

Early onset is another feature of autism illustrated by the case of John. Autism begins early in life, and in retrospect many parents recall abnormalities that seem to date back to birth. Because many autistic infants make few demands and have a normal physical appearance and development, the condition may not be accurately diagnosed for a few years. In the majority of cases, however, parents become aware of their child's profound disorder by the age of 3 (Short & Schopler, 1988). By this time, parents have noted the child's impaired communication abilities, one of the three classical symptoms of autism. The other two central symptoms are impairments in social interaction, and stereotyped patterns of behavior, interests, and activities. Disturbances in these three areas of functioning also characterize other pervasive developmental disorders, but the impairment typically is less severe than in autism.

IMPAIRED SOCIAL INTERACTION

The dictionary definition of the word *autism* is "absorption in one's own mental activity." Many mental health professionals view this inability to relate to others as the central feature of autism

and of all the pervasive developmental disorders. Social impairments range from relatively mild oddities such as a lack of social or emotional reciprocity, to extreme difficulties in which there is little awareness of the existence of others, let alone of their feelings (see Table 14–5). Children and adults with pervasive developmental disorders seem to treat other people as if they were confusing and foreign objects rather than as sources of protection, comfort, and reciprocal stimulation.

Some people with pervasive developmental disorders appear to be missing the basic, inborn tendency to form attachments with other people. As infants, they do not show many of the attachment behaviors that help normal children to form a special bond with their caregivers. In retrospect, many parents remember that their autistic children did not seek them out in times of distress, nor were they comforted by physical contact. These children find normal hugs and kisses disturbing, even painful, rather than reassuring.

Social impairments continue as the infants become toddlers and preschoolers. Children with pervasive developmental disorder show little interest in their peers. They do not engage in spontaneous social play, and they fail to develop friendships as they grow older. *Gaze aversion* is one characteristic feature of these social difficulties, as children and adults with pervasive developmental disorders actively avert eye contact.

Even those adults who achieve exceptionally good outcomes continue to show little understanding of, or empathy for,

▼ The movie *Rain Man* offered a realistic portrayal of autism in adult life. Dustin Hoffman played the role of Raymond, an autistic man, and Tom Cruise played the role of his brother, who tried but failed to establish a relationship with Raymond.

TABLE 14–5

DSM-IV Diagnostic Criteria for Autistic Disorder

A. A total of six (or more) items from (1), (2), and (3), with at least two from (1), and one each from (2) and (3):

    1. Qualitative impairment in social interaction, as manifested by at least two of the following:

        a. marked impairment in the use of multiple nonverbal behaviors such as eye-to-eye gaze, facial expression, body postures, and gestures to regulate social interaction

        b. failure to develop peer relationships appropriate to developmental level

        c. a lack of spontaneous seeking to share enjoyment, interests, or achievements with other people

        d. lack of social or emotional reciprocity

    2. Qualitative impairments in communication as manifested by at least one of the following:

        a. delay in, or total lack of, the development of spoken language (not accompanied by an attempt to compensate through alternative modes of communication such as gesture or mime)

        b. in individuals with adequate speech, marked impairment in the ability to initiate or sustain a conversation with others

        c. stereotyped and repetitive use of language or idiosyncratic language

        d. lack of varied, spontaneous make-believe play or social imitative play appropriate to developmental level

    3. Restricted repetitive and stereotyped patterns of behavior, interests, and activities, as manifested by at least one of the following:

        a. encompassing preoccupation with one or more stereotyped and restricted patterns of interest that is abnormal either in intensity or focus

        b. apparently inflexible adherence to specific, nonfunctional routines or rituals

        c. stereotyped and repetitive motor mannerisms

        d. persistent preoccupation with parts of objects

B. Delays or abnormal functioning in at least one of the following areas, with onset prior to age 3 years: (1) social interaction, (2) language as used in social communication, or (3) symbolic or imaginative play

other people. For example, extreme social difficulties still remained in what may be the most successful outcome of autism ever documented: a woman who was diagnosed autistic as a child but who nevertheless obtained a Ph.D. in animal science. This woman reported having to "compute" intellectually the feelings of other people based on such observations as whether they were smiling at her. At the same time, she maintained a need for some limited and predictable physical contact. As a means of providing this, she invented her own "squeeze machine." The device consisted of two long, padded boards that she lay between to receive a "hug" as the boards were gently pulled toward each other by a compressor. This remarkable woman reported feeling greatly calmed by lying in the machine for 20 minutes or so (Sacks, 1993/1994).

IMPAIRED COMMUNICATION

In addition to their dramatic social isolation, people with pervasive developmental disorders suffer from a variety of impairments in communication. (The one exception is Asperger's disorder, a subtype we discuss shortly.) The communication problems often are severe, but there can be a range of difficulties. Some children fail to speak at all between the ages of 1 and 2, the time when normal children typically learn their first words. Others learn a few rudimentary words such as "Mama," and then suddenly lose their language abilities. Still other children progress further in acquiring language, but either lose their abilities or stop progressing at the normal rate of language acquisition (Schreibman, 1988). Many autistic children remain mute, and about half never acquire functional language (Rutter, 1978).

Among those people with pervasive developmental disorder who learn to use speech, their language exhibits many unusual features. For one, the subtleties of speaking style often are unusual, a problem referred to as *dysprosody*. In dysprosody, speech production is disturbed in its rate, rhythm, and intonation. This makes the disturbed child or adult sound highly unusual to the normal listener, even when the content of their speech is normal.

Echolalia is another common language problem. People with autism or other pervasive developmental disorders frequently repeat phrases that are spoken to them, or sometimes repeatedly echo a phrase they heard at an earlier point in time. As with other problems, there is a dramatic contrast with normal development. When the mother of a 1½-year-old points to herself and says "Who is this?," normal toddlers will respond with "Mama." A 10-year-old autistic child with echolalia will respond to the same question by repeating "Who is this?"

Another common language problem is *pronoun reversal*. Children and adults with pervasive developmental disorder are especially likely to confuse the pronoun "you" with the pronoun "I." They say "You want a cookie" when they mean "I want a cookie." Some have speculated that this speech error reveals profound emotional confusion. According to one interpretation, pronoun reversal indicates that autistic children have failed to individuate, to become a separate person (Bettelheim, 1967). A much more parsimonious explanation is that pronoun reversal demonstrates a lack of understanding of speech. In hundreds of everyday conversations, people with pervasive developmental disorders are referred to as "you." Lacking a deeper understanding of the meaning of pronouns, they refer to themselves as "you," not "I."

The speech difficulties of autistic children and others with pervasive developmental disorders are not the products of auditory or other sensory problems, nor are they simply disturbances in the mechanics of speech. Rather, the difficulties stem from basic disturbances in the ability to communicate, and even more basically, in the ability to imitate or reciprocate interactions. Unlike infants and toddlers who are deaf or mute, these children do not use gestures as substitutes for speech. In fact, some children do not engage in the social imitation that is essential for learning basic skills, let alone for building relationships.

Even higher-functioning people with pervasive developmental disorders who imitate others and have relatively well-developed language skills nevertheless demonstrate a limited ability to imagine and think abstractly. They sometimes fail to generate or understand unique or imaginative speech, and they commonly have difficulty comprehending abstractions like metaphors.

The language problems in the pervasive developmental disorders apparently involve restrictions in thinking, not just in expression.

STEREOTYPED BEHAVIOR, INTERESTS, AND ACTIVITIES

The third major symptom of autism and other pervasive developmental disorders is restricted, repetitive, and stereotyped patterns of behavior, interests, and activities. Many children with autistic disorder literally spend hours spinning a top or flapping a string in front of their eyes. Others might become uncontrollably agitated if the arrangement of furniture in a room is changed even slightly. Compulsively rigid adherence to daily routines is yet another aspect of these restricted activities and interests.

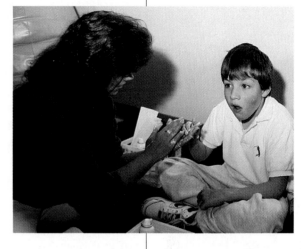

Not surprisingly, these odd preoccupations and rituals create social complications. People unfamiliar with the disorder are likely to find such behavior bizarre and perhaps frightening. The ritualistic behavior also causes numerous problems for those who are trying to manage and educate autistic children. How do you educate a child who is totally preoccupied with flapping a string in front of his or her face for hours?

What purpose does such stereotyped behavior serve for the disturbed individual? Rituals such as flapping a string or spinning a top seem to serve no other function than to provide sensory feedback. Thus, they are often referred to as *self-stimulation*. The common interpretation of self-stimulation is that the autistic child receives too little sensory input, and that the ritual self-stimulation increases sensation to a more desirable level. We prefer an alternative interpretation. The stimulation of everyday environments has been described as overwhelming by several high-functioning people with pervasive developmental disorders. Perhaps self-stimulation reduces rather than increases sensory input by making the stimulation monotonously predictable. This alternative interpretation suggests, in fact, that all of the stereotyped behavior found

▲ **Children with autistic disorder, like the child in this picture, are normal in physical appearance. The communication problems, autistic aloneness, and need to preserve sameness are readily apparent among children with autism, however.**

in pervasive developmental disorders can be viewed as a compulsive ritual. The repetitive actions may serve the function of making a terrifying world more constant and predictable and therefore less frightening.

In addition to impaired social interaction, communication, and activities, people with autism and other pervasive developmental disorders commonly exhibit other notable problems. The three most prominent are (1) apparent sensory deficits, (2) self-injurious behavior, and (3) highly specialized abilities in some rare cases.

APPARENT SENSORY DEFICITS

Some people with autism or other pervasive developmental disorders respond to auditory, tactile, or visual sensations in highly unusual and idiosyncratic manners. For example, some people with autistic disorder occasionally respond as if they were deaf even though their hearing is intact. This unresponsiveness is an example of an *apparent sensory deficit* (Lovaas et al., 1971). There is no impairment in the sense organ, but the individual's responding makes it appear otherwise. Even more puzzling is that the same person who fails to be startled by a sudden crack of thunder may scream in apparent pain in reaction to a small sound like the scratch of chalk on a blackboard (Schreibman, 1988). This inconsistency suggests that the problem lies at some higher level of perception rather than at a lower level of sensation. The autistic individual's sensory apparatus is intact, but some cortical abnormality in integrating and perceiving sensory input creates these unusual and varied reactions to sounds, sights, and touches.

SELF-INJURY

Self-injurious behavior is one of the most bizarre and dangerous difficulties that can accompany autism and other pervasive developmental disorders. The most common forms of self-injury are repeated head banging and biting of the fingers and wrists (Rutter, Greenfield, & Lockyer, 1967). The resultant injuries may involve only minor bruises, or they can be severe enough to cause broken bones, brain damage, and even death. It is important that this self-injury not be misinterpreted as suicidal behavior. The autistic child does not have enough self-awareness to be truly suicidal. Instead, self-injury seems to have several possible causes, the most widely accepted of which is self-stimulation (Carr,

1977). Fortunately, self-injury can be treated effectively with behavior modification techniques, as we discuss later.

SAVANT PERFORMANCE

One of the most intriguing of all of the fascinating characteristics of autism and pervasive developmental disorders is the occasional child who shows *savant performance*—an exceptional ability in a highly specialized area of functioning. Savant performance typically involves artistic, musical, or mathematical skills. The image on page 499 portrays the savant artistic abilities of Nadia, a young girl with autism. Nadia's artistic abilities at the age of 5 and 6 are impressive and fascinating. What is even more interesting is that Nadia's artistic abilities deteriorated as she improved in other areas of functioning as a result of intensive therapy (Selfe, 1977; see Further Thoughts).

No one has an adequate theory, let alone an explanation, for savant performance. Unfortunately, one thing does seems clear. Despite what many people had hoped, the existence of savant performance does not indicate that autistic children have superior intelligence. Most autistic children do not exhibit these special abilities, and savant performance sometimes is observed among mentally retarded and brain-injured people as well. More specifically, even when they are given intelligence tests that do not require verbal communication, 60 percent of autistic children have IQs below 50, 20 percent have IQs between 50 and 70, and only 20 percent have IQs over 70 (Ritvo & Freeman, 1978). In addition, the IQ scores of autistic children behave like the IQs of normal children: They are stable over time, and they predict future educational attainment (Schreibman, 1988). Interest has grown in a subgroup of people with pervasive developmental disorder who do have normal intelligence, however, as we discuss in the next section on classification.

Classification

BRIEF HISTORICAL PERSPECTIVE

The history of the classification of the pervasive developmental disorders is a very brief one. The syndrome of "early infantile autism" was first described in 1943 by psychiatrist Leo Kanner (1894–1981) of Johns Hopkins University. Kanner reported on 11 children whose unusual symptoms were strikingly similar and whose difficulties were dramatically different from those of other emotionally disturbed children. Among the characteristics that Kanner noted were an inability to form relationships with others, delayed or noncommunicative speech, a demand for sameness in the environment, stereotyped play activities, and lack of imagination (Kanner, 1943). To Kanner's credit, contemporary diagnostic criteria are very similar to the symptoms he described.

While Kanner's contributions are well-known, mental health professionals have only recently recognized that Viennese psychiatrist Hans Asperger (1944) identified a very similar condition to autism at virtually the same time as Kanner. One important difference, however, was that Asperger's patients evidenced higher intellectual functioning. For the first time, a distinction between the two sets of historically important observations has been introduced into the formal diagnostic nomenclature in DSM-IV. **Asperger's disorder** is now listed as a subtype of pervasive developmental disorder. Descriptively, it is identical to autism, with the exception that the disorder involves no clinically significant delay in language.

While Kanner's and Asperger's observations have stood the test of time, another event in the history of the classification of autism is memorable for the misunderstanding that it caused. For several decades, the term "childhood schizophrenia" was used to classify autism together with other severe forms of childhood psychopathology (Bender, 1947). However, the symptoms of autism and schizophrenia differ dramatically, and evidence indicates that autism and schizophrenia remain different over time (Rutter, Greenfield, & Lockyear, 1967). Moreover, the pervasive developmental disorders have an onset in the preschool years, while the incidence of schizophrenia does not become notable until the teen years. Some professionals continue to use the misleading term "childhood schizophrenia," but it has been appropriately abandoned by most investigators.

CONTEMPORARY CLASSIFICATION

Since the introduction of DSM-III, the term *pervasive developmental disorder* has been used as an umbrella classification that includes autism and a few similar disorders that failed to meet all the criteria for autism. DSM-IV has introduced some new distinctions, however. As noted, Asperger's disorder refers to people who show the symptoms of autism but do not have major problems in communication. *Childhood disintegrative disorder* refers to a condition characterized by problems in social interaction and communication, in addition to stereotyped behavior. The onset occurs after at least 2 years of normal development, and previously acquired skills are lost. Finally, *Rett's disorder* refers to a condition characterized by at least 5 months of normal development followed by (1) a deceleration in head growth, (2) loss of purposeful hand movements, (3) loss of social engagement, (4) poor coordination, and (5) a marked delay in language.

One reason for introducing these new diagnostic categories is to facilitate accurate research on etiology and treatment. Care also must be taken in distinguishing pervasive developmental disorders from *developmental aphasia*, a disorder characterized by delayed or absent speech. Children with developmental aphasia attempt to communicate through nonverbal signals, and they have normal social interests. Sociability also distinguishes mental retardation from pervasive developmental disorders. The major problem in distinguishing autism and mental retardation has been the failure to recognize autism. Autistic disorders have frequently been misdiagnosed as mental retardation.

Epidemiology

Autism is an extremely rare disorder. Only 4 or 5 out of every 10,000 children qualify for the diagnosis. Even the combined prevalence of autism and other pervasive developmental disorders is extremely low, perhaps 20 out of every 10,000 children (Wing & Gould, 1979).

At one time experts believed that autism was more common among the higher social classes, but research reveals that the apparent relation was created by referral bias (Gillberg & Schaumann, 1982). Parents with fewer resources may accept an initial misdiagnosis of mental

▲ Nadia, a girl with autism, drew this picture of a horse and rider when she was 5½ years old. Nadia's savant drawing ability diminished as she began to learn to communicate and relate to others.

▲ Leo Kanner (1894–1981) was a U.S. psychiatrist who promoted the study of psychological problems among children. Kanner was noted for his identification of autism as a distinct psychological disorder.

Savant Performance

Savant performance is one of the most intriguing observations in abnormal psychology. Several hundred cases of savant performance have been documented throughout the world in the last century. Such notable figures as Langdon Down and Alfred Binet wrote about one or more of their patients with savant abilities. Incredible, specialized abilities have been found among a small percentage of autistic people, the mentally retarded, and others suffering from mental handicaps or brain injuries (Treffert, 1988). The abilities are not just unusual relative to the mental disturbance or low IQ of the savant individual, but they far exceed normal performance in a highly specialized area of functioning.

There seem to be a limited number of categories of savant performance. Mathematical facility and calendar calculation is one of the more commonly noted areas of ability. Some savants are able to recite the day of the week for virtually any past or future date in a matter of several seconds; others can perform incredibly rapid mental arithmetic. Astonishing memory skills are another type of savant ability. Cases have been reported, for example, in which people who were otherwise mentally retarded could accurately recall the weather for any particular day extending back for years in time. Musical talents are a third type of relatively common savant ability. Several cases have been reported in which people of limited intelligence could play back entire complicated compositions after hearing them only once (Treffert, 1988). Finally, some savants possess advanced drawing abilities, as exemplified by the sketch by Nadia reproduced in this chapter.

Nadia was 6½ years old when she was first seen by British therapist Lorna Selfe (1977), who documented her drawing abilities. According to her mother, Nadia had begun to produce complex drawings by the age of 3½. Nadia drew frequently and quickly, working with her left hand while holding her face very close to the sheet of paper. She used no colors in her drawings, and she did not copy from picture books. Rather, Nadia typically would see a picture in a book, often a simple one, and a day or two later she would begin to draw a similar but more complex version of it. Her favorite subjects for drawing included horses, roosters, and human figures.

At the time she was first seen, Nadia had severely restricted language skills and met the criteria for a diagnosis of autism. She entered a school for autistic children at the age of 7½, and she had made some progress by the age of 9. For example, she learned to return a greeting rather than echoing "Hello Nadia" when greeted by others. A puzzling and somewhat sad consequence of her education was that her drawing interest and ability waned as her other skills developed (Selfe, 1977).

What allows savants like Nadia to perform their seemingly magical feats? Savants themselves are of little help in answering this question. They typically cannot describe their own mental processes. Scientific explanations are not much more satisfying. Some theorists have speculated that savant abilities are attributable to exceptional *eidetic imagery* or visual memory. Others have hypothesized that savant ability is a result of genetic influences. Finally, several theorists have suggested that savant performance is a way of compensating for sensory deprivation or limited cognitive abilities. One compensatory hypothesis is that damage to the left cerebral hemisphere heightens the functioning of the spatial and mathematical abilities localized in the right hemisphere of the brain.

Each of these speculations is far from being adequately developed or researched. At present, savant performance remains a fascinating and unexplained phenomenon. It poses a challenge both to abnormal psychologists and to cognitive scientists, who must somehow account for these unusual abilities in theories of normal cognitive functioning. ■

retardation, but wealthier and better educated parents continue to seek opinions from specialized professionals, who eventually recognize the autism (Schopler, Andrews, & Strapp, 1979). This process leads to a correlation between social class and autism among those patients treated at prestigious clinics, but when the general population is examined, no association is found. This epidemiological fact is important, because the supposed higher intelligence and social status of the parents of autistic children has been used as "evidence" to support the false views that autistic children have superior intellects and that the disorder is caused by successful but cold and distant parents.

A more promising epidemiological finding is that the risk for autism increases dramatically among the siblings of autistic children. The prevalence of autism among the overall population is about .04 percent, whereas the prevalence among children with an autistic sibling is 2 to 3 percent, a 50-fold increase (Smalley, Asarnow, & Spence, 1988). Although these statistics don't prove that autism has a genetic cause, they have encouraged research in this area. Finally, the fact that autism is 3 to 4 times more common among boys than among girls has prompted a search for a gender-linked etiology.

Etiological Considerations and Research

The unusual symptoms and low prevalence of autism imply that diagnosticians have identified a disorder that will prove to have a single, specific etiology. Autism, however, appears to have multiple causes. Several problems that we have already discussed as causes of mental retardation also appear to cause autism. In addition, recent findings suggest that genetic factors play an important role in the etiology of the disorder. Before discussing evidence on biological etiologies of autism, we first briefly consider—and reject—environmental explanations.

PSYCHOLOGICAL AND SOCIAL FACTORS

For many years after Kanner identified autism, a number of professionals asserted that the disorder was caused by poor parenting. In particular, the disorder was said to be caused by parents who were cold, distant, and subtly reject-

ing of their children. This view was once so popular that in 1960, *Time* magazine published an account of these "refrigerator parents." The article claimed that the parents of autistic children "just happened to defrost long enough to produce a child" (Schreibman, 1988).

Hypothesizing about a psychological etiology began with Kanner (1943) himself. To his credit, however, Kanner consistently argued that autism was caused by a combination of biological and psychosocial factors (Eisenberg & Kanner, 1956). Other theorists focused exclusively on parenting. Theories of parental causation ranged from purely psychoanalytic speculations that autism was a result of the infant's defense against maternal hostility (Bettelheim, 1967) to purely behavioral views that the disorder was caused by inappropriate parental reinforcement (Ferster, 1961).

Evidence to support these speculations either has crumbled or failed to emerge. The observation that many parents of autistic children came from higher socioeconomic backgrounds once formed a major part of the justification for theories about "refrigerator parents." But as noted earlier, research has demonstrated that autism is not associated with high parental intelligence and social status. More directly, researchers have found no differences in the child-rearing styles of the parents of autistic children when compared with those of the parents of normal children (Rutter et al., 1971).

The view that "refrigerator parents" cause autism also can be seriously challenged on logical grounds. How could a parent's emotional distance create such an extreme disturbance so early in life? As we saw in our discussion of mental retardation, even the heinous abuse of infants does not cause symptoms that approach the form or severity of the problems found among autistic children. And no one has ever suggested that autistic infants suffer anything approaching traumatic abuse. Moreover, if parents are emotionally distant from an autistic child, might this not be a reaction to a child who shows no interest in relationships? Attachment behaviors are maintained by reciprocal interaction. If an infant shows no normal interest in cuddling or mimicking, is it surprising if the parent becomes a bit distant?

Speculation that autism is caused by poor parenting can never be completely disproved. However, logic, the lack of empirical support for psychological hypotheses, and mounting research on biological causes suggest with virtual certainty that autism does not have a psychological cause. More basically, the rules of science require scientists to prove their hypotheses and not to force others to disprove them (see Research Methods). Parents have been unfairly blamed for causing autism, and we greet further assertions that poor parenting causes autism with extreme skepticism.

The Null Hypothesis and the Burden of Proof

Scientists have established a basic and extremely important rule for making and testing any new hypothesis: The scientist who makes a new prediction must prove it to be true. Scientists are not obligated to *dis*prove other researchers' assertions. Until a hypothesis is supported by empirical evidence, the community of scientists assumes that the new prediction is false.

The concepts of the experimental hypothesis and the null hypothesis are central to understanding this essential rule of science. An **experimental hypothesis** is any new prediction made by an investigator. Researchers must adopt and state their experimental hypothesis both in correlational studies and in experiments (see Research Methods in Chapters 2 and 3). In all scientific research, the **null hypothesis** is the alternative to the experimental hypothesis. The null hypothesis always predicts that the experimental hypothesis is not true. The rules of science dictate that scientists must assume that the null hypothesis iholds until research contradicts it. That is, the burden of proof falls upon the scientist who makes a new prediction—who offers an experimental hypothesis.

These rules of science are analogous to rules about the burden of proof that have been adopted in trial courts. In U.S. courtrooms, the law assumes that a defendant is innocent until proven guilty. Defendants do not need to prove their innocence; prosecutors need to prove the defendants' guilt. Thus, the null hypothesis is analogous to the assumption of innocence, and the burden of proof in science falls on any scientist who challenges the null hypothesis, just as it falls on the prosecutor in a court trial.

These rules in science and in law serve important purposes. Both are conservative principles designed to protect the field from false assertions.

Our legal philosophy is that "it is better to let ten guilty people go free than to punish one innocent person." Scientists adopt a similar philosophy—that false "scientific evidence" is more dangerous than undetected knowledge. Because of these safeguards, we can be confident when an experimental hypothesis *is* supported or when a defendant *is* found guilty.

We can easily apply these concepts and rules to a hypothesis discussed in this chapter, the idea that autism is caused by "refrigerator parents." In this example, the experimental hypothesis is that cold, distant, and aloof parents cause the pervasive developmental disorder. The null hypothesis is that autism is *not* caused by refrigerator parenting. According to the rules of science, a theorist who hypothesizes that autism is caused by "refrigerator parents" must prove that it is true. Scientists are not obligated to prove that the assertion is false, because the null hypothesis holds until it is rejected. The value of this conservative approach is obvious when we consider the needless blame and guilt caused by the false allegations that have been made about "refrigerator parents."

There is one more similarity between the rules of science and the rules of the courtroom. Courtroom verdicts do not lead to a judgment that the defendant is "innocent," but only to a decision that she or he is "not guilty." In theory, the possibility remains that a defendant who is found "not guilty" did indeed commit a crime. Similarly, scientific research does not lead to the conclusion that the null hypothesis is true. Scientists never prove the null hypothesis; they only fail to reject it. The reason for this position is that the philosophy of knowledge, *epistemology*, tells us that it is impossible ever to prove that an experimental hypothesis is false in every circumstance.

Returning to our example, in theory it therefore remains possible that in some circumstances "refrigerator parents" do cause autism. This is only a theoretical possibility, however. Like all experimental hypotheses, the assertion must be unequivocally proved by its proponents. Until then, the wise rules of science dictate that we reject the theory. ∎

BIOLOGICAL FACTORS

A number of findings indicate that biological abnormalities play an important role in the etiology of autism. These include the following:

- Nearly half of all children with autistic disorder develop seizure disorders by adolescence or early adult life (Wing, 1988).
- Substantial increases in the prevalence of autism are found among children who have certain known genetic and infectious diseases (Reiss, Feinstein, & Rosenbaum, 1986).
- The prevalence of autism is higher among immediate relatives of autistic individuals than among the general population. Prevalence is particularly high among twin pairs (Smalley et al., 1988; Bailey et al., in press).
- A disproportionate number of neurological abnormalities have been identified among autistic children by a variety of techniques ranging from evidence of pregnancy and birth complications to abnormal EEGs to findings based on postmortem examination of the brain (Schreibman, 1988).

Autism as a Consequence of Known Biological Disorders One view of these diverse findings is that autism has several different biological causes (Reiss, Feinstein, & Rosenbaum, 1986). In support of this, one epidemiological study found that over half the cases of autism were associated with various known biological difficulties or disorders (Wing, 1988). These illnesses include many established causes of mental retardation, in particular fragile-X syndrome, tuberous sclerosis, PKU, rubella, and encephalitis (Reiss, Feinstein, & Rosenbaum, 1986). Other causes of mental retardation, however, are not associated with an increased prevalence of autism. For example, autism is not related to Down syndrome, the most common known biological cause of mental retardation.

Thus, there are many brain pathologies that cause mental retardation but only a few specific disturbances that may cause both mental retardation and autism.

A Strongly Genetic Disorder? In recent years a handful of studies have suggested that genetic factors also may play an important role in the etiology of many, if not all, cases of autism. The prevalence of autism is as much as 50 times higher among the siblings of an autistic child, and researchers have found higher concordance rates for autism among MZ than DZ twins (Smalley et al., 1988). In one investigation, the concordance rate for MZ twins was reported to be 95.7 percent, in contrast to 23.5 percent for DZ twins (Ritvo et al., 1985). This result may have overestimated the true concordance rate, however, as the investigators recruited subjects through a national newsletter to parents, and parents with twins who are concordant for autism are more likely to respond to this method of recruitment (Le Couteur, 1988). Nevertheless, another report found a concordance rate of 91 percent for autism among MZ twin pairs in contrast to 0 percent among DZ twins (Steffenburg et al., 1989).

Somewhat different results have been reported by a group of British investigators who conducted two major studies of the behavior genetics of autism. In the first report, the concordance rate for autism was found to be 36 percent for MZ twins and 0 percent for DZ twins (Folstein & Rutter, 1977). Importantly, however, the MZ–DZ comparison jumped to 82 percent versus 10 percent when concordance for any form of cognitive or learning difficulty was computed. From these results, the investigators concluded that autism was an extreme manifestation of an underlying cognitive disorder that was strongly heritable.

This research group replicated and expanded these findings in a recent investigation that included a reevaluation of the original sample and recruitment of a new group of twins (Bailey et al., in press). In this largest study to date, concordance rates for autism were 60 percent for MZ twins and 0 percent for DZ twins. Concordance rates for a social or cognitive disorder were 92 percent for MZ pairs and 10 percent for DZ pairs. Importantly, all twins in this new study were carefully screened for known heritable conditions (like fragile-X) that may have distorted the results of earlier studies. The fact that only a few conditions were detected by screening suggests that most cases of autism are caused by a genetic abnormality that has yet to be detected, not by known genetic or infectious illnesses (Bailey et al., in press). If so, autism is strongly but not completely genetic.

Even if autism does not have a single specific etiology, it still may be produced by a common underlying pathology. That is, genetics, PKU, and tuberous sclerosis may be different routes to the same destination in that they produce similar abnormalities in brain function, structure, or development. In fact, different brain abnormalities may cause different symptoms of the disorder, and perhaps this accounts for differences in the presentation of pervasive developmental disorders (for example, autism versus Asperger's disorder). Detecting a common pathology could lead to the development of more effective means of preventing or treating the disorder. Toward these ends, researchers have developed several promising leads in understanding the neuropathology of autism.

Neurophysiology and Autism With respect to abnormal brain function, theorizing has focused on two major neurophysiological processes. The first theory concerns the neurotransmitter serotonin. About one-third of autistic children have elevated blood levels of serotonin (Kohler, 1988). However, elevated levels of neurotransmitters in the blood or other peripheral sites do not necessarily indicate higher levels in the brain.

A potentially more important finding concerns the effect of the medication *fenfluramine* in the treatment of autism. Commonly used as a diet aid in the general population, fenfluramine has been demonstrated to reduce brain serotonin levels in animals, and some pilot research suggested that the drug alleviates some symptoms of autism (Geller et al., 1982). Subsequent investigation of the clinical effectiveness of fenfluramine has produced much more mixed results, however, as we shall see in the treatment section. At this time the relationship of serotonin levels to autism is uncertain and requires further investigation.

Recent research has also focused on the possible role of the endorphins in the neurophysiology of autism. Some evidence indicates that endorphin levels are elevated among people with autistic disorder and that elevated blood levels of endorphins are associated with decreased pain sensitivity among autistic children. (Recall from Chapter 10 that the internally produced endorphins have effects similar to those of externally administered opiate drugs like morphine.) This suggests that elevated endorphin levels may be responsible for some unusual symptoms exhibited by autistic children, particularly their self-destructive behavior (Gillberg, 1988).

Neuroanatomy and Autism Other research has searched for abnormalities in brain structure among people with autism. Perhaps certain structures of the brain are damaged or develop abnormally in autistic children. The question is: Where are the abnormalities located?

Early theorizing suggested that the left cerebral hemisphere was a likely site of brain damage in autism, because speech typically is controlled by left hemisphere structures. Many experts have rejected this view, however, because the communication deficits that characterize autism are more basic than problems in language expression or comprehension. Based on this reasoning, it has been suggested that damage is more likely to be found in subcortical brain structures (Wing, 1988). Consistent with this reasoning, some research suggests that autistic people may have abnormalities in parts of the limbic system—the area of the brain that regulates emotions—and also in areas of the cerebellum, where sensorimotor input is integrated (Schreibman, 1988).

Although it is possible that the brains of autistic people have subcortical damage, no convincing evidence on structural abnormalities is currently available. If present, the abnormalities are considerably more subtle than the brain damage associated with most known organic causes of mental retardation. More fruitful evidence surely will come from research that uses new brain-imaging techniques, as well as from the postmortem examination of brains of autistic people.

As investigators search for sites of brain damage, one thing seems clear. Any structural abnormalities are likely to be the result of abnormal brain development, not of specific damage or lesions. This is because *plasticity* is a basic characteristic of the development of the infant's brain. If damage occurs in one site in the infant's brain, another area of the brain often takes over the function of the damaged location. Because most cases of autism begin at an age when the brain is still plastic, specific brain damage or lesions are unlikely causes (Rutter, 1978).

Treatment

Some controversy exists about the degree to which treatment can alter the prognosis for autistic children. Some people are optimistic about the possibilities of new or established treatments, whereas others are far more skeptical (see Research Close-up). Everyone acknowledges, however, that there is no cure for the disorder. Thus, the effectiveness of treatment must be compared against the natural course and outcome of autism.

COURSE AND OUTCOME

Unfortunately, autism is a lifelong disorder. In one study of 63 autistic children who were followed into adulthood, only 1 was functioning in what could be considered the normal range. Another 22 children achieved fair to good adjustment as adults. Even this group exhibited social isolation and odd behavior, however, and required some form of specialized supervision. The remainder of the autistic people in the study (over 60 percent) were living in institutions or other special settings at the time of follow-up (Rutter, 1970). This gloomy picture is consistent with the findings painted by several similar longitudinal investigations (Schreibman, 1988), although Asperger's disorder has a more optimistic prognosis (Gillberg, 1991).

Two developmental periods are especially important to the course of autism: the early preschool years and early adolescence. Children who have developed language skills by the age of 5 or 6 have a significantly more positive prognosis than do those who have no or severely limited speech at this age. Not surprisingly, higher IQ as measured during the early school years also is a positive prognostic indicator (Schreibman, 1988). This research was conducted before the diagnostic category of Asperger's disorder was introduced, but these findings would seem to indicate a more optimistic prognosis for that disorder.

The other key developmental period in autism is early adolescence. During the early teen years, the cognitive and social skills of some autistic children improve notably, whereas those of others decline. At this point, scientists cannot predict the pattern for any given child. Adolescence also is an important developmental period in that as many as half of all autistic children develop seizure disorders during their teen years (Wing, 1988).

Clinical case reports offer some insight into what is considered to be a good outcome for those very few autistic people who achieve adequate adult functioning. One such report is the case of Jerry, a 31-year-old man who had been diagnosed as autistic by Kanner (Bemporad, 1979). At the time of the case study, Jerry was living by himself in an apartment near his parents' home, where he went most evenings to eat dinner and watch television with his family. Watching television was Jerry's only leisure activity, and he spent most of his free time in front of the set. He did not enjoy reading, sports, or other diversions. At the time of the interview, Jerry was nearing completion of a college degree. He also held a part-time job. However, he needed extremely detailed instructions in order to complete his work, because he had great difficulty thinking of an original way to attack a problem.

At 31, Jerry had no friends and only a vague interest in social relationships. People seemed frightening to him, not so much because he feared ridicule or rejection, but because they were so unpredictable. Jerry compulsively needed routine, and people did not repeat identical behaviors over and over again. He apparently had little insight into his social isolation, blaming his social problems on the evils of society.

Other aspects of his early symptoms also continued into adult life. Although Jerry could communicate well, his imagination was severely constrained. He reported no fantasies or daydreams. His earlier need for sameness also stayed with him into adulthood. Much of his day was filled with rituals. It took him 2 hours to take a shower, for example, because of his need to arrange things just right. On occasion, he would still lose himself in self-stimulation, rocking back and forth repeatedly. Overall, however,

A Study of Facilitated Communication

acilitated communication is a technique that has created both excited optimism and extensive skepticism concerning the possibilities for treating autism. In facilitated communication, a "facilitator" supports the hand and arm of a disabled individual, thus allowing the child to type on a keyboard. The technique was developed in Australia by educator Rosemary Crossley, who originally used it with people with motor disabilities such as cerebral palsy (Crossley & McDonald, 1980). It was brought to the United States by the Australian special educator Douglas Biklen, who has used the technique with autistic individuals. Biklen (1992) has claimed that the technique allows autistic people to express themselves. He reports that autistic people show insight, awareness, and literary talent. He also maintains that they sometimes report traumatic experiences during facilitated communication.

Many popular media sources, including nationally televised programs, have portrayed facilitated communication enthusiastically and uncritically. Eager for a breakthrough cure, many relatives of autistic people have embraced the technique. Is facilitated communication a legitimate breakthrough?

Whereas Biklen (1992) embraces a case study approach to facilitated communication and invariably finds positive results (see Research Methods in Chapter 1), independent investigators have conducted more systematic studies of the technique. One such study was conducted by Eberlin, McConnachie, Igel, and Volpe (1993). These investigators studied facilitated communication in 21 adolescents diagnosed as autistic and 10 adult facilitators who were enthusiastic about the technique.

The research study involved four primary procedures. First, in the baseline condition the autistic adolescents were asked a variety of questions and allowed to type or otherwise communicate their answers to the best of their abilities. A special, alphabetically configured keyboard was used for typing in this and all other conditions. Second, in the pretest the adolescents responded to the same questions

as in the first condition, but they were encouraged to type their answers with the aid of the facilitator, who was screened from hearing or seeing the questions being asked. Third, in the free response condition the adolescents were asked to respond to questions with the aid of the facilitator after the facilitator had received 20 hours of training in the technique. In this condition, the facilitator could see and hear the questions being asked. Finally, in the posttest the autistic adolescents were asked to respond to the identical questions as in the first and second conditions with the aid of the facilitator. The facilitators were screened again in this last condition.

Test questions included items from an intelligence test and personal questions like "What is your favorite food?" Results indicated that, in fact, responses to the questions were *worse* during the facilitated communication pretest and posttest than they had been during baseline. (Some of the autistic adolescents were able to communicate with words or gestures, at least to a minimal degree.) For example, 14 of 21 subjects were able to answer at least one personal question correctly during the baseline, but only 3 subjects did so with facilitated communication at pretest. Five subjects answered at least one question correctly during the facilitated communication posttest. (A few subjects could type accurately on their own, thus explaining the correct answers.) Moreover, scoring of the typing was very liberal. For example, a response of "APPXYZ" was judged to be the correct answer "apple" on the pretest.

These results contrasted dramatically with results obtained from a few subjects during the free response condition. For example, before facilitated communication, one subject was able to communicate only by using two manual signs. When asked to define emotion, however, with the aid of a facilitator this same subject typed "EMOTION ZOMETHIN* FEEL EXPREZ." This response surely would be more impressive if we did not know the results of the controlled study.

Breakthrough treatments like facilitated communication have a ready audience. Mentally ill people and their relatives, frustrated professionals, and the popular media often are desperate for dramatic advances and therefore are uncritical and susceptible to inadequately documented claims. Although we share the desire for spectacular and successful treatments, once again we urge you to be healthy skeptics. The burden of proof falls upon the shoulders of the proponent of a treatment (see Research Methods). When a truly effective new treatment is discovered, it will not be difficult to demonstrate its effectiveness using sound scientific methods. ∎

Jerry was doing very well in comparison to most autistic adults.

Little is known about how autistic children experience their disorder, because of their social disinterest or aversion, impaired communication skills, and limited imaginative activities. Those autistics who achieve a good outcome sometimes can offer intriguing insights into the autistic child's phenomenological experience. Jerry's memories of his childhood are especially interesting. Although he had been seriously disturbed, Jerry was a high-functioning autistic child. When he was 8 years old, his IQ was measured at 101. Here are some of the interviewer's comments on Jerry's recollection of his childhood:

His childhood experience could be summarized as consisting of two predominant experiential states: confusion and terror. The recurrent theme that ran through all of Jerry's recollections was that of living in a frightening world presenting painful stimuli that could not be mastered. Noises were unbearably loud, smells overpowering. Nothing seemed constant; everything was unpredictable and strange. Animate beings were a particular problem. Dogs were remembered as eerie and terrifying. As a child, he believed they were somehow humanoid (since they moved of their own volition, etc.), yet they were not really human, a puzzle that mystified him. . . . He was also frightened of other children . . . he could never predict or understand their behavior. . . . He said that he realized he was a burden to his family because he stuttered so much. Obviously, among all of his problems the stuttering caused the least concern to his parents; yet, after all these years, Jerry could still not judge the relative significance of his various problems. (Bemporad, 1979, pp. 192–193)

The case of Jerry clearly indicates the persistence of many of the symptoms of autism into the adult years. Despite his many successes, Jerry continued to be isolated from other people and frightened and puzzled by much of the world around him. Still, he achieved a life that is far superior to the typical course of autism. Can treatment help other children with pervasive developmental disorders to lead more normal lives?

MEDICATION

A huge variety of medications have been used to treat autism, including antipsychotics, antidepressants, amphetamines, psychedelics, and megavitamins. Unfortunately, none of these medications is an effective treatment for autism, and few show much promise.

Of all the medications, fenfluramine has generated the most excitement. Fenfluramine was used initially as an experimental treatment for autism based on the hypothesis that some symptoms of autism are caused by excess levels of serotonin (Geller et al., 1982). In several studies by the UCLA group that first experimented with the drug, fenfluramine was reported to reduce blood serotonin levels and to improve the cognitive performance and social behavior of autistic children (Geller et al., 1982; Ritvo et al., 1984).

Some investigators replicated the positive findings of the UCLA group (for example, Campbell et al., 1986). Unfortunately, other researchers have found few positive benefits and several side effects associated with fenfluramine treatment. Fenfluramine does reduce serotonin blood levels, but several independent researchers have not found improved functioning among autistic children as a result (Ekman et al., 1989; Sherman et al., 1989).

Although controversy about the effectiveness of the drug will certainly continue, the effects of fenfluramine clearly are not dramatic. When effective, the drug seems to increase attention and social interest and decrease self-stimulation and irritability. As with certain antipsychotic medications, particularly haloperidol (Haldol), these changes may help in the management and education of autistic children, but they fall far short of "curing" the disorder (Schreibman, 1988). Given the mixed results, fenfluramine is best considered to be an experimental drug in the treatment of autism.

PSYCHOTHERAPY: INTENSIVE BEHAVIOR MODIFICATION

Several theorists and clinicians have attempted to treat autism with various types of psychodynamic therapy. Based on the "refrigerator parent" hypothesis, many of these treatments attempted to provide nurturing, supportive environments that would allow autistic children to form attachments with surrogate caretakers (for example, Bettelheim, 1967). Rejection of theories of psychological etiology, together with evidence on the ineffectiveness of psychodynamic therapies (Bartak & Rutter, 1973), have caused responsible professionals to abandon this avenue of treatment.

Intensive behavior modification using operant conditioning techniques is a much more promising approach, even though behavioral views of the cause of autism were equally misguided. Behavior therapists have focused on treating the specific symptoms of autism, including communication deficits, self-care skills, and self-stimulatory or self-destructive behavior. Even within these different symptom areas, behavior modification emphasizes very specific and small goals. In attempting to teach language to an autistic child, for example, the therapist might spend hours, days, or weeks teaching the pronunciation of a specific syllable. Months of intensive effort may be needed to teach a small number of words and phrases. The autistic child's lack of imitation is one reason why so much effort goes into achieving such modest goals.

If the first goal of behavior modification is to identify very specific target behaviors, the second is to gain control over these behaviors through the use of reinforcement and punishment. Unlike normal children, who are reinforced by social interest and approval, autistic children do not understand ordinary praise, or they may find social interaction aversive. For this reason, the autistic child's successful efforts must be rewarded repeatedly with primary reinforcers such as a favorite food, at least in the beginning phases of treatment.

An example helps to illustrate the level of detail of behavior modification programs. A common goal with an echolalic autistic child is to teach the child to respond by answering questions rather than repeating them. As an early step in treatment, a target behavior might be to teach the autistic child to respond to the question "What is your name?" with the correct answer "Joshua."

In order to bring this specific response under the control of the therapist, initially it may be necessary to reward the child for simply echoing. Therapist: "What is your name?" Child: "What is your name?" Reward. This first step may have to be repeated hundreds of times over the course of several days.

A logical next step would be to teach the child to echo both the question and the response. Therapist: "What is your name? . . . Joshua." Child: "What is your name? . . . Joshua." Reward. Again, hundreds of repetitions may be necessary.

Gradually, the behavior therapist sets slightly more difficult goals, rewarding only increasingly accurate approximations of the correct response. One such intermediate step might be to echo the question "What is your name?" in a whisper and repeat the response "Joshua" in a normal tone of voice. Over a period of days, even weeks, the autistic child learns to respond "Joshua" to the question, "What is your name?"

Similar detailed strategies are used to teach autistic children other language skills. In the hope of speeding the process, some therapists have used sign language to teach autistic children to communicate (Carr, 1982). Unfortunately, this method has not led to a breakthrough. The communication deficits in autism apparently are more basic than receptive or expressive problems with spoken language. Behavior modification remains a painfully slow process that differs greatly from the way in which children normally learn to speak. The intensity and detail of these necessary efforts remind us that normal children come into the world remarkably well equipped to acquire language.

In addition to teaching communication skills, behavior therapists who work with children with

▲ O. Ivar Lovaas, a psychologist at UCLA, is a leader in using behavior modification to treat children with autistic disorder.

pervasive developmental disorders have concentrated on reducing the excesses of self-stimulation, self-injurious behavior, and general disruptiveness, as well as teaching new skills to eliminate behavioral deficits in self-care and social behavior (Schreibman, 1988). Behavior modification programs have been successful with some behavioral excesses, particularly self-injury, but the treatments are controversial because they typically rely on punishment. A slap or a mild electric shock can reduce or eliminate such potentially dangerous behaviors as head banging, but are such aversive treatments justified? Obviously, we all would prefer an alternative that did not involve punishment, but this option is currently not available. What is the appropriate ethical choice? Should a self-injurious autistic child be punished as a means of eliminating head banging, or is it preferable to use restraints (such as having the child wear a helmet) to deal with the behavior? This is a question that confronts therapists, parents, and others concerned with the treatment and protection of autistic children. Which option would you choose?

In other areas of intervention, behavior therapists have been fairly successful in teaching autistic children self-care skills and less successful in teaching social responsiveness. As Schreibman (1988) noted in her review of attempts to modify the social isolation of autistic children, "It is perhaps prophetic that the behavior characteristic which most uniquely defines autism, is also the one that has proven the most difficult to understand and treat" (p. 118).

Although focusing on specific target behaviors is a basic principle of behavior therapy, the important question to ask about their effectiveness is: To what extent does treatment improve the entire syndrome of autism? Research has demonstrated that autistic children can learn specific target behaviors, but do intensive training efforts bring about improvements that are clinically significant?

An optimistic answer to this question has been provided by O. Ivar Lovaas, a psychologist at UCLA who is an acknowledged leader in behavior modification for autistic children. In a comprehensive report on the efforts of his research team, Lovaas (1987) compared the outcomes of three groups of autistic children: (a) 19 children who received intensive behavior modification, (b) 19 children who were referred to the program but who received less-intensive treatment

due to the unavailability of therapists; and (c) 21 children who were seen elsewhere. In this study, all children received independent diagnoses of autism. Children with extremely low IQ scores were excluded, and treatment began before the children were 4 years of age. The children in the treatment group received the types of interventions described above, including both reinforcement and punishment procedures. In fact, they were treated 40 hours a week for a period of more than 2 years.

No differences among the three groups of children were found before treatment began. Assessments following treatment were conducted between the ages of 6 and 7, at the time when the children ordinarily would have finished the first grade. In the intensive behavior modification group, 9 children (47 percent) completed first grade in a normal school. Eight more children (42 percent) passed first grade in a special class for children who cannot speak. In comparison, only 1 child (2 percent) in the two control groups completed first grade in a normal classroom. In addition, 18 children (45 percent) who received an alternative treatment completed first-grade classes for aphasic children. Data on these findings are summarized in Table 14–6. In examining this table, you should note the strong relation between IQ and outcomes. You also should note the low mean IQ levels of the children, despite the investigators' attempts to screen out the most severely impaired children.

These data provide a reason for some optimism, and the efforts of Lovaas and others who

TABLE 14–6

Educational Placement and IQ of Children with Autistic Disorder Following Behavior Modification or Alternative Treatments

Group		Classroom N	Mean IQ
Intensive Behavior Modification	Normal	9	107
	Aphasic	8	74
	Retarded	2	30
Limited Treatment	Normal	0	—
	Aphasic	8	74
	Retarded	11	36
No Treatment	Normal	1	99
	Aphasic	10	67
	Retarded	10	44

From O.I. Lovaas (1987). Behavioral treatment and normal educational and intellectual functioning in young autistic children. *Journal of Consulting and Clinical Psychology, 55*, 3–9.

have used behavior therapy to teach skills to autistic children should be applauded. Despite the fact that autism seems to be caused by neurological abnormalities, the most effective treatment for the disorder is highly structured and intensive operant behavior therapy (Schreibman, 1988). Still, cautions must be raised. Are the children who passed first grade functioning normally in other respects? Would treatment have been as effective if it had not begun so early in life? Because pretreatment IQ predicted outcome (Lovaas, 1987), does behavior modification produce dramatic changes only with autistic children who are relatively high-functioning? What about the 53 percent of children who received intensive therapy but who were not in normal classrooms?

Perhaps the most important question about the effectiveness of behavior modification is its cost. Remember that the children in the intensive behavior modification group were treated for 40 hours per week for a period of more than 2 years. At the same time, children in the "limited treatment" control group received almost 10 hours of weekly treatment, yet they showed few improvements. The expenses associated with early but effective treatment clearly are far less than those involved in a lifetime of care (Lovaas, 1987). Still, the question is this: How do we, as a society, justify devoting large amounts of resources to the rare problem of autism, when in comparison we neglect intervention efforts with the much more common—and in many ways more treatable—problem of mental retardation?

Summary

Mental retardation is defined by (1) significantly subaverage intellectual functioning, (2) existing concurrently with related limitations in adaptive skills, and (3) an onset before age 18. Intellectual functioning must be determined by an individualized **IQ** test. Many important criticisms have been raised about IQ tests, but they are reliable and valid (if imperfect) predictors of academic performance. Many people who have significantly subaverage IQs function adequately in the world, however, because they show no deficits in adaptive behavior. Such people are not considered to be mentally retarded.

KEY TERMS

- amniocentesis
- Asperger's disorder
- autistic disorder
- cultural-familial retardation
- Down syndrome
- experimental hypothesis
- fetal alcohol syndrome
- fragile-X syndrome
- intelligence quotient (IQ)
- lead poisoning
- mainstreaming
- mental retardation
- normalization
- null hypothesis
- pervasive developmental disorders
- phenylketonuria (PKU)
- reaction range

The DSM-IV divides **mental retardation** into four levels based on IQ scores. People with mild mental retardation complete their education at the sixth-grade level, and live in the community with little or no support. This is by far the most common category of mental retardation. People with moderate mental retardation reach a second-grade level of academic performance, and require careful supervision in independent living. Severe mental retardation is characterized by major limitations in development and communication and necessitates close supervision. Finally, profound mental retardation often is accompanied by many physical handicaps and sharply restricted development, and demands constant supervision in the community or in institutions.

The etiology of mental retardation can be grouped into cases caused by known biological abnormalities and cases resulting from normal variations in IQ. **Down syndrome**, which is caused by an extra chromosome on the 21st pair, is the most common of the known biological causes of mental retardation. **Fragile-X syndrome**, the second leading biological cause, is a genetic disorder indicated by a weakening of the X sex chromosome. Other known biological causes include **PKU**, an inherited metabolic deficiency; infectious diseases transmitted to the fetus during pregnancy or birth such as rubella, syphilis, and genital herpes; excessive maternal alcohol consumption or drug use during pregnancy; Rh incompatibility; and malnutrition, premature birth, and low birth weight.

So-called **"cultural-familial retardation"** comprises most cases of mental retardation. Retardation typically is mild, and there is no known specific etiology. An important debate about cultural-familial retardation is the relative importance of normal genetic variation and deprived psychosocial environments in its development.

Many cases of mental retardation can be prevented by adequate health care before and during pregnancy. Testing for chromosomal or genetic abnormalities in the fetus and considering selective abortion is a more problematic means of preventing retardation. Early psychoeducational programs also may prevent some cases of mental retardation by improving adaptive behavior if not by increasing IQ scores. Treatments for mental retardation include preschool stimulation programs, medical treatment of physical handicaps, and specialized educational services in school. Finally, a major policy goal is to **normalize** the lives of mentally retarded people through **mainstreaming** in public schools and promoting care in the community.

The **pervasive developmental disorders** involve profound disturbances in relationships, stereotyped activities, and communication difficulties. Autistic disorder is the most widely researched pervasive developmental disorder. Social impairments in autism may be relatively mild oddities, but they also may include extreme difficulties in which there is little awareness of the existence of others. About half of all autistic children fail to develop communicative speech, and the remainder have either highly restricted language abilities or striking oddities in speech. Finally, many autistic people spend hours engaging in self-stimulation. Compulsively rigid adherence to daily routines is another manifestation of their restricted activities and interests.

Other difficulties often are found in autism and the pervasive developmental disorders. Apparent sensory deficits involve a lack of responsiveness to stimuli. Self-injurious behavior is another unusual and potentially dangerous problem. Savant performance is an exceptional ability at performing mental feats such as rapid mathematical calculations. Despite such unusual abilities, most people with pervasive developmental disorders are mentally retarded. One exception is **Asperger's disorder**, characterized by the same difficulties as are found in autism except that language acquisition is not impaired.

The pervasive developmental disorders are rare conditions, and they almost certainly are caused by biological abnormalities. Several known causes of mental retardation may cause pervasive developmental disorders (for example, fragile-X syndrome). Recent evidence also suggests that genetics plays an important role. At this time, there is no easy, effective treatment for these conditions. Intensive behavior modification has shown much promise as a treatment, but the expense and effort involved are considerable. Without intensive treatment that is maintained over time, the prognosis for the pervasive developmental disorders is a gloomy one. The majority of people with these conditions require intensive, life-long care, often within an institution.

Critical Thinking

1. The concept of intelligence can be quite controversial. Is academic performance the same thing as intelligence? How would you define social or practical intelligence? Do you agree that people should be considered mentally retarded only if they have a significantly subaverage IQ *and* deficits in adaptive skills?

2. In some states, autistic children are able to receive more subsidized mental health services than are mentally retarded children. In part, this is because autism often is viewed as an illness that can be cured, whereas retardation is seen as an unchangeable characteristic of the person. Do you agree with these views? Do you think it is justifiable to spend more money per child to treat autism than to treat mental retardation?

Psychological Problems of Childhood and Eating Disorders

Children and adolescents suffer from most of the disorders covered in earlier chapters of this text. Children may develop mood disorders or anxiety disorders, for example. With the exception of mental retardation and pervasive developmental disorders, however, all the problems we have discussed are far more prevalent among adults than among children. Theory and research often link these disorders to childhood experiences, but the symptoms typically do not fully emerge until the patient reaches adulthood.

Overview

The psychological problems more commonly found among children are not simply miniature versions of adult disorders. Rather, they are unique in many ways. In fact, the DSM-IV contains a separate diagnostic category called "Disorders Usually First Diagnosed in Infancy, Childhood, or Adolescence." Other than mental retardation and pervasive developmental disorders (see Chapter 14), the most important psychological disorders of childhood are externalizing disorders and internalizing disorders.

Externalizing disorders are behavior problems that are directed toward the external world. Their disruptive nature is evident in the major subtypes of externalizing disorders: *attention-deficit/hyperactivity disorder*, *oppositional defiant disorder*, and *conduct disorder*. We discuss each of these problems in detail later in this chapter. For now, you need to know only two things about externalizing disorders: (1) these disorders are characterized by children's failure to control their behavior according to the expectations of others, particularly their parents and teachers; and (2) externalizing disorders are, by far, the most commonly diagnosed psychological problems among children.

Internalizing disorders are psychological problems of childhood that are directed inward toward the child rather than outward toward the world. Excessive anxiety and sadness are the major internalizing disorders that we consider in this chapter. The DSM-IV does not list internalizing problems as unique psychological disorders of childhood, but instead notes that children may qualify for the "adult" diagnoses

for anxiety and mood disorders. We think it is important for you to consider how children uniquely experience internalizing problems, however, because children do not interpret events or express emotions in the same manner as adults. Thus, in our discussion of internalizing disorders we suggest that the same diagnostic criteria may not apply to anxiety and mood disorders among children and among adults.

We discuss **eating disorders**—severe disturbances in eating behavior—in a separate section of this chapter. In particular, we highlight *anorexia nervosa*, a disorder characterized by drastically restricted eating and extreme emaciation, and *bulimia nervosa*, a disorder distinguished by frequent episodes of binge eating followed by intentional purging. Eating disorders once were considered to be psychological problems of childhood, but DSM-IV lists them in their own separate diagnostic category. We review eating disorders in this chapter because they typically develop during adolescence.

As we have discussed throughout the text, all abnormal behavior must constantly be evaluated by making comparisons with normal behavior. What is considered normal changes rapidly during the first 20 years of life. Is it normal to lie down on the floor, kick, scream, and cry if you don't get your way? This certainly is *not* normal behavior for a 19-year-old college student. It is normal, though sometimes obnoxious, for a 2-year-old child to throw a temper tantrum. Similarly, fears of monsters are developmentally normal at the age of 4, but not at the age of 14; and staying up until all hours is normal for 14-year-old adolescents, but not for 4-year-old children.

Thus, it is especially important to take a *developmental psychopathology* perspective in considering the psychological problems of infancy, childhood, and adolescence (see Chapter 2). In particular, we must consider *developmental norms* when deciding whether children's behavior is normal or abnormal. The first question we must ask in evaluating a potential psychological problem of childhood is: How old is the child? A given behavior may be normal at one age, but the same behavior may constitute an internalizing or externalizing problem at a different age. That is, psychologists become concerned when a child's behavior deviates substantially from developmental norms. In fact, some specific deviations from developmental norms create unique psychological difficulties for children

(for example, bedwetting). We briefly consider some of these specific problems when describing the classification of psychological disorders of childhood.

Developmental norms change rapidly during infancy, childhood, and adolescence, but development does not stop at the age of 18 or 21. In recognition of this important fact, we continue our discussion of psychological problems and changing developmental norms into Chapter 16. In Chapter 16, we review some common psychological difficulties experienced during the course of *adult* development—for example, problems in marital and family relationships. Together, Chapters 15 and 16 address the important issues of psychological distress and **life-span development**—continuities and changes in behavior from infancy through the last years of life.

Psychological Problems of Childhood

Identifying abnormal behavior among children can be a difficult and often a subjective task. Many of the concerns about defining abnormal behavior raised in Chapters 1 and 4 are particularly relevant to the psychological disorders of childhood (for example, labeling, dimensions versus categories). A unique complication stems from the fact that very few children or adolescents identify themselves as needing psychological help. Instead, some adult—a parent, teacher, legal authority, or mental health professional—typically decides that a child is emotionally disturbed.

This fact creates special problems for assessment. One core problem is that the adult's evaluation is potentially biased. In one sense, a child may serve as a "projective test" for an adult. For example, a depressed mother may overinterpret her daughter's actions as indicative of the daughter's sadness, or an intolerant teacher may conclude that normal misbehavior indicates that a boy has a conduct problem. In both examples, the evaluation of the child reflects something about the adult evaluator as well as about the child.

Difficulties in evaluating children's inner thoughts and feelings constitute another core

challenge for assessment. The daughter of a depressed mother may not recognize her own sadness, or she may want to protect her troubled mother by being stoic. The aggressive boy may or may not feel angry (or sad), but he is unlikely to admit either feeling to anyone, especially not to his teacher.

We can be assured that children are distressed when they freely acknowledge that they are worried or very sad. When children in difficult circumstances say that they have no inner troubles, however, psychologists face difficult questions in treatment and research. Is the child really troubled but unaware of, or unable to describe, the hidden emotions? Is the child painfully aware of the emotional struggles, but reluctant to admit these feelings? Or is the child really coping effectively? In attempting to answer such questions, psychologists also must be careful not to project their beliefs onto children.

Throughout the chapter, we consider the challenges to assessment and treatment that arise from the fact that it is adults who identify psychological problems and the need for psychological treatment among children. You should also keep these issues in mind as you read through the following case study.

CASE STUDY

Conflicts about Externalizing Behavior

Jeremy W., an 8-year-old boy, was brought to a clinical psychologist by his mother following the recommendations of his second-grade teacher and a school counselor. Mrs. W. came to the psychologist reluctantly, because she was not sure if she agreed with the suggestions of the school personnel. In fact, Mrs. W. wasn't sure if she agreed with her husband about what was going on with Jeremy.

According to Mrs. W., Jeremy was constantly in trouble at school. His teacher said that she was reprimanding Jeremy daily for disrupting the class, not paying attention, and failing to finish his work. The teacher felt that her attempts at discipline had little effect. Sometimes Jeremy would listen for awhile, but soon he would be pestering another child, talking out of turn, or simply staring off into space. Lately, Jeremy had begun to talk back when he was disciplined, and his teacher had sent him to the principal's office several times in the past month.

The psychologist confirmed this information in a subsequent telephone call to the school. At that time, the teacher also noted that Jeremy had no real friends in school, and that other kids thought of him as a "pain." The teacher had referred Jeremy to a school counselor, who gave him several academic tests. According to an individualized intelligence test, Jeremy had an IQ of 108. However, his achievement test scores indicated that he was achieving at a first-grade level, almost a year behind his current grade level. The school counselor suspected that Jeremy might have a learning disability, but she also thought that his behavior problems were interfering with his learning. She concluded that Jeremy should remain in his regular classroom for the present. As a first step, the counselor recommended therapy for Jeremy and perhaps for his parents. After treatment, she would reevaluate him for possible placement in a "resource room," a special class for students with learning problems.

Mrs. W. said that she was frightened by the counselor's suggestion that Jeremy might be "emotionally disturbed" or "learning-disabled." According to his mother, Jeremy was somewhat difficult to manage at home, but she had never considered the possibility that he needed psychological help. Jeremy had been a handful ever since the "terrible twos," but he had never been a *bad* child, in her view. Mrs. W. said that she had merely thought that Jeremy expressed himself better through actions than words. In this respect, he was the opposite of his 11-year-old sister, who was an A and B student. Mrs. W. was not convinced that Jeremy's teacher was the best person to work with him, but she did agree that he was having problems in school. In her mind, Jeremy was developing low self-esteem, and many of his actions were attempts to get attention.

According to Mrs. W., Jeremy's father spent very little time with him. Mr. W. worked long hours on his construction job, and he often was off with his friends on weekends. Mrs. W. said that her husband was of little help even when he was home. He would tell his wife that it was her job to take care of the kids—he needed his rest. With tears in her eyes, Mrs. W. said that she needed a rest, too.

In any case, Mr. W. was not concerned about Jeremy's behavior or his schoolwork. Instead, he thought that Jeremy was just "all boy" and not much of a student—just like Mr. W. was as a child. He refused to take time off from work to see a psychologist.

In confidence, Mrs. W. said that she too saw a lot of his father in Jeremy—too much of him, in fact. She got no support from her husband in disciplining Jeremy or in encouraging him in his schoolwork. She blamed her husband for Jeremy's problems, and she was secretly furious with him. She knew that Jeremy had to do well in school in order to live a better life, and she felt like a failure as a mother. She was willing to try anything to help Jeremy, but she doubted that there was anything she could do without her husband's help and support. ■

The case of Jeremy W. illustrates many of the complicated issues that arise in assessing and treating children's psychological problems. One essential issue is the need to reconcile adults' differing evaluations of the same child. Is Jeremy a disobedient child, as his teacher thinks? A learning-disabled child, as suggested by the school counselor? An emotionally disturbed child, as his mother fears? Or is he simply "all boy," as his father claims? What about Jeremy himself? How does he feel about himself, about his family, and about his schoolwork and his friendships at school?

Mental health professionals who treat children are constantly vexed by such difficult questions. In fact, treatment often begins with an attempt to get the adults to agree as to what the problem really is. Maybe the problem in the case history is not Jeremy alone. Perhaps the conflicts between the adults who supervise Jeremy are at least part of the problem. Mr. W. seems to be undercutting his wife's parenting, and they both may be failing to support Jeremy's teacher. Because of such possibilities, many psychologists prefer to see children in the context of family therapy rather than treating children alone. Mr. and Mrs. W. may need to learn to present a "united front" to Jeremy, for example, and they may need to resolve conflicts in their marriage in order to do so. Many psychologists also note the importance of coordinating treatment between the home and the school, and they therefore work to establish communication and cooperation between parents and teachers.

Of course, Jeremy is also at least part of the problem, and this raises another whole set of issues about the psychological problems of childhood. If we can trust his teacher's report—and experienced child psychologists do trust teachers—Jeremy clearly has some type of externalizing problem. The question is: What is the problem, and why does he have it? Perhaps Jeremy's behavior is simply a reaction to the adults' conflicts, and he will get better when the adults work out their differences. Or perhaps Jeremy is a troubled child who is causing some of these conflicts, not just reacting to them. Mr. and Mrs. W. both felt that Jeremy and his father were a lot alike. Could Jeremy have learned or inherited some of his father's characteristics?

We cannot answer these questions definitively in Jeremy's case, but in this chapter we do highlight a diagnostic distinction between externalizing disorders—a distinction that answers many of these questions implicitly. The diagnosis *oppositional defiant disorder* implies that an externalizing problem has environmental origins. In contrast, the diagnosis <u>*attention-deficit/hyperactivity disorder*</u> implies behavior and attentional problems with some sort of biological cause. In fact, you may have heard that "hyperactivity" has a biological cause and requires medication, whereas "conduct problems" are caused by family troubles and respond to psychological treatments.

As you will see when we discuss the etiology of externalizing disorders, researchers have not demonstrated that there are separate and distinct environmental and biological causes for oppositional defiant disorder versus attention-deficit/hyperactivity disorder. As our systems perspective indicates, biological, psychological, and social factors contribute to both disorders. More generally, you should recall the point we have made several times earlier in the text: Successful treatment does not imply cause. Attention-deficit/hyperactivity disorder improves when treated with medication, but this does *not* prove that the disorder has biological origins.

Typical Symptoms and Associated Features

A thorough consideration of the symptoms of all the psychological problems of infancy, childhood, and adolescence would repeat all the problems we discussed earlier in the text. As we have noted, children can and sometimes do suffer from "adult" disorders. In this section, we focus only on unique areas of disturbance among children: (1) externalizing symptoms; (2) internalizing symptoms; and (3) problems in relationships with peers.

EXTERNALIZING SYMPTOMS

As illustrated by Jeremy W., *externalizing symptoms* are characterized by violations of age-appropriate social rules. Rule violations may include disobedience, aggression, and perhaps legal violations (particularly during adolescence). All children violate at least some social rules, of course, and we often admire an innocent and clever rule breaker. For example, Mark Twain's fictional character Tom Sawyer broke all kinds of rules—but we still view Tom as the prototypical "all-American boy." Tom Sawyer decidedly was not a candidate for psychotherapy! Similarly, we see Calvin of the *Calvin and Hobbes* cartoons as devilish, but he is not really "bad," and we certainly do not view him as "sick."

Calvin and Hobbes by Bill Watterson

Several factors influence how adults evaluate children's rule violations. These include the frequency, intensity, duration, and cross-situational consistency of children's behavior. Externalizing behavior is a far greater concern when it is frequent, intense, lasting, and pervasive. That is, externalizing behavior is more problematic when it is part of a *syndrome* or cluster of problems than when it is a *symptom* that occurs in isolation. The existence of an externalizing syndrome has been demonstrated consistently by statistical analysis (factor analysis) of checklists on which parents or teachers rate children's psychological symptoms. Moreover, agreement among adult raters typically is high for this externalizing dimension (Achenbach, McConaughy, & Howell, 1987).

At least two additional considerations influence the evaluation of externalizing behavior. One is its *impact* on a victim, and the second is the *intent* of the perpetrator. We judge the identical act of aggression more harshly if it has a more harmful effect on a victim. We also judge rule violations harshly when they are uncaring, angry, and callous, but we chuckle at the innocent adventures of a Calvin or a Tom Sawyer. Of course, intent can be difficult to discern. You might wonder about Jeremy W.'s private motivations, for example.

In many respects, adults' judgments about children's externalizing problems parallel judgments about criminal responsibility made in our legal system. Review the factors we have just listed, and you will recognize that each one is a familiar consideration in criminal cases. Parents and teachers are the judge and jury for children's misconduct.

Seriousness of Children's Externalizing Behavior Some misconduct is normal, per-

haps even healthy, in children. In considering externalizing problems in the real world, however, it is essential to note that children's rule violations are not trivial and are far from "cute." Externalizing problems not only disrupt the lives of troubled children, but they also adversely affect the lives of people around the child. Many schoolteachers lament that they spend far too much time disciplining children—a circumstance that is frustrating to teachers and unfair to well-behaved youngsters in the classroom. Even more serious, the FBI reports that approximately 30 percent of arrests for *index offenses*—major crimes including murder, forcible rape, and robbery—are of juveniles under the age of 18 (FBI, 1985; see Figure 15–1). Other evidence indicates that the worst 5 percent of juvenile offenders account for approximately half of all juvenile arrests (Farrington, Ohlin, & Wilson, 1986).

Children's Age and Externalizing Problems
Very different rules and rule violations apply to children of different ages. A preschooler with an externalizing problem is likely to be disobedient to his parents and uncooperative with other children. During the school years, he or she is more likely to be disruptive in the classroom, aggressive on the playground, or defiant at home. By adolescence, the problem teenager may be failing in school, ignoring all discipline at home, hanging out with delinquent peers, and perhaps violating the law. Children's age also is important to consider in relation to the *timing* as well as the nature of rule violations. All children violate rules, but children with externalizing problems violate rules at a younger age than is developmentally normal (Loeber, 1988). For this reason, it is essential to consider the normal development of socialization.

Socialization in Normal Development
Socialization is the process of shaping children's behavior and attitudes to conform to the expectations of parents, teachers, and society as a whole (Hetherington & Parke, 1986). Many psychologists believe that parental explanation, example, and appropriate discipline are most important in socializing children, but other influences cannot be ignored. Peer groups exert strong if sometimes subtle conformity pressures that increase as children grow older. School and television also are powerful socialization agents.

Socialization is *not* a major task of development during the first year of life; what is most important at this age is the formation of a close bond between infants and caregivers. Research indicates that babies are not "spoiled" when they are picked up, cuddled, and loved in other ways. In fact, such natural interactions make infants easier, not more difficult, to manage—a fact demonstrated by psychologist Mary Ainsworth, an internationally reknowned expert on infant–mother attachments (Ainsworth, 1979). Rules do become a major issue, however, when infants become toddlers. It is developmentally normal for children to begin to test the limits of their world during the "terrible twos." Successful socialization during this age balances parental authority with children's developing sense of being able to control their world. For example, children may need to follow broad rules about eating a balanced diet, but they benefit from being permitted to exercise some autonomy in choosing what specific foods they will eat.

A major developmental goal of socialization during the preschool years is to begin to learn rules in peer relationships—rules about cooperating and sharing, for example. Learning to obey teachers and follow the rules of a small "society," the school, is an essential task for the school-aged child. Parents' and teachers' authority gradually declines, and peers become more important influences on the behavior of school-aged children and particularly of adolescents. Television, popular music, and other media also socialize children and adolescents by conveying rules about the popular culture.

Overall, the normal development of socialization moves from external control by parents, teachers, and other adults to the internal control of behavior. When a child internalizes social values and conforms to them with minimal external pressure, he or she is exhibiting *self-control*. Thus, self-control is the ultimate goal of socialization.

Adolescence-Limited versus Life-Course-Persistent Externalizing Behavior One stage of normal development—adolescence—borders on the abnormal, at least from the perspective of adults. Teenagers often violate the rules laid down by parents, teachers, and society as a means of asserting their independence and perhaps of conforming to the rules of their peer group. Because of this normative increase in externalizing behavior, it is essential to dis-

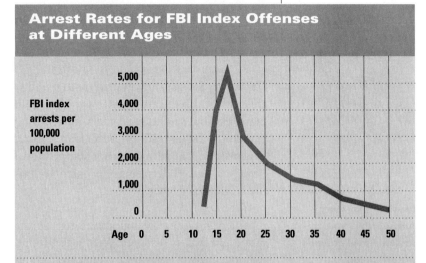

Arrest Rates for FBI Index Offenses at Different Ages

FBI index arrests per 100,000 population

Figure 15-1: Arrest rates across age for the Federal Bureau of Investigation's index offenses in 1980. Index offenses include homicide, forcible rape, robbery, aggravated assault, burglary, larceny, and auto theft.

Source: A. Blumstein, J. Cohen, and D.P. Farrington (1980). Criminal career research: Its value for criminology. *Criminology, 26,* 11.

tinguish between antisocial behavior that is *adolescent-limited*—that ends along with the teen years—and *life-course-persistent* antisocial behavior that continues into adult life (Moffitt, 1993).

This leads us to one of the most important findings about externalizing problems among children and adolescents: Externalizing problems that have an earlier onset are more likely to persist over the individual's life course. It is counterintuitive, but true, that scientists are better able to predict adult antisocial behavior from information obtained during childhood than from information obtained during adolescence (Farrington, Ohlin, & Wilson, 1986; Loeber, 1988; Moffitt, 1993).

By way of explanation, we must point out that it is *not* the case that antisocial adults were once well-behaved adolescents; in fact, the vast majority of antisocial adults have a history of antisocial behavior during the teen years (Robins, 1978). Rather, the explanation is the normative increase in externalizing behavior during adolescence. So many

▼ **Temper tantrums are a normal part of child development during the "terrible twos." Awareness of developmental norms is essential for evaluating abnormal behavior in children.**

▲ Canadian-American psychologist Mary Ainsworth is an internationally reknowned expert on infant-caregiver attachments. Ainsworth demonstrated the importance of parental warmth and responsiveness for healthy child development.

▲ Children experience sadness, anxiety, and other internalizing problems, but these problems are difficult to assess during the younger years. The diagnosis of depression becomes much more common during adolescence, especially among teenage girls.

adolescents engage in some form of antisocial behavior that, in order to identify teenagers most at risk, scientists need to look back in time to a stage of development (childhood) when conformity, not rebellion, is the norm (Moffitt, 1993).

INTERNALIZING SYMPTOMS

Internalizing symptoms involve psychological distress that is directed inward toward the child rather than outward toward others. Internalizing symptoms include sadness, fears, and somatic complaints, and perhaps other symptoms of mood and anxiety disorders—for example, feeling worthless or tense.

The DSM-IV identifies some unique ways in which children experience the symptoms of mood and anxiety disorders. When diagnosing major depressive episodes among children and adolescents, for example, the manual allows "irritable mood" to replace the "depressed mood" criterion. This exception recognizes that children sometimes act angry when they are feeling sad, and, more generally, that children may express their feelings in unique ways, or that they may mask their true emotions, especially when talking to adults.

Another example of an exception for children is the DSM-IV diagnosis of phobia. In contrast to the adult diagnostic criteria, children are not required to recognize that their fears are unreasonable. As implied by this exception, children may have limited insight into their problems. More generally, young children may lack the *cognitive capacity* to experience some of the internalizing symptoms found among adults.

In our view, questions about young children's cognitive capacities are particularly applicable to depression. Developmental psychopathologists have questioned whether children can experience many cognitive symptoms of depression, because their basic cognitive abilities are limited by their age (Rutter, 1986, 1988). For example, we wonder about ideas of suicide among preschoolers. Five-year-olds do not understand that death is permanent, because they have a limited understanding of the concept of time. Given this, can

preschoolers' (extremely rare) thoughts of suicide be equated with those of an adult?

Internalizing Symptoms and Normal Development A major problem in evaluating children's internalizing symptoms is that the course of children's normal emotional development is not well charted. One reason for this is that it is much more difficult for adults to assess children's inner experiences than it is to observe children's behavior. Children, in turn, often are not reliable or valid informants about their internal life. Children's capacity to recognize emotions in themselves and in others emerges slowly over the course of development, as does their ability to express—and to mask—their own feelings (Lewis & Michalson, 1983).

The difficulties in assessing internalizing problems are evident in psychological research. For example, in one study of 48 families in which a child was a psychiatric inpatient, a correlation of only .01 was found between identical measures of children's depression completed by parents and their children (Kazdin, French, & Unis, 1983). That is, there was no agreement between parents and children in rating the child's depression. In another study, children's and parents' ratings of depression were associated with different psychological symptoms. Children's ratings of their own depression were linked with their feelings of hopelessness, low self-esteem, internal attributions for negative events, and external locus of control (see Chapter 5). In contrast, parents' ratings of children's depression were not related to these internalizing symptoms but were correlated with the parents' evaluations of children's externalizing behavior (Kazdin, 1989). Finally, and perhaps of greatest concern, some researchers have found that parents underestimate the extent of depression reported by their children and adolescents (Kazdin & Petti, 1982; Rutter, 1989). For various reasons, adults are much more aware of what a child does—particularly what a child does wrong—than they are of how a child feels.

Problems in assessing internalizing problems constantly vex researchers. Clearly, there is a need for better measures of children's internalizing problems—and for more basic research on emotional development. At present, a conservative conclusion may be most prudent. There is cause for concern if either a parent or a child reports internalizing symptoms, and it is particularly important to assess children and adolescents with sensitivity and care.

Children's Fears in Developmental Perspective
Unlike most internalizing symptoms, children can identify specific fears fairly readily, and adults can also observe much of children's fearful behavior. For these reasons, psychologists have better, if still inadequate, evidence on the development of children's fears. This evidence is directly relevant to understanding internalizing disorders among children, and it also offers one example of why more basic research is needed on the development of internalizing symptoms.

Three developmental findings are especially important to note. First, the frequency of children's fears declines with age (King et al., 1989; Lapouse & Monk, 1959). Apparently, children outgrow many of their fears, probably by confronting them and overcoming them in daily life. Second, different fears develop for the first time at different ages. For example, infants typically develop a fear of strangers around the age of 7 to 8 months; preschoolers develop fears of monsters and the dark between the ages of 2 and 4; and children between ages 5 and 8 often develop fears related to school. (To cite one curious example, many children dream that they forgot to put on all of their clothes, and they are mortified to find themselves going to school in their underwear.) Such evidence implies that many fears are developmentally normal—a conclusion that can be particularly reassuring to parents who wonder about the origins of their children's worries. A third developmental finding of note is that some fears are common and apparently stable across different ages of childhood (King et al., 1989). Unlike other fears, these do not emerge suddenly, and they apparently are not outgrown. Table 15–1 contains a listing of some of these fears, all of which seem to focus on uncontrollable events.

Separation Anxiety Separation anxiety is one fear that is of unique importance among children. *Separation anxiety* is a normal fear that typically develops in the months just before a baby's first birthday. At this age it is not a psychological problem—in fact, it is a healthy response that indicates that an infant has a secure attachment to his or her caretakers (Ainsworth et al., 1978). Normal toddlers and preschoolers continue to show a degree of distress when sep-

TABLE 15–1
Some Fears that are Prevalent across Different Age Groups

8- to 10-year-olds		11- to 13-year-olds		14- to 16-year-olds	
Item Description	**Percent Endorsement**	**Item Description**	**Percent Endorsement**	**Item Description**	**Percent Endorsement**
Nuclear war	68	Nuclear war	80	Nuclear war	69
Being hit by a car or truck	72	Not being able to breathe	62	Not being able to breathe	55
Not being able to breathe	68	Being hit by a car or truck	62	Bombing attacks	
Bombing attacks		Bombing attack		—being invaded	53
—being invaded	65	—being invaded	62	Being hit by a car or truck	50
Earthquakes	62	Earthquakes	51	Fire—getting burned	48
Falling from high places	58	Fire—getting burned	51	Falling from high places	42
A burglar breaking into		A burglar breaking into		A burglar breaking into	
our house	56	our house	47	our house	39
Fire—getting burned	52	Falling from high places	46	Snakes	39
Being sent to the principal	47	Snakes	40	Spiders	36
Getting lost in a strange		Death or dead people	39	Earthquakes	35
place	46				

Source: Adapted from N.J. King, K. Ollier, R.Iacuone, S. Schuster, K. Bays, E. Gullone, & T.H. Ollendick (1989). Fears of children and adolescents: A cross-sectional Australian study using the Revised-Fear Survey Schedule for Children. *Journal of Child Psychology and Psychiatry, 30, 775–784.*

arated from attachment figures, and it is also normal for children to experience milder forms of separation anxiety at older ages.

Excessive separation anxiety can become a serious problem, however. In fact, the DSM-IV lists **separation anxiety disorder** as a psychological problem characterized by symptoms such as persistent and excessive worry for the safety of an attachment figure, fears of getting lost or being kidnapped, nightmares with separation themes, and refusal to be alone. In order to meet the criteria for separation anxiety disorder, at least three such symptoms must persist for at least 4 weeks.

It is normal for children to experience even very strong separation fears; thus the DSM-IV indicates that the anxiety also must interfere with a child's functioning. Separation anxiety clearly is the problem in such cases, particularly when it interferes with school attendance. **School refusal**, also known as *school phobia*, is characterized by an extreme reluctance to go to school, and is accompanied by various symptoms of anxiety, such as stomachaches and headaches.

▲ Separation anxiety is a normal fear that typically develops just before a baby's first birthday. Normal toddlers and preschoolers continue to show a degree of distress even during routine separations from their attachment figures.

Some children are literally phobic about aspects of attending school, but in many cases, school refusal can be traced to separation anxiety disorder (Last & Strauss, 1990). Whatever its origins, school refusal is a serious problem that has been reported to account for more than two-thirds of referrals to an anxiety disorders clinic for children (Last & Strauss, 1990). We illustrate separation anxiety disorder complicated by school refusal in the following case study.

CASE STUDY

Separation Anxiety Disorder and School Refusal

According to her mother, 5-year-old Sally K. had always been a shy child. From the time she was a toddler, Sally was much more interested in playing with her mother than in playing with her peers, at least in comparison with her two older brothers. She also was much more fearful than her brothers. Mrs. K. said that Sally had always been hesitant around strangers, and even now, she ran to her mother or hid behind the couch when unfamiliar adults came to the house. Sally played with one girl in her neighborhood, but her mother said that Sally shied away from new children as well as from adults.

In most respects, Mrs. K. felt there was no real problem with Sally's behavior. Sally just had a shy personality, and Mrs. K. liked having her around the house. Sally usually followed her mother from room to room as she did her housework, and Mrs. K. frequently would stop to play with Sally. In fact, Mrs. K. engaged in few activities apart from Sally, because Sally became so upset when her mother left her.

Mrs. K. seemed unconcerned about Sally's separation anxiety. She interpreted Sally's behavior as a sign that she loved her mother and not that Sally was overly dependent on her. She described Sally as her "baby girl" and said she was in no hurry for Sally to grow up. Mrs. K. wanted to "spoil" Sally.

Mrs. K. did note that kindergarten had become a problem. Sally was refusing to go to school. In fact, kindergarten had been a disaster from the beginning. Sally cried and protested when her mother dropped her off on the first day, and when Mrs. K. stopped by to check on her an hour later, Sally got so upset all over again that her mother decided to take her home. Episodes like this continued for about a month, and for the last 2 weeks, Sally had not attended school at all because of her headaches and stomachaches.

Mrs. K. said that she had wanted to hold Sally out of school for a year because her August birthday made her a bit young for her class. Her husband insisted that Sally was ready for kindergarten, and Mrs. K. had gone along with him. Mrs. K. still felt that Sally would be better off delaying kindergarten until next year. She was coming for an appointment with a clinical psychologist on the recommendation of the school principal and at the insistence of her husband. She told the psychologist that only one appointment would be needed if he wrote a letter agreeing with her position. ■

Sally's separation anxiety and school refusal were readily observed by the adults around her. Sally clearly was troubled and fearful. Still, you may wonder how Sally *really* felt. How much of the separation anxiety was Sally's problem and how much of it was her mother's problem? Mrs. K. certainly seemed to want Sally near her, and as a result, perhaps she made Sally more, not less, anxious about separation. As with other psychological disorders of childhood, many psychologists suggest that separation anxiety disorder is best understood in the context of children's family relationships (Berg, 1993).

TROUBLED PEER RELATIONSHIPS

Children with internalizing or externalizing problems often have troubled peer relationships. In fact, research demonstrates that troubled peer relationships predict future, as well as current, psychological problems among children (Parker & Asher, 1987; Rutter, 1989). Simply put, children who are aggressive and disobedient or shy and withdrawn often are not well liked by their peers. However, different patterns of peer relationship difficulties have been found among children with internalizing and externalizing problems.

Many recent research findings on psychological problems and peer relationships have used the **peer sociometric method** to assess children's relationships. Peer sociometrics evaluate children's relationships by obtaining information on who is "liked most" and who is "liked least" from a large group of children who know each other (for example, children in a classroom). Statistical procedures are then used to group children into one of five categories based on the ratings of their peers. *Popular* children receive many "liked most" and few "liked least" ratings. *Average* children also receive few "liked least" ratings, but they receive fewer "liked most" ratings than popular children. *Neglected* children receive few of either type of rating, and *rejected* children are the opposite of popular children: They receive many "liked least" ratings and few "liked most" nominations. Finally, *controversial* children receive many positive and many negative ratings from their peers (Coie & Kupersmidt, 1983; Newcomb, Bukowski, & Pattee, 1993).

The neglected and rejected classifications are especially relevant to the present discussion. Rejected children are considerably more likely to have externalizing problems in comparison to the other four peer status groups (Patterson, Kupersmidt, & Griesler, 1990). Still, it is important to note that children with externalizing problems are not completely isolated. They usually have some close friends, but unfortunately their friends are likely to be other children with behavior problems (Olweus, 1984). The rejected status is the category most strongly related to psychological difficulties, but neglected children also have more troubles than popular, average, and controversial children. Not surprisingly, neglected children are likely to have internalizing symptoms such as loneliness (Asher & Wheeler, 1985). In contrast to peer rejection, an optimistic research finding about the neglected sociometric status is that it is not particularly stable over time and across situations (Coie & Kupersmidt, 1983; Newcomb, Bukowski, & Pattee, 1993). Apparently, children who are left out of one social group often succeed in finding friends in new social circumstances.

ADULT REPORTS OF ABNORMAL CHILD BEHAVIOR

In concluding our discussion of typical symptoms and associated features, we must again consider the important fact that adults, not children, identify children's psychological problems. This means that, in research and in practice, child clinical psychologists must continually attempt to discern how much of a problem reported by an adult is real and how much exists only in the eye of the beholder.

Consider a study conducted by Lobitz and Johnson (1975). These researchers studied 28 families who had a child between the ages of 4 and 8 who was being treated for externalizing problems. They compared the treated families with a group of families with a young child who had never received (and apparently did not need) psychological treatment. The investigators found that they could correctly assign 90 percent of the children to either the treatment or normal group by using the parents' reports of child behavior problems. However, the researchers were much less accurate in assigning children to the correct group when the assignment was based on actual observations of the children's behavior.

These findings suggest that many of the children's externalizing symptoms were problems only in the eyes of the parents. We must be cautious in reaching this conclusion, however. The researchers had only limited opportunities to observe the children's misbehavior, and the observations surely were affected by **reactivity**—changes in behavior that occur simply as a result of being observed. Think about it: The clinic-referred children surely were on their best behavior when they were being observed, particularly because their parents had just brought them to the doctor for being bad! Nevertheless, the findings suggest that the referral decision was influenced by characteristics of the parents. It may be that parents are more likely to bring a child to a mental health professional when they themselves are depressed, unhappy in their marriage, parenting alone, or uninformed about normal child development. Child clinical psychologists must constantly consider such possibilities.

Classification of Psychological Disorders of Childhood

Until recent years, diagnosticians assumed that children suffered from the same psychological disorders as adults—a tendency that one author termed "adultomorphism" (Garber, 1984). Controversies still rage about the appropriate classification of the psychological disorders of childhood, but researchers at least agree now that children's psychological problems are *not* simply miniature versions of adult disorders. Many psychological disorders are unique to childhood, as are their causes and treatments.

Some continuity has been found between the psychological disorders of childhood and those of adult life. Antisocial behavior often continues into adult life, as we have already discussed. Evidence also indicates that depressed children are at risk for experiencing depression during adult life (Harrington et al., 1990).

The continuity of psychological difficulties between childhood and adult life is not necessarily **isomorphic**, or identical in form. Rather, transformations can occur in the way an underlying characteristic is expressed across the course of development. For example, shy children do not simply become shy adults. Instead, continuity has been demonstrated by evidence that shy (versus more outgoing) boys delay entry into marriage, parenthood, and careers, and they attain less occupational success. Shy girls, in turn, enter into more traditional homemaker roles than do their more assertive peers (Caspi, Elder, & Bem, 1988).

These data illustrate how psychological distress can differ in its expression or form in childhood and in adulthood. Classification systems therefore must be sensitive to the unique psychological problems of infancy, childhood, and adolescence. We begin our consideration of efforts to develop classifications of childhood disorders with a brief historical survey.

BRIEF HISTORICAL PERSPECTIVE

The beginnings of child clinical psychology as a discipline can be traced to 1896, when psychologist Lightner Witmer (1867–1956) established the first psychological clinic for children in the United States at the University of Pennsylvania. Witmer's efforts stemmed in part from the recent emergence of psychology as an academic discipline, but they also were part of a major change in societal attitudes toward children. Prior to the nineteenth century, life was harsh for children, who were expected to act and work (beginning around the age of 7) like little adults (Aries, 1962). Beginning in the latter half of the nineteenth century, however, child labor laws were passed, schooling was made mandatory, and special juvenile courts were created. In short, U.S. society began to recognize childhood as a stage of development requiring special social protection and nurturance.

Childhood continued to be overlooked in the formal classifications of mental disorders that were developed in the middle of the twentieth century. The DSM-I (1952) contained only two separate diagnoses for children, and DSM-II (1968) listed only seven childhood disorders. Prompted by earlier efforts made by the Group for Advancement of Psychiatry (GAP, 1966) and the World Health Organization (Rutter, Shaffer, & Shepherd, 1975), DSM-III recognized a much wider range of childhood disorders (1980). The DSM-III contained a proliferation of diagnostic categories for children, 40 in all. Although laudable, the new effort was overly ambitious. Many of the new diagnoses were severely criticized and were subsequently dropped. Despite numerous changes since 1980, the DSM-IV may still have too long a list of childhood disorders.

CONTEMPORARY CLASSIFICATIONS: SOME STRENGTHS AND WEAKNESSES IN DSM-IV

Table 15–2 summarizes the childhood disorders contained in DSM-IV (1994). You should note two broad features of this list. First, many of the numerous diagnoses listed in the table surely are new to you. Second, the broad category of "Attention-Deficit and Disruptive Behavior Disorders" in DSM-IV can be equated with externalizing disorders, but there is no category equivalent to internalizing disorders. Each of these points about the DSM-IV classification deserves careful consideration.

Rare Childhood Disorders One reason many of the DSM-IV diagnoses may be unfamiliar to you is that some of them are rare and unusual problems; we can consider most of these only briefly in this text. *Pica* is the persistent eating of nonnutritive substances such as paint or dirt. Many infants and toddlers put nonnutritive substances in their mouths, but the feeding disorder pica is rarely diagnosed, except among mentally retarded children. *Rumination disorder*, the repeated regurgitation and rechewing of food, is another infrequent feeding disorder. Rumination disorder is found primarily among infants, and it can be a serious problem that causes very low weight gain and can even lead to death.

Tourette's disorder is a rare problem (4 to 5 cases per 10,000 people) that is characterized by repeated motor and verbal tics. The tics can be voluntarily suppressed only for brief periods of time, and they can interfere substantially with life functioning. Other tic disorder classifications reflect the facts that children may develop verbal or motor tics in isolation, and that children's tics often last for only a brief period of time (see Table 15–2).

Selective mutism involves the consistent failure to speak in certain social situations (for example, in school), while speech is unrestricted in other situations (for example, at home). Selective mutism is found among less than 1 percent of the children treated for mental health disorders. *Reactive attachment disorder* is another rare problem; it is characterized by severely disturbed and developmentally inappropriate social relationships. Children may resist comfort and cuddling, for example, or may "freeze" and watch others from a safe distance. Reactive attachment disorder is caused by parenting that is so grossly neglectful that the infant or preschooler fails to develop a selective attachment relationship. (In Chapter 17 we discuss the topics of child abuse and neglect—social problems that unfortunately are not rare.) *Stereotypic movement disorder* is self-stimulation or self-injurious behavior that is sufficiently problematic to become the focus of treatment, as may be the case in mental retardation or pervasive developmental disorder (see Chapter 14).

Finally, *encopresis* and *enuresis* refer respectively to inappropriately controlled defecation and urination. Both problems are relatively common, especially bedwetting, which is found among approximately 5 percent of 5-year-olds, 2 to 3 percent of 10-year-olds, and 1 percent of 18-year-olds. Encopresis and enuresis typically are causes of, not reactions to, psychological distress. That is, symptoms like shyness or social anxiety, which sometimes accompany enuresis or encopresis, generally disappear once children learn to control their bowels or bladders. Encopresis and especially enuresis can be effectively treated with various biofeedback devices. The best-known such treatment is the *bell and pad*, a device that awakens children by setting off an alarm as they begin to wet the bed during the night. Research indicates that the bell and pad is about 75 percent effective in treating bedwetting among young school-aged children (Houts, 1991).

TABLE 15–2

DSM-IV Disorders Usually First Diagnosed in Infancy, Childood, or Adolescence[a]

Attention-Deficit and Disruptive Behavior Disorders
Attention-deficit/hyperactivity disorder
  Combined type
  Predominantly inattentive type
  Predominantly hyperactive-impulsive type
Conduct disorder
Oppositional defiant disorder

Learning Disorders
Reading disorder
Mathematics disorder
Disorder of written expression

Motor Skills Disorder
Developmental coordination disorder

Communication Disorders
Expressive language disorder
Mixed receptive-expressive language disorder
Phonological disorder
Stuttering

Feeding and Eating Disorders of Infancy or Early Childhood
Pica
Rumination disorder
Feeding disorder of infancy or early childhood

Tic Disorders
Tourette's disorder
Chronic motor or vocal tic disorder
Transient tic disorder

Elimination Disorders
Encopresis
  With constipation and overflow incontinence
  Without constipation and overflow incontinence
Enuresis

Other Disorders of Infancy, Childhood, and Adolescence
Separation anxiety disorder
Selective mutism
Reactive attachment disorder of infancy or early childhood
Stereotypic movement disorder

[a] Note: This listing does not include mental retardation or pervasive developmental disorders, which we discussed in Chapter 14. It also does not include "Not Otherwise Specified" (NOS) subtypes of the diagnoses. NOS subtypes exist for many of the disorders listed here, and they are used when a child meets many but not all of the diagnostic criteria for the specific disorder.

Overinclusive Listing of Disorders Another reason some of the disorders listed in Table 15–2 may be unfamiliar is the questionable nature of their status as "mental disorders." DSM-I and DSM-II clearly were underinclusive, as evidenced by their short list of childhood disorders. But has the DSM now gone too far the other way? Is bedwetting a mental disorder? A number of commentators believe that, beginning with DSM-III, the manual became overinclusive in its listing of childhood disorders. That is, in attempting to remedy its earlier neglect of children's psychological difficulties, the manual included too many "disorders" that are not in fact mental disorders (Garmezy, 1978).[†]

"Developmental coordination disorder" is perhaps the most obvious example of overinclusion in DSM-IV. The manual defines this problem as follows: "Performance in daily activities that require motor coordination is substantial-ly below that expected given the person's chronological age and measured intelligence" (p. 54). In poking fun at such diagnostic overzealousness, two pediatricians proposed a new diagnostic category they called "sports deficit disorder." The major diagnostic criterion for this "disorder" is always being the last one chosen for a sports team (Burke & McGee, 1990).

The "learning disorders" and "communication disorders" are more controversial examples of possible overinclusion in DSM-IV. Educators call these childhood problems *learning disabilities* (see Further Thoughts) and *speech and hearing problems*, respectively. Learning disabilities and speech and hearing problems both are common and serious difficulties experienced by children, but we question their status as mental disorders. We view both problems as involving educational more than mental health concerns.

FURTHER THOUGHTS

Learning Disabilities

The classification **learning disabilities** refers to a heterogeneous group of problems that are characterized by a difference between academic aptitude and academic performance. There are numerous ways of defining learning disabilities more specifically, but each method presents difficulties (Wicks-Nelson & Israel, 1991). The most common definition compares scores on intelligence tests, which measure academic aptitude, with scores on *academic achievement tests*—measures of performance in some academic subject area. Typically, a learning disability is defined as a difference of one or two standard deviations between aptitude and achievement. Thus, according to this definition, a child would be considered to have a learning disability if he or she scored a standard deviation above the mean on an intelligence test (an IQ of 115) but a standard deviation below the mean in reading (scoring well below the average for his or her grade level).

The DSM-IV includes learning disabilities (called learning disorders in the manual) in its list of mental disorders. The DSM-IV also includes subcategories of learning disorders in reading, arithmetic, and written expression. Learning disabilities typically are diagnosed by school professionals, however, and they almost always are treated in academic settings. Thus, mental health professionals typically work with children with learning disabilities only when the problems co-occur with other psychological disorders. In fact, there is a high degree of co-morbidity between learning disabilities and both attention-deficit/hyperactivity disorder and oppositional defiant disorder (Barkley, 1990).

The origins of learning disabilities have been traced to a number of problems, including perceptual distortions, attentional problems, language difficulties, and poor cognitive strategies. Typically, the etiology of the problems is attributed to some biological cause, and considerable research has been

---

[†] In response to criticisms of overinclusion, several questionable new disorders were dropped from DSM-III in the 1987 revision (DSM-III-R), and more disorders were dropped in revising DSM-III-R into DSM-IV.

conducted on brain functions in learning disabilities. This research, however, has not identified any psychological deficit or biological cause that is common to all learning disabilities (Wicks-Nelson & Israel, 1991).

Tremendous efforts have gone into attempts to treat learning disabilities. Interventions in schools were given tremendous impetus in 1975 when Congress passed the Education for All Handicapped Children Act. This law mandated that local school systems must provide special resources for educating handicapped children, including children with learning disabilities. The numerous interventions that have been attempted include intensive tutoring, individually or in small groups; behavior therapy programs in which academic success is systematically rewarded; psychostimulant medication; counseling for related problems (for example, low self-esteem); and various special efforts such as training in visual-motor skills. Unfortunately, no treatment has demonstrated consistent success (Wicks-Nelson & Israel, 1991).

We can conclude that a substantial number of children in the United States—perhaps 5 percent of all schoolchildren—do not achieve at a level consistent with their abilities. Controversy and uncertainty remain, however, about the definition, cause, and treatment of learning disabilities. ∎

Internalizing Disorders and Empirically-Derived Classification Systems In addition to the large number of childhood disorders listed, you also should note the absence of a diagnostic category for internalizing disorders in DSM-IV. This is a change from DSM-III-R, which listed three separate anxiety disorders of childhood. The absence of internalizing disorders is notable, because it is inconsistent with empirical evidence derived from the psychometric approach to classifying childhood disorders.

The **psychometric approach** to classification forms diagnostic categories based on statistical analysis of behavior problem checklists completed by parents and teachers. The most significant contribution of the psychometric approach is its identification of two broad categories of child behavior problems—the externalizing and internalizing dimensions introduced at the beginning of the chapter. These dimensions have been empirically derived with great consistency, and their reliability and validity have been well established (Achenbach, 1985; Achenbach et al., 1991; Cantwell, 1988). Thus, the absence of an internalizing category in DSM-IV is surprising, given the manual's goal of basing classification on empirical findings. We also are concerned because, as we discussed previously, children often experience and express anxiety and depression in very different ways than adults do. Thus, in this chapter we continue to consider anxiety and mood disorders as they uniquely apply to children.

SUBCLASSIFICATION OF EXTERNALIZING DISORDERS

How externalizing problems should be subdivided is an important, controversial, and frequently studied topic. For this reason, we review the subclassification of externalizing disorders in some detail.

Brief Historical Perspective Throughout most of history, children with externalizing disorders were categorized as having a weak moral character, not an emotional disorder. They were "bad," not "sick."

According to Ross and Ross (1982), the modern subclassification of externalizing disorders can be traced to British physician George Still, who wrote about the condition that we know today as *attention-deficit/hyperactivity disorder*. Still (1902) noted that some disruptive children had difficulties that seemed to stem from temperament or other biological causes. He particularly suspected brain damage. Still hypothesized that these children suffered from a physical disorder, not a moral failing; and he suggested that they needed medical care.

Still's hypothesis began a long line of inquiry. Subsequent researchers noted that overactivity was one of several common consequences of demonstrable brain damage in children, for example, following head trauma or encephalitis. Animal studies also documented that overactivity could be caused by brain damage such as that caused by oxygen deprivation during birth. These observations led to the hypothesis that hyperactivity in children was caused by **minimal brain damage** (MBD)—damage to the brain too slight to be detected except in a child's behavior (Ehrenfest, 1926).

The MBD hypothesis is reasonable as long as it is treated as a hypothesis. To support the hypothesis, experts need to document specific brain damage or dysfunctions among overly active children. Unfortunately, some professionals erroneously concluded that MBD could be inferred based solely on a child's hyperactive behavior (Ross & Ross, 1982). This tautology, or error of circular reasoning, should be apparent: What causes hyperactivity? Brain damage. How do you know of the brain damage? The child is hyperactive. Despite such mistaken logic, the MBD explanation of hyperactive behavior became accepted "fact" in the 1950s and 1960s (Ross & Ross, 1982), and even today, some professionals use MBD as a synonym for attention-deficit/hyperactivity disorder.

The MBD conclusion also was perpetuated by the supposed "paradoxical effect" of psychostimulants on hyperactive children. **Psychostimulants** are medications that heighten energy and alertness when taken in small dosages, and they lead to restless, even frenetic, behavior in larger dosages. (The effects are accurately conveyed by the street name for the drugs, "speed.") The U.S. psychiatrist Charles Bradley (1937) was one of the first to observe that stimulants seemingly had a paradoxical effect on overactive children. Psychostimulants seemed to speed up normal adults, but they slowed down hyperactive children—an outcome that might be explained by MBD (Ross & Ross, 1982).

The idea that psychostimulants have paradoxical effects on hyperactive children was not definitely proven wrong until the 1970s, in part because no one had studied the effects of psychostimulants on normal children. Although it was accepted practice to prescribe psychostimulants to millions of "abnormal" hyperactive children across the United States, it was deemed unethical to give experimental dosages to normal children. A study by a group of researchers at the National Institutes of Mental Health finally laid the "paradoxical effect" idea to rest (Rapoport et al., 1978). These investigators addressed the ethical problem by obtaining permission from colleagues in the medical

and mental health community to study the effects of psychostimulants on their exceptionally competent children. The researchers found that the psychostimulants affected the normal children in the same way that they affected overactive children. The medication improved the normal children's attention and decreased their motor activity (Rapoport et al., 1978).

Thus, there is no firm evidence that MBD is a specific cause of attention-deficit/hyperactivity disorder, and there is no paradoxical effect. Nevertheless, the assumption remains that hyperactivity is a distinct externalizing disorder with biological origins that is treated most appropriately with medication. It is also commonly assumed that a second major subclass of externalizing disorders, called oppositional defiant disorder, has an environmental origin and demands psychological intervention.

Contemporary Subclassification of Externalizing Disorders   DSM-IV lists three major subtypes of disruptive behavior disorders: oppositional defiant disorder (see Table 15–3), conduct disorder (see Table 15–4), and attention-deficit/hyperactivity disorder (see Table 15–5). At the outset, you should note two important links between oppositional defiant disorder and conduct disorder. First, the diagnoses are distinguished primarily by the seriousness of the rule violations listed in the diagnostic criteria. Second, the two disorders are developmentally related. Oppositional defiant disorder occurs primarily among school-aged children. It may develop into conduct disorder, a more serious problem found more commonly among preadolescents and teenagers (Loeber, Lahey, & Thomas, 1991).

Juvenile Delinquency   **Conduct disorder** is defined primarily by forms of behavior like stealing or assault that are illegal as well as antisocial. This is the sort of behavior that you may think of as juvenile delinquency. **Juvenile delinquency** is a legal classification, however, not a mental health term. Technically, youths are not classified as delinquents until they are found to be deliquent by a judge. Still, you can view conduct disorder as roughly comparable to what is sometimes called "hidden delinquency," or undetected lawbreaking among the young.

You also should note that some of the diagnostic criteria for conduct disorder are comparable to **status offenses**—acts that are illegal only because of the youth's status as a minor. Examples are running away from home and truancy from school. Status offenses stand in contrast to *criminal offenses*—actions such as armed robbery and forcible rape that are illegal at any age. Finally, DSM-IV includes a notation for age of onset in defining conduct disorders—a distinction between the adolescent-limited versus life-course patterns of antisocial behavior, as we discussed earlier.

Oppositional Defiant Disorder and Attention-Deficit/ Hyperactivity Disorder **Oppositional defiant disorder** involves minor transgressions such as refusing to obey adult requests, arguing, and acting angry. Such behavior is normal among adolescents, but it is a cause for concern among school-aged children. A basic controversy has been whether oppositional defiant disorder is distinct from attention-deficit/hyperactivity disorder.

Are these two conditions different psychological problems? The current consensus is that the two disorders are best conceived as separate but overlapping problems (Barkley, 1990; Hinshaw, 1987). Oppositional defiant disorder and attention-deficit/hyperactivity disorder can be differentiated reliably, but they are highly co-morbid conditions. Many children with one disorder also have the other problem. Closer consideration of the symptoms of attention-deficit/hyperactivity disorder suggests how the two problems differ.

Symptoms and Subtypes of Attention-Deficit/ Hyperactivity Disorder **Attention-deficit/hyperactivity disorder** is characterized by three distinction symptoms: (1) hyperactivity, (2) inattention, and (3) impulsivity. Hyperactivity is the aspect of the disorder that is most obvious to adults. Children's hyperactivity is found across situations, even during sleep, but it is much more notable in structured settings than in unstructured ones (Barkley, 1988, 1990). For example, adults notice hyperactive behavior much more readily in the classroom than on the playground. In fact, this is one reason why hyperactivity typically is diagnosed for the first time during the early school years. Parents may have thought that their preschooler was very active and energetic, but they are often shocked to hear the extent of a first- or second-grade teacher's com-

---

TABLE 15-3

DSM-IV Diagnostic Criteria for Oppositional Defiant Disorder

A. A pattern of negativistic, hostile, and defiant behavior lasting at least 6 months, during which four (or more) of the following are present:
1. Often loses temper.
2. Often argues with adults.
3. Often actively defies or refuses to comply with adults' requests or rules.
4. Often deliberately annoys people.
5. Often blames others for his or her mistakes or misbehavior.
6. Is often touchy or easily annoyed by others.
7. Is often angry and resentful.
8. Is often spiteful and vindictive.

B. The disturbance in behavior causes clinically significant impairment in social, academic, or occupational functioning.

TABLE 15-4

DSM-IV Diagnostic Criteria for Conduct Disorder

A. A repetitive and persistent pattern of behavior in which the basic rights of others or major age-appropriate societal norms or rules are violated, as manifested by the presence of three (or more) of the following criteria in the past 12 months, with at least one criterion present in the past 6 months:

Aggression to people and animals
1. Often bullies, threatens, or intimidates others.
2. Often initiates physical fights.
3. Has used a weapon that can cause serious physical harm to others.
4. Has been physically cruel to people.
5. Has been physically cruel to animals.
6. Has stolen while confronting a victim.
7. Has forced someone into sexual activity.

Destruction of property
8. Has deliberately engaged in fire setting with the intention of causing serious damage.
9. Has deliberately destroyed others' property.

Deceitfulness or theft
10. Has broken into someone else's house, building, or car.
11. Often lies to obtain goods or favors to avoid obligations.
12. Has stolen items of nontrivial value without confronting a victim.

Serious violations of rules
13. Often stays out at night despite parental prohibitions, beginning before age 13 years.
14. Has run away from home overnight at least twice while living in parental or parental surrogate home.
15. Is often truant from school, beginning before age 13 years.

B. The disturbance in behavior causes clinically significant impairment in social, academic, or occupational functioning.

Specify type based on age at onset:

Childhood-Onset Type: Onset of at least one criterion characteristic of Conduct Disorder prior to age 10 years.

Adolescent-Onset Type: Absence of any criteria characteristic of Conduct Disorder prior to age 10 years.

DSM-IV Diagnostic Criteria for Attention-Deficit/Hyperactivity Disorder

A. Either (I) or (II):

  (I) Inattention: Six (or more) of the following symptoms of inattention have persisted for at least 6 months to a degree that is maladaptive and inconsistent with developmental level:

    1. Often fails to give close attention to details or makes careless mistakes in schoolwork, work, or other activities.

    2. Often has difficulty sustaining attention in tasks or play activities.

    3. Often does not seem to listen when spoken to directly.

    4. Often does not follow through on instructions and fails to finish schoolwork, chores, or duties in the workplace.

    5. Often has difficulty organizing tasks and activities.

    6. Often avoids, dislikes, or is reluctant to engage in tasks that require sustained mental effort.

    7. Often loses things necessary for tasks or activities.

    8. Is often easily distracted by extraneous stimuli.

    9. Is often forgetful of daily activities.

  (II) Hyperactivity and Impulsivity: Six (or more) of the following symptoms of hyperactivity-impulsivity have persisted for at least 6 months to a degree that is maladaptive and inconsistent with developmental level:

    Hyperactivity

    1. Often fidgets with hands or feet or squirms in seat.

    2. Often leaves seat in classsroom or in other situations in which remaining seated is expected.

    3. Often runs about or climbs excessively in situations in which it is inappropriate.

    4. Often has difficulty playing or engaging in leisure activities quietly.

    5. Is often "on the go" or often acts as if "driven by a motor."

    6. Often talks excessively.

    Impulsivity

    7. Often blurts out answers before questions have been completed.

    8. Often has difficulty awaiting turn.

    9. Often interrupts or intrudes on others.

B. Some hyperactive-impulsive or inattentive symptoms that caused impairment were present before age 7 years.

C. Some impairment from the symptoms is present in two or more settings.

D. There must be clear evidence of clinically significant impairment in social, academic, or occupational functioning.

  ***Code* based on type:**

  Combined Type: Criteria for I and II are met for past 6 months.

  Predominantly Inattentive Type: Criteria for I are met but Criteria for II are not met for past 6 months.

  Predominantly Hyperactive-Impulsive Type: Criteria for II are met but Criteria for I are not met for past 6 months.

plaints.[†] As illustrated by the case of Jeremy, hyperactivity really becomes a problem in the classroom, and classroom problems are often intensified by the learning difficulties that commonly accompany the disorder (Barkley, 1990).

Situational influences can complicate the diagnosis of attention-deficit/hyperactivity disorder, because children who are extremely active in the classroom may be relatively controlled in the pediatrician's or the psychologist's office. In one study, only 20 percent of children with attention-deficit/hyperactivity disorder were overly active during an examination in the pediatrician's office (Sleator & Ullmann, 1981). Consequently, reports from teachers are critical in identifying the disorder.

Inattention is the second basic symptom of attention-deficit/hyperactivity disorder. A particular attentional problem is "staying on task," or what has been termed *sustained attention* (Douglas & Peters, 1979). Numerous studies have documented difficulties in sustained attention using the *continuous performance test*, a laboratory task that requires children to monitor and respond to numbers or letters presented on a computer screen (see Chapter 12). The performance of hyperactive children quickly deteriorates on this task—an indication of their difficulties in sustaining attention (Douglas, 1983).

Attentional problems became the major focus of the disorder in the 1970s and early 1980s. As an indication of this focus, attention-deficit/hyperactivity disorder was termed "attention-deficit disorder" in DSM-III—one more label in a series of terms for a disorder that has also been called MBD, hyperactivity, and hyperkinetic reaction of childhood (Barkley, 1990). We are less concerned about whether "attention deficit" or "hyperactivity" gets top billing in naming the disorder than we are about two facts. First, some children have problems primarily with only one of the two symptoms, as is evident in the subtypes listed in DSM-IV (see Table 15–5). Second, contrary to what has been asserted by some professionals, hyperactivity is not merely a consequence of inattention (Barkley, 1990).

Impulsivity, the third major characteristic of attention-deficit/hyperactivity disorder, has been studied much less frequently than have overactivity and inattention. Still, impulsivity is frequently noted by teachers and parents, who describe impulsive children as "acting before they think." At least one leading researcher has asserted that such impulsive tendencies may

---

[†] Hyperactivity in the classroom typically involves fidgeting and squirming, not large motor movements.

prove to be the hallmark symptom of attention-deficit/hyperactivity disorder (Barkley, 1990).

CONTEXTUAL CLASSIFICATIONS FOR ABNORMAL CHILD BEHAVIOR?

As a final note on classification, we remind you that children's behavior is intimately linked with family, school, and peer contexts. Because of this, some commentators have suggested that diagnosing individual children is misleading and misguided (Kazdin, 1989). Instead, children's psychological problems could be classified within the context of key interpersonal relationships. A classification system that diagnosed troubled relationships would seem to be potentially more valid than diagnoses for individual children. Parents, teachers, and peers often are part of a child's "individual" problem, as you saw in the cases of Jeremy and Sally.

We believe that classification in context is an important goal for future research and practice, and we discuss interpersonal classification more fully in Chapter 16. Given current research and theory, we follow the traditional approach to classification in this chapter. Still, we urge you to think about children's behavior problems in their social context.

Epidemiology of Psychological Disorders of Childhood

A panel of experts assembled by the National Academy of Sciences (1989) concluded that at least 12 percent of the 63 million children living in the United States suffer from a mental disorder. The panel found that a minimum of $1.5 billion was spent annually for the direct mental health treatment of children—and this figure excluded the additional costs of treating children's emotional problems in general medical settings, schools, welfare agencies, and juvenile courts (National Academy of Sciences, 1989). Clearly, children's mental health is a major national problem, but epidemiologic evidence is valuable for reasons other than documenting the extent of children's psychological difficulties. Factors correlated with higher prevalence rates identify subgroups of children at risk, and this information suggests possible causes of children's psychological disorders (see Research Methods).

RESEARCH METHODS

Samples and Sampling

Psychologists are very concerned with the samples that they study, and samples are often described in great detail in psychological research—a fact attested to by numerous examples throughout this text. However, psychologists often do not consider it necessary to obtain a **representative sample**—a sample that accurately represents some larger group of people. Instead, psychologists and other mental health researchers often obtain *convenience samples*—groups of people who are easily recruited and studied. In research in abnormal psychology, people who have sought psychological treatment often comprise the convenience sample.

The use of a convenience sample does not create problems for many of the questions that psy-

chologists wish to study. For example, there is no need to obtain a representative sample to study the effectiveness of medication for treating most psychological disorders. For other purposes, obtaining representative samples is essential. For example, researchers who have studied children in clinical settings have found that a disproportionate number of these children come from single-parent families. From this evidence, they conclude that single parenting causes the children's psychological problems. When more representative samples are studied, however, it becomes evident that the great majority of children from single-parent families do *not* have psychological problems. Therefore, single parenting alone cannot cause the children's troubles. A relationship exists between family status and children's psychological adjustment, but it is not near-ly as strong in representative samples as it appears to be in convenience samples (Emery, 1988).

Examples like this are one of the reasons why we have systematically addressed the topic of epidemiology throughout this text. When studying risk factors like family status, it often is informative to be able to *generalize*—to make accurate statements that extend beyond a specific sample to a larger population group. How do scientists select representative samples that allow them to generalize from a sample to a larger population? Theoretically, the methods for obtaining a representative sample are straightforward. First, the researcher must identify the *population* of interest, the entire group of people to whom the researcher wants to generalize—for example, children under the age of 18 living in the United States. Second, the researcher must *randomly select* research subjects from the sample and obtain a large enough sample to ensure that the results are statistically reliable. These two procedures allow researchers to make generalizations that sometimes seem remarkable, such as when the outcome of a political election is accurately predicted by polling a relatively small number of voters.

Errors can occur in either step of the process of selecting a representative sample. One of the most famous errors in sampling occurred in 1948 when newspaper headlines heralded Thomas E. Dewey's election over Harry S. Truman in the U.S. presidential election. Truman actually won the election, as you can easily discern from his smiling face in the accompanying photo. Where did the pollsters go wrong? They made a mistake in identifying the population of voters. The researchers sampled randomly and appropriately from the population of voters who owned telephones. In 1948, however, many less-affluent people did not own telephones, and the less wealthy voted overwhelmingly for Truman, a Democrat.

Political scientists have become much more sophisticated in their sampling strategies since 1948, but psychologists sometimes repeat earlier errors. Thus, as you read about psychological research, we urge you to think critically about samples and sampling methods. A fortunate trend in the study of child psychopathology is that sociologists and psychologists are beginning to collaborate in epidemiologic

research. An example is Nicholas Zill, a researcher who was trained as a psychologist but who conducts sociological studies with population samples. In a report on findings from a survey of 17,110 children—a representative sample of U.S. children 17 years of age and younger taken in 1988—the following data were obtained (Zill & Schoenborn, 1990):

1. Nearly 20 percent of young people in the United States between the ages of 3 and 17 had a learning, behavioral, or developmental disorder. About 4 percent had delays in growth or development, 6.5 percent had a learning disorder, and 13.4 percent had significant emotional or behavioral problems. (The percentages add up to more than 20 percent, because some children had more than one problem.)

2. About 2 percent of children received treatment or counseling for developmental delays, 5 percent for learning problems, and more than 10 percent for psychological problems.

3. Learning and emotional or behavior problems were associated with family income, but the relationship was a modest one. For example, 15.8 percent of the children whose parents earned under $10,000 a year had an emotional or behavior problem, com-

▲ **Pollsters incorrectly predicted a victory for Republican Thomas Dewey over Democrat Harry Truman in the 1948 presidential election. Polls were based on a random survey of people who owned telephones, an unrepresentative sample of the population. Telephone owners were wealthier and more conservative than the average voter in 1948.**

pared with 12.8 percent of children whose parents earned over $40,000.

4. Black and Latino parents reported fewer problems among their children than did white parents. This finding may be attributable to underreporting among members of these ethnic groups. Blacks and Latinos have lower average incomes than whites, and therefore more, not fewer, problems are expected among minority children. In fact, this is exactly what was found according to data taken from school records instead of parents' observations.

These findings are important in their own right, and they also illustrate the broader value of obtaining representative samples of the general population in some psychological research. Clinical and convenience samples are decidedly not representative of the general population. There often are compelling reasons for studying these unrepresentative groups, but researchers who rely on such samples must exercise great caution in generalizing to the larger population. Such inferences only can be drawn from studies of representative samples. ■

GENDER DIFFERENCES IN EXTERNALIZING AND INTERNALIZING PROBLEMS

Gender is one risk factor consistently correlated with an increased risk for psychological problems among children. The relationship between gender and psychological problems is interesting because it reverses itself across the course of development. Boys are treated more for psychological problems than girls are, but more women than men enter into therapy. Where is the turning point, and what is the explanation for this phenomenon? We can begin to answer this question by examining gender differences in externalizing and internalizing problems.

Epidemiological studies consistently find that boys have far more externalizing disorders than girls, and externalizing problems are more likely to bring children into contact with mental health professionals (National Academy of Sciences, 1989; Rutter, 1989). From 3 to 5 percent of children are estimated to have attention-deficit/hyperactivity disorder, and anywhere from 5 to 15 percent of youths may have oppositional defiant disorder and/or conduct disorder. These problems are from 2 to 10 times more common among boys than among girls.

Gender differences in externalizing are related both to biology and to socialization. Males have been found to be more aggressive than females across numerous cultures, and evidence from animal studies indicates that exposure to the male sex hormone *testosterone* increases aggression. At the same time, it is clear that boys and girls are socialized into very different gender

roles (Huston, 1983; Maccoby & Jacklin, 1974). Society accepts and encourages more aggressive behavior among boys than among girls. Thus, biological differences in externalizing behavior are accentuated by social interaction and societal expectations.

Except for the normative increase during adolescence, the prevalence of externalizing behavior declines with age. In contrast, the prevalence of internalizing problems increases with age. In particular, depression begins to emerge in preadolescence and adolescence (Achenbach & Edelbrock, 1981; Fleming & Offord, 1990; National Academy of Sciences, 1989; Rutter, 1989), and mood disorders become one of the most common psychological problems of adult life (see Chapter 5). Thus, parents, teachers, and other adults seek treatment of younger boys' antisocial behavior, but the increase in depression among teenagers, especially adolescent girls, begins to balance the relationship between gender and the prevalence of psychological problems (Lewinsohn et al., 1994). By early adult life, more females than males report psychological problems.

Suicide among Children and Adolescents
Because of their prevalence and disruptiveness, externalizing problems are the focus of much psychological attention. Adults also need to be sensitive to children's internal distress, however, as the evidence on suicide underscores in a dramatic fashion. Children and adolescents attempt suicide far less frequently than adults, but suicide still is the third leading cause of

death among teenagers—trailing only automobile accidents and natural causes (see Figure 15–2). Teenage suicide is a special concern because adolescent suicide rates have tripled since the 1960s. Suicide is extremely rare among children under the age of 10, but the rate of suicide has also increased among younger age groups (Hawton, 1986).

In comparison to adult suicide attempts, suicide attempts among adolescents are more

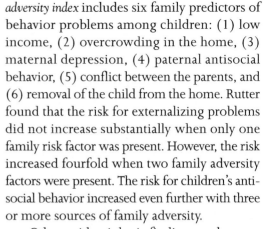

Major Causes of Adolescent (10–19 Years Old) Mortality, 1985

Motor vehicle accidents	
Natural causes*	
Suicide	
Other violence/Injury	
Homicide	
Drowning	
Fires	

0 5 10 15 20 30 25 30 35 40
Percent of total deaths

*Including neoplasms, congenital anomalies, and a number of relatively rare conditions.

Figure 15-2: Suicide is the third leading cause of death among adolescents.

Source: L. Fingerhut and J. Kleinman Trends and Current Status in Childhood Mortality, U.S., 1900–1985. *Vital and Health Statistics,* Series 3. No. 26 (DHHS Pub No. 89-1410). Hyattsville, MD: National Center for Health Statistics, 1989.

▲ **Michael Rutter, a British psychiatrist, is an international authority on the epidemiology of child psychopathology. Rutter was knighted by the Queen of England in recognition of his many contributions to the study of abnormal behavior among children.**

impulsive, are more likely to follow a family conflict, and are more often motivated by anger rather than depression (Hawton, 1986). *Cluster suicides* are also more common among teenagers than among adults (Spirito et al., 1989). When one teenager commits suicide, his or her peers are at an increased risk for suicide attempts. The risk sometimes stems from suicide pacts, but in addition the death may make suicide seem more acceptable to other teenagers. As suggested by some accounts of reactions to the 1994 suicide of rock star, Kurt Cobain, some adolescents may view a peer's suicide as understandable, even romantic.

FAMILY RISK FACTORS

The prevalence of psychological disorders among children is related to several factors in addition to gender. Family adversity is a particularly important risk factor, as has been highlighted by British psychiatrist Michael Rutter, an international authority on the epidemiology of child psychopathology. Rutter's (1978, 1989) *family*

adversity index includes six family predictors of behavior problems among children: (1) low income, (2) overcrowding in the home, (3) maternal depression, (4) paternal antisocial behavior, (5) conflict between the parents, and (6) removal of the child from the home. Rutter found that the risk for externalizing problems did not increase substantially when only one family risk factor was present. However, the risk increased fourfold when two family adversity factors were present. The risk for children's antisocial behavior increased even further with three or more sources of family adversity.

Other epidemiologic findings underscore the relationship between children's psychological problems and social disadvantage. For example, psychological disorders occur among over 20 percent of children living in urban inner-city neighborhoods (National Academy of Sciences, 1989), and are associated with divorce and single parenting (see Further Thoughts in Chapter 17). Family dysfunction and stressful life events are associated with internalizing as well as externalizing problems (Fleming & Offord, 1990). For these reasons, family adversity is a substantial concern in the etiology of children's psychological problems.

Etiological Considerations and Research

In reviewing the etiology of childhood disorders, we discuss psychological factors before biological factors; however, you should be aware of two cautions at the outset. First, bear in mind that families share genes as well as the family environment, as we have noted repeatedly throughout the text. Second, note that our discussion focuses on externalizing problems. Most research on the causes of anxiety or mood disorders among children is based on the same theories of etiology we discussed in relation to adults (see Chapters 5 and 6). For example, biological theories of mood disorders in children are virtually identical to those for adults (Puig-Antich, 1986). One exception is attachment theory—an approach that has special relevance to the development of both internalizing and externalizing disorders among children. We begin with this important topic.

PSYCHOLOGICAL FACTORS
Attachment Theory Together with psycholo-

gist Mary Ainsworth, British psychiatrist John Bowlby (1969, 1973, 1980) can be credited with developing *attachment theory*, a set of proposals about the importance to psychological development of close relationships, beginning with the relationships between infants and their caregivers (see Chapter 2). Bowlby, Ainsworth, and colleagues proposed that psychopathology is caused by troubled attachments, specifically when (1) no selective attachment is formed; (2) an insecure attachment develops; or (3) there are multiple and prolonged separations from (or the permanent loss of) an attachment figure.

As we noted earlier in the chapter, extreme parental neglect deprives infants of the opportunity to form a selective attachment. Such neglect can cause reactive attachment disorder, or what attachment researchers sometimes call "anaclitic depression"—the lack of social responsiveness found among infants who do not have a consistent attachment figure (Sroufe & Fleeson, 1986). Research on the consequences of extreme neglect for children is strongly buttressed by evidence from animal analogue research. Nonhuman primates who are raised in isolation without a parent or a substitute attachment figure have dramatically troubled social relationships (Suomi & Harlow, 1972). Thus, it has been clearly established that psychological problems can be caused by the failure to form an attachment relationship.

Variations in the quality of early attachments are also associated with children's emotional difficulties. Attachment quality can be roughly divided into secure (healthy) and anxious attachments. An infant with an **anxious attachment** has formed a selective attachment, but the attachment figure responds inadequately or inconsistently to the child's needs. As a result, the infant experiences anxiety about exploration and ambivalence about the attachment figure (Ainsworth et al., 1978). Children with anxious (versus secure) attachments have lower self-esteem, and they are less competent and more dependent on others (Cassidy, 1988; Sroufe & Fleeson, 1986). Still, it has not been established whether anxious attachment is linked with anxiety or mood disorders among children. Moreover, the correlation between anxious attachment and maladjustment may be caused by third variables. For example, a difficult temperament may both strain attachment relationships and increase the risk for psychological disorders among children.

Separation or loss is a third disruption in attachment—one that clearly causes distress among children, at least in the short run. Children move through a four-stage process akin to grief when they are separated from or lose an attachment figure. The process includes (1) numbed responsiveness, (2) yearning and protest, (3) disorganization and despair, and ultimately (4) reorganization and *detachment* or loss of interest in the former attachment figure (Bowlby, 1979). There is considerable controversy about the consequences of detachment. Bowlby (1972) asserted that detachment forms a predisposition for subsequent depression. He argued that detachment creates insecurity that causes depression when the person's needs go unfullfilled in subsequent relationships. Critics have suggested, however, that what Bowlby called detachment really is an indication of children's adjustment to the new circumstances (Rutter, 1981). This interpretation highlights children's **resilience** or ability to "bounce back" from adversity. It is consistent with research that has failed to find a consistent relationship between childhood loss and depression during adult life (Crook & Eliot, 1980; Tennant, Bebbington, & Hurry, 1980).

Inadequate Parenting and Parenting Styles

Theorists assert that disruptions in attachment cause externalizing as well as internalizing problems. Indeed, research in developmental psychology indicates that parental warmth and emotional responsiveness does facilitate children's socialization. But love alone is not enough. Parents are most effective when they are *authoritative*—that is, both loving and firm in disciplining their children.

In fact, parenting can be classified into four styles by combining the two dimensions of warmth and control (see Figure 15-3). In contrast to authoritative parents, *authoritarian* parents lack warmth, and while their discipline is strict, it is often harsh and undemocratic. Children of authoritarian parents generally are compliant, but they also may be anxious. *Indulgent* parents are the opposite of authoritarian parents; indulgent parents are affectionate but lax in their discipline. The children of indulgent parents tend to be impulsive and noncompliant, but they are not extremely antisocial. Finally, *neglectful* parents are unconcerned either with their children's emotional needs or with

▲ **British psychiatrist John Bowlby (1907–1990) can be credited with developing attachment theory, a set of proposals about the importance of infant-caregiver and other close relationships to children's psychological development.**

their needs for discipline. Children with serious conduct problems often have neglectful parents (Baumrind, 1971; Maccoby & Martin, 1983; see Figure 15–3).

A Classification of Parenting Styles

	Accepting, Responsive, Child-centered	Rejecting, Unresponsive, Parent-centered
Demanding, controlling	Authoritative	Authoritarian
Undemanding, low in control attempts	Indulgent	Neglectful

Figure 15-3: Four styles of parenting, based on dimensions of parental warmth and discipline efforts

Source: E.E. Maccoby & J.A. Martin (1983). Socialization in the context of the family: Parent-child interaction. In E.M. Hetherington (Ed.), *Socialization, personality, and social development* (Vol. 4), *Handbook of child psychology* (pp. 1-101). New York: Wiley.

Coercion More specific problems in parenting have also been studied in relationship to children's externalizing problems. Psychologist Gerald Patterson's (1982) concept of coercion is one of the most important examples of this line of research on social learning. **Coercion** occurs when unwitting parents positively reinforce children's misbehavior by giving in to their demands. The children, in turn, negatively reinforce their parents by ending their obnoxious behavior as soon as their parents capitulate. Thus, coercion describes a system of interaction in which parents and children reciprocally influence each other's behavior. The concept is illustrated in the following brief case study.

BRIEF CASE STUDY

Ms. B. finally admitted that she had lost all control of her 4-year-old son, Billy. Ms. B. was a single parent who was exhausted by her routine of working from 8 to 5:30 every day and managing Billy and the household in the evenings and on weekends. She had no parenting or financial support from Billy's father or anyone else, and Ms. B. was worn down. When it came time to discipline Billy, she usually gave in—either because this was the easiest thing to do, or because she felt too guilty to say no.

Ms. B. described many difficult interactions with Billy. One example stood out in the mind of the psychologist she consulted. Ms. B. would often stop at the grocery store with Billy after work, and he inevitably gave her trouble while they were shopping. Dealing with the candy aisle was a recent problem. Billy had asked for some candy when they first approached the aisle. Ms. B. told him no, but in an increasingly loud voice Billy protested, "I WANT CANDY!" Ms. B. attempted to stick to her guns, but soon she was embarrassed by the disapproving looks on the faces of other mothers. Feeling both resentful and resigned, she grabbed a bag of M&Ms and gave it to Billy. This gave her a few minutes of peace and quiet while she completed her shopping. ■

Clearly, Ms. B. rewarded Billy for his misbehavior in this interaction. As suggested by the coercion construct, Billy also negatively reinforced his mother by quieting down when she gave in to his demands. Because both parties were reinforced, the coercive interaction is predicted to continue over time (Patterson, 1982).

The coercion concept is appealing, in part, because it has direct, practical implications. Parents need to break the pattern of interaction by ignoring the misbehavior (extinction), punishing it, or rewarding more positive actions (Forehand & McMahon, 1981). We discuss such treatments of noncompliant behavior later in the chapter. In Billy's case, the psychologist recommended the use of **time-out**, the technique of briefly isolating a child following misbehavior. The next time Billy acted up in the grocery store, Ms. B. left her shopping cart, and she and Billy sat in the car until he quieted down. She then completed her shopping. Several trips to the car were needed the first day Ms. B. tried the new strategy, but Billy's behavior improved within a few trips to the store. He soon was earning rewards for being good—not for being bad—while shopping.

The Importance of Parental Love The coercion concept underscores the importance of parental discipline in managing children's behavior. As we have noted, however, children are better behaved when their parents are loving as well as firm. Why is this so? Attachment theory suggests that children who feel secure and valued by their parents are more compliant because they value their parents in return. That is, children *identify* with parents who are loving to them (Waters, Hay, & Richters, 1986).

More generally, children's noncompliance may not always stem from a lack of parental discipline. Sometimes children misbehave as a way of getting attention rather than as a way of getting what they want. Consider the social learning concept of *negative attention*, the idea that parents sometimes accidentally reinforce children's misbehavior that they intend to punish. Imagine, for example, a parent who scolds a child for misbehaving. The parent's objective is to stop the undesired behavior. In some circumstances, this attempt at punishment has the opposite effect: It increases the child's misbehavior. That is, the child is reinforced by the negative attention. Social learning theorists typically do not ask why the discipline attempt is reinforcing. They instead focus on finding a truly effective punishment. We think it is essential to try to understand negative attention, however. Many children may be reinforced by negative attention because they are not getting enough attention—enough love—in other ways. If this is so, some of children's behavior problems may be better treated by increasing parental affection than by tightening up on parental discipline (Emery, 1992).

Conflict and Inconsistent Parenting Inconsistent discipline is another frequent correlate of children's externalizing problems (Patterson, DeBaryshe, & Ramsey, 1989). Inconsistency can involve frequent changes in the style and standards of one parent, or two parents may be inconsistent in their differing expectations and rules for a child. For example, inconsistency between mothers and fathers often becomes a problem when parents have conflicts in their own relationship—as when they are unhappily married or divorced. In these circumstances, parents may deliberately undermine each other's discipline.

Yet another problem occurs when parents' actions are inconsistent with their words. For example, consider the contradiction inherent in angry and harsh physical punishment. On the one hand, such discipline teaches children to follow the rules. On the other hand, it teaches children that anger and aggression are acceptable means of solving problems. Parents socialize children by modeling appropriate behavior as well as by disciplining them, and children often imitate what their parents do, not what they say (Bandura, 1973).

Self-Control and Externalizing Problems To this point, our discussion has focused on the external control of children's behavior. Self-control is the ultimate goal of this socialization, and several investigators have found problems with self-control among children who have externalizing disorders.

One area of research on self-control has focused on *delay of gratification*—the adaptive ability to defer smaller but immediate rewards for larger long-term benefits. (An example of delay of gratification is studying for an exam rather than going out with friends.) In general, children with externalizing problems have been found to be lacking in the ability to delay gratification. They are more oriented to the present than are other children. They opt for immediate rewards rather than for long-term goals, a maladaptive characteristic for achieving educational and career goals (Mischel, 1983).

Children with externalizing problems also may fail to exert self-control because they misinterpret the intentions of others, particularly in ambiguous social situations. Several studies by psychologist Ken Dodge and his colleagues have indicated that aggressive children overinterpret the aggressive intentions of their peers (Dodge & Frame, 1982; Crick & Dodge, 1994). In a sense, some children with externalizing problems seem to believe that they need to "get you before you get me."

More broadly, some psychologists have raised questions about the moral reasoning of children with externalizing problems. Moral reasoning can be assessed by the explanations children give for their actions, and can be coded according to a hierarchy created by psychologist Lawrence Kohlberg (1985). Research indicates that children use increasingly abstract and sophisticated moral principles as they grow older. For example, a young boy may say that the reason he behaves well is because "Mommy will get mad." An older boy may explain that the reason he

▲ Clinical psychologist Gerald Patterson is a leader in studying children's aggression from a social learning perspective.

behaves well is because "You need to follow the rules." A teenager might explain that he behaves well because "It is the right thing to do."

According to Kohlberg, higher moral principles are based on values regarding appropriate conduct rather than on the immediate consequences of misbehavior. He has hypothesized that these more sophisticated guidelines, in turn, lead to more prosocial behavior. In support of his theorizing, some evidence does indicate that aggressive children follow the hedonic principles commonly used by children at younger ages (Kohlberg, 1985). They exhibit less self-control, or to put it in familiar terms, they may have less of a "conscience" than their peers.

Psychological Factors in Attention-Deficit/ Hyperactivity Disorder To this point, we have not distinguished between the etiology of oppositional defiant disorder and that of attention-deficit/hyperactivity disorder. In fact, none of the above findings purports to explain the unique development of attention-deficit/hyperactivity disorder. Scientists who study psychological factors in the development of externalizing problems seem to fall into one of two camps in this regard. One camp makes no diagnostic distinction between attention-deficit/hyperactivity disorder and oppositional defiant disorder, and these scientists therefore apply all the above findings to both problems. Another camp views attention-deficit/hyperactivity disorder as a biological problem, and these scientists therefore apply the above findings only to oppositional defiant disorder and conduct disorder. In other words, there are essentially no theories of how psychological factors might play a unique role in the development of attention-deficit/hyperactivity disorder.

Some researchers have found that the parents of children with attention-deficit/hyperactivity disorder are less effective than other parents. For example, mothers of children with attention-deficit/hyperactivity disorder have been observed to be more critical, demanding, and controlling when compared to the mothers of normal children (Mash & Johnston, 1982). However, problems in parenting may be a reaction to the children's troubles and not a cause of them.

Researchers have used a clever technique to document that mothers do react negatively to their children's behavior problems. They compare the interactions between mothers and their children with attention-deficit/hyperactivity disorder under two conditions: placebo versus medication. That is, the experimenter administers either a psychostimulant or a placebo in a triple-blind study (neither the child, the mother, nor the experimenter knows who received the real medication), and mother-child interactions are subsequently observed. Because psychostimulant medication directly alters the children's behavior, any differences between mother-child interactions in the two conditions are caused by changes in the children's behavior.

Several studies have found differences between the placebo and the psychostimulant conditions. Children with attention-deficit/hyperactivity disorder become more attentive and compliant while on medication, and their mothers' behavior "improves" as well. In comparison to the placebo group, mothers become less negative and less controlling when their children are medicated (Barkley et al., 1984; Danforth, Barkley, & Stokes, 1991). Children with attention-deficit/hyperactivity disorder make social interactions more difficult. At the same time, it is surely true that troubled parenting intensifies their problems.

BIOLOGICAL FACTORS

Genetic Influences Many scientists view a behavior genetics explanation as the most promising theory of the etiology of attention-deficit/hyperactivity disorder (Barkley, 1990). Evidence indicates that activity level and attentional capacities are influenced by genetic factors among normal children (Scarr, 1966; Willerman, 1973). More directly, researchers have found a 51 percent concordance rate for attention-deficit/hyperactivity disorder among MZ twins, compared with a 3"3 percent concordance rate for DZ pairs (Goodman & Stevenson, 1989).

These data suggest that genes contribute to attention-deficit/hyperactivity disorder, but that nongenetic factors are involved as well. A further complication is that heredity also plays a role in the etiology of other externalizing problems (Gottesman & Goldsmith, in press). One finding of interest, however, is that genetic factors explain less variation in delinquent behavior than in adult criminality (DiLalla & Gottesman, 1990). Apparently, there is more of a genetic contribution to life-course-persistent antisocial behavior than to adolescence-limited antisocial behavior.

If there are genetic contributions to externalizing disorders, an essential question is: What is the heritible mechanism? We might distinguish between attention-deficit/hyperactivity disorder and oppositional defiant disorder in this way. Hyperactivity or inattention may be directly heritable but oppositional behavior is not. (No one has suggested that there is a "crime gene," let alone an "argue with your teacher gene.")

One factor that has been hypothesized to cause oppositional defiant disorder and conduct disorder might be genetically mediated: chronic underarousal of the autonomic nervous system. That is, children with externalizing problems may be less emotionally reactive than other children. As a result, they may be more likely to engage in stimulation-seeking and less likely to learn from punishment (Quay, 1965).

Neurological Evidence Findings from neurological and neuropsychological research suggest other biological contributions to externalizing disorders, particularly to attention-deficit/hyperactivity disorder. We have already noted that brain damage can produce overactivity and inattention, but *hard signs* of brain damage, such as an abnormal CT scan, are found in less than 5 percent of cases (Rutter, 1983). Neurological *soft signs* such as delays in fine motor coordination—as may be evident in poor penmanship—have been found with greater frequency among children with attention-deficit/hyperactivity disorder. Soft signs are not considered strong evidence of neurological dysfunction, however. Moreover, evidence is inconsistent on the prevalence of soft signs among children with attention-deficit/hyperactivity disorder, and soft signs are found among many normal children (Barkley, 1990). Thus, the significance of the appearance of soft signs among children with attention-deficit/hyperactivity disorder is uncertain.

Other potential indicators of neuropathology in attention-deficit/hyperactivity disorder include a history of pregnancy and birth complications, minor anomalies in physical appearance, and delays in reaching developmental milestones. Still, no clear marker of biological vulnerability has been identified. Two promising avenues for investigation are (1) the search for selective dopamine deficits (psychostimulants are known to increase brain levels of dopamine); and (2) the possibility that impairments are localized in the prefrontal region of the right cerebral hemisphere, an area of the brain that may underlie attentional abilities and behavioral inhibition (Barkley, 1990).

Toxins and Diet A third set of hypotheses about biological factors in the etiology of attention-deficit/hyperactivity disorder has focused on diet and environmental toxins. With the exception of lead poisoning (see Chapter 14), research in this area is most notable for establishing the *lack* of an effect of ingested substances on children's behavior.

Consider research on the so-called "Feingold diet." In a popular book written for the parents of hyperactive children, physician Benjamin Feingold (1975) proposed that hyperactivity was caused by ingestion of food additives, particularly the *salicylates*, which are commonly found in processed foods. Feingold asserted that hyperactive children would become better behaved if they avoided salicylates, and tens of thousands of parents of hyperactive children embraced his recommended diet. The Feingold diet became so popular that Congress considered a ban on salicylates.

Many parents reported notable benefits of the Feingold diet, and they became staunch advocates despite the tremendous inconvenience of searching out natural foods. But the parents' great effort presented a problem. Could the diet simply have been a placebo? The answer to this question was yes, according to researchers who randomly assigned the families of 36 hyperactive boys either to the Feingold diet or to a sham diet that required a similar effort (Harley et al., 1978). With few exceptions, the investigators found no differences between the alternative diets on parent ratings or on observations of the children's behavior in a laboratory setting. Other research also revealed that, although a small subgroup of children may respond adversely to certain food additives, these dietary substances do not cause hyperactivity (Conners, 1980).

Food additives are not the only aspect of children's diets that have been suspected of causing hyperactivity. Parents and teachers often blame refined sugar, and physicians often recommend sugar-restricted diets to the parents of children with attention-deficit/hyperactivity disorder (Bennett & Sherman, 1983). Existing studies indicate that sugar does not cause hyperactive behavior, however, nor does the restriction of sugar lead to behavioral improvement (Milich, Wolraich, & Lindgren, 1986).

Subtypes of Externalizing Disorders Problems in classification surely have contributed to the limited success of research on biological factors in attention-deficit/hyperactivity disorder. One major problem stems from its co-morbidity with oppositional defiant disorder. Many research findings have been confounded by the fact that many of the affected children—approximately 50 percent—have both externalizing disorders. Thus, a major challenge for researchers is to compare diagnostically "pure" cases in an attempt to isolate the factors uniquely associated with one or the other disorder (Henker & Whalen, 1989; Hinshaw, 1987).

Even this strategy may not be sufficiently refined. Attention-deficit/hyperactivity disorder and oppositional defiant disorder are heterogeneous problems that have multiple causes. The externalizing disorders may need to be subclassified further in order to allow scientists to identify specific causes.

SOCIAL FACTORS

A number of social and societal factors also play a role in the etiology of internalizing and especially externalizing problems. As we noted earlier, more psychological problems are found among children who grow up in poor inner-

▼ This 3-year-old boy suffered a gunshot wound during a drive-by shooting involving gang members. Ironically, the boy plays with a toy pistol while recuperating in his hospital bed.

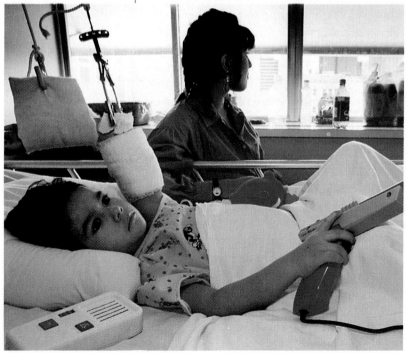

city neighborhoods. Professionals who wish to promote children's mental health therefore need to be concerned about poverty, inadequate schooling, and violence.

You should note, moreover, that parents are not solely responsible for socializing children. Violence is continually modeled on television, for example, and longitudinal evidence indicates that children learn aggression from television programs (Eron, 1982). Peer groups also can teach antisocial behavior, as is evident in inner-city gangs. In fact, some researchers have suggested that *socialized delinquency*, in which criminal acts occur in the company of others, is an important subtype of externalizing disorders.

Cross-cultural evidence also points to broad societal influences on externalizing behavior. Violence has become a major concern in the United States, and citizens of other countries often are horrified and puzzled by the extent of violence in our country. As summarized in Figure 15–4, there is good reason for their shock and fear. The rate of death by homicide among 15-to-24-year-old males in the United States far outstrips murder rates elsewhere in the world, a fact that undeniably points to a societal tolerance for violence and the availability of guns. The fact that young black men are far more likely to be murdered than young white men also points to the problems created by poverty, social disadvantage, and limited opportunities for achieving success.

Treatment of Psychological Disorders of Childhood

TREATMENT OF INTERNALIZING DISORDERS

Until recently, children were expected to "outgrow" most of their internalizing problems. Thus, few treatments for anxiety or mood disorders have been developed or studied specifically as they apply to children (Kazdin, 1994). Some children do suffer from disorders such as depression or obsessive-compulsive disorder. The prevalence of these problems is much lower among children than among adults, but recent findings indicate that the disorders are not "outgrown"—they persist across time, sometimes into adult life. Children's internalizing problems therefore require treatment, and treatments need to be developed and modified to meet children's unique needs.

Treatment research on children's internalizing disorders is still in its infancy. Initial findings indicate that children with obsessive-compulsive disorders respond positively to *clomipramine*, the same medication that is effective with adults (Leonard et al., 1989). However, antidepressant medications are no more effective than placebos in treating depression among children and adolescents (Kazdin, 1990). Some forms of psychotherapy for children's internalizing problems show promise (Kazdin, 1994), but the most accurate conclusion about the treatment of internalizing disorders is that research is needed on psychological and psychopharmacological treatments.

TREATMENT OF EXTERNALIZING DISORDERS

In contrast, numerous treatments have been developed in an attempt to alter children's externalizing disorders. Unfortunately, these problems are difficult to change (Kazdin, 1987). The most promising treatments include psychostimulants for attention-deficit/hyperactivity disorder, behavioral family therapy for oppositional defiant disorder, and various family and residential programs for treating conduct disorders and delinquent youth.

Psychostimulants Every year more than 600,000 children in the United States—between 1 and 2 percent of the school-age population—are treated with *psychostimulants* for attention-deficit/hyperactivity disorder (Safer & Kramer, 1988). This widespread usage may startle you, but medication is an inexpensive, carefully researched, and effective treatment for the disorder (Barkley, 1991; Henker & Whalen, 1989). Psychostimulants produce immediate benefits in the behavior of about 75 percent of children with attention-deficit/hyperactivity disorder, and these changes are substantial enough to be easily noted by parents and teachers. Still, these positive conclusions about the use of psychostimulants must be qualified on several grounds. Psychostimulants have only limited effects on learning; it is not clear whether they produce long-term benefits; and they have several side effects. Finally, the effectiveness of psychostimulants is not specific to attention-deficit/hyperactivity disorder. Let us examine each of these issues.

Usage and Effects The most commonly prescribed

psychostimulants are known by the trade names of Ritalin, Dexedrine, and Cylert. Each medication has the effect of increasing alertness and arousal. Psychostimulants usually are prescribed

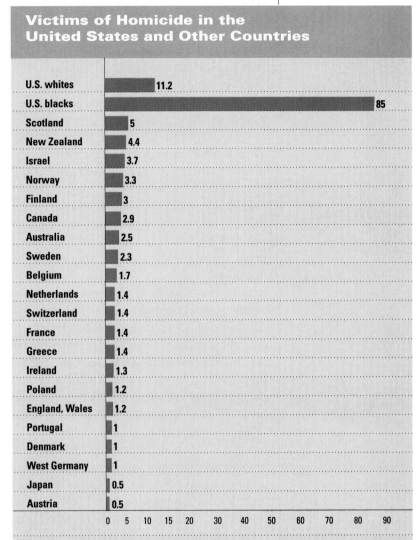

Victims of Homicide in the United States and Other Countries

Country	Rate
U.S. whites	11.2
U.S. blacks	85
Scotland	5
New Zealand	4.4
Israel	3.7
Norway	3.3
Finland	3
Canada	2.9
Australia	2.5
Sweden	2.3
Belgium	1.7
Netherlands	1.4
Switzerland	1.4
France	1.4
Greece	1.4
Ireland	1.3
Poland	1.2
England, Wales	1.2
Portugal	1
Denmark	1
West Germany	1
Japan	0.5
Austria	0.5

Figure 15-4: Rates of death by homicide among males 15 through 24 years of age in 1986 or 1987 for U.S. whites and blacks and for other countries.

Source: J.E. Richters (1993). Community violence and children's development: Toward a research agenda for the 1990s. *Psychiatry*, 56, 3-6.

by pediatricians, who typically are consulted following a child's difficulties in the early years of school. The central nature of school-related problems is evident in the fact that psychostimulants typically are prescribed around the school day. A pill is taken before school in the morning, and because the effects of the medication last for only 3 or 4 hours, another pill is taken at the lunch hour. A third pill may or may not be taken after school, but the medication typically is not taken on weekends or during school vacations because of concerns about side effects. Children take psychostimulants for years, not days or weeks. Traditionally, medication was discontinued in early adolescence, because it was believed that the problem was "outgrown" by that age. Follow-up studies, however, indicate that problems with inattention, impulsivity, and hyperactivity continue through adolescence and into adult life (Thorley, 1984; Weiss et al., 1985). Thus, the current trend is to continue psychostimulants through the teen years and perhaps into adulthood (Barkley, 1991; Campbell, Green, & Deutsch, 1985).

Psychostimulants indisputably improve children's attentiveness and decrease their disruptiveness (Barkley, 1991; Pelham et al., 1993). These benefits have been demonstrated in numerous double-blind, placebo-controlled studies, but they also are demonstrated more informally: Many teachers who are unaware of the new treatment send notes home about the improved behavior of one of their "problem" pupils. The benefits of psychostimulants for learning are less certain. On the one hand, psychostimulants lead to improved schoolwork, evident in more accurate completion of reading, spelling, and arithmetic assignments (Pelham et al., 1985). On the other hand, grades and achievement test scores do not improve dramatically, if they improve at all (Henker & Whalen, 1989; O'Leary, 1980).

Research on **dose-response effects**, the response to different dosages of medication, was once thought to explain the different effects on behavior and learning. Sprague and Sleator (1977) found that a lower dosage of psychostimulants produced maximum gains in learning, but that benefits began to deteriorate at higher dosages. These same higher doses produced maximum improvements in behavior—suggesting that some children received too much medication, because medication typically is increased gradually or *titrated* until maximum behavioral improvements are reached.

Dose-response effects have been inconsistent in subsequent research, however, and different children often respond uniquely to different dosages of medication. Thus, it remains uncertain why improved attention and behavior in the classroom does not translate into notably improved grades and achievement. An even more troubling and puzzling fact is that psychostimulants have not been found to lead to long-term improvements in behavior, learn-

ing, or other areas of functioning (Barkley, 1991; Dulcan, 1986).

Side Effects The side effects of psychostimulants also are somewhat troubling. Some side effects are relatively minor, such as decreased appetite, increased heart rate, and sleeping difficulties. Evidence that psychostimulants can slow physical growth is of much greater concern. Children maintained on psychostimulants fall somewhat behind expected gains in height and weight, although rebounds in growth occur when the medication is stopped. This is one reason why the medication often is discontinued when children are out of school. Still, careful monitoring of cases is necessary because of possible individual differences in growth effects (Campbell, Green, & Deutsch, 1985).

Another side effect that concerns some psychologists is that parents, teachers, and children often credit the pills, not the child, for the improved behavior (Whalen & Henker, 1976). When they are having an "off" day, for example, many children with attention-deficit/hyperactivity disorder are asked "Did you take your pill today?" Some research indicates that children do make internal attributions for their positive behavior (Hoza et al., 1993), but the question about attributions may reflect a more general concern: Should children's misbehavior be corrected with medication?

This is an important and reasonable question to ask, especially considering that the effects of psychostimulants are not specific to attention-deficit/hyperactivity disorder. Medication improves oppositional and defiant behavior as well (Klorman et al., 1994). Attention-deficit/hyperactivity disorder has not been proved to be a unique biological problem with a specific biological treatment. At the same time, psychostimulants are an inexpensive and effective treatment, especially in comparison with the alternatives. Many parents and professionals identify medication as the treatment of choice for attention deficit/hyperactivity disorder.

Behavioral Family Therapy Behavioral **family therapy** is the major alternative treatment for attention-deficit/hyperactivity disorder, and behavioral family therapy is also a common treatment for other externalizing problems. There are several variations of behavioral family therapy, but all approaches train parents and perhaps teachers to use the principles of operant conditioning to improve discipline in children's daily life.

Behavioral family therapy typically begins with *parent training*. Parents are taught to identify specific problematic behaviors, list preferred alternative behaviors, and set consequences for appropriate and inappropriate behavior. Parents also may be told to make a "star chart" for recording children's progress, and perhaps to develop a "daily report card" that the child will carry back home from school as a way of coordinating discipline in both settings.

Other aspects of parent training may include teaching parents about punishment strategies, such as the time-out technique discussed earlier. Conventional wisdom in parent training holds that punishment should be firm but not angry, and that rewards should far outweigh punishments as a strategy of discipline. These are reasonable goals, but some experts feel that parent training should directly emphasize increasing warmth as well as discipline in parent–child relationships. From this perspective, the goal of parent training is to teach parents to be authoritative.

Research with younger (Forehand, Wells, & Griest, 1980) and older (Patterson, 1982) children with oppositional defiant disorders supports the short-term effectiveness of behavioral family therapy. Some evidence also indicates that improvements are sustained over the course of a year (Patterson & Fleischman, 1979). A comprehensive review concluded that parent training was "one of the more promising treatments for conduct disorders" (Kazdin, 1987, p. 191). The same reviewer argued, however, that conduct disorders are chronic diseases that require intensive and repeated treatment. Behavior therapy leads to short-term improvements, but because externalizing problems are often chronic, treatment may need to be repeated over time.

A positive evaluation of behavioral family therapy is tempered further by several studies that have compared the treatment with psychostimulants. Medication has consistently been found to be more effective, although a combination of medication and behavior therapy may be better than either alone (Henker & Whalen, 1989; Pelham et al., 1993). In considering the challenges for behavioral family therapy, you should recall that the parents of children with externalizing problems are often living in adverse circumstances that make it difficult to alter their parenting (Emery, Fincham, & Cummings, 1992).

In fact, parent training has been found to be less effective when family troubles are greater (Kazdin, 1994). Parents can be effective in changing children's behavior, but psychologists need to develop more effective ways of helping parents to cope with difficult family environments.

Treatment of Conduct Disorders and Juvenile Delinquency Numerous programs have been developed to treat conduct disorders and juvenile delinquency. In fact, exciting claims about the effectiveness of new programs for difficult youth commonly are reported in the popular media. You should be cautious as you learn about these new approaches. Research indicates that conduct disorders among adolescents are even more resistant to treatment than are externalizing problems among younger children (Kazdin, 1994).

Some behavioral family therapy approaches have shown promise in treating young people with family or legal problems (Alexander & Parsons, 1982). These treatments are based on principles similar to those in programs for younger children, such as parent training. An important difference is that *negotiation*—a process in which young people are actively involved in defining rules—is central to behavioral family therapy with adolescents. Developmental psychology suggests numerous reasons why teenagers should assume this more active role in family therapy. An obvious reason is that parents have less direct control over adolescents than over younger children. Because of this, many mental health professionals advocate treating externalizing problems prior to adolescence.

A significant number of adolescents are treated in residential programs outside the home, because their conduct problems are severe, their

▼ Time out is a common and effective discipline technique. Discipline is most effective when it combines firm and consistent rules with warmth and responsiveness to children's needs.

families are dysfunctional, or they have been determined by the courts to be juvenile delinquents. One of the most actively researched residential programs is *Achievement Place*, a group home that operates according to highly structured behavior therapy principles. Achievement Place homes, like many similar residential programs, are very effective in improving aggression and noncompliance while the adolescent is living in the treatment setting. For this reason, professionals working in residential or inpatient settings are wise to adopt similar behavioral strategies. Unfortunately, the programs do not prevent **recidivism**, or repeat offending, once the adolescent leaves the residential placement (Emery & Marholin, 1977; Kazdin, 1987). Delinquent adolescents typically live in family, peer, and school environments that do not consistently reward prosocial behavior or monitor and punish antisocial behavior.

Of course, many delinquent youths are treated in the juvenile justice system, and treatment or *rehabilitation* is the explicit goal of most legal interventions with minors. The philosophy of the juvenile justice system in the United States is based on the principle of *parens patriae*—the state as parent. In theory, juvenile courts are designed to help troubled youth, not to punish them. This lofty goal is belied by research indicating that **diversion**—keeping problem youths out of the juvenile justice system—is a promising "treatment" (Davidson et al., 1987). The juvenile justice system often seems to create delinquency instead of curing it, and evidence indicates that recidivism is lower when delinquents are diverted away from the courts.

Our overview of the treatment of externalizing disorders is realistic, but we do not intend it to be pessimistic. Externalizing problems are of vast importance to children, families, and society, and the difficulties in treating antisocial youth should be seen as a challenge and not a defeat. Perhaps the best hope is to prevent some of these problems from developing in the first place by helping to ease some of the sources of family adversity that help to create them.

Eating Disorders

Eating disorders are characterized by severe disturbances in eating behavior. The eating disorders include **anorexia nervosa**, the refusal to maintain a minimally normal body weight, and **bulimia nervosa**, repeated episodes of binge eating followed by inappropriate compensatory behaviors such as self-induced vomiting. The term *anorexia* is derived from the Greek word for "loss of appetite"; *bulimia* is derived from the Greek word for "ox appetite." The linguistic origins of the terms bear only superficial similarities to the symptoms of these troublesome eating disorders.

Eating disorders typically develop during adolescence or early adult life; thus, we discuss these problems in this chapter together with psychological disorders of childhood. The problems often begin with a normal diet that goes awry. For example, a teenage girl of normal weight may attempt to lose a few pounds, perhaps with the encouragement of her family, but the successful diet does not end when she reaches this goal. The young woman remains on her diet, continually trying to lose a few more pounds. Family members become distressed by her increasingly emaciated appearance, but the teenager may insist that her appearance is fine or even a bit too "fat." The young woman with anorexia is not likely to be worried about her thinness. In fact, she may not recognize it.

Eating disorders are especially common among college women. In the United States today, a premium is placed on physical appearance, particularly among young women. Many theorists believe that eating disorders are one unfortunate consequence of this superficial societal value. Images in the popular media—and interactions with male and female peers—often seem to tell young women that they must attain the perfect weight, the perfect body, and the perfect appearance. The following brief case study illustrates the problem of bulimia nervosa in a college sophomore who also had a history of anorexia nervosa.

Bulimia Nervosa with a History of Anorexia Nervosa

Michelle was a sophomore at a state university when she first sought help for a humiliating problem: She binged and purged several times a week. When her roommate was gone, Michelle would buy a half-gallon of ice cream, bring it back to her room, and secretly gorge herself. When she was finished bingeing, Michelle would walk across the street to an empty bathroom in the psychology department, where she would force herself to vomit by sticking her finger down her throat. Michelle was disgusted by her actions, but she could not stop herself. In fact, the pattern had been going on for most of the school year. She decided to seek treatment when a friend from her psychology class discovered her purging in the bathroom. The friend also had a history of bulimia, but she had gotten her eating under control and convinced Michelle to try therapy.

Michelle's problems with eating actually began when she was in high school. She had studied ballet since she was 8 years old, and with the stern encouragement of her instructor, she struggled to maintain her willowy figure as she became an adolescent. At first she dieted openly, but her parents constantly criticized her inadequate eating. In order to appease them, she occasionally would eat a normal meal but force herself to vomit shortly afterwards. When she was a junior in high school,

Michelle's parents confronted her and brought her to a psychologist, who treated her for anorexia nervosa. She was 5 feet 6 inches tall at the time, but she weighed only 95 pounds. Michelle was furious at her parents and refused to talk in any depth with the therapist. She allowed herself to gain a few pounds—to about 105—only to convince her parents that she did not need treatment.

After this, Michelle planned her diet with great care. She starved herself all week so she could eat normally on dates during the weekend. Occasionally, she forced herself to vomit after eating too much, but she did not see this as a big problem. Until the past summer, she had maintained her weight at 105 pounds. Over the summer, however, Michelle gained about 15 pounds. This weight was normal for her height and body type, but she was trying to diet in addition to halting her bingeing and purging. She was extremely frustrated by her "lack of self-control" in both areas.

By all outward appearances, Michelle was a bright, attractive, successful, and happy young woman. Nevertheless, she admitted to her therapist that she felt like a failure and a "fake." She pretended to be happy and normal, but inside she felt as though she was going to explode. Secretly, she was miserable. ■

Typical Symptoms and Associated Features

Michelle presented a mixed picture that included many of the symptoms of both bulimia nervosa and anorexia nervosa. Her bingeing and purging was typical of bulimia nervosa, the diagnosis that was given to Michelle at the time. *Binges* are characterized by the rapid eating of a large quantity of food. The food often is high in calories and is easily purged. Vomiting is the most common way of *purging* the body of food to prevent weight gain after bingeing. Other compensatory behaviors include the misuse of laxatives, diuretics, or enemas; long periods of fasting;

and intense exercise. Occasional episodes of bingeing and purging are very common among college women. Although this obviously is unhealthy behavior, bulimia nervosa is diagnosed only when the problem is frequent and enduring (Yates, 1989).

Like Michelle, people with bulimia nervosa plan to purge after bingeing. Nevertheless, they feel out of control in their behavior. Their actions are secretive and a source of considerable shame. In contrast, people with anorexia nervosa take great pride in their self-control. Their eating is extremely restricted, and although the disorder may be punctuated by occasional episodes of bingeing and purging, they feel like masters of control. Thus, both eating disorders are characterized by a struggle for control. Bulimia is a failure of control and a constant struggle to regain it; anorexia is a dubious success in the striving for control. In Michelle's case, you can almost sense her struggle to regain the extreme control she once had over her eating and her weight.

Anorexics literally starve themselves to the point where they are extremely emaciated, yet they steadfastly deny problems with their weight. Professionals disagree as to whether this denial results from a *distorted body image*—a gross inaccuracy in self-perception. Professionals agree, however, that anorexia is a source of pride, not shame.

People with eating disorders are obsessed with food and with their body image, and they often follow detailed rituals about eating and diet. In fact, some evidence links anorexia nervosa with obsessive-compulsive disorder (Kasvikis et al., 1986). Another characteristic of people with anorexia and bulimia nervosa is that they believe that how they look is who they are. Given their constant dissatisfaction with their appearance, it is not surprising that they have low self-esteem. Eating disorders, especially bulimia nervosa, often are accompanied by depression, although it is uncertain whether depression causes eating disorders or is a reaction to them (Hsu, 1990).

▼ **This young woman with anorexia nervosa looks critically at her image in the mirror. She was dieting at the time despite her obviously protruding ribs and her weight of 89 pounds.**

Classification of Eating Disorders

BRIEF HISTORICAL PERSPECTIVE

Isolated cases of eating disorders have been reported throughout history. In fact, the term *anorexia nervosa* was coined in 1874 by a British physician, Sir William Withey Gull (1816–1890). Still, the history of professional concern with the dis-

orders is very brief. References to eating disorders were rare in the literature prior to 1960, and the disorders have received scientific attention only in recent decades (Hsu, 1990; Yates, 1989). The diagnoses first appeared in the DSM in 1980 (DSM-III), and while the diagnostic criteria have changed somewhat, the obvious problems in eating continue to be the central features of these disorders. The only change of note in DSM-IV was the creation of a separate diagnostic category for eating disorders. They previously had been listed as a subtype of the psychological disorders of childhood.

CONTEMPORARY CLASSIFICATION

The DSM-IV contains only two subtypes of eating disorders: anorexia nervosa and bulimia nervosa. Anorexia nervosa is defined by four symptoms: (1) a refusal to maintain weight at or above minimally normal weight for age and height (for example, less than 85 percent of expected body weight); (2) an intense fear of gaining weight; (3) a disturbance in the way weight or body shape is experienced, undue influence of weight or body shape on self-evaluation, or denial of the seriousness of low body weight; and (4) *amenorrhea*, the absence of menstruation, in postmenarcheal females (see Table 15–6).

Bulimia nervosa is defined by five symptoms: (1) recurrent episodes of binge eating that involve both large amounts of food and a feeling of lack of control over eating; (2) recurrent inappropriate compensatory behavior, especially purging; (3) a frequency of at least two episodes per day with a duration of at least 3 months; (4) undue influence of weight and body shape on self-evaluation; and (5) the disturbance does not occur solely during episodes of anorexia nervosa (see Table 15–6).

There has been some debate about whether other eating problems should be included in the DSM-IV list of eating disorders. Binge eating without compensatory behavior is one possible addition. Obesity is another problem that might be classified as an eating disorder. Some experts believe that anorexia nervosa and bulimia nervosa share essential features with these other eating problems as well as with normal dieting (Hsu, 1990). However, DSM-IV (1994) restricted the list to anorexia and bulimia nervosa, because evidence is equivocal on the role of psychological factors in binge eating, obesity, and other eating problems.

Epidemiology of Eating Disorders

Estimates of the epidemiology of anorexia and bulimia vary, but it is commonly accepted that the prevalence of both disorders has increased dramatically in recent years (Mitchell & Eckert, 1987). The DSM-IV indicates that anorexia ner-

The prevalence of eating disorders is notably higher, in fact, among groups of women for whom thinness is valued even more highly: ballet dancers, models, and gymnasts (Yates, 1989). The increased prevalence of eating disorders in recent decades also may be explained by gender roles, as beauty increasingly has been equated with thinness. Changes in the dimensions of

---

TABLE 15-6

DSM-IV Diagnostic Criteria for Anorexia Nervosa and Bulimia Nervosa

Anorexia Nervosa

A. Refusal to maintain body weight at or above a minimally normal weight for age and height (e.g., weight loss leading to maintenance of body weight less than 85% of that expected; or failure to make expected weight gain during period of growth, leading to body weight less than 85% of that expected).

B. Intense fear of gaining weight or becoming fat, even though underweight.

C. Disturbance in the way in which one's body weight or shape is experienced, undue influence of body weight or shape on self-evaluation, or denial of the seriousness of the current low body weight.

D. In postmenarcheal females, amenorrhea, i.e., the absence of at least three consecutive menstrual cycles.

Bulimia Nervosa

A. Recurrent episodes of binge eating. An episode of binge eating is characterized by both of the following:
  1. eating, in a discrete period of time (e.g., within any 2-hour period), an amount of food that is definitely larger than most people would eat during a similar period of time and under similar circumstances
  2. a sense of lack of control over eating during the episode (e.g., a feeling that one cannot stop eating or control what or how much one is eating)

B. Recurrent inappropriate compensatory behavior in order to prevent weight gain, such as self-induced vomiting; misuse of laxatives, diuretics, enemas, or other medications; fasting; or excessive exercise.

C. The binge eating and inappropriate compensatory behaviors both occur, on average, at least twice a week for 3 months.

D. Self-evaluation is unduly influenced by body shape and weight.

E. The disturbance does not occur exclusively during episodes of Anorexia Nervosa.

---

vosa is found among 0.5 to 1.0 percent of females in adolescence or early adult life, and bulimia occurs among 1 to 3 percent of the same population. There is a considerable degree of comorbidity between anorexia and bulimia. Many people with anorexia engage in episodes of bingeing and purging, and 30 to 80 percent of cases of bulimia have a history of anorexia (Yates, 1989).

GENDER ROLES

Both anorexia and bulimia nervosa are approximately 10 times more common among women than among men. Many scientists propose that this huge difference is accounted for by gender roles (Hsu, 1990). Popular attitudes toward women in the United States often propose that "looks are everything," and thinness is essential to our dominant cultural image of good looks.

Playboy centerfolds and Miss America Beauty Pageant contestants—cultural icons but dubious models for young women—document this trend. Between 1959 and 1978, the ratio of weight to height of these "ideal women" declined by 10 percent. Their body shapes also became more androgynous, as average bust and hip sizes decreased while waist sizes increased slightly (Garner et al., 1980).

Standards of beauty are relative, not absolute. Eating disorders are found almost exclusively in North America, Western Europe, and Japan; in other cultures, women who are more rounded are considered to be more beautiful (Hsu, 1990; Yates, 1989). In the United States, in fact, eating disorders are far less common among black Americans, who often hold a different standard of beauty than do white Americans. It is interesting and distressing to note that the prevalence of eating disorders may be rising among middle-class blacks. This may reflect a relationship between wealth and standards of beauty. In Third World countries, wealth is *positively* correlated with body weight. Being larger is a symbol of beauty and success. In industrialized nations, in contrast, wealth is *negatively* correlated with weight (Hsu, 1989). As the Western saying goes, "You can never be too rich or too thin."

AGE OF ONSET

Both anorexia and bulimia nervosa typically begin in late adolescence or early adulthood. A significant minority of cases of anorexia nervosa do begin during early adolescence, particularly as young girls approach or first reach puberty. The adolescent onset of eating disorders has provoked much speculation about their etiology. Certain characteristics of adolescence have been speculated to cause eating disorders; these include hormonal changes (Garfield & Garner, 1982), autonomy struggles (Minuchin, Rosman, & Baker, 1978), and problems with sexuality (Coovert et al., 1989). Consistent with the gender-roles interpretation of etiology, other theorists have noted that the young adolescent girl is the most idealized cultural image of beauty (Hsu, 1990). Each of these hypotheses may have some value in accounting for the onset of eating disorders, but consistent with our systems perspective, no single explanation is sufficient.

▼ Model Kate Moss. Contemporary images of women place a premium on slimness and suggest that women should be judged by their appearance. Both of these messages apparently contribute to the etiology of eating disorders.

Etiological Considerations and Research

The regulation of normal eating and body weight results from a combination of biological, psychological, and social factors, and researchers have focused on each of these levels of analysis in attempting to explain the etiology of anorexia nervosa and bulimia nervosa. Unlike most disorders we have discussed, sociocultural theories offer the most promising explanations of the high prevalence among young women in the U.S. today. We therefore begin by considering social factors in the etiology of eating disorders and move on to consider additional psychological and biological contributions.

SOCIAL FACTORS

The image of women and the value placed on women's appearance is an essential factor in causing eating disorders. This conclusion is supported by the epidemiological evidence we have noted: Eating disorders are more prevalent in industrialized societies, and in the United States they are more common among whites, higher socioeconomic classes, and women working in professions in which slimness is valued and rewarded. Other evidence also supports the importance of cultural values in causing eating disorders. The prevalence of eating disorders increases when members of relatively unaffected groups move into new cultures—for example, when Arab or Asian women move to Europe or North America (Yates, 1989).

Adolescent girls are at risk for developing eating disorders in part because teenagers attempt to shape themselves, quite literally, to fit the idealized image of women. Another problem is that the emphasis on appearance lessens the value of other roles filled by girls and women. Physical *attractiveness* predicts self-esteem among adolescent girls, whereas physical *competence* predicts self-esteem among adolescent boys (Lerner et al., 1986). Our culture needs to teach young women that who you are is much more than how you look.

Not every woman in the United States develops an eating disorder, of course, and some men do suffer from anorexia or bulimia nervosa. Other stressors, therefore, must interact with the cultural diathesis to produce eating disorders. Troubled family relationships may be one such contributing factor. Families of girls with eating disorders have been found to be less emotional and nurturant and more resistant to adolescent autonomy in comparison with other families (Humphrey, 1987). Other evidence indicates possible differences in the family patterns for anorexia and for bulimia. The families of girls with anorexia may be enmeshed and overprotective, whereas the families of girls with bulimia may be more angry and rejecting (Yates, 1989). Still, no clear and consistent family risk factors for eating disorders have been identified other than demographic characteristics such as race and income.

Speculation about psychological factors in eating disorders is wide-ranging, but, as is the case with research on family relationships, researchers have identified few consistent psychological characteristics of young women with eating disorders. We have noted that the struggle for control seems to be one central psychological issue, and some leading clinicians have hypothesized that control strivings are central to etiology (Bruch, 1982). Clinical reports suggest that girls with eating disorders are exceptionally "good": They are conforming and eager to please. Perhaps these exceptionally "good girls" give up too much of the normal adolescent struggle for autonomy and attempt to please others instead. If so, their efforts to control their eating and weight may be a way both of controlling themselves further and of gaining control over at least one aspect of their lives. Young women with eating disorders also may attempt to control their own emotions excessively. Some recent research indicates that they have difficulty identifying their feelings (Leon et al., 1994).

Depression is another psychological factor that may contribute to eating disorders, particularly to bulimia. An increased prevalence of depression has been found not only among people with eating disorders but also among the members of their families (Hsu, 1990). This has led some to speculate that the two problems are etiologically related. In support of this theorizing, research indicates that antidepressant medications are effective in reducing some symptoms of bulimia. Other experts suggest that depression may be a reaction to bulimia (Hsu, 1990; Yates, 1989), and research also indicates that depression improves markedly following successful group psychotherapy for bulimia (see Research Close-up).

BIOLOGICAL FACTORS

Eating disorders occasionally have been linked with a specific biological abnormality such as a hormonal disturbance or a lesion in the *hypothalamus*—the area of the brain that regulates routine biological functions including appetite (see Chapter 2). Such findings have promoted more general biological explanations of eating disorders. For example, twin studies suggest that genetics contributes to the etiology of eating disorders (Hsu, 1990).

Other evidence indicates that many biological abnormalities related to eating disorders apparently are reactions to the problems and not causes of them. These include elevations in endogenous opioids, low levels of serotonin, and diminished neuroendocrine functioning (Yates, 1990). Even some behavioral manifestations of the disorder appear to be reactions to starvation, not symptoms of an emotional problem. According to experimental studies conducted by the army during World War II, preoccupation with food, compulsive food rituals, and increased energy are documented consequences of starvation (Garfinkel & Garner, 1982).

Treatment of Eating Disorders

The treatment of anorexia nervosa usually follows a two-tiered approach. The first goal is to help the patient gain a minimal amount of weight. If weight loss is severe, treatment may occur in an inpatient setting, where strict behavior therapy programs make rewards (for example, social activities) contingent on weight gain. The second goal of treatment is more general—namely, to address the emotional difficulties that are thought to cause the disorder. Some clinicians have reported success with individual therapy (Bruch, 1982), and others advocate family therapy.

Structural family therapy is one approach that is commonly discussed in the clinical literature. Structural family therapists see parents' interference with adolescent autonomy as the central problem in anorexia nervosa. In family therapy they attempt to redefine the eating disorder as an interpersonal problem, get the anorexic out of the sick role, and encourage parents to confront their own conflicts (Liebman et al., 1983; Minuchin et al., 1978). Structural family therapy has only limited empirical support, and the effectiveness of other treatments for anorexia nervosa is also questionable. This skepticism extends to medication; several drugs have been used without much success as experimental treatments for the disorder (Hsu, 1990; Yates, 1990).

Research also is sparse on the treatment of bulimia nervosa, but available evidence is more encouraging. Both psychotherapy, which usually takes a cognitive behavioral approach, and medication have some demonstrated benefits. Antidepressants are the most effective medication for treating bulimia. In one investigation, 68 percent of patients on antidepressants were completely abstaining from bulimic episodes 10 weeks after treatment began (Hughes et al., 1986). Psychotherapy is also effective in treating many cases of bulimia. In one of the few studies that

RESEARCH CLOSE-UP

Intensive Group Psychotherapy and Medication in the Treatment of Bulimia Nervosa

Mental health professionals have developed a number of treatments in an attempt to address the dramatic increase in the prevalence of eating disorders. Systematic research on these treatments is still in its initial phases. Existing evidence indicates that anorexia nervosa is extremely difficult to treat, but some findings support the effectiveness of both psychotherapy and antidepressant medication in treating bulimia nervosa. These two approaches obviously differ greatly; thus, it is important to compare their effectiveness, as was done in a large study conducted at the University of Minnesota (Mitchell et al., 1990).

Women between the ages of 18 and 40 who met the DSM-III criteria for bulimia were included in this study. The 171 women who participated were assigned at random to one of four treatment conditions: (1) placebo only; (2) antidepressant medication only; (3) group therapy plus placebo; and (4) group therapy plus medication. Imipramine was the antidepressant medication used for all participants. Group psychotherapy followed a cognitive behavior therapy model, and it was short-term (10 weeks) but very intensive. The first 2 weeks of the program included two 2-hour group sessions during which the therapists introduced a system for planning meals and explained the cognitive behavior therapy approach. The subjects were told to attempt to avoid bingeing and purging during the next 4 weeks of the treatment. In order to monitor eating and provide support for efforts at controlling bulimia, the groups met for 3 hours 5 nights a week for the first week, but they tapered down to two meetings by the fourth week. The groups met for only one 1½ hour session for each of the final 4 weeks of the program.

Standardized measures of eating disorders, depression, and anxiety were admininstered at the end of treatment. This allowed the investigators to compare both medication and group psychotherapy against the placebo control group, as well as to examine whether the combination of treatments added to their individual effectiveness. The most striking finding was that group psychotherapy led to statistically significant improvements in eating behaviors, depression, and anxiety. Antidepressant medication alone also resulted in significantly more improvements than placebo on measures of depression and anxiety, but differences were not significant on all of the measures of eating behavior. Group therapy plus placebo was significantly and substantially more effective than antidepressant medication alone, even when the two treatments were compared on measures of depression and anxiety. Finally, the addition of antidepressant medication to group therapy (group therapy plus medication versus group therapy plus placebo) did not add significantly to the effectiveness of the group treatment, except that depression improved somewhat more on medication versus placebo.

Overall, group psychotherapy was found to be an effective treatment that resulted in about a 90 percent reduction in episodes of binge eating. Antidepressant medication also led to fewer episodes of binge eating—a reduction of about 65 percent—but the medication clearly was less effective than psychotherapy. Women who were taking medication also were significantly more likely to drop out of the study than were women in therapy, another indication of the superiority of group psychotherapy. Clearly, these results indicate that intensive group psychotherapy, not antidepressant medication, is the treatment of choice for bulimia nervosa. They also suggest that depression may be more of a reaction to the eating disorder than a cause of it. ■

compared medication with psychotherapy, intensive group psychotherapy was notably more effective than antidepressant medication (Mitchell et al., 1990; see Research Close-up).

COURSE AND OUTCOME

Several follow-up studies of anorexia nervosa have found a mixed outlook for the problem. At posttreatment follow-up assessments, 50 to 60 percent of patients have a weight within the normal range, 10 to 20 percent remain significantly below their expected body weight, and the remainder are intermediate in weight (Hsu, 1990). Anorexics do starve themselves, and perhaps as many as 5 percent literally starve themselves to death.

Although important, weight gain is not necessarily the best measure of the course of anorexia nervosa. In fact, about two-thirds of women with a history of anorexia nervosa continue to have difficulties related to the eating disorder notwithstanding gains in weight. Menstruation returns along with weight gain for most women, but preoccupation with diet, weight, and body shape typically continue. Patients may also develop new problems with social life, depression, or bulimia (Hsu, 1990).

Research on the course and long-term outcome of bulimia is inadequate. Consistent with evidence on treatment effectiveness, available data indicate more positive outcomes for bulimia nervosa than for anorexia nervosa. This must remain a cautious conclusion until more thorough research is available.

Summary

At least 12 percent of children living in the United States suffer from a mental disorder. Two well-established areas of disturbance among children and adolescents are externalizing problems and internalizing problems. **Externalizing disorders** are directed outward toward others and are characterized by violations of age-appropriate social rules. They are failures of **socialization**, the normal process of teaching children to conform to the values of family, school, and society. **Internalizing disorders** are directed inward toward the child and include sadness, fear, and other symptoms of mood and anxiety disorders.

The DSM-IV lists three major subtypes of externalizing disorders: **oppositional defiant disorder**, **conduct disorder**, and **attention-deficit/hyperactivity disorder.** The diagnosis of attention-deficit/hyperactivity disorder has a history marked by two errors that need correction: The problem cannot be equated with **minimal brain damage**, and **psychostimulants** do not have a paradoxical effect on children with this disorder. Oppositional defiant disorder often is a precursor of conduct disorder, which involves more serious rule violations including law-breaking or **juvenile delinquency**.

Oppositional defiant disorder and attention-deficit/hyperactivity disorder are best conceived as separate but overlapping problems. Attention-deficit/hyperactivity disorder is distinguished by symptoms of hyperactivity, inattention, and impulsivity. Hyperactivity is much more notable in structured settings like the classroom, and many problems with the disorder revolve around school. Inattention was once viewed as the central feature of the disorder, but researchers now recognize that either hyperactivity or inattention may be predominant.

Troubled attachments are one of the psy-

KEY TERMS

- anorexia nervosa
- anxious attachment
- attention-deficit/hyperactivity disorder
- behavioral family therapy
- bulimia nervosa
- coercion
- conduct disorder
- diversion
- dose-response effect
- eating disorders
- externalizing disorders
- internalizing disorders
- isomorphic
- juvenile delinquency
- learning disabilities
- life-span development
- minimal brain damage (MBD)
- oppositional defiant disorder
- peer sociometric method
- psychometric approach
- psychostimulants
- reactivity

chological factors that may play a role in causing children's emotional problems. Other research indicates that parents are most effective when they are authoritative: loving and firm in disciplining their children. **Coercion** is a more specific parenting problem that occurs when unwitting parents reinforce children's misbehavior by giving in to their demands. Inconsistent discipline is another parenting problem that may arise when parents are unhappily married or divorced. Yet another problem occurs when parents are poor models. Finally, self-control may be inadequate among children with externalizing disorders.

Biological factors are thought to be more critical to attention-deficit/hyperactivity disorder; these include genetics, neurological abnormalities, and dietary factors. Researchers have failed to identify a specific biological etiology, however, perhaps because of problems in classification. The co-morbidity of attention-deficit/hyperactivity disorder and oppositional defiant disorder make it difficult to interpret past research, and both problems are heterogeneous disorders that may require further subclassification. Finally, social factors contribute to the etiology of internalizing and especially of externalizing problems; these include television, peer groups, poverty, and attitudes about violence.

Few treatments for anxiety or mood disorders have been developed specifically for children. The most promising treatments for externalizing disorders include psychostimulants for attention-deficit/hyperactivity disorder, **behavioral family therapy** for oppositional defiant disorder, and various family and residential programs for treating conduct disorders and delinquent youth. Medication is more effective than behavioral family therapy, although a combination of medication and therapy may be better than either alone. The difficulty of changing externalizing problems is underscored by the limited success of numerous attempts to treat conduct disorders and juvenile delinquency in families, in group homes, and in the juvenile justice system.

Eating disorders include **anorexia nervosa,** the refusal to maintain a minimally normal body weight, and **bulimia nervosa,** repeated episodes of binge eating followed by inappropriate compensatory behaviors such as self-induced vomiting. The problems typically develop during adolescence or early adult life. People with bulimia nervosa feel out of control and are secretive and ashamed about their behavior. In contrast, people with anorexia nervosa take great pride in the extreme self-control that allows them to starve themselves.

Both eating disorders are often accompanied by depression, although it is uncertain whether depression is a cause of or a reaction to the eating problems. Both disorders are approximately 10 times more common among women than among men, a difference probably accounted for by gender roles.

Sociocultural theories offer the most promising explanations of the increased risk for the development of eating disorders. Adolescent girls attempt to shape themselves to fit the idealized image of women. In addition, the societal emphasis on appearance lessens the value of other roles filled by girls and women. Other stressors must interact with the cultural diathesis to produce eating disorders, and clinicians have emphasized family relationships, depression, and striving for control as contributing psychological factors.

The treatment of anorexia nervosa usually begins by helping patients gain a minimal amount of weight, and it later addresses the emotional difficulties that are thought to cause the disorder. Treatments for anorexia nervosa, including medication, have only limited effectiveness, however, as evidenced by the continuation of weight and psychological problems over time. Both psychotherapy, which usually takes a cognitive behavioral approach, and medication have some demonstrated effectiveness in treating bulimia. Available evidence indicates that psychotherapy is the more effective approach.

Critical Thinking

1. Special challenges exist in assessing psychological disorders of childhood. What biases do you think might intrude on adults' evaluations of children's psychological problems? How would you approach the assessments of children's inner thoughts and feelings? Think about these questions both as a scientist and as a clinician. How could you develop reliable and valid measures of children's problems, and how would you approach the individual child or family?

2. What are your personal thoughts on the use of psychostimulant medication? Do you think it is appropriate to use medication to help children behave in school? How might your feelings change if you had a child with attention-deficit/hyperactivity disorder?

3. Are children born with inherent tendencies toward aggression, or do they learn aggressive behaviors from social role models? What are the implications of your views (and of different theories) for important topics like warmth and control in parenting or restricting violence on television?

4. Consider how U.S. culture views women in movies, advertisements, "women's magazines," and other popular media. How are cultural views of women evident in your own attitudes and interactions? What items would you include on a measure of men's or women's attitudes about women's appearance?

5. Examine the image of men that is portrayed in the popular media (television, advertisements, "men's magazines"). What gender roles are men expected to fulfill? Are men valued for what they do, while women are valued for how they look?

Life Cycle Transitions and Adult Development

M ost of us struggle with painful and trying events at times during our adult lives. We may confront the death of a loved one, for example. The intense sadness of our grief may feel much like clinical depression, but grief is not the same as the syndrome of depression. Grief is an acceptable, normal, and healthy response to loss. We expect to flounder for a time when we lose someone close to us, and in fact, we may be concerned about the *absence* of emotional conflicts during difficult times in our lives. If our reactions are relatively mild, we may wonder, "What's wrong with me?"

Overview

In this chapter, we discuss grief and other painful but normal psychological experiences as a part of our overview of psychological distress and life-span development (see Chapter 15). This chapter focuses on difficult **life cycle transitions**—struggles in the process of moving from one social or psychological "stage" of adult development into a new one. We highlight three particular transitions in this discussion. The *transition to adult life* in the late teens and early twenties is a time for grappling with the major issues related to identity, career, and relationships. *Family transitions* in the middle years of life may include very happy events like the birth of the first child or very unhappy ones like a difficult divorce. Major changes in life roles such as retirement, grief over the death of loved ones, and the more abstract issue of facing our own mortality often accompany the inevitable process of aging and the *transition to later life*.

Life cycle transitions are periods of change between two stages of adult development. We use the term *stage* tentatively, however, because adult development is not characterized by a sequence of time-limited and qualitatively different experiences, as the term implies. Rather, theorists note common *developmental tasks of adult life*—fairly predictable challenges in relationships, work, life goals, and personal identity that occur during the course of the adult years (Havighurst, 1952). As we discuss shortly, we can only loosely identify the ages and events

that best mark the transitions between the developmental tasks of adult life. Several theorists divide adult development into three periods—early, middle, and later life. This rough division of stages of adult development is consistent with our focus on transitions into adulthood, in middle adulthood, and during later life.

Life cycle transitions are decidedly *not* mental disorders, and the DSM-IV contains only scattered references to various difficult transitions in normal development. However, several life cycle and relationship problems are listed in a section of the manual titled "Other Conditions That May Be a Focus of Clinical Attention." As indicated by this title, many people consult a mental health professional when they are struggling with difficult challenges in life. That is one reason why we review life cycle transitions in this chapter.

There are other important reasons for reviewing normal life cycle transitions in a text on abnormal psychology. As we have discussed at numerous points throughout the text, difficult life stressors often contribute to the etiology of a mental disorder. Similarly, theorists have suggested that mental disorders may be caused by inadequate coping with troublesome life events. For example, Freud theorized that depression was caused by the inadequate resolution of grief (see Chapter 5). Thus, one goal of this chapter is to better understand the etiology of mental disorders by examining certain life stressors in more detail.

We also highlight life cycle transitions because psychological theory and research on adult development suggest new ways of conceptualizing and treating emotional problems. The DSM is an evolving classification system, and we expect that future editions eventually will include more *interpersonal diagnoses*—psychological problems that are conceptualized as residing within the context of human relationships and not just within the individual (McLemore & Benjamin, 1979). We begin with a case study from our files.

CASE STUDY

Grief and Uncertainty over Divorce in Midlife

Chuck M. was 51 years old when his wife told him she wanted a divorce. Chuck and his wife had been married for 27 years, and he was totally unprepared for her pronouncement. He knew that his marriage was not perfect, but he had thought of his wife's complaints as normal "nagging." He had never thought of his marriage as either particularly troubled or particularly happy. He just had not thought about his marriage much at all. Chuck was content in his lifestyle, and he could not fathom what his wife was thinking. After having served in the Navy for 20 years, Chuck was collecting a pension and working as a technician for an electronics company. His two children were grown, the family was financially secure, and Chuck was planning to retire to Florida in another 10 or 15 years. His life was on the course he had set long ago.

At first, Chuck simply did not believe what was happening. His wife said that she had been unhappy for years, and that she had only recently gotten up the courage to leave him. This account clashed with Chuck's view of the history of their marriage. He openly wondered if the real problem was his wife's menopause, or what he called "the change of life."

Reality began to hit Chuck a few weeks after his wife moved out of their house and into an apartment. The move made the marriage problems impossible to dismiss. Chuck's wife said that she wanted a friendly divorce, and she telephoned him a few times a week just to talk. Chuck did not want a divorce, and if it was going to come to a divorce, he certainly did not want to be "friends." He was furious with his wife, but he still worked to avoid conflicts and keep his anger under control. Chuck wanted to avoid hard feelings, at least until he figured out what was going on with his wife and his marriage. Although he saw no need for it, he consulted a clin-ical psychologist at his wife's suggestion. She had been seeing a counselor, and she had found their discussions very helpful.

Chuck remained stoic throughout the first several therapy sessions. He freely discussed the events of his life and admitted that he now realized that he had taken his wife for granted. He grudgingly acknowl-edged that he was a "little upset" and "pretty angry," but he could not or would not describe his emotions with more intensity or much more detail. Mostly, he wanted the therapist to try to help him to figure out what was really going on with his wife.

Chuck's feelings came flooding out in therapy a few weeks later when his wife told him that she was in love with another man. Chuck raged to the ther-apist about how he felt used and cheated. He was stunned, but he was not going to let his wife get away with this. He immediately contacted a lawyer—he wanted to make sure that his wife "didn't get a dime" out of the divorce settlement. Chuck also called his children and told them all of the details about what had happened. He seemed bent on revenge.

Chuck admitted to his therapist that, in addition to anger, he felt intense hurt and pain—real, phys-ical pain as though someone had just punched him in the chest. When the therapist asked Chuck if any of these emotions were familiar to him, Chuck eventually recalled his feelings when he was 17 years old. His father died suddenly that year, and Chuck recalled feeling intense grief over the loss. He had controlled his feelings at the time, so he was sur-prised by the strong emotions he now felt in recall-ing the unfortunate event over 30 years later. His current feelings about his marital separation remind-ed him a lot of his sadness at his father's death, but his present grief was more volatile and he was much more angry than before.

Chuck began to talk more about his intense lone-liness and sadness as therapy continued over the next few months and as it became clearer that his marriage really was ending. He kept up his daily routine at home and at work, but he said that it seemed as if he was liv-ing in a dream. In the midst of his grief, he sometimes wondered if his entire marriage, maybe his entire life, had been a sham. How could he have been so blind? Who was this woman he had been married to? What was he supposed to do with himself and his life plans if the divorce really happened? ■

Typical Symptoms and Associated Features

The case of Chuck M. is complex in many ways. In reading through the case, you may have focused on who was at fault for the breakdown of the mar-riage, an issue that also preoccupies many divorc-ing couples. You may think that Chuck indeed was "blind"—insensitive—during his marriage. Or perhaps you wonder if his wife was involved in an affair prior to the separation. As impor-tant as these questions may be, we are not con-cerned with issues of fault. Instead, we focus on Chuck's reactions to the marital separation.

Are Chuck's reactions typical "symptoms" of life cycle transitions?[†] There is no DSM-IV list-ing of the psychological symptoms associated with life-span transitions, nor is there any other well-accepted listing of the troubles that accom-pany difficult life experiences. The various life cycle transitions obviously differ greatly, and it is also true that different people respond to the same stressor in unique ways (see Chapter 7). Thus, Chuck's reactions may have little in common with the feelings of other people who are getting divorced, let alone with people who are experiencing other major life changes such as going away to college or retiring.

At a more abstract level, however, there are some similarities across diverse life cycle transi-tions. Erik Erikson (1902–1994) highlighted con-flict as the common theme. For example, Erikson (1968) characterized the formation of a sense of self during the adolescent years in terms of a struggle between identity on the one hand and role confusion on the other. In fact, Erikson orga-nized each one of his eight stages of psychoso-cial development (see Chapter 2) around a central conflict, or what he termed a *crisis of the healthy personality*. According to Erikson (1959, 1980), "Each successive step . . . is a potential crisis because of a radical *change in perspective*" (p. 57, italics in original). Change creates tension both intrapsychically and interpersonally, as the com-fortable but predictable known is pitted against the fearsome but exciting unknown. The con-flict inherent in change is a central theme in each of Erikson's stages of psychosocial development; each crisis involves a conflict between stagnation and growth.

Conflict, therefore, is a common element across life cycle transitions. This is true if for no other reason than because transitions, by defi-nition, involve change, and conflict is a com-mon consequence of change. Conflict is not necessarily bad. In fact, conflict may be neces-sary in order for change to occur. Nevertheless, conflict and change often are psychologically distressing.

Many conflicts during life cycle transitions are interpersonal in nature. Chuck's growing conflict with his former wife is an obvious exam-ple. As Erikson suggested, other conflicts dur-ing life cycle transitions occur within the individual. Chuck experienced many conflict-ing emotions, including pain, sadness, and anger. Chuck's emotions were extremely intense and volatile, but similar emotional conflicts are com-mon during other major life changes. In fact, *grief*, the emotional process of coping with loss, is often characterized by conflicting feelings, as we discuss in more detail later in the chapter. Other internal conflicts are cognitive, not emo-tional, in nature. Broad cognitive uncertainties are reminiscent of the sort of questions many of us ask when we first become adults. Such ques-

▲ Psychologist Erik Erikson (1902–1994) characterized devel-opment in terms of stages extending throughout the life-span. A central conflict defines the transition between each of his stages of psychosocial development.

[†] Life cycle transitions involve normal distress, and we therefore frequently use the term "experience" instead of "symptom" in this chapter. We continue to use "typical symptoms" in chapter headings in order to be consistent with earlier chapters.

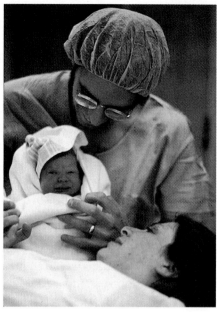

tions reflect a search for what Erikson (1968) called *identity*, our global sense of self.

Thus, conflict is a common theme found across very different life cycle transitions. In discussing conflict in this chapter, we often consider the behavioral, emotional, and cognitive components of conflict. Interpersonal conflicts often increase in frequency during life cycle transitions, particularly conflicts in close relationships. Emotional conflicts include grief and other reactions characterized by uncertain and opposing feelings. Cognitive conflicts involve a number of challenges to self-esteem, including broad doubts about identity.

Classification of Life Cycle Transitions

There is no official classification of life cycle transitions comparable to the categories of mental disorder listed in the DSM-IV. The DSM-IV contains a list of "Other Conditions That May Be a Focus of Clinical Attention," commonly referred to as "V codes."[†] Examples of V codes are "Partner Relational Problem," "Identity Problem," "Bereavement," and "Phase of Life Problem." The list of V codes is not an extensive summary of life difficulties. Instead, the DSM-IV offers only brief examples of the types of problems that it does not classify as mental disorders. Thus, we focus on other attempts to

categorize the major transitions and struggles of adult development.

BRIEF HISTORICAL PERSPECTIVE

The concept of adult development is a very recent idea when viewed from a historical perspective. Erikson (1959, 1980) first highlighted the notion in his work on the stages of psychosocial development. As we summarized in Table 2–4, Erikson suggested that there were eight stages of psychosocial development from birth until death.

Erikson's model includes four stages of adult development: (1) identity versus role confusion, (2) intimacy versus self-absorption, (3) generativity versus stagnation, and (4) integrity versus despair. Erikson viewed *identity versus role confusion* as the major challenge of adolescence and young adulthood. The young person's goal is to integrate various role identities into a global sense of self. The resolution of the **identity crisis**, this period of basic uncertainty about self, provides the first complete answer to the question "Who am I?" In Erikson's view, the resolution of the identity crisis allows young adults to embark on a journey toward achieving long-term life goals.

According to Erikson, one life goal is to form an intimate relationship early in adulthood. In his second stage of adult development, *intimacy versus self-absorption*, Erikson described the challenge in establishing intimate relationships

▲ **Development continues throughout the adult life cycle. "Stages" of adult development often are marked by key transitions in family relationships and academic or work roles.**

[†] The term "V code" has no special meaning; it refers to the letter of an appendix in the International Classification of Disease where the codes were once listed.

as achieving a balance between closeness and independence. Self-absorption characterizes people who either become dependent in intimate relationships or who remain aloof from others. Of course, people can remain aloof either inside or outside of close relationships.

People who succeed in establishing a truly intimate relationship are better prepared for their family and work lives. According to Erikson, they nevertheless eventually encounter the third crisis of adult life, *generativity versus stagnation*. Generativity is defined by accomplishments in middle adult life. These accomplishments include career achievements, but success in rearing children also is critical from Erikson's perspective. People who stagnate may have both a family and a job, but they steer their life course without a sense of purpose or direction in either of these principal areas of adult life.

A Model of Life Transitions during the Adult Years

Late Adult Transition: Age 60–65

| Culminating life structure for middle adulthood: 55–60 | Era of late adulthood: 60-? |

Age 50 transition: 50–55

Entry life structure for middle adulthood: 45–50

Midlife Transition: Age 40–45

| Culminating life structure for early adulthood: 33–40 | Era of middle adulthood: 40-65 |

Age 30 transition: 28–33

Entry life structure for early adulthood: 22–28

Early Adult Transition: Age 17–22

Era of early adulthood: 17-45

Era of preadulthood: 0-22

FIGURE 16-1: Levinson's three major transitions between different "eras" of adult life, and smaller changes within each "era."

Source: D.J. Levinson et al. (1978). The conception of adult development. From *The seasons of a man's life*. New York: Knopf.

Erikson's last stage of psychosocial development involves the conflict between *integrity and despair*. People can look back on their lives either with a sense of acceptance or a sense of despair or anger. Integrity comes from pride in life accomplishments and, more importantly, from the acceptance of our personal history. Despair comes from the impossible desire to change the past and from yearning for a second chance at life.

CONTEMPORARY VIEWS OF LIFE CYCLE TRANSITIONS

Erikson's views continue to be used to classify and comprehend life cycle transitions. He focused largely on the psychological side of psychosocial development, however, whereas many contemporary approaches emphasize the social aspects of life-span changes. For example, some contemporary researchers study the **family life cycle**—the developmental course of family relationships throughout life.

Family life cycle theorists classify adult development based on the tasks and transitions of family life rather than on the psychological challenges of adulthood. Their efforts to delineate the family life cycle typically define stages around major changes in children's developmental status. Shifts in children's development create marked changes not only for children as individuals but also for the family as a whole. Table 16–1 offers an example of one such approach to classifying the family life cycle. In reviewing these important and familiar transitions in family life, you should note that these stages of family development are not the same for everyone, and they focus mainly on the experience of white, middle-class families in the United States. We consider both common themes and diversity in family transitions in more detail later in this chapter.

Another example of a greater emphasis on social rather than purely psychological tasks of adult development has been offered by psychologist Daniel Levinson. Levinson (1986) emphasized three major (and many more minor) transitions between broad "eras" or "seasons" in adult life (see Figure 16–1). The *early adult transition* involves moving away from family and assuming adult roles. In Levinson's view, the *midlife transition* is a time for becoming less driven by internal and external demands and for developing more compassion for ourselves and others. This is his somewhat controversial idea of a "midlife crisis." The *late adult transition*, according to Levinson, is characterized by the changing roles and relationships of later life.

All these models of adult development are intriguing, but they must be considered with some caution. One caution is that history, culture, and personal values strongly influence views about which tasks are "normal" during the course of adult development. For example, Erikson's writing dates to the middle of the twentieth century. One reflection of cultural and historical influences on his model is that he assumed that normal adult development included forming an intimate heterosexual relationship and remaining in a life-long partnership. We can readily question his implicit assumption that deviations from this pattern were "abnormal" by pointing to the more diverse lifestyles and demographics of our times. In contrast to Erikson's perspective, contemporary life-span psychology notes that many diverse paths may be traveled in the journey through normal adult life.

Another caution is that transitions or "crises" may not be as predictable as the models imply. Once a transition is resolved, it is not necessarily resolved permanently. An identity crisis can occur at various stages of the life cycle (Waterman & Archer, 1990). In addition, some people may not pass through a particular stage of development. Not everyone forms a lasting intimate relationship, for instance. In short, adult development is more flexible than implied by the concept of stages. Nevertheless, the outlines offered by Erikson, Levinson, and family life cycle theorists do capture broad commonalities in the experiences of a great many people. At the very least, we all form age-related goals for ourselves, and we evaluate our achievements to the extent that we are "on time" or "off time" in achieving these goals. With appropriate cautions in mind, we turn to a closer examination of three major life cycle transitions: the transition to adulthood, family

transitions in the middle years of adult life, and the transition to later life.

TABLE 16–1

One Outline of Stages in the Family Life Cycle

Stage	Family Developmental Tasks
1. Married couple	Establishing a mutually satisfying marriage; adjusting to pregnancy and the promise of parenthood; fitting into kin network
2. Childbearing	Having, adjusting to, and encouraging the development of infants; establishing a satisfying home for both parents and infants
3. Preschool age	Adapting to the critical needs and interests of preschool children in stimulating, growth-promoting ways; coping with energy depletion and lack of privacy as parents
4. School age	Fitting into the community of school-aged families in constructive ways; encouraging children's educational achievement
5. Teenage	Balancing freedom with responsibility as teenagers mature and emancipate themselves; establishing postparental interests and careers
6. Launching center	Releasing young adults into work, military service, college, marriage, and so forth with appropriate rituals and assistance; maintaining a supportive home base.
7. Middle-aged parents	Rebuilding the marriage relationship; maintaining kin ties with older and younger generations
8. Aging family members	Coping with bereavement and living alone; closing the family home or adapting to aging; adjusting to retirement

Source: E.M. Duvall & B.C. Miller. (1985). *Marriage and family development* (p. 62). New York: Harper & Row.

The Transition to Adulthood

In the United States today, the transition to adult life typically begins late in the teen years, and it may continue into the middle twenties or even later. During this age range, young adults assume increasing independence, and many leave their family home. By the end of the transition, young adults have begun life roles in the central areas of adult development: love and work.

Typical Symptoms and Associated Features

In writing about the transition to adult life, Erikson (1959, 1980) argued that, in order to assume successful and lasting adult roles, young people need a **moratorium** or a time of uncertainty about themselves and their goals. In his words

The period can be viewed as a *psychosocial moratorium* during which the individual through free role experimentation may find a niche in some section of his society, a niche which is firmly defined and yet seems to be uniquely made for him. In finding it the young adult gains an assured sense of inner continuity and social sameness which will bridge what he *was* as a child and what he is *about to become*, and will reconcile his *conception of himself* and his community's recognition of him (pp. 119–120, italics in original).

IDENTITY CRISIS

As conveyed by this quotation, Erikson focused on the identity crisis as the central psychological conflict during the transition to adult life. Identity conflicts are epitomized by the searching and repeated question, "Who am I?" Erikson's focus on identity has much intuitive appeal, as it seems to capture many familiar experiences. In fact, the identity crisis is a frequent theme in novels like J. D. Salinger's *Catcher in the Rye* and movies such as *Reality Bites*. At this time of multiple changes in life roles, many of us feel unable to decide on a career, and our tentative choices are uncertain and volatile. We question our values and loyalties about religion, sex, relationships, and morality. We often doubt our ability to succeed in work or in relationships. Significantly, we also lack perspective on our experience. We feel as though we are confronting fundamental questions about who we are rather than merely passing through a stage.

CHANGES IN ROLES
AND RELATIONSHIPS

Of course, other things besides a person's identity change during the transition to adulthood. Young adults must make decisions about whether and where to go to college and what career paths to pursue. Such major decisions can permanently alter the course of life.

New boundaries also must be negotiated in the relationships between young adults and their parents. Finding the right balance between autonomy and relatedness is difficult. Conflicts in parent–child relationships increase during adolescence, as young people interpret parental control as an infringement on their independence (Smetana, 1989).

The theories of ego psychologist Karen Horney (1939) are helpful to understanding conflicted relationships between parents and young adults, as well as other relationship difficulties throughout the adult life cycle. Horney theorized that people have competing needs to move toward, to move away from, and to move against others. Moving toward others fulfills needs for love and acceptance. Moving away from others is a way of establishing independence and efficacy. Moving against others meets the individual's need for power and dominance. According to Horney, relationship difficulties come from conflicts among these three basic needs. Young adults want their parents' support; they also want their own independence; and at the same time, they may also want to outdo their parents.

Conflicts often increase in relationships with peers as well as with parents during the transition to adult life. Young adults become less certain about their friends as they become less certain about themselves. In fact, a sense of certainty about personal identity is correlated with both greater intimacy and the relative lack of conflict in peer relationships, including loving relationships (Fitch & Adams, 1983). Another important change is that relationships, especially intimate relationships, take on new meanings during the transition to adult life. Young adults seriously consider the possibility of making a lifelong commitment, a prospect that puts new pressures on love relationships.

The number of changing roles and relationships suggests that the search for self during the transition to adulthood may be less of an attempt to define a single "me" and more of a struggle to integrate new role identities with old ones. Experimentation with new roles may overwhelm the young person's ability to resolve cognitive dissonance. Given all of the real and practical changes during the transition to adult life, it is not surprising that many of us ask: "Who am I?"

EMOTIONAL TURMOIL

Emotional conflicts also mark the transition to adult life, as well as earlier adolescent transitions (Paikoff & Brooks-Gunn, 1991). Researchers have demonstrated that young people experience more intense and volatile emotions than adults do. In a clever series of studies, "beepers" were used to signal adolescents and adults at various times during the day and night in order to assess their activities and emotional states. In comparison to adults, young people between the ages of 13 and 18 reported emotions that were more intense, shorter lived, and more subject to change (Csikszentmihalyi & Larson, 1984; Larson, Csikszentmihalyi, Graef, 1980).

Relatively mild anxiety and depression often increase during the transition to adult life, but in our view many emotional conflicts stem from uncertainty about relationships. In particular, Horney's conflicting needs to move toward, away from, and against others may be experienced as emotional conflicts. That is, young people often experience the conflicting feelings of love (moving toward), sadness (moving away from), and anger (moving against). Their emotional struggles may stem both from conflicts among these competing feelings and also from the intensity with which young people feel each of these emotions.

Classification of Identity Conflicts

The DSM-III-R listed "identity disorder" as a psychological disorder of childhood, but the DSM-IV has wisely moved identity problems to the section on V codes. As with all of the V codes, the description of identity problems in the DSM-IV is much briefer than the detailed consideration of mental disorders. There is one sentence: "This category can be used when the focus of clinical attention is uncertainty about multiple issues relating to identity such as long-term goals, career choice, friendship patterns, sexual orientation and behavior, moral values, and group loyalties" (p. 685).

Other classification efforts have subcategorized styles of coping with identity conflicts. Based on Erikson's concepts, Marcia (1966) proposed several categories of identity conflict. Young people who have questioned their childhood identities but who are not actively searching for new adult roles, fall into the category of *identity diffusion. Identity foreclosure* describes young adults who never question themselves or their goals but who instead proceed along the predetermined course of their childhood commitments. People who are in the middle of an identity crisis and who are actively searching for adult roles, fall into a grouping called *identity moratorium.* Finally, young people who have questioned their identities and who have successfully decided on their own long-term goals have reached the stage of *identity achievement.*

Some research supports the validity of these categories. For example, the percentage of students classified as identity achievers increases between the first and last years of college (Waterman, Geary, & Waterman, 1974), and the percentage continues to increase in the years after college graduation (Waterman & Goldman, 1976). Consistent with Erikson's theory, identity achievers also are less conforming and more confident in social interaction than others are (Adams et al., 1985; Adams, Abraham, & Markstrom, 1987). At the same time, researchers have failed to detect a clear developmental sequence in Marcia's four categories; they do not appear to be actual stages of identity formation. What is most notable, however, is the general absence of research on the development of identity.

Epidemiology of Identity Conflicts

The epidemiology of the transition to adult life is easy to characterize. Given sufficient time, everyone eventually becomes an adult! More serious questions can be asked about this process: How many people experience significant distress during this phase of development? How many people never fully assume the responsibility of adult roles? To what extent are identity conflicts influenced by cultural expectations?

Unfortunately, psychologists have few empirical answers to these essential questions. Perhaps the most important epidemiological evidence pertains to cultural influences on identity formation. For example, research conducted during the 1960s, a time of social and political strife, particularly for college students, suggested that a new identity status was common during this historical period: *alienated*

▼ Uncertainty about identity, relationships, and life goals are common during the transition to adult life. The movie *Reality Bites* offered a contemporary portrayal of the struggles involved in assuming adult roles.

▼ Conflicts are common between parents and their adolescent or young adult children. Conflicts help young people establish their autonomy, and they are a part of a transition in family life for parents.

identity achievement. Young people with this status assumed an adult identity (they were identity achievers), but their definition of self was alienated; it conflicted with many values held by the larger society (Marcia, 1980). These people chose new adult roles that differed from traditional ones.

College students may be less alienated today than they were in the 1960s. Instead, demographic data suggest more reasons for alienation among a different group of young adults. The William T. Grant Foundation's Commission on Work, Family, and Citizenship (1988) brought particular attention to the status of the "Forgotten Half"—youth who do not attend college and who often assume marginal roles in U.S. society. The Commission concluded:

> Our 2-year study of 16- to-24-year-olds has convinced us that, as young Americans navigate the passage from youth to adulthood, far too many flounder and ultimately fail in their efforts. Although rich in material resources, our society seems unable to ensure that *all* our youth will mature into young men and women able to face their futures with a sense of confidence and security. This is especially true of the 20 million non-college-bound young people we have termed the Forgotten Half. . . . Opportunities for today's young workers who begin their careers with only a high school diploma or less are far more constrained than were those of their peers of 15 years ago. Typically, they cope with bleak job prospects by delaying marriage and the formation of their families. Many stop looking for work altogether. Disappointed in their ambitions and frustrated in their efforts to find a satisfying place in their communities, an unacceptably high number of young Americans give little in return to their families, their schools, and their work. (p. 1)

The report about the "Forgotten Half" highlights the influence of society on the transition of adult life. Young adults cannot form an enduring identity in their occupations if there are few attractive job opportunities. Identity diffusion may be a consequence of unresolved psychological conflicts, but delays in making commitments to work and family can also result from the limited opportunities available to some members of society.

Etiological Considerations and Research

Few psychologists have attempted to predict empirically who will have more difficulties with the transition to adulthood. Nevertheless, the broad influences of family and society appear to be of central importance. Psychological research suggests that the most successful young adults have parents who strike a balance between continuing to provide support and supervision of their children and allowing them increasing independence (Hill & Holmbeck, 1986). Identity achievers often have families that are characterized in this way, while identity diffusers may have rejecting and distant families, and identity foreclosers may have overprotective families (Adams & Adams, 1989). It also is of interest to note that young people who come from troubled families are more successful when they have developed a close and supportive relationship with some other adult (Werner & Smith, 1982).

Is the absence of an identity crisis a problem that foreshadows identity conflicts later in life? Little research has been conducted on this important question, but cross-cultural considerations imply that foreclosure may not be a problem. In fact, some commentators have suggested that the struggles of the transition to adult life are a consequence of the affluence, education, and alternative roles available to young people in industrialized societies. In less developed countries, people's life course may be determined by parental authority or economic necessity, neither of which allows for an identity crisis. In considering this, you should also note that adult roles were assumed at much younger ages in the United States in the not-too-distant past, as they still are in many nonindustrialized societies.

Gender roles also appear to influence the resolution of the identity crisis and the formation of identity. Erikson's theories have been criticized for focusing on men to the exclusion of women. As an alternative, it has been suggested that women often form identities based more on family relationships than on instrumental success in a career (Gilligan, 1982). Consistent with this perspective, some evidence indicates that the process of developing an identity is different among women with traditional gender-role orientations than it is among others. Men are thought to form identities first and subsequently enter into lasting relationships with others. Women in traditional roles, however, may define themselves in terms of their significant relationships with other people; that is, their identity develops out of their relationships, not vice versa. For these women, relationship intimacy may be fused with identity rather than being a consequence of it (Dyk & Adams, 1990).

Treatment During the Transition to Adult Life

No research has been conducted on alternative treatments for people who are experiencing distress during the transition to adult life. Clinical reports indicate that many young adults seek therapy at this time, an observation bolstered by the frequent utilization of college counseling services. As discussed in the clinical literature, treatment goals include validating the young person's distress and helping him or her to understand and clarify difficult life choices. In addition, it may be helpful to "normalize" the experience of identity conflict; that is, to conceptualize the individual's struggle as a part of the difficult but normal confusion that results from the search for self. Finally, many clinicians suggest that supportive, nondirective therapy is a particularly appropriate treatment approach, because seeking autonomy is a recurring theme of the transition to adulthood. Each of these observations holds intuitive appeal, but firm conclusions await empirical validation.

Family Transitions

Family transitions are major changes in family life and family relationships. Family transitions typically involve the addition or loss of members of a family household, including the transitions to marriage, parenting, and the *empty nest*—the adjustment that occurs when adult children leave the family home. Other family transitions may involve only changes in relationships and not in household composition, such as when an early adolescent assumes more independence. Divorce and remarriage also are common family transitions in the United States today, an observation that underscores the fact that families extend beyond the boundaries of a household.

Clearly, there are many different types of families, including married families, single-parent families, divorced families, remarried families, gay and lesbian families, childless families, and extended family groups. Nevertheless, social scientists find it helpful to consider the family life cycle, a fairly predictable sequence of development in family relationships across time (see Table 16–1). In fact, changes in family relationships are the focus of many of the key transitions in adult development in the middle years of life.

Typical Symptoms and Associated Features

All family transitions are characterized by change—changes in time demands, changing expectations, and changes in the degree of control or warmth in family relationships. Early in marriage, newlyweds must directly or indirectly negotiate their expectations about time together, emotional closeness, and who will assume authority and responsibility for performing different tasks inside and outside the household. The roles that couples assume in the first years of their marriage often set a pattern that lasts for a lifetime. Nevertheless, aspects of the marital roles must be renegotiated when children are born. Children place numerous demands on each partner's time, energy, and patience. Although it is a joyous event for many young couples, the birth of the first child also challenges the marital relationship. A spouse's needs may become second priority to the demands of parenting, and the birth of children also confronts young adults with the substantial dilemma of choosing between priorities in work and family (Cowan & Cowan, 1993).

As children grow older, parents must gradually allow their relationships with their children to change to meet the children's developmental needs. Maintaining warmth while loosening the reigns of control is the overriding theme of change in parent-child relationships. When the children leave the family home, adults must discover or rediscover interests inside their marriage and outside the home. These patterns are again altered by the birth of grandchildren, retirement, and the further family transitions of later life.

FAMILY CONFLICT

Increased family conflict is a common consequence of all of these changes in family relationships. The increase in conflict is illustrated by research on the relationship between children's age and parents' marital satisfaction. On average, marital satisfaction declines following the birth of the first child, and marital happiness does not rise again until the family nest begins to empty (Anderson, Russell, & Schumm, 1983; Rutter & Rutter, 1993).

Family members may fight about hundreds of different issues. However, psychologists generally have been more concerned with the process than with the content of family conflicts. One analysis suggests that all disputes during family transitions ultimately involve either power struggles or intimacy struggles. *Power struggles* are attempts to change dominance relations, whereas *intimacy struggles* are attempts to alter the degree of closeness in a relationship (Emery, 1992). Uncertainty about the *boundaries* or rules of the relationship may make conflicts particularly difficult during family transitions. Each dispute takes on added importance because it sets a precedent for the new roles that are being defined in the relationship. As family members move through the transition, they eventually negotiate new boundaries for their relationship. Conflict is reduced as they reach this broader understanding.

Increased conflict may be a normal part of family transitions, but conflict creates great difficulties for some families. One of the most consistent findings in the study of family interactions concerns the **reciprocity** or social exchange of cooperation and conflict (Jacobson, Follette, & McDonald, 1982; Margolin, 1981; Patterson, 1982). Family members who have happy relationships reciprocate each other's positive actions, but they overlook negative behavior. A grouchy

▼ The movie *Mrs. Doubtfire* conveyed some of the emotional conflict of divorce. In order to maintain contact with his children, the character played by Robin Williams dressed as an older woman and became a housekeeper for his children and former wife.

remark is dismissed as part of a "bad day," whereas a compliment is readily returned. In contrast, family members who have troubled relationships are caught in negative cycles of interaction. They ignore positive initiations but reciprocate negative ones. Pleasant comments may be seen as manipulative or may simply be ignored, whereas a sarcastic comment elicits retaliation in a game of one-upmanship. Conflict also causes more problems when it is frequent and angry, especially when disputes escalate into episodes of family violence (see Chapter 17).

EMOTIONAL DISTRESS

Whether family conflict is expressed through explosive outbursts, constant bickering, or the "silent treatment," fighting often causes emotional distress for all family members (Cummings & Davies, 1994). Arguments not only upset the opponents in a dispute, but they can reverberate throughout the family. Children are often upset by their parents' conflicts, for example. In fact, researchers have found that children's psychophysiological arousal increases in response to their parents' fighting (Gottman & Katz, 1989).

Increased emotional distress may be only a temporary, if trying, consequence of family transitions. However, unresolved conflicts may lead to more serious emotional problems. Ongoing family conflict, particularly marital conflict, is closely linked with depression, especially among women (Beach, Sandeen, & O'Leary, 1990). Marital distress also is associated with an increased risk for agoraphobia (Barlow, O'Brien, & Last, 1984), and parental conflict predicts increased behavior problems among children (Emery, 1982). As we saw in the case of Chuck M., moreover, emotional turmoil is a clear and painful consequence of separation and divorce. It is of interest to note that while marital conflict is more strongly related to women's depression, divorce is more closely linked with depression among men (Gotlib & McCabe, 1990). (See Further Thoughts in Chapter 17 for a discussion of children and divorce).

COGNITIVE CONFLICTS

Cognitive conflicts also may accompany difficult family transitions. Attribution of blame for family distress is one specific source of cognitive conflict. For example, happily married couples blame their marital disputes on difficult but temporary circumstances. In contrast, unhappily married couples blame each other for their disputes. Specifically, each partner tends to blame the conflict on difficulties in the other partner's personality (Fincham & Bradbury, 1987).

Family transitions also can cause broader cognitive conflicts. Identity conflicts may be renewed, especially because identity often is closely linked with family roles. For example, a divorce may challenge a family member's sense of self, especially when adults base much of their identity on their roles as spouse and parent. Marriage, childbirth, and the empty nest also lead to role changes that may create the need for a redefinition of self.

Classification of Family Relationships

As we noted earlier, family transitions can be classified according to different stages in the family life cycle (see Table 16–1). Other family theorists have developed very different typologies of family difficulties based on descriptions of key family relationships. For example, psychologist Lorna Benjamin (1993) has proposed that Sullivan's interpersonal theory of personality (see Chapter 2) can be used to classify personality disorders within the context of key relationships. Benjamin argues that there are two key dimensions of relationships, an affiliation dimension and an interdependence dimension. Her *affiliation* continuum is anchored by attack at one end and active love at the opposite extreme. Her *interdependence* dimension has control and emancipation at the two opposite extremes. From these two dimensions, she derives four basic styles of relationships, as portrayed in Figure 16–2.

Yet another way of classifying family relationships comes from the clinical literature on family therapy. This more informal approach categorizes constellations or patterns of family relationships. The scapegoating pattern is a commonly discussed example of this approach to family typology. A *scapegoat* is a family member who is held to blame for all of a family's troubles. The concept of scapegoating is akin to the idea of the "common enemy" in international relations. Common enemies can create alliances between enemies, as occurred in World War II when the United States and the Soviet Union joined forces in opposing Nazi Germany. Scapegoating in families is thought to serve a

similar function. For example, unhappily married parents may unite in their mutual blaming of family difficulties on a scapegoated child.

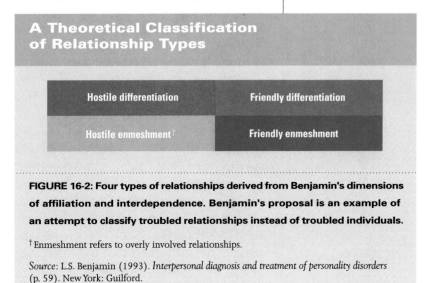

A Theoretical Classification of Relationship Types

Hostile differentiation	Friendly differentiation
Hostile enmeshment [†]	Friendly enmeshment

FIGURE 16-2: Four types of relationships derived from Benjamin's dimensions of affiliation and interdependence. Benjamin's proposal is an example of an attempt to classify troubled relationships instead of troubled individuals.

[†] Enmeshment refers to overly involved relationships.

Source: L.S. Benjamin (1993). *Interpersonal diagnosis and treatment of personality disorders* (p. 59). New York: Guilford.

The scapegoat is treated like an outsider in a family, as is illustrated in Figure 16–3, which portrays one boy's view of his family.

These and other approaches to classifying family relationships hold some appeal, but current attempts to classify families are inadequate both conceptually and empirically. Researchers first must demonstrate the reliability and validity of family classifications. Ultimately, they must prove that the family approach to classification is superior to categorizing individuals, at least in some areas of functioning. Such empirical efforts seem worthwhile, because many sources of emotional distress may be more adequately conceptualized within the context of key family relationships.

Epidemiology of Family Transitions

Epidemiological evidence is scant on the percentage of families who have difficulties with many life transitions. However, sound data are available on the number of people who pass through various family transitions with or without troubles. In fact, such data are considered to be so important to our national well-being that they often are collected by the United States Census Bureau.

Alternative lifestyles notwithstanding, evidence clearly indicates that most adults in the United States—over 90 percent—get married during their adult lives. Age at first marriage has increased in recent years, and nearly half of all people who get married today report a history of cohabitation prior to marriage (Cherlin, 1992). About five out of every six married women in the United States bear a child, but childbirth increasingly has taken place outside marriage.

Although probably very few people live "happily ever after," at any one point in time most people do report their marriage is happy. One national survey of the parents of children aged 7 to 11 found that 69 percent reported their marriage to be "very happy," 28 percent said it was "fairly happy," and 3 percent admitted it was "not too happy" (Zill, 1978). The extent to which marital happiness fluctuates is not known, nor do we know the number of couples who become extremely dissatisfied with their marriage at some point in their lives.

Miguel's "Sculpture" of His Family

FIGURE 16-3: Miguel, a boy who was a scapegoat in his family, arranged family members in this way when asked to make a "sculpture" of his family during a family therapy session. Some clinicians believe that family relationships should be classified according to patterns or constellations like those illustrated in Miguel's family sculpture.

Source: Illustration by Gaston Weisz. In R. Sherman & N. Fredman (1986). *Handbook of structured techniques in marriage and family therapy* (p. 76). New York: Brunner/Mazel.

Divorce rates have increased dramatically in the United States since the 1960s, and much research has focused on this important topic. Estimates indicate that about half of all of today's marriages will end in divorce. Most divorces occur early in a marriage, moreover, so that about half of all divorces take place within the first 7 years of marriage. Divorce is likely to be followed by remarriage, especially among whites. About three out of four whites, and perhaps one

out of two blacks, remarry following a divorce (Cherlin, 1992).

Etiological Considerations and Research

Most theories of the causes of difficulties in family transitions emphasize psychological and social factors. This focus is not surprising, given that family life obviously is an environmental event. However, it is also true that individuals make their own environments; thus environments are partially *heritable* (see Research Methods). For these reasons, it is important that we briefly examine biological contributions to family transitions after we consider psychological and social factors.

PSYCHOLOGICAL FACTORS

Family therapists and family researchers often blame difficulties in negotiating family transitions on problems with *communication*. Family members must be able to communicate their feelings and wishes in order to renegotiate family roles and relationships during routine times as well as during times of change. Communication not only includes direct conversation, but also nonverbal behaviors such as posture, voice tone, and affect that can convey hidden meanings. Think of the different meanings you can attach to a simple statement like "You look great today." Depending on your tone of voice, emphasis, and nonverbal gestures, the same statement might be an honest complement, a sarcastic insult, a sexual innuendo, or a disinterested observation.

Communication Problems There are many different potential problems in communication. Based on his extensive studies of marital interaction, John Gottman (1994), a clinical psychologist and noted marital interaction researcher, has identified four basic communication problems: criticism, contempt, defensiveness, and stonewalling. *Criticism* involves attacking someone's personality rather than his or her actions. According to Gottman, a criticism is a statement like, "You are unimaginative and boring!" A more adaptive complaint is, "I wish we could do something different once in a while." *Contempt* is an insult that may be motivated by anger and is intended to hurt the other person. *Defensiveness* is a form of self-justification such as denying responsibility, blaming the other person, or "yes-

The Concept of Heritability

Behavior genetics is the study of genetic contributions to complex behavior like psychopathology (see Chapter 2). The twin study is the most common method used in behavior genetics. We have reviewed numerous examples of twin research throughout this text, and we have noted that the evidence indicates numerous genetic contributions to abnormal behavior. When researchers find that MZ twins have higher concordance rates for a particular behavioral characteristic than do DZ twins, they rightly conclude that genes contribute to the development of the characteristic.

The value of twin studies for identifying genetic contributions to behavior is widely accepted, but it is less commonly recognized that twin studies also yield important information about environmental contributions to behavior. In particular, environmental factors are implicated in the etiology of a disorder when the concordance rate for MZ twins is less than 100 percent. Concordance rates for MZ twins would have to be perfect if a disorder was purely genetic, because MZ twins are genetically identical. Thus, imperfect MZ concordance rates demonstrate environmental contributions to the development of a behavioral characteristic—provided that the characteristic has been measured reliably and validly.

Because twin studies yield information about the contributions of both genes and environments, behavior geneticists have developed ways of measuring **heritability**, the relative contribution of genes to behavioral characteristics. Defined more formally, heritability is the proportion of variance in a trait that is attributable to genetic factors. Researchers often measure heritability by a statistic called the **heritability ratio**, which can be described according to the following simple formula:

$$\text{Heritability ratio} = \frac{\text{Variance due to genetic factors}}{\text{Total variance in a behavioral characteristic}}$$

Where:

Total variance = Variance due to genetic factors + Variance due to environmental factors + Variance due to the interaction of genes and environment[†]

The heritability ratio is a commonly used statistic for summarizing the genetic contributions to behavioral characteristics. It can be a useful summary when it is interpreted cautiously. You should particularly note two cautions. First, recall that the systems perspective indicates that genes and environments work together, not separately. Thus, in one sense it is erroneous even to attempt to calculate heritability, because all behavior is the product of genes and environments. That is, many experts assume that everything is an interaction between genes *and* environment. Second, any estimate of heritability is necessarily limited to the particular sample in a study. That is, we cannot generalize heritability estimates from one investigation to the population as a whole. When a researcher finds a heritability of 50 percent for some trait, this does not mean that the trait has the same heritability in the population as a whole or that heritability ratios are unchangeable.

This second point leads into a broader caution. Heritability estimates do not reflect the range of environments that are *theoretically* possible. Consider this point. One political goal in the United States is to provide everyone with the same rich and fullfilling environment. If we ever achieved the goal of providing everyone with the identical environment, all differences between people would be caused by genetics. You can see this by setting the variance due to environmental factors to zero in the above equation. In this case, heritability always equals 1.0. In short, heritability estimates in contemporary studies underestimate potential environmental

---

[†] The variance due to environments can be further divided into shared and unique (non-shared) environmental components. An example of a shared environment is family income; an example of a nonshared environment is being the favorite child.

contributions to a behavior. Although there are dramatic and frightening exceptions, contemporary environments vary relatively little from one another compared to what is possible in theory.

The practical implication of this theoretical point is that environments may matter more than we are able to detect in contemporary research. Consider, for example, that the environmental variation found in today's research does not include those historical changes in the average expected environment that have produced notable increases in life expectancy, education, and material resources for the population as a whole. Dramatic changes have occurred in the average expected environment in the United States in the past century or two. Thus, estimates of heritability in today's samples may be high in part because there is relatively limited environmental variation, notwithstanding ongoing social problems like poverty, racism, and sexism. Regardless of heritability estimates, both genes and environment are important to behavioral development, as we discuss further in the Research Close-up in this chapter. ∎

butting"—for example, "Okay, I understand how you feel, but . . . ." Finally, *stonewalling* is a pattern of isolation and withdrawal. Complaints are ignored, and for all practical purposes, communication is nonexistent.

Gottman's research has focused on married couples, but similar patterns of problematic communication would seem to apply to parents and children or even to divorced partners. Other researchers in the area of family interaction have focused on different problems in communication, but their findings share a basic feature in common. A consistent finding from empirical research is that communication difficulties distinguish distressed from nondistressed family relationships.

Family Roles Broader family roles also may be responsible for the development of some distressed family relationships. Many people believe, for example, that pressures to fulfill traditional marital roles—the wife as homemaker and the husband as breadwinner—may cause difficulties in some marriages. In studies of unhappily married couples, women often complain of feeling unsupported in their marriages, whereas men often report feeling disengaged from their family life. In contrast, one study found that androgynous couples—couples in which husbands and wives both scored high on measures of masculinity and femininity—had marriages that were happier and less distressed than more traditional unions (Baucom et al., 1990). Although nontraditional gender roles may lead to better long-term outcomes, it probably is also true that androgyny creates more conflict during the transition to marriage. Nontraditional couples must define the terms of their own relationship rather than assume clearly defined social roles; that is, the boundaries of their relationship are not defined by tradition.

SOCIAL FACTORS

Gender roles can be conceptualized in psychological terms, but they also reflect the influence of society on family relationships. Numerous other social influences contribute to the development of family distress. Poverty, crowded living conditions, and limited social support systems all can cause substantial distress in family life and family relationships. In fact, many family problems are major social concerns in the United States today. Teenage pregnancy, nonmarital childbirth, divorce, and family violence are social issues, not just psychological ones.

BIOLOGICAL FACTORS

Although their importance may be less obvious, biological factors also contribute to problematic family transitions. In fact, the potential contribution of biological factors to difficult family transitions bears on a central debate about individual development and family distress: Is family distress caused by dysfunctional individuals, or do troubled family relationships cause individual psychological problems? Clearly, family and individual problems are correlated, but it is not easy to determine the direction of causality or to rule out third variables. For example, marital status and marital distress are associated with an increased risk for individual psychopathology, but this correlation has several potential explanations. Marital distress may cause psychopathology, or marital happiness might protect individuals against it. On the other hand, people with emotional disorders may be less likely to get married or to remain in a marriage (Gotlib & McCabe, 1990).

Psychological research does not have any simple answers to untangling this and other correlations between individual and family distress. Rather, evidence points to different explanations for different disorders, and to reciprocal influences, such that each problem contributes to the other. It is clear, however, that biological factors contribute to family distress. Evidence even indicates that there are genetic contributions to family transitions such as divorce (McGue & Lykken, 1992). As we discuss in the accompanying Research Close-Up, this empirical finding should not only lead you to think more deeply about the causes of family distress, but it should also cause you to rethink the meanings and the methods of behavior genetic research.

RESEARCH CLOSE-UP

The Genetics of Divorce

Quite obviously, family transitions like marriage and divorce are changes that occur in the environment. For this reason, family transitions are commonly assumed to be determined purely by psychological and social factors. However, behavior geneticists have increasingly emphasized that people make their own environments (Scarr & McCarthy, 1982). That is, environmental events do not occur at random, but different people are more or less likely to seek out unique environments or respond to common environments in unique ways. For example, some people are risk-takers who constantly seek thrills in experience; other people are risk-adverse, and they seek stable and predictable environments. Thus, family transitions like marriage and divorce may be partially determined by the individual's personality, and personality and other individual characteristics may be influenced by genetic factors. In this way, family transitions may be partially determined by biology; in this sense, divorce may be genetic.

In fact, behavior genetics researchers have found genetic contributions to environmental experience. A study conducted by psychologists Matt McGue and David Lykken of the University of Minnesota provides one example of this line of evidence. McGue and Lykken (1992) gathered a sample of 1,516 MZ and DZ twin pairs to test the extent to which genetic factors play a role in divorce, a life event that few of us have typically conceived of as being "genetic."

These investigators found dramatically higher concordance rates for divorce among MZ than among DZ twin pairs. MZ twins with divorced co-twins were over 6 times as likely to be divorced as MZ twins with never-divorced probands. For DZ twins, the risk of divorce also was greater if the co-twin was divorced, but the risk was less than 2 times higher than when the DZ proband was never divorced. In fact, the investigators calculated that the heritability of divorce was .525 in their sample. This estimate is all the more remarkable because the researchers studied only one marital partner. Presumably, the twins' various spouses also contributed to marital longevity or divorce. Thus, genetic contributions to divorce may be even stronger than indicated by the heritability estimate.

How could divorce be genetic? Clearly, there is no divorce gene. Rather, McGue and Lykken (1992) speculated that divorce may be a consequence of personality factors that are partially shaped by genetics—for example, a tendency toward antisocial behavior. This is a very important suggestion. It implies, for instance, that researchers who compare children from married and divorced families are, to some extent, comparing apples and oranges. Divorce does not occur at random; thus children from divorced and married families differ in more ways than their parents' marital status. Genetically determined personality characteristics probably are among the differences between the two groups of children.

Thus, this intriguing study raises questions about research on the consequences of family environments. At the same time, however, it also raises questions about the interpretation of behavior genetics research. One question concerns whether genes and environment should be separated in calculating heritabilities or in conceptualizing etiology in any other way. Divorce rates in the United States 100 years ago were close to zero, and they still are in some parts of the world today (for example, Ireland, where divorce is still illegal). We certainly would be hard-pressed to explain such historical and cultural changes in divorce rates in terms of genetics. What does it mean to calculate the heritability of divorce when historical changes in the course of 100 years can change divorce rates from zero to over 50 percent? Genes may be important in determining who gets divorced, but environmental thresholds can eliminate divorce, or perhaps even increase divorce rates to 100 percent! In short, the issue is genes *and* environment, not genes *or* environment.

The findings also highlight the important question of explaining the *mechanisms* of genetic effects. Personality may be the genetically determined mechanism that explains these findings, as suggested by McGue and Lykken. The findings may also be explained by a host of other genetically determined factors, however, ranging from physical attractiveness to age at marriage. Finally, the findings raise questions about whether MZ and DZ twins always share the same trait-relevant environment, an essential assumption of the twin study method (see Chapter 2). Social influences may explain some of the difference in concordance rates in this study. For example, divorce often occurs in clusters, suggesting a process of social disinhibition. McGue and Lykken's findings may partially reflect that process. People may find divorce to be more socially acceptable if their identical rather than their fraternal co-twin has been divorced previously.

These observations are not intended as specific criticisms of the study by McGue and Lykken. In fact, the investigators themselves raised several of these issues in their important scientific report. Rather, the observations are intended to encourage you to think more deeply both about genetic contributions to environmental events—and about environmental contributions to behavior genetic findings. ■

Treatment During Family Transitions

A wide array of therapies have been developed for the treatment of family distress. These include both marital and family therapies and a variety of community action projects designed to prevent family problems. In the following sections we briefly introduce a few of these efforts.

PREVENTION PROGRAMS

Programs designed to prevent marital distress have a long and informal history. Perhaps the commonest attempts to promote successful marriages have been offered by various religious groups. As a requirement before performing a wedding, some religions encourage or require engaged couples to attend counseling sessions or discussion groups about family life. Unfortunately, little research has been conducted on the effectiveness of most of these programs.

Some research has been conducted on more psychologically oriented prevention efforts. One example is the Premarital Relationship Enhancement Program (PREP), a program originally designed from research with college students. PREP participants meet in small groups of couples, where they freely discuss their expectations about their marital relationships, including difficult topics such as sexuality. Couples also learn specific communication and problem-solving skills as a part of the training. In one study, couples randomly assigned to participate in PREP maintained their marital satisfaction 3 years later, while the marital happiness of control couples declined during this time (Markman et al., 1988).

The evidence on the success of the PREP is encouraging for the prevention of marital distress, but the systematic research illustrated by this study is of broader importance. Formal and informal prevention programs have been developed to help family members at nearly every transition in the family life cycle. There are childbirth programs, parenting programs, and support groups for parents whose children are infants, preschoolers, school-aged, or teenagers. Courts have programs for helping parents cope with separation, divorce, and remarriage (see Chapter 17). Creativity in developing programs is not lacking. What often is missing, however, is systematic research on the effectiveness of prevention efforts.

MARITAL AND FAMILY THERAPY
Marital and family therapy focuses on changing relationships, rather than on changing individuals. The marital or family therapist acts as an objective outsider who helps family members to identify and voice their disagreements, improve their communication, solve some specific problems, and ultimately alter and enhance troubled family relationships. This very different approach to therapy is illustrated in the following brief case history.

BRIEF CASE STUDY

**Conflict and Communication
in Marital Therapy**

Jan and Bill were seeking therapy for long-standing troubles in their marriage. Jan, a wife and homemaker, complained that Bill did not give her enough help with running the household or raising the couple's three children. More poignantly, Jan felt unloved, because Bill did not seem to enjoy being around her and the children. Bill countered that he loved being with his children, but said that Jan was a constant nag who did not appreciate the demands of his job as an insurance salesman. He also said that she was a "bottomless pit" in demanding his love and attention. The couple had been seen for several sessions when the following interaction occurred:

Jan: As you suggested, Bill and I were supposed to be working on a schedule so that he would only call on clients two evenings last week. But just like I knew would happen, Bill didn't follow through. (Jan begins to cry.) I just knew you wouldn't do it! Is that so much to ask? Couldn't you be home a few evenings during the week? Couldn't you at least tell me when you have to go out?
Bill: (in a monotone) I got some new clients this week, and there's a sales

push on. I couldn't reschedule. Next week will be better.
Jan: Next week won't be any different! Or the week after that. You aren't going to change. Why should you? You have everything your way!
Therapist: I can see you're upset, Jan, but let's give Bill a chance. Do you know your schedule for next week?
Bill: Pretty much, but you never know.
Therapist: Do you want to make a commitment to Jan right now about what nights you will be home in the evening next week?
Bill: I suppose I can be home around six or so on Tuesday . . .
Jan: You suppose! Go ahead and . . .
Therapist: One second, Jan. OK, Bill. Tuesday is a start, but do you see what your tone of voice says to Jan?
Bill: But she's always complaining about something! I said that I'd be home, OK? What else do you want me to do?
Jan: I want you to *want* to be home.
Therapist: Now we're getting to the real issue. Part of this is about schedules and time together, but part of this is about what it means to fight about these things. Jan, when it seems like Bill doesn't want to be around you and the kids, you feel unloved.
Jan: That's what I just said. You heard me, but he didn't.
Therapist: Bill, you feel controlled when Jan asks you about your work schedule. You have a lot to balance between work and home, and maybe you really don't want to be with Jan when you feel like she's forcing you to come home.
Bill: That's exactly how I feel.
Therapist: I want the two of you to talk with each other about these feelings. Then we will get back to work on the schedule—that might help to solve some practical problems. Jan, tell Bill how you feel—and Bill, I only want you to listen to her feelings. Try to understand what she says, and don't worry about a rebuttal. In a few minutes, we'll try this the other way around. ■

Several issues in marital therapy with Jan and Bill were evident in this brief exchange. At the most specific level, the goal was to help them solve the important problem of work and family schedules. Even an imperfect schedule might reduce some of the couple's conflict, because it would give them some clarity. Another goal was to break the couple's negative cycle of interaction by interrupting some fights, ignoring provocations, and encouraging Jan and Bill to talk about their own, deeper feelings. The discussion of feelings should be helpful in its own right. It also might allow the couple to develop a schedule, which, in turn, would alleviate some hard feelings. If they could mutually agree on a plan, Jan would have one less reason to feel rejected, and Bill would have one less reason to feel dominated.

Behavioral Marital Therapy Most research on marital therapy has examined behavior therapy approaches, the approach illustrated in the case of Bill and Jan. **Behavioral marital therapy** emphasizes the couple's moment-to-moment interaction, particularly their exchange of positive and negative behaviors, their style of communication, and their strategies for solving problems. Systematic research comparing the effectiveness of behavioral marital therapy versus no treatment indicates that marital therapy leads to significant, short-term improvements in marital satisfaction in about half of all couples treated. Still, approximately half of couples seen in behavioral marital therapy do not improve significantly. Relapse at follow-up is also common, and other treatment approaches appear to be about as effective as behavioral

marital therapy (Alexander, Holtzworth-Munroe, & Jameson, 1994).

Thus, there clearly is a need to expand on behavioral marital therapy and perhaps to integrate it with other approaches. Clinically, behavioral marital therapists are beginning to address emotion, the core issue for Jan and Bill (Margolin, 1987). This bodes well for future innovations. There is also a need to extend research efforts to include treatments for other difficult family transitions—for example, coping with divorce.

Treating Individual Problems with Marital and Family Therapy Marital therapy increasingly has been used not only to improve marriages, but also as an alternative to individual therapy in the treatment of psychological disorders. Marital or family therapy has been attempted as a primary or adjunctive treatment for almost every mental disorder, but most empirical work has focused on couples treatment for depression, anxiety, and alcoholism. In each area, research suggests that an improved marriage helps to alleviate individual disorders, particularly depression (Beach, Sandeen, & O'Leary, 1990; Jacobson, Holtzworth-Munroe, & Schmaling, 1989). These findings not only are important for treatment outcome, but they also underscore the reciprocal nature of individual and family relationships. In some cases, successful marital therapy removes the cause of an individual spouse's psychopathology. In other cases, successful marital therapy enables well-adjusted spouses to understand and cope with his or her partner's psychological troubles.

Aging and the Transition to Later Life

Adults in their forties and fifties become increasingly aware of their aging bodies. Men often worry about their physical performance in athletics and sex. Middle-aged men also become more concerned about their physical health, especially as they learn of events like a friend's unexpected heart attack. Women also worry about their physical performance and appearance in middle age, but women often are more concerned with their husbands' than with their own physical health. Men have a notably short-

er life expectancy than women—7 years shorter on average. Thus, even as they encourage their husbands to follow good health practices, many middle-aged women begin a mental "rehearsal for widowhood" (Neugarten, 1990).

Menopause, the cessation of menstruation, is an important physical focus for middle-aged women. Women in the United States have their last period at an average age of 51 years old, although menstruation typically is erratic for 2 or 3 years prior to its complete cessation. Many women experience physical symptoms such as "hot flashes" during menopause, and some experience emotional swings as well. For example, they may find themselves crying for no apparent reason. Episodes of depression also increase during menopause.

Psychological adjustments to aging and the loss of fertility contribute to emotional volatility during menopause, but so do the physical symptoms that result from fluctuations in the female sex hormone **estrogen**. In fact, *hormone replacement therapy*, the administration of artificial estrogen, alleviates many of the adverse physical symptoms of menopause. This eases some of the psychological strains associated with these symptoms. Hormone replacement therapy also reduces the subsequent risk for heart and bone disease, but it is a controversial treatment because it simultaneously increases the risk for cancer.

Hormone replacement therapy has no direct effect on depression, which is unrelated to estrogen levels during menopause, or on other broad psychological consequences of the "change of life" (Rutter & Rutter, 1993). Many women struggle with the challenges to identity that accompany the very real changes in their lives at the time of menopause. Still, we should note that menopause is *not* a trying time for other women. For example, women may find the freedom from fear of pregnancy liberating. Moreover, many middle-aged women enjoy the "empty nest"—they value the increased time they have for themselves as children move away from home (Rutter & Rutter, 1993).

Concerns about physical health increase for both men and women in their sixties, seventies, and eighties. Chronic diseases such as hypertension become common, all five sensory systems decline in acuity, and some cognitive abilities also can decline with advancing age (see Chapter 13). Major social transitions also typically occur during these years. Most people retire from lifelong occupations in their early to middle sixties, a transition that is eagerly anticipated by some people and dreaded by others. Whether retirement is seen as the end of a valued career or the beginning of a new life, it requires a redefinition of family roles as husbands and wives have more time and expectations for each other. Another family change is that parent-child relationships begin to reverse later in life. Children increasingly find themselves worrying about and caring for their older parents.

Death is an inevitability that also confronts older adults. With advancing age, we all must face both the abstraction of our own mortality and our specific fears about a painful and prolonged death. Death is a part of life for older adults, as friends fall ill and die. Women are particularly likely to become widows in their sixties and seventies. This loss is commonly followed by a period of intense grief, as is illustrated in the following case history.

▼ The transition to later life is *not* a time of despair for most people. Older adults who remain physically active and socially involved have better mental and physical health.

BRIEF CASE STUDY

Bereavement and Widowhood
Mrs. Sylvia J. was 78 years old when she consulted a clinical psychologist for the first time in her life. Mrs. J. was physically fit, intellectually sharp, and emotionally vital. She remained terribly distressed by her husband's death, how-

ever. Eighteen months earlier, the 83-year-old Mr. J. had suffered a stroke. After a few weeks in the hospital, he was transferred to a nursing home, where his recuperation progressed slowly over the course of several months. According to his wife, Mr. J.'s care in the nursing home bordered on malpractice. He died as a result of infections from pervasive bedsores that he developed lying in the same position for hours on end in the nursing home. The staff was supposed to shift his position frequently, but according to Mrs. J., they simply ignored her husband.

Mrs. J. was uncertain how to handle her grief, because she was stricken by many conflicting emotions. She had literally waited a lifetime to find the right man—she had married for the first time at the age of 71 after a long and successful career as a schoolteacher. She had been content throughout her life, but her marriage was bliss. She felt intensely sad over the loss of her husband, and she continued to make him part of her life. She would talk aloud to his picture when she awoke in the morning, and she visited his grave daily except when the weather was very bad.

Mrs. J. cried freely when discussing her loss, but she also chastised herself for not doing better in getting on with her life. She had several female friends with whom she played bridge several times a week. Mrs. J. enjoyed the company of her friends, who also were widowed and who seemed more accepting of their losses.

A greater problem than acceptance was the intense anger Mrs. J. often felt but rarely acknowledged. She was furious at the nursing home, and she was vaguely considering legal action against the institution. During her career as a teacher, she had never tolerated incompetence, and the incompetence of the nursing home had robbed her of her happiness. She was confused, however, because her minister said that her anger was wrong. He said that she

should forgive the nursing home and be happy to know that her husband was in heaven. Mrs. J. wanted to follow her minister's advice, but her emotions would not allow it. She wanted the psychologist to tell her if her feelings were wrong. ■

Typical Symptoms and Associated Features

Clearly, it was not wrong for Mrs. J. to be distraught over her husband's death, but were some of her other reactions abnormal? Having constant thoughts of another person might seem obsessional in some circumstances, and talking out loud to a picture might indicate delusions or hallucinations. Mrs. J. was showing normal reactions to grief, however, as similar responses are common among other grief-stricken older people. Frequent thoughts of a loved one are a normal part of grief, and it also is normal for intense grief to continue for a year or two, or perhaps longer. But what about Mrs. J.'s anger? Whether she should forgive the nursing home or sue them depends on many factors, of course, but she was not wrong—abnormal—for feeling angry. Evidence indicates that anger too is a common part of grief, and grief is a frequent experience among older adults.

GRIEF AND BEREAVEMENT

Grief is the emotional and social process of coping with a separation or a loss. **Bereavement** is a specific form of grieving in response to the death of a loved one. The process of grieving in bereavement is commonly described as proceeding in a series of stages. We considered Bowlby's (1979) four stages in Chapter 15: (1) numbing and denial, (2) yearning and searching, (3) depression and disorganization, and (4) reorganization. Bowlby based his model of grief on attachment theory and observations of children, but his stages are very similar to Elisabeth Kübler-Ross's popular model of grief. Kübler-Ross (1969) independently developed a model of bereavement in her work with terminally ill medical patients. She described their grief as occurring in five stages: (1) denial, (2) anger, (3) bargaining, (4) depression, and (5) acceptance.

The stage of bargaining, a period of attempting to negotiate for a longer life, is the only major difference between the models of Bowlby and Kübler-Ross. Perhaps bargaining is a unique reaction found among terminally ill patients, who understandably hope for some miracle cure. For our purposes, you should note that anger is a part of both models of grief. Bowlby's stage of yearning and searching involves frequent outbursts of protest or anger. Importantly, attachment theory offers an explanation for why someone might feel angry in the middle of intense sadness over a loss. Yearning and searching is a pursuit of, and a signal to, the missing attachment figure. Protest brings about reunion when the separation is temporary and the attachment figure is in proximity with the mourner. Of course, a reunion is impossible following the death of a loved one, as bereaved people understand intellectually. However, emotions, specifically anger, may not be rational at a time of loss.

Stage theories of grief have considerable intuitive appeal, but researchers have questioned whether bereavement follows any clear-cut series of stages. According to available evidence, few people experience grief in a fixed sequence of stages, but mourners instead vacillate between different emotions—for example, moving back and forth between sadness and anger. Other people apparently do not experience many of the stages described by Bowlby or Kübler-Ross, and still other people show few observable reactions to bereavement—they suffer in silence. In short, although denial, sadness, and anger may be normal reactions to loss, there is no one "right" way to grieve, nor should people be forced to express their unexpressed grief. In fact, research indicates that *less* intense bereavement predicts *better* long-term adjustment (Wortman & Silver, 1988).

OTHER ASPECTS OF THE MENTAL HEALTH AND EMOTIONAL WELL-BEING OF OLDER ADULTS

Erikson suggested that the conflict between integrity and despair was another common psychological struggle during the transition to later life. Experience suggests that many older adults struggle with the broad issue of the meaning of their lives when they look back from the perspective of their later years. Identity conflicts also may accompany less monumental tasks, such as the changes that come from becoming a grandparent or retiring from a long-term occupation. Unfortunately, little research has been conducted on Erikson's interesting conceptualization of the major psychosocial conflict of later life (see Further Thoughts).

FURTHER THOUGHTS

Reminiscence among Older Adults

It is difficult to operationalize and conduct research on the abstractions of Erikson's stages of psychosocial development, including his stage of integrity versus despair. Some researchers have made innovative attempts in this direction, however, by studying a common phenomenon among older adults: *reminiscence*—personal memories of the distant past. In fact, reminiscence may be helpful in facilitating adjustment during later life, as many senior centers in the community offer life-history discussion groups as a part of their services.

All memories of the past are not equal, as suggested by Erikson's conflict between integrity and despair. Older adults may recall their journey through life with pride and acceptance or with disappointment and regret. As a way of studying the manner in which memories of the past mark adjustment during later life, Canadian psychologists Paul Wong and Lisa Watt developed a taxonomy of six different categories of reminiscence.

Integrative reminiscence is an attempt to achieve a sense of self-worth, coherence, and reconciliation with the past. It includes a discussion of past conflicts and losses, but it is characterized by an overriding acceptance of events. *Instrumental reminiscence* involves the review of goal-directed activities and attainments. It reflects a sense of control and success in overcoming life's obstacles.

Transitive reminiscence serves the function of passing on cultural heritage and personal legacy, and it includes both direct moral instruction and storytelling that has clear moral implications. *Escapist reminiscence* is full of glorification of the past and deprecation of the present, a yearning for the "good old days." *Obsessive reminiscence* includes preoccupation with failure and is full of guilt, bitterness, and despair. Finally, *narrative reminiscence* is descriptive rather than interpretive. It involves "sticking to the facts" and does not serve clear intrapsychic or interpersonal functions.

Each of these styles of discussing the past has been found among older adults. In fact, initial evidence has found that integrative reminiscence and instrumental reminiscence are related to successful aging, whereas obsessive reminiscence is associated with less successful adjustment in later life (Wong & Watt, 1991). Reminiscence may have limited value as an intervention, however, because the amount of time elders spend discussing the past does not distinguish successful and unsuccessful older adults. Perhaps we are limited in the extent to which we can "rewrite" our personal histories in a more favorable light. ■

A much more frequently studied issue is the mental health of older adults. Mental health problems, including depression, anxiety, substance abuse, and paranoia are causes for legitimate concern among older adults. Nevertheless, epidemiological evidence indicates that the prevalence of mental disorders is lower, not higher, among adults 65 years of age and older (see Table 16–2). Contrary to some stereotypes, later life is *not* a time of fear, disappointment, dejection, and despair. With the exception of the cognitive disorders, which do increase with age (see Chapter 13), mood and anxiety disorders are the most common emotional problems among older adults. Affective disorders are less than half as common among older as among younger adults, and anxiety disorders also are less prevalent. Moreover, life satisfaction remains stable across the transition to later life.

Despite the lower prevalence rates, psychological disorders are an important concern among older adults. This is especially true of depression, which may be more profound, lasting, and debilitating among older than younger adults. Suicide risk is a particular concern, as adults over the age of 65 have the highest rate of completed suicide of any age group. The risk for completed suicide is notably higher among older white males, and in fact, suicide is one of the top 10 causes of death among older adults (Koenig & Blazer, 1990). Most experts view the increase in suicide as a consequence not only of the emotional problems and adverse social circumstances found among older adults, but also as a result of chronic pain, physical disease, and the prospect of a long terminal illness.

Ageism In considering some of the common experiences of the transition to later life, we all must be careful to guard against falling prey to common stereotypes about "old people." Older adults confront a form of social prejudice known as **ageism**, a term that encompasses a number of misconceptions and prejudices about aging. For example, young Americans, even mental health professionals, tend to view older adults as stubborn, irritable, bossy, and complaining (Thomas, 1980). Older adults are more different than they are alike, however, and stability rather than change in personality seems to be the rule across the transition to later life. Some research indicates that adults become more inwardly focused as they enter later life, but the major finding is that personality is consistent from middle age to old age (Clarke-Stewart, Perlmutter, & Friedman, 1988).

Classification of Adults in Later Life

There are no formal classifications of adults in later life. Distinctions based roughly on age and/or health status are used commonly, if rather informally, in **gerontology**, the multidisciplinary study of aging. One approach distinguishes between the young-old, the old-old, and the oldest-old.

The *young-old* are adults roughly between the ages of 65 and 75. However, the category is defined less by age than by health and vigor. Notwithstanding the normal physical problems of aging, the young-old are in good health and are active members of their communities. The majority of older adults belong to this group.

The *old-old* are adults between the ages of approximately 75 and 85 who suffer from major physical, psychological, or social (largely economic) problems. They require some routine assistance in living, although only about 6 percent of Americans in this age range live in a nursing home. Despite advanced age, a healthy and active 80-year-old adult would be considered to be young-old instead of old-old.

Finally, the *oldest-old* are adults 85 years old or older. People in this category are a diverse group and include some adults who maintain their vigor and others in need of constant assistance. Widowed women and low-income groups are found disproportionately among the oldest-old. Twenty-two percent of the oldest-old live in nursing homes (Neugarten, 1990).

Epidemiology of Aging

In 1990, approximately 1 out of every 8 persons living in the United States—over 31 million people—were 65 years of age or older. Approximately 10 percent, or 3 million, of these older adults were the oldest-old—people 85 years old or older (U.S. Census Bureau, 1992). One of the most important facts about older adults in the United States is that both the proportion and the absolute number of older Americans is expected to increase through the middle of the twenty-first century. The increase will occur partly as a result of medical advances but primarily due to the aging of the post-World War II "baby boom" generation (see Figure 16–4).

The proportion of the U.S. population 65 years of age or older should peak around the year 2030. At that time, 1 out of every 5 Americans will be at least 65 years old. During these years, increases in the prevalence of older adults in the U.S. will be most dramatic among the oldest of the old. In fact, the proportion and absolute number of adults in the oldest-old grouping will continue to rise until halfway through the twenty-first century. By the year 2050, the oldest-old may comprise one-fourth of the population of older adults (U.S. Census Bureau, 1986).

Most older Americans are women, and the ratio of women to men increases at older ages. Among adults 65 years of age or older, women outnumber men by 3 to 2, but women outnumber men 2 to 1 at the age of 85 or older (U.S. Census Bureau, 1992). One important con-

TABLE 16–2

Age Differences in the Six-Month Prevalence of Mood Disorder, Anxiety Disorder, and All Diagnoses

Diagnosis	Age Group (%)			
	18–24	25–44	45–64	65+
All diagnoses				
Baltimore	23.5	25.3	21.3	13.9
North Carolina	21.5	19.1	20.9	13.5
New Haven	19.8	20.4	11.1	7.5
St. Louis	15.2	18.1	12.4	5.8
Mood disorders				
Baltimore	2.5	5.6	4.3	1.7
North Carolina	3.7	4.2	4.2	2.1
New Haven	5.5	7.6	4.0	2.9
St. Louis	5.0	6.7	6.4	1.5
Anxiety disorders				
Baltimore	16.9	14.7	15.5	12.1
North Carolina	16.7	14.4	16.1	11.6
New Haven	7.0	9.2	5.8	4.5
St. Louis	7.5	8.5	5.2	3.0

Source: L.K. George, D.F. Blazer, I. Winfield-Laird, P.J. Leaf, & R.L. Fishbach (1988). Psychiatric disorders and mental health service use in later life: Evidence from the Epidemiologic Catchment Area Program. In J. Brody and G. Maddox, *Epidemiology and aging* (p. 205). New York: Springer.

sequence of gender differences in longevity is that the majority of older men are married, whereas the majority of older women live alone. Census data also indicate that poverty rates are higher among older Americans than among younger age groups (except children), and the percentage of older Americans living in poverty increases with advancing age. This is due, in part, to the lower economic status of widowed women.

Etiological Considerations and Research

Biological, psychological, and social factors all contribute to the adequacy of adjustment during the transition to later life. There is little doubt that the most important biological contribution to psychological well-being in later life is good physical health. In fact, a study of adults over the age of 70 found that both men and women listed poor health as the most common contribution to a negative quality of life in their later years (Flanagan, 1982).

Health behavior is particularly important to the physical well-being of older adults. Increased vigor and good health in later life are associated with proper diet, continued exercise, weight control, and the avoidance of cigarette smoking and excessive alcohol use (Bromley, 1990). More generally, it has been suggested that the overriding goal of gerontology in industrialized societies should be to promote healthy and active lifestyles among older adults and to decrease the period of illness and infirmity that precedes death (Fries, 1990). In industrialized societies, current life expectancies probably are very close to the biological limits of the human species; therefore, increasing longevity may be an unrealistic goal. Still, it may be possible to extend the number of vigorous and healthy years of life.

In addition to appropriate health behavior, important psychological contributions to adjustment in later life include the availability of close relationships and the experience of loss. Among men over the age of 70 the most frequently listed positive contributions to quality of life include relationships with spouses, friends, and children. Because so many women over the age of 70 are widowed, women mention relationships with spouses far less frequently than

men in describing contributions to their positive quality of life. Women do list relationships with friends, children, and general socializing among the most common positive contributions to quality of life (Flanagan, 1982).

As we discussed earlier, marital satisfaction is more closely related to women's than to men's mental health among younger adults, whereas marital status is more closely linked with men's than women's emotional well-being. Evidence on widowhood suggests that the pattern continues into later life. Bereavement and living alone are more strongly related to depression among men than among women (Siegel & Kuykendall, 1990). Men apparently benefit more from marriage, and women benefit more from happy relationships.

Numerous social factors are linked with a happier transition to later life, especially material well-being and participation in recreational activities. Religion is also very important to many older adults, and religious affiliations have been found to moderate the ill-effects of bereavement, particularly among men (Siegel & Kuykendall, 1990). Other research indicates that integration into a community is a major contribution to adjustment to later life. For example, rates of mental illnesses are notably higher among residents of nursing homes (Koenig & Blazer, 1990).

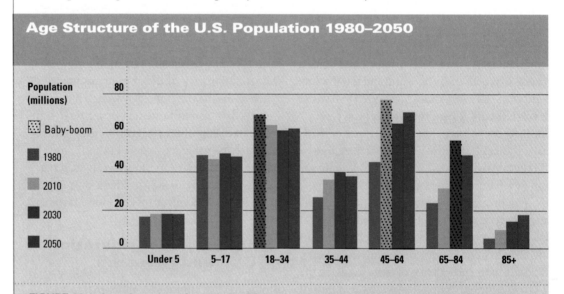

FIGURE 16-4: Actual number of people in different age groups in the United States population in 1980, and projections for the years 2010, 2030, and 2050. Note the aging of the population as the "baby boom" generation grows older.

Source: U.S. Census Bureau (1986). Age structure of the U.S. population in the 21st century. *Statistical Brief* (1–86). Washington, D.C.: U.S. Government Printing Office.

Treatment of Psychological Problems in Later Life

The availability and adequacy of medical care is of great importance to older adults, not only for treating disease but also for promoting physical health and psychological well-being. Because health behavior is critical to the quality of life among older adults, experts view health psychology and behavioral medicine as central components of medical care. In fact, a new subdiscipline of these fields called **behavioral gerontology** has been developed specifically for studying and treating the behavioral components of health and illness among older adults (Bromley, 1990).

The same psychological and biological therapies used to treat psychological disorders among younger adults can be used to treat these problems among the aged. Older adults may have misconceptions about psychotherapy. Thus, education about the process can be critical to its success. Some evidence also indicates that certain biological treatments may be more effective among older than among younger adults, particularly electroconvulsive therapy in the treatment of unremitting depression. In general, research is insufficient on the effectiveness of alternative treatments for mental disorders among older adults. Mental services designed specifically for this population also are inadequate.

Summary

Life cycle transitions are struggles in moving from one stage of adult development into a new one. We can only loosely identify the ages and events that best mark the transitions between the developmental tasks of adult life, but several theorists divide adult development into early, middle, and later life. Life cycle transitions are decidedly *not* mental disorders, but they are important to study because (1) they are a frequent focus of treatment, (2) they may be important to the etiology of specific emotional disorders, and (3) they suggest new ways of conceptualizing psychological problems.

The experiences associated with diverse life cycle transitions differ greatly, but there are some similarities. Conflict is one common theme. Many conflicts during life cycle transitions are interpersonal in nature; others reflect a search for identity, our global sense of self; and still others involve emotions.

The concept of adult development is a recent idea that was first highlighted by Erik Erikson's work on psychosocial development. In contrast, **family life cycle** theorists classify adult development in terms of transitions in family life, and other theorists emphasize the social as well as the psychological nature of adult development. All models must be considered with caution, however, because history, culture, and personal values strongly influence views of normality, and adult transitions are not as predictable as the models imply.

The transition to adult life begins late in the teen years and may continue into the middle twenties. The **identity crisis** is a central psychological conflict during the transition to adult life, a conflict epitomized by the question "Who am I?" Many things other than identity change during the transition to adulthood, however, including parent–child relationships, educational and career paths, and peer relationships. Emotional conflicts also mark the transition to adult life, as young people experience more intense and rapidly changing emotions than adults do.

KEY TERMS

- ageism
- behavioral gerontology
- behavioral marital therapy
- bereavement
- estrogen
- family life cycle
- family transitions
- gerontology
- grief
- heritability ratio
- identity crisis
- life cycle transitions
- menopause
- moratorium
- reciprocity

Family transitions are major changes in family relationships that typically involve the addition or loss of members of a family household. The family life cycle is a fairly predictable sequence of stages of family development such as marriage, the transition to parenthood, and the empty nest. Increased family conflict is a common consequence of all of these changes. Family members who have troubled relationships get caught in negative interactions. Ongoing family conflict is closely linked with individual psychological problems, especially among women. Some emotional distress may be better conceptualized within the context of family relationships, but classification of family types is only beginning.

Epidemiologic evidence on family transitions is collected by the U.S. Census Bureau. This evidence indicates that (a) about 90 percent of people get married, (b) five out of six married people have children, (c) an increasing proportion of children are born outside of marriage, and (d) divorce (which occurs in 50 percent of marriages) and remarriage are common transitions today. Family researchers often blame difficulties in negotiating family transitions on problems with communication, but broader family roles, such as traditional gender roles, also may be responsible for distressed family relationships. Social factors like poverty and even genetics also contribute to difficulties in family transitions. Both marital and family therapies and a variety of community action projects have been used to treat or prevent family problems. Some treatments show promise, but more innovation and more empirical evaluation are needed. One promising area is the use of marital and family therapy to treat individual psychological disorders.

Concerns about physical health increase for adults in their sixties, seventies, and eighties, and major social transitions also typically occur during these years. In addition, loss and **grief** are common experiences in the later years of life. **Bereavement** is grief in response to the death of a loved one that is commonly described as proceeding in a series of stages. According to available evidence, however, people do not need to experience grief in a fixed sequence of stages. Epidemiological evidence indicates that the prevalence of mental disorders is lower, not higher, among adults 65 years of age and older, but adults over the age of 65 do have the highest suicide rate of any age group.

One approach to classification distinguishes between the young-old, the old-old, and the oldest-old. Young-old adults are between the ages of 65 and 75, are in good health, and are active members of their communities. The old-old category is defined as adults between the ages of 75 and 85 who suffer from major physical, psychological, or social problems. The oldest-old are adults 85 years old or older. Approximately one out of every eight persons living in the United States is 65 years of age or older, and both the proportion and the absolute number of older Americans is expected to increase through the middle of the twenty-first century.

The most important biological contribution to psychological well-being in later life is good physical health, which is dependent on positive health behavior. Psychological contributions to adjustment in later life include the availability of close relationships and the experience of loss. Social factors linked with a happier transition include material well-being, participation in recreational activities, religious affiliation, and integration into the community. Finally, **behavioral gerontology** is a central component of medical care, and the same therapies can be used to treat psychological disorders among younger and older adults. Research is insufficient on the effectiveness of alternative treatments for older adults, however.

Critical Thinking

1. What are some of the benefits and limitations of a broad model like Erikson's stages of psychosocial development? Can psychologists ever hope to develop a clear model of adult development, or are the tasks of adult life too diverse to study systematically?

2. What are your personal thoughts about identity conflicts? Do you experience uncertainties about yourself or observe them in your friends? Do you think a moratorium is necessary for healthy development? Do you worry about people who vigorously pursue their childhood career paths?

3. Is communication overrated by psychologists? Are some things better left unsaid and some conflicts better left unresolved? Do gender differences exist in communication interests and styles?

4. What can the United States do to prepare for the aging of its population? Are the country's social, medical, and economic resources sufficient to provide for the coming "boom" in the population of older adults?

17

Mental Health
and the Law

You already have encountered many of the topics considered in this chapter—perhaps even in this morning's newspaper. A number of intriguing and often controversial issues are found at the intersection of abnormal psychology and the law. The *insanity defense* probably is the most familiar of these issues. Under certain circumstances, a person with a mental illness may be judged not guilty by reason of insanity. Perpetrators who are determined to be insane are not legally responsible for their actions, even though they have committed a crime. Instead of going to jail, insane defendants are likely to be confined in a mental institution. But what is insanity, and how does it differ from mental illness? As we address these and other questions in this chapter, you will learn that the legal system views abnormal behavior very differently from the way it is understood by mental health professionals.

Overview

▼ **One of several notes that John Hinckley wrote to actress Jodie Foster. Hinckley believed that he could win Foster's love by gaining notoriety, a delusion that apparently motivated him to attempt to assassinate former President Ronald Reagan.**

In addition to the insanity defense and related questions of criminal responsibility, the topics considered in this chapter include several issues related to mental hospitals, especially involuntary commitment, deinstitutionalization, and the rights of mental patients. The confinement of an individual against his or her will is a serious action that must balance broad societal values against the needs and rights of the individual. In order to gain a glimpse of the magnitude of this decision, recall that many political dissidents in the former Soviet Union were confined to institutions to "treat" their "mental illnesses."

We also discuss legal intervention in families based on mental health concerns, with an emphasis on the issues of child abuse and custody disputes after divorce. These legal cases can be vital to children's physical and emotional health. Concerns about serious mental illness are the exception, not the rule, in custody and abuse cases, but predictions about children's emotional well-being often are vital to the decisions that are reached.

Finally, we consider some of the legal responsibilities of mental health professionals to their clients, especially confidentiality and the limitations on it. Confidentiality and other topics in psychology and the law are not only of interest to legal and mental health professionals, but they also have broad implications for society. The manner in which we treat the most disturbed members of our society often marks the boundaries that define some of our most basic legal rights and responsibilities as citizens.

As a way of introducing the topic of mental health and the law, we consider one of the most infamous cases in which the insanity defense has been successfully used in recent years: the acquittal of John Hinckley. In 1981 Hinckley attempted to assassinate Ronald Reagan, the president of the United States. Our account is based on information in two detailed books on the assassination attempt (Clarke, 1990; Low, Jeffries, & Bonnie, 1986), and it is summarized in the following case study.

John Hinckley and the Insanity Defense

On March 30, 1981, John Hinckley stood outside of the Washington Hilton, drew a revolver from his raincoat pocket, and fired six shots at President Ronald Reagan. The president and three other men were wounded. The president rapidly recovered from his potentially fatal wound, but the presidential press secretary, James Brady, was permanently crippled by a shot that struck him just above the left eye. Hinckley was charged with attempted assassination, but his trial resulted in a verdict of "not guilty by reason of insanity."

Hinckley had never previously been convicted of a crime, and he came from a wealthy family. Hinckley had a history of unusual behavior, however, and had expressed violent intentions. He had read several books on famous assassinations and had joined the American Nazi Party. In fact, he was expelled from the Nazi Party in 1979 because of his continual advocacy of violence. A particular oddity was Hinckley's obsession with actress Jodie Foster, whom he had seen play the role of a child prostitute in the movie *Taxi Driver*. Apparently in an attempt to win her favor, Hinckley adopted much of the style of Foster's movie rescuer, Travis Bickle. This included acquiring weapons similar to those used by the movie character and stalking the president, much as the movie character had stalked a political candidate.

Hinckley repeatedly tried to contact Foster in real life and succeeded a few times, but his approaches were consistently rejected. He came to believe that the only way to win her over was through some dramatic action. Less than 2 hours before he shot the president, he completed a letter to Foster, which said:

Jodie, I would abandon this idea of getting Reagan in a second if I could only win your heart and live out the rest of my life with you, whether it be in total obscurity or whatever.

I will admit to you that the reason I'm going ahead with this attempt now is because I just cannot wait any longer to impress you. I've got to do something now to make you understand, in no uncertain terms, that I am doing all of this for your sake! By sacrificing my freedom and possibly my life, I hope to change your mind about me. This letter is being written only an hour before I leave for the Hilton Hotel. Jodie, I'm asking you to please look into your heart and at least give me the chance, with this historical deed, to gain your respect and love.

Hinckley's trial centered upon the question of his sanity, or as one author put it, whether he was "mad" or merely angry (Clarke, 1990). Numerous expert witnesses were called both by the defense and the prosecution to determine whether Hinckley was legally sane or insane. According to the federal law that was in effect at the time, the prosecution had to prove "beyond a reasonable doubt" that Hinckley was indeed sane. That is, the prosecution had to establish that mental disease had not either (1) created an irresistible impulse that made it impossible for Hinckley to resist attempting to kill the president, or (2) so impaired Hinckley's thinking that he did not appreciate the wrongfulness of his actions. (The burden of proof and the definition of insanity in the federal law subsequently were changed because of Hinckley's acquittal, as we discuss later in this chapter.)

All the prosecution's experts concluded that Hinckley was sane; all the defense's experts concluded that Hinckley was insane. The prosecution's experts called attention to the fact that Hinckley's actions were planned in advance and to Hinckley's awareness that his actions would have consequences, including possible imprisonment or death. He chose six deadly "devastator" bullets from an abundance of ammunition, and he fired them all accurately in less than 3 seconds. Defense experts emphasized his erratic behavior, particularly his obsession with Jodie Foster. One psychiatrist suggested, for example, that the president and other victims were merely "bit players" in Hinckley's delusion that through his "historic deed" he would be united with Foster in death.

Hinckley was found not guilty by reason of insanity. We don't know what factors influenced the jury to come to this decision or whether they found him insane based on the "irresistible impulse" or the "right from wrong" part of the insanity defense. In any event, the verdict meant that Hinckley received no prison sentence. Instead, he was ordered into a mental hospital to be treated in confinement for an unspecified period of time. At this time, Hinckley remains confined in St. Elizabeth's Hospital outside Washington, D.C. Theoretically, he could be released if he is considered by the hospital staff to no longer be dangerous to himself or to others. On the other hand, Hinckley could remain confined to the hospital for the rest of his life. In fact, he has unsuccessfully petitioned for release on several occasions. ∎

John Hinckley obviously was emotionally disturbed, and legally he was determined to be insane when he shot the president. As is illustrated in this case study, however, the insanity defense is an area of conflict between mental health and the law. One conflict involves the unreliability of expert testimony, as different mental health experts often disagree about a given defendant's sanity, thus creating a "battle of the experts" (Low, Jeffries, & Bonnie, 1986). A more basic conflict centers on the difference between the legal concept of sanity and the psychological concept of mental disorder, as we discuss shortly. An even more fundamental conflict involves the opposing assumptions that the legal and mental health systems make about the causes of and responsibility for human behavior; that is, free will versus determinism.

Free Will versus Determinism

Criminal law assumes that human behavior is the product of **free will**, the capacity to make choices and freely act upon them. Because behavior is assumed to be a product of free will, in the eyes of the law people are responsible for their own actions. When a person violates the law, the individual is held accountable. This is the legal concept known as **criminal responsibility**.

In contrast, mental health professionals assume that human behavior is determined by biological, psychological, and social forces. This assumption, known as **determinism**, is made by all psychologists (except humanists—see Chapter 2), but it is particularly obvious in the study of abnormal behavior. Mental disorders and the actions that stem from them are not viewed as choices but as conditions that are outside of voluntary control. Just as the concept of responsibility follows from an assumption of free will, a consequence of the deterministic view is that no one is ultimately "responsible" for his or her actions.

The assumption of determinism is not arbitrary. It is essential to make if psychology is to be a science. The causes of human behavior cannot be studied without assuming that behavior is determined by factors that can be measured and perhaps controlled. To draw an analogy, if meteorologists assumed that hurricanes were caused by "free will," they would have nothing to study. Imagine a weather forecast in which the meteorologist says, "Well, I wonder where Hurricane Bob will choose to head tonight." If meteorologists wish to have a scientific discipline, they must assume that the path of a hurricane is determined, that it is caused by forces that are potentially knowable. Similarly, free will is a concept that is foreign to psychologists when they are thinking as scientists, because it is an unscientific concept.

Assumptions about free will and determinism come into particular conflict in the case of the insanity defense. In the U.S. law, **insanity** is an exception to criminal responsibility. The legally insane individual is assumed not to be acting out of free will. As a result, like John Hinckley, the legally insane are not held to be criminally responsible for their actions. Ironically, the insanity defense thus reaffirms the legal system's view that people are responsible for their actions by calling attention to the rare exceptions when they are not.

Thus, debates about the insanity defense involve a broad conflict of philosophies, as well as differences about the specifics of a given case. Is human behavior a product of free will, or is it determined by biological, psychological, and social forces? Are people with mental disorders responsible for their actions, or are they not responsible?

IS MENTAL ILLNESS A MYTH?

American psychiatrist Thomas Szasz (1963; 1970) has adopted a provocative and controversial position about free will, mental illness, and the insanity defense. Szasz abandons the traditional deterministic view held by behavioral scientists. He instead adopts a humanistic philosophy that puts free will at the center of human behavior. In fact, Szasz asserts that the concept of mental illness is a myth. According to Szasz, abnormal behavior must be defined relative to some social or moral standard. Because there is no objective standard, there can be no objective mental disease. Thus, Szasz argues that mental disorders are subjective "problems in living," not objective diseases.

The logical conclusion of Szasz's view of free will is that all people—even people with emotional disorders—*are* responsible for their actions. Consistent with this position, Szasz has argued that the insanity defense should be abolished (Szasz, 1963). It also follows from Szasz's views that other exceptions made for mentally disturbed people in the legal system should be eliminated—for example, commitment to mental hospitals against their will (Moore, 1975).

RIGHTS AND RESPONSIBILITIES

In arguing for a broader concept of responsibility, Szasz also fights for broader recognition of human dignity and individual rights. In the law, rights and responsibilities go hand in hand. When responsibilities are lost, rights are lost too. When responsibilities are assumed, rights are gained. Thus, while opposing the insanity defense, Szasz simultaneously supports greater recognition of the rights of mental patients who become involved in either the legal or the mental health systems. The basic, human rights of mental patients sometimes have been trampled on, and much concern has been raised about protecting them better. Szasz argues that the mentally ill should be treated identically to the mentally healthy in terms of both social responsibility and social dignity.

Szasz's concerns about the "myth of mental illness" extend beyond the individual to broad social abuses. He asserts that the concept of mental illness can be invoked to obscure the logic of behavior that runs counter to social standards and to blame social deviance on disease instead of on society. This clearly happened in the former Soviet Union, where some dissidents were judged insane for holding political beliefs that conflicted with those of the Communist Party. Their "diagnosis" justified their confinement to mental hospitals. Szasz asserts that similar, albeit far more subtle abuses of the "myth of mental illness" occur in the United States.

Not surprisingly, Szasz's view that mental illness is a myth is generally seen as extreme. Whatever the reaction to his positions, however, Szasz has contributed greatly to issues in mental health and the law by cutting to the heart of philosophical assumptions. Differences in basic assumptions about free will and determinism are an inevitable source of conflict between the legal and mental health systems, and nowhere is the deterministic philosophy of psychology more evident than in its concepts of mental illness. Differences in views about the extent to which mental illness impairs free will in turn underscore debates about the rights and responsibilities of people suffering from a mental disorder. As we will see in numerous examples in this chapter, the core of the dilemma is how to reconcile concepts of individual rights and responsibilities, which follow from an assumption of free will, with the deterministic view that is at the core of a scientific approach to understanding human behavior.

▲ Psychiatrist Thomas Szasz has called attention to fundamental conflicts about individual rights and responsibilities in the philosophies of the legal and the mental health systems.

Mental Health, Criminal Responsibility, and Procedural Rights

Criminal law assumes that mental disorders sometimes may affect an individual's capacity to exercise his or her rights and responsibilities. Defendants who are judged *incompetent to stand* *trial* are thought to be unable to exercise their right to participate in their own trial defense. Defendants who are found not guilty by reason of insanity are determined not to be criminally responsibility for their actions. We consider each of these issues in this section.

The Insanity Defense

The idea that mental disability should limit criminal responsibility dates back to ancient Greek and Hebrew traditions and was evident in early English law. Records indicate cases where English kings pardoned murderers because of "madness," and later judicial decisions similarly excused some criminals who were "madmen" or "idiots" (Reisner & Slobogin, 1990). The emerging rationale underlying many of these insanity acquittals was that the defendant lacked the capacity to distinguish "good from evil" or what eventually became known as the inability to distinguish right from wrong. This ground for the **insanity defense** was codified in 1843, after Daniel M'Naghten was found not guilty of murder by reason of insanity.

M'Naghten was a British subject who claimed that the "voice of God" had ordered him to kill Prime Minister Robert Peel, but who mistakenly murdered Peel's private secretary instead. His insanity acquittal raised considerable controversy, and caused the House of Lords to devise the following insanity test:

> To establish a defense on the ground of insanity, it must be clearly proved that, at the time of the committing of the act, the party accused was laboring under such a defect of reason, from disease of the mind, as not to know the nature and quality of the act he was doing; or, if he did know it, that he did not know he was doing what was wrong. [*Regina* v. *M'Naghten*, 8 Eng. Rep. 718, 722 (1843)]

Subsequently known as the *M'Naghten test*, this rule clearly articulated the "right from wrong" principle for determining insanity. If at the time a criminal act is committed, a mental disease or defect prevents a criminal from knowing the wrongfulness of his or her actions, the criminal can be found to be *not guilty by reason of insanity* (NGRI). The "right from wrong" ground established in the M'Naghten case continues to be the major focus of the insanity defense in U.S. law today. However, subsequent developments first broadened and later narrowed the grounds for determining insanity.

After M'Naghten, the insanity defense was broadened in the United States when, later in the nineteenth century, a second ground for determining insanity was introduced—the so-called *irresistible impulse test* . The irresistible impulse test indicated that defendants also could be found insane if they were unable to control their actions because of mental disease. *Parsons* v. *State* was one of the first cases in which the irresistible impulse test was adopted [81 Ala. 577, 596, 2 So. 854 (1886)]. In this 1886 case, an Alabama court ruled that defendants could be judged insane if they could not "avoid doing the act in question" because of mental disease. The rationale for the irresistible impulse test was that when people are unable to control their behavior, the law can have no effect on deterring crimes. *Deterrence*, the idea that people will avoid committing crimes because they fear being punished for them, is a major public policy goal of criminal law. In the *Parsons* case, however, the court reasoned that convicting people for acts that they could not control would serve no deterrence purpose. In such cases, a finding of NGRI was justified.

A 1954 ruling by the Washington, D.C. federal circuit court in *Durham* v. *United States* further broadened the insanity defense [214 F.2d 862 (D.C. Cir. 1954)]. Known as the *product test*, the *Durham* opinion indicated that an accused is not criminally responsible if his unlawful act was the product of mental disease or defect. The ruling made no attempt to define either "product" or "mental disease." In fact, the terms were purposely designed to be very broad. The vague product test was justified as a way of allowing mental health professionals wide discretion in using their expertise in determining insanity and testifying in court.

Problems arose in applying the product test, however, including the fact that some mental health professionals decided to include psychopathy (antisocial personality disorder in DSM-IV) as one of the "mental diseases" that could be used as a basis for an insanity defense. This created a circular problem: Antisocial personality disorder is defined primarily by a pattern of criminal behavior, yet the same criminal behavior could be used to substantiate that the perpetrator was insane (Campbell, 1990). This and other problems with the definition of mental disease under the product test came to a halt when the *Durham* decision was overruled in 1972 (Reisner & Slobogin, 1990).

In 1955, a year after the original *Durham* decision, the American Law Institute drafted model legislation designed to address various problems with the previous rules for determining insanity. The model legislation is important because it subsequently was adopted by the majority of states. The rule indicates that

> A person is not responsible for criminal conduct if at the time of such conduct as a result of mental disease or defect he lacks substantial capacity either to appreciate the criminality [wrongfulness] of his conduct or to conform his conduct to the requirements of the law.

This definition of insanity combines the M'Naghten rule and the irresistible impulse test, although it softens the requirements somewhat with the term "substantial capacity." (Compare this with the language used in the M'Naghten rule.) A second component of the American Law Institute's model legislation, which also has been enacted by many states, excluded a history of criminal behavior from being used to define "mental disease or defect." This eliminates the problem of circularity caused by the antisocial personality disorder diagnosis.

The most recent developments in the law governing the insanity defense occurred as a result of the acquittal of John Hinckley. Following the controversy over this case, both the American Bar Association and the American Psychiatric Association recommended the elimination of the "irresistible impulse" component of the insanity defense. These organizations judged this strand of the insanity defense to be more controversial and unreliable than the "right from wrong" standard (Mackay, 1988). Consistent with these recommendations, federal legislation was changed in 1984 and defined the insanity defense as follows:

> It is an affirmative defense to a prosecution under any federal statute that, at the time of the commission of acts constituting the offense, the defendant, as a result of severe mental disease or defect, was unable to appreciate the nature and quality or the wrongfulness of his acts. Mental disease or defect does not otherwise constitute a defense (Title 18 of the United States Code).

GUILTY BUT MENTALLY ILL

Several states have since echoed this change in federal law by enacting similar legislation. Another change prompted by the Hinckley case was the promotion of the new verdict of *guilty but mentally ill* (GBMI), which has now been enacted by about a quarter of all states (Mackay, 1988). Defendants can be found to be guilty but mentally ill if it is demonstrated that they are guilty of the crime, were mentally ill at the time it was committed, but were not legally insane at that time. The GBMI verdict was designed as a compromise to NGRI. The GBMI verdict holds defendants criminally responsible for their crimes but acknowledges their mental disorder and helps ensure that they receive treatment. Thus, a defendant found GBMI can be sentenced in the same manner as any criminal, but the court can order treatment for the mental disorder as well. Some evidence indicates, however, that rather than replace NGRI verdicts, the GBMI verdict is most often used in cases in which defendants simply would have been found guilty in the past (Smith & Hall, 1982).

Recent developments clearly represent a move toward restricting the insanity defense. The furor surrounding the high-profile Hinckley case was not unlike the controversy that surrounded the high-profile M'Naghten case more than 100 years earlier. Ironically, the Hinckley case also led to revisions in the insanity defense that resemble the original M'Naghten test (Mackay, 1988). As it was for a time after 1843, the most common contemporary standard for determining legal insanity is the inability to distinguish right from wrong.

BURDEN OF PROOF

In addition to the definition of insanity, the *burden of proof* substantially influences the meaning and likely success of the insanity defense. Under U.S. criminal law, the defendant is assumed to be innocent until proven guilty "beyond a reasonable doubt." The burden of proof thus rests with the prosecution, and the *standard of proof* is a very high one—beyond a reasonable doubt. But must the prosecution also prove beyond a reasonable doubt that a defendant is sane?

In fact, about one-third of all states require the prosecution to prove a defendant's sanity beyond a reasonable doubt, and until 1984 this also was the practice in federal courts. In the Hinckley trial, the prosecution was obliged to prove that Hinckley was sane beyond a reasonable doubt, a case they failed to make. Changes implemented in federal law following the Hinckley case shifted the burden of proof, so that in federal courts the defense now must prove defendants' insanity rather than the prosecution having to prove their sanity. Insanity must be proven by the standard of "clear and convincing evidence," a stringent standard but not as exacting as "beyond a reasonable doubt." The majority of states also now place the burden of proof on the defense, but the standard of proof typically is less restrictive than that found in federal law—"the preponderance of the evidence." Thus, the insanity defense has been narrowed even further by shifting the burden of proof from the prosecution to the defense in federal law and in many states (Reisner & Slobogin, 1990).

DEFINING "MENTAL DISEASE OR DEFECT"

An issue of obvious importance to the mental health professions is the precise meaning of the term "mental disease or defect" that is used in one form or another in all the legal definitions of insanity. The American Law Institute's proposal specifically excluded antisocial personality disorder, but would any other diagnosis listed in the DSM qualify? The 1984 federal legislation indicated that the mental disease must be "severe," but what does this mean?

The question of which mental disorders qualify for the "mental disease or defect" component of the insanity defense is unresolved, although the legal definition of "mental disease" generally is more restrictive than the mental health definition (Campbell, 1990). Some legal and mental health professionals would allow any disorder listed in the DSM to qualify for the insanity defense, however, provided that the other criteria for the legal definition of insanity also were met (LaFave & Scott, 1986). Others have argued that some especially difficult circumstances should qualify defendants for the "mental disease or defect" component of the insanity defense, even if the problems are not listed as DSM diagnoses (see Further Thoughts on battered women later in this chapter). Still other commentators would sharply restrict the mental diseases or defects that can be used as a part of the insanity defense. One suggestion is to confine the insanity defense to mental retardation, schizophrenia, mood disorders, and cog-

nitive disorders, excluding cognitive disorders induced by substance use or abuse (Gerard, 1987). Finally, the American Psychiatric Association has stated that mental diseases or defects are limited to "those severely abnormal mental conditions that grossly and demonstrably impair a person's perception or understanding of reality that are not attributable primarily to the voluntary ingestion of alcohol or other psychoactive substances" (APA, 1983).

MENTAL HEALTH PROFESSIONALS AS EXPERT WITNESSES

Whether testifying about a defendant's mental disorders or about other mental health matters, mental health experts for the prosecution and the defense often present conflicting testimony. Such a "battle of the experts" can be an embarrassment to the profession and can raise questions about professional ethics. For example, a commonly asked question is whether an expert's testimony has been "bought" by one side or the other. This possibility sometimes seems feasible to juries when they learn about the fees paid to expert witnesses.

In fact, some psychologists have argued that mental health professionals should not be allowed to offer expert testimony at all. These critics assert that the mental health questions posed by the legal system cannot be answered with adequate reliability or validity, nor do mental health experts help judges and juries reach more accurate decisions (Faust & Ziskin, 1988). Reflect for a moment about the many concerns about diagnostic reliability raised throughout this textbook. If mental health professionals often disagree about the presence or absence of a carefully defined mental disorder, is it any wonder that they frequently disagree about the presence or absence of a poorly defined concept like insanity? And if the reliability of the "insanity diagnosis" is poor, is it unethical for an expert witness to testify about its presence or absence?

In considering these questions, it must be recognized that the procedures and goals of the legal system differ from those familiar to psychologists. Expert witnesses are expected to offer informed opinion, not to present the "truth" to the court. Lawyers expect questions to be raised about the credibility of an expert witness's testimony, and they also expect conflicting testimony to be presented by the opposing side's experts (Fitch, Petrella, & Wallace, 1987). The duty of the attorneys for the prosecution and for the defense is to present the most convincing case for their side, which is not the same thing as presenting the most objective case. Although courtroom procedure rules do not excuse inaccurate "expert testimony," they do leave room for testimony even in the face of imperfect empirical evidence. The end product of a trial is a judgment about truth made by a judge or a jury, not the establishment of a scientific fact.

Mental health professionals who act as expert witnesses serve their profession and the legal system best if their testimony adheres closely to their expertise. In insanity cases, for example, the mental health expert's job is to testify about defendants' mental health and state of mind, not to determine their sanity. The determination of a defendant's sanity is a decision to be made by a judge or a jury, not by the expert witness. In fact, the American Psychological Association specifically recommends that "since it is not within the professional competence of psychologists to offer conclusions on matters of law, psychologists should resist pressure to offer such conclusions" (Monahan, 1980). A lawyer may ask for the expert's opinion about the "ultimate issue" of insanity, but expert witnesses have an obligation not to answer such questions of law because these questions exceed their expertise.

USE AND CONSEQUENCES OF THE INSANITY DEFENSE

Given the tremendous controversy and important philosophical issues that surround the insanity defense, you might be surprised to learn how infrequently it is used. Evidence suggests that it is put forward in only about 1 percent of all criminal cases in the United States, and only about 25 percent of defendants who offer the defense are actually found to be NGRI (Callahan et al., 1991; Steadman, Pantle, & Pasewark, 1983). In addition, over 90 percent of these acquittals result from plea bargains rather than jury trials (Callahan et al., 1991). In England, where the M'Naghten rule still stands, the insanity defense is virtually nonexistent, being used in perhaps a handful of cases each year (Mackay, 1988).

The question also arises as to whether a successful insanity defense results in a shorter amount of time spent incarcerated. Some defendants found NGRI have been incarcerated in mental institutions for much shorter periods of time than they would have served if they had been sentenced to jail. Many defendants have actually been incarcerated for much longer periods of time, however—yet another reminder that rights are lost when responsibilities are not assumed. On the average, however, defendants who are found NGRI spend approximately the same amount of time confined in an institution as they would have if they had been given a prison sentence instead (Pantle, Pasewark, & Steadman, 1980).

Competence and Criminal Proceedings

Another important link between mental health and criminal law is the issue of competence. **Competence** concerns defendants' ability to understand the legal proceedings that are taking place against them and to participate in their own defense. If defendants have no such understanding—that is, if they are *incompetent*—the legal proceedings must be suspended until such time as they can be understood by the defendant. Competence has been defined as follows by the U.S. Supreme Court in *Dusky* v. *United States* [363 U.S. 402, 80 S. Ct. 788, 4 L. Ed. 2d. 824 (1960)]:

> The test must be whether he [the defendant] has sufficient present ability to consult with his attorney with a reasonable degree of rational understanding and a rational as well as factual understanding of proceedings against him.

Several features of the legal definition of competence should be noted. First, competence refers to the defendant's current mental state, whereas the insanity defense refers to the defendant's state of mind at the time of committing a crime. Second, as with insanity, the legal definition of incompetence is not the same as the psychologist's definition of mental illness. Even a psychotic individual may possess enough rational understanding to be deemed competent in the eyes of the law. Third, competence refers to defendants' ability to understand criminal proceedings, not their willingness to participate in them. For example, a defendant who simply refuses to consult with a court-appointed lawyer is not incompetent. Finally, the "reasonable degree" of understanding needed to establish competence is generally acknowledged to be fairly low. That is, only those who suffer from severe emotional disorders are likely to be found incompetent (Melton et al., 1987).

TABLE 17–1

Abilities Related to Competence to Stand Trial

Competence to stand trial may involve the defendant's ability to:

1. Understand his or her current legal situation.
2. Understand the charges against him or her.
3. Understand the facts relevant to his case.
4. Understand the legal issues and procedures in his case.
5. Understand legal defenses available in his behalf.
6. Understand the dispositions, pleas, and penalties possible.
7. Appraise likely outcomes.
8. Appraise the roles of defense counsel, the prosecuting attorney, the judge, the jury, the witnesses, and the defendant.
9. Identify and locate witnesses.
10. Relate to defense counsel.
11. Trust and communicate relevantly with his counsel.
12. Comprehend instructions and advice.
13. Make decisions after receiving advice.
14. Maintain a collaborative relationship with his attorney and help plan legal strategy.
15. Follow testimony for contradictions or errors.
16. Testify relevantly and be cross-examined if necessary.
17. Challenge prosecution witnesses.
18. Tolerate stress at the trial and while awaiting trial.
19. Refrain from irrational and unmanageable behavior during the trial.
20. Disclose pertinent facts surrounding the alleged offense.
21. Protect himself and utilize the legal safeguards available to him.

Source: Group for Advancement of Psychiatry (1974). *Misuse of psychiatry in the criminal courts: Competency to stand trial* (pp. 896–897).

Unlike the various definitions of insanity, the legal definition of incompetence contains no reference to "mental disease or defect." The role of expert witnesses in determining competency is therefore quite different from their role in determining sanity. The evaluation focuses much more on specific behaviors and capacities than on DSM disorders. One listing of the specific capacities that should be considered in a competency evaluation has been compiled by the Group for the Advancement of

Psychiatry. These areas of inquiry are summarized in Table 17–1.

The most common finding of incompetence occurs when defendants are found incompetent to stand trial, but the issue of incompetence may arise at several stages of the criminal process. Defendants must be competent to understand the *Miranda* warning issued during their arrest. (The *Miranda* warning details the suspect's rights to remain silent and to have an attorney present during police questioning.) Defendants also must be competent at the time of their sentencing, which takes place after they have been convicted of a crime. Finally, recent rulings indicate that defendants sentenced to death must be competent at the time of their execution, or the death sentence cannot be carried out.

Many more people accused of crimes are institutionalized because of findings of incompetence than because of insanity rulings. However, incompetence has received far less attention from both legal and mental health scholars. This may reflect the fact that competence determinations raise few broad social and philosophical issues, unlike the insanity defense.

The goal of ensuring fairness forms the rationale for requiring that defendants are competent before criminal actions can proceed. Unfortunately, determinations of incompetence have sometimes produced what would seem to be very unfair results. Defendants who are judged to be incompetent are confined to mental institutions until they are competent to understand the criminal proceedings, at which time the proceedings resume. In some cases, the length of time that defendants have been confined while awaiting their return to competence has greatly exceeded the time that they would have served if they had been convicted. Although there is little doubt that defendants who are found incompetent have severe mental disorders, people who are hospitalized because of incompetence do not always receive the same protections as people who are hospitalized through civil commitment procedures, the topic we turn to next.

Mental Hospitals and the Law

Mental health issues are important in civil law as well as in criminal law. In particular, the involuntary hospitalization of the severely mentally impaired raises questions of major importance in civil law. Three issues are of special relevance: (1) civil commitment, the legal process of sending someone to a mental hospital against his or her will; (2) patients' rights, especially their right to treatment, their right to treatment in the least restrictive alternative environment, and their right to refuse certain treatments; and (3) deinstitutionalization, the movement to treat patients in their communities instead of in mental hospitals. We begin our consideration of involuntary hospitalization with a brief review of the history of mental hospitals in the United States.

Historical Overview of Mental Hospitals in the United States

In 1842, the famous British author Charles Dickens toured the United States and visited several mental institutions while on his tour. In *American Notes and Pictures from Italy* (1842/1970), he wrote the following about one of the institutions that he visited:

> I cannot say that I derived much comfort from the inspection of this charity. The different wards might have been cleaner and better ordered; I saw nothing of that salutary system which had impressed me so favorably elsewhere; and everything had a lounging, listless, madhouse air, which was very painful. The moping idiot, cowering down with long dishevelled hair; the gibbering maniac, with his hideous laugh and pointed finger; the vacant eye, the fierce wild face, the gloomy picking of the hands and lips, and munching of the nails: there they were all without disguise, in naked ugliness and horror. In the dining-room, a bare, dull, dreary place, with nothing for the eye to rest on but the empty walls, a woman was locked up alone. She was bent, they told me, on committing suicide. If anything could have strengthened her in her resolution, it would certainly have been the insupportable monotony of such an existence. (p. 93)

Such cruel care of the mentally disturbed has been a problem throughout the course of history. In Europe during the Middle Ages, "lunatics" and "idiots," as the mentally ill and mentally retarded were commonly called, were given marginal care. Some were kept at home by their families, while others roamed freely as beggars. Mentally disturbed people who were violent or appeared dangerous often were imprisoned with criminals. A few were tried as witches. Those who could not subsist on their own were housed in almshouses for the poor.

In the 1600s and 1700s, "insane asylums" were established to house the mentally disturbed. The first asylum in the United States was founded in Williamsburg, Virginia, in 1773. Early asylums were little more than human warehouses, but as the nineteenth century began, the **moral treatment** movement led to improved conditions in at least some mental hospitals. Founded on a basic respect for human dignity and the belief that humanistic care would help to relieve mental illness, moral treatment reform efforts were instituted by leading mental health professionals such as Benjamin Rush in America, Phillipe Pinel in France, and William Tuke in England. Rather than simply confining mental patients, moral treatment offered support, care, and a degree of freedom.

Many of the large mental institutions that still dot the U.S. countryside were built in the nineteenth century to fulfill the philosophy of moral treatment. In the middle of the 1800s, mental health advocate Dorothea Dix gave particular impetus to this trend. Dix argued that treating the mentally ill in mental hospitals was both more humane and more economical than caring for them haphazardly in their communities, and she urged that special facilities be built to house mental patients. Dix and like-minded reformers were successful in their efforts. In 1830, there were only four public mental hospitals in the United States that housed a combined total of under 200 patients. By 1880, there were 75 public mental hospitals, with a total population of more than 35,000 residents (Torrey, 1988).

Despite laudable intentions, few patients were cured. As the moral treatment movement faded, many mental institutions simply became larger and more grotesque human warehouses. The number of patients living in mental hospitals continued to grow rapidly in the first half of the twentieth century, and the problems of large mental institutions grew along with their populations. The squalid conditions in state mental hospitals began to be revealed to the public shortly after World War II. Many conscientious objec-

▲ **Dorothea Dix (1802–1887) was an early advocate for the humane treatment of the mentally ill. Many mental institutions were built during the late 1800s due in large part to Dix's efforts.**

tors who worked in mental hospitals instead of serving in the armed forces revealed the horrors that they had observed to politicians and the popular media (Torrey, 1988).

As can be seen in Figure 17–1, the number of patients living in mental hospitals began to shrink dramatically in the 1950s. This was due in large part to the discovery of antipsychotic medications and to the deinstitutionalization movement—the attempt to care for the mentally ill in their communities—which owed no small debt to the public outcry started by the World War II conscientious objectors. Even today, however, some large institutions continue to exist and to offer inadequate care. Moreover, the laudable deinstitutionalization movement, which had the opposite goals of Dix's institutionalization efforts, has many problems, as we will soon see.

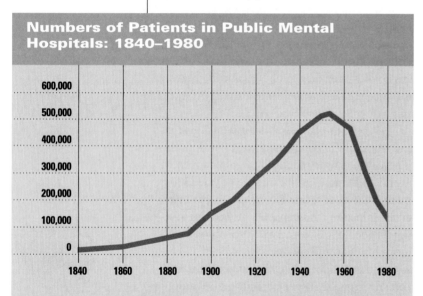

Numbers of Patients in Public Mental Hospitals: 1840–1980

FIGURE 17-1: This figure charts the changing numbers of patients living in mental hospitals. Note the steady increase from the last part of the 1800s, when large mental hospitals were built, and the steady decline associated with the development of antipsychotic medication and deinstitutionalization from the 1950s to the present.

Source: E.F. Torrey (1988). *Nowhere to go: The tragic odyssey of the homeless mentally ill,* p. 3. New York: HarperCollins.

Libertarianism versus Paternalism in Treating Mental Patients

What are society's legal and philosophical rationales for hospitalizing people against their will? As a general matter, debates about involuntary hospitalization highlight the philosophical tension between *libertarian* views, which emphasize protecting the rights of the individual, and *paternalist* approaches, which emphasize the state's duty to protect its citizens. This tension is evident in contemporary rationales for committing mental patients to institutions. For example, the involuntary hospitalization of someone who appears to be dangerous to others serves a protective, paternalist goal. Yet civil libertarians note that *preventive detention*—confinement before a crime is committed—can lead to substantial abuse. With the exception of **civil commitment** —the involuntary hospitalization of the mentally ill—our laws prohibit the confinement of someone simply on the suspicion that he or she is about to commit a crime, no matter how strong or how realistic this suspicion may be.

Many scholars have become embroiled in the debate between the libertarian and paternalist philosophies. Some of these scholars recognize few justifications for civil commitment (Durham & LaFond, 1988), whereas others argue that many such justifications exist (Torrey, 1988). Despite a recent swing of the pendulum back in the direction of paternalism, the major trend over the past several decades has been a libertarian one, including the closer scrutiny of civil commitment procedures, an increasing recognition of patients' rights, and the deinstitutionalization of patients from mental hospitals. Note that this increased concern for patient rights has run parallel to the increased emphasis on their criminal responsibility in the insanity defense. Rights and responsibilities do indeed go hand in hand.

Civil Commitment

American law contains two broad rationales for civil commitment. The first rationale is based on the state's *parens patriae* authority, the philosophy that the government has a humanitarian responsibility to care for its weaker members. (The literal translation of the Latin phrase *parens patriae* is the "state as parent.") The concept of *parens patriae* dates back to ancient Rome and has influenced U.S. law through English traditions. Under the state's *parens patriae* authority, civil commitment may be justified when the mentally disturbed are either dangerous to themselves or unable to care for themselves (Myers, 1983–84). In addition to the confinement of the mentally ill, the concept of *parens patriae* is used to justify the state's supervision of minors and physically incapacitated adults.

The second rationale for civil commitment is based on the state's *police power*—its duty to protect the public safety, health, and welfare. Our government restricts individual liberties for the public good in many ways. For the safety of others, we are restricted from yelling "Fire!" in a crowded theater or from driving an automobile at 100 miles an hour. The civil commitment of people who are dangerous to others is justified by similar police power rationales. Civil commitment obviously involves a dramatic restriction in individual liberty, however, as it constitutes confinement without having committed a crime. Thus, this severe restriction on individual liberty requires the highest degree of scrutiny.

The police power rationales for civil commitment have been invoked throughout the history of U.S. law, as the "furiously insane" could be detained in order to prevent them from doing harm to others even in Colonial times (Myers, 1983–84). Commitment under *parens patriae* rationales was virtually unknown in the United States until large mental institutions were built in the 1800s. Some evidence suggests that civil commitment standards were very lax during the same historical period that mental institutions were being built. For example, an 1842 New York state statute required the confinement of all "lunatics" irrespective of whether they were dangerous or able to care for themselves. The law commissioned "assessors" to round up lunatics and have them confined for a period of no less than 6 months (Reisner & Slobogin, 1990).

Legislation that more carefully defined the grounds for civil commitment and protected at least some of the rights of the mentally ill was not adopted until the latter part of the nineteenth century; its adoption was due in large part to the efforts of Mrs. E.P.W. Packard (Myers, 1983–84). Mrs. Packard was committed to a mental hospital by her husband under an Illinois law that allowed a man to commit his children or his wife to a mental hospital against their will and without the usual evidence of insanity. The commitment of Mrs. Packard was questionable at best. In presenting evidence in favor of her commitment, for example, one doctor noted that Mrs. Packard was rational but she was a "religious bigot" (Reisner & Slobogin, 1990). Following

her release 3 years after being committed, Mrs. Packard campaigned to revise commitment standards to prevent such abuses, and she succeeded in influencing the laws in many states.

Following the reforms begun by Mrs. Packard, civil commitment laws remained largely unchanged from the late 1800s until the 1960s and 1970s. During recent years, several notable cases set important precedents that have affected civil commitment laws and procedures. These developments are discussed shortly, but first we consider civil commitment procedures and philosophies in more detail.

GROUNDS AND PROCEDURES

Most states provide two types of civil commitment procedures: emergency procedures and formal procedures. *Emergency commitment procedures* allow an acutely disturbed individual to be temporarily confined in a mental hospital, typically for no more than a few days. Various states designate physicians, mental health professionals, or even police officers as being qualified to determine whether an emergency commitment is required. Obviously, such action is taken only when a mental disorder is very serious, and the risk that the patient is dangerous to self or others appears to be very high.

Formal commitment procedures can lead to involuntary hospitalization that lasts for much longer periods of time than an emergency commitment, and it can be ordered only by a court. An adversary hearing must be available to mental patients who object to involuntary hospitalization; all of their usual due process rights must be protected in formal commitment procedures, and the need for hospitalization must be demonstrated by "clear and convincing" evidence. Furthermore, once an individual is involuntarily committed to a mental institution through formal procedures, his or her case often is automatically reviewed after a set period of time— for example, every 6 months.

Because civil commitment is a matter of state law, the specific grounds for involuntary hospitalization vary from state to state. Still, three grounds tend to dominate commitment laws: (1) inability to care for self, (2) being dangerous to self, and (3) being dangerous to others. The broadest of these is *inability to care for self*. In some states, mental patients may be hospitalized against their will if they are unable to care for themselves adequately in the community or if they do not have family or friends who will care for them. The intention of this commitment standard is benevolent, but because it has been abused in some cases, newly articulated patient rights have been used to attack the "inability to care for self" ground for civil commitment (Durham & LaFond, 1988). Debates continue in courtrooms and in state legislatures. Is it better to be paternalist and sacrifice some individual rights by involuntarily committing mental patients who do not want but who clearly need inpatient treatment? Or is it better to protect civil liberties by not committing patients who obviously are severely disturbed but who manage to survive on their own outside of mental hospitals?

The two other grounds for justifying civil commitment generally have not been attacked on philosophical grounds. Few civil libertarians object to hospitalizing people against their will when they clearly are either *dangerous to self* or *dangerous to others*, provided that the danger is "imminent." Thus, a commonly accepted standard for civil commitment is "clear and convincing evidence of imminent danger to oneself or others." Questions have been raised about the ability of mental health professionals to predict dangerousness, however.

PREDICTING DANGEROUSNESS AND SUICIDAL RISK

The first question to ask about civil commitment and the prediction of dangerousness is: Are mentally disturbed people more dangerous than other people? To many laypeople, the obvious answer to this question is yes. Until recently, however, psychological research has suggested the opposite answer. John Monahan (1992), a psychologist and law professor who is the leading authority on the prediction of dangerousness, once concluded that there was no evidence that violence and mental illness were related. Recently, he has modified his position.

Monahan (1992) argues that new and methodologically sophisticated research suggests that violence and serious mental illness are related after all. In addressing the question about the link between violence and mental illness, he examines both the rate of violence among the mentally ill and the rate of mental disorder among criminals. Whichever way the question is asked, evidence supports the conclusion that the two problems are associated. The prevalence of bipolar disorder, major depression, and schizophrenia

has been found to be several times as high among prison inmates as among the general population. Similarly, the rate of violence is about 5 times higher among people diagnosed with one of these major mental disorders than among those with no diagnosis. People who abuse alcohol or drugs are even more likely to engage in violent behavior (see Table 17–2).

Although the finding of increased risk of dangerousness to others is important, this evidence does not directly translate into a policy of confining the mentally ill, for several reasons. For one, the data indicate that the risk for violence among the mentally ill is far lower than is publicly perceived. In fact, approximately 90 percent of the mentally disturbed are not violent (Monahan, 1992). Second, other research indicates that although current psychotic symptoms predict violence, a past history of psychosis is not associated with an increased risk (Link, Cullen, & Andrews, 1990). Finally and most importantly, numerous factors other than mental illness are known to predict an increased risk for violence, but they obviously do not justify involuntary confinement. For example, research has documented that people who live in poverty or who have a history of criminal behavior are more likely to be violent. Would anyone suggest that such a statistical risk justifies involuntary hospitalization?

Clinical Assessment and the Prediction of Dangerousness If mental illness is a relatively poor and philosophically problematic predictor of violence, the second question becomes: Can clinical assessments of the dangerousness of mental patients improve prediction? Researchers have concluded that clinical predictions that someone will be violent are wrong approximately 2 out of 3 three times (Ennis & Emery, 1978; Monahan, 1981; see Research Close-up). That is, the false-positive rate of a prediction of violence is about 67 percent. The clinical prediction of violence is sufficiently inaccurate that several commentators have asserted that it is unethical for mental health experts to offer predictions about dangerousness to the courts (Ewing, 1991; Foot, 1990; Melton et al., 1987).

In arguing in support of the expert prediction of dangerousness, other commentators have noted that the prediction of violence is above chance levels despite inaccuracies in prediction (Monahan, 1981). At first glance, being

▲ John Monahan, a psychologist at the University of Virginia School of Law, is a leader in the study of psychology and the law. Monahan is particularly noted for his work on the prediction of violence.

The Accuracy of Predictions of Violence to Others

Research has concluded that the clinical prediction of violence to others is inaccurate, but most studies of this topic are older and are flawed in various ways. Many studies, for example, assumed that the clinician had predicted violence only in cases where the patient was committed to a hospital. Clinicians do not commit every patient who they fear may be violent, however, and they sometimes commit patients who have a low likelihood of violence. Some dangerous patients allow themselves to be hospitalized voluntarily, moreover. Another problem with past research is the measurement of subsequent violence. Studies have used police reports, court records, and medical files to assess subsequent violence, but many acts of violence are not documented in these official records.

A recent study by Lidz, Mulvey, and Gardner (1993) sought to assess clinical predictions of violence more thoroughly than past research studies had done. These investigators studied 714 cases seen in the psychiatric emergency room of a large teaching hospital in an urban area. Half the cases were predicted to have some potential for violence by two clinicians who interviewed them (including at least one psychiatrist), and the other half were comparison cases that were not predicted to be violent by the clinicians. Clinicians were asked directly about their predictions, and the two groups of patients were matched on their age, sex, and race as well as on whether they were admitted to the hospital. Thus, any differences in actual violence between the groups had to be a result of the predictions, not of either the background factors or whether the patient was hospitalized.

Another innovation in methodology was to interview patients and someone who knew them about subsequent episodes of violence rather than to rely solely upon official records (although these records were also examined). At least three interviews were conducted with all 714 cases in the 6 months following their contact with the emergency room. Violence was judged to have occurred if, according to any source of information, a patient laid hands on another person with a violent intent or threatened another person with a weapon.

The investigators found that 53 percent of the predicted cases engaged in a subsequent episode of violence versus 36 percent of the comparison cases, a statistically significant difference. Clinicians were equally good at predicting violence among members of different ethnic groups and among people of different ages. Predictions of violence among women were less accurate than predictions for men, however. In fact, the clinical predictions of violence among women were no better than chance, as the clinicians greatly underestimated the base rate of violence among women (see Research Methods).

Among patients who had no prior history of violent behavior, clinical prediction still was found to be above chance levels. Apparently the clinicians made some accurate judgments based on information other than past behavior. Surprisingly, however, the accuracy of the clinical predictions was no greater when the risk of violence in a patient was judged to be higher versus lower. The critical distinction was the decision of whether the potential for violence was present or absent.

This research indicates that the clinical prediction of violence does have some value after all. Many inaccuracies are found in clinical prediction, but at least among men, clinicians were able to beat chance in predicting the potential for violence. A challenge for future research will be to find ways to improve the sensitivity and the specificity of the prediction of violence. This is an especially important goal given the damage wrought by both false positives—wrongly hospitalizing someone who is not dangerous; and by false negatives—releasing someone who is dangerous to others. ■

wrong in predicting violence 2 out of 3 times may seem worse than chance. This is not the case, however, as one must take **base rates** or population frequencies into account. When pre-

TABLE 17–2

Mental Illness and Violence

Current Prevalence of Mental Disorders Among Convicted Criminals and Normals

Diagnosis	Percentage with Diagnosis	
	Chicago Jail Detainees	Normals
Schizophrenia	2.7	0.9
Major Depression	3.9	1.1
Mania or Bipolar Disorder	1.4	0.1
Any Severe Disorder	6.4	1.8

Prevalence of Violence Among Normals and the Mentally Ill

Diagnosis	Percentage Violent
No Disorder	2.1
Schizophrenia	12.7
Major Depression	11.7
Mania or Bipolar Disorder	11.0
Alcohol Abuse/Dependence	24.6
Substance Abuse/Dependence	34.7

Adapted from J. Monahan (1992). Mental disorder and violent behavior: Perceptions and evidence. *American Psychologist, 47,* 516, 518; L. Teplin (1990). The prevalence of severe mental disorder among male urban jail detainees. *American Journal of Public Health , 80 ,* 665; and J. Swanson et al. (1990). Violence and psychiatric disorder in the community. *Hospital and Community Psychiatry , 41 ,* 765.

dicting an event that has a very low frequency, a false-positive rate of two-thirds is, in fact, better than chance (see Research Methods). This is an important if somewhat difficult point. United States Supreme Court Justice Blackmun failed to grasp the concept of base rates when considering evidence on the prediction of violence in a real case that was heard before the court. He wrongly claimed that a coin flip would be more accurate than clinical prediction (Reisner & Slobogin, 1990).

Another consideration is that the prediction of violence may be better in the short term than in the long run. This is an important distinction, because most research examines long-term outcomes (Monahan, 1981). Specifically, research indicates that 2 out of 3 people who are involuntarily hospitalized are not violent after they are released. This does not mean that they would not have been violent if they had never been committed. Obviously, clinicians commit only those people who they strongly believe will

become violent imminently, and they release the same people only if they are convinced that these people will not become violent. Such urgent, real-life decisions make it impossible to conduct unequivocal research. For obvious ethical reasons, no one has done or ever will do the true experiment that would best test the validity of short-term clinical predictions: Release or confine potentially violent people at random and compare their rates of actual violence with clinical predictions about violence.

In reconciling the conflicting viewpoints on the prediction of violence, perhaps the best advice comes from those who point to differences between the definitions and goals of the legal system and the mental health system. As with insanity assessments, clinicians who perform expert assessments of violence do best when they restrict their evaluation to their area of expertise. Research and clinical evidence can be used to determine a reasonable assessment of the likelihood of violence. However, it is the job of the legal system, not the mental health professional, to translate such probabilities into decisions about whether a given individual is "dangerous" in the legal sense of the term (Grisso & Appelbaum, in press).

Assessing Suicide Risk   Identical concerns apply to civil commitment and the assessment of suicide risk as to the assessment of dangerousness to others. As was discussed in Chapter 5, mental disorders, particularly depression, are related to an increased risk of suicide, but the risk of suicide clearly is far too small to justify civil commitment simply because of the presence of a mental disorder. Similarly, evidence on the clinical prediction of suicide risk also indicates very high false-positive rates (Pokony, 1983). Although these findings again raise concerns about the accuracy of clinical prediction, reassurance can be found in the actual procedures used for evaluating patients for civil commitment under either of the two dangerousness standards. In many cases in which a patient is involuntarily hospitalized, patients freely and directly acknowledge their intention to commit suicide or to physically harm others.

COMMITMENT OF MINORS

The caution that accompanies the civil commitment of adults stands in marked contrast to the process of institutionalizing juveniles who do not wish to be hospitalized. Technically, the involuntary hospitalization of minors is not a civil commitment issue because most minors are classified as "voluntary" patients even when they are hospitalized against their wishes. This is because parents, not minor children, have the right to commit children to hospitals. According to the 1979 Supreme Court ruling in *Parham* v. *J.R.* [442 U.S. 584 (1979)], minors, unlike adults, are not entitled to a full hearing before they can be committed to a mental hospital. Although state laws may add requirements, according to *Parham* parents can commit a minor against the minor's wishes, as long as an independent fact finder agrees. The staff of the hospital where parents have applied for admission qualify as independent fact finders, even though they have clear financial incentives to find reasons why inpatient care is needed (Weithorn, 1988).

Paternalists and libertarians find themselves in hot debate over the commitment of minors. Civil libertarians argue for an increased recognition of children's rights, while paternalists are reluctant to interfere with parents' rights or family autonomy. Perhaps the strongest libertarian argument is that many minors are committed to mental hospitals merely because they are troublesome to their parents and because hospitalization is profitable to private psychiatric hospitals.

Clinical psychologist and lawyer Lois Weithorn (1988) assembled some impressive evidence in support of this perspective. Among the facts that she documented are the following:

- Between 1980 and 1984 the number of juveniles admitted to private psychiatric hospitals increased by 450 percent.
- Advertisements suggesting hospitalization as an option for difficult or troubled adolescents were common in the popular media during the 1980s.
- The National Association of Private Psychiatric Hospitals adopted guidelines suggesting that hospitalization of teenagers is justified by "sexual promiscuity" and perhaps even by a preference for punk rock music over scout or church group activities.
- Less than one-third of all hospitalized adolescents suffered from severe disorders, such as psychosis or serious depression.
- The number of status offenders adjudicated in the juvenile justice system declined sharply during the same years that hospital admissions rose.

Weithorn (1988) concluded that these facts indicated that the former status offender (see Chapter 15) became the new adolescent inpatient in the 1980s. She sees the shift from the juvenile justice system to the mental health system in the treatment of troublesome adolescents as a worrisome change of emphasis from "badness" to "sickness." From her perspective, a basic problem with this shift is the lack of protection of the due process rights of minors who are hospitalized. Due process rights for teenagers accused of crimes were won in the juvenile courts in the 1960s, but, as the *Parham* decision made clear, adolescents are not entitled to the same procedural protections as adults in the mental health system. This lack of protection is a particular concern because many of the difficulties that lead to the hospitalization of adolescents do not seem to be "mental disorders" but instead seem like "problems in living with a teenager," to paraphrase Szasz.

The Rights of Mental Patients

Several important trials have clarified the rights of mental patients following their civil commitment to a mental hospital. These rights include: (1) the right to treatment; (2) the right to treatment in the least restrictive alternative environment; and (3) the right to refuse treatment.

THE RIGHT TO TREATMENT: *WYATT V. STICKNEY*

One of the most significant cases was *Wyatt* v. *Stickney*, which established that hospitalized mental patients have a constitutional *right to treatment*. *Wyatt* v. *Stickney* (1972) began as a dispute over the dismissal of 99 employees from Bryce Hospital in Tuscaloosa, Alabama. The state mental hospital had been built in the 1850s and housed nearly 5,000 patients when the much-needed staff members were released due to budget cuts. All accounts indicate that conditions in the hospital were very bad even before the layoffs. The buildings were fire hazards, the food was inedible, sanitation was neglected, avoidable sickness was rampant, abuse of patients was frequent, and confinement of patients with no apparent therapeutic goal occurred regularly.

Base Rates and Predictions

The validity with which an outcome like violence can be predicted depends upon a number of factors. One obvious influence is the magnitude of the relation between the predictor and the outcome. The stronger the relation, the better the prediction. Thus, the clinical prediction of violence seems highly flawed when we learn that clinicians are wrong two-thirds of the time that they predict that a patient will be violent. The validity of prediction also is affected by some conditions that are not obvious, however. *Base rates* or population frequencies are another very important influence (Meehl & Rosen, 1955).

We can use the prediction of violence to illustrate the general influence of base rates on the validity of prediction. We construct a hypothetical example in which we assume that (a) future, serious violence in our population has a base rate of 3 percent, (b) clinicians predict that violence will occur among 6 percent of the population, and (c) the clinical prediction of violence is wrong two-thirds of the time. These assumptions are portrayed in the following contingency table:

	Actually Violent	Actually Not Violent
Predicted Violent	2% (true positive)	4% (false positive)
Predicted Not Violent	1% (false negative)	93% (true negative)

A quick check of the figures will confirm for you that they meet all our assumptions. The prediction that patients will be violent is wrong two-thirds of the time in this example. But let us examine the prediction a bit more closely. What are the sensitivity and specificity (see Chapter 4) of the clinical prediction in this hypothetical example? The hypothetical example yields a sensitivity of 67 percent (true positives over the sum of true positives and false negatives) and a specificity of 96 percent (true negatives divided by the sum of the true negatives and false positives).

Now we can compare these figures with another hypothetical example: Supreme Court Justice Blackmun's prediction that a coin flip is as accurate as clinical prediction. Justice Blackmun assumed that a coin flip would be right half of the time—it would come up heads or tails—while clinical prediction was right only one-third of the time. The statistics are not as simple as Justice Blackmun assumed, however, as we can easily illustrate. For this example, we will assume that (a) the base rate of future, serious violence remains at 3 percent, (b) the coin will predict violence (heads) 50 percent of the time, and (c) the coin flip produces random predictions. These assumptions are portrayed in the following contingency table:

	Actually Violent	Actually Not Violent
Predicted Violent	1.5%	48.5%
Predicted Not Violent	1.5%	48.5%

Unlike what Justice Blackmun asserted, the coin flip does not beat clinical prediction in these hypothetical examples. The sensitivity and specificity of the coin flip both are 50 percent, figures that indicate random prediction and that are considerably lower than those obtained for clinical prediction. More basically, the percentage of false positives is much higher using Justice Blackmun's method than using clinical prediction (48.5 percent versus 4 percent). The clinical prediction of violence was wrong 67 percent of the time, as we forced it to be. Justice Blackmun's coin flip, however, was not wrong in predicting violence 50 percent of the time. It was wrong in predicting violence 97 percent of the time [48.5/(48.5 + 1.5)].

A key to understanding Justice Blackmun's error is to recognize that base rates affect the percentage of false positives and false negatives. The base rate of predicting violence using the clinical method (6 percent) was fairly close to the base rate of the actual occurrence of violence (3 percent). The base rate of predicting violence using the coin flip (50 percent) was much higher than its actual occurrence, however. In general, the statistical potential for accurate prediction is maximized when the predictor variable and the outcome variable have more similar base rates (Meehl & Rosen, 1955).

A low base rate is one reason why serious violence and other infrequent events are so difficult to predict. Predictions that the infrequent event will occur typically have a higher base rate than the actual outcomes. As a final illustration of how these differing base rates affect prediction, we can return to the coin flip example but alter one aspect of it. We set the base rate of the occurrence of violence as identical to the base rate with which it is predicted to occur (50 percent). This is illustrated in the following contingency table:

	Actually Violent	Actually Not Violent
Predicted Violent	50%	50%
Predicted Not Violent	50%	50%

The association between the coin flip and the occurrence of violence clearly is random in this example, as indicated by its specificity and sensitivity, which remain at 50 percent. In this hypothetical example, however, the coin flip "beats" the clinical prediction of violence. The coin flip is wrong in predicting violence only half of the time, which is better than being wrong two-thirds of the time. This is only a hypothetical example. In the real world, violence is a low-frequency event, and for statistical reasons alone, this makes it more difficult to predict validly (Meehl & Rosen, 1955). The clinical prediction of violence is far from perfect, but it is better than chance. Justice Blackmun did not understand the influence of base rates. We hope that you do now. ■

Litigation was filed on behalf of Ricky Wyatt, a resident in the institution, as part of a class action suit against the Alabama mental health commissioner, Dr. Stickney. The suit argued that institutionalized patients had a right to treatment that Bryce Hospital failed to fulfill. The commissioner was in the somewhat unusual position of being a proponent of a suit against him, as he wanted to improve the care of the mentally ill in the state but was faced with budget problems. The case was tried and appealed several times, and the patients' suit was upheld.

The victory forced the state of Alabama to provide services, but *Wyatt* had a broader impact that influenced mental patients and mental hospitals throughout the country. The judicial rulings clearly established that hospitalized mental patients have a right to treatment. Specifically, a federal district court ruled that at a minimum, public mental institutions must provide: (1) a humane psychological and physical environment, (2) qualified staff in numbers sufficient to administer adequate treatment, and (3) individualized treatment plans [334 F. Supp. 1341 (M.D. Ala. 1971) at 1343]. The court also ordered that the implementation of changes needed to fulfill these patient rights could not be delayed until funding was available.

The consequences of the *Wyatt* decision extended far beyond Bryce Hospital. The case helped to focus national attention on the treatment of the mentally ill and the mentally retard-ed and led to the filing of numerous "right to treatment" cases. The threat of litigation impelled the staff of numerous other mental hospitals to improve patient care. *Wyatt* also helped to spur the deinstitutionalization movement, because the level of care required by the ruling is impossible to provide in large, overcrowded institutions (Myers, 1983–84). As we will see, however, this has meant that some mental patients simply were released to the community without adequate care there either.

O'Connor* v. *Donaldson The Supreme Court acknowledged the right of mental patients to treatment in another landmark case, *O'Connor* v. *Donaldson* [422 U.S. 563 (1975)]. Kenneth Donaldson had been confined in a Florida mental hospital for nearly 15 years, despite his repeated requests for release based on his claims that he was not mentally ill, was not dangerous to himself or others, and was receiving no treatment in the hospital. Eventually, he sued the hospital's superintendent, Dr. J. B. O'Connor, for release based on the assertion that he had been deprived of his constitutional right to liberty.

The evidence presented at the trial indicated that Donaldson was not and never had been dangerous to himself or others. Testimony also revealed that reliable individuals and agencies in the community had made several offers to care for Donaldson, but superintendent O'Connor had repeatedly rejected them. O'Connor had insisted that Donaldson could be released only to the custody of his parents, who were very old and unable to care for him. O'Connor's position on Donaldson's supposed inability to care for himself was puzzling, because Donaldson was employed and had lived on his own for many years before being committed to the hospital. Other evidence documented that Donaldson had received nothing but custodial care while he was hospitalized.

After a series of trials and appeals, the Supreme Court eventually ruled that Donaldson was neither dangerous to himself nor dangerous to others. It further ruled that a state could not confine him as being in need of treatment and yet fail to provide him with that treatment. Specifically, it ordered that "the State cannot constitutionally confine . . . a non-dangerous individual who is capable of surviving safely in freedom by himself or with the help of willing and responsible family members or friends." Thus, O'Connor and similar cases not only underscored a patient's right to treatment, but it also set limitations on civil commitment standards. Commitment based on dangerousness to self or others remained unquestioned, but commitment based on inability to care for self became much more controversial, especially if institutionalization offered little treatment or therapeutic benefit.

▲ **Kenneth Donaldson proudly displaying a copy of the Supreme Court ruling in his case. The court held that nondangerous mental patients cannot be confined against their will, a decision that freed Donaldson and set an important precedent for other hospitalized mental patients.**

THE LEAST RESTRICTIVE ALTERNATIVE

The patient's right to be treated in the least restrictive alternative environment was first developed in the 1966 case of *Lake* v. *Cameron* [364 F. 2d 657 (D.C. Cir. 1966)], decided by the Washington, D.C., Circuit Court of Appeals. Catherine Lake was 60 years old when she was committed to St. Elizabeth's Hospital because of "a chronic brain syndrome associated with aging." A particular problem was her tendency to wander away from her home, which posed a threat to her life through exposure to the elements or other dangers.

In contesting the commitment, Mrs. Lake did not object to her need for treatment, but she argued that appropriate treatment was available in a less restrictive setting. The court agreed, suggesting several less restrictive alternatives to institutionalization. These alternatives ranged from having Mrs. Lake carry an identification card to treating her in a public nursing home.

Several additional cases following *Lake* firmly established the doctrine of the least restrictive alternative. Litigation was quickly followed by legislation, as numerous states incorporated the right to treatment in the least restrictive alternative environment into their mental health statutes (Hoffman & Foust, 1977). Although the concept was quickly embraced, no one was or is absolutely certain what the expression "*least restrictive alternative*" means.

In theory, the least restrictive alternative can be seen as an attempt to balance paternalist and libertarian concerns in the involuntary treatment of the mentally ill. The state provides mandatory care, but that care must restrict individual liberties to the minimal degree possible. Questions arise about how to define and implement the theory. Who should determine what alternative is the least restrictive? Is this the job of the mental health professional who is making treatment decisions? Should the court monitor the consideration of alternatives? Should an independent party supervise these decisions? The practical answer to these important questions generally has been to place the decisions in the hands of mental health professionals. Ironically, this was the arrangement before *Lake*; thus the case did not lead to the development of new procedural safeguards.

Perhaps the most important issue about the least restrictive alternative concerns the problem that developed in the original *Lake* case: the unavailability of less restrictive alternatives. No suitable community care was found for Mrs. Lake, who was returned to the institution. If a less restrictive alternative treatment is not available, must the service be developed and provided by the community? Some early cases suggested that the courts would mandate such a solution, but this trend quickly faded. Thus, *Lake* both established patients' right to treatment in the least restrictive alternative environment, and foreshadowed the problem of insufficient alternative treatments available in the community. The development of community resources has not kept up with the release of patients from mental hospitals (Hoffman & Foust, 1977). This is especially unfortunate, given that data suggest that community treatment can be more effective than inpatient care (Kiesler, 1982).

THE RIGHT TO REFUSE TREATMENT

The third and most recent development in litigation involving people committed to mental hospitals is the *right to refuse treatment*, particularly the right to refuse psychotropic medication. Several courts and state legislatures have concluded that mental patients have the right to refuse certain treatments under certain conditions, although this right is on less firm ground than the other two rights we have discussed. In particular, the Supreme Court has yet to establish whether there is a constitutional basis for the right to refuse treatment.

The very concept of a patient refusing treatment is problematic in that involuntary hospitalization itself is treatment against a patient's will. The patient who is committed involuntarily to a mental hospital has refused inpatient treatment but is receiving it anyway. On what grounds can subsequent treatment decisions be refused if the decision about hospitalization already has been taken out of the patient's hands? Many mental health professionals have noted this contradiction, and they argue that patients lose their right to refuse treatment once they are involuntarily hospitalized (Gutheil, 1986). After all, a mental health professional is in an awkward position if a patient is committed to a hospital for treatment yet retains the right to refuse medication. How can mental health professionals do their job in such a circumstance?

The question of the right to refuse treatment often turns on the issue of informed consent, one of several legal doctrines that can be used to justify a patient's refusal of mental health (or medical) treatments (Hermann, 1990). **Informed consent** requires that (1) a clinician tell a patient about a procedure and its associated risks, (2) the patient understands the information and freely consents to the treatment, and (3) the patient is competent to give consent. When the patient's competence to provide consent is in question, a common approach is to appoint an independent guardian who offers a *substituted judgment*, deciding not what is best for the patient, but what the patient would have been likely to do if he or she were competent (Gutheil, 1986).

The rationales for and parameters of patients' right to refuse treatment are still being debated in litigation and legislation. Several courts have ruled that patients retain their competence to make treatment decisions even if they have been committed through civil procedures. Moreover, half of the states have recognized the right to refuse psychotropic medications provided that patients are not dangerous to themselves or others (Hermann, 1990). The Supreme Court first ruled on this topic in the 1990 case of *Washington v. Harper* [110 S. Ct. 1028 (1990)]. This case involved a Washington state prison that overrode a patient's refusal of psychotropic medications. The court decided in favor of the prison, ruling that the prison's review process sufficiently protected the patient's right to refuse treatment. This process stipulated that the patient's wishes could be overruled only after review by a three-member panel consisting of a psychologist, a psychiatrist, and a deputy warden. The Supreme Court's decision may signal a greater willingness on the part of the courts to limit patients' right to refuse treatment.

Deinstitutionalization

Legal cases have restricted inpatient treatment of the mentally ill, but a broader influence has been the **deinstitutionalization** movement—the philosophy that many of the mentally ill and mentally retarded can be better cared for in their community than in large mental hospitals. Bertram Brown, a former director of the National Institute for Mental Health, defined the goals of deinstitutionalization as: "(1) the prevention of inappropriate mental hospital admissions through the provision of community alternatives for treatment, (2) the release to the community of all institutionalized patients who have been given adequate preparation for such a change, and (3) the establishment and maintenance of community support systems for noninstitutionalized people receiving mental health services in the community" (Braun, et al., 1981).

The establishment of mental health centers in communities was part of the effort to achieve these three goals. In 1963, the U.S. Congress passed the Community Mental Health Centers (CMHC) act with the strong support of President John F. Kennedy[†]. The act provided for the creation of community care facilities for the seriously mentally ill as alternatives to institutional

---

[†] President Kennedy had a special interest in mental health because of his sister, Rosemary. She was mildly mentally retarded as a child, but she became psychotic as a young adult and underwent a failed lobotomy that left her so impaired that she had to be confined to a nursing home.

care. This law began a broad change in the way mental health services are delivered in the United States. There were no community mental health centers in operation in 1965, but by 1981 nearly 800 were in existence (Torrey, 1988).

Deinstitutionalization has occurred in dramatic fashion. In 1955, some 559,000 people in the United States were confined to mental hospitals, but by 1985 that number had shrunk to 110,000 (NIMH, 1985). Unfortunately, CMHCs have not achieved many of their goals in helping deinstitutionalized patients. In fact, CMHCs generally have not focused their services on former inpatients with serious mental illness. As can be seen in Figure 17–2, the percentage of schizophrenic patients served by CMHCs is small and declining, while the percentage of patients with mild problems is larger and growing. In fact, many CMHCs do not even offer services for the seriously mentally ill, such as emergency treatment or inpatient care, despite the fact that they are mandated to do so by legislation (Torrey, 1988). Other community resources, such as halfway houses, simply have not been implemented in adequate numbers.

Other problems with the deinstitutionalization movement are evident. As public hospital-ization has declined, the number of mental patients living in nursing homes and other for-profit institutions has grown (Goldman, Adams, & Taube, 1983; Torrey, 1988). In addition, a *revolving door* phenomenon has developed in which more patients are admitted to psychiatric hospitals more frequently but for shorter periods of time. For example, one study found that 24 percent of inpatients in New York City had ten or more previous admissions (Karras & Otis, 1987). Moreover, the deinstitutionalized mentally ill constitute a large part of the homeless population (Fischer & Breakey, 1991). One study found that 31 percent of the homeless were in need of mental health services (Roth & Bean, 1986). In his stirring and disturbing book *Nowhere to Go,* psychiatrist E. Fuller Torrey (1988) notes eight major problems with deinstitutionalization.

1. There are at least twice as many seriously mentally ill individuals living on streets and in shelters as there are in public mental hospitals.
2. There are increasing numbers of seriously mentally ill individuals in the nation's jails and prisons.
3. Seriously mentally ill individuals are regularly released from hospitals with little or no provision for aftercare or follow-up treatment.
4. Violent acts perpetrated by untreated mentally ill individuals are increasing in number.
5. Housing and living conditions for mentally ill individuals in the community are grossly inadequate.
6. Community mental health centers, originally funded to provide community care for the mentally ill so that these individuals would no longer have to go to state mental hospitals, are almost complete failures in this regard.
7. Laws designed to protect the rights of the seriously mentally ill primarily protect their right to remain mentally ill.
8. The majority of mentally ill individuals discharged from hospitals have been officially lost. Nobody knows where they are.

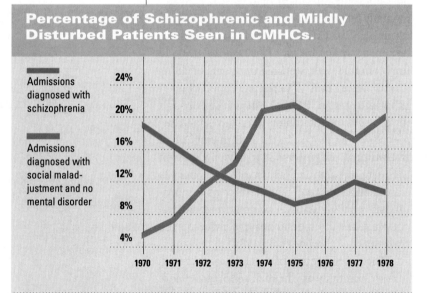

Percentage of Schizophrenic and Mildly Disturbed Patients Seen in CMHCs.

Admissions diagnosed with schizophrenia

Admissions diagnosed with social maladjustment and no mental disorder

FIGURE 17-2: This figure illustrates the percentages of both schizophrenic and mildly disturbed patients admitted to community mental health centers during the 1970s. The decline in the number of schizophrenic patients and rise in the number if mildly disturbed patients is one indication of the failure of CMHCs to compensate for deinstitutionalization.

Source: E.F. Torrey (1988). *Nowhere to go: The tragic odyssey of the homeless mentally ill,* p. 3. New York: HarperCollins.

HAS THE PENDULUM SWUNG TOO FAR?

Some advocates for the mentally ill, particularly those in mental health professions, feel that

◀ **These contrasting photos illustrate how mental patients often are neglected both inside and outside of institutions. The photo on the left, taken several decades ago, shows some of the depressing and dehumanizing conditions that characterized many institutions for the mentally ill. The photo on the right depicts the contemporary problem of homelessness. Many homeless people are deinstitutionalized mental patients.**

the pendulum between paternalism and libertarianism has swung too far in the direction of patient rights. Many mental patients who clearly are in need of treatment cannot be committed under existing statutes. Some of the problems of the deinstitutionalized mentally ill are compounded by restrictive civil commitment laws. One commentary graphically described the situation as one in which patients were "rotting with their rights on" (Appelbaum & Gutheil, 1979). Torrey (1988) argues, "Apparently drafted by the law firm of Franz Kafka and Lewis Carroll, the laws on the mentally ill that have emanated from the deinstitutionalization era are both absurd and tragic" (pp. 29–30). "Freedom to be insane is an illusory freedom, a cruel hoax perpetrated on those who cannot think clearly by those who will not think clearly" (p. 34).

As a means of balancing paternalist and libertarian concerns, some experts have suggested that more paternalism is needed in committing patients, but that commitment should be to involuntary treatment in the least restrictive environment, such as mandatory outpatient care (Myers, 1983–84). Hospitalization would be required only as a last resort. Others also support more paternalism in civil commitment laws, but argue that a reorientation is needed in the thinking—and funding—of mental health professionals. Most psychiatrists, clinical psychologists, and social workers only treat the "worried well," and perhaps new incentives are needed to direct more of their efforts toward helping the seriously mentally ill (Torrey, 1988).

Mental Health and Family Law

Both the insanity defense and civil commitment primarily involve people who have a serious mental illness. In contrast, mental health professionals who are involved with *family law* issues typically work with people whose problems are less severe, and they often are consulted about issues related to normal development. This is evident in the major issues that form the focus of family law: divorce, spousal abuse, foster care, adoption, juvenile delinquency, child custody disputes, and child abuse and neglect. Any one of these problems can involve serious psychopathology, but they more commonly involve family members who are only mildly disturbed or are functioning normally.

We consider both family law and mental health law issues together in this chapter, because the opinions and advice of mental health professionals are frequently sought by legal professionals working in both areas. However, family and mental health law are distinct in the legal system. The two areas have different roots and practices, and attorneys may specialize in one or the other area, but rarely both. In fact, family law cases typically are tried in different courts than are mental health law cases. These separate courts, known variously as "juvenile courts," "domestic relations courts," or "family courts," were first created at the turn of the century and adhere to a different philosophy than other

U.S. courts. Much of mental health law is based on the state's police power obligations, but virtually all of family law is premised on the government's *parens patriae* duties.

In theory, the functions of juvenile and family courts are to help and protect children and families. Thus, the goals of family courts historically have been more psychological than legal. In fact, the authors of a recent, comprehensive overview of the role of psychologists in the courts concluded, "Perhaps nowhere in the legal system is there as much deference to mental health professionals as in the juvenile court" (Melton et al., 1987, p. 291).

The importance of mental health professionals is particularly evident in the two family law topics considered in this chapter—child custody disputes following divorce, and cases of child abuse and neglect. Mental health professionals and psychological findings are of great importance not only because of the family court's philosophy, but also because terms like *child abuse* are poorly defined in the law. The laws governing judicial dispositions of these family concerns are similarly vague. In fact, the guiding principle for judicial decision making is the very general directive to make determinations according to what is in the "child's best interest" (Mnookin, 1975). Not surprisingly, family court judges frequently turn to mental health professionals for practical guidance in defining a given child's "best interests."

Balancing the Interests of Children, Parents, and the State

A general dilemma in family law is how to balance the potentially competing interests of children, parents, and the state (Mnookin, 1985). We alluded to this three-sided problem in our earlier discussion of the *Parham* decision on the commitment of minors to mental hospitals. People involved with such cases must address a number of difficult questions: Are children entitled to the same due process rights as adults? Should parental authority be respected above and beyond the wishes of either children or the state? Or should the state's *parens patriae* obligation overrule the desires of both children and parents?

One set of answers to these questions comes from advocates for children who consistently argue that children, or at least adolescents, are

entitled to the same basic rights as adults. Advocates for this position were upset by *Parham*, for example, because they want minors to have the same due process rights as adults. Different rationales come from paternalists who believe that children need vigorous protection by the state. Paternalists do not favor *Parham* either, because it limits state supervision by giving parents the power to make decisions about hospitalizing minors. A paternalist might instead advocate for increased government regulation of private mental hospitals. The winners in *Parham* were those people who hold a third position as advocates for parental rights or "family autonomy." Proponents of family autonomy want to minimize the involvement of the state in the family, whether that intrusion comes from state supervision or broader rights for children.

The tension among the rights and responsibilities of children, parents, and the state pervades controversies about child custody and child abuse. Advocates for children's rights want children to have a voice in the outcome of custody disputes and the disposition of abuse cases. Advocates for family autonomy want parents to resolve custody disputes themselves and to narrow the definition of abuse and neglect in order to minimize state intervention in the family. Advocates for state intervention want judges to determine custody arrangements, and they argue for earlier and more vigorous intervention in cases of child abuse.

Child Custody Disputes Following Divorce

Divorce is a common experience for children living in the United States (see Further Thoughts on children of divorce). Every year, approximately 2 percent of U.S. children experience a divorce (SCCYF, 1989), and demographers have estimated that 38 percent of white children and 75 percent of black children born to married parents will experience a parental divorce by the age of 16 (Bumpass, 1984). **Child custody** is one of the issues that must be decided when parents divorce. Although the legal terminology differs from state to state, in effect custody decisions involve two determinations: *physical custody*, or where the children will live at what times, and *legal custody*, or how the parents will make separate or joint decisions about their children's lives. *Sole custody* refers to a situation in which

The Psychological Health of Children of Divorce

The state's *parens patriae* duty to protect children is a major justification for its role in automatically assuming supervision over child custody following divorce. Obviously, this role was assumed long before psychological research was available on the question on how divorce affects children's well-being. Still, considerable research has been conducted on children from divorced families, and findings raise questions about the child protection justification for state intervention.

The psychological consequences of divorce for children have been and continue to be debated. Some commentators suggest that children cope successfully with divorce, while others conclude that divorce has severe, lasting, and damaging emotional consequences. However, empirical research clearly documents two important facts about the adjustment of children from divorced families: (1) on various measures of their psychological functioning, they differ only to a small degree from children whose parents are married, and (2) a substantial portion of the difficulties found among children after divorce actually begin long before the marital separation occurs.

Numerous studies have compared the psychological functioning of children whose parents have divorced with that of children whose parents remain married. Many of these investigations were included in a recent quantitative meta-analysis of 92 studies of divorce that involved over 13,000 children (Amato & Keith, 1991). When all studies of children from married and divorced families were compared on all measures, an average effect size of only .14 standard deviation units was found to distinguish the two groups of children, a difference that is equivalent to an IQ of 100 compared to an IQ of 102. The reviewers found that the largest effect size for any area of psychological difficulty was .23 standard deviation units for children's conduct problems.

The effect sizes attributable to divorce may be even smaller than those suggested by cross-sectional studies, because differences in children's psychological health may be present before divorce. Researchers typically have assessed children's psychological functioning after the divorce, but it is possible that the difficulties found among children after divorce actually began prior to divorce. If so, the problems obviously are not consequences of divorce.

This is exactly what several recent studies have found. The possibility was first documented in a small but intensive longitudinal study of normal children and their families (Block, Block, & Gjerde, 1986). The finding was recently confirmed in an investigation of two large, nationally representative samples, one of 14,476 British children and the second of 2,279 American children (Cherlin et al., 1991). Data were available on the behavior problems of children before and after divorce, thus allowing the investigators to compare children's adjustment following divorce with their adjustment prior to divorce. In fact, when various predivorce differences in children's functioning and family life were statistically controlled, the postdivorce differences were reduced to the point that they were no longer statistically reliable, even in these very large samples.

An independent analysis of the national sample of British children confirmed that problems found among children after divorce actually begin long before the marital separation (Elliott & Richards, 1991). Thus, recent research suggests that many of the psychological troubles found among children after divorce actually begin before divorce occurs. To the extent that they do, these problems cannot be "consequences of divorce." Together with the small magnitude of psychological disturbances that are typically found among children whose parents have divorced, this evidence raises questions about why courts automatically assume supervision of children whose parents divorce through their *parens patriae* powers. Rather than protecting children, courts may be providing divorcing parents with a forum for fighting when they get involved in the difficult transition of divorce. ■

only one parent retains physical or legal custody of the children; in contrast, in *joint custody* both parents retain custody.

The majority of custody decisions are made outside of court by attorneys who negotiate for the parents. A growing number of custody decisions are being made by parents themselves, however, typically with the help of a mediator—a neutral third party who facilitates the parents' discussions. Finally, a small but significant percentage of custody disputes are decided in court by a judge (Maccoby & Mnookin, 1992). Mental health professionals may be involved in providing recommendations during attorney negotiations, they may provide expert testimony in court, or they may act as mediators themselves.

EXPERT WITNESSES IN CUSTODY DETERMINATIONS

Mental health professionals who conduct custody evaluations typically consider a number of factors in evaluating a child's best interests. These include the quality of the child's relationship with each parent, the family environment provided by each parent, each parent's mental health, the relationship between the parents, and the child's expressed wishes, if any (Emery & Rogers, 1991). Mental health professionals face a tremendous obstacle in conducting a custody evaluation, however. The law that governs custody disputes, the *child's best interests standard*, is unclear about what a child's future best interests are, how they can be determined, or how they can be achieved. As law professor Robert Mnookin (1975) has pointed out:

> Deciding what is best for a child poses a question no less ultimate than the purposes and values of life itself. Should the judge be primarily concerned with the child's happiness? Or with the child's spiritual and religious training? Should the judge be concerned with the economic "productivity" of the child when he grows up? Are the primary values of life in warm interpersonal relationships, or in discipline and self-sacrifice? Is stability and security for a child more desirable than intellectual stimulation? These questions could be elaborated endlessly. And yet, where is the judge to look for the set of values that should inform the choice of what is best for the child? (pp. 260–261)

Because the child's best interests standard is so vague, Mnookin (1975) has argued further that it increases the likelihood that custody hearings will be acrimonious. Virtually any information that makes one parent look bad and the other look good may be construed as helping a parent's case, and people who have been married have access to much private and potentially damaging information about each other. The likelihood that the best interests standard increases acrimony is a particular problem, because a wide range of research indicates that conflict between parents is strongly related to maladjustment among children following divorce (Emery, 1982, 1988; Grych & Fincham, 1990). This raises the sad irony that parents and the legal system may be undermining a child's best interests by fighting for them in a custody battle (Emery & Wyer, 1987). For this reason, many mental health professionals feel that they serve children and the legal system better if they help parents to settle custody disputes outside of court rather than providing testimony in court.

CUSTODY MEDIATION

Mental health professionals, as well as many family lawyers, have begun to serve a new role in helping parents who dispute custody by working as custody *mediators* . Mediators meet with divorcing parents and help them to identify, negotiate, and ultimately resolve their disputes. The role of mediator is very different from the role that mental health professionals have traditionally fulfilled in evaluating children in custody disputes. Mediation also is a major change in the practice of the law, as mediators adopt a cooperative approach to dispute resolution rather than the usual adversary procedures (Emery & Wyer, 1987).

Custody mediation has been embraced rapidly in the United States, and a handful of states require that mediation be attempted before a custody dispute will be heard in court. Evidence consistently indicates that mediation dramatically reduces the number of custody hearings in court, helps parents reach decisions more quickly, and is viewed more favorably than litigation by parents, especially fathers (Emery, 1994; Emery, Matthews, & Wyer, 1991). Perhaps the most significant contribution of custody mediation, however, is that it suggests that mental health professionals need not limit their involvement in the legal system to providing evaluations. Rather, mental health professionals can help to develop alternatives to legal procedures when these procedures create undue distress for the people involved.

Child Abuse

The trend in child custody disputes is toward more family autonomy, but the state's role in regulating child abuse clearly has grown dramatically. Like spousal abuse (see Further Thoughts on battered women), historically child abuse was common and condoned, and only recently has it been "discovered" to be a problem. The first child protection efforts in the United States did not begin until 1875. A much publicized case of foster parents who physically beat a young girl in their care led to the founding of the New York Society for the Prevention of Cruelty to Children. The society was given the power to police child abuse, and other states rapidly followed New York's example by establishing similar organizations and legislation throughout the country (Lazoritz, 1990).

Although state governments assumed some jurisdiction over child abuse in the nineteenth century, consistent public attention was not brought to bear on the problem until 1962, when physician Henry Kempe wrote about the "battered child syndrome." Kempe documented tragic cases of child abuse in which children suffered repeated injuries, fractured bones, and, in a substantial number of cases, death (Kempe et al., 1962). Kempe's influential article prompted legislation that defined child abuse and required physicians to report suspected cases. This reporting requirement continues today, and in most states it extends to include mental health professionals, schoolteachers, and other professionals who have regular contact with children. In fact, mental health professionals not only can but they must break the confidentiality of psychotherapy if they suspect child abuse (Melton & Limber, 1989).

Four forms of **child abuse** generally are distinguished by mental health professionals and are treated separately in the law: physical abuse, sexual abuse, neglect, and psychological abuse. *Physical child abuse* involves the intentional use of physically painful and harmful actions. The definition of physical abuse is complicated by the fact that corporal punishments like spanking are widely accepted discipline practices (Emery,

1989; Wolfe, 1987). Only about 10 percent of physically abused children whose caretakers are reported to social service agencies sustain injuries serious enough to require professional care, but the danger to children can be considerable nevertheless. Estimates indicate that 2,000 to 5,000 children die every year because of maltreatment (Zigler & Hall, 1989).

Child sexual abuse involves sexual contact between an adult and a child. Reports of child sexual abuse have increased astronomically in recent years, as this important problem has been fully recognized only since the 1980s (Haugaard & Reppucci, 1988). The sexual abuse of children is now known to be far more prevalent than would have been believed a short time ago. For example, one survey of adult women living in an urban area found that 2.5 percent said that they had been coerced into oral, anal, or genital intercourse with their father, stepfather, or brother before the age of 18 (Russell, 1983).

Child neglect involves placing children at risk for serious physical or psychological harm by failing to provide basic and expected care. Some children are severely neglected, and they experience extreme failure in their growth and development as a result (Wolfe, 1987). Some children also suffer *psychological abuse*—repeated denigration in the absence of physical harm.

The number of reported cases of child abuse has increased dramatically in recent years. As indicated in Figure 17–3, the number of reports of child abuse made to social service agencies climbed from 669,000 in 1976 to 2,178,000 in 1987. There is debate about the reasons for the increased number of reports. The rate of child abuse could be increasing, but the real increase may be in *reports* of abuse (Besharov, 1992; Finkelhor, 1992). Over half of all reports of abuse are found to be unsubstantiated after an investigation, and some have suggested that the percentage of unsubstantiated reports is growing. One reason for this, according to some critics, is that the concept of neglect is applied too broadly (Besharov, 1986, 1988, 1992).

The increasing number of reports of child abuse and the large percentage of less-severe cases that are substantiated may create two problems. First, if social service agencies are overwhelmed with more minor cases, they are less able to deal with children who are living in circumstances of clear danger. Second, it may be that intervention in less-severe cases actually does more harm than good (Besharov, 1986, 1988, 1992).

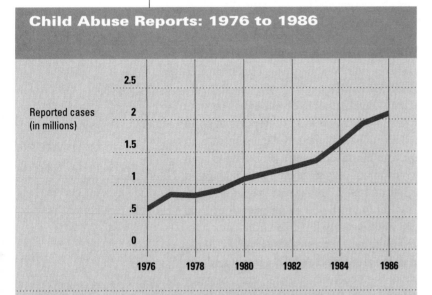

Child Abuse Reports: 1976 to 1986

Reported cases (in millions)

FIGURE 17-3: The number of official reports of child abuse made to social service agencies has grown steadily in recent years. Social scientists disagree about whether the prevalence of abuse has grown or more questionable reports are being made.

From D.J. Besharov (1992). A balanced approach to reporting child abuse. *The Child, Youth, and Family Services Quarterly, 15,* 5.

When an allegation of abuse is substantiated, one of the major questions is whether to remove the child from the home. Over 100,000 maltreated children are placed in *foster care* each year. Foster care obviously benefits children who are in physical danger, but as many as half of all children placed in foster care are in no immediate danger of physical injury (Besharov, 1988). Stable foster care can offer children psychological benefits, as well as physical protection (Wald, 1985). However, half of the children placed in foster care remain there for at least 2 years, almost one-third are separated from their parents for over 6 years, and a substantial proportion live in many different foster homes during this time (Besharov, 1986).

As with child custody decisions, judicial determinations about foster care and other possible dispositions of child abuse cases are guided by the "child's best interest" standard. Psychologists frequently play a role in these legal proceedings by investigating allegations of abuse in interviews with children, making recommendations to the court about appropriate placements for children, and providing treatment to children and families (Melton & Limber, 1989; Wolfe, 1987). The ambiguity in defining abuse, and the uncertainty about the benefits and costs of intervention, suggest perhaps a more important role psychologists can play in abuse cases: conducting more research that can be used to clarify and guide legal decision making in this important area.

Professional Responsibilities and the Law

The regulation of the mental health professions is the final area of psychology and the law that we consider in this chapter. Psychiatrists, clinical psychologists, and social workers all have **professional responsibilities** to meet the ethical standards of their profession and to uphold the laws of the states in which they practice. The duties of mental health professionals are numerous and varied, and we focus on only two important and illustrative professional issues: negligence and confidentiality.

Professional Negligence and Malpractice

Negligence occurs when a professional fails to perform in a manner that is consistent with the level of skill exercised by other professionals in the field. Simply put, negligence is substandard professional service. *Malpractice* refers to situations in which professional negligence results in harm to clients or patients. In the law, malpractice is demonstrated when: (1) a professional has a duty to conform to a standard of conduct, (2) the professional is negligent in that duty, (3) the professional's client experiences damages or loss, and (4) it is reasonably certain that the negligence caused the damages (Reisner & Slobogin, 1990). When professionals are found to be guilty of malpractice, they are subject to disciplinary action both from their professional organizations and through state licensing boards, as well as to civil suits and possibly to criminal actions.

The Battered Woman Syndrome as a Defense

For centuries large numbers of women have been physically beaten by their husbands or lovers. This fact is easy to document, because wife battering has been institutionalized for much of Western history—and it remains an accepted practice in parts of the world today. For example, the familiar phrase "rule of thumb" refers to the size of the stick, no thicker than a man's thumb, with which men were legitimately allowed to beat their wives according to common law.

Nevertheless, spousal abuse has been recognized as a social problem only in the last few decades. During these years, laws have been passed that for the first time protect wives from their husbands' physical and sexual abuse. Even today, however, in some states a husband cannot be charged with raping his wife no matter what the circumstances of forced sex might be. American laws have protected people from assaults by strangers much more stringently than they have protected people from assault by members of their own family.

The prevalence of spouse abuse in the United States today is a matter of political and scientific debate, in large part because of disagreements about what constitutes abuse. Some startling facts about family violence cannot be disputed, however. For example, FBI statistics indicate that approximately one-third of all female murder victims are killed by a husband or a boyfriend.

Battered women often remain in the abusive relationship for incomprehensibly long periods of time. To outsiders, the battered woman's reluctance to leave the relationship seems foolish, even masochistic. To the battered woman herself, however, leaving the relationship often seems wrong or impossible. She may feel trapped in an abusive relationship by finances or out of concern for her children; chronic abuse may cause her to lose perspective on the extent of her maltreatment; or she simply may see no viable alternative to subjecting herself to repeated abuse. Some women who have been constantly threatened, intimidated, and beaten by their husbands or boyfriends eventually escape the abuse only by killing their tormentors. (A few abused children also have killed a parent or stepparent.) Is this violence in response to violence justified?

The killing of an abuser clearly is justified in the U.S. law when the victim's life is in immediate danger. In such a circumstance, the action can easily be construed as self-defense. In other cases, however, the killing of a batterer takes place when the threat of abuse may be looming in the background but is not immediate. In this situation, a woman might still plead self-defense. According to contemporary trial practice, the defense may depend heavily on what has been called the battered woman syndrome.

The **battered woman syndrome** is a term coined by psychologist Lenore Walker (1979) to describe her observations about the psychological effects of being chronically abused by a husband or lover. Two aspects of the syndrome are especially crucial to its use as a defense. First, Walker discusses what she calls the "cycle of violence," which includes three stages: (1) a tension-building phase leading up to violence; (2) the battering incident itself; and (3) a stage of loving contrition, during which the batterer apologizes and attempts to make amends for his actions. A second crucial aspect of Walker's battered woman syndrome is her view that the abused woman experiences learned helplessness (see Chapter 5). Walker assumes that learned helplessness makes it impossible for some battered women to leave an abusive relationship. These two assertions are essential to a successful defense, because they imply that the battered woman expects to be beaten repeatedly but becomes immobilized and unable to leave the relationship.

Expert testimony on the battered woman's syndrome apparently has been very influential in successfully defending a number of battered women who have killed abusive men. This defense has become very controversial, however. A number of courts have determined that expert testimony on the battered woman syndrome is inadmissible on various grounds, although the trend appears to be toward increasing acceptance of such testimony by the legal system (Brown, 1990). Walker (1989) reported that members of her firm had testified in over 160 cases where a battered woman had killed her abuser. Others have raised questions about the scientific status of the battered woman syndrome, doubting the coherence of the theory and the evidence that supports it (Faigman, 1986). One question that has been asked, for example, is: How can someone who is suffering from learned helplessness bring herself to kill?

Questions like this can make it difficult to plead self-defense based on the battered woman syndrome. A defense of "temporary insanity" is an alternative that may be more easily proved in court. The legal definition of insanity refers to a defendant's mental state at the time of committing the criminal act; thus, it is possible for a defendant to suffer from "temporary insanity." An argument for temporary insanity based on the battered woman syndrome could be made on the basis of either the "right from wrong" or the "irresistible impulse" strand of the insanity defense. The essence of such an argument would be that the stress of the physical abuse so impaired the battered woman's thinking that either she was unable to appreciate the consequences of her actions or she was driven to the point where she could no longer control her behavior (Cipparone, 1987).

The questions of whether the woman was imminently threatened and why she did not leave the relationship usually play a lesser role in a temporary insanity defense than in a plea of self-defense. However, temporary insanity pleas appear to be used less frequently than self-defense in cases where women have killed their batterers, perhaps because the temporary insanity defense is less palatable. This defense carries the stigma of an insanity determination, as well as the possibility of confinement in a mental institution. Perhaps more importantly, advocates for battered women feel strongly that abused women are in a vulnerable and dangerous situation, and they wish to establish that the victims' actions are legitimate acts of self-defense. A successful insanity defense relieves one woman of criminal responsibility for her actions. When the defense of self-defense is successful, however, this makes a broader political statement: Women have a right to take extreme actions to protect themselves against chronic battering (Walker, 1989). ∎

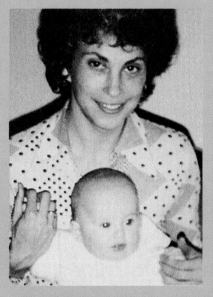 

▲ **Hedda Nussbaum before and after the repeated beatings inflicted by her partner, Joel Steinberg. Lisa, a 6-year-old girl whom Steinberg and Nussbaum illegally adopted, died following a beating by Steinberg. Nussbaum was granted immunity for serving as a witness against Steinberg, who was convicted of manslaughter for Lisa's death.**

While medical malpractice claims are common, malpractice claims against mental health professionals are relatively infrequent. For example, one survey found that claims against psychiatrists accounted for only 0.3 percent of all malpractice suits filed in the state of California between 1974 and 1978 (Slawson & Guggenheim, 1984). The inappropriate use of electroconvulsive therapy (ECT) and of medication are two of the more common reasons for malpractice claims against mental health professionals. These treatments are clearly defined, research on their appropriate use is more clear-cut than is psychotherapy research, and the treatments can result in physical as well as psychological damages. In other words, malpractice is easier to demonstrate for these treatments.

The existence of a sexual relationship between therapists and their clients is another common ground for successful malpractice suits. Although damages can be difficult to prove, it has become commonly accepted that sexual relationships between therapists and their clients are damaging in and of themselves. This is evident in the ethical codes of the American Psychological Association and the American Psychiatric Association, both of which prohibit sexual relationships between therapists and their clients. Other claims of professional negligence stem from the failure to prevent suicide, failure to prevent violence against others, and violations of confidentiality (Leesfield, 1987). Each of these areas of professional negligence is of considerable significance, and they dominate the malpractice claims that have been filed against mental health professionals. As the field continues to evolve, a new area of professional negligence may become important: the failure to offer adequate treatment and to inform clients about treatment alternatives.

INFORMED CONSENT ON THE EFFICACY OF ALTERNATIVE TREATMENTS

The choice of alternative treatments for mental disorders may depend on a number of chance factors ranging from the profession of the therapist to his or her theoretical orientation. Only psychiatrists can prescribe medication, and they surely are more likely to recommend this treatment than are psychologists and social workers. Similarly, behavior therapists are likely to offer behavior therapy, and psychoanalysts to offer psychoanalysis.

As we have argued in earlier chapters, however, the goal of research is to identify specific treatments for specific disorders. This scientific approach has been successful in identifying some approaches that are more effective than others in treating particular disorders. If evidence points to the superiority of one treatment over another, several questions arise. Does the mental health professional have an obligation to offer the more effective treatment, make a referral to another professional who can provide it, or at a minimum, obtain informed consent to pursue an alternative course of therapy?

This issue was raised in the case *Osheroff* v. *Chestnut Lodge* [62 Md. App. 519, 490 A. 2d. 720 (Md. App. 1985)]. In 1979, Dr. Rafael Osheroff, an internist, admitted himself to Chestnut Lodge, a private psychiatric hospital in Maryland that had long been famous as a center for psychoanalytic psychotherapy. Dr. Osheroff had a history of depression and anxiety, problems that previously had been treated on an outpatient basis with some success using tricyclic antidepressant medication. Apparently, Dr. Osheroff had not been taking his medication prior to his admission to Chestnut Lodge, and his condition had worsened. He was diagnosed by hospital staff as suffering primarily from a narcissistic personality disorder and secondarily from manic-depressive illness (Klerman, 1990; Malcolm, 1987).

Medication was not offered to Dr. Osheroff during his hospitalization because hospital staff hoped that he could achieve what they viewed as "more basic" changes in his personality through psychotherapy. As an alternative to medication, Dr. Osheroff was seen in individual, psychoanalytic psychotherapy 4 times a week, and he participated in group therapy as well. During Dr. Osheroff's 7 months of hospitalization, his condition did not improve and actually may have deteriorated somewhat. After this time, his family discharged him from Chestnut Lodge and admitted him to another private psychiatric hospital, Silver Hill in Connecticut. At Silver Hill, Dr. Osheroff was diagnosed as suffering from a psychotic depressive reaction, and he was treated with phenothiazines and tricyclic antidepressants. He began to improve within 3 weeks after treatment began, and he was discharged from the hospital within 3 months. Although he continued to experience some problems, following his discharge Dr. Osheroff was able to resume his medical practice with the help of outpatient psychotherapy and antidepressants (Klerman, 1990; Malcolm, 1987).

In 1982, Dr. Osheroff sued Chestnut Lodge for negligence. His claim stated that Chestnut Lodge had misdiagnosed his condition, failed to offer appropriate treatment, and failed to offer him informed consent about treatment alternatives (Malcolm, 1987). He argued that research available in 1979 provided clear support for the use of medication in the treatment of severe depression but offered no support for the use of psychoanalytic psychotherapy in the treatment of either depression or narcissistic personality disorder. As required by state law in Maryland, the matter was first heard by an arbitration panel. The panel initially awarded Dr. Osheroff $250,000 in damages, but later reduced the amount of the award. Both sides appealed the decision of the arbitration board, but the matter was eventually settled out of court (Klerman, 1990).

The private settlement of this case limits its precedent-setting value. Nevertheless, it suggests that mental health professionals will be held to increasingly higher standards in offering, or at least informing patients about the risks and benefits of alternative treatments. As researchers demonstrate that certain approaches are more or less effective in treating particular disorders, offering informed consent about treatment alternatives is likely to become a routine practice for mental health professionals. Informed consent means providing accurate information about risks and benefits in an understandable and noncoercive manner.

WHO IS THE CLIENT?

An issue closely related to the choice of a therapeutic approach is the choice of who is to receive treatment. Many psychological problems are closely linked with family difficulties, as we have discussed in previous chapters. Researchers continue to debate whether particular disorders cause family distress or whether family distress causes particular disorders, but some degree of reciprocal causality surely operates even for severe disorders like schizophrenia (Gotlib & McCabe, 1990). This raises the question of who should be targeted to receive psychological treatment as well as what sort of treatment they should receive.

The issue is not a minor one. Not only are certain treatments more effective than others for certain disorders, but the choice of a treatment can convey subtle but important messages about the cause of psychological problems and the responsibility for changing them. For example, individual therapy with a troubled child or a depressed wife can communicate both to the clients and their families that the problem rests within the individual, even though the difficulties might be a reaction to poor parenting or to an abusive marriage. Similarly, family therapy can falsely convey the impression that schizophrenia is caused by inadequate child rearing. Some of these impressions can be corrected by direct feedback from a therapist, but some are unavoidable consequences of the focus of treatment.

Another problem arises when therapists are unclear about who their client is. To whom do therapists owe confidentiality? Should information that therapists obtain from children be held in confidence, or are parents entitled to know what their children are saying in therapy? If a couple divorces after marital therapy, can a therapist testify at the request of one spouse and over the objection of the other? If a therapist sees a client in court-ordered treatment, must (or can) information on therapy be shared with the court? There are no easy solutions to such dilemmas. Clearly, the best approach is for therapists to decide who their client is before the question of disclosure arises, and to share their position on confidentiality with all involved parties. Confidentiality, however, is not an all-or-none proposition.

Confidentiality

Confidentiality—the ethical obligation not to reveal private communications—is basic to psychotherapy. The therapist's guarantee of privacy is essential to facilitating the disclosure of important, clinically relevant information, and the maintenance of confidentiality with past clients is essential to gaining the trust of future clients. For these reasons, confidentiality standards are a part of the professional ethics of all of the major mental health professions, and they are frequently addressed in state licensing regulations as well.

Despite the overriding importance of confidentiality, mental health professionals sometimes may be compelled by law to reveal confidential information. For example, all states require mental health professionals to break confidentiality and report suspected cases of child abuse. *Privileged communications* are confidential exchanges that legislation explicitly protects from being revealed. Various state statutes extend some privileged communication to psychologists and psychiatrists, as they do to physicians, lawyers, and the clergy (Morse, 1990), but child abuse must be reported in all states. This requirement can create dilemmas for therapists (Smith & Meyer, 1985). In order to provide fully informed consent, must a therapist make the limits on confidentiality clear before beginning therapy? If therapists tell their clients that their disclosures of child abuse will be reported to social service agencies, does this encourage clients to be something less than honest? Does reporting child abuse undermine the therapeutic relationship that might benefit an abused child?

Confidentiality also must be broken when clients are dangerous to themselves or others, so that civil commitment can proceed. The influential case of *Tarasoff* v. *Regents of the University of California* [551 P.2d 334 (1976)] identified another obligation that therapists may assume when a client expresses violent intentions: the duty to warn the potential victim.

TARASOFF AND THE DUTY TO PROTECT POTENTIAL VICTIMS

On October 27, 1969, a young woman named Tatiana Tarasoff was killed by Prosenjit Poddar, a foreign student at the University of California at Berkeley. Poddar had pursued a romantic relationship with Tarasoff, but after having been repeatedly rejected by her, he sought treatment at the Berkeley student health facility. Poddar was diagnosed as suffering from paranoid schizophrenia, and the clinical psychologist who treated Poddar concluded that he was dangerous to himself and others. After consulting with two psychiatrists, the psychologist decided to pursue civil commitment. He notified the campus police of his concerns, and asked them to detain Poddar for the purpose of an emergency commitment. The police concluded that Poddar was not dangerous, however, and released him after he agreed to stay away from Tarasoff. Poddar subsequently discontinued therapy, and no one notified Tarasoff of the threat that had been made on her life. Poddar had never mentioned Tatiana Tarasoff by name, but the information he related to the psychologist was sufficient to deduce

her identity. Two months after the police had questioned him, Poddar murdered Tarasoff after being rejected by her once more.

Tarasoff's parents sued the university, the therapists, and the police for negligence. The California Supreme Court ruled that the defendants were liable for failing to warn the woman of the impending danger. Specifically, the court ruled that therapists are liable if (1) they should have known about the dangerousness based on accepted professional standards of conduct, and (2) they failed to exercise reasonable care in warning the potential victim. Subsequent California cases have limited the duty to protect to cases that involve a specific, identifiable target of potential violence. A general statement of intended violence invokes no duty to protect (Goodman, 1985).

The *Tarasoff* case prompted subsequent litigation, and at least ten states have enacted laws that outline therapists' duty to protect potential victims of violence (Geske, 1989). Guidelines for evaluating and documenting assessments of dangerousness to others are rapidly becoming as important as policies for assessing suicide risk (Monahan, 1993). Still, the issues raised by *Tarasoff* are far from resolved. For example, we can easily foresee future cases in which questions will be raised about therapists' duty to protect the unwitting sexual partners of their clients who have AIDS.

(FX7-Oct.28)--MURDER VICTIM AND SUSPECT--Pretty Tatiana Tarasoff, 20-year old University of California junior, was brutally stabbed to death Monday on the doorstep of her Berkeley, Calif., home while nearly a dozen neighbors watched in horror. Police said Prosenjit Poddar (right), a U.C. graduate student, will be arraigned on charges of slaying the girl.

▲ Tatiana Tarasoff and Prosenjit Poddar, the man who killed her. The California Supreme Court ruled that Poddar's therapist should have warned Tarasoff that her life might be in danger.

Summary

The U.S. legal system assumes that behavior is the product of **free will,** the capacity to make choices and freely act upon them. The law therefore holds people responsible for their own actions. Psychology rejects the notion of free will and instead emphasizes **determinism,** the idea that behavior is caused by biological, psychological, and social forces. Assumptions about free will and determinism conflict strongly in the **insanity defense.** The legally insane individual is not assumed to be acting out of free will and therefore is not held responsible for his or her actions.

The M'Naghten test is one rule for finding a person not guilty by reason of insanity. According to this rule, legal insanity is established if a mental disease or defect prevents a criminal from knowing the wrongfulness of his or her actions. A second major rule, the irresistible impulse test, indicates that defendants are insane if they were unable to control their actions because of mental disease or defect. Controversies about the insanity defense have caused some states to drop the irresistible impulse test, as well as to shift the burden of proof from the prosecution to the defense. Another new development is the creation of the verdict of guilty but mentally ill, an outcome that holds defendants criminally responsible for their crimes but helps ensure that they receive treatment.

The precise meaning of the term *mental disease* or *mental defect* can be controversial. Some professionals would allow any DSM-IV disorder to qualify a defendant for the insanity defense; other commentators have argued for a broader view that would include some especially difficult life circumstances; and still others would sharply restrict the definition to the DSM diagnoses of mental retardation, schizophrenia, mood disorders, and cognitive disorders. Whatever definition is used, mental health professionals who serve as expert witnesses are responsible only for offering opinions about psychological well-being. The court, not the expert witness, is responsible for determining the ultimate issue of insanity.

Competence is the defendant's ability to understand legal proceedings and to participate in his or her own defense. Many more people accused of crimes are institutionalized because of findings of incompetence than because of insanity. Incompetence has received far less attention, perhaps because, unlike the insanity defense, competence determinations raise few broad philosophical issues about responsibility.

The issue of **civil commitment**—hospitalizing people against their will—reflects philosophical tensions within the law. On the one hand are libertarian views, which emphasize protecting the rights of the individual. On the other are paternalist approaches, which emphasize the state's duty to protect its citizens. Emergency commitment procedures allow an acutely disturbed individual to be temporarily confined in a mental hospital without a court order, typically for no more than a few days. Formal commitment procedures involve a formal legal hearing and lead to involuntary hospitalization that lasts for much longer periods of time. Three grounds dominate formal commitment laws: (1) inability to care for self, (2) dangerous to self, and (3) dangerous to others. Controversies abound, but a relation between mental illness and "dangerousness" does exist, and mental health professionals can predict dangerousness with some accuracy.

Paternalists and libertarians disagree concerning the commitment of minors who can be hospitalized by their parents. Admissions of adolescents to mental hospitals have increased dramatically, and some commentators have suggested that many minors are committed to mental hospitals merely because they are troublesome to their parents and because hospitalization is profitable to private psychiatric hospitals.

The rights of mental patients have received increased attention since the 1970s. The right to treatment indicates that hospitalized patients must receive therapy and not just custodial care. The right to treatment in the least restrictive environment indicates that therapy should be provided in community settings when it is possible and appropriate. The right to refuse treatment indicates that patients cannot be forced to receive certain treatments (for example, taking medications) without informed consent or careful substituted judgment. Concerns about patients' rights also have given impetus to the **deinstitutionalization** movement, the philosophy that many of the mentally ill and mentally retarded can be better cared for in their community than in large mental hospitals. Unfortunately, the lack of follow-up care in the community has undermined this laudable goal.

Family law focuses on such issues as divorce, spousal abuse, adoption, juvenile delinquency, child custody disputes, and child abuse and neglect. Family law and mental health law have different roots, and cases involving one are typically tried in different courts than are cases involving the other. A general dilemma in family law is how to balance the potentially competing interests of children, parents, and the state.

Child custody must be decided when parents divorce. These decisions involve determinations about both physical custody—where the children will live—and legal custody—how the parents will make decisions about their children. The law that governs custody determinations is the child's best interests standard, a vague directive that requires judgments as to what the child's best interests are and what the future will bring. Parents often make determinations about their own children's best interests privately in mediation or elsewhere.

Child abuse may involve physical abuse, sexual abuse, neglect, or psychological abuse. Reports of child abuse have increased greatly in recent years, but neither the law nor mental health professionals have reached consensus on how best to fulfill children's best interests in these cases.

Psychiatrists, clinical psychologists, and social workers all have **professional responsibilities** to meet the ethical standards of their profession and to uphold the laws of the states in which they practice. Key professional issues include obtaining **informed consent** about alternative treatment procedures, clearly identifying whom the professional is serving, and maintaining **confidentiality.** A relatively new concern is the duty to warn potential victims when a client reveals violent intentions.

Critical Thinking

1. What is your view on the insanity defense? Should we hold mentally ill criminals fully responsible for all of their actions? What about battered women who kill their husbands? What about abused children who kill a parent or stepparent?

2. What is your position on deinstitutionalization? Has the pendulum swung too far in the direction of releasing mental patients into communities with inadequate services? What do you think when you see someone who is clearly mentally ill living in the streets? How would you feel if a group home for the mentally ill was being planned for the neighborhood in which you live?

3. Do you think it is unethical for mental health professionals to offer treatments they prefer to use even when research indicates that other approaches are more effective?

Glossary

Abnormal psychology The application of psychological science to the study of mental disorders. Includes investigation of the causes and treatment of psychopathological conditions.

Abstinence violation effect The guilt and perceived loss of control that the person feels whenever he or she slips and finds himself or herself returning to drug use after an extended period of abstinence.

Addiction A term used to describe substance use problems such as alcoholism. Replaced in official terminology by the term *substance dependence*, with which it is synonymous.

Affect The pattern of observable behaviors that are associated with these subjective feelings. People express affect through changes in their facial expressions, the pitch of their voices, and their hand and body movements.

Agism A number of misconceptions and prejudices about aging and older adults.

Agnosia ("perception without meaning"). The inability to identify objects. The person's sensory functions are unimpaired, but he or she is unable to recognize the source of stimulation.

Agoraphobia An exaggerated fear of being in situations from which escape might be difficult. Literally means "fear of the market place" and is sometimes described as fear of public spaces.

Agreeableness A dimension of personality that describes the person's willingness to cooperate and empathize with other people.

Alogia A form of speech disturbance found in schizophrenia. Can include reductions in the amount of speech (poverty of speech) or speech that does not convey meaningful information (poverty of content of speech).

Alzheimer's disease A form of dementia in which cognitive impairment appears gradually and deterioration is progressive. A definite diagnosis of Alzheimer's dis-

ease requires the observation of two specific types of brain lesions: neurofibrillary tangles and senile plaques.

Amnestic disorder A form of cognitive disorder characterized by memory impairments that are more limited or circumscribed than those seen in dementia or delirium.

Amniocentesis The extraction of fluid from the amniotic sac in order to test for chromosomal and genetic defects in the developing fetus.

Analogue study A research procedure in which the investigator studies behaviors that resemble mental disorders—or isolated features of mental disorders. Usually employed in situations in which the investigator hopes to gain greater experimental control over the independent variable.

Androgyny The possession of both "female" and "male" gender-role characteristics.

Anhedonia The inability to experience pleasure. In contrast to blunted affect, which refers to the lack of outward expression, anhedonia is a lack of positive subjective feelings.

Anorexia nervosa A type of eating disorder characterized by the refusal to maintain a minimally normal body weight along with other symptoms related to eating and body image.

Anterograde amnesia The inability to learn or remember new material after a particular point in time.

Antisocial personality disorder A pervasive and persistent disregard for, and frequent violation of, the rights of other people. Also known as *psychopathy*. In DSM-IV, it is defined in terms of a persistent pattern of irresponsible and antisocial behavior that begins during childhood or adolescence and continues into the adult years.

Anxiety A diffuse emotional reaction that is out of proportion to threats from the environment. Rather than being

directed toward the person's present circumstances, anxiety is typically associated with the anticipation of future problems.

Anxious attachment An insecure relationship in which an infant or child shows ambivalence about seeking reassurance or security from an attachment figure.

Aphasia The loss or impairment of previously acquired abilities in language comprehension or production that cannot be explained by sensory or motor defects or by diffuse brain dysfunction.

Apraxia The loss of a previously acquired ability to perform purposeful movements in response to verbal commands. The problem cannot be explained by muscle weakness or simple incoordination.

Asperger's disorder A subtype of pervasive developmental disorder (new in DSM-IV) that is identical to autism (oddities in social interaction, stereotyped behavior), with the exception that there is no clinically significant delay in language.

Assessment The process of gathering and organizing information about a person's behavior.

Attachments Selective bonds that develop between infants and their caregivers, usually their parents, and are theorized to be related to later development. Analogous to the process imprinting which has been observed in many animals.

Attention-deficit/hyperactivity disorder A psychological disorder of childhood characterized by hyperactivity, inattention, and impulsivity. Typically has an onset by the early school years.

Attribution Perceived causes; people's beliefs about cause-effect relations.

Atypical antipsychotic A type of medication that is beneficial for psychotic patients but does not produce extrapyramidal motor side effects and may not be associated with increased risk of tardive dyskinesia.

Autistic disorder A severe form of pervasive developmental disorder characterized by oddities in social interaction (autistic aloneness), communication impairments, and stereotyped behavior, interests, and activities.

Autonomic nervous system The division of the peripheral nervous system that regulates the functions of various bodily organs such as the heart and stomach. The actions of the autonomic nervous system are largely involuntary, and it has two branches, the sympathetic and parasympathetic nervous systems.

Aversion therapy A classical conditioning technique for attempting to eliminate unwanted behavior by pairing an unpleasant (aversive) stimulus with the behavior, for example, inducing nausea when alcohol is consumed.

Avoidant personality disorder An enduring pattern of thinking and behavior that is characterized by pervasive social discomfort, fear of negative evaluation, and timidity. People with this disorder tend to be socially isolated outside of family circles. They want to be liked by others, but they are easily hurt by even minimal signs of disapproval from other people.

Avolition (lack of volition or will). A negative symptom of schizophrenia involving a loss of willpower, indecisiveness, and ambivalence. The person becomes apathetic and ceases to engage in purposeful actions.

Axon The trunk of the neuron where messages are transmitted outward toward other cells with which a given neuron communicates.

Balanced placebo design A research design that combines the placebo and antiplacebo methods. It can be used to assess the effect of alcohol, the effect of expectations, and the interaction of alcohol by expectation.

Base rates Population frequencies. Relative base rates set statistical limits on the degree to which two variables can be associated with each other.

Behavioral coding system (also known as a formal observation schedule). An observational assessment procedure that focuses on the frequency of specific behavioral events.

Behavioral family therapy A form of family treatment that may include several variations, but always trains parents to use the principles of operant conditioning as a way of improving child discipline.

Behavioral gerontology A subspecialty within behavioral medicine developed specifically for studying and treating the behavioral components of illness among older adults.

Behavioral marital therapy A variation on couples therapy that emphasizes the partners' moment-to-moment interaction, particularly their exchange of positive and negative behaviors, their style of communication, and their strategies for solving problems.

Behavioral medicine A multidisciplinary field concerned with studying and treating the behavioral components of physical illness.

Behavior genetics The study of broad genetic contributions to the development of normal and abnormal behavior.

Behavior therapy An approach to psychotherapy that focuses on behavior change in the present, not insight about the past. Behavior therapy includes a diverse array of techniques, many of which were developed from basic, psychological research.

Behaviorism The belief within scientific psychology that observable behaviors, not unobservable cognitive or emotional states, are the appropriate focus of psychological study. Movement begun by John B. Watson.

Bereavement Grieving in response to the death of a loved one.

Biofeedback Behavioral medicine treatment that uses laboratory equipment to monitor physiological processes (that generally occur outside of conscious awareness) and provide feedback about them. Hypothesized to help patients to gain conscious control over problematic physiological processes such as hypertension.

Biological reductionism The assumption that biological explanations are more useful than psychological explanations because they deal with smaller units—with brain chemistry, for example, instead of emotional experience.

Biopsychosocial model A view of the etiology of mental disorders which assumes that disorder can best be understood in terms of the interaction of biological, psychological, and social systems.

Bipolar mood disorder A form of mood disorder in which the person experiences episodes of mania as well as episodes of depression.

Blunted affect A flattening or restriction of the person's nonverbal display of emotional responses. Blunted patients fail to exhibit signs of emotion or feeling.

Body dysmorphic disorder A type of somatoform disorder characterized by constant preoccupation with some imagined defect in physical appearance.

Borderline personality disorder An enduring pattern of thinking and behavior whose essential feature is a pervasive instability in mood, self-image, and interpersonal relationships. Manifestations of this disorder include frantic efforts to avoid real or imagined abandonment. People who fit this description frequently hold opinions of significant others that vacillate between unrealistically positive and negative extremes.

Brief psychotic disorder A diagnostic category in DSM-IV that includes people who exhibit psychotic symptoms for at least one day but no more than one month. After the symptoms are resolved, the person returns to the same level of functioning that had been achieved prior to the psychotic episode.

Brief reactive psychosis A disorder that includes patients who exhibit transient symptoms of schizophrenia followed by a complete recovery.

Bulimia nervosa A type of eating disorder characterized by repeated episodes of binge eating followed by inappropriate compensatory behaviors (such as self-induced vomiting) together with other symptoms related to eating and body image.

Cardiovascular disease (CVD) A group of disorders that affect the heart and circulatory system. Hypertension (high blood pressure) and coronary heart disease are the most important forms of CVD.

Catatonia Motor symptoms that can include either immobility and marked muscular rigidity or excitement and over-activity.

Catatonic type A subtype of schizophrenia that is characterized by symptoms of motor immobility (including rigidity and posturing) or excessive and purposeless motor activity.

Categorical approach to classification A view of classification based on the assumption that there are qualitative differences between normal and abnormal behavior as well as between one form of abnormal behavior and other forms of abnormal behavior.

Central nervous system The major communication system in the body, which is comprised of the brain and the spinal cord.

Cerebellum Part of the hindbrain that serves as a control center in helping to coordinate physical movements. The cerebellum receives information on body movements and integrates this feedback with directives about desired actions from higher brain structures.

Cerebral cortex The uneven surface of the brain that lies just underneath the skull, and controls and integrates sophisticated memory, sensory, and motor functions.

Cerebral hemispheres The two major structures of the forebrain and the site of most sensory, emotional, and cognitive processes. The functions of the cerebral hemispheres are lateralized. In general, the left cerebral hemisphere is involved in language and related functions, and the right side is involved in spatial organization and analysis.

Child abuse A legal decision that a parent or other responsible adult has inflicted damage or offered inadequate care to a child; may include physical abuse, sexual abuse, neglect, and psychological abuse.

Child custody A legal decision, especially common in separation and divorce, that involves determining where children will reside and how parents will share legal rights and responsibilities for childrearing.

Chromosomes Chainlike structures found in the nucleus of cells that carry genes and information about heredity. Humans normally have 23 pairs of chromosomes.

Civil commitment The involuntary hospitalization of the mentally ill; the decision typically is justified based on dangerousness to self or others (or inability to care for self).

Classical conditioning Pavlov's form of learning through association. A conditioned response eventually is elicited by a conditioned stimulus after repeated pairings with an unconditioned stimulus (which produces an unconditioned response).

Classification system A system for grouping together objects or organisms that share certain properties in common. In psychopathology, the set of categories in DSM-IV that describes mental disorders.

Client-centered therapy Carl Rogers's humanistic therapy that follows the client's lead. Therapists offer warmth,

empathy, and genuineness, but clients solve their own problems.

Clinical psychology The profession and academic discipline that is concerned with the application of psychological science to the assessment and treatment of mental disorders.

Coercion A pattern of interaction in which unwitting parents positively reinforce children's misbehavior (by giving in to their demands), and children negatively reinforce parents' capitulation (by ending their obnoxious behavior).

Cognitive behavior therapy The expansion of the scope of behavior therapy to include cognition and research on human information processing. Includes various general techniques such as Beck's cognitive therapy and Ellis's RET.

Cognitive therapy A psychotherapy technique and important part of cognitive behavior therapy that was developed specifically as a treatment for depression by Aaron Beck. Beck's cognitive therapy involves challenging negative cognitive distortions through a technique called collaborative empiricism.

Community psychology An approach within clinical psychology that attempts to improve individual well-being by promoting social change.

Co-morbidity The simultaneous manifestation of more than one disorder.

Competence Defendants' ability to understand legal proceedings and act rationally in relation to them. Competence evaluations can take place at different points in the legal process, but competence to stand trial is particularly important (the ability to participate in one's own defense).

Compulsion A repetitive, ritualistic behavior that is aimed at the reduction of anxiety and distress or the prevention of some dreaded event. Compulsions are considered by the person to be senseless or irrational. The person feels compelled to perform the compulsion; he or she attempts to resist but cannot.

Concordance Agreement. In behavior genetic studies, concordance occurs when a relative has the same disorder as a proband (index case); for example, when twin pairs either both have the same disorder or both are free from the disorder.

Conditioned response A response that is elicited by a conditioned stimulus;

similar to but weaker than the unconditioned response. Central in classical conditioning.

Conditioned stimulus A neutral stimulus that, when repeatedly paired with an unconditioned stimulus, comes to produce a conditioned response. In Pavlov's experiments, the bell was the conditioned stimulus. Central in classical conditioning.

Conduct disorder A psychological disorder of childhood that is defined primarily by behavior that is illegal as well as antisocial.

Confidentiality The ethical obligation not to reveal private communications in psychotherapy and in other professional contacts between mental health professionals and their clients.

Conscientiousness A dimension of personality that reflects the person's persistence in the pursuit of goals, the ability to organize activities, and dependability in completing expected duties.

Construct (or hypothetical construct) A theoretical device that refer to events or states that reside within a person and are proposed to help understand or explain a person's behavior.

Construct validity The overall strength of the network of relations that have been observed among variables that are used to define a construct. The extent to which the construct possesses some systematic meaning.

Controlled drinking A controversial goal for some alcohol abusers. This concept refers to moderate consumption of alcohol in a pattern that avoids drinking to the point of intoxication.

Conversion disorder A type of somatoform disorder characterized by physical symptoms that often mimic those found in neurological diseases such as blindness, numbing, or paralysis. The symptoms often make no anatomical sense.

Coronary heart disease (CHD) A group of diseases of the heart that includes angina pectoris (chest pains) and myocardial infarction (heart attack).

Corpus callosum Connects the two cerebral hemispheres and is involved in coordinating the different functions performed by the left and the right sides of the brain.

Correlational method The scientific method which involves systematically studying the nature and the strength of the relation between two factors or variables (their co-relation).

Correlation coefficient A number that always ranges between -1.00 and +1.00 and indicates the strength and direction of the relation between two variables. A higher absolute value indicates a stronger relation, while a correlation coefficient of 0 indicates no relation. The sign indicates the direction of the correlation.

Countertransference The therapist's own feelings toward the client, particularly as described in psychoanalysis.

Couples therapy Partners who are involved in an intimate relationship are seen together in psychotherapy; sometimes called marital therapy or marriage counseling. Improving communication and negotiation are common goals.

Creutzfeldt-Jakob disease A type of dementia caused by a specific viral infection.

Criminal responsibility A legal concept that holds a person responsible for committing a crime if he or she (a) has been proven to have committed the act and (b) was legally sane at the time.

Cultural-familial retardation Typically mild mental retardation that runs in families and is linked with poverty. Thought to be the most common cause of mental retardation. There is controversy about the relative roles of genes or psychosocial disadvantage.

Cultural relativity The view that normal and abnormal behavior are defined by culture, and therefore the definitions are relative, not absolute.

Cybernetics A communication and control process that uses feedback loops in order to adjust progress toward a goal, for example, the operation of a thermostat.

Cyclothymia A chronic, less severe form of bipolar disorder. The bipolar equivalent of dysthymia.

Defense mechanisms Unconscious processes that service the ego and reduce conscious anxiety by distorting anxiety-producing memories, emotions, and impulses, for example, projection, displacement, or rationalization.

Deinstitutionalization The movement to treat the mentally ill and mentally retarded in communities rather than in large mental hospitals.

Delirium A confusional state that develops over a short period of time and is often associated with agitation and hyperactivity. The primary symptom is clouding of consciousness or reduced awareness of one's surroundings.

Delusion An obviously false and idiosyncratic belief that is rigidly held in spite of its preposterous nature.

Delusional disorder Describes persons who do not meet the full symptomatic criteria for schizophrenia, but they are preoccupied for at least one month with delusions that are not bizarre.

Dementia A gradually worsening loss of memory and related cognitive functions, including the use of language as well as reasoning and decision making.

Dementia praecox Kraepelin's original term for the disorder now known as schizophrenia. It referred to psychotic disorders which ended in severe intellectual deterioration (dementia) and which had an early or premature (praecox) onset, usually during adolescence.

Dendrites "Branches" out from the soma of the neuron that serve the primary function of receiving messages from other cells.

Dependent personality disorder An enduring pattern of dependent and submissive behavior. These people are exceedingly dependent on other people for advice and reassurance. Often unable to make everyday decisions on their own, they feel anxious and helpless when they are alone.

Dependent variable The outcome that is hypothesized to vary according to manipulations in the independent variable in an experiment.

Depersonalization disorder A type of dissociative disorder characterized by severe and persistent feelings of being detached from oneself (depersonalization experiences). For example, the repeated and profound sensation of floating above your body and observing yourself act.

Depression Can refer to a *symptom* (subjective feelings of sadness), a *mood* (sustained and pervasive feelings of despair), or to a clinical *syndrome* (in which the presence of a depressed mood is accompanied by several additional symptoms, such as fatigue, loss of energy, sleeping difficulties, and appetite changes).

Determinism The philosophical assumption (made by all psychologists except humanistic psychologists) that behavior is a potentially predictable consequence of biological, psychological, and social factors. Contrasts with the assumption that behavior is the product of free will.

Detoxification The process of short-term medical care (medication, rest, diets, flu-

ids, and so on) during removal of a drug upon which a person has become dependent. The aim is to minimize withdrawal symptoms.

Developmental psychopathology A new approach to abnormal psychology that emphasizes the importance of normal development to understanding abnormal behavior.

Diagnosis The process of determining the nature of a person's disorder. In the case of psychopathology, deciding that a person fits into a particular diagnostic category, such as schizophrenia or major depressive disorder.

Diagnostic efficiency The overall ability of a test to make correct and incorrect predictions.

Diathesis A predisposition to disorder. Also known as *vulnerability*. A diathesis only causes abnormal behavior when it is combined with a stress or challenging experience.

Diathesis-stress model A general view of the etiology of mental disorder which assumes that a disorder is produced by an interaction between some type of predisposition and a precipitating event.

Dimensional approach to classification A view of classification based on the assumption that behavior is distributed on a continuum from normal to abnormal. Also includes the assumption that differences between one type of behavior and another are quantitative rather than qualitative in nature.

Disorganized speech (also known as *formal thought disorder*) Severe disruptions of verbal communication, involving the form of the person's speech.

Disorganized type A subtype of schizophrenia (formerly known as hebephrenia) that is characterized by disorganized speech, disorganized behavior, and flat or inappropriate affect. If delusions or hallucinations are present, their content is not well organized.

Dissociation The separation of mental processes such as memory or consciousness that normally are integrated. Normal dissociative experiences include fleeting feelings of unreality and *deja vu* experiences—the feeling that an event has happened before. Extreme dissociative experiences characterize dissociative disorders.

Dissociative amnesia A type of dissociative disorder characterized by the sudden inability to recall extensive and important personal information. The onset often is sudden and may occur in response to trauma or extreme stress.

Dissociative disorders A category of psychological disorders characterized by persistent, maladaptive disruptions in the integration of memory, consciousness, or identity. Examples include dissociative fugue and dissociative identity disorder (multiple personality).

Dissociative fugue A rare dissociative disorder characterized by sudden, unplanned travel, the inability to remember details about the past, and confusion about identity or the assumption of a new identity. The onset typically follows a traumatic event.

Dissociative identity disorder An unusual dissociative disorder characterized by the existence of two or more distinct personalities in a single individual (also known as multiple personality disorder). At least two personalities repeatedly take control over the person's behavior, and some personalities have limited or no memory of the other.

Diversion A practice of directing problem youth away from the juvenile justice system and into some alternative treatment or program. For example, a juvenile offender may be referred to counseling instead of having a hearing held in court.

Dizygotic (DZ) twins Faternal twins produced from separate fertilized eggs. Like all siblings, DZ twins share an average of 50 percent of their genes.

Dominance The hierarchical ordering of a social group into more and less powerful members. Dominance rankings are indexed by the availability of uncontested privileges.

Dose-response effects Different treatment responses to different dosages of a medication.

Double blind, placebo-controlled study A study in which neither the therapist nor the patient knows whether the patient receives the real treatment (for example, a medication) or a placebo.

Down syndrome The most common known biological cause of mental retardation. It is caused by an extra chromosome (usually on the 21st pair) and associated with a characteristic physical appearance. It was termed *mongolism* by the nineteenth-century British physician Langdon Down.

Drug of abuse (also called a psychoactive substance) A chemical substance that alters a person's mood, level of perception, or brain functioning.

Dualism The philosophical view that the mind and body are separate. Dates to the writings of the philosopher René Descartes, who attempted to balance the dominant religious views of his times with emerging scientific reasoning. Descartes argued that many human functions have biological explanations, but some human experiences have no somatic representation. Thus, he argued for a distinction—a dualism—between mind and body.

Dyskinesia Involuntary movements such as tics, chorea, or tremors, that are often associated with certain types of dementia.

Dyspareunia Persistent genital pain during or after sexual intercourse. The problem can occur in either men or women.

Eating disorders A category of psychological disorders characterized by severe disturbances in eating behavior, specifically anorexia nervosa and bulimia nervosa.

Eclectic An approach of picking different treatments according to the needs of individual disorders and individual clients.

Ego One of Freud's three central personality structures. In Freudian theory, the ego must deal with reality as it attempts to fulfill id impulses as well as superego demands. The ego operates on the reality principle, and much of the ego resides in conscious awareness.

Ego analysis Originated in the work of different therapists trained in Freudian psychoanalysis, but who focused much more on the ego than on the id. Ego analysts are concerned with the patient's dealings with the external world.

Electra complex Freud's hypothesis of "penis envy," girls yearn for something their fathers have and that they are "missing." In Freudian theory, girls resolve the Electra complex by identifying with their mothers.

Electroconvulsive therapy (ECT) A treatment that involves the deliberate induction of a convulsion by passing electricity through one or both hemispheres of the brain. Modern ECT uses restraints, medication, and carefully controlled electrical stimulation to minimize adverse consequences. Can be an effective treatment for severe depression, especially following the failure of other approaches.

Emotion A state of arousal that is defined by subjective feeling states, such as sadness, anger, and disgust. Emotions are often accompanied by physiological changes, such as in heart rate and respiration rate.

Emotion-focused coping Internally oriented coping in an attempt to alter one's emotional or cognitive responses to a stressor.

Empathy Emotional understanding. Empathy involves understanding others' unique feelings and perspectives. Highlighted by Rogers but basic to most forms of psychotherapy.

Endocrine system A collection of glands found at various locations throughout the body, including the ovaries or testes and the pituitary, thyroid, and adrenal glands. Releases hormones that sometimes act as neuromodulators and affect responses to stress. Also important in physical growth and development.

Endorphins The term is a contraction formed from the words endogenous (meaning within) and morphine. They are relatively short chains of amino acids, or neuropeptides, that are naturally synthesized in the brain and are closely related to morphine (an opioid) in terms of their pharmacological properties.

Epidemiology The scientific study of the frequency and distribution of disorders within a population.

Erectile dysfunction Difficulty experienced by a man in obtaining an erection that is sufficient to accomplish intercourse or maintaining an erection long enough to satisfy himself or his partner during intercourse.

Estrogen The female sex hormone.

Etiology The causes or origins of a disorder.

Experiment A powerful scientific method that allows researchers to determine cause and effect relations. Key elements include random assignment, the manipulation of the independent variable, and careful measurement of the dependent variable.

Experimental hypothesis A new prediction made by an investigator to be tested in an experiment.

Expressed emotion (EE) A concept that refers to a collection of negative or intrusive attitudes sometimes displayed by relatives of patients who are being treated for a disorder. If at least one of a patient's relatives is hostile, critical, or emotionally overinvolved, the family environment typically is considered high in expressed emotion.

Externalizing disorders An empirically derived category of disruptive child behavior problems that create problems for the external world (for example, attention-deficit/hyperactivity disorder).

External validity Whether the findings of an experiment generalize to other people, places, and circumstances, particularly real-life situations.

Extinction The gradual elimination of a response when learning conditions change. In classical conditioning, extinction occurs when a conditioned stimulus no longer is paired with an unconditioned stimulus. In operant conditioning, extinction occurs when the contingent is removed between behavior and its consequences.

Extraversion A dimension of personality that describes a person's activity level, especially interest in interacting with other people, and the ease with which the person expresses positive emotions.

False negative A person whose response to a test indicated that the trait or disorder in question was not present, when it was, in fact, present.

False positive A person whose response to a test indicated that the trait or disorder in question was present when it was, in fact, not present.

Family life cycle The developmental course of family relationships throughout life; most family life cycle theories mark stages and transitions with major changes in family relationships and membership.

Family therapy Treatment that might include two, three, or more family members in the psychotherapy sessions. Improving communication and negotiation are common goals, although family therapy also may be used to help well members adjust to a family member's illness.

Family transitions Major changes in family life and family relationships that typically involve the addition or loss of members of a family household.

Fear An unpleasant emotional reaction experienced in the face of real, immediate danger. It builds quickly in intensity and helps to organize the person's responses to threats from the environment.

Fetal alcohol syndrome A disorder caused by heavy maternal alcohol consumption and repeated exposure of the developing fetus to alcohol. Infants have retarded physical development, a small head, narrow eyes, cardiac defects, and cognitive impairments. Intellectual functioning ranges from mild mental retardation to normal intelligence with learning disabilities.

Fetishism The use of nonliving objects as a focus of sexual arousal

Fight or flight A response to a threat in which psychophysiological reactions mobilize the body to take action against danger.

Fixation The psychodynamic concept that psychological development is arrested at a particular age or stage. The person stops growing emotionally.

Flashbacks Reexperienced memories of past events, particularly as occurs in post-traumatic stress disorder or following use of hallucinogenic drugs.

Flooding A treatment for fears and phobias that involves exposure to the feared stimulus at full intensity. Works through extinction.

Forebrain The major portion of the brain made up primarily of the two cerebral hemispheres. Location of most sensory, emotional, and cognitive processes.

Fragile-X syndrome The second most common known biological cause of mental retardation. Transmitted genetically and indicated by a weakening or break on one arm of the X sex chromosome.

Free will The capacity to make choices and freely act upon them. A philosophical counterpoint to determinism, which is the scientific assumption that behavior is a predictable consequence of internal and external events. Humanistic psychology and the American legal system assume people act out of free will.

Gender identity A person's sense of himself or herself as being either male or female.

Gender identity disorder A strong and persistent identification with the opposite sex coupled with a sense of discomfort with one's anatomic sex.

Gender roles Roles associated with social expectations about gendered behavior, for example, "masculine" or "feminine" activities.

General adaptation syndrome (GAS) Selye's three stages in reaction to stress: alarm, resistance, and exhaustion.

Generalization Making accurate statements that extend beyond a specific sample to a larger population.

General paresis (general paralysis) A set of severe symptoms including dementia, delusions of grandeur, and paralysis caused by the sexually transmitted disease syphilis. Discovery of the cause of general paresis spurred the biological model of mental illness.

Genes Ultramicroscopic units of DNA that carry information about heredity. Located on the chromosomes.

Genotype An individual's actual genetic structure, most of which cannot be observed directly at this time.

Gerontology The multidisciplinary study of aging and older adults.

Gestalt therapy A variation of the humanistic approach to psychotherapy that underscores affective awareness and expression, genuineness, and experiencing the moment (living in the "here and now").

Grief The emotional and social process of coping with a separation or a loss, often described as proceeding in stages.

Group therapy The treatment of three or more people in a group setting, often using group relationships as a central part of therapy.

Hallucination A perceptual experience in the absence of external stimulation, such as hearing voices that aren't really there.

Health behavior A wide range of activities that are essential to promoting good health, including positive actions such as proper diet and the avoidance of negative activities such as cigarette smoking.

Health psychology A subspecialty in psychology concerned with the study and promotion of healthy behavior.

Heritability The variability in a behavioral characteristic that is accounted for by genetic factors.

Heritability ratio A statistic for computing the proportion of variance in a behavioral characteristic that is accounted for by genetic factors in a given study or series of studies.

Hierarchy of needs Humanistic psychologist Abraham Maslow's ordering of human needs into more or less pressing priorities. Includes survival, safety, belongingness, esteem, and self-actualization needs.

Hindbrain The lower, rear portion of the brain near the brainstem which includes the medulla, pons, and cerebellum. Controls basic biological functions that sustain life.

Histrionic personality disorder An enduring pattern of thinking and behavior that is characterized by excessive emotionality and attention-seeking behavior. People with this disorder are self-centered, vain, and demanding. Their emotions tend to be shallow and may vacillate erratically.

Holism The assumption that the whole is more than the sum of its parts. A central tenet of systems theory, and counterpoint to reductionism.

Homeostasis The tendency to maintain a steady state. A familiar in biology that also is widely applicable in psychology.

Hormones Chemical substances that are released into the bloodstream by glands in the endocrine system. Hormones affect the functioning of distant body systems and sometimes act as neuromodulators.

Humanistic psychotherapy An approach that assumes that the most essential human quality is the ability to make choices and freely act on them (free will). Promoted as a "third force" to counteract the deterministic views of psychodynamic and the behavioral approaches to psychotherapy.

Huntington's disease A primary, differentiated dementia characterized by the presence of unusual involuntary muscle movements. Many Huntington's patients also exhibit a variety of personality changes and symptoms of mental disorders, including primarily depression and anxiety.

Hypochondriasis A type of somatoform disorder characterized by a persons preoccupying fear or belief that he or she is suffering from a physical illness.

Hypomania An episode of increased energy that is not sufficiently severe to qualify as a full-blown manic episode.

Hypothalamus A part of the limbic system that plays a role in sensation, but more importantly it controls basic biological urges such as eating, drinking, and sexual activity, as well as much of the functioning of the autonomic nervous system.

Hysteria An outdated but influential diagnostic category that included both somatoform and dissociative disorders. Attempts to treat hysteria had a major effect on Charcot, Freud, and Janet, among others. In Greek, *hystera* means "uterus," a reflection of ancient speculation that hysteria was restricted to women and caused by frustrated sexual desires.

Iatrogenesis A creation of a disorder by an attempt to treat it.

Id One of Freud's three central personality structures. In Freudian theory, the id is present at birth and is the source of basic drives and motivations. The id houses biological drives (such as hunger) as well as Freud's two key psychological drives, sex and aggression. Operates according to the pleasure principle.

Identification A process wherein children not only imitate adults but also want to be like them and adopt their values. In Freudian theory, identification is the resolution to the Oedipal and Electra conflicts. In developmental psychology, a similar but broader concept than modeling.

Identity Erikson's term for the broad definition of self; in his view, identity is the product of the adolescent's struggle to answer the question, "Who am I?"

Identity crisis Erikson's period of basic uncertainty about self during late adolescence and early adult life. A consequence of the psychosocial stage of identity versus role confusion.

Inappropriate affect A form of emotional disturbance seen in schizophrenia. The central features of inappropriate affect are incongruity and lack of adaptability in emotional expression.

Incidence The number of new cases of a disorder that appear in a population during a specific period of time.

Independent variable The variable in an experiment that is controlled and deliberately manipulated by the experimenter (for example, whether or not a subject receives a treatment). Affects the dependent variable.

Infarct The area of dead tissue produced by a stroke.

Informed consent A legal and ethical safeguard concerning risks in research and in treatment. Includes (a) accurate information about potential risks and benefits, (b) competence on the part of subjects/patients to understand them, and (c) the ability of subjects/patients to participate voluntarily.

Inhibited sexual arousal Difficulty experienced by a woman in achieving or maintaining genital responses, such as lubrication and swelling, that are necessary to complete sexual intercourse.

Insanity A legal term referring to a defendant's state of mind at the time of committing a crime. An insane individual is not held legally responsible for his or her actions because of a mental disease or defect.

Insanity defense An attempt to prove that a person with a mental illness did not meet the legal criteria for sanity at the time of committing a crime. The inability to tell right from wrong and an "irresistible impulse" are the two most common contemporary grounds for the defense.

Insight Self-understanding; the extent to which a person recognizes the nature (or understands the potential causes) of his or her disorder. In psychoanalysis, insight is the ultimate goal, specifically, to bring formerly unconscious material into conscious awareness.

Intelligence quotient (IQ) A measure of intellectual ability that typically has a mean of 100 and a standard deviation of 15. An individual's IQ is determined by comparisons with norms for same-aged peers.

Internalizing disorders An empirically derived category of psychological problems of childhood that affect the child more than the external world (for example, depression).

Internal validity Whether changes in the dependent variable can be accurately attributed to changes in the independent variable in an experiment, that is, there are no experimental confounds.

Interpretation A tool in psychotherapy and psychoanalysis in which the therapist suggests new meanings about a client's accounts of his or her past and present life.

Introspection Reflections on inner experiences. Wundt attempted to use the introspective method in research; Freud relied on it in treatment and exploration of his own memories.

In vivo desensitization A treatment for overcoming fears and phobias that involves gradual exposure to feared stimuli in real life while simultaneously maintaining a state of relaxation. Contrast with systematic desensitization.

Irrational beliefs Impossible, absolute standards, such as, "Everyone must love me all of the time." Discussed by Albert Ellis and central to his Rational Emotive Therapy.

Isomorphic Identical in form. Contrasts with characteristics that undergo transformations in appearance but maintain underlying consistencies. For example, antisocial behavior changes in form across age (it is not isomorphic), but the persistent violation of rules is an underlying consistency.

Juvenile delinquency A legal term that refers to a minor who has violated the law and been judged responsible for the law breaking.

Korsakoff's syndrome An amnestic disorder sometimes associated with chronic alcoholism. Memory is impaired but other cognitive functions are not.

Labeling theory A perspective on mental disorders that is primarily concerned with the social context in which abnormal behavior occurs. Labeling theory is more interested in social factors that determine whether or not a person will be given a psychiatric diagnosis than in psychological or biological reasons for the behaviors.

La belle indifference A flippant lack of concern about physical symptoms that may accompany somatoform disorders.

Lateralization The specialized functioning of each cerebral hemisphere. In general, the left hemisphere is involved in language and related functions, and the right side is involved in spatial organization and analysis.

Lead poisoning Ingestion of toxic levels of lead (mainly through environmental pollutants) that can cause brain damage and a number of adverse behavioral and cognitive impairments, including mental retardation.

Learning disabilities A heterogenous group of educational problems characterized by academic performance that is notably below academic aptitude.

Life cycle transitions Movements from one social or psychological "stage" of adult development into a new one; often characterized by interpersonal, emotional, and identity conflict.

Lifespan development The study of continuities and changes in behavior, affect, and cognition from infancy through the last years of life.

Limbic system A variety of brain structures, including the thalamus and hypothalamus, that are central to the regulation of emotion and basic learning processes.

Linkage A process used to locate the position of a gene on a particular chromosome. Two genetic loci are said to be linked if they are close together on the same chromosome.

Longitudinal study A type of research design in which subjects are studied over a period of time (contrasts with the cross-sectional approach of studying subjects only at one point in time). Longitudinal studies attempt to establish whether hypothesized causes precede their putative effects in time.

Mainstreaming The educational philosophy that mentally retarded children should be taught, as much as possible, in regular classrooms rather than in "special" classes.

Mania A disturbance in mood characterized by symptoms such as elation, inflated self-esteem, hyperactivity, and accelerated speaking and thinking. An exaggerated feeling of physical and emotional well-being.

Medulla The part of the hindbrain that controls various body functions involved in sustaining life, including heart rate, blood pressure, and respiration.

Melancholia A particularly severe type of depression. In DSM-IV, melancholia is described in terms of a number of specific features such as loss of pleasure in activities and lack of reactivity to events in the person's environment that are normally pleasurable.

Menopause The cessation of menstruation and the associated physical and psychological changes that occur among middle-aged women (the so-called "change of life").

Mental retardation Substantial limitations in present functioning characterized by significantly subaverage intellectual functioning (IQ of 70 to 75 or below), concurrent limitations in adaptive skills, and an onset before age 18.

Midbrain Part of the brain between the hindbrain and forebrain that is involved in the control of some motor activities, especially those related to fighting and sex.

Minimal brain damage (MBD) Damage to the brain too slight to be detected with objective instruments but sometimes inferred from behavior. Was once held to be the cause of attention-deficit/hyperactivity disorder, but now widely rejected.

Modeling A social learning concept describing the process of learning through imitation. Contrasts with the broader concept of identification.

Monothetic class A category that is defined in terms of features that are necessary and sufficient to identify members of the class.

Monozygotic (MZ) twins Identical twins produced from a single fertilized egg; thus MZ twins have identical genotypes.

Mood A pervasive and sustained emotional response which, in its extreme, can color the person's perception of the world.

Mood disorders A broad category of psychopathology that includes depressive disorders and bipolar disorders. These conditions are defined in terms of episodes in which the person's behavior is dominated by either clinical depression or mania.

Moral anxiety In Freudian theory, the result of conflict between the superego and the ego.

Moral treatment A historically important movement in the treatment of the mentally ill that led to improved hospital conditions. This movement was based on the belief that the mentally ill deserve adequate care and that good care would promote their recovery.

Moratorium A period of allowing oneself to be uncertain or confused about identity. Erikson advocated a moratorium as an important step in the formation of an enduring identity.

Multiaxial (classification system) A classification system in which the person is rated with regard to several separate aspects of behavior or adjustment.

Multifactorial causes The etiology of a disorder results from a combination of biological, psychological, and social factors rather than from a single cause.

Multiple personality disorder An unusual dissociative disorder characterized by the existence of two or more distinct personalities in a single individual (called dissociative identity disorder in DSM-IV).

Narcissistic personality disorder An enduring pattern of thinking and behavior that is characterized by pervasive grandiosity. Narcissistic people are preoccupied with their own achievements and abilities.

Nature–nurture controversy The debate that pits genetic and biological factors against life experience as causes of abnormal behavior.

Negative reinforcement Occurs when the cessation of a stimulus increases the frequency of behavior (for example, a friend's nagging ends when you give in).

Negative symptoms (of schizophrenia) Include flat or blunted affect, avolition, alogia, and anhedonia.

Neurofibrillary tangles A type of brain lesion found in the cerebral cortex and the hippocampus in patients with Alzheimer's disease. A pattern of disorganized neurofibrils, which provide structural support for the neurons and help transport chemicals that are used in the production of neurotransmitters.

Neuroleptic A type of antipsychotic medication which also induces side effects that resemble the motor symptoms of Parkinson's disease.

Neurologist A physician who deals primarily with diseases of the brain and nervous system.

Neuromodulators Chemicals such as endorphins that may be released from neurons or from endocrine glands. Neuromodulators can influence communication among many neurons, and they often affect regions of the brain that are quite distant from where they were released.

Neuron The nerve cells that form the basic building blocks of the brain. Each neuron is comprised of the soma or cell body, the dendrites, the axon, and the terminal buttons.

Neuropsychological assessment Assessment procedures focused on the examination of performance on psychological tests to indicate whether a person has a brain disorder. An example is the Halstead-Reitan Neuropsychological Test Battery.

Neurotic anxiety In Freudian theory, the result of conflict between the id and the ego.

Neuroticism A dimension of personality that is concerned with emotional stability, especially the expression of negative emotions, such as anxiety, depression, and anger.

Neurotransmitters Chemical substances that are released into the synapse between two neurons and carry signals from the terminal button of one neuron to the receptors of another.

Normalization The philosophy that mentally retarded or mentally ill people are entitled to live as much as possible like other members of the society. Often associated with deinstitutionalization in providing custodial care and mainstreaming in education.

Null hypothesis The prediction that an experimental hypothesis is not true. Scientists must assume that the null hypothesis holds until research contradicts it.

Obsession A repetitive, unwanted, intrusive cognitive event that may take the form of thoughts, images, or impulses. Obsessions intrude suddenly into consciousness and lead to an increase in subjective anxiety.

Obsessive-compulsive personality disorder An enduring pattern of thinking and behavior that is characterized by perfectionism and inflexibility. These people are preoccupied with rules and efficiency. They are excessively conscientious, moralistic, and judgmental.

Oedipal conflict Freud's view that boys harbor forbidden sexual desires for their mothers, and they typically resolve the dilemma between the ages of 4 and 6 by identifying with their fathers.

Openness to experience A dimension of personality that describes the person's willingness to consider and explore unfamiliar ideas, feelings, and activities.

Operant conditioning A learning theory asserting that behavior is a function of its consequences. Specifically, behavior increases if it is rewarded, and it decreases if it is punished.

Operational definition A procedure that is used to measure a theoretical construct.

Oppositional defiant disorder A psychological disorder of childhood characterized by persistent but relatively minor transgressions such as refusing to obey adult requests, arguing, and acting angry.

Pain disorder A type of somatoform disorder characterized by preoccupation with pain, and complaints are motivated at least in part by psychological factors.

Panic attack A sudden, overwhelming experience of terror or fright. While anxiety involves a blend of several negative emotions, panic is more focused.

Paradigm A set of assumptions both about the substance of a theory and about how scientists should collect data and test theoretical propositions. The term was applied to the progress of science by Thomas Kuhn (1962), an influential historian and philosopher.

Paranoid personality disorder An enduring pattern of thinking and behavior characterized by a pervasive tendency to be inappropriately suspicious of other people's motives and behaviors. People who fit the description for this disorder expect that other people are trying to harm them, and they take extraordinary precautions to avoid being exploited or injured.

Paranoid type A subtype of schizophrenia that is characterized by systematic delusions with persecutory or grandiose content. Preoccupation with frequent auditory hallucinations can also be associated with the paranoid type.

Paraphilias Forms of sexual disorder that involve sexual arousal in association with unusual objects and situations, such as inanimate objects, sexual contacts with children, exhibiting their genitals to strangers, and inflicting pain on another person.

Parasympathetic nervous system The branch of the autonomic nervous system that generally controls the slowing of psychophysiological arousal and energy conservation.

Parkinson's disease A disorder of the motor system that is caused by a degeneration of a specific area of the brain stem known as the *substantia nigra* and loss of the neurotransmitter dopamine, which is produced by cells in this area.

Peer sociometrics A method of assessing children's social relationships and categorizing children's social standing by obtaining information on who is "liked most" and who is "liked least" from a group of children who know each other.

Penile plethysmograph A physiological assessment tool used to measure male sexual arousal.

Peripheral nervous system Nerves that stem out from the central nervous system and connect to the body's muscles, sensory systems, and organs. Divided into two subdivisions, the somatic and the autonomic nervous systems.

Personality The combination of persistent traits or characteristics that, taken as a whole, describe a person's behavior. In DSM-IV, personality is defined as "enduring patterns of perceiving, relating to, and thinking about the environment and oneself, which are exhibited in a wide range of important social and personal contexts."

Personality disorder Inflexible and maladaptive patterns of personality that begin by early adulthood and result in either social or occupational problems or distress to the individual.

Pervasive developmental disorders A category of unusual psychological problems that begin early in life and involve severe impairments in a number of areas of functioning. Autistic disorder is one example.

Phenomenology The study of events and symptoms (including subjective experiences) in their own right rather than in terms of inferred causes.

Phenotype The observed expression of a given genotype or genetic structure, for example, eye color.

Phenylketonuria (PKU) A cause of mental retardation transmitted by the pairing of recessive genes that results in the deficiency of the enzyme that metabolizes phenylalanine. Infants have normal intelligence at birth, but the ingestion of foods containing phenylalanine causes phenylketonuria and produces brain damage. Can be prevented with a phenylalanine-free diet.

Phobia A persistent and irrational narrowly defined fear that is associated with a specific object or situation.

Pick's disease A form of primary dementia that is associated with atrophy of the frontal and temporal lobes of the brain. Very similar to Alzheimer's disease in terms of both behavioral symptoms and cognitive impairment.

Placebo In medicine, pills that are pharmacologically inert; more broadly, any type of treatment that contains no known "specific ingredients" for treating a given condition.

Placebo control group A group of subjects given a treatment with no known specific ingredients for the purpose of comparison with alternative treatments that are thought to contain specific, therapeutic benefits.

Placebo effect The improvement in a condition produced by a placebo (sometimes a substantial change). An overriding goal of scientific research is to identify treatments that exceed placebo effects.

Polygenic Caused by more than one gene. Characteristics become normally distributed as more genes are involved in the phenotypic expression of a trait.

Polysubstance abuse (also known as multidrug abuse) A disorder characterized by the abuse of at least three different psychoactive drugs (not including nicotine or caffeine). No single substance predominates in the pattern of abuse.

Polythetic class A category that is defined in terms of a set of criteria that are neither necessary nor sufficient. Each member of the category must possess a certain minimal number of the defining features, but none of the features has to be found in each member of the category.

Pons Part of the hindbrain that serves various functions in regulating stages of sleep.

Population The entire group of people about whom a researcher wants to generalize.

Positive predictive power The probability that a person who has a positive test response will actually have the disorder.

Positive reinforcement Occurs when the onset of a stimulus increases the frequency of behavior (for example, you get paid for your work).

Positive symptoms (of schizophrenia) Include hallucinations, delusions, disorganized speech, inappropriate affect, and disorganized behavior.

Posttraumatic stress disorder (PTSD) A psychological disorder characterized by recurring symptoms of numbing, reexperiencing, and hyperarousal following exposure to a traumatic stressor.

Prefrontal lobotomy A psychosurgery technique introduced in 1935 by Egas Moniz in which the two hemispheres of the brain were severed. Moniz won a Nobel Prize for the treatment, which has now been discredited.

Premorbid history A pattern of behavior that precedes the onset of an illness. Adjustment prior to the disorder.

Preparedness The notion that organisms are biologically prepared, on the basis of neural pathways in their central nervous systems, to learn certain types of associations (also known as biological constraints on learning).

Primary gain A psychoanalytic concept that a conversion symptom protects the mind by unconsciously expressing a psychological conflict. For example, a physical symptom (paralysis) may symbolize some underlying conflict (a desire to hurt someone). Contrasts with secondary gain or the direct reinforcement of a symptom.

Primary prevention An attempt to prevent new cases of disorder by improving the environment; promotes health, not just the treatment of illness.

Probands Index cases. In behavior genetic studies, probands are family members

who have a disorder, and the relatives of the index cases are examined for concordance.

Problem-focused coping Externally oriented coping in an attempt to change or otherwise control a stressor.

Prodromal phase Precedes the active phase of schizophrenia and is marked by an obvious deterioration in role functioning. Prodromal signs and symptoms are less dramatic than those seen during the active phase of the disorder.

Professional responsibilities A professional's obligation to follow the ethical standards of his or her profession and to uphold the laws of the states in which he or she practices, for example, confidentiality.

Prognosis Predictions about the future course of a disorder with or without treatment.

Psychiatry The branch of medicine that is concerned with the study and treatment of mental disorders.

Psychoactive drugs Various drugs—ranging from alcohol, tobacco, and caffeine to controlled substances—that affect the individual's psychological state.

Psychoactive substance A drug that alters a person's mood, level of perception, or brain functioning.

Psychoanalysis Freud's orthodox form of psychotherapy that is practiced rarely today because of its time, expense, and questionable effectiveness in treating mental disorders. Freud viewed the task of psychoanalysis as promoting insight by uncovering the unconscious conflicts and motivations that cause psychological difficulties.

Psychodynamic A variation on the Freudian approach which searches for unconscious conflicts and motivations, but does not adhere to Freud literally as in psychoanalysis.

Psychodynamic psychotherapy An "uncovering" form of psychotherapy in which the therapist typically is more engaged and directive; the process is considerably less lengthy than in psychoanalysis.

Psychology The science, profession, and academic discipline concerned with the study of mental processes and behavior in humans and animals.

Psychoneuroimmunology Research on the effects of stress on the functioning of the immune system.

Psychopathology The manifestations of (and the study of the causes of) mental disorders. Generally used as another term to describe abnormal behavior.

Psychopathy Another term for antisocial personality disorder. Usually associated with Cleckley's definition of that concept, which included features such as disregard for the truth, lack of empathy, and inability to learn from experience.

Psychopharmacology The study of the effects of psychoactive drugs on behavior. Clinical psychopharmacology involves the expert use of drugs in the treatment of mental disorders.

Psychophysiology The study of changes in the functioning of the body that result from psychological experiences.

Psychosexual development Freud's view that development proceeds in a series of stages marked by key psychosexual tasks, specifically the oral, anal, phallic, and genital stages.

Psychosis A term that refers to several types of severe mental disorder in which the person is out of contact with reality. Hallucinations and delusions are examples of psychotic symptoms.

Psychosomatic disorder A term indicating that a physical disease is a product both of the psyche (mind) and the soma (body).

Psychostimulants Medications that heighten energy and alertness when taken in small dosages, but lead to restless, even frenetic, behavior when misused. Often used in the treatment of attention-deficit/hyperactivity disorder.

Psychosurgery A controversial treatment that involves the surgical destruction of specific regions of the brain. Modern psychosurgery involves relatively little destruction of brain tissue, unlike the discredited prefrontal lobotomy.

Psychotherapy The use of psychological techniques in an attempt to produce change in the context of a special, helping relationship.

Punishment Occurs when the onset of a stimulus decreases the frequency of behavior (for example, your parents scold you).

Random assignment Any of several methods of ensuring that each subject has a statistically equal chance of being exposed to any level of an independent variable.

Random selection A method of selecting samples from a larger population that ensures that each subject has a statistically equal chance of being selected.

Rape Acts involving nonconsensual sexual penetration obtained by physical force, by threat of bodily harm, or when the victim is incapable of giving consent by virtue of mental illness, mental retardation, or intoxication.

Rating scale An assessment tool in which the observer is asked to make judgments that place the person somewhere along a dimension.

Rational-emotive therapy (RET) A cognitive behavior therapy technique designed to challenge irrational beliefs about oneself and the world. Developed by Albert Ellis as a treatment for anxiety, depression, and related problems.

Reactivity The influence of an observer's presence on the behavior of the person who is being observed.

Receptors Sites on the dendrites or soma of a neuron that are sensitive to certain neurotransmitters.

Recidivism Repeat offending in violating the law.

Reciprocal causality The concept of causality as bi-directional (or circular). Interaction is a process of mutual influence, not separable causes and effects.

Reciprocity The social exchange of cooperation and conflict. Family members with happy relationships reciprocate positive actions; family members with troubled relationships reciprocate negative ones.

Reductionism The scientific perspective that the whole is the sum of its parts, and that the task of scientists is to divide the world into its smaller and smaller components.

Regression A return or retreat to an earlier stage or style of coping or behaving.

Reliability The consistency of measurements, including diagnostic decisions. One index of reliability is agreement among clinicians. **Representative sample** A sample that accurately represents some larger group of people (the population of interest).

Residual phase Follows the active phase of a disorder such as schizophrenia. At this point, psychotic symptoms have improved, but the person continues to be impaired in various ways. Negative symptoms may be more pronounced during the residual phase.

Residual type A subtype of schizophrenia that includes patients who no longer meet the criteria for active phase symptoms but nevertheless demonstrate continued signs of negative symptoms or attenuated forms of delusions, hallucinations, or disorganized speech.

Resilience The ability to "bounce back" from adversity despite life stress and emotional distress.

Response cost Occurs when the removal of a stimulus decreases the frequency of behavior (for example, your parents take away the use of the car).

Reticular activating system Located in the midbrain, but extending into the pons and medulla as well. Regulates sleeping and waking and sexual behavior.

Retrograde amnesia The loss of memory for events prior to the onset of an illness or the experience of a traumatic event.

Retrospective reports Recollections about past experiences that are often questioned in terms of reliability and validity.

Reuptake The process of recapturing some neurotransmitters in the synapse before they reach the receptors of another cell and returning the chemical substances to the terminal button. The neurotransmitter then is reused in subsequent neural transmission.

Reverse causality Indicates that causation could be operating in the opposite direction: Y could be causing X instead of X causing Y. A threat to interpretation in correlational studies, and a basic reason why correlation does not mean causation.

Role playing Improvisational play acting that may be used in therapy to teach clients alternative ways of acting in problematic situations.

Schizoaffective disorder A disorder defined by a period of disturbance during which the symptoms of schizophrenia partially overlap with a major depressive episode or a manic episode.

Schizoid personality disorder An enduring pattern of thinking and behavior characterized by pervasive indifference to other people, coupled with a diminished range of emotional experience and expression. People who fit this description prefer social isolation to interactions with friends or family.

Schizophrenia A type of (or group of) psychotic disorders characterized by positive and negative symptoms and associated with a deterioration in role functioning. The term was originally coined by Eugen Bleuler to describe the *splitting of mental associations*, which he believed to be the fundamental disturbance in schizophrenia (previously known as dementia praecox).

Schizophrenic spectrum A group of disorders that, on the basis of family history and adoption study data, are presumed to be genetically related to schizophrenia. These disorders may include schizotypal personality disorder, schizoaffective disorder, and delusional disorder.

Schizophreniform disorder A condition characterized by the same symptoms as schizophrenia, in which the patient has exhibited symptoms for less than the 6 month period required by DSM-IV for a diagnosis of schizophrenia.

Schizotaxia According to Paul Meehl's theoretical model for schizophrenia, a subtle neurological defect of unknown form that is inherited by all individuals who are predisposed to schizophrenia.

Schizotypal personality disorder An enduring pattern of discomfort with other people coupled with peculiar thinking and behavior. The latter symptoms take the form of perceptual and cognitive disturbances. Considered by some experts to be part of the schizophrenic spectrum.

School refusal (*school phobia*) Extreme reluctance to go to school, accompanied by various symptoms of anxiety such as stomachaches and headaches. May be a fear of school or an expression of separation anxiety disorder.

Scientist-practitioner model A model of training and professional activity, particularly influential in clinical psychology, that emphasizes the integration of science and practice.

Seasonal affective disorder A type of mood disorder (either unipolar or bipolar) in which there has been a regular temporal relation between onset (or disappearance) of the person's episodes and a particular time of the year. For example, the person might become depressed in the winter.

Secondary gain The psychoanalytic concept that conversion (or other somatoform) symptoms can help a patient avoid responsibility or receive attention (reinforcement).

Secondary prevention Focuses on the early detection of emotional problems (for instance, "at risk" groups) in an attempt to prevent problems from becoming more serious and difficult to treat.

Self-concept Carl Rogers's core structure of personality in his humanistic approach; he viewed a strong and positive self-concept as essential to healthy psychological adjustment.

Self-control Appropriate behavior guided by internal (rather than external) rules.

Self-efficacy Albert Bandura's central cognitive concept, the belief that one can achieve desired goals.

Self-instruction training A cognitive behavior therapy technique for teaching children self-control which involves modeling and imitation of self-statements.

Self-schema Cognitions about oneself.

Senile plaques A type of brain lesion found in Alzheimer's disease that consists of a central core of homogeneous protein material known as *amyloid* surrounded by clumps of debris left over from destroyed neurons.

Sensate focus A procedure for the treatment of sexual dysfunction that involves a series of simple exercises in which the couple spends time in a quiet, relaxed setting, learning to touch each other.

Sensitivity The ability of a test to identify correctly people who have the disorder in question. Also called the *true positive rate*.

Separation anxiety disorder A psychological disorder of childhood characterized by persistent and excessive worry for the safety of an attachment figure and related fears such as getting lost, being kidnapped, nightmares, and refusal to be alone. Distinct from normal separation anxiety, which typically develops shortly before an infant's first birthday.

Sex roles Characteristics, behaviors, and skills that are defined within a specific culture as being either masculine or feminine.

Sexual dysfunctions Forms of sexual disorder that involve inhibitions of sexual desire or interference with the physiological responses leading to orgasm.

Socialization The process of shaping children's behavior and attitudes to conform to the expectations of parents, teachers, and society.

Social roles Characteristic styles of behaving according to the expectations of a social situation, for example, gender roles.

Social skills training A behavior therapy technique in which clients are taught new skills that are desirable and likely to be rewarded in the everyday world.

Social support The emotional and practical assistance received from others.

Soma The cell body and largest part of the neuron where most of the neuron's metabolism and maintenance is controlled and performed.

Somatic nervous system The division of the peripheral nervous system that governs voluntary muscular control (as opposed to the autonomic nervous system, which regulates relatively involuntary organ responses).

Somatization disorder A type of somatoform disorder characterized by multiple, somatic complaints in the absence of organic impairments.

Somatoform disorders A category of psychological disorders characterized by unusual physical symptoms that occur in the absence of a known physical pathology. Examples include hypochondriasis and conversion disorder. Somatoform disorders are somatic in form only, thus their name (note the distinction from psychosomatic disorders, which do involve real physical pathology).

Specificity The ability of a test to identify as being "negative" people who do not have the disorder.

Stage of development A period of continuous and relatively slow change focused on a particular set of psychological or social issues. Contrasts with developmental transition, a period of rapid change between stages of development.

State-dependent learning Learning that occurs in one state of affect or consciousness is best recalled in the same state of affect or consciousness.

Status offense An act that is illegal only because of a youth's status as a minor, for example, running away from home, truancy from school.

Stress An event that creates physiological or psychological strain for the individual. Stress has been defined differently by various scientists.

Stress management A treatment used in behavioral medicine and health psychology in an attempt to teach more effective coping skills, reduce adverse reactions to stress, and improve health behavior.

Substance abuse The less severe form of substance use disorder listed in DSM-IV. Describes a pattern of drug use which is defined in terms of interference with the person's ability to fulfill major role obligations, the recurrent use of a drug in dangerous situations, or the experience of repeated legal difficulties that are associated with drug use.

Substance dependence The more severe form of substance use disorder listed in DSM-IV. Refers to a pattern of repeated self-administration that results in tolerance, withdrawal, or compulsive drug-taking behavior.

Superego One of Freud's three central personality structures, roughly equivalent to the "conscience." In Freudian theory, the superego contains societal standards of behavior, particularly rules that children learn from identifying with their parents. The superego attempts to control id impulses.

Sympathetic nervous system The branch of the autonomic nervous system that generally controls psychophysiological activities associated with increased arousal and energy expenditure.

Symptom alleviation Reducing the dysfunctional symptoms of a disorder but not eliminating its root cause.

Synapse A small gap filled with fluid that lies between the axon of one neuron and a dendrite or soma of another neuron.

Syndrome A group of symptoms that appear together and are assumed to represent a specific type of disorder.

Systematic desensitization A treatment for overcoming fears and phobias developed by Joseph Wolpe. Involves learning relaxation skills, developing a fear hierarchy, and systematic exposure to imagined, feared events while simultaneously maintaining relaxation.

Systems theory An innovation in the philosophy of conceptualizing and conducting science which emphasizing interdependence, cybernetics, and especially holism—the idea that the whole is more than the sum of its parts. Often traced to biologist and philosopher Ludwig von Bertalanffy.

Tardive dyskinesia A motor syndrome produced as a side effect of neuroleptic medication. Consists of abnormal involuntary movements of the mouth and face, such as tongue protrusion, chewing, and lip-puckering, as well as spasmodic movements of the limbs and trunk of the body.

Temperament Characteristic styles of relating to the world that are often con-

ceptualized as inborn traits. Generally emphasizes the "how" as opposed to the "what" of behavior. See the "Big Five" temperamental characteristics.

Terminal buttons "Buds" found on the small branches at the end of the axon where messages are sent from one neuron out to other ones.

Tertiary prevention Involves treatment for a disorder, but also attempts to address some of the adverse consequences of mental illness (such as unemployment).

Thalamus A part of the limbic system that is involved in receiving and integrating sensory information both from the sense organs and from higher brain structures.

The person-situation debate The controversy over the assumption that a person's behavior is stable over time and across situations. Social learning theorists question this assumption, arguing that human behavior is often determined primarily by the specific context in which it occurs rather than by internal personality traits.

Third variable An unmeasured factor that may account for a correlation observed between any two variables. A threat to interpretation in correlational studies, and a basic reason why correlation does not mean causation.

Threshold model A perspective on etiology which holds that people can exhibit characteristics of a disorder without experiencing any adverse impact on their adjustment until they pass a critical threshold. Beyond that level, there is presumably a dramatic increase in the number of problems that are encountered.

Time-out A discipline technique that involves briefly isolating a child as a punishment for misbehavior.

Token economy A type of contingency management program that has been adopted in many institutional settings. Desired and undesired behaviors are identified, contingencies are defined, behavior is monitored, and rewards or punishments are given according to the rules of the economy.

Tolerance The process through which the nervous system becomes less sensitive to the effects of a psychoactive substance. As a result, the person needs to consume increased quantities of the drug to achieve the same subjective effect.

Transference In psychoanalysis, the process whereby patients transfer feelings about a key figure in their life onto the analyst. In psychotherapy, the client's feelings toward the therapist.

Transsexualism A severe form of gender identity disorder in adults.

Traumatic stress A catastrophic event that involves real or perceived threat to life or physical well-being.

Two-factor theory A combination of classical conditioning and operant conditioning that is hypothesized to explain the acquisition and maintenance of fear. Fears are acquired through classical conditioning and maintained through operant conditioning (the reduction in anxiety that stems from avoidance).

Type A behavior pattern A characterological response to challenge that is competitive, hostile, urgent, impatient, and achievement-striving. Linked to an increased risk for coronary heart disease.

Unconditioned response An automatic reaction to an event (unconditioned stimulus), as when an animal salivates in response to the sight of meat. Central in classical conditioning.

Unconditioned stimulus A stimulus that elicits an automatic reaction (an unconditioned response), as when the sight of meat produces salivation. Central in classical conditioning.

Unconscious Mental processes or contents that reside outside of awareness. In Freudian theory, the seat of many hidden memories, motivations, and defenses.

Undifferentiated type A subtype of schizophrenia that includes patients who display prominent psychotic symptoms and either meet the criteria for several subtypes or otherwise do not meet the criteria for the catatonic, paranoid, or disorganized types.

Vaginal photometer A physiological assessment tool used to measure female sexual arousal.

Vaginismus A form of sexual dysfunction in which the outer muscles of the vagina snap tightly shut when penetration is attempted, thus preventing insertion of any object.

Validity The meaning or systematic importance of a construct or a measurement.

Vascular dementia (also known as multi-infarct dementia) A type of dementia associated with vascular disease. The cognitive symptoms of vascular dementia are the same as those for Alzheimer's disease, but a gradual onset is not required.

Ventricles Four connected chambers in the brain filled with cerebrospinal fluid. The ventricles are enlarged in some psychological and neurological disorders.

Victimization A pattern of responses often observed among victims of violent crimes, particularly rape, that includes fear, guilt, self-blame, powerlessness, and lowered self-esteem.

Vulnerability marker A specific measure, such as a biochemical assay or a psychological test, that might be useful in identifying people who are vulnerable to a disorder such as schizophrenia.

Withdrawal The constellation of symptoms that are experienced shortly after a person stops taking a drug after heavy or prolonged use.

Worry A relatively uncontrollable sequence of negative, emotional thoughts and images that are concerned with possible future threats or danger.

References

Abel, G.G., & Gouleau, J.L. (1990). Male sex offenders. In M.E. Thase, B.A. Edelstein, and M. Hersen (Eds.), *Handbook of outpatient treatment of adults: Nonpsychotic mental disorders*. New York: Plenum. pp. 271-290.

Abel, G.G., & Osborn, C. (1992). The paraphilias: The extent and nature of sexually deviant and criminal behavior. *Psychiatric Clinics of North America*, 15, 675-687.

Abou-Saleh, M.T. (1992). Lithium. In E. S. Paykel (Ed.), *Handbook of affective disorders* (2nd edition) New York: Guilford. (pp. 369-386).

Abramson, L.Y., Seligman, M.E.P., & Teasdale, J. (1978). Learned helplessness in humans: Critique and reformulation. *Journal of Abnormal Psychology*, 87, 49-74.

Abramson, L.Y., Metalsky, G.I., & Alloy, L.B. (1989). Hopelessness depression: A theory based-subtype of depression. *Psychological Review*, 96, 358-372.

Achenbach, T.M. (1985). *Assessment and Taxonomy of Child and Adolescent Psychopathology*. Beverly Hills: Sage.

Achenbach, T.M. & Edelbrock, C.S. (1981). Behavioral problems and competencies reported by parents of normal and disturbed children aged four through sixteen. *Monographs of the Society for Research in Child Development*. Serial No. 188.

Achenbach, T.M., Howell, C.T., Quay, H.C., & Conners, C.K. (1991). National survey of problems and competencies among four- to sixteen-year-olds. *Monographs of the Society for Research in Child Development*, 56, No. 3, Serial No. 225.

Achenbach, T.M., McConaughy, S.H., & Howell, C.T. (1987). Child/adolescent behavioral and emotional problems: Implications of cross-informant correlations for situational specificity. *Psychological Bulletin*, 101, 213-232.

Adams, G.G., Abraham, K.G., & Markstrom, C.A. (1987). The relation among identity development, self-consciousness and self-focusing during middle and late adolescence. *Developmental psychology*, 23, 292-297.

Adams, G.R. & Adams, C.M. (1989). Developmental issues. In L.K.G. Hsu & M. Hersen (Eds). *Recent developments in adolescent psychiatry* (pp. 13-30). New York: Wiley.

Adams, G.R., Ryan, J.H., Hoffman, J.J., Dobson, W.R., & Nielsen, E.C. (1985). Ego identity status, conformity behavior and personality in late adolescence. *Journal of Personality and Social Psychology*, 47, 1091-1104.

Agras, W.S. (1993). The diagnosis and treatment of panic disorder. *Annual Review of Medicine*, 44, 39-51.

Ainsworth, M.D.S., (1979). Infant-mother attachment. *American Psychologist*, 34, 932-937.

Ainsworth, M.D.S., Blehar, M., Waters, E., & Wall, S. (1978). *Patterns of attachment*. Hillsdale, NJ: Erlbaum.

Akiskal, H.S. (1981). Subaffective disorders: dysthymic, cyclothymic, and bipolar II disorders in the "borderline" realm. *Psychiatric Clinics of North America*, 4, 25-46.

Akiskal, H.S. (1985). Anxiety: Definition, relationship to depression, and proposal for an integrative model. In A.H. Tuma and J.D. Maser (Eds.), *Anxiety and the anxiety disorders*. Hillsdale, N.J.: Erlbaum.

Akiskal, H.S., Chen, S.E., Davis, G.C., Puzantian, V.R., Kashgarian, M., & Bolinger, J.M. (1985). Borderline: An adjective in search of a noun. *Journal of Clinical Psychiatry*, 46, 41-48.

Al-Kubaisy, T., Marks, I.M., Logsdail, S., Marks, M.P., Lovell, K., Sungur, M., & Araya, R. (1992). Role of exposure homework in phobia reduction: A controlled study. *Behavior Therapy*, 23, 599-621.

Aldridge-Morris, R. (1989). *Multiple personality: An exercise in deception*. Hillsdale, NJ: Erlbaum.

Alessi, G. (1992). Models of proximate and ultimate causation in psychology. *American Psychologist*, 47, 1359-1370.

Alexander, F. (1950). *Psychosomatic medicine: Its principles and applications*. New York: Norton.

Alexander, F. & French, T.M. (1947). *Psychoanalytic therapy*. New York: Ronald Press.

Alexander, F., French, T.M., & Pollock, G.H. (1968). *Psychosomatic specificity*. Chicago: University of Chicago Press.

Alexander, J.F. & Parsons, B.V. (1982). *Functional family therapy*. Monterey, CA: Brooks/Cole.

Alexander, J.F., Holtzworth-Munroe, A., & Jameson, P.B. (1994). The process and outcome of marital and family therapy: Research, review, and evaluation. In A.E. Bergin & S.L. Garfield (Eds.), *Handbook of psychotherapy and behavior change*, (4th. Ed., pp. 595-630). New York: Wiley.

Allan, C.A., & Cooke, D.J. (1985). Stressful life events and alcohol misuses in women: A critical review. *Journal of Studies on Alcohol*, 46, 147-152.

Allen, A., & Blazer, D.G. (1991). Mood disorders. In Sadavoy, J., Lazarus, L.W., and Jarvik, L.F. (Eds.), *Comprehensive review of geriatric psychiatry*. Washington, D.C.: American Psychiatric Press. pp. 337-351.

Alloy, L.B., Abramson, L.Y., Metalsky, G.I., & Hartlage, S. (1988). The hopelessness theory of depression: Attributional aspects. *British Journal of Clinical Psychology*, 27, 5-21.

Amato, P.R. & Keith, B. (1991a). Parental divorce and the well-being of children: A meta-analysis. *Psychological Bulletin*, 110, 26-46.

Amato, P.R. & Keith, B. (1991b). Parental divorce and adult well-being: A meta-analysis. *Journal of Marriage and the Family*, 53, 43-58.

American Association on Mental Retardation (1992). *Mental retardation: Definition, classification, and systems of supports* (9th. Ed.). Washington, D.C.: AAMR.

American Psychiatric Association. (1980). *Psychiatric glossary*. Washington, D.C.: American Psychiatric Press.

American Psychiatric Association. (1994). *Diagnostic and statistical manual of mental disorders* First edition, 1952; second edition, 1968; third edition, 1980; revised third edition, 1987; fourth edition, 1994. Washington, D. C.: American Psychiatric Association.

American Psychiatric Association (1983). American Psychiatric Association statement on the insanity defense. *American Journal of Psychiatry*, 140, 681-688.

American Psychological Association (1991). The definition and description of clinical psychology. *The Clinical Psychologist*, 44, 5-11.

Ames, M.A., & Houston, D.A. (1990). Legal, social, and biological definitions of pedophilia. *Archives of Sexual Behavior*, 19, 333-342.

Anastasi, A. (1986). Evolving concepts of test validation. *Annual Review of Psychology*, 37, 1-15.

Anderson, A.A., Russell, C.S., & Schumm, W.R. (1983). Perceived marital quality and family life cycle categories: A further analysis. *Journal of Marriage and the Family*, 45, 127-139.

Anderson, N.B., & McNeilly, M. (1991). Age, gender, and ethnicity as variables in psychophysiological assessment: Sociodemographics in context. *Psychological Assessment*, 3, 376-384.

Andreasen, N. (1979). Thought, language and communication disorders: I. Clinical assessment, definition of terms, and evaluation of their reliability. *Archives of General Psychiatry*, 36, 1315-1321.

Andreasen, N.C. (1988). Brain imaging: Applications in psychiatry. *Science*, 239, 1381-1388.

Andreasen, N.C., & Carpenter, W.T., Jr. (1993). Diagnosis and classification of schizophrenia. *Schizophrenia Bulletin*, 19, 199-214.

Andreasen, N.C., & Olsen, S. (1982). Negative v. positive schizophrenia: Definition and validation. *Archives of General Psychiatry*, 39, 789-794.

Andreasen, N.C. (1984). *The broken brain: The biological revolution in psychiatry*. New York: Harper & Row.

Andreasen, N.C. (1985). Positive v. negative schizophrenia: A critical evaluation. *Schizophrenia Bulletin*, 11, 380-389.

Andreasen, N.C., Flaum, M. Swayze, V.W.II. Tyrell, G., Arndt, S. (1990). Positive and negative symptoms in schizophrenia: A critical reappraisal. *Archives of General Psychiatry*, 47, 615-621.

Andrews, G., MacMahon, S.W., Austin, A., & Byrne, D.G. (1984). Hypertension: Comparison of drug and non-drug treatments. *British Medical Journal*, 284, 1523-1530.

Anthony, J.C., & Helzer, J.E. (1991). Syndromes of drug abuse and dependence. In L.N. Robins and D.A. Regier (Eds.). *Psychiatric disorders in America: The epidemiologic catchment area study*. New York: Free Press. pp. 116-154.

Appelbaum, P.S. & Gutheil, T.G. (1979). Rotting with their rights on: Constitutional theory and clinical reality in drug refusal by psychiatric patients. *Bulletin of the American Academy of Psychiatry and Law*, 7, 308-317.

Arato, M., Frecska, E., Tekes, K., MacCrimmon, D.J. (1991). Serotonergic interhemispheric asymmetry: Gender differences in cortex. *Acta Psychiatrica Scandinavica*, 84, 110-111.

Archer, R.P. (1992). Review of the Minnesota Multiphasic Personality Inventory-2. In J.J. Kramer & J.C. Conoley (Eds.). *The eleventh mental measurements yearbook*. Lincoln, NB: University of Nebraska Press.

Aries, P. (1962). *Centuries of childhood: A social history of family life.* New York: Vintage Books.

Asher, S.R. & Wheeler, V.A. (1985). Children's loneliness: A comparison of rejected and neglected peer status. *Journal of Consulting and Clinical Psychology,* 53, 500-505.

Babor, T.F. (1992). Cross-cultural research on alcohol: A quoi bon? In J.E. Helzer & G.J. Canino (Eds.). *Alcoholism in North America, Europe, and Asia.* New York: Oxford. pp.33-52.

Bailey, A., Le Couteur, A., Gottesman, I., Bolton, P., Simonoff, E., Yuzda, E., & Rutter, M. (in press). Autism as a strongly genetic disorder: Evidence from a British twin study. *Psychological Medicine.*

Baker, C.D., & de Silva, P. (1988). The relationship between male sexual dysfunction and belief in Zilbergeld's myths: An empirical investigation. *Sexual and Marital Therapy,* 3, 229-238.

Baker, T.B., Morse, E., & Sherman, J.E. (1986). The motivation to sue drugs: A psychobiological analysis of urges. *Nebraska Symposium on Motivation,* 34, 257-323.

Baker, T.B., & Tiffany, S.T. (1985). Morphine tolerance as habituation. *Psychological Review,* 92, 78-108.

Ballenger, J.C. (1991). Long-term pharmacologic treatment of panic disorder. *Journal of Clinical Psychiatry,* 52 (suppl 2), 18-23.

Ballenger, J.C. Burrows, G.D., DuPont, R.L., Lesser, I.M., Noyes, R. et al. (1988). Alprazolam in panic disorder and agoraphobia: Results from a multicenter trial, I. Efficacy in short term treatment. *Archives of General Psychiatry,* 45, 413-422.

Baltes, M.M., Kuhl, K.P., & Sowarka, D. (1992). Testing for limits of cognitive reserve capacity: A promising strategy for early diagnosis of dementia? *Journal of Gerontology: Psychological Sciences,* 47, P165-P167.

Baltes, P.B. (1993). The aging mind: Potential and limits. *Gerontologist,* 33, 580-594.

Baltes, P.B., & Kliegl, R. (1992). Further testing of limits of cognitive plasticity: Negative age differences in a mnemonic skill are robust. *Developmental Psychology,* 28, 121-125.

Bancroft, J. (1989). *Human sexuality and its problems* (second edition). Edinburgh: Churchill Livingstone.

Bancroft, J., & Wu, F.C.W. (1983). Changes in erectile responsiveness during androgen therapy. *Archives of Sexual Behavior,* 12, 59-66.

Bancroft, J., Dickerson, M., Fairburn, C.G., Gray, J., Greenwood, J., Stevenson, N., & Warner, P. (1986). Sex therapy outcome research: A reappraisal of methodology. I. A treatment study of male sexual dysfunction. *Psychological Medicine,* 16, 851-863.

Bandura, A. (1973). *Aggression: A social learning analysis.* Englewood-Cliffs, NJ: Prentice Hall.

Bandura, A. (1977). Self-efficacy: Toward a unifying theory of behavior change. *Psychological Review,* 84, 191-215.

Bandura, A. & Walters, R.H. (1963). *Social learning and personality development.* New York: Ronald Press.

Barbaree, H.E., Seto, M.C., Serin, R.C., Amos, N.L., & Preston, D.L. (1994). Comparisons between sexual and nonsexual rapist subtypes: Sexual arousal to rape, offense precursors, and offense characteristics. *Criminal Justice and Behavior,* 21, 95-114.

Barker, J.G., & Howell, R.J. (1992). The plethysmograph: A review of recent literature. *Bulletin of the American Academy of Psychiatry and the Law,* 20, 13-25.

Barkley, R.A. (1990). *Hyperactive Children: A handbook for diagnosis and treatment* (2nd Ed). New York: Guilford.

Barkley, R.A. (1988). The effects of methylphenidate on the interactions of preschool ADHD children

with their mothers. *Journal of the American Academy of Child and Adolescent Psychiatry,* 27, 336-341.

Barkley, R.A., Karlsson, J., Strzelecki, E., & Murphy, J.V. (1984). Effects of age and Ritalin dosage on the mother-child interactions of hyperactive children. *Journal of Consulting and Clinical Psychology,* 52, 750-758.

Barlow, D.H., Hayes, S.C., & Nelson, R.O. (1984). *The scientist practitioner: Research and accountability in clinical and educational settings.* New York: Pergamon.

Barlow, D.H. (1991). Disorders of emotion. *Psychological Inquiry,* 2, 58-71.

Barlow, D.H. (1988). *Anxiety and its disorders: The nature and treatment of anxiety and panic.* New York: Guilford.

Barlow, D.H., & Cerny, J.A. (1988). *Psychological treatment of panic.* New York: Guilford.

Barlow, D.H., & Craske, M.G. (1988). The phenomenology of panic. In S. Rachman and J.D. Maser (Eds.), *Panic: Psychological perspectives.* Hillsdale, N.J.: Erlbaum.

Barlow, D.H. (1986). Causes of sexual dysfunction: The role of anxiety and cognitive interference. *Journal of Consulting and Clinical Psychology,* 54, 140-148.

Barlow, D.H., O'Brien, G.T., & Last, C.G. (1984). Couples treatment of agoraphobia. *Behavior Therapy,* 15, 41-58.

Barnett, P.A., & Gotlib, I.H. (1988). Psychosocial functioning and depression: Distinguishing among antecedents, concomitants, and consequences. *Psychological Bulletin,* 104, 97-126.

Baroff, G.S. (1986). *Mental retardation: Nature, cause, and management* (2nd. Ed.). Washington, DC: Hemisphere Publishing.

Barondes, S.H. (1993). *Molecules and mental illness.* New York: Scientific American.

Barr, R.F. (1973). Responses to erotic stimuli of transsexual and homosexual males. *British Journal of Psychiatry,* 123, 579-585.

Bartak, L. & Rutter, M. (1973). Special educational treatment of autistic children: A comparative study. I. Design of study and characteristics of units. *Journal of Child Psychology and Psychiatry,* 14, 217-222.

Baruth, L.G. & Huber, C.H. (1984). *An introduction to marital theory and therapy.* Monterey, CA: Brooks/Cole

Basoglu, M., Lax, T., Kasvikis, Y., & Marks, I. (1988). Predictors of improvement in obsessive-compulsive disorder. *Journal of Anxiety Disorders,* 2, 299-317.

Bass, E. & Davis, L. (1988). *The courage to heal.* New York: Harper & Row.

Baucom, D.H. & Epstein, N. (1990). *Cognitive-behavioral marital therapy.* New York: Brunner/Mazel.

Baucom, D.H., Notarius, C.I., Burnett, C.K., & Haefner, P. (1990). Gender differences and sex-role identity in marriage. In F.D. Fincham & T.N. Bradbury (Eds.), *The psychology of marriage: Basic issues and applications* (pp. 150-171). New York: Guilford.

Baum, A., Davidson, L.M., Singer, J.E., & Street, S.W. (1987). Stress as a psychophysiological response. In A. Baum & J.E. Singer (Eds.), *Handbook of psychology and health. Stress.* (Vol. 5, pp. 1-24). Hillsdale, NJ: Erlbaum.

Baumeister, R.F. (1990). Suicide as escape from self. *Psychological Review,* 97, 90-113.

Baumrind, D. (1971). Current patterns of parental authority. *Developmental Psychology Monograph,* 4(1, Pt.2).

Bayer, R. (1981). *Homosexuality and American psychiatry: The politics of diagnosis.* New York: Basic books.

Beach, S.R.H., Sandeen, E.E., & O'Leary, K.D. (1990). *Depression in marriage: A model for etiology and treatment.* New York: Guilford.

Bean, M.H. (1975). Alcoholics anonymous: AA. *Psychiatric Annals,* 5, 83-91.

Bebbington, P. Katz, R., & McGuffin, P. (199?). The familial aggregation of affective disorders: Relation to symptom severity and social provocation.

Bech, P. (1992). Symptoms and assessment of depression. In E. S. Paykel (Ed.), *Handbook of affective disorders* (2nd edition). New York: Guilford. (pp. 3-14)

Beck, A. (1976). *Cognitive therapy and the emotional disorders.* New York: International Universities Press.

Beck, A.T., & Emery, G. (1985). *Anxiety disorders and phobias: A cognitive perspective.* New York: Basic Books.

Beck, A.T. (1984). Cognition and therapy. *Archives of General Psychiatry,* 41, 1112-1114.

Beck, A.T. (1967). *Depression: Clinical, experimental, and theoretical aspects.* New York: Harper & Row.

Beck, A.T., Steer, R.A., & Garbin, M.G. (1988). Psychometric properties of the Beck Depression Inventory: Twenty-five years of evaluation. *Clinical Psychology Review,* 8, 77-100.

Beck, A.T. (1974). The development of depression. In R.J. Friedman & M.M. Katz (Eds.). *The psychology of depression: Contemporary theory and research* (pp. 3-20). New York: Winston-Wiley.

Beck, A.T., Rush, A.J., Shaw, B.F.,& Emery, G. (1979). *Cognitive therapy of depression.* New York: Guilford.

Beck, J.G. (1993). Vaginismus. In W. O'Donohue and J.H. Geer (Eds.), *Handbook of sexual dysfunctions: Assessment and treatment.* Boston: Allyn and Bacon. (pp. 381-397).

Becker, J.V. (1989). Impact of sexual abuse on sexual functioning. In S.R. Lieblum and R.C. Rosen (Eds.), *Principles and practice of sex therapy* (2nd edition). New York: Guilford.

Beidel, D.C., Turner, S.M., & Cooley, M.R. (1993). Assessing reliable and clinically significant change in social phobia: Validity of the social phobia and anxiety inventory. *Behaviour Research and Therapy,* 31, 331-337.

Belar, C.D., & Perry, N.W. (1992). The National Conference on Scientist-Practitioner Education and Training for the professional practice of psychology. *American Psychologist,* 47, 71-75.

Bell, R. Q. (1968). A reinterpretation of the direction of effects in studies of socialization. *Psychological Review,* 75, 81-95.

Bellack, A.S., & Mueser, K.T. (1993). Psychosocial treatment for schizophrenia. *Schizophrenia Bulletin,* 19, 317-336.

Bemporad, J.R. (1979). Adult recollections of a formerly autistic child. *Journal of Autism and Developmental Disorders,* 9, 179-197.

Bender, L. (1947). Childhood schizophrenia, clinical study of one hundred schizophrenic children. *American Journal of Orthopsychiatry,* 17, 40-56.

Benjamin, L.S. (1974). Structural analysis of social behavior. *Psychological Review,* 81, 392-425.

Benjamin, L.S. (1993). *Interpersonal diagnosis and treatment of personality disorders.* New York: Guilford.

Bennett, F.C. & Sherman, R. (1983). Management of childhood "hyperactivity" by primary care physicians. *Journal of Developmental and Behavioral Pediatrics,* 4, 88-93.

Benson, D.F. (1992). Neuropsychiatric aspects of aphasia and related language impairments. In S.C. Yudofsky and R.E. Hales (Eds.). *Textbook of neuropsychiatry* (2nd ed.). Washington, D.C.: American Psychiatric Press. pp. 311-327.

Berg, I. (1993). Aspects of school phobia. In C.G. Last (Ed.), *Anxiety across the lifespan: A developmental perspective* (pp. 78-93). New York: Springer.

Berkman, L.F., Seeman, T.E., Albert, M., Blazer, D., Kahn, R., Mohs, R., Finch, C., Schneider, E., Cotman, C., McClearn, G., Nesselroade, J., Featherman, D., Garmezy, N., McKhann, G., Brim, G., Prager, D., & Rowe, J. (1993). High, usual, and impaired functioning in community-dwelling older men and women: Findings from the MacArthur foundation research network on successful aging. *Journal of Clinical Epidemiology, 46,* 1129-1140.

Bernlef, J. (1988). *Out of mind.* London: Faber.

Bernstein, D.A., & Borkovec, T.D. (1973). *Progressive relaxation training: A manual for the helping professions.* Champaign, IL: Research Press.

Bernstein, D.P., Cohen, P., Velez, C.N., Schwab-Stone, M., Siever, L.J., & Shinsato, L. (1993). Prevalence and stability of the DSM-III-R personality disorders in a community-based survey of adolescents. *American Journal of Psychiatry, 150,* 1237-1243.

Bernstein, E.M. & Putnam, F.W. (1986). Development, reliability, and validity of a dissociation scale. *Journal of Nervous & Mental Disease, 174,* 727-735.

Berrios, G. (1990). Memory and the cognitive paradigm of dementia during the 19th century: A conceptual history. In R.M. Murray and T.H. Turner (Eds) *Lectures on the history of psychiatry.* Oxford: Gaskell/Royal College of Psychiatrists.

Berrios, G.E. (1990). Alzheimer's disease: A conceptual history. *International Journal of Geriatric Psychiatry, 5,* 355-365.

Berrios, G.E., & Hauser, R. (1988). The early development of Kraepelin's ideas on classification: A conceptual history. *Psychological Medicine, 18,* 813-821.

Berrios, G.E. (1992). Research into the history of psychiatry. In C. Freeman, and P. Tyrer (Eds.). *Research methods in psychiatry: A beginner's guide* (2nd ed). London: Gaskell.

Berrios, G.E. (1989). Obsessive-compulsive disorder: Its conceptual history in France during the 19th century. *Comprehensive Psychiatry, 30,* 283-295.

Bertelson, A., Harvald, B., & Hauge, M. (1977). A Danish twin study of manic-depressive disorders. *British Journal of Psychiatry, 130,* 330-351.

Besharov, D.J. (1988). How child abuse programs hurt poor children: The misuse of foster care. *Clearinghouse Review, 20,* 219-227.

Besharov, D.J. (1992). A balanced approach to reporting child abuse. *Child, Youth, and Family Services Quarterly, 15,* 5-7.

Besharov, D.J. (1986). The misuse of foster care: When the desire to help children outruns the ability to improve parental functioning. *Family Law Quarterly, 20,* 213-231.

Bettelheim, B. (1967). *The empty fortress.* New York: Free Press.

Beutler, L.E., Crago, M., & Arizmendi, T.G. (1986). Therapist variables in psychotherapy process and outcome. In S.L. Garfield & A.E. Bergin (Eds.), *Handbook of psychotherapy and behavior change* (3rd. Ed., pp. 257-310). New York: Wiley.

Beutler, L.E., Machado, P.P.P., & Neufeldt, S.A. (1994). Therapist variables. In A.E. Bergin & S.L. Garfield, *Handbook of psychotherapy and behavior change* (4th. Ed., pp. 229-269). New York: Wiley.

Bianchi, S. (1991). Family disruption and economic hardship: The short-run picture for children. *Current population reports* (Series p-70, No. 23). Washington, D.C.: U.S. Government Printing Office.

Bickel, H. (1980). Phenylketonuria: Past, present, future. *Journal of Inherited Metabolic Disease, 3,* 123-312.

Biggins, C.A., Boyd, J.L., Harrop, F.M., Madeley, P., Mindham, R.H.S., Randall, J.I., & Spokes, E.G.S. (1992). A controlled, longitudinal study of dementia in Parkinson's disease. *Journal of Neurology, Neurosurgery, and Psychiatry, 55,* 566-571.

Biklen, D. (1992). Autism orthodoxy versus free speech: A reply to Cummins and Prior. *Harvard Educational Review, 62,* 242-256.

Billings, A.G., & Moos, R.H. (1982). Psychosocial theory and research on depression: An integrative framework and review. *Clinical Psychology Review, 2,* 213-237.

Billy, J.O.G., Tanfer, K., Grady, W.R., & Klepinger, D.H. (1993). The sexual behavior of men in the United States. *Family Planning Perspectives, 25,* 52-60.

Bingham, W.V.D., & Moore, B.V. (1924). *How to interview.* New York: Harper and Row.

Binswanger, L. (1963). *Being-in-the-world: Selected papers of Ludwig Binswanger.* New York: Basic.

Black, D.W., Noyes, R., Goldstein, R.B., & Blum, N. (1992). A family study of obsessive-compulsive disorder. *Archives of General Psychiatry, 49,* 362-368.

Blackburn, R. (1990). Treatment of the psychopathic offender.

Blackburn, R. (1988). On moral judgements and personality disorders: The myth of psychopathic personality revisited. *British Journal of Psychiatry, 153,* 505-512.

Blader, J.C., & Marshall, W.L. (1989). Is assessment of sexual arousal in rapists worthwhile? A critique of current methods and the development of a response compatibility approach. *Clinical Psychology Review, 9,* 569-587.

Blair, C.D. & Lanyon, R.I. (1981). Exhibitionism: Etiology and treatment. *Psychological Bulletin, 89,* 439-463.

Blanchard, R. (1989). The classification and labeling of nonhomosexual gender dysphorias. *Archives of Sexual Behavior, 18,* 315-334.

Blanchard, E.B. (Ed.), (1992). Special issue on behavioral medicine. *Journal of Consulting and Clinical Psychology, 60.*

Blanchard, E.B. (1994). Behavioral medicine and health psychology. In A.E. Bergin & S.L. Garfield (Eds.), *Handbook of psychotherapy and behavior change* (4th. Ed., pp. 701-733). New York: Wiley.

Blashfield, R.K., Sprock, J., Haymaker, D. & Hodgin, J. (1989). The family resemblance hypothesis applied to psychiatric classification. *Journal of Nervous and Mental Disease, 177,* 492-497.

Blashfield, R.K., & McElroy, R.A. (1989). Ontology of personality disorder categories. *Psychiatric Annals, 19,* 126-131.

Blashfield, R.K. (1982). Feighner et al., invisible colleges, and the Matthew Effect. *Schizophrenia Bulletin, 8,* 1-6.

Blashfield, R.K., & Draguns, J.G. (1976). Evaluative criteria for psychiatric classification. *Journal of Abnormal Psychology, 85,* 140-150.

Blashfield, R.K. (1973). An evaluation of the DSM-II classification of schizophrenia as a nomenclature. *Journal of Abnormal Psychology, 82,* 382-389.

Blashfield, R.K. (1984). *The classification of psychopathology: Neo-Kraepelinian and quantitative approaches.* New York: Plenum.

Blashfield, R.K., & McElroy, R.A. (1987). The 1985 literature on the personality disorders. *Comprehensive Psychiatry, 28,* 536-546.

Blazer, D., Hughes, D., & George, L.K. (1987). Stressful life events and the onset of a generalized anxiety syndrome. *American Journal of Psychiatry, 144,* 1178-1183.

Blehar, M.C., & Rosenthal, N.E. (1989). Seasonal affective disorders and phototherapy: Report of a National Institute of Mental Health-sponsored workshop. *Archives of General Psychiatry, 46,* 469-474.

Bleuler, M. (1978). *The schizophrenic disorders: Long-term patient and family studies.* New Haven, CT: Yale University Press.

Bliss, E.L. (1986). *Multiple personality, allied disorders, and hypnosis.* New York: Oxford University Press.

Bloch, S. & Crouch, E. (1987). *Therapeutic factors in group psychotherapy.* New York: Oxford University Press.

Block, J.H., Block, J., & Gjerde, P.F. (1986). The personality of children prior to divorce: A prospective study. *Child Development, 57,* 827-840.

Blum, K., & Payne, J.E. (1991). *Alcohol and the addictive brain: New hope for alcoholics from biogenetic research.* New York: Free Press.

Blume, S.B. (1991). Women, alcohol, and drugs. In N.S. Miller (Ed.). *Comprehensive handbook of drug and alcohol addiction.* New York: Dekker. pp. 147-177.

Bolger, J.P., Carpenter, B.C., & Strauss, M.E. (1994). Behavior and affect in Alzheimer's disease. *Clinics in Geriatric Medicine, 10,* 315-337.

Booth-Kewley, S. & Friedman, H.S. (1987). Psychological predictors of heart Disease: A quantitative review. *Psychological Bulletin, 101,* 343-362.

Borkovec, T.D., & Costello, E. (1993). Efficacy of applied relaxation and cognitive-behavioral therapy in the treatment of generalized anxiety disorder. *Journal of Consulting and Clinical Psychology, 61,* 611-619.

Borkovec, T.D., & Inz, J. (1990). The nature of worry in generalized anxiety disorder: A predominance of thought activity. *Behavior Research and Therapy, 28,* 153-158.

Borkovec, T.D., Shadick, R., & Hopkins, M. (1990). The nature of normal versus pathological worry. In R. Rapee and D.H. Barlow (Eds.), *Chronic anxiety and generalized anxiety disorder.* New York: Guilford.

Bornstein, R.F., Klein, D.N., Mallon, J.C., & Slater, J.F. (1988). Schizotypal personality disorder in an outpatient population: Incidence and clinical characteristics. *Journal of Clinical Psychology, 44,* 322-325.

Børup, C., Kaiser, A., & Jensen, E. (1992). Long-term antabuse treatment: Tolerance and reasons for withdrawal. *Acta Psychiatrica Scandinavica, 86,* 47-49.

Boss, M. (1963). *Daseinsanalysis and psychoanalysis.* New York: Basic.

Bower, G.H. (1990). Awareness, the unconscious, and repression: An experimental psychologist's perspective. In J.L. Singer (Ed.), *Repression and dissociation* (pp. 209-232). Chicago: University of Chicago Press.

Bowers, K.S. & Meichenbaum, D. (Eds.), (1984). *The unconscious reconsidered.* New York: Wiley.

Bowlby, J. (1969). *Attachment.* New York: Basic Books.

Bowlby, J. (1973). *Separation: Anxiety and anger.* New York: Basic Books.

Bowlby, J. (1980). *Loss: Sadness and depression.* New York: Basic Books.

Bowlby, J. (1982). Attachment and loss: Retrospect and prospect. *American Journal of Orthopsychiatry, 52,* 664-678.

Boyer, W.F. (1992). Potential indications for the selective serotonin reuptake inhibitors. *International Clinical Psychopharmacology, 6 suppl 5,* 5-12.

Bradford, J.M.W., Boulet, J., & Pawlak, A. (1992). The paraphilias: A multiplicity of deviant behaviours. *Canadian Journal of Psychiatry, 37,* 104-107.

Bradford, J.M.W., & Pawlak, A. (1993). Double-blind placebo cross-over study of cyproterone acetate in the treatment of paraphilias. *Archives of Sexual Behavior, 22,* 383-402.

Bradley, C. (1937). The behavior of children receiving benezedrine. *American Journal of Psychiatry, 94,* 577-585.

Braun, P., Kochansky, G., Shapiro, R. et al., (1981). Overview: Deinstitutionalization of psychiatric patients, a critical review of outcome studies. *American Journal of Psychiatry, 138,* 736-749.

Braun, B.G. (1989). Psychotherapy of the survivor of incest with a dissociative disorder. *Psychiatric Clinics of North America, 12,* 307-324.

Brayne, C. (1993). Research and Alzheimer's disease: An epidemiological perspective. *Psychological Medicine, 23,* 287-296.

Brecher, E.M., & the editors of consumer reports. (1972). *Licit and illicit drugs.* Boston: Little, Brown and Co.

Bregman, J.D., Dykens, E., Watson, M., Ort, S.I., & Leckman, J.F. (1987). Fragile-X syndrome: Variability of phenotypic expression. *Journal of the American Academy of Child and Adolescent Psychiatry, 26,* 463-471.

Breier, A., Buchanan, R.W., Irish, D.I., & Carpenter, W.T., Jr. (1993). Clozapine treatment of outpatients with schizophrenia: Outcome and long-term response patterns. *Hospital and Community Psychiatry, 44,* 1145-1149.

Breitner, J.C.S., Gatz, M., Bergem, A.L.M., Christian, J.C., Mortimer, J.A., McClearn, G.E., Heston, L.L., Welsh, K.A., Anthony, J.C., Folstein, M.F., & Radebaugh, T.S. (1993). Use of twin cohorts for research in Alzheimer's disease. *Neurology, 43,* 261-267.

Brenner, D.E., Kukull, W.A., van Belle, G., Bowen, J.D., McCormick, W.C., Teri, L., & Larson, E.B. (1993). Relationship between cigarette smoking and Alzheimer's disease in a population-based case-control study. *Neurology, 43,* 293-300.

Brenner, M.H. (1973). *Mental illness and the economy.* Cambridge: Harvard University Press.

Breslau, N., Davis, G.C., Andreski, P., and Peterson, E. (1991). Traumatic events and posttraumatic stress disorder in an urban population of young adults. *Archives of General Psychiatry, 48,* 216-222.

Bretherton, I. (1992). The origins of attachment theory: John Bowlby and Mary Ainsworth. *Developmental Psychology, 28,* 759-775.

Bretherton, I. (1985). Attachment theory: Retrospect and prospect. In I. Bretherton and E. Waters (Eds.), Growing points in attachment theory and research. *Monographs of the Society for Research in Child Development, 56,* 1-14.

Brett, E.A., Spitzer, R.L., & Williams, J.B.W. (1988). DSM-III-R criteria for posttraumatic stress disorder. *American Journal of Psychiatry, 145,* 1232-1235.

Brewer, C. (1992). Controlled trials of antabuse in alcoholism: The importance of supervision and adequate dosage. *Acta Psychiatrica Scandinavica, 86,* 51-58.

Brewin, C.R. (1985). Depression and causal attributions: What is their relation? *Psychological Bulletin, 98,* 297-309.

Brewin, C.R., Andrews, B., & Gotlib, I.H. (1993) Psychopathology and early experience: A reappraisal of retrospective reports. *Psychological Bulletin, 113,* 82-98.

Brewin, C.R., MacCarthy, B., Duda, K. et al. (1991). Attributions and expressed emotion in the relatives of patients with schizophrenia. *Journal of Abnormal Psychology, 100,* 546-554.

Bridges, R.N. & Goldberg, D.P. (1985). Somatic presentation of DSM-III psychiatric disorders in primary care. *Journal of Psychosomatic Research, 29,* 563-569.

Brink, S. (1993). Singing the Prozac blues. *U.S. News and World Report,* November 8, 76-79.

British Medical Research Council (1965). Clinical trial of the treatment of depressive illness. *British Medical Journal, 1,* 881-886.

Brody, E.M. (1989). The family at risk. In E. Light and B.D. Lebowitz (Eds.), *Alzheimer's disease treatment and family stress: Directions for research.* U.S. Dept of Health and Human Services, DHHS Publication No. (ADM) 89-1569 pp. 2-49.

Brody, E.M., Saperstein, A.R., & Lawton, M.P. (1989). A multi-service respite program for caregivers of Alzheimer's patients. *Journal of Gerontological Social Work, 14,* 41-75.

Brom, D., Kleber, R.J., & Defares, P.B. (1989). Brief psychotherapy for posttraumatic stress disorders. *Journal of Consulting and Clinical Psychology, 57,* 607-612.

Bromley, D.B. (1990). *Behavioral gerontology: Central issues in the psychology of ageing.* New York: Wiley.

Bronfenbrenner, U. (1979). *The ecology of human development.* Cambridge, MA: Harvard University Press.

Brown, G.W., Bifulco, A., & Harris, T.O. (1987). Life events, vulnerability and onset of depression: Some refinements. *British Journal of Psychiatry, 150,* 30-42.

Brown, W.A. (1990). Is light treatment a placebo? *Psychopharmacology Bulletin, 26,* 527-530.

Brown, G.W., Bifulco, A., & Andrews, B. (1990). Self-esteem and depression: III. Aetiological issues. *Social Psychiatry and Psychiatric Epidemiology, 25,* 235-243.

Brown, S.A., Goldman, M.S., Inn, A., & Anderson, L. (1980). Expectations of reinforcement from alcohol: Their domain and relation to drinking patterns. *Journal of Consulting and Clinical Psychology, 48,* 419-426.

Brown, S.A. (1993). Drug effect expectancies and addictive behavior change. *Experimental and Clinical Psychopharmacology, 1,* 55-67.

Brown, L.S. (1992). A feminist critique of the personality disorders. In L.S. Brown & M. Ballou (Eds.), *Personality and psychopathology: Feminist reappraisals.* New York: Guilford.

Brown, T.A., & Barlow, D.H. (1992). Comorbidity among anxiety disorders: Implications for treatment and DSM-IV. *Journal of Consulting and Clinical Psychology, 60,* 835-844.

Brown, G.W., Birley, J.L.T., & Wing, J.K. (1972). Influence of family life on the course of schizophrenic disorders: A replication. *British Journal of Psychiatry, 121,* 241-258.

Brown, G.W. & Harris, T.O. (1978). *Social origins of depression: A study of psychiatric disorder in women.* Tavistock Publications: London.

Brown, R. (1990). Limitations on expert testimony on the battered woman syndrome in homicide cases: The return of the ultimate issue rule. *Arizona Law Review, 32,* 665-689.

Brownell, K.D., Marlatt, G.A., Lichtenstein, E., & Wilson, G.T., 1986). Understanding and preventing relapse. *American Psychologist, 41,* 765-782.

Bruch, H. (1982). Anorexia nervosa: Therapy and theory. *American Journal of Psychiatry, 132,* 1531-1538.

Buck, R. (1984). *The communication of emotion.* New York: Guilford.

Bulbena, A., & Berrios, G.E. (1986). Pseudodementia: Facts and figures. *British Journal of Psychiatry, 148,* 87-94.

Bullough, V.L. (1976). *Sexual variance in society and history.* New York: Wiley.

Bumpass, L., (1984). Children and marital disruption: A replication and update. *Demography, 21,* 71-82.

Burke, B.L. & McGee, D.P. (1990). Sports deficit disorder. *Pediatrics, 85,* 1118.

Busby, W.J., Campbell, A.J., Borrie, M.J., & Spears, G.F.S. (1988). Alcohol use in a community-based sample of subjects aged 70 years and older. *Journal of the American Geriatrics Society, 36,* 301-305.

Buss, D.M. (1992). Mate preference mechanisms: Consequences for partner choice and intrasexual competition. In J.H. Barkow, L. Cosmides, and J. Tooby (Eds.), *The adapted mind: Evolutionary psychology and the generation of culture.* New York: Oxford University Press.

Buss, A.H., & Plomin, R. (1986). The EAS approach to temperament. In R. Plomin and J. Dunn (Eds.). *The study of temperament: Changes, continuities, and challenges.* Hillsdale, NJ: Erlbaum.

Butters, N. (1992). Memory remembered: 1970-1991. *Archives of Clinical Neuropsychology, 7,* 285-295.

Buydens-Branchey, L., Branchey, M.H., Noumair, D., & Lieber, C.S. (1989). Age of alcoholism onset: II. Relationship to susceptibility to serotonin precursor availability. *Archives of General Psychiatry, 46,* 231-236.

Byerley, W.F., Reimherr, F.W., Wood, D.R., & Grosser, B.I. (1988). Fluoxetine, a selective serotonin uptake inhibitor, for the treatment of outpatients with major depression. *Journal of Clinical Psychopharmacology, 8,* 112-115.

Cacioppo, J.T. & Bernston, G.G. (1992). Social psychological contributions to the decade of the brain: Doctrine of multilevel analysis. *American Psychologist, 47,* 1019-1028.

Cado, S., & Leitenberg, H. (1990). Guilt reactions to sexual fantasies during intercourse. *Archives of Sexual Behavior, 19,* 49-63.

Cairns, R.B. & Green, J.A. (1979). How to assess personality and social patterns: Observations or ratings? In R.B. Cairns (Ed.) *The analysis of social interactions: Methods, issues, and illustrations.* Hillsdale, NJ: Erlbaum.

Caldwell, C., & Gottesman, I.I. (1992). Schizophrenia—A high-risk factor for suicide: Clues to risk reduction. *Suicide and Life-Threatening Behavior, 2,* 479-493.

Callahan, L.A., Steadman, H.J., McGreevy, M.A., & Robbins, P.C. (1991). The volume and characteristics of insanity defense pleas: An eight-state study. *Bulletin of the American Academy of Psychiatry and the Law, 19,* 331-338.

Cameron, O.G., & Hill, E.M. (1989). Women and anxiety. *Psychiatric Clinics of North America, 12,* 175-186.

Cameron, H.M., & McGoogan, E. (1981). A prospective study of 1152 hospital autopsies: II. Analysis of inaccuracies in clinical diagnoses and their significance. *Journal of Pathology, 133,* 285-300.

Cameron, N. & Rychlak, J.F. (1985). *Personality development and psychopathology: A dynamic approach.* Boston: Houghton Mifflin.

Campbell, E. (1990). The psychopath and the definition of "mental disease of defect" under the Model Penal Code test of insanity: A question of psychology or a question of law? *Nebraska Law Review, 69,* 190-229.

Campbell, M., Green, W.H., & Deutsch, S.I. (1985). *Child and adolescent psychopharmacology.* Beverly Hills: Sage.

Campos, J.J., Barrett, K.C., Lamb, M.E., Goldsmith, H.H., & Sternberg, C. (1983). Socioemotional development. In M.M. Haith & J. Campos (Eds). *Infancy and developmental psychobiology (Vol. 2) Mussen's handbook of child psychology.* New York: Wiley.

Canino, G.L., Bird, H.R. et al. (1987). Prevalence of specific psychiatric disorders in Puerto Rico. *Archives of General Psychiatry, 44,* 727-735.

Cannon, T.D., Mednick, S.A., Parnas, J., Schulsinger, F., Praestholm, J., & Vestergaard, A. (1993). Developmental brain abnormalities in the offspring of schizophrenic mothers. I. Contributions of genetic and perinatal factors. *Archives of General Psychiatry, 50,* 551-564.

Cannon, T.D., Mednick, S.A., & Parnas, J. (1990). Antecedents of predominantly negative and predominantly positive-symptom schizophrenia in a high-risk population. *Archives of General Psychiatry, 47,* 622-632.

Cannon, W.B. (1935). Stress and strains of homeostasis. *American Journal of Medical Science*, 189, 1-14.

Cantwell, D.P. (1988). DSM-III studies. In M. Rutter, A.H. Tuma, & I.S. Lann (Eds.), *Assessment and diagnosis in child psychopathology* (pp.3-36). New York: Guilford.

Caplan, G. (1964). *Principles of preventive psychiatry.* New York: Basic Books.

Capron, C. & Duyme, M. (1989). Assessment of effects of socioeconomic status on IQ in a full cross-fostering study. *Nature*, 340, 552-554.

Caracci, G., & Miller, N.S. (1991). Alcohol and drug addiction in the elderly. In N.S. Miller (Ed.). *Comprehensive handbook of drug and alcohol addiction.* New York: Dekker. pp. 179-191.

Carey, G., & Gottesman, I.I. (1981). Twin and family studies of anxiety, phobic, and obsessive disorders. In D.F. Klein and J.G. Rabkin (Eds.), *Anxiety: New research and changing concepts.* New York: Raven Press.

Carey, G., & Gottesman, I.I. (1978). Reliability and validity in binary ratings: Areas of common misunderstanding in diagnosis and symptom rating. *Archives of General Psychiatry*, 35, 1454-1459.

Carlsson, A. (1988). The current status of the dopamine hypothesis of schizophrenia. *Neuropsychopharmacology*, 1, 179-186.

Carpenter, W.T., & Strauss, J.S. (1991). The prediction of outcome in schizophrenia IV: Eleven-year follow-up of the Washington IPSS cohort. *Journal of Nervous and Mental Disease*, 179, 517-525.

Carpenter, W.T., Jr., & Stephens, J.H. (1979). An attempted integration of information relevant to schizophrenic subtypes. *Schizophrenia Bulletin*, 5, 490-506.

Carr, E.G. (1977). The motivation of self-injurious behavior: A review of some hypotheses. *Psychological Bulletin*, 84, 800-816.

Carr, E.G. (1982). *How to teach sign language to developmentally disabled children.* Lawrence, KS: H & H Enterprises.

Carroll, M.A., Schneider, H.G., & Wesley, G.R. (1985). *Ethics in the practice of psychology.* Englewood-Cliffs, NJ: Prentice-Hall.

Caspi, A., Elder, G.H., & Bem, D.J. (1988). Moving away from the world: Life-course patterns of shy children. *Developmental Psychology*, 24, 824-831.

Cassidy, J. (1988). Child-mother attachment and the self in six-year olds. *Child Development*, 59, 121-134.

Chalkey, A.J., & Powell, G.E. (1983). The clinical description of forty-eight cases of sexual fetishism. *British Journal of Psychiatry*, 142, 292-295.

Chambless, D.L., Cherney, J., Caputo, G.C., & Rheinstein, B.J. (1987). Anxiety disorders and alcoholism: A study with inpatient alcoholics. *Journal of Anxiety Disorders*, 1, 29-40.

Chambless, D.L., & Gillis, M.M. (1993). Cognitive therapy of anxiety disorders. *Journal of Consulting and Clinical Psychology*, 61, 248-260.

Chappel, J.N. (1992). Effective use of alcoholics anonymous and narcotics anonymous in treating patients. *Psychiatric Annals*, 22, 409-418.

Chappel, J.N. (1993). Long-term recovery from alcoholism. *Psychiatric Clinics of North America*, 16, 177-187.

Charvat, J., Dell, P.P., Golkow, P., & Folkow, B. (1964). Mental factors in cardiovascular disease. *Cardiology*, 44, 124-141.

Chassin, L. (1984). Adolescent substance use and abuse. In P. Karoly and J.J. Steffen (Eds.), *Adolescent behavior disorders: Foundations and contemporary concerns* [Advances in Child Behavioral Analysis and Therapy (volume 3)]. pp. 99-152.

Chassin, L., Pillow, D.R., Curran, P.J., Molina, B.S.G., & Barrera, M., Jr. (1993). Relation of parental alcoholism to early adolescent substance use: A test of three mediating mechanisms. *Journal of Abnormal Psychology*, 102, 3-19.

Chen, C.S. (1972). A further note on studies of acquired behavioral tolerance to alcohol. *Psychopharmacologia*, 27, 265-274.

Cherlin, A.J., Furstenberg, F.F., Chase-Lansdale, P.L., Kiernan, K.E., Robins, P.K., Morrison, D.R., & Teitler, J.O. (1991). Longitudinal studies of effects of divorce on children in Great Britain and the United States. *Science*, 252, 1386-1389.

Cherlin, A.J., (1991). *Marriage, divorce, remarriage* (2nd. Ed.). Cambridge, MA: Harvard University Press.

Chess, S. & Thomas, A. (1984). *Origins and evolution of behavior disorders.* New York: Bruner-Mazel.

Chodoff, P. (1982). Hysteria and women. *American Journal of Psychiatry*, 139, 545-551.

Christensen, A. & Jacobson, N.S. (1994). Who (or what) can do psychotherapy: The status and challenge of nonprofessional therapies. *Psychological Science*, 5, 8-14.

Christiansen, B.A., Smith, G.T., Roehling, P.V., & Goldman, M.S. (1989). Using alcohol expectancies to predict adolescent drinking behavior after one year. *Journal of Consulting and Clinical Psychology*, 57, 93-99.

Cicchetti, D. & Beegly, M. (1990). *Children with Down syndrome: A developmental perspective.* New York: Cambridge University Press.

Cicchetti, D. & Cohen, D. (in press). *Manual of developmental psychopathology.* New York: Wiley.

Cipparone, R.C. (1987). The defense of battered women who kill. *University of Pennsylvania Law Review*, 135, 427-452.

Clark, L.A., McEwen, J.L., Collard, L.M., & Hickok, L.G. (1993). Symptoms and traits of personality disorder: Two new methods for their assessment. *Psychological Assessment*, 5, 81-91.

Clark, L.A., & Watson, D. (1991). Tripartite model of anxiety and depression: Psychometric evidence and taxonomic implications. *Journal of Abnormal Psychology*, 100, 316-336.

Clark, D.M. (1986). A cognitive approach to panic. *Behaviour Research and Therapy*, 24, 461-470.

Clark, D.B., & Sayette, M.A. (1993). Anxiety and the development of alcoholism: Clinical and scientific issues. *American Journal on Addictions*, 2, 59-76.

Clark, D.M. (1986). Cognitive therapy for anxiety. *Behavioral Psychotherapy*, 14, 283-294.

Clarke, J.W. (1990). *On being mad or merely angry.* Princeton, NJ: Princeton University Press.

Clarke-Stewart, A., Perlmutter, M., & Friedman, S. (1988). *Lifelong human development.* New York: Wiley.

Cleckley, H. (1976). *The mask of sanity* (5th ed.). St. Louis: Mosby.

Clementz, B.A., & Sweeney, J.A. (1990). Is eye movement dysfunction a biological marker for schizophrenia? A methodological review. *Psychological Bulletin*, 108, 77-92.

Clementz, B.A., Grove, W.M., Iacono, W.G., & Sweeney, J.A. (1992). Smooth-pursuit eye movement dysfunction and liability for schizophrenia: Implications for genetic modeling. *Journal of Abnormal Psychology*, 101, 117-129.

Cloninger, C.R. (1987). Neurogenetic adaptive mechanisms in alcoholism. *Science*, 236, 410-416.

Cloninger, C.R., Sigvardsson, S., Bohman, M., & von Knorring, A.L. (1982). Predisposition to petty criminality in Swedish adoptees, II. Cross-fostering analysis of gene-environment interaction. *Archives of General Psychiatry*, 39, 1242-1249.

Cloninger, C.R., & Gottesman, I.I. (1987). Genetic and environmental factors in antisocial behav-ior disorders. In S.A. Mednick, T.E. Moffitt, & S.A. Stack (Eds). *The causes of crime: New biological approaches.* Cambridge, England: Cambridge University Press. pp. 92-109.

Cohen, S. (1988). *The chemical brain: The neurochemistry of addictive disorders.* Irvine, CA: CareInstitute.

Cohen, S., Kaplan, J.R., Cunnick, J.E., Manuck, S.B., & Rabin, B.S. (1992). Chronic social stress, affiliation, and cellular immune response in nonhuman primates. *Psychological Science*, 3, 301-304.

Cohen, S. & Wills, T.A. (1985). Stress, social support, and the buffering process. *Psychological Bulletin*, 98, 310-357.

Cohen, S. & Williamson. G.M. (1991). Stress and infectious disease in humans. *Psychological Bulletin*, 109, 5-24.

Coie, J. & Kupersmidt, J., (1983). A behavioral analysis of emerging social status in boys' groups. *Child Development*, 54, 1400-1416.

Colby, K.M. (1975). *Artificial paranoia: A computer simulation of paranoid processes.* New York: Pergamon.

Cole, M. (1985). Sex therapy — A critical appraisal. *British Journal of Psychiatry*, 147, 337-351.

Cole, J.O. (1964). Phenothiazine treatment in acute schizophrenia. *Archives of General Psychiatry*, 10, 246-261.

Comfort, A. (1987). Deviation and variation. In G.D. Wilson (Ed.), *Variant sexuality: Research and theory.* London: Croom Helm. pp. 1-20.

Conger, J.J. (1956). Alcoholism: Theory, problem, and challenge. II. Reinforcement theory and the dynamics of alcoholism. *Quarterly Journal of Studies on Alcohol*, 17, 296-305.

Conners, C.K. (1980). Artificial colors and the diet of disruptive behavior: Current status of research. In R.M. Knights & D. J. Bakker (Eds.). *Treatment of hyperactive and learning disabled children.* Baltimore: University Park Press.

Consensus Conference on electroconvulsive therapy. (1985). *Journal of the American Medical Association*, 254, 103-108.

Cook, D.R. (1985). Craftsman versus professional: Analysis of the controlled drinking controversy. *Journal of Studies on Alcohol*, 46, 433-442.

Cook, W.L., Strachan, A.M., Goldstein, M.J., & Miklowitz, D.J. (1989). Expressed emotion and reciprocal affective relationships in families of disturbed adolescents. *Family Process*, 28, 337-348.

Cook, M., & Mineka, S. (1989). Observational conditioning of fear to fear-relevant versus fear-irrelevant stimuli in Rhesus monkeys. *Journal of Abnormal Psychology*, 98, 448-459.

Coons, P. (1986). The prevalence of multiple personality disorder. *Newsletter of the International Society for the Study of Multiple Personality and Dissociation*, 4, 6-8

Coons, P. & Milstein, V. (1988). Psychogenic amnesia: A clinical investigation of 25 consecutive cases. Unpublished data cited in D. Spiegel & E. Cardena (1991). Disintegrated experience: The dissociative disorders revisited. *Journal of Abnormal Psychology*, 100, 366-378.

Cooper, J.E., Kendell, R.E., Gurland, B.J., Sharpe, L., Copeland, J. R. M., & Simon, R. (1972). *Psychiatric diagnosis in New York and London.* London: Oxford University Press.

Coovert, D.L., Kinder, B.N., & Thompson, J.K. (1989). The psychosexual aspects of anorexia nervosa and bulimia nervosa: A review of the literature. *Clinical Psychology Review*, 9, 169-180.

Copestake, P. (1993). Aluminum and Alzheimer's disease: An update. *Food and Chemical Toxicology*, 31, 670-683.

Cornblatt, B.A., Lenzenweger, M.F., Dworkin, R.H., & Erlenmeyer-Kimling, L. (1992). Childhood attentional dysfunctions predict social deficits in unaffected adults at risk for schizophrenia. *British Journal of Psychiatry*, 16 (suppl. 18) 59-64.

Corning, W.C. (1986). Bootstrapping toward a classification system. In T. Millon and G. Klerman (Eds.). *Contemporary directions in psychopathology: Toward the DSM-IV.* NY: Guilford. pp. 279-306.

Corse, C.D., Manuck, S.B., Cantwell, J.D., Giordani, B., & Matthews, K.A. (1982). Coronary-prone behavior pattern and cardiovascular response in persons with and without coronary heart disease. *Psychosomatic Medicine*, 44, 449-459.

Coryell, W., & Winokur, G. (1992). Course and outcome. In E. S. Paykel (Ed.), *Handbook of affective disorders* (2nd edition) New York: Guilford. (pp. 89-110).

Coryell, W., Endicott, J., Andreasen, N., Keller, M. (1985). Bipolar I, bipolar II, and nonbipolar major depression among the relatives of affectively ill probands. *American Journal of Psychiatry*, 142, 817-821.

Costa, P.T., & McCrea, R.R. (1992). The five-factor model of personality and its relevance to personality disorders. *Journal of Personality Disorders*, 6, 343-359.

Costello, C.G. (1982). Fears and phobias in women: A community study. *Journal of Abnormal Psychology*, 91, 280-286.

Costello, C.G. (1993). Advantages of the symptom approach to schizophrenia. In C.G. Costello (Ed.) *Symptoms of schizophrenia.* New York: Wiley, p. 1-26.

Costello, C.G. (1992). Problems in recent tests of two cognitive theories of panic. *Behaviour Research and Therapy*, 30, 1-5.

Costello, C.G. (1976). *Anxiety and depression: The adaptive emotions.* Montreal: McGill-Queen's University Press.

Coyne, J.C. (1992). Cognition in depression: A paradigm in crisis. *Psychological Inquiry*, 3, 232-235.

Coyne, J.C., Downey, G., & Boergers, J. (1993). Depression in families: A systems perspective. In D. Cichetti & S.L. Toth (eds) *Rochester symposium on developmental psychopathology: Vol 4, Developmental approaches to the affective disorders.* Rochester, NY: University of Rochester.

Coyne, J. (1985). Ambiguity and controversy: An introduction. In J. Coyne (Ed.). *Essential papers on depression.* New York: NYU Press.

Coyne, J.C., & Gotlib, I.H. (1983). The role of cognition in depression: A critical appraisal. *Psychological Bulletin*, 94, 472-505.

Coyne, J. (1976). Toward an interactional description of depression. *Psychiatry.* 39, 28-40.

Craddock, N., & McGuffin, P. (1993). Approaches to the genetics of affective disorders. *Annals of Medicine*, 317-322.

Cranston-Cuebas, M.A., Barlow, D.H., Mitchell, W., & Athanasiou, R. (1993). Differential effects of a misattribution manipulation on sexually functional and dysfunctional men. *Journal of Abnormal Psychology*, 102, 525-533.

Cranston-Cuebas, M.A., Barlow, D.H. (1990). Cognitive and affective contributions to sexual functioning. In J. Bancroft, D.M. Davis, & D. Weinstein (Eds). *Annual review of sex research, vol 1: An integrative and interdisciplinary review.* Lake Mills, IA: Stoyles Graphic Services. pp 119-161.

Craske, M.G., Sanderson, W.C., & Barlow, D.H. (1987). The relationships among panic, fear, and avoidance. *Journal of Anxiety Disorders*, 1, 153-160.

Craske, M.G., Rapee, R.M., Jackel, L., & Barlow, D.H. (1989). Qualitative dimensions of worry in DSM-III-R generalized anxiety disorder subjects and nonanxious controls. *Behaviour Research and Therapy*, 27, 397-402.

Creese, I., Burt, D.R., & Snyder, S.H. (1976). Dopamine receptor binding predicts clinical and pharmacological potencies of antischizophrenic drugs. *Science*, 192, 481-483.

Crick, N.R. & Dodge, K.A. (1994). A review and reformulation of social information-processing mechanisms in children's social adjustment. *Psychological Bulletin*, 115, 74-101.

Critelli, J.W. & Neumann, K.F. (1984). The placebo: Conceptual analysis of a construct in transition. *American Psychologist*, 39, 32-39.

Crocker, J., & Major, B. (1989). Social stigma and self-esteem: The self-protective properties of stigma. *Psychological Review*, 96, 608-630.

Cronbach, L.J., & Meehl, P.E. (1955). Construct validity in psychological tests. *Psychological Bulletin*, 52, 281-302.

Crook, T. & Eliot, J. (1980). Parental death during childhood and adult depression: A critical review of the literature. *Psychological Bulletin*, 87, 252-259.

Cross-National Collaborative Panic Study. Second Phase Investigators. (1992). Drug treatment of panic disorder: Comparative efficacy of alprazolam, imipramine, and placebo. *British Journal of Psychiatry*, 160, 191-202.

Crossley, R. & McDonald, A. (1980). *Annie's coming out.* New York: Penguin.

Crow, T.J. (1980). Molecular pathology of schizophrenia: More than one disease process? *British Medical Journal*, 280, 66-68.

Crow, T.J. (1985). The two-syndrome concept: Origins and current status. *Schizophrenia Bulletin*, 11, 471-486.

Crowe, R.R. (1983). Antisocial personality disorder. In R.E. Tarter (Ed) *The child at psychiatric risk.* New York: Oxford. pp. 214-227.

Crowell, J.A., Waters, E., Kring, A., & Riso, L.P. (1993). The psychosocial etiologies of personality disorders: What is the answer like? *Journal of Personality Disorders*, suppl., 118-128.

Cummings, J.L. (1992). Neuropsychiatric aspects of Alzheimer's disease and other dementing illnesses. In S.C. Yudofsky and R.E. Hales (Eds). *Textbook of neuropsychiatry* (2nd edition). Washington, D.C.: American Psychiatric Press. pp. 605-620.

Cummings, E.M. & Davies, P. (1994). *Children and marital conflict.* New York: Guilford Press.

Cutting, J. (1986). *The Psychology of schizophrenia.* London: Churchill Livingstone.

Cutting, J., & McClelland, R. (1986). Psychiatric manifestations of organic illness. In P. Hill, R. Murray, & A. Thorley (Eds.), *Essentials of postgraduate psychiatry* (2nd ed.), London: Grune & Stratton. pp. 461-493.

D'Emilio, J. & Freedman, E.B. (1988). *Intimate matters: A history of sexuality in America.* New York: Harper and Row.

D'Zurilla, T. & Goldfried, M. (1971). Problem solving and behavior modification. *Journal of Abnormal Psychology*, 78, 107-126.

Dackis, C.A., & Gold, M.S. (1991). Inpatient treatment of drug and alcohol addiction. In N.S. Miller (Ed) *Comprehensive handbook of drug and alcohol addiction.* New York: Dekker. pp. 1233-1244.

Dadds, M.R., Schwartz, S., & Sanders, M.R. (1987). Marital discord and treatment outcome in behavioral treatment of child conduct disorders. *Journal of Consulting and Clinical Psychology*, 55, 396-403.

Dalayeun, J.F., Nores, J.M., & Bergal, S. (1993). Physiology of beta-endorphins: A close-up view and a review of the literature. *Biomedicine & Pharmacotherapy*, 47, 311-320.

Danforth, J.S., Barkley, R.A., & Stokes, T.F. (1991). Observations of parent-child interactions with hyperactive children: Research and clinical implications. *Clinical Psychology Review*, 11, 703-727.

Darkes, J., & Goldman, M.S. (1993). Expectancy challenge and drinking reduction: Experimental evidence for a mediational process. *Journal of Consulting and Clinical Psychology*, 61, 344-353.

Davey, G.C.L. (1989). UCS revaluation and conditioning models of acquired fears. *Behaviour Research and Therapy*, 27, 521-528.

Davidson, J.M. (19__). Sexual emotions, hormones, and behavior. *Advances* (Institute for the advancement of health), 6, 56-58.

Davidson, J., Kudler, H., Smith, R., Mahorney, S.L., Lipper, S., Hammett, E., Saunders, W.B., & Cavenar, J.O. (1990). Treatment of posttraumatic stress disorder with amitriptyline and placebo. *Archives of General Psychiatry*, 47, 259-266.

Davidson, J.R. & Foa, E.B. (1991). Diagnostic issues in posttraumatic stress disorder: Considerations for the DSM-IV. *Journal of Abnormal Psychology*, 100, 346-355.

Davidson, W.S., Redner, R., Blakely, C.H., Mitchell, C.M., & Emshoff, J.G. (1987). Diversion of juvenile offenders: An experimental comparison. *Journal of Consulting and Clinical Psychology*, 55, 68-75.

Davidson, M. (1982). *Uncommon sense: The life and thought of Ludwig von Bertalanffy (1901-1972), father of general systems theory.* Boston: Houghton Mifflin.

Davis, G.C., & Akiskal, H.S. (1986). Descriptive, biological, and theoretical aspects of borderline personality disorder. *Hospital and Community Psychiatry*, 37, 685-692.

Davis, K.L., & Haroutunian, V. (1993). Strategies for the treatment of Alzheimer's disease. *Neurology*, 43 (suppl 4), S52-S55.

Davis, K.L., Kahn, R.S., Ko, G., & Davidson, M. (1991). Dopamine in schizophrenia: A review and reconceptualization. *American Journal of Psychiatry*, 148, 1474-1486.

Davis, R.H. (1978). Review of the Rorschach Test. In O.K. Burros (Ed.). *Mental measurements yearbook* 8th edition. Highland Park, NJ: Gryphon Press. pp. 1045.

Davis, V.E., & Walsh, M.J. (1970). Alcohol, amines and alkaloids: A possible biochemical basis for alcohol addiction. *Science*, 167, 1005-1007.

Davis, J.M., & Casper, R. (1977). Anti-psychotic drugs: Clinical pharmacology and therapeutic use. *Drugs*, 14, 260-282.

Dawes, R.M. (1994). *House of cards: The collapse of modern psychotherapy.* New York: Free Press.

Dawes, R.M., Faust, D., & Meehl, P.E. (1989). Clinical versus actuarial judgment. *Science*, 243, 1668-1674.

Deblinger, E., McLeer, S.V., Atkins, M.S., Ralphe, D., & Foa, E. (1989). Post-traumatic stress in sexually abused, physically abused, and nonabused children. *Child Abuse and Neglect*, 13, 403-408.

DeLeon, P.H., Fox, R.E., & Graham, S.R. (1991). Prescription privileges: Psychology's next frontier? *American Psychologist*, 46, 384-393.

Deltito, J.A., & Perugi, G. (1986). A case of social phobia with avoidant personality disorder treated with MAOI. *Comprehensive Psychiatry*, 27, 255-258.

Depue, R.A., & Iacono, W.G. (1989). Neurobehavioral aspects of affective disorders. *Annual Review of Psychology*, 40, 457-492.

Depue, R.A., & Monroe, S.M. (1978). The unipolar-bipolar distinction in the depressive disorders. *Psychological Bulletin*, 85, 1001-1029.

deSilva, P. (1988). Phobias and preparedness: Replication and extension. *Behaviour Research and Therapy*, 26, 97-98.

Deutsch, A. (1949). *The mentally ill in America: A history of their care and treatment from Colonial times.* New York: Columbia University Press.

Deutsch, M. (1973). *The resolution of conflict.* New Haven: Yale University Press.

DeVeaugh-Geiss, J. (1993). Diagnosis and treatment of obsessive-compulsive disorder. *Annual Review of Medicine, 44,* 53-61.

Dickens, C. (1842/1970). *American notes and pictures from Italy.* New York: Oxford University Press.

Dienstbier, R.A. (1989). Arousal and physiological toughness: Implications for mental and physical health. *Psychological Review, 96,* 84-100.

Dijkman-Caes, D.I., Kraan, H.F., & DeVries, M.W. (1993). Research on panic disorder and agoraphobia in daily life: A review of current studies. *Journal of Anxiety Disorders, 7,* 235-247.

DiLalla, L.F., & Gottesman, I.I. (1991). Biological and genetic contributors to violence — Widom's untold tale. *Psychological Bulletin, 109,* 125-129.

DiLalla, L.F. & Gottesman, I.I. (1990). Heterogeneity of causes for delinquency and criminality: Lifespan perspectives. *Development and Psychopathology, 1,* 339-349.

DiNardo, P.A.. Moras, K., Barlow, D.H., Rapee, R.M., & Brown, T.A. (1993). Reliability of DSM-III-R anxiety disorder categories: Using the Anxiety Disorders Interview Schedule-Revised (ADIS-R). *Archives of General Psychiatry, 50,* 251-256.

DiNardo, P.A., O'Brien, G.T., Barlow, D.H., Waddell, M.T., & Blanchard, E.B. (1988). *Anxiety Disorders Interview Schedule —Revised (ADIS-R).* Albany, NY: Phobia and Anxiety Disorders Clinic, State University of New York at Albany.

Dodge, K.A. & Frame, C.L., (1982). Social-cognitive biases and deficits in aggressive boys. *Child Development, 53,* 620-635.

Dohrenwend, B.P., Levav, I., Shrout, P.E., Schwartz, S., Naveh, G., Link, B.G., Skodol, A.E., & Stueve, A. (1992). Socioeconomic status and psychiatric disorders: The causation-selection issue. *Science, 255,* 946-952.

Dohrenwend, B.P., Link, B.G., Kern, R., Shrout, P.E., & Markowitz, J. (1990). Measuring life events: The problem of variability within event categories. *Stress Medicine, 6,* 179-187.

Dolan, B. (1991). Cross-cultural aspects of anorexia nervosa and bulimia: A review. *International Journal of Eating Disorders, 10,* 67-78.

Donahey, K.M., & Carroll, R.A. (1993). Gender differences in factors associated with hypoactive sexual desire. *Journal of Sex and Marital Therapy, 19,* 25-40.

Douglas, V.I. (1983). Attention and cognitive problems. In M. Rutter (Ed.), *Developmental neuropsychiatry* (pp. 280-329). New York: Guilford.

Douglas, V.I. & Peters, K.G. (1979). Toward a clearer definition of the attentional deficit of hyperactive children. In G.A. Hale & M. Lewis (Eds.), *Attention and the development of cognitive skills* (pp. 173-248). New York: Plenum.

Drake, R.E., & Vaillant, G.E. (1985). A validity study of axis II of DSM-III. *American Journal of Psychiatry, 142,* 553-558.

Dryden, W. & DiGiuseppe, R. (1990). *A primer on rational-emotive therapy.* Champaign, Il: Research Press.

Dulcan, M.K. (1986). Comprehensive treatment of children and adolescents with attention deficit disorders: The state of the art. *Clinical Psychology Review, 6,* 539-569.

Durham, R.C., & Allan, T. (1993). Psychological treatment of generalized anxiety disorder: A review of the clinical significance of results in outcome studies since 1980. *British Journal of Psychiatry, 163,* 19-26.

Durham, M.L. & LaFond, J.Q. (1988). A search for the missing premise of involuntary therapeutic commitment: Effective treatment of the mentally ill. *Rutgers Law Review, 40,* 303-368.

Dyk, P.H. & Adams, G.R. (1990). Identity and intimacy: An initial investigation of three theoretical models using cross-lag panel correlations. *Journal of Youth and Adolescence, 19,* 91-110.

Eagle, M., & Wolitzky, D.L. (1988). Psychodynamics. In C.G. Last and M. Hersen (Eds.), *Handbook of anxiety disorders.* New York: Pergamon.

Eaton, W.W., Dryman, A., & Weissman, M.M. (1991). Panic and phobia. In L.N. Robins and D.A. Regier (Eds.), *Psychiatric disorders in America: The epidemiologic catchment area study.* New York: Free Press. pp. 155-179.

Eaton, W.W., Mortensen, P.B., Herrman, H., Freeman, H. et al. (1992). Long-term course of hospitalization for schizophrenia: I. Risk for rehospitalization. *Schizophrenia Bulletin, 18,* 217-228.

Eberlin, M., McConnachie, G., Igel, S., & Volpe, L. (1993). Facilitated communication: A failure to replicate the phenomenon. *Journal of Autism and Developmental Disorders, 23,* 507-530.

Edelbrock, C., & Costello, A.J. (1984). Structured psychiatric interviews for children and adolescents. In G.R. Goldstein & M. Hersen (Eds.), *Handbook of psychological assessment.* London: Pergamon. pp. 276-290.

Egeland, J.A., Gerhard, D.S., Pauls, D.L., Sussex, J.N., Kidd, K.K., Allen, C.R., Hostetter, A.M., & Housman, D.E. (1987). Bipolar affective disorders linked to DNA markers on chromosome 11. *Nature, 325,* 783-787.

Ehrenfest, H. (1926). Birth injuries of the child. *Gynecological and Obstretrical Monographs.* New York: Appleton.

Ehrman, R., Ternes, J., O'Brien, C.P., & McLellan, A.T. (1992). Conditioned tolerance in human opiate addicts. *Psychopharmacology, 108,* 218-224.

Eisenberg, L. & Kanner, L. (1956). Early infantile autism: 1943-1955. *American Journal of Orthopsychiatry, 26,* 55-65.

Eisenthal, S., Emery, R., Lazare, A. & Udin, H. (1979). 'Adherence' and the negotiated approach to patienthood. *Archives of General Psychiatry, 36,* 393-398.

Eklund, P.L.E., Gooren, L.J.G., & Bezemer, P.D. (1988). Prevalence of transsexualism in the Netherlands. *British Journal of Psychiatry, 152,* 638-640.

Ekman, G., Miranda-Linne, F., Gillberg, C., Garle, M., & Wetterberg, L. (1989). *Journal of Autism and Developmental Disorders, 19,* 511-531.

Elkin, I., Shea, T., Watkins, J.T., Imber, S.D., Sotsky, S.M., Collins, J.F., Glass,D.R., Pikonis, P.A., Leber, W.R., Docherty, J.P., Fiester, S.J., & Parloff, M.B. (1989). National Institute of Mental Health treatment of depression collaborative research program: General effectiveness of treatments. *Archives of General Psychiatry, 46,* 971-982.

Ellenbroek, B.A. (1993). Treatment of schizophrenia: A clinical and preclinical evaluation of neuroleptic drugs. *Pharmacological Therapy, 57,* 1-78.

Elliott, G. (1989). Stress and illness. In S. Cheren (Ed.), *Psychosomatic medicine: Theory, physiology, and practice* (Vol. 1, pp. 45-90). Madison, CT: International Universities Press.

Elliott, B.J. & Richards, M.P.M. (1991). Children and divorce: Educational performance and behaviour before and after parental separation. *International Journal of Law and the Family, 5,* 258-276.

Ellis, A. (1962). *Reason and emotion in psychotherapy.* New York: Lyle Stuart.

Ellis, A. (1973). *Humanistic psychotherapy: The rational-emotive approach.* New York: McGraw-Hill.

Ellis, A. (1970). *Reason and emotion in psychotherapy.* New York: Lyle Stuart.

Emery, R.E., Fincham, F.D., & Cummings, E.M. (1992). Parenting in context: Systemic thinking about parental conflict and its influence on children. *Journal of Consulting and Clinical Psychology, 60,* 909-912.

Emery, R.E. & Marholin, D. (1977). An applied behavior analysis of delinquency: The irrelevancy of relevant behavior. *American Psychologist, 32,* 860-873.

Emery, R.E. (1994). *Renegotiating family relationships: Divorce, child custody, and mediation.* New York: Guilford.

Emery, R.E., & Rogers, K.C. (1990). The role of behavior therapists in child custody cases. In M. Hersen & R.M. Eisler (Eds.), *Progress in behavior modification* (pp. 60-89). Beverly Hills: Sage.

Emery, R. E., Matthews, S., & Wyer (1991). Child custody mediation and litigation: Further evidence on the differing views of mothers and fathers. *Journal of Consulting and Clinical Psychology 59,* 410-418.

Emery, R.E. & Wyer, M.M. (1987). Divorce mediation. *American Psychologist, 42,* 472-480.

Emery, R.E. (1982). Interparental conflict and the children of discord and divorce. *Psychological Bulletin, 92,* 310-330.

Emery, R.E. (1988). *Marriage, divorce, and children's adjustment.* Newbury Park, CA: Sage Publications.

Emery, R.E. (1989). Family violence. *American Psychologist, 44,* 321-328.

Emery, R.E. (1992). Family conflict and its developmental implications: A conceptual analysis of deep meanings and systemic processes. In C.U. Shantz & W.W. Hartup (Eds.), *Conflict in Child and Adolescent Development,* (pp. 270-298) London: Cambridge.

Emmelkamp, P.M.G., & Beens, H. (1991). Cognitive therapy with obsessive-compulsive disorder: A comparative evaluation. *Behaviour Research and Therapy, 29,* 293-300.

Engel, G.L. (1977). The need for a new medical model: A challenge for biomedicine. *Science, 196,* 129-136.

Ennis, B. & Emery, R. (1978). *The rights of mental patients.* New York: Avon.

Epstein, S. (1980). The stability of behavior: II. Implications for psychological research. *American Psychologist, 35,* 790-806.

Epstein, S. (1979). The stability of behavior: I. On predicting most of the people much of the time. *Journal of Personality and Social Psychology, 37,* 1097-1126.

Erdelyi, M.H. (1990). Repression, reconstruction, and defense: History and integration of the psychoanalytic and experimental frameworks. In J.L. Singer (Ed.), *Repression and dissociation* (pp. 1-32). Chicago: University of Chicago Press.

Erikson, E.H. (1959, 1980). *Identity and the life cycle.* New York: Norton.

Erikson, E.H. (1968). *Identity: Youth and crisis.* New York: Norton.

Erlenmeyer-Kimling, L., & Cornblatt, B.A. (1992). A summary of attentional findings in the New York high-risk project. Journal of Psychiatric Research, 26, 405-426.

Eron, L.D. (1982). Parent-child interaction, television violence, and aggression in children. *American Psychologist, 37,* 197-211.

Ewing, C. (1991). Preventive detention and execution: The constitutionality of punishing future crimes. *Law and Human Behavior, 15,* 139-163.

Exner, J.E. (1986). *The Rorschach: A comprehensive system.* (vol 1, 2nd edition). New York: Wiley.

Eysenck, H.J. (1979). The conditioning model of neurosis. *Behavioral and Brain Sciences, 2,* 155-199.

Eysenck, H.J. (1952). The effects of psychotherapy: An evaluation. *Journal of Consulting Psychology, 16,* 319-324.

Fabrega, H. (1991). The culture and history of psychiatric stigma in early modern and modern Western societies: A review of recent literature. *Comprehensive Psychiatry*, 32, 97-119.

Faigman, D.L. (1986). The battered woman syndrome and self-defense: A legal and empirical dissent. *Virginia Law Review*, 72, 619-647.

Falloon, I., Boyd, J.L., & McGill, C.W. (1985). *Family care of schizophrenia*. New York: Guilford.

Farah, M.J., O'Reilly, R.C., & Vecera, S.P. (1993). Dissociated overt and covert recognition as an emergent property of a lesioned neural network. *Psychological Review*, 100, 571-588.

Farde, L. & Nordstrom, A.L. (1992). PET analysis indicates atypical central dopamine receptor occupancy in clozapine-treated patients. *British Journal of Psychiatry*, 160 (suppl 17), 30-33.

Faris, R.E.L. & Dunham, H.W. (1939). *Mental disorders in urban areas: An ecological study of schizophrenia and other psychoses*. Chicago: University of Chicago Press.

Farmer, A.E., McGuffin, P., & Gottesman, I.I. (1984). Searching for the split in schizophrenia: A twin study perspective. *Psychiatry Research*, 13, 109-118.

Farmer, A.E., & Griffiths, H. (1992). Labeling and illness in primary care: Comparing factors influencing general practitioners' and psychiatrists' decisions regarding patient referral to mental illness services. *Psychological Medicine*, 22, 717-723.

Farmer, A.E., McGuffin, P., & Gottesman, I.I. (1987). Twin concordance for DSM-III schizophrenia: Scrutinizing the validity of the definition. *Archives of General Psychiatry*, 44, 634-641.

Farmer, A.E., & Blewett, A. (1993). Drug treatment of resistant schizophrenia: Limitations and recommendations. *Drugs*, 45, 374-383.

Farquhar, J.W., Macoby, N., Wood, P.D. et al., (1977). Community education for cardiovascular health. *Lancet*, i, 1192-1195.

Farrington, D., Ohlin, J. & Wilson, J.Q. (1986). *Understanding and controlling crime*. New York: Springer-Verlag.

Faust, D. & Ziskin, J. (1988). The expert witness in psychology and psychiatry. *Science*, 241, 31-35.

Fawcett, J., Clark, D.C., & Busch, K.A. (1993). Assessing and treating the patient at risk for suicide. *Psychiatric Annals*, 23, 244-255.

Federal Bureau of Investigation. *Sourcebook of criminal justice statistics*. Washington: U.S. Government Printing Office.

Feingold, B.F. (1975). *Why your child is hyperactive*. New York: Random House.

Ferreira, L., & Soares-da-Silva, P. (1991). 5-hydroxytryptamine and alcoholism. *Human Psychopharmacology: Clinical and Experimental*, 6 (suppl), 21-24.

Ferster, C.B. (1961). Positive reinforcement and behavioral deficits of autistic children. *Child Development*, 32, 437-456.

Figley, C.R. (1978). *Stress disorders among vietnam veterans*. New York: Bruner/Mazel.

Fillmore, K.M. (1987). Women's drinking across the adult life course as compared to men's British *Journal of Addiction*, 82, 801-811.

Fincham, F.D. & Bradbury, T.N. (1990). *The psychology of marriage: Basic issues and applications*. New York: Guilford.

Fincham, F.D. & Bradbury, T.N. (1987). The impact of attributions in marriage: A longitudinal analysis. *Journal of Personality and Social Psychology*, 53, 510-517.

Fingarette, H. (1988). *Heavy drinking: The myth of alcoholism as a disease*. Berkeley: University of California Press.

Fink, M. (1992). Electroconvulsive therapy. In E. S. Paykel (Ed.), *Handbook of affective disorders* (2nd edition) New York: Guilford. (pp. 359-367).

Fink, P.J., & Tasman, A. (Eds.) (1992). *Stigma and mental illness*. Washington, D.C.: American Psychiatric Press.

Finkelhor, D. (1992). New myths about the child welfare system. *Child, Youth, and Family Services Quarterly*, 15, 3-5.

Finlay-Jones, R., & Brown, G.W. (1981). Types of stressful life event and the onset of anxiety and depressive disorders. *Psychological Medicine*, 11, 803-815.

Finney, J.W., & Moos, R.H. (1991). The long-term course of treated alcoholism: I. Mortality, relapse and remission rates and comparisons with community controls. *Journal of Studies on Alcohol*, 52, 44-54.

Finney, J.S., & Moos, R.H. (1992). The long-term course of treated alcoholism: II. Predictors and correlates of 10-year functioning and mortality. *Journal of Studies on Alcohol*, 53, 142-153.

Fisher, P.J. & Breakey, W.R. (1991). The epidemiology of alcohol, drug, and mental disorders among homeless persons. *American Psychologist*, 46, 1115-1128.

Fitch, S.A. & Adams, G.R. (1983). Ego-identity and intimacy status: Replication and extension. *Developmental Psychology*, 19, 839-845.

Fitch, W.L., Petrella, R.C., & Wallace, J. (1987). Legal ethics and the use of mental health experts in criminal cases. *Behavioral Sciences and the Law*, 5, 105-117.

Flanagan, J.C. (1982). *New insights to improve the quality of life at age 70*. Palo Alto, CA: American Institutes for Research.

Fleming, J.E. & Offord, D.R. (1990). Epidemiology of childhood depressive disorders: A critical review. *Journal of American Academy of Child and Adolescent Psychiatry*, 29, 571-580.

Foa, E.B., Rothbaum, B.O., Riggs, D.S., & Murdock, T.B. (1991). Treatment of posttraumatic stress disorder in rape victims: A comparison between cognitive-behavioral procedures and counseling. *Journal of Consulting and Clinical Psychology,*, 59, 715-723.

Foa, E.B., Steketee, G., & Rothbaum, B.O. (1989). Behavioral/cognitive conceptualizations of posttraumatic stress disorder. *Behavior Therapy*, 20, 155-176.

Folstein, S. & Rutter, M. (1977). Infantile autism: A genetic study of 21 twin pairs. *Journal of Child Psychology and Psychiatry*, 18, 291-321.

Fontana, A. (1966). Familial etiology of schizophrenia: Is a scientific methodology possible? *Psychological Bulletin*, 66, 214-228.

Foot, P. (1990). Ethics and the death penalty: Participation of forensic psychiatrists in capital trials. In R. Rosner & R. Weinstock (Eds.), *Ethical practice in psychiatry and the law* (pp. 202-217). New York: Plenum.

Ford, C., & Beach, F. (1951). *Patterns of sexual behavior*. New York: Harper & Row.

Ford, D.H. & Lerner, R.M. (1992). *Developmental systems theory: An integrative approach*. Newbury Park, CA: Sage.

Fordyce, W.E. (1976). *Behavioral methods for chronic pain and illness*. St. Louis: C.V. Mosby.

Forehand, R. & McMahon, R.J. (1981). *Helping the noncompliant child: A clinician's guide to parent training*. New York: Guilford.

Forehand, R., Wells, K., & Griest, D. (1980). An examination of the social validity of a parent training program. *Behavior Therapy*, 11, 488-502.

Foster, S.L., & Cone, J.D. (1986). Design and use of direct observation procedures. In A.R. Ciminero, K.S. Calhoun, and H.E. Adams (Eds.), *Handbook of behavioral assessment* (2nd edition). New York: Wiley.

Fowles, D.C. (1992). Schizophrenia: Diathesis-stress revisited. *Annual Review of Psychology*, 43, 303-336.

Foy, D.W., Resnick, H.S., Sipprelle, R.C., & Carroll, E.M. (1987). Premilitary, military, and post-military factors in the development of combat-related posttraumatic stress disorder. *The Behavior Therapist*, 10, 3-9.

Frances, A. (1980). The DSM-III personality disorders section: A commentary. *American Journal of Psychiatry*, 137, 1050-1054.

Frances, A. (1985). Validating schizotypal personality disorders: Problems with the schizophrenia connection. *Schizophrenia Bulletin*, 11, 595-597.

Frances, A.J., Widiger, T.A., & Pincus, H.A. (1989). The development of DSM-IV. *Archives of General Psychiatry*, 46, 373-375.

Frank, E., Anderson, C., & Rubenstein, D. (1978). Frequency of sexual dysfunction in normal couples. *New England Journal of Medicine*, 299, 111-115.

Frank, J.D. & Frank, J.B. (1991). *Persuasion and healing* (3rd. Ed.). Baltimore: Johns Hopkins University Press.

Frank, J.D. (1973). *Persuasion and healing* (2nd. Ed.). Baltimore: Johns Hopkins University Press.

Frank, E., Turner, S.M., Stewart, B.D., Jacob, M., & West, D. (1981). Past psychiatric symptoms and the response to sexual assault. *Comprehensive Psychiatry*, 22, 479-487.

Frank, J.D. (1961). *Persuasion and healing*. Baltimore: Johns Hopkins University Press.

Frankel, F.H. (1990). Hypnotizability and dissociation. *American Journal of Psychiatry*, 147, 823-829.

Frasure-Smith, N. & Prince, R. (1985). Long-term follow-up of the ischemic heart disease life stress monitoring program. *Psychosomatic Medicine*, 51, 485-513.

Freeman, P.S., & Gunderson, J.G. (1989). Treatment of personality disorders. *Psychiatric Annals*, 19, 147-153.

Freidman, M. & Rosenman, R.H. (1959). Association of specific overt behavior pattern with blood and cardiovascular findings: Blood cholesterol level, blood clotting time, incidence of arcus senilis and clinical coronary artery disease. *Journal of the American Medical Association*, 169, 1286-1296.

Freud, S. (1894/1957). On the grounds for detaching a particular syndrome from neurasthenia under the description "anxiety neurosis." In J. Strachey (Ed.), *Standard edition of the complete psychological works of Sigmund Freud* (Vol 1). London: Hogarth Press.

Freud, S. (1926/1959). Inhibitions, symptoms, and anxiety. In J. Strachey (Ed.), *Standard edition of the complete psychological works of Sigmund Freud*. (Vol 20). London: Hogarth Press.

Freud, S. (1917/1961). Mourning and melancholia. In J. Strachey (Ed. and Trans.). *The standard edition of the complete psychological works of Sigmund Freud* (Vol 14). London: Hogarth Press.

Freud, S. (1930/1961). *Civilization and its Discontents*. J. Strachey (Ed. & Trans.). *The standard edition of the complete psychological works of Sigmund Freud* (Vol. 21). London: Hogarth Press.

Freud, S. (1917/1955). *A Difficulty in the Path of Psychoanalysis*. J. Strachey (Ed. & Trans.), *The standard edition of the complete psychological works of Sigmund Freud* (Vol. 17). London: Hogarth Press.

Freud, S. (1962/1924). The aetiology of hysteria. In J. Strachey (Ed. and Trans.), *The standard edition of the complete psychological works of Sigmund Freud* (Vol. 3, pp. 191-221). London: Hogarth Press.

Freud, S. (1940/1969). *An outline of psycho-analysis*. New York: Norton.

Freud, S. (1912/1957). Recommendations for physicians on the psycho-analytic method for treatment. *Standard Edition*, 12, 109-120. London: Hogarth Press.

Freund, K., & Blanchard, R. (1986). The concept of courtship disorder. *Journal of Sex and Marital Therapy*, 12, 79-92.

Freund, K., & Watson, R.J. (1991). Assessment of the sensitivity and specificity of a phallometric test: An update of phallometric diagnosis of pedophilia. *Psychological Assessment*, 3, 254-260.

Friedland, R.P. (1993). Epidemiology, education, and the ecology of Alzheimer's disease. *Neurology*, 43, 246-248.

Friedman, E.S., Clark, D.B., & Gershon, S. (1992). Stress, anxiety, and depression: Review of biological, diagnostic, and nosologic issues. *Journal of Anxiety Disorders*, 6, 337-363.

Friedman, M., Thoresen, C.D., Gill, J.J., et al., (1986). Alteration of Type A behavior and its effect on cardiac recurrences in post-myocardial infarction patients: Summary results of the recurrent coronary prevention project. *American Heart Journal*, 112, 653-665.

Fuller, R.K., & Roth, H.P. (1979). Disulfiram for the treatment of alcoholism: An evaluation of 128 men. *Annals of Internal Medicine*, 90, 901-904.

Funder, D.C., & Colvin, C.R. (1991). Explorations in behavioral consistency: Properties of persons, situations, and behaviors. *Journal of Personality and Social Psychology*, 60, 773-794.

Furby, L., Weinrott, M.R., & Blackshaw, L. (1989). Sex offenders recidivism: A review. *Psychological Bulletin*, 105, 3-30.

Gagnon, J.H., & Simon, W. (1973). *Sexual conduct: The social sources of human sexuality*. Chicago: Aldine.

Garber, J., & Hollon, S.D. (1991). What can specificity designs say about causality in psychopathology research? *Psychological Bulletin*, 110, 129-136.

Garber, H.I. (1988). *The Milwaukee project: Preventing Mental Retardation in Children at risk*. Washington: American association on Mental Retardation.

Garber, J. (1984). Classification of childhood psychopathology: A developmental perspective. *Child Development*, 55, 30-48.

Garfield, S.L. (1989). *The practice of brief psychotherapy*. New York: Pergamon.

Garfield, S. & Kurtz, R. (1974). A survey of clinical psychologists: Characteristics, activities, and orientations. *The Clinical Psychologist*, 28, 7-10.

Garfinkel, P.E. & Garner, D.M. (1982). *Anorexia nervosa: A multidimensional perspective*. New York: Basic Books.

Garmezy, N. (1978). DSM-III: Never mind the psychologists; Is it good for the children? *The Clinical Psychologist*, 31, 1-6.

Garner, D.M., Garfinkel, P.E., Schwartz, D., & Thompson, M. (1980). Cultural expectations of thinness in women. *Psychological Reports*, 47, 483-491.

Gaylord, S.A., & Zung, W.W.K. (1987). Affective disorders among the aging. In L.L. Carstensen & B.A. Edelstein (Eds.). *Handbook of clinical gerontology*. New York: Plenum.

Geer, J., Heiman, J., & Leitenberg, H. (1984). *Human sexuality*. Englewood Cliffs, N.J.: Prentice-Hall.

Gehlbach, S.H. (1988). *Interpreting the medical literature: Practical epidemiology for clinicians* (2nd edition). New York: Macmillan.

Geller, E., Ritvo, E.R., Freeman, B.J., & Yuwiler, A. (1982). Preliminary observations on the effect of fenfluramine on blood serotonin and symptoms in three autistic Boys. *New England Journal of Medicine*, 307, 165-169.

Gerardi, R.J., Blanchard, E.B., & Kolb, L.C. (1989). Ability of Vietnam veterans to dissimulate a psychophysiological assessment for posttraumatic stress disorder. *Behavior Therapy*, 20, 229-244.

Gerstley, L., McLellan, T., Alterman, A.I., Woody, G.E., Luborsky, L, & Prout, M. (1989). Ability to form an alliance with the therapist: A possible marker of prognosis for patients with antisocial personality disorder. *American Journal of Psychiatry*, 146, 508-512.

Geske, M.R. (1989). Statutes limiting mental health professionals' liability for the violent acts of their patients. *Indiana Law Journal*, 64, 391-422.

Gianoulakis, C. (1993). Endogenous opioids and excessive alcohol-consumption. *Journal of Psychiatry and Neuroscience*, 18, 148-156.

Gilbert, D.G., Hagen, R.L., D'Agostino, J.A. (1986). The effects of cigarette smoking on human sexual potency. *Addictive Behaviors*, 11, 431-434.

Gillberg, C. (1991). Outcome in autism and autistic-like conditions. *Journal of the American Academy of Child and Adolescent Psychiatry*, 30, 375-382.

Gillberg, C. & Schaumann, H. (1982). Social class and infantile autism. *Journal of Autism and Developmental Disorders*, 12, 223-228.

Gillberg, C. (1988). The role of the endogenous opioids in autism and possible relationships to clinical features. In L. Wing (Ed.), *Aspects of autism: Biological Research* (pp. 31-37). Gaskell: London.

Gilligan, C. (1982). *In a different voice*. Cambridge: Harvard University Press.

Gitlin, M.J. (1993). Pharmacotherapy of personality disorders: Conceptual framework and clinical strategies. *Journal of Clinical Psychopharmacology*, 13, 343-353.

Gittelman-Klein, R. (1988). Questioning the clinical usefulness of projective psychological tests for children. *Developmental and Behavioral Pediatrics*, 7, 378-382.

Glaser, R., Rice, J., Sheridan, J., Fertel, R., Stout, J., Speicher, C.E., Pinsky, D., Kotur, M., Post., A., Beck., M., & Kiecolt-Glaser, J.K. (1987). Stress-related immune suppression: Health implications. *Brain, Behavior, and Immunity*, 1, 7-20.

Glass, D.C. (1977). *Behavior patterns, stress, and coronary disease*. Hillsdale, NJ: Erlbaum.

Gleick, J. (1987). *Chaos: Making of a new science*. New York: Viking Press.

Goldberg, S. (1991). Recent developments in attachment theory and research. *Canadian Journal of Psychiatry*, 36, 393-400.

Goldberg, E.M., & Morrison, S.L. (1963). Schizophrenia and social class. *British Journal of Psychiatry*, 109, 785-802.

Goldberg, E.M. (1970). *Helping the aged: A field experiment in social work*. London: Allen & Unwin.

Goldberg, L.R. (1990). An alternative "description of personality": The Big Five factor structure. *Journal of Personality and Social Psychology*, 59, 1216-1229.

Goldberg, S.C., Schulz, S.C., Schulz, P.M et al (1986). Borderline and schizotypal personality disorders treated with low-dose thiothizene vs placebo. *Archives of General Psychiatry*, 43, 680-686.

Goldfried, M.R., & Kent, R.N. (1972). Traditional versus behavioral personality assessment: A comparison of methodological and theoretical assumptions. *Psychological Bulletin*, 77, 409-420.

Goldfried, M.R. (Ed.), (1982). *Converging themes in psychotherapy*. New York: Springer.

Goldfried, M.R. & Castonguay, L.G. (1993). Behavior therapy: Redefining strengths and limitations. *Behavior Therapy*, 24, 505-526.

Goldman, M.S., Brown, S.A., & Christiansen. B.A. (1987). Expectancy theory: Thinking about drinking. In H.T. Blane and K.E. Leonard (Eds.). *Psychological theories of drinking and alcoholism*. New York: Guilford. pp. 181-226.

Goldman, H.H., Skodol, A.E., & Lave, T.R. (1992). Revising axis V for DSM-IV: A review of measures of social functioning. *American Journal of Psychiatry*, 149, 1148-1156.

Goldman, M.S., Brown, S.A., Christiansen, B.A., & Smith, G.T. (1991). Alcoholism and memory: Broadening the scope of alcohol-expectancy research. *Psychological Bulletin*, 110, 137-146.

Goldman, H.H., Adams, N.H., & Taube, C.A. (1983). Deinstitutionalization: The data demythologized. *Hospital and Community Psychiatry*, 34, 129-134.

Goldsmith, H.H., Buss, A.H., Plomin, R., Rothbart, M.K., Thomas, A., & Chess, S. (1987). What is temperament? Four approaches. *Child Development*, 58, 505-529.

Goldsmith, H. (1988). Roundtable: What is temperament? Four approaches. *Child Development*, 58, 505-529.

Goldstein, M.J., & Kant, H.S. (1973). *Pornography and sexual deviance*. Berkeley: University of California Press.

Goldstein, A.J., & Chambless, D.L. (1978). A reanalysis of agoraphobia. *Behavior Therapy*, 9, 47-59.

Goldstein, M.J. (1988). The family and psychopathology. *Annual Review of Psychology*, 39, 283-299.

Golomb, J., de Leon, M.J., Kluger, A., George, A.E., Tarshish, C., & Ferris, S.H. (1993). Hippocampal atrophy in normal aging: An association with recent memory impairment. *Archives of Neurology*, 50, 967-973.

Golwyn, D.H., & Sevlie, C.P. (1992). Paraphilias, nonparaphilic sexual addictions, and social phobia. *Journal of Clinical Psychiatry*, 53, 330.

Gomberg, E.S.L. (1988). Alcoholic women in treatment: The question of stigma and age. *Alcohol and Alcoholism*, 23, 507-514.

Gomberg, E.S.L. (1993). Women and alcohol: Use and abuse. *Journal of Nervous and Mental Disease*, 181, 211-219.

Gomberg, E.S.L. (1987). Drug and alcohol problems of elderly persons. In T.D. Nirenberg, & S.A. Maisto (Eds.), *Developments in the assessment and treatment of addictive behaviors*. Norwood, NJ: Ablex Publishing Corp.

Good, B., & Kleinman, A. (1985). Culture and anxiety: cross-cultural evidence for the patterning of anxiety disorders. In A.H. Tuma and J. Maser (Eds.), *Anxiety and the anxiety disorders*. Hillsdale, NJ: Erlbaum.

Good, B., & Kleinman, A. (1985). Culture and depression. In A. Kleinman and B. Good (Eds.). *Culture and depression: Studies in the anthropology and cross-cultural psychiatry of affect and disorder*. Berkeley: University of California Press. pp. 491-506.

Goodman, W.K., Price, L.H., Rasmussen, S.A., Mazure, C., Fleischman, R.L., Hill, C.L., Heninger, G.R., & Charmey, D.S. (1989). The Yale-Brown Obsessive Compulsive Scale: 1. Development, use, and reliability. *Archives of General Psychiatry*, 46, 1006-1011.

Goodman, L.A., Koss, M.P., Fitzgerald, L.F., Russo, N.F., & Keita, G.P. (1993). Male violence against women: Current research and future directions. *American Psychologist*, 48, 1054-1058.

Goodman, R. & Stevenson, J. (1989). A twin study of hyperactivity: II. The aetiologyical role of genes, family relationships, and perinatal adversity. *Journal of Child Clinical Psychology and Psychiatry*, 30, 691-709.

Goodman, L.A., Koss, M.P., & Russo, N.F. (1993b). Violence against women: Mental health effects. Part II: Conceptualizations of posttraumatic stress. *Applied and Preventive Psychology*, 2, 123-130.

Goodman, T.A. (1985). From Tarasoff to Hopper: The evolution of the therapist's duty to protect third parties. *Behavioral Sciences and the Law*, 3, 195-225.

Goodman, L.A., Koss, M.P., & Russo, N.F. (1993a). Violence against women: Physical and mental health effects. Part I: Research findings. *Applied and Preventive Psychology, 2,* 79-79.

Goodwin, D.W. (1991). The genetics of alcoholism. In P.R. McHugh & V.A. McKusick (Eds.). *Genes, Brain, and Behavior.* New York: Raven Press.

Goodwin, D.W. (1984b). Studies of familial alcoholism: A review. *Journal of Clinical Psychiatry, 45,* 14-17.

Goodwin, G.M. (1992). Tricyclic and newer antidepressants. In E. S. Paykel (Ed.), *Handbook of affective disorders* (2nd edition) New York: Guilford. (pp. 327-344).

Goodwin, D.W. (1984a). Speculations on the cause(s) of alcoholism. *Journal of Clinical Psychiatry, 45,* 491-493.

Goodwin, D.W. (1988). *Alcohol and the writer.* New York: Penguin Books.

Goodwin, D.W. & Guze, S.B. (1979). *Psychiatric diagnosis* (2nd. Ed.). New York: Oxford University Press.

Gorenstein, E.E. (1992). *The science of mental illness.* San Diego: Academic Press.

Gorton, G., & Akhtar, S. (1990). The literature on personality disorders, 1985-88: Trends, issues, and controversies. *Hospital and Community Psychiatry, 41,* 39-51.

Gosselin, C.C., & Wilson, G.D. (1980). *Sexual variations.* London: Faber & Faber.

Gotlib, I.H., & Lee. C.M. (1989). The social functioning of depressed patients: A longitudinal assessment. *Journal of Social and Clinical Psychology, 8,* 223-237.

Gotlib, I.H., & Hammen, C. (1992). *Psychological aspects of depression: Toward a cognitive-interpersonal integration.* New York: Wiley.

Gotlib, I.H., & Robinson, L.A. (1982). Responses to depressed individuals: Discrepancies between self-report and observer-rated behavior. *Journal of Abnormal Psychology, 91,* 231-240.

Gotlib, I.H., & Meltzer, S.J. (1987). Depression and the perception of social skill in dyadic interaction. *Cognitive Therapy and Research, 11,* 41-53.

Gotlib, I.H., & Colby, C.A. (1987). *Treatment of depression: An interpersonal systems approach.* New York: Pergamon.

Gotlib, I.H. & McCabe, S.B. (1990). Marriage and psychopathology. In F.D. Fincham & T.N. Bradbury (Eds.), *The psychology of marriage: Basic issues and applications* (pp. 226-257). New York: Guilford.

Gottesman, I.I. (1987). The psychotic hinterlands or, the fringes of lunacy. *British Medical Bulletin, 43,* 1-13.

Gottesman, I.I., McGuffin, P., & Farmer, A. (1987). Clinical genetics as clues to the "real" genetics of schizophrenia. *Schizophrenia Bulletin, 13,* 23-47.

Gottesman, I.I. (1991). *Schizophrenia genesis: The origins of madness.* New York: Freeman.

Gottesman, I.G. (1963). Genetic aspects of intelligent behavior. In N. Ellis (Ed.), *The Handbook of Mental Deficiency: Psychological Theory and Research* (pp.253-296). New York: McGraw Hill.

Gottesman, I.I. & Goldsmith, H.H. (in press). Developmental psychopathology of antisocial behavior: Inserting genes into its ontogenesis and epigenesis. In C.A. Nelson (Ed.), *Threats to optimal development: Integrating biological, psychological, and social risk factors.* Hillsdale, NJ: Erlbaum.

Gottfries, C.G. (1991). Classifying organic mental disorders and dementia — A review of historical perspectives. *International Psychogeriatrics, 3* (suppl), 9-17.

Gottman, J.M., & Levenson, R.W. (1986). Assessing the role of emotion in marriage. *Behavioral Assessment, 8,* 31-48.

Gottman, J.M. (1985). Observational measures of behavior therapy outcome: A reply to Jacobsen. *Behavioral Assessment, 7,* 317-321.

Gottman, J.M., & Levenson, R.W. (1992). Marital processes predictive of later dissolution: Behavior, physiology, and health. *Journal of Personality and Social Psychology, 63,* 221-233.

Gottman, J., Notarius, C., Gonso, J., & Markman, H. (1976). *A couple's guide to communication.* Champaign, IL: Research Press.

Gottman, J. M., & Katz, L. F. (1989). Effects of marital discord on young children's peer interaction and health. *Developmental Psychology, 25,* 373-381.

Gottman, J.M. (1994). *Why marriages succeed or fail.* New York: Simon and Schuster.

Goudie, A.J. (1990). Conditioned opponent processes in the development of tolerance to psychoactive drugs. *Progress in Neuro-Psychopharmacology and Biological Psychiatry, 14,* 675-688.

Gove, W.R. (1990). Labeling theory's explanation of mental illness: An update of recent evidence. In M. Nagler (Ed.), *Perspectives on disability.* Palo Alto, CA: Health Markets Research.

Gove, W.R. (1970). Societal reaction as an explanation of mental illness: An evaluation. *American Sociological Review, 35,* 873-884.

Gove, W.R., Hughes, M., & Styles, C.B. (1983). Does marriage have positive effects on the psychological well-being of the individual? *Journal of Health and Social Behavior, 24,* 122-132.

Graham, J.R. (1990). *MMPI-2. Assessing personality and psychopathology.* New York: Oxford.

Granville-Grossman, K. (1983). Mind and body. In M.H. Lader (Ed.), *Handbook of psychiatry 2: Mental disorders and somatic illness* (pp. 5-13). London: Cambridge University Press.

Gray, J.A. (1990). Brain systems that mediate both emotion and cognition. *Cognition and Emotion, 4,* 269-288.

Greaves, G.B. (1980). Multiple personality disorder: 165 years after Mary Reynolds. *Journal of Nervous and Mental Disease, 168,* 577-596.

Greenberg, L.S., Elliott, R.K., & Lietaer, G. (1994). In A.E. Bergin & S.L. Garfield, *Handbook of psychotherapy and behavior change* (4th. Ed., pp. 509-542). New York: Wiley.

Greenblatt, M., Grosser, G.H., & Wechsler, H. (1964). Differential response of hospitalized depressed patients to somatic therapy. *American Journal of Psychiatry, 120,* 935-943.

Greene, R.L. (1991). *The MMPI-2/MMPI: An interpretive manual.* Boston: Allyn and Bacon.

Greenough, W.T. (1987). Experience effects on the developing and the mature brain: Dendritic branching and synaptogenesis. In N.A. Krasnegor, E.M. Blass, and M.A. Hofer (Eds.). *Perinatal development: A psychobiological perspective.* Orlando, FL: Academic Press. pp. 195-221.

Griffitt, W. (1987). Females, males, and sexual responses. In K. Kelley (Ed.). *Females, males, and sexuality.* Albany: State University of New York Press.

Grisso, T. & Appelbaum, P.S. (in press). Is it unethical to offer predictions of future violence? *Law and Human Behavior.*

Grossman, H.J. (1983). *Classification in mental retardation.* Washington: American Association on Mental Deficiency.

Grotevant, H.D., & Carlson, C.I. (1989). *Family assessment: A guide to methods and measures.* New York: Guilford.

Group for Advancement of Psychiatry (1966). *Psychopathological disorders of childhood: Theoretical considerations and a proposed classification.* Report 62. New York: Mental Health Memorials Center.

Grove, W.M., & Tellegen, A. (1991). Problems in the classification of personality disorders. *Journal of Personality Disorders, 5,* 31-41.

Grove, W.M., & Andreasen, N.C. (1992). Concepts, diagnosis and classification. In E.S. Paykel (Ed.). *Handbook of affective disorders* (2nd edition). New York: Guilford. (pp. 25-42).

Grove, W.M., Lebow, B.S., Clementz, B.A., Cerri, A. et al. (1991). Familial prevalence and coaggregation of schizotypy indicators: A multitrait family study. *Journal of Abnormal Psychology, 100,* 115-121.

Grove, W.M., Andreasen, N.C., Young, M., Endicott, J., Keller, M.B., Hirschfeld, R.M.A., & Reich, T. (1987). Isolation and characterization of a nuclear depressive syndrome. *Psychological Medicine, 17,* 471-484.

Grove, W.M., Andreasen, N.C., McDonald-Scott, P., Keller, M., B., & Shapiro, R.W. (1981). Reliability studies of psychiatric diagnosis. *Archives of General Psychiatry, 38,* 408-413.

Growdon, J.H. (1992). Treatment for Alzheimer's disease? *New England Journal of Medicine, 327,* 1306-1308.

Grych, J.H., & Fincham, F.D. (1990). Marital conflict and children's adjustment: A cognitive-contextual framework. *Psychological Bulletin, 101,* 267-290.

Guggenmoos-Holzmann, I. (1993). How reliable are chance-corrected measures of agreement. *Statistics in Medicine, 12,* 2191-2205.

Gunderson, J. (1984). *Borderline personality disorder.* Washington, D.C.: American Psychiatric Press.

Gunderson, J.G., & Singer, M.T. (1975). Defining borderline patients: An overview. *American Journal of Psychiatry, 132,* 1-10.

Gunderson, J., Kolb, J., Austin, V. (1981). The diagnostic interview for borderline patients. *American Journal of Psychiatry, 138,* 896-903.

Gunderson, J., & Singer, M.T. (1975). Defining borderline patients: An overview. *American Journal of Psychiatry, 132,* 1-10.

Gur, R.E. (1985). Regional cerebral blood flow in schizophrenia. In M. Alpert (Ed.). *Controversies in schizophrenia: changes and constancies.* New York: Guilford.

Gur, R.E., & Pearlson, G.D. (1993). Neuroimaging in schizophrenia research. *Schizophrenia Bulletin, 19,* 337-353.

Gurland, B.J. (1976). The comparative frequency of depression in various adult age groups. *Journal of Gerontology, 31,* 283-392.

Gurman, A.S. & Kniskern, D.P. (Eds.), (1991). *Handbook of family therapy* (Vol.II. New York: Brunner/Mazel.

Gusella, J.F., Wexler, N.S., Conneally, P.M., Naylor, S.L., Anderson, M.A., Tanzi, R.E., Watkins, P.C., Ottina, K., Wallace, M.R., Sakaguchi, A.Y., Young, A.B. et al. (1983). A polymorphic DNA marker genetically linked to Huntington's disease. *Nature, 306,* 234-238.

Gutheil, T.G. (1986). The right to refuse treatment: Paradox, pendulum and the quality of care. *Behavioral Sciences and the Law, 4,* 265-277.

Guze, S.B., & Robins, E. (1970). Suicide and primary affective disorders. *British Journal of Psychiatry, 117,* 437-438.

Hafner, H. (1990). Primary dementia of Alzheimer's type —epidemiology and risk factors. *Psychiatria Fennica, 21,* 145-162.

Halford, W.K. (1991). Beyond expressed emotion: Behavioral assessment of family interaction associated with the course of schizophrenia. *Behavioral Assessment, 13,* 99-123.

Hamilton, M. (1982). Symptoms and assessment of depression. In E. S. Paykel (Ed.), *Handbook of affective disorders* (pp. 3-11). New York: Guilford.

Hammen, C. (1991). The generation of stress in the course of unipolar depression. *Journal of Abnormal Psychology, 100,* 555-561.

Hankoff, I.D. (1982). Suicide and attempted suicide. In E. S. Paykel (Ed.), *Handbook of affective disorders* (pp. 416-428). New York: Guilford.

Hanson, D.R., Gottesman, I.I., & Heston, L.L. (1990). Long range schizophrenia forecasting: Many a slip twixt cup and lip. In J. Rolf, K. Nuechterlein, A. Masten, and D. Cicchetti (Eds). *Risk and protective factors in the development of schizophrenia.* New York: Cambridge University Press. pp. 424-444.

Hanson, D.R., Gottesman, I.I., & Heston, L.L. (1976). Some possible childhood indications of adult schizophrenia inferred from children of schizophrenics. *British Journal of Psychiatry, 129,* 142-154.

Harding, C.M., Zubin, J., & Strauss, J.S. (1992). Chronicity in schizophrenia: Revisited. *British Journal of Psychiatry, 161* (suppl. 18), 27-37.

Hare, R.D. (1985). Comparison of procedures for the assessment of psychopathy. *Journal of Consulting and Clinical Psychology, 53,* 7-16.

Hare, R.D. (1983). Diagnosis of antisocial personality disorder in two prison populations. *American Journal of Psychiatry, 140,* 887-890.

Hare, R.D. (1978). Electrodermal and cardiovascular correlates of psychopathy. In R.D. Hare & D.Schalling (Eds.), *Psychopathic behavior: Approaches to research.* New York: Wiley.

Hare, R.D., Hart, S.D., & Harpur, T.J. (1991). Psychopathy and the DSM-IV criteria for antisocial personality disorder. *Journal of Abnormal Psychology, 100,* 391-398.

Hare, R.D., McPherson, L.M., & Forth, A.E. (1988). Male psychopaths and their criminal careers. *Journal of Consulting and Clinical Psychology, 56,* 710-714.

Harley, J.P., Ray, R.S., Tomasi, L., Eichman, P.L., Matthews, C.G., Chun, R., Cleeland, C.S., & Traisman, E. (1978). Hyperkinesis and food additives: Testing the Feingold hypothesis. *Pediatrics, 6,* 818-828

Harpur, T.J., & Hare, R.D. (1990). Psychopathy and attention. In J. Enns (Ed.). *The development of attention: Research and theory.* Amsterdam: New Holland.

Harrington, R., Fudge, H., Rutter, M., Pickles, A., & Hill, J. (1990). Adult outcomes of childhood and adolescent depression. I. Psychiatric status. *Archives of General Psychiatry, 47,* 465-473.

Harris, G.T., Rice, M.E., Quinsey, V.L., Chaplin, T.C., et al. (1992). Maximizing the discriminant validity of phallometric assessment data. *Psychological Assessment, 4,* 502-511.

Harris, T., Brown, G.W., & Bifulco, A. (1986). Loss of parent in childhood and adult psychiatric disorder: The role of lack of adequate parental care. *Psychological Medicine, 16,* 641-659.

Harrow, M., Rattenbury, F., & Stoll, F. (1988). Schizophrenic delusions: An analysis of their persistence, of related premorbid ideas, and of three major dimensions. In T.F. Oltmanns & B.A. Maher (Eds.), *Delusional beliefs.* New York: Wiley. pp. 184-211.

Hartmann, H., Kris, E., & Loewenstein, R.W. (1947). Comments on the formation of psychic structure. In A. Freud, et al. (Eds.) *The psychoanalytic study of the child .* New York: International Universities Press.

Haugaard, J.J. & Reppucci, N.D. (1988). *The sexual abuse of children.* San Francisco: Jossey-Bass.

Havighurst, R.J. (1952). *Developmental tasks and education.* New York: McKay.

Hawley, T.L. & Disney, E.R. (1992). Crack's children: The consequences of maternal cocaine abuse. *Social Policy Report: Society for Research in Child Development, 6,* 1-22.

Hawton, K. (1986). *Suicide and attempted suicide among children and adolescents.* Beverly Hills: Sage.

Hayes, S.C., Nelson, R.O., & Jarrett, R.B. (1987). The treatment utility of assessment: A functional approach to evaluating assessment quality. *American Psychologist, 42,* 963-974.

Haynes, S.G. & Feinleib, M. (1980). Women, work, and coronary heart disease: Prospective findings from the Framingham heart study. *American Journal of Public Health, 70,* 133-141.

Heath, A.C., Jardine, R., & Martin, N.G. (1989). Interactive effects of genotype and social environment on alcohol consumption in female twins. *Journal of Studies on Alcohol, 50,* 38-48.

Heath, D.B. (1991). Uses and misuses of the concept of ethnicity in alcohol studies: An essay in deconstruction. *International Journal of the Addictions, 25,* 607-628.

Heber, R. (1959). A manual on terminology and classification in mental deficiency. *American Journal on Mental Deficiency, 64* (Monograph Supplement).

Heberbrand, J. (1992). A critical appraisal of X-linked bipolar illness. Evidence for the assumed mode of transmission is lacking. *British Journal of Psychiatry, 160,* 7-11.

Heilbrun, A.B., Jr. (1993). Hallucinations. In C.G. Costello (Ed.), *Symptoms of schizophrenia.* New York: Wiley. pp. 56-91.

Heiman, J.R., & Grafton-Becker, V. (1989). Orgasmic disorders in women. In S.R. Leiblum, & R.C. Rosen (Eds.), *Principles and practice of sex therapy: Update for the 1990s* (2nd ed.). New York: Guilford. pp. 51-88.

Heiman, J.R. (1983). Women and sexuality: Loosening the double binds. In G.W. Albee, S. Gordon, & H. Leitenberg (Eds.), *Promoting sexual responsibility and preventing sexual problems.* Hanover, NH: New England Press.

Heiman,J.R. (1980). Female sexual response patterns: Interactions of physiological, affective, and contextual cues. *Archives of General Psychiatry, 37,* 1311-1316.

Heimberg, R.G., Holt, C.S., Schneier, F.R., Spitzer, R.L., & Liebowitz, M.R. (1993). The issue of subtyping in the diagnosis of social phobia. *Journal of Anxiety Disorders, 7,* 249-269.

Heindel, W.C., Salmon, D.P., Shults, C.W., Walicke, P.A., & Butters, N. (1989). Neuropsychological evidence for multiple implicit memory systems: A comparison of Alzheimer's, Huntington's, and Parkinson's disease patients. *Journal of Neuroscience, 9,* 582-587.

Heitler, S.M. (1992). *From conflict to resolution: Strategies for diagnosis and treatment of distressed individuals, couples, and families.* New York: Norton.

Helmes, E., & Reddon, J.R. (1993). A perspective on developments in assessing psychopathology: A critical review of the MMPI and MMPI-2. *Psychological Bulletin, 113,* 453-471.

Helzer, J.E. (1987). Epidemiology of alcoholism. *Journal of Consulting and Clinical Psychology, 55,* 284-292.

Helzer, J.E., Bucholz, K., & Robins, L.N. (1992). Five communities in the United States: Results of the epidemiologic catchment area survey. In J.E. Helzer & G.J. Canino (Eds). *Alcoholism in North America, Europe, and Asia.* New York: Oxford. pp. 71-95.

Helzer, J.E., Burnam, A., & McEvoy, L.T. (1991). Alcohol abuse and dependence. In L.N. Robins and D.A. Regier (Eds.). *Psychiatric disorders in America: The epidemiologic catchment area study.* New York: Free Press. pp. 81-115.

Helzer, J.E., & Canino, G.J. (Eds). (1992). *Alcoholism in North America, Europe, and Asia.* New York: Oxford.

Helzer, J.E., Robins, L.N., & McEvoy, L. (1987). Posttraumatic stress disorder in the general population: Findings of the epidemiologic catchment area survey. *New England Journal of Medicine, 317,* 1630-1634.

Hempel, C.G. (1961). Introduction to problems of taxonomy. In J. Zubin (Ed.). *Field studies in the mental disorders.* New York: Grune & Stratton.

Henker, B. & Whalen, C.K. (1989). Hyperactivity and attention deficits. *American Psychologist, 44,* 216-223.

Herbert, T.B. & Cohen, S. (1993). Depression and immunity: A meta-analytic review. *Psychological Bulletin, 113,* 472-486.

Herdt, G., & Stoller, R.J. (1990). *Intimate communications: Erotics and the study of culture.* New York: Columbia University Press.

Herdt, G.H., & Davidson, J. (1988). The Sambia "Turnim-Man": Sociocultural and clinical aspects of gender formation in male pseudohermaphrodites with 5-alpha-reductase deficiency in Papua New Guinea. *Archives of Sexual Behavior, 17,* 33-56.

Hermann, D.H.J. (1990). Autonomy, self determination, the right of involuntarily committed persons to refuse treatment, and the use of substituted judgment in medication decisions involving incompetent persons. *International Journal of Law and Psychiatry, 13,* 361-385.

Hesselbrock, V., & Hesselbrock, M. (1990). Behavioral/social factors that may enhance or attenuate genetic effects. In C.R. Cloninger & H. Begleiter (Eds). *Genetics and biology of alcoholism.* Cold Spring Harbor: Cold Spring Harbor Laboratory Press. pp. 75-86.

Heston, L.L., & White, J.A. (1991). The vanishing mind: A practical guide to Alzheimer's disease and other dementias. New York: Freeman.

Heston, L.L. (1966). Psychiatric disorders in foster home reared children of schizophrenic mothers. *British Journal of Psychiatry, 112,* 819-825.

Hetherington, E.M. & Parke, R.D. (1986). *Child psychology: A contemporary perspective.* New York: McGraw-Hill.

Hill, J., & Holmbeck, G. (1986). Attachment and autonomy during adolescence. In G. Whitehurst (Ed.), *Annals of child development* (Vol. 3., 145-189). Greenwich, CT: JAI.

Hill, M.A. (1992). Light, circadian rhythms, and mood disorders: A review. *Annals of Clinical Psychiatry, 4,* 131-146.

Hinde, R.A. (1992). Developmental psychology in the context of other behavioral sciences. *Developmental Psychology, 28,* 1018-1029.

Hinshaw, S.P. (1987). On the distinction between attentional deficits/hyperactivity and conduct problems/aggression in child psychopathology. *Psychological Bulletin, 101,* 443-463.

Hirschfeld, R.M.A. (1993). Personality disorders: Definition and diagnosis. *Journal of Personality Disorders,* supplement, 9-17

Hite, S. (1976). *The Hite report.* New York: Macmillan.

Hoch, P.H., & Polatin, P. (1949). Pseudoneurotic forms of schizophrenia. *Psychiatric Quarterly, 23,* 248-276.

Hoehn-Saric, R., & NcLeod, D.R. (1991). Clinical management of generalized anxiety disorder. In W. Coryell & G. Winokur (Eds.). *The clinical management of anxiety disorders.* New York: Oxford University Press. pp. 79-100.

Hoenig, J. (1985). Etiology of transsexualism. In B.W. Steiner (Ed.) *Gender dysphoria: Development, research, management.* New York: Plenum. pp. 33-74.

Hoffman, P.B. & Foust, L.L. (1977). Least restrictive treatment of the mentally ill: A doctrine in search of its senses. *San Diego Law Review, 14,* 1100-1154.

Hogan, D.R. (1990). Sexual dysfunctions: A historical perspective. In Walker (Ed) *History of clinical psychology.* pp. 279-309.

Hogarty, G.E. (1993). Prevention of relapse in chronic schizophrenic patients. *Journal of Clinical Psychiatry*, 54 (suppl), 18-23.

Hogarty, G.E., Anderson, C.M., Reiss, D.J. et al. (1991). Family psychoeducation, social skills training, and maintenance chemotherapy in the aftercare treatment of schizophrenia. II: two-year effects of a controlled study on relapse and adjustment. *Archives of General Psychiatry*, 48, 340-347.

Hole, J.W., Jr. (1984). *Human anatomy and physiology* (3rd Edition). Dubuque, IA: Wm C. Brown.

Hollon, S.D., & Beck, A.T. (1986). Cognitive and cognitive-behavior therapies. In S.L. Garfield & A.E. Bergin (Eds.), *Handbook of psychotherapy and behavior change: An empirical analysis* (3rd ed., pp. 443-482). New York: Wiley.

Hollon, S.D., Shelton, R.C., & Davis, D.D. (1993). Cognitive therapy for depression: Conceptual issues and clinical efficacy. *Journal of Consulting and Clinical Psychology*, 61, 270-275.

Hollon, S.D., DeRubeis, R.J., & Evans, M.D. (1987). Causal medication of change in treatment for depression: Discriminating between nonspecificity and noncausality. *Psychological Bulletin*, 102, 139-149.

Hollon, S.D. & Beck, A.T. (1986). Cognitive and cognitive-behavioral therapies. In S.L. Garfield & A.E. Bergin (Eds.), *Handbook of psychotherapy and behavior change* (3rd. Ed., pp.443-482). New York: Wiley.

Holman, J.E., & Caston, R.J. (1987). Interorganizational influences on mental health diagnoses: A macrolevel study of labeling processes. *Sociological Perspectives*, 30, 180-200.

Holmes, T.H. & Rahe, R.H. (1967). The social readjustment rating scale. *Journal of Psychosomatic Research*, 11, 213-218.

Holtzworth-Munroe, A., & Jacobson, N.S. (1991). Behavioral marital therapy. In A.S. Gurman & D.P. Kniskern (Eds.), *Handbook of family therapy* (Vol.II, pp. 96-133). New York: Brunner/Mazel.

Holzman, P.S. (1989). The use of eye movement dysfunctions in exploring the genetic transmission of schizophrenia. *European Archives of Psychiatry and Neurological Sciences*, 239, 43-48.

Holzman, P.S. (1985). Eye movement dysfunctions and psychosis. *International Review of Neurobiology*, 27, 179-205.

Holzman, P.S. et al. (1974). Eye-tracking dysfunctions in schizophrenic patients and their relatives. *Archives of General Psychiatry*, 31, 143-151.

Hooley, J.M. (1985). Expressed emotion: A review of the critical literature. *Clinical Psychology Review*, 5, 119-139.

Hooley, J.M., & Teasdale, J.D. (1989). Predictors of relapse in unipolar depressives: expressed emotion, marital distress, and perceived criticism. *Journal of Abnormal Psychology*, 98, 229-235.

Hooley, J.M. (1986). Expressed emotion and depression: Interactions between patients and high- versus low-expressed emotion spouses. *Journal of Abnormal Psychology*, 95, 237-246.

Hopps, J.G., & Pinderhughes, E.B. (1987). Profession of social work: Contemporary characteristics. In A. Minehan (Ed.), *Encyclopedia of social work* (18th ed.). Silverspring, MD: National Association of Social Work.

Horn, J.M., Loehlin, J.C. & Willerman, L. (1979). Intellectual resemblance among adoptive and biological relatives: The Texas Adoption Project. *Behavior Genetics*, 9, 177-205.

Horney, K. (1939). *New ways in psychoanalysis*. New York: International Universities Press.

Horvath, T.B., Siever, L.J., Mohs, R.C., & Davis, K. (1991). Organic mental syndromes and disorders. In H.I. Kaplan and B.J. Sadock (Eds.),

Comprehensive textbook of psychiatry (5th edition). Volume 1, pp. 599-641.

Hotchner, A.E. (1966). *Papa Hemingway: A personal memoir*. New York: Random House.

Houts, A.C. (1991). Nocturnal enuresis as a biobehavioral problem. *Behavior Therapy*, 22, 133-151.

Howard, K.I., Kopta, S.M., Krause, M.S., & Orlinsky, D.E. (1986). The dose-effect relationship in psychotherapy. *American Psychologist*, 41, 159-164.

Hoza, B., Pelham, W.E., Milich, R., Pillow, D., & McBride, K. (1993). The self-perceptions and attributions of attention deficit hyperactivity disordered and nonreferred boys. *Journal of Abnormal Child Psychology*, 21, 271-286.

Hsu, L.K. (1989). The gender gap in eating disorders: Why are the eating disorders more common among women? *Clinical Psychology Review*, 9, 393-407.

Hsu, L.K.G. (1990). *Eating disorders*. New York: Guilford.

Hughes, P.L., Wells, L.A., Cunningham, C.J., & Ilstrup, D.M. (1986). Treatment of bulimia with desipramine: A double-blind, placebo-controlled study. *Archives of General Psychiatry*, 43, 182-186.

Hull, J.G., & Bond, C.F., Jr. (1986). Social and behavioral consequences of alcohol consumption and expectancy: A meta-analysis. *Psychological Bulletin*, 99, 347-360.

Humphrey, L.L. (1987). Comparison of bulimic-anorexic and nondistressed families using structural analysis of social behavior. *Journal of the American Academy of Child and Adolescent Psychiatry*, 26, 248-255.

Huntington's Disease Collaborative Research Group (1993). A novel gene containing a trinucleotide repeat that is expanded and unstable on Huntington's disease chromosomes. *Cell*, 72, 971-983.

Hurt, S.W., Reznikoff, M. & Clarkin, J.F. (1991). *Psychological assessment, psychiatric diagnosis, and treatment planning*. New York: Brunner/Mazel.

Huston, A.C. (1983). Sextyping. In E.M. Hetherington (Ed.), *Socialization, personality, and social development* (Vol. 4), *Handbook of child psychology* (pp. 388-467). New York: Wiley.

Hyler, S.E., Williams, J.B.W., & Spitzer, R.L. (1982). Reliability in the DSM-III field trials. *Archives of General Psychiatry*, 39, 1275-1278.

Iacono, W.G., & Grove, W.M. (1993). Schizophrenia reviewed: Toward an integrative genetic model. *Psychological Science*, 4, 273-276.

Iacono, W.G., Moreau, M., Beiser, M., Fleming, J.A. et al. (1992). Smooth-pursuit eye tracking in first-episode psychotic patients and their relatives. *Journal of Abnormal Psychology*, 101, 104-116.

Iacono, W.G. (1985). Psychophysiologic markers of psychopathology: A review. *Canadian Psychology*, 26, 96-112.

Iacono, W.G. (1991). Psychophysiological assessment of psychopathology. *Psychological Assessment*, 3, 309-320.

Iacono, W.G., & Clementz, B.A. (1993). A strategy for elucidating genetic influences on complex psychopathological syndromes (with special reference to ocular motor functioning and schizophrenia). In L.J. Chapman, J.P. Chapman, & D. Fowles (Eds.) *Progress in experimental personality and psychopathology research*. pp. 11-65.

Imperato-McGinley, J., Guerrero, L., Gautier, T., & Peterson, R.E. (1974). Steroid 5a-reductase deficiency in man: An inherited form of male pseudohermaphroditism. *Science*, 186, 1213-1215.

Jablensky, A. (1986). Epidemiology of schizophrenia: A European perspective. *Schizophrenia Bulletin*, 12, 52-73.

Jablensky, A. (1985). Approaches to the definition and classification of anxiety and related disorders

in European psychiatry. In A.H. Tuma and J. Maser (Eds.), *Anxiety and the anxiety disorders*. Hillsdale, N.J.: Erlbaum.

Jablensky, A., Sartorius, N., Ernberg, G., Anker, M., Korten, A., Cooper, J.E., Day, R., & Bertelsen, A. (1992). Schizophrenia: manifestations, incidence and course in different cultures: A World Health Organization ten-country study. *Psychological Medicine*, Mono Suppl 20, 1-97.

Jacob, T. (1975). Family interaction in disturbed and normal families: A methodological and substantive review. *Psychological Bulletin*, 82, 33-65.

Jacobson, R.R., Acker, C.F., & Lishman, W.A. (1990). Patterns of neuropsychological deficit in alcoholic Korsakoff's Syndrome. *Psychological Medicine*, 20, 321-334.

Jacobson, E. (1938). *Progressive relaxation*. Chicago: University of Chicago Press.

Jacobson, N.S. (1985). The role of observational measures in behavior therapy outcome research. *Behavioral Assessment*, 7, 297-308.

Jacobson, N.S., Follette, W.C., & McDonald, D.W. (1982). Reactivity to positive and negative behavior in distressed and nondistressed married couples. *Journal of Consulting and Clinical Psychology*, 50, 706-714.

Jacobson, N.S., Holtzworth-Munroe, A., & Schmaling, K.B. (1989). Marital therapy and spouse involvement in the treatment of depression, agoraphobia, and alcoholism. *Journal of Consulting and Clinical Psychology*, 57, 5-10.

Jacoby, R., & Bergmann, K. (1986). The psychiatry of old age. In P. Hill, R. Murray, and A. Thorley (Eds.), *Essentials of postgraduate psychiatry* (2nd ed.). London: Grune & Stratton. pp. 495-526.

Jacqmin, H., Commenges, D., Letenneur, L., Barbergergateau, P., & Dartigues, J.F. (1994). Components of drinking water and risk of cognitive impairment in the elderly. *American Journal of Epidemiology*, 139, 48-57.

Janet, P. (1915/1915). Psychoanalysis. *Journal of Abnormal Psychology*, 1-35; 253-187.

Jarvis, T.J. (1992). Implications of gender for alcohol treatment research: A quantitative and qualitative review. *British Journal of Addiction*, 87, 1249-1261.

Jellinek, E.M. (1960). *The disease concept of alcoholism*. New Haven, CT: Hillhouse Press.

Jellinek, E.M. (1952). Phases of alcohol addiction. *Quarterly Journal of Studies on Alcohol*, 13, 673-684.

Jenkins, C.D. (1988). Epidemiology of cardiovascular diseases. *Journal of Consulting and Clinical Psychology*, 56, 324-332.

Jeste, D.V., & Caligiuri, M.P. (1993). Tardive dyskinesia. *Schizophrenia Bulletin*, 19, 303-316.

Johnson, D. (1990). Long-term drug treatment of psychosis: Observations on some current issues. *International Review of Psychiatry*, 2, 341-353.

Johnson, P. (1989). Hemingway: Portrait of the artist as an intellectual. *Commentary*, 87, 49-59.

Johnston, D.W. (1989). Prevention of cardiovascular disease by psychological methods. *British Journal of Psychiatry*, 154, 183-194.

Johnston, D.W. (1985). Psychological interventions in cardiovascular disease. *Journal of Psychsomatic Research*, 29, 447-456.

Jones, B.M., & Jones, M.K. (1976). Women and alcohol: Intoxication, metabolism, and the menstrual cycle. In M. Greenblatt and M.A. Schuckit (Eds.). *Alcohol problems in women and children*. New York, Grune & Stratton. pp. 103-136.

Jones, R.R., Reid, J.B., & Patterson, G.R. (1975). Naturalistic observation in clinical assessment. In p. McReynolds, (Ed), *Advances in psychological assessment* (Vol. 3). San Francisco: Jossey-Bass.

Jones, J.C. & Barlow, D.H. (1990). The etiology of posttraumatic stress disorder. *Clinical Psychology Review, 10,* 299-328.

Josephs, R.A., & Steele, C.M. (1990). The two faces of alcohol myopia: Attentional mediation of psychological stress. *Journal of Abnormal Psychology, 99,* 115-126.

Joyce, P. (1992). Prediction of treatment response. In E. S. Paykel (Ed.), *Handbook of affective disorders* (2nd edition) New York: Guilford. (pp. 453-462).

Kagan, J., Reznick, S., & Snidman, N. (1987). The physiology and psychology of behavioral inhibition in children. *Child Development, 58,* 1459-1473.

Kagan, J. (1958). The concept of identification. *Psychological Review, 65,* 296-305.

Kamarck, T. & Jennings, J.R. (1991). Biobehavioral factors in sudden cardiac death. *Psychological Bulletin, 109,* 42-75.

Kane, J.M., & Marder, S.R. (1993). Psychopharmacologic treatment of schizophrenia. *Schizophrenia Bulletin, 19,* 287-302.

Kane, J.M. Woerner, M., & Lieberman, J. (1985). Tardive dyskinesis: Prevalence, incidence and risk factors. In D.E. Casey, T.N. Chase, A.V. Christensen, and J. Gerlach (Eds.), *Dyskinesis: Research and treatment.* Berlin: Springer-Verlag, pp. 72-78.

Kane, J.M., Woerner, M., Lieberman, J., & Rabiner, C.J. (1984). Studies on the long-term treatment of schizophrenia. *Psychiatric Hospital, 15,* 179-183.

Kanner, L. (1943). Autistic disturbances of affective contact. *Nervous Child, 2,* 217-250.

Kaplan, H.S. (1988). Anxiety and sexual dysfunction. *Journal of Clinical Psychiatry, 49,* 21-25.

Kaplan, L.J. (1989). *Female perversions: The temptations of Emma Bovary.* New York: Doubleday.

Kaplan, H.S. (1979). *Disorders of sexual desire and other new concepts and techniques in sex therapy.* New York: Brunner/Mazel.

Kaplan, H.S. (1974). *The new sex therapy: Active treatment of sexual dysfunctions.* New York: Brunner/Mazel.

Kapur, S., & Mann, J.J. (1992). Role of the dopaminergic system in depression. *Biological Psychiatry, 32,* 1-17.

Karasek, R.A., Theorell, T.G., Schwartz, J., Pieper, C., & Alfredsson, L. (1982). Job, psychological factors and coronary heart disease: Swedish prospective findings and U.S. prevalence findings using a new occupational inference method. *Advances in Cardiology, 29,* 62-67.

Karler, R., Calder, L.D., Chaudhry, I.A., & Turkanis, S.A. (1989). Blockade of "reverse tolerance" to cocaine and amphetamine by MK-801. *Life Sciences, 45,* 599-606.

Karno, M., & Golding, J.M. (1991). Obsessive compulsive disorder. In L.N. Robins and D.A. Regier (Eds.), *Psychiatric disorders in America: The epidemiologic catchment area study.* New York: Free Press.

Karras, A. & Otis, D.B. (1987). A comparison of inpatients in an urban state hospital in 1975 and 1982. *Hospital and Community Psychiatry, 38,* 963-967.

Kass, F., Charles, E., Klein, D.F., & Cohen, P. (1983). Discordance between the SCL-90 and therapists' psychopathology ratings: Implications for clinical assessment. *Archives of General Psychiatry, 40,* 389-392.

Kasvikis, Y.G., Tsakiris, F., Marks, I.M., Basogulu, M., & Noshirvani, H.V. (1986). Past history of anorexia nervosa in women with obsessive-compulsive disorders. *International Journal of Eating Disorders, 5,* 1069-1075.

Katon, W., & Roy-Byrne, P.P. (1991). Mixed anxiety and depression. *Journal of Abnormal Psychology, 100,* 337-345.

Katsanis, J., & Iacono, W.G. (1991). Clinical, neuropsychological, and brain structural correlates of smooth-pursuit eye tracking performance in chronic schizophrenia. *Journal of Abnormal Psychology, 100,* 526-534.

Katschnig, H. & Amering, M. (1990). Panic attacks and panic disorder in cross-cultural perspective. In J.C. Ballenger (Ed.), *Clinical aspects of panic disorder.* New York: Wiley.

Katz, R., & McGuffin, P. (1993). The genetics of affective disorders. In D. Fowles (Ed) *Progress in experimental personality and psychopathology research.*

Katz, R.J., DeVeaugh-Geiss, J., & Landau, P. (1990). Clomipramine in obsessive-compulsive disorder. *Biological Psychiatry, 28,* 401-414.

Katzman, R. (1976). The prevalence and malignancy of Alzheimer's disease. *Archives of Neurology, 33,* 217-218.

Katzman, R. (1993). Education and the prevalence of dementia and Alzheimer's disease. *Neurology, 43,* 13-20.

Kaul, T.J. & Bednar, R.L. (1986). Experiential group research: Results, questions, and suggestions. In S.L. Garfield & A.E. Bergin (Eds.), *Handbook of psychotherapy and behavior change* (3rd. Ed., pp. 671-714). New York: Wiley.

Kavanagh, D.J. (1992). Recent developments in expressed emotion and schizophrenia. *British Journal of Psychiatry, 160,* 601-620.

Kazdin, A.E., French, N.H., & Unis, A.S. (1983). Child, mother, and father evaluations of depression in psychiatric inpatient children. *Journal of Abnormal Child Psychology, 11,* 167-180.

Kazdin, A.E. (1994). Psychotherapy for children and adolescents. In A.E. Bergin & S.L. Garfield (Eds.), *Handbook of psychotherapy and behavior change,* (4th. Ed., pp. 543-594). New York: Wiley.

Kazdin, A.E. & Petti, T.A. (1982). Self-report and interview measures of childhood and adolescent depression. *Journal of Child Psychology and Psychiatry, 23,* 437-457.

Kazdin, A.E. & Wilcoxon, L.A. (1976). Systematic desensitization and nonspecific treatment effects: A methodological evaluation. *Psychological Bulletin, 83,* 729-758.

Kazdin, A.E. (1987). Treatment of antisocial behavior in children: Current status and future directions. *Psychological Bulletin, 102,* 187-203.

Kazdin, A.E. (1989). Identifying depression in children: A comparison of alternative selection criteria. *Journal of Abnormal Child Psychology, 17,* 437-454.

Kazdin, A.E. (1990). Childhood depression. *Journal of Child Psychology and Psychiatry, 31,* 121-160.

Keane, T.M., Zimering, R.T., & Caddell, J.M. (1985). A behavioral formulation of posttraumatic stress disorder in Vietnam veterans. *the Behavior Therapist, 8,* 9-12.

Keane, T.M., Fairbank, J.A., Caddell, J.M., & Zimering, R.T. (1989). Implosive (flooding) therapy reduces symptoms of PTSD in Vietnam combat veterans. *Behavior Therapy, 20,* 245-260.

Keith, S.J., Regier, D.A., & Rae, D.S. (1991). Schizophrenic disorders. In L.N. Robins and D.A. Regier (Eds.). *Psychiatric disorders in America: The epidemiologic catchment area study.* New York: Free Press. pp.33-52.

Keller, M.B., Lavori, P.W., Coryell, W., Endicott, J., & Mueller, (1993). Bipolar I: A five-year prospective follow-up. *Journal of Nervous and Mental Disease, 181,* 238-245.

Keller, M.B. (1988). Diagnostic issues and clinical course of unipolar illness. *The American Psychiatric Association Annual Review,* Volume 6.

Keller, M.B. (1987). Differential diagnosis, natural course and epidemiology of bipolar disorder. *The American Psychiatric Association Annual Review,* Volume 6.

Keller, M. (1970). Tribute to E.M. Jellinek. In R.E. Popham (Ed.). *Alcohol & alcoholism.* Toronto: University of Toronto Press. pp. xi-xvi.

Kellner, R. (1985). Functional somatic symptoms in hypochondriasis. *Archives of General Psychiatry, 42,* 821-833.

Kelly, M.P., Strassberg, D.S., & Kircher, J.R. (1990). Attitudinal and experiential correlates of anorgasmia. *Archives of Sexual Behavior, 19,* 165-177.

Kelly, T., Soloff, P.H., Cornelius, J., George, A., Lis, J.A., & Ulrich, R. (1992). Can we study (treat) borderline patients? Attrition from research and open treatment. *Journal of Personality Disorders, 6,* 417-433.

Kelly, T.A. (1990). The role of values in psychotherapy: A critical review of process and outcome effects. *Clinical Psychology Review, 10,* 171-186.

Kempe, C.H., Silverman, F., Steele, B., Droegueller, W., & Silver, H. (1962). The battered child syndrome. *Journal of the American Medical Association, 181,* 17-24.

Kendall, P.C., & Ingram, R.E. (1989). Cognitive-behavioral perspectives: Theory and research on depression and anxiety. In P.C. Kendall & D. Watson (Eds.), *Anxiety and depression: Distinctive and overlapping features.* San Diego, CA: Academic Press, pp. 27-53.

Kendall, P.C., & Watson, D. (Eds.) (1989). *Anxiety and depression: Distinctive and overlapping features.* San Diego: CA: Academic Press.

Kendell, R.E. (1989). Clinical validity. *Psychological Medicine, 19,* 45-55.

Kendell, R.E. (1981). The present status of electroconvulsive therapy. *British Journal of Psychiatry, 139,* 265-283.

Kendell, R.E. (1975). The concept of disease and its implications for psychiatry. *British Journal of Psychiatry, 127,* 305-315.

Kendell, R.E. (1984). Reflections on psychiatric classification —For the architects of DSM-IV and ICD-10. *Integrative Psychiatry, 2,* 43-47.

Kendell, R.E. (1991). Relationship between the DSM-IV and the ICD-10. *Journal of Abnormal Psychology, 100,* 297-301.

Kendell, R.E. (1975). *The role of diagnosis in psychiatry.* Oxford: Blackwell Scientific Publications.

Kendell, R.E. (1968). *The classification of depressive illnesses.* London: Oxford University Press.

Kendell, R.E. (1976). The classification of depression: A review of contemporary confusion. *British Journal of Psychiatry, 129,* 15-28.

Kendler, K.S. (1985). Diagnostic approaches to schizotypal personality disorder: A historical perspective. *Schizophrenia Bulletin, 11,* 538-553.

Kendler, K.S., Neale, M.C., Kessler, R.C., Heath, A.C., & Eaves, L.J. (1992a). Generalized anxiety disorder in women: A population-based twin study. *Archives of General Psychiatry, 49,* 267-272.

Kendler, K.S., & Diehl, S.R. (1993). The genetics of schizophrenia: A current, genetic-epidemiologic perspective. *Schizophrenia Bulletin, 19,* 261-285.

Kendler, K.S., Kessler, R.C., Neale, M.C., Heath, A.C., & Eaves, L.J. (1993). The prediction of major depression in women: Toward an integrated etiologic model. *American Journal of Psychiatry, 150,* 1139-1148.

Kendler, K.S., Neale, M.C., Kessler, R.C., Heath, A.C., & Eaves, L.J. (1993). A longitudinal twin study of 1-year prevalence of major depression in women. *Archives of General Psychiatry, 50,* 843-852.

Kendler, K.S., Neale, M.C., Kessler, R.C., Heath, A.C., & Eaves, L.J. (1992b). The genetic epidemiology of phobias in women: The interrelationship of agoraphobia, social phobia, situational phobia, and simple phobia. *Archives of General Psychiatry*, 49, 273-281.

Kendler, K.S., Heath, A.C., Neale, M.C., Kessler, R.C., & Eaves, L.J. (1992). A population-based twin study of alcoholism in women. *Journal of the American Medical Association*, 268, 1877-1882.

Kendler, K.S. (1988). Familial aggregation of schizophrenia and schizophrenia spectrum disorders. *Archives of General Psychiatry*, 45, 377-383.

Kendler, K.S. (1990). The super-normal control group in psychiatric genetics: Possible artifactual evidence for coaggregation. *Psychiatric Genetics*, 1, 45-53.

Kendler, K.S., Gruenberg, A.M., & Tsuang, M.T. (1985). Subtype stability in schizophrenia. *American Journal of Psychiatry*, 142, 827-832.

Kennedy, J.L., Giuffra, L.A., Moises, H.W., Cavalli-Sforza, L.L., Pakstis, A.J., Kidd, J.R., Castiglione, C.M., Sjorgren, B., Wetterberg, L., & Kidd, K.K. (1988). Evidence against linkage of schizophrenia to markers on chromosome 5 in a northern Swedish pedigree. *Nature*, 336, 167-170.

Kenrick, D.T., & Funder, D.C. (1988). Profiting from controversy: Lessons from the person-situation debate. *American Psychologist*, 43, 23-34.

Kent, T.A., Campbell, J.R., & Goodwin, D.W. (1985). Blood platelet uptake of serotonin in men alcoholics. *Journal of Studies on Alcohol*, 46, 357-359.

Kernberg, O.F. (1975). *Borderline conditions and pathological narcissism*. New York: Aronson.

Kernberg, O.F. (1967). Borderline personality organization. *Journal of the American Psychoanalytic Association*, 15, 641-685.

Kessel, J.B., & Zimmerman, M. (1993). Reporting errors in studies of the diagnostic performance of self-administered questionnaires: Extent of the problem, recommendations for standardized presentation of results, and implications for the peer review process. *Psychological Assessment*, 5, 395-399.

Kessler, R.C., McGonagle, K.A., Zhao, S., Nelson, C.R., Highes, M., Eshleman, S., Wittchen, H., & Kendler, K.S. (1994). Lifetime and 12-month prevalence of DSM-III-R psychiatric disorders in the United States: Results from the National Comorbidity Survey. *Archives of General Psychiatry*, 51, 8-19.

Kessler, R.C., & McLeod, J.D. (1984). Sex differences in vulnerability to undesirable life events. *American Sociological Review*, 49, 620-631.

Kety, S.S., Rosenthal, D., Wender, P.H., Schulsinger, F., & Jacobsen, B. (1975). Mental illness in the biological and adoptive families of adopted individuals who have become schizophrenic: A preliminary report based on psychiatric interviews. In R.R. Fieve, D. Rosenthal, and H. Brill (Eds.), *Genetic research in psychiatry*. Baltimore: Johns Hopkins University Press.

Kety, S.S. (1987). The significance of genetic factors in the etiology of schizophrenia: Results from the national study of adoptees in Denmark. *Journal of Psychiatric Research*, 21, 423-429.

Keys, A., Taylor, H.L., Blackburn, H., Brozek, J., Anderson, H., & Simonson, E. (1971). Mortality and coronary heart disease among men studied for 23 years. *Archives of Internal Medicine*, 128, 201-214.

Kiesler, C. (1982). Mental hospitals and alternative care: Noninstitutionalization as potential public policy for mental patients. *American Psychologist*, 37, 349-360.

Kihlstrom, J.F. (1984). Conscious, subconscious, unconscious: A cognitive perspective. In K.S. Bowers & D. Meichenbaum (Eds.), *The unconscious reconsidered* (pp. 149-211). New York: Wiley.

Kihlstrom, J.F. & Hoyt, I.P. (1990). Repression, dissociation, and hypnosis. In J.L. Singer (Ed.), *Repression and dissociation* (pp. 181-208). Chicago: University of Chicago Press.

Kihlstrom, J.F., Glisky, M.L., & Angiulo, M.J. (1994). Dissociative tendencies and dissociative disorders. *Journal of Abnormal Psychology*, 103, 117-124.

Kilmann, P.R. et al. (1982). The treatment of sexual paraphilias: A review of the outcome research. *Journal of Sex Research*, 18, 193-252.

Kilpatrick, D.G., Saunders, B.E., Amick-McMullan, A., Best, C.L., Veronen, L.J., & Resnick, H.S. (1989). Victim and crime factors associated with the development of crime-related posttraumatic stress disorder. *Behavior Therapy*, 20, 199-214.

Kimble, G.A. (1989). Psychology from the standpoint of a generalist. *American Psychologist*, 44, 491-499.

King, N.J., Ollier, K., Iacuone, R., Schuster, S., Bays, K., Gullone, E., & Ollendick, T.H. (1989). Fears of children and adolescents: A cross-sectional Australian study using the Revised-Fear Survey Schedule for Children. *Journal of Child Psychology and Psychiatry*, 30, 775-784.

Kinsey, A.C., Pomeroy, W., Martin, C., & Gebhard, P. (1953). *Sexual behavior in the human female*. Philadelphia: Saunders.

Kinsey, A.C., Pomeroy, W.B., & Martin, C.E. (1948). *Sexual behavior in the human male*. Philadelphia: Saunders.

Kirk, S.A., & Kutchins, H. (1992). *The selling of DSM: The rhetoric of science in psychiatry*. New York: Aldine de Gruyter.

Kirmayer, L.J. (1984). Culture, affect and somatization. *Transcultural Psychiatric Research Review*, 21, 159-188.

Kissin, B. & Hanson, M. (1982). The bio-psych-social perspective in alcoholism. In J. Solomon (Ed.), *Alcoholism and clinical psychiatry*. New York: Plenum.

Kivlahan, D.R., Marlatt, G.A., Fromme, K., Coppel, D.B., & Williams, E. (1990). Secondary prevention with college drinkers: Evaluation of an alcohol skills training program. *Journal of Consulting and Clinical Psychology*, 58, 805-810.

Kleiger, J.H. (1992). A conceptual critique of the EA:es comparison in the Comprehensive Rorschach System. *Psychological Assessment*, 4, 288-296.

Klein, D.F. (1993). False suffocation alarms, spontaneous panics, and related conditions: An integrative hypothesis. *Archives of General Psychiatry*, 50, 306-317.

Klein, D.F., & Klein, H.M. (1989). The definition and psychopharmacology of spontaneous panic and phobia. In P. Tyrer (Ed.), *Psychopharmacology of anxiety*. New York: Oxford University Press.

Klein, D.F. (1981). Anxiety reconceptualized. In D.F. Klein and J. Rabkin (Eds) *Anxiety: New research and changing concepts*. New York: Raven Press, pp. 235-263.

Kleinman, A. (1982). Neurasthenia and depression: A study of somatization and culture in China. *Culture, Medicine, and Psychiatry*, 6, 117-189.

Klerman, G.L., Weissman, M.M., Rounsaville, B.J., & Chevron, E.S. (1984). *Interpersonal psychotherapy of depression*. New York: Basic Books.

Klerman, G.L. (1986). Historical perspectives on contemporary schools of psychopathology. In T. Millon and G. Klerman (Eds.), *Contemporary directions in psychopathology: Toward the DSM-IV*. New York: Guilford.

Klerman, G.L. (1990). History and development of modern concepts of anxiety and panic. In J. Ballenger (Ed.), *Clinical aspects of panic disorder*. New York: Wiley. pp. 3-12.

Klerman, G.L. (1984). The advantages of DSM-III. *American Journal of Psychiatry*, 141, 539-545.

Klerman, G.L., Weissman, M.M., Rounsaville, B.J., & Chevron, E.S. (1984). *Interpersonal psychotherapy of depression*. New York: Basic Books. Kovacs, M., & Beck, A.T. (1978). Maladaptive cognitive structures in depression. *American Journal of Psychiatry*, 135, 525-533.

Klerman, G. (1990). The psychiatric patient's right to effective treatment: Implications of *Osheroff vs. Chestnut Lodge*, *American Journal of Psychiatry*, 147, 409-418.

Klerman, G.L., Weissman, M.M., Markowitz, J.C., Glick, I., Wilner, P.J., Mason, B., & Shear, M.K. (1994). Medication and psychotherapy. In A.E. Bergin & S.L. Garfield (Eds.), *Handbook of psychotherapy and behavior change* (4th. Ed., pp. 734-782). New York: Wiley.

Klorman, R., Brumaghim, J.T., Fitzpatrick, P.A., Borgstedt, A.D., & Strauss, J. (1994). Clinical and cognitive effects of methylphenidate on children with attention deficit disorder as a function of aggression/oppositionality and age. *Journal of Abnormal Psychology*, 103, 206-221.

Kluft, R.P. (1987). An update on multiple personality disorder. *Hospital and Community Psychiatry*, 38, 363-373.

Kluznik, J.C., Speed, N., Van Valkenburg, C., & Magraw, R. (1986). Forty-year follow-up of United States prisoners of war. *American Journal of Psychiatry*, 143, 1443-1446.

Knight, R.A., & Prentky, R.A. (1990). Classifying sexual offenders: The development and corroboration of taxonomic models. In W.L. Marshall, D.R. Laws, & H.E. Barbaree (Eds.). *Handbook of sexual assault: Issues, theories, and treatment of the offender*. New York: Plenum.

Knight, R.A., Prentky, R.A., & Cerce, D.D., (1994). The development, reliability, and validity of an inventory for the multidimensional assessment of sex and aggression. *Criminal Justice and Behavior*, 21, 72-94.

Koch, H., & Knapp, D.E. (1987). Highlights of drug utilization in office practice. National Ambulatory Medical Survey, 1885. *Advance data from vital and health statistics*, No. 134, Dept of Health and Human Services Publication No. (PHS) 87-1250 Maryland: Public Health Service.

Koenig, H.G. & Blazer, D.G. (1990). Depression and other affective disorders. In C.K. Cassel, D.E. Riesenberg, L.B. Sorenson, & J.R. Walsh (Eds.), *Geriatric medicine* (2nd Ed., pp. 473-489). New York: Springer-Verlag.

Kohlberg, L. (1985). *The psychology of moral development*. San Francisco: Harper and Row.

Kohler, J.A. (1988). The role of serotonin in autism. In L. Wing (Ed.), *Aspects of autism: Biological Research* (pp. 53-58). Gaskell: London.

Kohut, J. (1971). *The analysis of the self*. New York: International Universities.

Kohut, J. (1977). *The restoration of the self*. New York: International Universities.

Kokmen, E., Beard, C.M., O'Brien, P.C., Offord, K.P., & Kurland, L.T. (1993). Is the incidence of dementing illness changing?: A 25-year time trend study in Rochester, Minnesota (1960-1984). *Neurology*, 43, 1887-1993.

Kolb, B., & Whishaw, I.Q. (1990). *Fundamentals of human neuropsychology* (3rd ed.). New York: Freeman.

Kolb, L.C. (1987). A neuropsychological hypothesis explaining posttraumatic stress disorder. *American Journal of Psychiatry*, 144, 989-995.

Koluchova, J. (1972). Severe deprivation in twins: A case study of marked IQ change after age 7. *Journal of Child Psychology and Psychiatry*, 13, 107-114.

Koran, L.J. (1975). The reliability of clinical methods, data and judgements. *New England Journal of Medicine*, 293, 642-646, 695-701.

Koranyi, E.K. (1989). Physiology of stress reviewed. In S. Cheren (Ed.), *Psychosomatic medicine: Theory, physiology, and practice* (Vol. 1, pp. 241-278). Madison, CT: International Universities Press.

Kornhuber, J., Riederer, P. et al. (1989). 3H-spiperone binding sites in post-mortem brains from schizophrenic patients: Relationship to neuroleptic drug treatment, abnormal movements, and positive symptoms. *Journal of Neural Transmission*, 75, 1-10.

Koskenvuo, M., Kaprio, J., Rose, R.J., Kesaniemi, A., Sarna, S., Heikkila, K., & Langinvainio, H. (1988). Hostility as a risk factor for mortality and ischemic heart disease in men. *Psychosomatic Medicine*, 50, 330-340.

Koss, M.P. (1992). The underdetection of rape. *Journal of Social Issues*, 48, 63-75.

Koss, M.P. (1993). Rape: Scope, impact, interventions, and public policy responses. *American Psychologist*, 48, 1062-1069.

Koss, M.P. & Butcher, J.M. (1986). Research on brief psychotherapy. In S.L. Garfield & A.E. Bergin (Eds.), *Handbook of psychotherapy and behavior change* (3rd. Ed., pp. 627-670.). New York: Wiley.

Kosson, D.S., & Newman, J.P. (1986). Psychopathy and the allocation of attentional capacity in a divided-attention situation. *Journal of Abnormal Psychology*, 95, 257-263.

Kovacs, M., Feinberg, T.L., Crouse-Novak, M.A., Paulaukas, S., Pollock, M., & Finkelstein, R. (1984). Depressive disorders in childhood: II. A longitudinal study of the risk for a subsequent major depression. *Archives of General Psychiatry*, 41, 643-649.

Kovelman, J.A., & Scheibel, A.B. (1986). Biological substrates of schizophrenia. *Acta Neurologica Scandinavica*, 73, 1-32.

Kozel, N.J., & Adams, E.H. (1986). Epidemiology of drug abuse: An overview. *Science*, 234, 970-974.

Kraepelin, E. (1921). *Manic-depressive insanity and paranoia*. Edinburgh: E. and S. Livingstone.

Krafft-Ebing, R. (1892). *Psychopathia sexualis, with especial reference to contrary sexual instinct: A medico-legal study.* (translation of the 7th edition). Philadelphia: F.A. Davies.

Krantz, D.S., Contrada, R.J., Hill, D.R., & Friedler, E. (1988). Environmental stress and biobehavioral antecedents of coronary heart disease. *Journal of Consulting and Clinical Psychology*, 56, 333-341.

Kristenson, H. (1992). Long-term antabuse treatment of alcohol-dependent patients. *Acta Psychiatrica Scandinavica*, 86, 41-45.

Krohn, A. (1980). Some clinical manifestations of structural defects in a borderline personality. *International Journal of Psychoanalytic Psychotherapy*, 8, 337-362.

Krystal, J.H., Kosten, T.R., Southwick, S., Mason, J.W., Perry, B.D., & Giller, E.L. (1989). Neurobiological aspects of PTSD: Review of clinical and preclinical studies. *Behavior Therapy*, 20, 199-214.

Kuhn, T.S. (1962). *The structure of scientific revolutions*. Chicago: Chicago University Press.

Kuiper, B., & Cohen-Kettenis, P. (1988). Sex reassignment surgery: A study of 141 Dutch transsexuals. *Archives of Sexual Behavior*, 17, 439-457.

Kuipers, L. (1992). Expressed emotion research in Europe. *British Journal of Clinical Psychology*, 31, 429-443.

Kuipers, L., & Bebbington, P. (1988). Expressed emotion research in schizophrenia: theoretical and clinical implications. *Psychological Medicine*, 18, 893-909.

Kupfer, D.J., & Thase, M.E. (1989). Laboratory studies and validity of psychiatric diagnosis: Has there

been progress? In L.N. Robins & J.E. Barrett (Eds.), *The validity of psychiatric diagnosis*. New York: Raven Press. pp. 177-197.

Kushner, M.B., Sher, K.J., & Beitman, B.D. (1990). The relation between alcohol problems and the anxiety disorders. *American Journal of Psychiatry*, 147, 685-695.

Kutchins, H., & Kirk, S.A. (1986). The reliability of DSM-III: A critical review. *Social Work Research and Abstracts*, 22, 3-12.

L'Abate, L., & Bagarozzi, D.A. (1993). *Sourcebook of marriage and family evaluation*. New York: Brunner/Mazel.

Lacey, J.I. (1967). Somatic response patterning and stress: Some revisions of activation theory. In M.H. Appley & R. Trumball (Eds.), *Psychological stress*. New York: McGraw-Hill.

LaCroix, A.Z. & Haynes, S.G. (1987). Gender differences in the stressfulness of workplace roles: A focus on work and health. In R. Barnett, G. Baruch, & L. Biener (Eds.), *Gender and stress* (pp. 96-121). New York: Free Press.

Lam, D. (1991). Psychosocial family intervention in schizophrenia: A review of empirical studies. *Psychological Medicine*, 21, 423-441.

Lamb, M.E., Thompson, R.A., & Gardner, W.P et al. (1984). Security of infantile attachment as assessed in the "strange situation": Its study and biological interpretation. *Behavioral and Brain Sciences*, 7, 127-147.

Lambert, M.J., Shapiro, D.A., & Bergin, A.E. (1986). The effectiveness of psychotherapy. In S.L. Garfield & A.E. Bergin (Eds.), *Handbook of psychotherapy and behavior change* (3rd. Ed., pp. 157-212). New York: Wiley.

Lancet, Editors of. (1952). *Disabilities and how to live with them*. London: Lancet. [cited in C. Landis (1964). *Varieties of psychopathological experience*. New York: Holt, Rinehart, & Winston. pp. 241-242.]

Landy, F.J. (1986). Stamp collecting versus science: Validation as hypothesis testing. *American Psychologist*, 41, 1183-11192.

Lang, A.R., Pelham, W.E., Johnston, C., & Gelernter, S. (1989). Levels of adult alcohol consumption induced by interaction with child confederate exhibiting normal versus externalizing behaviors. *Journal of Abnormal Psychology*, 98, 294- .

Lang, P.J. (1979). A bio-informational theory of emotional imagery. *Psychophysiology*, 16, 495-512.

Lang, A.R. (1983). Addictive personality: A viable construct? In P. Levison, D. Gerstein, & D. Masloof (Eds.), *Commonalities in substance abuse and habitual behavior*. Lexington, MA: Lexington Books of D.C. Heath.

Lange, A.J. & Jakubowski, P. (1976). *Responsible assertive behavior*. Campaign, IL: Research Press.

Lapouse, R. & Monk, M. (1958). An epidemiologic study of behavior characteristics in children. *American Journal of Public Health*, 48, 1134-1144.

Larsen, J.K. (1991). MAOIs in the treatment of depression: A review. *European Journal of Psychiatry*, 5, 79-88).

Larson, E.W., Olinsky, A., Rummens, T.A., & Morse, R.M. (1992). Disulfiram treatment of patients with both alcohol dependence and other psychiatric disorders: A review. *Alcoholism: Clinical and Experimental Research*, 16, 125-130.

Larson, R., Csikszentmihalyi, M., & Graef, R. (1980). Mood variability and the psychosocial adjustment of adolescents. *Journal of Youth and Adolescence*, 9, 469-490.

Last, C.G. & Strauss, C.C. (1990). School refusal in anxiety-disordered children and adolescents. *Journal of the American Academy of Child and Adolescent Psychiatry*, 29, 31-35.

Lavori, P.W., Klerman, G.L., Keller, M.B., Reich, T., Rice, J., & Endicott, J. (1987). Age-period-

cohort analysis of secular trends in onset of major depression: Findings in siblings of patients with major affective disorder. *Journal of Psychiatric Research*, 21, 23-35.

Lawton, M.P. (1989). Environmental approaches to research and treatment of Alzheimer's disease. In E. Light and B.D. Lebowitz (Eds.), *Alzheimer's disease treatment and family stress: Directions for research*. U.S. Dept of Health and Human Services, DHHS Publication No. (ADM) 89-1569 pp. 340-362.

Lazarus, A. (1988). Dyspareunia: A multimodal psychotherapeutic perspective. In S. Leiblum and R.C. Rosen (Eds.), *Principles and practice of sex therapy* (2nd ed.). New York: Guilford.

Lazarus, R.S. & Folkman, S. (1984). *Stress, appraisal, and coping*. New York: Springer.

Lazarus, R.S. (1966). *Psychological stress and the coping process*. New York: McGraw-Hill.

Lazoritz, S. (1990). What ever happened to Mary Ellen? *Child Abuse and Neglect*, 14, 143-149.

Le Couteur, A. (1988). The role of genetics in the aetiology of autism, including findings of the links with the fragile X syndrome. In L. Wing (Ed.), *Aspects of autism: Biological Research* (pp. 38-52). Gaskell: London.

Leary, T. (1957). *Interpersonal diagnosis of personality*. New York: The Ronald Press.

Lee, C.L., & Bates, J.E. (1985). Mother-child interaction at age two years and perceived difficult temperament. *Child Development*, 56, 1314-1325.

Leesfield, I.H. (1987). Negligence of mental health professionals. *Trial*, 23, 57-61.

Leff, J.P. (1988). *Psychiatry around the globe: A transcultural view*. London: Royal College of Psychiatrists.

Leff, J., & Vaughn, C. (1985). *Expressed emotion in families: Its significance for Mental illness*. New York: Guilford.

Leff, J. (1992). Transcultural aspects. In E. S. Paykel (Ed.), *Handbook of affective disorders* (2nd edition). New York: Guilford. (pp. 539-550).

Leff, J., Wig, N.N., Bedi. H. et al. (1990). Relatives' expressed emotion and the course of schizophrenia in Chandigarh: A two-year follow-up of a first-contact sample. *British Journal of Psychiatry*, 156, 351-356.

Leff, J., Sartorius, N., Jablensky, A., Korten, A., & Ernberg, G. (1992). The International Pilot Study of Schizophrenia: Five-year follow-up findings. *Psychological Medicine*, 22, 131-145).

Lefley, H.P. (1992). Expressed emotion: Conceptual, clinical, and social policy issues. *Hospital and Community Psychiatry*, 43, 591-598.

Leiblum, S.R., & Rosen, R.C. (1989). *Principles and practice of sex therapy: Update for the 1990s*. New York: Guilford.

Leichtman, M. (1989). Evolving concepts of borderline personality disorders. *Bulletin of the Menninger Clinic*, 53, 229-249.

Leigh, B.C. (1989). In search of the seven dwarves: Issues of measurement and meaning in alcohol expectancy research. *Psychological Bulletin*, 105, 361-373.

Leigh, B.C., & Stacy, A.W. (1993). Alcohol outcome expectancies: Scale construction and predictive utility in higher order confirmatory models. *Psychological Assessment*, 5, 216-229.

Lenzenweger, M.F., Cornblatt, B.A., & Putnick, M. (1991). Schizotypy and sustained attention. *Journal of Abnormal Psychology*, 100, 84-89.

Leon, G., Fulkerson, J.A., Perry, C.L., & Cudeck, R. (1993). Personality and behavioral vulnerabilities associated with risk status for eating disorders in adolescent girls. *Journal of Abnormal Psychology*, 102, 438-444.

Leonard, H.L., Swedo, S.E., Rapoport, J.L., Koby, E.V., Lenane, M.C., Cheslow, D.L., & Hamburger,

S.D. (1989). Treatment of obsessive-compulsive disorder with clomipramine and desipramine in children and adolescents: A double-blind crossover comparison. *Archives of General Psychiatry, 46,* 1088-1092.

Leonhard, K. (1986). Different causative factors in different forms of schizophrenia. *British Journal of Psychiatry, 149,* 1-6.

Leonhard, K. (1979). *The classification of endogenous psychoses* (5th edition). New York: Wiley.

Lerner, R.M., Orlos, J.B., & Knapp, J.R. (1976). Physical attractiveness, physical effectiveness, and self concept in late adolescents. *Adolescent, 11,* 313-326.

Letourneau, E. & O'Donohue, W. (1993). Sexual desire disorders. In W. O'Donohue and J.H. Geer (Eds.), *Handbook of sexual dysfunctions: Assessment and treatment.* Boston: Allyn and Bacon. pp. 53-82.

Lettieri, D.J. (1987). Stress and stages of addiction. In E. Gottheil, K.A. Druley, S. Pashko, & S.P. Weinstein (Eds.). *Stress and addiction.* New York: Brunner/Mazel.

Levenson, R.W. (1987). Alcohol, affect, and physiology: Positive effects in the early stages of drinking. In E. Gottheil, K.A. Druley, S. Pashko, & S.P. Weinstein (Eds.). *Stress and Addiction.* New York: Brunner/Mazel. pp. 173-196.

Levenson, M.R. (1992). Rethinking psychopathy. *Theory and Psychology, 2,* 51-71.

Levin, S. (1984). Frontal lobe dysfunction in schizophrenia: I. Eye movement impairments. *Journal of Psychiatric Research, 18,* 27-55.

Levine, S.B. (1987). More on the nature of sexual desire. *Journal of Sex and Marital Therapy, 13,* 35-44.

Levine, S.B., Risen, C.B., & Althof, S.E. (1990). Essay on the diagnosis and nature of paraphilia. *Journal of Sex and Marital Therapy, 16,* 89-102.

Levine, M., & Perkins, D.V. (1987). *Principles of community psychology: Perspectives and applications.* New York: Oxford University Press.

Levine, H.G. (1978). The discovery of addiction: Changing conceptions of habitual drunkenness in America. *Journal of Studies on Alcohol, 39,* 143-174.

Levy, D.L., Holzman, P.S., Matthysse, S., & Mendell, N.R. (1993). Eye tracking dysfunction and schizophrenia: A critical perspective. *Schizophrenia Bulletin, 19,* 461-537.

Lewander, T. (1992). Differential development of therapeutic drugs for psychosis. *Clinical Neuropharmacology, 15* (suppl 1), 654-655.

Lewine, R.J. (1981). Sex differences in schizophrenia: Timing or subtypes? *Psychological Bulletin, 90,* 432-444.

Lewine, R.J. (1988). Gender and schizophrenia. In H.A. Nasrallah (Ed.). *Handbook of schizophrenia,* volume 3. Amsterdam: Elsevier. pp 379-397.

Lewine, R.J., & Sommers, A.A. (1985). Clinical definition of negative symptoms as a reflection of theory and methodology. In Murray Alpert (Ed.), *Controversies in schizophrenia: Changes and constancies.* New York: Guilford.

Lewinsohn, P.M., Hoberman, H.M., & Rosenbaum, M. (1988). A prospective study of risk factors for unipolar depression. *Journal of Abnormal Psychology, 97,* 251-264.

Lewinsohn, P.M., Mischel, W., Chaplin, W., & Barton, R. (1980). Social competence and depression: The role of illusory self-perceptions. *Journal of Abnormal Psychology, 89,* 203-212.

Lewinsohn, P.M. (1974). A behavioral approach to depression. In R.J. Friedman & M.M. Katz (Eds.). *The psychology of depression: Contemporary theory and research* (pp. 157-178) . New York: Winston-Wiley.

Lewinsohn, P.M., Steinmetz, J.L., Larson, D.W., & Franklin, J. (1981). Depression-related cognitions: Antecedent or consequence? *Journal of Abnormal Psychology, 90,* 213-219.

Lewinsohn, P.M., Hoberman, H.M., Teri, L., & Hautzinger, M. (1985). An integrative theory of depression. In S. Reiss & R.R. Bootzin (Eds.). *Theoretical issues in behavior therapy.* New San Diego: Academic Press.

Lewinsohn, P.M., Roberts, R.E., Seeley, J.R., Rohde, P., Gotlib, I.H., & Hops, H. (1994). Adolescent psychopathology: II. Psychosocial risk factors for depression. *Journal of Abnormal Psychology, 103,* 302-315.

Lewis, A.J. (1938). States of depression: Their clinical and aetiological differentiation. *British Medical Journal,* 4060ff.

Lewis, M. & Michalson, L. (1983). *Children's emotions and moods: Developmental theory and measurement.* New York: Plenum.

Liberman, R.P., Cardin, V., McGill, C.W., Falloon, I.R.H., & Evans, C.D. (1987). Behavioral family management of schizophrenia: Clinical outcome and costs. *Psychiatric Annals, 17,* 610-619.

Liberman, R.P., DeRisi, W.J., & Mueser, K.T. (1989). *Social skills training for psychiatric patients.* New York: Pergamon.

Lidz, C.W., Mulvey, E.P., & Gardner, W. (1993). The accuracy of predictions of violence to others. *Journal of the American Medical Association, 269,* 1007-1011.

Lieberman, J.A., & Koreen, A.R. (1993). Neurochemistry and neuroendocrinology of schizophrenia: A selective review. *Schizophrenia Bulletin, 19,* 371-429.

Liebowitz, M.R. (1993). Mixed anxiety and depression: Should it be included in DSM-IV? *Journal of Clinical Psychiatry, 54* (suppl 5), 4-7.

Liebowitz, M.R., Schneier, F.R., Hollander, E., Welkowitz, L.A. et al. (1991). Treatment of social phobia with drugs other than benzodiazepines. *Journal of Clinical Psychiatry, 52* (suppl), 10-15.

Liebowitz, M.R., Gorman, J.M., Fyer, A.J., & Klein, D.F. (1985). Social phobia: Review of a neglected anxiety disorder. *Archives of General Psychiatry, 42,* 729-736.

Liem, J.H. (1974). Effects of verbal communications of parents and children: A comparison of normal and schizophrenic families. *Journal of Consulting and Clinical Psychology, 42,* 438-450.

Light, L.L. (1991). Memory and aging: Four hypotheses in search of data. *Annual Review of Psychology, 42,* 333-376.

Lilienfeld, S.O. (1992). The association between antisocial personality and somatization disorders: A review and integration of theoretical models. *Clinical Psychology Review, 12,* 641-662.

Lindenmayer, J.P. (1993). Recent advances in pharmacotherapy of schizophrenia. *Psychiatric Annals, 23,* 201-208.

Linehan, M.M., Hubert, A.E., Suarez, A., Doublas, A., & Heard, H.L. (1991). Cognitive-behavioral treatment of chronically parasuicidal borderline patients. *Archives of General Psychiatry, 48,* 1060-1064.

Linehan, M.M. (1987). Dialectical behavior therapy for borderline personality disorder. *Bulletin of the Menninger Clinic, 51,* 261-276.

Link, B.G., Mirotznik, J., & Cullen, F.T. (1991). The effectiveness of stigma coping orientations: Can negative consequences of mental illness labeling be avoided? *Journal of Health and Social Behavior, 32,* 302-320.

Link, B.G., Cullen, F.T., Struening, E., Shrout, P.E., & Dohrenwend, B.P. (1989). A modified labeling theory approach to mental disorders: An empirical assessment. *American Sociological Review, 54,* 400-423.

Link, B., Cullen, F., & Andrews, H. (1990, August). Violent and illegal behavior of current and for-mer mental patients compared to community controls. Paper presented at the meeting of the Society for the Study of Social Problems.

Lipowski, Z.J. (1989). Delirium in the elderly patient. *New England Journal of Medicine, 320,* 578-582.

Lipowski, Z.J. (1988). Somatization: The concept and its clinical applications. *American Journal of Psychiatry, 145,* 1358-1368.

Lipsey, M.W. & Wilson, D.B. (1993). The efficacy of psychological, educational, and behavioral treatment: Confirmation for meta-analysis. *American Psychologist, 48,* 1181-1209.

Lipton, D.N., McDonei, E.C., & McFall, R.M. (1987). Heterosocial perception in rapists. *Journal of Consulting and Clinical Psychology, 55,* 17-21.

Lishman, W.A. (1987). *Organic psychiatry: The psychological consequences of cerebral disorder* (2nd edition). Oxford: Blackwell Scientific Publications.

Litten, R.E., & Allen, E.R. (1991). Pharmacotherapies for alcoholism: Promising agents and clinical issues. *Alcoholism: Clinical and Experimental Research, 15,* 620-633.

Livesley, W.J. (1989). Classifying personality disorders: Ideal types, prototypes, or dimensions? *Psychiatric Clinics of North America, 12,* 531-539.

Livesley, W.J., & West, M. (1986). The DSM-III distinction between schizoid and avoidant personality disorders. *Canadian Journal of Psychiatry, 31,* 59-62.

Livesley, W.J., Jang, K.L, Jackson, D.N., & Vernon, P.A. (1993). Genetic and environmental contributions to dimensions of personality disorder. *American Journal of Psychiatry, 150,* 1826-1831.

Livesley, W.J., Schroeder, M.L., Jackson, D.N., & Jang, K.L (1994). Categorical distinctions in the study of personality disorder: Implications for classification. *Journal of Abnormal Psychology, 103,* 6-17.

Lobitz, G.K. & Johnson, S.M. (1975). Normal versus deviant children: A multimethod comparison. *Journal of Abnormal Child Psychology, 3,* 353-374.

Loeber, R. (1988). Natural histories of conduct problems, delinquency, and associated substance use: Evidence for developmental progression. In B.B. Lahey & A.E. Kazdin (Eds.), *Advances in clinical child psychology* (Vol. 11, pp. 73-118). New York: Plenum.

Loeber, R., Lahey, B.B., & Thomas, C. (1991). Diagnostic conundrum of oppositional defiant disorder and conduct disorder. *Journal of Abnormal Psychology, 100,* 379-390.

Loeber, R (1982). The stability of antisocial and delinquent child behavior: A review. *Psychological Bulletin, 53,* 1431-1446.

Loftus, E.F. & Klinger, M.R. (1992). Is the unconscious smart or dumb? *American Psychologist, 47,* 761-765.

Loftus, E.F. (1993). The reality of repressed memories. *American Psychologist, 48,* 518-537.

London, P. (1964). *The modes and morals of psychotherapy.* New York: Holt, Rinehart and Winston.

LoPiccolo, J. (1991). Sexual dysfunction. In Hersen and Bellack (Eds.). *International handbook of behavior modification.* pp. 547-564.

LoPiccolo, J., & Stock, W.E. (1986). Treatment of sexual dysfunction. *Journal of Consulting and Clinical Psychology, 54,* 158-167.

Lorion, R.P. & Felner, R.D. (1986). Research on psychotherapy with the disadvantaged. In S.L. Garfield & A.E. Bergin (Eds.), *Handbook of psychotherapy and behavior change* (3rd. Ed., pp. 739-776). New York: Wiley.

Lovaas, O.I. (1987). Behavioral treatment and normal educational and intellectual functioning in young autistic children. *Journal of Consulting and Clinical Psychology, 55,* 3-9.

Lovaas, O.I., Schreibman, L., Koegel, R.L., & Rehm, R. (1971). Selective responding by autistic children to multiple sensory input. *Journal of Abnormal Psychology*, 77, 211-222.

Low, P.W., Jeffries, J.C., & Bonnie, R.J. (1986). *The trial of John W. Hinckley, Jr.: A case study in the insanity defense*. Mineola, NY: Foundation Press.

Luborsky, L., Singer, B., & Luborsky, L. (1975). Comparative studies of psychotherapy. *Archives of General Psychiatry*, 32, 995-1008.

Luborsky, L., Barber, J.P., & Beutler, L. (1993). Introduction to special section: A briefing on curative factors in dynamic psychotherapy. *Journal of Consulting and Clinical Psychology*, 61, 539-541.

Luborsky, L. (1984). *Principles of psychoanalytic psychotherapy: A manual for supportive-expressive treatment*. New York: Basic.

Luborsky, L., Diguer, L., Luborsky, E., McLellan, A.T., Woody, G., & Alexander, L. (1993). Psychological health-sickness (PHS) as a predictor of outcomes in dynamic and other psychotherapies. *Journal of Consulting and Clinical Psychology*, 61, 542-548.

Lubs, M. & Maes, J. (1977). Recurrence risk in mental retardation. In P. Mittler (Ed.), *Research to practice in mental retardation* (Vol. 3). Baltimore: University Park Press.

Lubs, H.A. (1969). A marker X chromosome. *American Journal of Human Genetics*, 21, 231-244.

Ludolph, P.S., Westen, D., Misle, B., Jackson, A., Wixom, J., & Wiss, F.C. (1990). The borderline diagnosis in adolescents: Symptoms and developmental history. *American Journal of Psychiatry*, 147, 470-476.

Luepnitz, D.A. (1982). *Child custody: A study of families after divorce*. Lexington, MA: Lexington Books.

Lukoff, D., Nuechterlein, K.H., & Ventura, J. (1986). Manual for expanded Brief Psychiatric Rating Scale (BPRS). *Schizophrenia Bulletin*, 12, 594-602.

Luria, A. (1961). *The role of speech in the regulation of normal and abnormal behaviors*. New York: Liveright.

Lykken, D.T. (1957). A study of anxiety in the sociopathic personality. *Journal of Abnormal and Social Psychology*, 55, 6-10.

Maccoby, E.E., & Jacklin, C.N. (1983). The "person" characteristics of children and the family as environment. In D. Magnusson & V.L. Allen (Eds.), *Human development: An interactional perspective*. San Diego, CA: Academic Press. pp. 75-92.

Maccoby, E.E. & Mnookin, R.H. (1992). *Dividing the Child: Social and Legal Dilemmas of Custody*. Cambridge, MA: Harvard University Press.

Maccoby, E.E. & Martin, J.A. (1983). Socialization in the context of the family: Parent-child interaction. In E.M. Hetherington (Ed.), *Socialization, personality, and social development* (Vol. 4), Handbook of child psychology (pp. 1-101). New York: Wiley.

Maccoby, E.E. (1992). The role of parents in the socialization of children: An historical overview. *Developmental Psychology*, 28, 1006-1017.

Maccoby, E.E. (1991). Gender and relationships: A reprise. *American Psychologist*, 46, 538-539.

Maccoby, E.E. & Jacklin, C.N. (1974). *The psychology of sex differences*. Stanford: Stanford University Press.

Mackay, A.V.P., Iversen, L.L., Rossor, M., Spokes, E., Bird, E., Arregui, A., Creese, I., & Snyder, S.H. (1982). Increased brain dopamine and dopamine receptors in schizophrenia. *Archives of General Psychiatry*, 39, 991-997.

Mackay, R.D. (1988). Post-Hinckley insanity in the U.S.A. *Criminal Law Review*, 88-96

Maddi, S.R. (1980). *Personality theories: A comparative analysis* (4th. Ed.). Homewood, IL: Dorsey.

Magnusson, D. (1981). *Toward a psychology of situations: An interactional perspective*. Hillsdale, NJ: Erlbaum.

Maher, B.A., & Spitzer, M. (1993). Delusions. In C.G. Costello (Ed.) *Symptoms of schizophrenia*. New York: Wiley, p. 92-120.

Mahoney, M.J. (1991). *Human change processes: The scientific foundations of psychotherapy*. New York: Basic Books.

Maier, W., Lichtermann, D., Klingler, T., Heun, R., & Hallmayer, J. (1992). Prevalence of personality disorders (DSM-III-R) in the community. *Journal of Personality Disorders*, 6, 187-196.

Major, B., & Crocker, J. (1993). Social stigma: The consequences of attributional ambiguity. In D.M. Mackie and D.L. Hamilton (Eds). *Affect, cognition, and stereotyping: Interactive processes in group perception*. San Diego, CA: Academic Press. pp. 345-370.

Mäkelä, K. (1986). Attitudes toward drinking and drunkenness in four Scandinavian countries. In T.F. Babor (Ed). *Alcohol and culture: Comparative perspectives from Europe and America*, vol 472. New York: New York Academy of Sciences, pp. 21-32.

Mäkelä, K. (1994). Rates of attrition among the membership of Alcoholics Anonymous in Finland. *Journal of Studies on Alcohol*, 55, 91-95.

Malcolm, J.G. (1987). Treatment choices and informed consent in psychiatry: Implications of the Osheroff case for the profession. *Journal of Psychiatry and the Law*, 15, 9-81.

Maltzman, I. (1989). A reply to Cook, "Craftsman versus professional: Analysis of the controlled drinking controversy." *Journal of Studies on Alcohol*, 50, 466-472).

Mandler, G. (1966). Anxiety. In D.L. Sills (Ed.), *International encyclopedia of the social sciences*. New York: Macmillan.

Mandler, G. (1975). *Mind and emotion*. New York: Wiley.

Mangone, C.A., Sanguinetti, R.M., Baumann, P.D., Gonzalez, R.C., et al. (1993). Influence of feelings of burden on the caregiver's perception of the patient's functional status. *Dementia*, 4, 287-294.

Mankoo, B., Sherrington, R., Brynjolfsson, J., Kalsi, G., Petursson, J., Sigmundsson, T., Read, T., Murphy, P., Curtis, D. Melmer. G. & Gurling, H. (1991). New microsatellite polymorphisms provide a highly polymorphic map of chromosome 5 bands q11.2-q13.3 for linkage analysis of Icelandic and English families affected by schizophrenia. *Psychiatric Genetics*, 2, 17.

Manschreck, T.C. (1993). Psychomotor abnormalities. In C.G. Costello (Ed.), *Symptoms of schizophrenia*. New York: Wiley. pp. 261-290.

Marcia, J.E. (1966). Development and validation of ego-identity status. *Journal of personality and Social Psychology*, 24, 551-558.

Marder, S.R., Ames, D., Wirshing, W.C., & Van Putten, T. (1993). Schizophrenia. *Psychiatric Clinics of North America*, 16, 567-587.

Marengo, J.T., & Harrow, M. (1993). Thought disorder. In C.G. Costello (Ed.) *Symptoms of schizophrenia*. New York: Wiley, p. 27-55.

Margolin, G. (1981). Behavior exchange in happy and unhappy marriages: A family cycle perspective. *Behavior Therapy*, 12, 329-343.

Margolin, G. (1987). Marital therapy: A cognitive-behavioral approach. In N.S. Jacobson (Ed.), *Psychotherapists in clinical practice* (pp. 232-285). New York: Guilford.

Margraf, J., Barlow, D.H., Clark, D.M., & Telch, M.J. (1993). Psychological treatment of panic: Work in progress on outcome, active ingredients, and follow-up. *Behaviour Research and Therapy*, 31, 1-8.

Margraf, J., Taylor, C.B., Ehlers, A., Roth, W.T., & Agras, W.S. (1987). Panic attacks in the natural environment. *Journal of Nervous and Mental Disease*, 175, 558-565.

Margulis, L., & Sagan, D. (1991). *Mystery dance: On the evolution of human sexuality*. New York: Summit Books.

Markman, H.J., Floyd, F.J., Stanley, S.M., & Storaasli, R.D. (1988). Prevention of marital distress: A longitudinal investigation. *Journal of Consulting and Clinical Psychology*, 56, 210-217.

Markova, I.S., & Berrios, G.E. (1992). The meaning of insight in clinical psychiatry. *British Journal of Psychiatry*, 160, 850-860.

Markovitz, P.J., Calabrese, J.R., Schulz, C.S., Meltzer, H.Y. (1991). Fluoxetine in the treatment of borderline and schizotypal personality disorders. *American Journal of Psychiatry*, 148, 1064-1067.

Marks, I.M., Swinson, R.P., Basoglu, M., Kuch, K., Noshirvani, H., O'SUllivan, G. Lelliott, P.T., Kirby, M., McNamee, G., Sengun, S., & Wickwire, K. (1993). Alprazolam and exposure alone and combined in panic disorder with agoraphobia: A controlled study in London and Toronto. *British Journal of Psychiatry*, 162, 776-787.

Marks, I.M. (1987). *Fears, phobias, and rituals: Panic, anxiety, and their disorders*. New York: Oxford University Press.

Marks, P.A., Seeman, W. & Haller, D.L. (1974). *The actuarial use of the MMPI with adolescents and adults*. New York: Oxford.

Marlatt, G.A. (1985). Relapse prevention: Theoretical rationale and overview of the model. In G.A. Marlatt & J.R. Gordon (Eds). *Relapse prevention*. New York: Guilford.

Marlatt, G.A., & Rohsenow, D.J. (1980). Cognitive processes in alcohol use: Expectancy and the balanced placebo design. In N.K. Mello (Ed.), *Advances in substance abuse*, (Vol 1). Greenwich, Conn: JAl Press, Inc. pp. 159-199.

Marlatt, G.A. (1987). Alcohol, the magic elixir: Stress, expectancy, and the transformation of emotional states. In E. Gottheil, K.A. Druley, S. Pashko, & S.P. Weinstein (Eds.). *Stress and Addiction*. New York: Brunner/Mazel. pp. 302-322.

Marlatt, G.A., Baer, J.S., Donovan, D.M., & Kivlahan, D.R. (1988). Addictive behaviors: Etiology and treatment. *Annual Review of Psychology*, 39, 223-252.

Marlatt, G.A., & Baer, J.S. (1988). Addictive behaviors: Etiology and treatment. *Annual Review of Psychology*, 39, 223-252.

Marques, J.K., Day, D.M., Nelson, C., & West, M.A. (1994). Effects of cognitive-behavioral treatment on sex offender recidivism: Preliminary results of a longitudinal study. *Criminal Justice and Behavior*, 21, 28-54.

Marques, J.K., Day, D.M., Nelson, C., & West, M.A. (1993). Findings and recommendations from California's experimental treatment program. In G.C.N. Hall, R. Hirschman, J.R. Graham, and M.S. Zaragoza (Eds), *Sexual aggression: Issues in etiology, assessment, and treatment*. Washington, D.C.: Hemisphere. pp. 197-214.

Marsella, A.J., Sartorius, N., Jablensky, A., & Fenton, F.R. (1985). Cross-cultural studies of depressive disorders: An overview. In A. Kleinman and B. Good (Eds.). *Culture and depression: Studies in the anthropology and cross-cultural psychiatry of affect and disorder*. Berkeley, CA: University of California. pp. 299-324.

Marshall, W.L. (1989). Intimacy, loneliness, and sexual offenders. *Behaviour Research and Therapy*, 27, 491-503.

Marshall, W.L., Eccles, A., & Barbaree, H.E. (1991). The treatment of exhibitionists: A focus on sexual deviance versus cognitive and relationship features. *Behaviour Research and Therapy*, 29, 129-135.

Marshall, W.L., & Pithers, W.D. (1994). A reconsideration of treatment outcome with sex offenders. *Criminal Justice and Behavior, 21*, 10-27.

Marshall, W.L., Payne, K., Barbaree, H.E., & Eccles, A. (1991). Exhibitionists: Sexual preferences for exposing. *Behaviour Research and Therapy, 29*, 37-40.

Marshall, W.L., Hudson, S.M., & Ward, T. (1992). Sexual deviance. In P.H. Wilson (Ed.), *Principles and practice of relapse prevention*. New York: Guilford.

Martin, C.S., & Sayette, M.A. (1993). Experimental design in alcohol administration research: Limitations and alternatives in the manipulation of dosage-set. *Journal of Studies on Alcohol, 54*, 750-761.

Mash, E.J. & Johnston, C. (1982). A comparison of the mother-child interactions of younger and older hyperactive and normal children. *Child Development, 53*, 1371-1381.

Maslow, A.H. (1970). *Motivation and personality* (2nd.Ed.). New York: Harper & Row.

Mason, J.W. (1975). A historical view of the "stress" field (Part II). *Journal of Human Stress, 1*, 12-16.

Masters, W.H., & Johnson, V.E. (1966). *Human sexual response*. Boston: Little-Brown.

Masters, W.H., & Johnson, V.E. (1970). *Human sexual inadequacy*. Boston: Little-Brown.

Matarazzo, J.D. (1983). The reliability of psychiatric and psychological diagnosis. *Clinical Psychology Review, 3*, 103-145.

Mate-Kole, C., Freschi, M., & Robin, A. (1988). Aspects of psychiatric symptoms at different stages in the treatment of transsexualism. *British Journal of Psychiatry, 152*, 550-553.

Mathews, A. (1990). Why worry: The cognitive function of anxiety. *Behaviour Research and Therapy, 28*, 455-468.

Matson, J.L. & Frame, C.L. (1986). *Psychopathology among mentally retarded children and adolescents*. Beverly Hills, CA: Sage.

Matthews, K.A. (1988). Coronary heart disease and Type A behaviors: Update on and alternative to the Booth-Kewley and Friedman (1987) quantitative review. *Psychological Bulletin, 1988*, 373-380.

Matthysse, S. & Pope, A. (1986). The neuropathology of psychiatric disorders. In P. Berger & K.H. Brodie (Eds.), *American handbook of psychiatry* (Vol. 8, 2nd Ed., 151-159). New York: Basic Books.

Max, W. (1993). The economic impact of Alzheimer's disease. *Neurology, 43* (suppl 4), S6-S10.

May, R. (1967). *Psychology and the human dilemma*. New York: Van Nostrand Reinhold.

McAnulty, R.D., & Adams, H.E. (1992). Validity and ethics of penile circumference measures of sexual arousal: A reply to McConaghy. *Archives of Sexual Behavior, 21*, 177-195.

McBride, W.J., Murphy, J.M., Yoshimoto, K., Lumeng, L. & Li, T.K. (1993). Serotonin mechanisms in alcohol-drinking behavior. *Drug Development Research, 30*, 170-177.

McCarthy, B.W. (1989). Cognitive-behavioral strategies and techniques in the treatment of early ejaculation. In S.R. Lieblum and R.C. Rosen (Eds.). *Principles and practice of sex therapy* (2nd edition). New York: Guilford.

McCaul, M.E., Turkkan, J.S., & Stitzer, J.L. (1989). Conditioned opponent responses: Effects of placebo challenge in alcoholic subjects. *Alcoholism: Clinical and Experimental Research, 13*, 631-635.

McConaghy, N. (1989). Validity and ethics of penile circumference measures of sexual arousal: A critical review. *Archives of Sexual Behavior, 18*, 357-369.

McConaghy, N. (1990). Sexual deviation. In A.S. Bellack, M. Hersen, and A.E. Kazdin (Eds.). *International handbook of behavior modification and therapy* (2nd ed) New York: Plenum.

McFall, R.M. (1991). Manifesto for a science of clinical psychology. *The Clinical Psychologist, 44*, 75-88.

McFall, R.M. (1990). The enhancement of social skills: An information-processing analysis. In W.L. Marshall, D.R. Laws, and H.E. Barbaree (Eds.). *Handbook of sexual assault: Issues, theories, and treatment of the offender*. New York: Plenum.

McFall, R.M., & McDonel, E.C. (1986). The continuing search for units of analysis in psychology: Beyond persons, situations, and their interactions. In R.O. Nelson & S.C. Hayes (Eds.). *Conceptual foundations of behavioral assessment*. New York: Guilford. pp. 201-241.

McFall, R.M. (1982). A review and reformulation of the concept of social skills. *Behavioral Assessment, 4*, 1-33.

McGlashan, T. (1986). The Chestnut Lodge follow up study. III. Long-term outcome of borderline personalities. *Archives of General Psychiatry, 43*, 20-30.

McGlashan, T. (1986). Schizotypal personality disorder: Chestnut Lodge Follow-up Study: VI. Long-term follow-up perspectives. *Archives of General Psychiatry, 43*, 329-334.

McGlashan, T.H. (1992). The longitudinal profile of borderline personality disorder: Contributions from the Chestnut Lodge follow-up study. In D. Silver & M. Rosenbluth (Eds.), *Handbook of borderline disorders*. Madison, CT: International Universities Press. pp. 53-83.

McGlashan, T.H., & Fenton, W.S. (1991). Classical subtypes for schizophrenia: Literature review for DSM-IV. *Schizophrenia Bulletin, 17*, 609-623.

McGowin, D.F. (1993). *Living in the labyrinth: A personal journey through the maze of Alzheimer's*. New York: Delacorte Press.

McGue, M. (1993). From proteins to cognitions: The behavioral genetics of alcoholism. In R. Plomin and G.E. McClearn (Eds.), *Nature, nurture and psychology*. Washington, D.C.: American Psychological Association.

McGue, M., Pickins, R.W., & Svikis, D.S. (1992). Sex and age effects on the inheritance of alcohol problems: A twin study. *Journal of Abnormal Psychology, 101*, 3-17.

McGue, M. & Lykken, D.T. (1992). Genetic influence on risk of divorce. *Psychological Science, 3*, 368-373.

McGuffin, P., Owen, M.J., O'Donovan, M.C., Thapar, A., & Gottesman, I.I. (1994). *Seminars in psychiatry genetics*. London: Gaskell.

McGuffin, P., Katz, R., & Rutherford, J. (1991). Nature, nurture, and depression: A twin study. *Psychological Medicine, 21*, 329-335.

McGuffin, P., Farmer, A.E., Gottesman, I.I., Murray, R.M., & Reveley, A.M. (1984) Twin concordance for operationally defined schizophrenia. *Archives of General Psychiatry, 41*, 541-545.

McGuffin, P., Farmer, A.E., & Gottesman, I.I. (1987) Is there really a split in schizophrenia? The genetic evidence. *British Journal of Psychiatry, 150*, 581-592.

McGuffin, P., Sargeant, M., Hett, G., Tidmarsh, S., Whatley, S., & Marchbanks, R.M. (1990). Exclusion of a schizophrenia susceptibility gene from the chromosome 5q11-q13 region. New data and a reanalysis of previous reports. *American Journal of Human Genetics, 47*, 524-535.

McGuffin, P., Reveley, A., & Holland, A. (1982). Identical triplets: Non-identical psychosis? *British Journal of Psychiatry, 140*, 1-6.

McGuffin, P. & Gottesman, I.I. (1985). Genetic influences on normal and abnormal development. In M. Rutter & L. Hersov (Eds.), *Child and adolescent psychiatry* (pp. 17-33). Oxford: Blackwell Scientific.

McKey, R.H., Condelli, L., Granson, H., Barrett, B. McConkey, C., & Plantz, M. (1985, June). *The impact of Head Start on children, families, and communities* (final report of the Head Start Evaluation, Synthesis and Utilization Project). Washington: CSR.

McLellan, A.T., O'Brien, C.P., Metzger, D., Alterman, A.I., Cornish, J., & Urschel, H. (1992). How effective is substance abuse treatment — Compared to what? In C.P. O'Brien and J.H. Jaffe (Eds). *Addictive states*. New York: Raven. pp. 231-251.

McLemore, C.W. & Benjamin, L.A. (1979). Whatever happened to interpersonal diagnosis? A psychosocial alternative to DSM-III. *American Psychologist, 34*, 17-34.

McNally, R.J. (1990). Psychological approaches to panic disorder: A review. *Psychological Bulletin, 108*, 403-419.

McNally, R.J. (1987). Preparedness and phobias: A review. *Psychological Bulletin, 101*, 283-303.

McNeal, E.T., & Cimbolic, P. (1986). Antidepressants and biochemical theories of depression. *Psychological Bulletin, 99*, 361-374.

McReynolds, P. (1986). History of assessment in clinical and educational settings. In R.O. Nelson, & S.C. Hayes (Eds.). *Conceptual foundations of behavioral assessment*. New York: Guilford.

Mechanic, D. (1986). The concept of illness behavior: Culture, situation and personal predisposition. *Psychological Medicine, 16*, 1-7.

Mednick, S.A., & Schulsinger, F. (1968). Some premorbid characteristics related to breakdown in children with schizophrenic mothers. *Journal of Psychiatric Research* (Suppl. 1), 6, 354-362.

Mednick, S.A., & McNeil, T. (1968). Current methodology in research on the etiology of schizophrenia. *Psychological Bulletin, 70*, 681-693.

Meehl, P.E. (1993). The origins of some of my conjectures concerning schizophrenia. In L.J. Chapman, J.P. Chapman, & D. Fowles (Eds). *Progress in experimental personality and psychopathology research*. pp. 1-11.

Meehl, P.E. (1990). Toward an integrated theory of schizotaxia, schizotypy, and schizophrenia. *Journal of Personality Disorders, 4*, 1-99.

Meehl, P.E. (1962). Schizotaxia, schizotypy, schizophrenia. *American Psychologist, 17*, 827-838.

Meehl, P.E. & Rosen, A. (1955). Antecedent probability and the efficiency of psychometric signs, patterns, or cutting scores. *Psychological Bulletin, 52*, 194-216.

Meichenbaum, D. (1977). *Cognitive behavior modification*. New York: Plenum Press.

Melchior, C.L., & Tabakoff, B. (1985). Features of environment-dependent tolerance to ethanol. *Psychopharmacology, 87*, 94-100.

Mellor, C.S. (1982). The present status of first rank symptoms. *British Journal of Psychiatry, 140*, 423-424.

Melman, A., Tiefer, L., & Pedersen, R. (1988). Evaluation of first 406 patients in urology department based center for male sexual dysfunction. *Urology, 32*, 6-10.

Melton, G., Petrila, J., Poythress, N., & Slobogin, C. (1987). *Psychological evaluations for the courts*. New York: Guilford.

Melton, G.B. & Limber, S. (1989). Psychologists' involvement in cases of child maltreatment: Limits of roles and expertise. *American Psychologist, 44*, 1225-1233.

Meltzer, H.Y. (1992). The role of dopamine in schizophrenia. In J Lindenmayer and S.R. Kay (Eds.), *New biological vistas on schizophrenia*. New York: Brunner/Mazel.

Meltzer, H.Y. (1987). Biological studies in schizophrenia. *Schizophrenia Bulletin, 13*, 77-114.

Meltzer, H.Y. (1990). Clozapine: Mechanisms of action in relation to its clinical advantages. In A.

Kales, C.N. Stefanis, J. Talbott (Eds.), *Recent advances in schizophrenia.* New York: Springer-Verlag, pp. 237-256.

Meltzer, H.Y. (1985). Dopamine and negative symptoms in schizophrenia: Critique of the Type I-II hypothesis. In M. Alpert (Ed.), *Controversies in schizophrenia: Changes and constancies.* New York: Guilford. pp. 110-136.

Meltzer, H.Y. (1993). Serotonin-dopamine interactions and atypical antipsychotic drugs. *Psychiatric Annals, 23,* 193-200.

Mendelson, J.H., & Mello, N.K. (1989). Studies of alcohol: Past, present and future. *Journal of Studies on Alcohol, 50,* 293-296.

Mendez, M.F., Selwood, A., Mastri, A.R., & Frey, W.H. (1993). Pick's disease versus Alzheimer's disease: A comparison of clinical characteristics. *Neurology, 43,* 289-292.

Merckelbach, H., de Ruiter, C., van den Hout, M.A., & Hoekstra, R. (1989). Conditioning experiences and phobias. *Behaviour Research and Therapy, 27,* 657-662.

Merikangas, K.R. (1990). The genetic epidemiology of alcoholism. *Psychological Medicine, 20,* 11-22.

Merikangas, K.R., & Gelernter, C.S. (1990). Comorbidity for alcoholism and depression. *Psychiatric Clinics of North America, 13,* 613-632.

Mersky, H. (1992). The manufacture of personalities: The production of multiple personality disorder. *British Journal of Psychiatry, 160,* 327-340.

Messick, S. (1989). Validity. In R.L. Linn (Ed.). *Educational measurement* (3rd edition). New York: American Council on Education, MacMillan Publishing Co.

Mesulam, M. (1981). Dissociative states with abnormal temporal lobe EEG. *Archives of Neurology, 38,* 176-181.

Metalsky, G.I., Joiner, T.E., Hardin, T.S., & Abramson, L.Y. (1993). Depressive reactions to failure in a naturalistic setting: A test of the hopelessness and self-esteem theories of depression. *Journal of Abnormal Psychology, 102,* 101-109.

Miklowitz, D.J., Goldstein, M.J., Faloon, I.R.H., & Doane, J.A. (1984). Interactional correlates of expressed emotion in the families of schizophrenics. *British Journal of Psychiatry, 144,* 482-487.

Miklowitz, D.J., Goldstein, M.J., et al. (1988). Family factors and the course of bipolar affective disorder. *Archives of General Psychiatry, 45,* 225-231.

Miklowtiz, D.J., Doane, J.A., et al. (1989). Is expressed emotion an index of a transactional process? I. Parents' affective style. *Family Process, 28,* 153-167.

Milich, R., Wolraich, M., & Lindgren, S. (1986). Sugar and hyperactivity: A critical review of empirical findings. *Clinical Psychology Review, 6,* 493-513.

Miller, G.A., & Kozak, M.J. (1993). Three-systems assessment and the construct of emotion. In N. Birbaumer and A. Ohman (Eds.), *The structure of emotion: Psychophysiological, cognitive, and clinical aspects.* Seattle: Hogrefe & Huber, pp. 31-47.

Miller & Lief (1976). Masturbatory attitudes, knowledge and experience: Data from the Sex Knowledge and Attitude Test (SKAT). *Archives of Sexual Behavior, 5,* 447-468.

Miller, M.E. & Bowers, K.S. (1986). Hypnotic analgesia and stress inoculation in the reduction of pain. *Journal of Abnormal Psychology, 95,* 6-14.

Miller, N.S., Belkin, B.M., & Gold, M.S. (1991). Alcohol and drug dependence among the elderly: Epidemiology, diagnosis, and treatment. *Comprehensive Psychiatry, 32,* 153-165.

Miller, N.S. (1991). *Comprehensive handbook of drug and alcohol addiction.* New York: Marcel Dekker.

Miller, P.M. (1987). Commonalities of addictive behaviors. In T.D. Nirenberg, & S.A. Maisto

(Eds.), *Developments in the assessment and treatment of addictive behaviors.* Norwood, NJ: Ablex Publishing Corp.

Miller, T.Q., Turner, C.W., Tindale, R.S., Posavac, E.J., & Dugoni, B.L. (1991). Reasons for the trend toward null findings in research on Type A behavior. *Psychological Bulletin, 110,* 469-485.

Miller, T.W. (1989). *Stressful life events.* Madison, CT: International Universities Press.

Miller, W.R., & Kurtz, E. (1994). Models of alcoholism used in treatment: Contrasting AA and other perspectives with which it is often confused. *Journal of Studies on Alcohol, 55,* 159-166.

Miller-Johnson, S., Emery, R.E., Marvin, R.S., Clarke, W., Lovinger, R., & Martin, M. (1994). Parent-child relationships and the management of insulin-dependent diabetes mellitus. *Journal of Consulting and Clinical Psychology, 62,* 603-610.

Millon, T. (1981). *Disorders of personality.* New York: Wiley.

Millon, T., & Everly, G.S. (1985). *Personality and its disorders.* New York: Wiley.

Mineka, S. (1985). Animal models of anxiety-based disorders: Their usefulness and limitations. In A.H. Tuma and J. Maser (Eds.), *Anxiety and the anxiety disorders.* Hillsdale, N.J.: Erlbaum.

Mineka, S. & Zinbarg, R. (1991). Animal models of psychopathology. In C. E. Walker (Ed). *Clinical psychology.*

Mineka, S., & Kihlstrom, J.F. (1978). Unpredictable and uncontrollable events: A new perspective on experimental neurosis. *Journal of Abnormal Psychology, 87,* 256-271.

Minuchin, S., Rosman, B.L., & Baker, L. (1978). *Psychosomatic families.* Cambridge, MA: Harvard University Press.

Minuchin, P., (1985). Families and individual development: Provocations from the field of family therapy. *Child Development, 56,* 289-302.

Minuchin, S. (1974). *Families and family therapy.* Cambridge, MA: Harvard University Press.

Mischel, W. (1968). *Personality and assessment.* New York: Wiley.

Mischel, W. (1983). Delay of gratification as process and as person variable in development. In D. Magnusson & V.L. Allen (Eds.), *Human development: An interactional perspective.* New York: Academic Press.

Mishler, E.G., & Waxler, N.E. (1968). *Interaction in families: An experimental study of family processes and schizophrenia.* New York: Wiley.

Mitchell, P., Waters, B., Morrison, N. et al. (1991). Close linkage of bipolar disorder to chromosome 11 markers is excluded in two large Australian pedigrees. *Journal of Affective Disorders, 21,* 23-32.

Mitchell, J.E., Pyle, R.L., Eckert, E.D., Hatsukami, D., Pomeroy, C., & Zimmerman, R. (1990). A comparison study of antidepressants and structured intensive group psychotherapy in the treatment of bulimia nervosa. *Archives of General Psychiatry, 47,* 149-157.

Mnookin, R.H. (1985). *In the interest of children: Advocacy, law reform, and public policy.* New York: Freeman.

Mnookin, R.H., (1975). Child-custody adjudication: Judicial functions in the face of indeterminancy. *Law and Contemporary Problems, 88,* 226-293.

Moffitt, T.E. (1993). Adolescence-limited and life-course-persistent antisocial behavior: A developmental taxonomy. *Psychological Review, 100,* 674-701.

Mohr, D.C., & Beutler, L.E. (1990). Erectile dysfunction: A review of diagnostic and treatment procedures. *Clinical Psychology Review, 10,* 123-150.

Moldin, S.O., Reich, T., & Rice, J.P. (1991). Current perspectives on the genetics of unipolar depression. *Behavior Genetics, 21,* 211-242.

Monahan, J. (1993). Limiting therapist exposure to *Tarasoff* liability: Guidelines for risk containment. *American Psychologist, 48,* 242-250.

Monahan, J. (1980). *Who is the client?: The ethics of psychological intervention in the criminal justice system.* Washington, DC: American Psychological Association.

Monahan, J. (1981). *The clinical prediction of violent behavior.* Rockville, MD: NIMH.

Monahan, J. (1992). Mental disorder and violent behavior: Perceptions and evidence. *American Psychologist, 47,* 511-521.

Money, J. (1987). Masochism: On the childhood origin of paraphilia, opponent-process theory, and antiandrogen therapy. *Journal of Sex Research, 23,* 273-275.

Money, J. (1984). Paraphilias: Phenomenology and classification. *American Journal of Psychotherapy, 38,* 164-179.

Monroe, S.M., & Wade, S.L. (1988). Life events. In C.G. Last and M. Hersen (Eds.), *Handbook of anxiety disorders.* New York: Pergamon.

Monroe, S.M., & Simons, A.D. (1991). Diathesis-stress theories in the context of life stress research: Implications for the depressive disorders. *Psychological Bulletin, 110,* 406-425.

Montgomery, H.A., Miller, W.R., & Tonigan, J.S. (1993). Differences among AA groups: Implications for research. *Journal of Studies on Alcohol, 54,* 502-504.

Moore, M. (1975). Some myths about "mental illness". *Inquiry, 18,* 233-240.

Moos, R.H. (1974). *Family Environment Scale (Form R).* Palo Alto, CA: Consulting Psychologists Press.

Moos, R.H. (1974). *Evaluating treatment environments: A social ecological approach.* New York: Wiley.

Moos, R.H. (1981). *Work environment scale manual.* Palo Alto, CA: Consulting Psychologists Press.

Morey, L.C. (1988). Personality disorders in DSM-III and DSM-III-R: Convergence, coverage, and internal consistency. *American Journal of Psychiatry, 145,* 573-577.

Morokoff, P.J., & Heiman, J.R. (1980). Effects of erotic stimuli on sexually functional and dysfunctional women: Multiple measures before and after sex therapy. *Behaviour Research and Therapy, 18,* 127-137.

Morokoff, P.J. (1989). Sex bias and POD. *American Psychologist, 73-75.*

Morokoff, P.J. (1978). Determinants of female orgasm. In J. LoPiccolo & L. LoPiccolo (Eds.), *Handbook of sex therapy.* New York: Plenum.

Morrison, J. & Herbstein, J. (1988). Secondary affective disorder in women with somatization disorder. *Comprehensive Psychiatry, 29,* 433-440.

Morrow, J., & Nolen-Hoeksema, S. (1989). The effects of response sets for depression: The remediation of depressive affect. *Journal of Personality and Social Psychology.*

Morse, K.L. (1990). A uniform testimonial privilege for mental health professionals. *Ohio State Law Journal, 51,* 741-757.

Mueser, K.T., Bellack, A.S., Douglas, M.S., & Morrison, R.L. (1991). Prevalence and stability of social skill deficits in schizophrenia. *Schizophrenia Research, 5,* 167-176.

Mulligan, T., Retchin, S.M., Chinchilli, V.M., & Bettinger, C.B. (1988). The role of aging and chronic disease in sexual dysfunction. *JAGS, 36,* 520-524.

Multiple Risk Factor Intervention Trial Research Group (1982). Multiple Risk Factor Intervention Trial: Risk factor changes and mortality results. *Journal of the American Medical Association, 248,* 1465-1477.

Murphy, G.E., Simons, A.D., Wetzel, R.D., & Lustman, P.J. (1984). Cognitive therapy and pharmacotherapy, singly and together, in the treatment of depression. *Archives of General Psychiatry, 41,* 33-41.

Murphy, J.M. (1976). Psychiatric labeling in cross-cultural perspective. *Science,*

Murphy, E., & Macdonald, A. (1992). Affective disorders in old age. In E. S. Paykel (Ed.), *Handbook of affective disorders* (2nd edition). New York: Guilford. (pp. 601-618).

Myers, J.K., & Weissman, M.M. (1980). Screening for depression in a community sample: The use of a self-report scale to detect the depressive syndrome. *American Journal of Psychiatry, 137,* 1081-1084.

Myers, J.E.B. (1983-84). Involuntary civil commitment of the mentally ill: A system in need of change. *Villanova Law Review, 29,* 367-433.

Nakawatase, T.V., Yamamoto, J., & Sasao, T. (1993). The association between fast-flushing response and alcohol use among Japanese Americans. *Journal of Studies on Alcohol, 54,* 48-53.

Nathan, P.E. (1993). Alcoholism: Psychopathology, etiology, and treatment. In P.B. Sutker and H.E. Adams (Eds.) *Comprehensive handbook of psychopathology* (2nd edition). New York: Plenum. pp. 451-476.

Nathan, S.G. (1986). The epidemiology of the DSM-III psychosexual dysfunctions. *Journal of Sex and Marital Therapy, 12,* 267-281.

National Victim Center. (1992). *Crime and victimization in America: Statistical overview.* Arlington, VA: National Victim Center.

National Institute of Mental Health (1985). *Annual survey of patient characteristics—1985 state and county mental hospital inpatient services.* Rockville, MD: NIMH.

National Academy of Sciences, Institute of Medicine (1989). *Research on children & adolescents with mental, behavioral, and developmental disorders.* Washington: National Academy Press.

Neal, A.M., & Turner, S.M. (1991). Anxiety disorders research with African Americans: Current status. *Psychological Bulletin, 109,* 400-410.

Neale, J.M., & Oltmanns, T.F. (1980). *Schizophrenia.* New York: Wiley.

Neale, J.M., Cox, D.S., Valdimarsdottir, H., & Stone, A.A. (1988). The relation between immunity and health: Comment on Pennebaker, Kiecolt-Glaser, and Glaser. *Journal of Consulting and Clinical Psychology, 56,* 636-637.

Neibuhr, R. (1951). To be abased and to abound. *Messenger,* Feb. 13, p.7.

Neisser, U & Harsch, N. (1992). Phantom flashbulbs: False recollections of hearing the news about Challenger. In E. Winograd & U. Neisser (Eds.), *Affect and accuracy in recall: Studies of "flashbulb" memories* (pp. 9-31). New York: Cambridge University Press.

Nemeroff, C.B. & Bissette, G. (1986). Neuropeptides in psychiatric disorders. In P. Berger & K.H. Brodie (Eds.), *Biological psychiatry* (pp.64-110). New York: Basic.

Nestadt, G., Romanoski, A.J., Chahal, R., Merchant, A., Folstein, J.F., Gruenberg, E.M., & McHugh, P.R. (1990). An epidemiological study of histrionic personality disorder. *Psychological Medicine, 20,* 413-422.

Nestadt, G., Romanoski, A.J., Brown, C.H., Chahal, R., Merchant, A., Folstein, M.F., Gruenberg, E.M., & McHugh, P.R. (1991). DSM-III compulsive personality disorder: An epidemiological study. *Psychological Medicine, 21,* 461-471.

Neugebauer, R. (1979). Medieval and early modern theories of mental illness. *Archives of General Psychiatry, 36,* 477-483.

Newcomb, M.D. (1993). 4 Theories of rape in American society. *Archives of Sexual Behavior, 22,* 373-377.

Newcomb, A.F., Bukowski, W.M., & Pattee, L. (1993). Children's peer relations: A meta-analytic review of popular, rejected, neglected, controversial, and average sociometric status. *Psychological Bulletin, 113,* 99-128.

Newlin, D.B. (1989). The skin-flushing response: Autonomic, self-report, and conditioned responses to repeated administrations of alcohol in Asian men. *Journal of Abnormal Psychology, 98,* 421-425.

Newlin, D.B., & Thomson, J.B. (1991). Chronic tolerance and sensitization to alcohol in sons of alcoholics. *Alcoholism: Clinical and Experimental Research, 15,* 399-405.

Newman, J.P. & Kosson, D.S. (1986). Passive avoidance learning in psychopathic and nonpsychopathic offenders. *Journal of Abnormal Psychology, 95,* 257-263.

Newman, J.P., Kosson, D.S., & Patterson, C.M. (1992). Delay of gratification in psychopathic and nonpsychopathic offenders. *Journal of Abnormal Psychology, 101,* 630-636.

Newton, R.D. (1948). The identity of Alzheimer's disease and senile dementia and their relationship to senility. *Journal of Mental Science, 94,* 225-249.

Nietzel, M.T., Bernstein, D.A., & Milich, R. (1994). *Introduction to clinical psychology* (4th ed.). Englewood Cliffs, NJ: Prentice-Hall.

Nisbett, R.E. & Wilson, T.D. (1977). Telling more than we can know: Verbal reports on mental processes. *Psychological Review, 84,* 231-259.

Nolen-Hoeksema, S. (1990). *Sex differences in depression.* Stanford, CA: Stanford University Press.

Nolen-Hoeksema, S., Morrow, J., & Fredrickson, B.L. (1993). Response styles and the duration of episodes of depressed mood. *Journal of Abnormal Psychology, 102,* 20-28.

Nolen-Hoeksema, S. (1989). Life-span views on depression. In P.B. Baltes, D.L. Featherman, & R.M. Lerner (Eds.). *Life-span development and behavior* (Vol. 9) (pp. 203-241). Hillsdale, NJ: Erlbaum.

Noyes, R. Jr. (1991). Treatments of choice for anxiety disorders. In W. Coryell & G. Winokur (Eds.). *The clinical management of anxiety disorders.* New York: Oxford University Press. pp. 140-153.

Noyes, R., Jr., Clarkson, C., Crowe, R.R., Yates, W.R., & McChesney, C.M. (1987). A family study of generalized anxiety disorder. *American Journal of Psychiatry, 144,* 1019-1024.

Noyes, R., Garvey, M.J., & Cook, B.L. (1989). Follow-up study of patients with panic disorder and agoraphobia with panic attacks treated with tricyclic antidepressants. *Journal of Affective Disorders, 16,* 249-257.

Nuechterlein, K.H. (1991). Vigilance in schizophrenia and related disorders. In S.R. Steinhauer, J.H. Gruzelier, and J. Zubin (Eds.). *Handbook of schizophrenia: Neuropsychology, psychophysiology, and information processing.* Volume 5. Amsterdam, The Netherlands: Elsevier, pp. 397-433.

Nuechterlein, K.H., & Dawson, M.E. (1984). Vulnerability and stress factors in the developmental course of schizophrenic disorders. *Schizophrenia Bulletin, 10,* 158-159.

Nuechterlein, K.H., Snyder, K.S., & Mintz, J. (1992). Paths to relapse: Possible transactional processes connecting patient illness onset, expressed emotion, and psychotic relapse. *British Journal of Psychiatry, 161* (suppl 18), 88-96.

Nunes, E.V., Frank, K.A., & Kornfeld, J. (1987). Psychologic treatment for the Type A behavior pattern and for coronary heart disease: A meta-analysis of the literature. *Psychosomatic Medicine, 48,* 159-173.

O'Connor, G.T., Buring, J.E., Yusuf, S., Goldhaber, S.Z., Olmstead, E.M., Paffenbarger, R.S., & Hennekens, C.H. (1989). An overview of randomized trials of rehabilitation with exercise after myocardial infarction. *Circulation, 80,* 234-244.

O'Donohue, W., & Geer, J.H. (1993). *Handbook of sexual dysfunctions: Assessment and treatment.* Boston: Allyn & Bacon.

O'Grady, J.C. (1990). The prevalence and diagnostic significance of Schneiderian first-rank symptoms in a random sample of acute psychiatric in-patients. *British Journal of Psychiatry, 156,* 496-500.

O'Leary, K.D. (1980). Pills or skills for hyperactive children. *Journal of Applied Behavior Analysis, 13,* 191-204.

O'Leary, K.D. & Borkovec, T.D. (1978). Conceptual, methodological, and ethical problems of placebo groups in psychotherapy research. *American Psychologist, 31,* 821-830.

O'Leary, K.D. & Wilson, G.T. (1987). *Behavior therapy: Application and outcome.* Englewood-Cliffs, NJ: Prentice Hall.

O'Shea, B., & Falvey, J. (1988). Huntington's disease: Update of the literature. *British Journal of Psychological Medicine, 5,* 61-70.

O'Sullivan, G., Noshirvani, H., Marks, I., Monteiro, W., & Lelliott, P. (1991). Six-year follow-up after exposure and clomipramine therapy for obsessive compulsive disorder. *Journal of Clinical Psychiatry, 52,* 150-155.

O'Sullivan, G., & Marks, I. (1991). Follow-up studies of behavioral treatment of phobic and obsessive compulsive neuroses. *Psychiatric Annals, 21,* 368-373.

Oatley, K., & Bolton, W. (1985). A social-cognitive theory of depression in reaction to life events. *Psychological Review, 92,* 372-388.

Oei, T.P.S., Lim, B., & Hennessy, B. (1990). Psychological dysfunction in battle: Combat stress reactions and posttraumatic stress disorder. *Clinical Psychology Review, 10,* 355-388.

Öhman, A. (1986). Face the beast and fear the face: Animal and social fears as prototypes for evolutionary analyses of emotion. *Psychophysiology, 23,* 123-145.

Oliver, J.M., & Simmons, M.E. (1984). Depression as measured by the DSM-III and the Beck Depression Inventory in an unselected adult population. *Journal of Consulting and Clinical Psychology, 52,* 892-898.

Oltmanns, T.F. (1988). Defining delusional beliefs. In T.F. Oltmanns and B.A. Maher (Eds.) *Delusional beliefs.* New York: Wiley.

Oltmanns, T.F., Neale, J.M., & Davison, G.C. (1991). *Case studies in abnormal psychology* (3rd Ed.). New York: Wiley.

Olweus, D. (1984). Aggressors and their victims: Bullying at school. In N. Frude & H. Gault (Eds.), *Disruptive behavior in schools* (pp. 57-76). New York: Wiley.

Onstad, S., Skre, I., Torgersen, S., & Kringlen, E. (1991). Twin concordance for DSM-III-R schizophrenia. *Acta Psychiatrica Scandinavica, 83,* 395-401.

Oren, D.A., & Rosenthal, N.E. (1992). Seasonal affective disorders. In E.S. Paykel (Ed.). *Handbook of affective disorders* (2nd edition). New York: Guilford. (pp. 551-568).

Orford, J. (1985). *Excessive appetites: A psychological view of addictions.* New York: Wiley.

Öst, L.G., & Hugdahl, K. (1981). Acquisition of phobias and anxiety response patterns in clinical patients. *Behaviour Research and Therapy, 19,* 439-447.

Öst, L. (1987). Applied relaxation: Description of a coping technique and review of controlled studies. *Behaviour Research and Therapy, 25,* 397-409.

Overstreet, D.H., Rezvani, A.H., & Janowsky, D.S. (1992). Genetic animal models of depression and ethanol preference provide support for cholinergic and serotonergic involvement in depression and alcoholism. *Biological Psychiatry*, 31, 919-936.

Page, P.B. (1988). The origins of alcohol studies: E.M. Jellinek and the documentation of the alcohol research literature. *British Journal of Addiction*, 83, 1095-1103.

Paikoff, R.L., & Brooks-Gunn, J. (1991). Do parent-child relationships change during puberty? *Psychological Bulletin*, 110, 47-66.

Panksepp, J. (1988). Brain emotional circuits and psychopathologies. In M. Clynes & J. Panksepp (Eds.), *Emotions and psychopathology* (pp. 37-76). New York: Plenum.

Pantle, M., Pasewark, R., & Steadman, H. (1980). Comparing institutionalization periods and subsequent arrests of insanity acquittees and convicted felons. *Journal of Psychiatry and the Law*, 8, 305-316.

Paris, J. (1993). Personality disorders: A biopsychosocial model. *Journal of Personality Disorders*, 7, 255-264.

Paris, J. (1992). Social factors in borderline personality disorder: A review and a hypothesis. *Canadian Journal of Psychiatry*, 37, 480-486.

Parker, J.G. & Asher, S.R. (1987). Peer relations and later personality adjustment: Are low-accepted children at risk? *Psychological Bulletin*, 102, 357-389.

Parloff, M.B., Waskow, I.E., & Wolfe, B.E. (1978). Research on therapist variables in relation to process and outcome. In S.L. Garfield & A.E. Bergin (Eds.), *Handbook of psychotherapy and behavior change* (2nd. Ed., pp. 233-282). New York: Wiley.

Parnas, J., Cannon, T.D., Jacobsen, B., Schulsinger, H., Schulsinger, F., & Mednick, S.A. (1993). Lifetime DSM-III-R diagnostic outcomes in the offspring of schizophrenic mothers: Results from the Copenhagen high-risk study. *Archives of General Psychiatry*, 50, 707-714.

Pato, M.T., Zohar-Kadouch, R., Zohar, J., & Murphy, D.L. (1988). Return of symptoms after discontinuation of clomipramine in patients with obsessive-compulsive disorder. *American Journal of Psychiatry*, 145, 1521-1525.

Patterson, C.J., Kupersmidt, J.B., & Griesler, P.C. (1990). Children's perceptions of self and of relationships with others as a function of sociometric status. *Child Development*, 61, 1335-1349.

Patterson, C.M., & Newman, J.P. (1993). Reflectivity and learning from aversive events: Toward a psychological mechanism for the syndromes of disinhibition. *Psychological Review*, 100, 716-736.

Patterson, G.R. (1982). *Coercive family process*. Eugene, OR: Castalia.

Patterson, G.R. & Fleischman, M.J. (1979). Maintenance of treatment effects: Some considerations concerning family systems and follow-up data. *Behavior Therapy*, 10, 168-185.

Patterson, G.R., DeBaryshe, B.D., & Ramsey, E. (1989). A developmental perspective on antisocial behavior. *American Psychologist*, 44, 329-325.

Patton, J.R., Beirne-Smith, M., & Payne, J.S. (1990). *Mental retardation* (3rd ed) Columbus, OH: Merrill Publishing.

Paul, G.L., & Lentz, R.J. (1977). *Psychosocial treatment of chronic mental patients: Milieu versus social-learning programs*. Cambridge: Harvard University Press.

Pedersen, N.L., & Gatz, M. (1991). Twin studies as a tool for bridging the gap between genetics and epidemiology of dementia: The study of dementia in Swedish twins [abstract]. *Gerontologist*, 31, 333.

Peele, S. (1992b). Why is everybody always pickin' on me? A response to comments. *Addictive Behaviors*, 17, 83-93.

Peele, S. (1992a). Alcoholism, politics, and bureaucracy: The consensus against controlled drinking therapy in America. *Addictive Behaviors*, 17, 49-62.

Pelham, W.E., Carlson, C., Sams, S.E., Vallano, G., Dixon, M.J., & Hoza, B. (1993). Separate and combined effects of methylphenidate and behavior modification with attention deficit-hyperactivity disorder in the classroom. *Journal of Consulting and Clinical Psychology*, 61, 506-515.

Pendery, M.L., Maltzman, I.M., & West, L.J. (1982). Controlled drinking by alcoholics? New findings and a reevaluation of a major affirmative study. *Science*, 217, 169-175.

Pennebaker, J.W., Kiecolt-Glaser, J. & Glaser, R. (1988). Disclosure of traumas and immune function: Health implications for psychotherapy. *Journal of Consulting and Clinical Psychology*, 56, 239-245.

Pennebaker, J.W. (1990). *Opening up: The healing power of confiding in others*. New York: Morrow.

Perilstein, R.D., Lipper, S., Friedman, L.J. (1991). Three cases of paraphilias responsive to fluoxetine treatment. *Journal of Clinical Psychiatry*, 52, 169-170.

Perls, F. (1969). *Gestalt therapy verbatim*. Lafayette, CA: Real People Press.

Perris, C. (1992). Bipolar-unipolar distinction. In E.S. Paykel (Ed.). *Handbook of affective disorders* (2nd edition). New York: Guilford. (pp. 57-75).

Perry, J.C. (1993). Longitudinal studies of personality disorders. *Journal of Personality Disorders*, supplement, 63-85.

Perry, J.C. (1990). Challenges in validating personality disorders: Beyond description. *Journal of Personality Disorders*, 4, 273-289.

Perry, C. & Laurence, J. (1984). Mental processing outside of awareness: The contributions of Freud and Janet. In K.S. Bowers & D. Meichenbaum (Eds.), *The unconscious reconsidered* (pp. 9-48). New York: Wiley.

Person, E.S., Terestman, N., Myers, W.A., Goldberg, E.L., & Salvadori, C. (1989). Gender differences in sexual behaviors and fantasies in a college population. *Journal of Sex and Marital Therapy*, 15, 187-198.

Persons, J.B. (1986). The advantages of studying psychological phenomena rather than psychiatric diagnoses. *American Psychologist*, 41, 1252-1260.

Peselow, E.D., Stanley, M., Filippi. A.M., Barouche, F., Goodnick, P., & Fieve, R.P. (1989). The predictive value of the dexamethasone suppression test. A placebo-controlled study. *British Journal of Psychiatry*, 155, 667-672.

Peterson, C. & Seligman, M.E.P. (1984). Causal explanations as a risk factor for depression: Theory and evidence. *Psychological Review*, 91, 347-374.

Pfohl, B., Coryell, W., Zimmerman, M., & Stangl, D. (1986). DSM-III personality disorders: Diagnostic overlap and internal consistency of individual DSM-III criteria. *Comprehensive Psychiatry*, 27, 21-34.

Phillips, K.A. (1991). Body dysmorphic disorder: The distress of imagined ugliness. *American Journal of Psychiatry*, 148, 1138-1149.

Phillips, E.L., Phillips, E.A., Wolf, M.M., & Fixsen, D.L. (1973). Achievement Place: Development of the elected manager system. *Journal of Applied Behavior Analysis*, 6, 541-561.

Pickens, R.W., Svikis, D.S., McGue, M., Lykken, D.T., Heston, L.L., & Clayton, P.J. (1991). Heterogeneity in the inheritance of alcoholism: A study of male and female twins. *Archives of General Psychiatry*, 48, 19-28.

Pisani, V.C., Fawcett, J., Clark, D.C., & McGuire, M. (1993). The relative contributions of medication adherence and AA meeting attendance to abstinent outcome for chronic alcoholics. *Journal of Studies on Alcohol*, 54, 115-119.

Pitman, R.K. (1984). Janet's obsessions and psychasthenia: A synopsis. *Psychiatric Quarterly*, 56, 291-314.

Pitman, R.K. (1987). Pierre Janet on obsessive-compulsive disorder (1903). Review and commentary. *Archives of General Psychiatry*, 44, 226-232.

Pitman, R.K., van der Kolk, B.A., Orr, S.P., & Greenberg, M. (1990). Naloxone-reversible analgesic response to combat-related stimuli in posttraumatic stress disorder. *Archives of General Psychiatry*, 47, 541-544.

Pitts, F.N., Jr., & McClure, J.N., Jr. (1967). Lactate metabolism in anxiety neurosis. *New England Journal of Medicine*, 277, 1329-1336.

Plomin, R. (1990). *Nature and nurture: An introduction to human behavioral genetics*. Pacific Grove, CA: Brooks/Cole.

Plomin, R., DeFries, J.C., & McClearn, G.E. (1990). *Behavioral genetics* (2nd Ed). New York: Freeman.

Plomin, R. (1990). The role of inheritance in behavior. *Science*, 248, 183-188.

Plomin, R. & Daniels, D. (1987). Why are children in the same family so different from one another? *Behavioral and Brain Sciences*, 10, 1-60

Pogue-Geile, M.F., & Harrow, M. (1984). Negative and positive symptoms in schizophrenia and depression: A follow-up. *Schizophrenia Bulletin*, 10, 371-387.

Pokony, A. (1983). Prediction of suicide in psychiatric patients: A prospective study. *Archives of General Psychiatry*, 40, 249-257.

Pollen, D.A. (1993). *Hannah's heirs: The quest for the genetic origins of Alzheimer's disease*. New York: Oxford University Press.

Pollitt, R.J. (1987). Amino acid disorders. In J.B. Holton (Ed.), *The inherited metabolic diseases*. Edinburgh: Churchill Livingstone. p. 96.

Poon, L.W., Kaszniak, A.W., & Dudley, W.N. (1992). Approaches in the experimental neuropsychology of dementia: A methodological and model review. In M. Bergener, K. Hasegawa, S.I. Finkel, and T. Nishimura (Eds.), *Aging and mental disorders: International perspectives*. New York: Springer.

Porrino, L.J., Rapoport, J.L., Behar, D., Sceery, W., Ismond, D.R., & Bunney, W.E. (1983). A naturalistic assessment of the motor activity of hyperactive boys I. Comparisons with normal controls. *Archives of General Psychiatry*, 40, 681-687.

Post, F. (1982). Affective disorders in old age. In E. S. Paykel (Ed.), *Handbook of affective disorders* (pp. 393-402). New York: Guilford.

Poulos, C.X., & Cappell, H. (1991). Homeostatic theory of drug tolerance: A general model of physiological adaptation. *Psychological Review*, 98, 390-408.

Power, C. (1979). The time-sample behavior checklist: Observational assessment of patient functioning. *Journal of Behavioral Assessment*, 1, 199-210.

Prescott, C.A., Hewitt, J.K., Heath, A.C., Truett, K.R., Neale, M.C., & Eaves, L.J. (1994a). Environmental and genetic influences on alcohol use in a volunteer sample of older twins. *Journal of Studies on Alcohol*, 55, 18-32.

Prescott, C.A., Hewitt, J.K., Truett, K.R., Heath, A.C., Neale, M.C., & Eaves, L.J. (1994b). Genetic and environmental influences on lifetime alcohol-related problems in a volunteer sample of older twins. *Journal of Studies on Alcohol*, 55, 184-202.

Prestige, B.R. & Lake, C.R. (1987). Prevalence and recognition of depression among primary care outpatients. *Journal of Family Practice*, 25, 67-72.

Prince, M. (1906). *The dissociation of a personality*. New York: Longmans, Green, & Co.

Prochaska, J.O. (1984). *Systems of psychotherapy: A transtheoretical analysis*. Homewood, IL: Dorsey.

Pruzinsky, T., & Borkovec, T.D. (1990). Cognitive and personality characteristics of worriers. *Behaviour Research and Therapy, 28*, 507-512.

Puig-Antich, J. (1986). Psychobiological markers: Effects of age and puberty. In M. Rutter, C. Izard, & P. Read (Eds.), *Depression in young people* (pp. 341-382). New York: Guilford.

Putnam, F.W., Curoff, J.J., et al. (1986). The clinical phenomenology of multiple personality disorder: Review of 100 recent cases. *Journal of Clinical Psychiatry, 47*, 285-293.

Quality Assurance Project. (1991). Treatment outlines for antisocial personality disorder. *Australian and New Zealand Journal of Psychiatry, 25*, 541-547.

Quay, H.C. (1965). Psychopathic personality as pathological stimulation-seeking. *American Journal of Psychiatry, 122*, 180-183.

Quevillon, R.P. (1993). Dyspareunia. In W. O'Donohue and J.H. Geer (Eds.). *Handbook of sexual dysfunctions: Assessment and treatment*. Boston: Allyn and Bacon. pp. 367-380.

Rachlin, H. (1992). Teleological behaviorism. *American Psychologist, 47*, 1371-1382.

Rachman, S. (1990). The determinants and treatment of simple phobias. *Advances in Behaviour Research and Therapy, 12*, 1-30.

Rachman, S.J., & Hodgson, R.J. (1980). *Obsessions and compulsions*. Englewood Cliffs, N.J.: Prentice-Hall.

Rachman, S., & deSilva, P. (1978). Abnormal and normal obsessions. *Behaviour Research and Therapy, 16*, 233-248.

Rachman, S. (1991). *Fear and courage* (2nd edition). San Francisco: Freeman.

Ramey, C.T. & Bryant, D. (1982). Evidence for primary prevention of developmental retardation. *Journal of the Division of Early Childhood, 5*, 73-78.

Rapee, R.M. (1991). Generalized anxiety disorder: A review of clinical features and theoretical concepts. *Clinical Psychology Review, 11*, 419-440.

Rapoport, J.L., Buchsbaum, M.S., Zahn, T.P., Weingartner, H., Ludlow, C., & Mikkelsen, E.J. (1978). Dextroamphetamine: Cognitive and behavioral effects in normal prepubertal boys. *Science, 199*, 560-563.

Raz, S., & Raz, N. (1990). Structural brain abnormalities in the major psychoses: A quantitative review of the evidence from computerized imaging. *Psychological Bulletin, 108*, 93-108.

Regier, D.A., Myers, J.K., Kramer, M., Robins, L.N., Blazer, D.G., Hough, R.L., Eaton, W.W., & Locke, B.Z. (1984). The NIMH Epidemiologic Catchment Area Program: Historical context, major objectives, and study population characteristics. *Archives of General Psychiatry, 41*, 934-941.

Reich, J., Yates, W., & Nduaguba, M. (1987). Prevalence of DSM-III personality disorders in the community. *Social Psychiatry and Psychiatric Epidemiology, 24*, 12-16.

Reich, J., & Thompson, W.D. (1987). DSM-III personality disorder clusters in three populations. *British Journal of Psychiatry, 150*, 471-475.

Reid, J.B. (Ed.). (1978). *A social learning approach to family intervention: Vol. 2. Observation in home settings*. Eugene, OR: Castalia.

Reiman, E.M., Raichle, M.E., Robins, E., Mintun, M.A., Fusselman, M.J., Fox, P.T., Price, J.L., & Hackman, K.A. (1989). Neuroanatomical correlates of a lactate-induced anxiety attack. *Archives of General Psychiatry, 46*, 493-500.

Reisman, J.M. (1990). *A history of clinical psychology* (2nd edition). New York: Hemisphere.

Reisner, R. & Slobogin, C. (1990). *Law and the mental health system* (2d.Ed.). St. Paul, MN: West.

Reiss, A.L., Feinstein, C., & Rosenbaum, K.N. (1986). Autism and genetic disorders. *Schizophrenia Bulletin, 12*, 724-738.

Rey, J.M., Stewart, G.W., Plapp, J.M. Bashir, M.R. et al. (1988). DSM-III Axis IV revisited. *American Journal of Psychiatry, 145*, 286-292.

Richters, J.E. (1993). Community violence and children's development: Toward a research agenda for the 1990s. *Psychiatry, 56*, 3-6.

Riecher, A., Maurer, K., Loffler, W., Fatkenheuer, B., an der Heiden, W., Munk-Jorgensen, P., Stromgren, E., & Hafner, H. (1991). Gender differences in age at onset and course of schizophrenic disorders. In H. Hafner and W.F. Gattaz (Eds.). *Search for the causes of schizophrenia, volume II*. Berlin: Springer-Verlag. pp. 14-33.

Ritvo, E.R., Freeman, B.J., Yuwiler, A., Geller, E., Yokota, A., Schroth, P., & Novak, P. (1984). Study of fenfluramine in outpatients with the syndrome of autism. *Journal of Pediatrics, 105*, 823-828.

Roberts, J. & Rowland, M. (1981). Hypertension in adults 25-74 years of age: United States, 1971-75 (Vital and Health Statistics Series 11, No 221); DHEW Publication No. PHS 81-1671). Washington: US Government Printing Office.

Robin, A.L., Koepke, T., & Nayar, M. (1986). Conceptualizing, assessing, and treating parent-adolescent conflict. In B.Lahey and A.Kazdin (Eds.), *Advances in Clinical Child Psychology, 9*, 87-124.

Robins, L.N. (1966). *Deviant children grown up: A sociological and psychiatric study of sociopathic personality*. Baltimore: Williams & Wilkins.

Robins, E., & Guze, S. (1989). Establishment of diagnostic validity in psychiatric illness. In L.N. Robins & J.E. Barrett (Eds.), *The validity of psychiatric diagnosis*. New York: Raven Press. pp. 177-197.

Robins, L.N., Helzer, J.E., Weissman, M.M., Orvaschel, H., Gruenberg, E., Burke, J.D., & Regier, D.A. (1984). Lifetime prevalence of specific psychiatric disorders in three sites. *Archives of General Psychiatry, 41*, 949-958.

Robins, L.N., Locke, B.Z., & Regier, D.A. (1991). An overview of psychiatric disorders in America. In L.N. Robins and D.A. Regier (Eds.), *Psychiatric disorders in America: The Epidemiologic Catchment Area Study*. New York: Free Press. pp. 328-366.

Robins, L.N., & McEvoy, L. (1992). Conduct problems as predictors of substance abuse. In C.P. O'Brien and J.J. Jaffe (Eds.) *Addictive states*. New York: Raven Press.

Robins, L.N., & Regier, D.A. (1991). *Psychiatric disorders in America: The Epidemiologic Catchment Area Study*. New York: Free Press.

Robins, L.N., Tipp, J., & Przybeck, T. (1991). Antisocial personality. In L.N. Robins, & D.A. Regier (Eds), *Psychiatric disorders in America: The epidemiologic catchment area study*. New York: Free Press. pp. 258-290.

Robinson, P. (1976). *The modernization of sex: Havelock Ellis, Alfred Kinsey, William Masters and Virginia Johnson*. New York: Harper and Row.

Roemer, L., & Borkovec, T.D. (1993). Worry: Unwanted cognitive activity that controls unwanted somatic experience. In D.M. Wegner and J.W. Pennebaker (Eds.), *Handbook of mental control*. Englewood Cliffs, NJ: Prentice-Hall.

Rogers, M.P. (1989). The interaction between brain, behavior, and immunity. In S. Cheren (Ed.), *Psychosomatic medicine: Theory, physiology, and practice* (Vol. 1, pp. 279-330). Madison, CT: International Universities Press.

Rogers, C.R. (1961). *On becoming a person: A therapist's view of psychotherapy*. Boston: Houghton Mifflin.

Rogers, C.R. (1951). *Client-centered therapy*. Boston: Houghton-Mifflin.

Rogers, R., Bloom, M., & Manson, S. (1984). Insanity defenses: Contested or conceded? *American Journal of Psychiatry, 141*, 885-888.

Rogers, C.R. (1957). The necessary and sufficient conditions of therapeutic personality change. *Journal of Consulting Psychology, 21*, 95-103.

Rohde, P., Lewinsohn, P., & Seeley, J. (1990). Are people changed by the experience of having an episode of depression? A further test of the scar hypothesis. *Journal of Abnormal Psychology, 99*, 264-271.

Roman, P.M., & Blum, T.C. (1987). Notes on the new epidemiology of alcoholism in the USA. *The Journal of Drug Issues, 17*, 321-332.

Roman, G.C., Tatemichi, T.K., Erkinjuntti, T., Cummings, J.L., Masdeu, J.C., Garcia, J.H., Amaducci, L., Orgogozo, J.M., Brun, A., Hofman, A. et al. (1993). Vascular dementia: Diagnostic criteria for research studies: Report of the NINDS-AIREN International Workshop. *Neurology, 43*, 250-260.

Rook, K.S. & Dooley, D. (1985). Applying social support research: Theoretical problems and future directions. *Journal of Social Issues, 41*, 5-28.

Room, R. (1987). Alcohol control, addiction and processes of change: Comment on "The limitations of control-of-supply models for explaining and preventing alcoholism and drug addiction." *Journal of Studies on Alcohol, 48*, 78-83.

Rosenberg, R. (1993). Drug treatment of panic disorder. *Psychopharmacology and Toxicology, 72*, 344-353.

Rosenthal, D., & Quinn, O.W. (1977). Quadruplet hallucinations: Phenotypic variations of a schizophrenic genotype. *Archives of General Psychiatry, 34*, 817-827.

Rosenthal, N.E., Sack, D.A., Gillin, J.C. et al (1984). Seasonal affective disorder: A description of the syndrome and preliminary findings with light therapy. *Archives of General Psychiatry, 41*, 72-80.

Rosenthal, D. (Ed.). (1963). *The Genain quadruplets*. New York: Basic Books.

Rosenthal, R. (1983). Assessing the statistical importance of the effects of psychotherapy. *Journal of Consulting and Clinical Psychology, 51*, 4-13.

Rosenthal, R. (1966). *Experimenter bias in behavioral research*. New York: Appleton-Century-Crofts.

Rosenthal, R. & Rosnow, R.L. (1969). *Artifact in behavioral science research*. New York: Academic Press.

Rosin, A.J., & Glatt, M.M. (1971). Alcohol excess in the elderly. *Quarterly Journal of Studies on Alcohol, 32*, 53-59.

Ross, H.E. (1989). Alcohol and drug abuse in treated alcoholics: A comparison of men and women. *Alcohol: Clinical and Experimental Research, 13*, 810-816.

Ross, D.M. & Ross, S.A. (1982). *Hyperactivity: Current issues, research, and theory*. New York: Wiley.

Ross, C.A., Norton, G.R., & Wozney, K. (1989). Multiple personality disorder: An analysis of 236 cases. *Canadian Journal of Psychiatry, 34*, 413-418.

Ross, C.A. (1991). Epidemiology of multiple personality disorder and dissociation. *Psychiatric Clinics of North America, 14*, 503-516.

Roth, M., & Argyle, N. (1988). Anxiety, panic, and phobic disorders: An overview. *Journal of Psychiatric Research, 22*, 33-54.

Roth, D. & Bean, J. (1986). New perspectives on homelessness: Findings from a statewide epidemiological study. *Hospital and Community Psychiatry, 37*, 712-723.

Rounsaville, B.J., Spitzer, R.L., & Williams, J.B.W. (1986). Proposed changes in DSM-III substance use disorders: Description and rationale. *American Journal of Psychiatry, 143*, 463-468.

Royal College of Psychiatrists. (1989). *The practical administration of electroconvulsive therapy (EDT)*. London: Gaskell.

Rubonis, A.V. & Bickman, L. (1991). Psychological impairment in the wake of disaster: The disaster-psychopathology relationship. *Psychological Bulletin*, 109, 384-399.

Rush, A.J. (1993). Clinical practice guidelines: Good news, bad news, or no news? *Archives of General Psychiatry*, 50, 483-490.

Rush, A.J., Beck, A.T., Kovacs, M., & Hollon, S.D. (1977). Comparative efficacy of cognitive therapy and pharmacotherapy in the treatment of depressed outpatients. *Cognitive Therapy and Research*, 1, 17-38.

Rush, A.J., Giles, D.E., Jarrett, R.B., Feldman-Koffler, F., Debus, J.R. Weissenburger, J. Orsulak, P.J., Roffwarg, H.P. (1989). Reduced REM latency predicts response to tricyclic medication in depressed outpatients. *Biological Psychiatry*, 26, 61-72.

Rush, B. (1943/1785). An inquiry into the effects of ardent spirits upon the human body and mind with an account of the means of preventing and of the remedies for curing them. Reprinted with an introduction by the editor, *Quarterly Journal of Studies on Alcohol*, 4, 321-341.

Russell, D.E.H. (1984). *Sexual exploitation: Rape, child sexual abuse, and workplace harassment*. Beverly Hills, CA: Sage.

Russell, D.E.H. (1983). The incidence and prevalence of intrafamilial and extrafamilial sexual abuse of female children. *Child Abuse and Neglect*, 7, 133-146.

Rutter, M. (1987). Temperament, personality, and personality disorder. *British Journal of Psychiatry*, 150, 443-458.

Rutter, M. & Garmezy, N. (1983). Developmental psychopathology. In E.M. Hetherington (Ed.), *Handbook of child psychology* (Vol. 4, pp. 775-912). New York: Wiley.

Rutter, M., Greenfield, D., & Lockyer, L. (1967). A five- to fifteen year follow-up study of infantile psychosis. II. Social and behavioral outcome. *British Journal of Psychiatry*, 113, 1187-1199.

Rutter, M.L. (1989). Isle of Wight revisited: Twenty-five years of child psychiatric epidemiology. *Journal of the American Academy of Child Psychiatry*, 28, 633-653.

Rutter, M., Shaffer, D., & Shepard, M. (1975). *A multiaxial classification of child psychiatric disorders. An evaluation and proposal*. Geneva: World Health Organization.

Rutter, M. & Rutter, M. (1993). *Developing minds*. New York: Basic Books.

Rutter, M. (1970). Autistic children: Infancy to adulthood. *Seminars in Psychiatry*, 2, 435-450.

Rutter, M.L. (1986). The developmental psychopathology of depression: Issues and perspectives. In M. Rutter, C. Izard, & P. Read (Eds.), *Depression in young people* (pp. 3-32). New York: Guilford.

Rutter, M.L. (1978b). Family, area and school influences in the genesis of conduct disorders. In L. Hersov, M. Berger, & D. Shaffer (Eds.), *Aggression and anti-social behavior in childhood and adolescence*. Oxford: Pergamon.

Rutter, M. (1978a). Diagnosis and definition of child autism. *Journal of Autism and Childhood Schizophrenia*, 8, 139-161.

Rutter, M.L. (1981). *Maternal deprivation reassessed* (2nd. Ed.). London: Penguin.

Rutter, M. (1983). Introduction: Concepts of brain dysfunction syndromes. In M. Rutter (Ed.), *Developmental neuropsychiatry* (pp. 1-14). New York: Guilford Press.

Ryland, D.H., & Kruesi, M.J.P. (1992). Suicide among adolescents. *International Review of Psychiatry*, 4, 117-129.

Sabshin, M. (1990). Turning points in twentieth-century American psychiatry. *American Journal of Psychiatry*, 147, 1267-1274.

Sackett, D. (1992). A primer on the precision and accuracy of the clinical examination. *Journal of the American Medical Association*, 267, 2638-2644.

Sackheim, H.A. (1989). Mechanisms of action. *Convulsive Therapy*, 6, 207-310.

Sacks, O. (1985). *The man who mistook his wife for a hat and other clinical tales*. New York: Summit books.

Sacks, O. (1993/1994). An anthropologist on Mars. *New Yorker*, Dec 27/Jan 3, pp. 107-124.

Safer, D.J. & Krager, J.M. (1988). A survey of medication treatment for hyperactive/inattentive students. *Journal of the American Medical Association*, 260, 2256-2258.

Sainsbury, P. (1982). Suicide: Epidemiology and relationship to depression. In J.K. Wing & L. Wing (Eds.), *Cambridge handbook of psychiatry: Psychoses of uncertain aetiology* (pp. 134-140). Cambridge University Press.

Salkovskis, P.M. & Harrison, J. (1984). Abnormal and normal obsessions—a replication. *Behaviour Research and Therapy*, 22, 549-552.

Sanders, S.A., Reinisch, J.M., & McWhirter, D.P. (1990). Homosexuality/heterosexuality: An overview. In D.P. McWhirter, S.A. Sanders, & J.M. Reinisch (Eds). *Homosexuality/heterosexuality: Concepts of sexual orientation*. New York: Oxford.

Sanderson, W.C., Rapee, R.M., & Barlow, D.H. (1989). The influence of an illusion of control on panic attacks induced via inhalation of 5.5% carbon dioxide-enriched air. *Archives of General Psychiatry*, 46, 157-162.

Sapolsky, R.M. (1992). Neuroendocrinology of the stress response. In J.B. Becker, S.M. Breedlove, & D. Crews (Eds.), *Behavioral endocrinology* (pp. 288-324). Cambridge, MA: MIT Press.

Sargent, T.O. (1988). Fetishism. *Journal of Social Work and Human Sexuality*, 7, 27-42.

Sartorius, N., Jablensky, A., Lorton, A., Ernberg, G., Anker, M., Cooper, J. E., & Day, R. (1986). Early manifestations and first-contact incidence of schizophrenia in different cultures. *Psychological Medicine*, 16, 909-928.

Sartorius, N., Kaelber, C.T., Cooper, J.E., Roper, M.T., Rae, D.S., Gulbinat, W., Ustun, B, & Regier, D.A. (1993). Progress toward achieving a common language in psychiatry: Results from the field trial of the clinical guidelines accompanying the WHO classification of mental and behavioral disorders in ICD-10. *Archives of General Psychiatry*, 50, 115-124.

Sartory, G. (1989). Obsessional-compulsive disorder. In G. Turpin (Ed.), *Handbook of clinical psychophysiology*. New York: Wiley. pp. 329-356.

Sato, M. (1992). A lasting vulnerability to psychosis in patients with previous methamphetamine psychosis. In P.W. Kalivas and H.H. Samson (Eds). *Neurobiology of drug and alcohol addiction. Annals of the New York Academy of Sciences*. Vo. 654. pp. 160-170.

Satterfield, S.B. (1988). Transsexualism. *Journal of Social Work and Human Sexuality*, 7, 77-87.

Sayer, N.A., Sackeim, H.A., Moeller, J.R., Prudic, J., Devanand, D.P., Coleman, E.A., & Kiersky, J.E. (1993). The relations between observer-rating and self-report of depressive symptomatology. *Psychological Assessment*, 5, 350-360.

Sayette, M.A. (1993). An appraisal-disruption model of alcohol's effects on stress responses in social drinkers. *Psychological Bulletin*, 114, 459-476.

Scarone, S., Gambini, O. Hafele, E., Bellodi, L., & Smeraldi, E. (1987). Neurofunctional assessment of schizophrenia: A preliminary investigation of the presence of eye-tracking (SPEMs) and qual-ity extinction test (QET) abnormalities in a sample of schizophrenic patients. *Biological Psychology*, 24, 253-259.

Scarr, S. & McCartney, K. (1983). How people make their own environments: A theory of genotype-environment effects. *Child Development*, 54, 424-435.

Scarr, S. (1966). Genetic factors in activity motivation. *Child development*, 37, 663-673.

Scarr, S. (1992). Developmental theories for the 1990s: Development and individual differences. *Child Development*, 63, 1-19.

Schacht, T., & Nathan, P. (1977). But is it good for psychologists? Appraisal and status of DSM-III. *American Psychologist*, 32, 1017-1025.

Schacht, T.E. (1985). DSM-III and the politics of truth. *American Psychologist*, 40, 513-521.

Scheff, T.J. (1966). *Being mentally ill: A sociological theory*. Chicago: Aldine.

Scheff, T.J. (1984). *Being mentally ill: A sociological theory*. 2nd edition. Chicago: Aldine.

Schellenberg, G.D., Payami, H., Wijsman, E.M., Orr, H.T., Goddard, K.A.B., Anderson, L., Nemens, E., White, J.A., Alonso, M.E., Ball, M.J., Kaye, J., Morris, J.C., Chui, H., Sadovnick, A.D., Heston, L.L., Martin, G.M., & Bird, T.D. (1993). Chromosome 14 and late-onset familial Alzheimer disease (FAD). *American Journal of Human Genetics*, 53, 619-628.

Schiff, M., Duyme, M., Dumaret, A., & Tomkiewicz, S. (1982), How much could we boost scholastic achievement and IQ scores? A direct answer from a French adoption study. *Cognition*, 12, 165-196.

Schneider, K. (1959). *Clinical psychopathology* (M. W. Hamilton, Trans.). New York: Grune & Stratton.

Schneiderman, N., Chesney, M.A., & Krantz, D.S. (1989). Biobehavioral aspects of cardiovascular disease: Progress and prospects. *Health Psychology*, 8, 649-676.

Schneller, J. (1988). Terror on the A-train: Anatomy of a panic attack. *Mademoiselle*, 94, 148-159.

Schopler, E.M., Andrews, C.E. & Strupp, K. (1979). Do autistic children come from upper-middle-class parents? *Journal of Autism and Developmental Disorders*, 9, 139-152.

Schotti, J.R., Evans, I.M., Meyer, L.H., & Walker, P. (1991). A meta-analysis of intervention research with problem behavior: Treatment validity and standards of practice. *American Journal on Mental Retardation*, 96, 233-256.

Schreibman, L. (1988). *Autism*. Beverly Hills: Sage.

Schreiner-Engel, P., & Schiavi, R.C. (1986). Lifetime psychopathology in individuals with low sexual desire. *Journal of Nervous and Mental Disease*, 174, 646-651.

Schuckit, M.A. (1994). A clinical model of genetic influences in alcohol dependence. *Journal of Studies on Alcohol*, 55, 5-17.

Schuckit, M.A. (1987). Biological vulnerability to alcoholism. *Journal of Consulting and Clinical Psychology*, 55, 301-309.

Schuckit, M.A. (1989). *Drug and alcohol abuse: A clinical guide to diagnosis and treatment* (3rd edition). New York: Plenum.

Schuyler, D. (1991). *A practical guide to cognitive therapy*. New York: Norton.

Schwartz, G.E. (1989). Dysregulation Theory and disease: Toward a general model for psychosomatic medicine. In S. Cheren (Ed.), *Psychosomatic medicine: Theory, physiology, and practice* (Vol. 1, pp. 91-118). Madison, CT: International Universities Press.

Schwartz, G.E. (1982). Testing the biopsychosocial model: The ultimate challenge facing behavioral medicine. *Journal of Consulting and Clinical Psychology*, 50, 1040-1053.

Scurfield, R.M. (1985). Posttrauma stress assessment and treatment: Overview and formulations. In C.R. Figley (Ed.), *Trauma and its wake* (pp. 219-259). New York: Brunner/Mazel.

Searles, J.S. (1990). Methodological limitations of research on the genetics of alcoholism. In C.R. Cloninger & H. Begleiter (Eds.). *Genetics and biology of alcoholism*. Cold Spring Harbor: Cold Spring Harbor Laboratory Press. pp. 89-100.

Searles, J.S. (1988). The role of genetics in the pathogenesis of alcoholism. *Journal of Abnormal Psychology*, 97, 153-167.

Sedgwick, P. (1981). Illness—mental and otherwise. In A.L. Caplan, H.T. Engelhardt, Jr., & J.J. McCartney (Eds.). *Concepts of health and disease: Interdisciplinary perspectives* (pp. 119-129).

Segal, Z.V., & Dobson, K.S. (1992). Cognitive models of depression: Report from a consensus development conference. *Psychological Inquiry*, 3, 219-224.

Segraves, R.T., & Segraves, K.B. (1990). Categorical and multi-axial diagnosis of male erectile disorder. *Journal of Sex and Marital Therapy*, 16, 208-213.

Segraves, R.T. (1988). Psychiatric drugs and inhibited female orgasm. *Journal of Sex and Marital Therapy*, 14, 202-206.

Seidman, L.J. (1983). Schizophrenia and brain dysfunction: An integration of recent neurodiagnostic findings. *Psychological Bulletin*, 94, 195-238.

Select Committee on Children, Youth, and Families (SCCYF) of the United States House of Representatives, (1989). *U.S. children and their families: Current conditions and recent trends.* Washington: Government Printing Office.

Selfe, L. (1977). *Nadia: A case of extraordinary drawing ability in an autistic child*. London: Academic Press.

Seligman, M.E.P. (1971). Phobias and preparedness. *Behavior Therapy*, 2, 307-320.

Seligman, M.E.P. (1975). *Helplessness: On depression, development, and death*. San Francisco: Freeman.

Seligman, M.E.P. (1974). Depression and learned helplessness. In R.J. Friedman & M.M. Katz (Eds.). *The psychology of depression: Contemporary theory and research* (pp.83-113). NY: Winston-Wiley.

Selye, H. (1936). A syndrome produced by diverse nocuous agents. *Nature*, 13, 32.

Selye, H. (1956). *The stress of life*. New York: McGraw-Hill.

Serbin, L.A., & Sprafkin, C.H. (1987). A developmental approach: Sexuality from infancy through adolescence. In J.H. Geer and W.T. O'Donohue (Eds.). *Theories of human sexuality*. New York: Plenum. pp. 163-196.

Shalev, A. & Munitz, H. (1986). Conversion without hysteria: A case report and review of the literature. *British Journal of Psychiatry*, 148, 198-203.

Shapiro, A.K. & Morris, L.A. (1978). The placebo effect in medical and psychological therapies. In S.L. Garfield & A.E. Bergin (Eds.), *Handbook of psychotherapy and behavior change* (2nd. Ed., pp.369-410). New York: Wiley.

Shapiro, D.A. & Shapiro, D. (1982). Meta-analysis of comparative therapy outcome studies: A replication and refinement. *Psychological Bulletin*, 92, 581-604.

Sharif, Z., Gewirtz, G., & Iqbal, N. (1993). Brain imaging in schizophrenia: A review. *Psychiatric Annals*, 23, 123-134.

Shea, M.T. (1993). Psychosocial treatment of personality disorders. *Journal of Personality Disorders*, supplement, 167-180.

Shea, M.T. (1991). Standardized approaches to individual psychotherapy of patients with borderline personality disorder. *Hospital and Community Psychiatry*, 42, 1034-1038.

Shearer, D.E. & Shearer, M.S. (1976). The Portage Project: A model for early childhood intervention. In T.D. Tjossem (Ed.), *Intervention strategies for high risk infants and young children*. Baltimore: University Park Press.

Shedler, J., Mayman, M., & Manis, M. (1993). The illusion of mental health. *American Psychologist*, 48, 1117-1131.

Shenton, M.E., Kikinis, R., Jolesz, F.A., Pollak, S.D. et al. (1992). Abnormalities of the left temporal lobe and thought disorder in schizophrenia: A quantitative magnetic resonance imaging study. *New England Journal of Medicine*, 327, 604-612.

Sher, K.J. (1991). *Children of alcoholics: A critical appraisal of theory and research*. Chicago: University of Chicago Press.

Sherman, J., Factor, D.C., Swinson, R., & Darjes, R.W. (1989). The effects of fenfluramine (hydrochloride) on the behaviors of fifteen autistic children. *Journal of Autism and Developmental Disorders*, 19, 533-543.

Sherrington, R., Brynjolfsson, J., Petursson, H., Potter, M., Dudleston, K., Barraclough, B., Wasmuth, J., Cobbs, M., & Gurling, H. (1988). Localization of a susceptibility locus for schizophrenia on chromosome 5. *Nature*, 336, 164-170.

Shneidman, E.S, (1986). Some essentials of suicide and some implications for response. In A. Roy (Ed.), *Suicide*. Baltimore: Williams & Wilkins.

Shontz, F.C., & Green, P. (1992). Trends in research on the Rorschach: Review and recommendations. *Applied and Preventive Psychology*, 1, 149-156.

Short, A.B. & Schopler, E. (1988). Factors relating to age of onset in autism. *Journal of Autism and Developmental Disorders*, 18, 207-216.

Shorter, E. (1992). *From paralysis to fatigue: A history of psychosomatic illness in the modern era*. New York: Free Press.

Shoulson, I. (1990). Huntington's disease: Cognitive and psychiatric features. *Neuropsychiatry, Neuropsychology, and Behavioral Neurology*, 3, 15-22.

Shover, L.R., Friedman, J.M., Weiler, S.J., Heiman, J.R., & LoPiccolo, J. (1982). Multiaxial problem-oriented system for sexual dysfunctions. *Archives of General Psychiatry*, 39, 614-619.

Shrout, P.E., Link, B.G., Dohrenwend, B.P. Skodal, A.E., Stueve, A., & Mirttznik, J. (1989). Characterizing life events as risk factors for depression: The role of fateful loss events. *Journal of Abnormal Psychology*, 98, 460-467.

Siegel, J.M. & Kuykendall, D.H. (1990). Loss, widowhood, and psychological distress among the elderly. *Journal of Consulting and Clinical Psychology*, 58, 519-524.

Siegel, S., Hinson, R.E., Krank, M.D., & McCully, J. (1982). Heroin "overdose" death: The contribution of drug-associated environmental cues. *Science*, 216, 436-437.

Siegel, S. (1988). Drug anticipation and drug tolerance. In M. Lader (Ed.). *The psychopharmacology of addiction*.

Siever, L.J., Coursey, R.D., Alterman, I.S., Zahn, T. et al. (1989). Clinical, psychophysiological, and neurological characteristics of volunteers with impaired smooth pursuit eye movements. *Biological Psychiatry*, 26, 35-51.

Siever, L.J., & Klar, H. (1986). A review of DSM-III criteria for the Personality Disorders. *Annual Review of Psychiatry*, 5, 279-XXX.

Siever, L.J., & Davis, K.L. (1985). Overview: Toward a dysregulation hypothesis of depression. *American Journal of Psychiatry*, 142, 1017-1031.

Siever, L.J., Bernstein, D.P., & Silverman, J.M. (1991). Schizotypal personality disorder: A review of its current status. *Journal of Personality Disorders*, 5, 178-193.

Sifneos, P.E. (1987). *Short-term dynamic psychotherapy: Evaluation and technique*. New York: Plenum.

Signorielli, N. (1989). The stigma of mental illness on television. *Journal of Broadcasting and electronic media*, 33, 325-331.

Silove, D., Manicavasagar, V., O'Connell, D., & Blaszczynski, A. (1993). Reported early separation anxiety symptoms in patients with panic and generalized anxiety disorders. *Australian and New Zealand Journal of Psychiatry*, 27, 489-494.

Silverstone, T. (1992). New aspects in the treatment of depression. *International Clinical Psychopharmacology*, 6 (Suppl. 5), 41-44.

Simonoff, E., McGuffin, P., & Gottesman, I.I. (1994). Genetic influences on normal and abnormal development. In M. Rutter, E. Taylor, & L. Hersov (Eds.), *Child and adolescent psychiatry* (3rd. Ed.). London: Blackwell Scientific.

Simons, A.D., Garfield, S.L., & Murphy, G.E. (1984). The process of change in cognitive therapy and pharmacotherapy for depression. *Archives of General Psychiatry*, 41, 45-51.

Singer, M.T., & Wynne, L.C. (1965). Thought disorder and family relations of schizophrenics: IV. Results and implications. *Archives of General Psychiatry*, 12, 201-212.

Singer, J.L. (Ed.), (1990). *Repression and dissociation*. Chicago: University of Chicago Press.

Singh, N.N., Guernsey, T.F., & Ellis, C.R. (1992). Drug therapy for persons with developmental disabilities: Legislation and litigation. *Clinical Psychology Review*, 12, 665-679.

Sizemore, C.C. & Pittillo, E.S. (1977). I'm Eve!. New York: Doubleday.

Sizemore, C.C. (1989). *A mind of her own*. New York: William Morrow.

Skinner, B.F. (1953). *Science and human behavior*. New York: Macmillan.

Skodol, A.E., Dohrenwend, B.P., Link, B.G., & Shrout, P.E. (1990). The nature of stress: Problems of measurement. In J.D. Noshpit, & K.D. Coddington (Eds.), *Stressors and the adjustment disorders* (pp. 3-20). New York: Wiley.

Slaby, A.E., & Martin, S.D. (1991). Drug and alcohol emergencies. In N.S. Miller (Ed.) *Comprehensive handbook of drug and alcohol addiction*. New York: Dekker. pp. 1003-1030.

Slade, P.D., & Bentall, R.P. (1988). *Sensory deception: A scientific analysis of hallucination*. Baltimore: Johns Hopkins University Press.

Slater, E. (1965). Diagnosis of hysteria. *British Medical Journal*, 1, 1395-1399.

Slawson, G. & Guggenheim, H. (1984). Psychiatric malpractice: A review of the national loss experience. *American Journal of Psychiatry*, 141, 979-981.

Sleator, E.K. & Ullmann, R.K. (1981). Can the physician diagnose hyperactivity in the office? *Pediatrics*, 67, 13-17.

Sloane, R.B., Staples, F.R., Cristo, A.H., Yorkston, N.J., & Whipple, K. (1975). *Psychotherapy versus behavior therapy*. Cambridge, MA: Harvard University Press.

Sloman, L., Gardner, R., & Price, J. (1989). Biology of family systems and mood disorders. *Family Process*, 28, 387-398.

Smalley, S.L., Asarnow, R.F., & Spence, M.A. (1988). Autism and genetics: A decade of research. *Archives of General Psychiatry*, 45, 953-961.

Smart, R.G., & Mann, R.E. (1993). Recent liver cirrhosis declines: Estimates of the impact of alcohol abuse treatment and alcoholics anonymous. *Addiction*, 88, 193-198.

Smetana, J.G. (1989). Adolescents' and parents' reasoning about actually family conflict. *Child Development*, 60, 1052-1067.

Smith, A.L., & Weissman, M.M. (1992). Epidemiology. In E. S. Paykel (Ed.), *Handbook of affective disorders* (2nd edition). New York: Guilford. (pp. 111-130).

Smith, G. & Hall, M. (1982). Evaluating Michigan's guilty but mentally ill verdict: An empirical study. *University of Michigan Journal of Law Reform, 16*, 77-114.

Smith, G.N., Iacono, W.G., Moreau, M., Tallman, K., Beiser, M., & Flak, B. (1988). Choice of comparison group and findings of computerized tomography in schizophrenia. *British Journal of Psychiatry, 153*, 667-674.

Smith, M.L., Glass, G.V., & Miller, T.I. (1980). *The benefits of psychotherapy*. Baltimore: John Hopkins University Press.

Smith, S.R. & Meyer, R.G. (1985). Child abuse reporting laws and psychotherapy: A time for reconsideration. *International Journal of Law and Psychiatry, 7*, 351-366.

Snowdon, D., Ostwald, S., & Kane, R. (1989). Education, survival, and independence in elderly catholic sisters, 1936-1988. *American Journal of Epidemiology, 130*, 999-1012.

Sobell, L.C., Sobell, M.B., Toneatto, T., & Leo, G.I. (1993). What triggers the resolution of alcohol problems without treatment? *Alcoholism: Clinical and Experimental Research, 17*, 217-224.

Sobell, M.B., & Sobell, L.C. (1989). Moratorium on Maltzman: An appeal to reason. *Journal of Studies on Alcohol, 50*, 473-480.

Sobell, M.B., & Sobell, L.C. (1976). Second year treatment outcome of alcoholics treated by individualized behavior therapy: Results. *Behaviour Research and Therapy, 11*, 195-215.

Sobell, M.B., & Sobell, L.C. (1973). Alcoholics treated by individualized behavior therapy: One year treatment outcomes. *Behaviour Research and Therapy, 11*, 599-618.

Solomon, K., Manepalli, J., Ireland, G.A., & Mahon, G.M. (1993). Alcoholism and prescription drug abuse in the elderly: St. Louis University grand rounds. *Journal of the American Geriatrics Society, 41*, 57-69.

Solstad, K., & Hertoft, P. (1993). Frequency of sexual problems and sexual dysfunction in middle-aged Danish men. *Archives of Sexual Behavior, 22*, 51-58.

Sorensen, D.J., Paul, G.L., & Mariotto, M.J. (1988). Inconsistencies in paranoid functioning, premorbid adjustment, and chronicity: Question of diagnostic criteria. *Schizophrenia Bulletin, 14*, 323-336.

Spanos, N.P., Weekes, J.R., Menary, E., & Bertrand, L.D. (1986). Hypnotic interview and age regression procedures in the elicitation of multiple personality symptoms: A simulation study. *Psychiatry, 49*, 298-311.

Spanos, N.P., Weekes, J.R., & Betrand, L.D. (1985). Multiple personality: A social psychological perspective. *Journal of Abnormal Psychology, 94*, 362-376.

Spanos, N.P. (1986). Hypnotic behavior: A social-psychological interpretation of amnesia, analgesia, and "trance logic". *Behavioral and Brain Sciences, 9*, 449-467.

Spaulding, W. (1986). Assessment of adult-onset pervasive behavior disorders. In A.R. Ciminero, K.S. Calhoun, and H.E. Adams (Eds.), *Handbook of behavioral assessment* (2nd edition). New York: Wiley. pp. 631-669.

Spector, I.P., & Carey, M.P. (1990). Incidence and prevalence of the sexual dysfunctions: A critical review of the empirical literature. *Archives of Sexual Behavior, 19*, 389-408.

Spiegel, D. & Cardena, E. (1991). Disintegrated experience: The dissociative disorders revisited. *Journal of Abnormal Psychology, 100*, 366-378.

Spirito, A., Brown, L., Overholser, J., & Fritz, G. (1989). Attempted suicide in adolescence: A review and critique of the literature. *Clinical Psychology Review, 9*, 335-363.

Spitz, R.A. (1946). Anaclitic depression. *Psychoanalytic study of the child, 2*, 53-74.

Spitzer, R.L., Foreman, J., & Nee, J. (1979). DSM-III field trials: I. Initial interrater diagnostic reliability. *American Journal of Psychiatry, 136*, 815-817.

Spitzer, R.L. (1985). DSM-III and the politics-science dichotomy syndrome. *American Psychologist, 40*, 522-526.

Spitzer, R.L., First, M.B., Williams, J.B.W., Kendler, K., Pincus, H.A., & Tucker, G. (1992). Now is the time to retire the term "organic mental disorders." *American Journal of Psychiatry, 149*, 240-244.

Spitzer, R.L, & Fleiss, J.L. (1974). A re-analysis of the reliability of psychiatric diagnosis. *British Journal of Psychiatry, 125*, 341-347.

Spivack, G. & Shure, M.B. (1974). *Social adjustment of young children: A cognitive approach to solving real-life problems*. Washington: Jossey-Bass.

Squire, L.R. (1992). Memory and the hippocampus: A synthesis from findings with rats, monkeys, and humans. *Psychological Review, 99*, 195-231.

Squires-Wheeler, E., Skodol, A., Bassett, A., & Erlenmeyer-Kimling, L. (1989). DSM-III-R schizotypal personality traits in offspring of schizophrenic disorder, affective disorder, and normal control parents. *Journal of Psychiatric Research, 23*, 229-239.

Sroufe, L.A. (1983). Infant-caregiver attachment and patterns of adaptation in the preschool: The roots of maladaptation and competence. In M. Perlmutter (Ed), *Minnesota Symposium in Child Psychology, 16*, 41-83.

Sroufe, L.A. & Fleeson, J. (1986). Attachment and the construction of relationships. In W.W. Hartup & Z. Rubin (Eds.), *Relationships and development* (pp. 51-72). Hillsdale, NJ: Erlbaum.

Stacey, A.W., Widaman, K.F., & Marlatt, G.A. (1990). Expectancy models of alcohol use. *Journal of Personality and Social Psychology, 58*, 918-928.

Stacy A.W., Newcomb, M.D., & Bentler, P.W. (1991). Cognitive motivation and drug use: A 9-year longitudinal study. *Journal of Abnormal Psychology, 100*, 502-515.

Stahl, S.M., & Wets, K.M. (1988). Clinical pharmacology of schizophrenia. In P. Bebbington & P. McGuffin (Eds.), *Schizophrenia: The major issues*. Oxford: Heineman. pp. 135-157.

Starr, P. (1982). *The social transformation of American medicine*. New York: Basic.

Steadman, H., Pantle, R., & Pasewark, S. (1983). Factors associated with a successful insanity defense. *American Journal of Psychiatry, 140*, 401-405.

Steele, C.M., & Josephs, R.A. (1990). Alcohol myopia: Its prized and dangerous effects. *American Psychologist, 45*, 921-933.

Steele, C.M., & Josephs, R.A. (1988). Drinking your troubles away II: An attention-allocation model of alcohol's effect on psychological stress. *Journal of Abnormal Psychology, 97*, 196-205.

Steffenburg, S., Gillberg, C., Hellgren, L., Andersson, L., Gillberg, I., Jakobsson, G., & Bohman, M. (1989). A twin study of autism in Denmark, Finland, Iceland, Norway and Sweden. *Journal of Child Psychology and Psychiatry, 30*, 405-416.

Steketee, F., & Foa, E.B. (1985). Obsessive-compulsive disorder. In D.H. Barlow (Ed.), *Clinical handbook of psychological disorders*. New York: Guilford. pp. 69-144.

Stiles, W.B., Shapiro, D.A., & Elliott, R. (1986). Are all psychotherapies equivalent? *American Psychologist, 41*, 165-180.

Still, G.F. (1902). The Coulstonian Lectures on some abnormal physical conditions in children. *Lancet, 1*, 1008-1012, 1077-1082, 1163-1168.

Stokes, P. (1993). Fluoxetine: A five-year review. *Clinical Therapeutics, 15*, 216-243.

Stokols, D. (1992). Establishing and maintaining healthy environments: Toward a social ecology of health promotion. *American Psychologist, 47*, 6-22.

Stoller, R.J. (1991). *Pain and passion: A psychoanalyst explores the world of S & M*. New York: Plenum.

Stoller, R.J. (1975). *Perversion: The erotic form of hatred*. New York: Random House.

Stone, M.H. (1993). Long-term outcome in personality disorders. *British Journal of Psychiatry, 162*, 299-313.

Stone, M. (1985). Schizotypal personality: Psychotherapeutic aspects. *Schizophrenia Bulletin, 11*, 576-589.

Strauss, M.E. (1993). Relations of symptoms to cognitive deficits in schizophrenia. *Schizophrenia Bulletin, 19*, 215-231.

Strauss, J.S., Carpenter, W.T., & Bartko, J.J. (1974). Schizophrenic signs and symptoms. *Schizophrenia Bulletin, 2*, 61-69.

Strauss, J.S., & Carpenter, W.T., Jr. (1981). *Schizophrenia*. New York: Plenum.

Strauss, J.S. (1969). Hallucinations and delusions as points on continua function: Rating scale evidence. *Archives of General Psychiatry, 21*, 581-586.

Strauss, J.S., & Carpenter, W.T. (1978). The prognosis of schizophrenia: Rationale for a multidimensional concept. *Schizophrenia Bulletin, 4*, 56-67.

Stricker, G. & Healey, B.J. (1990). Projective assessment of object relations: A review of the empirical evidence. *Psychological Assessment, 2*, 219-230.

Strober, M. (1991). Family-genetic studies of eating disorders. *Journal of Clinical Psychiatry, 52* (suppl), 9-12.

Strong, S.R. (1978). Social psychological approach to psychotherapy research. In S.L. Garfield & A.E. Bergin (Eds.), *Handbook of psychotherapy and behavior change* (2nd. Ed., pp.101-136). New York: Wiley.

Strupp, H.H. (1986). Psychotherapy: Research, practice, and public policy (how to avoid dead ends). *American Psychologist, 41*, 120-130.

Strupp, H.H. (1971). *Psychotherapy and the modification of abnormal behavior*. New York: McGraw-Hill.

Stuart, F.M., Hammond, D.C., & Pett, M.A. (1987). Inhibited sexual desire in women. *Archives of Sexual Behavior, 16*, 91-106.

Styron, W. (1990). *Darkness visible: A memoir of madness*. New York: Vintage Books.

Suomi, S.J. (1983). Social development in rhesus monkey: Considerations of individual differences. In A. Oliverio & M. Zappella (Eds.), *The behavior of human infants*. New York: Plenum.

Suomi, S.J. & Harlow, H.F. (1972). Social rehabilitation of isolate-reared monkeys. *Developmental Psychology, 6*, 487-496.

Sussman, N., & Chou, J.C.Y. (1988). Current issues in benzodiazepine use for anxiety disorders. *Psychiatric Annals, 18*, 139-145.

Swanson, J., Holzer, C., Ganju, V., & Jono, R. (1990). Violence and psychiatric disorder in the community: Evidence from the Epidemiologic Catchment Area Surveys. *Hospital and Community Psychiatry, 41*, 761-770.

Swartz, M.S., Hughes, D., Blazer, D.G., & George, L.K. (1987). Somatization disorder in the community: A study of diagnostic concordance among three diagnostic systems. *Journal of Nervous and Mental Disorder, 175*, 26-33.

Swinson, R.P., & Kuch, K. (1990). Clinical features of panic and related disorders. In J.C. Ballenger (Ed.), *Clinical aspects of panic disorder*. New York: Wiley.

Szasz, T. (1960). The myth of mental illness. *American Psychologist*, 15, 113-118.

Szasz, T. (1971). *Psychiatric justice*. New York: Collier Books.

Szasz, T. (1963). *Law, liberty, and psychiatry: An inquiry into the social uses of mental health practices*. New York: Macmillan.

Szasz, T. (1970). *Ideology and insanity: Essays on the psychiatric dehumanization of man*. New York: Doubleday.

Tanfer, K. (1993). National survey of men: Design and Execution. *Family Planning Perspectives*, 25, 83-86.

Tarter, R.E., Alterman, A.I., & Edwards, K.L. (1985). Vulnerability to alcoholism in men: A behavior-genetic perspective. *Journal of Studies on Alcohol*, 46, 329-356.

Taylor, S.E. (1990). Health psychology: The science and the field. *American Psychologist*, 45, 40-50.

Tearnan, B.H., & Telch, M.J. (1988). Etiology of agoraphobia: An investigation of perceived childhood and parental factors. *Phobia Practice and Research Journal*, 1, 13-24.

Teicher, M.H., Glod, C., & Cole, J.O. (1990). Emergence of intense suicidal preoccupation during fluoxetine treatment. *American Journal of Psychiatry*, 147, 207-210.

Telch,, M.J., Brouillard, M., Telch, C.F., Agras, W.S., & Taylor, C.B. (1989). Role of cognitive appraisal in panic-related avoidance. *Behaviour Research and Therapy*, 27, 373-383.

Tellegen, A. (1985). Structures of mood and personality and their relevance to assessing anxiety, with an emphasis on self-report. In A.H. Tuma, & J.D. Maser (Eds.), *Anxiety and the anxiety disorders*. Hillsdale, NJ: Erlbaum. pp. 681-706.

Tennant, C., Bebbington, P. & Hurry, J. (1980). Parental death in childhood and risk of adult depressive disorders: A review. *Psychological Medicine*, 10, 289-299.

Teplin, L. (1990). The prevalence of severe mental disorder among male urban jail detainees: Comparison with the Epidemiologic Catchment Area Program. *American Journal of Public Health*, 80, 663-669.

Teri, L., & Gallagher-Thompson, D. (1991). Cognitive-behavioral interventions for treatment of depression in Alzheimer's patients. *Gerontologist*, 31, 413-416.

Teri, L., & Wagner, A. (1992). Alzheimer's disease and depression. *Journal of Consulting and Clinical Psychology*, 60, 379-391.

Terman, M., Terman, J.S., Quitkin, F.M. et al. (1989). Light therapy for seasonal affective disorder: A review of efficacy. *Neuropsychopharmacology*, 2, 1-22.

Test, M.A., Knoedler, W.H., Allness, D.J.,, Burke, S.S., Brown, R.L., & Wallisch, L.S. (1991). Long-term community treatment through an assertive continuous treatment team. In C.A. Tamminga, & S.C. Schulz (eds.). *Schizophrenia research: Advances in neuropsychiatry and psychopharmacology*. New York: Raven Press. pp. 239-246.

Thase, M.E. (1989). Comparison between seasonal affective and other forms of recurrent depression. In N.E. Rosenthal et al (Eds.) *Seasonal affective disorders and phototherapy*. New York: Guilford. pp. 64-78.

Thase, M. (1988). The relationship between Down syndrome and Alzheimer's disease. In L. Nadel (Ed.), *The psychobiology of down Syndrome*. Cambridge, MA: MIT Press.

Thigpen, C.H. & Cleckley, H.M. (1957). *The three faces of Eve*. New York: McGraw-Hill

Thomas, A. & Chess, S. (1977). *Temperament and development*. New York: Brunner/Mazel.

Thompson, T. (1993). The wizard of Prozac: A pilgrimage to the center of a medical debate. *Washington Post*, November 21, F1-F5.

Thoresen, C.E. & Powell, L.H. (1992). Type A behavior pattern: New perspectives on theory, assessment, and intervention. *Journal of Consulting and Clinical Psychology*, 60, 595-604.

Thorley, G. (1984). Review of follow-up and follow-back studies of childhood hyperactivity. *Psychological Bulletin*, 96, 116-132.

Ticehurst, S. (1990). Alcohol and the elderly. *Australian and New Zealand Journal of Psychiatry*, 24, 252-260.

Tiefer, L. (1988). A feminist critique of the sexual dysfunction nomenclature. *Women and Therapy*, 7, 5-21.

Tienari, P. (1991). Interaction between genetic vulnerability and family environment: The Finnish adoptive family study of schizophrenia. *Acta Psychiatrica Scandinavica*, 84, 460-465.

Tienari, P. Sorri, A., Lahti, I. et al. (1987). Genetic and psychosocial factors in schizophrenia: the Finnish adoptive family study. *Schizophrenia Bulletin*, 13, 477-484.

Tiffany, S.T., & Baker, T.B. (1986). Tolerance to alcohol: Psychological models and their application to alcoholism. *Annals of Behavioral Medicine*, 8, 7-12.

Tollefson, G.D. (1991). Anxiety and alcoholism: A serotonin link. *British Journal of Psychiatry*, 159 (suppl 12), 34-39.

Torgersen, S. (1988). Genetics. In C.G. Last and M. Hersen (Eds.), *Handbook of anxiety disorders*. New York: Pergamon.

Torgersen, S., Onstad, S., Skre, I., Edvardsen, J., & Kringlen, E. (1993). "True" schizotypal personality disorder: A study of co-twins and relatives of schizophrenic probands. *American Journal of Psychiatry*, 150, 1661-1667.

Torgersen, S. (1986). Genetic factors in moderately severe and mild affective disorders. *Archives of General Psychiatry*, 43, 222-226.

Torgersen, S. (1985). Relationship of schizotypal personality disorder to schizophrenia: Genetics. *Schizophrenia Bulletin*, 11, 554-563.

Torrey, E.F., Bowler, A.E., Taylor, E.H., & Gottesman, I.I. (1994). *Schizophrenia and manic-depressive disorder: The biological roots of mental illness as revealed by the landmark study of identical twins*. New York: Basic Books.

Torrey, E.F. (1988). *Nowhere to go: The tragic odyssey of the homeless mentally ill*. New York: Harper & Row.

Trachtenberg, M.C., & Blum, K. (1987). Alcohol and opioid peptides: Neuropharmacological rationale for physical craving of alcohol. *American Journal of Drug and Alcohol Abuse*, 13, 365-372.

Treffert, D.A. (1988). The idiot savant: A review of the syndrome. *American Journal of Psychiatry*, 145, 563-572.

Truax, C. & Carkhuff, R. (1967). *Toward effective counseling and psychotherapy: Training and practice*. Hawthorne, NY: Aldine Publishing.

Trull, T.J., Widiger, T.A., & Guthrie, P. (1990). Categorical versus dimensional status of borderline personality disorder. *Journal of Abnormal Psychology*, 99, 40-48.

Tsuang, M.T., Simpson, J.C., & Fleming, J.A. (1992). Epidemiology of suicide. *International Review of Psychiatry*, 4, 117-129.

Tsuang, M.T., Woolson, R.F., Fleming, J.A. (1979). Long-term outcome of major psychoses: I. Schizophrenia and affective disorders compared with psychiatrically symptom-free surgical conditions. *Archives of General Psychiatry*, 36, 1295-1301.

Turkat, I.D., & Carlson, C.R. (1984). Date-based versus symptomatic formulation of treatment: The case of a dependent personality. *Journal of Behavior Therapy and Experimental Psychiatry*, 15, 153-160.

Turkheimer, E. (1991). Individual and Group Differences in Adoption studies of IQ. *Psychological Bulletin*, 110, 392-405.

Turner, R.J., & Wagonfeld, M.O. (1967). Occupational mobility and schizophrenia: An assessment of the social causation and social selection hypotheses. *American Sociological Review*, 32, 104-113.

Turner, S.M., & Beidel, D.C. (1988). *Treating obsessive-compulsive disorder*. New York: Pergamon.

Turpin, G. (1991). The psychophysiological assessment of anxiety disorders: Three-systems measurement and beyond. *Psychological Assessment*, 3, 366-375.

Tyrer, P., Casey, P. & Gall, J. (1983). Relationship between neurosis and personality disorder. *British Journal of Psychiatry*, 142, 404-408.

Tyrer, P. (1989). Choice of treatment in anxiety. In P. Tyrer (Ed.), *Psychopharmacology of anxiety*. New York: Oxford University Press.

Tyrer, P., Candy, J. & Kelly, D. (1973). A study of the clinical effects of phenelzine and placebo in the treatment of phobic anxiety. *Psychopharmacology*, 32, 237-254.

Tyrer, P., & Ferguson, B. (1987). Problems in the classification of personality disorder. *Psychological Medicine*, 17, 15-20.

Tyrer, P., Seivewright, N., Ferguson, B., Murphy, S., Darling, C., Brothwell, J., Kingdon, D., & Johnson, A.L. (1990). The Nottingham Study of Neurotic Disorder: Relationship between personality status and symptoms. *Psychological Medicine*, 20, 423-431.

U.S. Census Bureau (1992). Growth of America's oldest-old population. *Profiles of America's Elderly*, No. 2. Washington: U.S. Government Printing Office.

U.S. Census Bureau (1986). Age structure of the U.S. population in the 21st century. *Statistical Brief* (1-86). Washington: U.S. Government Printing Office.

Vaillant, G.E. (1983). *The natural history of alcoholism: causes, patterns, and paths to recovery*. Cambridge: Harvard University Press.

Vaillant, G.E. (1992). Is there a natural history of addiction? In C.P. O'Brien & J.H. Jaffe (Eds.). *Addictive states*. New York: Raven Press. pp. 41-58.

Vaillant, G.E. (1984). The disadvantages of DSM-III outweigh its advantages. *American Journal of Psychiatry*, 141, 542-545.

van der Hart, O. & Friedman, B. (1989). A reader's guide to dissociation: A neglected intellectual heritage. *Dissociation*, 2, 13-16.

Van der Molen, G.M., Van den Hout, M.A., Van Dieren, A.C., & Griez, E. (1989). Childhood separation anxiety and adult onset panic disorders. *Journal of Anxiety Disorders*, 3, 97-106.

Van der Kolk, B.A., Boyd, H., Krystal, J., & Greenburg, M. (1984). Posttraumatic stress disorder as a biologically based disorder: Implications of the animal model of inescapable shock. In B.A. Van der Kolk (Ed.), *Posttraumatic stress disorder: Psychological and biological sequelae* (pp. 124-134). Washington: American Psychiatric Press.

Vasey, M.W., & Borkovec, T.D. (1992). A catastrophizing assessment of worrisome thoughts. *Cognitive Therapy and Research*, 16, 505-520.

Vaughn, C.E., & Leff, J.P. (1976). The influence of family and social factors on the course of psychiatric illness: A comparison of schizophrenic and depressed neurotic patients. *British Journal of Psychiatry*, 129, 125-137.

Verebey, K. (1991). Laboratory methodology for drug and alcohol addiction. In N.S. Miller (Ed.) *Comprehensive handbook of drug and alcohol addiction*. New York: Dekker. pp. 809-824.

Vogel, F. & Motulsky, A.G. (1986). *Human genetics: Problems and approaches* (2nd Ed.). New York: Springer-Verlag.

Vogel-Sprott, M. (1992). *Alcohol tolerance and social drinking: Learning the consequences.* New York: Guilford.

Vogler, G.P., Gottesman, I.I., McGue, M.K., & Rao, D.C. (1990). Mixed model segregation analysis of schizophrenia in the Lindelius Swedish pedigrees. *Behavior Genetics, 20,* 461-472.

von Bertalanffy, L. (1968). *General systems theory.* New York: Braziller.

Von Korff, M., Eaton, W., Keyl, P. (1985). The epidemiology of panic attacks and disorder: Results from three community surveys. *American Journal of Epidemiology, 122,* 970-981.

Vuchinich, S., Emery, R.E., & Cassidy, J. (1988). Family members as third parties in dyadic family conflict: Strategies, alliances, and outcomes. *Child Development, 59,* 1293-1302.

Wakefield, J. (1988). Female primary orgasmic dysfunction: Masters and Johnson versus DSM-III-R on diagnosis and incidence. *Journal of Sex Research, 24,* 363-377.

Walker, E., Davis, D., & Baum, K. (1993). Social withdrawal. In C.G. Costello (Ed.) *Symptoms of schizophrenia.* New York: Wiley, p. 227-260.

Walker, L. (1989). Psychology and violence against women. *American Psychologist, 44,* 695-702.

Walker, L. (1979). *The battered woman.* New York: Harper & Row.

Wall, T.L., Thomasson, H.R., Schuckit, M.A., & Ehlers, C.L. (1992). Subjective feelings of alcohol intoxication in Asians with genetic variations of ALDH2 alleles. *Alcoholism: Clinical and Experimental Research, 16,* 991-993.

Wallis, C.J., Rezazadeh, S.M., & Lal, H. (1993). Role of serotonin in ethanol abuse. *Drug Development and Research, 30,* 178-188.

Walsh, J. (1990). Assessment and treatment of the schizotypal personality disorder. *Journal of Independent Social Work, 4,* 41-59.

Walsh, D.C., Hingson, R.W., Merrigan, D.M., et al. (1991). A randomized trial of treatment options for alcohol abusing workers. *New England Journal of Medicine, 325,* 775-782.

Warheit, G.J., & Auth, J.B. (1985). Epidemiology of alcohol abuse in adulthood. In J.O. Cavendar (Ed.), *Psychiatry* (Vol. 3, pp. 1-18). Philadelphia, PA: Lippincott.

Warner, P., & Bancroft, J. (1986). Sex therapy outcome research: A reappraisal of methodology. 2. Methodological considerations—The importance of prognostic variability. *Psychological Medicine, 16,* 855-863.

Waterman, G., Geary, P., & Waterman, C. (1974). Longitudinal study of changes in ego identity status from the freshman to the senior year at college. *Developmental Psychology, 10,* 387-392.

Waterman, A.S. & Goldman, J.A. (1976). A longitudinal study of changes in ego identity development at a liberal arts college. *Journal of Youth and Adolescence, 5,* 361-370.

Waterman, A.S. & Archer, S. (1990). A life-span perspective on identity formation: Development in form, function, and process. In P.B. Baltes, D.L. Featherman, & R.M. Lerner (Eds.), *Life-span development and behavior* (Vol. 10, pp. 29-57). Hillsdale, NJ: Erlbaum.

Waters, E., Hay, D., & Richters, J. (1986). Infant-parent attachment and the origins of prosocial and antisocial behavior. In D. Olweus, J. Block, & M. Radke-Yarrow (Eds.), *Development of antisocial and prosocial behavior: Research, theories, and issues* (pp. 97-126). Orlando, FL: Academic.

Watkins, J.G. (1984). The Bianchi (L.A. Hillside Strangler) case: Sociopath or multiple personality. *International Journal of Clinical and Experimental Hypnosis, 32,* 67-101.

Watson, D., & Clark, L.A. (1984). Negative affectivity: The disposition to experience aversive emotional states. *Psychological Bulletin, 96,* 465-490.

Watson, D., & Clark, L.A. (1990). *The Positive and Negative Affect Schedule-Expanded Form.* Unpublished manuscript. Southern Methodist University.

Watson, J.B. & Rayner, R. (1920). Conditioned emotional reactions. *Journal of Experimental Psychology, 3,* 1-14.

Watson, I.P.B., Hoffman, L., & Wilson, G.V. (1988). The neuropsychiatry of post-traumatic stress disorder. *British Journal of Psychiatry, 152,* 164-173.

Watson, J.B. (1913). Psychology as the behaviorist views it. *Psychological Review, 20,* 158-177.

Watt, N. F. (1984). In a nutshell: The first two decades of high-risk research in schizophrenia. In N.F. Watt, E.J. Anthony, L.C. Wynne, and J.E. Rolf (Eds). *Children at risk for schizophrenia: A longitudinal perspective.* Cambridge: Cambridge University Press.

Watt, N.F., Anthony, E.J., Wynne, L.C., & Rolf, J.E. (Eds.). (1984). *Children at risk for schizophrenia: A longitudinal perspective.* Cambridge: Cambridge University Press.

Watt, L.M. & Wong, P.T. (1991). A taxonomy of reminiscence and therapeutic implications. *Journal of Gerontological Social Work, 16,* 37-57.

Weddington, W.W. (1992). Use of pharmacologic agents in the treatment of addiction. *Psychiatric Annals, 22,* 425-429.

Wegner, D.M. (1989). *White bears and other unwanted thoughts: Suppression, obsession, and the psychology of mental control.* New York: Viking.

Wegner, D.M., Shortt, J.W., Blake, A.W., & Page, M.S. (1990). The suppression of exciting thoughts. *Journal of Personality and Social Psychology, 58,* 409-418.

Wegner, D.M. (1994). Ironic processes of mental control. *Psychological Review, 101,* 34-52.

Wehr, T.A. (1989). Seasonal affective disorder: A historical overview. In Rosenthal, N.E., & Blehar, M.C. (Eds.) *Seasonal affective disorders and phototherapy.* New York: Guilford.

Weinberger, D.R., Berman, K.F., Suddath, R., & Torrey, E.F. (1992). Evidence of dysfunction of a prefrontal-limbic network in schizophrenia: A magnetic resonance imaging and regional cerebral blood flow study of discordant monozygotic twins. *American Journal of Psychiatry, 149,* 890-897.

Weinberger, D.R., Berman, K.F., & Zec, R.F. (1986). Physiologic dysfunction of dorsolateral prefrontal cortex in schizophrenia: I. Regional cerebral blood flow evidence. *Archives of General Psychiatry, 43,* 114-124.

Weinberger, D.R. (1987). Implications of normal brain development for the pathogenesis of schizophrenia. *Archives of General Psychiatry, 44,* 660-669.

Weiner, H. & Fawzy, F.I. (1989). An integrative model of health, disease, and illness. In S. Cheren (Ed.), *Psychosomatic medicine: Theory, physiology, and practice* (Vol. 1, pp. 9-44). Madison, CT: International Universities Press.

Weinstein, R.M. (1983). Labeling theory and the attitudes of mental patients: A review. *Journal of Health and Social Behavior, 24,* 70-84.

Weishaar, M.E., & Beck, A.T. (1992). Hopelessness and suicide. *International Review of Psychiatry, 4,* 177-184.

Weiss, J.M., & Simson, P.G. (1985). Neurochemical basis of stress-induced depression. *Psychopharmacology Bulletin, 21,* 447-457.

Weiss, G., Hechtman, L., Milroy, T., & Perlman, T. (1985). Psychiatric status of hyperactives as adults: A controlled prospective 15-year follow-up of 63 hyperactive children. *Journal of the American Academy of Child Psychiatry. 24,* 211-220.

Weissman, J. (1988). Anxiety and alcoholism. *Journal of Clinical Psychiatry, 49* (suppl), 17-19.

Weissman, M.M. (1988). Epidemiology of panic disorder and agoraphobia. In A.J. Francis and R.E. Hales (Eds.), *Annual Review of Psychiatry,* vol. 7. Washington, D.C.: American Psychiatric Press.

Weissman, M.M. (1993). The epidemiology of personality disorders: A 1990 update. *Journal of Personality Disorders,* supplement, 44-62.

Weissman, M.M., Bruce, M.L., Leaf, P.J., Florio, L.P., & Holzer, C. (1991). Affective disorders. In L.N. Robins & D.A. Regier (Eds.), *Psychiatric disorders in America: The epidemiologic catchment area study.* New York: Free Press. pp. 53-80.

Weissman, M., Meyers, J., & Harding, P. (1978). Psychiatric disorders in a U.S. urban community: 1975-1976. *American Journal of Psychiatry, 135,* 459-462.

Weithorn, L.A. (1988). Mental hospitalization of troublesome youth: An analysis of skyrocketing admission rates. *Stanford Law Review, 40,* 773-838.

Wenzlaff, R.M., Wegner, D.M., & Klein, S.B. (1991). The role of thought suppression in the bonding of thought and mood. *Journal of Personality and Social Psychology, 60,* 500-508.

Werner, J.S. & Smith, R.S. (1982). *Vulnerable but invincible: A longitudinal study of resilient children and youth.* New York: McGraw-Hill.

Werner, E.E. (1992). *Overcoming the odds: High risk children from birth to adulthood.* Ithaca, NY: Cornell University Press.

Wertheimer, J. (1991). Affective disorders and organic mental disorders. *International Psychogeriatrics, 3,* 19-27.

Westermeyer, J. (1987). Cultural factors in clinical assessment. *Journal of Consulting and Clinical Psychology, 55,* 471-478.

Weston, D., Ludolph, P., Misle, B., Ruffins, S., & Block, J. (1990). Physical and sexual abuse in adolescent girls with borderline personality disorder. *American Journal of Orthopsychiatry, 60,* 55-66.

Whalen, R.E., Geary, D.C., & Johnson, F. (1990). Models of sexuality. In D.P. McWhirter, S.A. Sanders, & J.M. Reinisch (Eds). *Homosexuality/heterosexuality: Concepts of sexual orientation.* New York: Oxford. pp. 61-70.

Whybrow, P.C., Akiskal, H.S., & McKinney, W.T., Jr. (1984). *Mood disorders: Toward a new psychobiology.* New York: Plenum.

Wicks-Nelson, R. & Israel, A.C. (1991). *Behavior disorders of childhood* (2nd Ed). Englewood Cliffs, NJ: Prentice-Hall.

Widiger, T.A., & Rogers, J.H. (1989). Prevalence and comorbidity of personality disorders. *Psychiatric Annals, 19,* 132-136.

Widiger, T.A., Frances, A., Warner, L., & Bluhm, C. (1986). Diagnostic criteria for the borderline and schizotypal personality disorders. *Journal of Abnormal Psychology, 95,* 43-51.

Widiger, T.A., & Trull, T.J. (1992). Personality and psychopathology: An application of the five-factor model. *Journal of Personality, 60,* 363-393.

Widiger, T.A., & Costa, P.T., Jr. (1994). Personality and personality disorders. *Journal of Abnormal Psychology, 103,* 78-91.

Widiger, T.A., & Frances, A. (1985). The DSM-III personality disorders: Perspectives from psychology. *Archives of General Psychiatry, 42,* 615-623.

Widiger, T.A., Frances, A.J., Pincus, H.A., Davis, W.W., & First, M.B. (1991). Toward an empirical classification for the DSM-IV. *Journal of Abnormal Psychology, 100,* 280-288.

Widiger, T.A. (1993). The DSM-III-R categorical personality disorder diagnoses: A critique and an alternative. *Psychological Inquiry, 4,* 75-90.

Widiger, T.A., & Frances, A. (1987). Interviews and inventories for the measurement of personality disorders. *Clinical Psychology Review, 7*, 49-75.

Wierzbicki, M. (1993). *Issues in clinical psychology: Subjective versus objective approaches.* Boston: Allyn and Bacon.

Wiggins, J.S., & Pincus, A.L. (1992). Personality: Structure and assessment. *Annual Review of Psychology, 43*, 473-504.

Wiggins, J.S. (1973). *Personality and prediction: Principles of personality assessment.* Reading, MA: Addison-Wesley.

Wiggins, J.S. (1982). Circumplex models of interpersonal behavior in clinical psychology. In P.C. Kendall & J.N. Butcher (Eds.), *Handbook of research methods in clinical psychology* (pp. 183-221). New York: Wiley.

Willerman, L. (1973). Activity level and hyperactivity in twins. *Child Development, 44*, 288-293.

William T. Grant Foundation (1988). *The forgotten half: Pathways to success for America's youth and young families.* Washington, DC: Youth and America's Future: The William T. Grant Foundation Commission on Work, Family and Citizenship.

Williams, J.B.W., Gibbon, M., First, M.B., Spitzer, R.L, Davies, M., Borus, J., Howes, J.M., Kane, J., Pope, H.G., Rounsaville, B., Wittchen, H. (1992). The structured clinical interview for DSM-III-R (SCID), II: Multisite test-retest reliability. *Archives of General Psychiatry, 49*, 630-636.

Williams, J.B.W. (1985). The multiaxial system of DSM-III: Where did it come from and where should it go? *Archives of General Psychiatry, 42*, 175-180.

Wilsnack, S.C., & Wilsnack, R.W. (1991). Epidemiology of women's drinking. *Journal of Substance Abuse, 3*, 133-158.

Wilsnack, S.C. (1984). Drinking, sexuality and sexual dysfunction in women. In S.C. Wilsnack and L.J. Beckman (Eds). *Alcohol problems in women.* New York: Guilford. pp. 189-227.

Wilsnack, R.W., Wilsnack, S.C., & Klassen, A.D. (1984). Women's drinking and drinking problems: Patterns from a 1981 national survey. *American Journal of Public Health, 74*, 1231-1238.

Wilson, G.D. (1987). An ethological approach to sexual deviation. In G.D. Wilson (Ed.). *Variant sexuality: research and theory.* London: Croom Helm. pp. 84-115.

Wilson, T.D. & Linville, P.W. (1982). Improving the academic performance of college freshman: Attribution therapy revisited. *Journal of Personality and Social Psychology, 42*, 367-376.

Wilson, M. (1989). The Black extended family: An analytical review. *Developmental Psychology, 22*, 246-258.

Wincze, J.P., & Carey, M.P. (1991). *Sexual dysfunction: A guide for assessment and treatment.* New York: Guilford.

Wincze, J.P. (1989). Assessment and treatment of atypical sexual behavior. In S.R. Lieblum and R.C. Rosen (Eds.). *Principles and practice of sex therapy* (2nd edition). New York: Guilford. pp. 382-404.

Wing, L. & Gould, HJ. (1979). Severe impairments of social interaction and associate abnormalities in children: Epidemiology and classification. *Journal of Autism and Developmental Disorders, 9*, 11-29.

Wing, L. (1988). Autism: Possible clues to the underlying pathology - 1. Clinical facts. In L. Wing (Ed.), *Aspects of autism: Biological Research* (pp. 11-18). Gaskell: London.

Winger, G., Hofmann, F.G., & Woods, J.H. (1992). *A handbook on drug and alcohol abuse: The biomedical aspects* (3rd Ed.). New York: Oxford.

Winograd, E. & Killinger, W.A. (1983). Relating age at encoding in early childhood to adult recall: Development of flashbulb memories. *Journal of Experimental Psychology: General, 112*, 413-422.

Winokur, G., Zimmerman, M., & Cadoret, R. (1988). 'Cause the Bible tells me so. *Archives of General Psychiatry, 45*, 683-684.

Wolf, S., & Chick, J. (1980). Schizoid personality in childhood: A controlled follow-up study. *Psychological Medicine, 10*, 85-100.

Wolfe, D. (1987). *Child abuse: Implications for child development and psychopathology.* Beverly Hills: Sage.

Wolpe, J., & Rachman, S.J. (1960). Psychoanalytic "evidence," A critique based on Freud's case of Little Hans. *Journal of Nervous and Mental Disease, 131*, 135-147.

Wolpe, J. (1990). *The practice of behavior therapy* (4th Ed.). New York: Pergamon.

Wolpe, J. (1958). *Psychotherapy and reciprocal inhibition.* Stanford, CA: Stanford University Press.

Wong, D.F., Wagner, H.N., Jr., Tune, L.E., Dannals, R.F., Pearlson, G.D., Links, J.M. et al. (1986). Positron emission tomography reveals elevated D₂ dopamine receptors in drug-naive schizophrenics. *Science, 234*, 1558-1563.

Woody, G.E., McLellan, A.T., Luborsky, L., & O'Brien, C.P. (1985). Sociopathy and psychotherapy outcome. *Archives of General Psychiatry, 42*, 1081-1086.

World Health Organization. (1992). *The ICD-10 classification of mental and behavioural disorders: Clinical descriptions and diagnostic guidelines.* Geneva, Switzerland: World Health Organization.

World Health Organization. (1983). *Depressive disorders in different cultures.* Geneva, Switzerland: World Health Organization.

Wortman, C.B. & Silver, R.C. (1989). The myths of coping with loss. *Journal of Consulting and Clinical Psychology, 57*, 349-357.

Wynne, L.C., & Singer, M.T. (1963). Thought disorder and family relations of schizophrenics: II. A classification of forms of thinking. *Archives of General Psychiatry, 9*, 199-206.

Yalom, I.D. (1985). *Theory and practice of group psychotherapy* (3rd Ed.). New York: Basic.

Yang, B., Stack, S., & Lester, D. (1992). Suicide and unemployment: Predicting the smoothed trend and yearly fluctuations. *Journal of Socio-Economics, 21*, 39-41.

Yates, A. (1989). Current perspectives on the eating disorders: I. History, psychological, and biological aspects. *Journal of the American Academy of Child and Adolescent Psychiatry, 28*, 813-828.

Yates, A. (1990). Current perspectives on the eating disorders: II. Treatment, outcome, and research directions. *Journal of the American Academy of Child and Adolescent Psychiatry, 29*, 1-9.

Yi, D. (1991). Alcohol. In N.S. Miller (Ed.). *Comprehensive handbook of drug and alcohol addiction.* New York: Marcel Dekker, Inc.

Zajecka, J., Fawcett, J., Schaff, M., Jeffriess, H., & Guy, C. (1991). The role of serotonin in sexual dysfunction: Fluoxetine-associated orgasm dysfunction. *Journal of Clinical Psychiatry, 52*, 66-68.

Zarit, S.H., Zarit, J.M., & Rosenberg-Thompson, S. (1990). A special treatment unit for Alzheimer's disease: Medical, behavioral, and environmental features. *Clinical Gerontologist, 9*, 47-63.

Zatta, P.F. (1993). Controversial aspects of aluminum accumulation and subcompartmentation in Alzheimer's disease. *Trace Elements in Medicine, 10*, 120-128.

Zeiss, A.M., Lewinsohn, P.M., & Munoz, R.F. (1979). Nonspecific improvement effects in depression using interpersonal skills training, pleasant activity schedules, or cognitive training. *Journal of Consulting and Clinical Psychology, 47*, 427-439.

Zemishlany, Z., Siever, L.J., & Coccaro, E.F. (1988). Biologic factors in personality disorders. *Israel Journal of Psychiatry and Related Sciences, 25*, 12-23.

Zigler, E. & Hodapp, R.M. (1986). *Understanding mental retardation.* New York: Cambridge University Press.

Zigler, E. & Styfco, S.J. (1993). Using research and theory to justify and inform Head Start expansion. *Social Policy Report for the Society for Research in Child Development, 7* (2), 1-20.

Zigler, E. & Hall, N.W. (1989). Physical abuse in America: Past, present, and future. In D. Cicchetti, & V. Carlson (Eds.), *Child maltreatment: Theory and research on the causes and consequences of child abuse and neglect* (pp. 38-77). Cambridge: University of Cambridge Press.

Zigler, E. (1967). Familial mental retardation: A continuing dilemma. *Science, 155*, 292-298.

Zilbergeld, B. (1978). *Male sexuality.* New York: Bantam.

Zill, N. & Schoenborn, C.A. (1990). Developmental, learning, and emotional problems: Health of our nation's children, United States, 1988. *Advance data from vital and health statistics; no 190.* Hyattsville, MD: National Center for Health Statistics.

Zill, N. (1978). Divorce, marital happiness, and the mental health of children: Findings from the FCD National Survey of Children. Paper presented at the NIMH workshop on divorce and children. Bethesda, MD.

Zimmerman, M., & Coryell, W.H. (1990). Diagnosing personality disorders in the community: A comparison of self-report and interview measures. *Archives of General Psychiatry, 47*, 527-531.

Zimmerman, M., & Spitzer, R.L. (1989). Melancholia: From DSM-III to DSM-III-R. *American Journal of Psychiatry, 146*, 20-28.

Zimmerman, M., & Coryell, W.H. (1989). DSM-III personality disorder diagnoses in a nonpatient sample. *Archives of General Psychiatry, 46*, 682-689.

Zinbarg, R.E., Barlow, D.H., Brown, T.A., & Hertz, R.M. (1992). Cognitive-behavioral approaches to the nature and treatment of anxiety disorders. *Annual Review of Psychology, 43*, 235-267.

Ziskin, J. & Faust, D. (1989). Psychiatric and psychological evidence in child custody cases. *Trial*, 45-49.

Zoccolillo, M. & Cloninger, C.R. (1985). Parental breakdown associated with somatization disorder (hysteria). *British Journal of Psychiatry, 147*, 443-446.

Zola-Morgan, S., Squire, L.R., & Amaral, D.G. (1986). Human amnesia and the medial temporal region: Enduring memory impairment following a bilateral lesion limited to field CA1 of the hippocampus. *Journal of Neuroscience, 6*, 2950-2967.

Zook, A. & Walton, J.M. (1989). Theoretical orientations and work settings of clinical and counseling psychologists: A current perspective. *Professional Psychology, 20*, 23-31.

Zubin, J., & Spring, B. (1977). Vulnerability - A new view of schizophrenia. *Journal of Abnormal Psychology, 86*, 103-126.

Zucker, K.J. (1985). Cross-gender-identified children. In B.W. Steiner (Ed), *Gender dysphoria: Development, research, management.* New York: Plenum. pp. 75-174.

Zuckerman, M. (1990). Some dubious premises in research and theory on racial differences: Scientific, social, and ethical issues. *American Psychologist, 45*, 1297-1303.

Credits

PHOTOGRAPHS

All portraits Illustrated by Van Howell

Chapter 1: Page 3, Bettmann; **p. 7**, Heron/Monkmeyer Press; **p. 8**, Tri-Star Pictures, Inc./Everett Collection; **p. 9**, Lester Sloan/Woodfin Camp & Associates; **p. 13**, Earl Dotter/Impact Visuals; **p. 14**, Portrait based on photo from courtesy of Lee Robins; **p. 21**, Robert Capa/Magnum Photos, Inc.; **p. 25**, Dan Habib/Impact Visuals.

Chapter 2: Page 36, Portrait based on photo from Who/Photo; **p. 39**, Boris of Boston; **p. 48**, CNRI/Phototake; **p. 52**, Bob Daemmrich/The Image Works; **p. 52**, Art Gingert/Comstock; **p. 55**, Paramount Pictures; **p. 56**, Photofest; **p. 65**, Richard Hutchings/Photo Researchers, Inc.; **p. 65**, Wasyl Szkodzinsky/Photo Researchers, Inc.; **p. 66**, Culver Pictures, Inc.

Chapter 3: Page 77, Loren McIntyre/Woodfin Camp & Associates; **p. 82**, Gary Retherford/Photo Researchers, Inc.; **p. 86**, Portrait based on photo from Bettmann; **p. 88**, Portrait based on photo from courtesy of Joseph Wolpe; **p. 91**, Portrait based on photo from courtesy of Albert Bandura; **p. 92**, Portrait based on photo from Carl Rogers Memorial Library; **p. 98**, Portrait based on photo from Bettmann; **p. 100**, Wasyl Szkodzinsky/Photo Researchers, Inc.; **p. 102**, Bob Daemmrich/Stock Boston, Inc.; **p. 103**, Andy Levin/Photo Researchers, Inc.

Chapter 4: Page 113, Rosamund Purscell; **p. 114**, UPI/Bettmann; **p. 115**, J.P. Fizet/Sygma; **p. 116**, Portrait based on photo from the Archives of the American Psychiatric Association, Washington, D.C., Copyright 1994; **p. 122**, Faye Ellman; **p. 125**, Vanessa Vick/Photo Researchers, Inc.; **p. 133**, Ray Stott/The Image Works; **p. 136**, Portrait based on photo from courtesy of G.B. Peterson; **p. 142**, Ken Karp; **p. 147**, Will & Deni McIntyre/Photo Researchers, Inc.

Chapter 5: Page 155, Mel Digiacomo/The Image Bank; **p. 156**, Bernard Gotfryd/Woodfin Camp & Associates; **p. 158**, Blake Discher/Sygma; **p. 160**, Jeffrey Markowitz/Sygma; **p. 165**, Portrait based on photo from courtesy of Myrna Weissman; **p. 166**, Lester Sloan/Woodfin Camp & Associates; **p. 166**, Teri Stratford; **p. 171**, Crandall/The Image Works; **p. 176**, Portrait based on photo from courtesy of Peter Lewinson; **p. 177**, Collins/Monkmeyer Press; **p. 184**, Portrait based on photo from courtesy of Aaron Beck; **p. 187**, James D. Wilson/Woodfin Camp & Associates.

Chapter 6: Page 198, Rick Friedman/Black Star; **p. 201**, Schneps/The Image Bank; **p. 206**, Portrait based on photo from courtesy of Donald Klein; **p. 206**, Frederick Ayer/Photo Researchers, Inc.; **p. 207**, Pamela Frank/Everett Collection; **p. 210**, Burt Ghan/Magnum Photos, Inc.; **p. 213**, Ellis Herwig/Stock Boston, Inc.; **p. 216**, Andrew Lichtenstein/Impact Visuals; **p. 223**, Reprinted from Psychology Today Magazine, Pg. 32, 4/85/American Psychological Association; **p. 225**, Jacques M. Chenet/Woodfin Camp & Associates.

Chapter 7: Page 239, Portrait based on photo from Bettmann; **p. 239**, Portrait based on photo from Bettmann; **p. 239**, Portrait based on photo from Bettmann; **p. 243**, Malcolm S. Kirk; **p. 243**, Elizabeth Crews/The Image Works; **p. 243**, David W. Hamilton/The Image Bank; **p. 249**, Benelux Press B.V./Photo Researchers, Inc.; **p. 252**, David Alan Harvey/Woodfin Camp & Associates; **p. 256**, Gerd Ludwig/Woodfin Camp & Associates; **p. 258**, M. Bernsau/The Image Works; **p. 261**, Alan Hawes/Sygma; **p. 266**, Rhoda Sidney; **p. 267**, Portrait based on photo from courtesy of Edna Foa.

Chapter 8: Page 274, National Library of Medicine/Mark Marten/Photo Researchers, Inc.; **p. 277**, Portrait based on photo from Bettmann; **p. 277**, Bart Bartholomew/Black Star; **p. 279**, Scott Applewhite/AP/Wide World Photos; **p. 280**, Tim Jonke/The Image Bank; **p. 282**, Everett Collection; **p. 286**, Olga Shelygin/AP/Wide World Photos; **p. 289**, Robbie Marantz/The Image Bank; **p. 290**, Photofest.

Chapter 9: Page 307, Lester Sloan/Woodfin Camp & Associates; **p. 311**, Photofest; **p. 312**, M. Grecco/Stock Boston, Inc.; **p. 313**, Photofest; **p. 314**, Owen Franken/Stock Boston, Inc.; **p. 318**, Everett Collection; **p. 318**, Everett Collection; **p. 324**, Portrait based on photo from courtesy of John Gunderson; **p. 326**, Mary Ellen Mark Library; **p. 328**, AP/Wide World Photos.

Chapter 10: Page 338, Robert Cohen/The Commercial Appeal; **p. 343**, Andrew Cooper/Sygma; **p. 347**, Photo Researchers, Inc.; **p. 347**, Portrait based on photo from courtesy of Center of Alcohol Studies, Rutgers University; **p. 349**, Portrait based on photo from courtesy of George Vaillant; **p. 351**, Everett Collection; **p. 355**, R. Lucas/The Image Works; **p. 355**, J.P. Laffont/Sygma; **p. 363**, Richard Hutchings/Photo Researchers, Inc.; **p. 364**, Bachmann/The Image Works; **p. 366**, Sygma.

Chapter 11: Page 375, Portrait based on photo from Bettmann; **p. 378**, UPI/Portrait based on photo from Bettmann; **p. 385**, W. Hill/The Image Works; **p. 392**, Brian Lantelme; **p. 397**, Michael Weisbrot/The Image Works; **p. 399**, Catherine Karnow/Woodfin Camp & Associates; **p. 402**, UPI/Bettman.

Chapter 12: Page 410, Weisbrot/The Image Works; **p. 411**, Mary Ellen Mark Library; **p. 414**, Courtesy of The New York Academy of Medicine Library, from the book "Dementia Praecox and Paraphrenia" by Emil Kraepelin, publisher E.S. Livingstone, Edinburgh, 1919; **p. 414**, Bettmann; **p. 416**, Mary Ellen Mark Library; **p. 422**, Portrait based on photo from courtesy of Dr. I. Gottesseman; **p. 424**, Portrait based on photo from courtesy of Paul Meehl; **p. 425**, MIH/Science Source/Photo Researchers, Inc.; **p. 428**, Monte Buchsbaum, M.D.; **p. 438**, William G. Iacono, Ph. D.; **p. 440**, Focus on Sports.

Chapter 13: Page 450, Ira Wyman/Sygma; **p. 453**, Wally McNamee/Woodfin Camp & Associates; **p. 456**, SIU/Science Source/Photo Researchers, Inc.; **p. 460**, Courtesy of Dr. Paul Hoff, Psychiatric Hospital, Ludwig-Maximilian University, Munich, Germany; **p. 464**, Martin M. Rotker/Science Source/Photo Researchers, Inc.; **p. 470**, Tim Beddow/Science Photo Library/Photo Researchers, Inc.; **p. 470**, Tim Beddow/Science Photo Library/Photo Researchers, Inc.; **p. 472**, Jacques Chenet/Woodfin Camp & Associates; **p. 473**, Richard Falco/Black Star.

Chapter 14: Page 478, Everett Collection; **p. 486**, Elaine Rebman/Photo Researchers, Inc.; **p. 488**, J. Griffin/The Image Works; **p. 491**, Bob Adelman/Magnum Photos, Inc.; **p. 492**, Will & Deni McIntyre/Photo Researchers, Inc.; **p. 495**, AP/Wide World Photos; **p. 497**, Goodwin/Monkmeyer Press; **p. 499**, Print from "Nadia" book, pg. 24 by Lorna Selfe, © Academic Press, 1977; **p. 499**, The Alan Mason Chesney Medical Archives of the John Hopkins Medical Institutions; **p. 508**, Portrait based on photo from courtesy of Ivar Lovaas; **p. 00, Portrait based on photo from Bettmann.**

Chapter 15: Page 519, Lew Merrim/Monkmeyer Press; **p. 520**, Portrait based on photo from courtesy of Mary Ainsworth; **p. 520**, Jeff Greenberg/Picture Cube; **p. 521**, Tom McCarthy/Picture Cube; **p. 532**, UPI/Bettmann; **p. 534**, Chris Steele Perkins/Portrait based on photo from Magnum Photos, Inc.; **p. 535**, Portrait based on photo from courtesy of the Tavistock Clinic, Mrs. J. Hopkins; **p. 537**, Rick Hunter/Sygma; **p. 540**, Bob Daemmrich/The Image Works; **p. 543**, Brian Plonka/Impact Visuals; **p. 546**, Pierre Vauthey/Sygma; **p. 548**, Portrait based on photo from courtesy of G.R. Patterson.

Chapter 16: Page 558, Portrait based on photo from courtesy of Jon Erikson; **p. 559**, Leduc/Monkmeyer Press; **p. 559**, Simon Cherpitel/Magnum Photos, Inc.; **p. 559**, Dollarhide/Monkmeyer Press; **p. 563**, Sygma; **p. 563**, Mark Burnett/Photo Researchers, Inc.; **p. 566**, Arthur Grace/Sygma; **p. 575**, Jon L. Barkan/Picture Cube; **p. 575**, Bob Daemmrich/The Image Works.

Chapter 17: Page 586, Sygma; **p. 589**, Portrait based on photo from courtesy of Thomas Szasz; **p. 595**, Portrait based on photo from Bettmann; **p. 598**, Portrait based on photo from courtesy of John Monahan; **p. 604**, AP/Wide World Photos; **p. 607**, Jerry Cooke/Photo Researchers, Inc.; **p. 607**, Eugene Richards/Magnum Photos, Inc.; **p. 614**, AP/Wide World Photos; **p. 614**, AP/Wide World Photos; **p. 617**, AP/Wide World Photos; **p. 617**, AP/Wide World Photos.

FIGURES

Chapter 2: Cartoon 2-1 *Calvin and Hobbes* copyright 1993 Watterson. Reprinted with permission of *Universal Press Syndicate*. All rights reserved. **Fig. 2-2** John G. Seamon and Douglas T. Kenrick, *Psychology*, 2nd Edition, © 1994, p. 44. Reprinted by permission of Prentice Hall, Inc., Englewood Cliffs, N.J. **Fig. 2-3** John G. Seamon and Douglas T. Kenrick, *Psychology*, 2nd Edition. © 1994, p. 51. Reprinted by permission of Prentice Hall, Inc., Englewood Cliffs, N.J. **Fig. 2.4** John G. Seamon and Douglas T. Kenrick, *Psychology*, 2nd Edition, © 1994, p. 67. Reprinted by permission of Prentice Hall, Inc., Englewood Cliffs, N.J. **Fig. 2.6** Reproduced by permission of Blackwell Scientific Publications Limited.

Chapter 3: Cartoon 3-1 Drawing by Mankoff; © 1991 The New Yorker Magazine, Inc. **Fig. 3.1** M.L. Smith, G.V. Glass and T.I. Miller, *The Benefits of Psychotherapy* (1980). Reprinted by permission of Johns Hopkins University Press. **Fig.3.2** From K.I. Howard, S.M. Kopta, M.S. Krause and D.E. Orlinsky (1986). The dose-effect relationship in psychotherapy. *American Psychologist*, 41, 159-164. Reprinted with permission from K.I. Howard.

Chapter 4: Cartoon 4-1 *Calvin and Hobbes* copyright 1993 Watterson. Reprinted with permission of *Universal Press Syndicate*. All rights reserved. **MMPI Profile** Sundberg/Tyler/Taplin, *Clinical Psychology: Expanding Horizons*, Second Edition, © 1973, p. 101. Reprinted by permission of Prentice-Hall, Inc., Englewood Cliffs, N.J.

Chapter 5: Cartoon 5-1 BILL SCHORR reprinted by permission of UFS, Inc. **Fig. 5.1** Arthur Kleinman and Byron Good, *Culture and Depression: Studies in the Overview*. Copyright © 1985 The Regents of the University of California. Reprinted with permission.

Chapter 6: Cartoon 6-1 Copyright, USA TODAY. Reprinted with permission. **Fig. 6.1** Reprinted with permission from *Behavior Research and Therapy*, Vol. 30, C.G. Costello, *Problems in Recent Tests of Two Cognitive Theories of Panic*, 1992, Elsevier Science Ltd., Pergamon Imprint, Oxford, England. **Cartoon 6-2** *Far Side* copyright 1990 FARWORKS, INC./Dist. by Universal Press Syndicate. Reprinted with permission. All rights reserved. **Fig. 6.2** Reprinted with permission from *Behavior Research and Therapy*, Vol. 30, C.G. Costello, *Problems in Recent Tests of Two Cognitive Theories of Panic*, 1986, Elsevier Science Ltd., Pergamon Imprint, Oxford, England.

Chapter 7: Fig. 7.1 From *Biology*, Fourth Edition, by Willis H. Johnson, Louis E. Delanney, Thomas A. Cole, and Austin E. Brooks, copyright © 1972 by Holt, Rinehart and Winston,

Inc. Reproduced by permission of the publisher. **Fig. 7.2** *Handbook of Psychology and Health Stress,* Vol. 5, pp. 1-24, A. Baum and J.E. Singer (eds.), © 1987. Reprinted with permission of Lawrence Erlbaum Associates, Inc. **Fig. 7.3** Copyright © 1983 by The New York Times Company. Reprinted by permission. **Fig. 7.4** *Archives of General Psychiatry,* 1991, 48, 216-22. Copyright © 1991, American Medical Association.

Chapter 8: Fig. 8.1 Adapted from D.M. Kaufman (1985) *Clinical Neurology for Psychiatrists,* Second Edition. Reprinted with permission of W.B. Saunders Company.

Chapter 9: Cartoon 9-1 *Far Side* copyright 1990 FARWORKS, INC./Dist. by Universal Press Syndicate. Reprinted with permission. All rights reserved. **Fig. 9.1** American Psychiatric Association: *Diagnostic and Statistical Manual of Mental Disorders,* 3rd ed., Revised. Washington, D.C., American Psychiatric Association, 1987.

Chapter 11: Fig. 11-1 Adapted from Frederic Martini, *Fundamentals of Anatomy and Physiology,* 2nd ed. Englewood Cliffs, NJ: Prentice Hall, 1992. Drawing (A) by Craig Luce. Drawing (B) by William C. Ober, M.D., and Claire W. Garrison, R.N. **Fig. 11.2** G.D. Wilson (1987). An ethological approach to sexual deviation. In G.G. Wilson (Ed.), *Variant sexuality: Research and theory* (p. 92). London: Croom Helm.

Chapter 12: Fig. 12.1 From *Schizophrenia Genesis: The Origins of Madness* by Irving I. Gottesman. Copyright © 1991 by Irving I. Gottesman. Reprinted with permission of W.H. Freeman and Company. **Fig. 12-2** Adapted from M. Martini and M. Timmons (1995). *Human Anatomy,* p. 381. Englewood Cliffs, NJ: Prentice Hall.

Chapter 13: Fig. 13-2 Adapted from W.C. Heindel et al (1989). Neuropsychological evidence for multiple implicit memory systems: A comparison of Alzheimer's, Huntington's, and Parkinson's disease patients. *Journal of Neuroscience,* 9, 586. **Fig. 13-3** Adapted from F. Martini and M. Timmons (1995). *Human Anatomy,* p. 378. Englewood Cliffs, NJ: Prentice Hall. **Fig. 13.5** From *The Vanishing Mind* by L.L. Heston and J.A. White. Copyright © 1991 by W.H. Freeman and Company. Used with permission.

Chapter 14: Fig. 14.1 E. Zigler, Familial mental retardation: A continuing dilemma. *Science,* 1967, 155, 292-98. Copyright © 1967 by the American Association for the Advancement of Science. **Fig. 14.2** G.S. Baroff (1986). *Mental Retardation: Nature, Cause and Management.* Washington D.C.: Hemisphere Publishing Corp. Reproduced with permission. All rights reserved.

Chapter 15: Cartoon 15-1 *Calvin and Hobbes* copyright © 1990 Watterson. Reprinted with permission of Universal Press Syndicate. All rights reserved. **Fig. 15.1** A. Blumstein, J. Cohen, and D.P. Farrington, *Criminal Career Research: Its Value for Criminology. Criminology,* 26, p. 11, 1980. Reprinted with permission.

Chapter 16: Fig. 16.1 From *The Seasons of a Man's Life* by Daniel J. Levinson et al. Copyright © 1978 by Daniel J. Levinson. Reprinted by permission of Alfred A. Knopf, Inc. **Fig. 16.2** L.S. Benjamin, *Interpersonal diagnosis and treatment of personality disorders* ((1993). Reprinted with permission of Guilford Publications. **Fig. 16.3** Illustration by Gaston Weisz in R. Sherman and N. Fredman (1986). *Handbook of Structured Techniques In Marriage and Family Therapy,* p. 76. Reprinted with permission of Brunner/Mazel, Inc.

Chapter 17: Fig. 17.1 From *Nowhere to Go* by E. Fuller Torrey. Copyright © 1988 by E. Fuller Torrey. Reprinted by permission of HarperCollins Publishers, Inc. **Fig. 17.2** From *Nowhere to Go* by E. Fuller Torrey. Copyright © 1988 by E. Fuller Torrey. Reprinted by permission of Harper Collins Publishers, Inc. **Fig. 17.3** D.J. Besharov (1992). *A Balanced Approach to Reporting Child Abuse in The Child, Youth and Family Services Quarterly,* 15, p. 5.

TABLES

Chapter 2: Tab. 2.3 Based on G.E. Schwartz (1987). Testing the biopsychosocial model: The ultimate challenge facing behavioral medicine. *Journal of Consulting and Clinical Psychology,* 50, 1040-1053.

Chapter 3: Tab. 3.1 A.E. Bergin and S.L. Garfield (Eds.), *Handbook of Psychotherapy and Behavior Change,* 4th Edition. Copyright © 1994 by John Wiley & Sons. Reprinted by permission of John Wiley & Sons, Inc. **Tab. 3.2** Reprinted by permission of the publishers from *Psychotherapy versus Behavior Therapy* by R. Bruce Sloane et al. Cambridge Mass.: Harvard University Press. Copyright © 1975 by the President and Fellows of Harvard College. **Tab. 3.3** A.E. Bergin and S.L. Garfield (Eds.), *Handbook of Psychotherapy and Behavior Change,* 4th Edition. Copyright © 1994 by John Wiley & Sons. Reprinted by permission of John Wiley & Sons, Inc.

Chapter 4: Tab. 4.4 Adapted from R.E. Kendall, "Clinical Validity," in *Psychological Medicine,* 19 (1989), p. 47. Reprinted with permission from Cambridge University Press. **Tab.

4.10 From A. Ciminero et al. (Eds.), *Handbook of Behavioral Assessment,* 2nd ed., 1986. New York: Wiley Interscience.

Chapter 5: Tab. 5.1 P.C. Whybrow, H.S. Akiskal, and W.T. McKinney, Jr., *Mood Disorders: Toward a New Psychobiology* (1984). Reprinted with permission of Plenum Publishing Corporation. **Tab. 5.6** L.J. Chapman, J.P. Chapman, and D. Fowles (eds.) *Progress in Experimental Personality and Psychopathology Research,* © 1995. Reprinted with permission of Springer Publishing Company, Inc., New York, NY 10012.

Chapter 6: Tab. 6.5 Adapted and reprinted with the permission of The Free Press, Macmillan Publishing from *Psychiatric Disorders in America: The Epidemiologic Catchment Area Study* by Lee N. Robins and Darrel A. Regier. Copyright © 1991 by Lee N. Robins and Darrel A. Regier. **Tab. 6.6** *American Journal of Psychiatry,* 144, 1019-1024, 1987. Copyright © 1987, The American Psychiatric Association. Reprinted by permission. **Tab. 6.8** *The Clinical Management of Anxiety Disorders,* W. Coryell and G. Winokur (eds.), 1991. Reprinted with permission of the publisher, Oxford University Press.

Chapter 7: Tab. 7.1 Reprinted with permission from *Journal of Psychosomatic Research* Vol. 11, Thomas H. Holmes and R.H. Rahe, "The Social Readjustment Rating Scale." 1967, Elsevier Science Ltd., Pergamon Imprint, Oxford, England.

Chapter 9: Tab. 9.2 Reproduced by special permission of the publisher, Psychological Assessment Resources, Inc., 16204 North Florida Avenue, Lutz, Florida 33549, from the NEO Personality Inventory-Revised, by Paul Costa and Rpbert McCrae, Copyright © 1978, 1985, 1989, 1992 by PAR, Inc. Further reproduction is prohibited without permission of PAR, Inc. **Tab. 9.9** *Archives of General Psychiatry,* 1982, 39, 1242-1249. Copyright © 1982, American Medical Association.

Chapter 10: Tab. 10.1 M.A. Schuckit, *Drug and Alcohol Abuse,* Third Edition, 1989. Reprinted by permission of Plenum Publishing Corporation. **Tab. 10.2** Reprinted with permission from the Diagnostic and Statistical Manual of Mental Disorders, Fourth Edition. Copyright © 1994 American Psychiatric Association. **Tab 10.4** G.E. Vaillant (1992). Is There a Natural History of Addiction? In C.P. O'Brien and J.H. Jaffee (Eds.). *Addictive States.* Reprinted with permission of Raven Press. **Tab. 10.5** Helzer, J.E., Burnam, A. and McEvoy, L.T., Alcohol abuse and dependence. In L.N. Robins and D.A. Regier (Eds.): *Psychiatric Disorders in America: The Epidemiologic Catchment Area Study,* p. 91. Copyright © 1991 by L.N. Robins and D.A. Regier. Adapted with permission of The Free Press, an imprint of Simon & Schuster.

Chapter 11: Tab. 11.1 Reprinted with permission from the Diagnostic and Statistical Manual of Mental Disorders, Fourth Edition. Copyright © 1994 American Psychiatric Association. **Tab 11.2** Reprinted by permission of the New England Journal of Medicine, 299, 111-115, 1978. **Tab. 11.5** Reprinted with permission from the Diagnostic and Statistical Manual of Mental Disorders, Fourth Edition. Copyright © 1994 American Psychiatric Association. **Tab. 11.6** D.R. Laws and H.E. Barbaree (eds.), *Handbook of Sexual Assault,* 1990. Reprinted by permission of Plenum Publishing Corporation.

Chapter 13: Tab. 13-1 Reprinted with permission from *Journal of Psychiatric Research,* Vol. 12. Folstein et al., Mini-Mental State: A Practical Method for Grading the Cognitive State of Patients for the Clinician (1975), Elsevier Science Ltd., Pergamon Imprint, Oxford, England. **Tab. 13-4** *The Vanishing Mind* by L.L. Heston and J.A. White. Copyright (c)1991 by W.H. Freeman and Company. Used with permission.

Chapter 14: Tab. 14.2 Vineland Adaptive Behavior Scales by Sara S. Sparrow, David A. Balla, Domenic V. Cicchetti © 1984 American Guidance Service, Inc., 4201 Woodland Rd. Circle Pines, Minnesota 55914-1796. Reproduced with permission of the publisher. All rights reserved. **Tab. 14.4** Adapted from T.J. Bouchard, Jr., and M. McGue. Familial Studies of Intelligence: A Review. *Science* 1981, 212, 1055-1059. Copyright © 1981 by the American Association for the Advancement of Science. **Tab. 14.6** Copyright © 1987 by the American Phychological Association. Reprinted by permission.

Chapter 15: Tab. 15.1 Adapted from *Journal of Child Psychology and Psychiatry,* 30, 5, p. 781. Copyright (c)1989 by the Association for Child Psychology and Psychiatry. Reprinted by permission.

Chapter 16: Tab. 16.1 From *Marriage and Family Development,* 6th Ed. by Evelyn Millis Duvall and Brent C. Miller. Copyright © 1985 by Harper & Row, Publishers, Inc. Reprinted by permission of HarperCollins Publishers, Inc. **Tab. 16.3** L.K. George, D.F. Blazer, I. Winfield-Laird, P.J. Leaf, & R.L. Fishbach, 1988, in J. Brody and G. Maddox, *Epidemiology and Aging,* New York: Springer. Copyright © 1988 by Springer Publishing Company. Used by permission.

Chapter 17: Tab. 17.1 Table from *Misuse of Psychiatry in the Criminal Courts: Competence to Stand Trial,* 1974, pp. 896-897. Reprinted with permission from *Group for Advancement of Psychiatry.*

Name Index

Subject Index

Decision Trees
for Differential Diagnosis

One of the appendices in DSM-IV includes a set of decision trees that can help a clinician understand the organization and hierarchal structure of this classification system. We have reproduced two of these decision trees as examples that may be a useful for students. One is for psychotic disorders and the other is for mood disorders. Each tree begins with a set of symptoms that the clinician has presumably observed in a patient, such as delusions and hallucinations. From this starting point, the clinician follows a series of questions which either rule in or rule out the presence of various types of disorders. Remember that these decision trees are drawn in very general terms; the diagnostic criteria for specific disorders are more complex and detailed than the way they are portrayed in this diagram. Note: NOS stands for "not otherwise specified."

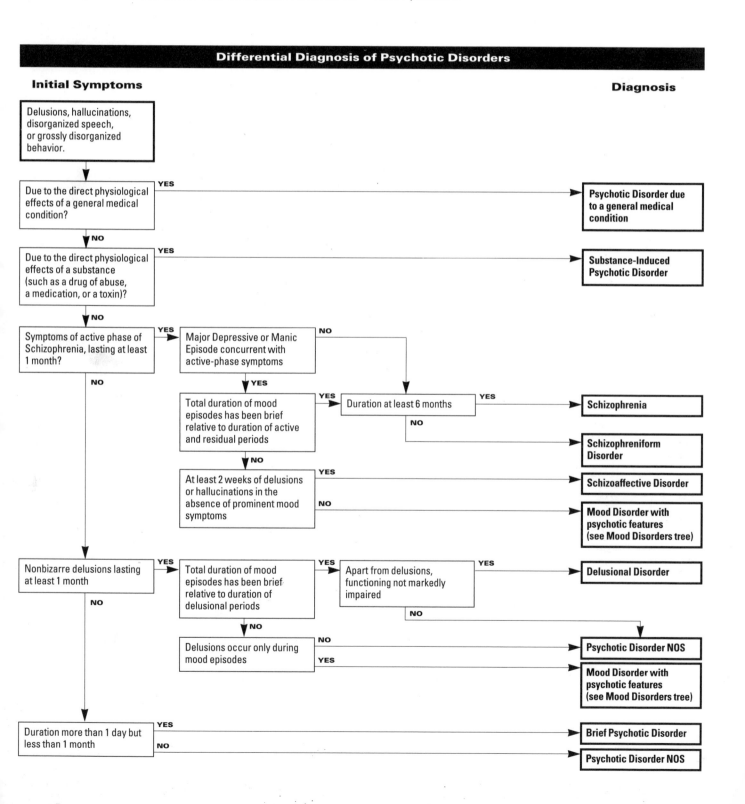